TEX: The Program

COMPUTERS & TYPESETTING / B

TEX: The Program

DONALD E. KNUTH *Stanford University*

Illustrations by
DUANE BIBBY

**ADDISON WESLEY
PUBLISHING COMPANY**

Reading, Massachusetts
Menlo Park, California
Don Mills, Ontario
Wokingham, England
Amsterdam · Mexico City
San Juan · Bogotá · Sydney
Santiago · Singapore · Tokyo

TEX is a trademark of the American Mathematical Society.

METAFONT is a trademark of Addison Wesley Publishing Company.

The program for TEX is in the public domain, and readers may freely incorporate the algorithms of this book into their own programs. However, use of the name 'TEX' is restricted to software systems that agree exactly with the program presented here.

Library of Congress Cataloging-in-Publication Data

```
Knuth, Donald Ervin, 1938-
   TeX : The program.

   (Computers & Typesetting ; B)
   Includes index.
   1. TeX (Computer system).  2. Computerized
typesetting.  3. Mathematics printing.  I. Title.
II. Series: Knuth, Donald Ervin, 1938-
Computers & typesetting ; B.
Z253.4.T47K578  1986        686.2'25544        86-1232
ISBN 0-201-13437-3
```

ISBN 0-201-13437-3
BCDEFGHIJ-HA-89876

To David R. Fuchs:
Who fixed everything

Preface

G ENUINE EXAMPLES of large software programs are rarely found in books; yet students of computer science will get a warped perspective of the subject if they experience only "toy programs" of textbook proportions. I hope that the program for TeX, which occupies the bulk of this volume, will therefore prove to be an instructive case study.

My goal in this work has been to write a computer program of which a professor of computer science might be proud, in spite of the fact that it meets real-world constraints and compromises. I have tried to explain thousands of details as well as possible, using the best documentation tools available. Since I have learned much in the past from reading other people's programs, I have also tried to make my own program sufficiently stimulating that it might give a bit of pleasure to its readers. There aren't many jokes, but several of the algorithms are amusing and/or amazing.

I believe that the final bug in TeX was discovered and removed on November 27, 1985. But if, somehow, an error still lurks in the code, I shall gladly pay a finder's fee of $20.48 to the first person who discovers it. (This is twice the previous amount, and I plan to double it again in a year; you see, I really am confident!)

The number of people who have voluntarily helped me get TeX into its present state is almost incredible; nearly everyone I know has made vital contributions, so I can't possibly list the names of everybody I wish to thank. On the other hand there is one person whose continuing support has been indispensible, and he deserves a special acknowledgment: David R. Fuchs has truly been my "right-hand man" as a partner in the TeX project for many years. I would also like to thank the National Science Foundation and the System Development Foundation for their generous support of this research over many years.

Boston, Massachusetts   — D. E. K.
December 1985

Supplementary Bibliography

Readers who want to pursue TeX further may find a number of additional documents helpful. A complete bibliography of relevant literature would be extremely long; therefore this list has been limited to publications of the TeX project at Stanford University. Further information can be found in *TUGboat* (the journal of the TeX Users Group, published since 1980), and in the papers cited in the bibliographies of the papers cited here.

- "Mathematical Typography" by Donald E. Knuth, *Bulletin of the American Mathematical Society* (new series) **1** (March 1979), 337–372. [Reprinted as part 1 of *TeX and METAFONT: New Directions in Typesetting* (Providence, R.I.: American Mathematical Society, and Bedford, Mass.: Digital Press, 1979).] *Discusses the author's motivation for starting to work on TeX, and traces the early history of computer typesetting.*

- "Tau Epsilon Chi, a system for technical text" by Donald E. Knuth, Stanford Computer Science Report 675 (Stanford, California, September 1978), 198 pp. [Reprinted as part 2 of *TeX and METAFONT*, the book cited above.] *The first user manual. Describes the TeX78 system, which is now obsolete but possibly of interest to historians.*

- The TeXbook by Donald E. Knuth (Reading, Mass.: Addison Wesley, 1984), x+483 pp. [The third printing, 1986, is also published as *Computers and Typesetting*, Volume A.] *The definitive user manual; a prerequisite for reading the program in the present book. Includes numerous examples, exercises, lies, and jokes.*

- "The WEB system of structured documentation" by Donald E. Knuth, Stanford Computer Science Report 980 (Stanford, California, September 1983), 206 pp. *A ten-page user manual for WEB, followed by complete programs for WEB in its own language. Also includes instructions for installation of TeX, given the file TeX.WEB.*

- "Literate programming" by Donald E. Knuth, *The Computer Journal* **27** (1984), 97–111. *An expository introduction to WEB and its underlying philosophy.*

- "A torture test for TeX" by Donald E. Knuth, Stanford Computer Science Report 1027 (Stanford, California, November 1984), 142 pp. *The TRIP test suite; defines the criteria by which a program can qualify to use the name 'TeX'.*

- "TeXware" by Donald E. Knuth and David R. Fuchs, Stanford Computer Science Report (to appear). *The WEB programs for four utility programs that are often used with TEX:* `POOLtype, TFtoPL, PLtoTF, and DVItype.`

■ "Breaking paragraphs into lines" by Michael F. Plass and Donald E. Knuth, *Software—Practice and Experience* **11** (1981), 1119–1184. *Develops the theory underlying TEX's line-breaking algorithm and applies it to a variety of practical problems; includes an illustrated history of line-breaking techniques in the printing industry. An appendix discusses a simplified algorithm suitable for word processors.*

■ "Choosing better line breaks" by Michael F. Plass and Donald E. Knuth, in *Document Preparation Systems*, Nievergelt et al., eds. (Amsterdam: North-Holland, 1982), 221–242. *A shorter version of the preceding paper. Introduces the notion of a "kerf," which unifies and generalizes TEX's primitive operations of glue, penalties, and discretionary breaks.*

■ "Optimal pagination techniques for automatic typesetting systems" by Michael Frederick Plass, Stanford Computer Science report 870 (Stanford, California, June 1981), vi+72 pp. *This Ph.D. dissertation extends TEX's line-breaking algorithm to page breaking, and proves that certain more complex extensions would be computationally intractable (i.e., NP-complete). The document was produced by a special two-pass extension of TEX78 in which all page breaks were determined by the new method.*

■ "Word hy-phen-a-tion by com-pu-ter" by Franklin Mark Liang, Stanford Computer Science report 977 (Stanford, California, August 1983), v+85 pp. *This Ph.D. dissertation introduces TEX's hyphenation algorithm and the underlying data structures. It includes a history of previous approaches and a method of preparing hyphenation patterns from a given dictionary.*

■ "How to run TEX in French" by Jacques Désarménien, Stanford Computer Science report 1013 (Stanford, California, August 1984), 42 pp; partially reprinted in *TUGboat* **5**,2 (November 1984), 91–108. *Presents macros and hyphenation tables that adapt TEX to* la mode de Paris.

■ "TEX incunabula" by Donald E. Knuth, *TUGboat* **5**, 1 (May 1984), 4–11. *A record of the first publications that were produced with TEX.*

■ "The errors of TEX" by Donald E. Knuth, *Software—Practice and Experience*, to appear. *An analysis of what the author learned while implementing and maintaining TEX; tabulates and classifies every bug that was discovered and every improvement that was made during eight years of development.*

How to Read a Web

The program in this book was prepared with the WEB system of structured documentation. A WEB program is a Pascal program that has been cut up into pieces and rearranged into an order that is easier for a human being to understand. A Pascal program is a WEB program that has been rearranged into an order that is easier for a computer to understand.

In other words, WEB programs and Pascal programs are essentially the same kinds of things, but their parts are arranged differently. You should be able to understand a Pascal program better when you see it in its WEB form, if the author of the WEB form has chosen a good order of presentation.

Before you try to read a WEB program, you should be familiar with the Pascal language. The following paragraphs describe how a WEB document can be mechanically translated into Pascal code. Thus, the WEB form serves as a high-level description that can be converted to ordinary Pascal by a preprocessing routine. The preprocessor expands macros and does a few other things that compensate for Pascal's limitations; although Pascal was not originally designed to be a language for system programming, WEB enriches it so that production software can be constructed and documented in a pleasant way.

A WEB program consists of numbered sections: First comes §1, then §2, and so on. Each section is intended to be small enough that it can be understood by itself, and the WEB format indicates how each section relates to other sections. In this way, an entire program can be regarded as a web or network, consisting of little pieces and interconnections between pieces. The complex whole can be understood by understanding each simple part and by understanding the simple relationships between neighboring parts.

Large software programs are inherently complex, and there is no "royal road" to instant comprehension of their subtle features. But if you read a well-written WEB program one section at a time, starting with §1, you will find that its ideas are not difficult to assimilate.

Every section of a WEB program begins with commentary about the purpose of that section, or about some noteworthy feature of that part of the program; such comments are in English, and informality is the rule. Then the section concludes with a formal part that is expressed in Pascal language; this is what actually counts, and you should be able to convince yourself that the formal Pascal code actually does what the informal comments imply.

Between the introductory comments and the Pascal code, there may also be one or more macro definitions, which are explained below. Thus, each section has three parts:

- informal commentary;
- macro definitions;
- Pascal code;

and these three parts always occur in the stated order. In practice, the individual parts are sometimes empty: Some sections have no opening comments, some have no macro definitions, and some have no Pascal code.

Every section is either *named* or *unnamed*. The Pascal code in a named section begins with '⟨ Name of section ⟩ ≡' in angle brackets, and the section name is followed by its so-called replacement text. For example, the Pascal code in §23 might be

$$\langle \text{Clear the arrays } 23 \rangle \equiv$$
$$\textbf{for } k \leftarrow 1 \textbf{ to } n \textbf{ do}$$
$$\qquad \textbf{begin } a[k] \leftarrow 0; \quad b[k] \leftarrow 0;$$
$$\qquad \textbf{end}$$

and this means that the section name is 'Clear the arrays' while the replacement text is 'FOR K:=1 TO N DO BEGIN A[K]:=0; B[K]:=0;END'.

This example illustrates the fact that WEB descriptions of replacement texts are formatted in a special way, intended to make the Pascal code easy to read. For example, lowercase letters are used instead of uppercase; reserved words like '**begin**' are set in boldface type, while identifiers like 'k' are set in italics. Program structure is shown by indentation. A few special symbols are also used to enhance readability:

'$\leftarrow$'	stands for	':=';
'$\leq$'	stands for	'<=';
'$\geq$'	stands for	'>=';
'$\neq$'	stands for	'<>';
'$\wedge$'	stands for	'AND';
'$\vee$'	stands for	'OR';
'$\neg$'	stands for	'NOT';
'$\in$'	stands for	'IN';
'$5 \cdot 10^{20}$'	stands for	'5E20'.

When the name of a section appears in another section, it stands for the corresponding replacement text. For example, suppose the Pascal code for §20 is

$$\langle \text{Initialize the data structures } 20 \rangle \equiv$$
$$sum \leftarrow 0; \ \langle \text{Clear the arrays } 23 \rangle;$$

this means that the replacement text for 'Clear the arrays' should be inserted as part of the replacement text for 'Initialize the data structures'. The name of a section generally provides a short summary of what that section does; therefore the full details won't distract your attention unless you need to know them. But if you do need further details, the subscript '23' in '$\langle$ Clear the arrays 23 $\rangle$' makes it easy for you to locate the subsidiary replacement text. Incidentally, §23 in our example will contain a footnote that says 'This code is used in section 20'; thus you can move easily from a replacement text to its context or vice versa.

The process of converting a WEB program to a Pascal program is quite simple, at least conceptually: First you put together all the Pascal code that appears in *unnamed* sections, preserving the relative order. Then you substitute the replacement texts for all macros and named sections that appear in the resulting code; and you continue to do this until only pure Pascal remains.

It's possible to give the same name to several different sections. Continuing our example, let's suppose that the Pascal code of §30 is

$$\langle \text{Initialize the data structures } 20 \rangle \ +\equiv$$
$$reset(source\_file);$$

The '$+\equiv$' here indicates that the name 'Initialize the data structures' has appeared before; the Pascal code following '$+\equiv$' will be *appended* to the previous replacement text for that name. Thus, if 'Initialize the data structures' is defined only in §20 and §30, the actual replacement text for $\langle$ Initialize the data structures 20 $\rangle$ will be

$$sum \leftarrow 0; \ \langle \text{Clear the arrays } 23 \rangle; \ reset(source\_file);$$

Section 20 will also contain a footnote: 'See also section 30'.

Incidentally, the identifier '*source_file*' in this example contains an *underline* symbol; but its Pascal equivalent is just 'SOURCEFILE', because Pascal doesn't allow underlines to appear in names. When you're reading a WEB program, you might as well imagine that the underlines are really present, since they make the program more readable; but you should realize that '*write_ln*' is the same as Pascal's 'WRITELN'.

Macros in WEB are introduced by the keyword '**define**', and they act rather like section names but on a smaller scale. For example, the definitions

> **define** *exit* $\equiv$ 10   { go here to leave a procedure }
> **define** *return* $\equiv$ **goto** *exit*   { terminate a procedure call }

say that the identifier '*return*' should be replaced by 'GOTO 10' when it appears in Pascal code. A macro might also have a parameter, denoted by '#'; for example, after

> **define** *print_ln* (#) $\equiv$ *write_ln* (*print_file*, #)

the preprocessor will expand a text like '*print_ln*('Hello.')' into

> WRITELN(PRINTFILE,'Hello.')

Macros with parameters must be followed by an argument in parentheses whenever they are used; this argument is substituted for all #'s in the right-hand side of the macro definition.

WEB also has *numeric macros*, which are defined with an '=' sign instead of '$\equiv$'. For example, definitions like

> **define** *buf_size* = 80
> **define** *double_buf_size* = *buf_size* + *buf_size*

associate numbers with identifiers; the numbers are substituted for later appearances of the identifiers in subsequent Pascal texts. The preprocessor also adds and subtracts adjacent numbers before generating Pascal code; for example, '**array** [0 .. *double_buf_size* − 1] **of** *char*' will become 'ARRAY[0..159]OF CHAR' after the definitions above.

Hundreds of identifiers generally appear in a long program, and it's hard to keep them straight. Therefore the WEB system provides a comprehensive index that lists all sections where a given identifier appears. Entries in the index are underlined if the identifier was defined in the corresponding section. Furthermore, the right-hand pages of this book contain mini-indexes that will make it unnecessary for you to look at the big index very often. Every identifier that is used somewhere on a pair of facing pages is listed in a footnote on the right-hand page, unless it is explicitly defined or declared somewhere on the left-hand or right-hand page you are reading. These footnote entries tell you whether the identifier is a procedure or a macro or a boolean, etc.

Constants in a `WEB` program might be specified in octal or hexadecimal notation; the preprocessor will convert them into decimal form as required by Pascal. An octal constant starts with a single prime symbol followed by digits in italics; a hexadecimal constant starts with a double prime symbol followed by digits in typewriter type. For example, ´*10000* and ˝`1000` both represent the number 2^{12}, which is 4096 in decimal notation.

Alphabetic constants for ASCII codes can be represented in `WEB` programs by double-quoted strings of length 1. For example, `"A"` stands for 65 and `"a"` stands for 97. Double-quoted strings of other lengths are also permitted; the preprocessor converts these into numeric constants that are 128 or more. This makes it possible to circumvent Pascal's limited string-manipulation capabilities.

OK! You know enough now about `WEB` conventions to understand 99% of the program in this book. Just a few more rules are needed to make the system work in practice and to make your knowledge 100% complete. These remaining technicalities are given here in fine print so that you can come back to them if necessary; but you should really turn now to the program and start reading it first, so that you can see how natural the `WEB` format turns out to be. Then you'll find it easy to understand the few nitty-gritty details that remain.

Detail #1, forced comments. Comments that appear in braces within Pascal code are not included in the Pascal program output by the preprocessor. But the special symbols `@{` and `@}` stand for braces that do get through to the Pascal program. This makes it possible to "comment out" certain code that is not necessary in a production system, using `WEB`'s primitive macro capabilities.

Detail #2, verbatim text. A string of symbols that's enclosed in a box, e.g., ' verbatim ', is included in the Pascal program without any preprocessing.

Detail #3, concatenation. Two consecutive identifiers or constants are usually separated by spaces in the Pascal program. This space is suppressed if the symbol `@&` appears between them in the `WEB` program.

Detail #4, the string pool. The preprocessor creates a file that lists all the double-quoted strings of length $\neq 1$, so that the program can manipulate these strings. This file contains one line per string, starting with string number 128, then number 129, and so on. Each line begins with a two-digit number **nn**, which is followed by **nn** characters for the string in question. After the final string, the file ends with a special line containing an asterisk in the first column, followed by a nine-digit "check sum." For example, suppose that the **WEB** program uses only two special strings, namely "" (the empty string) and "This longer string". Then the pool file will contain a total of three lines,

```
00
18This longer string
*519788345
```

In this case, occurrences of "" in the **WEB** program will be replaced by 128; occurrences of "This longer string" will be replaced by 129. The symbol @$ stands for the numeric value of the check sum (in this case 519788345); a program can test if it has read the correct string pool by comparing the file's check sum with @$.

Detail #5, format changes. The macro-definition part of a **WEB** section might contain '**format**' specifications mixed in with the instructions that '**define**' macros. Format specs have no affect on the corresponding Pascal program, but they do influence the appearance of the **WEB** program. For example, the specification

format *return* $\equiv$ *nil*

means that the identifier '*return*' should get the same typographic treatment as Pascal's reserved word '**nil**'. Therefore we will henceforth see '**return**' in boldface type, even though it is not a reserved word of Pascal. Format specifications are appropriate for macros that don't behave as ordinary variables in the Pascal program.

Contents

The Program

1.   Introduction.   This is TEX, a document compiler intended to produce typesetting of high quality. The Pascal program that follows is the definition of TEX82, a standard version of TEX that is designed to be highly portable so that identical output will be obtainable on a great variety of computers.

The main purpose of the following program is to explain the algorithms of TEX as clearly as possible. As a result, the program will not necessarily be very efficient when a particular Pascal compiler has translated it into a particular machine language. However, the program has been written so that it can be tuned to run efficiently in a wide variety of operating environments by making comparatively few changes. Such flexibility is possible because the documentation that follows is written in the `WEB` language, which is at a higher level than Pascal; the preprocessing step that converts `WEB` to Pascal is able to introduce most of the necessary refinements. Semi-automatic translation to other languages is also feasible, because the program below does not make extensive use of features that are peculiar to Pascal.

A large piece of software like TEX has inherent complexity that cannot be reduced below a certain level of difficulty, although each individual part is fairly simple by itself. The `WEB` language is intended to make the algorithms as readable as possible, by reflecting the way the individual program pieces fit together and by providing the cross-references that connect different parts. Detailed comments about what is going on, and about why things were done in certain ways, have been liberally sprinkled throughout the program. These comments explain features of the implementation, but they rarely attempt to explain the TEX language itself, since the reader is supposed to be familiar with *The TEXbook*.

2. The present implementation has a long ancestry, beginning in the summer of 1977, when Michael F. Plass and Frank M. Liang designed and coded a prototype based on some specifications that the author had made in May of that year. This original protoTEX included macro definitions and elementary manipulations on boxes and glue, but it did not have line-breaking, page-breaking, mathematical formulas, alignment routines, error recovery, or the present semantic nest; furthermore, it used character lists instead of token lists, so that a control sequence like \halign was represented by a list of seven characters. A complete version of TEX was designed and coded by the author in late 1977 and early 1978; that program, like its prototype, was written in the SAIL language, for which an excellent debugging system was available. Preliminary plans to convert the SAIL code into a form somewhat like the present "web" were developed by Luis Trabb Pardo and the author at the beginning of 1979, and a complete implementation was created by Ignacio A. Zabala in 1979 and 1980. The TEX82 program, which was written by the author during the latter part of 1981 and the early part of 1982, also incorporates ideas from the 1979 implementation of TEX in MESA that was written by Leonidas Guibas, Robert Sedgewick, and Douglas Wyatt at the Xerox Palo Alto Research Center. Several hundred refinements were introduced into TEX82 based on the experiences gained with the original implementations, so that essentially every part of the system has been substantially improved. After the appearance of "Version 0" in September 1982, this program benefited greatly from the comments of many other people, notably David R. Fuchs and Howard W. Trickey.

No doubt there still is plenty of room for improvement, but the author is firmly committed to keeping TEX82 "frozen" from now on; stability and reliability are to be its main virtues.

On the other hand, the WEB description can be extended without changing the core of TEX82 itself, and the program has been designed so that such extensions are not extremely difficult to make. The *banner* string defined here should be changed whenever TEX undergoes any modifications, so that it will be clear which version of TEX might be the guilty party when a problem arises.

If this program is changed, the resulting system should not be called 'TEX'; the official name 'TEX' by itself is reserved for software systems that are fully compatible with each other. A special test suite called the "TRIP test" is available for helping to determine whether a particular implementation deserves to be known as 'TEX' [cf. Stanford Computer Science report CS1027, November 1984].

define *banner* ≡ ´This␣is␣TeX,␣Version␣2.0´   { printed when TEX starts }

3. Different Pascals have slightly different conventions, and the present program expresses TEX in terms of the Pascal that was available to the author in 1982. Constructions that apply to this particular compiler, which we shall call Pascal-H, should help the reader to see how to make an appropriate interface for other systems if necessary. (Pascal-H is Charles Hedrick's modification of a compiler for the DECsystem-10 that was originally developed at the University of Hamburg; cf. *SOFTWARE—Practice & Experience* **6** (1976), 29–42. The TEX program below is intended to be adaptable, without extensive changes, to most other versions of Pascal, so it does not fully use the admirable features of Pascal-H. Indeed, a conscious effort has been made here to avoid using several idiosyncratic features of standard Pascal itself, so that most of the code can be translated mechanically into other high-level languages. For example, the '**with**' and '*new*' features are not used, nor are pointer types, set types, or enumerated scalar types; there are no '**var**' parameters, except in the case of files; there are no tag fields on variant records; there are no assignments *real* ← *integer*; no procedures are declared local to other procedures.)

The portions of this program that involve system-dependent code, where changes might be necessary because of differences between Pascal compilers and/or differences between operating systems, can be identified by looking at the sections whose numbers are listed under 'system dependencies' in the index. Furthermore, the index entries for 'dirty Pascal' list all places where the restrictions of Pascal have not been followed perfectly, for one reason or another.

4. The program begins with a normal Pascal program heading, whose components will be filled in later, using the conventions of WEB. For example, the portion of the program called '⟨ Global variables 13 ⟩' below will be replaced by a sequence of variable declarations that starts in §13 of this documentation. In this way, we are able to define each individual global variable when we are prepared to understand what it means; we do not have to define all of the globals at once. Cross references in §13, where it says "See also sections 20, 26, . . . ," also make it possible to look at the set of all global variables, if desired. Similar remarks apply to the other portions of the program heading.

Actually the heading shown here is not quite normal: The **program** line does not mention any *output* file, because Pascal-H would ask the TEX user to specify a file name if *output* were specified here.

> **define** *mtype* ≡ *t@&y@&p@&e*   { this is a WEB coding trick: }
> **format** *mtype* ≡ *type*   { 'mtype' will be equivalent to 'type' }
> **format** *type* ≡ *true*   { but '*type*' will not be treated as a reserved word }

⟨ Compiler directives 9 ⟩
program *TEX*;   { all file names are defined dynamically }
  label ⟨ Labels in the outer block 6 ⟩
  const ⟨ Constants in the outer block 11 ⟩
  mtype ⟨ Types in the outer block 18 ⟩
  var ⟨ Global variables 13 ⟩
  procedure *initialize*;   { this procedure gets things started properly }
    var ⟨ Local variables for initialization 19 ⟩
    begin ⟨ Initialize whatever TEX might access 8 ⟩
    end;
⟨ Basic printing procedures 57 ⟩
⟨ Error handling procedures 78 ⟩

5. The overall TEX program begins with the heading just shown, after which comes a bunch of procedure declarations and function declarations. Finally we will get to the main program, which begins with the comment '*start_here*'. If you want to skip down to the main program now, you can look up '*start_here*' in the index. But the author suggests that the best way to understand this program is to follow pretty much the order of TEX's components as they appear in the WEB description you are now reading, since the present ordering is intended to combine the advantages of the "bottom up" and "top down" approaches to the problem of understanding a somewhat complicated system.

---

start_here, §1332.

6. Three labels must be declared in the main program, so we give them symbolic names.

define *start_of_TEX* = 1   { go here when TEX's variables are initialized }
define *end_of_TEX* = 9998   { go here to close files and terminate gracefully }
define *final_end* = 9999   { this label marks the ending of the program }

⟨ Labels in the outer block 6 ⟩ ≡
  start_of_TEX, *end_of_TEX*, *final_end*;   { key control points }

This code is used in section 4.

7. Some of the code below is intended to be used only when diagnosing the strange behavior that sometimes occurs when TEX is being installed or when system wizards are fooling around with TEX without quite knowing what they are doing. Such code will not normally be compiled; it is delimited by the codewords '**debug**...**gubed**', with apologies to people who wish to preserve the purity of English.

Similarly, there is some conditional code delimited by '**stat**...**tats**' that is intended for use when statistics are to be kept about TEX's memory usage. The **stat** ... **tats** code also implements diagnostic information for \tracingparagraphs and \tracingpages.

define *debug* ≡ @{   { change this to '*debug* ≡ ' when debugging }
define *gubed* ≡ @}   { change this to '*gubed* ≡ ' when debugging }
format *debug* ≡ *begin*
format *gubed* ≡ *end*

define *stat* ≡ @{   { change this to '*stat* ≡ ' when gathering usage statistics }
define *tats* ≡ @}   { change this to '*tats* ≡ ' when gathering usage statistics }
format *stat* ≡ *begin*
format *tats* ≡ *end*

8. This program has two important variations: (1) There is a long and slow version called INITEX, which does the extra calculations needed to initialize TEX's internal tables; and (2) there is a shorter and faster production version, which cuts the initialization to a bare minimum. Parts of the program that are needed in (1) but not in (2) are delimited by the codewords '**init**...**tini**'.

define *init* ≡   { change this to '*init* ≡ @{' in the production version }
define *tini* ≡   { change this to '*tini* ≡ @}' in the production version }
format *init* ≡ *begin*
format *tini* ≡ *end*

⟨ Initialize whatever TEX might access 8 ⟩ ≡
  ⟨ Set initial values of key variables 21 ⟩
  init ⟨ Initialize table entries (done by INITEX only) 164 ⟩ **tini**

This code is used in section 4.

9.   If the first character of a Pascal comment is a dollar sign, Pascal-H treats the comment as a list of "compiler directives" that will affect the translation of this program into machine language. The directives shown below specify full checking and inclusion of the Pascal debugger when TeX is being debugged, but they cause range checking and other redundant code to be eliminated when the production system is being generated. Arithmetic overflow will be detected in all cases.

⟨ Compiler directives 9 ⟩ ≡
  @{@&$C−, A+, D−@}   { no range check, catch arithmetic overflow, no debug overhead }
  debug @{@&$C+, D+@} **gubed**   { but turn everything on when debugging }

This code is used in section 4.

10.   This TeX implementation conforms to the rules of the *Pascal User Manual* published by Jensen and Wirth in 1975, except where system-dependent code is necessary to make a useful system program, and except in another respect where such conformity would unnecessarily obscure the meaning and clutter up the code: We assume that **case** statements may include a default case that applies if no matching label is found. Thus, we shall use constructions like

> **case** x **of**
> 1: ⟨ code for $x = 1$ ⟩;
> 3: ⟨ code for $x = 3$ ⟩;
> **othercases** ⟨ code for $x \neq 1$ and $x \neq 3$ ⟩
> **endcases**

since most Pascal compilers have plugged this hole in the language by incorporating some sort of default mechanism. For example, the Pascal-H compiler allows '*others:*' as a default label, and other Pascals allow syntaxes like '**else**' or '**otherwise**' or '*otherwise:*', etc. The definitions of **othercases** and **endcases** should be changed to agree with local conventions. Note that no semicolon appears before **endcases** in this program, so the definition of **endcases** should include a semicolon if the compiler wants one. (Of course, if no default mechanism is available, the **case** statements of TeX will have to be laboriously extended by listing all remaining cases. People who are stuck with such Pascals have, in fact, done this, successfully but not happily!)

  define *othercases* ≡ *others*:   { default for cases not listed explicitly }
  define *endcases* ≡ **end**   { follows the default case in an extended **case** statement }
  format *othercases* ≡ *else*
  format *endcases* ≡ *end*

11. The following parameters can be changed at compile time to extend or reduce TeX's capacity. They may have different values in INITEX and in production versions of TeX.

⟨ Constants in the outer block 11 ⟩ ≡

$mem\_max = 30000$; { greatest index in TeX's internal mem array; must be strictly less than $max\_halfword$; must be equal to mem_top in INITEX, otherwise $\geq mem\_top$ }

$mem\_min = 0$; { smallest index in TeX's internal mem array; must be $min\_halfword$ or more; must be equal to mem_bot in INITEX, otherwise $\leq mem\_bot$ }

$buf\_size = 500$; { maximum number of characters simultaneously present in current lines of open files and in control sequences between \csname and \endcsname; must not exceed $max\_halfword$ }

$error\_line = 72$; { width of context lines on terminal error messages }

$half\_error\_line = 42$; { width of first lines of contexts in terminal error messages; should be between 30 and $error\_line - 15$ }

$max\_print\_line = 79$; { width of longest text lines output; should be at least 60 }

$stack\_size = 200$; { maximum number of simultaneous input sources }

$max\_in\_open = 6$;
{ maximum number of input files and error insertions that can be going on simultaneously }

$font\_max = 75$; { maximum internal font number; must not exceed $max\_quarterword$ and must be at most $font\_base + 256$ }

$font\_mem\_size = 20000$; { number of words of $font\_info$ for all fonts }

$param\_size = 60$; { maximum number of simultaneous macro parameters }

$nest\_size = 40$; { maximum number of semantic levels simultaneously active }

$max\_strings = 3000$; { maximum number of strings; must not exceed $max\_halfword$ }

$string\_vacancies = 8000$; { the minimum number of characters that should be available for the user's control sequences and font names, after TeX's own error messages are stored }

$pool\_size = 32000$; { maximum number of characters in strings, including all error messages and help texts, and the names of all fonts and control sequences; must exceed $string\_vacancies$ by the total length of TeX's own strings, which is currently about 23000 }

$save\_size = 600$; { space for saving values outside of current group; must be at most $max\_halfword$ }

$trie\_size = 8000$; { space for hyphenation patterns; should be larger for INITEX than it is in production versions of TeX }

$dvi\_buf\_size = 800$; { size of the output buffer; must be a multiple of 8 }

$file\_name\_size = 40$; { file names shouldn't be longer than this }

$pool_name = $ ´TeXformats:TEX.POOL␣␣␣␣␣␣␣␣␣␣␣␣␣␣␣␣␣␣␣␣␣␣␣␣´;
{ string of length $file\_name\_size$; tells where the string pool appears }

This code is used in section 4.

12. Like the preceding parameters, the following quantities can be changed at compile time to extend or reduce TeX's capacity. But if they are changed, it is necessary to rerun the initialization program INITEX to generate new tables for the production TeX program. One can't simply make helter-skelter changes to the following constants, since certain rather complex initialization numbers are computed from them. They are defined here using WEB macros, instead of being put into Pascal's **const** list, in order to emphasize this distinction.

define $mem\_bot = 0$
{ smallest index in the mem array dumped by INITEX; must not be less than mem_min }

define $mem\_top \equiv 30000$
{ largest index in the mem array dumped by INITEX; must be substantially larger than mem_bot and not greater than mem_max }

define *font_base* = 0   { smallest internal font number; must not be less than *min_quarterword* }
define *hash_size* = 2100   { maximum number of control sequences; it should be at most about
            (*mem_max* − *mem_min*)/10, but 2100 is already quite generous }
define *hash_prime* = 1777   { a prime number equal to about 85% of *hash_size* }
define *hyph_size* = 307   { another prime; the number of \hyphenation exceptions }

13.   In case somebody has inadvertently made bad settings of the "constants," TEX checks them
using a global variable called *bad*.

This is the first of many sections of TEX where global variables are defined.

⟨ Global variables 13 ⟩ ≡
bad: *integer*;   { is some "constant" wrong? }

See also sections 20, 26, 30, 32, 39, 50, 54, 73, 76, 79, 96, 104, 115, 116, 117, 118, 124, 165, 173, 181, 213, 246,
    253, 256, 271, 286, 297, 301, 304, 305, 308, 309, 310, 333, 361, 382, 387, 388, 410, 438, 447, 480, 489, 493,
    512, 513, 520, 527, 532, 539, 549, 550, 555, 592, 595, 605, 616, 646, 647, 661, 684, 719, 724, 764, 770, 814,
    821, 823, 825, 828, 833, 839, 847, 872, 892, 900, 905, 921, 926, 943, 945, 946, 950, 971, 980, 982, 989, 1074,
    1266, 1281, 1299, 1305, 1331, 1342, and 1345.

This code is used in section 4.

14.   Later on we will say 'if *mem_max* ≥ *max_halfword* **then** *bad* ← 14', or something similar.
(We can't do that until *max_halfword* has been defined.)

⟨ Check the "constant" values for consistency 14 ⟩ ≡
    bad ← 0;
    if (*half_error_line* < 30) ∨ (*half_error_line* > *error_line* − 15) **then** *bad* ← 1;
    if *max_print_line* < 60 **then** *bad* ← 2;
    if *dvi_buf_size* **mod** 8 ≠ 0 **then** *bad* ← 3;
    if *mem_bot* + 1100 > *mem_top* **then** *bad* ← 4;
    if *hash_prime* > *hash_size* **then** *bad* ← 5;

See also sections 111, 290, 522, and 1249.

This code is used in section 1332.

---

font_info: **array**, §549.   *max_quarterword* = 255, §110.   *min_halfword* = macro, §110.
max_halfword = macro, §110.   *mem*: **array**, §116.   *min_quarterword* = 0, §110.

15. Labels are given symbolic names by the following definitions, so that occasional **goto** statements will be meaningful. We insert the label '*exit:*' just before the '**end**' of a procedure in which we have used the '**return**' statement defined below; the label '*restart*' is occasionally used at the very beginning of a procedure; and the label '*reswitch*' is occasionally used just prior to a **case** statement in which some cases change the conditions and we wish to branch to the newly applicable case. Loops that are set up with the **loop** construction defined below are commonly exited by going to '*done*' or to '*found*' or to '*not_found*', and they are sometimes repeated by going to '*continue*'. If two or more parts of a subroutine start differently but end up the same, the shared code may be gathered together at '*common_ending*'.

Incidentally, this program never declares a label that isn't actually used, because some fussy Pascal compilers will complain about redundant labels.

define *exit* = 10   { go here to leave a procedure }
define *restart* = 20   { go here to start a procedure again }
define *reswitch* = 21   { go here to start a case statement again }
define *continue* = 22   { go here to resume a loop }
define *done* = 30   { go here to exit a loop }
define *done1* = 31   { like *done*, when there is more than one loop }
define *done2* = 32   { for exiting the second loop in a long block }
define *done3* = 33   { for exiting the third loop in a very long block }
define *done4* = 34   { for exiting the fourth loop in an extremely long block }
define *done5* = 35   { for exiting the fifth loop in an immense block }
define *done6* = 36   { for exiting the sixth loop in a block }
define *found* = 40   { go here when you've found it }
define *found1* = 41   { like *found*, when there's more than one per routine }
define *found2* = 42   { like *found*, when there's more than two per routine }
define *not_found* = 45   { go here when you've found nothing }
define *common_ending* = 50   { go here when you want to merge with another branch }

16. Here are some macros for common programming idioms.

define $incr(\texttt{\#}) \equiv \texttt{\#} \leftarrow \texttt{\#} + 1$ { increase a variable by unity }
define $decr(\texttt{\#}) \equiv \texttt{\#} \leftarrow \texttt{\#} - 1$ { decrease a variable by unity }
define $negate(\texttt{\#}) \equiv \texttt{\#} \leftarrow -\texttt{\#}$ { change the sign of a variable }
define *loop* ≡ **while** *true* **do**   { repeat over and over until a **goto** happens }
format *loop* ≡ *xclause*   { WEB's **xclause** acts like '**while** *true* **do**' }
define *do_nothing* ≡   { empty statement }
define *return* ≡ **goto** *exit*   { terminate a procedure call }
format *return* ≡ *nil*
define *empty* = 0   { symbolic name for a null constant }

17.   The character set.   In order to make TeX readily portable to a wide variety of computers, all of its input text is converted to an internal seven-bit code that is essentially standard ASCII, the "American Standard Code for Information Interchange." This conversion is done immediately when each character is read in. Conversely, characters are converted from ASCII to the user's external representation just before they are output to a text file.

Such an internal code is relevant to users of TeX primarily because it governs the positions of characters in the fonts. For example, the character 'A' has ASCII code $65 = \,'101$, and when TeX typesets this letter it specifies character number 65 in the current font. If that font actually has 'A' in a different position, TeX doesn't know what the real position is; the program that does the actual printing from TeX's device-independent files is responsible for converting from ASCII to a particular font encoding.

TeX's internal code also defines the value of constants that begin with a reverse apostrophe; and it provides an index to the \catcode, \mathcode, \uccode, \lccode, and \delcode tables.

18.   Characters of text that have been converted to TeX's internal form are said to be of type *ASCII_code*, which is a subrange of the integers.

⟨ Types in the outer block 18 ⟩ ≡
    ASCII_code = 0 . . 127;   { seven-bit numbers }

See also sections 25, 38, 101, 109, 113, 150, 212, 269, 300, 548, 594, 920, and 925.

This code is used in section 4.

19.   The original Pascal compiler was designed in the late 60s, when six-bit character sets were common, so it did not make provision for lowercase letters. Nowadays, of course, we need to deal with both capital and small letters in a convenient way, especially in a program for typesetting; so the present specification of TeX has been written under the assumption that the Pascal compiler and run-time system permit the use of text files with more than 64 distinguishable characters. More precisely, we assume that the character set contains at least the letters and symbols associated with ASCII codes $\,'40$ through $\,'176$; all of these characters are now available on most computer terminals.

Since we are dealing with more characters than were present in the first Pascal compilers, we have to decide what to call the associated data type. Some Pascals use the original name *char* for the characters in text files, even though there now are more than 64 such characters, while other Pascals consider *char* to be a 64-element subrange of a larger data type that has some other name.

In order to accommodate this difference, we shall use the name *text_char* to stand for the data type of the characters that are converted to and from *ASCII_code* when they are input and output. We shall also assume that *text_char* consists of the elements $chr(first\_text\_char)$ through $chr(last\_text\_char)$, inclusive. The following definitions should be adjusted if necessary.

    define *text_char* ≡ *char*   { the data type of characters in text files }
    define *first_text_char* = 0   { ordinal number of the smallest element of *text_char* }
    define *last_text_char* = 127   { ordinal number of the largest element of *text_char* }

⟨ Local variables for initialization 19 ⟩ ≡
i: 0 . . *last_text_char*;

See also sections 163 and 927.

This code is used in section 4.

20. The TEX processor converts between ASCII code and the user's external character set by means of arrays *xord* and *xchr* that are analogous to Pascal's *ord* and *chr* functions.

⟨ Global variables 13 ⟩ +≡
xord: **array** [*text_char*] **of** *ASCII_code*;   { specifies conversion of input characters }
xchr: **array** [*ASCII_code*] **of** *text_char*;   { specifies conversion of output characters }

21. Since we are assuming that our Pascal system is able to read and write the visible characters of standard ASCII (although not necessarily using the ASCII codes to represent them), the following assignment statements initialize most of the *xchr* array properly, without needing any system-dependent changes. On the other hand, it is possible to implement TEX with less complete character sets, and in such cases it will be necessary to change something here.

⟨ Set initial values of key variables 21 ⟩ ≡
  xchr[´40] ← ´␣´; *xchr*[´41] ← ´!´; *xchr*[´42] ← ´"´; *xchr*[´43] ← ´#´; *xchr*[´44] ← ´$´;
  xchr[´45] ← ´%´; *xchr*[´46] ← ´&´; *xchr*[´47] ← ´´´;
  xchr[´50] ← ´(´; *xchr*[´51] ← ´)´; *xchr*[´52] ← ´*´; *xchr*[´53] ← ´+´; *xchr*[´54] ← ´,´;
  xchr[´55] ← ´-´; *xchr*[´56] ← ´.´; *xchr*[´57] ← ´/´;
  xchr[´60] ← ´0´; *xchr*[´61] ← ´1´; *xchr*[´62] ← ´2´; *xchr*[´63] ← ´3´; *xchr*[´64] ← ´4´;
  xchr[´65] ← ´5´; *xchr*[´66] ← ´6´; *xchr*[´67] ← ´7´;
  xchr[´70] ← ´8´; *xchr*[´71] ← ´9´; *xchr*[´72] ← ´:´; *xchr*[´73] ← ´;´; *xchr*[´74] ← ´<´;
  xchr[´75] ← ´=´; *xchr*[´76] ← ´>´; *xchr*[´77] ← ´?´;
  xchr[´100] ← ´@´; *xchr*[´101] ← ´A´; *xchr*[´102] ← ´B´; *xchr*[´103] ← ´C´; *xchr*[´104] ← ´D´;
  xchr[´105] ← ´E´; *xchr*[´106] ← ´F´; *xchr*[´107] ← ´G´;
  xchr[´110] ← ´H´; *xchr*[´111] ← ´I´; *xchr*[´112] ← ´J´; *xchr*[´113] ← ´K´; *xchr*[´114] ← ´L´;
  xchr[´115] ← ´M´; *xchr*[´116] ← ´N´; *xchr*[´117] ← ´O´;
  xchr[´120] ← ´P´; *xchr*[´121] ← ´Q´; *xchr*[´122] ← ´R´; *xchr*[´123] ← ´S´; *xchr*[´124] ← ´T´;
  xchr[´125] ← ´U´; *xchr*[´126] ← ´V´; *xchr*[´127] ← ´W´;
  xchr[´130] ← ´X´; *xchr*[´131] ← ´Y´; *xchr*[´132] ← ´Z´; *xchr*[´133] ← ´[´; *xchr*[´134] ← ´\´;
  xchr[´135] ← ´]´; *xchr*[´136] ← ´^´; *xchr*[´137] ← ´_´;
  xchr[´140] ← ´`´; *xchr*[´141] ← ´a´; *xchr*[´142] ← ´b´; *xchr*[´143] ← ´c´; *xchr*[´144] ← ´d´;
  xchr[´145] ← ´e´; *xchr*[´146] ← ´f´; *xchr*[´147] ← ´g´;
  xchr[´150] ← ´h´; *xchr*[´151] ← ´i´; *xchr*[´152] ← ´j´; *xchr*[´153] ← ´k´; *xchr*[´154] ← ´l´;
  xchr[´155] ← ´m´; *xchr*[´156] ← ´n´; *xchr*[´157] ← ´o´;
  xchr[´160] ← ´p´; *xchr*[´161] ← ´q´; *xchr*[´162] ← ´r´; *xchr*[´163] ← ´s´; *xchr*[´164] ← ´t´;
  xchr[´165] ← ´u´; *xchr*[´166] ← ´v´; *xchr*[´167] ← ´w´;
  xchr[´170] ← ´x´; *xchr*[´171] ← ´y´; *xchr*[´172] ← ´z´; *xchr*[´173] ← ´{´; *xchr*[´174] ← ´|´;
  xchr[´175] ← ´}´; *xchr*[´176] ← ´~´;
  xchr[0] ← ´␣´; *xchr*[´177] ← ´␣´;   { ASCII codes 0 and ´177 do not appear in text }

See also sections 23, 24, 74, 77, 80, 97, 166, 215, 254, 257, 272, 287, 383, 439, 481, 490, 521, 551, 556, 593, 596, 606, 648, 662, 685, 771, 928, 990, 1267, 1282, 1300, and 1343.

This code is used in section 8.

22. Some of the ASCII codes without visible characters have been given symbolic names in this program because they are used with a special meaning.

  define *null_code* = ´0   { ASCII code that might disappear }
  define *carriage_return* = ´15   { ASCII code used at end of line }
  define *invalid_code* = ´177   { ASCII code that should not appear }

23.   The ASCII code is "standard" only to a certain extent, since many computer installations have found it advantageous to have ready access to more than 94 printing characters. Appendix C of *The TeXbook* gives a complete specification of the intended correspondence between characters and TeX's internal representation.

If TeX is being used on a garden-variety Pascal for which only standard ASCII codes will appear in the input and output files, it doesn't really matter what codes are specified in $xchr[1 \; .. \; '37]$, but the safest policy is to blank everything out by using the code shown below.

However, other settings of $xchr$ will make TeX more friendly on computers that have an extended character set, so that users can type things like '≠' instead of '\ne'. At MIT, for example, it would be more appropriate to substitute the code

$$\textbf{for } i \leftarrow 1 \textbf{ to } '37 \textbf{ do } xchr[i] \leftarrow chr(i);$$

TeX's character set is essentially the same as MIT's, even with respect to characters less than $'40$. People with extended character sets can assign codes arbitrarily, giving an $xchr$ equivalent to whatever characters the users of TeX are allowed to have in their input files. It is best to make the codes correspond to the intended interpretations as shown in Appendix C whenever possible; but this is not necessary. For example, in countries with an alphabet of more than 26 letters, it is usually best to map the additional letters into codes less than $'40$.

⟨ Set initial values of key variables 21 ⟩ +≡
    for $i \leftarrow 1$ **to** $'37$ **do** $xchr[i] \leftarrow \; \hat{} \sqcup \hat{} \, ;$

24.   The following system-independent code makes the $xord$ array contain a suitable inverse to the information in $xchr$. Note that if $xchr[i] = xchr[j]$ where $i < j < '177$, the value of $xord[xchr[i]]$ will turn out to be j or more; hence, standard ASCII code numbers will be used instead of codes below $'40$ in case there is a coincidence.

⟨ Set initial values of key variables 21 ⟩ +≡
    for $i \leftarrow first\_text\_char$ **to** $last\_text\_char$ **do** $xord[chr(i)] \leftarrow invalid\_code;$
    for $i \leftarrow 1$ **to** $'176$ **do** $xord[xchr[i]] \leftarrow i;$

$ASCII\_code = 0 \; .. \; 127, \; \S18.$ $i \colon 0 \; .. \; last\_text\_char, \; \S19.$ $text\_char = \text{macro}, \; \S19.$
$first\_text\_char = 0, \; \S19.$ $last\_text\_char = 127, \; \S19.$

25. Input and output. The bane of portability is the fact that different operating systems treat input and output quite differently, perhaps because computer scientists have not given sufficient attention to this problem. People have felt somehow that input and output are not part of "real" programming. Well, it is true that some kinds of programming are more fun than others. With existing input/output conventions being so diverse and so messy, the only sources of joy in such parts of the code are the rare occasions when one can find a way to make the program a little less bad than it might have been. We have two choices, either to attack I/O now and get it over with, or to postpone it until near the end. Neither prospect is very attractive, so let's get it over with.

The basic operations we need to do are (1) inputting and outputting of text, to or from a file or the user's terminal; (2) inputting and outputting of eight-bit bytes, to or from a file; (3) instructing the operating system to initiate ("open") or to terminate ("close") input or output from a specified file; (4) testing whether the end of an input file has been reached.

TeX needs to deal with two kinds of files. We shall use the term *alpha_file* for a file that contains textual data, and the term *byte_file* for a file that contains eight-bit binary information. These two types turn out to be the same on many computers, but sometimes there is a significant distinction, so we shall be careful to distinguish between them. Standard protocols for transferring such files from computer to computer, via high-speed networks, are now becoming available to more and more communities of users.

The program actually makes use also of a third kind of file, called a *word_file*, when dumping and reloading base information for its own initialization. We shall define a word file later; but it will be possible for us to specify simple operations on word files before they are defined.

⟨ Types in the outer block 18 ⟩ +≡
　　eight_bits = 0 .. 255;　{ unsigned one-byte quantity }
　　alpha_file = **packed file of** *text_char*;　{ files that contain textual data }
　　byte_file = **packed file of** *eight_bits*;　{ files that contain binary data }

26. Most of what we need to do with respect to input and output can be handled by the I/O facilities that are standard in Pascal, i.e., the routines called *get*, *put*, *eof*, and so on. But standard Pascal does not allow file variables to be associated with file names that are determined at run time, so it cannot be used to implement TeX; some sort of extension to Pascal's ordinary *reset* and *rewrite* is crucial for our purposes. We shall assume that *name_of_file* is a variable of an appropriate type such that the Pascal run-time system being used to implement TeX can open a file whose external name is specified by *name_of_file*.

⟨ Global variables 13 ⟩ +≡
name_of_file: **packed array** [1 .. *file_name_size*] **of** *char*;
　　{ on some systems this may be a **record** variable }
name_length: 0 .. *file_name_size*;
　　{ this many characters are actually relevant in *name_of_file* (the rest are blank) }

27. The Pascal-H compiler with which the present version of TeX was prepared has extended the rules of Pascal in a very convenient way. To open file f, we can write

$$reset(f, name, \text{'}/0\text{'})　　\text{for input;}$$
$$rewrite(f, name, \text{'}/0\text{'})　　\text{for output.}$$

The '*name*' parameter, which is of type '**packed array** [⟨*any*⟩] **of** *text_char*', stands for the name of the external file that is being opened for input or output. Blank spaces that might appear in *name* are ignored.

The '/0' parameter tells the operating system not to issue its own error messages if something goes wrong. If a file of the specified name cannot be found, or if such a file cannot be opened for some other reason (e.g., someone may already be trying to write the same file), we will have $erstat(f) \neq 0$ after an unsuccessful *reset* or *rewrite*. This allows TEX to undertake appropriate corrective action.

TEX's file-opening procedures return *false* if no file identified by *name_of_file* could be opened.

define *reset_OK* (#) ≡ *erstat*(#) = 0
define *rewrite_OK* (#) ≡ *erstat*(#) = 0

function *a_open_in*(**var** *f* : *alpha_file*): *boolean*;   { open a text file for input }
  begin *reset*(*f*, *name_of_file*, ´/0´); *a_open_in* ← *reset_OK* (*f*);
  end;

function *a_open_out*(**var** *f* : *alpha_file*): *boolean*;   { open a text file for output }
  begin *rewrite*(*f*, *name_of_file*, ´/0´); *a_open_out* ← *rewrite_OK* (*f*);
  end;

function *b_open_in*(**var** *f* : *byte_file*): *boolean*;   { open a binary file for input }
  begin *reset*(*f*, *name_of_file*, ´/0´); *b_open_in* ← *reset_OK* (*f*);
  end;

function *b_open_out*(**var** *f* : *byte_file*): *boolean*;   { open a binary file for output }
  begin *rewrite*(*f*, *name_of_file*, ´/0´); *b_open_out* ← *rewrite_OK* (*f*);
  end;

function *w_open_in*(**var** *f* : *word_file*): *boolean*;   { open a word file for input }
  begin *reset*(*f*, *name_of_file*, ´/0´); *w_open_in* ← *reset_OK* (*f*);
  end;

function *w_open_out*(**var** *f* : *word_file*): *boolean*;   { open a word file for output }
  begin *rewrite*(*f*, *name_of_file*, ´/0´); *w_open_out* ← *rewrite_OK* (*f*);
  end;

---

file_name_size = **const**, §11.   *text_char* = macro, §19.   *word_file* = **file**, §113.

28. Files can be closed with the Pascal-H routine '*close*(*f*)', which should be used when all input or output with respect to *f* has been completed. This makes *f* available to be opened again, if desired; and if *f* was used for output, the *close* operation makes the corresponding external file appear on the user's area, ready to be read.

These procedures should not generate error messages if a file is being closed before it has been successfully opened.

procedure *a_close*(**var** *f* : *alpha_file*);   { close a text file }
  begin *close*(*f*);
  end;

procedure *b_close*(**var** *f* : *byte_file*);   { close a binary file }
  begin *close*(*f*);
  end;

procedure *w_close*(**var** *f* : *word_file*);   { close a word file }
  begin *close*(*f*);
  end;

29. Binary input and output are done with Pascal's ordinary *get* and *put* procedures, so we don't have to make any other special arrangements for binary I/O. Text output is also easy to do with standard Pascal routines. The treatment of text input is more difficult, however, because of the necessary translation to *ASCII_code* values. TeX's conventions should be efficient, and they should blend nicely with the user's operating environment.

30. Input from text files is read one line at a time, using a routine called *input_ln*. This function is defined in terms of global variables called *buffer*, *first*, and *last* that will be described in detail later; for now, it suffices for us to know that *buffer* is an array of *ASCII_code* values, and that *first* and *last* are indices into this array representing the beginning and ending of a line of text.

⟨ Global variables 13 ⟩ +≡
buffer: **array** [0 .. *buf_size*] **of** *ASCII_code*;   { lines of characters being read }
first: 0 .. *buf_size*;   { the first unused position in *buffer* }
last: 0 .. *buf_size*;   { end of the line just input to *buffer* }
max_buf_stack: 0 .. *buf_size*;   { largest index used in *buffer* }

31. The *input_ln* function brings the next line of input from the specified field into available positions of the buffer array and returns the value *true*, unless the file has already been entirely read, in which case it returns *false* and sets *last* ← *first*. In general, the *ASCII_code* numbers that represent the next line of the file are input into *buffer*[*first*], *buffer*[*first* + 1], ..., *buffer*[*last* − 1]; and the global variable *last* is set equal to *first* plus the length of the line. Trailing blanks are removed from the line; thus, either *last* = *first* (in which case the line was entirely blank) or *buffer*[*last* − 1] ≠ "␣".

An overflow error is given, however, if the normal actions of *input_ln* would make *last* ≥ *buf_size*; this is done so that other parts of TeX can safely look at the contents of *buffer*[*last* + 1] without overstepping the bounds of the *buffer* array. Upon entry to *input_ln*, the condition *first* < *buf_size* will always hold, so that there is always room for an "empty" line.

The variable *max_buf_stack*, which is used to keep track of how large the *buf_size* parameter must be to accommodate the present job, is also kept up to date by *input_ln*.

If the *bypass_eoln* parameter is *true*, *input_ln* will do a *get* before looking at the first character of the line; this skips over an *eoln* that was in $f\uparrow$. The procedure does not do a *get* when it reaches the end of the line; therefore it can be used to acquire input from the user's terminal as well as from ordinary text files.

Standard Pascal says that a file should have *eoln* immediately before *eof*, but TeX needs only a weaker restriction: If *eof* occurs in the middle of a line, the system function *eoln* should return a *true* result (even though $f\uparrow$ will be undefined).

Since the inner loop of *input_ln* is part of TeX's "inner loop"—each character of input comes in at this place—it is wise to reduce system overhead by making use of special routines that read in an entire array of characters at once, if such routines are available. The following code uses standard Pascal to illustrate what needs to be done, but finer tuning is often possible at well-developed Pascal sites.

```
function input_ln(var f : alpha_file; bypass_eoln : boolean): boolean;
        { inputs the next line or returns false }
   var last_nonblank: 0 .. buf_size;   { last with trailing blanks removed }
   begin if bypass_eoln then
      if ¬eof(f) then get(f);   { input the first character of the line into f↑ }
   last ← first;   { cf. Matthew 19 : 30 }
   if eof(f) then input_ln ← false
   else begin last_nonblank ← first;
      while ¬eoln(f) do
         begin if last ≥ max_buf_stack then
            begin max_buf_stack ← last + 1;
            if max_buf_stack = buf_size then overflow("buffer␣size", buf_size);
            end;
         buffer[last] ← xord[f↑]; get(f); incr(last);
         if buffer[last − 1] ≠ "␣" then last_nonblank ← last;
         end;
      last ← last_nonblank; input_ln ← true;
      end;
   end;
```

32.   The user's terminal acts essentially like other files of text, except that it is used both for input and for output. When the terminal is considered an input file, the file variable is called *term_in*, and when it is considered an output file the file variable is *term_out*.

⟨ Global variables 13 ⟩ +≡
term_in: *alpha_file*;   { the terminal as an input file }
term_out: *alpha_file*;   { the terminal as an output file }

33.   Here is how to open the terminal files in Pascal-H. The '/I' switch suppresses the first *get*.

define *t_open_in* ≡ *reset*(*term_in*, ˋTTY:ˊ, ˋ/O/Iˊ)   { open the terminal for text input }
define *t_open_out* ≡ *rewrite*(*term_out*, ˋTTY:ˊ, ˋ/Oˊ)   { open the terminal for text output }

---

alpha_file = **packed file**, §25.
ASCII_code = 0 .. 127, §18.
buf_size = **const**, §11.

byte_file = **packed file**, §25.
incr = macro, §16.
overflow: **procedure**, §94.

word_file = **file**, §113.
xord: **array**, §20.

34. Sometimes it is necessary to synchronize the input/output mixture that happens on the user's terminal, and three system-dependent procedures are used for this purpose. The first of these, *update_terminal*, is called when we want to make sure that everything we have output to the terminal so far has actually left the computer's internal buffers and been sent. The second, *clear_terminal*, is called when we wish to cancel any input that the user may have typed ahead (since we are about to issue an unexpected error message). The third, *wake_up_terminal*, is supposed to revive the terminal if the user has disabled it by some instruction to the operating system. The following macros show how these operations can be specified in Pascal-H:

define *update_terminal* ≡ *break*(*term_out*)   { empty the terminal output buffer }
define *clear_terminal* ≡ *break_in*(*term_in*, *true*)   { clear the terminal input buffer }
define *wake_up_terminal* ≡ *do_nothing*   { cancel the user's cancellation of output }

35. We need a special routine to read the first line of TeX input from the user's terminal. This line is different because it is read before we have opened the transcript file; there is sort of a "chicken and egg" problem here. If the user types '\input paper' on the first line, or if some macro invoked by that line does such an \input, the transcript file will be named 'paper.log'; but if no \input commands are performed during the first line of terminal input, the transcript file will acquire its default name 'texput.log'. (The transcript file will not contain error messages generated by the first line before the first \input command.)

The first line is even more special if we are lucky enough to have an operating system that treats TeX differently from a run-of-the-mill Pascal object program. It's nice to let the user start running a TeX job by typing a command line like 'tex paper'; in such a case, TeX will operate as if the first line of input were 'paper', i.e., the first line will consist of the remainder of the command line, after the part that invoked TeX.

36. Different systems have different ways to get started. But regardless of what conventions are adopted, the routine that initializes the terminal should satisfy the following specifications:

1) It should open file *term_in* for input from the terminal. (The file *term_out* will already be open for output to the terminal.)

2) If the user has given a command line, this line should be considered the first line of terminal input. Otherwise the user should be prompted with '**', and the first line of input should be whatever is typed in response.

3) The first line of input, which might or might not be a command line, should appear in locations *first* to *last* − 1 of the *buffer* array.

4) The global variable *loc* should be set so that the character to be read next by TeX is in *buffer*[*loc*]. This character should not be blank, and we should have *loc* < *last*.

(It may be necessary to prompt the user several times before a non-blank line comes in. The prompt is '**' instead of the later '*' because the meaning is slightly different: '\input' need not be typed immediately after '**'.)

define *loc* ≡ *cur_input.loc_field*   { location of first unread character in *buffer* }

37.   The following program does the required initialization without retrieving a possible command line. It should be clear how to modify this routine to deal with command lines, if the system permits them.

```
function init_terminal: boolean;   { gets the terminal input started }
  label exit;
  begin t_open_in;
  loop begin wake_up_terminal; write(term_out, `**´); update_terminal;
    if ¬input_ln(term_in, true) then   { this shouldn't happen }
      begin write_ln(term_out); write(term_out, `!␣End␣of␣file␣on␣the␣terminal...␣why?´);
      init_terminal ← false; return;
      end;
    loc ← first;
    while (loc < last) ∧ (buffer[loc] = "␣") do  incr(loc);
    if loc < last then
      begin init_terminal ← true; return;   { return unless the line was all blank }
      end;
    write_ln(term_out, `Please␣type␣the␣name␣of␣your␣input␣file.´);
    end;
exit: end;
```

buffer: **array**, §30.
cur_input: *in_state_record*, §301.
do_nothing = macro, §16.
exit = 10, §15.

first: 0 .. *buf_size*, §30.
incr = macro, §16.
last: 0 .. *buf_size*, §30.
loc_field: *halfword*, §300.

t_open_in = macro, §33.
term_in: *alpha_file*, §32.
term_out: *alpha_file*, §32.

38. String handling. Control sequence names and diagnostic messages are variable-length strings of seven-bit characters. Since Pascal does not have a well-developed string mechanism, TeX does all of its string processing by homegrown methods.

Elaborate facilities for dynamic strings are not needed, so all of the necessary operations can be handled with a simple data structure. The array *str_pool* contains all of the (seven-bit) ASCII codes in all of the strings, and the array *str_start* contains indices of the starting points of each string. Strings are referred to by integer numbers, so that string number s comprises the characters *str_pool*$[j]$ for *str_start*$[s] \leq j < $ *str_start*$[s+1]$. Additional integer variables *pool_ptr* and *str_ptr* indicate the number of entries used so far in *str_pool* and *str_start*, respectively; locations *str_pool*$[pool\_ptr]$ and *str_start*$[str\_ptr]$ are ready for the next string to be allocated.

String numbers 0 to 127 are reserved for strings that correspond to single ASCII characters. This is in accordance with the conventions of WEB, which converts single-character strings into the ASCII code number of the single character involved, while it converts other strings into integers and builds a string pool file. Thus, when the string constant "." appears in the program below, WEB converts it into the integer 46, which is the ASCII code for a period, while WEB will convert a string like "hello" into some integer greater than 127. String number 46 will presumably be the single character '.'; but some ASCII codes have no standard visible representation, and TeX sometimes needs to be able to print an arbitrary ASCII character, so the first 128 strings are used to specify exactly what should be printed for each of the 128 possibilities.

Elements of the *str_pool* array must be ASCII codes that can actually be printed; i.e., they must have an *xchr* equivalent in the local character set. (However, the names of control sequences need not meet this restriction, when they appear in *str_pool*.)

⟨ Types in the outer block 18 ⟩ +≡
    pool_pointer = 0 .. *pool_size*; { for variables that point into *str_pool* }
    str_number = 0 .. *max_strings*; { for variables that point into *str_start* }

39. ⟨ Global variables 13 ⟩ +≡
str_pool: **packed array** $[pool\_pointer]$ **of** *ASCII_code*; { the characters }
str_start: **array** $[str\_number]$ **of** *pool_pointer*; { the starting pointers }
pool_ptr: *pool_pointer*; { first unused position in *str_pool* }
str_ptr: *str_number*; { number of the current string being created }
init_pool_ptr: *pool_pointer*; { the starting value of *pool_ptr* }
init_str_ptr: *str_number*; { the starting value of *str_ptr* }

40. Several of the elementary string operations are performed using WEB macros instead of Pascal procedures, because many of the operations are done quite frequently and we want to avoid the overhead of procedure calls. For example, here is a simple macro that computes the length of a string.

    define *length*(#) ≡ (*str_start*$[\# + 1]$ − *str_start*$[\#]$)   { the number of characters in string number # }

41. The length of the current string is called *cur_length*:

    define *cur_length* ≡ (*pool_ptr* − *str_start*$[str\_ptr]$)

42. Strings are created by appending character codes to *str_pool*. The *append_char* macro, defined here, does not check to see if the value of *pool_ptr* has gotten too high; this test is supposed to be made before *append_char* is used. There is also a *flush_char* macro, which erases the last character appended.

To test if there is room to append l more characters to *str_pool*, we shall write *str_room*(l), which aborts TEX and gives an apologetic error message if there isn't enough room.

define *append_char*(#) ≡   { put *ASCII_code* # at the end of *str_pool* }
        begin *str_pool*[*pool_ptr*] ← #; *incr*(*pool_ptr*);
        end
define *flush_char* ≡ *decr*(*pool_ptr*)   { forget the last character in the pool }
define *str_room*(#) ≡   { make sure that the pool hasn't overflowed }
            begin if *pool_ptr* + # > *pool_size* **then** *overflow*("pool␣size", *pool_size* − *init_pool_ptr*);
            end

43.   Once a sequence of characters has been appended to *str_pool*, it officially becomes a string when the function *make_string* is called. This function returns the identification number of the new string as its value.

function *make_string*: *str_number*;   { current string enters the pool }
    begin if *str_ptr* = *max_strings* **then** *overflow*("number␣of␣strings", *max_strings* − *init_str_ptr*);
    incr(*str_ptr*); *str_start*[*str_ptr*] ← *pool_ptr*; *make_string* ← *str_ptr* − 1;
    end;

44.   To destroy the most recently made string, we say *flush_string*.

define *flush_string* ≡
            begin *decr*(*str_ptr*); *pool_ptr* ← *str_start*[*str_ptr*];
            end

45.   The following subroutine compares string s with another string of the same length that appears in *buffer* starting at position k; the result is *true* if and only if the strings are equal. Empirical tests indicate that *str_eq_buf* is used in such a way that it tends to return *true* about 80 percent of the time.

function *str_eq_buf*(s : *str_number*; k : *integer*): *boolean*;   { test equality of strings }
    label *not_found*;   { loop exit }
    var j: *pool_pointer*;   { running index }
        result: *boolean*;   { result of comparison }
    begin j ← *str_start*[s];
    while j < *str_start*[s + 1] **do**
        begin if *str_pool*[j] ≠ *buffer*[k] **then**
            begin *result* ← *false*; **goto** *not_found*;
            end;
        incr(j); *incr*(k);
        end;
    result ← *true*;
not_found: *str_eq_buf* ← *result*;
    end;

ASCII_code = 0 .. 127, §18.
buffer: **array**, §30.
decr = macro, §16.

incr = macro, §16.
max_strings = **const**, §11.
not_found = 45, §15.

overflow: **procedure**, §94.
pool_size = **const**, §11.
xchr: **array**, §20.

46. Here is a similar routine, but it compares two strings in the string pool, and it does not assume that they have the same length.

function $str\_eq\_str(s, t : str\_number)$: $boolean$;   { test equality of strings }
  label not_found;   { loop exit }
  var j, k: $pool\_pointer$;   { running indices }
    $result$: $boolean$;   { result of comparison }
  begin $result \leftarrow false$;
  if $length(s) \neq length(t)$ **then goto** not_found;
  $j \leftarrow str\_start[s]$; $k \leftarrow str\_start[t]$;
  while $j < str\_start[s + 1]$ **do**
    begin if $str\_pool[j] \neq str\_pool[k]$ **then goto** not_found;
    $incr(j)$; $incr(k)$;
    end;
  $result \leftarrow true$;
not_found: $str\_eq\_str \leftarrow result$;
  end;

47. The initial values of str_pool, str_start, $pool\_ptr$, and str_ptr are computed by the INITEX program, based in part on the information that WEB has output while processing TeX.

  init function $get\_strings\_started$: $boolean$;
        { initializes the string pool, but returns $false$ if something goes wrong }
  label $done, exit$;
  var k, l: $0 .. 127$;   { small indices or counters }
    m, n: $text\_char$;   { characters input from $pool\_file$ }
    g: str_number;   { garbage }
    a: $integer$;   { accumulator for check sum }
    c: $boolean$;   { check sum has been checked }
  begin $pool\_ptr \leftarrow 0$; $str\_ptr \leftarrow 0$; $str\_start[0] \leftarrow 0$; ⟨ Make the first 128 strings 48 ⟩;
  ⟨ Read the other strings from the TEX.POOL file and return $true$, or give an error message and return
      $false$ 51 ⟩;
$exit$: **end**;
  tini

48. ⟨ Make the first 128 strings 48 ⟩ ≡
  for $k \leftarrow 0$ **to** 127 **do**
    begin if (⟨ Character k cannot be printed 49 ⟩) **then**
      begin $append\_char("\hat{\ }")$; $append\_char("\hat{\ }")$;
      if $k < '100$ **then** $append\_char(k + '100)$
      else $append\_char(k - '100)$;
      end
    else $append\_char(k)$;
    $g \leftarrow make\_string$;
    end

This code is used in section 47.

49. The first 128 strings will contain 95 standard ASCII characters, and the other 33 characters will be printed in three-symbol form like '^^A' unless a system-dependent change is made here. Installations that have an extended character set, where for example $xchr['32] = '\neq'$, would like string ´32 to be the single character ´32 instead of the three characters ´136, ´136, ´132 (^^Z). On the other hand, even people with an extended character set will want to represent string ´15 by ^^M, since ´15 is *carriage_return*; the idea is to produce visible strings instead of tabs or line-feeds or carriage-returns or bell-rings or characters that are treated anomalously in text files.

The boolean expression defined here should be *true* unless TEX internal code number k corresponds to a non-troublesome visible symbol in the local character set. At MIT, for example, the appropriate formula would be '$k \in [0, ´10 .. ´12, ´14, ´15, ´33, ´177]$'. If character k cannot be printed, then character $k + ´100$ or $k - ´100$ must be printable; thus, at least 64 printable characters are needed.

⟨ Character k cannot be printed 49 ⟩ ≡
    $(k < "␣") \vee (k > "~")$

This code is used in section 48.

50.   When the WEB system program called TANGLE processes the TEX.WEB description that you are now reading, it outputs the Pascal program TEX.PAS and also a string pool file called TEX.POOL. The INITEX program reads the latter file, where each string appears as a two-digit decimal length followed by the string itself, and the information is recorded in TEX's string memory.

⟨ Global variables 13 ⟩ +≡
    init *pool_file*: *alpha_file*;   { the string-pool file output by TANGLE }
    tini

51.   **define** *bad_pool*(#) ≡
                begin *wake_up_terminal*; *write_ln*(*term_out*, #); *a_close*(*pool_file*);
                get_strings_started ← *false*; **return**;
                end

⟨ Read the other strings from the TEX.POOL file and return *true*, or give an error message and return
        false 51 ⟩ ≡
    name_of_file ← *pool_name*;   { we needn't set *name_length* }
    if *a_open_in*(*pool_file*) **then**
        begin c ← *false*;
        repeat ⟨ Read one string, but return *false* if the string memory space is getting too tight for
                comfort 52 ⟩;
        until c;
        a_close(*pool_file*); *get_strings_started* ← *true*;
        end
    else *bad_pool*(´!␣I␣can´´t␣read␣TEX.POOL.´)

This code is used in section 47.

---

a_close: **procedure**, §28.
a_open_in: **function**, §27.
alpha_file = **packed file**, §25.
append_char = macro, §42.
carriage_return = 13, §22.
done = 30, §15.
exit = 10, §15.

incr = macro, §16.
length = macro, §40.
make_string: **function**, §43.
name_length: 0 .. *file_name_size*,
    §26.
name_of_file: **packed array**, §26.
not_found = 45, §15.

pool_name = string", §11.
pool_pointer = 0 .. *pool_size*, §38.
str_number = 0 .. *max_strings*, §38.
term_out: *alpha_file*, §32.
text_char = macro, §19.
wake_up_terminal = macro, §34.
xchr: **array**, §20.

52. ⟨ Read one string, but return *false* if the string memory space is getting too tight for comfort 52 ⟩ ≡

    begin if $eof(pool\_file)$ **then** $bad\_pool(\text{`!}\sqcup\texttt{TEX.POOL}\sqcup\texttt{has}\sqcup\texttt{no}\sqcup\texttt{check}\sqcup\texttt{sum.`})$;

    $read(pool\_file, m, n)$; { read two digits of string length }

    if $m = \text{`*`}$ **then** ⟨ Check the pool check sum 53 ⟩

    else begin if $(xord[m] < \text{"0"}) \vee (xord[m] > \text{"9"}) \vee (xord[n] < \text{"0"}) \vee (xord[n] > \text{"9"})$ **then**

        $bad\_pool(\text{`!}\sqcup\texttt{TEX.POOL}\sqcup\texttt{line}\sqcup\texttt{doesn''t}\sqcup\texttt{begin}\sqcup\texttt{with}\sqcup\texttt{two}\sqcup\texttt{digits.`})$;

        $l \leftarrow xord[m] * 10 + xord[n] - \text{"0"} * 11$; { compute the length }

        if $pool\_ptr + l + string\_vacancies > pool\_size$ **then**

            $bad\_pool(\text{`!}\sqcup\texttt{You}\sqcup\texttt{have}\sqcup\texttt{to}\sqcup\texttt{increase}\sqcup\texttt{POOLSIZE.`})$;

        for $k \leftarrow 1$ **to** l **do**

            begin if $eoln(pool\_file)$ **then** $m \leftarrow \text{`}\sqcup\text{`}$ **else** $read(pool\_file, m)$;

            $append\_char(xord[m])$;

            end;

        $read\_ln(pool\_file)$; $g \leftarrow make\_string$;

        end;

    end

This code is used in section 51.

53. The WEB operation @$ denotes the value that should be at the end of this TEX.POOL file; any other value means that the wrong pool file has been loaded.

⟨ Check the pool check sum 53 ⟩ ≡

    begin $a \leftarrow 0$; $k \leftarrow 1$;

    loop begin if $(xord[n] < \text{"0"}) \vee (xord[n] > \text{"9"})$ **then**

        $bad\_pool(\text{`!}\sqcup\texttt{TEX.POOL}\sqcup\texttt{check}\sqcup\texttt{sum}\sqcup\texttt{doesn''t}\sqcup\texttt{have}\sqcup\texttt{nine}\sqcup\texttt{digits.`})$;

    $a \leftarrow 10 * a + xord[n] - \text{"0"}$;

    if $k = 9$ **then goto** $done$;

    $incr(k)$; $read(pool\_file, n)$;

    end;

$done$: **if** $a \neq$ @$ **then** $bad\_pool(\text{`!}\sqcup\texttt{TEX.POOL}\sqcup\texttt{doesn''t}\sqcup\texttt{match;}\sqcup\texttt{TANGLE}\sqcup\texttt{me}\sqcup\texttt{again.`})$;

    $c \leftarrow true$;

    end

This code is used in section 52.

54. On-line and off-line printing.   Messages that are sent to a user's terminal and to the transcript-log file are produced by several '*print*' procedures. These procedures will direct their output to a variety of places, based on the setting of the global variable *selector*, which has the following possible values:

term_and_log, the normal setting, prints on the terminal and on the transcript file.

log_only, prints only on the transcript file.

term_only, prints only on the terminal.

no_print, doesn't print at all. This is used only in rare cases before the transcript file is open.

pseudo, puts output into a cyclic buffer that is used by the *show_context* routine; when we get
     to that routine we shall discuss the reasoning behind this curious mode.

new_string, appends the output to the current string in the string pool.

0 to 15, prints on one of the sixteen files for \write output.

The symbolic names '*term_and_log*', etc., have been assigned numeric codes that satisfy the convenient relations $no\_print + 1 = term\_only$, $no\_print + 2 = log\_only$, $term\_only + 2 = log\_only + 1 = term\_and\_log$.

Three additional global variables, *tally* and *term_offset* and *file_offset*, record the number of characters that have been printed since they were most recently cleared to zero. We use *tally* to record the length of (possibly very long) stretches of printing; *term_offset* and *file_offset*, on the other hand, keep track of how many characters have appeared so far on the current line that has been output to the terminal or to the transcript file, respectively.

> **define** $no\_print = 16$ { *selector* setting that makes data disappear }
> **define** $term\_only = 17$ { printing is destined for the terminal only }
> **define** $log\_only = 18$ { printing is destined for the transcript file only }
> **define** $term\_and\_log = 19$ { normal *selector* setting }
> **define** $pseudo = 20$ { special *selector* setting for *show_context* }
> **define** $new\_string = 21$ { printing is deflected to the string pool }
> **define** $max\_selector = 21$ { highest selector setting }

⟨ Global variables 13 ⟩ +≡

log_file: *alpha_file*;   { transcript of TEX session }

selector: $0 .. max\_selector$;   { where to print a message }

dig: **array** $[0 .. 22]$ **of** $0 .. 15$;   { digits in a number being output }

tally: *integer*;   { the number of characters recently printed }

term_offset: $0 .. max\_print\_line$;   { the number of characters on the current terminal line }

file_offset: $0 .. max\_print\_line$;   { the number of characters on the current file line }

trick_buf: **array** $[0 .. error\_line]$ **of** *ASCII_code*;   { circular buffer for pseudoprinting }

trick_count: *integer*;   { threshold for pseudoprinting, explained later }

first_count: *integer*;   { another variable for pseudoprinting }

55.   ⟨ Initialize the output routines 55 ⟩ ≡
   selector ← *term_only*; *tally* ← 0; *term_offset* ← 0; *file_offset* ← 0;

See also sections 61, 528, and 533.

This code is used in section 1332.

56.   Macro abbreviations for output to the terminal and to the log file are defined here for convenience. Some systems need special conventions for terminal output, and it is possible to adhere to those conventions by changing *wterm*, *wterm_ln*, and *wterm_cr* in this section.

> **define** $wterm(\texttt{\#}) \equiv write(term\_out, \texttt{\#})$
> **define** $wterm\_ln(\texttt{\#}) \equiv write\_ln(term\_out, \texttt{\#})$
> **define** $wterm\_cr \equiv write\_ln(term\_out)$
> **define** $wlog(\texttt{\#}) \equiv write(log\_file, \texttt{\#})$
> **define** $wlog\_ln(\texttt{\#}) \equiv write\_ln(log\_file, \texttt{\#})$
> **define** $wlog\_cr \equiv write\_ln(log\_file)$

57.   To end a line of text output, we call $print\_ln$.

⟨ Basic printing procedures 57 ⟩ ≡

procedure $print\_ln$;   { prints an end-of-line }
  begin case $selector$ **of**
  $term\_and\_log$: **begin** $wterm\_cr$; $wlog\_cr$; $term\_offset \leftarrow 0$; $file\_offset \leftarrow 0$;
    end;
  log_only: **begin** $wlog\_cr$; $file\_offset \leftarrow 0$;
    end;
  $term\_only$: **begin** $wterm\_cr$; $term\_offset \leftarrow 0$;
    end;
  $no\_print, pseudo, new\_string$: $do\_nothing$;
  othercases $write\_ln(write\_file[selector])$
  endcases;
  end;   { $tally$ is not affected }

See also sections 58, 59, 60, 62, 63, 64, 65, 262, 263, 518, 699, and 1355.

This code is used in section 4.

$alpha_file = $ **packed file**, §25.	$error_line = $ **const**, §11.	$show\_context$: **procedure**, §311.
$ASCII\_code = 0 \mathrel{..} 127$, §18.	$max_print_line = $ **const**, §11.	$term\_out$: $alpha\_file$, §32.
$do_nothing = $ macro, §16.	$print$: **procedure**, §59.	$write\_file$: **array**, §1342.

58. The *print_char* procedure sends one character to the desired destination, using the *xchr* array to map it into an external character compatible with *input_ln*. All printing comes through *print_ln* or *print_char*.

⟨ Basic printing procedures 57 ⟩ +≡
procedure *print_char*(*s* : *ASCII_code*);   { prints a single character }
  label *exit*;
  begin if ⟨ Character *s* is the current new-line character 244 ⟩ **then**
    if *selector* < *pseudo* **then**
      begin *print_ln*; **return**;
      end;
  case *selector* **of**
  term_and_log: **begin** *wterm*(*xchr*[*s*]); *wlog*(*xchr*[*s*]); *incr*(*term_offset*); *incr*(*file_offset*);
    if *term_offset* = *max_print_line* **then**
      begin *wterm_cr*; *term_offset* ← 0;
      end;
    if *file_offset* = *max_print_line* **then**
      begin *wlog_cr*; *file_offset* ← 0;
      end;
    end;
  log_only: **begin** *wlog*(*xchr*[*s*]); *incr*(*file_offset*);
    if *file_offset* = *max_print_line* **then** *print_ln*;
    end;
  term_only: **begin** *wterm*(*xchr*[*s*]); *incr*(*term_offset*);
    if *term_offset* = *max_print_line* **then** *print_ln*;
    end;
  no_print: *do_nothing*;
  pseudo: **if** *tally* < *trick_count* **then** *trick_buf*[*tally* **mod** *error_line*] ← *s*;
  new_string: **begin if** *pool_ptr* < *pool_size* **then** *append_char*(*s*);
    end;   { we drop characters if the string space is full }
  othercases *write*(*write_file*[*selector*], *xchr*[*s*])
  endcases;
  incr(*tally*);
exit: **end**;

59. An entire string is output by calling *print*. Note that if we are outputting the single standard ASCII character c, we could call *print*("c"), since "c" = 99 is the number of a single-character string, as explained above. But *print_char*("c") is quicker, so TEX goes directly to the *print_char* routine when it knows that this is safe. (The present implementation assumes that it is always safe to print a visible ASCII character.)

⟨ Basic printing procedures 57 ⟩ +≡
procedure *print*(*s* : *integer*);   { prints string *s* }
  label *exit*;
  var *j*: *pool_pointer*;   { current character code position }
  begin if *s* ≥ *str_ptr* **then** *s* ← "???"   { this can't happen }
  else if *s* < 128 **then**
    if *s* < 0 **then** *s* ← "???"   { can't happen }
    else if (⟨ Character *s* is the current new-line character 244 ⟩) **then**

```
            if selector < pseudo then
                begin print_ln; return;
                end;
        j ← str_start[s];
        while j < str_start[s + 1] do
          begin print_char(str_pool[j]); incr(j);
          end;
exit: end;
```

60. Control sequence names might contain *ASCII_code* values that can't be printed using *print_char*. Therefore we use *slow_print* for them:

⟨ Basic printing procedures 57 ⟩ +≡
```
procedure slow_print(s : integer);   { prints string s }
  label exit;
  var j: pool_pointer;   { current character code position }
  begin if s ≥ str_ptr then  s ← "???"   { this can't happen }
  else if s < 128 then
      if s < 0 then  s ← "???"   { can't happen }
      else if (⟨ Character s is the current new-line character 244 ⟩) then
          if selector < pseudo then
              begin print_ln; return;
              end;
    j ← str_start[s];
    while j < str_start[s + 1] do
      begin print(str_pool[j]); incr(j);
      end;
exit: end;
```

61. Here is the very first thing that TEX prints: a headline that identifies the version number and format package. The *term_offset* variable is temporarily incorrect, but the discrepancy is not serious since we assume that the banner and format identifier together will occupy at most *max_print_line* character positions.

⟨ Initialize the output routines 55 ⟩ +≡
```
  wterm(banner);
  if format_ident = 0 then  wterm_ln(´␣(no␣format␣preloaded)´)
  else begin print(format_ident); print_ln;
    end;
  update_terminal;
```

---

append_char = macro, §42.
ASCII_code = 0 . . 127, §18.
banner = macro, §2.
do_nothing = macro, §16.
error_line = **const**, §11.
exit = 10, §15.
file_offset: 0 . . *max_print_line*, §54.
format_ident: *str_number*, §1299.
incr = macro, §16.
log_only = 18, §54.
max_print_line = **const**, §11.

new_string = 21, §54.
no_print = 16, §54.
pool_pointer = 0 . . *pool_size*, §38.
pool_size = **const**, §11.
print_ln: **procedure**, §57.
pseudo = 20, §54.
selector: 0 . . 21, §54.
tally: *integer*, §54.
term_and_log = 19, §54.
term_offset: 0 . . *max_print_line*, §54.

term_only = 17, §54.
trick_buf: **array**, §54.
trick_count: *integer*, §54.
update_terminal = macro, §34.
wlog = macro, §56.
wlog_cr = macro, §56.
write_file: **array**, §1342.
wterm = macro, §56.
wterm_cr = macro, §56.
wterm_ln = macro, §56.
xchr: **array**, §20.

62. The procedure *print_nl* is like *print*, but it makes sure that the string appears at the beginning of a new line.

⟨Basic printing procedures 57⟩ +≡

procedure *print_nl*(*s* : *str_number*);   { prints string *s* at beginning of line }
  begin if ((*term_offset* > 0) ∧ (*odd*(*selector*))) ∨ ((*file_offset* > 0) ∧ (*selector* ≥ *log_only*)) **then**
    print_ln;
  print(*s*);
  end;

63. The procedure *print_esc* prints a string that is preceded by the user's escape character (which is usually a backslash).

⟨Basic printing procedures 57⟩ +≡

procedure *print_esc*(*s* : *str_number*);   { prints escape character, then *s* }
  var *c*: *integer*;   { the escape character code }
  begin ⟨Set variable *c* to the current escape character 243⟩;
  if *c* ≥ 0 **then**
    if *c* < 128 **then** *print*(*c*);
  print(*s*);
  end;

64. An array of digits in the range 0 .. 15 is printed by *print_the_digs*.

⟨Basic printing procedures 57⟩ +≡

procedure *print_the_digs*(*k* : *eight_bits*);   { prints *dig*[*k* − 1] ... *dig*[0] }
  begin while *k* > 0 **do**
    begin *decr*(*k*);
    if *dig*[*k*] < 10 **then** *print_char*("0" + *dig*[*k*])
    else *print_char*("A" − 10 + *dig*[*k*]);
    end;
  end;

65. The following procedure, which prints out the decimal representation of a given integer *n*, has been written carefully so that it works properly if *n* = 0 or if (−*n*) would cause overflow. It does not apply **mod** or **div** to negative arguments, since such operations are not implemented consistently by all Pascal compilers.

⟨Basic printing procedures 57⟩ +≡

procedure *print_int*(*n* : *integer*);   { prints an integer in decimal form }
  var *k*: 0 .. 23;   { index to current digit; we assume that *n* < 10^{23} }
    m: *integer*;   { used to negate *n* in possibly dangerous cases }
  begin *k* ← 0;
  if *n* < 0 **then**
    begin *print_char*("-");
    if *n* > −100000000 **then** *negate*(*n*)
    else begin *m* ← −1 − *n*; *n* ← *m* **div** 10; *m* ← (*m* **mod** 10) + 1; *k* ← 1;
      if *m* < 10 **then** *dig*[0] ← *m*
      else begin *dig*[0] ← 0; *incr*(*n*);
        end;
      end;
    end;

repeat $dig[k] \leftarrow n \bmod 10; \; n \leftarrow n \textbf{ div } 10; \; incr(k);$
until $n = 0;$
$print\_the\_digs(k);$
end;

66. Here is a trivial procedure to print two digits; it is usually called with a parameter in the range $0 \leq n \leq 99$.

procedure $print\_two(n : integer);$ { prints two least significant digits }
   begin $n \leftarrow abs(n) \bmod 100; \; print\_char(\text{"0"} + (n \textbf{ div } 10)); \; print\_char(\text{"0"} + (n \bmod 10));$
   end;

67. Hexadecimal printing of nonnegative integers is accomplished by $print\_hex$.

procedure $print\_hex(n : integer);$ { prints a positive integer in hexadecimal form }
   var k: $0 .. 22;$ { index to current digit; we assume that $0 \leq n < 16^{22}$ }
   begin $k \leftarrow 0; \; print\_char(\text{""""});$
   repeat $dig[k] \leftarrow n \bmod 16; \; n \leftarrow n \textbf{ div } 16; \; incr(k);$
   until $n = 0;$
   $print\_the\_digs(k);$
   end;

68. In certain situations, TeX prints either a standard visible ASCII character or its hexadecimal ASCII code.

procedure $print\_ASCII(c : integer);$ { prints a character or its code }
   begin if $(c \geq 0) \wedge (c \leq 127)$ **then** $print(c)$
   else begin $print\_char(\text{"["});$
     if $c < 0$ **then** $print\_int(c)$ **else** $print\_hex(c);$
     $print\_char(\text{"]"});$
     end;
   end;

69. Roman numerals are produced by the *print_roman_int* routine. Readers who like puzzles might enjoy trying to figure out how this tricky code works; therefore no explanation will be given. Notice that 1990 yields `mcmxc`, not `mxm`.

procedure *print_roman_int*(n : *integer*);
  label *exit*;
  var j, k: *pool_pointer*; { mysterious indices into *str_pool* }
    u, v: *nonnegative_integer*; { mysterious numbers }
  begin $j \leftarrow$ *str_start*["m2d5c2l5x2v5i"]; $v \leftarrow 1000$;
  loop begin while $n \geq v$ **do**
      begin *print_char*(*str_pool*[j]); $n \leftarrow n - v$;
      end;
    if $n \leq 0$ **then return**; { nonpositive input produces no output }
    $k \leftarrow j + 2$; $u \leftarrow v$ **div** (*str_pool*[$k - 1$] − "0");
    if *str_pool*[$k - 1$] = "2" **then**
      begin $k \leftarrow k + 2$; $u \leftarrow u$ **div** (*str_pool*[$k - 1$] − "0");
      end;
    if $n + u \geq v$ **then**
      begin *print_char*(*str_pool*[k]); $n \leftarrow n + u$;
      end
    else begin $j \leftarrow j + 2$; $v \leftarrow v$ **div** (*str_pool*[$j - 1$] − "0");
      end;
    end;
exit: **end**;

70. The *print* subroutine will not print a string that is still being created. The following procedure will.

procedure *print_current_string*; { prints a yet-unmade string }
  var j: *pool_pointer*; { points to current character code }
  begin $j \leftarrow$ *str_start*[*str_ptr*];
  while $j <$ *pool_ptr* **do**
    begin *print_char*(*str_pool*[j]); *incr*(j);
    end;
  end;

71. Here is a procedure that asks the user to type a line of input, assuming that the *selector* setting is either *term_only* or *term_and_log*. The input is placed into locations *first* through *last* − 1 of the *buffer* array, and echoed on the transcript file if appropriate.

  This procedure is never called when *interaction* < *scroll_mode*.

define *prompt_input*(#) ≡
        begin *wake_up_terminal*; *print*(#); *term_input*;
        end { prints a string and gets a line of input }
procedure *term_input*; { gets a line from the terminal }
  var k: $0 \mathinner{\ldotp\ldotp} buf\_size$; { index into *buffer* }
  begin *update_terminal*; { Now the user sees the prompt for sure }
  if ¬*input_ln*(*term_in*, *true*) **then** *fatal_error*("End␣of␣file␣on␣the␣terminal!");
  term_offset ← 0; { the user's line ended with ⟨return⟩ }
  decr(*selector*); { prepare to echo the input }

if $last \neq first$ **then**
    for $k \leftarrow first$ **to** $last - 1$ **do** $print(buffer[k])$;
$print\_ln$; $incr(selector)$;   { restore previous status }
end;

72. Reporting errors. When something anomalous is detected, TeX typically does something like this:

$$print\_err(\texttt{"Something\textvisiblespace anomalous\textvisiblespace has\textvisiblespace been\textvisiblespace detected"});$$
$$help3\,(\texttt{"This\textvisiblespace is\textvisiblespace the\textvisiblespace first\textvisiblespace line\textvisiblespace of\textvisiblespace my\textvisiblespace offer\textvisiblespace to\textvisiblespace help."})$$
$$(\texttt{"This\textvisiblespace is\textvisiblespace the\textvisiblespace second\textvisiblespace line.\textvisiblespace I\textquotesingle m\textvisiblespace trying\textvisiblespace to"})$$
$$(\texttt{"explain\textvisiblespace the\textvisiblespace best\textvisiblespace way\textvisiblespace for\textvisiblespace you\textvisiblespace to\textvisiblespace proceed."});$$
$$error;$$

A two-line help message would be given using *help2*, etc.; these informal helps should use simple vocabulary that complements the words used in the official error message that was printed. (Outside the U.S.A., the help messages should preferably be translated into the local vernacular. Each line of help is at most 60 characters long, in the present implementation, so that *max_print_line* will not be exceeded.)

The *print_err* procedure supplies a '!' before the official message, and makes sure that the terminal is awake if a stop is going to occur. The *error* procedure supplies a '.' after the official message, then it shows the location of the error; and if *interaction* = *error_stop_mode*, it also enters into a dialog with the user, during which time the help message may be printed.

73. The global variable *interaction* has four settings, representing increasing amounts of user interaction:

define *batch_mode* = 0   { omits all stops and omits terminal output }
define *nonstop_mode* = 1   { omits all stops }
define *scroll_mode* = 2   { omits error stops }
define *error_stop_mode* = 3   { stops at every opportunity to interact }
define *print_err*(**#**) ≡
        begin if *interaction* = *error_stop_mode* **then** *wake_up_terminal*;
        print_nl(`"!␣"`); *print*(**#**);
        end

⟨ Global variables 13 ⟩ +≡
interaction: *batch_mode* .. *error_stop_mode*;   { current level of interaction }

74.   ⟨ Set initial values of key variables 21 ⟩ +≡
  interaction ← *error_stop_mode*;

75. TeX is careful not to call *error* when the print *selector* setting might be unusual. The only possible values of *selector* at the time of error messages are

no_print (when *interaction* = *batch_mode* and *log_file* not yet open);
term_only (when *interaction* > *batch_mode* and *log_file* not yet open);
log_only (when *interaction* = *batch_mode* and *log_file* is open);
term_and_log (when *interaction* > *batch_mode* and *log_file* is open).

⟨ Initialize the print *selector* based on *interaction* 75 ⟩ ≡
  if *interaction* = *batch_mode* **then** *selector* ← *no_print* **else** *selector* ← *term_only*

This code is used in sections 1265 and 1337.

76.   A global variable *deletions_allowed* is set *false* if the *get_next* routine is active when *error* is called; this ensures that *get_next* and related routines like *get_token* will never be called recursively.

The global variable *history* records the worst level of error that has been detected. It has four possible values: *spotless*, *warning_issued*, *error_message_issued*, and *fatal_error_stop*.

Another global variable, *error_count*, is increased by one when an *error* occurs without an interactive dialog, and it is reset to zero at the end of every paragraph. If *error_count* reaches 100, TeX decides that there is no point in continuing further.

> **define** *spotless* $= 0$ { *history* value when nothing has been amiss yet }
> **define** *warning_issued* $= 1$ { *history* value when *begin_diagnostic* has been called }
> **define** *error_message_issued* $= 2$ { *history* value when *error* has been called }
> **define** *fatal_error_stop* $= 3$ { *history* value when termination was premature }

⟨ Global variables 13 ⟩ $+\equiv$
deletions_allowed: *boolean*;   { is it safe for *error* to call *get_token*? }
history: *spotless* .. *fatal_error_stop*;   { has the source input been clean so far? }
error_count: $-1 .. 100$;   { the number of scrolled errors since the last paragraph ended }

77.   The value of *history* is initially *fatal_error_stop*, but it will be changed to *spotless* if TeX survives the initialization process.

⟨ Set initial values of key variables 21 ⟩ $+\equiv$
   deletions_allowed $\leftarrow$ *true*; *error_count* $\leftarrow 0$;   { *history* is initialized elsewhere }

---

begin_diagnostic: **procedure**, §245.
error: **procedure**, §82.
get_next: **procedure**, §341.
get_token: **procedure**, §365.
help2 = macro, §79.
help3 = macro, §79.

log_file: *alpha_file*, §54.
log_only = 18, §54.
max_print_line = **const**, §11.
no_print = 16, §54.
print: **procedure**, §59.

print_nl: **procedure**, §62.
selector: 0 .. 21, §54.
term_and_log = 19, §54.
term_only = 17, §54.
wake_up_terminal = macro, §34.

78. Since errors can be detected almost anywhere in TeX, we want to declare the error procedures near the beginning of the program. But the error procedures in turn use some other procedures, which need to be declared *forward* before we get to *error* itself.

It is possible for *error* to be called recursively if some error arises when *get_token* is being used to delete a token, or if some fatal error occurs while TeX is trying to fix a non-fatal one. But such recursion is never more than one level deep.

⟨ Error handling procedures 78 ⟩ ≡
procedure *normalize_selector*; *forward*;
procedure *get_token*; *forward*;
procedure *term_input*; *forward*;
procedure *show_context*; *forward*;
procedure *begin_file_reading*; *forward*;
procedure *open_log_file*; *forward*;
procedure *close_files_and_terminate*; *forward*;
procedure *clear_for_error_prompt*; *forward*;
procedure *give_err_help*; *forward*;
debug procedure *debug_help*; *forward*; **gubed**

See also sections 81, 82, 93, 94, and 95.

This code is used in section 4.

79. Individual lines of help are recorded in the array *help_line*, which contains entries in positions $0 \ldots (help\_ptr - 1)$. They should be printed in reverse order, i.e., with $help\_line[0]$ appearing last.

define $hlp1(\#) \equiv help\_line[0] \leftarrow \#;$ **end**
define $hlp2(\#) \equiv help\_line[1] \leftarrow \#;$ $hlp1$
define $hlp3(\#) \equiv help\_line[2] \leftarrow \#;$ $hlp2$
define $hlp4(\#) \equiv help\_line[3] \leftarrow \#;$ $hlp3$
define $hlp5(\#) \equiv help\_line[4] \leftarrow \#;$ $hlp4$
define $hlp6(\#) \equiv help\_line[5] \leftarrow \#;$ $hlp5$
define $help0 \equiv help\_ptr \leftarrow 0$ { sometimes there might be no help }
define $help1 \equiv$ **begin** $help\_ptr \leftarrow 1;$ $hlp1$ { use this with one help line }
define $help2 \equiv$ **begin** $help\_ptr \leftarrow 2;$ $hlp2$ { use this with two help lines }
define $help3 \equiv$ **begin** $help\_ptr \leftarrow 3;$ $hlp3$ { use this with three help lines }
define $help4 \equiv$ **begin** $help\_ptr \leftarrow 4;$ $hlp4$ { use this with four help lines }
define $help5 \equiv$ **begin** $help\_ptr \leftarrow 5;$ $hlp5$ { use this with five help lines }
define $help6 \equiv$ **begin** $help\_ptr \leftarrow 6;$ $hlp6$ { use this with six help lines }

⟨ Global variables 13 ⟩ +≡
help_line: **array** $[0 \ldots 5]$ **of** *str_number*; { helps for the next *error* }
help_ptr: $0 \ldots 6$; { the number of help lines present }
use_err_help: *boolean*; { should the *err_help* list be shown? }

80. ⟨ Set initial values of key variables 21 ⟩ +≡
  $help\_ptr \leftarrow 0;$ $use\_err\_help \leftarrow false;$

81. The *jump_out* procedure just cuts across all active procedure levels and goes to *end_of_TeX*. This is the only nonlocal **goto** statement in the whole program. It is used when there is no recovery from a particular error.

Some Pascal compilers do not implement non-local **goto** statements. In such cases the body of *jump_out* should simply be '*close_files_and_terminate*;' followed by a call on some system procedure that quietly terminates the program.

⟨ Error handling procedures 78 ⟩ +≡
procedure *jump_out*;
  begin goto *end_of_TEX* ;
  end;

82. Here now is the general *error* routine.

⟨ Error handling procedures 78 ⟩ +≡
procedure *error*; { completes the job of error reporting }
  label *continue*, *exit*;
  var *c*: *ASCII_code*; { what the user types }
    s1, *s2*, *s3*, *s4*: *integer*; { used to save global variables when deleting tokens }
  begin if *history* < *error_message_issued* **then** *history* ← *error_message_issued*;
  print_char("."); *show_context*;
  if *interaction* = *error_stop_mode* **then** ⟨ Get user's advice and **return** 83 ⟩;
  incr(*error_count*);
  if *error_count* = 100 **then**
    begin *print_nl*("(That␣makes␣100␣errors;␣please␣try␣again.)"); *history* ← *fatal_error_stop*;
    jump_out;
    end;
  ⟨ Put help message on the transcript file 90 ⟩;
exit: **end**;

83. ⟨ Get user's advice and **return** 83 ⟩ ≡
  loop begin *continue*: *clear_for_error_prompt*; *prompt_input*("?␣");
    if *last* = *first* **then return**;
    c ← *buffer*[*first*];
    if *c* ≥ "a" **then** *c* ← *c* + "A" − "a"; { convert to uppercase }
    ⟨ Interpret code *c* and **return** if done 84 ⟩;
    end
This code is used in section 82.

ASCII_code = 0 .. 127, §18.
begin_file_reading: **procedure**, §328.
buffer: **array**, §30.
clear_for_error_prompt: **procedure**, §330.
close_files_and_terminate: **procedure**, §1333.
continue = 22, §15.
debug_help: **procedure**, §1338.
end_of_TEX = 9998, §6.

err_help = macro, §230.
error_count: −1 .. 100, §76.
error_message_issued = 2, §76.
exit = 10, §15.
fatal_error_stop = 3, §76.
first: 0 .. *buf_size*, §30.
get_token: **procedure**, §365.
give_err_help: **procedure**, §1284.
history: 0 .. 3, §76.
incr = macro, §16.

last: 0 .. *buf_size*, §30.
normalize_selector: **procedure**, §92.
open_log_file: **procedure**, §534.
print_char: **procedure**, §58.
print_nl: **procedure**, §62.
prompt_input = macro, §71.
show_context: **procedure**, §311.
str_number = 0 .. *max_strings*, §38.
term_input: **procedure**, §71.

84. It is desirable to provide an 'E' option here that gives the user an easy way to return from TeX to the system editor, with the offending line ready to be edited. But such an extension requires some system wizardry, so the present implementation simply types out the name of the file that should be edited and the relevant line number.

There is a secret 'D' option available when the debugging routines haven't been commented out.

⟨ Interpret code c and **return** if done 84 ⟩ ≡
  case c **of**
  "0","1","2","3","4","5","6","7","8","9": **if** *deletions_allowed* **then**
    ⟨ Delete $c -$ "0" tokens and **goto** *continue* 88 ⟩;
  debug "D": **begin** *debug_help*; **goto** *continue*; **end**; **gubed**
  "E": **if** *base_ptr* > 0 **then**
    begin *print_nl*("You␣want␣to␣edit␣file␣"); *print*(*input_stack*[*base_ptr*].*name_field*);
    print("␣at␣line␣"); *print_int*(*line*); *interaction* ← *scroll_mode*; *jump_out*;
    end;
  "H": ⟨ Print the help information and **goto** *continue* 89 ⟩;
  "I": ⟨ Introduce new material from the terminal and **return** 87 ⟩;
  "Q","R","S": ⟨ Change the interaction level and **return** 86 ⟩;
  "X": **begin** *interaction* ← *scroll_mode*; *jump_out*;
    end;
  othercases *do_nothing*
  endcases;
  ⟨ Print the menu of available options 85 ⟩
This code is used in section 83.

85. ⟨ Print the menu of available options 85 ⟩ ≡
  begin *print*("Type␣<return>␣to␣proceed,␣S␣to␣scroll␣future␣error␣messages,");
  print_nl("R␣to␣run␣without␣stopping,␣Q␣to␣run␣quietly,");
  print_nl("I␣to␣insert␣something,␣");
  if *base_ptr* > 0 **then** *print*("E␣to␣edit␣your␣file,");
  if *deletions_allowed* **then**
    print_nl("1␣or␣...␣or␣9␣to␣ignore␣the␣next␣1␣to␣9␣tokens␣of␣input,");
  print_nl("H␣for␣help,␣X␣to␣quit.");
  end
This code is used in section 84.

86. Here the author of TeX apologizes for making use of the numerical relation between "Q", "R", "S", and the desired interaction settings *batch_mode*, *nonstop_mode*, *scroll_mode*.

⟨ Change the interaction level and **return** 86 ⟩ ≡
  begin *error_count* ← 0; *interaction* ← *batch_mode* + $c -$ "Q"; *print*("OK,␣entering␣");
  case c **of**
  "Q": **begin** *print_esc*("batchmode"); *decr*(*selector*);
    end;
  "R": *print_esc*("nonstopmode");
  "S": *print_esc*("scrollmode");
  end; { there are no other cases }
  print("..."); *print_ln*; *update_terminal*; **return**;
  end
This code is used in section 84.

87. When the following code is executed, $buffer[(first+1)\mathrel{..}(last-1)]$ may contain the material inserted by the user; otherwise another prompt will be given. In order to understand this part of the program fully, you need to be familiar with TeX's input stacks.

⟨ Introduce new material from the terminal and **return** 87 ⟩ ≡
  begin *begin_file_reading*;   { enter a new syntactic level for terminal input }
    { now *state* = *mid_line*, so an initial blank space will count as a blank }
  if *last* > *first* + 1 **then**
    begin *loc* ← *first* + 1; *buffer*[*first*] ← "␣";
    end
  else begin *prompt_input*("insert>"); *loc* ← *first*;
    end;
  first ← *last*; *cur_input.limit_field* ← *last* − 1;   { no *end_line_char* ends this line }
  return;
  end

This code is used in section 84.

88. We allow deletion of up to 99 tokens at a time.

⟨ Delete *c* − "0" tokens and **goto** *continue* 88 ⟩ ≡
  begin *s1* ← *cur_tok*; *s2* ← *cur_cmd*; *s3* ← *cur_chr*; *s4* ← *align_state*; *align_state* ← 1000000;
  OK_to_interrupt ← *false*;
  if (*last* > *first* + 1) ∧ (*buffer*[*first* + 1] ≥ "0") ∧ (*buffer*[*first* + 1] ≤ "9") **then**
    c ← *c* * 10 + *buffer*[*first* + 1] − "0" * 11
  else *c* ← *c* − "0";
  while *c* > 0 **do**
    begin *get_token*;   { one-level recursive call of *error* is possible }
    decr(*c*);
    end;
  cur_tok ← *s1*; *cur_cmd* ← *s2*; *cur_chr* ← *s3*; *align_state* ← *s4*; *OK_to_interrupt* ← *true*;
  help2("I␣have␣just␣deleted␣some␣text,␣as␣you␣asked.")
  ("You␣can␣now␣delete␣more,␣or␣insert,␣or␣whatever."); *show_context*; **goto** *continue*;
  end

This code is used in section 84.

---

align_state: *integer*, §309.
base_ptr: 0 .. *stack_size*, §310.
batch_mode = 0, §73.
begin_file_reading: **procedure**, §328.
buffer: **array**, §30.
c: *ASCII_code*, §82.
continue = 22, §15.
cur_chr: *halfword*, §297.
cur_cmd: *eight_bits*, §297.
cur_input: *in_state_record*, §301.
cur_tok: *halfword*, §297.
debug_help: **procedure**, §1338.
decr = macro, §16.
deletions_allowed: *boolean*, §76.
do_nothing = macro, §16.

end_line_char = macro, §236.
error_count: −1 .. 100, §76.
first: 0 .. *buf_size*, §30.
get_token: **procedure**, §365.
help2 = macro, §79.
input_stack: **array**, §301.
jump_out: **procedure**, §81.
last: 0 .. *buf_size*, §30.
limit_field: *halfword*, §300.
line: *integer*, §304.
loc = macro, §36.
mid_line = 1, §303.
name_field: *halfword*, §300.
nonstop_mode = 1, §73.
OK_to_interrupt: *boolean*, §96.

print: **procedure**, §59.
print_esc: **procedure**, §63.
print_int: **procedure**, §65.
print_ln: **procedure**, §57.
print_nl: **procedure**, §62.
prompt_input = macro, §71.
s1: *integer*, §82.
s2: *integer*, §82.
s3: *integer*, §82.
s4: *integer*, §82.
scroll_mode = 2, §73.
selector: 0 .. 21, §54.
show_context: **procedure**, §311.
state = macro, §302.
update_terminal = macro, §34.

89. ⟨Print the help information and **goto** *continue* 89⟩ ≡

  begin if *use_err_help* **then**
    begin *give_err_help*; *use_err_help* ← *false*;
    end
  else begin if *help_ptr* = 0 **then** *help2* ("Sorry,␣I␣don´t␣know␣how␣to␣help␣in␣this␣situation.")
    ("Maybe␣you␣should␣try␣asking␣a␣human?");
    repeat *decr*(*help_ptr*); *print*(*help_line*[*help_ptr*]); *print_ln*;
    until *help_ptr* = 0;
    end;
  help4 ("Sorry,␣I␣already␣gave␣what␣help␣I␣could...")
  ("Maybe␣you␣should␣try␣asking␣a␣human?")
  ("An␣error␣might␣have␣occurred␣before␣I␣noticed␣any␣problems.")
  ("``If␣all␣else␣fails,␣read␣the␣instructions.´´");
  goto *continue*;
  end

This code is used in section 84.

90. ⟨Put help message on the transcript file 90⟩ ≡

  if *interaction* > *batch_mode* **then** *decr*(*selector*); { avoid terminal output }
  if *use_err_help* **then**
    begin *print_ln*; *give_err_help*;
    end
  else while *help_ptr* > 0 **do**
    begin *decr*(*help_ptr*); *print_nl*(*help_line*[*help_ptr*]);
    end;
  print_ln;
  if *interaction* > *batch_mode* **then** *incr*(*selector*); { re-enable terminal output }
  print_ln

This code is used in section 82.

91. A dozen or so error messages end with a parenthesized integer, so we save a teeny bit of program space by declaring the following procedure:

procedure *int_error*(*n* : *integer*);
  begin *print*("␣("); *print_int*(*n*); *print_char*(")"); *error*;
  end;

92. In anomalous cases, the print selector might be in an unknown state; the following subroutine is called to fix things just enough to keep running a bit longer.

  The normal idea of *batch_mode* is that nothing at all should be written on the terminal. However, in the unusual case that a fatal error has occurred but no log file could be opened, we make an exception and allow an explanatory message to be seen.

procedure *normalize_selector*;
  begin if *job_name* > 0 **then** *selector* ← *term_and_log*
  else *selector* ← *term_only*;
  if *job_name* = 0 **then** *open_log_file*;
  if *interaction* = *batch_mode* **then** *decr*(*selector*);
  end;

93.   The following procedure prints TeX's last words before dying.

> **define** *succumb* ≡
>> **begin if** *interaction* = *error_stop_mode* **then** *interaction* ← *scroll_mode*;
>>> { no more interaction }
>>
>> *error*;
>> **debug if** *interaction* > *batch_mode* **then** *debug_help*;
>> **gubed**
>> *history* ← *fatal_error_stop*; *jump_out*;   { irrecoverable error }
>> **end**

⟨ Error handling procedures 78 ⟩ +≡
procedure *fatal_error*(*s* : *str_number*);   { prints *s*, and that's it }
  begin *normalize_selector*;
  print_err("Emergency␣stop"); *help1*(*s*); *succumb*;
  end;

94.   Here is the most dreaded error message.

⟨ Error handling procedures 78 ⟩ +≡
procedure *overflow*(*s* : *str_number*; *n* : *integer*);   { stop due to finiteness }
  begin *normalize_selector*; *print_err*("TeX␣capacity␣exceeded,␣sorry␣["); *print*(*s*);
  print_char("="); *print_int*(*n*); *print_char*("]");
  help2("If␣you␣really␣absolutely␣need␣more␣capacity,")
  ("you␣can␣ask␣a␣wizard␣to␣enlarge␣me."); *succumb*;
  end;

---

batch_mode = 0, §73.
continue = 22, §15.
debug_help: **procedure**, §1338.
decr = macro, §16.
fatal_error_stop = 3, §76.
give_err_help: **procedure**, §1284.
help_line: **array**, §79.
help_ptr: 0 . . 6, §79.
help1 = macro, §79.

help2 = macro, §79.
help4 = macro, §79.
history: 0 . . 3, §76.
incr = macro, §16.
job_name: *str_number*, §527.
jump_out: **procedure**, §81.
open_log_file: **procedure**, §534.
print: **procedure**, §59.
print_char: **procedure**, §58.

print_int: **procedure**, §65.
print_ln: **procedure**, §57.
print_nl: **procedure**, §62.
scroll_mode = 2, §73.
selector: 0 . . 21, §54.
str_number = 0 . . *max_strings*, §38.
term_and_log = 19, §54.
term_only = 17, §54.
use_err_help: *boolean*, §79.

95.   The program might sometime run completely amok, at which point there is no choice but
to stop. If no previous error has been detected, that's bad news; a message is printed that is really
intended for the TEX maintenance person instead of the user (unless the user has been particularly
diabolical). The index entries for 'this can't happen' may help to pinpoint the problem.

⟨ Error handling procedures 78 ⟩ +≡
procedure *confusion*(*s* : *str_number*);   { consistency check violated; *s* tells where }
  begin *normalize_selector*;
  if *history* < *error_message_issued* **then**
    begin *print_err*("This␣can´t␣happen␣("); *print*(*s*); *print_char*(")");
    help1("I´m␣broken.␣Please␣show␣this␣to␣someone␣who␣can␣fix␣can␣fix");
    end
  else begin *print_err*("I␣can´t␣go␣on␣meeting␣you␣like␣this");
    help2("One␣of␣your␣faux␣pas␣seems␣to␣have␣wounded␣me␣deeply...")
    ("in␣fact,␣I´m␣barely␣conscious.␣Please␣fix␣it␣and␣try␣again.");
    end;
  succumb;
  end;

96.   Users occasionally want to interrupt TEX while it's running. If the Pascal runtime system
allows this, one can implement a routine that sets the global variable *interrupt* to some nonzero
value when such an interrupt is signalled. Otherwise there is probably at least a way to make
interrupt nonzero using the Pascal debugger.

  define *check_interrupt* ≡
        begin if *interrupt* ≠ 0 **then** *pause_for_instructions*;
        end

⟨ Global variables 13 ⟩ +≡
interrupt: *integer*;   { should TEX pause for instructions? }
OK_to_interrupt: *boolean*;   { should interrupts be observed? }

97.   ⟨ Set initial values of key variables 21 ⟩ +≡
  interrupt ← 0; *OK_to_interrupt* ← *true*;

98.   When an interrupt has been detected, the program goes into its highest interaction level
and lets the user have the full flexibility of the *error* routine. TEX checks for interrupts only at
times when it is safe to do this.

procedure *pause_for_instructions*;
  begin if *OK_to_interrupt* **then**
    begin *interaction* ← *error_stop_mode*;
    if (*selector* = *log_only*) ∨ (*selector* = *no_print*) **then** *incr*(*selector*);
    print_err("Interruption"); *help3*("You␣rang?")
    ("Try␣to␣insert␣some␣instructions␣for␣me␣(e.g.,␣`I\showlists´),")
    ("unless␣you␣just␣want␣to␣quit␣by␣typing␣`X´."); *deletions_allowed* ← *false*; *error*;
    deletions_allowed ← *true*; *interrupt* ← 0;
    end;
  end;

99.   Arithmetic with scaled dimensions.   The principal computations performed by TₑX are done entirely in terms of integers less than 2^{31} in magnitude; and divisions are done only when both dividend and divisor are nonnegative. Thus, the arithmetic specified in this program can be carried out in exactly the same way on a wide variety of computers, including some small ones. Why? Because the arithmetic calculations need to be spelled out precisely in order to guarantee that TₑX will produce identical output on different machines. If some quantities were rounded differently in different implementations, we would find that line breaks and even page breaks might occur in different places. Hence the arithmetic of TₑX has been designed with care, and systems that claim to be implementations of TₑX82 should follow precisely the calculations as they appear in the present program.

(Actually there are three places where TₑX uses **div** with a possibly negative numerator. These are harmless; see **div** in the index. Also if the user sets the \time or the \year to a negative value, some diagnostic information will involve negative-numerator division. The same remarks apply for **mod** as well as for **div**.)

100.   Here is a routine that calculates half of an integer, using an unambiguous convention with respect to signed odd numbers.

function $half(x : integer)$: $integer$;
  begin if $odd(x)$ **then** $half \leftarrow (x + 1) \textbf{ div } 2$
  else $half \leftarrow x \textbf{ div } 2$;
  end;

101.   Fixed-point arithmetic is done on *scaled integers* that are multiples of 2^{-16}. In other words, a binary point is assumed to be sixteen bit positions from the right end of a binary computer word.

  define $unity \equiv \text{'}200000$ $\{\, 2^{16}, \text{ represents } 1.00000 \,\}$
  define $two \equiv \text{'}400000$ $\{\, 2^{17}, \text{ represents } 2.00000 \,\}$

⟨ Types in the outer block 18 ⟩ +≡
  $scaled = integer$;   { this type is used for scaled integers }
  $nonnegative\_integer = 0 \mathinner{\ldotp\ldotp} \text{'}17777777777$; $\{\, 0 \le x < 2^{31} \,\}$
  $small\_number = 0 \mathinner{\ldotp\ldotp} 63$;   { this type is self-explanatory }

102.   The following function is used to create a scaled integer from a given decimal fraction $(.d_0 d_1 \ldots d_{k-1})$, where $0 \le k \le 17$. The digit d_i is given in $dig[i]$, and the calculation produces a correctly rounded result.

function $round\_decimals(k : small\_number)$: $scaled$;   { converts a decimal fraction }
  var a: $integer$;   { the accumulator }
  begin $a \leftarrow 0$;
  while $k > 0$ **do**
    begin $decr(k)$; $a \leftarrow (a + dig[k] * two) \textbf{ div } 10$;
    end;
  $round\_decimals \leftarrow (a + 1) \textbf{ div } 2$;
  end;

103.   Conversely, here is a procedure analogous to *print_int*. If the output of this procedure is subsequently read by TₑX and converted by the *round_decimals* routine above, it turns out that the original value will be reproduced exactly; the "simplest" such decimal number is output, but there is always at least one digit following the decimal point.

The invariant relation in the **repeat** loop is that a sequence of decimal digits yet to be printed will yield the original number if and only if they form a fraction f in the range $s - \delta \leq 10 \cdot 2^{16} f < s$. We can stop if and only if $f = 0$ satisfies this condition; the loop will terminate before s can possibly become zero.

procedure *print_scaled* (s : *scaled*);   { prints scaled real, rounded to five digits }
   var *delta*: *scaled*;   { amount of allowable inaccuracy }
   begin if $s < 0$ **then**
      begin *print_char* ("-"); *negate* (s);   { print the sign, if negative }
      end;
   print_int (s **div** *unity*);   { print the integer part }
   print_char ("."); $s \leftarrow 10 * (s \bmod unity) + 5$; *delta* $\leftarrow 10$;
   repeat if *delta* $>$ *unity* **then** $s \leftarrow s + '100000 - (delta \textbf{ div } 2)$;   { round the last digit }
      print_char ("0" + (s **div** *unity*)); $s \leftarrow 10 * (s \bmod unity)$; *delta* $\leftarrow delta * 10$;
   until $s \leq delta$;
   end;

104.   Physical sizes that a TEX user specifies for portions of documents are represented internally as scaled points. Thus, if we define an 'sp' (scaled point) as a unit equal to 2^{-16} printer's points, every dimension inside of TEX is an integer number of sp. There are exactly 4,736,286.72 sp per inch. Users are not allowed to specify dimensions larger than $2^{30} - 1$ sp, which is a distance of about 18.892 feet (5.7583 meters); two such quantities can be added without overflow on a 32-bit computer.

The present implementation of TEX does not check for overflow when dimensions are added or subtracted. This could be done by inserting a few dozen tests of the form '**if** $x \geq '10000000000$ **then** *report_overflow*', but the chance of overflow is so remote that such tests do not seem worthwhile.

TEX needs to do only a few arithmetic operations on scaled quantities, other than addition and subtraction, and the following subroutines do most of the work. A single computation might use several subroutine calls, and it is desirable to avoid producing multiple error messages in case of arithmetic overflow; so the routines set the global variable *arith_error* to *true* instead of reporting errors directly to the user. Another global variable, *remainder*, holds the remainder after a division.

⟨ Global variables 13 ⟩ +≡
arith_error: *boolean*;   { has arithmetic overflow occurred recently? }
remainder: *scaled*;   { amount subtracted to get an exact division }

---

decr = macro, §16.   *negate* = macro, §16.   *print_int*: **procedure**, §65.
dig: **array**, §54.   *print_char*: **procedure**, §58.

105.　　The first arithmetical subroutine we need computes $nx + y$, where x and y are *scaled* and n is an integer.

```
function nx_plus_y(n : integer; x, y : scaled): scaled;
  begin if n < 0 then
    begin negate(x); negate(n);
    end;
  if n = 0 then nx_plus_y ← y
  else if ((x ≤ ('7777777777 − y) div n) ∧ (−x ≤ ('7777777777 + y) div n)) then nx_plus_y ← n ∗ x + y
    else begin arith_error ← true; nx_plus_y ← 0;
      end;
  end;
```

106.　　We also need to divide scaled dimensions by integers.

```
function x_over_n(x : scaled; n : integer): scaled;
  var negative: boolean;   { should remainder be negated? }
  begin negative ← false;
  if n = 0 then
    begin arith_error ← true; x_over_n ← 0; remainder ← x;
    end
  else begin if n < 0 then
      begin negate(x); negate(n); negative ← true;
      end;
    if x ≥ 0 then
      begin x_over_n ← x div n; remainder ← x mod n;
      end
    else begin x_over_n ← −((−x) div n); remainder ← −((−x) mod n);
      end;
    end;
  if negative then negate(remainder);
  end;
```

107.　　Then comes the multiplication of a scaled number by a fraction n/d, where n and d are nonnegative integers $\leq 2^{16}$ and d is positive. It would be too dangerous to multiply by n and then divide by d, in separate operations, since overflow might well occur; and it would be too inaccurate to divide by d and then multiply by n. Hence this subroutine simulates 1.5-precision arithmetic.

```
function xn_over_d(x : scaled; n, d : integer): scaled;
  var positive: boolean;   { was x ≥ 0? }
    t, u, v: nonnegative_integer;   { intermediate quantities }
  begin if x ≥ 0 then positive ← true
  else begin negate(x); positive ← false;
    end;
  t ← (x mod '100000) ∗ n;  u ← (x div '100000) ∗ n + (t div '100000);
  v ← (u mod d) ∗ '100000 + (t mod '100000);
  if u div d ≥ '100000 then arith_error ← true
  else u ← '100000 ∗ (u div d) + (v div d);
```

if *positive* **then**
　begin *xn_over_d* ← *u*; *remainder* ← *v* **mod** *d*;
　end
else begin *xn_over_d* ← −*u*; *remainder* ← −(*v* **mod** *d*);
　end;
end;

108.　　The next subroutine is used to compute the "badness" of glue, when a total *t* is supposed to be made from amounts that sum to *s*. According to *The TeXbook*, the badness of this situation is $100(t/s)^3$; however, badness is simply a heuristic, so we need not squeeze out the last drop of accuracy when computing it. All we really want is an approximation that has similar properties.

The actual method used to compute the badness is easier to read from the program than to describe in words. It produces an integer value that is a reasonably close approximation to $100(t/s)^3$, and all implementations of TeX should use precisely this method. Any badness of 2^{13} or more is treated as infinitely bad, and represented by 10000.

It is not difficult to prove that

$$badness(t+1, s) \geq badness(t, s) \geq badness(t, s+1).$$

The badness function defined here is capable of computing at most 1095 distinct values, but that is plenty.

define *inf_bad* = 10000　　{ infinitely bad value }

function *badness*(*t, s* : *scaled*): *halfword*;　　{ compute badness, given $t \geq 0$ }
　var *r*: *integer*;　　{ approximation to $\alpha t/s$, where $\alpha^3 \approx 100 \cdot 2^{18}$ }
　begin if *t* = 0 **then** *badness* ← 0
　else if *s* ≤ 0 **then** *badness* ← *inf_bad*
　　else begin if *t* ≤ 7230584 **then** *r* ← (*t* ∗ 297) **div** *s*　　{ $297^3 = 99.94 \times 2^{18}$ }
　　　else if *s* ≥ 1663497 **then** *r* ← *t* **div** (*s* **div** 297)
　　　　else *r* ← *t*;
　　　if *r* > 1290 **then** *badness* ← *inf_bad*　　{ $1290^3 < 2^{31} < 1291^3$ }
　　　else *badness* ← (*r* ∗ *r* ∗ *r* + ´400000) **div** ´1000000;
　　　end;　　{ that was $r^3/2^{18}$, rounded to the nearest integer }
　end;

---

arith_error: *boolean*, §104.　　　　*negate* = macro, §16.　　　　*remainder*: *scaled*, §104.
halfword = *min_halfword* ..　　　　*nonnegative_integer*, §101.　　*scaled* = *integer*, §101.
　max_halfword, §113.

109. When TeX "packages" a list into a box, it needs to calculate the proportionality ratio by which the glue inside the box should stretch or shrink. This calculation does not affect TeX's decision making, so the precise details of rounding, etc., in the glue calculation are not of critical importance for the consistency of results on different computers.

We shall use the type *glue_ratio* for such proportionality ratios. A glue ratio should take the same amount of memory as an *integer* (usually 32 bits) if it is to blend smoothly with TeX's other data structures. Thus *glue_ratio* should be equivalent to *short_real* in some implementations of Pascal. Alternatively, it is possible to deal with glue ratios using nothing but fixed-point arithmetic; see *TUGboat* **3**,1 (February 1982), 10–27. (But the routines cited there must be modified to allow negative glue ratios.)

define *set_glue_ratio_zero*(#) ≡ # ← 0.0 { store the representation of zero ratio }
define *set_glue_ratio_one*(#) ≡ # ← 1.0 { store the representation of unit ratio }
define *float*(#) ≡ # { convert from *glue_ratio* to type *real* }
define *unfloat*(#) ≡ # { convert from *real* to type *glue_ratio* }
define *float_constant*(#) ≡ #.0 { convert *integer* constant to *real* }

⟨ Types in the outer block 18 ⟩ +≡
    glue_ratio = *real*; { one-word representation of a glue expansion factor }

110.   Packed data.   In order to make efficient use of storage space, TₑX bases its major data structures on a *memory_word*, which contains either a (signed) integer, possibly scaled, or an (unsigned) *glue_ratio*, or a small number of fields that are one half or one quarter of the size used for storing integers.

If x is a variable of type *memory_word*, it contains up to four fields that can be referred to as follows:

$$
\begin{array}{ll}
x.int & (\text{an } integer\,) \\
x.sc & (\text{a } scaled \text{ integer}) \\
x.gr & (\text{a } glue\_ratio\,) \\
x.hh.lh,\ x.hh.rh & (\text{two halfword fields}) \\
x.hh.b0,\ x.hh.b1,\ x.hh.rh & (\text{two quarterword fields, one halfword field}) \\
x.qqqq.b0,\ x.qqqq.b1,\ x.qqqq.b2,\ x.qqqq.b3 & (\text{four quarterword fields})
\end{array}
$$

This is somewhat cumbersome to write, and not very readable either, but macros will be used to make the notation shorter and more transparent. The Pascal code below gives a formal definition of *memory_word* and its subsidiary types, using packed variant records. TₑX makes no assumptions about the relative positions of the fields within a word.

Since we are assuming 32-bit integers, a halfword must contain at least 16 bits, and a quarterword must contain at least 8 bits. But it doesn't hurt to have more bits; for example, with enough 36-bit words you might be able to have *mem_max* as large as 262142, which is eight times as much memory as anybody had during the first four years of TₑX's existence.

N.B.: Valuable memory space will be dreadfully wasted unless TₑX is compiled by a Pascal that packs all of the *memory_word* variants into the space of a single integer. This means, for example, that *glue_ratio* words should be *short_real* instead of *real* on some computers. Some Pascal compilers will pack an integer whose subrange is '0 .. 255' into an eight-bit field, but others insist on allocating space for an additional sign bit; on such systems you can get 256 values into a quarterword only if the subrange is '−128 .. 127'.

The present implementation tries to accommodate as many variations as possible, so it makes few assumptions. If integers having the subrange '*min_quarterword* .. *max_quarterword*' can be packed into a quarterword, and if integers having the subrange '*min_halfword* .. *max_halfword*' can be packed into a halfword, everything should work satisfactorily.

It is usually most efficient to have *min_quarterword* = *min_halfword* = 0, so one should try to achieve this unless it causes a severe problem. The values defined here are recommended for most 32-bit computers.

define *min_quarterword* = 0   { smallest allowable value in a *quarterword* }
define *max_quarterword* = 255   { largest allowable value in a *quarterword* }
define *min_halfword* ≡ 0   { smallest allowable value in a *halfword* }
define *max_halfword* ≡ 65535   { largest allowable value in a *halfword* }

---

halfword = *min_halfword* ..   *mem_max* = **const**, §11.   *quarterword* = 0 .. 255, §113.
  max_halfword, §113.   *memory_word* = **record**, §113.

111. Here are the inequalities that the quarterword and halfword values must satisfy (or rather, the inequalities that they mustn't satisfy):

⟨ Check the "constant" values for consistency 14 ⟩ +≡

 init if $(mem\_min \neq mem\_bot) \vee (mem\_max \neq mem\_top)$ **then** $bad \leftarrow 10$;

 tini

 if $(mem\_min > mem\_bot) \vee (mem\_max < mem\_top)$ **then** $bad \leftarrow 10$;

 if $(min\_quarterword > 0) \vee (max\_quarterword < 127)$ **then** $bad \leftarrow 11$;

 if $(min\_halfword > 0) \vee (max\_halfword < 32767)$ **then** $bad \leftarrow 12$;

 if $(min\_quarterword < min\_halfword) \vee (max\_quarterword > max\_halfword)$ **then** $bad \leftarrow 13$;

 if $(mem\_min < min\_halfword) \vee (mem\_max \geq max\_halfword) \vee$

   $(mem\_bot - mem\_min > max\_halfword + 1)$ **then** $bad \leftarrow 14$;

 if $(font\_base < min\_quarterword) \vee (font\_max > max\_quarterword)$ **then** $bad \leftarrow 15$;

 if $font\_max > font\_base + 256$ **then** $bad \leftarrow 16$;

 if $(save\_size > max\_halfword) \vee (max\_strings > max\_halfword)$ **then** $bad \leftarrow 17$;

 if $buf\_size > max\_halfword$ **then** $bad \leftarrow 18$;

 if $max\_quarterword - min\_quarterword < 255$ **then** $bad \leftarrow 19$;

112. The operation of adding or subtracting $min\_quarterword$ occurs quite frequently in TEX, so it is convenient to abbreviate this operation by using the macros qi and qo for input and output to and from quarterword format.

The inner loop of TEX will run faster with respect to compilers that don't optimize expressions like '$x+0$' and '$x-0$', if these macros are simplified in the obvious way when $min\_quarterword = 0$.

 define $qi(\#) \equiv \# + min\_quarterword$ { to put an *eight_bits* item into a quarterword }

 define $qo(\#) \equiv \# - min\_quarterword$ { to take an *eight_bits* item out of a quarterword }

 define $hi(\#) \equiv \# + min\_halfword$ { to put a sixteen-bit item into a halfword }

 define $ho(\#) \equiv \# - min\_halfword$ { to take a sixteen-bit item from a halfword }

113. The reader should study the following definitions closely:

 define $sc \equiv int$ { *scaled* data is equivalent to *integer* }

⟨ Types in the outer block 18 ⟩ +≡

 $quarterword = min\_quarterword \mathinner{.\,.} max\_quarterword$;   { 1/4 of a word }

 $halfword = min\_halfword \mathinner{.\,.} max\_halfword$;   { 1/2 of a word }

 $two\_choices = 1 \mathinner{.\,.} 2$;   { used when there are two variants in a record }

 $four\_choices = 1 \mathinner{.\,.} 4$;   { used when there are four variants in a record }

 $two_halves = $ **packed record** rh: $halfword$;

  case $two\_choices$ **of**

  1: (lh : $halfword$);

  2: ($b0$: $quarterword$; $b1$: $quarterword$);

  end;

 $four_quarters = $ **packed record** $b0$: $quarterword$;

  $b1$: $quarterword$;

  $b2$: $quarterword$;

  $b3$: $quarterword$;

  end;

$memory\_word$ = **record**
  case $four\_choices$ **of**
  1: ($int : integer$);
  2: ($gr : glue\_ratio$);
  3: ($hh : two\_halves$);
  4: ($qqqq : four\_quarters$);
  end;
$word\_file$ = **file of** $memory\_word$;

114.   When debugging, we may want to print a $memory\_word$ without knowing what type it is; so we print it in all modes.

debug procedure $print\_word(w : memory\_word)$;   { prints w in all ways }
begin $print\_int(w.int)$; $print\_char("\sqcup")$;
$print\_scaled(w.sc)$; $print\_char("\sqcup")$;
$print\_scaled(round(unity * float(w.gr)))$; $print\_ln$;
$print\_int(w.hh.lh)$; $print\_char("=")$; $print\_int(w.hh.b0)$; $print\_char(":")$; $print\_int(w.hh.b1)$;
$print\_char(";")$; $print\_int(w.hh.rh)$; $print\_char("\sqcup")$;
$print\_int(w.qqqq.b0)$; $print\_char(":")$; $print\_int(w.qqqq.b1)$; $print\_char(":")$; $print\_int(w.qqqq.b2)$;
$print\_char(":")$; $print\_int(w.qqqq.b3)$;
end;
gubed

---

bad: $integer$, §13.
buf_size = **const**, §11.
$eight\_bits$ = 0 .. 255, §25.
$float$ = macro, §109.
$font\_max$ = **const**, §11.
$glue\_ratio$ = $real$, §109.
$max\_halfword$ = macro, §110.

$max\_quarterword$ = 255, §110.
$max\_strings$ = **const**, §11.
mem_max = **const**, §11.
mem_min = **const**, §11.
$min\_halfword$ = macro, §110.
$min\_quarterword$ = 0, §110.
$print\_char$: **procedure**, §58.

$print\_int$: **procedure**, §65.
$print\_ln$: **procedure**, §57.
$print\_scaled$: **procedure**, §103.
$save\_size$ = **const**, §11.
$scaled$ = $integer$, §101.
$unity$ = macro, §101.

115. Dynamic memory allocation.   The TeX system does nearly all of its own memory allocation, so that it can readily be transported into environments that do not have automatic facilities for strings, garbage collection, etc., and so that it can be in control of what error messages the user receives. The dynamic storage requirements of TeX are handled by providing a large array *mem* in which consecutive blocks of words are used as nodes by the TeX routines.

Pointer variables are indices into this array, or into another array called *eqtb* that will be explained later. A pointer variable might also be a special flag that lies outside the bounds of *mem*, so we allow pointers to assume any *halfword* value. The minimum halfword value represents a null pointer. TeX does not assume that *mem*[*null*] exists.

> **define** *pointer* ≡ *halfword*   { a flag or a location in *mem* or *eqtb* }
> **define** *null* ≡ *min_halfword*   { the null pointer }

⟨ Global variables 13 ⟩ +≡
temp_ptr: *pointer*;   { a pointer variable for occasional emergency use }

116.   The *mem* array is divided into two regions that are allocated separately, but the dividing line between these two regions is not fixed; they grow together until finding their "natural" size in a particular job. Locations less than or equal to *lo_mem_max* are used for storing variable-length records consisting of two or more words each. This region is maintained using an algorithm similar to the one described in exercise 2.5–19 of *The Art of Computer Programming*. However, no size field appears in the allocated nodes; the program is responsible for knowing the relevant size when a node is freed. Locations greater than or equal to *hi_mem_min* are used for storing one-word records; a conventional AVAIL stack is used for allocation in this region.

Locations of *mem* between *mem_bot* and *mem_top* may be dumped as part of preloaded format files, by the INITEX preprocessor. Production versions of TeX may extend the memory at both ends in order to provide more space; locations between *mem_min* and *mem_bot* are always used for variable-size nodes, and locations between *mem_top* and *mem_max* are always used for single-word nodes.

The key pointers that govern *mem* allocation have a prescribed order:

$$null \le mem\_min \le mem\_bot < lo\_mem\_max < hi\_mem\_min < mem\_top \le mem\_end \le mem\_max.$$

Empirical tests show that the present implementation of TeX tends to spend about 9% of its running time allocating nodes, and about 6% deallocating them after their use.

⟨ Global variables 13 ⟩ +≡
mem: **array** [*mem_min* .. *mem_max*] **of** *memory_word*;   { the big dynamic storage area }
lo_mem_max: *pointer*;   { the largest location of variable-size memory in use }
hi_mem_min: *pointer*;   { the smallest location of one-word memory in use }

117.   In order to study the memory requirements of particular applications, it is possible to prepare a version of TeX that keeps track of current and maximum memory usage. When code between the delimiters **stat** ... **tats** is not "commented out," TeX will run a bit slower but it will report these statistics when *tracing_stats* is sufficiently large.

⟨ Global variables 13 ⟩ +≡
var_used, *dyn_used*: *integer*;   { how much memory is in use }

118. Let's consider the one-word memory region first, since it's the simplest. The pointer variable *mem_end* holds the highest-numbered location of *mem* that has ever been used. The free locations of *mem* that occur between *hi_mem_min* and *mem_end*, inclusive, are of type *two_halves*, and we write *info*(p) and *link*(p) for the *lh* and *rh* fields of *mem*[p] when it is of this type. The single-word free locations form a linked list

$$avail, \ link(avail), \ link(link(avail)), \ \ldots$$

terminated by *null*.

> **define** *link*(#) ≡ *mem*[#].*hh*.*rh*   { the *link* field of a memory word }
> **define** *info*(#) ≡ *mem*[#].*hh*.*lh*   { the *info* field of a memory word }

⟨ Global variables 13 ⟩ +≡
avail: *pointer*;   { head of the list of available one-word nodes }
mem_end: *pointer*;   { the last one-word node used in *mem* }

119. If memory is exhausted, it might mean that the user has forgotten a right brace. We will define some procedures later that try to help pinpoint the trouble.

⟨ Declare the procedure called *show_token_list* 292 ⟩
⟨ Declare the procedure called *runaway* 306 ⟩

---

eqtb: **array**, §253.
halfword = *min_halfword* ..
   max_halfword, §113.
hh: *two_halves*, §113.
lh: *halfword*, §113.

mem_max = **const**, §11.
mem_min = **const**, §11.
memory_word = **record**, §113.
min_halfword = macro, §110.
rh: *halfword*, §113.

runaway: **procedure**, §306.
show_token_list: **procedure**, §292.
tracing_stats = macro, §236.
two_halves = **packed record**, §113.

120. The function *get_avail* returns a pointer to a new one-word node whose *link* field is null. However, TeX will halt if there is no more room left.

If the available-space list is empty, i.e., if *avail* = *null*, we try first to increase *mem_end*. If that cannot be done, i.e., if *mem_end* = *mem_max*, we try to decrease *hi_mem_min*. If that cannot be done, i.e., if *hi_mem_min* = *low_mem_max* + 1, we have to quit.

function *get_avail*: *pointer*;   { single-word node allocation }
  var *p*: *pointer*;   { the new node being got }
  begin *p* ← *avail*;   { get top location in the *avail* stack }
  if *p* ≠ *null* **then** *avail* ← *link*(*avail*)   { and pop it off }
  else if *mem_end* < *mem_max* **then**   { or go into virgin territory }
      begin *incr*(*mem_end*); *p* ← *mem_end*;
      end
    else begin *decr*(*hi_mem_min*); *p* ← *hi_mem_min*;
      if *hi_mem_min* ≤ *lo_mem_max* **then**
        begin *runaway*;   { if memory is exhausted, display possible runaway text }
        overflow("main␣memory␣size", *mem_max* + 1 − *mem_min*);
            { quit; all one-word nodes are busy }
        end;
      end;
  link(*p*) ← *null*;   { provide an oft-desired initialization of the new node }
  stat *incr*(*dyn_used*); **tats**   { maintain statistics }
  get_avail ← *p*;
  end;

121. Conversely, a one-word node is recycled by calling *free_avail*. This routine is part of TeX's "inner loop," so we want it to be fast.

define *free_avail*(**#**) ≡   { single-word node liberation }
        begin *link*(**#**) ← *avail*; *avail* ← **#**;
        stat *decr*(*dyn_used*); **tats**
        end

122. There's also a *fast_get_avail* routine, which saves the procedure-call overhead at the expense of extra programming. This routine is used in the places that would otherwise account for the most calls of *get_avail*.

define *fast_get_avail*(**#**) ≡
        begin **#** ← *avail*;   { avoid *get_avail* if possible, to save time }
        if **#** = *null* **then** **#** ← *get_avail*
        else begin *avail* ← *link*(**#**); *link*(**#**) ← *null*;
          stat *incr*(*dyn_used*); **tats**
          end;
        end

123. The procedure $flush\_list(p)$ frees an entire linked list of one-word nodes that starts at position p.

procedure $flush\_list(p : pointer)$;   { makes list of single-word nodes available }
  var q, r: $pointer$;   { list traversers }
  begin if $p \neq null$ **then**
    begin $r \leftarrow p$;
    repeat $q \leftarrow r$; $r \leftarrow link(r)$;
      stat $decr(dyn\_used)$; **tats**
    until $r = null$;   { now q is the last node on the list }
    $link(q) \leftarrow avail$; $avail \leftarrow p$;
    end;
  end;

124. The available-space list that keeps track of the variable-size portion of mem is a nonempty, doubly-linked circular list of empty nodes, pointed to by the roving pointer $rover$.

Each empty node has size 2 or more; the first word contains the special value $max\_halfword$ in its $link$ field and the size in its $info$ field; the second word contains the two pointers for double linking.

Each nonempty node also has size 2 or more. Its first word is of type two_halves, and its $link$ field is never equal to $max\_halfword$. Otherwise there is complete flexibility with respect to the contents of its other fields and its other words.

(We require $mem\_max < max\_halfword$ because terrible things can happen when $max\_halfword$ appears in the $link$ field of a nonempty node.)

  define $empty\_flag \equiv max\_halfword$ { the $link$ of an empty variable-size node }
  define $is\_empty(\#) \equiv (link(\#) = empty\_flag)$ { tests for empty node }
  define $node\_size \equiv info$ { the size field in empty variable-size nodes }
  define $llink(\#) \equiv info(\# + 1)$ { left link in doubly-linked list of empty nodes }
  define $rlink(\#) \equiv link(\# + 1)$ { right link in doubly-linked list of empty nodes }

⟨ Global variables 13 ⟩ +≡
$rover$: $pointer$;   { points to some node in the list of empties }

$avail$: $pointer$, §118.
$decr$ = macro, §16.
dyn_used: $integer$, §117.
hi_mem_min: $pointer$, §116.
$incr$ = macro, §16.
$info$ = macro, §118.

$link$ = macro, §118.
lo_mem_max: $pointer$, §116.
$max\_halfword$ = macro, §110.
mem_max = **const**, §11.
mem_min = **const**, §11.

$null$ = macro, §115.
$overflow$: **procedure**, §94.
$pointer$ = macro, §115.
$runaway$: **procedure**, §306.
two_halves = **packed record**, §113.

125. A call to *get_node* with argument *s* returns a pointer to a new node of size *s*, which must be 2 or more. The *link* field of the first word of this new node is set to null. An overflow stop occurs if no suitable space exists.

If *get_node* is called with $s = 2^{30}$, it simply merges adjacent free areas and returns the value *max_halfword*.

```
function get_node(s : integer): pointer;   { variable-size node allocation }
  label found, exit, restart;
  var p: pointer;   { the node currently under inspection }
    q: pointer;   { the node physically after node p }
    r: integer;   { the newly allocated node, or a candidate for this honor }
    t: integer;   { temporary register }
  begin restart: p ← rover;   { start at some free node in the ring }
  repeat ⟨ Try to allocate within node p and its physical successors, and goto found if allocation was
        possible 127 ⟩;
    p ← rlink(p);   { move to the next node in the ring }
  until p = rover;   { repeat until the whole list has been traversed }
  if s = ´10000000000 then
    begin get_node ← max_halfword; return;
    end;
  if lo_mem_max + 2 < hi_mem_min then
    if lo_mem_max + 2 ≤ mem_bot + max_halfword then
      ⟨ Grow more variable-size memory and goto restart 126 ⟩;
  overflow("main␣memory␣size", mem_max + 1 − mem_min);   { sorry, nothing satisfactory is left }
found: link(r) ← null;   { this node is now nonempty }
  stat var_used ← var_used + s;   { maintain usage statistics }
  tats
  get_node ← r;
exit: end;
```

126. The lower part of *mem* grows by 1000 words at a time, unless we are very close to going under. When it grows, we simply link a new node into the available-space list. This method of controlled growth helps to keep the *mem* usage consecutive when TEX is implemented on "virtual memory" systems.

```
⟨ Grow more variable-size memory and goto restart 126 ⟩ ≡
  begin if lo_mem_max + 1000 < hi_mem_min then t ← lo_mem_max + 1000
  else t ← (lo_mem_max + hi_mem_min + 2) div 2;   { lo_mem_max + 2 ≤ t < hi_mem_min }
  p ← llink(rover); q ← lo_mem_max; rlink(p) ← q; link(rover) ← q;
  if t > mem_bot + max_halfword then t ← mem_bot + max_halfword;
  rlink(q) ← rover; llink(q) ← p; link(q) ← empty_flag; node_size(q) ← t − lo_mem_max;
  lo_mem_max ← t; link(lo_mem_max) ← null; info(lo_mem_max) ← null; rover ← q; goto restart;
  end
```

This code is used in section 125.

127. Empirical tests show that the routine in this section performs a node-merging operation about 0.75 times per allocation, on the average, after which it finds that $r > p + 1$ about 95% of the time.

⟨ Try to allocate within node p and its physical successors, and **goto** *found* if allocation was
        possible 127 ⟩ ≡
  $q \leftarrow p + node\_size(p);$ { find the physical successor }
  while *is_empty*(q) **do**   { merge node p with node q }
    begin $t \leftarrow rlink(q);$
    if $q = rover$ **then** $rover \leftarrow t;$
    $llink(t) \leftarrow llink(q);\ rlink(llink(q)) \leftarrow t;$
    $q \leftarrow q + node\_size(q);$
    end;
  $r \leftarrow q - s;$
  if $r > p + 1$ **then** ⟨ Allocate from the top of node p and **goto** *found* 128 ⟩;
  if $r = p$ **then**
    if $((rlink(p) \neq rover) \vee (llink(p) \neq rover))$ **then** ⟨ Allocate entire node p and **goto** *found* 129 ⟩;
  $node\_size(p) \leftarrow q - p$ { reset the size in case it grew }
This code is used in section 125.

128.   ⟨ Allocate from the top of node p and **goto** *found* 128 ⟩ ≡
  begin $node\_size(p) \leftarrow r - p;$ { store the remaining size }
  $rover \leftarrow p;$ { start searching here next time }
  goto *found*;
  end
This code is used in section 127.

129.   Here we delete node p from the ring, and let *rover* rove around.

⟨ Allocate entire node p and **goto** *found* 129 ⟩ ≡
  begin $rover \leftarrow rlink(p);\ t \leftarrow llink(p);\ llink(rover) \leftarrow t;\ rlink(t) \leftarrow rover;$ **goto** *found*;
  end
This code is used in section 127.

130.   Conversely, when some variable-size node p of size s is no longer needed, the operation
free_node(p, s) will make its words available, by inserting p as a new empty node just before
where *rover* now points.

procedure *free_node*(p : pointer; s : halfword);   { variable-size node liberation }
  var q : pointer;   { $llink(rover)$ }
  begin $node\_size(p) \leftarrow s;\ link(p) \leftarrow empty\_flag;\ q \leftarrow llink(rover);\ llink(p) \leftarrow q;\ rlink(p) \leftarrow rover;$
    { set both links }
  $llink(rover) \leftarrow p;\ rlink(q) \leftarrow p;$ { insert p into the ring }
  stat $var\_used \leftarrow var\_used - s;$ **tats**   { maintain statistics }
  end;

$empty\_flag$ = macro, §124.
$exit$ = 10, §15.
$found$ = 40, §15.
$halfword$ = $min\_halfword$ ..
    $max\_halfword$, §113.
hi_mem_min: *pointer*, §116.
$info$ = macro, §118.
is_empty = macro, §124.

$link$ = macro, §118.
$llink$ = macro, §124.
lo_mem_max: *pointer*, §116.
$max\_halfword$ = macro, §110.
mem_max = **const**, §11.
mem_min = **const**, §11.
$node\_size$ = macro, §124.

$null$ = macro, §115.
$overflow$: **procedure**, §94.
$pointer$ = macro, §115.
$restart$ = 20, §15.
$rlink$ = macro, §124.
$rover$: *pointer*, §124.
var_used: *integer*, §117.

131. Just before INITEX writes out the memory, it sorts the doubly linked available space list. The list is probably very short at such times, so a simple insertion sort is used. The smallest available location will be pointed to by *rover*, the next-smallest by *rlink*(*rover*), etc.

> **init procedure** *sort_avail*;   { sorts the available variable-size nodes by location }
> **var** *p, q, r*: *pointer*;   { indices into *mem* }
>   *old_rover*: *pointer*;   { initial *rover* setting }
> **begin** *p* ← *get_node*(´10000000000´);   { merge adjacent free areas }
> *p* ← *rlink*(*rover*); *rlink*(*rover*) ← *max_halfword*; *old_rover* ← *rover*;
> **while** *p* ≠ *old_rover* **do** ⟨ Sort *p* into the list starting at *rover* and advance *p* to *rlink*(*p*) 132 ⟩;
> *p* ← *rover*;
> **while** *rlink*(*p*) ≠ *max_halfword* **do**
>   **begin** *llink*(*rlink*(*p*)) ← *p*; *p* ← *rlink*(*p*);
>   **end**;
> *rlink*(*p*) ← *rover*; *llink*(*rover*) ← *p*;
> **end**;
> **tini**

132. The following **while** loop is guaranteed to terminate, since the list that starts at *rover* ends with *max_halfword* during the sorting procedure.

⟨ Sort *p* into the list starting at *rover* and advance *p* to *rlink*(*p*) 132 ⟩ ≡
>   **if** *p* < *rover* **then**
>   **begin** *q* ← *p*; *p* ← *rlink*(*q*); *rlink*(*q*) ← *rover*; *rover* ← *q*;
>   **end**
>   **else begin** *q* ← *rover*;
>   **while** *rlink*(*q*) < *p* **do** *q* ← *rlink*(*q*);
>   *r* ← *rlink*(*p*); *rlink*(*p*) ← *rlink*(*q*); *rlink*(*q*) ← *p*; *p* ← *r*;
>   **end**

This code is used in section 131.

133.   Data structures for boxes and their friends.   From the computer's standpoint, TeX's chief mission is to create horizontal and vertical lists. We shall now investigate how the elements of these lists are represented internally as nodes in the dynamic memory.

A horizontal or vertical list is linked together by *link* fields in the first word of each node. Individual nodes represent boxes, glue, penalties, or special things like discretionary hyphens; because of this variety, some nodes are longer than others, and we must distinguish different kinds of nodes. We do this by putting a '*type*' field in the first word, together with the link and an optional '*subtype*'.

> **define** *type*(#) ≡ *mem*[#].*hh*.*b0*   { identifies what kind of node this is }
> **define** *subtype*(#) ≡ *mem*[#].*hh*.*b1*   { secondary identification in some cases }

134.   A *char_node*, which represents a single character, is the most important kind of node because it accounts for the vast majority of all boxes. Special precautions are therefore taken to ensure that a *char_node* does not take up much memory space. Every such node is one word long, and in fact it is identifiable by this property, since other kinds of nodes have at least two words, and they appear in *mem* locations less than *hi_mem_min*. This makes it possible to omit the *type* field in a *char_node*, leaving us room for two bytes that identify a *font* and a *character* within that font.

Note that the format of a *char_node* allows for up to 256 different fonts and up to 256 characters per font; but most implementations will probably limit the total number of fonts to fewer than 75 per job, and most fonts will stick to characters whose codes are less than 128 (since higher codes are accessed outside of math mode only via ligatures and the \char operator).

Extensions of TeX intended for oriental languages will need even more than 256×256 possible characters, when we consider different sizes and styles of type. It is suggested that Chinese and Japanese fonts be handled by representing such characters in two consecutive *char_node* entries: The first of these would identify the font and the character dimensions, and it would also link to the second, where the full halfword *info* field would address the desired character. Such an extension of TeX would not be difficult; further details are left to the reader. The saving feature about oriental characters is that most of them have the same box dimensions.

In order to make sure that the *character* code fits in a quarterword, TeX adds the quantity *min_quarterword* to the actual code.

Character nodes appear only in horizontal lists, never in vertical lists.

> **define** *is_char_node*(#) ≡ (# ≥ *hi_mem_min*)   { does the argument point to a *char_node*? }
> **define** *font* ≡ *type*   { the font code in a *char_node* }
> **define** *character* ≡ *subtype*   { the character code in a *char_node* }

---

b0: *quarterword*, §113.
b1: *quarterword*, §113.
get_node: **function**, §125.
hh: *two_halves*, §113.
hi_mem_min: *pointer*, §116.

info = macro, §118.
link = macro, §118.
llink = macro, §124.
max_halfword = macro, §110.

min_quarterword = 0, §110.
pointer = macro, §115.
rlink = macro, §124.
rover: *pointer*, §124.

135. An *hlist_node* stands for a box that was made from a horizontal list. Each *hlist_node* is seven words long, and contains the following fields (in addition to the mandatory *type* and *link*, which we shall not mention explicitly when discussing the other node types): The *height* and *width* and *depth* are scaled integers denoting the dimensions of the box. There is also a *shift_amount* field, a scaled integer indicating how much this box should be lowered (if it appears in a horizontal list), or how much it should be moved to the right (if it appears in a vertical list). There is a *list_ptr* field, which points to the beginning of the list from which this box was fabricated; if *list_ptr* is *null*, the box is empty. Finally, there are three fields that represent the setting of the glue: *glue_set*(p) is a word of type *glue_ratio* that represents the proportionality constant for glue setting; *glue_sign*(p) is *stretching* or *shrinking* or *normal* depending on whether or not the glue should stretch or shrink or remain rigid; and *glue_order*(p) specifies the order of infinity to which glue setting applies (*normal*, *fil*, *fill*, or *filll*). The *subtype* field is not used.

> **define** *hlist_node* = 0   { *type* of hlist nodes }
> **define** *box_node_size* = 7   { number of words to allocate for a box node }
> **define** *width_offset* = 1   { position of *width* field in a box node }
> **define** *depth_offset* = 2   { position of *depth* field in a box node }
> **define** *height_offset* = 3   { position of *height* field in a box node }
> **define** *width*(#) ≡ *mem*[# + *width_offset*].*sc*   { width of the box, in sp }
> **define** *depth*(#) ≡ *mem*[# + *depth_offset*].*sc*   { depth of the box, in sp }
> **define** *height*(#) ≡ *mem*[# + *height_offset*].*sc*   { height of the box, in sp }
> **define** *shift_amount*(#) ≡ *mem*[# + 4].*sc*   { repositioning distance, in sp }
> **define** *list_offset* = 5   { position of *list_ptr* field in a box node }
> **define** *list_ptr*(#) ≡ *link*(# + *list_offset*)   { beginning of the list inside the box }
> **define** *glue_order*(#) ≡ *subtype*(# + *list_offset*)   { applicable order of infinity }
> **define** *glue_sign*(#) ≡ *type*(# + *list_offset*)   { stretching or shrinking }
> **define** *normal* = 0   { the most common case when several cases are named }
> **define** *stretching* = 1   { glue setting applies to the stretch components }
> **define** *shrinking* = 2   { glue setting applies to the shrink components }
> **define** *glue_offset* = 6   { position of *glue_set* in a box node }
> **define** *glue_set*(#) ≡ *mem*[# + *glue_offset*].*gr*   { a word of type *glue_ratio* for glue setting }

136. The *new_null_box* function returns a pointer to an *hlist_node* in which all subfields have the values corresponding to '\hbox{}'. The *subtype* field is set to *min_quarterword*, since that' the desired *span_count* value if this *hlist_node* is changed to an *unset_node*.

function *new_null_box*: *pointer*;   { creates a new box node }
> **var** *p*: *pointer*;   { the new node }
> **begin** *p* ← *get_node*(*box_node_size*); *type*(p) ← *hlist_node*; *subtype*(p) ← *min_quarterword*;
> *width*(p) ← 0; *depth*(p) ← 0; *height*(p) ← 0; *shift_amount*(p) ← 0; *list_ptr*(p) ← *null*;
> *glue_sign*(p) ← *normal*; *glue_order*(p) ← *normal*; *set_glue_ratio_zero*(*glue_set*(p)); *new_null_box* ← *p*;
> **end**;

137. A *vlist_node* is like an *hlist_node* in all respects except that it contains a vertical list.

> **define** *vlist_node* = 1   { *type* of vlist nodes }

138. A *rule_node* stands for a solid black rectangle; it has *width*, *depth*, and *height* fields just as in an *hlist_node*. However, if any of these dimensions is -2^{30}, the actual value will be determined by running the rule up to the boundary of the innermost enclosing box. This is called a "running dimension." The *width* is never running in an hlist; the *height* and *depth* are never running in a vlist.

> **define** *rule_node* = 2   { *type* of rule nodes }
> **define** *rule_node_size* = 4   { number of words to allocate for a rule node }
> **define** *null_flag* ≡ − ´10000000000   { −2^{30}, signifies a missing item }
> **define** *is_running*(#) ≡ (# = *null_flag*)   { tests for a running dimension }

139.   A new rule node is delivered by the *new_rule* function. It makes all the dimensions "running," so you have to change the ones that are not allowed to run.

function *new_rule*: *pointer*;
  var *p*: *pointer*;   { the new node }
  begin *p* ← *get_node*(*rule_node_size*); *type*(*p*) ← *rule_node*; *subtype*(*p*) ← 0;
      { the *subtype* is not used }
  width(*p*) ← *null_flag*; *depth*(*p*) ← *null_flag*; *height*(*p*) ← *null_flag*; *new_rule* ← *p*;
  end;

140.   Insertions are represented by *ins_node* records, where the *subtype* indicates the corresponding box number. For example, '\insert 250' leads to an *ins_node* whose *subtype* is 250 + *min_quarterword*. The *height* field of an *ins_node* is slightly misnamed; it actually holds the natural height plus depth of the vertical list being inserted. The *depth* field holds the *split_max_depth* to be used in case this insertion is split, and the *split_top_ptr* points to the corresponding *split_top_skip*. The *float_cost* field holds the *floating_penalty* that will be used if this insertion floats to a subsequent page after a split insertion of the same class. There is one more field, the *ins_ptr*, which points to the beginning of the vlist for the insertion.

> **define** *ins_node* = 3   { *type* of insertion nodes }
> **define** *ins_node_size* = 5   { number of words to allocate for an insertion }
> **define** *float_cost*(#) ≡ *mem*[# + 1].*int*   { the *floating_penalty* to be used }
> **define** *ins_ptr*(#) ≡ *info*(# + 4)   { the vertical list to be inserted }
> **define** *split_top_ptr*(#) ≡ *link*(# + 4)   { the *split_top_skip* to be used }

141.   A *mark_node* has a *mark_ptr* field that points to the reference count of a token list that contains the user's \mark text. This field occupies a full word instead of a halfword, because there's nothing to put in the other halfword; it is easier in Pascal to use the full word than to risk leaving garbage in the unused half.

> **define** *mark_node* = 4   { *type* of a mark node }
> **define** *small_node_size* = 2   { number of words to allocate for most node types }
> **define** *mark_ptr*(#) ≡ *mem*[# + 1].*int*   { head of the token list for a mark }

---

fil = 1, §150.
fill = 2, §150.
filll = 3, §150.
floating_penalty = macro, §236.
get_node: **function**, §125.
glue_ratio = *real*, §109.
gr: *glue_ratio*, §113.

info = macro, §118.
int: *integer*, §113.
link = macro, §118.
min_quarterword = 0, §110.
null = macro, §115.
pointer = macro, §115.
sc = macro, §113.

set_glue_ratio_zero = macro, §109.
span_count = macro, §159.
split_max_depth = macro, §247.
split_top_skip = macro, §224.
subtype = macro, §133.
type = macro, §133.
unset_node = 13, §159.

142. An *adjust_node*, which occurs only in horizontal lists, specifies material that will be moved out into the surrounding vertical list; i.e., it is used to implement TeX's '\vadjust' operation. The *adjust_ptr* field points to the vlist containing this material.

define *adjust_node* = 5 { *type* of an adjust node }
define *adjust_ptr* ≡ *mark_ptr*   { vertical list to be moved out of horizontal list }

143. A *ligature_node*, which occurs only in horizontal lists, specifies a composite character that was formed from two or more actual characters. The second word of the node, which is called the *lig_char* word, contains *font* and *character* fields just as in a *char_node*. The characters that generated the ligature have not been forgotten, since they are needed for diagnostic messages and for hyphenation; the *lig_ptr* field points to a linked list of character nodes for those characters.

define *ligature_node* = 6 { *type* of a ligature node }
define *lig_char*(#) ≡ # + 1   { the word where the ligature is to be found }
define *lig_ptr*(#) ≡ *link*(*lig_char*(#))   { the list of characters }

144. The *new_ligature* function creates a ligature node having given contents of the *font*, *character*, and *lig_ptr* fields.

function *new_ligature*(*f*, *c* : *quarterword*; *q* : *pointer*): *pointer*;
  var *p*: *pointer*;   { the new node }
  begin *p* ← *get_node*(*small_node_size*); *type*(*p*) ← *ligature_node*; *subtype*(*p*) ← 0;
      { the *subtype* is not used }
  font(*lig_char*(*p*)) ← *f*; *character*(*lig_char*(*p*)) ← *c*; *lig_ptr*(*p*) ← *q*; *new_ligature* ← *p*;
  end;

145. A *disc_node*, which occurs only in horizontal lists, specifies a "discretionary" line break. If such a break occurs at node *p*, the text that starts at *pre_break*(*p*) will precede the break, the text that starts at *post_break*(*p*) will follow the break, and text that appears in the next *replace_count*(*p*) nodes will be ignored. For example, an ordinary discretionary hyphen, indicated by '\-', yields a *disc_node* with *pre_break* pointing to a *char_node* containing a hyphen, *post_break* = *null*, and *replace_count* = 0. All three of the discretionary texts must be lists that consist entirely of character, kern, box, rule, and ligature nodes.

If *pre_break*(*p*) = *null*, the *ex_hyphen_penalty* will be charged for this break. Otherwise the *hyphen_penalty* will be charged. The texts will actually be substituted into the list by the line-breaking algorithm if it decides to make the break, and the discretionary node will disappear at that time; thus, the output routine sees only discretionaries that were not chosen.

define *disc_node* = 7   { *type* of a discretionary node }
define *replace_count* ≡ *subtype*   { how many subsequent nodes to replace }
define *pre_break* ≡ *llink*   { text that precedes a discretionary break }
define *post_break* ≡ *rlink*   { text that follows a discretionary break }

function *new_disc*: *pointer*;   { creates an empty *disc_node* }
  var *p*: *pointer*;   { the new node }
  begin *p* ← *get_node*(*small_node_size*); *type*(*p*) ← *disc_node*; *replace_count*(*p*) ← 0;
  pre_break(*p*) ← *null*; *post_break*(*p*) ← *null*; *new_disc* ← *p*;
  end;

146. A *whatsit_node* is a wild card reserved for extensions to TeX. The *subtype* field in its first word says what '*whatsit*' it is, and implicitly determines the node size (which must be 2 or more) and the format of the remaining words. When a *whatsit_node* is encountered in a list, special actions are invoked; knowledgeable people who are careful not to mess up the rest of TEX are able to make TEX do new things by adding code at the end of the program. For example, there might be a 'TEXnicolor' extension to specify different colors of ink, and the whatsit node might contain the desired parameters.

The present implementation of TEX treats the features associated with '\write' and '\special' as if they were extensions, in order to illustrate how such routines might be coded. We shall defer further discussion of extensions until the end of this program.

> **define** *whatsit_node* $= 8$ { *type* of special extension nodes }

147. A *math_node*, which occurs only in horizontal lists, appears before and after mathematical formulas. The *subtype* field is *before* before the formula and *after* after it. There is a *width* field, which represents the amount of surrounding space inserted by \mathsurround.

> **define** *math_node* $= 9$ { *type* of a math node }
> **define** *before* $= 0$ { *subtype* for math node that introduces a formula }
> **define** *after* $= 1$ { *subtype* for math node that winds up a formula }

function *new_math*($w : scaled$; $s : small\_number$): *pointer*;
 var p: *pointer*; { the new node }
 begin $p \leftarrow get\_node(small\_node\_size)$; $type(p) \leftarrow math\_node$; $subtype(p) \leftarrow s$; $width(p) \leftarrow w$;
 $new\_math \leftarrow p$;
 end;

148. TEX makes use of the fact that *hlist_node*, *vlist_node*, *rule_node*, *ins_node*, *mark_node*, *adjust_node*, *ligature_node*, *disc_node*, *whatsit_node*, and *math_node* are at the low end of the type codes, by permitting a break at glue in a list if and only if the *type* of the previous node is less than *math_node*. Furthermore, a node is discarded after a break if its type is *math_node* or more.

> **define** *precedes_break*(**#**) $\equiv (type(\text{\#}) < math\_node)$
> **define** *non_discardable*(**#**) $\equiv (type(\text{\#}) < math\_node)$

---

char_node, §134.
character = macro, §134.
ex_hyphen_penalty = macro, §236.
font = macro, §134.
get_node: **function**, §125.
hlist_node = 0, §135.
hyphen_penalty = macro, §236.
ins_node = 3, §140.

link = macro, §118.
llink = macro, §124.
mark_node = 4, §141.
mark_ptr = macro, §141.
null = macro, §115.
pointer = macro, §115.
quarterword = 0 .. 255, §113.
rlink = macro, §124.

rule_node = 2, §138.
scaled = *integer*, §101.
small_node_size = 2, §141.
small_number = 0 .. 63, §101.
subtype = macro, §133.
type = macro, §133.
vlist_node = 1, §137.
width = macro, §135.

149. A *glue_node* represents glue in a list. However, it is really only a pointer to a separate glue specification, since TeX makes use of the fact that many essentially identical nodes of glue are usually present. If p points to a *glue_node*, *glue_ptr*(p) points to another packet of words that specify the stretch and shrink components, etc.

Glue nodes also serve to represent leaders; the *subtype* is used to distinguish between ordinary glue (which is called *normal*) and the three kinds of leaders (which are called *a_leaders*, *c_leaders*, and *x_leaders*). The *leader_ptr* field points to a rule node or to a box node containing the leaders; it is set to *null* in ordinary glue nodes.

Many kinds of glue are computed from TeX's "skip" parameters, and it is helpful to know which parameter has led to a particular glue node. Therefore the *subtype* is set to indicate the source of glue, whenever it originated as a parameter. We will be defining symbolic names for the parameter numbers later (e.g., *line_skip_code* = 0, *baseline_skip_code* = 1, etc.); it suffices for now to say that the *subtype* of parametric glue will be the same as the parameter number, plus one.

In math formulas there are two more possibilities for the *subtype* in a glue node: *mu_glue* denotes an \mskip (where the units are scaled mu instead of scaled pt); and *cond_math_glue* denotes the '\nonscript' feature that cancels the glue node immediately following if it appears in a subscript.

define *glue_node* = 10   { *type* of node that points to a glue specification }
define *cond_math_glue* = 98   { special *subtype* to suppress glue in the next node }
define *mu_glue* = 99   { *subtype* for math glue }
define *a_leaders* = 100   { *subtype* for aligned leaders }
define *c_leaders* = 101   { *subtype* for centered leaders }
define *x_leaders* = 102   { *subtype* for expanded leaders }
define *glue_ptr* $\equiv$ *llink*   { pointer to a glue specification }
define *leader_ptr* $\equiv$ *rlink*   { pointer to box or rule node for leaders }

150. A glue specification has a halfword reference count in its first word, representing *null* plus the number of glue nodes that point to it (less one). Note that the reference count appears in the same position as the *link* field in list nodes; this is the field that is initialized to *null* when a node is allocated, and it is also the field that is flagged by *empty_flag* in empty nodes.

Glue specifications also contain three *scaled* fields, for the *width*, *stretch*, and *shrink* dimensions. Finally, there are two one-byte fields called *stretch_order* and *shrink_order*; these contain the orders of infinity (*normal*, *fil*, *fill*, or *filll*) corresponding to the stretch and shrink values.

define *glue_spec_size* = 4   { number of words to allocate for a glue specification }
define *glue_ref_count*(#) $\equiv$ *link*(#)   { reference count of a glue specification }
define *stretch*(#) $\equiv$ *mem*[# + 2].*sc*   { the stretchability of this glob of glue }
define *shrink*(#) $\equiv$ *mem*[# + 3].*sc*   { the shrinkability of this glob of glue }
define *stretch_order* $\equiv$ *type*   { order of infinity for stretching }
define *shrink_order* $\equiv$ *subtype*   { order of infinity for shrinking }
define *fil* = 1   { first-order infinity }
define *fill* = 2   { second-order infinity }
define *filll* = 3   { third-order infinity }

⟨ Types in the outer block 18 ⟩ +$\equiv$
  glue_ord = *normal* .. *filll*;   { infinity to the 0, 1, 2, or 3 power }

151. Here is a function that returns a pointer to a copy of a glue spec. The reference count in the copy is *null*, because there is assumed to be exactly one reference to the new specification.

function *new_spec*(*p* : *pointer*): *pointer*;   { duplicates a glue specification }
  var *q*: *pointer*;   { the new spec }
  begin *q* ← *get_node*(*glue_spec_size*);
  mem[*q*] ← *mem*[*p*]; *glue_ref_count*(*q*) ← *null*;
  width(*q*) ← *width*(*p*); *stretch*(*q*) ← *stretch*(*p*); *shrink*(*q*) ← *shrink*(*p*); *new_spec* ← *q*;
  end;

152. And here's a function that creates a glue node for a given parameter identified by its code number; for example, *new_param_glue*(*line_skip_code*) returns a pointer to a glue node for the current \lineskip.

function *new_param_glue*(*n* : *small_number*): *pointer*;
  var *p*: *pointer*;   { the new node }
    q: *pointer*;   { the glue specification }
  begin *p* ← *get_node*(*small_node_size*); *type*(*p*) ← *glue_node*; *subtype*(*p*) ← *n* + 1;
  leader_ptr(*p*) ← *null*;
  q ← ⟨ Current *mem* equivalent of glue parameter number *n* 224 ⟩; *glue_ptr*(*p*) ← *q*;
  incr(*glue_ref_count*(*q*)); *new_param_glue* ← *p*;
  end;

153. Glue nodes that are more or less anonymous are created by *new_glue*, whose argument points to a glue specification.

function *new_glue*(*q* : *pointer*): *pointer*;
  var *p*: *pointer*;   { the new node }
  begin *p* ← *get_node*(*small_node_size*); *type*(*p*) ← *glue_node*; *subtype*(*p*) ← *normal*;
  leader_ptr(*p*) ← *null*; *glue_ptr*(*p*) ← *q*; *incr*(*glue_ref_count*(*q*)); *new_glue* ← *p*;
  end;

154. Still another subroutine is needed: this one is sort of a combination of *new_param_glue* and *new_glue*. It creates a glue node for one of the current glue parameters, but it makes a fresh copy of the glue specification, since that specification will probably be subject to change, while the parameter will stay put. The global variable *temp_ptr* is set to the address of the new spec.

function *new_skip_param*(*n* : *small_number*): *pointer*;
  var *p*: *pointer*;   { the new node }
  begin *temp_ptr* ← *new_spec*(⟨ Current *mem* equivalent of glue parameter number *n* 224 ⟩);
  p ← *new_glue*(*temp_ptr*); *glue_ref_count*(*temp_ptr*) ← *null*; *subtype*(*p*) ← *n* + 1; *new_skip_param* ← *p*;
  end;

---

baseline_skip_code = 1, §224.
empty_flag = macro, §124.
get_node: **function**, §125.
incr = macro, §16.
line_skip_code = 0, §224.
link = macro, §118.
llink = macro, §124.

normal = 0, §135.
null = macro, §115.
pointer = macro, §115.
rlink = macro, §124.
sc = macro, §113.
scaled = *integer*, §101.

small_node_size = 2, §141.
small_number = 0 . . 63, §101.
subtype = macro, §133.
temp_ptr: *pointer*, §115.
type = macro, §133.
width = macro, §135.

155.   A *kern_node* has a *width* field to specify a (normally negative) amount of spacing. This spacing correction appears in horizontal lists between letters like A and V when the font designer said that it looks better to move them closer together or further apart. A kern node can also appear in a vertical list, when its '*width*' denotes additional spacing in the vertical direction. The *subtype* is either *normal* (for kerns inserted from font information or math mode calculations) or *explicit* (for kerns inserted from \kern and \/ commands) or *acc_kern* (for kerns inserted from non-math accents) or *mu_glue* (for kerns inserted from \mkern specifications in math formulas).

define *kern_node* = 11   { *type* of a kern node }
define *explicit* = 1   { *subtype* of kern nodes from \kern and \/ }
define *acc_kern* = 2   { *subtype* of kern nodes from accents }

156.   The *new_kern* function creates a kern node having a given width.

function *new_kern*(*w* : *scaled*): *pointer*;
  var *p*: *pointer*;   { the new node }
  begin *p* ← *get_node*(*small_node_size*); *type*(*p*) ← *kern_node*; *subtype*(*p*) ← *normal*; *width*(*p*) ← *w*;
  new_kern ← *p*;
  end;

157.   A *penalty_node* specifies the penalty associated with line or page breaking, in its *penalty* field. This field is a fullword integer, but the full range of integer values is not used: Any penalty ≥ 10000 is treated as infinity, and no break will be allowed for such high values. Similarly, any penalty ≤ -10000 is treated as negative infinity, and a break will be forced.

define *penalty_node* = 12   { *type* of a penalty node }
define *inf_penalty* = *inf_bad*   { "infinite" penalty value }
define *eject_penalty* = −*inf_penalty*   { "negatively infinite" penalty value }
define *penalty*(**#**) ≡ *mem*[**#** + 1].*int*   { the added cost of breaking a list here }

158.   Anyone who has been reading the last few sections of the program will be able to guess what comes next.

function *new_penalty*(*m* : *integer*): *pointer*;
  var *p*: *pointer*;   { the new node }
  begin *p* ← *get_node*(*small_node_size*); *type*(*p*) ← *penalty_node*; *subtype*(*p*) ← 0;
    { the *subtype* is not used }
  penalty(*p*) ← *m*; *new_penalty* ← *p*;
  end;

159.   You might think that we have introduced enough node types by now. Well, almost, but there is one more: An *unset_node* has nearly the same format as an *hlist_node* or *vlist_node*; it is used for entries in \halign or \valign that are not yet in their final form, since the box dimensions are their "natural" sizes before any glue adjustment has been made. The *glue_set* word is not present; instead, we have a *glue_stretch* field, which contains the total stretch of order *glue_order* that is present in the hlist or vlist being boxed. Similarly, the *shift_amount* field is replaced by a *glue_shrink* field, containing the total shrink of order *glue_sign* that is present. The *subtype* field is called *span_count*; an unset box typically contains the data for *qo*(*span_count*) + 1 columns. Unset nodes will be changed to box nodes when alignment is completed.

define *unset_node* = 13   { *type* for an unset node }
define *glue_stretch*(**#**) ≡ *mem*[**#** + *glue_offset*].*sc*   { total stretch in an unset node }

define *glue_shrink* ≡ *shift_amount*   { total shrink in an unset node }
define *span_count* ≡ *subtype*   { indicates the number of spanned columns }

160.   In fact, there are still more types coming. When we get to math formula processing we will see that a *style_node* has *type* = 14; and a number of larger type codes will also be defined, for use in math mode only.

161.   Warning: If any changes are made to these data structure layouts, such as changing any of the node sizes or even reordering the words of nodes, the *copy_node_list* procedure and the memory initialization code below may have to be changed. Such potentially dangerous parts of the program are listed in the index under 'data structure assumptions'. However, other references to the nodes are made symbolically in terms of the WEB macro definitions above, so that format changes will leave TEX's other algorithms intact.

162. Memory layout. Some areas of *mem* are dedicated to fixed usage, since static allocation is more efficient than dynamic allocation when we can get away with it. For example, locations *mem_bot* to *mem_bot* + 3 are always used to store the specification for glue that is 'Opt plus Opt minus Opt'. The following macro definitions accomplish the static allocation by giving symbolic names to the fixed positions. Static variable-size nodes appear in locations *mem_bot* through *lo_mem_stat_max*, and static single-word nodes appear in locations *hi_mem_stat_min* through *mem_top*, inclusive. It is harmless to let *lig_trick*, *garbage*, and *backup_head* share the same location of *mem*.

> **define** *zero_glue* ≡ *mem_bot* { specification for Opt plus Opt minus Opt }
> **define** *fil_glue* ≡ *zero_glue* + *glue_spec_size* { Opt plus 1fil minus Opt }
> **define** *fill_glue* ≡ *fil_glue* + *glue_spec_size* { Opt plus 1fill minus Opt }
> **define** *ss_glue* ≡ *fill_glue* + *glue_spec_size* { Opt plus 1fil minus 1fil }
> **define** *fil_neg_glue* ≡ *ss_glue* + *glue_spec_size* { Opt plus -1fil minus Opt }
> **define** *lo_mem_stat_max* ≡ *fil_neg_glue* + *glue_spec_size* − 1
> { largest statically allocated word in the variable-size *mem* }

> **define** *page_ins_head* ≡ *mem_top* { list of insertion data for current page }
> **define** *contrib_head* ≡ *mem_top* − 1 { vlist of items not yet on current page }
> **define** *page_head* ≡ *mem_top* − 2 { vlist for current page }
> **define** *temp_head* ≡ *mem_top* − 3 { head of a temporary list of some kind }
> **define** *hold_head* ≡ *mem_top* − 4 { head of a temporary list of another kind }
> **define** *adjust_head* ≡ *mem_top* − 5 { head of adjustment list returned by *hpack* }
> **define** *active* ≡ *mem_top* − 7 { head of active list in *line_break*, needs two words }
> **define** *align_head* ≡ *mem_top* − 8 { head of preamble list for alignments }
> **define** *end_span* ≡ *mem_top* − 9 { tail of spanned-width lists }
> **define** *omit_template* ≡ *mem_top* − 10 { a constant token list }
> **define** *null_list* ≡ *mem_top* − 11 { permanently empty list }
> **define** *lig_trick* ≡ *mem_top* − 12 { a ligature masquerading as a *char_node* }
> **define** *garbage* ≡ *mem_top* − 12 { used for scrap information }
> **define** *backup_head* ≡ *mem_top* − 13 { head of token list built by *scan_keyword* }
> **define** *hi_mem_stat_min* ≡ *mem_top* − 13 { smallest statically allocated word in the one-word *mem* }
> **define** *hi_mem_stat_usage* = 14 { the number of one-word nodes always present }

163. The following code gets *mem* off to a good start, when TeX is initializing itself the slow way.

⟨ Local variables for initialization 19 ⟩ +≡
k: *integer*; { index into *mem*, *eqtb*, etc. }

164. ⟨ Initialize table entries (done by INITEX only) 164 ⟩ ≡
  for *k* ← *mem_bot* + 1 **to** *lo_mem_stat_max* **do** *mem*[*k*].*sc* ← 0; { all glue dimensions are zeroed }
  k ← *mem_bot*; **while** *k* ≤ *lo_mem_stat_max* **do** { set first words of glue specifications }
    begin *glue_ref_count*(*k*) ← *null* + 1; *stretch_order*(*k*) ← *normal*; *shrink_order*(*k*) ← *normal*;
    k ← *k* + *glue_spec_size*;
    end;
  stretch(*fil_glue*) ← *unity*; *stretch_order*(*fil_glue*) ← *fil*;
  stretch(*fill_glue*) ← *unity*; *stretch_order*(*fill_glue*) ← *fill*;
  stretch(*ss_glue*) ← *unity*; *stretch_order*(*ss_glue*) ← *fil*;
  shrink(*ss_glue*) ← *unity*; *shrink_order*(*ss_glue*) ← *fil*;

$stretch(fil\_neg\_glue) \leftarrow -unity$; $stretch\_order(fil\_neg\_glue) \leftarrow fil$;
$rover \leftarrow lo\_mem\_stat\_max + 1$; $link(rover) \leftarrow empty\_flag$; { now initialize the dynamic memory }
$node\_size(rover) \leftarrow 1000$; { which is a 1000-word available node }
$llink(rover) \leftarrow rover$; $rlink(rover) \leftarrow rover$;
$lo\_mem\_max \leftarrow rover + 1000$; $link(lo\_mem\_max) \leftarrow null$; $info(lo\_mem\_max) \leftarrow null$;
for $k \leftarrow hi\_mem\_stat\_min$ **to** mem_top **do** $mem[k] \leftarrow mem[lo\_mem\_max]$; { clear list heads }
⟨ Initialize the special list heads and constant nodes 790 ⟩;
$avail \leftarrow null$; $mem\_end \leftarrow mem\_top$; $hi\_mem\_min \leftarrow hi\_mem\_stat\_min$;
        { initialize the one-word memory }
$var\_used \leftarrow lo\_mem\_stat\_max + 1 - mem\_bot$; $dyn\_used \leftarrow hi\_mem\_stat\_usage$; { initialize statistics }

See also sections 222, 228, 232, 240, 250, 258, 552, 952, 1216, 1301, and 1369.

This code is used in section 8.

165. If TeX is extended improperly, the *mem* array might get screwed up. For example, some pointers might be wrong, or some "dead" nodes might not have been freed when the last reference to them disappeared. Procedures *check_mem* and *search_mem* are available to help diagnose such problems. These procedures make use of two arrays called *free* and *was_free* that are present only if TeX's debugging routines have been included. (You may want to decrease the size of *mem* while you are debugging.)

⟨ Global variables 13 ⟩ +≡
    debug *free*: **packed array** [*mem_min* .. *mem_max*] **of** *boolean*; { free cells }
    was_free: **packed array** [*mem_min* .. *mem_max*] **of** *boolean*; { previously free cells }
    was_mem_end, *was_lo_max*, *was_hi_min*: *pointer*;
            { previous *mem_end*, *lo_mem_max*, and *hi_mem_min* }
    panicking: *boolean*; { do we want to check memory constantly? }
    gubed

166. ⟨ Set initial values of key variables 21 ⟩ +≡
    debug *was_mem_end* ← *mem_min*; { indicate that everything was previously free }
    was_lo_max ← *mem_min*; *was_hi_min* ← *mem_max*; *panicking* ← *false*;
    gubed

---

avail: *pointer*, §118.
char_node, §134.
check_mem: **procedure**, §167.
dyn_used: *integer*, §117.
empty_flag = macro, §124.
eqtb: **array**, §253.
fil = 1, §150.
fill = 2, §150.
glue_ref_count = macro, §150.
glue_spec_size = 4, §150.
hi_mem_min: *pointer*, §116.
hpack: **function**, §649.

info = macro, §118.
line_break: **procedure**, §815.
link = macro, §118.
llink = macro, §124.
lo_mem_max: *pointer*, §116.
mem_max = **const**, §11.
mem_min = **const**, §11.
node_size = macro, §124.
normal = 0, §135.
null = macro, §115.
pointer = macro, §115.

rlink = macro, §124.
rover: *pointer*, §124.
sc = macro, §113.
scan_keyword: **function**, §407.
search_mem: **procedure**, §172.
shrink = macro, §150.
shrink_order = macro, §150.
stretch = macro, §150.
stretch_order = macro, §150.
unity = macro, §101.
var_used: *integer*, §117.

167.   Procedure *check_mem* makes sure that the available space lists of *mem* are well formed, and it optionally prints out all locations that are reserved now but were free the last time this procedure was called.

```
debug procedure check_mem(print_locs : boolean);
label done1, done2;   { loop exits }
var p, q: pointer;   { current locations of interest in mem }
   clobbered: boolean;   { is something amiss? }
begin for p ← mem_min to lo_mem_max do free[p] ← false;   { you can probably do this faster }
for p ← hi_mem_min to mem_end do free[p] ← false;   { ditto }
⟨ Check single-word avail list 168 ⟩;
⟨ Check variable-size avail list 169 ⟩;
⟨ Check flags of unavailable nodes 170 ⟩;
if print_locs then ⟨ Print newly busy locations 171 ⟩;
for p ← mem_min to lo_mem_max do was_free[p] ← free[p];
for p ← hi_mem_min to mem_end do was_free[p] ← free[p];   { was_free ← free might be faster }
was_mem_end ← mem_end;  was_lo_max ← lo_mem_max;  was_hi_min ← hi_mem_min;
end;
gubed
```

168.   ⟨ Check single-word *avail* list 168 ⟩ ≡
```
p ← avail;  q ← null;  clobbered ← false;
while p ≠ null do
   begin if (p > mem_end) ∨ (p < hi_mem_min) then  clobbered ← true
   else if free[p] then  clobbered ← true;
   if clobbered then
      begin print_nl("AVAIL␣list␣clobbered␣at␣");  print_int(q);  goto done1;
      end;
   free[p] ← true;  q ← p;  p ← link(q);
   end;
done1:
```
This code is used in section 167.

169.   ⟨ Check variable-size *avail* list 169 ⟩ ≡
```
p ← rover;  q ← null;  clobbered ← false;
repeat if (p ≥ lo_mem_max) ∨ (p < mem_min) then  clobbered ← true
   else if (rlink(p) ≥ lo_mem_max) ∨ (rlink(p) < mem_min) then  clobbered ← true
      else if ¬(is_empty(p)) ∨ (node_size(p) < 2) ∨ (p + node_size(p) > lo_mem_max) ∨
            (llink(rlink(p)) ≠ p) then  clobbered ← true;
   if clobbered then
      begin print_nl("Double-AVAIL␣list␣clobbered␣at␣");  print_int(q);  goto done2;
      end;
   for q ← p to p + node_size(p) − 1 do   { mark all locations free }
      begin if free[q] then
         begin print_nl("Doubly␣free␣location␣at␣");  print_int(q);  goto done2;
         end;
      free[q] ← true;
      end;
```

$q \leftarrow p; \; p \leftarrow rlink(p);$
   until $p = rover;$
done2:

This code is used in section 167.

170. ⟨ Check flags of unavailable nodes 170 ⟩ ≡
   $p \leftarrow mem\_min;$
   while $p \leq lo\_mem\_max$ **do**   { node p should not be empty }
      begin if $is\_empty(p)$ **then**
         begin $print\_nl(\texttt{"Bad}_{\sqcup}\texttt{flag}_{\sqcup}\texttt{at}_{\sqcup}\texttt{"}); \; print\_int(p);$
         end;
      while $(p \leq lo\_mem\_max) \wedge \neg free[p]$ **do** $incr(p);$
      while $(p \leq lo\_mem\_max) \wedge free[p]$ **do** $incr(p);$
      end

This code is used in section 167.

171. ⟨ Print newly busy locations 171 ⟩ ≡
   begin $print\_nl(\texttt{"New}_{\sqcup}\texttt{busy}_{\sqcup}\texttt{locs:"});$
   for $p \leftarrow mem\_min$ **to** lo_mem_max **do**
      if $\neg free[p] \wedge ((p > was\_lo\_max) \vee was\_free[p])$ **then**
         begin $print\_char(\texttt{"}_{\sqcup}\texttt{"}); \; print\_int(p);$
         end;
   for $p \leftarrow hi\_mem\_min$ **to** mem_end **do**
      if $\neg free[p] \wedge ((p < was\_hi\_min) \vee (p > was\_mem\_end) \vee was\_free[p])$ **then**
         begin $print\_char(\texttt{"}_{\sqcup}\texttt{"}); \; print\_int(p);$
         end;
   end

This code is used in section 167.

---

avail: **pointer**, §118.
done1 = 31, §15.
done2 = 32, §15.
free: **packed array**, §165.
hi_mem_min: *pointer*, §116.
incr = macro, §16.
is_empty = macro, §124.
link = macro, §118.

llink = macro, §124.
lo_mem_max: *pointer*, §116.
mem_min = **const**, §11.
node_size = macro, §124.
null = macro, §115.
pointer = macro, §115.
print_char: **procedure**, §58.
print_int: **procedure**, §65.

print_nl: **procedure**, §62.
rlink = macro, §124.
rover: *pointer*, §124.
was_free: **packed array**, §165.
was_hi_min: *pointer*, §165.
was_lo_max: *pointer*, §165.
was_mem_end: *pointer*, §165.

172. The *search_mem* procedure attempts to answer the question "Who points to node p?" In doing so, it fetches *link* and *info* fields of *mem* that might not be of type *two_halves*. Strictly speaking, this is undefined in Pascal, and it can lead to "false drops" (words that seem to point to p purely by coincidence). But for debugging purposes, we want to rule out the places that do *not* point to p, so a few false drops are tolerable.

```
debug procedure search_mem(p : pointer);   { look for pointers to p }
var q: integer;   { current position being searched }
begin for q ← mem_min to lo_mem_max do
  begin if link(q) = p then
    begin print_nl("LINK("); print_int(q); print_char(")");
    end;
  if info(q) = p then
    begin print_nl("INFO("); print_int(q); print_char(")");
    end;
  end;
for q ← hi_mem_min to mem_end do
  begin if link(q) = p then
    begin print_nl("LINK("); print_int(q); print_char(")");
    end;
  if info(q) = p then
    begin print_nl("INFO("); print_int(q); print_char(")");
    end;
  end;
⟨ Search eqtb for equivalents equal to p 255 ⟩;
⟨ Search save_stack for equivalents that point to p 285 ⟩;
⟨ Search hyph_list for pointers to p 933 ⟩;
end;
gubed
```

173. Displaying boxes. We can reinforce our knowledge of the data structures just introduced by considering two procedures that display a list in symbolic form. The first of these, called *short_display*, is used in "overfull box" messages to give the top-level description of a list. The other one, called *show_node_list*, prints a detailed description of exactly what is in the data structure.

The philosophy of *short_display* is to ignore the fine points about exactly what is inside boxes, except that ligatures and discretionary breaks are expanded. As a result, *short_display* is a recursive procedure, but the recursion is never more than one level deep.

A global variable *font_in_short_display* keeps track of the font code that is assumed to be present when *short_display* begins; deviations from this font will be printed.

⟨ Global variables 13 ⟩ +≡
font_in_short_display: *integer*;   { an internal font number }

174.   Boxes, rules, inserts, whatsits, marks, and things in general that are sort of "complicated" are indicated only by printing '[]'.

procedure *short_display*(*p* : *integer*);   { prints highlights of list *p* }
  var *n*: *integer*;   { for replacement counts }
  begin while *p* > *null* **do**
    begin if *is_char_node*(*p*) **then**
      begin if *p* ≤ *mem_end* **then**
        begin if *font*(*p*) ≠ *font_in_short_display* **then**
          begin if (*font*(*p*) < *font_base*) ∨ (*font*(*p*) > *font_max*) **then** *print_char*("*")
          else ⟨ Print the font identifier for *font*(*p*) 267 ⟩;
          print_char("␣"); *font_in_short_display* ← *font*(*p*);
          end;
        print_ASCII(*qo*(*character*(*p*)));
        end;
      end
    else ⟨ Print a short indication of the contents of node *p* 175 ⟩;
    p ← *link*(*p*);
    end;
  end;

---

character = macro, §134.
eqtb: **array**, §253.
font = macro, §134.
font_max = **const**, §11.
hi_mem_min: *pointer*, §116.
hyph_list: **array**, §926.
info = macro, §118.

is_char_node = macro, §134.
link = macro, §118.
lo_mem_max: *pointer*, §116.
mem_min = **const**, §11.
null = macro, §115.
pointer = macro, §115.
print_ASCII: **procedure**, §68.

print_char: **procedure**, §58.
print_int: **procedure**, §65.
print_nl: **procedure**, §62.
qo = macro, §112.
save_stack: **array**, §271.
show_node_list: **procedure**, §182.
two_halves = **packed record**, §113.

175. ⟨ Print a short indication of the contents of node p 175 ⟩ ≡

  case $type(p)$ **of**

$hlist\_node, vlist\_node, ins\_node, whatsit\_node, mark\_node, adjust\_node, unset\_node$: $print("[]")$;

$rule\_node$: $print\_char("|")$;

$glue\_node$: **if** $glue\_ptr(p) \neq zero\_glue$ **then** $print\_char("\textvisiblespace")$;

$math\_node$: $print\_char("\$")$;

$ligature\_node$: $short\_display(lig\_ptr(p))$;

$disc\_node$: **begin** $short\_display(pre\_break(p))$; $short\_display(post\_break(p))$;

    $n \leftarrow replace\_count(p)$;

    while $n > 0$ **do**

      begin if $link(p) \neq null$ **then** $p \leftarrow link(p)$;

      $decr(n)$;

      end;

    end;

  othercases $do\_nothing$

  endcases

This code is used in section 174.

176.   The $show\_node\_list$ routine requires some auxiliary subroutines: one to print a font-and-character combination, one to print a token list without its reference count, and one to print a rule dimension.

procedure $print\_font\_and\_char(p : integer)$;   { prints $char\_node$ data }

  begin if $p > mem\_end$ **then** $print\_esc("CLOBBERED.")$

  else begin if $(font(p) < font\_base) \vee (font(p) > font\_max)$ **then** $print\_char("*")$

    else ⟨ Print the font identifier for $font(p)$ 267 ⟩;

    $print\_char("\textvisiblespace")$; $print\_ASCII(qo(character(p)))$;

    end;

  end;

procedure $print\_mark(p : integer)$;   { prints token list data in braces }

  begin $print\_char("\{")$;

  if $(p < hi\_mem\_min) \vee (p > mem\_end)$ **then** $print\_esc("CLOBBERED.")$

  else $show\_token\_list(link(p), null, max\_print\_line - 10)$;

  $print\_char("\}")$;

  end;

procedure $print\_rule\_dimen(d : scaled)$;   { prints dimension in rule node }

  begin if $is\_running(d)$ **then** $print\_char("*")$

  else $print\_scaled(d)$;

  end;

177.   Then there is a subroutine that prints glue stretch and shrink, possibly followed by the name of finite units:

procedure $print\_glue(d : scaled; order : integer; s : str\_number)$;   { prints a glue component }

  begin $print\_scaled(d)$;

  if $(order < normal) \vee (order > filll)$ **then** $print("foul")$

  else if $order > normal$ **then**

    begin $print("fil")$;

    while $order > fil$ **do**

```
      begin print_char("l"); decr(order);
      end;
    end
  else if s ≠ 0 then  print(s);
end;
```

178.   The next subroutine prints a whole glue specification.

procedure *print_spec*(*p* : *integer*; *s* : *str_number*);   { prints a glue specification }
  begin if (*p* < *mem_min*) ∨ (*p* ≥ *lo_mem_max*) **then** *print_char*("*")
  else begin *print_scaled*(*width*(*p*));
    if *s* ≠ 0 **then** *print*(*s*);
    if *stretch*(*p*) ≠ 0 **then**
      begin *print*("␣plus␣"); *print_glue*(*stretch*(*p*), *stretch_order*(*p*), *s*);
      end;
    if *shrink*(*p*) ≠ 0 **then**
      begin *print*("␣minus␣"); *print_glue*(*shrink*(*p*), *shrink_order*(*p*), *s*);
      end;
    end;
  end;

179.   We also need to declare some procedures that appear later in this documentation.

⟨ Declare procedures needed for displaying the elements of mlists 691 ⟩
⟨ Declare the procedure called *print_skip_param* 225 ⟩

180. Since boxes can be inside of boxes, *show_node_list* is inherently recursive, up to a given maximum number of levels. The history of nesting is indicated by the current string, which will be printed at the beginning of each line; the length of this string, namely *cur_length*, is the depth of nesting.

Recursive calls on *show_node_list* therefore use the following pattern:

> **define** *node_list_display*(**#**) ≡
>   **begin** *append_char*("."); *show_node_list*(**#**); *flush_char*;
>   **end**   { *str_room* need not be checked; see *show_box* below }

181. A global variable called *depth_threshold* is used to record the maximum depth of nesting for which *show_node_list* will show information. If we have *depth_threshold* = 0, for example, only the top level information will be given and no sublists will be traversed. Another global variable, called *breadth_max*, tells the maximum number of items to show at each level; *breadth_max* had better be positive, or you won't see anything.

⟨ Global variables 13 ⟩ +≡
depth_threshold: *integer*; { maximum nesting depth in box displays }
breadth_max: *integer*; { maximum number of items shown at the same list level }

182. Now we are ready for *show_node_list* itself. This procedure has been written to be "extra robust" in the sense that it should not crash or get into a loop even if the data structures have been messed up by bugs in the rest of the program. You can safely call its parent routine *show_box*(*p*) for arbitrary values of *p* when you are debugging TeX. However, in the presence of bad data, the procedure may fetch a *memory_word* whose variant is different from the way it was stored; for example, it might try to read *mem*[*p*].*hh* when *mem*[*p*] contains a scaled integer, if *p* is a pointer that has been clobbered or chosen at random.

procedure *show_node_list*(*p* : *pointer*); { prints a node list symbolically }
  label *exit*;
  var *n*: *integer*; { the number of items already printed at this level }
    g: *real*; { a glue ratio, as a floating point number }
  begin if *cur_length* > *depth_threshold* **then**
    begin if *p* > *null* **then** *print*("␣[]"); { indicate that there's been some truncation }
    return;
    end;
  n ← 0;
  while *p* > *null* **do**
    begin *print_ln*; *print_current_string*; { display the nesting history }
    if *p* > *mem_end* **then** { pointer out of range }
      begin *print*("Bad␣link,␣display␣aborted."); **return**;
      end;
    incr(*n*);
    if *n* > *breadth_max* **then** { time to stop }
      begin *print*("etc."); **return**;
      end;
    ⟨ Display node *p* 183 ⟩;
    p ← *link*(*p*);
    end;
exit: **end**;

183. ⟨ Display node p 183 ⟩ ≡
  if *is_char_node*(p) **then** *print_font_and_char*(p)
  else case *type*(p) **of**
    hlist_node, *vlist_node*, *unset_node*: ⟨ Display box p 184 ⟩;
    rule_node: ⟨ Display rule p 187 ⟩;
    ins_node: ⟨ Display insertion p 188 ⟩;
    whatsit_node: ⟨ Display the whatsit node p 1356 ⟩;
    glue_node: ⟨ Display glue p 189 ⟩;
    kern_node: ⟨ Display kern p 191 ⟩;
    math_node: ⟨ Display math node p 192 ⟩;
    ligature_node: ⟨ Display ligature p 193 ⟩;
    penalty_node: ⟨ Display penalty p 194 ⟩;
    disc_node: ⟨ Display discretionary p 195 ⟩;
    mark_node: ⟨ Display mark p 196 ⟩;
    adjust_node: ⟨ Display adjustment p 197 ⟩;
    ⟨ Cases of *show_node_list* that arise in mlists only 690 ⟩
    othercases *print*("Unknown␣node␣type!")
  endcases

This code is used in section 182.

184. ⟨ Display box p 184 ⟩ ≡
  begin if *type*(p) = *hlist_node* **then** *print_esc*("h")
  else if *type*(p) = *vlist_node* **then** *print_esc*("v")
    else *print_esc*("unset");
  print("box("); *print_scaled*(*height*(p)); *print_char*("+"); *print_scaled*(*depth*(p)); *print*(")x");
  print_scaled(*width*(p));
  if *type*(p) = *unset_node* **then** ⟨ Display special fields of the unset node p 185 ⟩
  else begin ⟨ Display the value of *glue_set*(p) 186 ⟩;
    if *shift_amount*(p) ≠ 0 **then**
      begin *print*(",␣shifted␣"); *print_scaled*(*shift_amount*(p));
      end;
    end;
  node_list_display(*list_ptr*(p));   { recursive call }
  end

This code is used in section 183.

---

adjust_node = 5, §142.
append_char = macro, §42.
cur_length = macro, §41.
depth = macro, §135.
disc_node = 7, §145.
exit = 10, §15.
flush_char = macro, §42.
glue_node = 10, §149.
glue_set = macro, §135.
height = macro, §135.
hh: *two_halves*, §113.
hlist_node = 0, §135.
incr = macro, §16.
ins_node = 3, §140.
is_char_node = macro, §134.

kern_node = 11, §155.
ligature_node = 6, §143.
link = macro, §118.
list_ptr = macro, §135.
mark_node = 4, §141.
math_node = 9, §147.
memory_word = **record**, §113.
null = macro, §115.
penalty_node = 12, §157.
pointer = macro, §115.
print: **procedure**, §59.
print_char: **procedure**, §58.
print_current_string: **procedure**,
  §70.

print_esc: **procedure**, §63.
print_font_and_char: **procedure**,
  §176.
print_ln: **procedure**, §57.
print_scaled: **procedure**, §103.
rule_node = 2, §138.
shift_amount = macro, §135.
show_box: **procedure**, §198.
str_room = macro, §42.
type = macro, §133.
unset_node = 13, §159.
vlist_node = 1, §137.
whatsit_node = 8, §146.
width = macro, §135.

185. ⟨ Display special fields of the unset node p 185 ⟩ ≡
  begin if $span\_count(p) \neq min\_quarterword$ **then**
    begin $print("\_(")$; $print\_int(qo(span\_count(p)) + 1)$; $print("\_columns)")$;
    end;
  if $glue\_stretch(p) \neq 0$ **then**
    begin $print(",\_stretch\_")$; $print\_glue(glue\_stretch(p), glue\_order(p), 0)$;
    end;
  if $glue\_shrink(p) \neq 0$ **then**
    begin $print(",\_shrink\_")$; $print\_glue(glue\_shrink(p), glue\_sign(p), 0)$;
    end;
  end

This code is used in section 184.

186. The code will have to change in this place if $glue\_ratio$ is a structured type instead of an ordinary *real*. Note that this routine should avoid arithmetic errors even if the $glue\_set$ field holds an arbitrary random value. The following code assumes that a properly formed nonzero *real* number has absolute value 2^{20} or more when it is regarded as an integer; this precaution was adequate to prevent floating point underflow on the author's computer.

⟨ Display the value of $glue\_set(p)$ 186 ⟩ ≡
  $g \leftarrow float(glue\_set(p))$;
  if $(g \neq float\_constant(0)) \wedge (glue\_sign(p) \neq normal)$ **then**
    begin $print(",\_glue\_set\_")$;
    if $glue\_sign(p) = shrinking$ **then** $print("-\_")$;
    if $abs(mem[p + glue\_offset].int) < '4000000$ **then** $print("?.?")$
    else if $abs(g) > float\_constant(20000)$ **then**
        begin if $g > float\_constant(0)$ **then** $print\_char(">")$
        else $print("<\_-")$;
        $print\_glue(20000 * unity, glue\_order(p), 0)$;
        end
      else $print\_glue(round(unity * g), glue\_order(p), 0)$;
    end

This code is used in section 184.

187. ⟨ Display rule p 187 ⟩ ≡
  begin $print\_esc("rule(")$; $print\_rule\_dimen(height(p))$; $print\_char("+")$;
  $print\_rule\_dimen(depth(p))$; $print(")x")$; $print\_rule\_dimen(width(p))$;
  end

This code is used in section 183.

188. ⟨ Display insertion p 188 ⟩ ≡
  begin $print\_esc("insert")$; $print\_int(qo(subtype(p)))$; $print(",\_natural\_size\_")$;
  $print\_scaled(height(p))$; $print(";\_split(")$; $print\_spec(split\_top\_ptr(p), 0)$; $print\_char(",")$;
  $print\_scaled(depth(p))$; $print(");\_float\_cost\_")$; $print\_int(float\_cost(p))$;
  $node\_list\_display(ins\_ptr(p))$;   { recursive call }
  end

This code is used in section 183.

189.   ⟨ Display glue p 189 ⟩ ≡
   if $subtype(p) \geq a\_leaders$ **then** ⟨ Display leaders p 190 ⟩
   else begin $print\_esc(\texttt{"glue"})$;
      if $subtype(p) \neq normal$ **then**
         begin $print\_char(\texttt{"("})$;
         if $subtype(p) < cond\_math\_glue$ **then** $print\_skip\_param(subtype(p) - 1)$
         else if $subtype(p) = cond\_math\_glue$ **then** $print\_esc(\texttt{"nonscript"})$
            else $print\_esc(\texttt{"mskip"})$;
         $print\_char(\texttt{")"})$;
         end;
      if $subtype(p) \neq cond\_math\_glue$ **then**
         begin $print\_char(\texttt{"␣"})$;
         if $subtype(p) < cond\_math\_glue$ **then** $print\_spec(glue\_ptr(p), 0)$
         else $print\_spec(glue\_ptr(p), \texttt{"mu"})$;
         end;
      end

This code is used in section 183.

190.   ⟨ Display leaders p 190 ⟩ ≡
   begin $print\_esc(\texttt{""})$;
   if $subtype(p) = c\_leaders$ **then** $print\_char(\texttt{"c"})$
   else if $subtype(p) = x\_leaders$ **then** $print\_char(\texttt{"x"})$;
   $print(\texttt{"leaders␣"})$; $print\_spec(glue\_ptr(p), 0)$; $node\_list\_display(leader\_ptr(p))$;   { recursive call }
   end

This code is used in section 189.

$a\_leaders = 100, \S149.$
$c\_leaders = 101, \S149.$
$cond\_math\_glue = 98, \S149.$
$depth = $ macro, $\S135.$
$float = $ macro, $\S109.$
$float_constant = $ macro, $\S109.$
$float_cost = $ macro, $\S140.$
$g: real, \S182.$
$glue\_offset = 6, \S135.$
$glue_order = $ macro, $\S135.$
$glue_ptr = $ macro, $\S149.$
$glue\_ratio = real, \S109.$
$glue_set = $ macro, $\S135.$
$glue_shrink = $ macro, $\S159.$
$glue_sign = $ macro, $\S135.$

$glue_stretch = $ macro, $\S159.$
$height = $ macro, $\S135.$
$ins_ptr = $ macro, $\S140.$
$int: integer, \S113.$
$leader_ptr = $ macro, $\S149.$
$min\_quarterword = 0, \S110.$
$node_list_display = $ macro, $\S180.$
$normal = 0, \S135.$
$p: pointer, \S182.$
$print:$ **procedure**, $\S59.$
$print\_char:$ **procedure**, $\S58.$
$print\_esc:$ **procedure**, $\S63.$
$print\_glue:$ **procedure**, $\S177.$
$print\_int:$ **procedure**, $\S65.$

$print\_rule\_dimen:$ **procedure**, $\S176.$
$print\_scaled:$ **procedure**, $\S103.$
$print\_skip\_param:$ **procedure**, $\S225.$
$print\_spec:$ **procedure**, $\S178.$
$qo = $ macro, $\S112.$
$shrinking = 2, \S135.$
$span_count = $ macro, $\S159.$
$split_top_ptr = $ macro, $\S140.$
$subtype = $ macro, $\S133.$
$unity = $ macro, $\S101.$
$width = $ macro, $\S135.$
$x\_leaders = 102, \S149.$

191.   An "explicit" kern value is indicated implicitly by an explicit space.

⟨ Display kern p 191 ⟩ ≡

   if $subtype(p) \neq mu\_glue$ **then**

      begin $print\_esc(\texttt{"kern"})$;

      if $subtype(p) \neq normal$ **then** $print\_char(\texttt{"␣"})$;

      $print\_scaled(width(p))$;

      if $subtype(p) = acc\_kern$ **then** $print(\texttt{"␣(for␣accent)"})$;

      end

   else begin $print\_esc(\texttt{"mkern"})$; $print\_scaled(width(p))$; $print(\texttt{"mu"})$;

      end

This code is used in section 183.

192.   ⟨ Display math node p 192 ⟩ ≡

   begin $print\_esc(\texttt{"math"})$;

   if $subtype(p) = before$ **then** $print(\texttt{"on"})$

   else $print(\texttt{"off"})$;

   if $width(p) \neq 0$ **then**

      begin $print(\texttt{",␣surrounded␣"})$; $print\_scaled(width(p))$;

      end;

   end

This code is used in section 183.

193.   ⟨ Display ligature p 193 ⟩ ≡

   begin $print\_font\_and\_char(lig\_char(p))$; $print(\texttt{"␣(ligature␣"})$;

   $font\_in\_short\_display \leftarrow font(lig\_char(p))$; $short\_display(lig\_ptr(p))$; $print\_char(\texttt{")"})$;

   end

This code is used in section 183.

194.   ⟨ Display penalty p 194 ⟩ ≡

   begin $print\_esc(\texttt{"penalty␣"})$; $print\_int(penalty(p))$;

   end

This code is used in section 183.

195.   The $post\_break$ list of a discretionary node is indicated by a prefixed '|' instead of the '.' before the pre_break list.

⟨ Display discretionary p 195 ⟩ ≡

   begin $print\_esc(\texttt{"discretionary"})$;

   if $replace\_count(p) > 0$ **then**

      begin $print(\texttt{"␣replacing␣"})$; $print\_int(replace\_count(p))$;

      end;

   $node\_list\_display(pre\_break(p))$;   { recursive call }

   $append\_char(\texttt{"|"})$; $show\_node\_list(post\_break(p))$; $flush\_char$;   { recursive call }

   end

This code is used in section 183.

196.   ⟨ Display mark p 196 ⟩ ≡

   begin $print\_esc(\texttt{"mark"})$; $print\_mark(mark\_ptr(p))$;

   end

This code is used in section 183.

197. ⟨ Display adjustment p 197 ⟩ ≡
    begin *print_esc*("vadjust"); *node_list_display*(*adjust_ptr*(*p*));   { recursive call }
    end

This code is used in section 183.

198.   The recursive machinery is started by calling *show_box*.

procedure *show_box*(*p* : *pointer*);
    begin ⟨ Assign the values *depth_threshold* ← *show_box_depth* and *breadth_max* ← *show_box_breadth* 236 ⟩;
    if *breadth_max* ≤ 0 **then** *breadth_max* ← 5;
    if *pool_ptr* + *depth_threshold* ≥ *pool_size* **then** *depth_threshold* ← *pool_size* − *pool_ptr* − 1;
        { now there's enough room for prefix string }
    show_node_list(*p*);   { the show starts at *p* }
    print_ln;
    end;

acc_kern = 2, §155.
adjust_ptr = macro, §142.
append_char = macro, §42.
before = 0, §147.
breadth_max: *integer*, §181.
depth_threshold: *integer*, §181.
flush_char = macro, §42.
font = macro, §134.
font_in_short_display: *integer*, §173.
lig_char = macro, §143.
lig_ptr = macro, §143.
mark_ptr = macro, §141.

mu_glue = 99, §149.
node_list_display = macro, §180.
normal = 0, §135.
p: *pointer*, §182.
penalty = macro, §157.
pointer = macro, §115.
pool_size = **const**, §11.
post_break = macro, §145.
pre_break = macro, §145.
print: **procedure**, §59.
print_char: **procedure**, §58.
print_esc: **procedure**, §63.

print_font_and_char: **procedure**,
   §176.
print_int: **procedure**, §65.
print_ln: **procedure**, §57.
print_mark: **procedure**, §176.
print_scaled: **procedure**, §103.
replace_count = macro, §145.
show_box_breadth = macro, §236.
show_box_depth = macro, §236.
subtype = macro, §133.
width = macro, §135.

199.   **Destroying boxes.**   When we are done with a node list, we are obliged to return it to free storage, including all of its sublists. The recursive procedure *flush_node_list* does this for us.

200.   First, however, we shall consider two non-recursive procedures that do simpler tasks. The first of these, *delete_token_ref*, is called when a pointer to a token list's reference count is being removed. This means that the token list should disappear if the reference count was *null*, otherwise the count should be decreased by one.

> **define** *token_ref_count*(**#**) ≡ *info*(**#**)   { reference count preceding a token list }

procedure *delete_token_ref*(*p* : *pointer*);
>   { *p* points to the reference count of a token list that is losing one reference }
> **begin if** *token_ref_count*(*p*) = *null* **then** *flush_list*(*p*)
> **else** *decr*(*token_ref_count*(*p*));
> **end**;

201.   Similarly, *delete_glue_ref* is called when a pointer to a glue specification is being withdrawn.

> **define** *fast_delete_glue_ref*(**#**) ≡
>>   **begin if** *glue_ref_count*(**#**) = *null* **then** *free_node*(**#**, *glue_spec_size*)
>>   **else** *decr*(*glue_ref_count*(**#**));
>>   **end**

procedure *delete_glue_ref*(*p* : *pointer*);   { *p* points to a glue specification }
>   *fast_delete_glue_ref*(*p*);

202.   Now we are ready to delete any node list, recursively. In practice, the nodes deleted are usually charnodes (about 2/3 of the time), and they are glue nodes in about half of the remaining cases.

procedure *flush_node_list*(*p* : *pointer*);   { erase list of nodes starting at *p* }
>   **label** *done*;   { go here when node *p* has been freed }
>   **var** *q*: *pointer*;   { successor to node *p* }
>   **begin while** *p* ≠ *null* **do**
>>   **begin** *q* ← *link*(*p*);
>>   **if** *is_char_node*(*p*) **then** *free_avail*(*p*)
>>   **else begin case** *type*(*p*) **of**
>>>   *hlist_node*, *vlist_node*, *unset_node*: **begin** *flush_node_list*(*list_ptr*(*p*)); *free_node*(*p*, *box_node_size*);
>>>   **goto** *done*;
>>>   **end**;
>>>   *rule_node*: **begin** *free_node*(*p*, *rule_node_size*); **goto** *done*;
>>>   **end**;
>>>   *ins_node*: **begin** *flush_node_list*(*ins_ptr*(*p*)); *delete_glue_ref*(*split_top_ptr*(*p*));
>>>   *free_node*(*p*, *ins_node_size*); **goto** *done*;
>>>   **end**;
>>>   *whatsit_node*: ⟨ Wipe out the whatsit node *p* and **goto** *done* 1358 ⟩;
>>>   *glue_node*: **begin** *fast_delete_glue_ref*(*glue_ptr*(*p*));
>>>   **if** *leader_ptr*(*p*) ≠ *null* **then** *flush_node_list*(*leader_ptr*(*p*));
>>>   **end**;
>>>   *kern_node*, *math_node*, *penalty_node*: *do_nothing*;
>>>   *ligature_node*: *flush_node_list*(*lig_ptr*(*p*));

$mark\_node$: $delete\_token\_ref(mark\_ptr(p))$;

$disc\_node$: **begin** $flush\_node\_list(pre\_break(p))$; $flush\_node\_list(post\_break(p))$;
    end;

$adjust\_node$: $flush\_node\_list(adjust\_ptr(p))$;

⟨ Cases of $flush\_node\_list$ that arise in mlists only 698 ⟩

othercases $confusion("\texttt{flushing}")$

endcases;

$free\_node(p, small\_node\_size)$;

$done$: **end**;

$p \leftarrow q$;

end;

end;

$adjust\_node = 5$, §142.
$adjust\_ptr =$ macro, §142.
$box\_node\_size = 7$, §135.
$confusion$: **procedure**, §95.
$decr =$ macro, §16.
$disc\_node = 7$, §145.
$do\_nothing =$ macro, §16.
$done = 30$, §15.
$flush\_list$: **procedure**, §123.
$free\_avail =$ macro, §121.
$free\_node$: **procedure**, §130.
$glue\_node = 10$, §149.
$glue\_ptr =$ macro, §149.
$glue\_ref\_count =$ macro, §150.
$glue\_spec\_size = 4$, §150.

$hlist\_node = 0$, §135.
$info =$ macro, §118.
$ins\_node = 3$, §140.
$ins\_node\_size = 5$, §140.
$ins\_ptr =$ macro, §140.
$is\_char\_node =$ macro, §134.
$kern\_node = 11$, §155.
$leader\_ptr =$ macro, §149.
$lig\_ptr =$ macro, §143.
$ligature\_node = 6$, §143.
$link =$ macro, §118.
$list\_ptr =$ macro, §135.
$mark\_node = 4$, §141.
$mark\_ptr =$ macro, §141.

$math\_node = 9$, §147.
$null =$ macro, §115.
$penalty\_node = 12$, §157.
$pointer =$ macro, §115.
$post\_break =$ macro, §145.
$pre\_break =$ macro, §145.
$rule\_node = 2$, §138.
$rule\_node\_size = 4$, §138.
$small\_node\_size = 2$, §141.
$split\_top\_ptr =$ macro, §140.
$type =$ macro, §133.
$unset\_node = 13$, §159.
$vlist\_node = 1$, §137.
$whatsit\_node = 8$, §146.

203.   Copying boxes.   Another recursive operation that acts on boxes is sometimes needed: The procedure *copy_node_list* returns a pointer to another node list that has the same structure and meaning as the original. Note that since glue specifications and token lists have reference counts, we need not make copies of them. Reference counts can never get too large to fit in a halfword, since each pointer to a node is in a different memory address, and the total number of memory addresses fits in a halfword.

(Well, there actually are also references from outside *mem*; if the *save_stack* is made arbitrarily large, it would theoretically be possible to break TEX by overflowing a reference count. But who would want to do that?)

> **define** *add_token_ref*(#) ≡ *incr*(*token_ref_count*(#))   { new reference to a token list }
> **define** *add_glue_ref*(#) ≡ *incr*(*glue_ref_count*(#))   { new reference to a glue spec }

204.   The copying procedure copies words en masse without bothering to look at their individual fields. If the node format changes—for example, if the size is altered, or if some link field is moved to another relative position—then this code may need to be changed too.

function *copy_node_list*(*p* : *pointer*): *pointer*;
        { makes a duplicate of the node list that starts at *p* and returns a pointer to the new list }
  var *h*: *pointer*;   { temporary head of copied list }
    q: *pointer*;   { previous position in new list }
    r: *pointer*;   { current node being fabricated for new list }
    words: 0 .. 5;   { number of words remaining to be copied }
  begin *h* ← *get_avail*; *q* ← *h*;
  while *p* ≠ *null* **do**
    begin ⟨ Make a copy of node *p* in node *r* 205 ⟩;
    link(*q*) ← *r*; *q* ← *r*; *p* ← *link*(*p*);
    end;
  link(*q*) ← *null*; *q* ← *link*(*h*); *free_avail*(*h*); *copy_node_list* ← *q*;
  end;

205.   ⟨ Make a copy of node *p* in node *r* 205 ⟩ ≡
  words ← 1;   { this setting occurs in more branches than any other }
  if *is_char_node*(*p*) **then** *r* ← *get_avail*
  else ⟨ Case statement to copy different types and set *words* to the number of initial words not yet
        copied 206 ⟩;
  while *words* > 0 **do**
    begin *decr*(*words*); *mem*[*r* + *words*] ← *mem*[*p* + *words*];
    end
This code is used in section 204.

206.   ⟨ Case statement to copy different types and set *words* to the number of initial words not yet
        copied 206 ⟩ ≡
  case *type*(*p*) **of**
  hlist_node, *vlist_node*, *unset_node*: **begin** *r* ← *get_node*(*box_node_size*); *mem*[*r* + 6] ← *mem*[*p* + 6];
    mem[*r* + 5] ← *mem*[*p* + 5];   { copy the last two words }
    list_ptr(*r*) ← *copy_node_list*(*list_ptr*(*p*));   { this affects *mem*[*r* + 5] }
    words ← 5;
    end;

$rule\_node$: **begin** $r \leftarrow get\_node(rule\_node\_size)$; $words \leftarrow rule\_node\_size$;
   end;
ins_node: **begin** $r \leftarrow get\_node(ins\_node\_size)$; $mem[r+4] \leftarrow mem[p+4]$;
   $add\_glue\_ref(split\_top\_ptr(p))$; $ins\_ptr(r) \leftarrow copy\_node\_list(ins\_ptr(p))$;   { this affects $mem[r+4]$ }
   $words \leftarrow ins\_node\_size - 1$;
   end;
$whatsit\_node$: ⟨ Make a partial copy of the whatsit node p and make r point to it; set $words$ to the
       number of initial words not yet copied 1357 ⟩;
$glue\_node$: **begin** $r \leftarrow get\_node(small\_node\_size)$; $add\_glue\_ref(glue\_ptr(p))$;
   $glue\_ptr(r) \leftarrow glue\_ptr(p)$; $leader\_ptr(r) \leftarrow copy\_node\_list(leader\_ptr(p))$;
   end;
$kern\_node, math\_node, penalty\_node$: **begin** $r \leftarrow get\_node(small\_node\_size)$; $words \leftarrow small\_node\_size$;
   end;
$ligature\_node$: **begin** $r \leftarrow get\_node(small\_node\_size)$; $mem[lig\_char(r)] \leftarrow mem[lig\_char(p)]$;
      { copy *font* and *character* }
   $lig\_ptr(r) \leftarrow copy\_node\_list(lig\_ptr(p))$;
   end;
$disc\_node$: **begin** $r \leftarrow get\_node(small\_node\_size)$; $pre\_break(r) \leftarrow copy\_node\_list(pre\_break(p))$;
   $post\_break(r) \leftarrow copy\_node\_list(post\_break(p))$;
   end;
$mark\_node$: **begin** $r \leftarrow get\_node(small\_node\_size)$; $add\_token\_ref(mark\_ptr(p))$;
   $words \leftarrow small\_node\_size$;
   end;
$adjust\_node$: **begin** $r \leftarrow get\_node(small\_node\_size)$; $adjust\_ptr(r) \leftarrow copy\_node\_list(adjust\_ptr(p))$;
   end;   { $words = 1 = small\_node\_size - 1$ }
othercases $confusion(\texttt{"copying"})$
endcases

This code is used in section 205.

$adjust\_node = 5$, §142.
$adjust\_ptr$ = macro, §142.
$box\_node\_size = 7$, §135.
$character$ = macro, §134.
$confusion$: **procedure**, §95.
$decr$ = macro, §16.
$disc\_node = 7$, §145.
$font$ = macro, §134.
$free\_avail$ = macro, §121.
get_avail: **function**, §120.
get_node: **function**, §125.
$glue\_node = 10$, §149.
$glue\_ptr$ = macro, §149.
$glue\_ref\_count$ = macro, §150.
$hlist\_node = 0$, §135.

$incr$ = macro, §16.
$ins\_node = 3$, §140.
$ins\_node\_size = 5$, §140.
ins_ptr = macro, §140.
is_char_node = macro, §134.
$kern\_node = 11$, §155.
$leader\_ptr$ = macro, §149.
lig_char = macro, §143.
lig_ptr = macro, §143.
$ligature\_node = 6$, §143.
$link$ = macro, §118.
$list\_ptr$ = macro, §135.
$mark\_node = 4$, §141.
$mark\_ptr$ = macro, §141.
$math\_node = 9$, §147.

$null$ = macro, §115.
$penalty\_node = 12$, §157.
$pointer$ = macro, §115.
$post\_break$ = macro, §145.
pre_break = macro, §145.
$rule\_node = 2$, §138.
$rule\_node\_size = 4$, §138.
$save\_stack$: **array**, §271.
$small\_node\_size = 2$, §141.
$split\_top\_ptr$ = macro, §140.
$token\_ref\_count$ = macro, §200.
$type$ = macro, §133.
$unset\_node = 13$, §159.
$vlist\_node = 1$, §137.
$whatsit\_node = 8$, §146.

207.   The command codes.   Before we can go any further, we need to define symbolic names for the internal code numbers that represent the various commands obeyed by TEX. These codes are somewhat arbitrary, but not completely so. For example, the command codes for character types are fixed by the language, since a user says, e.g., '\catcode `\$ = 3' to make $ a math delimiter, and the command code *math_shift* is equal to 3. Some other codes have been made adjacent so that **case** statements in the program need not consider cases that are widely spaced, or so that **case** statements can be replaced by **if** statements.

At any rate, here is the list, for future reference. First come the "catcode" commands, several of which share their numeric codes with ordinary commands when the catcode cannot emerge from TEX's scanning routine.

define *escape* $= 0$ { escape delimiter (called \ in *The TEXbook*) }
define *relax* $= 0$ { do nothing (\relax) }
define *left_brace* $= 1$ { beginning of a group ({) }
define *right_brace* $= 2$ { ending of a group (}) }
define *math_shift* $= 3$ { mathematics shift character ($) }
define *tab_mark* $= 4$ { alignment delimiter (&, \span) }
define *car_ret* $= 5$ { end of line (*carriage_return*, \cr, \crcr) }
define *out_param* $= 5$ { output a macro parameter }
define *mac_param* $= 6$ { macro parameter symbol (#) }
define *sup_mark* $= 7$ { superscript (^) }
define *sub_mark* $= 8$ { subscript (_) }
define *ignore* $= 9$ { characters to ignore (^^J) }
define *endv* $= 9$ { end of $\langle v_j \rangle$ list in alignment template }
define *spacer* $= 10$ { characters equivalent to blank space (␣) }
define *letter* $= 11$ { characters regarded as letters (A..Z, a..z) }
define *other_char* $= 12$ { none of the special character types }
define *active_char* $= 13$ { characters that invoke macros (^^[ ) }
define *par_end* $= 13$ { end of paragraph (\par) }
define *match* $= 13$ { match a macro parameter }
define *comment* $= 14$ { characters that introduce comments (%) }
define *end_match* $= 14$ { end of parameters to macro }
define *stop* $= 14$ { end of job (\end, \dump) }
define *invalid_char* $= 15$ { characters that shouldn't appear (^^?) }
define *delim_num* $= 15$ { specify delimiter numerically (\delimiter) }
define *max_char_code* $= 15$ { largest catcode for individual characters }

208.   Next are the ordinary run-of-the-mill command codes. Codes that are *min_internal* or more represent internal quantities that might be expanded by '\the'.

define *char_num* $= 16$ { character specified numerically (\char) }
define *math_char_num* $= 17$ { explicit math code (\mathchar) }
define *mark* $= 18$ { mark definition (\mark) }
define *xray* $= 19$ { peek inside of TEX (\show, \showbox, etc.) }
define *make_box* $= 20$ { make a box (\box, \copy, \hbox, etc.) }
define *hmove* $= 21$ { horizontal motion (\moveleft, \moveright) }
define *vmove* $= 22$ { vertical motion (\raise, \lower) }
define *un_hbox* $= 23$ { unglue a box (\unhbox, \unhcopy) }
define *un_vbox* $= 24$ { unglue a box (\unvbox, \unvcopy) }

define *remove_item* = 25   { nullify last item (`\unpenalty`, `\unkern`, `\unskip`) }
define *hskip* = 26   { horizontal glue (`\hskip`, `\hfil`, etc.) }
define *vskip* = 27   { vertical glue (`\vskip`, `\vfil`, etc.) }
define *mskip* = 28   { math glue (`\mskip`) }
define *kern* = 29   { fixed space (`\kern`) }
define *mkern* = 30   { math kern (`\mkern`) }
define *leader_ship* = 31   { use a box (`\shipout`, `\leaders`, etc.) }
define *halign* = 32   { horizontal table alignment (`\halign`) }
define *valign* = 33   { vertical table alignment (`\valign`) }
define *no_align* = 34   { temporary escape from alignment (`\noalign`) }
define *vrule* = 35   { vertical rule (`\vrule`) }
define *hrule* = 36   { horizontal rule (`\hrule`) }
define *insert* = 37   { vlist inserted in box (`\insert`) }
define *vadjust* = 38   { vlist inserted in enclosing paragraph (`\vadjust`) }
define *ignore_spaces* = 39   { gobble *spacer* tokens (`\ignorespaces`) }
define *after_assignment* = 40   { save till assignment is done (`\afterassignment`) }
define *after_group* = 41   { save till group is done (`\aftergroup`) }
define *break_penalty* = 42   { additional badness (`\penalty`) }
define *start_par* = 43   { begin paragraph (`\indent`, `\noindent`) }
define *ital_corr* = 44   { italic correction (`\/`) }
define *accent* = 45   { attach accent in text (`\accent`) }
define *math_accent* = 46   { attach accent in math (`\mathaccent`) }
define *discretionary* = 47   { discretionary texts (`\-`, `\discretionary`) }
define *eq_no* = 48   { equation number (`\eqno`, `\leqno`) }
define *left_right* = 49   { variable delimiter (`\left`, `\right`) }
define *math_comp* = 50   { component of formula (`\mathbin`, etc.) }
define *limit_switch* = 51   { diddle limit conventions (`\displaylimits`, etc.) }
define *above* = 52   { generalized fraction (`\above`, `\atop`, etc.) }
define *math_style* = 53   { style specification (`\displaystyle`, etc.) }
define *math_choice* = 54   { choice specification (`\mathchoice`) }
define *non_script* = 55   { conditional math glue (`\nonscript`) }
define *vcenter* = 56   { vertically center a vbox (`\vcenter`) }
define *case_shift* = 57   { force specific case (`\lowercase`, `\uppercase`) }
define *message* = 58   { send to user (`\message`, `\errmessage`) }
define *extension* = 59   { extensions to TeX (`\write`, `\special`, etc.) }
define *in_stream* = 60   { files for reading (`\openin`, `\closein`) }
define *begin_group* = 61   { begin local grouping (`\begingroup`) }
define *end_group* = 62   { end local grouping (`\endgroup`) }
define *omit* = 63   { omit alignment template (`\omit`) }
define *ex_space* = 64   { explicit space (`\␣`) }
define *radical* = 65   { square root and similar signs (`\radical`) }
define *end_cs_name* = 66   { end control sequence (`\endcsname`) }
define *min_internal* = 67   { the smallest code that can follow `\the` }
define *char_given* = 67   { character code defined by `\chardef` }
define *math_given* = 68   { math code defined by `\mathchardef` }
define *last_item* = 69   { most recent item (`\lastpenalty`, `\lastkern`, `\lastskip`) }
define *max_non_prefixed_command* = 69   { largest command code that can't be `\global` }

209. The next codes are special; they all relate to mode-independent assignment of values to TeX's internal registers or tables. Codes that are *max_internal* or less represent internal quantities that might be expanded by '\the'.

> **define** *toks_register* = 70   { token list register (\toks) }
> **define** *assign_toks* = 71   { special token list (\output, \everypar, etc.) }
> **define** *assign_int* = 72   { user-defined integer (\tolerance, \day, etc.) }
> **define** *assign_dimen* = 73   { user-defined length (\hsize, etc.) }
> **define** *assign_glue* = 74   { user-defined glue (\baselineskip, etc.) }
> **define** *assign_mu_glue* = 75   { user-defined muglue (\thinmuskip, etc.) }
> **define** *assign_font_dimen* = 76   { user-defined font dimension (\fontdimen) }
> **define** *assign_font_int* = 77   { user-defined font integer (\hyphenchar, \skewchar) }
> **define** *set_aux* = 78   { specify state info (\spacefactor, \prevdepth) }
> **define** *set_prev_graf* = 79   { specify state info (\prevgraf) }
> **define** *set_page_dimen* = 80   { specify state info (\pagegoal, etc.) }
> **define** *set_page_int* = 81   { specify state info (\deadcycles, \insertpenalties) }
> **define** *set_box_dimen* = 82   { change dimension of box (\wd, \ht, \dp) }
> **define** *set_shape* = 83   { specify fancy paragraph shape (\parshape) }
> **define** *def_code* = 84   { define a character code (\catcode, etc.) }
> **define** *def_family* = 85   { declare math fonts (\textfont, etc.) }
> **define** *set_font* = 86   { set current font (font identifiers) }
> **define** *def_font* = 87   { define a font file (\font) }
> **define** *register* = 88   { internal register (\count, \dimen, etc.) }
> **define** *max_internal* = 88   { the largest code that can follow \the }
> **define** *advance* = 89   { advance a register or parameter (\advance) }
> **define** *multiply* = 90   { multiply a register or parameter (\multiply) }
> **define** *divide* = 91   { divide a register or parameter (\divide) }
> **define** *prefix* = 92   { qualify a definition (\global, \long, \outer) }
> **define** *let* = 93   { assign a command code (\let, \futurelet) }
> **define** *shorthand_def* = 94   { code definition (\chardef, \countdef, etc.) }
> **define** *read_to_cs* = 95   { read into a control sequence (\read) }
> **define** *def* = 96   { macro definition (\def, \gdef, \xdef, \edef) }
> **define** *set_box* = 97   { set a box (\setbox) }
> **define** *hyph_data* = 98   { hyphenation data (\hyphenation, \patterns) }
> **define** *set_interaction* = 99   { define level of interaction (\batchmode, etc.) }
> **define** *max_command* = 99   { the largest command code seen at *big_switch* }

210. The remaining command codes are extra special, since they cannot get through TeX's scanner to the main control routine. They have been given values higher than *max_command* so that their special nature is easily discernable. The "expandable" commands come first.

> **define** *undefined_cs* = *max_command* + 1   { initial state of most *eq_type* fields }
> **define** *expand_after* = *max_command* + 2   { special expansion (\expandafter) }
> **define** *no_expand* = *max_command* + 3   { special nonexpansion (\noexpand) }
> **define** *input* = *max_command* + 4   { input a source file (\input, \endinput) }
> **define** *if_test* = *max_command* + 5   { conditional text (\if, \ifcase, etc.) }
> **define** *fi_or_else* = *max_command* + 6   { delimiters for conditionals (\else, etc.) }
> **define** *cs_name* = *max_command* + 7   { make a control sequence from tokens (\csname) }
> **define** *convert* = *max_command* + 8   { convert to text (\number, \string, etc.) }
> **define** *the* = *max_command* + 9   { expand an internal quantity (\the) }

define $top\_bot\_mark = max\_command + 10$ { inserted mark (\topmark, etc.) }
define $call = max\_command + 11$ { non-long, non-outer control sequence }
define $long\_call = max\_command + 12$ { long, non-outer control sequence }
define $outer\_call = max\_command + 13$ { non-long, outer control sequence }
define $long\_outer\_call = max\_command + 14$ { long, outer control sequence }
define $end\_template = max\_command + 15$ { end of an alignment template }
define $dont\_expand = max\_command + 16$ { the following token was marked by \noexpand }
define $glue\_ref = max\_command + 17$ { the equivalent points to a glue specification }
define $shape\_ref = max\_command + 18$ { the equivalent points to a parshape specification }
define $box\_ref = max\_command + 19$ { the equivalent points to a box node, or is *null* }
define $data = max\_command + 20$ { the equivalent is simply a halfword number }

$big\_switch = 60, \S1030.$ $eq_type = $ macro, $\S221.$ $null = $ macro, $\S115.$

211. The semantic nest. TeX is typically in the midst of building many lists at once. For example, when a math formula is being processed, TeX is in math mode and working on an mlist; this formula has temporarily interrupted TeX from being in horizontal mode and building the hlist of a paragraph; and this paragraph has temporarily interrupted TeX from being in vertical mode and building the vlist for the next page of a document. Similarly, when a \vbox occurs inside of an \hbox, TeX is temporarily interrupted from working in restricted horizontal mode, and it enters internal vertical mode. The "semantic nest" is a stack that keeps track of what lists and modes are currently suspended.

At each level of processing we are in one of six modes:

vmode stands for vertical mode (the page builder);

hmode stands for horizontal mode (the paragraph builder);

mmode stands for displayed formula mode;

$-vmode$ stands for internal vertical mode (e.g., in a \vbox);

$-hmode$ stands for restricted horizontal mode (e.g., in an \hbox);

$-mmode$ stands for math formula mode (not displayed).

The mode is temporarily set to zero while processing \write texts in the *ship_out* routine.

Numeric values are assigned to *vmode*, *hmode*, and *mmode* so that TeX's "big semantic switch" can select the appropriate thing to do by computing the value $abs(mode) + cur\_cmd$, where *mode* is the current mode and *cur_cmd* is the current command code.

define $vmode = 1$ { vertical mode }
define $hmode = vmode + max\_command + 1$ { horizontal mode }
define $mmode = hmode + max\_command + 1$ { math mode }

procedure *print_mode*(m : *integer*);   { prints the mode represented by m }
  begin if $m > 0$ **then**
    case m **div** $(max\_command + 1)$ **of**
    0: *print*("vertical");
    1: *print*("horizontal");
    2: *print*("display␣math");
    end
  else if $m = 0$ **then** *print*("no")
    else case $(-m)$ **div** $(max\_command + 1)$ **of**
      0: *print*("internal␣vertical");
      1: *print*("restricted␣horizontal");
      2: *print*("math");
      end;
  print("␣mode");
  end;

212. The state of affairs at any semantic level can be represented by five values:

mode is the number representing the semantic mode, as just explained.

head is a *pointer* to a list head for the list being built; *link*(*head*) therefore points to the first element of the list, or to *null* if the list is empty.

tail is a *pointer* to the final node of the list being built; thus, *tail* = *head* if and only if the list is empty.

prev_graf is the number of lines of the current paragraph that have already been put into the present vertical list.

aux is an auxiliary integer that gives further information that is needed to characterize the situation.

In vertical mode, *aux* is also known as *prev_depth*; it is the scaled value representing the depth of the previous box, for use in baseline calculations, or it is ≤ -1000pt if the next box on the vertical list is to be exempt from baseline calculations. In horizontal mode, *aux* is also known as *space_factor*; it holds the current space factor used in spacing calculations. In math mode, *aux* is also known as *incompleat_noad*; if not *null*, it points to a record that represents the numerator of a generalized fraction for which the denominator is currently being formed in the current list.

There is also a sixth quantity, *mode_line*, which is used to correlate the semantic nest with the user's input; *mode_line* contains the source line number at which the current level of nesting was entered. The negative of this line number is used as the *mode_line* at the level of the user's output routine.

The semantic nest is an array called *nest* that holds the *mode*, *head*, *tail*, *prev_graf*, *aux*, and *mode_line* values for all semantic levels below the currently active one. Information about the currently active level is kept in the global quantities *mode*, *head*, *tail*, *prev_graf*, *aux*, and *mode_line*, which live in a Pascal record that is ready to be pushed onto *nest* if necessary.

define *ignore_depth* $\equiv -65536000$ { *prev_depth* value that is ignored }

⟨ Types in the outer block 18 ⟩ +≡
  list_state_record = **record** *mode_field*: −*mmode* .. *mmode*;
    head_field, *tail_field*: *pointer*;
    pg_field, *aux_field*, *ml_field*: *integer*;
  end;

213. **define** *mode* ≡ *cur_list.mode_field* { current mode }
  define *head* ≡ *cur_list.head_field* { header node of current list }
  define *tail* ≡ *cur_list.tail_field* { final node on current list }
  define *prev_graf* ≡ *cur_list.pg_field* { number of paragraph lines accumulated }
  define *aux* ≡ *cur_list.aux_field* { auxiliary data about the current list }
  define *prev_depth* ≡ *aux* { the name of *aux* in vertical mode }
  define *space_factor* ≡ *aux* { the name of *aux* in horizontal mode }
  define *incompleat_noad* ≡ *aux* { the name of *aux* in math mode }
  define *mode_line* ≡ *cur_list.ml_field* { source file line number at beginning of list }

⟨ Global variables 13 ⟩ +≡
nest: **array** [0 .. *nest_size*] **of** *list_state_record*;
nest_ptr: 0 .. *nest_size*; { first unused location of *nest* }
max_nest_stack: 0 .. *nest_size*; { maximum of *nest_ptr* when pushing }
cur_list: *list_state_record*; { the "top" semantic state }
shown_mode: −*mmode* .. *mmode*; { most recent mode shown by \tracingcommands }

---

cur_cmd: *eight_bits*, §297.
link = macro, §118.
max_command = 99, §209.

nest_size = **const**, §11.
null = macro, §115.
pointer = macro, §115.

print: **procedure**, §59.
ship_out: **procedure**, §638.

214.   Here is a common way to make the current list grow:

define $tail\_append(\#) \equiv$
            begin $link(tail) \leftarrow \#;\ \ tail \leftarrow link(tail);$
            end

215.   We will see later that the vertical list at the bottom semantic level is split into two parts; the "current page" runs from $page\_head$ to $page\_tail$, and the "contribution list" runs from $contrib\_head$ to $tail$ of semantic level zero. The idea is that contributions are first formed in vertical mode, then "contributed" to the current page (during which time the page-breaking decisions are made). For now, we don't need to know any more details about the page-building process.

⟨ Set initial values of key variables 21 ⟩ +≡
    $nest\_ptr \leftarrow 0;\ \ max\_nest\_stack \leftarrow 0;\ \ mode \leftarrow vmode;\ \ head \leftarrow contrib\_head;\ \ tail \leftarrow contrib\_head;$
    $prev\_depth \leftarrow ignore\_depth;\ \ mode\_line \leftarrow 0;\ \ prev\_graf \leftarrow 0;\ \ shown\_mode \leftarrow 0;$
    ⟨ Start a new current page 991 ⟩;

216.   When TEX's work on one level is interrupted, the state is saved by calling $push\_nest$. This routine changes $head$ and $tail$ so that a new (empty) list is begun; it does not change $mode$ or aux.

procedure $push\_nest$;   { enter a new semantic level, save the old }
    begin if $nest\_ptr > max\_nest\_stack$ **then**
        begin $max\_nest\_stack \leftarrow nest\_ptr;$
        if $nest\_ptr = nest\_size$ **then** $overflow(\text{"semantic}_\sqcup\text{nest}_\sqcup\text{size"}, nest\_size);$
        end;
    $nest[nest\_ptr] \leftarrow cur\_list;$ { stack the record }
    $incr(nest\_ptr);\ \ head \leftarrow get\_avail;\ \ tail \leftarrow head;\ \ prev\_graf \leftarrow 0;\ \ mode\_line \leftarrow line;$
    end;

217.   Conversely, when TEX is finished on the current level, the former state is restored by calling pop_nest. This routine will never be called at the lowest semantic level, nor will it be called unless $head$ is a node that should be returned to free memory.

procedure pop_nest;   { leave a semantic level, re-enter the old }
    begin $free\_avail(head);\ \ decr(nest\_ptr);\ \ cur\_list \leftarrow nest[nest\_ptr];$
    end;

218.   Here is a procedure that displays what TEX is working on, at all levels.

procedure $print\_totals$; $forward$;
procedure $show\_activities$;
    var p: $0\mathinner{\ldotp\ldotp}nest\_size$;   { index into $nest$ }
        m: $-mmode\mathinner{\ldotp\ldotp}mmode$;   { mode }
        a: $integer$;   { auxiliary }
        q, r: $pointer$;   { for showing the current page }
        t: $integer$;   { ditto }
    begin $nest[nest\_ptr] \leftarrow cur\_list;$ { put the top level into the array }
    $print\_nl(\text{""});\ \ print\_ln;$
    for $p \leftarrow nest\_ptr$ **downto** 0 **do**
        begin $m \leftarrow nest[p].mode\_field;\ \ a \leftarrow nest[p].aux\_field;\ \ print\_nl(\text{"\#\#\#}_\sqcup\text{"});\ \ print\_mode(m);$
        $print(\text{"}_\sqcup\text{entered}_\sqcup\text{at}_\sqcup\text{line}_\sqcup\text{"});\ \ print\_int(abs(nest[p].ml\_field));$

```
    if nest[p].ml_field < 0 then print("␣(\output␣routine)");
    if p = 0 then
        begin ⟨ Show the status of the current page 986 ⟩;
        if link(contrib_head) ≠ null then print_nl("###␣recent␣contributions:");
        end;
    show_box(link(nest[p].head_field)); ⟨ Show the auxiliary field, a 219 ⟩;
    end;
    end;
```

219. ⟨ Show the auxiliary field, *a* 219 ⟩ ≡
```
case abs(m) div (max_command + 1) of
0: begin print_nl("prevdepth␣");
    if a ≤ ignore_depth then print("ignored")
    else print_scaled(a);
    if nest[p].pg_field ≠ 0 then
        begin print(",␣prevgraf␣"); print_int(nest[p].pg_field); print("␣line");
        if nest[p].pg_field ≠ 1 then print_char("s");
        end;
    end;
1: begin print_nl("spacefactor␣"); print_int(a);
    end;
2: if a ≠ null then
    begin print("this␣will␣be␣denominator␣of:"); show_box(a);
    end;
end   { there are no other cases }
```
This code is used in section 218.

---

220.   The table of equivalents.   Now that we have studied the data structures for TeX's semantic routines, we ought to consider the data structures used by its syntactic routines. In other words, our next concern will be the tables that TeX looks at when it is scanning what the user has written.

The biggest and most important such table is called *eqtb*. It holds the current "equivalents" of things; i.e., it explains what things mean or what their current values are, for all quantities that are subject to the nesting structure provided by TeX's grouping mechanism. There are six parts to *eqtb*:

1) *eqtb*[*active_base* .. (*hash_base* − 1)] holds the current equivalents of single-character control sequences.

2) *eqtb*[*hash_base* .. (*glue_base* −1)] holds the current equivalents of multiletter control sequences.

3) *eqtb*[*glue_base* .. (*local_base* − 1)] holds the current equivalents of glue parameters like the current baselineskip.

4) *eqtb*[*local_base* .. (*int_base* − 1)] holds the current equivalents of local halfword quantities like the current box registers, the current "catcodes," the current font, and a pointer to the current paragraph shape.

5) *eqtb*[*int_base* .. (*dimen_base* −1)] holds the current equivalents of fullword integer parameters like the current hyphenation penalty.

6) *eqtb*[*dimen_base* .. *eqtb_size*] holds the current equivalents of fullword dimension parameters like the current hsize or amount of hanging indentation.

Note that, for example, the current amount of baselineskip glue is determined by the setting of a particular location in region 3 of *eqtb*, while the current meaning of the control sequence '\baselineskip' (which might have been changed by \def or \let) appears in region 2.

221.   Each entry in *eqtb* is a *memory_word*. Most of these words are of type *two_halves*, and subdivided into three fields:

1) The *eq_level* (a quarterword) is the level of grouping at which this equivalent was defined. If the level is *level_zero*, the equivalent has never been defined; *level_one* refers to the outer level (outside of all groups), and this level is also used for global definitions that never go away. Higher levels are for equivalents that will disappear at the end of their group.

2) The *eq_type* (another quarterword) specifies what kind of entry this is. There are many types, since each TeX primitive like \hbox, \def, etc., has its own special code. The list of command codes above includes all possible settings of the *eq_type* field.

3) The *equiv* (a halfword) is the current equivalent value. This may be a font number, a pointer into *mem*, or a variety of other things.

> **define** *eq_level_field*(#) ≡ #.*hh.b1*
> **define** *eq_type_field*(#) ≡ #.*hh.b0*
> **define** *equiv_field*(#) ≡ #.*hh.rh*
> **define** *eq_level*(#) ≡ *eq_level_field*(*eqtb*[#])   { level of definition }
> **define** *eq_type*(#) ≡ *eq_type_field*(*eqtb*[#])   { command code for equivalent }
> **define** *equiv*(#) ≡ *equiv_field*(*eqtb*[#])   { equivalent value }
> **define** *level_zero* = *min_quarterword*   { level for undefined quantities }
> **define** *level_one* = *level_zero* + 1   { outermost level for defined quantities }

222. Many locations in *eqtb* have symbolic names. The purpose of the next paragraphs is to define these names, and to set up the initial values of the equivalents.

In the first region we have 128 equivalents for single-character control sequences, followed by 128 equivalents for "active characters" that act as control sequences.

Then comes region 2, which corresponds to the hash table that we will define later. The maximum address in this region is used for a dummy control sequence that is perpetually undefined. There also are several locations for control sequences that are perpetually defined (since they are used in error recovery).

define $active\_base = 1$ { beginning of region 1, for active character equivalents }
define $single\_base = active\_base + 128$ { equivalents of one-letter control sequences }
define $null\_cs = single\_base + 128$ { equivalent of \csname\endcsname }
define $hash\_base = null\_cs + 1$ { beginning of region 2, for the hash table }
define $frozen\_control\_sequence = hash\_base + hash\_size$ { for error recovery }
define $frozen\_protection = frozen\_control\_sequence$ { inaccessible but definable }
define $frozen\_cr = frozen\_control\_sequence + 1$ { permanent '\cr' }
define $frozen\_end\_group = frozen\_control\_sequence + 2$ { permanent '\endgroup' }
define $frozen\_right = frozen\_control\_sequence + 3$ { permanent '\right' }
define $frozen\_fi = frozen\_control\_sequence + 4$ { permanent '\fi' }
define $frozen\_end\_template = frozen\_control\_sequence + 5$ { permanent '\endtemplate' }
define $frozen\_endv = frozen\_control\_sequence + 6$ { second permanent '\endtemplate' }
define $frozen\_relax = frozen\_control\_sequence + 7$ { permanent '\relax' }
define $end\_write = frozen\_control\_sequence + 8$ { permanent '\endwrite' }
define $frozen\_dont\_expand = frozen\_control\_sequence + 9$ { permanent '\notexpanded:' }
define $frozen\_null\_font = frozen\_control\_sequence + 10$ { permanent '\nullfont' }
define $font\_id\_base = frozen\_null\_font - font\_base$ { begins table of 257 permanent font identifiers }
define $undefined\_control\_sequence = frozen\_null\_font + 257$ { dummy location }
define $glue\_base = undefined\_control\_sequence + 1$ { beginning of region 3 }

⟨ Initialize table entries (done by INITEX only) 164 ⟩ +≡
    $eq\_type(undefined\_control\_sequence) \leftarrow undefined\_cs$; $equiv(undefined\_control\_sequence) \leftarrow null$;
    $eq\_level(undefined\_control\_sequence) \leftarrow level\_zero$;
    for $k \leftarrow active\_base$ **to** $undefined\_control\_sequence - 1$ **do** $eqtb[k] \leftarrow eqtb[undefined\_control\_sequence]$;

$b0$: *quarterword*, §113.
$b1$: *quarterword*, §113.
dimen_base = 4801, §236.
eqtb: **array**, §253.
eqtb_size = 5076, §247.
font_base = 0, §12.

hash_size = 2100, §12.
hh: *two_halves*, §113.
int_base = 4367, §230.
k: *integer*, §163.
local_base = 3156, §224.
mem: **array**, §116.

memory_word = **record**, §113.
min_quarterword = 0, §110.
null = macro, §115.
rh: *halfword*, §113.
two_halves = **packed record**, §113.
undefined_cs = 100, §210.

223. Here is a routine that displays the current meaning of an *eqtb* entry in region 1 or 2. (Similar routines for the other regions will appear below.)

⟨ Show equivalent *n*, in region 1 or 2 223 ⟩ ≡
 begin *sprint_cs*(*n*); *print_char*("="); *print_cmd_chr*(*eq_type*(*n*), *equiv*(*n*));
 if *eq_type*(*n*) ≥ *call* **then**
  begin *print_char*(":"); *show_token_list*(*link*(*equiv*(*n*)), *null*, 32);
  end;
 end

This code is used in section 252.

224. Region 3 of *eqtb* contains the 256 \skip registers, as well as the glue parameters defined here. It is important that the "muskip" parameters have larger numbers than the others.

 define *line_skip_code* = 0 { interline glue if *baseline_skip* is infeasible }
 define *baseline_skip_code* = 1 { desired glue between baselines }
 define *par_skip_code* = 2 { extra glue just above a paragraph }
 define *above_display_skip_code* = 3 { extra glue just above displayed math }
 define *below_display_skip_code* = 4 { extra glue just below displayed math }
 define *above_display_short_skip_code* = 5 { glue above displayed math following short lines }
 define *below_display_short_skip_code* = 6 { glue below displayed math following short lines }
 define *left_skip_code* = 7 { glue at left of justified lines }
 define *right_skip_code* = 8 { glue at right of justified lines }
 define *top_skip_code* = 9 { glue at top of main pages }
 define *split_top_skip_code* = 10 { glue at top of split pages }
 define *tab_skip_code* = 11 { glue between aligned entries }
 define *space_skip_code* = 12 { glue between words (if not *zero_glue*) }
 define *xspace_skip_code* = 13 { glue after sentences (if not *zero_glue*) }
 define *par_fill_skip_code* = 14 { glue on last line of paragraph }
 define *thin_mu_skip_code* = 15 { thin space in math formula }
 define *med_mu_skip_code* = 16 { medium space in math formula }
 define *thick_mu_skip_code* = 17 { thick space in math formula }
 define *glue_pars* = 18 { total number of glue parameters }
 define *skip_base* = *glue_base* + *glue_pars* { table of 256 "skip" registers }
 define *mu_skip_base* = *skip_base* + 256 { table of 256 "muskip" registers }
 define *local_base* = *mu_skip_base* + 256 { beginning of region 4 }

 define *skip*(#) ≡ *equiv*(*skip_base* + #) { *mem* location of glue specification }
 define *mu_skip*(#) ≡ *equiv*(*mu_skip_base* + #) { *mem* location of math glue spec }
 define *glue_par*(#) ≡ *equiv*(*glue_base* + #) { *mem* location of glue specification }
 define *line_skip* ≡ *glue_par*(*line_skip_code*)
 define *baseline_skip* ≡ *glue_par*(*baseline_skip_code*)
   ⋮
 define *thick_mu_skip* ≡ *glue_par*(*thick_mu_skip_code*)

⟨ Current *mem* equivalent of glue parameter number *n* 224 ⟩ ≡
 glue_par(*n*)

This code is used in sections 152 and 154.

225. Sometimes we need to convert TeX's internal code numbers into symbolic form. The *print_skip_param* routine gives the symbolic name of a glue parameter.

⟨ Declare the procedure called *print_skip_param* 225 ⟩ ≡
procedure *print_skip_param*(*n* : *integer*);
  begin case *n* **of**
  line_skip_code: *print_esc*("lineskip");
  baseline_skip_code: *print_esc*("baselineskip");
              ⋮
  thick_mu_skip_code: *print_esc*("thickmuskip");
  othercases *print*("[unknown␣glue␣parameter!]")
  endcases;
  end;

This code is used in section 179.

226.   The symbolic names for glue parameters are put into TEX's hash table by using the routine called *primitive*, defined below. Let us enter them now, so that we don't have to list all those parameter names anywhere else.

⟨ Put each of TEX's primitives into the hash table 226 ⟩ ≡
  primitive("lineskip", *assign_glue*, *glue_base* + *line_skip_code*);
  primitive("baselineskip", *assign_glue*, *glue_base* + *baseline_skip_code*);
              ⋮
  primitive("thickmuskip", *assign_mu_glue*, *glue_base* + *thick_mu_skip_code*);

See also sections 230, 238, 248, 265, 334, 376, 384, 411, 416, 468, 487, 491, 553, 780, 983, 1052, 1058, 1071, 1088, 1107, 1114, 1141, 1156, 1169, 1178, 1188, 1208, 1219, 1222, 1230, 1250, 1254, 1262, 1272, 1277, 1286, 1291, and 1344.

This code is used in section 1336.

227.   ⟨ Cases of *print_cmd_chr* for symbolic printing of primitives 227 ⟩ ≡
assign_glue, *assign_mu_glue*: **if** *chr_code* < *skip_base* **then** *print_skip_param*(*chr_code* − *glue_base*)
  else if *chr_code* < *mu_skip_base* **then**
      begin *print_esc*("skip"); *print_int*(*chr_code* − *skip_base*);
      end
  else begin *print_esc*("muskip"); *print_int*(*chr_code* − *mu_skip_base*);
      end;

See also sections 231, 239, 249, 266, 335, 377, 385, 412, 417, 469, 488, 492, 781, 984, 1053, 1059, 1072, 1089, 1108, 1115, 1143, 1157, 1170, 1179, 1189, 1209, 1220, 1223, 1231, 1251, 1255, 1261, 1263, 1273, 1278, 1287, 1292, 1295, and 1346.

This code is used in section 298.

---

assign_glue = 74, §209.
assign_mu_glue = 75, §209.
call = 110, §210.
chr_code: *halfword*, §298.
eq_type = macro, §221.
eqtb: **array**, §253.
equiv = macro, §221.
link = macro, §118.

mem: **array**, §116.
n: *small_number*, §152.
n: *small_number*, §154.
n: *pointer*, §252.
null = macro, §115.
primitive: **procedure**, §264.
print: **procedure**, §59.

print_char: **procedure**, §58.
print_cmd_chr: **procedure**, §298.
print_esc: **procedure**, §63.
print_int: **procedure**, §65.
show_token_list: **procedure**, §292.
sprint_cs: **procedure**, §263.
zero_glue = macro, §162.

228.   All glue parameters and registers are initially '0pt plus0pt minus0pt'.

⟨ Initialize table entries (done by **INITEX** only) 164 ⟩ +≡
  $equiv(glue\_base) \leftarrow zero\_glue$; $eq\_level(glue\_base) \leftarrow level\_one$; $eq\_type(glue\_base) \leftarrow glue\_ref$;
  for $k \leftarrow glue\_base + 1$ **to** $local\_base - 1$ **do** $eqtb[k] \leftarrow eqtb[glue\_base]$;
  $glue\_ref\_count(zero\_glue) \leftarrow glue\_ref\_count(zero\_glue) + local\_base - glue\_base$;

229.   ⟨ Show equivalent n, in region 3 229 ⟩ ≡
  if $n < skip\_base$ **then**
    begin $print\_skip\_param(n - glue\_base)$; $print\_char("=")$;
    if $n < glue\_base + thin\_mu\_skip\_code$ **then** $print\_spec(equiv(n), "pt")$
    else $print\_spec(equiv(n), "mu")$;
    end
  else if $n < mu\_skip\_base$ **then**
      begin $print\_esc("skip")$; $print\_int(n - skip\_base)$; $print\_char("=")$; $print\_spec(equiv(n), "pt")$;
      end
    else begin $print\_esc("muskip")$; $print\_int(n - mu\_skip\_base)$; $print\_char("=")$;
      $print\_spec(equiv(n), "mu")$;
      end

This code is used in section 252.

230.   Region 4 of *eqtb* contains the local quantities defined here. The bulk of this region is taken up by five tables that are indexed by seven-bit characters; these tables are important to both the syntactic and semantic portions of TeX. There are also a bunch of special things like font and token parameters, as well as the tables of \toks and \box registers.

  define $par\_shape\_loc = local\_base$ { specifies paragraph shape }
  define $output\_routine\_loc = local\_base + 1$ { points to token list for \output }
  define $every\_par\_loc = local\_base + 2$ { points to token list for \everypar }
  define $every\_math\_loc = local\_base + 3$ { points to token list for \everymath }
  define $every\_display\_loc = local\_base + 4$ { points to token list for \everydisplay }
  define $every\_hbox\_loc = local\_base + 5$ { points to token list for \everyhbox }
  define $every\_vbox\_loc = local\_base + 6$ { points to token list for \everyvbox }
  define $every\_job\_loc = local\_base + 7$ { points to token list for \everyjob }
  define $every\_cr\_loc = local\_base + 8$ { points to token list for \everycr }
  define $err\_help\_loc = local\_base + 9$ { points to token list for \errhelp }
  define $toks\_base = local\_base + 10$ { table of 256 token list registers }
  define $box\_base = toks\_base + 256$ { table of 256 box registers }
  define $cur\_font\_loc = box\_base + 256$ { internal font number outside math mode }
  define $math\_font\_base = cur\_font\_loc + 1$ { table of 48 math font numbers }
  define $cat\_code\_base = math\_font\_base + 48$ { table of 128 command codes (the "catcodes") }
  define $lc\_code\_base = cat\_code\_base + 128$ { table of 128 lowercase mappings }
  define $uc\_code\_base = lc\_code\_base + 128$ { table of 128 uppercase mappings }
  define $sf\_code\_base = uc\_code\_base + 128$ { table of 128 spacefactor mappings }
  define $math\_code\_base = sf\_code\_base + 128$ { table of 128 math mode mappings }
  define $int\_base = math\_code\_base + 128$ { beginning of region 5 }

  define $par\_shape\_ptr \equiv equiv(par\_shape\_loc)$
  define $output\_routine \equiv equiv(output\_routine\_loc)$
  define $every\_par \equiv equiv(every\_par\_loc)$

$\vdots$

define $err\_help \equiv equiv(err\_help\_loc)$
define $toks(\#) \equiv equiv(toks\_base + \#)$
define $box(\#) \equiv equiv(box\_base + \#)$
define $cur\_font \equiv equiv(cur\_font\_loc)$
define $fam\_fnt(\#) \equiv equiv(math\_font\_base + \#)$
define $cat\_code(\#) \equiv equiv(cat\_code\_base + \#)$
define $lc\_code(\#) \equiv equiv(lc\_code\_base + \#)$
define $uc\_code(\#) \equiv equiv(uc\_code\_base + \#)$
define $sf\_code(\#) \equiv equiv(sf\_code\_base + \#)$
define $math\_code(\#) \equiv equiv(math\_code\_base + \#)$
{ Note: $math\_code(c)$ is the true math code plus $min\_halfword$ }

⟨ Put each of TₑX's primitives into the hash table 226 ⟩ +≡
$primitive(\texttt{"output"}, assign\_toks, output\_routine\_loc)$;
$primitive(\texttt{"everypar"}, assign\_toks, every\_par\_loc)$;
$\vdots$
$primitive(\texttt{"errhelp"}, assign\_toks, err\_help\_loc)$;

231. ⟨ Cases of $print\_cmd\_chr$ for symbolic printing of primitives 227 ⟩ +≡
$assign\_toks$: **if** $chr\_code \geq toks\_base$ **then**
  begin $print\_esc(\texttt{"toks"})$; $print\_int(chr\_code - toks\_base)$;
  end
else case chr_code **of**
  $output\_routine\_loc$: $print\_esc(\texttt{"output"})$;
  $every\_par\_loc$: $print\_esc(\texttt{"everypar"})$;
  $every\_math\_loc$: $print\_esc(\texttt{"everymath"})$;
  $every\_display\_loc$: $print\_esc(\texttt{"everydisplay"})$;
  $every\_hbox\_loc$: $print\_esc(\texttt{"everyhbox"})$;
  $every\_vbox\_loc$: $print\_esc(\texttt{"everyvbox"})$;
  $every\_job\_loc$: $print\_esc(\texttt{"everyjob"})$;
  $every\_cr\_loc$: $print\_esc(\texttt{"everycr"})$;·
  othercases $print\_esc(\texttt{"errhelp"})$
  endcases;

$assign\_toks = 71$, §209.
chr_code: $halfword$, §298.
eq_level = macro, §221.
eq_type = macro, §221.
$eqtb$: **array**, §253.
$equiv$ = macro, §221.
$glue\_ref = 116$, §210.
$glue\_ref\_count$ = macro, §150.
k: $integer$, §163.

$level\_one = 1$, §221.
$local\_base = 3156$, §224.
$min\_halfword$ = macro, §110.
$mu\_skip\_base = 2900$, §224.
n: $pointer$, §252.
$primitive$: **procedure**, §264.
$print\_char$: **procedure**, §58.
$print\_cmd\_chr$: **procedure**, §298.

$print\_esc$: **procedure**, §63.
$print\_int$: **procedure**, §65.
$print\_skip\_param$: **procedure**, §225.
$print\_spec$: **procedure**, §178.
$skip\_base = 2644$, §224.
$thin\_mu\_skip\_code = 15$, §224.
$zero\_glue$ = macro, §162.

232. We initialize most things to null or undefined values. An undefined font is represented by the internal code *font_base*.

However, the character code tables are given initial values based on the conventional interpretation of ASCII code. These initial values should not be changed when TeX is adapted for use with non-English languages; all changes to the initialization conventions should be made in format packages, not in TeX itself, so that global interchange of formats is possible.

> **define** *null_font* $\equiv$ *font_base*
> **define** *var_code* $\equiv$ *'70000*   { math code meaning "use the current family" }

$\langle$ Initialize table entries (done by **INITEX** only) 164 $\rangle$ +$\equiv$

> *par_shape_ptr* $\leftarrow$ *null*; *eq_type*(*par_shape_loc*) $\leftarrow$ *shape_ref*; *eq_level*(*par_shape_loc*) $\leftarrow$ *level_one*;
> **for** $k \leftarrow$ *output_routine_loc* **to** *toks_base* + 255 **do** *eqtb*[k] $\leftarrow$ *eqtb*[*undefined_control_sequence*];
> *box*(0) $\leftarrow$ *null*; *eq_type*(*box_base*) $\leftarrow$ *box_ref*; *eq_level*(*box_base*) $\leftarrow$ *level_one*;
> **for** $k \leftarrow$ *box_base* + 1 **to** *box_base* + 255 **do** *eqtb*[k] $\leftarrow$ *eqtb*[*box_base*];
> *cur_font* $\leftarrow$ *null_font*; *eq_type*(*cur_font_loc*) $\leftarrow$ *data*; *eq_level*(*cur_font_loc*) $\leftarrow$ *level_one*;
> **for** $k \leftarrow$ *math_font_base* **to** *math_font_base* + 47 **do** *eqtb*[k] $\leftarrow$ *eqtb*[*cur_font_loc*];
> *equiv*(*cat_code_base*) $\leftarrow$ 0; *eq_type*(*cat_code_base*) $\leftarrow$ *data*; *eq_level*(*cat_code_base*) $\leftarrow$ *level_one*;
> **for** $k \leftarrow$ *cat_code_base* + 1 **to** *int_base* − 1 **do** *eqtb*[k] $\leftarrow$ *eqtb*[*cat_code_base*];
> **for** $k \leftarrow$ 0 **to** 127 **do**
> > **begin** *cat_code*(k) $\leftarrow$ *other_char*; *math_code*(k) $\leftarrow$ *hi*(k); *sf_code*(k) $\leftarrow$ 1000;
> > **end**;
>
> *cat_code*(*carriage_return*) $\leftarrow$ *car_ret*; *cat_code*("␣") $\leftarrow$ *spacer*; *cat_code*("\\") $\leftarrow$ *escape*;
> *cat_code*("%") $\leftarrow$ *comment*; *cat_code*(*invalid_code*) $\leftarrow$ *invalid_char*; *cat_code*(*null_code*) $\leftarrow$ *ignore*;
> **for** $k \leftarrow$ "0" **to** "9" **do** *math_code*(k) $\leftarrow$ *hi*(k + *var_code*);
> **for** $k \leftarrow$ "A" **to** "Z" **do**
> > **begin** *cat_code*(k) $\leftarrow$ *letter*; *cat_code*(k + "a" − "A") $\leftarrow$ *letter*;
> > *math_code*(k) $\leftarrow$ *hi*(k + *var_code* + *"100*);
> > *math_code*(k + "a" − "A") $\leftarrow$ *hi*(k + "a" − "A" + *var_code* + *"100*);
> > *lc_code*(k) $\leftarrow$ k + "a" − "A"; *lc_code*(k + "a" − "A") $\leftarrow$ k + "a" − "A";
> > *uc_code*(k) $\leftarrow$ k; *uc_code*(k + "a" − "A") $\leftarrow$ k;
> > *sf_code*(k) $\leftarrow$ 999;
> > **end**;

233. $\langle$ Show equivalent n, in region 4 233 $\rangle$ $\equiv$

> **if** n = *par_shape_loc* **then**
> > **begin** *print_esc*("parshape"); *print_char*("=");
> > **if** *par_shape_ptr* = *null* **then** *print_char*("0")
> > **else** *print_int*(*info*(*par_shape_ptr*));
> > **end**
> **else if** $n <$ *toks_base* **then**
> > **begin** *print_cmd_chr*(*assign_toks*, n); *print_char*("=");
> > **if** *equiv*(n) $\neq$ *null* **then** *show_token_list*(*link*(*equiv*(n)), *null*, 32);
> > **end**
> > **else if** $n <$ *box_base* **then**
> > > **begin** *print_esc*("toks"); *print_int*(n − *toks_base*); *print_char*("=");
> > > **if** *equiv*(n) $\neq$ *null* **then** *show_token_list*(*link*(*equiv*(n)), *null*, 32);
> > > **end**
> > > **else if** $n <$ *cur_font_loc* **then**

$\textbf{begin}\ print\_esc(\texttt{"box"});\ print\_int(n - box\_base);\ print\_char(\texttt{"="});$
$\textbf{if}\ equiv(n) = null\ \textbf{then}\ print(\texttt{"void"})$
$\textbf{else begin}\ depth\_threshold \leftarrow 0;\ breadth\_max \leftarrow 1;\ show\_node\_list(equiv(n));$
$\quad\quad \textbf{end};$
$\textbf{end}$
$\textbf{else if}\ n < cat\_code\_base\ \textbf{then}\ \langle\text{Show the font identifier in } eqtb[n]\ 234\rangle$
$\quad\textbf{else}\ \langle\text{Show the halfword code in } eqtb[n]\ 235\rangle$

This code is used in section 252.

234. $\langle\text{Show the font identifier in } eqtb[n]\ 234\rangle \equiv$
$\textbf{begin if}\ n = cur\_font\_loc\ \textbf{then}\ print(\texttt{"current}_{\sqcup}\texttt{font"})$
$\textbf{else if}\ n < math\_font\_base + 16\ \textbf{then}$
$\quad\textbf{begin}\ print\_esc(\texttt{"textfont"});\ print\_int(n - math\_font\_base);$
$\quad\textbf{end}$
$\ \ \textbf{else if}\ n < math\_font\_base + 32\ \textbf{then}$
$\quad\textbf{begin}\ print\_esc(\texttt{"scriptfont"});\ print\_int(n - math\_font\_base - 16);$
$\quad\textbf{end}$
$\ \ \textbf{else begin}\ print\_esc(\texttt{"scriptscriptfont"});\ print\_int(n - math\_font\_base - 32);$
$\quad\textbf{end};$
$print\_char(\texttt{"="});$
$print\_esc(hash[font\_id\_base + equiv(n)].rh);\quad \{\text{ that's } text(font\_id\_base + equiv(n))\ \}$
$\textbf{end}$

This code is used in section 233.

$assign\_toks = 71,\ §209.$
$box = \textbf{macro},\ §230.$
$box\_base = 3422,\ §230.$
$box\_ref = 118,\ §210.$
$breadth\_max\colon integer,\ §181.$
$car\_ret = 5,\ §207.$
$carriage\_return = 13,\ §22.$
$cat\_code = \textbf{macro},\ §230.$
$cat\_code\_base = 3727,\ §230.$
$comment = 14,\ §207.$
$cur\_font = \textbf{macro},\ §230.$
$cur\_font\_loc = 3678,\ §230.$
$data = 119,\ §210.$
$depth\_threshold\colon integer,\ §181.$
$eq\_level = \textbf{macro},\ §221.$
$eq\_type = \textbf{macro},\ §221.$
$eqtb\colon \textbf{array},\ §253.$
$equiv = \textbf{macro},\ §221.$
$escape = 0,\ §207.$
$font\_base = 0,\ §12.$

$font\_id\_base = 2368,\ §222.$
$hash\colon \textbf{array},\ §256.$
$hi = \textbf{macro},\ §112.$
$ignore = 9,\ §207.$
$info = \textbf{macro},\ §118.$
$int\_base = 4367,\ §230.$
$invalid\_char = 15,\ §207.$
$invalid\_code = 127,\ §22.$
$k\colon integer,\ §163.$
$lc\_code = \textbf{macro},\ §230.$
$letter = 11,\ §207.$
$level\_one = 1,\ §221.$
$link = \textbf{macro},\ §118.$
$math\_code = \textbf{macro},\ §230.$
$math\_font\_base = 3679,\ §230.$
$n\colon pointer,\ §252.$
$null = \textbf{macro},\ §115.$
$null\_code = 0,\ §22.$
$other\_char = 12,\ §207.$

$output\_routine\_loc = 3157,\ §230.$
$par\_shape\_loc = 3156,\ §230.$
$par\_shape\_ptr = \textbf{macro},\ §230.$
$print\colon \textbf{procedure},\ §59.$
$print\_char\colon \textbf{procedure},\ §58.$
$print\_cmd\_chr\colon \textbf{procedure},\ §298.$
$print\_esc\colon \textbf{procedure},\ §63.$
$print\_int\colon \textbf{procedure},\ §65.$
$rh\colon halfword,\ §113.$
$sf\_code = \textbf{macro},\ §230.$
$shape\_ref = 117,\ §210.$
$show\_node\_list\colon \textbf{procedure},\ §182.$
$show\_token\_list\colon \textbf{procedure},\ §292.$
$spacer = 10,\ §207.$
$text = \textbf{macro},\ §256.$
$toks\_base = 3166,\ §230.$
$uc\_code = \textbf{macro},\ §230.$
$undefined\_control\_sequence = 2625,$
$\quad §222.$

235. ⟨Show the halfword code in $eqtb[n]$ 235⟩ ≡

if $n < math\_code\_base$ **then**
   begin if $n < lc\_code\_base$ **then**
     begin $print\_esc("catcode")$; $print\_int(n - cat\_code\_base)$; **end**
   else if $n < uc\_code\_base$ **then**
       begin $print\_esc("lccode")$; $print\_int(n - lc\_code\_base)$; **end**
     else if $n < sf\_code\_base$ **then**
         begin $print\_esc("uccode")$; $print\_int(n - uc\_code\_base)$; **end**
       else begin $print\_esc("sfcode")$; $print\_int(n - sf\_code\_base)$; **end**;
   $print\_char("=")$; $print\_int(equiv(n))$; **end**
else begin $print\_esc("mathcode")$; $print\_int(n - math\_code\_base)$; $print\_char("=")$;
  $print\_int(ho(equiv(n)))$;
  end

This code is used in section 233.

236. Region 5 of $eqtb$ contains the integer parameters and registers defined here, as well as the del_code table. The latter table differs from the cat_code .. $math\_code$ tables that precede it, since delimiter codes are fullword integers while the other kinds of codes occupy at most a halfword. This is what makes region 5 different from region 4. We will store the eq_level information in an auxiliary array of quarterwords that will be defined later.

define $pretolerance\_code = 0$ { badness tolerance before hyphenation }
define $tolerance\_code = 1$ { badness tolerance after hyphenation }
define $line\_penalty\_code = 2$ { added to the badness of every line }
define $hyphen\_penalty\_code = 3$ { penalty for break after discretionary hyphen }
define $ex\_hyphen\_penalty\_code = 4$ { penalty for break after explicit hyphen }
define $club\_penalty\_code = 5$ { penalty for creating a club line }
define $widow\_penalty\_code = 6$ { penalty for creating a widow line }
define $display\_widow\_penalty\_code = 7$ { ditto, just before a display }
define $broken\_penalty\_code = 8$ { penalty for breaking a page at a broken line }
define $bin\_op\_penalty\_code = 9$ { penalty for breaking after a binary operation }
define $rel\_penalty\_code = 10$ { penalty for breaking after a relation }
define $pre\_display\_penalty\_code = 11$ { penalty for breaking just before a displayed formula }
define $post\_display\_penalty\_code = 12$ { penalty for breaking just after a displayed formula }
define $inter\_line\_penalty\_code = 13$ { additional penalty between lines }
define $double\_hyphen\_demerits\_code = 14$ { demerits for double hyphen break }
define $final\_hyphen\_demerits\_code = 15$ { demerits for final hyphen break }
define $adj\_demerits\_code = 16$ { demerits for adjacent incompatible lines }
define $mag\_code = 17$ { magnification ratio }
define $delimiter\_factor\_code = 18$ { ratio for variable-size delimiters }
define $looseness\_code = 19$ { change in number of lines for a paragraph }
define $time\_code = 20$ { current time of day }
define $day\_code = 21$ { current day of the month }
define $month\_code = 22$ { current month of the year }
define $year\_code = 23$ { current year of our Lord }
define $show\_box\_breadth\_code = 24$ { nodes per level in $show\_box$ }
define $show\_box\_depth\_code = 25$ { maximum level in $show\_box$ }
define $hbadness\_code = 26$ { hboxes exceeding this badness will be shown by $hpack$ }
define $vbadness\_code = 27$ { vboxes exceeding this badness will be shown by $vpack$ }

define $pausing\_code = 28$ { pause after each line is read from a file }
define $tracing\_online\_code = 29$ { show diagnostic output on terminal }
define $tracing\_macros\_code = 30$ { show macros as they are being expanded }
define $tracing\_stats\_code = 31$ { show memory usage if TEX knows it }
define $tracing\_paragraphs\_code = 32$ { show line-break calculations }
define $tracing\_pages\_code = 33$ { show page-break calculations }
define $tracing\_output\_code = 34$ { show boxes when they are shipped out }
define $tracing\_lost\_chars\_code = 35$ { show characters that aren't in the font }
define $tracing\_commands\_code = 36$ { show command codes at big_switch }
define $tracing\_restores\_code = 37$ { show equivalents when they are restored }
define $uc\_hyph\_code = 38$ { hyphenate words beginning with a capital letter }
define $output\_penalty\_code = 39$ { penalty found at current page break }
define $max\_dead\_cycles\_code = 40$ { bound on consecutive dead cycles of output }
define $hang\_after\_code = 41$ { hanging indentation changes after this many lines }
define $floating\_penalty\_code = 42$ { penalty for insertions heldover after a split }
define $global\_defs\_code = 43$ { override \global specifications }
define $cur\_fam\_code = 44$ { current family }
define $escape\_char\_code = 45$ { escape character for token output }
define $default\_hyphen\_char\_code = 46$ { value of \hyphenchar when a font is loaded }
define $default\_skew\_char\_code = 47$ { value of \skewchar when a font is loaded }
define $end\_line\_char\_code = 48$ { character placed at the right end of the buffer }
define $new\_line\_char\_code = 49$ { character that prints as $print\_ln$ }
define $int\_pars = 50$ { total number of integer parameters }
define $count\_base = int\_base + int\_pars$ { 256 user \count registers }
define $del\_code\_base = count\_base + 256$ { 128 delimiter code mappings }
define $dimen\_base = del\_code\_base + 128$ { beginning of region 6 }

define $del\_code(\#) \equiv eqtb[del\_code\_base + \#].int$
define $count(\#) \equiv eqtb[count\_base + \#].int$
define $int\_par(\#) \equiv eqtb[int\_base + \#].int$ { an integer parameter }
define $pretolerance \equiv int\_par(pretolerance\_code)$
define $tolerance \equiv int\_par(tolerance\_code)$
$$\vdots$$
define $new\_line\_char \equiv int\_par(new\_line\_char\_code)$

⟨ Assign the values $depth\_threshold \leftarrow show\_box\_depth$ and $breadth\_max \leftarrow show\_box\_breadth$ 236 ⟩ ≡
   $depth\_threshold \leftarrow show\_box\_depth$; $breadth\_max \leftarrow show\_box\_breadth$
This code is used in section 198.

$big\_switch = 60, \S 1030.$
$breadth\_max$: *integer*, §181.
$cat_code = $ macro, §230.
$cat\_code\_base = 3727, \S 230.$
$depth\_threshold$: *integer*, §181.
$eq_level = $ macro, §221.
$eqtb$: **array**, §253.
$equiv = $ macro, §221.

$ho = $ macro, §112.
$hpack$: **function**, §649.
int: *integer*, §113.
$int\_base = 4367, \S 230.$
$lc\_code\_base = 3855, \S 230.$
$math_code = $ macro, §230.
$math\_code\_base = 4239, \S 230.$
n: *pointer*, §252.

$print\_char$: **procedure**, §58.
$print\_esc$: **procedure**, §63.
$print\_int$: **procedure**, §65.
$print\_ln$: **procedure**, §57.
$sf\_code\_base = 4111, \S 230.$
$show\_box$: **procedure**, §198.
$uc\_code\_base = 3983, \S 230.$
$vpack = $ macro, §668.

237.   We can print the symbolic name of an integer parameter as follows.

procedure $print\_param(n : integer)$;
  begin case n **of**
  $pretolerance\_code$: $print\_esc($"`pretolerance`"$)$;
  $tolerance\_code$: $print\_esc($"`tolerance`"$)$;
$$\vdots$$
  $new\_line\_char\_code$: $print\_esc($"`newlinechar`"$)$;
  othercases $print($"`[unknown␣integer␣parameter!]`"$)$
  endcases;
  end;

238.   The integer parameter names must be entered into the hash table.

⟨ Put each of TEX's primitives into the hash table 226 ⟩ +≡
  $primitive($"`pretolerance`"$, assign\_int, int\_base + pretolerance\_code)$;
  $primitive($"`tolerance`"$, assign\_int, int\_base + tolerance\_code)$;
$$\vdots$$
  $primitive($"`newlinechar`"$, assign\_int, int\_base + new\_line\_char\_code)$;

239.   ⟨ Cases of $print\_cmd\_chr$ for symbolic printing of primitives 227 ⟩ +≡
$assign\_int$: **if** $chr\_code < count\_base$ **then** $print\_param(chr\_code - int\_base)$
  else begin $print\_esc($"`count`"$)$; $print\_int(chr\_code - count\_base)$;
      end;

240.   The integer parameters should really be initialized by a macro package; the following initialization does the minimum to keep TEX from complete failure.

⟨ Initialize table entries (done by **INITEX** only) 164 ⟩ +≡
  for $k \leftarrow int\_base$ **to** $del\_code\_base - 1$ **do** $eqtb[k].int \leftarrow 0$;
  $mag \leftarrow 1000$; $tolerance \leftarrow 10000$; $hang\_after \leftarrow 1$; $max\_dead\_cycles \leftarrow 25$; $escape\_char \leftarrow$ "`\`";
  $end\_line\_char \leftarrow carriage\_return$;
  for $k \leftarrow 0$ **to** 127 **do** $del\_code(k) \leftarrow -1$;
  $del\_code($"`.`"$) \leftarrow 0$;   { this null delimiter is used in error recovery }

241.   The following procedure, which is called just before TEX initializes its input and output, establishes the initial values of the date and time. Since standard Pascal cannot provide such information, something special is needed. The program here simply specifies July 4, 1776, at noon; but users probably want a better approximation to the truth.

procedure $fix\_date\_and\_time$;
  begin $time \leftarrow 12 * 60$;   { minutes since midnight }
  $day \leftarrow 4$;   { fourth day of the month }
  $month \leftarrow 7$;   { seventh month of the year }
  $year \leftarrow 1776$;   { Anno Domini }
  end;

242.   ⟨ Show equivalent n, in region 5 242 ⟩ ≡
  begin if $n < count\_base$ **then** $print\_param(n - int\_base)$
  else if $n < del\_code\_base$ **then**
      begin $print\_esc($"`count`"$)$; $print\_int(n - count\_base)$; **end**
    else begin $print\_esc($"`delcode`"$)$; $print\_int(n - del\_code\_base)$; **end**;

$print\_char(\texttt{"="});\ print\_int(eqtb[n].int);$
end

This code is used in section 252.

243. ⟨ Set variable c to the current escape character 243 ⟩ ≡
$c \leftarrow escape\_char$

This code is used in section 63.

244. ⟨ Character s is the current new-line character 244 ⟩ ≡
$s = new\_line\_char$

This code is used in sections 58, 59, and 60.

245. TeX is occasionally supposed to print diagnostic information that goes only into the transcript file, unless *tracing_online* is positive. Here are two routines that adjust the destination of print commands:

procedure *begin_diagnostic*;   { prepare to do some tracing }
  begin $old\_setting \leftarrow selector$;
  if $(tracing\_online \leq 0) \wedge (selector = term\_and\_log)$ **then**
    begin $decr(selector)$; **if** $history = spotless$ **then** $history \leftarrow warning\_issued$;
    end;
  end;

procedure *end_diagnostic*(*blank_line* : *boolean*);   { restore proper conditions after tracing }
  begin $print\_nl(\texttt{""})$; **if** *blank_line* **then** $print\_ln$;
  $selector \leftarrow old\_setting$;
  end;

246. Of course we had better declare another global variable, if the previous routines are going to work.

⟨ Global variables 13 ⟩ +≡
$old\_setting:\ 0\ ..\ max\_selector$;

---

247. The final region of *eqtb* contains the dimension parameters defined here, and the 256 \dimen registers.

> **define** *par_indent_code* = 0   { indentation of paragraphs }
> **define** *math_surround_code* = 1   { space around math in text }
> **define** *line_skip_limit_code* = 2   { threshold for *line_skip* instead of *baseline_skip* }
> **define** *hsize_code* = 3   { line width in horizontal mode }
> **define** *vsize_code* = 4   { page height in vertical mode }
> **define** *max_depth_code* = 5   { maximum depth of boxes on main pages }
> **define** *split_max_depth_code* = 6   { maximum depth of boxes on split pages }
> **define** *box_max_depth_code* = 7   { maximum depth of explicit vboxes }
> **define** *hfuzz_code* = 8   { tolerance for overfull hbox messages }
> **define** *vfuzz_code* = 9   { tolerance for overfull vbox messages }
> **define** *delimiter_shortfall_code* = 10   { maximum amount uncovered by variable delimiters }
> **define** *null_delimiter_space_code* = 11   { blank space in null delimiters }
> **define** *script_space_code* = 12   { extra space after subscript or superscript }
> **define** *pre_display_size_code* = 13   { length of text preceding a display }
> **define** *display_width_code* = 14   { length of line for displayed equation }
> **define** *display_indent_code* = 15   { indentation of line for displayed equation }
> **define** *overfull_rule_code* = 16   { width of rule that identifies overfull hboxes }
> **define** *hang_indent_code* = 17   { amount of hanging indentation }
> **define** *h_offset_code* = 18   { amount of horizontal offset when shipping pages out }
> **define** *v_offset_code* = 19   { amount of vertical offset when shipping pages out }
> **define** *dimen_pars* = 20   { total number of dimension parameters }
> **define** *scaled_base* = *dimen_base* + *dimen_pars*   { table of 256 user-defined \dimen registers }
> **define** *eqtb_size* = *scaled_base* + 255   { largest subscript of *eqtb* }
>
> **define** *dimen*(#) ≡ *eqtb*[*scaled_base* + #].*sc*
> **define** *dimen_par*(#) ≡ *eqtb*[*dimen_base* + #].*sc*   { a scaled quantity }
> **define** *par_indent* ≡ *dimen_par*(*par_indent_code*)
> **define** *math_surround* ≡ *dimen_par*(*math_surround_code*)
> $$\vdots$$
> **define** *v_offset* ≡ *dimen_par*(*v_offset_code*)

procedure *print_length_param*(*n* : *integer*);
  begin case *n* **of**
  par_indent_code: *print_esc*("parindent");
  math_surround_code: *print_esc*("mathsurround");
$$\vdots$$
  v_offset_code: *print_esc*("voffset");
  othercases *print*("[unknown␣dimen␣parameter!]")
  endcases;
  end;

248. ⟨ Put each of TeX's primitives into the hash table 226 ⟩ +≡
  primitive("parindent", *assign_dimen*, *dimen_base* + *par_indent_code*);
  primitive("mathsurround", *assign_dimen*, *dimen_base* + *math_surround_code*);
$$\vdots$$
  primitive("voffset", *assign_dimen*, *dimen_base* + *v_offset_code*);

249. ⟨Cases of *print_cmd_chr* for symbolic printing of primitives 227⟩ +≡

assign_dimen: **if** *chr_code* < *scaled_base* **then** *print_length_param*(*chr_code* − *dimen_base*)

   else begin *print_esc*("dimen"); *print_int*(*chr_code* − *scaled_base*);
     end;

250. ⟨Initialize table entries (done by INITEX only) 164⟩ +≡

   for *k* ← *dimen_base* **to** *eqtb_size* **do** *eqtb*[*k*].*sc* ← 0;

251. ⟨Show equivalent *n*, in region 6 251⟩ ≡

   begin if *n* < *scaled_base* **then** *print_length_param*(*n* − *dimen_base*)
   else begin *print_esc*("dimen"); *print_int*(*n* − *scaled_base*);
     end;
  print_char("="); *print_scaled*(*eqtb*[*n*].*sc*); *print*("pt");
  end

This code is used in section 252.

252. Here is a procedure that displays the contents of *eqtb*[*n*] symbolically.

⟨Declare the procedure called *print_cmd_chr* 298⟩
   stat procedure *show_eqtb*(*n* : *pointer*);
   begin if *n* < *active_base* **then** *print_char*("?")   { this can't happen }
   else if *n* < *glue_base* **then** ⟨Show equivalent *n*, in region 1 or 2 223⟩
     else if *n* < *local_base* **then** ⟨Show equivalent *n*, in region 3 229⟩
       else if *n* < *int_base* **then** ⟨Show equivalent *n*, in region 4 233⟩
         else if *n* < *dimen_base* **then** ⟨Show equivalent *n*, in region 5 242⟩
           else if *n* ≤ *eqtb_size* **then** ⟨Show equivalent *n*, in region 6 251⟩
             else *print_char*("?");   { this can't happen either }
  end;
  tats

---

assign_dimen = 73, §209.
baseline_skip = macro, §224.
chr_code: *halfword*, §298.
dimen_base = 4801, §236.
eqtb: **array**, §253.
int_base = 4367, §230.
k: *integer*, §163.

line_skip = macro, §224.
local_base = 3156, §224.
n: *pointer*, §252.
pointer = macro, §115.
primitive: **procedure**, §264.
print: **procedure**, §59.

print_char: **procedure**, §58.
print_cmd_chr: **procedure**, §298.
print_esc: **procedure**, §63.
print_int: **procedure**, §65.
print_scaled: **procedure**, §103.
sc = macro, §113.

253. The last two regions of *eqtb* have fullword values instead of the three fields *eq_level*, *eq_type*, and *equiv*. An *eq_type* is unnecessary, but TEX needs to store the *eq_level* information in another array called *xeq_level*.

⟨ Global variables 13 ⟩ +≡
eqtb: **array** [*active_base* .. *eqtb_size*] **of** *memory_word*;
xeq_level: **array** [*int_base* .. *eqtb_size*] **of** *quarterword*;

254. ⟨ Set initial values of key variables 21 ⟩ +≡
   for $k \leftarrow int\_base$ **to** *eqtb_size* **do** $xeq\_level[k] \leftarrow level\_one$;

255. When the debugging routine *search_mem* is looking for pointers having a given value, it is interested only in regions 1 to 3 of *eqtb*, and in the first part of region 4.

⟨ Search *eqtb* for equivalents equal to *p* 255 ⟩ ≡
   for $q \leftarrow active\_base$ **to** $box\_base + 255$ **do**
     begin if $equiv(q) = p$ **then**
       begin *print_nl*("EQUIV("); *print_int*(*q*); *print_char*(")");
       end;
     end
This code is used in section 172.

256. The hash table.   Control sequences are stored and retrieved by means of a fairly standard hash table algorithm called the method of "coalescing lists" (cf. Algorithm 6.4C in *The Art of Computer Programming*). Once a control sequence enters the table, it is never removed, because there are complicated situations involving \gdef where the removal of a control sequence at the end of a group would be a mistake preventable only by the introduction of a complicated reference-count mechanism.

The actual sequence of letters forming a control sequence identifier is stored in the *str_pool* array together with all the other strings. An auxiliary array *hash* consists of items with two halfword fields per word. The first of these, called *next*(*p*), points to the next identifier belonging to the same coalesced list as the identifier corresponding to *p*; and the other, called *text*(*p*), points to the *str_start* entry for *p*'s identifier. If position *p* of the hash table is empty, we have *text*(*p*) = 0; if position *p* is either empty or the end of a coalesced hash list, we have *next*(*p*) = 0. An auxiliary pointer variable called *hash_used* is maintained in such a way that all locations *p* ≥ *hash_used* are nonempty. The global variable *cs_count* tells how many multiletter control sequences have been defined, if statistics are being kept.

A global boolean variable called *no_new_control_sequence* is set to *true* during the time that new hash table entries are forbidden.

> **define** $next(\#) \equiv hash[\#].lh$ { link for coalesced lists }
> **define** $text(\#) \equiv hash[\#].rh$ { string number for control sequence name }
> **define** $hash\_is\_full \equiv (hash\_used = hash\_base)$ { test if all positions are occupied }
> **define** $font\_id\_text(\#) \equiv text(font\_id\_base + \#)$ { a frozen font identifier's name }

⟨ Global variables 13 ⟩ +≡
hash: **array** [*hash_base* .. *undefined_control_sequence* − 1] **of** *two_halves*;   { the hash table }
hash_used: *pointer*;   { allocation pointer for *hash* }
no_new_control_sequence: *boolean*;   { are new identifiers legal? }
cs_count: *integer*;   { total number of known identifiers }

257.   ⟨ Set initial values of key variables 21 ⟩ +≡
no_new_control_sequence ← *true*;   { new identifiers are usually forbidden }
next(*hash_base*) ← 0; *text*(*hash_base*) ← 0;
for *k* ← *hash_base* + 1 **to** *undefined_control_sequence* − 1 **do** *hash*[*k*] ← *hash*[*hash_base*];

258.   ⟨ Initialize table entries (done by INITEX only) 164 ⟩ +≡
hash_used ← *frozen_control_sequence*;   { nothing is used }
cs_count ← 0; *eq_type*(*frozen_dont_expand*) ← *dont_expand*;
text(*frozen_dont_expand*) ← "notexpanded:";

---

box_base = 3422, §230.
dont_expand = 115, §210.
eq_level = macro, §221.
eq_type = macro, §221.
eqtb_size = 5076, §247.
equiv = macro, §221.
font_id_base = 2368, §222.
frozen_control_sequence = 2358,
 §222.
frozen_dont_expand = 2367, §222.

int_base = 4367, §230.
k: integer, §163.
level_one = 1, §221.
lh: halfword, §113.
memory_word = **record**, §113.
p: 0 .. nest_size, §218.
pointer = macro, §115.
print_char: **procedure**, §58.
print_int: **procedure**, §65.
print_nl: **procedure**, §62.

q: pointer, §218.
quarterword = 0 .. 255, §113.
rh: halfword, §113.
search_mem: **procedure**, §172.
str_pool: **packed array**, §39.
str_start: **array**, §39.
two_halves = **packed record**, §113.
undefined_control_sequence = 2625,
 §222.

259.   Here is the subroutine that searches the hash table for an identifier that matches a given string of length $l > 1$ appearing in $buffer[j \mathrel{..} (j+l-1)]$. If the identifier is found, the corresponding hash table address is returned. Otherwise, if the global variable *no_new_control_sequence* is *true*, the dummy address *undefined_control_sequence* is returned. Otherwise the identifier is inserted into the hash table and its location is returned.

function *id_lookup*(j, l : *integer*): *pointer*; { search the hash table }
  label *found*; { go here if you found it }
  var h: *integer*; { hash code }
    p: *pointer*; { index in *hash* array }
    k: *pointer*; { index in *buffer* array }
  begin ⟨ Compute the hash code h 261 ⟩;
  $p \leftarrow h + hash\_base$; { we start searching here; note that $0 \le h < hash\_prime$ }
  loop begin if $text(p) > 0$ **then**
      if $length(text(p)) = l$ **then if** $str\_eq\_buf(text(p), j)$ **then goto** *found*;
    if $next(p) = 0$ **then**
      begin if *no_new_control_sequence* **then** $p \leftarrow undefined\_control\_sequence$
      else ⟨ Insert a new control sequence after p, then make p point to it 260 ⟩;
      goto *found*;
      end;
    $p \leftarrow next(p)$;
    end;
found: *id_lookup* $\leftarrow p$;
  end;

260.   ⟨ Insert a new control sequence after p, then make p point to it 260 ⟩ ≡
  begin if $text(p) > 0$ **then**
    begin repeat if *hash_is_full* **then** *overflow*("hash␣size", *hash_size*);
      decr(*hash_used*);
    until $text(hash\_used) = 0$; { search for an empty location in *hash* }
    $next(p) \leftarrow hash\_used$; $p \leftarrow hash\_used$;
    end;
  str_room(l);
  for $k \leftarrow j$ **to** $j + l - 1$ **do** *append_char*(*buffer*[k]);
  $text(p) \leftarrow make\_string$;
  stat *incr*(*cs_count*); **tats**
  end
This code is used in section 259.

261.   The value of *hash_prime* should be roughly 85% of *hash_size*, and it should be a prime number. The theory of hashing tells us to expect fewer than two table probes, on the average, when the search is successful. [See J. S. Vitter, *Journal of the ACM* **30** (1983), 231–258.]

⟨ Compute the hash code h 261 ⟩ ≡
  $h \leftarrow buffer[j]$;
  for $k \leftarrow j + 1$ **to** $j + l - 1$ **do**
    begin $h \leftarrow h + h + buffer[k]$;
    while $h \ge hash\_prime$ **do** $h \leftarrow h - hash\_prime$;
    end
This code is used in section 259.

262.   Single-character control sequences do not need to be looked up in a hash table, since we can use the character code itself as a direct address. The procedure *print_cs* prints the name of a control sequence, given a pointer to its address in *eqtb*. A space is printed after the name unless it is a single nonletter or an active character. This procedure might be invoked with invalid data, so it is "extra robust." The individual characters must be printed one at a time using *print*, since they may be unprintable.

⟨ Basic printing procedures 57 ⟩ +≡
procedure *print_cs*(*p* : *integer*);   { prints a purported control sequence }
  begin if *p* < *hash_base* **then**   { single character }
    if *p* ≥ *single_base* **then**
      if *p* = *null_cs* **then**
        begin *print_esc*("csname"); *print_esc*("endcsname");
        end
      else begin *print_esc*(*p* − *single_base*);
        if *cat_code*(*p* − *single_base*) = *letter* **then** *print_char*("␣");
      end
    else if *p* < *active_base* **then** *print_esc*("IMPOSSIBLE.")
      else *print*(*p* − *active_base*)
  else if *p* ≥ *undefined_control_sequence* **then** *print_esc*("IMPOSSIBLE.")
    else if (*text*(*p*) < 0) ∨ (*text*(*p*) ≥ *str_ptr*) **then** *print_esc*("NONEXISTENT.")
      else begin *print_esc*(""); *slow_print*(*text*(*p*)); *print_char*("␣");
        end;
  end;

263.   Here is a similar procedure; it avoids the error checks, and it never prints a space after the control sequence.

⟨ Basic printing procedures 57 ⟩ +≡
procedure *sprint_cs*(*p* : *pointer*);   { prints a control sequence }
  begin if *p* < *hash_base* **then**
    if *p* < *single_base* **then** *print*(*p* − *active_base*)
    else if *p* < *null_cs* **then** *print_esc*(*p* − *single_base*)
      else begin *print_esc*("csname"); *print_esc*("endcsname");
        end
  else begin *print_esc*(""); *slow_print*(*text*(*p*));
    end;
  end;

---

append_char = macro, §42.
buffer: **array**, §30.
cat_code = macro, §230.
cs_count: *integer*, §256.
decr = macro, §16.
eqtb: **array**, §253.
found = 40, §15.
hash: **array**, §256.
hash_is_full = macro, §256.
hash_prime = 1777, §12.
hash_size = 2100, §12.

hash_used: *pointer*, §256.
incr = macro, §16.
length = macro, §40.
letter = 11, §207.
make_string: **function**, §43.
next = macro, §256.
no_new_control_sequence: *boolean*, §256.
null_cs = 257, §222.
overflow: **procedure**, §94.
pointer = macro, §115.

print: **procedure**, §59.
print_char: **procedure**, §58.
print_esc: **procedure**, §63.
single_base = 129, §222.
slow_print: **procedure**, §60.
str_eq_buf: **function**, §45.
str_ptr: *str_number*, §39.
str_room = macro, §42.
text = macro, §256.
undefined_control_sequence = 2625, §222.

264. We need to put TeX's "primitive" control sequences into the hash table, together with their command code (which will be the *eq_type*) and an operand (which will be the *equiv*). The *primitive* procedure does this, in a way that no TeX user can. The global value *cur_val* contains the new *eqtb* pointer after *primitive* has acted.

init procedure *primitive*(s : *str_number*; c : *quarterword*; o : *halfword*);
var k: *pool_pointer*;   { index into *str_pool* }
   j: *small_number*;   { index into *buffer* }
   l: *small_number*;   { length of the string }
begin if $s < 128$ **then**   *cur_val* ← s + *single_base*
else begin k ← *str_start*[s]; l ← *str_start*[$s+1$] − k;   { we will move s into the (empty) *buffer* }
   for j ← 0 **to** $l − 1$ **do**   *buffer*[j] ← *str_pool*[$k + j$];
   cur_val ← *id_lookup*(0, l);   { *no_new_control_sequence* is *false* }
   flush_string; *text*(*cur_val*) ← s;   { we don't want to have the string twice }
   end;
eq_level(*cur_val*) ← *level_one*; *eq_type*(*cur_val*) ← c; *equiv*(*cur_val*) ← o;
end;
tini

265. Many of TeX's primitives need no *equiv*, since they are identifiable by their *eq_type* alone. These primitives are loaded into the hash table as follows:

⟨ Put each of TeX's primitives into the hash table 226 ⟩ +≡
   primitive("␣", *ex_space*, 0);
   primitive("/", *ital_corr*, 0);
   primitive("accent", *accent*, 0);
   primitive("advance", *advance*, 0);
   primitive("afterassignment", *after_assignment*, 0);
   primitive("aftergroup", *after_group*, 0);
   primitive("begingroup", *begin_group*, 0);
   primitive("char", *char_num*, 0);
   primitive("csname", *cs_name*, 0);
   primitive("delimiter", *delim_num*, 0);
   primitive("divide", *divide*, 0);
   primitive("endcsname", *end_cs_name*, 0);
   primitive("endgroup", *end_group*, 0); *text*(*frozen_end_group*) ← "endgroup";
   eqtb[*frozen_end_group*] ← *eqtb*[*cur_val*];
   primitive("expandafter", *expand_after*, 0);
   primitive("font", *def_font*, 0);
   primitive("fontdimen", *assign_font_dimen*, 0);
   primitive("halign", *halign*, 0);
   primitive("hrule", *hrule*, 0);
   primitive("ignorespaces", *ignore_spaces*, 0);
   primitive("insert", *insert*, 0);
   primitive("mark", *mark*, 0);
   primitive("mathaccent", *math_accent*, 0);
   primitive("mathchar", *math_char_num*, 0);
   primitive("mathchoice", *math_choice*, 0);
   primitive("multiply", *multiply*, 0);
   primitive("noalign", *no_align*, 0);

$primitive(\texttt{"noexpand"}, no\_expand, 0);$
$primitive(\texttt{"nonscript"}, non\_script, 0);$
$primitive(\texttt{"omit"}, omit, 0);$
$primitive(\texttt{"parshape"}, set\_shape, 0);$
$primitive(\texttt{"penalty"}, break\_penalty, 0);$
$primitive(\texttt{"prevgraf"}, set\_prev\_graf, 0);$
$primitive(\texttt{"radical"}, radical, 0);$
$primitive(\texttt{"read"}, read\_to\_cs, 0);$
$primitive(\texttt{"relax"}, relax, 256);$ { cf. $scan\_file\_name$ }
$text(frozen\_relax) \leftarrow \texttt{"relax"}; \; eqtb[frozen\_relax] \leftarrow eqtb[cur\_val];$
$primitive(\texttt{"setbox"}, set\_box, 0);$
$primitive(\texttt{"the"}, the, 0);$
$primitive(\texttt{"toks"}, toks\_register, 0);$
$primitive(\texttt{"vadjust"}, vadjust, 0);$
$primitive(\texttt{"valign"}, valign, 0);$
$primitive(\texttt{"vcenter"}, vcenter, 0);$
$primitive(\texttt{"vrule"}, vrule, 0);$

$accent = 45$, §208.
$advance = 89$, §209.
$after\_assignment = 40$, §208.
$after\_group = 41$, §208.
$assign\_font\_dimen = 76$, §209.
$begin\_group = 61$, §208.
$break\_penalty = 42$, §208.
$buffer$: **array**, §30.
$char\_num = 16$, §208.
$cs\_name = 106$, §210.
cur_val: $integer$, §410.
$def\_font = 87$, §209.
$delim\_num = 15$, §207.
$divide = 91$, §209.
$end\_cs\_name = 66$, §208.
$end\_group = 62$, §208.
$eq\_level =$ macro, §221.
$eq\_type =$ macro, §221.
$eqtb$: **array**, §253.
$equiv =$ macro, §221.
$ex\_space = 64$, §208.
$expand\_after = 101$, §210.

$flush\_string =$ macro, §44.
$frozen\_end\_group = 2360$, §222.
$frozen\_relax = 2365$, §222.
$halfword = min\_halfword$ ..
  $max\_halfword$, §113.
$halign = 32$, §208.
$hrule = 36$, §208.
id_lookup: **function**, §259.
$ignore\_spaces = 39$, §208.
$insert = 37$, §208.
$ital\_corr = 44$, §208.
$level\_one = 1$, §221.
$mark = 18$, §208.
$math\_accent = 46$, §208.
$math\_char\_num = 17$, §208.
$math\_choice = 54$, §208.
$multiply = 90$, §209.
$no\_align = 34$, §208.
$no\_expand = 102$, §210.
$no\_new\_control\_sequence$: $boolean$,
  §256.
$non\_script = 55$, §208.

$omit = 63$, §208.
$pool\_pointer = 0$ .. $pool\_size$, §38.
$quarterword = 0$ .. 255, §113.
$radical = 65$, §208.
$read\_to\_cs = 95$, §209.
$relax = 0$, §207.
$scan\_file\_name$: **procedure**, §526.
$set\_box = 97$, §209.
$set\_prev\_graf = 79$, §209.
$set\_shape = 83$, §209.
$single\_base = 129$, §222.
$small\_number = 0$ .. 63, §101.
$str\_number = 0$ .. $max\_strings$, §38.
str_pool: **packed array**, §39.
str_start: **array**, §39.
$text =$ macro, §256.
$the = 108$, §210.
$toks\_register = 70$, §209.
$vadjust = 38$, §208.
$valign = 33$, §208.
$vcenter = 56$, §208.
$vrule = 35$, §208.

266. Each primitive has a corresponding inverse, so that it is possible to display the cryptic numeric contents of *eqtb* in symbolic form. Every call of *primitive* in this program is therefore accompanied by some straightforward code that forms part of the *print_cmd_chr* routine below.

⟨ Cases of *print_cmd_chr* for symbolic printing of primitives 227 ⟩ +≡

accent: *print_esc*("accent");
advance: *print_esc*("advance");
after_assignment: *print_esc*("afterassignment");
after_group: *print_esc*("aftergroup");
assign_font_dimen: *print_esc*("fontdimen");
begin_group: *print_esc*("begingroup");
break_penalty: *print_esc*("penalty");
char_num: *print_esc*("char");
cs_name: *print_esc*("csname");
def_font: *print_esc*("font");
delim_num: *print_esc*("delimiter");
divide: *print_esc*("divide");
end_cs_name: *print_esc*("endcsname");
end_group: *print_esc*("endgroup");
ex_space: *print_esc*("␣");
expand_after: *print_esc*("expandafter");
halign: *print_esc*("halign");
hrule: *print_esc*("hrule");
ignore_spaces: *print_esc*("ignorespaces");
insert: *print_esc*("insert");
ital_corr: *print_esc*("/");
mark: *print_esc*("mark");
math_accent: *print_esc*("mathaccent");
math_char_num: *print_esc*("mathchar");
math_choice: *print_esc*("mathchoice");
multiply: *print_esc*("multiply");
no_align: *print_esc*("noalign");
no_expand: *print_esc*("noexpand");
non_script: *print_esc*("nonscript");
omit: *print_esc*("omit");
radical: *print_esc*("radical");
read_to_cs: *print_esc*("read");
relax: *print_esc*("relax");
set_box: *print_esc*("setbox");
set_prev_graf: *print_esc*("prevgraf");
set_shape: *print_esc*("parshape");
the: *print_esc*("the");
toks_register: *print_esc*("toks");
vadjust: *print_esc*("vadjust");
valign: *print_esc*("valign");
vcenter: *print_esc*("vcenter");
vrule: *print_esc*("vrule");

267.   We will deal with the other primitives later, at some point in the program where their *eq_type* and *equiv* values are more meaningful. For example, the primitives for math mode will be loaded when we consider the routines that deal with formulas. It is easy to find where each particular primitive was treated by looking in the index at the end; for example, the section where "radical" entered *eqtb* is listed under '\radical primitive'. (Primitives consisting of a single nonalphabetic character, like '\/', are listed under 'Single-character primitives'.)

Meanwhile, this is a convenient place to catch up on something we were unable to do before the hash table was defined:

⟨ Print the font identifier for *font*(*p*) 267 ⟩ ≡
  print_esc(*font_id_text*(*font*(*p*)))

This code is used in sections 174 and 176.

268. Saving and restoring equivalents. The nested structure provided by '{ . . . }' groups in TeX means that *eqtb* entries valid in outer groups should be saved and restored later if they are overridden inside the braces. When a new *eqtb* value is being assigned, the program therefore checks to see if the previous entry belongs to an outer level. In such a case, the old value is placed on the *save_stack* just before the new value enters *eqtb*. At the end of a grouping level, i.e., when the right brace is sensed, the *save_stack* is used to restore the outer values, and the inner ones are destroyed.

Entries on the *save_stack* are of type *memory_word*. The top item on this stack is *save_stack*[p], where $p = save\_ptr - 1$; it contains three fields called *save_type*, *save_level*, and *save_index*, and it is interpreted in one of four ways:

1) If *save_type*(p) = *restore_old_value*, then *save_index*(p) is a location in *eqtb* whose current value should be destroyed at the end of the current group and replaced by *save_stack*[$p-1$]. Furthermore if *save_index*(p) $\geq$ *int_base*, then *save_level*(p) should replace the corresponding entry in *xeq_level*.

2) If *save_type*(p) = *restore_zero*, then *save_index*(p) is a location in *eqtb* whose current value should be destroyed at the end of the current group, when it should be replaced by the current value of *eqtb*[*undefined_control_sequence*].

3) If *save_type*(p) = *insert_token*, then *save_index*(p) is a token that should be inserted into TeX's input when the current group ends.

4) If *save_type*(p) = *level_boundary*, then *save_level*(p) is a code explaining what kind of group we were previously in, and *save_index*(p) points to the level boundary word at the bottom of the entries for that group.

define *save_type*(**#**) $\equiv$ *save_stack*[**#**]*.hh.b0*   { classifies a *save_stack* entry }
define *save_level*(**#**) $\equiv$ *save_stack*[**#**]*.hh.b1*   { saved level for regions 5 and 6, or group code }
define *save_index*(**#**) $\equiv$ *save_stack*[**#**]*.hh.rh*   { *eqtb* location or *save_stack* location }
define *restore_old_value* = 0   { *save_type* when a value should be restored later }
define *restore_zero* = 1   { *save_type* when an undefined entry should be restored }
define *insert_token* = 2   { *save_type* when a token is being saved for later use }
define *level_boundary* = 3   { *save_type* corresponding to beginning of group }

269. Here are the group codes that are used to discriminate between different kinds of groups. They allow TeX to decide what special actions, if any, should be performed when a group ends.

Some groups are not supposed to be ended by right braces. For example, the '$' that begins a math formula causes a *math_shift_group* to be started, and this should be terminated by a matching '$'. Similarly, a group that starts with \left should end with \right, and one that starts with \begingroup should end with \endgroup.

define *bottom_level* = 0   { group code for the outside world }
define *simple_group* = 1   { group code for local structure only }
define *hbox_group* = 2   { code for '\hbox{...}' }
define *adjusted_hbox_group* = 3   { code for '\hbox{...}' in vertical mode }
define *vbox_group* = 4   { code for '\vbox{...}' }
define *vtop_group* = 5   { code for '\vtop{...}' }
define *align_group* = 6   { code for '\halign{...}', '\valign{...}' }
define *no_align_group* = 7   { code for '\noalign{...}' }

define *output_group* = 8 { code for output routine }
define *math_group* = 9 { code for, e.g, `'^{...}'` }
define *disc_group* = 10 { code for '\discretionary{...}{...}{...}' }
define *insert_group* = 11 { code for '\insert{...}', '\vadjust{...}' }
define *vcenter_group* = 12 { code for '\vcenter{...}' }
define *math_choice_group* = 13 { code for '\mathchoice{...}{...}{...}{...}' }
define *semi_simple_group* = 14 { code for '\begingroup...\endgroup' }
define *math_shift_group* = 15 { code for '$...$' }
define *math_left_group* = 16 { code for '\left...\right' }
define *max_group_code* = 16

⟨ Types in the outer block 18 ⟩ +≡
  group_code = 0 .. *max_group_code*; { *save_index* for a level boundary }

270. The global variable *cur_group* keeps track of what sort of group we are currently in. Another global variable, *cur_boundary*, points to the topmost *level_boundary* word. And *cur_level* is the current depth of nesting. The routines are designed to preserve the condition that no entry in the *save_stack* or in *eqtb* ever has a level greater than *cur_level*.

271. ⟨ Global variables 13 ⟩ +≡
save_stack: **array** [0 .. *save_size*] **of** *memory_word*;
save_ptr: 0 .. *save_size*; { first unused entry on *save_stack* }
max_save_stack: 0 .. *save_size*; { maximum usage of save stack }
cur_level: *quarterword*; { current nesting level for groups }
cur_group: *group_code*; { current group type }
cur_boundary: 0 .. *save_size*; { where the current level begins }

272. At this time it might be a good idea for the reader to review the introduction to *eqtb* that was given above just before the long lists of parameter names. Recall that the "outer level" of the program is *level_one*, since undefined control sequences are assumed to be "defined" at *level_zero*.

⟨ Set initial values of key variables 21 ⟩ +≡
  save_ptr ← 0; *cur_level* ← *level_one*; *cur_group* ← *bottom_level*; *cur_boundary* ← 0;
  max_save_stack ← 0;

273. The following macro is used to test if there is room for up to six more entries on *save_stack*. By making a conservative test like this, we can get by with testing for overflow in only a few places.

  define *check_full_save_stack* ≡
          if *save_ptr* > *max_save_stack* **then**
              begin *max_save_stack* ← *save_ptr*;
              if *max_save_stack* > *save_size* − 6 **then** *overflow*("save␣size", *save_size*);
              end

---

b0: *quarterword*, §113.
b1: *quarterword*, §113.
eqtb: **array**, §253.
hh: *two_halves*, §113.
int_base = 4367, §230.

level_one = 1, §221.
level_zero = 0, §221.
memory_word = **record**, §113.
overflow: **procedure**, §94.
quarterword = 0 .. 255, §113.

rh: *halfword*, §113.
save_size = **const**, §11.
undefined_control_sequence = 2625,
    §222.
xeq_level: **array**, §253.

274. Procedure *new_save_level* is called when a group begins. The argument is a group identification code like '*hbox_group*'. After calling this routine, it is safe to put five more entries on *save_stack*.

In some cases integer-valued items are placed onto the *save_stack* just below a *level_boundary* word, because this is a convenient place to keep information that is supposed to "pop up" just when the group has finished. For example, when '\hbox to 100pt{...}' is being treated, the 100pt dimension is stored on *save_stack* just before *new_save_level* is called.

We use the notation *saved*(k) to stand for an integer item that appears in location *save_ptr* + k of the save stack.

define *saved*(**#**) ≡ *save_stack*[*save_ptr* + **#**].*int*

procedure *new_save_level*(*c* : *group_code*);   { begin a new level of grouping }
 begin *check_full_save_stack*; *save_type*(*save_ptr*) ← *level_boundary*;
 save_level(*save_ptr*) ← *cur_group*; *save_index*(*save_ptr*) ← *cur_boundary*;
 if *cur_level* = *max_quarterword* **then**
  overflow("grouping␣levels", *max_quarterword* − *min_quarterword*);
    { quit if (*cur_level* + 1) is too big to be stored in *eqtb* }
 cur_boundary ← *save_ptr*; *incr*(*cur_level*); *incr*(*save_ptr*); *cur_group* ← *c*;
 end;

275. Just before an entry of *eqtb* is changed, the following procedure should be called to update the other data structures properly. It is important to keep in mind that reference counts in *mem* include references from within *save_stack*, so these counts must be handled carefully.

procedure *eq_destroy*(*w* : *memory_word*);   { gets ready to forget *w* }
 var *q*: *pointer*;   { *equiv* field of *w* }
 begin case *eq_type_field*(*w*) **of**
 call, *long_call*, *outer_call*, *long_outer_call*: *delete_token_ref*(*equiv_field*(*w*));
 glue_ref: *delete_glue_ref*(*equiv_field*(*w*));
 shape_ref: **begin** *q* ← *equiv_field*(*w*);   { we need to free a \parshape block }
  if *q* ≠ *null* **then** *free_node*(*q*, *info*(*q*) + *info*(*q*) + 1);
  end;   { such a block is $2n + 1$ words long, where $n = info(q)$ }
 box_ref: *flush_node_list*(*equiv_field*(*w*));
 othercases *do_nothing*
 endcases;
 end;

276. To save a value of *eqtb*[*p*] that was established at level *l*, we can use the following subroutine.

procedure *eq_save*(*p* : *pointer*; *l* : *quarterword*);   { saves *eqtb*[*p*] }
 begin *check_full_save_stack*;
 if *l* = *level_zero* **then** *save_type*(*save_ptr*) ← *restore_zero*
 else begin *save_stack*[*save_ptr*] ← *eqtb*[*p*]; *incr*(*save_ptr*); *save_type*(*save_ptr*) ← *restore_old_value*;
  end;
 save_level(*save_ptr*) ← *l*; *save_index*(*save_ptr*) ← *p*; *incr*(*save_ptr*);
 end;

277. The procedure *eq_define* defines an *eqtb* entry having specified *eq_type* and *equiv* fields, and saves the former value if appropriate. This procedure is used only for entries in the first four regions of *eqtb*, i.e., only for entries that have *eq_type* and *equiv* fields. After calling this routine, it is safe to put four more entries on *save_stack*, provided that there was room for four more entries before the call, since *eq_save* makes the necessary test.

procedure *eq_define*(p : *pointer*; t : *quarterword*; e : *halfword*);   { new data for *eqtb* }
    begin if *eq_level*(p) = *cur_level* **then** *eq_destroy*(*eqtb*[p])
    else if *cur_level* > *level_one* **then** *eq_save*(p, *eq_level*(p));
    eq_level(p) ← *cur_level*; *eq_type*(p) ← t; *equiv*(p) ← e;
    end;

278. The counterpart of *eq_define* for the remaining (fullword) positions in *eqtb* is called *eq_word_define*. Since *xeq_level*[p] ≥ *level_one* for all p, a '*restore_zero*' will never be used in this case.

procedure *eq_word_define*(p : *pointer*; w : *integer*);
    begin if *xeq_level*[p] ≠ *cur_level* **then**
        begin *eq_save*(p, *xeq_level*[p]); *xeq_level*[p] ← *cur_level*;
        end;
    eqtb[p].*int* ← w;
    end;

279. The *eq_define* and *eq_word_define* routines take care of local definitions. Global definitions are done in almost the same way, but there is no need to save old values, and the new value is associated with *level_one*.

procedure *geq_define*(p : *pointer*; t : *quarterword*; e : *halfword*);   { global *eq_define* }
    begin *eq_destroy*(*eqtb*[p]); *eq_level*(p) ← *level_one*; *eq_type*(p) ← t; *equiv*(p) ← e;
    end;

procedure *geq_word_define*(p : *pointer*; w : *integer*);   { global *eq_word_define* }
    begin *eqtb*[p].*int* ← w; *xeq_level*[p] ← *level_one*;
    end;

280. Subroutine *save_for_after* puts a token on the stack for save-keeping.

procedure *save_for_after*(t : *halfword*);
    begin *check_full_save_stack*; *save_type*(*save_ptr*) ← *insert_token*; *save_level*(*save_ptr*) ← *level_zero*;
    save_index(*save_ptr*) ← t; *incr*(*save_ptr*);
    end;

---

281.   The *unsave* routine goes the other way, taking items off of *save_stack*. This routine takes care of restoration when a level ends; everything belonging to the topmost group is cleared off of the save stack.

⟨ Declare the procedure called *restore_trace* 284 ⟩
procedure *back_input*; *forward*;
procedure *unsave*;   { pops the top level off the save stack }
  label *done*;
  var *p*: *pointer*;   { position to be restored }
    l: *quarterword*;   { saved level, if in fullword regions of *eqtb* }
    t: *halfword*;   { saved value of *cur_tok* }
  begin if *cur_level* > *level_one* **then**
    begin *decr*(*cur_level*); ⟨ Clear off top level from *save_stack* 282 ⟩;
    end
  else *confusion*("curlevel");   { *unsave* is not used when *cur_group* = *bottom_level* }
  end;

282.   ⟨ Clear off top level from *save_stack* 282 ⟩ ≡
  loop begin *decr*(*save_ptr*);
    if *save_type*(*save_ptr*) = *level_boundary* **then goto** *done*;
    p ← *save_index*(*save_ptr*);
    if *save_type*(*save_ptr*) = *insert_token* **then** ⟨ Insert token *p* into TeX's input 326 ⟩
    else begin if *save_type*(*save_ptr*) = *restore_old_value* **then**
        begin *l* ← *save_level*(*save_ptr*); *decr*(*save_ptr*);
        end
      else *save_stack*[*save_ptr*] ← *eqtb*[*undefined_control_sequence*];
      ⟨ Store *save_stack*[*save_ptr*] in *eqtb*[*p*], unless *eqtb*[*p*] holds a global value 283 ⟩;
      end;
    end;
done: *cur_group* ← *save_level*(*save_ptr*); *cur_boundary* ← *save_index*(*save_ptr*)
This code is used in section 281.

283.   A global definition, which sets the level to *level_one*, will not be undone by *unsave*. If at least one global definition of *eqtb*[*p*] has been carried out within the group that just ended, the last such definition will therefore survive.

⟨ Store *save_stack*[*save_ptr*] in *eqtb*[*p*], unless *eqtb*[*p*] holds a global value 283 ⟩ ≡
  if *p* < *int_base* **then**
    if *eq_level*(*p*) = *level_one* **then**
      begin *eq_destroy*(*save_stack*[*save_ptr*]);   { destroy the saved value }
      stat if *tracing_restores* > 0 **then** *restore_trace*(*p*, "retaining");
      tats
      end
    else begin *eq_destroy*(*eqtb*[*p*]);   { destroy the current value }
      eqtb[*p*] ← *save_stack*[*save_ptr*];   { restore the saved value }
      stat if *tracing_restores* > 0 **then** *restore_trace*(*p*, "restoring");
      tats
      end
  else if *xeq_level*[*p*] ≠ *level_one* **then**
      begin *eqtb*[*p*] ← *save_stack*[*save_ptr*]; *xeq_level*[*p*] ← *l*;

```
      stat if tracing_restores > 0 then restore_trace(p, "restoring");
      tats
      end
   else begin stat if tracing_restores > 0 then restore_trace(p, "retaining");
      tats
      end
```

This code is used in section 282.

284. ⟨ Declare the procedure called *restore_trace* 284 ⟩ ≡

```
   stat procedure restore_trace(p : pointer; s : str_number);
         { eqtb[p] has just been restored or retained }
   begin begin_diagnostic; print_char("{"); print(s); print_char("␣"); show_eqtb(p); print_char("}");
   end_diagnostic(false);
   end;
   tats
```

This code is used in section 281.

285. When looking for possible pointers to a memory location, it is helpful to look for references from *eqtb* that might be waiting on the save stack. Of course, we might find spurious pointers too; but this routine is merely an aid when debugging, and at such times we are grateful for any scraps of information, even if they prove to be irrelevant.

⟨ Search *save_stack* for equivalents that point to *p* 285 ⟩ ≡

```
   if save_ptr > 0 then
      for q ← 0 to save_ptr − 1 do
         begin if equiv_field(save_stack[q]) = p then
            begin print_nl("SAVE("); print_int(q); print_char(")");
            end;
         end
```

This code is used in section 172.

286. Most of the parameters kept in *eqtb* can be changed freely, but there's an exception: The magnification should not be used with two different values during any TEX job, since a single magnification is applied to an entire run. The global variable *mag_set* is set to the current magnification whenever it becomes necessary to "freeze" it at a particular value.

⟨ Global variables 13 ⟩ +≡

mag_set: *integer*;   { if nonzero, this magnification should be used henceforth }

---

287. ⟨ Set initial values of key variables 21 ⟩ +≡
$mag\_set \leftarrow 0$;

288. The *prepare_mag* subroutine is called whenever TeX wants to use *mag* for magnification.

procedure *prepare_mag*;
  begin if $(mag\_set > 0) \wedge (mag \neq mag\_set)$ **then**
    begin *print_err*("Incompatible␣magnification␣("); *print_int*(*mag*); *print*(");");
    print_nl("␣the␣previous␣value␣will␣be␣retained");
    help2("I␣can␣handle␣only␣one␣magnification␣ratio␣per␣job.␣So␣I´ve")
    ("reverted␣to␣the␣magnification␣you␣used␣earlier␣on␣this␣run.");
    int_error(*mag_set*); *geq_word_define*(*int_base* + *mag_code*, *mag_set*);   { *mag* ← *mag_set* }
    end;
  if $(mag \leq 0) \vee (mag > 32768)$ **then**
    begin *print_err*("Illegal␣magnification␣has␣been␣changed␣to␣1000");
    help1("The␣magnification␣ratio␣must␣be␣between␣1␣and␣32768."); *int_error*(*mag*);
    geq_word_define(*int_base* + *mag_code*, 1000);
    end;
  $mag\_set \leftarrow mag$;
  end;

289.   Token lists.   A TeX token is either a character or a control sequence, and it is represented internally in one of two ways: (1) A character whose ASCII code number is c and whose command code is m is represented as the number $2^8 m + c$; the command code is in the range $1 \le m \le 14$. (2) A control sequence whose *eqtb* address is p is represented as the number $cs\_token\_flag + p$. Here $cs\_token\_flag = 2^{12}$ is larger than $2^8 m + c$, yet it is small enough that $cs\_token\_flag + p < max\_halfword$; thus, a token fits comfortably in a halfword.

A token t represents a *left_brace* command if and only if $t < \mathit{left\_brace\_limit}$; it represents a *right_brace* command if and only if we have $\mathit{left\_brace\_limit} \le t < \mathit{right\_brace\_limit}$; and it represents a *match* or *end_match* command if and only if $\mathit{match\_token} \le t \le \mathit{end\_match\_token}$. The following definitions take care of these token-oriented constants and a few others.

define $cs\_token\_flag \equiv \ '10000$ { amount added to the *eqtb* location in a token that stands for a control sequence; is a multiple of 256 }
define $left\_brace\_token = \ '0400$ { $2^8 \cdot \mathit{left\_brace}$ }
define $left\_brace\_limit = \ '1000$ { $2^8 \cdot (\mathit{left\_brace} + 1)$ }
define $right\_brace\_token = \ '1000$ { $2^8 \cdot \mathit{right\_brace}$ }
define $right\_brace\_limit = \ '1400$ { $2^8 \cdot (\mathit{right\_brace} + 1)$ }
define $math\_shift\_token = \ '1400$ { $2^8 \cdot \mathit{math\_shift}$ }
define $tab\_token = \ '2000$ { $2^8 \cdot \mathit{tab\_mark}$ }
define $out\_param\_token = \ '2400$ { $2^8 \cdot \mathit{out\_param}$ }
define $space\_token = \ '5040$ { $2^8 \cdot \mathit{spacer} + $ "␣" }
define $letter\_token = \ '5400$ { $2^8 \cdot \mathit{letter}$ }
define $other\_token = \ '6000$ { $2^8 \cdot \mathit{other\_char}$ }
define $match\_token = \ '6400$ { $2^8 \cdot \mathit{match}$ }
define $end\_match\_token = \ '7000$ { $2^8 \cdot \mathit{end\_match}$ }

290.   ⟨ Check the "constant" values for consistency 14 ⟩ +≡
if $cs\_token\_flag + undefined\_control\_sequence > max\_halfword$ **then** $bad \leftarrow 21$;

291.   A token list is a singly linked list of one-word nodes in *mem*, where each word contains a token and a link. Macro definitions, output-routine definitions, marks, and \write texts are kept in TeX's memory in the form of token lists, preceded by a node that has a reference count in its *token_ref_count* field. The token stored in location p is called $info(p)$.

Three special commands appear in the token lists of macro definitions. When $m = match$, it means that TeX should scan a parameter for the current macro; when $m = end\_match$, it means that parameter matching should end and TeX should start reading the macro text; and when $m = out\_param$, it means that TeX should insert parameter number c into the text at this point.

The enclosing { and } characters of a macro definition are omitted, but the final right brace of an output routine is included at the end of its token list.

Here is an example macro definition that illustrates these conventions. After TeX processes the text

$$\def\mac a\#1\#2 \ b \ \{\#1\-a \ \#\#1\#2 \ \#2\}$$

the definition of \mac is represented as a token list containing

(reference count), *letter* a, *match* #, *match* #, *spacer* ␣, \b, *end_match*,
out_param 1, \-, *letter* a, *spacer* ␣, *mac_param* #, *other_char* 1,
out_param 2, *spacer* ␣, *out_param* 2.

The procedure *scan_toks* builds such token lists, and *macro_call* does the parameter matching.
     Examples such as

$$\verb|\def\m{\def\m{a}_b}|$$

explain why reference counts would be needed even if TEX had no \let operation: When the token list for \m is being read, the redefinition of \m changes the *eqtb* entry before the token list has been fully consumed, so we dare not simply destroy a token list when its control sequence is being redefined.

     If the parameter-matching part of a definition ends with '#{', the corresponding token list will have '{' just before the '*end_match*' and also at the very end. The first '{' is used to delimit the parameter; the second one keeps the first from disappearing.

292.   The procedure *show_token_list*, which prints a symbolic form of the token list that starts at a given node p, illustrates these conventions. The token list being displayed should not begin with a reference count. However, the procedure is intended to be robust, so that if the memory links are awry or if p is not really a pointer to a token list, nothing catastrophic will happen.

An additional parameter q is also given; this parameter is either null or it points to a node in the token list where a certain magic computation takes place that will be explained later. (Basically, q is non-null when we are printing the two-line context information at the time of an error message; q marks the place corresponding to where the second line should begin.)

For example, if p points to the node containing the first a in the token list above, then *show_token_list* will print the string

$$\text{`a\#1\#2}_\sqcup\backslash\text{b}_\sqcup\text{->\#1}\backslash\text{-a}_\sqcup\text{\#\#1\#2}_\sqcup\text{\#2'};$$

and if q points to the node containing the second a, the magic computation will be performed just before the second a is printed.

The generation will stop, and '\ETC.' will be printed, if the length of printing exceeds a given limit l. Anomalous entries are printed in the form of control sequences that are not followed by a blank space, e.g., '\BAD.'; this cannot be confused with actual control sequences because a real control sequence named BAD would come out '\BAD$_\sqcup$'.

⟨ Declare the procedure called *show_token_list* 292 ⟩ ≡
procedure *show_token_list*(*p, q* : *integer*; *l* : *integer*);
  label *exit*;
  var *m, c*: *integer*;   { pieces of a token }
    match_chr: *ASCII_code*;   { character used in a '*match*' }
    n: *ASCII_code*;   { the highest parameter number, as an ASCII digit }
  begin *match_chr* ← "#"; *n* ← "0"; *tally* ← 0;
  while (*p* ≠ *null*) ∧ (*tally* < *l*) **do**
    begin if *p* = *q* **then** ⟨ Do magic computation 320 ⟩;
    ⟨ Display token *p*, and **return** if there are problems 293 ⟩;
    p ← *link*(*p*);
    end;
  if *p* ≠ *null* **then** *print_esc*("ETC.");
exit: **end**;
This code is used in section 119.

293.   ⟨ Display token *p*, and **return** if there are problems 293 ⟩ ≡
  if (*p* < *hi_mem_min*) ∨ (*p* > *mem_end*) **then**
    begin *print_esc*("CLOBBERED."); **return**;
    end;
  if *info*(*p*) ≥ *cs_token_flag* **then** *print_cs*(*info*(*p*) − *cs_token_flag*)
  else begin *m* ← *info*(*p*) **div** ´400; *c* ← *info*(*p*) **mod** ´400;
    if (*info*(*p*) < 0) ∨ (*c* > 127) **then** *print_esc*("BAD.")
    else ⟨ Display the token (*m, c*) 294 ⟩;
    end
This code is used in section 292.

294. The procedure usually "learns" the character code used for macro parameters by seeing one in a *match* command before it runs into any *out_param* commands.

⟨ Display the token (m, c) 294 ⟩ ≡
  case m **of**
  left_brace, *right_brace*, *math_shift*, *tab_mark*, *sup_mark*, *sub_mark*, *spacer*, *letter*, *other_char*: *print*(*c*);
  mac_param: **begin** *print*(*c*); *print*(*c*);
    end;
  out_param: **begin** *print*(*match_chr*);
    if $c \leq 9$ **then** *print_char*(*c* + "0")
    else begin *print_char*("!"); **return**;
      end;
    end;
  match: **begin** *match_chr* ← *c*; *print*(*c*); *incr*(*n*); *print_char*(*n*);
    if $n >$ "9" **then return**;
    end;
  end_match: *print*("->");
  othercases *print_esc*("BAD.")
  endcases

This code is used in section 293.

295. Here's the way we sometimes want to display a token list, given a pointer to its reference count; the pointer may be null.

procedure *token_show*(*p* : *pointer*);
  begin if $p \neq null$ **then** *show_token_list*(*link*(*p*), *null*, 1000);
  end;

296. The *print_meaning* subroutine displays *cur_cmd* and *cur_chr* in symbolic form, including the expansion of a macro or mark.

procedure *print_meaning*;
  begin *print_cmd_chr*(*cur_cmd*, *cur_chr*);
  if $cur\_cmd \geq call$ **then**
    begin *print_char*(":"); *print_ln*; *token_show*(*cur_chr*);
    end
  else if $cur\_cmd = top\_bot\_mark$ **then**
      begin *print_char*(":"); *print_ln*; *token_show*(*cur_mark*[*cur_chr*]);
      end;
  end;

ASCII_code = 0 .. 127, §18.
call = 110, §210.
cs_token_flag = macro, §289.
cur_chr: *halfword*, §297.
cur_cmd: *eight_bits*, §297.
cur_mark: **array**, §382.
end_match = 14, §207.
exit = 10, §15.
hi_mem_min: *pointer*, §116.
incr = macro, §16.
info = macro, §118.
left_brace = 1, §207.

letter = 11, §207.
link = macro, §118.
mac_param = 6, §207.
match = 13, §207.
math_shift = 3, §207.
mem_end: *pointer*, §118.
null = macro, §115.
other_char = 12, §207.
out_param = 5, §207.
pointer = macro, §115.
print: **procedure**, §59.
print_char: **procedure**, §58.

print_cmd_chr: **procedure**, §298.
print_cs: **procedure**, §262.
print_esc: **procedure**, §63.
print_ln: **procedure**, §57.
right_brace = 2, §207.
spacer = 10, §207.
sub_mark = 8, §207.
sup_mark = 7, §207.
tab_mark = 4, §207.
tally: *integer*, §54.
top_bot_mark = 109, §210.

297. Introduction to the syntactic routines. Let's pause a moment now and try to look at the Big Picture. The TeX program consists of three main parts: syntactic routines, semantic routines, and output routines. The chief purpose of the syntactic routines is to deliver the user's input to the semantic routines, one token at a time. The semantic routines act as an interpreter responding to these tokens, which may be regarded as commands. And the output routines are periodically called on to convert box-and-glue lists into a compact set of instructions that will be sent to a typesetter. We have discussed the basic data structures and utility routines of TeX, so we are good and ready to plunge into the real activity by considering the syntactic routines.

Our current goal is to come to grips with the *get_next* procedure, which is the keystone of TeX's input mechanism. Each call of *get_next* sets the value of three variables *cur_cmd*, *cur_chr*, and *cur_cs*, representing the next input token.

> *cur_cmd* denotes a command code from the long list of codes given above;
> *cur_chr* denotes a character code or other modifier of the command code;
> *cur_cs* is the *eqtb* location of the current control sequence,
>   if the current token was a control sequence, otherwise it's zero.

Underlying this external behavior of *get_next* is all the machinery necessary to convert from character files to tokens. At a given time we may be only partially finished with the reading of several files (for which \input was specified), and partially finished with the expansion of some user-defined macros and/or some macro parameters, and partially finished with the generation of some text in a template for \halign, and so on. When reading a character file, special characters must be classified as math delimiters, etc.; comments and extra blank spaces must be removed, paragraphs must be recognized, and control sequences must be found in the hash table. Furthermore there are occasions in which the scanning routines have looked ahead for a word like 'plus' but only part of that word was found, hence a few characters must be put back into the input and scanned again.

To handle these situations, which might all be present simultaneously, TeX uses various stacks that hold information about the incomplete activities, and there is a finite state control for each level of the input mechanism. These stacks record the current state of an implicitly recursive process, but the *get_next* procedure is not recursive. Therefore it will not be difficult to translate these algorithms into low-level languages that do not support recursion.

⟨ Global variables 13 ⟩ +≡
cur_cmd: *eight_bits*;   { current command set by *get_next* }
cur_chr: *halfword*;   { operand of current command }
cur_cs: *pointer*;   { control sequence found here, zero if none found }
cur_tok: *halfword*;   { packed representative of *cur_cmd* and *cur_chr* }

298. The *print_cmd_chr* routine prints a symbolic interpretation of a command code and its modifier. This is used in certain 'You can´t' error messages, and in the implementation of diagnostic routines like \show.

The body of *print_cmd_chr* is a rather tedious listing of print commands, and most of it is essentially an inverse to the *primitive* routine that enters a TeX primitive into *eqtb*. Therefore much of this procedure appears elsewhere in the program, together with the corresponding *primitive* calls.

define $chr\_cmd(\texttt{\#}) \equiv$
            begin $print(\texttt{\#});\ print\_ASCII(chr\_code);$
            end
⟨ Declare the procedure called $print\_cmd\_chr$ 298 ⟩ $\equiv$
procedure $print\_cmd\_chr(cmd : quarterword;\ chr\_code : halfword);$
    begin case cmd **of**
    $left\_brace:\ chr\_cmd(\texttt{"begin-group␣character␣"});$
    $right\_brace:\ chr\_cmd(\texttt{"end-group␣character␣"});$
    $math\_shift:\ chr\_cmd(\texttt{"math␣shift␣character␣"});$
    $mac\_param:\ chr\_cmd(\texttt{"macro␣parameter␣character␣"});$
    $sup\_mark:\ chr\_cmd(\texttt{"superscript␣character␣"});$
    $sub\_mark:\ chr\_cmd(\texttt{"subscript␣character␣"});$
    $endv:\ print(\texttt{"end␣of␣alignment␣template"});$
    $spacer:\ chr\_cmd(\texttt{"blank␣space␣"});$
    $letter:\ chr\_cmd(\texttt{"the␣letter␣"});$
    $other\_char:\ chr\_cmd(\texttt{"the␣character␣"});$
    ⟨ Cases of $print\_cmd\_chr$ for symbolic printing of primitives 227 ⟩
    othercases $print(\texttt{"[unknown␣command␣code!]"})$
    endcases;
    end;
This code is used in section 252.

299.   Here is a procedure that displays the current command.

procedure $show\_cur\_cmd\_chr;$
    begin $begin\_diagnostic;\ print\_nl(\texttt{"\{"});$
    if $mode \neq shown\_mode$ **then**
        begin $print\_mode(mode);\ print(\texttt{":␣"});\ shown\_mode \leftarrow mode;$
        end;
    $print\_cmd\_chr(cur\_cmd, cur\_chr);\ print\_char(\texttt{"\}"});\ end\_diagnostic(false);$
    end;

300. Input stacks and states. This implementation of TeX uses two different conventions for representing sequential stacks.

1) If there is frequent access to the top entry, and if the stack is essentially never empty, then the top entry is kept in a global variable (even better would be a machine register), and the other entries appear in the array $stack[0 .. (ptr - 1)]$. For example, the semantic stack described above is handled this way, and so is the input stack that we are about to study.

2) If there is infrequent top access, the entire stack contents are in the array $stack[0 .. (ptr - 1)]$. For example, the *save_stack* is treated this way, as we have seen.

The state of TeX's input mechanism appears in the input stack, whose entries are records with six fields, called *state*, *index*, *start*, *loc*, *limit*, and *name*. This stack is maintained with convention (1), so it is declared in the following way:

⟨ Types in the outer block 18 ⟩ +≡
  $in\_state\_record =$ **record** $state\_field, index\_field: quarterword;$
    $start\_field, loc\_field, limit\_field, name\_field: halfword;$
    end;

301. ⟨ Global variables 13 ⟩ +≡
input_stack: **array** $[0 .. stack\_size]$ **of** *in_state_record*;
input_ptr: $0 .. stack\_size$; { first unused location of *input_stack* }
max_in_stack: $0 .. stack\_size$; { largest value of *input_ptr* when pushing }
cur_input: *in_state_record*; { the "top" input state, according to convention (1) }

302. We've already defined the special variable $loc \equiv cur\_input.loc\_field$ in our discussion of basic input-output routines. The other components of *cur_input* are defined in the same way:

  define $state \equiv cur\_input.state\_field$ { current scanner state }
  define $index \equiv cur\_input.index\_field$ { reference for buffer information }
  define $start \equiv cur\_input.start\_field$ { starting position in *buffer* }
  define $limit \equiv cur\_input.limit\_field$ { end of current line in *buffer* }
  define $name \equiv cur\_input.name\_field$ { name of the current file }

303. Let's look more closely now at the control variables (*state*, *index*, *start*, *loc*, *limit*, *name*), assuming that TeX is reading a line of characters that have been input from some file or from the user's terminal. There is an array called *buffer* that acts as a stack of all lines of characters that are currently being read from files, including all lines on subsidiary levels of the input stack that are not yet completed. TeX will return to the other lines when it is finished with the present input file.

(Incidentally, on a machine with byte-oriented addressing, it would be appropriate to combine *buffer* with the *str_pool* array, letting the buffer entries grow downward from the top of the string pool and checking that these two tables don't bump into each other.)

The line we are currently working on begins in position *start* of the buffer; the next character we are about to read is $buffer[loc]$; and *limit* is the location of the last character present. If $loc > limit$, the line has been completely read. Usually $buffer[limit]$ is the *end_line_char*, denoting the end of a line, but this is not true if the current line is an insertion that was entered on the user's terminal in response to an error message.

The *name* variable is a string number that designates the name of the current file, if we are reading a text file. It is zero if we are reading from the terminal; it is $n + 1$ if we are reading from input stream n, where $0 \leq n \leq 16$. (Input stream 16 stands for an invalid stream number; in such cases the input is actually from the terminal, under control of the procedure *read_toks*.)

The *state* variable has one of three values, when we are scanning such files:

        1) *state* = *mid_line* is the normal state.

        2) *state* = *skip_blanks* is like *mid_line*, but blanks are ignored.

        3) *state* = *new_line* is the state at the beginning of a line.

These state values are assigned numeric codes so that if we add the state code to the next character's command code, we get distinct values. For example, '*mid_line* + *spacer*' stands for the case that a blank space character occurs in the middle of a line when it is not being ignored; after this case is processed, the next value of *state* will be *skip_blanks*.

    define *mid_line* = 1   { *state* code when scanning a line of characters }
    define *skip_blanks* = 2 + *max_char_code*   { *state* code when ignoring blanks }
    define *new_line* = 3 + *max_char_code* + *max_char_code*   { *state* code at start of line }

---

buffer: **array**, §30.
end_line_char = macro, §236.
halfword = *min_halfword* . .
  max_halfword, §113.

loc = macro, §36.
max_char_code = 15, §207.
quarterword = 0 . . 255, §113.
read_toks: **procedure**, §482.

spacer = 10, §207.
stack_size = **const**, §11.
str_pool: **packed array**, §39.

304. Additional information about the current line is available via the *index* variable, which counts how many lines of characters are present in the buffer below the current level. We have $index = 0$ when reading from the terminal and prompting the user for each line; then if the user types, e.g., '\input paper', we will have $index = 1$ while reading the file paper.tex. However, it does not follow that *index* is the same as the input stack pointer, since many of the levels on the input stack may come from token lists. For example, the instruction '\input paper' might occur in a token list.

The global variable *in_open* is equal to the *index* value of the highest non-token-list level. Thus, the number of partially read lines in the buffer is $in\_open + 1$, and we have $in\_open = index$ when we are not reading a token list.

If we are not currently reading from the terminal, or from an input stream, we are reading from the file variable *input_file*[*index*]. We use the notation *terminal_input* as a convenient abbreviation for $name = 0$, and *cur_file* as an abbreviation for *input_file*[*index*].

The global variable *line* contains the line number in the topmost open file, for use in error messages. If we are not reading from the terminal, *line_stack*[*index*] holds the line number for the enclosing level, so that *line* can be restored when the current file has been read. Line numbers should never be negative, since the negative of the current line number is used to identify the user's output routine in the *mode_line* field of the semantic nest entries.

If more information about the input state is needed, it can be included in small arrays like those shown here. For example, the current page or segment number in the input file might be put into a variable *page*, maintained for enclosing levels in '*page_stack*: **array** $[1 .. max\_in\_open]$ **of** *integer*' by analogy with *line_stack*.

> **define** *terminal_input* $\equiv$ (*name* = 0)   { are we reading from the terminal? }
> **define** *cur_file* $\equiv$ *input_file*[*index*]   { the current *alpha_file* variable }

⟨ Global variables 13 ⟩ +≡
in_open: 0 .. *max_in_open*;   { the number of lines in the buffer, less one }
input_file: **array** $[1 .. max\_in\_open]$ **of** *alpha_file*;
line: *integer*;   { current line number in the current source file }
line_stack: **array** $[1 .. max\_in\_open]$ **of** *integer*;

305. Users of TEX sometimes forget to balance left and right braces properly, and one of the ways TEX tries to spot such errors is by considering an input file as broken into subfiles by control sequences that are declared to be \outer.

A variable called *scanner_status* tells TEX whether or not to complain when a subfile ends. This variable has five possible values:

normal, means that a subfile can safely end here without incident.

skipping, means that a subfile can safely end here, but not a file, because we're reading past some conditional text that was not selected.

defining, means that a subfile shouldn't end now because a macro is being defined.

matching, means that a subfile shouldn't end now because a macro is being used and we are searching for the end of its arguments.

aligning, means that a subfile shouldn't end now because we are not finished with the preamble of an \halign or \valign.

absorbing, means that a subfile shouldn't end now because we are reading a balanced token list
for \message, \write, etc.

If the *scanner_status* is not *normal*, the variable *warning_index* points to the *eqtb* location for
the relevant control sequence name to print in an error message.

define *skipping* = 1   { *scanner_status* when passing conditional text }
define *defining* = 2   { *scanner_status* when reading a macro definition }
define *matching* = 3   { *scanner_status* when reading macro arguments }
define *aligning* = 4   { *scanner_status* when reading an alignment preamble }
define *absorbing* = 5   { *scanner_status* when reading a balanced text }

⟨ Global variables 13 ⟩ +≡
scanner_status: *normal* .. *absorbing*;   { can a subfile end now? }
warning_index: *pointer*;   { identifier relevant to non-*normal* scanner status }
def_ref: *pointer*;   { reference count of token list being defined }

306.   Here is a procedure that uses *scanner_status* to print a warning message when a subfile
has ended, and at certain other crucial times:

⟨ Declare the procedure called *runaway* 306 ⟩ ≡
procedure *runaway*;
  var *p*: *pointer*;   { head of runaway list }
  begin if *scanner_status* > *skipping* **then**
    begin *print_nl*("Runaway␣");
    case *scanner_status* **of**
    defining: **begin** *print*("definition"); *p* ← *def_ref*;
      end;
    matching: **begin** *print*("argument"); *p* ← *temp_head*;
      end;
    aligning: **begin** *print*("preamble"); *p* ← *hold_head*;
      end;
    absorbing: **begin** *print*("text"); *p* ← *def_ref*;
      end;
    end;   { there are no other cases }
    print_char("?"); *print_ln*; *show_token_list*(*link*(*p*), *null*, *error_line* − 10);
    end;
  end;

This code is used in section 119.

---

alpha_file = **packed file**, §25.
eqtb: **array**, §253.
error_line = **const**, §11.
hold_head = macro, §162.
link = macro, §118.
max_in_open = **const**, §11.

mode_line = macro, §213.
normal = 0, §135.
null = macro, §115.
pointer = macro, §115.
print: **procedure**, §59.

print_char: **procedure**, §58.
print_ln: **procedure**, §57.
print_nl: **procedure**, §62.
show_token_list: **procedure**, §292.
temp_head = macro, §162.

307. However, all this discussion about input state really applies only to the case that we are inputting from a file. There is another important case, namely when we are currently getting input from a token list. In this case *state* = *token_list*, and the conventions about the other state variables are different:

loc is a pointer to the current node in the token list, i.e., the node that will be read next. If *loc* = *null*, the token list has been fully read.

start points to the first node of the token list; this node may or may not contain a reference count, depending on the type of token list involved.

token_type, which takes the place of *index* in the discussion above, is a code number that explains what kind of token list is being scanned.

name points to the *eqtb* address of the control sequence being expanded, if the current token list is a macro.

param_start, which takes the place of *limit*, tells where the parameters of the current macro begin in the *param_stack*, if the current token list is a macro.

The *token_type* can take several values, depending on where the current token list came from:

parameter, if a parameter is being scanned;

u_template, if the $\langle u_j \rangle$ part of an alignment template is being scanned;

v_template, if the $\langle v_j \rangle$ part of an alignment template is being scanned;

backed_up, if the token list being scanned has been inserted as 'to be read again'.

inserted, if the token list being scanned has been inserted as the text expansion of a \count or similar variable;

macro, if a user-defined control sequence is being scanned;

output_text, if an \output routine is being scanned;

every_par_text, if the text of \everypar is being scanned;

every_math_text, if the text of \everymath is being scanned;

every_display_text, if the text of \everydisplay is being scanned;

every_hbox_text, if the text of \everyhbox is being scanned;

every_vbox_text, if the text of \everyvbox is being scanned;

every_job_text, if the text of \everyjob is being scanned;

every_cr_text, if the text of \everycr is being scanned;

mark_text, if the text of a \mark is being scanned;

write_text, if the text of a \write is being scanned.

The codes for *output_text*, *every_par_text*, etc., are equal to a constant plus the corresponding codes for token list parameters *output_routine_loc*, *every_par_loc*, etc. The token list begins with a reference count if and only if *token_type* ≥ *macro*.

> **define** *token_list* = 0 { *state* code when scanning a token list }
> **define** *token_type* ≡ *index* { type of current token list }
> **define** *param_start* ≡ *limit* { base of macro parameters in *param_stack* }
> **define** *parameter* = 0 { *token_type* code for parameter }
> **define** *u_template* = 1 { *token_type* code for $\langle u_j \rangle$ template }
> **define** *v_template* = 2 { *token_type* code for $\langle v_j \rangle$ template }
> **define** *backed_up* = 3 { *token_type* code for text to be reread }
> **define** *inserted* = 4 { *token_type* code for inserted texts }

define $macro = 5$ { *token_type* code for defined control sequences }
define $output\_text = 6$ { *token_type* code for output routines }
define $every\_par\_text = 7$ { *token_type* code for \everypar }
define $every\_math\_text = 8$ { *token_type* code for \everymath }
define $every\_display\_text = 9$ { *token_type* code for \everydisplay }
define $every\_hbox\_text = 10$ { *token_type* code for \everyhbox }
define $every\_vbox\_text = 11$ { *token_type* code for \everyvbox }
define $every\_job\_text = 12$ { *token_type* code for \everyjob }
define $every\_cr\_text = 13$ { *token_type* code for \everycr }
define $mark\_text = 14$ { *token_type* code for \topmark, etc. }
define $write\_text = 15$ { *token_type* code for \write }

308. The *param_stack* is an auxiliary array used to hold pointers to the token lists for parameters at the current level and subsidiary levels of input. This stack is maintained with convention (2), and it grows at a different rate from the others.

⟨ Global variables 13 ⟩ +≡
param_stack: **array** $[0 .. param\_size]$ **of** *pointer*;   { token list pointers for parameters }
param_ptr: $0 .. param\_size$;   { first unused entry in *param_stack* }
max_param_stack: *integer*;   { largest value of *param_ptr*, will be $\leq param\_size + 9$ }

309. The input routines must also interact with the processing of \halign and \valign, since the appearance of tab marks and \cr in certain places is supposed to trigger the beginning of special ⟨v_j⟩ template text in the scanner. This magic is accomplished by an *align_state* variable that is increased by 1 when a '{' is scanned and decreased by 1 when a '}' is scanned. The *align_state* is nonzero during the ⟨u_j⟩ template, after which it is set to zero; the ⟨v_j⟩ template begins when a tab mark or \cr occurs at a time that *align_state* = 0.

⟨ Global variables 13 ⟩ +≡
align_state: *integer*;   { group level with respect to current alignment }

310. Thus, the "current input state" can be very complicated indeed; there can be many levels and each level can arise in a variety of ways. The *show_context* procedure, which is used by TEX's error-reporting routine to print out the current input state on all levels down to the most recent line of characters from an input file, illustrates most of these conventions. The global variable *base_ptr* contains the lowest level that was displayed by this procedure.

⟨ Global variables 13 ⟩ +≡
base_ptr: $0 .. stack\_size$;   { shallowest level shown by *show_context* }

---

eqtb: **array**, §253.
every_par_loc = 3158, §230.
loc = macro, §36.

null = macro, §115.
output_routine_loc = 3157, §230.
param_size = **const**, §11.

pointer = macro, §115.
show_context: **procedure**, §311.
stack_size = **const**, §11.

311. The status at each level is indicated by printing two lines, where the first line indicates what was read so far and the second line shows what remains to be read. The context is cropped, if necessary, so that the first line contains at most *half_error_line* characters, and the second contains at most *error_line*. Non-current input levels whose *token_type* is 'backed_up' are shown only if they have not been fully read.

procedure *show_context*; { prints where the scanner is }
  label *done*;
  var *old_setting*: 0 .. *max_selector*; { saved *selector* setting }
    ⟨ Local variables for formatting calculations 315 ⟩
  begin *base_ptr* ← *input_ptr*; *input_stack*[*base_ptr*] ← *cur_input*; { store current state }
  loop begin *cur_input* ← *input_stack*[*base_ptr*]; { enter into the context }
    ⟨ Display the current context 312 ⟩;
    if (*state* ≠ *token_list*) **then**
      if (*name* > 17) ∨ (*base_ptr* = 0) **then goto** *done*;
    decr(*base_ptr*);
    end;
done: *cur_input* ← *input_stack*[*input_ptr*]; { restore original state }
  end;

312. ⟨ Display the current context 312 ⟩ ≡
  if (*base_ptr* = *input_ptr*) ∨ (*state* ≠ *token_list*) ∨ (*token_type* ≠ *backed_up*) ∨ (*loc* ≠ *null*) **then**
      { we omit backed-up token lists that have already been read }
    begin *tally* ← 0; { get ready to count characters }
    old_setting ← *selector*;
    if *state* ≠ *token_list* **then**
      begin ⟨ Print location of current line 313 ⟩;
      ⟨ Pseudoprint the line 318 ⟩;
      end
    else begin ⟨ Print type of token list 314 ⟩;
      ⟨ Pseudoprint the token list 319 ⟩;
      end;
    selector ← *old_setting*; { stop pseudoprinting }
    ⟨ Print two lines using the tricky pseudoprinted information 317 ⟩;
    end
This code is used in section 311.

313. This routine should be changed, if necessary, to give the best possible indication of where the current line resides in the input file. For example, on some systems it is best to print both a page and line number.

⟨ Print location of current line 313 ⟩ ≡
  if *name* ≤ 17 **then**
    if *terminal_input* **then**
      if *base_ptr* = 0 **then** *print_nl*("<*>")
      else *print_nl*("<insert>␣")
    else begin *print_nl*("<read␣");
      if *name* = 17 **then** *print_char*("*") **else** *print_int*(*name* − 1);
      print_char(">");
      end

    else begin $print\_nl(\texttt{"l."})$; $print\_int(line)$;
      end;
$print\_char(\texttt{"}\sqcup\texttt{"})$

This code is used in section 312.

314. ⟨ Print type of token list 314 ⟩ ≡
    case $token\_type$ **of**
    $parameter$: $print\_nl(\texttt{"<argument>}\sqcup\texttt{"})$;
    $u\_template, v\_template$: $print\_nl(\texttt{"<template>}\sqcup\texttt{"})$;
    $backed\_up$: **if** $loc = null$ **then** $print\_nl(\texttt{"<recently}\sqcup\texttt{read>}\sqcup\texttt{"})$
      else $print\_nl(\texttt{"<to}\sqcup\texttt{be}\sqcup\texttt{read}\sqcup\texttt{again>}\sqcup\texttt{"})$;
    $inserted$: $print\_nl(\texttt{"<inserted}\sqcup\texttt{text>}\sqcup\texttt{"})$;
    $macro$: **begin** $print\_ln$; $print\_cs(name)$;
      end;
    $output\_text$: $print\_nl(\texttt{"<output>}\sqcup\texttt{"})$;
    $every\_par\_text$: $print\_nl(\texttt{"<everypar>}\sqcup\texttt{"})$;
    $every\_math\_text$: $print\_nl(\texttt{"<everymath>}\sqcup\texttt{"})$;
    $every\_display\_text$: $print\_nl(\texttt{"<everydisplay>}\sqcup\texttt{"})$;
    $every\_hbox\_text$: $print\_nl(\texttt{"<everyhbox>}\sqcup\texttt{"})$;
    $every\_vbox\_text$: $print\_nl(\texttt{"<everyvbox>}\sqcup\texttt{"})$;
    $every\_job\_text$: $print\_nl(\texttt{"<everyjob>}\sqcup\texttt{"})$;
    $every\_cr\_text$: $print\_nl(\texttt{"<everycr>}\sqcup\texttt{"})$;
    $mark\_text$: $print\_nl(\texttt{"<mark>}\sqcup\texttt{"})$;
    $write\_text$: $print\_nl(\texttt{"<write>}\sqcup\texttt{"})$;
    othercases $print\_nl(\texttt{"?"})$ { this should never happen }
    endcases

This code is used in section 312.

$backed\_up = 3$, §307.
$base\_ptr$: $0 \mathinner{\ldotp\ldotp} stack\_size$, §310.
cur_input: in_state_record, §301.
$decr = $ **macro**, §16.
$done = 30$, §15.
$error_line = $ **const**, §11.
$every\_cr\_text = 13$, §307.
$every\_display\_text = 9$, §307.
$every\_hbox\_text = 10$, §307.
$every\_job\_text = 12$, §307.
$every\_math\_text = 8$, §307.
$every\_par\_text = 7$, §307.
$every\_vbox\_text = 11$, §307.

$half_error_line = $ **const**, §11.
$input\_ptr$: $0 \mathinner{\ldotp\ldotp} stack\_size$, §301.
$input\_stack$: **array**, §301.
$inserted = 4$, §307.
$line$: $integer$, §304.
$loc = $ **macro**, §36.
$macro = 5$, §307.
$mark\_text = 14$, §307.
$max\_selector = 21$, §54.
$null = $ **macro**, §115.
$output\_text = 6$, §307.
$parameter = 0$, §307.
$print\_char$: **procedure**, §58.

$print\_cs$: **procedure**, §262.
$print\_int$: **procedure**, §65.
$print\_ln$: **procedure**, §57.
$print\_nl$: **procedure**, §62.
$selector$: $0 \mathinner{\ldotp\ldotp} 21$, §54.
$tally$: $integer$, §54.
$terminal_input = $ **macro**, §304.
$token\_list = 0$, §307.
$token_type = $ **macro**, §307.
$u\_template = 1$, §307.
$v\_template = 2$, §307.
$write\_text = 15$, §307.

315. Here it is necessary to explain a little trick. We don't want to store a long string that corresponds to a token list, because that string might take up lots of memory; and we are printing during a time when an error message is being given, so we dare not do anything that might overflow one of TeX's tables. So 'pseudoprinting' is the answer: We enter a mode of printing that stores characters into a buffer of length $error\_line$, where character $k + 1$ is placed into $trick\_buf[k \bmod error\_line]$ if $k < trick\_count$, otherwise character k is dropped. Initially we set $tally \leftarrow 0$ and $trick\_count \leftarrow 1000000$; then when we reach the point where transition from line 1 to line 2 should occur, we set $first\_count \leftarrow tally$ and $trick\_count \leftarrow \max(error\_line, tally + 1 + error\_line - half\_error\_line)$. At the end of the pseudoprinting, the values of $first\_count$, $tally$, and $trick\_count$ give us all the information we need to print the two lines, and all of the necessary text is in $trick\_buf$.

Namely, let l be the length of the descriptive information that appears on the first line. The length of the context information gathered for that line is $k = first\_count$, and the length of the context information gathered for line 2 is $m = \min(tally, trick\_count) - k$. If $l + k \leq h$, where $h = half\_error\_line$, we print $trick\_buf[0 \mathbin{..} k-1]$ after the descriptive information on line 1, and set $n \leftarrow l + k$; here n is the length of line 1. If $l + k > h$, some cropping is necessary, so we set $n \leftarrow h$ and print '...' followed by

$$trick\_buf[(l + k - h + 3) \mathbin{..} k - 1],$$

where subscripts of $trick\_buf$ are circular modulo $error\_line$. The second line consists of n spaces followed by $trick\_buf[k \mathbin{..} (k + m - 1)]$, unless $n + m > error\_line$; in the latter case, further cropping is done. This is easier to program than to explain.

⟨ Local variables for formatting calculations 315 ⟩ ≡
i: $0 \mathbin{..} buf\_size$;   { index into $buffer$ }
j: $0 \mathbin{..} buf\_size$;   { end of current line in $buffer$ }
l: $0 \mathbin{..} half\_error\_line$;   { length of descriptive information on line 1 }
m: $integer$;   { context information gathered for line 2 }
n: $0 \mathbin{..} error\_line$;   { length of line 1 }
p: $integer$;   { starting or ending place in $trick\_buf$ }
q: $integer$;   { temporary index }
This code is used in section 311.

316. The following code sets up the print routines so that they will gather the desired information.

define $begin\_pseudoprint \equiv$
        begin $l \leftarrow tally$; $tally \leftarrow 0$; $selector \leftarrow pseudo$; $trick\_count \leftarrow 1000000$;
        end
define $set\_trick\_count \equiv$
        begin $first\_count \leftarrow tally$; $trick\_count \leftarrow tally + 1 + error\_line - half\_error\_line$;
        if $trick\_count < error\_line$ **then** $trick\_count \leftarrow error\_line$;
        end

317. And the following code uses the information after it has been gathered.

⟨ Print two lines using the tricky pseudoprinted information 317 ⟩ ≡
  if $trick\_count = 1000000$ **then** set_trick_count;   { set_trick_count must be performed }

if $tally < trick\_count$ **then** $m \leftarrow tally - first\_count$
else $m \leftarrow trick\_count - first\_count$;   { context on line 2 }
if $l + first\_count \leq half\_error\_line$ **then**
   begin $p \leftarrow 0$; $n \leftarrow l + first\_count$;
   end
else begin $print(\texttt{"..."})$; $p \leftarrow l + first\_count - half\_error\_line + 3$; $n \leftarrow half\_error\_line$;
   end;
for $q \leftarrow p$ **to** $first\_count - 1$ **do** $print\_char(trick\_buf[q \bmod error\_line])$;
$print\_ln$;
for $q \leftarrow 1$ **to** n **do** $print\_char(\texttt{"}\sqcup\texttt{"})$;   { print n spaces to begin line 2 }
if $m + n \leq error\_line$ **then** $p \leftarrow first\_count + m$
else $p \leftarrow first\_count + (error\_line - n - 3)$;
for $q \leftarrow first\_count$ **to** $p - 1$ **do** $print\_char(trick\_buf[q \bmod error\_line])$;
if $m + n > error\_line$ **then** $print(\texttt{"..."})$

This code is used in section 312.

318.   But the trick is distracting us from our current goal, which is to understand the input state. So let's concentrate on the data structures that are being pseudoprinted as we finish up the *show_context* procedure.

⟨ Pseudoprint the line 318 ⟩ ≡
  $begin\_pseudoprint$;
  if $buffer[limit] = end\_line\_char$ **then** $j \leftarrow limit$
  else $j \leftarrow limit + 1$;   { determine the effective end of the line }
  if $j > 0$ **then**
    for $i \leftarrow start$ **to** $j - 1$ **do**
      begin if $i = loc$ **then** set_trick_count;
      $print(buffer[i])$;
      end

This code is used in section 312.

319.   ⟨ Pseudoprint the token list 319 ⟩ ≡
  $begin\_pseudoprint$;
  if $token\_type < macro$ **then** $show\_token\_list(start, loc, 100000)$
  else $show\_token\_list(link(start), loc, 100000)$ { avoid reference count }

This code is used in section 312.

320.   Here is the missing piece of *show_token_list* that is activated when the token beginning line 2 is about to be shown:

⟨ Do magic computation 320 ⟩ ≡
  set_trick_count

This code is used in section 292.

$buf_size = $ **const**, §11.
$buffer$: **array**, §30.
$end_line_char = $ macro, §236.
$error_line = $ **const**, §11.
$first\_count$: *integer*, §54.
$half_error_line = $ **const**, §11.
$link = $ macro, §118.

$loc = $ macro, §36.
$macro = 5$, §307.
$print$: **procedure**, §59.
$print\_char$: **procedure**, §58.
$print\_ln$: **procedure**, §57.
$pseudo = 20$, §54.
$selector$: $0 .. 21$, §54.

$show\_context$: **procedure**, §311.
$show\_token\_list$: **procedure**, §292.
$tally$: *integer*, §54.
$token_type = $ macro, §307.
$trick\_buf$: **array**, §54.
$trick\_count$: *integer*, §54.

321. Maintaining the input stacks. The following subroutines change the input status in commonly needed ways.

First comes *push_input*, which stores the current state and creates a new level (having, initially, the same properties as the old).

> **define** *push_input* ≡   { enter a new input level, save the old }
>   **begin if** *input_ptr* > *max_in_stack* **then**
>   **begin** *max_in_stack* ← *input_ptr*;
>   **if** *input_ptr* = *stack_size* **then** *overflow*("input␣stack␣size", *stack_size*);
>   **end**;
>   *input_stack*[*input_ptr*] ← *cur_input*;   { stack the record }
>   *incr*(*input_ptr*);
>   **end**

322. And of course what goes up must come down.

> **define** *pop_input* ≡   { leave an input level, re-enter the old }
>   **begin** *decr*(*input_ptr*); *cur_input* ← *input_stack*[*input_ptr*];
>   **end**

323. Here is a procedure that starts a new level of token-list input, given a token list p and its type t. If t = *macro*, the calling routine should set *name* and *loc*.

> **define** *back_list*(#) ≡ *begin_token_list*(#, *backed_up*)   { backs up a simple token list }
> **define** *ins_list*(#) ≡ *begin_token_list*(#, *inserted*)   { inserts a simple token list }

procedure *begin_token_list*(*p* : *pointer*; *t* : *quarterword*);
  begin *push_input*; *state* ← *token_list*; *start* ← *p*; *token_type* ← *t*;
  if *t* ≥ *macro* **then**   { the token list starts with a reference count }
    begin *add_token_ref*(*p*);
    if *t* = *macro* **then** *param_start* ← *param_ptr*
    else begin *loc* ← *link*(*p*);
      if *tracing_macros* > 1 **then**
        begin *begin_diagnostic*; *print_nl*("");
        case *t* **of**
        mark_text: *print_esc*("mark");
        write_text: *print_esc*("write");
        othercases *print_cmd_chr*(*assign_toks*, *t* − *output_text* + *output_routine_loc*)
        endcases;
        print("->"); *token_show*(*p*); *end_diagnostic*(*false*);
        end;
      end;
    end
  else *loc* ← *p*;
  end;

324. When a token list has been fully scanned, the following computations should be done as we leave that level of input. The *token_type* tends to be equal to either *backed_up* or *inserted* about 2/3 of the time.

procedure *end_token_list*;   { leave a token-list input level }
  begin if *token_type* ≥ *backed_up* **then**   { token list to be deleted }

begin if *token_type* ≤ *inserted* **then** *flush_list*(*start*)
  else begin *delete_token_ref*(*start*);   { update reference count }
    if *token_type* = *macro* **then**   { parameters must be flushed }
      while *param_ptr* > *param_start* **do**
        begin *decr*(*param_ptr*); *flush_list*(*param_stack*[*param_ptr*]);
        end;
    end;
  end
  else if *token_type* = *u_template* **then** *align_state* ← 0;
  pop_input; *check_interrupt*;
  end;

325.   Sometimes TeX has read too far and wants to "unscan" what it has seen. The *back_input* procedure takes care of this by putting the token just scanned back into the input stream, ready to be read again. This procedure can be used only if *cur_tok* represents the token to be replaced. Some applications of TeX use this procedure a lot, so it has been slightly optimized for speed.

procedure *back_input*;   { undoes one token of input }
  var *p*: *pointer*;   { a token list of length one }
  begin while (*state* = *token_list*) ∧ (*loc* = *null*) **do** *end_token_list*;   { conserve stack space }
  p ← *get_avail*; *info*(*p*) ← *cur_tok*;
  if *cur_tok* < *right_brace_limit* **then**
    if *cur_tok* < *left_brace_limit* **then** *decr*(*align_state*)
    else *incr*(*align_state*);
  push_input; *state* ← *token_list*; *start* ← *p*; *token_type* ← *backed_up*; *loc* ← *p*;
    { that was *back_list*(*p*), without procedure overhead }
  end;

326.   ⟨ Insert token *p* into TeX's input 326 ⟩ ≡
  begin *t* ← *cur_tok*; *cur_tok* ← *p*; *back_input*; *cur_tok* ← *t*;
  end

This code is used in section 282.

---

327. The *back_error* routine is used when we want to replace an offending token just before issuing an error message. This routine, like *back_input*, requires that *cur_tok* has been set. We disable interrupts during the call of *back_input* so that the help message won't be lost.

procedure *back_error*;   { back up one token and call *error* }
  begin *OK_to_interrupt* ← *false*; *back_input*; *OK_to_interrupt* ← *true*; *error*;
  end;

procedure *ins_error*;   { back up one inserted token and call *error* }
  begin *OK_to_interrupt* ← *false*; *back_input*; *token_type* ← *inserted*; *OK_to_interrupt* ← *true*; *error*;
  end;

328. The *begin_file_reading* procedure starts a new level of input for lines of characters to be read from a file, or as an insertion from the terminal. It does not take care of opening the file, nor does it set *loc* or *limit* or *line*.

procedure *begin_file_reading*;
  begin if *in_open* = *max_in_open* **then** *overflow*("text␣input␣levels", *max_in_open*);
  if *first* = *buf_size* **then** *overflow*("buffer␣size", *buf_size*);
  incr(*in_open*); *push_input*; *index* ← *in_open*; *line_stack*[*index*] ← *line*; *start* ← *first*;
  state ← *mid_line*; *name* ← 0;   { *terminal_input* is now *true* }
  end;

329. Conversely, the variables must be downdated when such a level of input is finished:

procedure *end_file_reading*;
  begin *first* ← *start*; *line* ← *line_stack*[*index*];
  if *name* > 17 **then** *a_close*(*cur_file*);   { forget it }
  pop_input; *decr*(*in_open*);
  end;

330. In order to keep the stack from overflowing during a long sequence of inserted '\show' commands, the following routine removes completed error-inserted lines from memory.

procedure *clear_for_error_prompt*;
  begin while (*state* ≠ *token_list*) ∧ *terminal_input* ∧ (*input_ptr* > 0) ∧ (*loc* > *limit*) **do**
    end_file_reading;
  print_ln; *clear_terminal*;
  end;

331. To get TeX's whole input mechanism going, we perform the following actions.

⟨ Initialize the input routines 331 ⟩ ≡
  begin *input_ptr* ← 0; *max_in_stack* ← 0; *in_open* ← 0; *max_buf_stack* ← 0; *param_ptr* ← 0;
  max_param_stack ← 0; *first* ← *buf_size*;
  repeat *buffer*[*first*] ← 0; *decr*(*first*);
  until *first* = 0;
  scanner_status ← *normal*; *warning_index* ← *null*; *first* ← 1; *state* ← *new_line*; *start* ← 1;
  index ← 0; *line* ← 0; *name* ← 0; *force_eof* ← *false*; *align_state* ← 1000000;
  if ¬*init_terminal* **then goto** *final_end*;
  limit ← *last*; *first* ← *last* + 1;   { *init_terminal* has set *loc* and *last* }
  end

This code is used in section 1337.

332. Getting the next token. The heart of TₑX's input mechanism is the *get_next* procedure, which we shall develop in the next few sections of the program. Perhaps we shouldn't actually call it the "heart," however, because it really acts as TₑX's eyes and mouth, reading the source files and gobbling them up. And it also helps TₑX to regurgitate stored token lists that are to be processed again.

The main duty of *get_next* is to input one token and to set *cur_cmd* and *cur_chr* to that token's command code and modifier. Furthermore, if the input token is a control sequence, the *eqtb* location of that control sequence is stored in *cur_cs*; otherwise *cur_cs* is set to zero.

Underlying this simple description is a certain amount of complexity because of all the cases that need to be handled. However, the inner loop of *get_next* is reasonably short and fast.

When *get_next* is asked to get the next token of a `\read` line, it sets *cur_cmd* = *cur_chr* = *cur_cs* = 0 in the case that no more tokens appear on that line. (There might not be any tokens at all, if the *end_line_char* has *ignore* as its catcode.)

333. The value of *par_loc* is the *eqtb* address of '`\par`'. This quantity is needed because a blank line of input is supposed to be exactly equivalent to the appearance of `\par`; we must set *cur_cs* ← *par_loc* when detecting a blank line.

⟨ Global variables 13 ⟩ +≡
par_loc: *pointer*;   { location of '`\par`' in *eqtb* }
par_token: *halfword*;   { token representing '`\par`' }

334. ⟨ Put each of TₑX's primitives into the hash table 226 ⟩ +≡
   primitive("`par`", *par_end*, 0); *par_loc* ← *cur_val*; *par_token* ← *cs_token_flag* + *par_loc*;

335. ⟨ Cases of *print_cmd_chr* for symbolic printing of primitives 227 ⟩ +≡
par_end: *print_esc*("`par`");

---

a_close: **procedure**, §28.
align_state: *integer*, §309.
back_input: **procedure**, §325.
buf_size = **const**, §11.
buffer: **array**, §30.
clear_terminal = macro, §34.
cs_token_flag = macro, §289.
cur_chr: *halfword*, §297.
cur_cmd: *eight_bits*, §297.
cur_cs: *pointer*, §297.
cur_file = macro, §304.
cur_tok: *halfword*, §297.
cur_val: *integer*, §410.
decr = macro, §16.
end_line_char = macro, §236.
eqtb: **array**, §253.
error: **procedure**, §82.
final_end = 9999, §6.
first: 0 .. *buf_size*, §30.

force_eof: *boolean*, §361.
get_next: **procedure**, §341.
halfword = *min_halfword* ..
   max_halfword, §113.
ignore = 9, §207.
in_open: 0 .. *max_in_open*, §304.
incr = macro, §16.
init_terminal: **function**, §37.
input_ptr: 0 .. *stack_size*, §301.
inserted = 4, §307.
last: 0 .. *buf_size*, §30.
line: *integer*, §304.
line_stack: **array**, §304.
loc = macro, §36.
max_buf_stack: 0 .. *buf_size*, §30.
max_in_open = **const**, §11.
max_in_stack: 0 .. *stack_size*, §301.
max_param_stack: *integer*, §308.
mid_line = 1, §303.

new_line = 33, §303.
normal = 0, §135.
null = macro, §115.
OK_to_interrupt: *boolean*, §96.
overflow: **procedure**, §94.
par_end = 13, §207.
param_ptr: 0 .. *param_size*, §308.
pointer = macro, §115.
pop_input = macro, §322.
primitive: **procedure**, §264.
print_cmd_chr: **procedure**, §298.
print_esc: **procedure**, §63.
print_ln: **procedure**, §57.
push_input = macro, §321.
scanner_status: 0 .. 5, §305.
terminal_input = macro, §304.
token_list = 0, §307.
token_type = macro, §307.
warning_index: *pointer*, §305.

336. Before getting into *get_next*, let's consider the subroutine that is called when an '\outer' control sequence has been scanned or when the end of a file has been reached. These two cases are distinguished by *cur_cs*, which is zero at the end of a file.

procedure *check_outer_validity*;
  var *p*: *pointer*; { points to inserted token list }
    q: *pointer*; { auxiliary pointer }
  begin if *scanner_status* ≠ *normal* **then**
    begin *deletions_allowed* ← *false*; ⟨ Back up an outer control sequence so that it can be reread 337 ⟩;
    if *scanner_status* > *skipping* **then** ⟨ Tell the user what has run away and try to recover 338 ⟩
    else begin *print_err*("Incomplete␣"); *print_cmd_chr*(*if_test*, *cur_if*);
      print(";␣all␣text␣was␣ignored␣after␣line␣"); *print_int*(*skip_line*);
      help3("A␣forbidden␣control␣sequence␣occurred␣in␣skipped␣text.")
      ("This␣kind␣of␣error␣happens␣when␣you␣say␣`\if...´␣and␣forget")
      ("the␣matching␣`\fi´.␣I´ve␣inserted␣a␣`\fi´;␣this␣might␣work.");
      if *cur_cs* ≠ 0 **then** *cur_cs* ← 0
      else *help_line*[2] ← "The␣file␣ended␣while␣I␣was␣skipping␣conditional␣text.";
      cur_tok ← *cs_token_flag* + *frozen_fi*; *ins_error*;
      end;
    deletions_allowed ← *true*;
    end;
  end;

337. An outer control sequence that occurs in a \read will not be reread, since the error recovery for \read is not very powerful.

⟨ Back up an outer control sequence so that it can be reread 337 ⟩ ≡
  if *cur_cs* ≠ 0 **then**
    begin if (*state* = *token_list*) ∨ (*name* < 1) ∨ (*name* > 17) **then**
      begin *p* ← *get_avail*; *info*(*p*) ← *cs_token_flag* + *cur_cs*; *back_list*(*p*);
        { prepare to read the control sequence again }
      end;
    cur_cmd ← *spacer*; *cur_chr* ← "␣"; { replace it by a space }
    end

This code is used in section 336.

338. ⟨ Tell the user what has run away and try to recover 338 ⟩ ≡
  begin *runaway*; { print a definition, argument, or preamble }
  if *cur_cs* = 0 **then** *print_err*("File␣ended")
  else begin *cur_cs* ← 0; *print_err*("Forbidden␣control␣sequence␣found");
    end;
  print("␣while␣scanning␣"); ⟨ Print either 'definition' or 'use' or 'preamble' or 'text', and insert
    tokens that should lead to recovery 339 ⟩;
  print("␣of␣"); *sprint_cs*(*warning_index*);
  help4("I␣suspect␣you␣have␣forgotten␣a␣`}´,␣causing␣me")
  ("to␣read␣past␣where␣you␣wanted␣me␣to␣stop.")
  ("I´ll␣try␣to␣recover;␣but␣if␣the␣error␣is␣serious,")
  ("you´d␣better␣type␣`E´␣or␣`X´␣now␣and␣fix␣your␣file.");
  error;

end

This code is used in section 336.

339. The recovery procedure can't be fully understood without knowing more about the TEX routines that should be aborted, but we can sketch the ideas here: For a runaway definition we will insert a right brace; for a runaway preamble, we will insert a special \cr token and a right brace; and for a runaway argument, we will set *long_state* to *outer_call* and insert \par.

⟨ Print either 'definition' or 'use' or 'preamble' or 'text', and insert tokens that should lead to recovery 339 ⟩ ≡

$p \leftarrow get\_avail$;

case *scanner_status* **of**

defining: **begin** $print("definition")$; $info(p) \leftarrow right\_brace\_token + "\}"$;
  end;

matching: **begin** $print("use")$; $info(p) \leftarrow par\_token$; $long\_state \leftarrow outer\_call$;
  end;

aligning: **begin** $print("preamble")$; $info(p) \leftarrow right\_brace\_token + "\}"$; $q \leftarrow p$; $p \leftarrow get\_avail$;
  $link(p) \leftarrow q$; $info(p) \leftarrow cs\_token\_flag + frozen\_cr$; $align\_state \leftarrow -1000000$;
  end;

absorbing: **begin** $print("text")$; $info(p) \leftarrow right\_brace\_token + "\}"$;
  end;

end;   { there are no other cases }

$ins\_list(p)$

This code is used in section 338.

340. We need to mention a procedure here that may be called by *get_next*.

procedure *firm_up_the_line*; *forward*;

---

absorbing = 5, §305.
align_state: *integer*, §309.
aligning = 4, §305.
back_list = macro, §323.
cs_token_flag = macro, §289.
cur_chr: *halfword*, §297.
cur_cmd: *eight_bits*, §297.
cur_cs: *pointer*, §297.
cur_if: *small_number*, §489.
cur_tok: *halfword*, §297.
defining = 2, §305.
deletions_allowed: *boolean*, §76.
error: **procedure**, §82.
firm_up_the_line: **procedure**, §363.
frozen_cr = 2359, §222.

frozen_fi = 2362, §222.
get_avail: **function**, §120.
get_next: **procedure**, §341.
help_line: **array**, §79.
help3 = macro, §79.
help4 = macro, §79.
if_test = 104, §210.
info = macro, §118.
ins_error: **procedure**, §327.
ins_list = macro, §323.
link = macro, §118.
long_state: 110 .. 113, §387.
matching = 3, §305.
normal = 0, §135.
outer_call = 112, §210.

par_token: *halfword*, §333.
pointer = macro, §115.
print: **procedure**, §59.
print_cmd_chr: **procedure**, §298.
print_err = macro, §73.
print_int: **procedure**, §65.
right_brace_token = 512, §289.
runaway: **procedure**, §306.
scanner_status: 0 .. 5, §305.
skip_line: *integer*, §493.
skipping = 1, §305.
spacer = 10, §207.
sprint_cs: **procedure**, §263.
token_list = 0, §307.
warning_index: *pointer*, §305.

341.   Now we're ready to take the plunge into *get_next* itself. Parts of this routine are executed more often than any other instructions of TeX.

> **define** *switch* = 25   { a label in *get_next* }
> **define** *start_cs* = 26   { another }

> **procedure** *get_next*;   { sets *cur_cmd*, *cur_chr*, *cur_cs* to next token }
>   **label** *restart*,   { go here to get the next input token }
>   *switch*,   { go here to eat the next character from a file }
>   *reswitch*,   { go here to digest it again }
>   *start_cs*,   { go here to start looking for a control sequence }
>   *found*,   { go here when a control sequence has been found }
>   *exit*;   { go here when the next input token has been got }
>   **var** *k*: 0 .. *buf_size*;   { an index into *buffer* }
>   *t*: *halfword*;   { a token }
>   *cat*: 0 .. 15;   { *cat_code*(*cur_chr*), usually }
>   **begin** *restart*: *cur_cs* ← 0;
>   **if** *state* ≠ *token_list* **then** ⟨ Input from external file, **goto** *restart* if no input found 343 ⟩
>   **else** ⟨ Input from token list, **goto** *restart* if end of list or if a parameter needs to be expanded 357 ⟩;
>   ⟨ If an alignment entry has just ended, take appropriate action 342 ⟩;
> *exit*: **end**;

342.   An alignment entry ends when a tab or \cr occurs, provided that the current level of braces is the same as the level that was present at the beginning of that alignment entry; i.e., provided that *align_state* has returned to the value it had after the ⟨u_j⟩ template for that entry.

⟨ If an alignment entry has just ended, take appropriate action 342 ⟩ ≡
>   **if** *cur_cmd* ≤ *car_ret* **then**
>   **if** *cur_cmd* ≥ *tab_mark* **then**
>   **if** *align_state* = 0 **then** ⟨ Insert the ⟨v_j⟩ template and **goto** *restart* 789 ⟩

This code is used in section 341.

343.   ⟨ Input from external file, **goto** *restart* if no input found 343 ⟩ ≡
>   **begin** *switch*: **if** *loc* ≤ *limit* **then**   { current line not yet finished }
>   **begin** *cur_chr* ← *buffer*[*loc*]; *incr*(*loc*);
>   *reswitch*: *cur_cmd* ← *cat_code*(*cur_chr*); ⟨ Change state if necessary, and **goto** *switch* if the current
>   character should be ignored, or **goto** *reswitch* if the current character changes to another 344 ⟩;
>   **end**
>   **else begin** *state* ← *new_line*;
>   ⟨ Move to next line of file, or **goto** *restart* if there is no next line, or **return** if a \read line has
>   finished 360 ⟩;
>   *check_interrupt*; **goto** *switch*;
>   **end**;
>   **end**

This code is used in section 341.

344.   The following 48-way switch accomplishes the scanning quickly, assuming that a decent Pascal compiler has translated the code. Note that the numeric values for *mid_line*, *skip_blanks*, and *new_line* are spaced apart from each other by *max_char_code* + 1, so we can add a character's command code to the state to get a single number that characterizes both.

define $any\_state\_plus(\#) \equiv mid\_line + \#, skip\_blanks + \#, new\_line + \#$

⟨ Change state if necessary, and **goto** *switch* if the current character should be ignored, or **goto** *reswitch*
    if the current character changes to another 344 ⟩ ≡
case $state + cur\_cmd$ **of**
⟨ Cases where character is ignored 345 ⟩: **goto** *switch*;
$any\_state\_plus(escape)$: ⟨ Scan a control sequence and set $state \leftarrow skip\_blanks$ or mid_line 354 ⟩;
$any\_state\_plus(active\_char)$: ⟨ Process an active-character control sequence and set
        $state \leftarrow mid\_line$ 353 ⟩;
$any\_state\_plus(sup\_mark)$: ⟨ If this sup_mark starts a control character like `^^A`, then **goto** *reswitch*,
        otherwise set $state \leftarrow mid\_line$ 352 ⟩;
$any\_state\_plus(invalid\_char)$: ⟨ Decry the invalid character and **goto** *restart* 346 ⟩;
⟨ Handle situations involving spaces, braces, changes of state 347 ⟩
othercases $do\_nothing$
endcases

This code is used in section 343.

345.   ⟨ Cases where character is ignored 345 ⟩ ≡
$any\_state\_plus(ignore), skip\_blanks + spacer, new\_line + spacer$

This code is used in section 344.

346.   We go to *restart* instead of to *switch*, because *state* might equal *token_list* after the error
has been dealt with (cf. *clear_for_error_prompt*).

⟨ Decry the invalid character and **goto** *restart* 346 ⟩ ≡
    begin $print\_err($ `"Text␣line␣contains␣an␣invalid␣character"` $)$;
    $help2($ `"A␣funny␣symbol␣that␣I␣can´t␣read␣has␣just␣been␣input."` $)$
    $($ `"Continue,␣and␣I´ll␣forget␣that␣it␣ever␣happened."` $)$;
    $deletions\_allowed \leftarrow false$; *error*; $deletions\_allowed \leftarrow true$; **goto** *restart*;
    end

This code is used in section 344.

$active\_char = 13$, §207.
$align\_state$: *integer*, §309.
$buf\_size =$ **const**, §11.
$buffer$: **array**, §30.
$car\_ret = 5$, §207.
$cat\_code =$ macro, §230.
$check\_interrupt =$ macro, §96.
$clear\_for\_error\_prompt$: **procedure**,
    §330.
cur_chr: *halfword*, §297.
cur_cmd: *eight_bits*, §297.
cur_cs: *pointer*, §297.

$deletions\_allowed$: *boolean*, §76.
$do\_nothing =$ macro, §16.
$error$: **procedure**, §82.
$escape = 0$, §207.
$exit = 10$, §15.
$found = 40$, §15.
$halfword = min\_halfword$ ..
    $max\_halfword$, §113.
$help2 =$ macro, §79.
$ignore = 9$, §207.
$incr =$ macro, §16.
$invalid\_char = 15$, §207.

$loc =$ macro, §36.
$max\_char\_code = 15$, §207.
$mid\_line = 1$, §303.
$new\_line = 33$, §303.
$print\_err =$ macro, §73.
$restart = 20$, §15.
$reswitch = 21$, §15.
$skip\_blanks = 17$, §303.
$spacer = 10$, §207.
$sup\_mark = 7$, §207.
$tab\_mark = 4$, §207.
$token\_list = 0$, §307.

347. **define** $add\_delims\_to(\texttt{\#}) \equiv \texttt{\#} + math\_shift, \texttt{\#} + tab\_mark, \texttt{\#} + mac\_param, \texttt{\#} + sub\_mark,$
$\qquad \texttt{\#} + letter, \texttt{\#} + other\_char$

⟨ Handle situations involving spaces, braces, changes of state 347 ⟩ ≡
$mid\_line + spacer$: ⟨ Enter $skip\_blanks$ state, emit a space 349 ⟩;
$mid\_line + car\_ret$: ⟨ Finish line, emit a space 348 ⟩;
$skip\_blanks + car\_ret, any\_state\_plus(comment)$: ⟨ Finish line, **goto** $switch$ 350 ⟩;
$new\_line + car\_ret$: ⟨ Finish line, emit a \par 351 ⟩;
$mid\_line + left\_brace$: $incr(align\_state)$;
$skip\_blanks + left\_brace, new\_line + left\_brace$: **begin** $state \leftarrow mid\_line$; $incr(align\_state)$;
$\quad$ **end**;
$mid\_line + right\_brace$: $decr(align\_state)$;
$skip\_blanks + right\_brace, new\_line + right\_brace$: **begin** $state \leftarrow mid\_line$; $decr(align\_state)$;
$\quad$ **end**;
$add\_delims\_to(skip\_blanks), add\_delims\_to(new\_line)$: $state \leftarrow mid\_line$;

This code is used in section 344.

348. When a character of type $spacer$ gets through, its character code is changed to "␣" = ´40. This means that the ASCII codes for tab and space, and for the space inserted at the end of a line, will be treated alike when macro parameters are being matched. We do this since such characters are indistinguishable on most computer terminal displays.

⟨ Finish line, emit a space 348 ⟩ ≡
$\quad$ **begin** $loc \leftarrow limit + 1$; $cur\_cmd \leftarrow spacer$; $cur\_chr \leftarrow$ "␣";
$\quad$ **end**

This code is used in section 347.

349. The following code is performed only when $cur\_cmd = spacer$.

⟨ Enter $skip\_blanks$ state, emit a space 349 ⟩ ≡
$\quad$ **begin** $state \leftarrow skip\_blanks$; $cur\_chr \leftarrow$ "␣";
$\quad$ **end**

This code is used in section 347.

350. ⟨ Finish line, **goto** $switch$ 350 ⟩ ≡
$\quad$ **begin** $loc \leftarrow limit + 1$; **goto** $switch$;
$\quad$ **end**

This code is used in section 347.

351. ⟨ Finish line, emit a \par 351 ⟩ ≡
$\quad$ **begin** $loc \leftarrow limit + 1$; $cur\_cs \leftarrow par\_loc$; $cur\_cmd \leftarrow eq\_type(cur\_cs)$; $cur\_chr \leftarrow equiv(cur\_cs)$;
$\quad$ **if** $cur\_cmd \geq outer\_call$ **then** $check\_outer\_validity$;
$\quad$ **end**

This code is used in section 347.

352. ⟨If this *sup_mark* starts a control character like `^^A`, then **goto** *reswitch*, otherwise set
        state ← *mid_line* 352⟩ ≡
  begin if (*cur_chr* = *buffer*[*loc*]) ∧ (*loc* < *limit*) **then**
      begin if *buffer*[*loc* + 1] < ´100 **then** *cur_chr* ← *buffer*[*loc* + 1] + ´100
      else *cur_chr* ← *buffer*[*loc* + 1] − ´100;
      loc ← *loc* + 2; **goto** *reswitch*;
      end;
  state ← *mid_line*;
  end

This code is used in section 344.

353. ⟨Process an active-character control sequence and set *state* ← *mid_line* 353⟩ ≡
  begin *cur_cs* ← *cur_chr* + *active_base*; *cur_cmd* ← *eq_type*(*cur_cs*); *cur_chr* ← *equiv*(*cur_cs*);
  state ← *mid_line*;
  if *cur_cmd* ≥ *outer_call* **then** *check_outer_validity*;
  end

This code is used in section 344.

---

align_state: *integer*, §309.
any_state_plus = macro, §344.
buffer: **array**, §30.
car_ret = 5, §207.
check_outer_validity: **procedure**,
  §336.
comment = 14, §207.
cur_chr: *halfword*, §297.
cur_cmd: *eight_bits*, §297.
cur_cs: *pointer*, §297.
decr = macro, §16.

eq_type = macro, §221.
equiv = macro, §221.
incr = macro, §16.
left_brace = 1, §207.
letter = 11, §207.
loc = macro, §36.
mac_param = 6, §207.
math_shift = 3, §207.
mid_line = 1, §303.
new_line = 33, §303.
other_char = 12, §207.

outer_call = 112, §210.
par_loc: *pointer*, §333.
reswitch = 21, §15.
right_brace = 2, §207.
skip_blanks = 17, §303.
spacer = 10, §207.
sub_mark = 8, §207.
sup_mark = 7, §207.
switch = 25, §341.
tab_mark = 4, §207.

354. Control sequence names are scanned only when they appear in some line of a file; once they have been scanned the first time, their *eqtb* location serves as a unique identification, so TEX doesn't need to refer to the original name any more except when it prints the equivalent in symbolic form.

The program that scans a control sequence has been written carefully in order to avoid the blowups that might otherwise occur if a malicious user tried something like '\catcode´15=0'. The algorithm might look at *buffer*[*limit* + 1], but it never looks at *buffer*[*limit* + 2].

If expanded control characters like '^^A' appear in or just following a control sequence name, they are converted to single characters in the buffer and the process is repeated, slowly but surely.

⟨Scan a control sequence and set *state* ← *skip_blanks* or *mid_line* 354⟩ ≡
  begin if *loc* > *limit* **then** *cur_cs* ← *null_cs* { *state* is irrelevant in this case }
  else begin *start_cs*: *k* ← *loc*; *cur_chr* ← *buffer*[*k*]; *cat* ← *cat_code*(*cur_chr*); *incr*(*k*);
    if *cat* = *letter* **then** *state* ← *skip_blanks*
    else if *cat* = *spacer* **then** *state* ← *skip_blanks*
      else *state* ← *mid_line*;
    if (*cat* = *letter*) ∧ (*k* ≤ *limit*) **then** ⟨Scan ahead in the buffer until finding a nonletter; if an
        expanded control code is encountered, reduce it and **goto** *start_cs*; otherwise if a multiletter
        control sequence is found, adjust *cur_cs* and *loc*, and **goto** *found* 356⟩
    else ⟨If an expanded control code is present, reduce it and **goto** *start_cs* 355⟩;
    cur_cs ← *single_base* + *buffer*[*loc*]; *incr*(*loc*);
    end;
found: *cur_cmd* ← *eq_type*(*cur_cs*); *cur_chr* ← *equiv*(*cur_cs*);
  if *cur_cmd* ≥ *outer_call* **then** *check_outer_validity*;
  end

This code is used in section 344.

355. Whenever we reach the following piece of code, we will have *cur_chr* = *buffer*[*k* − 1] and *k* ≤ *limit* + 1 and *cat* = *cat_code*(*cur_chr*). If an expanded control code like ^^A appears in *buffer*[(*k* − 1) .. (*k* + 1)], we will store the corresponding code in *buffer*[*k* − 1] and shift the rest of the buffer left two places. The value of *cur_chr* may be changed here, but not the value of *cat*.

⟨If an expanded control code is present, reduce it and **goto** *start_cs* 355⟩ ≡
  begin if *buffer*[*k*] = *cur_chr* **then**
    if *cat* = *sup_mark* **then**
      if *k* < *limit* **then**
        begin *cur_chr* ← *buffer*[*k* + 1];
        if *cur_chr* < ´100 **then** *buffer*[*k* − 1] ← *cur_chr* + ´100
        else *buffer*[*k* − 1] ← *cur_chr* − ´100;
        limit ← *limit* − 2; *first* ← *first* − 2;
        while *k* ≤ *limit* **do**
          begin *buffer*[*k*] ← *buffer*[*k* + 2]; *incr*(*k*);
          end;
        goto *start_cs*;
        end;
  end

This code is used in sections 354 and 356.

356. ⟨ Scan ahead in the buffer until finding a nonletter; if an expanded control code is encountered, reduce it and **goto** *start_cs*; otherwise if a multiletter control sequence is found, adjust *cur_cs* and *loc*, and **goto** *found* 356 ⟩ ≡
  begin repeat $cur\_chr \leftarrow buffer[k]$; $cat \leftarrow cat\_code(cur\_chr)$; $incr(k)$;
  until $(cat \neq letter) \vee (k > limit)$;
  ⟨ If an expanded control code is present, reduce it and **goto** *start_cs* 355 ⟩;
  if $cat \neq letter$ **then** $decr(k)$;   { now k points to first nonletter }
  if $k > loc + 1$ **then**   { multiletter control sequence has been scanned }
    begin $cur\_cs \leftarrow id\_lookup(loc, k - loc)$; $loc \leftarrow k$; **goto** *found*;
    end;
  end

This code is used in section 354.

---

buffer: **array**, §30.
cat: 0 .. 15, §341.
cat_code = macro, §230.
check_outer_validity: **procedure**, §336.
cur_chr: *halfword*, §297.
cur_cmd: *eight_bits*, §297.
cur_cs: *pointer*, §297.
decr = macro, §16.

eq_type = macro, §221.
eqtb: **array**, §253.
equiv = macro, §221.
first: 0 .. *buf_size*, §30.
found = 40, §15.
id_lookup: **function**, §259.
incr = macro, §16.
k: 0 .. *buf_size*, §341.
letter = 11, §207.

loc = macro, §36.
mid_line = 1, §303.
null_cs = 257, §222.
outer_call = 112, §210.
single_base = 129, §222.
skip_blanks = 17, §303.
spacer = 10, §207.
start_cs = 26, §341.
sup_mark = 7, §207.

357.   Let's consider now what happens when *get_next* is looking at a token list.

⟨ Input from token list, **goto** *restart* if end of list or if a parameter needs to be expanded 357 ⟩ ≡
  if *loc* ≠ *null* **then**   { list not exhausted }
    begin *t* ← *info*(*loc*); *loc* ← *link*(*loc*);   { move to next }
    if *t* ≥ *cs_token_flag* **then**   { a control sequence token }
      begin *cur_cs* ← *t* − *cs_token_flag*; *cur_cmd* ← *eq_type*(*cur_cs*); *cur_chr* ← *equiv*(*cur_cs*);
      if *cur_cmd* ≥ *outer_call* **then**
        if *cur_cmd* = *dont_expand* **then** ⟨ Get the next token, suppressing expansion 358 ⟩
        else *check_outer_validity*;
      end
    else begin *cur_cmd* ← *t* **div** ´400; *cur_chr* ← *t* **mod** ´400;
      case *cur_cmd* **of**
      left_brace: *incr*(*align_state*);
      right_brace: *decr*(*align_state*);
      out_param: ⟨ Insert macro parameter and **goto** *restart* 359 ⟩;
      othercases *do_nothing*
      endcases;
      end;
    end
  else begin   { we are done with this token list }
    end_token_list; **goto** *restart*;   { resume previous level }
    end

This code is used in section 341.

358.   The present point in the program is reached only when the *no_expand* routine has inserted a special marker into the input. In this special case, *info*(*loc*) is known to be a control sequence token, and *link*(*loc*) = *null*.

  define *no_expand_flag* = 257   { this characterizes a special variant of *relax* }

⟨ Get the next token, suppressing expansion 358 ⟩ ≡
  begin *cur_cs* ← *info*(*loc*) − *cs_token_flag*; *loc* ← *null*;
  cur_cmd ← *eq_type*(*cur_cs*); *cur_chr* ← *equiv*(*cur_cs*);
  if *cur_cmd* > *max_command* **then**
    begin *cur_cmd* ← *relax*; *cur_chr* ← *no_expand_flag*;
    end;
  end

This code is used in section 357.

359.   ⟨ Insert macro parameter and **goto** *restart* 359 ⟩ ≡
  begin *begin_token_list*(*param_stack*[*param_start* + *cur_chr* − 1], *parameter*); **goto** *restart*;
  end

This code is used in section 357.

360.   All of the easy branches of *get_next* have now been taken care of. There is one more branch.

⟨ Move to next line of file, or **goto** *restart* if there is no next line, or **return** if a \read line has finished 360 ⟩ ≡
  if *name* > 17 **then** ⟨ Read next line of file into *buffer*, or **goto** *restart* if the file has ended 362 ⟩

else begin if ¬*terminal_input* **then**   { \read line has ended }
      begin *cur_cmd* ← 0; *cur_chr* ← 0; **return**;
      end;
if *input_ptr* > 0 **then**   { text was inserted during error recovery }
      begin *end_file_reading*; **goto** *restart*;   { resume previous level }
      end;
if *selector* < *log_only* **then**   *open_log_file*;
if *interaction* > *nonstop_mode* **then**
      begin if *limit* = *start* **then**   { previous line was empty }
        print_nl("(Please␣type␣a␣command␣or␣say␣`\end´)");
      print_ln; *first* ← *start*; *prompt_input*("*");   { input on-line into *buffer* }
      limit ← *last*;
      if (*end_line_char* < 0) ∨ (*end_line_char* > 127) **then**   *decr*(*limit*)
      else *buffer*[*limit*] ← *end_line_char*;
      first ← *limit* + 1; *loc* ← *start*;
      end
else *fatal_error*("***␣(job␣aborted,␣no␣legal␣\end␣found)");   { nonstop mode, which is
        intended for overnight batch processing, never waits for on-line input }
end

This code is used in section 343.

---

361.   The global variable *force_eof* is normally *false*; it is set *true* by an \endinput command.
⟨ Global variables 13 ⟩ +≡
force_eof: *boolean*;   { should the next \input be aborted early? }

---

align_state: *integer*, §309.
begin_token_list: **procedure**, §323.
buffer: **array**, §30.
check_outer_validity: **procedure**,
    §336.
cs_token_flag = macro, §289.
cur_chr: *halfword*, §297.
cur_cmd: *eight_bits*, §297.
cur_cs: *pointer*, §297.
decr = macro, §16.
do_nothing = macro, §16.
dont_expand = 115, §210.
end_file_reading: **procedure**, §329.
end_line_char = macro, §236.
end_token_list: **procedure**, §324.
eq_type = macro, §221.

equiv = macro, §221.
fatal_error: **procedure**, §93.
first: 0 .. *buf_size*, §30.
get_next: **procedure**, §341.
incr = macro, §16.
info = macro, §118.
input_ptr: 0 .. *stack_size*, §301.
interaction: 0 .. 3, §73.
last: 0 .. *buf_size*, §30.
left_brace = 1, §207.
link = macro, §118.
loc = macro, §36.
log_only = 18, §54.
max_command = 99, §209.
no_expand = 102, §210.
nonstop_mode = 1, §73.

null = macro, §115.
open_log_file: **procedure**, §534.
out_param = 5, §207.
outer_call = 112, §210.
param_start = macro, §307.
parameter = 0, §307.
print_ln: **procedure**, §57.
print_nl: **procedure**, §62.
prompt_input = macro, §71.
relax = 0, §207.
restart = 20, §15.
right_brace = 2, §207.
selector: 0 .. 21, §54.
t: *halfword*, §341.
terminal_input = macro, §304.

362. ⟨ Read next line of file into *buffer*, or **goto** *restart* if the file has ended 362 ⟩ ≡
  begin *incr*(*line*); *first* ← *start*;
  if ¬*force_eof* **then**
    begin if *input_ln*(*cur_file*, *true*) **then**   { not end of file }
      firm_up_the_line { this sets *limit* }
    else *force_eof* ← *true*;
    end;
  if *force_eof* **then**
    begin *print_char*(")"); *force_eof* ← *false*; *update_terminal*;   { show user that file has been read }
    end_file_reading;   { resume previous level }
    check_outer_validity; **goto** *restart*;
    end;
  if (*end_line_char* < 0) ∨ (*end_line_char* > 127) **then** *decr*(*limit*)
  else *buffer*[*limit*] ← *end_line_char*;
  first ← *limit* + 1; *loc* ← *start*;   { ready to read }
  end

This code is used in section 360.

363. If the user has set the *pausing* parameter to some positive value, and if nonstop mode has not been selected, each line of input is displayed on the terminal and the transcript file, followed by '=>'. TeX waits for a response. If the response is simply *carriage_return*, the line is accepted as it stands, otherwise the line typed is used instead of the line in the file.

procedure *firm_up_the_line*;
  var *k*: 0 .. *buf_size*; { an index into *buffer* }
  begin *limit* ← *last*;
  if *pausing* > 0 **then**
    if *interaction* > *nonstop_mode* **then**
      begin *wake_up_terminal*; *print_ln*;
      if *start* < *limit* **then**
        for *k* ← *start* **to** *limit* − 1 **do** *print*(*buffer*[*k*]);
      first ← *limit*; *prompt_input*("=>");   { wait for user response }
      if *last* > *first* **then**
        begin for *k* ← *first* **to** *last* − 1 **do**   { move line down in buffer }
          buffer[*k* + *start* − *first*] ← *buffer*[*k*];
        limit ← *start* + *last* − *first*;
        end;
      end;
  end;

364. Since *get_next* is used so frequently in TeX, it is convenient to define three related procedures that do a little more:

get_token not only sets *cur_cmd* and *cur_chr*, it also sets *cur_tok*, a packed halfword version of the current token.

get_x_token, meaning "get an expanded token," is like *get_token*, but if the current token turns out to be a user-defined control sequence (i.e., a macro call), or a conditional, or something like \topmark or \expandafter or \csname, it is eliminated from the input by beginning the expansion of the macro or the evaluation of the conditional.

x_token is like *get_x_token* except that it assumes that *get_next* has already been called.

In fact, these three procedures account for *all* uses of *get_next*, except for two places in the "inner loop" when *cur_tok* need not be set, and except when the arguments to \ifx are being scanned.

365.   No new control sequences will be defined except during a call of *get_token*, or when \csname compresses a token list, because *no_new_control_sequence* is always *true* at other times.

procedure *get_token*;   { sets *cur_cmd*, *cur_chr*, *cur_tok* }
    begin *no_new_control_sequence* ← *false*; *get_next*; *no_new_control_sequence* ← *true*;
    if *cur_cs* = 0 **then** *cur_tok* ← (*cur_cmd* ∗ ´400´) + *cur_chr*
    else *cur_tok* ← *cs_token_flag* + *cur_cs*;
    end;

366. **Expanding the next token.** Only a dozen or so command codes $> max\_command$ can possibly be returned by get_next; in increasing order, they are $undefined\_cs$, $expand\_after$, no_expand, $input$, if_test, fi_or_else, cs_name, $convert$, the, top_bot_mark, $call$, $long\_call$, $outer\_call$, $long\_outer\_call$, and $end\_template$.

The $expand$ subroutine is used when $cur\_cmd > max\_command$. It removes a "call" or a conditional or one of the other special operations just listed. It follows that $expand$ might invoke itself recursively. In all cases, $expand$ destroys the current token, but it sets things up so that the next get_next will deliver the appropriate next token. The value of cur_tok need not be known when $expand$ is called.

Since several of the basic scanning routines communicate via global variables, their values are saved as local variables of $expand$ so that recursive calls don't invalidate them.

⟨ Declare the procedure called $macro\_call$ 389 ⟩
⟨ Declare the procedure called $insert\_relax$ 379 ⟩
procedure $pass\_text$; $forward$;
procedure $start\_input$; $forward$;
procedure $conditional$; $forward$;
procedure get_x_token; $forward$;
procedure $conv\_toks$; $forward$;
procedure ins_the_toks; $forward$;
procedure $expand$;
    var t: $halfword$;   { token that is being "expanded after" }
        p, q, r: $pointer$;   { for list manipulation }
        j: $0 .. buf\_size$;   { index into $buffer$ }
        cv_backup: $integer$;   { to save the global quantity cur_val }
        cvl_backup, $radix\_backup$: $small\_number$;   { to save cur_val_level and $radix$ }
        $backup\_backup$: $pointer$;   { to save $link(backup\_head)$ }
        $save\_scanner\_status$: $small\_number$;   { temporary storage of $scanner\_status$ }
    begin $cv\_backup \leftarrow cur\_val$; $cvl\_backup \leftarrow cur\_val\_level$; $radix\_backup \leftarrow radix$;
    $backup\_backup \leftarrow link(backup\_head)$;
    if $cur\_cmd < call$ **then** ⟨ Expand a nonmacro 367 ⟩
    else if $cur\_cmd < end\_template$ **then** $macro\_call$
        else ⟨ Insert a $frozen\_endv$ token 375 ⟩;
    $cur\_val \leftarrow cv\_backup$; $cur\_val\_level \leftarrow cvl\_backup$; $radix \leftarrow radix\_backup$;
    $link(backup\_head) \leftarrow backup\_backup$;
    end;

367. ⟨ Expand a nonmacro 367 ⟩ ≡
    begin if $tracing\_commands > 1$ **then** $show\_cur\_cmd\_chr$;
    case cur_cmd **of**
    top_bot_mark: ⟨ Insert the appropriate mark text into the scanner 386 ⟩;
    $expand\_after$: ⟨ Expand the token after the next token 368 ⟩;
    no_expand: ⟨ Suppress expansion of the next token 369 ⟩;
    cs_name: ⟨ Manufacture a control sequence name 372 ⟩;
    $convert$: $conv\_toks$;   { this procedure is discussed in Part 27 below }
    the: ins_the_toks;   { this procedure is discussed in Part 27 below }
    if_test: $conditional$;   { this procedure is discussed in Part 28 below }
    fi_or_else: ⟨ Terminate the current conditional and skip to \fi 510 ⟩;

input: ⟨ Initiate or terminate input from a file 378 ⟩;
othercases ⟨ Complain about an undefined macro 370 ⟩
endcases;
end

This code is used in section 366.

368.   It takes only a little shuffling to do what TₑX calls `\expandafter`.

⟨ Expand the token after the next token 368 ⟩ ≡
   begin *get_token*; *t* ← *cur_tok*; *get_token*;
   if *cur_cmd* > *max_command* **then** *expand* **else** *back_input*;
   cur_tok ← *t*; *back_input*;
   end

This code is used in section 367.

369.   The implementation of `\noexpand` is a bit trickier, because it is necessary to insert a special '*dont_expand*' marker into TₑX's reading mechanism. This special marker is processed by *get_next*, but it does not slow down the inner loop.

   Since `\outer` macros might arise here, we must also clear the *scanner_status* temporarily.

⟨ Suppress expansion of the next token 369 ⟩ ≡
   begin *save_scanner_status* ← *scanner_status*; *scanner_status* ← *normal*; *get_token*;
   scanner_status ← *save_scanner_status*; *t* ← *cur_tok*; *back_input*;
        { now *start* and *loc* point to the backed-up token *t* }
   if *t* ≥ *cs_token_flag* **then**
      begin *p* ← *get_avail*; *info*(*p*) ← *cs_token_flag* + *frozen_dont_expand*; *link*(*p*) ← *loc*; *start* ← *p*;
      loc ← *p*;
      end;
   end

This code is used in section 367.

---

back_input: **procedure**, §325.
backup_head = macro, §162.
buf_size = **const**, §11.
buffer: **array**, §30.
call = 110, §210.
conditional: **procedure**, §498.
conv_toks: **procedure**, §470.
convert = 107, §210.
cs_name = 106, §210.
cs_token_flag = macro, §289.
cur_cmd: *eight_bits*, §297.
cur_tok: *halfword*, §297.
cur_val: *integer*, §410.
cur_val_level: 0 .. 5, §410.
dont_expand = 115, §210.
end_template = 114, §210.
expand_after = 101, §210.

fi_or_else = 105, §210.
frozen_dont_expand = 2367, §222.
frozen_endv = 2364, §222.
get_avail: **function**, §120.
get_next: **procedure**, §341.
get_x_token: **procedure**, §380.
halfword = *min_halfword* ..
   max_halfword, §113.
if_test = 104, §210.
info = macro, §118.
input = 103, §210.
ins_the_toks: **procedure**, §467.
insert_relax: **procedure**, §379.
link = macro, §118.
loc = macro, §36.
long_call = 111, §210.
long_outer_call = 113, §210.

macro_call: **procedure**, §389.
max_command = 99, §209.
no_expand = 102, §210.
normal = 0, §135.
outer_call = 112, §210.
pass_text: **procedure**, §494.
pointer = macro, §115.
radix: *small_number*, §438.
scanner_status: 0 .. 5, §305.
show_cur_cmd_chr: **procedure**,
   §299.
small_number = 0 .. 63, §101.
start_input: **procedure**, §537.
the = 108, §210.
top_bot_mark = 109, §210.
tracing_commands = macro, §236.
undefined_cs = 100, §210.

370. ⟨Complain about an undefined macro 370⟩ ≡
 begin *print_err*("Undefined␣control␣sequence");
 help5("The␣control␣sequence␣at␣the␣end␣of␣the␣top␣line")
 ("of␣your␣error␣message␣was␣never␣\def´ed.␣If␣you␣have")
 ("misspelled␣it␣(e.g.,␣`\hobx´),␣type␣`I´␣and␣the␣correct")
 ("spelling␣(e.g.,␣`I\hbox´).␣Otherwise␣just␣continue,")
 ("and␣I´ll␣forget␣about␣whatever␣was␣undefined."); *error*;
 end

This code is used in section 367.

371. The *expand* procedure and some other routines that construct token lists find it convenient to use the following macros, which are valid only if the variables p and q are reserved for token-list building.

 define *store_new_token*(#) ≡
    begin $q \leftarrow$ *get_avail*; *link*(p) $\leftarrow q$; *info*(q) $\leftarrow$ #; $p \leftarrow q$; { *link*(p) is *null* }
    end
 define *fast_store_new_token*(#) ≡
    begin *fast_get_avail*(q); *link*(p) $\leftarrow q$; *info*(q) $\leftarrow$ #; $p \leftarrow q$; { *link*(p) is *null* }
    end

372. ⟨Manufacture a control sequence name 372⟩ ≡
 begin $r \leftarrow$ *get_avail*; $p \leftarrow r$; { head of the list of characters }
 repeat *get_x_token*;
  if *cur_cs* = 0 **then** *store_new_token*(*cur_tok*);
 until *cur_cs* ≠ 0;
 if *cur_cmd* ≠ *end_cs_name* **then** ⟨Complain about missing \endcsname 373⟩;
 ⟨Look up the characters of list r in the hash table, and set *cur_cs* 374⟩;
 flush_list(r);
 if *eq_type*(*cur_cs*) = *undefined_cs* **then**
  begin *eqtb*[*cur_cs*] $\leftarrow$ *eqtb*[*frozen_relax*];
  end; { the control sequence will now match `\relax` }
 cur_tok $\leftarrow$ *cur_cs* + *cs_token_flag*; *back_input*;
 end

This code is used in section 367.

373. ⟨Complain about missing \endcsname 373⟩ ≡
 begin *print_err*("Missing␣"); *print_esc*("endcsname"); *print*("␣inserted");
 help2("The␣control␣sequence␣marked␣<to␣be␣read␣again>␣should")
 ("not␣appear␣between␣\csname␣and␣\endcsname."); *back_error*;
 end

This code is used in section 372.

374. ⟨Look up the characters of list r in the hash table, and set *cur_cs* 374⟩ ≡
 $j \leftarrow$ *first*; $p \leftarrow$ *link*(r);
 while p ≠ *null* **do**
  begin if $j \geq$ *max_buf_stack* **then**
   begin *max_buf_stack* $\leftarrow j + 1$;
   if *max_buf_stack* = *buf_size* **then** *overflow*("buffer␣size", *buf_size*);
   end;

$buffer[j] \leftarrow info(p) \bmod \ '400; \ incr(j); \ p \leftarrow link(p);$
end;
if $j > first + 1$ **then**
    begin $no\_new\_control\_sequence \leftarrow false; \ cur\_cs \leftarrow id\_lookup(first, j - first);$
    $no\_new\_control\_sequence \leftarrow true;$
    end
else if $j = first$ **then** $cur\_cs \leftarrow null\_cs$ { the list is empty }
    else $cur\_cs \leftarrow single\_base + buffer[first]$ { the list has length one }

This code is used in section 372.

375. An *end_template* command is effectively changed to an *endv* command by the following code. (The reason for this is discussed below; the *frozen_end_template* at the end of the template has passed the *check_outer_validity* test, so its mission of error detection has been accomplished.)

⟨ Insert a *frozen_endv* token 375 ⟩ ≡
    begin $cur\_tok \leftarrow cs\_token\_flag + frozen\_endv; \ back\_input;$
    end

This code is used in section 366.

376. The processing of \input involves the *start_input* subroutine, which will be declared later; the processing of \endinput is trivial.

⟨ Put each of TEX's primitives into the hash table 226 ⟩ +≡
    $primitive("input", input, 0);$
    $primitive("endinput", input, 1);$

377. ⟨ Cases of *print_cmd_chr* for symbolic printing of primitives 227 ⟩ +≡
$input:$ **if** $chr\_code = 0$ **then** $print\_esc("input")$ **else** $print\_esc("endinput");$

378. ⟨ Initiate or terminate input from a file 378 ⟩ ≡
    if $cur\_chr > 0$ **then** $force\_eof \leftarrow true$
    else if $name\_in\_progress$ **then** $insert\_relax$
        else $start\_input$

This code is used in section 367.

---

back_error: **procedure**, §327.
back_input: **procedure**, §325.
buf_size = **const**, §11.
buffer: **array**, §30.
check_outer_validity: **procedure**,
  §336.
chr_code: *halfword*, §298.
cs_token_flag = macro, §289.
cur_chr: *halfword*, §297.
cur_cmd: *eight_bits*, §297.
cur_cs: *pointer*, §297.
cur_tok: *halfword*, §297.
end_cs_name = 66, §208.
end_template = 114, §210.
endv = 9, §207.
eq_type = macro, §221.
eqtb: **array**, §253.
error: **procedure**, §82.
expand: **procedure**, §366.

fast_get_avail = macro, §122.
first: 0 .. *buf_size*, §30.
flush_list: **procedure**, §123.
force_eof: *boolean*, §361.
frozen_end_template = 2363, §222.
frozen_endv = 2364, §222.
frozen_relax = 2365, §222.
get_avail: **function**, §120.
get_x_token: **procedure**, §380.
help2 = macro, §79.
help5 = macro, §79.
id_lookup: **function**, §259.
incr = macro, §16.
info = macro, §118.
input = 103, §210.
insert_relax: **procedure**, §379.
j: 0 .. *buf_size*, §366.
link = macro, §118.

max_buf_stack: 0 .. *buf_size*, §30.
name_in_progress: *boolean*, §527.
no_new_control_sequence: *boolean*,
  §256.
null = macro, §115.
null_cs = 257, §222.
overflow: **procedure**, §94.
p: *pointer*, §366.
primitive: **procedure**, §264.
print: **procedure**, §59.
print_cmd_chr: **procedure**, §298.
print_err = macro, §73.
print_esc: **procedure**, §63.
q: *pointer*, §366.
r: *pointer*, §366.
single_base = 129, §222.
start_input: **procedure**, §537.
undefined_cs = 100, §210.

379. Sometimes the expansion looks too far ahead, so we want to insert a harmless \relax into the user's input.

⟨ Declare the procedure called *insert_relax* 379 ⟩ ≡

procedure *insert_relax*;
  begin *cur_tok* ← *cs_token_flag* + *cur_cs*; *back_input*; *cur_tok* ← *cs_token_flag* + *frozen_relax*;
  back_input; *token_type* ← *inserted*;
  end;

This code is used in section 366.

380. Here is a recursive procedure that is TEX's usual way to get the next token of input. It has been slightly optimized to take account of common cases.

procedure *get_x_token*; { sets *cur_cmd*, *cur_chr*, *cur_tok*, and expands macros }
  label *restart*, *done*;
  begin *restart*: *get_next*;
  if *cur_cmd* ≤ *max_command* **then goto** *done*;
  if *cur_cmd* ≥ *call* **then**
    if *cur_cmd* < *end_template* **then** *macro_call*
    else begin *cur_cs* ← *frozen_endv*; *cur_cmd* ← *endv*; **goto** *done*; { *cur_chr* = *null_list* }
      end
  else *expand*;
  goto *restart*;
done: **if** *cur_cs* = 0 **then** *cur_tok* ← (*cur_cmd* * ´400) + *cur_chr*
  else *cur_tok* ← *cs_token_flag* + *cur_cs*;
  end;

381. The *get_x_token* procedure is equivalent to two consecutive procedure calls: *get_next*; *x_token*.

procedure *x_token*; { *get_x_token* without the initial *get_next* }
  begin while *cur_cmd* > *max_command* **do**
    begin *expand*; *get_next*;
    end;
  if *cur_cs* = 0 **then** *cur_tok* ← (*cur_cmd* * ´400) + *cur_chr*
  else *cur_tok* ← *cs_token_flag* + *cur_cs*;
  end;

382. A control sequence that has been \def'ed by the user is expanded by TEX's *macro_call* procedure.

Before we get into the details of *macro_call*, however, let's consider the treatment of primitives like \topmark, since they are essentially macros without parameters. The token lists for such marks are kept in a global array of five pointers; we refer to the individual entries of this array by symbolic names *top_mark*, etc. The value of *top_mark* is either *null* or a pointer to the reference count of a token list.

  define *top_mark_code* = 0   { the mark in effect at the previous page break }
  define *first_mark_code* = 1   { the first mark between *top_mark* and *bot_mark* }
  define *bot_mark_code* = 2   { the mark in effect at the current page break }
  define *split_first_mark_code* = 3   { the first mark found by \vsplit }
  define *split_bot_mark_code* = 4   { the last mark found by \vsplit }

define *top_mark* ≡ *cur_mark*[*top_mark_code*]
define *first_mark* ≡ *cur_mark*[*first_mark_code*]
define *bot_mark* ≡ *cur_mark*[*bot_mark_code*]
define *split_first_mark* ≡ *cur_mark*[*split_first_mark_code*]
define *split_bot_mark* ≡ *cur_mark*[*split_bot_mark_code*]

⟨ Global variables 13 ⟩ +≡
cur_mark: **array** [*top_mark_code* .. *split_bot_mark_code*] **of** *pointer*;   { token lists for marks }

383.   ⟨ Set initial values of key variables 21 ⟩ +≡
top_mark ← *null*; *first_mark* ← *null*; *bot_mark* ← *null*; *split_first_mark* ← *null*;
split_bot_mark ← *null*;

384.   ⟨ Put each of TEX's primitives into the hash table 226 ⟩ +≡
primitive("topmark", *top_bot_mark*, *top_mark_code*);
primitive("firstmark", *top_bot_mark*, *first_mark_code*);
primitive("botmark", *top_bot_mark*, *bot_mark_code*);
primitive("splitfirstmark", *top_bot_mark*, *split_first_mark_code*);
primitive("splitbotmark", *top_bot_mark*, *split_bot_mark_code*);

385.   ⟨ Cases of *print_cmd_chr* for symbolic printing of primitives 227 ⟩ +≡
top_bot_mark: **case** *chr_code* **of**
first_mark_code: *print_esc*("firstmark");
bot_mark_code: *print_esc*("botmark");
split_first_mark_code: *print_esc*("splitfirstmark");
split_bot_mark_code: *print_esc*("splitbotmark");
othercases *print_esc*("topmark")
endcases;

386.   The following code is activated when *cur_cmd* = *top_bot_mark* and when *cur_chr* is a code like *top_mark_code*.

⟨ Insert the appropriate mark text into the scanner 386 ⟩ ≡
begin if *cur_mark*[*cur_chr*] ≠ *null* **then** *begin_token_list*(*cur_mark*[*cur_chr*], *mark_text*);
end

This code is used in section 367.

back_input: **procedure**, §325.
begin_token_list: **procedure**, §323.
call = 110, §210.
chr_code: *halfword*, §298.
cs_token_flag = macro, §289.
cur_chr: *halfword*, §297.
cur_cmd: *eight_bits*, §297.
cur_cs: *pointer*, §297.
cur_tok: *halfword*, §297.
done = 30, §15.
end_template = 114, §210.
endv = 9, §207.
expand: **procedure**, §366.
frozen_endv = 2364, §222.
frozen_relax = 2365, §222.
get_next: **procedure**, §341.
inserted = 4, §307.
macro_call: **procedure**, §389.
mark_text = 14, §307.
max_command = 99, §209.
null = macro, §115.
null_list = macro, §162.
pointer = macro, §115.
primitive: **procedure**, §264.
print_cmd_chr: **procedure**, §298.
print_esc: **procedure**, §63.
restart = 20, §15.
token_type = macro, §307.
top_bot_mark = 109, §210.

387. Now let's consider *macro_call* itself, which is invoked when TEX is scanning a control sequence whose *cur_cmd* is either *call*, *long_call*, *outer_call*, or *long_outer_call*. The control sequence definition appears in the token list whose reference count is in location *cur_chr* of *mem*.

The global variable *long_state* will be set to *call* or to *long_call*, depending on whether or not the control sequence disallows \par in its parameters. The *get_next* routine will set *long_state* to *outer_call* and emit \par, if a file ends or if an \outer control sequence occurs in the midst of an argument.

⟨ Global variables 13 ⟩ +≡
long_state: *call* .. *long_outer_call*;   { governs the acceptance of \par }

388. The parameters, if any, must be scanned before the macro is expanded. Parameters are token lists without reference counts. They are placed on an auxiliary stack called *pstack* while they are being scanned, since the *param_stack* may be losing entries during the matching process. (Note that *param_stack* can't be gaining entries, since *macro_call* is the only routine that puts anything onto *param_stack*, and it is not recursive.)

⟨ Global variables 13 ⟩ +≡
pstack: **array** [0 .. 8] **of** *pointer*;   { arguments supplied to a macro }

389. After parameter scanning is complete, the parameters are moved to the *param_stack*. Then the macro body is fed to the scanner; in other words, *macro_call* places the defined text of the control sequence at the top of the TEX's input stack, so that *get_next* will proceed to read it next.

The global variable *cur_cs* contains the *eqtb* address of the control sequence being expanded, when *macro_call* begins. If this control sequence has not been declared \long, i.e., if its command code in the *eq_type* field is not *long_call* or *long_outer_call*, its parameters are not allowed to contain the control sequence \par. If an illegal \par appears, the macro call is aborted, and the \par will be rescanned.

⟨ Declare the procedure called *macro_call* 389 ⟩ ≡
procedure *macro_call*;   { invokes a user-defined control sequence }
  label *exit*, *continue*, *done*, *done1*, *found*;
  var *r*: *pointer*;   { current node in the macro's token list }
    p: *pointer*;   { current node in parameter token list being built }
    q: *pointer*;   { new node being put into the token list }
    s: *pointer*;   { backup pointer for parameter matching }
    t: *pointer*;   { cycle pointer for backup recovery }
    u, v: *pointer*;   { auxiliary pointers for backup recovery }
    rbrace_ptr: *pointer*;   { one step before the last *right_brace* token }
    n: *small_number*;   { the number of parameters scanned }
    unbalance: *halfword*;   { unmatched left braces in current parameter }
    m: *halfword*;   { the number of tokens or groups (usually) }
    ref_count: *pointer*;   { start of the token list }
    save_scanner_status: *small_number*;   { *scanner_status* upon entry }
    save_warning_index: *pointer*;   { *warning_index* upon entry }
    match_chr: *ASCII_code*;   { character used in parameter }
  begin *save_scanner_status* ← *scanner_status*; *save_warning_index* ← *warning_index*;
    warning_index ← *cur_cs*; *ref_count* ← *cur_chr*; *r* ← *link*(*ref_count*); *n* ← 0;

if *tracing_macros* > 0 then ⟨ Show the text of the macro being expanded 401 ⟩;
if *info*(*r*) ≠ *end_match_token* then ⟨ Scan the parameters and make *link*(*r*) point to the macro body;
        but **return** if an illegal \par is detected 391 ⟩;
⟨ Feed the macro body and its parameters to the scanner 390 ⟩;
exit: *scanner_status* ← *save_scanner_status*; *warning_index* ← *save_warning_index*;
   end;
This code is used in section 366.

390.   Before we put a new token list on the input stack, it is wise to clean off all token lists that
have recently been depleted. Then a user macro that ends with a call to itself will not require
unbounded stack space.

⟨ Feed the macro body and its parameters to the scanner 390 ⟩ ≡
   while (*state* = *token_list*) ∧ (*loc* = *null*) **do** *end_token_list*; { conserve stack space }
   begin_token_list(*ref_count*, *macro*); *name* ← *warning_index*; *loc* ← *link*(*r*);
   if *n* > 0 **then**
      begin if *param_ptr* + *n* > *max_param_stack* **then**
         begin *max_param_stack* ← *param_ptr* + *n*;
         if *max_param_stack* > *param_size* **then** *overflow*("parameter␣stack␣size", *param_size*);
         end;
      for *m* ← 0 **to** *n* − 1 **do** *param_stack*[*param_ptr* + *m*] ← *pstack*[*m*];
      param_ptr ← *param_ptr* + *n*;
      end
This code is used in section 389.

ASCII_code = 0 . . 127, §18.
begin_token_list: **procedure**, §323.
call = 110, §210.
continue = 22, §15.
cur_chr: *halfword*, §297.
cur_cmd: *eight_bits*, §297.
cur_cs: *pointer*, §297.
done = 30, §15.
done1 = 31, §15.
end_match_token = 3584, §289.
end_token_list: **procedure**, §324.
eq_type = macro, §221.
eqtb: **array**, §253.

exit = 10, §15.
found = 40, §15.
get_next: **procedure**, §341.
halfword = *min_halfword* . .
   max_halfword, §113.
info = macro, §118.
link = macro, §118.
loc = macro, §36.
long_call = 111, §210.
long_outer_call = 113, §210.
macro = 5, §307.
max_param_stack: *integer*, §308.
mem: **array**, §116.

null = macro, §115.
outer_call = 112, §210.
overflow: **procedure**, §94.
param_ptr: 0 . . *param_size*, §308.
param_size = **const**, §11.
pointer = macro, §115.
right_brace = 2, §207.
scanner_status: 0 . . 5, §305.
small_number = 0 . . 63, §101.
token_list = 0, §307.
tracing_macros = macro, §236.
warning_index: *pointer*, §305.

391. At this point, the reader will find it advisable to review the explanation of token list format that was presented earlier, since many aspects of that format are of importance chiefly in the *macro_call* routine.

The token list might begin with a string of compulsory tokens before the first *match* or *end_match*. In that case the macro name is supposed to be followed by those tokens; the following program will set $s = null$ to represent this restriction. Otherwise s will be set to the first token of a string that will delimit the next parameter.

⟨ Scan the parameters and make $link(r)$ point to the macro body; but **return** if an illegal \par is detected 391 ⟩ ≡
  begin $scanner\_status \leftarrow matching$; $unbalance \leftarrow 0$; $long\_state \leftarrow eq\_type(cur\_cs)$;
  if $long\_state \geq outer\_call$ **then** $long\_state \leftarrow long\_state - 2$;
  repeat if $(info(r) > match\_token + 127) \vee (info(r) < match\_token)$ **then** $s \leftarrow null$
    else begin $match\_chr \leftarrow info(r) - match\_token$; $s \leftarrow link(r)$; $r \leftarrow s$; $p \leftarrow temp\_head$;
      $link(p) \leftarrow null$; $m \leftarrow 0$;
      end;
    ⟨ Scan a parameter until its delimiter string has been found; or, if $s = null$, simply scan the delimiter string 392 ⟩;
      { now $info(r)$ is a token whose command code is either *match* or *end_match* }
  until $info(r) = end\_match\_token$;
  end

This code is used in section 389.

392. If $info(r)$ is a *match* or *end_match* command, it cannot be equal to any token found by *get_token*. Therefore an undelimited parameter—i.e., a *match* that is immediately followed by *match* or *end_match*—will always fail the test '$cur\_tok = info(r)$' in the following algorithm.

⟨ Scan a parameter until its delimiter string has been found; or, if $s = null$, simply scan the delimiter string 392 ⟩ ≡
continue: get_token; { set cur_tok to the next token of input }
  if $cur\_tok = info(r)$ **then** ⟨ Advance r; **goto** *found* if the parameter delimiter has been fully matched, otherwise **goto** *continue* 394 ⟩;
  ⟨ Contribute the recently matched tokens to the current parameter, and **goto** *continue* if a partial match is still in effect; but abort if $s = null$ 397 ⟩;
  if $cur\_tok = par\_token$ **then**
    if $long\_state \neq long\_call$ **then** ⟨ Report a runaway argument and abort 396 ⟩;
  if $cur\_tok < right\_brace\_limit$ **then**
    if $cur\_tok < left\_brace\_limit$ **then** ⟨ Contribute an entire group to the current parameter 399 ⟩
    else ⟨ Report an extra right brace and **goto** *continue* 395 ⟩
  else ⟨ Store the current token, but **goto** *continue* if it is a blank space that would become an undelimited parameter 393 ⟩;
  $incr(m)$;
  if $info(r) > end\_match\_token$ **then goto** *continue*;
  if $info(r) < match\_token$ **then goto** *continue*;
found: **if** $s \neq null$ **then** ⟨ Tidy up the parameter just scanned, and tuck it away 400 ⟩

This code is used in section 391.

393. ⟨ Store the current token, but **goto** *continue* if it is a blank space that would become an undelimited parameter 393 ⟩ ≡

begin if $cur\_tok = space\_token$ **then**
  if $info(r) \leq end\_match\_token$ **then**
    if $info(r) \geq match\_token$ **then goto** $continue$;
$store\_new\_token(cur\_tok)$;
end

This code is used in section 392.

394. A slightly subtle point arises here: When the parameter delimiter ends with '#{', the token list will have a left brace both before and after the *end_match*. Only one of these should affect the *align_state*, but both will be scanned, so we must make a correction.

⟨ Advance r; **goto** *found* if the parameter delimiter has been fully matched, otherwise **goto**
      continue 394 ⟩ ≡
begin $r \leftarrow link(r)$;
if $(info(r) \geq match\_token) \wedge (info(r) \leq end\_match\_token)$ **then**
  begin if $cur\_tok < left\_brace\_limit$ **then** $decr(align\_state)$;
  goto *found*;
  end
else goto *continue*;
end

This code is used in section 392.

395. ⟨ Report an extra right brace and **goto** *continue* 395 ⟩ ≡
begin $back\_input$; $print\_err("Argument␣of␣")$; $sprint\_cs(warning\_index)$;
$print("␣has␣an␣extra␣}")$;
$help6("I´ve␣run␣across␣a␣`}´␣that␣doesn´t␣seem␣to␣match␣anything.")$
$("For␣example,␣`\def\a#1{...}´␣and␣`\a´␣would␣produce")$
$("this␣error.␣If␣you␣simply␣proceed␣now,␣the␣`\par´␣that")$
$("I´ve␣just␣inserted␣will␣cause␣me␣to␣report␣a␣runaway")$
$("argument␣that␣might␣be␣the␣root␣of␣the␣problem.␣But␣if")$
$("your␣`}´␣was␣spurious,␣just␣type␣`2´␣and␣it␣will␣go␣away.")$; $incr(align\_state)$;
$long\_state \leftarrow call$; $cur\_tok \leftarrow par\_token$; ins_error;
end

This code is used in section 392.

$align\_state$: *integer*, §309.
$back\_input$: **procedure**, §325.
$call = 110$, §210.
$continue = 22$, §15.
cur_cs: *pointer*, §297.
cur_tok: *halfword*, §297.
$decr$ = macro, §16.
$end\_match = 14$, §207.
$end\_match\_token = 3584$, §289.
eq_type = macro, §221.
$found = 40$, §15.
$help6$ = macro, §79.
$incr$ = macro, §16.
$info$ = macro, §118.

ins_error: **procedure**, §327.
$left\_brace\_limit = 512$, §289.
$link$ = macro, §118.
$long\_call = 111$, §210.
$long\_state$: $110 .. 113$, §387.
m: *halfword*, §389.
$match = 13$, §207.
$match\_chr$: *ASCII_code*, §389.
$match\_token = 3328$, §289.
$matching = 3$, §305.
$null$ = macro, §115.
$outer\_call = 112$, §210.
p: *pointer*, §389.

par_token: *halfword*, §333.
$print$: **procedure**, §59.
$print\_err$ = macro, §73.
r: *pointer*, §389.
$right\_brace\_limit = 768$, §289.
s: *pointer*, §389.
$scanner\_status$: $0 .. 5$, §305.
$space\_token = 2592$, §289.
$sprint\_cs$: **procedure**, §263.
$store\_new\_token$ = macro, §371.
$temp\_head$ = macro, §162.
$unbalance$: *halfword*, §389.
$warning\_index$: *pointer*, §305.

396. If $long\_state = outer\_call$, a runaway argument has already been reported.

⟨ Report a runaway argument and abort 396 ⟩ ≡
    begin if $long\_state = call$ **then**
        begin $runaway$; $print\_err($"Paragraph␣ended␣before␣"$)$; $sprint\_cs(warning\_index)$;
        $print($"␣was␣complete"$)$;
        $help3($"I␣suspect␣you´ve␣forgotten␣a␣`}´,␣causing␣me␣to␣apply␣this"$)$
        $($"control␣sequence␣to␣too␣much␣text.␣How␣can␣we␣recover?"$)$
        $($"My␣plan␣is␣to␣forget␣the␣whole␣thing␣and␣hope␣for␣the␣best."$)$; $back\_error$;
        end;
    $pstack[n] \leftarrow link(temp\_head)$; $align\_state \leftarrow align\_state - unbalance$;
    for $m \leftarrow 0$ **to** n **do** $flush\_list(pstack[m])$;
    return;
    end

This code is used in sections 392 and 399.

397. When the following code becomes active, we have matched tokens from s to the predecessor of r, and we have found that $cur\_tok \neq info(r)$. An interesting situation now presents itself: If the parameter is to be delimited by a string such as 'ab', and if we have scanned 'aa', we want to contribute one 'a' to the current parameter and resume looking for a 'b'. The program must account for such partial matches and for others that can be quite complex. But most of the time we have $s = r$ and nothing needs to be done.

Incidentally, it is possible for \par tokens to sneak in to certain parameters of non-\long macros. For example, consider a case like '\def\a#1\par!{...}' where the first \par is not followed by an exclamation point. In such situations it does not seem appropriate to prohibit the \par, so TeX keeps quiet about this bending of the rules.

⟨ Contribute the recently matched tokens to the current parameter, and **goto** *continue* if a partial match is still in effect; but abort if $s = null$ 397 ⟩ ≡
    if $s \neq r$ **then**
        if $s = null$ **then** ⟨ Report an improper use of the macro and abort 398 ⟩
        else begin $t \leftarrow s$;
            repeat $store\_new\_token(info(t))$; $incr(m)$; $u \leftarrow link(t)$; $v \leftarrow s$;
                loop begin if $u = r$ **then**
                    if $cur\_tok \neq info(v)$ **then goto** *done*
                    else begin $r \leftarrow link(v)$; **goto** *continue*;
                        end;
                    if $info(u) \neq info(v)$ **then goto** *done*;
                    $u \leftarrow link(u)$; $v \leftarrow link(v)$;
                    end;
                done: $t \leftarrow link(t)$;
            until $t = r$;
            $r \leftarrow s$; { at this point, no tokens are recently matched }
            end

This code is used in section 392.

398. ⟨ Report an improper use of the macro and abort 398 ⟩ ≡
    begin $print\_err($"Use␣of␣"$)$; $sprint\_cs(warning\_index)$; $print($"␣doesn´t␣match␣its␣definition"$)$;
    $help4($"If␣you␣say,␣e.g.,␣`\def\a1{...}´,␣then␣you␣must␣always"$)$

("put␣`1´␣after␣`\a´,␣since␣control␣sequence␣names␣are")
("made␣up␣of␣letters␣only.␣The␣macro␣here␣has␣not␣been")
("followed␣by␣the␣required␣stuff,␣so␣I´m␣ignoring␣it."); *error*; **return**;
end

This code is used in section 397.

399.   ⟨ Contribute an entire group to the current parameter 399 ⟩ ≡
begin *unbalance* ← 1;
loop begin *fast_store_new_token*(*cur_tok*); *get_token*;
   if *cur_tok* = *par_token* **then**
      if *long_state* ≠ *long_call* **then** ⟨ Report a runaway argument and abort 396 ⟩;
   if *cur_tok* < *right_brace_limit* **then**
      if *cur_tok* < *left_brace_limit* **then** *incr*(*unbalance*)
      else begin *decr*(*unbalance*);
         if *unbalance* = 0 **then goto** *done1*;
         end;
   end;
done1: *rbrace_ptr* ← *p*; *store_new_token*(*cur_tok*);
   end

This code is used in section 392.

400. If the parameter consists of a single group enclosed in braces, we must strip off the enclosing braces. That's why *rbrace_ptr* was introduced.

⟨ Tidy up the parameter just scanned, and tuck it away 400 ⟩ ≡

    begin if $(m = 1) \wedge (info(p) < right\_brace\_limit) \wedge (p \neq temp\_head)$ **then**

        begin $link(rbrace\_ptr) \leftarrow null$; $free\_avail(p)$; $p \leftarrow link(temp\_head)$; $pstack[n] \leftarrow link(p)$;
$free\_avail(p)$;

        end

    else $pstack[n] \leftarrow link(temp\_head)$;

    $incr(n)$;

    if $tracing\_macros > 0$ **then**

        begin $begin\_diagnostic$; $print\_nl(match\_chr)$; $print\_int(n)$; $print(\texttt{"<-"})$;
$show\_token\_list(pstack[n-1], null, 1000)$; $end\_diagnostic(false)$;

        end;

    end

This code is used in section 392.

401. ⟨ Show the text of the macro being expanded 401 ⟩ ≡

    begin $begin\_diagnostic$; $print\_ln$; $print\_cs(warning\_index)$; $token\_show(ref\_count)$;
$end\_diagnostic(false)$;

    end

This code is used in section 389.

402.   Basic scanning subroutines.   Let's turn now to some procedures that TeX calls upon frequently to digest certain kinds of patterns in the input. Most of these are quite simple; some are quite elaborate. Almost all of the routines call *get_x_token*, which can cause them to be invoked recursively.

403.   The *scan_left_brace* routine is called when a left brace is supposed to be the next non-blank token. (The term "left brace" means, more precisely, a character whose catcode is *left_brace*.) TeX allows \relax to appear before the *left_brace*.

procedure *scan_left_brace*;   { reads a mandatory *left_brace* }
   begin ⟨ Get the next non-blank non-relax non-call token 404 ⟩;
   if *cur_cmd* ≠ *left_brace* **then**
      begin *print_err*("Missing␣{␣inserted");
      help4 ("A␣left␣brace␣was␣mandatory␣here,␣so␣I´ve␣put␣one␣in.")
      ("You␣might␣want␣to␣delete␣and/or␣insert␣some␣corrections")
      ("so␣that␣I␣will␣find␣a␣matching␣right␣brace␣soon.")
      ("(If␣you´re␣confused␣by␣all␣this,␣try␣typing␣`I}´␣now.)"); *back_error*;
      cur_tok ← *left_brace_token* + "{"; *cur_cmd* ← *left_brace*; *cur_chr* ← "{"; *incr*(*align_state*);
      end;
   end;

404.   ⟨ Get the next non-blank non-relax non-call token 404 ⟩ ≡
   repeat *get_x_token*;
   until (*cur_cmd* ≠ *spacer*) ∧ (*cur_cmd* ≠ *relax*)
This code is used in sections 403, 1078, 1084, 1151, 1160, 1211, 1226, and 1270.

405.   The *scan_optional_equals* routine looks for an optional '=' sign preceded by optional spaces; '\relax' is not ignored here.

procedure *scan_optional_equals*;
   begin ⟨ Get the next non-blank non-call token 406 ⟩;
   if *cur_tok* ≠ *other_token* + "=" **then** *back_input*;
   end;

---

align_state: *integer*, §309.
back_error: **procedure**, §327.
back_input: **procedure**, §325.
begin_diagnostic: **procedure**, §245.
cur_chr: *halfword*, §297.
cur_cmd: *eight_bits*, §297.
cur_tok: *halfword*, §297.
end_diagnostic: **procedure**, §245.
free_avail = macro, §121.
get_x_token: **procedure**, §380.
help4 = macro, §79.
incr = macro, §16.
info = macro, §118.

left_brace = 1, §207.
left_brace_token = 256, §289.
link = macro, §118.
m: *halfword*, §389.
match_chr: *ASCII_code*, §389.
n: *small_number*, §389.
null = macro, §115.
other_token = 3072, §289.
p: *pointer*, §389.
print: **procedure**, §59.
print_cs: **procedure**, §262.
print_err = macro, §73.
print_int: **procedure**, §65.

print_ln: **procedure**, §57.
print_nl: **procedure**, §62.
pstack: **array**, §388.
rbrace_ptr: *pointer*, §389.
ref_count: *pointer*, §389.
relax = 0, §207.
right_brace_limit = 768, §289.
show_token_list: **procedure**, §292.
spacer = 10, §207.
temp_head = macro, §162.
token_show: **procedure**, §295.
tracing_macros = macro, §236.
warning_index: *pointer*, §305.

406. ⟨ Get the next non-blank non-call token 406 ⟩ ≡
   repeat *get_x_token*;
   until *cur_cmd* ≠ *spacer*

This code is used in sections 405, 441, 455, 503, 526, 577, 785, 791, and 1045.

407. In case you are getting bored, here is a slightly less trivial routine: Given a string of lowercase letters, like 'pt' or 'plus' or 'width', the *scan_keyword* routine checks to see whether the next tokens of input match this string. The match must be exact, except that uppercase letters will match their lowercase counterparts; uppercase equivalents are determined by subtracting "a" − "A", rather than using the *uc_code* table, since TeX uses this routine only for its own limited set of keywords.

If a match is found, the characters are effectively removed from the input and *true* is returned. Otherwise *false* is returned, and the input is left essentially unchanged (except for the fact that some macros may have been expanded, etc.).

function *scan_keyword*(*s* : *str_number*): *boolean*;   { look for a given string }
   label *exit*;
   var *p*: *pointer*;   { tail of the backup list }
      q: *pointer*;   { new node being added to the token list via *store_new_token* }
      k: *pool_pointer*;   { index into *str_pool* }
   begin *p* ← *backup_head*; *link*(*p*) ← *null*; *k* ← *str_start*[*s*];
   while *k* < *str_start*[*s* + 1] **do**
      begin *get_x_token*;   { recursion is possible here }
      if (*cur_cs* = 0) ∧ ((*cur_chr* = *str_pool*[*k*]) ∨ (*cur_chr* = *str_pool*[*k*] − "a" + "A")) **then**
         begin *store_new_token*(*cur_tok*); *incr*(*k*);
         end
      else if (*cur_cmd* ≠ *spacer*) ∨ (*p* ≠ *backup_head*) **then**
            begin *back_input*;
            if *p* ≠ *backup_head* **then** *back_list*(*link*(*backup_head*));
            scan_keyword ← *false*; **return**;
            end;
      end;
   flush_list(*link*(*backup_head*)); *scan_keyword* ← *true*;
exit: **end**;

408. Here is a procedure that sounds an alarm when mu and non-mu units are being switched.

procedure *mu_error*;
   begin *print_err*("Incompatible␣glue␣units");
   help1("I'm␣going␣to␣assume␣that␣1mu=1pt␣when␣they're␣mixed."); *error*;
   end;

409. The next routine '*scan_something_internal*' is used to fetch internal numeric quantities like '\hsize', and also to handle the '\the' when expanding constructions like '\the\toks0' and '\the\baselineskip'. Soon we will be considering the *scan_int* procedure, which calls *scan_something_internal*; on the other hand, *scan_something_internal* also calls *scan_int*, for constructions like '\catcode`\$' or '\fontdimen 3 \ff'. So we have to declare *scan_int* as a *forward* procedure. A few other procedures are also declared at this point.

procedure *scan_int*; *forward*;   { scans an integer value }

⟨ Declare procedures that scan restricted classes of integers 432 ⟩
⟨ Declare procedures that scan font-related stuff 577 ⟩

410. TeX doesn't know exactly what to expect when *scan_something_internal* begins. For example, an integer or dimension or glue value could occur immediately after '\hskip'; and one can even say \the with respect to token lists in constructions like '\xdef\o{\the\output}'. On the other hand, only integers are allowed after a construction like '\count'. To handle the various possibilities, *scan_something_internal* has a *level* parameter, which tells the "highest" kind of quantity that *scan_something_internal* is allowed to produce. Six levels are distinguished, namely *int_val*, *dimen_val*, *glue_val*, *mu_val*, *ident_val*, and *tok_val*.

The output of *scan_something_internal* (and of the other routines *scan_int*, *scan_dimen*, and *scan_glue* below) is put into the global variable *cur_val*, and its level is put into *cur_val_level*. The highest values of *cur_val_level* are special: *mu_val* is used only when *cur_val* points to something in a "muskip" register, or to one of the three parameters \thinmuskip, \midmuskip, \thickmuskip; *ident_val* is used only when *cur_val* points to a font identifier; *tok_val* is used only when *cur_val* points to *null* or to the reference count of a token list. The last two cases are allowed only when *scan_something_internal* is called with *level* = *tok_val*.

If the output is glue, *cur_val* will point to a glue specification, and the reference count of that glue will have been updated to reflect this reference; if the output is a nonempty token list, *cur_val* will point to its reference count, but in this case the count will not have been updated. Otherwise *cur_val* will contain the integer or scaled value in question.

define *int_val* = 0   { integer values }
define *dimen_val* = 1   { dimension values }
define *glue_val* = 2   { glue specifications }
define *mu_val* = 3   { math glue specifications }
define *ident_val* = 4   { font identifier }
define *tok_val* = 5   { token lists }

⟨ Global variables 13 ⟩ +≡
cur_val: *integer*;   { value returned by numeric scanners }
cur_val_level: *int_val* .. *tok_val*;   { the "level" of this value }

---

411.   The hash table is initialized with '\count', '\dimen', '\skip', and '\muskip' all having *register* as their command code; they are distinguished by the *chr_code*, which is either *int_val*, *dimen_val*, *glue_val*, or *mu_val*.

⟨ Put each of TEX's primitives into the hash table 226 ⟩ +≡
 primitive("count", *register*, *int_val*); *primitive*("dimen", *register*, *dimen_val*);
 primitive("skip", *register*, *glue_val*); *primitive*("muskip", *register*, *mu_val*);

412.   ⟨ Cases of *print_cmd_chr* for symbolic printing of primitives 227 ⟩ +≡
register: **if** *chr_code* = *int_val* **then** *print_esc*("count")
 else if *chr_code* = *dimen_val* **then** *print_esc*("dimen")
  else if *chr_code* = *glue_val* **then** *print_esc*("skip")
   else *print_esc*("muskip");

413.   OK, we're ready for *scan_something_internal* itself. A second parameter, *negative*, is set *true* if the value that is found should be negated. It is assumed that *cur_cmd* and *cur_chr* represent the first token of the internal quantity to be scanned; an error will be signalled if *cur_cmd* < *min_internal* or *cur_cmd* > *max_internal*.

 define *scanned_result_end*(#) ≡ *cur_val_level* ← #; **end**
 define *scanned_result*(#) ≡ **begin** *cur_val* ← #; *scanned_result_end*

procedure *scan_something_internal*(*level* : *small_number*; *negative* : *boolean*);
   { fetch an internal parameter }
 var *m*: *halfword*; { *chr_code* part of the operand token }
  p: 0 . . *nest_size*; { index into *nest* }
 begin *m* ← *cur_chr*;
 case *cur_cmd* **of**
 def_code: ⟨ Fetch a character code from some table 414 ⟩;
 toks_register, *assign_toks*, *def_family*, *set_font*, *def_font*: ⟨ Fetch a token list or font identifier, provided
   that *level* = *tok_val* 415 ⟩;
 assign_int: *scanned_result*(*eqtb*[*m*].*int*)(*int_val*);
 assign_dimen: *scanned_result*(*eqtb*[*m*].*sc*)(*dimen_val*);
 assign_glue: *scanned_result*(*equiv*(*m*))(*glue_val*);
 assign_mu_glue: *scanned_result*(*equiv*(*m*))(*mu_val*);
 set_aux: ⟨ Fetch the *space_factor* or the *prev_depth* 418 ⟩;
 set_prev_graf: ⟨ Fetch the *prev_graf* 422 ⟩;
 set_page_int: ⟨ Fetch the *dead_cycles* or the *insert_penalties* 419 ⟩;
 set_page_dimen: ⟨ Fetch something on the *page_so_far* 421 ⟩;
 set_shape: ⟨ Fetch the *par_shape* size 423 ⟩;
 set_box_dimen: ⟨ Fetch a box dimension 420 ⟩;
 char_given, *math_given*: *scanned_result*(*cur_chr*)(*int_val*);
 assign_font_dimen: ⟨ Fetch a font dimension 425 ⟩;
 assign_font_int: ⟨ Fetch a font integer 426 ⟩;
 register: ⟨ Fetch a register 427 ⟩;
 last_item: ⟨ Fetch an item in the current node, if appropriate 424 ⟩;
 othercases ⟨ Complain that \the can't do this; give zero result 428 ⟩
 endcases;
 while *cur_val_level* > *level* **do** ⟨ Convert *cur_val* to a lower level 429 ⟩;
 ⟨ Fix the reference count, if any, and negate *cur_val* if *negative* 430 ⟩;
 end;

414. ⟨Fetch a character code from some table 414⟩ ≡
  begin *scan_seven_bit_int*;
  if $m = math\_code\_base$ **then** *scanned_result*(*ho*(*math_code*(*cur_val*)))(*int_val*)
  else if $m < math\_code\_base$ **then** *scanned_result*(*equiv*($m + cur\_val$))(*int_val*)
    else *scanned_result*(*eqtb*[$m + cur\_val$].*int*)(*int_val*);
  end

This code is used in section 413.

415. ⟨Fetch a token list or font identifier, provided that $level = tok\_val$ 415⟩ ≡
  if $level \neq tok\_val$ **then**
    begin *print_err*("Missing␣number,␣treated␣as␣zero");
    help3("A␣number␣should␣have␣been␣here;␣I␣inserted␣`0`.")
    ("(If␣you␣can´t␣figure␣out␣why␣I␣needed␣to␣see␣a␣number,")
    ("look␣up␣`weird␣error`␣in␣the␣index␣to␣The␣TeXbook.)"); *back_error*;
    scanned_result(0)(*dimen_val*);
    end
  else if $cur\_cmd \leq assign\_toks$ **then**
      begin if $cur\_cmd < assign\_toks$ **then**   { $cur\_cmd = toks\_register$ }
        begin *scan_eight_bit_int*; $m \leftarrow toks\_base + cur\_val$;
        end;
      scanned_result(*equiv*(*m*))(*tok_val*);
      end
    else begin *back_input*; *scan_font_ident*; *scanned_result*(*font_id_base* + *cur_val*)(*ident_val*);
      end

This code is used in section 413.

---

416. Users refer to '\the\spacefactor' only in horizontal mode, and to '\the\prevdepth' only in vertical mode; so we put the associated mode in the modifier part of the *set_aux* command. The *set_page_int* command has modifier 0 or 1, for '\deadcycles' and '\insertpenalties', respectively. The *set_box_dimen* command is modified by either *width_offset*, *height_offset*, or *depth_offset*. The *last_item* command is modified by either *int_val*, *dimen_val*, or *glue_val*.

⟨ Put each of TEX's primitives into the hash table 226 ⟩ +≡
 primitive("spacefactor", *set_aux*, *hmode*); *primitive*("prevdepth", *set_aux*, *vmode*);
 primitive("deadcycles", *set_page_int*, 0); *primitive*("insertpenalties", *set_page_int*, 1);
 primitive("wd", *set_box_dimen*, *width_offset*); *primitive*("ht", *set_box_dimen*, *height_offset*);
 primitive("dp", *set_box_dimen*, *depth_offset*); *primitive*("lastpenalty", *last_item*, *int_val*);
 primitive("lastkern", *last_item*, *dimen_val*); *primitive*("lastskip", *last_item*, *glue_val*);

417. ⟨ Cases of *print_cmd_chr* for symbolic printing of primitives 227 ⟩ +≡
set_aux: **if** *chr_code* = *vmode* **then** *print_esc*("prevdepth")
 else *print_esc*("spacefactor");
set_page_int: **if** *chr_code* = 0 **then** *print_esc*("deadcycles")
 else *print_esc*("insertpenalties");
set_box_dimen: **if** *chr_code* = *width_offset* **then** *print_esc*("wd")
 else if *chr_code* = *height_offset* **then** *print_esc*("ht")
  else *print_esc*("dp");
last_item: **if** *chr_code* = *int_val* **then** *print_esc*("lastpenalty")
 else if *chr_code* = *dimen_val* **then** *print_esc*("lastkern")
  else *print_esc*("lastskip");

418. ⟨ Fetch the *space_factor* or the *prev_depth* 418 ⟩ ≡
 if *abs*(*mode*) ≠ *m* **then**
  begin *print_err*("Improper␣"); *print_cmd_chr*(*set_aux*, *m*);
  help4("You␣can␣refer␣to␣\spacefactor␣only␣in␣horizontal␣mode;")
  ("you␣can␣refer␣to␣\prevdepth␣only␣in␣vertical␣mode;␣and")
  ("neither␣of␣these␣is␣meaningful␣inside␣\write.␣So")
  ("I´m␣forgetting␣what␣you␣said␣and␣using␣zero␣instead."); *error*;
  if *level* ≠ *tok_val* **then** *scanned_result*(0)(*dimen_val*)
  else *scanned_result*(0)(*int_val*);
  end
 else begin *cur_val* ← *aux*;
  if *m* = *vmode* **then** *cur_val_level* ← *dimen_val* **else** *cur_val_level* ← *int_val*;
  end
This code is used in section 413.

419. ⟨ Fetch the *dead_cycles* or the *insert_penalties* 419 ⟩ ≡
 begin if *m* = 0 **then** *cur_val* ← *dead_cycles* **else** *cur_val* ← *insert_penalties*;
 cur_val_level ← *int_val*;
 end
This code is used in section 413.

420. ⟨ Fetch a box dimension 420 ⟩ ≡
  begin *scan_eight_bit_int*;
  if *box*(*cur_val*) = *null* **then** *cur_val* ← 0 **else** *cur_val* ← *mem*[*box*(*cur_val*) + *m*].*sc*;
  cur_val_level ← *dimen_val*;
  end

This code is used in section 413.

421.   define *max_dimen* ≡ ´7777777777   { $2^{30} - 1$ }
⟨ Fetch something on the *page_so_far* 421 ⟩ ≡
  begin if *page_contents* = *empty* **then**
    if *m* = 0 **then** *cur_val* ← *max_dimen* **else** *cur_val* ← 0
  else *cur_val* ← *page_so_far*[*m*];
  cur_val_level ← *dimen_val*;
  end

This code is used in section 413.

422. ⟨ Fetch the *prev_graf* 422 ⟩ ≡
  begin *nest*[*nest_ptr*] ← *cur_list*; *p* ← *nest_ptr*;
  while *abs*(*nest*[*p*].*mode_field*) ≠ *vmode* **do** *decr*(*p*);
  scanned_result(*nest*[*p*].*pg_field*)(*int_val*);
  end

This code is used in section 413.

423. ⟨ Fetch the *par_shape* size 423 ⟩ ≡
  begin if *par_shape_ptr* = *null* **then** *cur_val* ← 0 **else** *cur_val* ← *info*(*par_shape_ptr*);
  cur_val_level ← *int_val*;
  end

This code is used in section 413.

---

aux = macro, §213.
box = macro, §230.
chr_code: *halfword*, §298.
cur_list: *list_state_record*, §213.
cur_val: *integer*, §410.
cur_val_level: 0 . . 5, §410.
dead_cycles: *integer*, §592.
decr = macro, §16.
depth_offset = 2, §135.
dimen_val = 1, §410.
empty = 0, §16.
error: **procedure**, §82.
glue_val = 2, §410.
height_offset = 3, §135.
help4 = macro, §79.
hmode = 101, §211.
info = macro, §118.

insert_penalties: *integer*, §982.
int_val = 0, §410.
last_item = 69, §208.
level: *small_number*, §413.
m: *halfword*, §413.
mem: **array**, §116.
mode = macro, §213.
mode_field: −201 . . 201, §212.
nest: **array**, §213.
nest_ptr: 0 . . *nest_size*, §213.
null = macro, §115.
p: 0 . . *nest_size*, §413.
page_contents: 0 . . 2, §980.
page_so_far: **array**, §982.
par_shape_ptr = macro, §230.
pg_field: *integer*, §212.
prev_depth = macro, §213.

prev_graf = macro, §213.
primitive: **procedure**, §264.
print_cmd_chr: **procedure**, §298.
print_err = macro, §73.
print_esc: **procedure**, §63.
sc = macro, §113.
scan_eight_bit_int: **procedure**,
  §433.
scanned_result = macro, §413.
set_aux = 78, §209.
set_box_dimen = 82, §209.
set_page_int = 81, §209.
space_factor = macro, §213.
tok_val = 5, §410.
vmode = 1, §211.
width_offset = 1, §135.

424. Here is where \lastpenalty, \lastkern, and \lastskip are implemented. The reference count for \lastskip will be updated later.

⟨ Fetch an item in the current node, if appropriate 424 ⟩ ≡
> **begin if** *cur_chr* = *glue_val* **then** *cur_val* ← *zero_glue* **else** *cur_val* ← 0;
> *cur_val_level* ← *cur_chr*;
> **if** ¬*is_char_node*(*tail*) ∧ (*mode* ≠ 0) **then**
> > **case** *cur_chr* **of**
> > *int_val*: **if** *type*(*tail*) = *penalty_node* **then** *cur_val* ← *penalty*(*tail*);
> > *dimen_val*: **if** *type*(*tail*) = *kern_node* **then** *cur_val* ← *width*(*tail*);
> > *glue_val*: **if** *type*(*tail*) = *glue_node* **then**
> > > **begin** *cur_val* ← *glue_ptr*(*tail*);
> > > **if** *subtype*(*tail*) = *mu_glue* **then** *cur_val_level* ← *mu_val*;
> > > **end**;
> > **end** { there are no other cases }
> **else if** (*mode* = *vmode*) ∧ (*tail* = *head*) **then**
> > **case** *cur_chr* **of**
> > *int_val*: *cur_val* ← *last_penalty*;
> > *dimen_val*: *cur_val* ← *last_kern*;
> > *glue_val*: **if** *last_glue* ≠ *max_halfword* **then** *cur_val* ← *last_glue*;
> > **end**; { there are no other cases }
> **end**

This code is used in section 413.

425. ⟨ Fetch a font dimension 425 ⟩ ≡
> **begin** *find_font_dimen*(*false*); *font_info*[*fmem_ptr*].*sc* ← 0;
> *scanned_result*(*font_info*[*cur_val*].*sc*)(*dimen_val*);
> **end**

This code is used in section 413.

426. ⟨ Fetch a font integer 426 ⟩ ≡
> **begin** *scan_font_ident*;
> **if** *m* = 0 **then** *scanned_result*(*hyphen_char*[*cur_val*])(*int_val*)
> **else** *scanned_result*(*skew_char*[*cur_val*])(*int_val*);
> **end**

This code is used in section 413.

427. ⟨ Fetch a register 427 ⟩ ≡
> **begin** *scan_eight_bit_int*;
> **case** *m* **of**
> *int_val*: *cur_val* ← *count*(*cur_val*);
> *dimen_val*: *cur_val* ← *dimen*(*cur_val*);
> *glue_val*: *cur_val* ← *skip*(*cur_val*);
> *mu_val*: *cur_val* ← *mu_skip*(*cur_val*);
> **end**; { there are no other cases }
> *cur_val_level* ← *m*;
> **end**

This code is used in section 413.

428. ⟨Complain that \the can't do this; give zero result 428⟩ ≡
  begin *print_err*("You␣can␣t␣use␣`"); *print_cmd_chr*(*cur_cmd*, *cur_chr*); *print*("␣after␣");
  print_esc("the"); *help1*("I´m␣forgetting␣what␣you␣said␣and␣using␣zero␣instead."); *error*;
  if *level* ≠ *tok_val* **then** *scanned_result*(0)(*dimen_val*)
  else *scanned_result*(0)(*int_val*);
  end

This code is used in section 413.

429. When a *glue_val* changes to a *dimen_val*, we use the width component of the glue; there is no need to decrease the reference count, since it has not yet been increased. When a *dimen_val* changes to an *int_val*, we use scaled points so that the value doesn't actually change. And when a *mu_val* changes to a *glue_val*, the value doesn't change either.

⟨Convert *cur_val* to a lower level 429⟩ ≡
  begin if *cur_val_level* = *glue_val* **then** *cur_val* ← *width*(*cur_val*)
  else if *cur_val_level* = *mu_val* **then** *mu_error*;
  decr(*cur_val_level*);
  end

This code is used in section 413.

430. If *cur_val* points to a glue specification at this point, the reference count for the glue does not yet include the reference by *cur_val*. If *negative* is *true*, *cur_val_level* is known to be ≤ *mu_val*.

⟨Fix the reference count, if any, and negate *cur_val* if *negative* 430⟩ ≡
  if *negative* **then**
    if *cur_val_level* ≥ *glue_val* **then**
      begin *cur_val* ← *new_spec*(*cur_val*); ⟨Negate all three glue components of *cur_val* 431⟩;
      end
    else *negate*(*cur_val*)
  else if (*cur_val_level* ≥ *glue_val*) ∧ (*cur_val_level* ≤ *mu_val*) **then** *add_glue_ref*(*cur_val*)

This code is used in section 413.

---

add_glue_ref = macro, §203.
count = macro, §236.
cur_chr: *halfword*, §297.
cur_cmd: *eight_bits*, §297.
cur_val: *integer*, §410.
cur_val_level: 0 . . 5, §410.
decr = macro, §16.
dimen = macro, §247.
dimen_val = 1, §410.
error: **procedure**, §82.
find_font_dimen: **procedure**, §578.
fmem_ptr: 0 . . *font_mem_size*, §549.
font_info: **array**, §549.
glue_node = 10, §149.
glue_ptr = macro, §149.
glue_val = 2, §410.
head = macro, §213.
help1 = macro, §79.
hyphen_char: **array**, §549.

int_val = 0, §410.
is_char_node = macro, §134.
kern_node = 11, §155.
last_glue: *pointer*, §982.
last_kern: *scaled*, §982.
last_penalty: *integer*, §982.
level: *small_number*, §413.
m: *halfword*, §413.
max_halfword = macro, §110.
mode = macro, §213.
mu_error: **procedure**, §408.
mu_glue = 99, §149.
mu_skip = macro, §224.
mu_val = 3, §410.
negate = macro, §16.
negative: *boolean*, §413.
new_spec: **function**, §151.
penalty = macro, §157.
penalty_node = 12, §157.

print: **procedure**, §59.
print_cmd_chr: **procedure**, §298.
print_err = macro, §73.
print_esc: **procedure**, §63.
sc = macro, §113.
scan_eight_bit_int: **procedure**, §433.
scan_font_ident: **procedure**, §577.
scanned_result = macro, §413.
skew_char: **array**, §549.
skip = macro, §224.
subtype = macro, §133.
tail = macro, §213.
tok_val = 5, §410.
type = macro, §133.
vmode = 1, §211.
width = macro, §135.
zero_glue = macro, §162.

431. ⟨Negate all three glue components of *cur_val* 431⟩ ≡
  begin *negate*(*width*(*cur_val*)); *negate*(*stretch*(*cur_val*)); *negate*(*shrink*(*cur_val*));
  end

This code is used in section 430.

432. Our next goal is to write the *scan_int* procedure, which scans anything that TeX treats as an integer. But first we might as well look at some simple applications of *scan_int* that have already been made inside of *scan_something_internal*:

⟨Declare procedures that scan restricted classes of integers 432⟩ ≡
procedure *scan_seven_bit_int*;
  begin *scan_int*;
  if (*cur_val* < 0) ∨ (*cur_val* > 127) **then**
    begin *print_err*("Bad␣character␣code");
    help2("The␣numeric␣code␣for␣a␣character␣must␣be␣between␣0␣and␣127.")
    ("I␣changed␣this␣one␣to␣zero."); *int_error*(*cur_val*); *cur_val* ← 0;
    end;
  end;

See also sections 433, 434, 435, 436, and 437.

This code is used in section 409.

433. ⟨Declare procedures that scan restricted classes of integers 432⟩ +≡
procedure *scan_eight_bit_int*;
  begin *scan_int*;
  if (*cur_val* < 0) ∨ (*cur_val* > 255) **then**
    begin *print_err*("Bad␣register␣code");
    help2("A␣register␣number␣must␣be␣between␣0␣and␣255.")
    ("I␣changed␣this␣one␣to␣zero."); *int_error*(*cur_val*); *cur_val* ← 0;
    end;
  end;

434. ⟨Declare procedures that scan restricted classes of integers 432⟩ +≡
procedure *scan_four_bit_int*;
  begin *scan_int*;
  if (*cur_val* < 0) ∨ (*cur_val* > 15) **then**
    begin *print_err*("Bad␣number");
    help2("Since␣I␣expected␣to␣read␣a␣number␣between␣0␣and␣15,")
    ("I␣changed␣this␣one␣to␣zero."); *int_error*(*cur_val*); *cur_val* ← 0;
    end;
  end;

435. While we're at it, we might as well deal with similar routines that will be needed later.

⟨Declare procedures that scan restricted classes of integers 432⟩ +≡
procedure *scan_char_num*;
  begin *scan_int*;
  if (*cur_val* < 0) ∨ (*cur_val* > 255) **then**
    begin *print_err*("Bad␣character␣code");
    help2("A␣character␣number␣must␣be␣between␣0␣and␣255.")
    ("I␣changed␣this␣one␣to␣zero."); *int_error*(*cur_val*); *cur_val* ← 0;

        end;
    end;

436. ⟨ Declare procedures that scan restricted classes of integers 432 ⟩ +≡
procedure *scan_fifteen_bit_int*;
    begin *scan_int*;
    if (*cur_val* < 0) ∨ (*cur_val* > ´77777) **then**
        begin *print_err*("Bad␣math␣code");
        help2("A␣numeric␣math␣code␣must␣be␣between␣0␣and␣32767.")
        ("I␣changed␣this␣one␣to␣zero."); *int_error*(*cur_val*); *cur_val* ← 0;
        end;
    end;

437. ⟨ Declare procedures that scan restricted classes of integers 432 ⟩ +≡
procedure *scan_twenty_seven_bit_int*;
    begin *scan_int*;
    if (*cur_val* < 0) ∨ (*cur_val* > ´7777777777) **then**
        begin *print_err*("Bad␣delimiter␣code");
        help2("A␣numeric␣delimiter␣code␣must␣be␣between␣0␣and␣2^{27}-1.")
        ("I␣changed␣this␣one␣to␣zero."); *int_error*(*cur_val*); *cur_val* ← 0;
        end;
    end;

438. An integer number can be preceded by any number of spaces and '+' or '-' signs. Then comes either a decimal constant (i.e., radix 10), an octal constant (i.e., radix 8, preceded by ´), a hexadecimal constant (radix 16, preceded by "), an alphabetic constant (preceded by `), or an internal variable. After scanning is complete, *cur_val* will contain the answer, which must be at most $2^{31} - 1 = 2147483647$ in absolute value. The value of *radix* is set to 10, 8, or 16 in the cases of decimal, octal, or hexadecimal constants, otherwise *radix* is set to zero. An optional space follows a constant.

define *octal_token* = *other_token* + "´"   { apostrophe, indicates an octal constant }
define *hex_token* = *other_token* + """"   { double quote, indicates a hex constant }
define *alpha_token* = *other_token* + "`"   { reverse apostrophe, precedes alpha constants }
define *point_token* = *other_token* + "."   { decimal point }
define *continental_point_token* = *other_token* + ","   { decimal point, Eurostyle }

⟨ Global variables 13 ⟩ +≡
radix: *small_number*;   { *scan_int* sets this to 8, 10, 16, or zero }

439. We initialize the following global variables just in case *expand* comes into action before any of the basic scanning routines has assigned them a value.

⟨ Set initial values of key variables 21 ⟩ +≡
    cur_val ← 0; *cur_val_level* ← *int_val*; *radix* ← 0;

---

cur_val: *integer*, §410.
cur_val_level: 0 . . 5, §410.
expand: **procedure**, §366.
help2 = macro, §79.
int_error: **procedure**, §91.
int_val = 0, §410.

negate = macro, §16.
other_token = 3072, §289.
print_err = macro, §73.
scan_int: **procedure**, §440.
scan_something_internal:

procedure, §413.
shrink = macro, §150.
small_number = 0 . . 63, §101.
stretch = macro, §150.
width = macro, §135.

440. The *scan_int* routine is used also to scan the integer part of a fraction; for example, the '3' in '3.14159' will be found by *scan_int*. The *scan_dimen* routine assumes that *cur_tok* = *point_token* after the integer part of such a fraction has been scanned by *scan_int*, and that the decimal point has been backed up to be scanned again.

procedure *scan_int*; { sets *cur_val* to an integer }
  label *done*;
  var *negative*: *boolean*; { should the answer be negated? }
    m: *integer*; { 2^{31} **div** *radix*, the threshold of danger }
    d: *small_number*; { the digit just scanned }
    vacuous: *boolean*; { have no digits appeared? }
    OK_so_far: *boolean*; { has an error message been issued? }
  begin *radix* ← 0; *OK_so_far* ← *true*;
  ⟨ Get the next non-blank non-sign token; set *negative* appropriately 441 ⟩;
  if *cur_tok* = *alpha_token* **then** ⟨ Scan an alphabetic character code into *cur_val* 442 ⟩
  else if (*cur_cmd* ≥ *min_internal*) ∧ (*cur_cmd* ≤ *max_internal*) **then**
      scan_something_internal(*int_val*, *false*)
    else ⟨ Scan a numeric constant 444 ⟩;
  if *negative* **then** *negate*(*cur_val*);
  end;

441. ⟨ Get the next non-blank non-sign token; set *negative* appropriately 441 ⟩ ≡
  negative ← *false*;
  repeat ⟨ Get the next non-blank non-call token 406 ⟩;
    if *cur_tok* = *other_token* + "-" **then**
      begin *negative* ← ¬*negative*; *cur_tok* ← *other_token* + "+";
      end;
  until *cur_tok* ≠ *other_token* + "+"

This code is used in sections 440, 448, and 461.

442. A space is ignored after an alphabetic character constant, so that such constants behave like numeric ones.

⟨ Scan an alphabetic character code into *cur_val* 442 ⟩ ≡
  begin *get_token*; { suppress macro expansion }
  if *cur_tok* < *cs_token_flag* **then**
    begin *cur_val* ← *cur_chr*;
    if *cur_cmd* ≤ *right_brace* **then**
      if *cur_cmd* = *right_brace* **then** *incr*(*align_state*)
      else *decr*(*align_state*);
    end
  else if *cur_tok* < *cs_token_flag* + *single_base* **then** *cur_val* ← *cur_tok* − *cs_token_flag* − *active_base*
    else *cur_val* ← *cur_tok* − *cs_token_flag* − *single_base*;
  if *cur_val* > 127 **then**
    begin *print_err*("Improper␣alphabetic␣constant");
    help2("A␣one-character␣control␣sequence␣belongs␣after␣a␣`␣mark.")
    ("So␣I´m␣essentially␣inserting␣\0␣here."); *cur_val* ← "0"; *back_error*;
    end
  else ⟨ Scan an optional space 443 ⟩;

end

This code is used in section 440.

443. ⟨ Scan an optional space 443 ⟩ ≡
    begin *get_x_token*;
    if *cur_cmd* ≠ *spacer* **then** *back_input*;
    end

This code is used in sections 442, 448, 455, and 1200.

444. ⟨ Scan a numeric constant 444 ⟩ ≡
    begin *radix* ← 10; *m* ← 214748364;
    if *cur_tok* = *octal_token* **then**
        begin *radix* ← 8; *m* ← ′2000000000; *get_x_token*;
        end
    else if *cur_tok* = *hex_token* **then**
          begin *radix* ← 16; *m* ← ′1000000000; *get_x_token*;
          end;
    vacuous ← *true*; *cur_val* ← 0;
    ⟨ Accumulate the constant until *cur_tok* is not a suitable digit 445 ⟩;
    if *vacuous* **then** ⟨ Express astonishment that no number was here 446 ⟩
    else if *cur_cmd* ≠ *spacer* **then** *back_input*;
    end

This code is used in section 440.

---

align_state: *integer*, §309.
alpha_token = 3168, §438.
back_error: **procedure**, §327.
back_input: **procedure**, §325.
cs_token_flag = macro, §289.
cur_chr: *halfword*, §297.
cur_cmd: *eight_bits*, §297.
cur_tok: *halfword*, §297.
cur_val: *integer*, §410.
decr = macro, §16.
done = 30, §15.

get_x_token: **procedure**, §380.
help2 = macro, §79.
hex_token = 3106, §438.
incr = macro, §16.
int_val = 0, §410.
max_internal = 88, §209.
min_internal = 67, §208.
negate = macro, §16.
octal_token = 3111, §438.
other_token = 3072, §289.

point_token = 3118, §438.
print_err = macro, §73.
radix: *small_number*, §438.
right_brace = 2, §207.
scan_dimen: **procedure**, §448.
scan_something_internal:
    procedure, §413.
single_base = 129, §222.
small_number = 0 .. 63, §101.
spacer = 10, §207.

445. **define** *infinity* ≡ ´17777777777   { the largest positive value that TEX knows }
   define *zero_token* = *other_token* + "0"   { zero, the smallest digit }
   define *A_token* = *letter_token* + "A"   { the smallest special hex digit }
   define *other_A_token* = *other_token* + "A"   { special hex digit of type *other_char* }

⟨ Accumulate the constant until *cur_tok* is not a suitable digit 445 ⟩ ≡
   loop begin if (*cur_tok* < *zero_token* + *radix*) ∧ (*cur_tok* ≥ *zero_token*) ∧ (*cur_tok* ≤ *zero_token* + 9)
         then *d* ← *cur_tok* − *zero_token*
      else if *radix* = 16 **then**
         if (*cur_tok* ≤ *A_token* + 5) ∧ (*cur_tok* ≥ *A_token*) **then** *d* ← *cur_tok* − *A_token* + 10
         else if (*cur_tok* ≤ *other_A_token* + 5) ∧ (*cur_tok* ≥ *other_A_token*) **then**
            d ← *cur_tok* − *other_A_token* + 10
         else goto *done*
      else goto *done*;
   vacuous ← *false*;
   if (*cur_val* ≥ *m*) ∧ ((*cur_val* > *m*) ∨ (*d* > 7) ∨ (*radix* ≠ 10)) **then**
      begin if *OK_so_far* **then**
         begin *print_err*("Number␣too␣big");
         help2("I␣can␣only␣go␣up␣to␣2147483647=´17777777777=""7FFFFFFF,")
         ("so␣I´m␣using␣that␣number␣instead␣of␣yours.");
         error; *cur_val* ← *infinity*; *OK_so_far* ← *false*;
         end;
      end
   else *cur_val* ← *cur_val* ∗ *radix* + *d*;
   get_x_token;
   end;
done:

This code is used in section 444.

446.   ⟨ Express astonishment that no number was here 446 ⟩ ≡
   begin *print_err*("Missing␣number,␣treated␣as␣zero");
   help3("A␣number␣should␣have␣been␣here;␣I␣inserted␣`0´.")
   ("(If␣you␣can´t␣figure␣out␣why␣I␣needed␣to␣see␣a␣number,")
   ("look␣up␣`weird␣error´␣in␣the␣index␣to␣The␣TeXbook.)"); *back_error*;
   end

This code is used in section 444.

447.   The *scan_dimen* routine is similar to *scan_int*, but it sets *cur_val* to a *scaled* value, i.e., an integral number of sp. One of its main tasks is therefore to interpret the abbreviations for various kinds of units and to convert measurements to scaled points.

   There are three parameters: *mu* is *true* if the finite units must be 'mu', while *mu* is *false* if 'mu' units are disallowed; *inf* is *true* if the infinite units 'fil', 'fill', 'filll' are permitted; and *shortcut* is *true* if *cur_val* already contains an integer and only the units need to be considered.

   The order of infinity that was found in the case of infinite glue is returned in the global variable *cur_order*.

⟨ Global variables 13 ⟩ +≡
cur_order: *glue_ord*;   { order of infinity found by *scan_dimen* }

448.   Constructions like '$-\,'77$ pt' are legal dimensions, so *scan_dimen* may begin with *scan_int*. This explains why it is convenient to use *scan_int* also for the integer part of a decimal fraction.

Several branches of *scan_dimen* work with *cur_val* as an integer and with an auxiliary fraction f, so that the actual quantity of interest is $cur\_val + f/2^{16}$. At the end of the routine, this "unpacked" representation is put into the single word *cur_val*, which suddenly switches significance from *integer* to *scaled*.

> **define** *attach_fraction* $= 88$ { go here to pack *cur_val* and f into *cur_val* }
> **define** *attach_sign* $= 89$ { go here when *cur_val* is correct except perhaps for sign }
> **define** *scan_normal_dimen* $\equiv$ *scan_dimen*(*false*, *false*, *false*)

procedure *scan_dimen*(*mu*, *inf*, *shortcut* : *boolean*);   { sets *cur_val* to a dimension }
> **label** *done*, *done1*, *done2*, *found*, *not_found*, *attach_fraction*, *attach_sign*;
> **var** *negative*: *boolean*;   { should the answer be negated? }
> > f: *integer*;   { numerator of a fraction whose denominator is 2^{16} }
> > ⟨ Local variables for dimension calculations 450 ⟩

> **begin** $f \leftarrow 0$; *arith_error* $\leftarrow$ *false*; *cur_order* $\leftarrow$ *normal*; *negative* $\leftarrow$ *false*;
> **if** $\neg$*shortcut* **then**
> > **begin** ⟨ Get the next non-blank non-sign token; set *negative* appropriately 441 ⟩;
> > **if** (*cur_cmd* $\geq$ *min_internal*) $\wedge$ (*cur_cmd* $\leq$ *max_internal*) **then**
> > > ⟨ Fetch an internal dimension and **goto** *attach_sign*, or fetch an internal integer 449 ⟩
> > **else begin** *back_input*;
> > > **if** *cur_tok* $=$ *continental_point_token* **then** *cur_tok* $\leftarrow$ *point_token*;
> > > **if** *cur_tok* $\neq$ *point_token* **then** *scan_int*
> > > **else begin** *radix* $\leftarrow$ 10; *cur_val* $\leftarrow$ 0; **end**;
> > > **if** *cur_tok* $=$ *continental_point_token* **then** *cur_tok* $\leftarrow$ *point_token*;
> > > **if** (*radix* $=$ 10) $\wedge$ (*cur_tok* $=$ *point_token*) **then** ⟨ Scan decimal fraction 452 ⟩;
> > > **end**;
> > **end**;
> **if** *cur_val* < 0 **then**   { in this case $f = 0$ }
> > **begin** *negative* $\leftarrow$ $\neg$*negative*; *negate*(*cur_val*);
> > **end**;
> ⟨ Scan units and set *cur_val* to $x \cdot (cur\_val + f/2^{16})$, where there are x units per sp; **goto** *attach_sign* if the units are internal 453 ⟩;
> ⟨ Scan an optional space 443 ⟩;
> *attach_sign*: **if** *arith_error* $\vee$ (*abs*(*cur_val*) $\geq$ $'10000000000$) **then**
> > ⟨ Report that this dimension is out of range 460 ⟩;
> **if** *negative* **then** *negate*(*cur_val*);
> **end**;

---

arith_error: *boolean*, §104.
back_error: **procedure**, §327.
back_input: **procedure**, §325.
continental_point_token, §438.
cur_cmd: *eight_bits*, §297.
cur_tok: *halfword*, §297.
cur_val: *integer*, §410.
d: *small_number*, §440.
done = 30, §15.
done1 = 31, §15.
done2 = 32, §15.

error: **procedure**, §82.
found = 40, §15.
get_x_token: **procedure**, §380.
glue_ord = 0 .. 3, §150.
help2 = macro, §79.
help3 = macro, §79.
letter_token = 2816, §289.
m: *integer*, §440.
max_internal = 88, §209.
min_internal = 67, §208.
negate = macro, §16.

normal = 0, §135.
not_found = 45, §15.
OK_so_far: *boolean*, §440.
other_char = 12, §207.
other_token = 3072, §289.
point_token = 3118, §438.
print_err = macro, §73.
radix: *small_number*, §438.
scaled = *integer*, §101.
scan_int: **procedure**, §440.
vacuous: *boolean*, §440.

449. ⟨ Fetch an internal dimension and **goto** *attach_sign*, or fetch an internal integer 449 ⟩ ≡
  if *mu* **then**
    begin *scan_something_internal*(*mu_val*, *false*); ⟨Coerce glue to a dimension 451⟩;
    if *cur_val_level* = *mu_val* **then goto** *attach_sign*;
    if *cur_val_level* ≠ *int_val* **then** *mu_error*;
    end
  else begin *scan_something_internal*(*dimen_val*, *false*);
    if *cur_val_level* = *dimen_val* **then goto** *attach_sign*;
    end
This code is used in section 448.

450. ⟨ Local variables for dimension calculations 450 ⟩ ≡
num, *denom*: 1 .. 65536;   { conversion ratio for the scanned units }
k: *small_number*;   { number of digits in a decimal fraction }
v: *scaled*;   { an internal dimension }
save_cur_val: *integer*;   { temporary storage of *cur_val* }
This code is used in section 448.

451.   The following code is executed when *scan_something_internal* was called asking for *mu_val*, when we really wanted a "mudimen" instead of "muglue."

⟨ Coerce glue to a dimension 451 ⟩ ≡
  if *cur_val_level* ≥ *glue_val* **then**
    begin *v* ← *width*(*cur_val*); *delete_glue_ref*(*cur_val*); *cur_val* ← *v*;
    end
This code is used in sections 449 and 455.

452.   When the following code is executed, we have *cur_tok* = *point_token*, but this token has been backed up using *back_input*; we must first discard it.
  It turns out that a decimal point all by itself is equivalent to '0.0'. Let's hope people don't use that fact.

⟨ Scan decimal fraction 452 ⟩ ≡
  begin *k* ← 0; *get_token*;   { *point_token* is being re-scanned }
  loop begin *get_x_token*;
    if (*cur_tok* > *zero_token* + 9) ∨ (*cur_tok* < *zero_token*) **then goto** *done1*;
    if *k* < 17 **then**   { digits for *k* ≥ 17 cannot affect the result }
      begin *dig*[*k*] ← *cur_tok* − *zero_token*; *incr*(*k*);
      end;
    end;
done1: *f* ← *round_decimals*(*k*);
  if *cur_cmd* ≠ *spacer* **then** *back_input*;
  end
This code is used in section 448.

453.   Now comes the harder part: At this point in the program, *cur_val* is a nonnegative integer and $f/2^{16}$ is a nonnegative fraction less than 1; we want to multiply the sum of these two quantities by the appropriate factor, based on the specified units, in order to produce a *scaled* result, and we want to do the calculation with fixed point arithmetic that does not overflow.

⟨ Scan units and set *cur_val* to $x \cdot (cur\_val + f/2^{16})$, where there are x units per sp; **goto** *attach_sign* if the units are internal 453 ⟩ ≡

    if *inf* **then** ⟨ Scan for `fil` units; **goto** *attach_fraction* if found 454 ⟩;

    ⟨ Scan for units that are internal dimensions; **goto** *attach_sign* with *cur_val* set if found 455 ⟩;

    if *mu* **then** ⟨ Scan for `mu` units and **goto** *attach_fraction* 456 ⟩;

    if *scan_keyword*("true") **then** ⟨ Adjust for the magnification ratio 457 ⟩;

    if *scan_keyword*("pt") **then goto** *attach_fraction*;   { the easy case }

    ⟨ Scan for all other units and adjust *cur_val* and *f* accordingly; **goto** *done* in the case of scaled points 458 ⟩;

attach_fraction: **if** $cur\_val \geq \text{'40000}$ **then** *arith_error* ← *true*

    else *cur_val* ← *cur_val* ∗ *unity* + *f*;

done:

This code is used in section 448.

454. A specification like 'filll1l' or 'fill L L L' will lead to two error messages (one for each additional keyword "l").

    ⟨ Scan for `fil` units; **goto** *attach_fraction* if found 454 ⟩ ≡

    if *scan_keyword*("fil") **then**

      begin *cur_order* ← *fil*;

      while *scan_keyword*("l") **do**

        begin if *cur_order* = *filll* **then**

          begin *print_err*("Illegal␣unit␣of␣measure␣("); *print*("replaced␣by␣filll)");

          help1("I␣dddon´t␣go␣any␣higher␣than␣filll."); *error*;

        end

        else *incr*(*cur_order*);

        end;

      goto *attach_fraction*;

      end

This code is used in section 453.

---

arith_error: *boolean*, §104.
attach_fraction = 88, §448.
attach_sign = 89, §448.
back_input: **procedure**, §325.
cur_cmd: *eight_bits*, §297.
cur_order: *glue_ord*, §447.
cur_tok: *halfword*, §297.
cur_val: *integer*, §410.
cur_val_level: 0 .. 5, §410.
delete_glue_ref: **procedure**, §201.
dig: **array**, §54.
dimen_val = 1, §410.
done = 30, §15.

done1 = 31, §15.
error: **procedure**, §82.
f: *integer*, §448.
fil = 1, §150.
filll = 3, §150.
get_x_token: **procedure**, §380.
glue_val = 2, §410.
help1 = macro, §79.
incr = macro, §16.
int_val = 0, §410.
mu_error: **procedure**, §408.
mu_val = 3, §410.
point_token = 3118, §438.

print: **procedure**, §59.
print_err = macro, §73.
round_decimals: **function**, §102.
scaled = *integer*, §101.
scan_keyword: **function**, §407.
scan_something_internal:
    procedure, §413.
small_number = 0 .. 63, §101.
spacer = 10, §207.
unity = macro, §101.
width = macro, §135.
zero_token = 3120, §445.

455. ⟨ Scan for units that are internal dimensions; **goto** *attach_sign* with *cur_val* set if found 455 ⟩ ≡
    save_cur_val ← *cur_val*; ⟨ Get the next non-blank non-call token 406 ⟩;
    if (*cur_cmd* < *min_internal*) ∨ (*cur_cmd* > *max_internal*) **then** *back_input*
    else begin if *mu* **then**
        begin *scan_something_internal*(*mu_val*, *false*); ⟨ Coerce glue to a dimension 451 ⟩;
        if *cur_val_level* ≠ *mu_val* **then** *mu_error*;
        end
      else *scan_something_internal*(*dimen_val*, *false*);
      v ← *cur_val*; **goto** *found*;
      end;
    if *mu* **then goto** *not_found*;
    if *scan_keyword*("em") **then** *v* ← (⟨ The em width for *cur_font* 558 ⟩)
    else if *scan_keyword*("ex") **then** *v* ← (⟨ The x-height for *cur_font* 559 ⟩)
      else goto *not_found*;
    ⟨ Scan an optional space 443 ⟩;
found: *cur_val* ← *nx_plus_y*(*save_cur_val*, *v*, *xn_over_d*(*v*, *f*, ´200000)); **goto** *attach_sign*;
not_found:
This code is used in section 453.

456. ⟨ Scan for **mu** units and **goto** *attach_fraction* 456 ⟩ ≡
    if *scan_keyword*("mu") **then goto** *attach_fraction*
    else begin *print_err*("Illegal␣unit␣of␣measure␣("); *print*("mu␣inserted)");
    help4("The␣unit␣of␣measurement␣in␣math␣glue␣must␣be␣mu.")
    ("To␣recover␣gracefully␣from␣this␣error,␣it´s␣best␣to")
    ("delete␣the␣erroneous␣units;␣e.g.,␣type␣`2´␣to␣delete")
    ("two␣letters.␣(See␣Chapter␣27␣of␣The␣TeXbook.)"); *error*; **goto** *attach_fraction*;
    end
This code is used in section 453.

457. ⟨ Adjust for the magnification ratio 457 ⟩ ≡
    begin *prepare_mag*;
    if *mag* ≠ 1000 **then**
      begin *cur_val* ← *xn_over_d*(*cur_val*, 1000, *mag*); *f* ← (1000 ∗ *f* + ´200000 ∗ *remainder*) **div** *mag*;
      cur_val ← *cur_val* + (*f* **div** ´200000); *f* ← *f* **mod** ´200000;
      end;
    end
This code is used in section 453.

458. The necessary conversion factors can all be specified exactly as fractions whose numerator and denominator are 32768 or less. According to the definitions here, 2660 dd ≈ 1000.33297 mm; this agrees well with the value 1000.333 mm cited by Bosshard in *Technische Grundlagen zur Satzherstellung* (Bern, 1980).

    define *set_conversion_end*(#) ≡ *denom* ← #;
        end
    define *set_conversion*(#) ≡ **begin** *num* ← #; *set_conversion_end*
⟨ Scan for all other units and adjust *cur_val* and *f* accordingly; **goto** *done* in the case of scaled
    points 458 ⟩ ≡
    if *scan_keyword*("in") **then** *set_conversion*(7227)(100)

else if $scan\_keyword($"pc"$)$ **then** $set\_conversion(12)(1)$
    else if $scan\_keyword($"cm"$)$ **then** $set\_conversion(7227)(254)$
      else if $scan\_keyword($"mm"$)$ **then** $set\_conversion(7227)(2540)$
        else if $scan\_keyword($"bp"$)$ **then** $set\_conversion(7227)(7200)$
          else if $scan\_keyword($"dd"$)$ **then** $set\_conversion(1238)(1157)$
            else if $scan\_keyword($"cc"$)$ **then** $set\_conversion(14856)(1157)$
              else if $scan\_keyword($"sp"$)$ **then goto** $done$
                else ⟨ Complain about unknown unit and **goto** $done2$ 459 ⟩;
$cur\_val \leftarrow xn\_over\_d(cur\_val, num, denom)$; $f \leftarrow (num * f + \,'200000 * remainder)$ **div** $denom$;
$cur\_val \leftarrow cur\_val + (f$ **div** $'200000)$; $f \leftarrow f$ **mod** $'200000$;
$done2$:

This code is used in section 453.

459. ⟨ Complain about unknown unit and **goto** $done2$ 459 ⟩ ≡
  begin $print\_err($"Illegal␣unit␣of␣measure␣("$)$; $print($"pt␣inserted)"$)$;
  $help6($"Dimensions␣can␣be␣in␣units␣of␣em,␣ex,␣in,␣pt,␣pc,"$)$
  $($"cm,␣mm,␣dd,␣cc,␣bp,␣or␣sp;␣but␣yours␣is␣a␣new␣one!"$)$
  $($"I´ll␣assume␣that␣you␣meant␣to␣say␣pt,␣for␣printers´␣points."$)$
  $($"To␣recover␣gracefully␣from␣this␣error,␣it´s␣best␣to"$)$
  $($"delete␣the␣erroneous␣units;␣e.g.,␣type␣`2´␣to␣delete"$)$
  $($"two␣letters.␣(See␣Chapter␣27␣of␣The␣TeXbook.)"$)$; $error$; **goto** $done2$;
  end

This code is used in section 458.

460. ⟨ Report that this dimension is out of range 460 ⟩ ≡
  begin $print\_err($"Dimension␣too␣large"$)$;
  $help2($"I␣can´t␣work␣with␣sizes␣bigger␣than␣about␣19␣feet."$)$
  $($"Continue␣and␣I´ll␣use␣the␣largest␣value␣I␣can."$)$;
  $error$; $cur\_val \leftarrow max\_dimen$; $arith\_error \leftarrow false$;
  end

This code is used in section 448.

$arith\_error$: *boolean*, §104.
$attach\_fraction = 88$, §448.
$attach\_sign = 89$, §448.
$back\_input$: **procedure**, §325.
cur_cmd: *eight_bits*, §297.
$cur_font = $ macro, §230.
cur_val: *integer*, §410.
cur_val_level: $0 .. 5$, §410.
$denom$, §450.
$dimen\_val = 1$, §410.
$done = 30$, §15.
$done2 = 32$, §15.
$error$: **procedure**, §82.

f: *integer*, §448.
$found = 40$, §15.
$help2 = $ macro, §79.
$help4 = $ macro, §79.
$help6 = $ macro, §79.
$mag = $ macro, §236.
$max_dimen = $ macro, §421.
$max\_internal = 88$, §209.
$min\_internal = 67$, §208.
mu_error: **procedure**, §408.
$mu\_val = 3$, §410.
$not\_found = 45$, §15.

num, §450.
nx_plus_y: **function**, §105.
$prepare\_mag$: **procedure**, §288.
$print$: **procedure**, §59.
$print_err = $ macro, §73.
$remainder$: *scaled*, §104.
$save\_cur\_val$: *integer*, §450.
$scan\_keyword$: **function**, §407.
$scan\_something\_internal$:
  procedure, §413.
v: *scaled*, §450.
xn_over_d: **function**, §107.

461. The final member of TeX's value-scanning trio is *scan_glue*, which makes *cur_val* point to a glue specification. The reference count of that glue spec will take account of the fact that *cur_val* is pointing to it.

The *level* parameter should be either *glue_val* or *mu_val*.

Since *scan_dimen* was so much more complex than *scan_int*, we might expect *scan_glue* to be even worse. But fortunately, it is very simple, since most of the work has already been done.

procedure *scan_glue*(*level* : *small_number*); { sets *cur_val* to a glue spec pointer }
  label *exit*;
  var *negative*: *boolean*; { should the answer be negated? }
    q: *pointer*; { new glue specification }
    mu: *boolean*; { does *level* = *mu_val*? }
  begin *mu* ← (*level* = *mu_val*);
  ⟨ Get the next non-blank non-sign token; set *negative* appropriately 441 ⟩;
  if (*cur_cmd* ≥ *min_internal*) ∧ (*cur_cmd* ≤ *max_internal*) **then**
    begin *scan_something_internal*(*level*, *negative*);
    if *cur_val_level* ≥ *glue_val* **then**
      begin if *cur_val_level* ≠ *level* **then** *mu_error*;
      return;
      end;
    if *cur_val_level* = *int_val* **then** *scan_dimen*(*mu*, *false*, *true*)
    else if *level* = *mu_val* **then** *mu_error*;
    end
  else begin *back_input*; *scan_dimen*(*mu*, *false*, *false*);
    if *negative* **then** *negate*(*cur_val*);
    end;
  ⟨ Create a new glue specification whose width is *cur_val*; scan for its stretch and shrink
      components 462 ⟩;
exit: **end**;

462. ⟨ Create a new glue specification whose width is *cur_val*; scan for its stretch and shrink
      components 462 ⟩ ≡
  q ← *new_spec*(*zero_glue*); *width*(*q*) ← *cur_val*;
  if *scan_keyword*("plus") **then**
    begin *scan_dimen*(*mu*, *true*, *false*); *stretch*(*q*) ← *cur_val*; *stretch_order*(*q*) ← *cur_order*;
    end;
  if *scan_keyword*("minus") **then**
    begin *scan_dimen*(*mu*, *true*, *false*); *shrink*(*q*) ← *cur_val*; *shrink_order*(*q*) ← *cur_order*;
    end;
  cur_val ← *q*

This code is used in section 461.

463.   Here's a similar procedure that returns a pointer to a rule node. This routine is called just after TeX has seen \hrule or \vrule; therefore *cur_cmd* will be either *hrule* or *vrule*. The idea is to store the default rule dimensions in the node, then to override them if 'height' or 'width' or 'depth' specifications are found (in any order).

> **define** *default_rule* = 26214   { 0.4 pt }

function *scan_rule_spec*: *pointer*;
  label *reswitch*;
  var *q*: *pointer*;   { the rule node being created }
  begin *q* ← *new_rule*;   { *width*, *depth*, and *height* all equal *null_flag* now }
  if *cur_cmd* = *vrule* **then** *width*(*q*) ← *default_rule*
  else begin *height*(*q*) ← *default_rule*; *depth*(*q*) ← 0;
    end;
reswitch: **if** *scan_keyword*("width") **then**
    begin *scan_normal_dimen*; *width*(*q*) ← *cur_val*; **goto** *reswitch*;
    end;
  if *scan_keyword*("height") **then**
    begin *scan_normal_dimen*; *height*(*q*) ← *cur_val*; **goto** *reswitch*;
    end;
  if *scan_keyword*("depth") **then**
    begin *scan_normal_dimen*; *depth*(*q*) ← *cur_val*; **goto** *reswitch*;
    end;
  scan_rule_spec ← *q*;
  end;

---

back_input: **procedure**, §325.
cur_cmd: *eight_bits*, §297.
cur_order: *glue_ord*, §447.
cur_val: *integer*, §410.
cur_val_level: 0 .. 5, §410.
depth = macro, §135.
exit = 10, §15.
glue_val = 2, §410.
height = macro, §135.
hrule = 36, §208.
int_val = 0, §410.
max_internal = 88, §209.

min_internal = 67, §208.
mu_error: **procedure**, §408.
mu_val = 3, §410.
negate = macro, §16.
new_rule: **function**, §139.
new_spec: **function**, §151.
null_flag = macro, §138.
pointer = macro, §115.
reswitch = 21, §15.
scan_int: **procedure**, §440.
scan_keyword: **function**, §407.

scan_normal_dimen = macro, §448.
scan_something_internal:
  procedure, §413.
shrink = macro, §150.
shrink_order = macro, §150.
small_number = 0 .. 63, §101.
stretch = macro, §150.
stretch_order = macro, §150.
vrule = 35, §208.
width = macro, §135.
zero_glue = macro, §162.

464. Building token lists. The token lists for macros and for other things like \mark and \output and \write are produced by a procedure called *scan_toks*.

Before we get into the details of *scan_toks*, let's consider a much simpler task, that of converting the current string into a token list. The *str_toks* function does this; it classifies spaces as type *spacer* and everything else as type *other_char*.

The token list created by *str_toks* begins at *link*(*temp_head*) and ends at the value *p* that is returned. (If *p* = *temp_head*, the list is empty.)

function *str_toks*: *pointer*;   { changes the current string to a token list }
  var *p*: *pointer*;   { tail of the token list }
    q: *pointer*;   { new node being added to the token list via *store_new_token* }
    t: *halfword*;   { token being appended }
    k: *pool_pointer*;   { index into *str_pool* }
  begin *str_room*(1); *p* ← *temp_head*; *link*(*p*) ← *null*; *k* ← *str_start*[*str_ptr*];
  while *k* < *pool_ptr* **do**
    begin *t* ← *str_pool*[*k*];
    if *t* = "␣" **then** *t* ← *space_token*
    else *t* ← *other_token* + *t*;
    fast_store_new_token(*t*); *incr*(*k*);
    end;
  pool_ptr ← *str_start*[*str_ptr*]; *str_toks* ← *p*;
  end;

465. The main reason for wanting *str_toks* is the next function, *the_toks*, which has similar input/output characteristics.

This procedure is supposed to scan something like '\skip\count12', i.e., whatever can follow '\the', and it constructs a token list containing something like '-3.0pt minus 0.5fill'.

function *the_toks*: *pointer*;
  var *old_setting*: 0 .. *max_selector*;   { holds *selector* setting }
    p, q, r: *pointer*;   { used for copying a token list }
  begin *get_x_token*; *scan_something_internal*(*tok_val*, *false*);
  if *cur_val_level* ≥ *ident_val* **then** ⟨ Copy the token list 466 ⟩
  else begin *old_setting* ← *selector*; *selector* ← *new_string*;
    case *cur_val_level* **of**
    int_val: *print_int*(*cur_val*);
    dimen_val: **begin** *print_scaled*(*cur_val*); *print*("pt");
      end;
    glue_val: **begin** *print_spec*(*cur_val*, "pt"); *delete_glue_ref*(*cur_val*);
      end;
    mu_val: **begin** *print_spec*(*cur_val*, "mu"); *delete_glue_ref*(*cur_val*);
      end;
    end;   { there are no other cases }
    selector ← *old_setting*; *the_toks* ← *str_toks*;
    end;
  end;

466. ⟨ Copy the token list 466 ⟩ ≡
  begin *p* ← *temp_head*; *link*(*p*) ← *null*;
  if *cur_val_level* = *ident_val* **then** *store_new_token*(*cs_token_flag* + *cur_val*)

else if $cur\_val \neq null$ **then**
     begin $r \leftarrow link(cur\_val)$; { do not copy the reference count }
     while $r \neq null$ **do**
       begin $fast\_store\_new\_token(info(r))$; $r \leftarrow link(r)$;
       end;
     end;
 $the\_toks \leftarrow p$;
end

This code is used in section 465.

467.   Here's part of the *expand* subroutine that we are now ready to complete:

procedure *ins_the_toks*;
  begin $link(garbage) \leftarrow the\_toks$; $ins\_list(link(temp\_head))$;
  end;

468.   The primitives \number, \romannumeral, \string, \meaning, \fontname, and \jobname are defined as follows.

  define $number\_code = 0$ { command code for \number }
  define $roman\_numeral\_code = 1$ { command code for \romannumeral }
  define $string\_code = 2$ { command code for \string }
  define $meaning\_code = 3$ { command code for \meaning }
  define $font\_name\_code = 4$ { command code for \fontname }
  define $job\_name\_code = 5$ { command code for \jobname }

⟨ Put each of TEX's primitives into the hash table 226 ⟩ +≡
  $primitive(\texttt{"number"}, convert, number\_code)$;
  $primitive(\texttt{"romannumeral"}, convert, roman\_numeral\_code)$;
  $primitive(\texttt{"string"}, convert, string\_code)$;
  $primitive(\texttt{"meaning"}, convert, meaning\_code)$;
  $primitive(\texttt{"fontname"}, convert, font\_name\_code)$;
  $primitive(\texttt{"jobname"}, convert, job\_name\_code)$;

---

convert = 107, §210.
cs_token_flag = macro, §289.
cur_val: *integer*, §410.
cur_val_level: 0 .. 5, §410.
delete_glue_ref: **procedure**, §201.
dimen_val = 1, §410.
expand: **procedure**, §366.
fast_store_new_token = macro, §371.
garbage = macro, §162.
get_x_token: **procedure**, §380.
glue_val = 2, §410.
halfword = *min_halfword* ..
  max_halfword, §113.
ident_val = 4, §410.
incr = macro, §16.
info = macro, §118.

ins_list = macro, §323.
int_val = 0, §410.
link = macro, §118.
max_selector = 21, §54.
mu_val = 3, §410.
new_string = 21, §54.
null = macro, §115.
other_char = 12, §207.
other_token = 3072, §289.
pointer = macro, §115.
pool_pointer = 0 .. *pool_size*, §38.
pool_ptr: *pool_pointer*, §39.
primitive: **procedure**, §264.
print: **procedure**, §59.
print_int: **procedure**, §65.

print_scaled: **procedure**, §103.
print_spec: **procedure**, §178.
scan_something_internal:
  procedure, §413.
scan_toks: **function**, §473.
selector: 0 .. 21, §54.
space_token = 2592, §289.
spacer = 10, §207.
store_new_token = macro, §371.
str_pool: **packed array**, §39.
str_ptr: *str_number*, §39.
str_room = macro, §42.
str_start: **array**, §39.
temp_head = macro, §162.
tok_val = 5, §410.

469. ⟨Cases of *print_cmd_chr* for symbolic printing of primitives 227⟩ +≡
convert: **case** *chr_code* **of**
  number_code: *print_esc*("number");
  roman_numeral_code: *print_esc*("romannumeral");
  string_code: *print_esc*("string");
  meaning_code: *print_esc*("meaning");
  font_name_code: *print_esc*("fontname");
  othercases *print_esc*("jobname")
  endcases;

470. The procedure *conv_toks* uses *str_toks* to insert the token list for *convert* functions into the scanner; '\outer' control sequences are allowed to follow '\string' and '\meaning'.

procedure *conv_toks*;
  var *old_setting*: 0 .. *max_selector*; {holds *selector* setting}
    c: *number_code* .. *job_name_code*; {desired type of conversion}
    save_scanner_status: *small_number*; {*scanner_status* upon entry}
  begin *c* ← *cur_chr*; ⟨Scan the argument for command *c* 471⟩;
  old_setting ← *selector*; *selector* ← *new_string*; ⟨Print the result of command *c* 472⟩;
  selector ← *old_setting*; *link*(*garbage*) ← *str_toks*; *ins_list*(*link*(*temp_head*));
  end;

471. ⟨Scan the argument for command *c* 471⟩ ≡
  case *c* **of**
  number_code, *roman_numeral_code*: *scan_int*;
  string_code, *meaning_code*: **begin** *save_scanner_status* ← *scanner_status*; *scanner_status* ← *normal*;
    get_token; *scanner_status* ← *save_scanner_status*;
    end;
  font_name_code: *scan_font_ident*;
  job_name_code: **if** *job_name* = 0 **then** *open_log_file*;
  end {there are no other cases}
This code is used in section 470.

472. ⟨Print the result of command *c* 472⟩ ≡
  case *c* **of**
  number_code: *print_int*(*cur_val*);
  roman_numeral_code: *print_roman_int*(*cur_val*);
  string_code: **if** *cur_cs* ≠ 0 **then** *sprint_cs*(*cur_cs*)
    else *print_char*(*cur_chr*);
  meaning_code: *print_meaning*;
  font_name_code: **begin** *print*(*font_name*[*cur_val*]);
    if *font_size*[*cur_val*] ≠ *font_dsize*[*cur_val*] **then**
      begin *print*("␣at␣"); *print_scaled*(*font_size*[*cur_val*]); *print*("pt");
      end;
    end;
  job_name_code: *print*(*job_name*);
  end {there are no other cases}
This code is used in section 470.

473. Now we can't postpone the difficulties any longer; we must bravely tackle *scan_toks*. This function returns a pointer to the tail of a new token list, and it also makes *def_ref* point to the reference count at the head of that list.

There are two boolean parameters, *macro_def* and *xpand*. If *macro_def* is true, the goal is to create the token list for a macro definition; otherwise the goal is to create the token list for some other TeX primitive: \mark, \output, \everypar, \lowercase, \uppercase, \message, \errmessage, \write, or \special. In the latter cases a left brace must be scanned next; this left brace will not be part of the token list, nor will the matching right brace that comes at the end. If *xpand* is false, the token list will simply be copied from the input using *get_token*. Otherwise all expandable tokens will be expanded until unexpandable tokens are left, except that the results of expanding '\the' are not expanded further. If both *macro_def* and *xpand* are true, the expansion applies only to the macro body (i.e., to the material following the first *left_brace* character).

The value of *cur_cs* when *scan_toks* begins should be the *eqtb* address of the control sequence to display in "runaway" error messages.

function *scan_toks*(*macro_def*, *xpand* : *boolean*): *pointer*;
  label *found*, *done*, *done1*, *done2*;
  var *t*: *halfword*; { token representing the highest parameter number }
    s: *halfword*; { saved token }
    p: *pointer*; { tail of the token list being built }
    q: *pointer*; { new node being added to the token list via *store_new_token* }
    unbalance: *halfword*; { number of unmatched left braces }
    hash_brace: *halfword*; { possible '#{' token }
  begin if *macro_def* **then** *scanner_status* ← *defining* **else** *scanner_status* ← *absorbing*;
  warning_index ← *cur_cs*; *def_ref* ← *get_avail*; *token_ref_count*(*def_ref*) ← *null*; *p* ← *def_ref*;
  hash_brace ← 0; *t* ← *zero_token*;
  if *macro_def* **then** ⟨Scan and build the parameter part of the macro definition 474⟩
  else *scan_left_brace*; { remove the compulsory left brace }
  ⟨Scan and build the body of the token list; **goto** *found* when finished 477⟩;
found: *scanner_status* ← *normal*;
  if *hash_brace* ≠ 0 **then** *store_new_token*(*hash_brace*);
  scan_toks ← *p*;
  end;

474. ⟨Scan and build the parameter part of the macro definition 474⟩ ≡
  begin loop
    begin *get_token*; { set *cur_cmd*, *cur_chr*, *cur_tok* }
    if *cur_tok* < *right_brace_limit* **then goto** *done1*;
    if *cur_cmd* = *mac_param* **then**
      ⟨If the next character is a parameter number, make *cur_tok* a *match* token; but if it is a left
        brace, store '*left_brace*, *end_match*', set *hash_brace*, and **goto** *done* 476⟩;
    store_new_token(*cur_tok*);
    end;
done1: *store_new_token*(*end_match_token*);
  if *cur_cmd* = *right_brace* **then** ⟨Express shock at the missing left brace; **goto** *found* 475⟩;
done: **end**
This code is used in section 473.

475. ⟨ Express shock at the missing left brace; **goto** *found* 475 ⟩ ≡
    begin *print_err*("Missing␣{␣inserted"); *incr*(*align_state*);
    help2("Where␣was␣the␣left␣brace?␣You␣said␣something␣like␣`\def\a}´,")
    ("which␣I´m␣going␣to␣interpret␣as␣`\def\a{}´."); *error*; **goto** *found*;
    end

This code is used in section 474.

476. ⟨ If the next character is a parameter number, make *cur_tok* a *match* token; but if it is a left
      brace, store '*left_brace*, *end_match*', set *hash_brace*, and **goto** *done* 476 ⟩ ≡
    begin $s \leftarrow match\_token + cur\_chr$; *get_token*;
    if $cur\_cmd = left\_brace$ **then**
        begin $hash\_brace \leftarrow cur\_tok$; *store_new_token*(*cur_tok*); *store_new_token*(*end_match_token*);
        goto *done*;
        end;
    if $t = zero\_token + 9$ **then**
        begin *print_err*("You␣already␣have␣nine␣parameters");
        help1("I´m␣going␣to␣ignore␣the␣#␣sign␣you␣just␣used."); *error*;
        end
    else begin *incr*(*t*);
        if $cur\_tok \neq t$ **then**
            begin *print_err*("Parameters␣must␣be␣numbered␣consecutively");
            help2("I´ve␣inserted␣the␣digit␣you␣should␣have␣used␣after␣the␣#.")
            ("Type␣`1´␣to␣delete␣what␣you␣did␣use."); *back_error*;
            end;
        $cur\_tok \leftarrow s$;
        end;
    end

This code is used in section 474.

---

absorbing = 5, §305.
align_state: *integer*, §309.
back_error: **procedure**, §327.
cur_chr: *halfword*, §297.
cur_cmd: *eight_bits*, §297.
cur_cs: *pointer*, §297.
cur_tok: *halfword*, §297.
def_ref: *pointer*, §305.
defining = 2, §305.
done = 30, §15.
done1 = 31, §15.
done2 = 32, §15.
end_match = 14, §207.
end_match_token = 3584, §289.

eqtb: **array**, §253.
error: **procedure**, §82.
found = 40, §15.
get_avail: **function**, §120.
get_token: **procedure**, §365.
halfword = *min_halfword* ..
  max_halfword, §113.
help1 = macro, §79.
help2 = macro, §79.
incr = macro, §16.
left_brace = 1, §207.
mac_param = 6, §207.
match = 13, §207.

match_token = 3328, §289.
normal = 0, §135.
null = macro, §115.
pointer = macro, §115.
print_err = macro, §73.
right_brace = 2, §207.
right_brace_limit = 768, §289.
scan_left_brace: **procedure**, §403.
scanner_status: 0 .. 5, §305.
store_new_token = macro, §371.
token_ref_count = macro, §200.
warning_index: *pointer*, §305.
zero_token = 3120, §445.

477. ⟨Scan and build the body of the token list; **goto** *found* when finished 477⟩ ≡
  unbalance ← 1;
  loop begin if *xpand* **then** ⟨Expand the next part of the input 478⟩
    else *get_token*;
    if *cur_tok* < *right_brace_limit* **then**
      if *cur_cmd* < *right_brace* **then** *incr*(*unbalance*)
      else begin *decr*(*unbalance*);
        if *unbalance* = 0 **then goto** *found*;
        end
    else if *cur_cmd* = *mac_param* **then**
      if *macro_def* **then** ⟨Look for parameter number or ## 479⟩;
    store_new_token(*cur_tok*);
    end
This code is used in section 473.

478. Here we insert an entire token list created by *the_toks* without expanding it further.
⟨Expand the next part of the input 478⟩ ≡
  begin loop
    begin *get_next*;
    if *cur_cmd* ≤ *max_command* **then goto** *done2*;
    if *cur_cmd* ≠ *the* **then** *expand*
    else begin *q* ← *the_toks*;
      if *link*(*temp_head*) ≠ *null* **then**
        begin *link*(*p*) ← *link*(*temp_head*); *p* ← *q*;
        end;
      end;
    end;
done2: *x_token*
  end
This code is used in section 477.

479. ⟨Look for parameter number or ## 479⟩ ≡
  begin *s* ← *cur_tok*;
  if *xpand* **then** *get_x_token*
  else *get_token*;
  if *cur_cmd* ≠ *mac_param* **then**
    if (*cur_tok* ≤ *zero_token*) ∨ (*cur_tok* > *t*) **then**
      begin *print_err*("Illegal␣parameter␣number␣in␣definition␣of␣");
      sprint_cs(*warning_index*); *help3*("You␣meant␣to␣type␣##␣instead␣of␣#,␣right?")
      ("Or␣maybe␣a␣}␣was␣forgotten␣somewhere␣earlier,␣and␣things")
      ("are␣all␣screwed␣up?␣I´m␣going␣to␣assume␣that␣you␣meant␣##."); *back_error*;
      cur_tok ← *s*;
      end
    else *cur_tok* ← *out_param_token* − "0" + *cur_chr*;
  end
This code is used in section 477.

480. Another way to create a token list is via the \read command. The sixteen files potentially usable for reading appear in the following global variables. The value of *read_open*[*n*] will be *closed* if stream number n has not been opened or if it has been fully read; *just_open* if an \openin but not a \read has been done; and *normal* if it is open and ready to read the next line.

> **define** *closed* = 2   { not open, or at end of file }
> **define** *just_open* = 1   { newly opened, first line not yet read }

⟨ Global variables 13 ⟩ +≡
read_file: **array** [0 .. 15] **of** *alpha_file*;   { used for \read }
read_open: **array** [0 .. 16] **of** *normal .. closed*;   { state of *read_file*[n] }

481.   ⟨ Set initial values of key variables 21 ⟩ +≡
> **for** $k \leftarrow 0$ **to** 16 **do** *read_open*[k] ← *closed*;

482.   The *read_toks* procedure constructs a token list like that for any macro definition, and makes *cur_val* point to it. Parameter r points to the control sequence that will receive this token list.

procedure *read_toks*(n : *integer*; r : *pointer*);
> **label** *done*;
> **var** p: *pointer*;   { tail of the token list }
> > q: *pointer*;   { new node being added to the token list via *store_new_token* }
> > s: *integer*;   { saved value of *align_state* }
> > m: *small_number*;   { stream number }
>
> **begin** *scanner_status* ← *defining*; *warning_index* ← r; *def_ref* ← *get_avail*;
> *token_ref_count*(*def_ref*) ← *null*; p ← *def_ref*;   { the reference count }
> *store_new_token*(*end_match_token*);
> **if** (n < 0) ∨ (n > 15) **then** m ← 16 **else** m ← n;
> s ← *align_state*; *align_state* ← 1000000;   { disable tab marks, etc. }
> **repeat** ⟨ Input and store tokens from the next line of the file 483 ⟩;
> **until** *align_state* = 1000000;
> *cur_val* ← *def_ref*; *scanner_status* ← *normal*; *align_state* ← s;
> **end**;

---

align_state: *integer*, §309.
alpha_file = **packed file**, §25.
back_error: **procedure**, §327.
cur_chr: *halfword*, §297.
cur_cmd: *eight_bits*, §297.
cur_tok: *halfword*, §297.
cur_val: *integer*, §410.
decr = macro, §16.
def_ref: *pointer*, §305.
defining = 2, §305.
done = 30, §15.
done2 = 32, §15.
end_match_token = 3584, §289.
expand: **procedure**, §366.
found = 40, §15.
get_avail: **function**, §120.
get_next: **procedure**, §341.

get_token: **procedure**, §365.
get_x_token: **procedure**, §380.
help3 = macro, §79.
incr = macro, §16.
k: *integer*, §163.
link = macro, §118.
mac_param = 6, §207.
macro_def: *boolean*, §473.
max_command = 99, §209.
normal = 0, §135.
null = macro, §115.
out_param_token = 1280, §289.
p: *pointer*, §473.
pointer = macro, §115.
print_err = macro, §73.
q: *pointer*, §473.
right_brace = 2, §207.

right_brace_limit = 768, §289.
s: *halfword*, §473.
scanner_status: 0 .. 5, §305.
small_number = 0 .. 63, §101.
sprint_cs: **procedure**, §263.
store_new_token = macro, §371.
t: *halfword*, §473.
temp_head = macro, §162.
the = 108, §210.
the_toks: **function**, §465.
token_ref_count = macro, §200.
unbalance: *halfword*, §473.
warning_index: *pointer*, §305.
x_token: **procedure**, §381.
xpand: *boolean*, §473.
zero_token = 3120, §445.

483. ⟨Input and store tokens from the next line of the file 483⟩ ≡
  begin_file_reading; *name* ← *m* + 1;
  if *read_open*[*m*] = *closed* **then** ⟨Input for \read from the terminal 484⟩
  else if *read_open*[*m*] = *just_open* **then** ⟨Input the first line of *read_file*[*m*] 485⟩
    else ⟨Input the next line of *read_file*[*m*] 486⟩;
  limit ← *last*;
  if (*end_line_char* < 0) ∨ (*end_line_char* > 127) **then** *decr*(*limit*)
  else *buffer*[*limit*] ← *end_line_char*;
  first ← *limit* + 1; *loc* ← *start*; *state* ← *new_line*;
  loop begin *get_token*;
    if *cur_tok* = 0 **then goto** *done*; { *cur_cmd* = *cur_chr* = 0 will occur at the end of the line }
    store_new_token(*cur_tok*);
    end;
done: *end_file_reading*

This code is used in section 482.

484. Here we input on-line into the *buffer* array, prompting the user explicitly if $n \geq 0$. The value of n is set negative so that additional prompts will not be given in the case of multi-line input.

⟨Input for \read from the terminal 484⟩ ≡
  if *interaction* > *nonstop_mode* **then**
    if *n* < 0 **then** *prompt_input*("")
    else begin *wake_up_terminal*; *print_ln*; *sprint_cs*(*r*); *prompt_input*("="); *n* ← −1;
      end
  else *fatal_error*("***␣(cannot␣\read␣from␣terminal␣in␣nonstop␣modes)")

This code is used in section 483.

485. The first line of a file must be treated specially, since *input_ln* must be told not to start with *get*.

⟨Input the first line of *read_file*[*m*] 485⟩ ≡
  if *input_ln*(*read_file*[*m*], *false*) **then** *read_open*[*m*] ← *normal*
  else begin *a_close*(*read_file*[*m*]); *read_open*[*m*] ← *closed*;
    end

This code is used in section 483.

486. An empty line is appended at the end of a *read_file*.

⟨Input the next line of *read_file*[*m*] 486⟩ ≡
  begin if ¬*input_ln*(*read_file*[*m*], *true*) **then**
    begin *a_close*(*read_file*[*m*]); *read_open*[*m*] ← *closed*;
    if *align_state* ≠ 1000000 **then**
      begin *runaway*; *print_err*("File␣ended␣within␣"); *print_esc*("read");
      help1("This␣\read␣has␣unbalanced␣braces."); *align_state* ← 1000000; *error*;
      end;
    end;
  end

This code is used in section 483.

487.   Conditional processing.   We consider now the way TₑX handles various kinds of \if commands.

> **define** *if_char_code* = 0   { '\if' }
> **define** *if_cat_code* = 1   { '\ifcat' }
> **define** *if_int_code* = 2   { '\ifnum' }
> **define** *if_dim_code* = 3   { '\ifdim' }
> **define** *if_odd_code* = 4   { '\ifodd' }
> **define** *if_vmode_code* = 5   { '\ifvmode' }
> **define** *if_hmode_code* = 6   { '\ifhmode' }
> **define** *if_mmode_code* = 7   { '\ifmmode' }
> **define** *if_inner_code* = 8   { '\ifinner' }
> **define** *if_void_code* = 9   { '\ifvoid' }
> **define** *if_hbox_code* = 10   { '\ifhbox' }
> **define** *if_vbox_code* = 11   { '\ifvbox' }
> **define** *ifx_code* = 12   { '\ifx' }
> **define** *if_eof_code* = 13   { '\ifeof' }
> **define** *if_true_code* = 14   { '\iftrue' }
> **define** *if_false_code* = 15   { '\iffalse' }
> **define** *if_case_code* = 16   { '\ifcase' }

⟨ Put each of TₑX's primitives into the hash table 226 ⟩ +≡
  primitive("if", *if_test*, *if_char_code*); *primitive*("ifcat", *if_test*, *if_cat_code*);
  primitive("ifnum", *if_test*, *if_int_code*); *primitive*("ifdim", *if_test*, *if_dim_code*);
  primitive("ifodd", *if_test*, *if_odd_code*); *primitive*("ifvmode", *if_test*, *if_vmode_code*);
  primitive("ifhmode", *if_test*, *if_hmode_code*); *primitive*("ifmmode", *if_test*, *if_mmode_code*);
  primitive("ifinner", *if_test*, *if_inner_code*); *primitive*("ifvoid", *if_test*, *if_void_code*);
  primitive("ifhbox", *if_test*, *if_hbox_code*); *primitive*("ifvbox", *if_test*, *if_vbox_code*);
  primitive("ifx", *if_test*, *ifx_code*); *primitive*("ifeof", *if_test*, *if_eof_code*);
  primitive("iftrue", *if_test*, *if_true_code*); *primitive*("iffalse", *if_test*, *if_false_code*);
  primitive("ifcase", *if_test*, *if_case_code*);

---

a_close: **procedure**, §28.
align_state: *integer*, §309.
begin_file_reading: **procedure**,
    §328.
buffer: **array**, §30.
closed = 2, §480.
cur_chr: *halfword*, §297.
cur_cmd: *eight_bits*, §297.
cur_tok: *halfword*, §297.
decr = macro, §16.
done = 30, §15.
end_file_reading: **procedure**, §329.
end_line_char = macro, §236.
error: **procedure**, §82.
fatal_error: **procedure**, §93.

first: 0 .. *buf_size*, §30.
get_token: **procedure**, §365.
help1 = macro, §79.
if_test = 104, §210.
input_ln: **function**, §31.
interaction: 0 .. 3, §73.
just_open = 1, §480.
last: 0 .. *buf_size*, §30.
limit = macro, §302.
loc = macro, §36.
m: *small_number*, §482.
n: *integer*, §482.
name = macro, §302.
new_line = 33, §303.
nonstop_mode = 1, §73.

normal = 0, §135.
primitive: **procedure**, §264.
print_err = macro, §73.
print_esc: **procedure**, §63.
print_ln: **procedure**, §57.
prompt_input = macro, §71.
r: *pointer*, §482.
read_file: **array**, §480.
read_open: **array**, §480.
runaway: **procedure**, §306.
sprint_cs: **procedure**, §263.
start = macro, §302.
state = macro, §302.
store_new_token = macro, §371.
wake_up_terminal = macro, §34.

488. ⟨Cases of *print_cmd_chr* for symbolic printing of primitives 227⟩ +≡
if_test: **case** *chr_code* **of**
  if_cat_code: *print_esc*("ifcat");
  if_int_code: *print_esc*("ifnum");
  if_dim_code: *print_esc*("ifdim");
  if_odd_code: *print_esc*("ifodd");
  if_vmode_code: *print_esc*("ifvmode");
  if_hmode_code: *print_esc*("ifhmode");
  if_mmode_code: *print_esc*("ifmmode");
  if_inner_code: *print_esc*("ifinner");
  if_void_code: *print_esc*("ifvoid");
  if_hbox_code: *print_esc*("ifhbox");
  if_vbox_code: *print_esc*("ifvbox");
  ifx_code: *print_esc*("ifx");
  if_eof_code: *print_esc*("ifeof");
  if_true_code: *print_esc*("iftrue");
  if_false_code: *print_esc*("iffalse");
  if_case_code: *print_esc*("ifcase");
  othercases *print_esc*("if")
  endcases;

489. Conditions can be inside conditions, and this nesting has a stack that is independent of the *save_stack*.

Four global variables represent the top of the condition stack: *cond_ptr* points to pushed-down entries, if any; *if_limit* specifies the largest code of a *fi_or_else* command that is syntactically legal; *cur_if* is the name of the current type of conditional; and *if_line* is the line number at which it began.

If no conditions are currently in progress, the condition stack has the special state *cond_ptr* = *null*, *if_limit* = *normal*, *cur_if* = 0, *if_line* = 0. Otherwise *cond_ptr* points to a two-word node; the *type*, *subtype*, and *link* fields of the first word contain *if_limit*, *cur_if*, and *cond_ptr* at the next level, and the second word contains the corresponding *if_line*.

  define *if_node_size* = 2   {number of words in stack entry for conditionals}
  define *if_line_field*(#) ≡ *mem*[# + 1].*int*
  define *if_code* = 1   {code for \if... being evaluated}
  define *fi_code* = 2   {code for \fi}
  define *else_code* = 3   {code for \else}
  define *or_code* = 4   {code for \or}
⟨Global variables 13⟩ +≡
cond_ptr: *pointer*;   {top of the condition stack}
if_limit: *normal* .. *or_code*;   {upper bound on *fi_or_else* codes}
cur_if: *small_number*;   {type of conditional being worked on}
if_line: *integer*;   {line where that conditional began}

490. ⟨Set initial values of key variables 21⟩ +≡
  cond_ptr ← *null*; *if_limit* ← *normal*; *cur_if* ← 0; *if_line* ← 0;

491. ⟨ Put each of TₑX's primitives into the hash table 226 ⟩ +≡
  primitive("fi", *fi_or_else*, *fi_code*); *text*(*frozen_fi*) ← "fi"; *eqtb*[*frozen_fi*] ← *eqtb*[*cur_val*];
  primitive("or", *fi_or_else*, *or_code*); *primitive*("else", *fi_or_else*, *else_code*);

492. ⟨ Cases of *print_cmd_chr* for symbolic printing of primitives 227 ⟩ +≡
fi_or_else: **if** *chr_code* = *fi_code* **then** *print_esc*("fi")
  else if *chr_code* = *or_code* **then** *print_esc*("or")
    else *print_esc*("else");

493. When we skip conditional text, we keep track of the line number where skipping began, for use in error messages.

⟨ Global variables 13 ⟩ +≡
skip_line: *integer*; { skipping began here }

494. Here is a procedure that ignores text until coming to an \or, \else, or \fi at level zero of \if ... \fi nesting. After it has acted, *cur_chr* will indicate the token that was found, but *cur_tok* will not be set (because this makes the procedure run faster).

procedure *pass_text*;
  label *done*;
  var *l*: *integer*; { level of \if ... \fi nesting }
    save_scanner_status: *small_number*; { *scanner_status* upon entry }
  begin *save_scanner_status* ← *scanner_status*; *scanner_status* ← *skipping*; *l* ← 0; *skip_line* ← *line*;
  loop begin *get_next*;
    if *cur_cmd* = *fi_or_else* **then**
      begin if *l* = 0 **then goto** *done*;
      if *cur_chr* = *fi_code* **then** *decr*(*l*);
      end
    else if *cur_cmd* = *if_test* **then** *incr*(*l*);
    end;
done: *scanner_status* ← *save_scanner_status*;
  end;

---

chr_code: *halfword*, §298.
cur_chr: *halfword*, §297.
cur_cmd: *eight_bits*, §297.
cur_tok: *halfword*, §297.
cur_val: *integer*, §410.
decr = macro, §16.
done = 30, §15.
eqtb: **array**, §253.
fi_or_else = 105, §210.
frozen_fi = 2362, §222.
get_next: **procedure**, §341.
if_case_code = 16, §487.
if_cat_code = 1, §487.
if_dim_code = 3, §487.
if_eof_code = 13, §487.
if_false_code = 15, §487.

if_hbox_code = 10, §487.
if_hmode_code = 6, §487.
if_inner_code = 8, §487.
if_int_code = 2, §487.
if_mmode_code = 7, §487.
if_odd_code = 4, §487.
if_test = 104, §210.
if_true_code = 14, §487.
if_vbox_code = 11, §487.
if_vmode_code = 5, §487.
if_void_code = 9, §487.
ifx_code = 12, §487.
incr = macro, §16.
int: *integer*, §113.
line: *integer*, §304.

link = macro, §118.
mem: **array**, §116.
normal = 0, §135.
null = macro, §115.
pointer = macro, §115.
primitive: **procedure**, §264.
print_cmd_chr: **procedure**, §298.
print_esc: **procedure**, §63.
save_stack: **array**, §271.
scanner_status: 0 .. 5, §305.
skipping = 1, §305.
small_number = 0 .. 63, §101.
subtype = macro, §133.
text = macro, §256.
type = macro, §133.

495. When we begin to process a new \if, we set $if\_limit \leftarrow if\_code$; then if \or or \else or \fi occurs before the current \if condition has been evaluated, \relax will be inserted. For example, a sequence of commands like '\ifvoid1\else...\fi' would otherwise require something after the '1'.

⟨ Push the condition stack 495 ⟩ ≡
    begin $p \leftarrow get\_node(if\_node\_size)$; $link(p) \leftarrow cond\_ptr$; $type(p) \leftarrow if\_limit$; $subtype(p) \leftarrow cur\_if$;
    $if\_line\_field(p) \leftarrow if\_line$; $cond\_ptr \leftarrow p$; $cur\_if \leftarrow cur\_chr$; $if\_limit \leftarrow if\_code$; $if\_line \leftarrow line$;
    end

This code is used in section 498.

496. ⟨ Pop the condition stack 496 ⟩ ≡
    begin $p \leftarrow cond\_ptr$; $if\_line \leftarrow if\_line\_field(p)$; $cur\_if \leftarrow subtype(p)$; $if\_limit \leftarrow type(p)$;
    $cond\_ptr \leftarrow link(p)$; $free\_node(p, if\_node\_size)$;
    end

This code is used in sections 498, 500, 509, and 510.

497. Here's a procedure that changes the if_limit code corresponding to a given value of $cond\_ptr$.

procedure $change\_if\_limit(l : small\_number; p : pointer)$;
    label $exit$;
    var q: $pointer$;
    begin if $p = cond\_ptr$ **then** $if\_limit \leftarrow l$ { that's the easy case }
    else begin $q \leftarrow cond\_ptr$;
      loop begin if $q = null$ **then** $confusion("if")$;
        if $link(q) = p$ **then**
          begin $type(q) \leftarrow l$; **return**;
          end;
        $q \leftarrow link(q)$;
        end;
      end;
$exit$: **end**;

498.   A condition is started when the *expand* procedure encounters an *if_test* command; in that case *expand* reduces to *conditional*, which is a recursive procedure.

> **procedure** *conditional*;
>   **label** *exit*, *common_ending*;
>   **var** *b*: *boolean*;   { is the condition true? }
>   *r*: `"<"` .. `">"`;   { relation to be evaluated }
>   *m, n*: *integer*;   { to be tested against the second operand }
>   *p, q*: *pointer*;   { for traversing token lists in `\ifx` tests }
>   *save_scanner_status*: *small_number*;   { *scanner_status* upon entry }
>   *save_cond_ptr*: *pointer*;   { *cond_ptr* corresponding to this conditional }
>   *this_if*: *small_number*;   { type of this conditional }
>   **begin** ⟨ Push the condition stack 495 ⟩; *save_cond_ptr* ← *cond_ptr*; *this_if* ← *cur_chr*;
>   ⟨ Either process `\ifcase` or set *b* to the value of a boolean condition 501 ⟩;
>   **if** *tracing_commands* > 1 **then** ⟨ Display the value of *b* 502 ⟩;
>   **if** *b* **then**
>   **begin** *change_if_limit*(*else_code*, *save_cond_ptr*); **return**;   { wait for `\else` or `\fi` }
>   **end**;
>   ⟨ Skip to `\else` or `\fi`, then **goto** *common_ending* 500 ⟩;
> *common_ending*: **if** *cur_chr* = *fi_code* **then** ⟨ Pop the condition stack 496 ⟩
>   **else** *if_limit* ← *fi_code*;   { wait for `\fi` }
> *exit*: **end**;

499.   In a construction like '`\if\iftrue abc\else d\fi`', the first `\else` that we come to after learning that the `\if` is false is not the `\else` we're looking for. Hence the following curious logic is needed.

500.   ⟨ Skip to `\else` or `\fi`, then **goto** *common_ending* 500 ⟩ ≡
>   **loop begin** *pass_text*;
>   **if** *cond_ptr* = *save_cond_ptr* **then**
>   **begin if** *cur_chr* ≠ *or_code* **then goto** *common_ending*;
>   *print_err*(`"Extra␣"`); *print_esc*(`"or"`);
>   *help1*(`"I´m␣ignoring␣this;␣it␣doesn´t␣match␣any␣\if."`); *error*;
>   **end**
>   **else if** *cur_chr* = *fi_code* **then** ⟨ Pop the condition stack 496 ⟩;
>   **end**

This code is used in section 498.

---

common_ending = 50, §15.
cond_ptr: *pointer*, §489.
confusion: **procedure**, §95.
cur_chr: *halfword*, §297.
cur_if: *small_number*, §489.
else_code = 3, §489.
error: **procedure**, §82.
exit = 10, §15.
expand: **procedure**, §366.
fi_code = 2, §489.
free_node: **procedure**, §130.

get_node: **function**, §125.
help1 = macro, §79.
if_code = 1, §489.
if_limit: 0 .. 4, §489.
if_line: *integer*, §489.
if_line_field = macro, §489.
if_node_size = 2, §489.
if_test = 104, §210.
line: *integer*, §304.
link = macro, §118.
null = macro, §115.

or_code = 4, §489.
p: *pointer*, §366.
pass_text: **procedure**, §494.
pointer = macro, §115.
print_err = macro, §73.
print_esc: **procedure**, §63.
scanner_status: 0 .. 5, §305.
small_number = 0 .. 63, §101.
subtype = macro, §133.
tracing_commands = macro, §236.
type = macro, §133.

501. ⟨ Either process \ifcase or set b to the value of a boolean condition 501 ⟩ ≡
  case $this\_if$ **of**
  if_char_code, if_cat_code: ⟨ Test if two characters match 506 ⟩;
  if_int_code, if_dim_code: ⟨ Test relation between integers or dimensions 503 ⟩;
  if_odd_code: ⟨ Test if an integer is odd 504 ⟩;
  if_vmode_code: $b \leftarrow (abs(mode) = vmode)$;
  if_hmode_code: $b \leftarrow (abs(mode) = hmode)$;
  if_mmode_code: $b \leftarrow (abs(mode) = mmode)$;
  if_inner_code: $b \leftarrow (mode < 0)$;
  if_void_code, if_hbox_code, if_vbox_code: ⟨ Test box register status 505 ⟩;
  ifx_code: ⟨ Test if two tokens match 507 ⟩;
  if_eof_code: **begin** $scan\_four\_bit\_int$; $b \leftarrow (read\_open[cur\_val] = closed)$;
    end;
  if_true_code: $b \leftarrow true$;
  if_false_code: $b \leftarrow false$;
  if_case_code: ⟨ Select the appropriate case and **return** or **goto** $common\_ending$ 509 ⟩;
  end { there are no other cases }

This code is used in section 498.

502. ⟨ Display the value of b 502 ⟩ ≡
  begin $begin\_diagnostic$;
  if b **then** $print($"{true}"$)$ **else** $print($"{false}"$)$;
  $end\_diagnostic(false)$;
  end

This code is used in section 498.

503. Here we use the fact that "<", "=", and ">" are consecutive ASCII codes.

⟨ Test relation between integers or dimensions 503 ⟩ ≡
  begin if $this\_if = if\_int\_code$ **then** $scan\_int$ **else** $scan\_normal\_dimen$;
  $n \leftarrow cur\_val$; ⟨ Get the next non-blank non-call token 406 ⟩;
  if $(cur_tok \geq other_token + $ "<"$) \wedge (cur_tok \leq other_token + $ ">"$)$ **then** $r \leftarrow cur\_tok - other\_token$
  else begin $print\_err($"Missing␣=␣inserted␣for␣"$)$; $print\_cmd\_chr(if\_test, this\_if)$;
    $help1($"I␣was␣expecting␣to␣see␣`<´,␣`=´,␣or␣`>´.␣Didn´t."$)$; $back\_error$; $r \leftarrow$ "="；
    end;
  if $this\_if = if\_int\_code$ **then** $scan\_int$ **else** $scan\_normal\_dimen$;
  case r **of**
  "<": $b \leftarrow (n < cur\_val)$;
  "=": $b \leftarrow (n = cur\_val)$;
  ">": $b \leftarrow (n > cur\_val)$;
  end;
  end

This code is used in section 501.

504. ⟨ Test if an integer is odd 504 ⟩ ≡
  begin $scan\_int$; $b \leftarrow odd(cur\_val)$;
  end

This code is used in section 501.

505. ⟨ Test box register status 505 ⟩ ≡
  begin *scan_eight_bit_int*; $p \leftarrow box(cur\_val)$;
  if *this_if* = *if_void_code* **then** $b \leftarrow (p = null)$
  else if $p = null$ **then** $b \leftarrow false$
      else if *this_if* = *if_hbox_code* **then** $b \leftarrow (type(p) = hlist\_node)$
          else $b \leftarrow (type(p) = vlist\_node)$;
  end

This code is used in section 501.

506. An active character will be treated as category 13 following \if\noexpand or following
\ifcat\noexpand. We use the fact that active characters have the smallest tokens, among all
control sequences.

  define *get_x_token_or_active_char* ≡
          begin *get_x_token*;
          if *cur_cmd* = *relax* **then**
              if *cur_chr* = *no_expand_flag* **then**
                  begin *cur_cmd* ← *active_char*; *cur_chr* ← *cur_tok* − *cs_token_flag* − *active_base*;
                  end;
          end

⟨ Test if two characters match 506 ⟩ ≡
  begin *get_x_token_or_active_char*;
  if (*cur_cmd* > *active_char*) ∨ (*cur_chr* > 127) **then**
      begin $m \leftarrow relax$; $n \leftarrow 256$; **end**
  else begin $m \leftarrow cur\_cmd$; $n \leftarrow cur\_chr$; **end**;
  get_x_token_or_active_char;
  if (*cur_cmd* > *active_char*) ∨ (*cur_chr* > 127) **then**
      begin *cur_cmd* ← *relax*; *cur_chr* ← 256; **end**;
  if *this_if* = *if_char_code* **then** $b \leftarrow (n = cur\_chr)$ **else** $b \leftarrow (m = cur\_cmd)$;
  end

This code is used in section 501.

---

active_base = 1, §222.
active_char = 13, §207.
b: *boolean*, §498.
back_error: **procedure**, §327.
begin_diagnostic: **procedure**, §245.
box = macro, §230.
closed = 2, §480.
common_ending = 50, §15.
cs_token_flag = macro, §289.
cur_chr: *halfword*, §297.
cur_cmd: *eight_bits*, §297.
cur_tok: *halfword*, §297.
cur_val: *integer*, §410.
end_diagnostic: **procedure**, §245.
get_x_token: **procedure**, §380.
help1 = macro, §79.
hlist_node = 0, §135.
hmode = 101, §211.
if_case_code = 16, §487.
if_cat_code = 1, §487.

if_char_code = 0, §487.
if_dim_code = 3, §487.
if_eof_code = 13, §487.
if_false_code = 15, §487.
if_hbox_code = 10, §487.
if_hmode_code = 6, §487.
if_inner_code = 8, §487.
if_int_code = 2, §487.
if_mmode_code = 7, §487.
if_odd_code = 4, §487.
if_test = 104, §210.
if_true_code = 14, §487.
if_vbox_code = 11, §487.
if_vmode_code = 5, §487.
if_void_code = 9, §487.
ifx_code = 12, §487.
m: *integer*, §498.
mmode = 201, §211.
mode = macro, §213.

n: *integer*, §498.
no_expand_flag = 257, §358.
null = macro, §115.
other_token = 3072, §289.
print: **procedure**, §59.
print_cmd_chr: **procedure**, §298.
print_err = macro, §73.
r = string", §498.
read_open: **array**, §480.
relax = 0, §207.
scan_eight_bit_int: **procedure**,
    §433.
scan_four_bit_int: **procedure**, §434.
scan_int: **procedure**, §440.
scan_normal_dimen = macro, §448.
this_if: *small_number*, §498.
type = macro, §133.
vlist_node = 1, §137.
vmode = 1, §211.

507. Note that '`\ifx`' will declare two macros different if one is *long* or *outer* and the other isn't, even though the texts of the macros are the same.

We need to reset *scanner_status*, since `\outer` control sequences are allowed, but we might be scanning a macro definition or preamble.

⟨ Test if two tokens match 507 ⟩ ≡
  begin *save_scanner_status* ← *scanner_status*; *scanner_status* ← *normal*; *get_next*; *n* ← *cur_cs*;
  p ← *cur_cmd*; *q* ← *cur_chr*; *get_next*;
  if *cur_cmd* ≠ *p* **then** *b* ← *false*
  else if *cur_cmd* < *call* **then** *b* ← (*cur_chr* = *q*)
    else ⟨ Test if two macro texts match 508 ⟩;
  scanner_status ← *save_scanner_status*;
  end

This code is used in section 501.

508. Note also that '`\ifx`' decides that macros `\a` and `\b` are different in examples like this:

$$\texttt{\textbackslash def\textbackslash a\{\textbackslash c\}}$$
$$\texttt{\textbackslash def\textbackslash b\{\textbackslash d\}}$$
$$\texttt{\textbackslash def\textbackslash c\{\}}$$
$$\texttt{\textbackslash def\textbackslash d\{\}}$$

⟨ Test if two macro texts match 508 ⟩ ≡
  begin *p* ← *link*(*cur_chr*); *q* ← *link*(*equiv*(*n*));   { omit reference counts }
  while (*p* ≠ *null*) ∧ (*q* ≠ *null*) **do**
    if *info*(*p*) ≠ *info*(*q*) **then** *p* ← *null*
    else begin *p* ← *link*(*p*); *q* ← *link*(*q*);
      end;
  b ← ((*p* = *null*) ∧ (*q* = *null*));
  end

This code is used in section 507.

509. ⟨ Select the appropriate case and **return** or **goto** *common_ending* 509 ⟩ ≡
  begin *scan_int*; *n* ← *cur_val*;   { *n* is the number of cases to pass }
  if *tracing_commands* > 1 **then**
    begin *begin_diagnostic*; *print*("{case␣"); *print_int*(*n*); *print_char*("}"); *end_diagnostic*(*false*);
    end;
  while *n* ≠ 0 **do**
    begin *pass_text*;
    if *cond_ptr* = *save_cond_ptr* **then**
      if *cur_chr* = *or_code* **then** *decr*(*n*)
      else goto *common_ending*
    else if *cur_chr* = *fi_code* **then** ⟨ Pop the condition stack 496 ⟩;
    end;
  change_if_limit(*or_code*, *save_cond_ptr*); **return**;   { wait for `\or`, `\else`, or `\fi` }
  end

This code is used in section 501.

510. The processing of conditionals is complete except for the following code, which is actually part of *expand*. It comes into play when \or, \else, or \fi is scanned.

⟨ Terminate the current conditional and skip to \fi 510 ⟩ ≡

   if *cur_chr* > *if_limit* **then**

      if *if_limit* = *if_code* **then** *insert_relax*   { condition not yet evaluated }

      else begin *print_err*("Extra␣"); *print_cmd_chr*(*fi_or_else*, *cur_chr*);

         help1("I´m␣ignoring␣this;␣it␣doesn´t␣match␣any␣\if."); *error*;

      end

   else begin while *cur_chr* ≠ *fi_code* **do** *pass_text*; { skip to \fi }

      ⟨ Pop the condition stack 496 ⟩;

      end

This code is used in section 367.

---

b: *boolean*, §498.
begin_diagnostic: **procedure**, §245.
call = 110, §210.
change_if_limit: **procedure**, §497.
common_ending = 50, §15.
cond_ptr: *pointer*, §489.
cur_chr: *halfword*, §297.
cur_cmd: *eight_bits*, §297.
cur_cs: *pointer*, §297.
cur_val: *integer*, §410.
decr = macro, §16.
end_diagnostic: **procedure**, §245.
equiv = macro, §221.
error: **procedure**, §82.

expand: **procedure**, §366.
fi_code = 2, §489.
fi_or_else = 105, §210.
get_next: **procedure**, §341.
help1 = macro, §79.
if_code = 1, §489.
if_limit: 0 . . 4, §489.
info = macro, §118.
insert_relax: **procedure**, §379.
link = macro, §118.
n: *integer*, §498.
normal = 0, §135.
null = macro, §115.
or_code = 4, §489.

pass_text: **procedure**, §494.
print: **procedure**, §59.
print_char: **procedure**, §58.
print_cmd_chr: **procedure**, §298.
print_err = macro, §73.
print_int: **procedure**, §65.
q: *pointer*, §498.
save_cond_ptr: *pointer*, §498.
save_scanner_status: *small_number*,
   §498.
scan_int: **procedure**, §440.
scanner_status: 0 . . 5, §305.
tracing_commands = macro, §236.

511. File names. It's time now to fret about file names. Besides the fact that different operating systems treat files in different ways, we must cope with the fact that completely different naming conventions are used by different groups of people. The following programs show what is required for one particular operating system; similar routines for other systems are not difficult to devise.

TeX assumes that a file name has three parts: the name proper; its "extension"; and a "file area" where it is found in an external file system. The extension of an input file or a write file is assumed to be '.tex' unless otherwise specified; it is '.log' on the transcript file that records each run of TeX; it is '.tfm' on the font metric files that describe characters in the fonts TeX uses; it is '.dvi' on the output files that specify typesetting information; and it is '.fmt' on the format files written by INITEX to initialize TeX. The file area can be arbitrary on input files, but files are usually output to the user's current area. If an input file cannot be found on the specified area, TeX will look for it on a special system area; this special area is intended for commonly used input files like webhdr.tex.

Simple uses of TeX refer only to file names that have no explicit extension or area. For example, a person usually says '\input paper' or '\font\tenrm = helvetica' instead of '\input paper.new' or '\font\tenrm = <csd.knuth>test'. Simple file names are best, because they make the TeX source files portable; whenever a file name consists entirely of letters and digits, it should be treated in the same way by all implementations of TeX. However, users need the ability to refer to other files in their environment, especially when responding to error messages concerning unopenable files; therefore we want to let them use the syntax that appears in their favorite operating system.

512. In order to isolate the system-dependent aspects of file names, the system-independent parts of TeX are expressed in terms of three system-dependent procedures called *begin_name*, *more_name*, and *end_name*. In essence, if the user-specified characters of the file name are $c_1 \ldots c_n$, the system-independent driver program does the operations

$$begin\_name; \; more\_name(c_1); \; \ldots ; \; more\_name(c_n); \; end\_name.$$

These three procedures communicate with each other via global variables. Afterwards the file name will appear in the string pool as three strings called *cur_name*, *cur_area*, and *cur_ext*; the latter two are null (i.e., ""), unless they were explicitly specified by the user.

Actually the situation is slightly more complicated, because TeX needs to know when the file name ends. The *more_name* routine is a function (with side effects) that returns *true* on the calls *more_name*(c_1), ..., *more_name*(c_{n-1}). The final call *more_name*(c_n) returns *false*; or, it returns *true* and the token following c_n is something like '\hbox' (i.e., not a character). In other words, *more_name* is supposed to return *true* unless it is sure that the file name has been completely scanned; and *end_name* is supposed to be able to finish the assembly of *cur_name*, *cur_area*, and *cur_ext* regardless of whether *more_name*(c_n) returned *true* or *false*.

⟨ Global variables 13 ⟩ +≡
cur_name: *str_number*;   { name of file just scanned }
cur_area: *str_number*;   { file area just scanned, or "" }
cur_ext: *str_number*;   { file extension just scanned, or "" }

513.   The file names we shall deal with for illustrative purposes have the following structure: If the name contains '>' or ':', the file area consists of all characters up to and including the final such character; otherwise the file area is null. If the remaining file name contains '.', the file extension consists of all such characters from the first remaining '.' to the end, otherwise the file extension is null.

We can scan such file names easily by using two global variables that keep track of the occurrences of area and extension delimiters:

⟨ Global variables 13 ⟩ +≡
area_delimiter: *pool_pointer*;   { the most recent '>' or ':', if any }
ext_delimiter: *pool_pointer*;   { the relevant '.', if any }

514.   Input files that can't be found in the user's area may appear in a standard system area called *TₑX_area*. Font metric files whose areas are not given explicitly are assumed to appear in a standard system area called *TₑX_font_area*. These system area names will, of course, vary from place to place.

> **define** *TₑX_area* ≡ `"TeXinputs:"`
> **define** *TₑX_font_area* ≡ `"TeXfonts:"`

515.   Here now is the first of the system-dependent routines for file name scanning.

procedure *begin_name*;
  begin *area_delimiter* ← 0; *ext_delimiter* ← 0;
  end;

516.   And here's the second.

function *more_name*(*c* : *ASCII_code*): *boolean*;
  begin if *c* = `"␣"` **then** *more_name* ← *false*
  else begin if (*c* = `">"`) ∨ (*c* = `":"`) **then**
      begin *area_delimiter* ← *pool_ptr*; *ext_delimiter* ← 0;
      end
    else if (*c* = `"."`) ∧ (*ext_delimiter* = 0) **then** *ext_delimiter* ← *pool_ptr*;
    str_room(1); *append_char*(*c*);   { contribute *c* to the current string }
    more_name ← *true*;
    end;
  end;

---

append_char = macro, §42.
ASCII_code = 0 . . 127, §18.
end_name: **procedure**, §517.

pool_pointer = 0 . . *pool_size*, §38.
pool_ptr: *pool_pointer*, §39.

str_number = 0 . . *max_strings*, §38.
str_room = macro, §42.

517. The third.

procedure *end_name*;
  begin if *str_ptr* + 3 > *max_strings* **then** *overflow*("number␣of␣strings", *max_strings* − *init_str_ptr*);
  if *area_delimiter* = 0 **then** *cur_area* ← ""
  else begin *cur_area* ← *str_ptr*; *incr*(*str_ptr*); *str_start*[*str_ptr*] ← *area_delimiter* + 1;
    end;
  if *ext_delimiter* = 0 **then**
    begin *cur_ext* ← ""; *cur_name* ← *make_string*;
    end
  else begin *cur_name* ← *str_ptr*; *incr*(*str_ptr*); *str_start*[*str_ptr*] ← *ext_delimiter*;
    cur_ext ← *make_string*;
    end;
  end;

518. Conversely, here is a routine that takes three strings and prints a file name that might have produced them. (The routine is system dependent, because some operating systems put the file area last instead of first.)

⟨ Basic printing procedures 57 ⟩ +≡
procedure *print_file_name*(*n, a, e* : *integer*);
  begin *print*(*a*); *print*(*n*); *print*(*e*);
  end;

519. Another system-dependent routine is needed to convert three internal TEX strings into the *name_of_file* value that is used to open files. The present code allows both lowercase and uppercase letters in the file name.

  define *append_to_name*(#) ≡
      begin *c* ← #; *incr*(*k*);
      if *k* ≤ *file_name_size* **then** *name_of_file*[*k*] ← *xchr*[*c*];
      end
procedure *pack_file_name*(*n, a, e* : *str_number*);
  var *k*: *integer*;   { number of positions filled in *name_of_file* }
    c: *ASCII_code*;   { character being packed }
    j: *pool_pointer*;   { index into *str_pool* }
  begin *k* ← 0;
  for *j* ← *str_start*[*a*] **to** *str_start*[*a* + 1] − 1 **do** *append_to_name*(*str_pool*[*j*]);
  for *j* ← *str_start*[*n*] **to** *str_start*[*n* + 1] − 1 **do** *append_to_name*(*str_pool*[*j*]);
  for *j* ← *str_start*[*e*] **to** *str_start*[*e* + 1] − 1 **do** *append_to_name*(*str_pool*[*j*]);
  if *k* ≤ *file_name_size* **then** *name_length* ← *k* **else** *name_length* ← *file_name_size*;
  for *k* ← *name_length* + 1 **to** *file_name_size* **do** *name_of_file*[*k*] ← ´␣´;
  end;

520. A messier routine is also needed, since format file names must be scanned before TEX's string mechanism has been initialized. We shall use the global variable *TEX_format_default* to supply the text for default system areas and extensions related to format files.

  define *format_default_length* = 20   { length of the *TEX_format_default* string }
  define *format_area_length* = 11   { length of its area part }
  define *format_ext_length* = 4   { length of its '.fmt' part }

⟨ Global variables 13 ⟩ +≡

$T_{E}X\_format\_default$: **packed array** $[1 .. format\_default\_length]$ **of** $char$;

521. ⟨ Set initial values of key variables 21 ⟩ +≡

   $T_{E}X\_format\_default \leftarrow$ `'TeXformats:plain.fmt'`;

522. ⟨ Check the "constant" values for consistency 14 ⟩ +≡

   if $format\_default\_length > file\_name\_size$ **then** $bad \leftarrow 31$;

523. Here is the messy routine that was just mentioned. It sets *name_of_file* from the first n
characters of $T_{E}X\_format\_default$, followed by $buffer[a .. b]$, followed by the last $format\_ext\_length$
characters of $T_{E}X\_format\_default$.

We dare not give error messages here, since TeX calls this routine before the *error* routine
is ready to roll. Instead, we simply drop excess characters, since the error will be detected in
another way when a strange file name isn't found.

procedure $pack\_buffered\_name(n : small\_number; a, b : integer)$;
   var k: $integer$;   { number of positions filled in *name_of_file* }
      c: $ASCII\_code$;   { character being packed }
      j: $integer$;   { index into *buffer* or $T_{E}X\_format\_default$ }
   begin if $n + b - a + 1 + format\_ext\_length > file\_name\_size$ **then**
      $b \leftarrow a + file\_name\_size - n - 1 - format\_ext\_length$;
   $k \leftarrow 0$;
   for $j \leftarrow 1$ **to** n **do** $append\_to\_name(xord[T_{E}X\_format\_default[j]])$;
   for $j \leftarrow a$ **to** b **do** $append\_to\_name(buffer[j])$;
   for $j \leftarrow format\_default\_length - format\_ext\_length + 1$ **to** $format\_default\_length$ **do**
      $append\_to\_name(xord[T_{E}X\_format\_default[j]])$;
   if $k \leq file\_name\_size$ **then** $name\_length \leftarrow k$ **else** $name\_length \leftarrow file\_name\_size$;
   for $k \leftarrow name\_length + 1$ **to** $file\_name\_size$ **do** $name\_of\_file[k] \leftarrow$ `'␣'`;
   end;

---

area_delimiter: *pool_pointer*, §513.
ASCII_code = 0 .. 127, §18.
bad: *integer*, §13.
buffer: **array**, §30.
cur_area: *str_number*, §512.
cur_ext: *str_number*, §512.
cur_name: *str_number*, §512.
error: **procedure**, §82.
ext_delimiter: *pool_pointer*, §513.

file_name_size = **const**, §11.
incr = macro, §16.
init_str_ptr: *str_number*, §39.
make_string: **function**, §43.
max_strings = **const**, §11.
name_length: 0 .. *file_name_size*,
   §26.
name_of_file: **packed array**, §26.
overflow: **procedure**, §94.

pool_pointer = 0 .. *pool_size*, §38.
print: **procedure**, §59.
small_number = 0 .. 63, §101.
str_number = 0 .. *max_strings*, §38.
str_pool: **packed array**, §39.
str_ptr: *str_number*, §39.
str_start: **array**, §39.
xchr: **array**, §20.
xord: **array**, §20.

524. Here is the only place we use *pack_buffered_name*. This part of the program becomes active when a "virgin" TEX is trying to get going, just after the preliminary initialization, or when the user is substituting another format file by typing '&' after the initial '**' prompt. The buffer contains the first line of input in $buffer[loc .. (last - 1)]$, where $loc < last$ and $buffer[loc] \neq$ "␣".

⟨ Declare the function called *open_fmt_file* 524 ⟩ ≡

```
function open_fmt_file: boolean;
  label found, exit;
  var j: 0 .. buf_size;   { the first space after the format file name }
  begin j ← loc;
  if buffer[loc] = "&" then
     begin incr(loc);  j ← loc;  buffer[last] ← "␣";
     while buffer[j] ≠ "␣" do  incr(j);
     pack_buffered_name(0, loc, j − 1);   { try first without the system file area }
     if w_open_in(fmt_file) then goto found;
     pack_buffered_name(format_area_length, loc, j − 1);   { now try the system format file area }
     if w_open_in(fmt_file) then goto found;
     wake_up_terminal; wterm_ln(´Sorry,␣I␣can´´t␣find␣that␣format;´, ´␣will␣try␣PLAIN.´);
     update_terminal;
     end;   { now pull out all the stops: try for the system plain file }
  pack_buffered_name(format_default_length − format_ext_length, 1, 0);
  if ¬w_open_in(fmt_file) then
     begin wake_up_terminal; wterm_ln(´I␣can´´t␣find␣the␣PLAIN␣format␣file!´);
     open_fmt_file ← false; return;
     end;
found: loc ← j;  open_fmt_file ← true;
exit: end;
```

This code is used in section 1303.

525. Operating systems often make it possible to determine the exact name (and possible version number) of a file that has been opened. The following routine, which simply makes a TEX string from the value of *name_of_file*, should ideally be changed to deduce the full name of file f, which is the file most recently opened, if it is possible to do this in a Pascal program.

This routine might be called after string memory has overflowed, hence we dare not use '*str_room*'.

```
function make_name_string: str_number;
  var k: 1 .. file_name_size;   { index into name_of_file }
  begin if (pool_ptr + name_length > pool_size) ∨ (str_ptr = max_strings) then
     make_name_string ← "?"
  else begin for k ← 1 to name_length do  append_char(xord[name_of_file[k]]);
     make_name_string ← make_string;
     end;
  end;
function a_make_name_string(var f : alpha_file): str_number;
  begin a_make_name_string ← make_name_string;
  end;
function b_make_name_string(var f : byte_file): str_number;
  begin b_make_name_string ← make_name_string;
```

end;
function $w\_make\_name\_string(\textbf{var } f : word\_file): str\_number;$
  begin $w\_make\_name\_string \leftarrow make\_name\_string;$
  end;

526. Now let's consider the "driver" routines by which TeX deals with file names in a system-independent manner. First comes a procedure that looks for a file name in the input by calling *get_x_token* for the information.

procedure *scan_file_name*;
  label *done*;
  begin $name\_in\_progress \leftarrow true;$ *begin_name*; ⟨ Get the next non-blank non-call token 406 ⟩;
  loop begin if $(cur\_cmd > other\_char) \vee (cur\_chr > 127)$ **then** { not a character }
    begin *back_input*; **goto** *done*;
    end;
  if $\neg more\_name(cur\_chr)$ **then goto** *done*;
  get_x_token;
  end;
done: *end_name*; $name\_in\_progress \leftarrow false;$
  end;

527. The global variable *name_in_progress* is used to prevent recursive use of *scan_file_name*, since the *begin_name* and other procedures communicate via global variables. Recursion would arise only by devious tricks like '\input\input f'; such attempts at sabotage must be thwarted. Furthermore, *name_in_progress* prevents \input from being initiated when a font size specification is being scanned.

Another global variable, *job_name*, contains the file name that was first \input by the user. This name is extended by 'log' and 'dvi' and 'fmt' in the names of TeX's output files.

⟨ Global variables 13 ⟩ +≡
name_in_progress: *boolean*; { is a file name being scanned? }
job_name: *str_number*; .{ principal file name }

528. Initially *job_name* = 0; it becomes nonzero as soon as the true name is known. We have *job_name* = 0 if and only if the 'log' file has not been opened, except of course for a short time just after *job_name* has become nonzero.

⟨ Initialize the output routines 55 ⟩ +≡
  $job\_name \leftarrow 0;$ $name\_in\_progress \leftarrow false;$

---

alpha_file = **packed file**, §25.
append_char = macro, §42.
back_input: **procedure**, §325.
buf_size = **const**, §11.
buffer: **array**, §30.
byte_file = **packed file**, §25.
cur_chr: *halfword*, §297.
cur_cmd: *eight_bits*, §297.
done = 30, §15.
end_name: **procedure**, §517.
exit = 10, §15.
file_name_size = **const**, §11.
fmt_file: *word_file*, §1305.
format_area_length = 11, §520.

format_default_length = 20, §520.
format_ext_length = 4, §520.
found = 40, §15.
get_x_token: **procedure**, §380.
incr = macro, §16.
last: 0 .. *buf_size*, §30.
loc = macro, §36.
make_string: **function**, §43.
max_strings = **const**, §11.
name_length: 0 .. *file_name_size*, §26.
name_of_file: **packed array**, §26.
other_char = 12, §207.

pack_buffered_name: **procedure**, §523.
pool_ptr: *pool_pointer*, §39.
pool_size = **const**, §11.
str_number = 0 .. *max_strings*, §38.
str_ptr: *str_number*, §39.
str_room = macro, §42.
update_terminal = macro, §34.
w_open_in: **function**, §27.
wake_up_terminal = macro, §34.
word_file = **file**, §113.
wterm_ln = macro, §56.
xord: **array**, §20.

529. Here is a routine that manufactures the output file names, assuming that $job\_name \neq 0$. It ignores and changes the current settings of cur_area and cur_ext.

define $pack\_cur\_name \equiv pack\_file\_name(cur\_name, cur\_area, cur\_ext)$

procedure $pack\_job\_name(s : str\_number)$;   { $s =$ ".log", ".dvi", or ".fmt" }
  begin $cur\_area \leftarrow$ ""; $cur\_ext \leftarrow s$; $cur\_name \leftarrow job\_name$; $pack\_cur\_name$;
  end;

530. If some trouble arises when TEX tries to open a file, the following routine calls upon the user to supply another file name. Parameter s is used in the error message to identify the type of file; parameter e is the default extension if none is given. Upon exit from the routine, variables cur_name, cur_area, cur_ext, and $name\_of\_file$ are ready for another attempt at file opening.

procedure $prompt\_file\_name(s, e : str\_number)$;
  label $done$;
  var $k: 0 .. buf\_size$;   { index into $buffer$ }
  begin if $interaction = scroll\_mode$ **then** $wake\_up\_terminal$;
  if $s =$ "input␣file␣name" **then** $print\_err($"I␣can´t␣find␣file␣`"$)$
  else $print\_err($"I␣can´t␣write␣on␣file␣`"$)$;
  $print\_file\_name(cur\_name, cur\_area, cur\_ext)$; $print($"´."$)$;
  if $e =$ ".tex" **then** $show\_context$;
  $print\_nl($"Please␣type␣another␣"$)$; $print(s)$;
  if $interaction < scroll\_mode$ **then**
    $fatal\_error($"***␣(job␣aborted,␣file␣error␣in␣nonstop␣mode)"$)$;
  $clear\_terminal$; $prompt\_input($":␣"$)$; ⟨Scan file name in the buffer 531⟩;
  if $cur\_ext =$ "" **then** $cur\_ext \leftarrow e$;
  $pack\_cur\_name$;
  end;

531. ⟨Scan file name in the buffer 531⟩ ≡
  begin $begin\_name$; $k \leftarrow first$;
  while $(buffer[k] =$ "␣"$) \wedge (k < last)$ **do** $incr(k)$;
  loop begin if $k = last$ **then goto** $done$;
    if $\neg more\_name(buffer[k])$ **then goto** $done$;
    $incr(k)$;
    end;
$done$: end_name;
  end

This code is used in section 530.

532. Here's an example of how these conventions are used. Whenever it is time to ship out a box of stuff, we shall use the macro $ensure\_dvi\_open$.

define *ensure_dvi_open* ≡
      if *output_file_name* = 0 **then**
        begin if *job_name* = 0 **then** *open_log_file*;
        pack_job_name(".dvi");
        while ¬*b_open_out*(*dvi_file*) **do** *prompt_file_name*("file␣name␣for␣output",".dvi");
        output_file_name ← *b_make_name_string*(*dvi_file*);
        end

⟨ Global variables 13 ⟩ +≡
dvi_file: *byte_file*; { the device-independent output goes here }
output_file_name: *str_number*; { full name of the output file }
log_name: *str_number*; { full name of the log file }

533. ⟨ Initialize the output routines 55 ⟩ +≡
  output_file_name ← 0;

534. The *open_log_file* routine is used to open the transcript file and to help it catch up to what has previously been printed on the terminal.

procedure *open_log_file*;
  var *old_setting*: 0 .. *max_selector*; { previous *selector* setting }
    k: 0 .. *buf_size*; { index into *months* and *buffer* }
    l: 0 .. *buf_size*; { end of first input line }
    months: **packed array** [1 .. 36] **of** *char*; { abbreviations of month names }
  begin *old_setting* ← *selector*;
  if *job_name* = 0 **then** *job_name* ← "texput";
  pack_job_name(".log");
  while ¬*a_open_out*(*log_file*) **do** ⟨ Try to get a different log file name 535 ⟩;
  log_name ← *a_make_name_string*(*log_file*); *selector* ← *log_only*;
  ⟨ Print the banner line, including the date and time 536 ⟩;
  input_stack[*input_ptr*] ← *cur_input*; { make sure bottom level is in memory }
  print_nl("**"); *l* ← *input_stack*[0].*limit_field*; { last position of first line }
  if *buffer*[*l*] = *end_line_char* **then** *decr*(*l*);
  for *k* ← 1 **to** *l* **do** *print*(*buffer*[*k*]);
  print_ln; { now the transcript file contains the first line of input }
  selector ← *old_setting* + 2; { *log_only* or *term_and_log* }
  end;

---

a_make_name_string: **function**, §525.
a_open_out: **function**, §27.
b_make_name_string: **function**, §525.
b_open_out: **function**, §27.
buf_size = **const**, §11.
buffer: **array**, §30.
byte_file = **packed file**, §25.
clear_terminal = macro, §34.
cur_area: *str_number*, §512.
cur_ext: *str_number*, §512.
cur_input: *in_state_record*, §301.
cur_name: *str_number*, §512.
decr = macro, §16.

done = 30, §15.
end_line_char = macro, §236.
end_name: **procedure**, §517.
fatal_error: **procedure**, §93.
first: 0 .. *buf_size*, §30.
incr = macro, §16.
input_ptr: 0 .. *stack_size*, §301.
input_stack: **array**, §301.
interaction: 0 .. 3, §73.
job_name: *str_number*, §527.
last: 0 .. *buf_size*, §30.
limit_field: *halfword*, §300.
log_file: *alpha_file*, §54.
log_only = 18, §54.
max_selector = 21, §54.

name_of_file: **packed array**, §26.
pack_file_name: **procedure**, §519.
print: **procedure**, §59.
print_err = macro, §73.
print_file_name: **procedure**, §518.
print_ln: **procedure**, §57.
print_nl: **procedure**, §62.
prompt_input = macro, §71.
scroll_mode = 2, §73.
selector: 0 .. 21, §54.
show_context: **procedure**, §311.
str_number = 0 .. *max_strings*, §38.
term_and_log = 19, §54.
wake_up_terminal = macro, §34.

535. Sometimes *open_log_file* is called at awkward moments when TEX is unable to print error messages or even to *show_context*. Therefore the program is careful not to call *prompt_file_name* if a fatal error could result.

Incidentally, the program always refers to the log file as a '**transcript file**', because some systems cannot use the extension '.log' for this file.

⟨ Try to get a different log file name 535 ⟩ ≡
  begin if *interaction* < *scroll_mode* **then** { bypass *fatal_error* }
    begin *print_err*("I␣can´t␣write␣on␣file␣`"); *print_file_name*(*cur_name*, *cur_area*, *cur_ext*);
    print("´.");
    job_name ← 0; *history* ← *fatal_error_stop*; *jump_out*;
    end; { abort the program without a log file }
  prompt_file_name("transcript␣file␣name", ".log");
  end

This code is used in section 534.

536. ⟨ Print the banner line, including the date and time 536 ⟩ ≡
  begin *wlog*(*banner*); *print*(*format_ident*); *print*("␣␣"); *print_int*(*day*); *print_char*("␣");
  months ← ´JANFEBMARAPRMAYJUNJULAUGSEPOCTNOVDEC´;
  for *k* ← 3 * *month* − 2 **to** 3 * *month* **do** *wlog*(*months*[*k*]);
  print_char("␣"); *print_int*(*year*); *print_char*("␣"); *print_two*(*time* **div** 60); *print_char*(":");
  print_two(*time* **mod** 60);
  end

This code is used in section 534.

537. Let's turn now to the procedure that is used to initiate file reading when an '\input' command is being processed.

procedure *start_input*; { TEX will \input something }
  label *done*;
  begin *scan_file_name*; { set *cur_name* to desired file name }
  if *cur_ext* = "" **then** *cur_ext* ← ".tex";
  pack_cur_name;
  loop begin *begin_file_reading*; { set up *cur_file* and new level of input }
    if *a_open_in*(*cur_file*) **then goto** *done*;
    if *cur_area* = "" **then**
      begin *pack_file_name*(*cur_name*, TEX_*area*, *cur_ext*);
      if *a_open_in*(*cur_file*) **then goto** *done*;
      end;
    end_file_reading; { remove the level that didn't work }
    prompt_file_name("input␣file␣name", ".tex");
    end;
done: *name* ← *a_make_name_string*(*cur_file*);
  if *job_name* = 0 **then**
    begin *job_name* ← *cur_name*; *open_log_file*;
    end;
      { *open_log_file* doesn't *show_context*, so *limit* and *loc* needn't be set to meaningful values yet }
  if *term_offset* + *length*(*name*) > *max_print_line* − 2 **then** *print_ln*
  else if (*term_offset* > 0) ∨ (*file_offset* > 0) **then** *print_char*("␣");
  print_char("("); *print*(*name*); *update_terminal*; *state* ← *new_line*;

if $name = str\_ptr - 1$ **then**   { we can conserve string pool space now }
   begin $flush\_string$; $name \leftarrow cur\_name$;
   end;
⟨ Read the first line of the new file 538 ⟩;
end;

538.   Here we have to remember to tell the $input\_ln$ routine not to start with a get. If the file is empty, it is considered to contain a single blank line.

⟨ Read the first line of the new file 538 ⟩ ≡
   begin if $\neg input\_ln(cur\_file, false)$ **then** $do\_nothing$;
   $firm\_up\_the\_line$;
   if $(end\_line\_char < 0) \vee (end\_line\_char > 127)$ **then** $decr(limit)$
   else $buffer[limit] \leftarrow end\_line\_char$;
   $first \leftarrow limit + 1$; $loc \leftarrow start$; $line \leftarrow 1$;
   end

This code is used in section 537.

$a\_make\_name\_string$: **function**,
  §525.
a_open_in: **function**, §27.
$banner$ = macro, §2.
$begin\_file\_reading$: **procedure**,
  §328.
$buffer$: **array**, §30.
cur_area: str_number, §512.
cur_ext: str_number, §512.
cur_file = macro, §304.
cur_name: str_number, §512.
day = macro, §236.
$decr$ = macro, §16.
$do\_nothing$ = macro, §16.
$done$ = 30, §15.
$end\_file\_reading$: **procedure**, §329.
end_line_char = macro, §236.
$fatal\_error$: **procedure**, §93.
$fatal\_error\_stop$ = 3, §76.
$file\_offset$: $0 .. max\_print\_line$, §54.
$firm\_up\_the\_line$: **procedure**, §363.

$first$: $0 .. buf\_size$, §30.
$flush\_string$ = macro, §44.
$format\_ident$: str_number, §1299.
$history$: $0 .. 3$, §76.
$input\_ln$: **function**, §31.
$interaction$: $0 .. 3$, §73.
job_name: str_number, §527.
$jump\_out$: **procedure**, §81.
k: $0 .. buf\_size$, §534.
$length$ = macro, §40.
$limit$ = macro, §302.
$line$: $integer$, §304.
loc = macro, §36.
max_print_line = **const**, §11.
$month$ = macro, §236.
$months$: **packed array**, §534.
$name$ = macro, §302.
new_line = 33, §303.
$pack\_cur\_name$ = macro, §529.
$pack\_file\_name$: **procedure**, §519.
$print$: **procedure**, §59.

$print\_char$: **procedure**, §58.
$print\_err$ = macro, §73.
$print\_file\_name$: **procedure**, §518.
$print\_int$: **procedure**, §65.
$print\_ln$: **procedure**, §57.
$print\_two$: **procedure**, §66.
$prompt\_file\_name$: **procedure**,
  §530.
$scan\_file\_name$: **procedure**, §526.
$scroll\_mode$ = 2, §73.
$show\_context$: **procedure**, §311.
$start$ = macro, §302.
$state$ = macro, §302.
str_ptr: str_number, §39.
$term\_offset$: $0 .. max\_print\_line$,
  §54.
TEX_area = macro, §514.
$time$ = macro, §236.
$update\_terminal$ = macro, §34.
$wlog$ = macro, §56.
$year$ = macro, §236.

539.   Font metric data.   TeX gets its knowledge about fonts from font metric files, also called **TFM** files; the 'T' in 'TFM' stands for TeX, but other programs know about them too.

The information in a **TFM** file appears in a sequence of 8-bit bytes. Since the number of bytes is always a multiple of 4, we could also regard the file as a sequence of 32-bit words, but TeX uses the byte interpretation. The format of **TFM** files was designed by Lyle Ramshaw in 1980. The intent is to convey a lot of different kinds of information in a compact but useful form.

⟨ Global variables 13 ⟩ +≡
tfm_file: *byte_file*;

540.   The first 24 bytes (6 words) of a **TFM** file contain twelve 16-bit integers that give the lengths of the various subsequent portions of the file. These twelve integers are, in order:

$$lf = \text{length of the entire file, in words};$$
$$lh = \text{length of the header data, in words};$$
$$bc = \text{smallest character code in the font};$$
$$ec = \text{largest character code in the font};$$
$$nw = \text{number of words in the width table};$$
$$nh = \text{number of words in the height table};$$
$$nd = \text{number of words in the depth table};$$
$$ni = \text{number of words in the italic correction table};$$
$$nl = \text{number of words in the lig/kern table};$$
$$nk = \text{number of words in the kern table};$$
$$ne = \text{number of words in the extensible character table};$$
$$np = \text{number of font parameter words}.$$

They are all nonnegative and less than 2^{15}. We must have $bc - 1 \le ec \le 255$, and

$$lf = 6 + lh + (ec - bc + 1) + nw + nh + nd + ni + nl + nk + ne + np.$$

Note that a font may contain as many as 256 characters (if $bc = 0$ and $ec = 255$), and as few as 0 characters (if $bc = ec + 1$).

Incidentally, when two or more 8-bit bytes are combined to form an integer of 16 or more bits, the most significant bytes appear first in the file. This is called BigEndian order.

541.   The rest of the **TFM** file may be regarded as a sequence of ten data arrays having the informal specification

$$header : \textbf{array} \; [0 .. \, lh - 1] \; \textbf{of} \; stuff$$
$$char\_info : \textbf{array} \; [bc .. \, ec] \; \textbf{of} \; char\_info\_word$$
$$width : \textbf{array} \; [0 .. \, nw - 1] \; \textbf{of} \; fix\_word$$
$$height : \textbf{array} \; [0 .. \, nh - 1] \; \textbf{of} \; fix\_word$$
$$depth : \textbf{array} \; [0 .. \, nd - 1] \; \textbf{of} \; fix\_word$$
$$italic : \textbf{array} \; [0 .. \, ni - 1] \; \textbf{of} \; fix\_word$$
$$lig\_kern : \textbf{array} \; [0 .. \, nl - 1] \; \textbf{of} \; lig\_kern\_command$$
$$kern : \textbf{array} \; [0 .. \, nk - 1] \; \textbf{of} \; fix\_word$$
$$exten : \textbf{array} \; [0 .. \, ne - 1] \; \textbf{of} \; extensible\_recipe$$
$$param : \textbf{array} \; [1 .. \, np] \; \textbf{of} \; fix\_word$$

The most important data type used here is a *fix_word*, which is a 32-bit representation of a binary fraction. A *fix_word* is a signed quantity, with the two's complement of the entire word used to represent negation. Of the 32 bits in a *fix_word*, exactly 12 are to the left of the binary point; thus, the largest *fix_word* value is $2048 - 2^{-20}$, and the smallest is -2048. We will see below, however, that all but two of the *fix_word* values must lie between -16 and $+16$.

542.   The first data array is a block of header information, which contains general facts about the font. The header must contain at least two words, *header*[0] and *header*[1], whose meaning is explained below. Additional header information of use to other software routines might also be included, but TₑX82 does not need to know about such details. For example, 16 more words of header information are in use at the Xerox Palo Alto Research Center; the first ten specify the character coding scheme used (e.g., 'XEROX text' or 'TeX math symbols'), the next five give the font identifier (e.g., 'HELVETICA' or 'CMSY'), and the last gives the "face byte." The program that converts DVI files to Xerox printing format gets this information by looking at the TFM file, which it needs to read anyway because of other information that is not explicitly repeated in DVI format. Extensions of TₑX for oriental languages should be able to identify oriental fonts by means of this additional header information.

header[0] is a 32-bit check sum that TₑX will copy into the DVI output file. Later on when the DVI file is printed, possibly on another computer, the actual font that gets used is supposed to have a check sum that agrees with the one in the TFM file used by TₑX. In this way, users will be warned about potential incompatibilities. (However, if the check sum is zero in either the font file or the TFM file, no check is made.) The actual relation between this check sum and the rest of the TFM file is not important; the check sum is simply an identification number with the property that incompatible fonts almost always have distinct check sums.

header[1] is a *fix_word* containing the design size of the font, in units of TₑX points. This number must be at least 1.0; it is fairly arbitrary, but usually the design size is 10.0 for a "10 point" font, i.e., a font that was designed to look best at a 10-point size, whatever that really means. When a TₑX user asks for a font 'at δ pt', the effect is to override the design size and replace it by δ, and to multiply the x and y coordinates of the points in the font image by a factor of δ divided by the design size. *All other dimensions in the* TFM *file are fix_word numbers in design-size units*, with the exception of *param*[1] (which denotes the slant ratio). Thus, for example, the value of *param*[6], which defines the em unit, is often the *fix_word* value $2^{20} = 1.0$, since many fonts have a design size equal to one em. The other dimensions must be less than 16 design-size units in absolute value; thus, *header*[1] and *param*[1] are the only *fix_word* entries in the whole TFM file whose first byte might be something besides 0 or 255.

byte_file = **packed file**, §25.   *extensible_recipe*, §546.   *param* = macro, §558.
char_info_word, §543.   *lig_kern_command*, §545.

543. Next comes the *char_info* array, which contains one *char_info_word* per character. Each word in this part of the file contains six fields packed into four bytes as follows.

first byte: *width_index* (8 bits)
second byte: *height_index* (4 bits) times 16, plus *depth_index* (4 bits)
third byte: *italic_index* (6 bits) times 4, plus *tag* (2 bits)
fourth byte: *remainder* (8 bits)

The actual width of a character is *width*[*width_index*], in design-size units; this is a device for compressing information, since many characters have the same width. Since it is quite common for many characters to have the same height, depth, or italic correction, the TFM format imposes a limit of 16 different heights, 16 different depths, and 64 different italic corrections.

The italic correction of a character has two different uses. (a) In ordinary text, the italic correction is added to the width only if the TeX user specifies '\/' after the character. (b) In math formulas, the italic correction is always added to the width, except with respect to the positioning of subscripts.

Incidentally, the relation $width[0] = height[0] = depth[0] = italic[0] = 0$ should always hold, so that an index of zero implies a value of zero. The *width_index* should never be zero unless the character does not exist in the font, since a character is valid if and only if it lies between *bc* and *ec* and has a nonzero *width_index*.

544. The *tag* field in a *char_info_word* has four values that explain how to interpret the *remainder* field.

$tag = 0$ (*no_tag*) means that *remainder* is unused.

$tag = 1$ (*lig_tag*) means that this character has a ligature/kerning program starting at position *remainder* in the *lig_kern* array.

$tag = 2$ (*list_tag*) means that this character is part of a chain of characters of ascending sizes, and not the largest in the chain. The *remainder* field gives the character code of the next larger character.

$tag = 3$ (*ext_tag*) means that this character code represents an extensible character, i.e., a character that is built up of smaller pieces so that it can be made arbitrarily large. The pieces are specified in *exten*[*remainder*].

Characters with $tag = 2$ and $tag = 3$ are treated as characters with $tag = 0$ unless they are used in special circumstances in math formulas. For example, the \sum operation looks for a *list_tag*, and the \left operation looks for both *list_tag* and *ext_tag*.

define *no_tag* = 0   { vanilla character }
define *lig_tag* = 1   { character has a ligature/kerning program }
define *list_tag* = 2   { character has a successor in a charlist }
define *ext_tag* = 3   { character is extensible }

545. The *lig_kern* array contains instructions in a simple programming language that explains what to do for special letter pairs. Each word in this array is a *lig_kern_command* of four bytes.

first byte: *stop_bit*, indicates that this is the final program step if the byte is 128 or more.

second byte: *next_char*, "if *next_char* follows the current character, then perform the operation and stop, otherwise continue."

third byte: *op_bit*, indicates a ligature step if less than 128, a kern step otherwise.

fourth byte: *remainder*.

In a ligature step the current character and *next_char* are replaced by the single character whose code is *remainder*. In a kern step, an additional space equal to *kern*[*remainder*] is inserted between the current character and *next_char*. (The value of *kern*[*remainder*] is often negative, so that the characters are brought closer together by kerning; but it might be positive.)

define *stop_flag* = 128 + *min_quarterword*   { value indicating 'STOP' in a lig/kern program }
define *kern_flag* = 128 + *min_quarterword*   { op code for a kern step }
define *stop_bit*(**#**) ≡ **#**.*b0*
define *next_char*(**#**) ≡ **#**.*b1*
define *op_bit*(**#**) ≡ **#**.*b2*
define *rem_byte*(**#**) ≡ **#**.*b3*

546. Extensible characters are specified by an *extensible_recipe*, which consists of four bytes called *top*, *mid*, *bot*, and *rep* (in this order). These bytes are the character codes of individual pieces used to build up a large symbol. If *top*, *mid*, or *bot* are zero, they are not present in the built-up result. For example, an extensible vertical line is like an extensible bracket, except that the top and bottom pieces are missing.

Let T, M, B, and R denote the respective pieces, or an empty box if the piece isn't present. Then the extensible characters have the form $TR^k MR^k B$ from top to bottom, for some $k \geq 0$, unless M is absent; in the latter case we can have $TR^k B$ for both even and odd values of k. The width of the extensible character is the width of R; and the height-plus-depth is the sum of the individual height-plus-depths of the components used, since the pieces are butted together in a vertical list.

define *ext_top*(**#**) ≡ **#**.*b0*   { *top* piece in a recipe }
define *ext_mid*(**#**) ≡ **#**.*b1*   { *mid* piece in a recipe }
define *ext_bot*(**#**) ≡ **#**.*b2*   { *bot* piece in a recipe }
define *ext_rep*(**#**) ≡ **#**.*b3*   { *rep* piece in a recipe }

---

b0: *quarterword*, §113.   *b3*: *quarterword*, §113.   *ec*: *halfword*, §560.
b1: *quarterword*, §113.   *bc*: *halfword*, §560.   *min_quarterword* = 0, §110.
b2: *quarterword*, §113.   *char_info* = macro, §554.

547. The final portion of a TFM file is the *param* array, which is another sequence of *fix_word* values.

param[1] = *slant* is the amount of italic slant, which is used to help position accents. For example, *slant* = .25 means that when you go up one unit, you also go .25 units to the right. The *slant* is a pure number; it's the only *fix_word* other than the design size itself that is not scaled by the design size.

param[2] = *space* is the normal spacing between words in text. Note that character "␣" in the font need not have anything to do with blank spaces.

param[3] = *space_stretch* is the amount of glue stretching between words.

param[4] = *space_shrink* is the amount of glue shrinking between words.

param[5] = *x_height* is the size of one ex in the font; it is also the height of letters for which accents don't have to be raised or lowered.

param[6] = *quad* is the size of one em in the font.

param[7] = *extra_space* is the amount added to *param*[2] at the ends of sentences.

If fewer than seven parameters are present, TeX sets the missing parameters to zero. Fonts used for math symbols are required to have additional parameter information, which is explained later.

> **define** *slant_code* = 1
> **define** *space_code* = 2
> **define** *space_stretch_code* = 3
> **define** *space_shrink_code* = 4
> **define** *x_height_code* = 5
> **define** *quad_code* = 6
> **define** *extra_space_code* = 7

548. So that is what TFM files hold. Since TeX has to absorb such information about lots of fonts, it stores most of the data in a large array called *font_info*. Each item of *font_info* is a *memory_word*; the *fix_word* data gets converted into *scaled* entries, while everything else goes into words of type *four_quarters*.

When the user defines \font\f, say, TeX assigns an internal number to the user's font \f. Adding this number to *font_id_base* gives the *eqtb* location of a "frozen" control sequence that will always select the font.

⟨ Types in the outer block 18 ⟩ +≡
  internal_font_number = *font_base* .. *font_max*; { *font* in a *char_node* }

549. Here now is the (rather formidable) array of font arrays.

⟨ Global variables 13 ⟩ +≡
font_info: **array** [0 .. *font_mem_size*] **of** *memory_word*; { the big collection of font data }
fmem_ptr: 0 .. *font_mem_size*; { first unused word of *font_info* }
font_ptr: *internal_font_number*; { largest internal font number in use }
font_check: **array** [*internal_font_number*] **of** *four_quarters*; { check sum }
font_size: **array** [*internal_font_number*] **of** *scaled*; { "at" size }
font_dsize: **array** [*internal_font_number*] **of** *scaled*; { "design" size }
font_params: **array** [*internal_font_number*] **of** *halfword*; { how many font parameters are present }
font_name: **array** [*internal_font_number*] **of** *str_number*; { name of the font }
font_area: **array** [*internal_font_number*] **of** *str_number*; { area of the font }
font_bc: **array** [*internal_font_number*] **of** *eight_bits*; { beginning (smallest) character code }

font_ec: **array** [*internal_font_number*] **of** *eight_bits*;   { ending (largest) character code }
font_glue: **array** [*internal_font_number*] **of** *pointer*;
          { glue specification for interword space, *null* if not allocated }
font_used: **array** [*internal_font_number*] **of** *boolean*;
          { has a character from this font actually appeared in the output? }
hyphen_char: **array** [*internal_font_number*] **of** *integer*;   { current \hyphenchar values }
skew_char: **array** [*internal_font_number*] **of** *integer*;   { current \skewchar values }

550.   Besides the arrays just enumerated, we have directory arrays that make it easy to get at the individual entries in *font_info*. For example, the *char_info* data for character c in font f will be in *font_info*[*char_base*[f] + c].*qqqq*; and if w is the *width_index* part of this word (the *b0* field), the width of the character is *font_info*[*width_base*[f] + w].*sc*. (These formulas assume that *min_quarterword* has already been added to c and to w, since TeX stores its quarterwords that way.)

⟨ Global variables 13 ⟩ +≡
char_base: **array** [*internal_font_number*] **of** *integer*;   { base addresses for *char_info* }
width_base: **array** [*internal_font_number*] **of** *integer*;   { base addresses for widths }
height_base: **array** [*internal_font_number*] **of** *integer*;   { base addresses for heights }
depth_base: **array** [*internal_font_number*] **of** *integer*;   { base addresses for depths }
italic_base: **array** [*internal_font_number*] **of** *integer*;   { base addresses for italic corrections }
lig_kern_base: **array** [*internal_font_number*] **of** *integer*;
          { base addresses for ligature/kerning programs }
kern_base: **array** [*internal_font_number*] **of** *integer*;   { base addresses for kerns }
exten_base: **array** [*internal_font_number*] **of** *integer*;   { base addresses for extensible recipes }
param_base: **array** [*internal_font_number*] **of** *integer*;   { base addresses for font parameters }

551.   ⟨ Set initial values of key variables 21 ⟩ +≡
     for k ← *font_base* **to** *font_max* **do** *font_used*[k] ← *false*;

---

b0: *quarterword*, §113.
char_info = macro, §554.
char_node, §134.
eight_bits = 0 . . 255, §25.
eqtb: **array**, §253.
extra_space = macro, §558.
fix_word, §541.
font = macro, §134.
font_base = 0, §12.
font_id_base = 2368, §222.
font_max = **const**, §11.

font_mem_size = **const**, §11.
four_quarters = **packed record**,
     §113.
halfword = *min_halfword* . .
     max_halfword, §113.
k: *integer*, §163.
memory_word = **record**, §113.
min_quarterword = 0, §110.
null = macro, §115.
param = macro, §558.
pointer = macro, §115.

qqqq: *four_quarters*, §113.
quad = macro, §558.
sc = macro, §113.
scaled = *integer*, §101.
slant = macro, §558.
space = macro, §558.
space_shrink = macro, §558.
space_stretch = macro, §558.
str_number = 0 . . *max_strings*, §38.
width_index, §543.
x_height = macro, §558.

552. TₑX always knows at least one font, namely the null font. It has no characters, and its seven parameters are all equal to zero.

⟨ Initialize table entries (done by INITEX only) 164 ⟩ +≡
  $font\_ptr \leftarrow null\_font$; $fmem\_ptr \leftarrow 7$; $font\_name[null\_font] \leftarrow$ "nullfont";
  $font\_area[null\_font] \leftarrow$ ""; $hyphen\_char[null\_font] \leftarrow$ "-"; $skew\_char[null\_font] \leftarrow -1$;
  $font\_bc[null\_font] \leftarrow 1$; $font\_ec[null\_font] \leftarrow 0$; $font\_size[null\_font] \leftarrow 0$; $font\_dsize[null\_font] \leftarrow 0$;
  $char\_base[null\_font] \leftarrow 0$; $width\_base[null\_font] \leftarrow 0$; $height\_base[null\_font] \leftarrow 0$;
  $depth\_base[null\_font] \leftarrow 0$; $italic\_base[null\_font] \leftarrow 0$; $lig\_kern\_base[null\_font] \leftarrow 0$;
  $kern\_base[null\_font] \leftarrow 0$; $exten\_base[null\_font] \leftarrow 0$; $font\_glue[null\_font] \leftarrow null$;
  $font\_params[null\_font] \leftarrow 7$; $param\_base[null\_font] \leftarrow -1$;
  for $k \leftarrow 0$ **to** 6 **do** $font\_info[k].sc \leftarrow 0$;

553. ⟨ Put each of TₑX's primitives into the hash table 226 ⟩ +≡
  $primitive($"nullfont"$, set\_font, null\_font)$; $text(frozen\_null\_font) \leftarrow$ "nullfont";
  $eqtb[frozen\_null\_font] \leftarrow eqtb[cur\_val]$;

554. Of course we want to define macros that suppress the detail of how font information is actually packed, so that we don't have to write things like

$$font\_info[width\_base[f] + font\_info[char\_base[f] + c].qqqq.b0].sc$$

too often. The WEB definitions here make $char\_info(f)(c)$ the $four\_quarters$ word of font information corresponding to character c of font f. If q is such a word, $char\_width(f)(q)$ will be the character's width; hence the long formula above is at least abbreviated to

$$char\_width(f)(char\_info(f)(c)).$$

Usually, of course, we will fetch q first and look at several of its fields at the same time.

The italic correction of a character will be denoted by $char\_italic(f)(q)$, so it is analogous to $char\_width$. But we will get at the height and depth in a slightly different way, since we usually want to compute both height and depth if we want either one. The value of $height\_depth(q)$ will be the 8-bit quantity

$$b = height\_index \times 16 + depth\_index,$$

and if b is such a byte we will write $char\_height(f)(b)$ and $char\_depth(f)(b)$ for the height and depth of the character c for which $q = char\_info(f)(c)$. Got that?

The tag field will be called $char\_tag(q)$; the remainder byte will be called $rem\_byte(q)$, using a macro that we have already defined above.

Access to a character's $width$, $height$, $depth$, and tag fields is part of TₑX's inner loop, so we want these macros to produce code that is as fast as possible under the circumstances.

  define $char\_info\_end(\#) \equiv \# \ ] \ .qqqq$
  define $char\_info(\#) \equiv font\_info \ [\ char\_base[\#] + char\_info\_end$
  define $char\_width\_end(\#) \equiv \#.b0 \ ] \ .sc$
  define $char\_width(\#) \equiv font\_info \ [\ width\_base[\#] + char\_width\_end$
  define $char\_exists(\#) \equiv (\#.b0 > min\_quarterword)$
  define $char\_italic\_end(\#) \equiv (qo(\#.b2)) \ \textbf{div} \ 4 \ ] \ .sc$
  define $char\_italic(\#) \equiv font\_info \ [\ italic\_base[\#] + char\_italic\_end$

define $height\_depth(\#) \equiv qo(\#.b1)$
define $char\_height\_end(\#) \equiv (\#) \textbf{ div } 16 \;] \; .sc$
define $char\_height(\#) \equiv font\_info \; [\; height\_base[\#] + char\_height\_end$
define $char\_depth\_end(\#) \equiv (\#) \textbf{ mod } 16 \;] \; .sc$
define $char\_depth(\#) \equiv font\_info \; [\; depth\_base[\#] + char\_depth\_end$
define $char\_tag(\#) \equiv ((qo(\#.b2)) \textbf{ mod } 4)$

555. The global variable *null_character* is set up to be a word of *char_info* for a character that doesn't exist. Such a word provides a convenient way to deal with erroneous situations.

⟨ Global variables 13 ⟩ +≡
$null\_character: four\_quarters;$ { nonexistent character information }

556. ⟨ Set initial values of key variables 21 ⟩ +≡
$null\_character.b0 \leftarrow min\_quarterword; \; null\_character.b1 \leftarrow min\_quarterword;$
$null\_character.b2 \leftarrow min\_quarterword; \; null\_character.b3 \leftarrow min\_quarterword;$

557. Here are some macros that help process ligatures and kerns. We write $char\_kern(f)(j)$ to find the amount of kerning specified by kerning command j in font f.

define $lig\_kern\_start(\#) \equiv lig\_kern\_base[\#] + rem\_byte$ { beginning of lig/kern program }
define $char\_kern\_end(\#) \equiv rem\_byte(\#) \;] \; .sc$
define $char\_kern(\#) \equiv font\_info \; [\; kern\_base[\#] + char\_kern\_end$

---

b0: *quarterword*, §113.
b1: *quarterword*, §113.
b2: *quarterword*, §113.
b3: *quarterword*, §113.
char_base: **array**, §550.
cur_val: *integer*, §410.
depth_base: **array**, §550.
depth_index, §543.
eqtb: **array**, §253.
exten_base: **array**, §550.
fmem_ptr: 0 .. *font_mem_size*, §549.
font_area: **array**, §549.
font_bc: **array**, §549.
font_dsize: **array**, §549.
font_ec: **array**, §549.

font_glue: **array**, §549.
font_name: **array**, §549.
font_params: **array**, §549.
font_ptr: *internal_font_number*, §549.
font_size: **array**, §549.
four_quarters = **packed record**, §113.
frozen_null_font = 2368, §222.
height_base: **array**, §550.
height_index, §543.
hyphen_char: **array**, §549.
italic_base: **array**, §550.
k: *integer*, §163.
kern_base: **array**, §550.

lig_kern_base: **array**, §550.
min_quarterword = 0, §110.
null = macro, §115.
null_font = macro, §232.
param_base: **array**, §550.
primitive: **procedure**, §264.
qo = macro, §112.
qqqq: *four_quarters*, §113.
rem_byte = macro, §545.
sc = macro, §113.
set_font = 86, §209.
skew_char: **array**, §549.
tag, §543.
text = macro, §256.
width_base: **array**, §550.

558.   Font parameters are referred to as *slant*(*f*), *space*(*f*), etc.

> **define** *param_end*(#) ≡ *param_base*[#]] .*sc*
> **define** *param*(#) ≡ *font_info* [# + *param_end*
> **define** *slant* ≡ *param*(*slant_code*)   { slant to the right, per unit distance upward }
> **define** *space* ≡ *param*(*space_code*)   { normal space between words }
> **define** *space_stretch* ≡ *param*(*space_stretch_code*)   { stretch between words }
> **define** *space_shrink* ≡ *param*(*space_shrink_code*)   { shrink between words }
> **define** *x_height* ≡ *param*(*x_height_code*)   { one ex }
> **define** *quad* ≡ *param*(*quad_code*)   { one em }
> **define** *extra_space* ≡ *param*(*extra_space_code*)   { additional space at end of sentence }

⟨ The em width for *cur_font* 558 ⟩ ≡ *quad*(*cur_font*)

This code is used in section 455.

559.   ⟨ The x-height for *cur_font* 559 ⟩ ≡ *x_height*(*cur_font*)

This code is used in section 455.

560.   TEX checks the information of a **TFM** file for validity as the file is being read in, so that no further checks will be needed when typesetting is going on. The somewhat tedious subroutine that does this is called *read_font_info*. It has four parameters: the user font identifier *u*, the file name and area strings *nom* and *aire*, and the "at" size *s*. If *s* is negative, its the negative of a scale factor to be applied to the design size; $s = -1000$ is the normal case. Otherwise *s* will be substituted for the design size; in this case, *s* must be positive and less than 2048 pt (i.e., it must be less than 2^{27} when considered as an integer).

The subroutine opens and closes a global file variable called *tfm_file*. It returns the value of the internal font number that was just loaded. If an error is detected, an error message is issued and no font information is stored; *null_font* is returned in this case.

> **define** *bad_tfm* = 11   { label for *read_font_info* }
> **define** *abort* ≡ **goto** *bad_tfm*   { do this when the **TFM** data is wrong }

function *read_font_info*(*u* : *pointer*; *nom*, *aire* : *str_number*; *s* : *scaled*): *internal_font_number*;
      { input a **TFM** file }
  label *done*, *bad_tfm*, *not_found*;
  var *k*: 0 .. *font_mem_size*;   { index into *font_info* }
    file_opened: *boolean*;   { was *tfm_file* successfully opened? }
    lf, *lh*, *bc*, *ec*, *nw*, *nh*, *nd*, *ni*, *nl*, *nk*, *ne*, *np*: *halfword*;   { sizes of subfiles }
    f: *internal_font_number*;   { the new font's number }
    g: *internal_font_number*;   { the number to return }
    a, *b*, *c*, *d*: *eight_bits*;   { byte variables }
    qw: *four_quarters*; *sw*: *scaled*;   { accumulators }
    z: *scaled*;   { the design size or the "at" size }
    alpha: *integer*; *beta*: 1 .. 16;   { auxiliary quantities used in fixed-point multiplication }
  begin *g* ← *null_font*;
⟨ Read and check the font data; *abort* if the **TFM** file is malformed; if there's no room for this font, say
    so and **goto** *done*; otherwise *incr*(*font_ptr*) and **goto** *done* 562 ⟩;
bad_tfm: ⟨ Report that the font won't be loaded 561 ⟩;
done: *b_close*(*tfm_file*); *read_font_info* ← *g*;
  end;

561.   There are programs called TFtoPL and PLtoTF that convert between the TFM format and a symbolic property-list format that can be easily edited. These programs contain extensive diagnostic information, so TeX does not have to bother giving precise details about why it rejects a particular TFM file.

> **define** *start_font_error_message* ≡ *print_err*("Font␣"); *sprint_cs*(*u*); *print_char*("=");
>   *print_file_name*(*nom*, *aire*, "");
>   **if** *s* ≥ 0 **then**
>   **begin** *print*("␣at␣"); *print_scaled*(*s*); *print*("pt");
>   **end**
>   **else if** *s* ≠ −1000 **then**
>   **begin** *print*("␣scaled␣"); *print_int*(−*s*);
>   **end**

⟨ Report that the font won't be loaded 561 ⟩ ≡
  start_font_error_message;
  if *file_opened* **then** *print*("␣not␣loadable:␣Bad␣metric␣(TFM)␣file")
  else *print*("␣not␣loadable:␣Metric␣(TFM)␣file␣not␣found");
  help5("I␣wasn´t␣able␣to␣read␣the␣size␣data␣for␣this␣font,")
  ("so␣I␣will␣ignore␣the␣font␣specification.")
  ("[Wizards␣can␣fix␣TFM␣files␣using␣TFtoPL/PLtoTF.]")
  ("You␣might␣try␣inserting␣a␣different␣font␣spec;")
  ("e.g.,␣type␣`I\font<same␣font␣id>=<substitute␣font␣name>´."); *error*

This code is used in section 560.

---

b_close: **procedure**, §28.
cur_font = macro, §230.
done = 30, §15.
eight_bits = 0 .. 255, §25.
error: **procedure**, §82.
extra_space_code = 7, §547.
font_mem_size = **const**, §11.
font_ptr: *internal_font_number*,
    §549.
four_quarters = **packed record**,
    §113.
halfword = *min_halfword* ..
    max_halfword, §113.

help5 = macro, §79.
incr = macro, §16.
internal_font_number = 0 .. *font_max*,
    §548.
not_found = 45, §15.
null_font = macro, §232.
param_base: **array**, §550.
pointer = macro, §115.
print: **procedure**, §59.
print_char: **procedure**, §58.
print_err = macro, §73.
print_file_name: **procedure**, §518.
print_int: **procedure**, §65.

print_scaled: **procedure**, §103.
quad_code = 6, §547.
sc = macro, §113.
scaled = *integer*, §101.
slant_code = 1, §547.
space_code = 2, §547.
space_shrink_code = 4, §547.
space_stretch_code = 3, §547.
sprint_cs: **procedure**, §263.
str_number = 0 .. *max_strings*, §38.
tfm_file: *byte_file*, §539.
x_height_code = 5, §547.

562. ⟨ Read and check the font data; *abort* if the TFM file is malformed; if there's no room for this
font, say so and **goto** *done*; otherwise *incr*(*font_ptr*) and **goto** *done* 562 ⟩ ≡
⟨ Open *tfm_file* for input 563 ⟩;
⟨ Read the TFM size fields 565 ⟩;
⟨ Use size fields to allocate font information 566 ⟩;
⟨ Read the TFM header 568 ⟩;
⟨ Read character data 569 ⟩;
⟨ Read box dimensions 571 ⟩;
⟨ Read ligature/kern program 573 ⟩;
⟨ Read extensible character recipes 574 ⟩;
⟨ Read font parameters 575 ⟩;
⟨ Make final adjustments and **goto** *done* 576 ⟩

This code is used in section 560.

563. ⟨ Open *tfm_file* for input 563 ⟩ ≡
file_opened ← *false*;
if *aire* = "" **then** *pack_file_name*(*nom*, $T_{E}X\_font\_area$, ".tfm")
else *pack_file_name*(*nom*, *aire*, ".tfm");
if ¬*b_open_in*(*tfm_file*) **then** *abort*;
file_opened ← *true*

This code is used in section 562.

564. Note: A malformed TFM file might be shorter than it claims to be; thus *eof*(*tfm_file*) might
be true when *read_font_info* refers to *tfm_file*↑ or when it says *get*(*tfm_file*). If such circumstances
cause system error messages, you will have to defeat them somehow, for example by defining *fget*
to be '**begin** *get*(*tfm_file*); **if** *eof*(*tfm_file*) **then** *abort*; **end**'.

define *fget* ≡ *get*(*tfm_file*)
define *fbyte* ≡ *tfm_file*↑
define *read_sixteen*(#) ≡
            begin # ← *fbyte*;
            if # > 127 **then** *abort*;
            fget; # ← # ∗ ´400 + *fbyte*;
            end
define *store_four_quarters*(#) ≡
            begin *fget*; *a* ← *fbyte*; *qw.b0* ← *qi*(*a*); *fget*; *b* ← *fbyte*; *qw.b1* ← *qi*(*b*); *fget*; *c* ← *fbyte*;
            qw.b2 ← *qi*(*c*); *fget*; *d* ← *fbyte*; *qw.b3* ← *qi*(*d*); # ← *qw*;
            end

565. ⟨ Read the TFM size fields 565 ⟩ ≡
begin *read_sixteen*(*lf*); *fget*; *read_sixteen*(*lh*); *fget*; *read_sixteen*(*bc*); *fget*; *read_sixteen*(*ec*);
if (*bc* > *ec* + 1) ∨ (*ec* > 255) **then** *abort*;
fget; *read_sixteen*(*nw*); *fget*; *read_sixteen*(*nh*); *fget*; *read_sixteen*(*nd*); *fget*; *read_sixteen*(*ni*); *fget*;
read_sixteen(*nl*); *fget*; *read_sixteen*(*nk*); *fget*; *read_sixteen*(*ne*); *fget*; *read_sixteen*(*np*);
if *lf* ≠ 6 + *lh* + (*ec* − *bc* + 1) + *nw* + *nh* + *nd* + *ni* + *nl* + *nk* + *ne* + *np* **then** *abort*;
end

This code is used in section 562.

566. The preliminary settings of the index-offset variables $char\_base$, $width\_base$, lig_kern_base, $kern\_base$, and $exten\_base$ will be corrected later by subtracting $min\_quarterword$ from them; and we will subtract 1 from $param\_base$ too. It's best to forget about such anomalies until later.

⟨ Use size fields to allocate font information 566 ⟩ ≡

 $lf \leftarrow lf - 6 - lh$; { lf words should be loaded into $font\_info$ }

 if $np < 7$ **then** $lf \leftarrow lf + 7 - np$; { at least seven parameters will appear }

 if $(font\_ptr = font\_max) \vee (fmem\_ptr + lf > font\_mem\_size)$ **then**

  ⟨ Apologize for not loading the font, **goto** *done* 567 ⟩;

 $f \leftarrow font\_ptr + 1$; $char\_base[f] \leftarrow fmem\_ptr - bc$; $width\_base[f] \leftarrow char\_base[f] + ec + 1$;

 $height\_base[f] \leftarrow width\_base[f] + nw$; $depth\_base[f] \leftarrow height\_base[f] + nh$;

 $italic\_base[f] \leftarrow depth\_base[f] + nd$; $lig\_kern\_base[f] \leftarrow italic\_base[f] + ni$;

 $kern\_base[f] \leftarrow lig\_kern\_base[f] + nl$; $exten\_base[f] \leftarrow kern\_base[f] + nk$;

 $param\_base[f] \leftarrow exten\_base[f] + ne$

This code is used in section 562.

567. ⟨ Apologize for not loading the font, **goto** *done* 567 ⟩ ≡

 begin $start\_font\_error\_message$; $print$("␣not␣loaded:␣Not␣enough␣room␣left");

 $help4$("I´m␣afraid␣I␣won´t␣be␣able␣to␣make␣use␣of␣this␣font,")

 ("because␣my␣memory␣for␣character-size␣data␣is␣too␣small.")

 ("If␣you´re␣really␣stuck,␣ask␣a␣wizard␣to␣enlarge␣me.")

 ("Or␣maybe␣try␣`I\font<same␣font␣id>=<name␣of␣loaded␣font>´."); $error$; **goto** *done*;

 end

This code is used in section 566.

---

a: $eight\_bits$, §560.

$abort$ = macro, §560.

$aire$: str_number, §560.

b: $eight\_bits$, §560.

b_open_in: **function**, §27.

$b0$: $quarterword$, §113.

$b1$: $quarterword$, §113.

$b2$: $quarterword$, §113.

$b3$: $quarterword$, §113.

bc: $halfword$, §560.

c: $eight\_bits$, §560.

$char\_base$: **array**, §550.

d: $eight\_bits$, §560.

$depth\_base$: **array**, §550.

$done$ = 30, §15.

ec: $halfword$, §560.

$error$: **procedure**, §82.

$exten\_base$: **array**, §550.

f: $internal\_font\_number$, §560.

$file\_opened$: $boolean$, §560.

$fmem\_ptr$: $0 .. font\_mem\_size$, §549.

$font\_max$ = **const**, §11.

$font\_mem\_size$ = **const**, §11.

$font\_ptr$: $internal\_font\_number$,
 §549.

$height\_base$: **array**, §550.

$help4$ = macro, §79.

$incr$ = macro, §16.

$italic\_base$: **array**, §550.

$kern\_base$: **array**, §550.

lf: $halfword$, §560.

lh: $halfword$, §560.

lig_kern_base: **array**, §550.

$min\_quarterword$ = 0, §110.

nd: $halfword$, §560.

ne: $halfword$, §560.

nh: $halfword$, §560.

ni: $halfword$, §560.

nk: $halfword$, §560.

nl: $halfword$, §560.

nom: str_number, §560.

np: $halfword$, §560.

nw: $halfword$, §560.

$pack\_file\_name$: **procedure**, §519.

$param\_base$: **array**, §550.

$print$: **procedure**, §59.

qi = macro, §112.

qw: $four\_quarters$, §560.

$read\_font\_info$: **function**, §560.

$start\_font\_error\_message$ = macro,
 §561.

T$_{E}$X$\_font\_area$ = macro, §514.

tfm_file: $byte\_file$, §539.

$width\_base$: **array**, §550.

568. Only the first two words of the header are needed by TEX82.

⟨ Read the TFM header 568 ⟩ ≡
  begin if $lh < 2$ **then** *abort*;
  store_four_quarters(*font_check*[f]); *fget*; *read_sixteen*(z); { this rejects a negative design size }
  fget; $z \leftarrow z * '400 + \textit{fbyte}$; *fget*; $z \leftarrow (z * '20) + (\textit{fbyte}\ \mathbf{div}\ '20)$;
  if $z < \textit{unity}$ **then** *abort*;
  while $lh > 2$ **do**
    begin *fget*; *fget*; *fget*; *fget*; *decr*(lh); { ignore the rest of the header }
    end;
  font_dsize[f] $\leftarrow z$;
  if $s \neq -1000$ **then**
    if $s \geq 0$ **then** $z \leftarrow s$
    else $z \leftarrow \textit{xn\_over\_d}(z, -s, 1000)$;
  font_size[f] $\leftarrow z$;
  end

This code is used in section 562.

569. ⟨ Read character data 569 ⟩ ≡
  for $k \leftarrow \textit{fmem\_ptr}$ **to** *width_base*[f] $- 1$ **do**
    begin *store_four_quarters*(*font_info*[k].*qqqq*);
    if $(a \geq nw) \vee (b\ \mathbf{div}\ '20 \geq nh) \vee (b\ \mathbf{mod}\ '20 \geq nd) \vee (c\ \mathbf{div}\ 4 \geq ni)$ **then** *abort*;
    case $c\ \mathbf{mod}\ 4$ **of**
    lig_tag: **if** $d \geq nl$ **then** *abort*;
    ext_tag: **if** $d \geq ne$ **then** *abort*;
    list_tag: ⟨ Check for charlist cycle 570 ⟩;
    othercases *do_nothing*   { *no_tag* }
    endcases;
    end

This code is used in section 562.

570. We want to make sure that there is no cycle of characters linked together by *list_tag* entries, since such a cycle would get TEX into an endless loop. If such a cycle exists, the routine here detects it when processing the largest character code in the cycle.

  define *check_byte_range*(#) ≡
        begin if (# < *bc*) ∨ (# > *ec*) **then** *abort*
        end
  define *current_character_being_worked_on* ≡ $k + bc - \textit{fmem\_ptr}$
⟨ Check for charlist cycle 570 ⟩ ≡
  begin *check_byte_range*(d);
  while $d < \textit{current\_character\_being\_worked\_on}$ **do**
    begin $qw \leftarrow \textit{char\_info}(f)(d)$; { N.B.: not $qi(d)$, since *char_base*[f] hasn't been adjusted yet }
    if *char_tag*(qw) $\neq$ *list_tag* **then goto** *not_found*;
    $d \leftarrow qo(\textit{rem\_byte}(qw))$;   { next character on the list }
    end;
  if $d = \textit{current\_character\_being\_worked\_on}$ **then** *abort*;   { yes, there's a cycle }
not_found: **end**

This code is used in section 569.

571. A *fix_word* whose four bytes are (a, b, c, d) from left to right represents the number

$$x = \begin{cases} b \cdot 2^{-4} + c \cdot 2^{-12} + d \cdot 2^{-20}, & \text{if } a = 0; \\ -16 + b \cdot 2^{-4} + c \cdot 2^{-12} + d \cdot 2^{-20}, & \text{if } a = 255. \end{cases}$$

(No other choices of a are allowed, since the magnitude of a number in design-size units must be less than 16.) We want to multiply this quantity by the integer z, which is known to be less than 2^{27}. Let $\alpha = 16z$. If $z < 2^{23}$, the individual multiplications $b \cdot z$, $c \cdot z$, $d \cdot z$ cannot overflow; otherwise we will divide z by 2, 4, 8, or 16, to obtain a multiplier less than 2^{23}, and we can compensate for this later. If z has thereby been replaced by $z' = z/2^e$, let $\beta = 2^{4-e}$; we shall compute

$$\lfloor (b + c \cdot 2^{-8} + d \cdot 2^{-16}) \, z'/\beta \rfloor$$

if $a = 0$, or the same quantity minus α if $a = 255$. This calculation must be done exactly, in order to guarantee portability of TeX between computers.

> **define** *store_scaled*(#) $\equiv$
>   **begin** *fget*; $a \leftarrow$ *fbyte*; *fget*; $b \leftarrow$ *fbyte*; *fget*; $c \leftarrow$ *fbyte*; *fget*; $d \leftarrow$ *fbyte*;
> $sw \leftarrow (((((d * z) \, \textbf{div} \, \text{'}400) + (c * z)) \, \textbf{div} \, \text{'}400) + (b * z)) \, \textbf{div} \, beta$;
>   **if** $a = 0$ **then** # $\leftarrow sw$ **else if** $a = 255$ **then** # $\leftarrow sw - alpha$ **else** *abort*;
>   **end**

$\langle$ Read box dimensions 571 $\rangle \equiv$
> **begin** $\langle$ Replace z by z' and compute α, β 572 $\rangle$;
> **for** $k \leftarrow$ *width_base*[*f*] **to** *lig_kern_base*[*f*] $- 1$ **do** *store_scaled*(*font_info*[*k*].*sc*);
> **if** *font_info*[*width_base*[*f*]].*sc* $\neq 0$ **then** *abort*; { *width*[0] must be zero }
> **if** *font_info*[*height_base*[*f*]].*sc* $\neq 0$ **then** *abort*; { *height*[0] must be zero }
> **if** *font_info*[*depth_base*[*f*]].*sc* $\neq 0$ **then** *abort*; { *depth*[0] must be zero }
> **if** *font_info*[*italic_base*[*f*]].*sc* $\neq 0$ **then** *abort*; { *italic*[0] must be zero }
> **end**

This code is used in section 562.

---

a: *eight_bits*, §560.
abort = macro, §560.
alpha: *integer*, §560.
b: *eight_bits*, §560.
bc: *halfword*, §560.
beta: 1 .. 16, §560.
c: *eight_bits*, §560.
char_base: **array**, §550.
char_info = macro, §554.
char_tag = macro, §554.
d: *eight_bits*, §560.
decr = macro, §16.
depth_base: **array**, §550.
do_nothing = macro, §16.
ec: *halfword*, §560.
ext_tag = 3, §544.
f: *internal_font_number*, §560.
fbyte = macro, §564.

fget = macro, §564.
fix_word, §541.
fmem_ptr: 0 .. *font_mem_size*, §549.
font_check: **array**, §549.
font_dsize: **array**, §549.
font_size: **array**, §549.
height_base: **array**, §550.
italic_base: **array**, §550.
k: 0 .. *font_mem_size*, §560.
lh: *halfword*, §560.
lig_kern_base: **array**, §550.
lig_tag = 1, §544.
list_tag = 2, §544.
nd: *halfword*, §560.
ne: *halfword*, §560.
nh: *halfword*, §560.
ni: *halfword*, §560.
nl: *halfword*, §560.

no_tag = 0, §544.
not_found = 45, §15.
nw: *halfword*, §560.
qi = macro, §112.
qo = macro, §112.
qqqq: *four_quarters*, §113.
qw: *four_quarters*, §560.
read_sixteen = macro, §564.
rem_byte = macro, §545.
s: *scaled*, §560.
sc = macro, §113.
store_four_quarters = macro, §564.
sw: *scaled*, §560.
unity = macro, §101.
width_base: **array**, §550.
xn_over_d: **function**, §107.
z: *scaled*, §560.

572. ⟨ Replace z by z' and compute α, β 572 ⟩ ≡
  begin *alpha* ← 16 * z; *beta* ← 16;
  while $z \geq$ *'40000000* **do**
    begin $z ←z$ **div** 2; *beta* ← *beta* **div** 2;
    end;
  end

This code is used in section 571.

573. ⟨ Read ligature/kern program 573 ⟩ ≡
  begin for $k ← lig\_kern\_base[f]$ **to** $kern\_base[f] - 1$ **do**
    begin *store_four_quarters*(*font_info*[k].*qqqq*); *check_byte_range*(b);
    if $c < 128$ **then** *check_byte_range*(d)   { check ligature }
    else if $d \geq nk$ **then** *abort*;   { check kern }
    end;
  if $(nl > 0) \wedge (a < 128)$ **then** *abort*;   { check for stop bit on last command }
  for $k ← kern\_base[f]$ **to** $exten\_base[f] - 1$ **do** *store_scaled*(*font_info*[k].*sc*);
  end

This code is used in section 562.

574. ⟨ Read extensible character recipes 574 ⟩ ≡
  for $k ← exten\_base[f]$ **to** $param\_base[f] - 1$ **do**
    begin *store_four_quarters*(*font_info*[k].*qqqq*);
    if $a \neq 0$ **then** *check_byte_range*(a);
    if $b \neq 0$ **then** *check_byte_range*(b);
    if $c \neq 0$ **then** *check_byte_range*(c);
    check_byte_range(d);
    end

This code is used in section 562.

575. We check to see that the TFM file doesn't end prematurely; but no error message is given for files having more than *lf* words.

⟨ Read font parameters 575 ⟩ ≡
  begin for $k ← 1$ **to** np **do**
    if $k = 1$ **then**   { the *slant* parameter is a pure number }
      begin *fget*; *sw* ← *fbyte*;
      if *sw* > 127 **then** *sw* ← *sw* − 256;
      fget; *sw* ← *sw* * *'400* + *fbyte*; *fget*; *sw* ← *sw* * *'400* + *fbyte*; *fget*;
      font_info[*param_base*[f]].*sc* ← (*sw* * *'20*) + (*fbyte* **div** *'20*);
      end
    else *store_scaled*(*font_info*[*param_base*[f] + k − 1].*sc*);
  if *eof*(*tfm_file*) **then** *abort*;
  for $k ← np + 1$ **to** 7 **do** *font_info*[*param_base*[f] + k − 1].*sc* ← 0;
  end

This code is used in section 562.

576. Now to wrap it up, we have checked all the necessary things about the TFM file, and all we need to do is put the finishing touches on the data for the new font.

  define *adjust*(#) ≡ #[f] ← *qo*(#[f])   { correct for the excess *min_quarterword* that was added }

231 FONT METRIC DATA

⟨ Make final adjustments and **goto** *done* 576 ⟩ ≡
    if $np \geq 7$ **then** $font\_params[f] \leftarrow np$ **else** $font\_params[f] \leftarrow 7$;
    $hyphen\_char[f] \leftarrow default\_hyphen\_char$; $skew\_char[f] \leftarrow default\_skew\_char$; $font\_name[f] \leftarrow nom$;
    $font\_area[f] \leftarrow aire$; $font\_bc[f] \leftarrow bc$; $font\_ec[f] \leftarrow ec$; $font\_glue[f] \leftarrow null$; $adjust(char\_base)$;
    $adjust(width\_base)$; $adjust(lig\_kern\_base)$; $adjust(kern\_base)$; $adjust(exten\_base)$;
    $decr(param\_base[f])$; $fmem\_ptr \leftarrow fmem\_ptr + lf$; $font\_ptr \leftarrow f$; $g \leftarrow f$; **goto** *done*

This code is used in section 562.

577.   Before we forget about the format of these tables, let's deal with two of TeX's basic scanning routines related to font information.

⟨ Declare procedures that scan font-related stuff 577 ⟩ ≡
procedure *scan_font_ident*;
    var f: *internal_font_number*; m: *halfword*;
    begin ⟨ Get the next non-blank non-call token 406 ⟩;
    if $cur\_cmd = def\_font$ **then** $f \leftarrow cur\_font$
    else if $cur\_cmd = set\_font$ **then** $f \leftarrow cur\_chr$
        else if $cur\_cmd = def\_family$ **then**
            begin $m \leftarrow cur\_chr$; $scan\_four\_bit\_int$; $f \leftarrow equiv(m + cur\_val)$;
            end
        else begin $print\_err($"Missing␣font␣identifier"$)$;
        $help2($"I␣was␣looking␣for␣a␣control␣sequence␣whose"$)$
        $($"current␣meaning␣has␣been␣defined␣by␣\font."$)$; $back\_error$; $f \leftarrow null\_font$;
        end;
    $cur\_val \leftarrow f$;
    end;

See also section 578.

This code is used in section 409.

---

a: *eight_bits*, §560.
abort = macro, §560.
aire: *str_number*, §560.
alpha: *integer*, §560.
b: *eight_bits*, §560.
back_error: **procedure**, §327.
bc: *halfword*, §560.
beta: 1 .. 16, §560.
c: *eight_bits*, §560.
char_base: **array**, §550.
check_byte_range = macro, §570.
cur_chr: *halfword*, §297.
cur_cmd: *eight_bits*, §297.
cur_font = macro, §230.
cur_val: *integer*, §410.
d: *eight_bits*, §560.
decr = macro, §16.
def_family = 85, §209.
def_font = 87, §209.
default_hyphen_char = macro, §236.
default_skew_char = macro, §236.
done = 30, §15.
ec: *halfword*, §560.
equiv = macro, §221.

exten_base: **array**, §550.
f: *internal_font_number*, §560.
fbyte = macro, §564.
fget = macro, §564.
fmem_ptr: 0 .. *font_mem_size*, §549.
font_area: **array**, §549.
font_bc: **array**, §549.
font_ec: **array**, §549.
font_glue: **array**, §549.
font_name: **array**, §549.
font_params: **array**, §549.
font_ptr: *internal_font_number*,
  §549.
g: *internal_font_number*, §560.
halfword = *min_halfword* ..
  max_halfword, §113.
help2 = macro, §79.
hyphen_char: **array**, §549.
internal_font_number = 0 .. *font_max*,
  §548.
k: 0 .. *font_mem_size*, §560.
kern_base: **array**, §550.
lf: *halfword*, §560.

lig_kern_base: **array**, §550.
min_quarterword = 0, §110.
nk: *halfword*, §560.
nl: *halfword*, §560.
nom: *str_number*, §560.
np: *halfword*, §560.
null = macro, §115.
null_font = macro, §232.
param_base: **array**, §550.
print_err = macro, §73.
qo = macro, §112.
qqqq: *four_quarters*, §113.
sc = macro, §113.
scan_four_bit_int: **procedure**, §434.
set_font = 86, §209.
skew_char: **array**, §549.
slant = macro, §558.
store_four_quarters = macro, §564.
store_scaled = macro, §571.
sw: *scaled*, §560.
tfm_file: *byte_file*, §539.
width_base: **array**, §550.
z: *scaled*, §560.

578. The following routine is used to implement '\fontdimen n f'. The boolean parameter *writing* is set *true* if the calling program intends to change the parameter value.

⟨ Declare procedures that scan font-related stuff 577 ⟩ +≡
procedure *find_font_dimen*(*writing* : *boolean*);   { sets *cur_val* to *font_info* location }
  var f: *internal_font_number*; n: *integer*;   { the parameter number }
  begin *scan_int*; $n \leftarrow cur\_val$; *scan_font_ident*; $f \leftarrow cur\_val$;
  if $n \leq 0$ **then** $cur\_val \leftarrow fmem\_ptr$
  else begin if $writing \wedge (n \leq space\_shrink\_code) \wedge (n \geq space\_code) \wedge (font\_glue[f] \neq null)$ **then**
      begin *delete_glue_ref*(*font_glue*[f]); *font_glue*[f] $\leftarrow null$;
      end;
    if $n > font\_params[f]$ **then**
      if $f < font\_ptr$ **then** $cur\_val \leftarrow fmem\_ptr$
      else ⟨ Increase the number of parameters in the last font 580 ⟩
    else $cur\_val \leftarrow n + param\_base[f]$;
    end;
  ⟨ Issue an error message if $cur\_val = fmem\_ptr$ 579 ⟩;
  end;

579. ⟨ Issue an error message if $cur\_val = fmem\_ptr$ 579 ⟩ ≡
  if $cur\_val = fmem\_ptr$ **then**
    begin *print_err*("Font␣"); *print_esc*(*font_id_text*(f)); *print*("␣has␣only␣");
    print_int(*font_params*[f]); *print*("␣fontdimen␣parameters");
    help2("To␣increase␣the␣number␣of␣font␣parameters,␣you␣must")
    ("use␣\fontdimen␣immediately␣after␣the␣\font␣is␣loaded."); *error*;
    end
This code is used in section 578.

580. ⟨ Increase the number of parameters in the last font 580 ⟩ ≡
  begin repeat if $fmem\_ptr = font\_mem\_size$ **then** *overflow*("font␣memory", *font_mem_size*);
    font_info[*fmem_ptr*].*sc* $\leftarrow 0$; *incr*(*fmem_ptr*); *incr*(*font_params*[f]);
  until $n = font\_params[f]$;
  $cur\_val \leftarrow fmem\_ptr - 1$;   { this equals $param\_base[f] + font\_params[f]$ }
  end
This code is used in section 578.

581. When TeX wants to typeset a character that doesn't exist, the character node is not created; thus the output routine can assume that characters exist when it sees them. The following procedure prints a warning message unless the user has suppressed it.

procedure *char_warning*(f : *internal_font_number*; c : *eight_bits*);
  begin if *tracing_lost_chars* > 0 **then**
    begin *begin_diagnostic*; *print_nl*("Missing␣character:␣There␣is␣no␣"); *print_ASCII*(c);
    print("␣in␣font␣"); *print*(*font_name*[f]); *print_char*("!"); *end_diagnostic*(*false*);
    end;
  end;

582.   Here is a function that returns a pointer to a character node for a given character in a given font. If that character doesn't exist, *null* is returned instead.

function *new_character*(f : *internal_font_number*; c : *eight_bits*): *pointer*;
   label *exit*;
   var p: *pointer*;   { newly allocated node }
   begin if *font_bc*[f] $\leq c$ **then**
     if *font_ec*[f] $\geq c$ **then**
       if *char_exists*(*char_info*(f)(*qi*(c))) **then**
         begin $p \leftarrow$ *get_avail*; *font*(p) $\leftarrow f$; *character*(p) $\leftarrow$ *qi*(c); *new_character* $\leftarrow p$; **return**;
         end;
    char_warning(f, c); *new_character* $\leftarrow$ *null*;
exit: **end**;

583. Device-independent file format.   The most important output produced by a run of
TEX is the "device independent" (DVI) file that specifies where characters and rules are to appear
on printed pages. The form of these files was designed by David R. Fuchs in 1979. Almost any
reasonable typesetting device can be driven by a program that takes DVI files as input, and dozens
of such DVI-to-whatever programs have been written. Thus, it is possible to print the output of
TEX on many different kinds of equipment, using TEX as a device-independent "front end."

A DVI file is a stream of 8-bit bytes, which may be regarded as a series of commands in a
machine-like language. The first byte of each command is the operation code, and this code
is followed by zero or more bytes that provide parameters to the command. The parameters
themselves may consist of several consecutive bytes; for example, the '*set_rule*' command has two
parameters, each of which is four bytes long. Parameters are usually regarded as nonnegative
integers; but four-byte-long parameters, and shorter parameters that denote distances, can be
either positive or negative. Such parameters are given in two's complement notation. For
example, a two-byte-long distance parameter has a value between -2^{15} and $2^{15} - 1$. As in
TFM files, numbers that occupy more than one byte position appear in BigEndian order.

A DVI file consists of a "preamble," followed by a sequence of one or more "pages," followed
by a "postamble." The preamble is simply a *pre* command, with its parameters that define
the dimensions used in the file; this must come first. Each "page" consists of a *bop* command,
followed by any number of other commands that tell where characters are to be placed on a
physical page, followed by an *eop* command. The pages appear in the order that TEX generated
them. If we ignore *nop* commands and *fnt_def* commands (which are allowed between any two
commands in the file), each *eop* command is immediately followed by a *bop* command, or by a
post command; in the latter case, there are no more pages in the file, and the remaining bytes
form the postamble. Further details about the postamble will be explained later.

Some parameters in DVI commands are "pointers." These are four-byte quantities that give the
location number of some other byte in the file; the first byte is number 0, then comes number 1,
and so on. For example, one of the parameters of a *bop* command points to the previous *bop*;
this makes it feasible to read the pages in backwards order, in case the results are being directed
to a device that stacks its output face up. Suppose the preamble of a DVI file occupies bytes 0
to 99. Now if the first page occupies bytes 100 to 999, say, and if the second page occupies bytes
1000 to 1999, then the *bop* that starts in byte 1000 points to 100 and the *bop* that starts in byte
2000 points to 1000. (The very first *bop*, i.e., the one starting in byte 100, has a pointer of -1.)

584. The DVI format is intended to be both compact and easily interpreted by a machine. Compactness is achieved by making most of the information implicit instead of explicit. When a DVI-reading program reads the commands for a page, it keeps track of several quantities: (a) The current font f is an integer; this value is changed only by *fnt* and *fnt_num* commands. (b) The current position on the page is given by two numbers called the horizontal and vertical coordinates, h and v. Both coordinates are zero at the upper left corner of the page; moving to the right corresponds to increasing the horizontal coordinate, and moving down corresponds to increasing the vertical coordinate. Thus, the coordinates are essentially Cartesian, except that vertical directions are flipped; the Cartesian version of (h, v) would be $(h, -v)$. (c) The current spacing amounts are given by four numbers w, x, y, and z, where w and x are used for horizontal spacing and where y and z are used for vertical spacing. (d) There is a stack containing (h, v, w, x, y, z) values; the DVI commands *push* and *pop* are used to change the current level of operation. Note that the current font f is not pushed and popped; the stack contains only information about positioning.

The values of h, v, w, x, y, and z are signed integers having up to 32 bits, including the sign. Since they represent physical distances, there is a small unit of measurement such that increasing h by 1 means moving a certain tiny distance to the right. The actual unit of measurement is variable, as explained below; TeX sets things up so that its DVI output is in sp units, i.e., scaled points, in agreement with all the *scaled* dimensions in TeX's data structures.

$bop = 139$, §586. $pop = 142$, §586. $push = 141$, §586.
$eop = 140$, §586. $post = 248$, §586. $scaled = integer$, §101.
$nop = 138$, §586. $pre = 247$, §586. $set\_rule = 132$, §586.

585. Here is a list of all the commands that may appear in a DVI file. Each command is specified by its symbolic name (e.g., *bop*), its opcode byte (e.g., 139), and its parameters (if any). The parameters are followed by a bracketed number telling how many bytes they occupy; for example, '$p[4]$' means that parameter p is four bytes long.

set_char_0 0. Typeset character number 0 from font f such that the reference point of the character is at (h, v). Then increase h by the width of that character. Note that a character may have zero or negative width, so one cannot be sure that h will advance after this command; but h usually does increase.

set_char_1 through *set_char_127* (opcodes 1 to 127). Do the operations of *set_char_0*; but use the character whose number matches the opcode, instead of character 0.

set1 128 $c[1]$. Same as *set_char_0*, except that character number c is typeset. TEX82 uses this command for characters in the range $128 \leq c < 256$.

set2 129 $c[2]$. Same as *set1*, except that c is two bytes long, so it is in the range $0 \leq c < 65536$. TEX82 never uses this command, but it should come in handy for extensions of TEX that deal with oriental languages.

set3 130 $c[3]$. Same as *set1*, except that c is three bytes long, so it can be as large as $2^{24} - 1$. Not even the Chinese language has this many characters, but this command might prove useful in some yet unforeseen extension.

set4 131 $c[4]$. Same as *set1*, except that c is four bytes long. Imagine that.

set_rule 132 $a[4]$ $b[4]$. Typeset a solid black rectangle of height a and width b, with its bottom left corner at (h, v). Then set $h \leftarrow h + b$. If either $a \leq 0$ or $b \leq 0$, nothing should be typeset. Note that if $b < 0$, the value of h will decrease even though nothing else happens. See below for details about how to typeset rules so that consistency with METAFONT is guaranteed.

put1 133 $c[1]$. Typeset character number c from font f such that the reference point of the character is at (h, v). (The 'put' commands are exactly like the 'set' commands, except that they simply put out a character or a rule without moving the reference point afterwards.)

put2 134 $c[2]$. Same as *set2*, except that h is not changed.

put3 135 $c[3]$. Same as *set3*, except that h is not changed.

put4 136 $c[4]$. Same as *set4*, except that h is not changed.

put_rule 137 $a[4]$ $b[4]$. Same as *set_rule*, except that h is not changed.

nop 138. No operation, do nothing. Any number of *nop*'s may occur between DVI commands, but a *nop* cannot be inserted between a command and its parameters or between two parameters.

bop 139 $c_0[4]$ $c_1[4]$ ... $c_9[4]$ $p[4]$. Beginning of a page: Set $(h, v, w, x, y, z) \leftarrow (0, 0, 0, 0, 0, 0)$ and set the stack empty. Set the current font f to an undefined value. The ten c_i parameters hold the values of \count0 ... \count9 in TEX at the time \shipout was invoked for this page; they can be used to identify pages, if a user wants to print only part of a DVI file. The parameter p points to the previous *bop* in the file; the first *bop* has $p = -1$.

eop 140. End of page: Print what you have read since the previous *bop*. At this point the stack should be empty. (The DVI-reading programs that drive most output devices will have kept a buffer of the material that appears on the page that has just ended. This material is largely, but not entirely, in order by v coordinate and (for fixed v) by h coordinate; so it usually needs to be sorted into some order that is appropriate for the device in question.)

push 141. Push the current values of (h, v, w, x, y, z) onto the top of the stack; do not change any of these values. Note that f is not pushed.

pop 142. Pop the top six values off of the stack and assign them respectively to (h, v, w, x, y, z). The number of pops should never exceed the number of pushes, since it would be highly embarrassing if the stack were empty at the time of a *pop* command.

right1 143 $b[1]$. Set $h \leftarrow h + b$, i.e., move right b units. The parameter is a signed number in two's complement notation, $-128 \leq b < 128$; if $b < 0$, the reference point moves left.

right2 144 $b[2]$. Same as *right1*, except that b is a two-byte quantity in the range $-32768 \leq b < 32768$.

right3 145 $b[3]$. Same as *right1*, except that b is a three-byte quantity in the range $-2^{23} \leq b < 2^{23}$.

right4 146 $b[4]$. Same as *right1*, except that b is a four-byte quantity in the range $-2^{31} \leq b < 2^{31}$.

w0 147. Set $h \leftarrow h + w$; i.e., move right w units. With luck, this parameterless command will usually suffice, because the same kind of motion will occur several times in succession; the following commands explain how w gets particular values.

w1 148 $b[1]$. Set $w \leftarrow b$ and $h \leftarrow h + b$. The value of b is a signed quantity in two's complement notation, $-128 \leq b < 128$. This command changes the current w spacing and moves right by b.

w2 149 $b[2]$. Same as *w1*, but b is two bytes long, $-32768 \leq b < 32768$.

w3 150 $b[3]$. Same as *w1*, but b is three bytes long, $-2^{23} \leq b < 2^{23}$.

w4 151 $b[4]$. Same as *w1*, but b is four bytes long, $-2^{31} \leq b < 2^{31}$.

x0 152. Set $h \leftarrow h + x$; i.e., move right x units. The 'x' commands are like the 'w' commands except that they involve x instead of w.

x1 153 $b[1]$. Set $x \leftarrow b$ and $h \leftarrow h + b$. The value of b is a signed quantity in two's complement notation, $-128 \leq b < 128$. This command changes the current x spacing and moves right by b.

x2 154 $b[2]$. Same as *x1*, but b is two bytes long, $-32768 \leq b < 32768$.

x3 155 $b[3]$. Same as *x1*, but b is three bytes long, $-2^{23} \leq b < 2^{23}$.

x4 156 $b[4]$. Same as *x1*, but b is four bytes long, $-2^{31} \leq b < 2^{31}$.

585. (continued)

down1 157 *a*[1]. Set $v \leftarrow v + a$, i.e., move down *a* units. The parameter is a signed number in two's complement notation, $-128 \leq a < 128$; if $a < 0$, the reference point actually moves up.

down2 158 *a*[2]. Same as *down1*, except that *a* is a two-byte quantity in the range $-32768 \leq a < 32768$.

down3 159 *a*[3]. Same as *down1*, except that *a* is a three-byte quantity in the range $-2^{23} \leq a < 2^{23}$.

down4 160 *a*[4]. Same as *down1*, except that *a* is a four-byte quantity in the range $-2^{31} \leq a < 2^{31}$.

y0 161. Set $v \leftarrow v + y$; i.e., move down *y* units. With luck, this parameterless command will usually suffice, because the same kind of motion will occur several times in succession; the following commands explain how *y* gets particular values.

y1 162 *a*[1]. Set $y \leftarrow a$ and $v \leftarrow v + a$. The value of *a* is a signed quantity in two's complement notation, $-128 \leq a < 128$. This command changes the current *y* spacing and moves down by *a*.

y2 163 *a*[2]. Same as *y1*, but *a* is two bytes long, $-32768 \leq a < 32768$.

y3 164 *a*[3]. Same as *y1*, but *a* is three bytes long, $-2^{23} \leq a < 2^{23}$.

y4 165 *a*[4]. Same as *y1*, but *a* is four bytes long, $-2^{31} \leq a < 2^{31}$.

z0 166. Set $v \leftarrow v + z$; i.e., move down *z* units. The 'z' commands are like the 'y' commands except that they involve *z* instead of *y*.

z1 167 *a*[1]. Set $z \leftarrow a$ and $v \leftarrow v + a$. The value of *a* is a signed quantity in two's complement notation, $-128 \leq a < 128$. This command changes the current *z* spacing and moves down by *a*.

z2 168 *a*[2]. Same as *z1*, but *a* is two bytes long, $-32768 \leq a < 32768$.

z3 169 *a*[3]. Same as *z1*, but *a* is three bytes long, $-2^{23} \leq a < 2^{23}$.

z4 170 *a*[4]. Same as *z1*, but *a* is four bytes long, $-2^{31} \leq a < 2^{31}$.

fnt_num_0 171. Set $f \leftarrow 0$. Font 0 must previously have been defined by a *fnt_def* instruction, as explained below.

fnt_num_1 through *fnt_num_63* (opcodes 172 to 234). Set $f \leftarrow 1, \ldots, f \leftarrow 63$, respectively.

fnt1 235 *k*[1]. Set $f \leftarrow k$. TEX82 uses this command for font numbers in the range $64 \leq k < 256$.

fnt2 236 *k*[2]. Same as *fnt1*, except that *k* is two bytes long, so it is in the range $0 \leq k < 65536$. TEX82 never generates this command, but large font numbers may prove useful for specifications of color or texture, or they may be used for special fonts that have fixed numbers in some external coding scheme.

fnt3 237 *k*[3]. Same as *fnt1*, except that *k* is three bytes long, so it can be as large as $2^{24} - 1$.

fnt4 238 *k*[4]. Same as *fnt1*, except that *k* is four bytes long; this is for the really big font numbers (and for the negative ones).

xxx1 239 *k*[1] *x*[*k*]. This command is undefined in general; it functions as a $(k + 2)$-byte *nop* unless special DVI-reading programs are being used. TEX82 generates *xxx1* when a short enough \special appears, setting k to the number of bytes being sent. It is recommended that x be a string having the form of a keyword followed by possible parameters relevant to that keyword.

xxx2 240 $k[2]$ $x[k]$. Like *xxx1*, but $0 \leq k < 65536$.

xxx3 241 $k[3]$ $x[k]$. Like *xxx1*, but $0 \leq k < 2^{24}$.

xxx4 242 $k[4]$ $x[k]$. Like *xxx1*, but k can be ridiculously large. TEX82 uses *xxx4* when sending a string of length 256 or more.

fnt_def1 243 $k[1]$ $c[4]$ $s[4]$ $d[4]$ $a[1]$ $l[1]$ $n[a+l]$. Define font k, where $0 \leq k < 256$; font definitions will be explained shortly.

fnt_def2 244 $k[2]$ $c[4]$ $s[4]$ $d[4]$ $a[1]$ $l[1]$ $n[a+l]$. Define font k, where $0 \leq k < 65536$.

fnt_def3 245 $k[3]$ $c[4]$ $s[4]$ $d[4]$ $a[1]$ $l[1]$ $n[a+l]$. Define font k, where $0 \leq k < 2^{24}$.

fnt_def4 246 $k[4]$ $c[4]$ $s[4]$ $d[4]$ $a[1]$ $l[1]$ $n[a+l]$. Define font k, where $-2^{31} \leq k < 2^{31}$.

pre 247 $i[1]$ *num*$[4]$ *den*$[4]$ *mag*$[4]$ $k[1]$ $x[k]$. Beginning of the preamble; this must come at the very beginning of the file. Parameters i, *num*, *den*, *mag*, k, and x are explained below.

post 248. Beginning of the postamble, see below.

post_post 249. Ending of the postamble, see below.

Commands 250–255 are undefined at the present time.

---

bop = 139, §586.	*post_post* = 249, §586.	*w1* = 148, §586.
den, §587.	*pre* = 247, §586.	*x0* = 152, §586.
down1 = 157, §586.	*push* = 141, §586.	*x1* = 153, §586.
eop = 140, §586.	*put_rule* = 137, §586.	*xxx1* = 239, §586.
fnt_def1 = 243, §586.	*put1* = 133, §586.	*xxx4* = 242, §586.
fnt_num_0 = 171, §586.	*right1* = 143, §586.	*y0* = 161, §586.
fnt1 = 235, §586.	*set_char_0* = 0, §586.	*y1* = 162, §586.
nop = 138, §586.	*set_rule* = 132, §586.	*z0* = 166, §586.
pop = 142, §586.	*set1* = 128, §586.	*z1* = 167, §586.
post = 248, §586.	*w0* = 147, §586.	

586. **define** *set_char_0* = 0   { typeset character 0 and move right }
  define *set1* = 128   { typeset a character and move right }
  define *set_rule* = 132   { typeset a rule and move right }
  define *put1* = 133   { typeset a character }
  define *put_rule* = 137   { typeset a rule }
  define *nop* = 138   { no operation }
  define *bop* = 139   { beginning of page }
  define *eop* = 140   { ending of page }
  define *push* = 141   { save the current positions }
  define *pop* = 142   { restore previous positions }
  define *right1* = 143   { move right }
  define *w0* = 147   { move right by w }
  define *w1* = 148   { move right and set w }
  define *x0* = 152   { move right by x }
  define *x1* = 153   { move right and set x }
  define *down1* = 157   { move down }
  define *y0* = 161   { move down by y }
  define *y1* = 162   { move down and set y }
  define *z0* = 166   { move down by z }
  define *z1* = 167   { move down and set z }
  define *fnt_num_0* = 171   { set current font to 0 }
  define *fnt1* = 235   { set current font }
  define *xxx1* = 239   { extension to DVI primitives }
  define *xxx4* = 242   { potentially long extension to DVI primitives }
  define *fnt_def1* = 243   { define the meaning of a font number }
  define *pre* = 247   { preamble }
  define *post* = 248   { postamble beginning }
  define *post_post* = 249   { postamble ending }

587. The preamble contains basic information about the file as a whole. As stated above, there are six parameters:

$$i[1]\ num[4]\ den[4]\ mag[4]\ k[1]\ x[k].$$

The i byte identifies DVI format; currently this byte is always set to 2. (Some day we will set $i = 3$, when DVI format makes another incompatible change—perhaps in 1992.)

The next two parameters, *num* and *den*, are positive integers that define the units of measurement; they are the numerator and denominator of a fraction by which all dimensions in the DVI file could be multiplied in order to get lengths in units of 10^{-7} meters. Since 7227pt = 254cm, and since TeX works with scaled points where there are 2^{16} sp in a point, TeX sets $num/den = (254 \cdot 10^5)/(7227 \cdot 2^{16}) = 25400000/473628672$.

The *mag* parameter is what TeX calls \mag, i.e., 1000 times the desired magnification. The actual fraction by which dimensions are multiplied is therefore $mag \cdot num/1000den$. Note that if a TeX source document does not call for any 'true' dimensions, and if you change it only by specifying a different \mag setting, the DVI file that TeX creates will be completely unchanged except for the value of *mag* in the preamble and postamble. (Fancy DVI-reading programs allow users to override the *mag* setting when a DVI file is being printed.)

Finally, k and x allow the DVI writer to include a comment, which is not interpreted further.

The length of comment x is k, where $0 \leq k < 256$.

define $id\_byte = 2$ { identifies the kind of DVI files described here }

588.   Font definitions for a given font number k contain further parameters

$$c[4]\ s[4]\ d[4]\ a[1]\ l[1]\ n[a + l].$$

The four-byte value c is the check sum that TEX found in the TFM file for this font; c should match the check sum of the font found by programs that read this DVI file.

Parameter s contains a fixed-point scale factor that is applied to the character widths in font k; font dimensions in TFM files and other font files are relative to this quantity, which is called the "at size" elsewhere in this documentation. The value of s is always positive and less than 2^{27}. It is given in the same units as the other DVI dimensions, i.e., in sp when TEX82 has made the file. Parameter d is similar to s; it is the "design size," and it is given in DVI units that have not been corrected for the magnification *mag* found in the preamble. Thus, font k is to be used at $mag \cdot s/1000d$ times its normal size.

The remaining part of a font definition gives the external name of the font, which is an ASCII string of length $a + l$. The number a is the length of the "area" or directory, and l is the length of the font name itself; the standard local system font area is supposed to be used when $a = 0$. The n field contains the area in its first a bytes.

Font definitions must appear before the first use of a particular font number. Once font k is defined, it must not be defined again; however, we shall see below that font definitions appear in the postamble as well as in the pages, so in this sense each font number is defined exactly twice, if at all. Like *nop* commands and *xxx* commands, font definitions can appear before the first *bop*, or between an *eop* and a *bop*.

589.   Sometimes it is desirable to make horizontal or vertical rules line up precisely with certain features in characters of a font. It is possible to guarantee the correct matching between DVI output and the characters generated by METAFONT by adhering to the following principles: (1) The METAFONT characters should be positioned so that a bottom edge or left edge that is supposed to line up with the bottom or left edge of a rule appears at the reference point, i.e., in row 0 and column 0 of the METAFONT raster. This ensures that the position of the rule will not be rounded differently when the pixel size is not a perfect multiple of the units of measurement in the DVI file. (2) A typeset rule of height $a > 0$ and width $b > 0$ should be equivalent to a METAFONT-generated character having black pixels in precisely those raster positions whose METAFONT coordinates satisfy $0 \leq x < \alpha b$ and $0 \leq y < \alpha a$, where α is the number of pixels per DVI unit.

590. The last page in a DVI file is followed by '*post*'; this command introduces the postamble, which summarizes important facts that TEX has accumulated about the file, making it possible to print subsets of the data with reasonable efficiency. The postamble has the form

$$post\ p[4]\ num[4]\ den[4]\ mag[4]\ l[4]\ u[4]\ s[2]\ t[2]$$
$$\langle\,\text{font definitions}\,\rangle$$
$$post\_post\ q[4]\ i[1]\ 223\text{'s}[\geq 4]$$

Here p is a pointer to the final *bop* in the file. The next three parameters, *num*, *den*, and *mag*, are duplicates of the quantities that appeared in the preamble.

Parameters l and u give respectively the height-plus-depth of the tallest page and the width of the widest page, in the same units as other dimensions of the file. These numbers might be used by a DVI-reading program to position individual "pages" on large sheets of film or paper; however, the standard convention for output on normal size paper is to position each page so that the upper left-hand corner is exactly one inch from the left and the top. Experience has shown that it is unwise to design DVI-to-printer software that attempts cleverly to center the output; a fixed position of the upper left corner is easiest for users to understand and to work with. Therefore l and u are often ignored.

Parameter s is the maximum stack depth (i.e., the largest excess of *push* commands over *pop* commands) needed to process this file. Then comes t, the total number of pages (*bop* commands) present.

The postamble continues with font definitions, which are any number of *fnt_def* commands as described above, possibly interspersed with *nop* commands. Each font number that is used in the DVI file must be defined exactly twice: Once before it is first selected by a *fnt* command, and once in the postamble.

591. The last part of the postamble, following the *post_post* byte that signifies the end of the font definitions, contains q, a pointer to the *post* command that started the postamble. An identification byte, i, comes next; this currently equals 2, as in the preamble.

The i byte is followed by four or more bytes that are all equal to the decimal number 223 (i.e., *'337* in octal). TEX puts out four to seven of these trailing bytes, until the total length of the file is a multiple of four bytes, since this works out best on machines that pack four bytes per word; but any number of 223's is allowed, as long as there are at least four of them. In effect, 223 is a sort of signature that is added at the very end.

This curious way to finish off a DVI file makes it feasible for DVI-reading programs to find the postamble first, on most computers, even though TEX wants to write the postamble last. Most operating systems permit random access to individual words or bytes of a file, so the DVI reader can start at the end and skip backwards over the 223's until finding the identification byte. Then it can back up four bytes, read q, and move to byte q of the file. This byte should, of course, contain the value 248 (*post*); now the postamble can be read, so the DVI reader can discover all the information needed for typesetting the pages. Note that it is also possible to skip through the DVI file at reasonably high speed to locate a particular page, if that proves desirable. This saves a lot of time, since DVI files used in production jobs tend to be large.

Unfortunately, however, standard Pascal does not include the ability to access a random position in a file, or even to determine the length of a file. Almost all systems nowadays provide the necessary capabilities, so DVI format has been designed to work most efficiently with modern operating systems. But if DVI files have to be processed under the restrictions of standard Pascal, one can simply read them from front to back, since the necessary header information is present in the preamble and in the font definitions. (The l and u and s and t parameters, which appear only in the postamble, are "frills" that are handy but not absolutely necessary.)

bop = 139, §586.
den, §587.
i, §587.
mag, §587.

nop = 138, §586.
num, §587.
pop = 142, §586.

post = 248, §586.
post_post = 249, §586.
push = 141, §586.

592. Shipping pages out. After considering TeX's eyes and stomach, we come now to the bowels.

The *ship_out* procedure is given a pointer to a box; its mission is to describe that box in DVI form, outputting a "page" to *dvi_file*. The DVI coordinates $(h, v) = (0, 0)$ should correspond to the upper left corner of the box being shipped.

Since boxes can be inside of boxes inside of boxes, the main work of *ship_out* is done by two mutually recursive routines, *hlist_out* and *vlist_out*, which traverse the hlists and vlists inside of horizontal and vertical boxes.

As individual pages are being processed, we need to accumulate information about the entire set of pages, since such statistics must be reported in the postamble. The global variables *total_pages*, *max_v*, *max_h*, *max_push*, and *last_bop* are used to record this information.

The variable *doing_leaders* is *true* while leaders are being output. The variable *dead_cycles* contains the number of times an output routine has been initiated since the last *ship_out*.

A few additional global variables are also defined here for use in *vlist_out* and *hlist_out*. They could have been local variables, but that would waste stack space when boxes are deeply nested, since the values of these variables are not needed during recursive calls.

⟨ Global variables 13 ⟩ +≡
total_pages: *integer*;   { the number of pages that have been shipped out }
max_v: *scaled*;   { maximum height-plus-depth of pages shipped so far }
max_h: *scaled*;   { maximum width of pages shipped so far }
max_push: *integer*;   { deepest nesting of *push* commands encountered so far }
last_bop: *integer*;   { location of previous *bop* in the DVI output }
dead_cycles: *integer*;   { recent outputs that didn't ship anything out }
doing_leaders: *boolean*;   { are we inside a leader box? }

c, f: *quarterword*;   { character and font in current *char_node* }
rule_ht, *rule_dp*, *rule_wd*: *scaled*;   { size of current rule being output }
g: *pointer*;   { current glue specification }
lq, lr: *integer*;   { quantities used in calculations for leaders }

593. ⟨ Set initial values of key variables 21 ⟩ +≡
total_pages ← 0; *max_v* ← 0; *max_h* ← 0; *max_push* ← 0; *last_bop* ← −1; *doing_leaders* ← *false*;
dead_cycles ← 0;

594. The DVI bytes are output to a buffer instead of being written directly to the output file. This makes it possible to reduce the overhead of subroutine calls, thereby measurably speeding up the computation, since output of DVI bytes is part of TeX's inner loop. And it has another advantage as well, since we can change instructions in the buffer in order to make the output more compact. For example, a '*down2*' command can be changed to a '*y2*', thereby making a subsequent '*y0*' command possible, saving two bytes.

The output buffer is divided into two parts of equal size; the bytes found in *dvi_buf*[0 .. *half_buf* − 1] constitute the first half, and those in *dvi_buf*[*half_buf* .. *dvi_buf_size* − 1] constitute the second. The global variable *dvi_ptr* points to the position that will receive the next output byte. When *dvi_ptr* reaches *dvi_limit*, which is always equal to one of the two values *half_buf* or *dvi_buf_size*, the half buffer that is about to be invaded next is sent to the output and *dvi_limit* is changed to its other value. Thus, there is always at least a half buffer's worth of information present, except at the very beginning of the job.

Bytes of the DVI file are numbered sequentially starting with 0; the next byte to be generated will be number $dvi\_offset + dvi\_ptr$. A byte is present in the buffer only if its number is $\geq dvi\_gone$.

⟨ Types in the outer block 18 ⟩ +≡
    $dvi\_index = 0 \,..\, dvi\_buf\_size$;   { an index into the output buffer }

595. Some systems may find it more efficient to make dvi_buf a **packed** array, since output of four bytes at once may be facilitated.

⟨ Global variables 13 ⟩ +≡
dvi_buf: **array** [dvi_index] **of** $eight\_bits$;   { buffer for DVI output }
$half\_buf$: dvi_index;   { half of dvi_buf_size }
dvi_limit: dvi_index;   { end of the current half buffer }
dvi_ptr: dvi_index;   { the next available buffer address }
dvi_offset: $integer$;   { dvi_buf_size times the number of times the output buffer has been fully emptied }
dvi_gone: $integer$;   { the number of bytes already output to dvi_file }

596. Initially the buffer is all in one piece; we will output half of it only after it first fills up.

⟨ Set initial values of key variables 21 ⟩ +≡
    $half\_buf \leftarrow dvi\_buf\_size$ **div** 2; $dvi\_limit \leftarrow dvi\_buf\_size$; $dvi\_ptr \leftarrow 0$; $dvi\_offset \leftarrow 0$; $dvi\_gone \leftarrow 0$;

597. The actual output of $dvi\_buf\,[a\,..\,b]$ to dvi_file is performed by calling $write\_dvi(a,b)$. For best results, this procedure should be optimized to run as fast as possible on each particular system, since it is part of TeX's inner loop. It is safe to assume that a and $b + 1$ will both be multiples of 4 when $write\_dvi(a,b)$ is called; therefore it is possible on many machines to use efficient methods to pack four bytes per word and to output an array of words with one system call.

procedure $write\_dvi(a, b : dvi\_index)$;
    var k: dvi_index;
    begin for $k \leftarrow a$ **to** b **do** $write(dvi\_file, dvi\_buf\,[k])$;
    end;

$bop = 139$, §586.
$char\_node$, §134.
$down2$, §585.
$dvi_buf_size = $ **const**, §11.
dvi_file: $byte\_file$, §532.

$eight\_bits = 0 \,..\, 255$, §25.
$hlist\_out$: **procedure**, §619.
$pointer = $ macro, §115.
$push = 141$, §586.
$quarterword = 0 \,..\, 255$, §113.

$scaled = integer$, §101.
$ship\_out$: **procedure**, §638.
$vlist\_out$: **procedure**, §629.
$y0 = 161$, §586.
$y2$, §585.

598. To put a byte in the buffer without paying the cost of invoking a procedure each time, we use the macro *dvi_out*.

> **define** *dvi_out*(#) ≡ **begin** *dvi_buf*[*dvi_ptr*] ← #; *incr*(*dvi_ptr*);
>   **if** *dvi_ptr* = *dvi_limit* **then** *dvi_swap*;
>   **end**

procedure *dvi_swap*; { outputs half of the buffer }
  begin if *dvi_limit* = *dvi_buf_size* **then**
    begin *write_dvi*(0, *half_buf* − 1); *dvi_limit* ← *half_buf*; *dvi_offset* ← *dvi_offset* + *dvi_buf_size*;
    dvi_ptr ← 0;
    end
  else begin *write_dvi*(*half_buf*, *dvi_buf_size* − 1); *dvi_limit* ← *dvi_buf_size*;
    end;
  dvi_gone ← *dvi_gone* + *half_buf*;
  end;

599. Here is how we clean out the buffer when TeX is all through; *dvi_ptr* will be a multiple of 4.

⟨ Empty the last bytes out of *dvi_buf* 599 ⟩ ≡
  if *dvi_limit* = *half_buf* **then** *write_dvi*(*half_buf*, *dvi_buf_size* − 1);
  if *dvi_ptr* > 0 **then** *write_dvi*(0, *dvi_ptr* − 1)

This code is used in section 642.

600. The *dvi_four* procedure outputs four bytes in two's complement notation, without risking arithmetic overflow.

procedure *dvi_four*(*x* : *integer*);
  begin if $x \geq 0$ **then** *dvi_out*(*x* **div** ′100000000)
  else begin *x* ← *x* + ′10000000000; *x* ← *x* + ′10000000000; *dvi_out*((*x* **div** ′100000000) + 128);
    end;
  x ← *x* **mod** ′100000000; *dvi_out*(*x* **div** ′200000); *x* ← *x* **mod** ′200000; *dvi_out*(*x* **div** ′400);
  dvi_out(*x* **mod** ′400);
  end;

601. A mild optimization of the output is performed by the *dvi_pop* routine, which issues a *pop* unless it is possible to cancel a '*push pop*' pair. The parameter to *dvi_pop* is the byte address following the old *push* that matches the new *pop*.

procedure *dvi_pop*(*l* : *integer*);
  begin if (*l* = *dvi_offset* + *dvi_ptr*) ∧ (*dvi_ptr* > 0) **then** *decr*(*dvi_ptr*)
  else *dvi_out*(*pop*);
  end;

602. Here's a procedure that outputs a font definition. Since TeX82 uses at most 256 different fonts per job, *fnt_def1* is always used as the command code.

procedure *dvi_font_def*(*f* : *internal_font_number*);
  var *k*: *pool_pointer*; { index into *str_pool* }
  begin *dvi_out*(*fnt_def1*); *dvi_out*(*f* − *font_base* − 1);
  dvi_out(*qo*(*font_check*[*f*].*b0*)); *dvi_out*(*qo*(*font_check*[*f*].*b1*)); *dvi_out*(*qo*(*font_check*[*f*].*b2*));
  dvi_out(*qo*(*font_check*[*f*].*b3*));

$dvi\_four(font\_size[f]); \quad dvi\_four(font\_dsize[f]);$
$dvi\_out(length(font\_area[f])); \quad dvi\_out(length(font\_name[f]));$
⟨ Output the font name whose internal number is f 603 ⟩;
end;

603. ⟨ Output the font name whose internal number is f 603 ⟩ ≡
  for $k \leftarrow str\_start[font\_area[f]]$ **to** $str\_start[font\_area[f] + 1] - 1$ **do** $dvi\_out(str\_pool[k]);$
  for $k \leftarrow str\_start[font\_name[f]]$ **to** $str\_start[font\_name[f] + 1] - 1$ **do** $dvi\_out(str\_pool[k])$

This code is used in section 602.

$b0$: *quarterword*, §113.
$b1$: *quarterword*, §113.
$b2$: *quarterword*, §113.
$b3$: *quarterword*, §113.
decr = macro, §16.
dvi_buf_size = **const**, §11.
fnt_def1 = 243, §586.
font_area: **array**, §549.

font_base = 0, §12.
font_check: **array**, §549.
font_dsize: **array**, §549.
font_name: **array**, §549.
font_size: **array**, §549.
incr = macro, §16.
internal_font_number = 0 .. *font_max*, §548.

length = macro, §40.
pool_pointer = 0 .. *pool_size*, §38.
pop = 142, §586.
push = 141, §586.
qo = macro, §112.
str_pool: **packed array**, §39.
str_start: **array**, §39.
write_dvi: **procedure**, §597.

604. Versions of TeX intended for small computers might well choose to omit the ideas in the next few parts of this program, since it is not really necessary to optimize the DVI code by making use of the *w0*, *x0*, *y0*, and *z0* commands. Furthermore, the algorithm that we are about to describe does not pretend to give an optimum reduction in the length of the DVI code; after all, speed is more important than compactness. But the method is surprisingly effective, and it takes comparatively little time.

We can best understand the basic idea by first considering a simpler problem that has the same essential characteristics. Given a sequence of digits, say $3\,1\,4\,1\,5\,9\,2\,6\,5\,3\,5\,8\,9$, we want to assign subscripts d, y, or z to each digit so as to maximize the number of "y-hits" and "z-hits"; a y-hit is an instance of two appearances of the same digit with the subscript y, where no y's intervene between the two appearances, and a z-hit is defined similarly. For example, the sequence above could be decorated with subscripts as follows:

$$3_z\,1_y\,4_d\,1_y\,5_y\,9_d\,2_d\,6_d\,5_y\,3_z\,5_y\,8_d\,9_d.$$

There are three y-hits ($1_y \ldots 1_y$ and $5_y \ldots 5_y \ldots 5_y$) and one z-hit ($3_z \ldots 3_z$); there are no d-hits, since the two appearances of 9_d have d's between them, but we don't count d-hits so it doesn't matter how many there are. These subscripts are analogous to the DVI commands called *down*, y, and z, and the digits are analogous to different amounts of vertical motion; a y-hit or z-hit corresponds to the opportunity to use the one-byte commands *y0* or *z0* in a DVI file.

TeX's method of assigning subscripts works like this: Append a new digit, say δ, to the right of the sequence. Now look back through the sequence until one of the following things happens: (a) You see δ_y or δ_z, and this was the first time you encountered a y or z subscript, respectively. Then assign y or z to the new δ; you have scored a hit. (b) You see δ_d, and no y subscripts have been encountered so far during this search. Then change the previous δ_d to δ_y (this corresponds to changing a command in the output buffer), and assign y to the new δ; it's another hit. (c) You see δ_d, and a y subscript has been seen but not a z. Change the previous δ_d to δ_z and assign z to the new δ. (d) You encounter both y and z subscripts before encountering a suitable δ, or you scan all the way to the front of the sequence. Assign d to the new δ; this assignment may be changed later.

The subscripts $3_z\,1_y\,4_d\ldots$ in the example above were, in fact, produced by this procedure, as the reader can verify. (Go ahead and try it.)

605. In order to implement such an idea, TeX maintains a stack of pointers to the *down*, y, and z commands that have been generated for the current page. And there is a similar stack for *right*, w, and x commands. These stacks are called the down stack and right stack, and their top elements are maintained in the variables *down_ptr* and *right_ptr*.

Each entry in these stacks contains four fields: The *width* field is the amount of motion down or to the right; the *location* field is the byte number of the DVI command in question (including the appropriate *dvi_offset*); the *link* field points to the next item below this one on the stack; and the *info* field encodes the options for possible change in the DVI command.

    define *movement_node_size* = 3   { number of words per entry in the down and right stacks }
    define *location*(#) ≡ *mem*[# + 2].*int*   { DVI byte number for a movement command }
⟨ Global variables 13 ⟩ +≡
down_ptr, *right_ptr*: *pointer*;   { heads of the down and right stacks }

606. ⟨ Set initial values of key variables 21 ⟩ +≡
   down_ptr ← *null*; *right_ptr* ← *null*;

607. Here is a subroutine that produces a DVI command for some specified downward or rightward motion. It has two parameters: w is the amount of motion, and o is either *down1* or *right1*. We use the fact that the command codes have convenient arithmetic properties: $y1 - down1 = w1 - right1$ and $z1 - down1 = x1 - right1$.

procedure *movement*(w : *scaled*; o : *eight_bits*);
   label *exit*, *found*, *not_found*, 2, 1;
   var *mstate*: *small_number*;   { have we seen a y or z? }
      p, q: *pointer*;   { current and top nodes on the stack }
      k: *integer*;   { index into *dvi_buf*, modulo *dvi_buf_size* }
   begin q ← *get_node*(*movement_node_size*);   { new node for the top of the stack }
   width(q) ← w; *location*(q) ← *dvi_offset* + *dvi_ptr*;
   if $o = down1$ **then**
      begin *link*(q) ← *down_ptr*; *down_ptr* ← q;
      end
   else begin *link*(q) ← *right_ptr*; *right_ptr* ← q;
      end;
   ⟨ Look at the other stack entries until deciding what sort of DVI command to generate; **goto** *found* if node p is a "hit" 611 ⟩;
   ⟨ Generate a *down* or *right* command for w and **return** 610 ⟩;
found: ⟨ Generate a *y0* or *z0* command in order to reuse a previous appearance of w 609 ⟩;
exit: **end**;

---

down1 = 157, §586.
dvi_buf_size = **const**, §11.
eight_bits = 0 .. 255, §25.
exit = 10, §15.
found = 40, §15.
get_node: **function**, §125.
info = macro, §118.
int: *integer*, §113.
link = macro, §118.

mem: **array**, §116.
not_found = 45, §15.
null = macro, §115.
pointer = macro, §115.
right1 = 143, §586.
scaled = *integer*, §101.
small_number = 0 .. 63, §101.
w0 = 147, §586.

w1 = 148, §586.
width = macro, §135.
x0 = 152, §586.
x1 = 153, §586.
y0 = 161, §586.
y1 = 162, §586.
z0 = 166, §586.
z1 = 167, §586.

608.　The *info* fields in the entries of the down stack or the right stack have six possible settings: *y_here* or *z_here* mean that the DVI command refers to y or z, respectively (or to w or x, in the case of horizontal motion); *yz_OK* means that the DVI command is *down* (or *right*) but can be changed to either y or z (or to either w or x); *y_OK* means that it is *down* and can be changed to y but not z; *z_OK* is similar; and *d_fixed* means it must stay *down*.

The four settings *yz_OK*, *y_OK*, *z_OK*, *d_fixed* would not need to be distinguished from each other if we were simply solving the digit-subscripting problem mentioned above. But in TeX's case there is a complication because of the nested structure of *push* and *pop* commands. Suppose we add parentheses to the digit-subscripting problem, redefining hits so that $\delta_y \ldots \delta_y$ is a hit if all y's between the δ's are enclosed in properly nested parentheses, and if the parenthesis level of the right-hand δ_y is deeper than or equal to that of the left-hand one. Thus, '(' and ')' correspond to '*push*' and '*pop*'. Now if we want to assign a subscript to the final 1 in the sequence

$$2_y\, 7_d\, 1_d\, (\, 8_z\, 2_y\, 8_z\,)\, 1$$

we cannot change the previous 1_d to 1_y, since that would invalidate the $2_y \ldots 2_y$ hit. But we can change it to 1_z, scoring a hit since the intervening 8_z's are enclosed in parentheses.

The program below removes movement nodes that are introduced after a *push*, before it outputs the corresponding *pop*.

define *y_here* $= 1$　{ *info* when the movement entry points to a y command }
define *z_here* $= 2$　{ *info* when the movement entry points to a z command }
define *yz_OK* $= 3$　{ *info* corresponding to an unconstrained *down* command }
define *y_OK* $= 4$　{ *info* corresponding to a *down* that can't become a z }
define *z_OK* $= 5$　{ *info* corresponding to a *down* that can't become a y }
define *d_fixed* $= 6$　{ *info* corresponding to a *down* that can't change }

609.　When the *movement* procedure gets to the label *found*, the value of *info*(p) will be either *y_here* or *z_here*. If it is, say, *y_here*, the procedure generates a *y0* command (or a *w0* command), and marks all *info* fields between q and p so that y is not OK in that range.

⟨ Generate a *y0* or *z0* command in order to reuse a previous appearance of w 609 ⟩ ≡
　info(q) ← *info*(p);
　if *info*(q) = *y_here* **then**
　　begin *dvi_out*(o + *y0* − *down1*);　{ *y0* or *w0* }
　　while *link*(q) ≠ p **do**
　　　begin q ← *link*(q);
　　　case *info*(q) **of**
　　　yz_OK: *info*(q) ← *z_OK*;
　　　y_OK: *info*(q) ← *d_fixed*;
　　　othercases *do_nothing*
　　　endcases;
　　　end;
　　end
　else begin *dvi_out*(o + *z0* − *down1*);　{ *z0* or *x0* }
　　while *link*(q) ≠ p **do**
　　　begin q ← *link*(q);
　　　case *info*(q) **of**

yz_OK: $info(q) \leftarrow y\_OK$;
z_OK: $info(q) \leftarrow d\_fixed$;
othercases $do\_nothing$
endcases;
  end;
end

This code is used in section 607.

610. ⟨ Generate a *down* or *right* command for w and **return** 610 ⟩ ≡
  $info(q) \leftarrow yz\_OK$;
  if $abs(w) \geq \prime40000000$ **then**
    begin $dvi\_out(o + 3)$;   { *down4* or *right4* }
    $dvi\_four(w)$; **return**;
    end;
  if $abs(w) \geq \prime100000$ **then**
    begin $dvi\_out(o + 2)$;   { *down3* or *right3* }
    if $w < 0$ **then** $w \leftarrow w + \prime100000000$;
    $dvi\_out(w \textbf{ div } \prime200000)$; $w \leftarrow w \bmod \prime200000$; **goto** 2;
    end;
  if $abs(w) \geq \prime200$ **then**
    begin $dvi\_out(o + 1)$;   { *down2* or *right2* }
    if $w < 0$ **then** $w \leftarrow w + \prime200000$;
    goto 2;
    end;
  $dvi\_out(o)$;   { *down1* or *right1* }
  if $w < 0$ **then** $w \leftarrow w + \prime400$;
  goto 1;
2: $dvi\_out(w \textbf{ div } \prime400)$;
1: $dvi\_out(w \bmod \prime400)$; **return**

This code is used in section 607.

$do\_nothing$ = macro, §16.
$down1$ = 157, §586.
$down2$, §585.
$down3$, §585.
$down4$, §585.
dvi_four: **procedure**, §600.
dvi_out = macro, §598.
$found$ = 40, §15.

$info$ = macro, §118.
$link$ = macro, §118.
$movement$: **procedure**, §607.
o: $eight\_bits$, §607.
p: $pointer$, §607.
pop = 142, §586.
$push$ = 141, §586.

q: $pointer$, §607.
$right1$ = 143, §586.
w: $scaled$, §607.
$w0$ = 147, §586.
$x0$ = 152, §586.
$y0$ = 161, §586.
$z0$ = 166, §586.

611. As we search through the stack, we are in one of three states, y_seen, z_seen, or $none\_seen$, depending on whether we have encountered y_here or z_here nodes. These states are encoded as multiples of 6, so that they can be added to the $info$ fields for quick decision-making.

> **define** $none\_seen = 0$ { no y_here or z_here nodes have been encountered yet }
> **define** $y\_seen = 6$ { we have seen y_here but not z_here }
> **define** $z\_seen = 12$ { we have seen z_here but not y_here }

⟨ Look at the other stack entries until deciding what sort of DVI command to generate; **goto** *found* if node p is a "hit" 611 ⟩ ≡

> $p \leftarrow link(q)$; $mstate \leftarrow none\_seen$;
> **while** $p \neq null$ **do**
> > **begin if** $width(p) = w$ **then** ⟨ Consider a node with matching width; **goto** *found* if it's a hit 612 ⟩
> > **else case** $mstate + info(p)$ **of**
> > > $none\_seen + y\_here$: $mstate \leftarrow y\_seen$;
> > > $none\_seen + z\_here$: $mstate \leftarrow z\_seen$;
> > > $y\_seen + z\_here, z\_seen + y\_here$: **goto** not_found;
> > > **othercases** $do\_nothing$
> > > **endcases**;
> > $p \leftarrow link(p)$;
> > **end**;
> not_found:

This code is used in section 607.

612. We might find a valid hit in a y or z byte that is already gone from the buffer. But we can't change bytes that are gone forever; "the moving finger writes, ..."

⟨ Consider a node with matching width; **goto** *found* if it's a hit 612 ⟩ ≡

> **case** $mstate + info(p)$ **of**
> $none\_seen + yz\_OK, none\_seen + y\_OK, z\_seen + yz\_OK, z\_seen + y\_OK$:
> > **if** $location(p) < dvi\_gone$ **then goto** not_found
> > **else** ⟨ Change buffered instruction to y or w and **goto** *found* 613 ⟩;
> $none\_seen + z\_OK, y\_seen + yz\_OK, y\_seen + z\_OK$:
> > **if** $location(p) < dvi\_gone$ **then goto** not_found
> > **else** ⟨ Change buffered instruction to z or x and **goto** *found* 614 ⟩;
> $none\_seen + y\_here, none\_seen + z\_here, y\_seen + z\_here, z\_seen + y\_here$: **goto** *found*;
> **othercases** $do\_nothing$
> **endcases**

This code is used in section 611.

613. ⟨ Change buffered instruction to y or w and **goto** *found* 613 ⟩ ≡

> **begin** $k \leftarrow location(p) - dvi\_offset$;
> **if** $k < 0$ **then** $k \leftarrow k + dvi\_buf\_size$;
> $dvi\_buf[k] \leftarrow dvi\_buf[k] + y1 - down1$; $info(p) \leftarrow y\_here$; **goto** *found*;
> **end**

This code is used in section 612.

614. ⟨Change buffered instruction to z or x and **goto** *found* 614⟩ ≡
    begin $k \leftarrow location(p) - dvi\_offset$;
    if $k < 0$ **then** $k \leftarrow k + dvi\_buf\_size$;
    $dvi\_buf[k] \leftarrow dvi\_buf[k] + z1 - down1$; $info(p) \leftarrow z\_here$; **goto** *found*;
    end

This code is used in section 612.

615. In case you are wondering when all the movement nodes are removed from TeX's memory, the answer is that they are recycled just before *hlist_out* and *vlist_out* finish outputting a box. This restores the down and right stacks to the state they were in before the box was output, except that some *info*'s may have become more restrictive.

procedure *prune_movements*(l : *integer*);   {delete movement nodes with *location* $\geq l$}
  label *done*, *exit*;
  var p: *pointer*;   {node being deleted}
  begin while $down\_ptr \neq null$ **do**
    begin if $location(down\_ptr) < l$ **then goto** *done*;
    $p \leftarrow down\_ptr$; $down\_ptr \leftarrow link(p)$; $free\_node(p, movement\_node\_size)$;
    end;
done: **while** $right\_ptr \neq null$ **do**
    begin if $location(right\_ptr) < l$ **then return**;
    $p \leftarrow right\_ptr$; $right\_ptr \leftarrow link(p)$; $free\_node(p, movement\_node\_size)$;
    end;
exit: **end**;

---

do_nothing = macro, §16.
done = 30, §15.
down_ptr: *pointer*, §605.
down1 = 157, §586.
dvi_buf_size = **const**, §11.
exit = 10, §15.
found = 40, §15.
free_node: **procedure**, §130.
hlist_out: **procedure**, §619.
info = macro, §118.
k: *integer*, §607.

link = macro, §118.
location = macro, §605.
movement_node_size = 3, §605.
mstate: *small_number*, §607.
not_found = 45, §15.
null = macro, §115.
p: *pointer*, §607.
pointer = macro, §115.
q: *pointer*, §607.
right_ptr: *pointer*, §605.

vlist_out: **procedure**, §629.
w: *scaled*, §607.
width = macro, §135.
y_here = 1, §608.
y_OK = 4, §608.
y1 = 162, §586.
yz_OK = 3, §608.
z_here = 2, §608.
z_OK = 5, §608.
z1 = 167, §586.

616. The actual distances by which we want to move might be computed as the sum of several separate movements. For example, there might be several glue nodes in succession, or we might want to move right by the width of some box plus some amount of glue. More importantly, the baselineskip distances are computed in terms of glue together with the depth and height of adjacent boxes, and we want the DVI file to lump these three quantities together into a single motion.

Therefore, TeX maintains two pairs of global variables: dvi_h and dvi_v are the h and v coordinates corresponding to the commands actually output to the DVI file, while cur_h and cur_v are the coordinates corresponding to the current state of the output routines. Coordinate changes will accumulate in cur_h and cur_v without being reflected in the output, until such a change becomes necessary or desirable; we can call the *movement* procedure whenever we want to make $dvi\_h = cur\_h$ or $dvi\_v = cur\_v$.

The current font reflected in the DVI output is called dvi_f; there is no need for a 'cur_f' variable.

The depth of nesting of *hlist_out* and *vlist_out* is called cur_s; this is essentially the depth of *push* commands in the DVI output.

define $synch\_h \equiv$
    if $cur\_h \neq dvi\_h$ **then**
        begin $movement(cur\_h - dvi\_h, right1)$; $dvi\_h \leftarrow cur\_h$;
        end
define $synch\_v \equiv$
    if $cur\_v \neq dvi\_v$ **then**
        begin $movement(cur\_v - dvi\_v, down1)$; $dvi\_v \leftarrow cur\_v$;
        end

⟨ Global variables 13 ⟩ +≡
dvi_h, dvi_v: *scaled*; { a DVI reader program thinks we are here }
cur_h, cur_v: *scaled*; { TeX thinks we are here }
dvi_f: *internal_font_number*; { the current font }
cur_s: *integer*; { current depth of output box nesting }

617. ⟨ Initialize variables as *ship_out* begins 617 ⟩ ≡
  $dvi\_h \leftarrow 0$; $dvi\_v \leftarrow 0$; $cur\_h \leftarrow h\_offset$; $dvi\_f \leftarrow null\_font$; $cur\_s \leftarrow -1$; *ensure_dvi_open*;
  if $total\_pages = 0$ **then**
    begin $dvi\_out(pre)$; $dvi\_out(id\_byte)$; { output the preamble }
    $dvi\_four(25400000)$; $dvi\_four(473628672)$; { conversion ratio for sp }
    prepare_mag; $dvi\_four(mag)$; { magnification factor is frozen }
    $old\_setting \leftarrow selector$; $selector \leftarrow new\_string$; $print("\sqcup TeX\sqcup output\sqcup")$; $print\_int(year)$;
    $print\_char(".")$; $print\_two(month)$; $print\_char(".")$; $print\_two(day)$; $print\_char(":")$;
    $print\_two(time$ **div** $60)$; $print\_two(time$ **mod** $60)$; $selector \leftarrow old\_setting$; $dvi\_out(cur\_length)$;
    for $s \leftarrow str\_start[str\_ptr]$ **to** $pool\_ptr - 1$ **do** $dvi\_out(str\_pool[s])$;
    $pool\_ptr \leftarrow str\_start[str\_ptr]$; { flush the current string }
    end
This code is used in section 640.

618. When *hlist_out* is called, its duty is to output the box represented by the *hlist_node* pointed to by *temp_ptr*. The reference point of that box has coordinates (cur_h, cur_v).

Similarly, when *vlist_out* is called, its duty is to output the box represented by the *vlist_node* pointed to by *temp_ptr*. The reference point of that box has coordinates (*cur_h*, *cur_v*).

procedure *vlist_out*; *forward*;   { *hlist_out* and *vlist_out* are mutually recursive }

619. The recursive procedures *hlist_out* and *vlist_out* each have local variables *save_h* and *save_v* to hold the values of *dvi_h* and *dvi_v* just before entering a new level of recursion. In effect, the values of *save_h* and *save_v* on TeX's run-time stack correspond to the values of h and v that a DVI-reading program will push onto its coordinate stack.

define *move_past* = 13 { go to this label when advancing past glue or a rule }
define *fin_rule* = 14 { go to this label to finish processing a rule }
define *next_p* = 15 { go to this label when finished with node p }
⟨ Declare procedures needed in *hlist_out*, *vlist_out* 1368 ⟩
procedure *hlist_out*; { output an *hlist_node* box }
  label *reswitch*, *move_past*, *fin_rule*, *next_p*;
  var *base_line*: *scaled*; { the baseline coordinate for this box }
    left_edge: *scaled*; { the left coordinate for this box }
    save_h, *save_v*: *scaled*; { what *dvi_h* and *dvi_v* should pop to }
    this_box: *pointer*; { pointer to containing box }
    g_order: *glue_ord*; { applicable order of infinity for glue }
    g_sign: *normal* .. *shrinking*; { selects type of glue }
    p: *pointer*; { current position in the hlist }
    save_loc: *integer*; { DVI byte location upon entry }
    leader_box: *pointer*; { the leader box being replicated }
    leader_wd: *scaled*; { width of leader box being replicated }
    lx: *scaled*; { extra space between leader boxes }
    outer_doing_leaders: *boolean*; { were we doing leaders? }
    edge: *scaled*; { left edge of sub-box, or right edge of leader space }
  begin *this_box* ← *temp_ptr*; *g_order* ← *glue_order*(*this_box*); *g_sign* ← *glue_sign*(*this_box*);
  p ← *list_ptr*(*this_box*); *incr*(*cur_s*);
  if *cur_s* > 0 **then** *dvi_out*(*push*);
  if *cur_s* > *max_push* **then** *max_push* ← *cur_s*;
  save_loc ← *dvi_offset* + *dvi_ptr*; *base_line* ← *cur_v*; *left_edge* ← *cur_h*;
  while *p* ≠ *null* **do** ⟨ Output node p for *hlist_out* and move to the next node, maintaining the condition *cur_v* = *base_line* 620 ⟩;
  prune_movements(*save_loc*);
  if *cur_s* > 0 **then** *dvi_pop*(*save_loc*);
  decr(*cur_s*);
  end;

620.　We ought to give special care to the efficiency of one part of *hlist_out*, since it belongs to TeX's inner loop. When a *char_node* is encountered, we save a little time by processing several nodes in succession until reaching a non-*char_node*. The program uses the fact that $set\_char\_0 = 0$.

⟨Output node p for *hlist_out* and move to the next node, maintaining the condition
　　　　$cur\_v = base\_line$ 620⟩ ≡
reswitch: **if** *is_char_node*(p) **then**
　　begin *synch_h*; *synch_v*;
　　repeat $f \leftarrow font(p)$; $c \leftarrow character(p)$;
　　　　if $f \neq dvi\_f$ **then** ⟨Change font *dvi_f* to f 621⟩;
　　　　if $c < qi(128)$ **then** *dvi_out*($qo(c)$)
　　　　else begin *dvi_out*(*set1*); *dvi_out*($qo(c)$);
　　　　　　end;
　　　　$cur\_h \leftarrow cur\_h + char\_width(f)(char\_info(f)(c))$; $p \leftarrow link(p)$;
　　until ¬*is_char_node*(p);
　　$dvi\_h \leftarrow cur\_h$;
　　end
　　else ⟨Output the non-*char_node* p for *hlist_out* and move to the next node 622⟩

This code is used in section 619.

621.　⟨Change font *dvi_f* to f 621⟩ ≡
　begin if ¬*font_used*[f] **then**
　　begin *dvi_font_def*(f); *font_used*[f] ← *true*;
　　end;
　if $f \leq 64 + font\_base$ **then** *dvi_out*($f - font\_base - 1 + fnt\_num\_0$)
　else begin *dvi_out*(*fnt1*); *dvi_out*($f - font\_base - 1$);
　　end;
　$dvi\_f \leftarrow f$;
　end

This code is used in section 620.

---

c: *quarterword*, §592.
char_info = macro, §554.
char_node, §134.
char_width = macro, §554.
character = macro, §134.
cur_h: *scaled*, §616.
cur_s: *integer*, §616.
cur_v: *scaled*, §616.
decr = macro, §16.
dvi_f: *internal_font_number*, §616.
dvi_font_def: **procedure**, §602.
dvi_h: *scaled*, §616.
dvi_out = macro, §598.
dvi_pop: **procedure**, §601.
dvi_v: *scaled*, §616.
f: *quarterword*, §592.

fnt_num_0 = 171, §586.
fnt1 = 235, §586.
font = macro, §134.
font_base = 0, §12.
font_used: **array**, §549.
glue_ord = 0 .. 3, §150.
glue_order = macro, §135.
glue_sign = macro, §135.
hlist_node = 0, §135.
incr = macro, §16.
is_char_node = macro, §134.
link = macro, §118.
list_ptr = macro, §135.
max_push: *integer*, §592.
normal = 0, §135.
null = macro, §115.

pointer = macro, §115.
prune_movements: **procedure**, §615.
push = 141, §586.
qi = macro, §112.
qo = macro, §112.
reswitch = 21, §15.
scaled = *integer*, §101.
set_char_0 = 0, §586.
set1 = 128, §586.
shrinking = 2, §135.
synch_h = macro, §616.
synch_v = macro, §616.
temp_ptr: *pointer*, §115.
vlist_out: **procedure**, §629.

622. ⟨Output the non-*char_node* p for *hlist_out* and move to the next node 622⟩ ≡
   begin case *type*(p) **of**
   hlist_node, *vlist_node*: ⟨Output a box in an hlist 623⟩;
   rule_node: **begin** *rule_ht* ← *height*(p); *rule_dp* ← *depth*(p); *rule_wd* ← *width*(p); **goto** *fin_rule*;
      end;
   whatsit_node: ⟨Output the whatsit node p in an hlist 1366⟩;
   glue_node: ⟨Move right or output leaders 625⟩;
   kern_node, *math_node*: *cur_h* ← *cur_h* + *width*(p);
   ligature_node: ⟨Make node p look like a *char_node* and **goto** *reswitch* 652⟩;
   othercases *do_nothing*
   endcases;
   goto *next_p*;
fin_rule: ⟨Output a rule in an hlist 624⟩;
move_past: *cur_h* ← *cur_h* + *rule_wd*;
next_p: p ← *link*(p);
   end

This code is used in section 620.

623. ⟨Output a box in an hlist 623⟩ ≡
   if *list_ptr*(p) = *null* **then** *cur_h* ← *cur_h* + *width*(p)
   else begin *save_h* ← *dvi_h*; *save_v* ← *dvi_v*; *cur_v* ← *base_line* + *shift_amount*(p);
         { shift the box down }
      temp_ptr ← p; *edge* ← *cur_h*;
      if *type*(p) = *vlist_node* **then** *vlist_out* **else** *hlist_out*;
      dvi_h ← *save_h*; *dvi_v* ← *save_v*; *cur_h* ← *edge* + *width*(p); *cur_v* ← *base_line*;
      end

This code is used in section 622.

624. ⟨Output a rule in an hlist 624⟩ ≡
   if *is_running*(*rule_ht*) **then** *rule_ht* ← *height*(*this_box*);
   if *is_running*(*rule_dp*) **then** *rule_dp* ← *depth*(*this_box*);
   rule_ht ← *rule_ht* + *rule_dp*;   { this is the rule thickness }
   if (*rule_ht* > 0) ∧ (*rule_wd* > 0) **then**   { we don't output empty rules }
      begin *synch_h*; *cur_v* ← *base_line* + *rule_dp*; *synch_v*; *dvi_out*(*set_rule*); *dvi_four*(*rule_ht*);
      dvi_four(*rule_wd*); *cur_v* ← *base_line*; *dvi_h* ← *dvi_h* + *rule_wd*;
      end

This code is used in section 622.

625. ⟨Move right or output leaders 625⟩ ≡
   begin g ← *glue_ptr*(p); *rule_wd* ← *width*(g);
   if *g_sign* ≠ *normal* **then**
      begin if *g_sign* = *stretching* **then**
         begin if *stretch_order*(g) = *g_order* **then**
            rule_wd ← *rule_wd* + *round*(*float*(*glue_set*(*this_box*)) ∗ *stretch*(g));
         end
      else begin if *shrink_order*(g) = *g_order* **then**
            rule_wd ← *rule_wd* − *round*(*float*(*glue_set*(*this_box*)) ∗ *shrink*(g));
         end;
      end;

if $subtype(p) \geq a\_leaders$ **then**
    $\langle$ Output leaders in an hlist, **goto** fin_rule if a rule or to $next\_p$ if done 626 $\rangle$;
goto $move\_past$;
end

This code is used in section 622.

626. $\langle$ Output leaders in an hlist, **goto** fin_rule if a rule or to $next\_p$ if done 626 $\rangle \equiv$
  begin $leader\_box \leftarrow leader\_ptr(p)$;
  if $type(leader\_box) = rule\_node$ **then**
    begin $rule\_ht \leftarrow height(leader\_box)$; $rule\_dp \leftarrow depth(leader\_box)$; **goto** fin_rule;
    end;
  $leader\_wd \leftarrow width(leader\_box)$;
  if $(leader\_wd > 0) \wedge (rule\_wd > 0)$ **then**
    begin $edge \leftarrow cur\_h + rule\_wd$; $lx \leftarrow 0$; $\langle$ Let cur_h be the position of the first box, and set
      $leader\_wd + lx$ to the spacing between corresponding parts of boxes 627 $\rangle$;
    while $cur\_h + leader\_wd \leq edge$ **do**
      $\langle$ Output a leader box at cur_h, then advance cur_h by $leader\_wd + lx$ 628 $\rangle$;
    $cur\_h \leftarrow edge$; **goto** $next\_p$;
    end;
  end

This code is used in section 625.

$a\_leaders = 100$, §149.
$base\_line$: $scaled$, §619.
$char\_node$, §134.
cur_h: $scaled$, §616.
cur_v: $scaled$, §616.
$depth$ = macro, §135.
$do\_nothing$ = macro, §16.
dvi_four: **procedure**, §600.
dvi_h: $scaled$, §616.
dvi_out = macro, §598.
dvi_v: $scaled$, §616.
$edge$: $scaled$, §619.
$fin\_rule = 14$, §619.
$float$ = macro, §109.
g: $pointer$, §592.
g_order: $glue\_ord$, §619.
g_sign: $0..2$, §619.
$glue\_node = 10$, §149.
$glue\_ptr$ = macro, §149.
$glue\_set$ = macro, §135.
$height$ = macro, §135.

$hlist\_node = 0$, §135.
$hlist\_out$: **procedure**, §619.
$is\_running$ = macro, §138.
$kern\_node = 11$, §155.
$leader\_box$: $pointer$, §619.
$leader\_ptr$ = macro, §149.
$leader\_wd$: $scaled$, §619.
$ligature\_node = 6$, §143.
$link$ = macro, §118.
$list\_ptr$ = macro, §135.
lx: $scaled$, §619.
$math\_node = 9$, §147.
$move\_past = 13$, §619.
$next\_p = 15$, §619.
$normal = 0$, §135.
$null$ = macro, §115.
p: $pointer$, §619.
$reswitch = 21$, §15.
$rule\_dp$: $scaled$, §592.
$rule\_ht$: $scaled$, §592.
$rule\_node = 2$, §138.

$rule\_wd$: $scaled$, §592.
$save\_h$: $scaled$, §619.
$save\_v$: $scaled$, §619.
$set\_rule = 132$, §586.
$shift\_amount$ = macro, §135.
$shrink$ = macro, §150.
$shrink\_order$ = macro, §150.
$stretch$ = macro, §150.
$stretch\_order$ = macro, §150.
$stretching = 1$, §135.
$subtype$ = macro, §133.
$synch\_h$ = macro, §616.
$synch\_v$ = macro, §616.
$temp\_ptr$: $pointer$, §115.
$this\_box$: $pointer$, §619.
$type$ = macro, §133.
$vlist\_node = 1$, §137.
$vlist\_out$: **procedure**, §629.
$whatsit\_node = 8$, §146.
$width$ = macro, §135.

627. The calculations related to leaders require a bit of care. First, in the case of *a_leaders* (aligned leaders), we want to move *cur_h* to *left_edge* plus the smallest multiple of *leader_wd* for which the result is not less than the current value of *cur_h*; i.e., *cur_h* should become *left_edge* + *leader_wd* × $\lceil (cur\_h - left\_edge)/leader\_wd \rceil$. The program here should work in all cases even though some implementations of Pascal give nonstandard results for the **div** operation when *cur_h* is less than *left_edge*.

In the case of *c_leaders* (centered leaders), we want to increase *cur_h* by half of the excess space not occupied by the leaders; and in the case of case of *x_leaders* (expanded leaders) we increase *cur_h* by $1/(q+1)$ of this excess space, where q is the number of times the leader box will be replicated. Slight inaccuracies in the division might accumulate; half of this rounding error is placed at each end of the leaders.

⟨ Let *cur_h* be the position of the first box, and set *leader_wd* + *lx* to the spacing between corresponding parts of boxes 627 ⟩ ≡
  if *subtype*(*p*) = *a_leaders* **then**
    begin *save_h* ← *cur_h*; *cur_h* ← *left_edge* + *leader_wd* * ((*cur_h* − *left_edge*) **div** *leader_wd*);
    if *cur_h* < *save_h* **then** *cur_h* ← *cur_h* + *leader_wd*;
    end
  else begin *lq* ← *rule_wd* **div** *leader_wd*; { the number of box copies }
    lr ← *rule_wd* **mod** *leader_wd*; { the remaining space }
    if *subtype*(*p*) = *c_leaders* **then** *cur_h* ← *cur_h* + (*lr* **div** 2)
    else begin *lx* ← (2 * *lr* + *lq* + 1) **div** (2 * *lq* + 2); { round(*lr*/(*lq* + 1)) }
      cur_h ← *cur_h* + ((*lr* − (*lq* − 1) * *lx*) **div** 2);
      end;
    end
This code is used in section 626.

628. The '*synch*' operations here are intended to decrease the number of bytes needed to specify horizontal and vertical motion in the DVI output.

⟨ Output a leader box at *cur_h*, then advance *cur_h* by *leader_wd* + *lx* 628 ⟩ ≡
  begin *cur_v* ← *base_line* + *shift_amount*(*leader_box*); *synch_v*; *save_v* ← *dvi_v*;
  synch_h; *save_h* ← *dvi_h*; *temp_ptr* ← *leader_box*; *outer_doing_leaders* ← *doing_leaders*;
  doing_leaders ← *true*;
  if *type*(*leader_box*) = *vlist_node* **then** *vlist_out* **else** *hlist_out*;
  doing_leaders ← *outer_doing_leaders*; *dvi_v* ← *save_v*; *dvi_h* ← *save_h*; *cur_v* ← *save_v*;
  cur_h ← *save_h* + *leader_wd* + *lx*;
  end
This code is used in section 626.

629. The *vlist_out* routine is similar to *hlist_out*, but a bit simpler.

procedure *vlist_out*; { output a *vlist_node* box }
  label *move_past*, *fin_rule*, *next_p*;
  var *left_edge*: *scaled*; { the left coordinate for this box }
    top_edge: *scaled*; { the top coordinate for this box }
    save_h, *save_v*: *scaled*; { what *dvi_h* and *dvi_v* should pop to }
    this_box: *pointer*; { pointer to containing box }
    g_order: *glue_ord*; { applicable order of infinity for glue }
    g_sign: *normal* .. *shrinking*; { selects type of glue }

p: *pointer*;   { current position in the vlist }
save_loc: *integer*;   { DVI byte location upon entry }
leader_box: *pointer*;   { the leader box being replicated }
leader_ht: *scaled*;   { height of leader box being replicated }
lx: *scaled*;   { extra space between leader boxes }
outer_doing_leaders: *boolean*;   { were we doing leaders? }
edge: *scaled*;   { bottom boundary of leader space }
begin *this_box* $\leftarrow$ *temp_ptr*; *g_order* $\leftarrow$ *glue_order*(*this_box*); *g_sign* $\leftarrow$ *glue_sign*(*this_box*);
$p \leftarrow$ *list_ptr*(*this_box*); *incr*(*cur_s*);
if *cur_s* > 0 **then** *dvi_out*(*push*);
if *cur_s* $>$ *max_push* **then** *max_push* $\leftarrow$ *cur_s*;
save_loc $\leftarrow$ *dvi_offset* + *dvi_ptr*; *left_edge* $\leftarrow$ *cur_h*; *cur_v* $\leftarrow$ *cur_v* $-$ *height*(*this_box*);
top_edge $\leftarrow$ *cur_v*;
while $p \neq$ *null* **do** $\langle$ Output node p for *vlist_out* and move to the next node, maintaining the
        condition *cur_h* = *left_edge* 630 $\rangle$;
prune_movements(*save_loc*);
if *cur_s* > 0 **then** *dvi_pop*(*save_loc*);
decr(*cur_s*);
end;

---

a_leaders = 100, §149.
base_line: *scaled*, §619.
c_leaders = 101, §149.
cur_h: *scaled*, §616.
cur_s: *integer*, §616.
cur_v: *scaled*, §616.
decr = macro, §16.
doing_leaders: *boolean*, §592.
dvi_h: *scaled*, §616.
dvi_out = macro, §598.
dvi_pop: **procedure**, §601.
dvi_v: *scaled*, §616.
fin_rule = 14, §619.
glue_ord = 0 . . 3, §150.
glue_order = macro, §135.
glue_sign = macro, §135.
height = macro, §135.

hlist_out: **procedure**, §619.
incr = macro, §16.
leader_box: *pointer*, §619.
leader_wd: *scaled*, §619.
left_edge: *scaled*, §619.
list_ptr = macro, §135.
lq: *integer*, §592.
lr: *integer*, §592.
lx: *scaled*, §619.
max_push: *integer*, §592.
move_past = 13, §619.
next_p = 15, §619.
normal = 0, §135.
null = macro, §115.
outer_doing_leaders: *boolean*, §619.
p: *pointer*, §619.
pointer = macro, §115.

prune_movements: **procedure**,
   §615.
push = 141, §586.
rule_wd: *scaled*, §592.
save_h: *scaled*, §619.
save_v: *scaled*, §619.
scaled = *integer*, §101.
shift_amount = macro, §135.
shrinking = 2, §135.
subtype = macro, §133.
synch_h = macro, §616.
synch_v = macro, §616.
temp_ptr: *pointer*, §115.
type = macro, §133.
vlist_node = 1, §137.
x_leaders = 102, §149.

630. ⟨Output node p for *vlist_out* and move to the next node, maintaining the condition
$cur\_h = left\_edge$ 630⟩ ≡
begin if *is_char_node*(p) **then** *confusion*("vlistout")
else ⟨Output the non-*char_node* p for *vlist_out* 631⟩;
next_p: $p \leftarrow link(p)$;
end

This code is used in section 629.

631. ⟨Output the non-*char_node* p for *vlist_out* 631⟩ ≡
begin case *type*(p) **of**
hlist_node, *vlist_node*: ⟨Output a box in a vlist 632⟩;
rule_node: **begin** $rule\_ht \leftarrow height(p)$; $rule\_dp \leftarrow depth(p)$; $rule\_wd \leftarrow width(p)$; **goto** *fin_rule*;
   end;
whatsit_node: ⟨Output the whatsit node p in a vlist 1365⟩;
glue_node: ⟨Move down or output leaders 634⟩;
kern_node: $cur\_v \leftarrow cur\_v + width(p)$;
othercases *do_nothing*
endcases;
goto *next_p*;
fin_rule: ⟨Output a rule in a vlist, **goto** *next_p* 633⟩;
move_past: $cur\_v \leftarrow cur\_v + rule\_ht$;
end

This code is used in section 630.

632. The *synch_v* here allows the DVI output to use one-byte commands for adjusting v in most cases, since the baselineskip distance will usually be constant.
⟨Output a box in a vlist 632⟩ ≡
  if *list_ptr*(p) = *null* **then** $cur\_v \leftarrow cur\_v + height(p) + depth(p)$
  else begin $cur\_v \leftarrow cur\_v + height(p)$; *synch_v*; $save\_h \leftarrow dvi\_h$; $save\_v \leftarrow dvi\_v$;
    $cur\_h \leftarrow left\_edge + shift\_amount(p)$; { shift the box right }
    $temp\_ptr \leftarrow p$;
    if *type*(p) = *vlist_node* **then** *vlist_out* **else** *hlist_out*;
    $dvi\_h \leftarrow save\_h$; $dvi\_v \leftarrow save\_v$; $cur\_v \leftarrow save\_v + depth(p)$; $cur\_h \leftarrow left\_edge$;
    end

This code is used in section 631.

633. ⟨Output a rule in a vlist, **goto** *next_p* 633⟩ ≡
  if *is_running*(*rule_wd*) **then** $rule\_wd \leftarrow width(this\_box)$;
  $rule\_ht \leftarrow rule\_ht + rule\_dp$; { this is the rule thickness }
  $cur\_v \leftarrow cur\_v + rule\_ht$;
  if ($rule\_ht > 0$) ∧ ($rule\_wd > 0$) **then** { we don't output empty rules }
    begin *synch_h*; *synch_v*; *dvi_out*(*put_rule*); *dvi_four*(*rule_ht*); *dvi_four*(*rule_wd*);
    end;
  goto *next_p*

This code is used in section 631.

634. ⟨Move down or output leaders 634⟩ ≡
  begin $g \leftarrow glue\_ptr(p)$; $rule\_ht \leftarrow width(g)$;
  if $g\_sign \neq normal$ **then**

> **begin if** $g\_sign = stretching$ **then**
>   **begin if** $stretch\_order(g) = g\_order$ **then**
> $rule\_ht \leftarrow rule\_ht + round(\mathit{float}(glue\_set(this\_box)) * stretch(g));$
>   **end**
> **else begin if** $shrink\_order(g) = g\_order$ **then**
> $rule\_ht \leftarrow rule\_ht - round(\mathit{float}(glue\_set(this\_box)) * shrink(g));$
>   **end**;
>   **end**;
> **if** $subtype(p) \geq a\_leaders$ **then**
>   ⟨ Output leaders in a vlist, **goto** fin_rule if a rule or to $next\_p$ if done 635 ⟩;
> **goto** $move\_past$;
> **end**

This code is used in section 631.

635. ⟨ Output leaders in a vlist, **goto** fin_rule if a rule or to $next\_p$ if done 635 ⟩ ≡
  begin $leader\_box \leftarrow leader\_ptr(p)$;
  if $type(leader\_box) = rule\_node$ **then**
    begin $rule\_wd \leftarrow width(leader\_box)$; $rule\_dp \leftarrow 0$; **goto** fin_rule;
    end;
  $leader\_ht \leftarrow height(leader\_box) + depth(leader\_box)$;
  if $(leader\_ht > 0) \wedge (rule\_ht > 0)$ **then**
    begin $edge \leftarrow cur\_v + rule\_ht$; $lx \leftarrow 0$; ⟨ Let cur_v be the position of the first box, and set
      $leader\_ht + lx$ to the spacing between corresponding parts of boxes 636 ⟩;
    while $cur\_v + leader\_ht \leq edge$ **do**
      ⟨ Output a leader box at cur_v, then advance cur_v by $leader\_ht + lx$ 637 ⟩;
    $cur\_v \leftarrow edge$; **goto** $next\_p$;
    end;
  end

This code is used in section 634.

$a\_leaders = 100$, §149.
$char\_node$, §134.
$confusion$: **procedure**, §95.
cur_h: $scaled$, §616.
cur_v: $scaled$, §616.
$depth = $ macro, §135.
$do_nothing = $ macro, §16.
dvi_four: **procedure**, §600.
dvi_h: $scaled$, §616.
$dvi_out = $ macro, §598.
dvi_v: $scaled$, §616.
$edge$: $scaled$, §629.
$fin\_rule = 14$, §619.
$\mathit{float} = $ macro, §109.
g: $pointer$, §592.
g_order: $glue\_ord$, §629.
g_sign: $0 .. 2$, §629.
$glue\_node = 10$, §149.
$glue_ptr = $ macro, §149.
$glue_set = $ macro, §135.

$height = $ macro, §135.
$hlist\_node = 0$, §135.
$hlist\_out$: **procedure**, §619.
$is_char_node = $ macro, §134.
$is_running = $ macro, §138.
$kern\_node = 11$, §155.
$leader\_box$: $pointer$, §629.
$leader\_ht$: $scaled$, §629.
$leader_ptr = $ macro, §149.
$left\_edge$: $scaled$, §629.
$link = $ macro, §118.
$list_ptr = $ macro, §135.
lx: $scaled$, §629.
$move\_past = 13$, §619.
$next\_p = 15$, §619.
$normal = 0$, §135.
$null = $ macro, §115.
p: $pointer$, §629.
$put\_rule = 137$, §586.
$rule\_dp$: $scaled$, §592.

$rule\_ht$: $scaled$, §592.
$rule\_node = 2$, §138.
$rule\_wd$: $scaled$, §592.
$save\_h$: $scaled$, §629.
$save\_v$: $scaled$, §629.
$shift_amount = $ macro, §135.
$shrink = $ macro, §150.
$shrink_order = $ macro, §150.
$stretch = $ macro, §150.
$stretch_order = $ macro, §150.
$stretching = 1$, §135.
$subtype = $ macro, §133.
$synch_h = $ macro, §616.
$synch_v = $ macro, §616.
$temp\_ptr$: $pointer$, §115.
$this\_box$: $pointer$, §629.
$type = $ macro, §133.
$vlist\_node = 1$, §137.
$whatsit\_node = 8$, §146.
$width = $ macro, §135.

636. ⟨ Let cur_v be the position of the first box, and set $leader\_ht + lx$ to the spacing between corresponding parts of boxes 636 ⟩ ≡

if $subtype(p) = a\_leaders$ **then**

    begin $save\_v \leftarrow cur\_v$; $cur\_v \leftarrow top\_edge + leader\_ht * ((cur\_v - top\_edge) \textbf{ div } leader\_ht)$;

    if $cur\_v < save\_v$ **then** $cur\_v \leftarrow cur\_v + leader\_ht$;

    end

else begin $lq \leftarrow rule\_ht \textbf{ div } leader\_ht$;   { the number of box copies }

    $lr \leftarrow rule\_ht \textbf{ mod } leader\_ht$;   { the remaining space }

    if $subtype(p) = c\_leaders$ **then** $cur\_v \leftarrow cur\_v + (lr \textbf{ div } 2)$

    else begin $lx \leftarrow (2 * lr + lq + 1) \textbf{ div } (2 * lq + 2)$;   { round$(lr/(lq + 1))$ }

      $cur\_v \leftarrow cur\_v + ((lr - (lq - 1) * lx) \textbf{ div } 2)$;

      end;

    end

This code is used in section 635.

637. When we reach this part of the program, cur_v indicates the top of a leader box, not its baseline.

⟨ Output a leader box at cur_v, then advance cur_v by $leader\_ht + lx$ 637 ⟩ ≡

    begin $cur\_h \leftarrow left\_edge + shift\_amount(leader\_box)$; $synch\_h$; $save\_h \leftarrow dvi\_h$;

    $cur\_v \leftarrow cur\_v + height(leader\_box)$; $synch\_v$; $save\_v \leftarrow dvi\_v$; $temp\_ptr \leftarrow leader\_box$;

    $outer\_doing\_leaders \leftarrow doing\_leaders$; $doing\_leaders \leftarrow true$;

    if $type(leader\_box) = vlist\_node$ **then** $vlist\_out$ **else** $hlist\_out$;

    $doing\_leaders \leftarrow outer\_doing\_leaders$; $dvi\_v \leftarrow save\_v$; $dvi\_h \leftarrow save\_h$; $cur\_h \leftarrow save\_h$;

    $cur\_v \leftarrow save\_v - height(leader\_box) + leader\_ht + lx$;

    end

This code is used in section 635.

638. The $hlist\_out$ and $vlist\_out$ procedures are now complete, so we are ready for the $ship\_out$ routine that gets them started in the first place.

procedure $ship\_out(p : pointer)$;   { output the box p }

    label $done$;

    var $page\_loc$: $integer$;   { location of the current bop }

      j, k: $0 .. 9$;   { indices to first ten count registers }

      s: $pool\_pointer$;   { index into str_pool }

      $old\_setting$: $0 .. max\_selector$;   { saved $selector$ setting }

    begin if $tracing\_output > 0$ **then**

      begin $print\_nl("")$; $print\_ln$; $print("\texttt{Completed\_box\_being\_shipped\_out}")$;

      end;

    if $term\_offset > max\_print\_line - 9$ **then** $print\_ln$

    else if $(term\_offset > 0) \vee (file\_offset > 0)$ **then** $print\_char("\texttt{\_}")$;

    $print\_char("\texttt{[}")$; $j \leftarrow 9$;

    while $(count(j) = 0) \wedge (j > 0)$ **do** $decr(j)$;

    for $k \leftarrow 0$ **to** j **do**

      begin $print\_int(count(k))$;

      if $k < j$ **then** $print\_char("\texttt{.}")$;

      end;

    $update\_terminal$;

if $tracing\_output > 0$ then
    begin $print\_char("]")$; $begin\_diagnostic$; $show\_box(p)$; $end\_diagnostic(true)$;
    end;
⟨ Ship box p out 640 ⟩;
if $tracing\_output \leq 0$ then $print\_char("]")$;
$dead\_cycles \leftarrow 0$; $update\_terminal$; { progress report }
⟨ Flush the box from memory, showing statistics if requested 639 ⟩;
end;

639. ⟨ Flush the box from memory, showing statistics if requested 639 ⟩ ≡
  stat if $tracing\_stats > 1$ then
    begin $print\_nl("Memory␣usage␣before:␣")$; $print\_int(var\_used)$; $print\_char("&")$;
    $print\_int(dyn\_used)$; $print\_char(";")$;
    end;
  tats
  $flush\_node\_list(p)$;
  stat if $tracing\_stats > 1$ then
    begin $print("␣after:␣")$; $print\_int(var\_used)$; $print\_char("&")$; $print\_int(dyn\_used)$;
    $print(";␣still␣untouched:␣")$; $print\_int(hi\_mem\_min - lo\_mem\_max - 1)$; $print\_ln$;
    end;
  tats

This code is used in section 638.

$a\_leaders = 100$, §149.
$begin\_diagnostic$: **procedure**, §245.
$bop = 139$, §586.
$c\_leaders = 101$, §149.
$count = $ macro, §236.
cur_h: $scaled$, §616.
cur_v: $scaled$, §616.
$dead\_cycles$: $integer$, §592.
$decr = $ macro, §16.
$doing\_leaders$: $boolean$, §592.
$done = 30$, §15.
dvi_h: $scaled$, §616.
dvi_v: $scaled$, §616.
dyn_used: $integer$, §117.
$end\_diagnostic$: **procedure**, §245.
$file\_offset$: $0 .. max\_print\_line$, §54.
$flush\_node\_list$: **procedure**, §202.
$height = $ macro, §135.
hi_mem_min: $pointer$, §116.
$hlist\_out$: **procedure**, §619.

$leader\_box$: $pointer$, §629.
$leader\_ht$: $scaled$, §629.
$left\_edge$: $scaled$, §629.
lo_mem_max: $pointer$, §116.
lq: $integer$, §592.
lr: $integer$, §592.
lx: $scaled$, §629.
$max_print_line = $ **const**, §11.
$max\_selector = 21$, §54.
$outer\_doing\_leaders$: $boolean$, §629.
p: $pointer$, §629.
$pointer = $ macro, §115.
$pool\_pointer = 0 .. pool\_size$, §38.
$print$: **procedure**, §59.
$print\_char$: **procedure**, §58.
$print\_int$: **procedure**, §65.
$print\_ln$: **procedure**, §57.
$print\_nl$: **procedure**, §62.
$rule\_ht$: $scaled$, §592.

$save\_h$: $scaled$, §629.
$save\_v$: $scaled$, §629.
$selector$: $0 .. 21$, §54.
$shift_amount = $ macro, §135.
$show\_box$: **procedure**, §198.
str_pool: **packed array**, §39.
$subtype = $ macro, §133.
$synch_h = $ macro, §616.
$synch_v = $ macro, §616.
$temp\_ptr$: $pointer$, §115.
$term\_offset$: $0 .. max\_print\_line$, §54.
top_edge: $scaled$, §629.
$tracing_output = $ macro, §236.
$tracing_stats = $ macro, §236.
$type = $ macro, §133.
$update_terminal = $ macro, §34.
var_used: $integer$, §117.
$vlist\_node = 1$, §137.

640.   ⟨ Ship box p out 640 ⟩ ≡
  ⟨ Update the values of max_h and max_v; but if the page is too large, **goto** $done$ 641 ⟩;
  ⟨ Initialize variables as $ship\_out$ begins 617 ⟩;
  $page\_loc \leftarrow dvi\_offset + dvi\_ptr$; $dvi\_out(bop)$;
  for $k \leftarrow 0$ **to** 9 **do** $dvi\_four(count(k))$;
  $dvi\_four(last\_bop)$; $last\_bop \leftarrow page\_loc$; $cur\_v \leftarrow height(p) + v\_offset$; $temp\_ptr \leftarrow p$;
  if $type(p) = vlist\_node$ **then** $vlist\_out$ **else** $hlist\_out$;
  $dvi\_out(eop)$; $incr(total\_pages)$;
$done$:

This code is used in section 638.

641.   Sometimes the user will generate a huge page because other error messages are being ignored. Such pages are not output to the dvi file, since they may confuse the printing software.

⟨ Update the values of max_h and max_v; but if the page is too large, **goto** $done$ 641 ⟩ ≡
  if $(height(p) > max\_dimen) \vee (depth(p) > max\_dimen) \vee$
        $(height(p) + depth(p) + v\_offset > max\_dimen) \vee (width(p) + h\_offset > max\_dimen)$ **then**
    begin $print\_err("Huge\_page\_cannot\_be\_shipped\_out")$;
    $help2("The\_page\_just\_created\_is\_more\_than\_18\_feet\_tall\_or")$
    $("more\_than\_18\_feet\_wide,\_so\_I\_suspect\_something\_went\_wrong.")$; $error$;
    if $tracing\_output \leq 0$ **then**
      begin $begin\_diagnostic$; $print\_nl("The\_following\_box\_has\_been\_deleted:")$; $show\_box(p)$;
      $end\_diagnostic(true)$;
      end;
    goto $done$;
    end;
  if $height(p) + depth(p) + v\_offset > max\_v$ **then** $max\_v \leftarrow height(p) + depth(p) + v\_offset$;
  if $width(p) + h\_offset > max\_h$ **then** $max\_h \leftarrow width(p) + h\_offset$

This code is used in section 640.

642.   At the end of the program, we must finish things off by writing the postamble. If $total\_pages = 0$, the DVI file was never opened.

An integer variable k will be declared for use by this routine.

⟨ Finish the DVI file 642 ⟩ ≡
  if $total\_pages = 0$ **then** $print\_nl("No\_pages\_of\_output.")$
  else begin $dvi\_out(post)$; { beginning of the postamble }
    $dvi\_four(last\_bop)$; $last\_bop \leftarrow dvi\_offset + dvi\_ptr - 5$; { $post$ location }
    $dvi\_four(25400000)$; $dvi\_four(473628672)$; { conversion ratio for sp }
    $prepare\_mag$; $dvi\_four(mag)$; { magnification factor }
    $dvi\_four(max\_v)$; $dvi\_four(max\_h)$;
    $dvi\_out(max\_push$ **div** $256)$; $dvi\_out(max\_push$ **mod** $256)$;
    $dvi\_out(total\_pages$ **div** $256)$; $dvi\_out(total\_pages$ **mod** $256)$;
    ⟨ Output the font definitions for all fonts that were used 643 ⟩;
    $dvi\_out(post\_post)$; $dvi\_four(last\_bop)$; $dvi\_out(id\_byte)$;
    $k \leftarrow 4 + ((dvi\_buf\_size - dvi\_ptr)$ **mod** $4)$; { the number of 223's }
    while $k > 0$ **do**
      begin $dvi\_out(223)$; $decr(k)$;
      end;
    ⟨ Empty the last bytes out of dvi_buf 599 ⟩;

$print\_nl$("Output␣written␣on␣"); $print$($output\_file\_name$); $print$("␣("); $print\_int$($total\_pages$);
$print$("␣**page**");
if $total\_pages \neq 1$ **then** $print\_char$("s");
$print$(",␣"); $print\_int$($dvi\_offset + dvi\_ptr$); $print$("␣**bytes).**"); b_close(dvi_file);
end

This code is used in section 1333.

643. ⟨Output the font definitions for all fonts that were used 643⟩ ≡
  while $font\_ptr > font\_base$ **do**
    begin if $font\_used[font\_ptr]$ **then** $dvi\_font\_def(font\_ptr)$;
    $decr(font\_ptr)$;
  end

This code is used in section 642.

644. Packaging.   We're essentially done with the parts of TeX that are concerned with the input (*get_next*) and the output (*ship_out*). So it's time to get heavily into the remaining part, which does the real work of typesetting.

After lists are constructed, TeX wraps them up and puts them into boxes. Two major subroutines are given the responsibility for this task: *hpack* applies to horizontal lists (hlists) and *vpack* applies to vertical lists (vlists). The main duty of *hpack* and *vpack* is to compute the dimensions of the resulting boxes, and to adjust the glue if one of those dimensions is pre-specified. The computed sizes normally enclose all of the material inside the new box; but some items may stick out if negative glue is used, if the box is overfull, or if a \vbox includes other boxes that have been shifted left.

The subroutine call *hpack*(*p*, *w*, *m*) returns a pointer to an *hlist_node* for a box containing the hlist that starts at *p*. Parameter *w* specifies a width; and parameter *m* is either '*exactly*' or '*additional*'. Thus, *hpack*(*p*, *w*, *exactly*) produces a box whose width is exactly *w*, while *hpack*(*p*, *w*, *additional*) yields a box whose width is the natural width plus *w*. It is convenient to define a macro called '*natural*' to cover the most common case, so that we can say *hpack*(*p*, *natural*) to get a box that has the natural width of list *p*.

Similarly, *vpack*(*p*, *w*, *m*) returns a pointer to a *vlist_node* for a box containing the vlist that starts at *p*. In this case *w* represents a height instead of a width; the parameter *m* is interpreted as in *hpack*.

define *exactly* = 0   { a box dimension is pre-specified }
define *additional* = 1   { a box dimension is increased from the natural one }
define *natural* ≡ 0, *additional*   { shorthand for parameters to *hpack* and *vpack* }

645.   The parameters to *hpack* and *vpack* correspond to TeX's primitives like '\hbox to 300pt', '\hbox spread 10pt'; note that '\hbox' with no dimension following it is equivalent to '\hbox spread 0pt'. The *scan_spec* subroutine scans such constructions in the user's input, including the mandatory left brace that follows them, and it puts the specification onto *save_stack* so that the desired box can later be obtained by executing the following code:

$$save\_ptr \leftarrow save\_ptr - 2;$$
$$hpack(p, saved(1), saved(0)).$$

procedure *scan_spec*;   { scans a box specification and left brace }
   label *found*;
   begin if *scan_keyword*("to") **then**   *saved*(0) ← *exactly*
   else if *scan_keyword*("spread") **then**   *saved*(0) ← *additional*
      else begin *saved*(0) ← *additional*;   *saved*(1) ← 0;   **goto** *found*;
         end;
   scan_normal_dimen;   *saved*(1) ← *cur_val*;
found: *save_ptr* ← *save_ptr* + 2;   *scan_left_brace*;
   end;

646.   To figure out the glue setting, *hpack* and *vpack* determine how much stretchability and shrinkability are present, considering all four orders of infinity. The highest order of infinity that has a nonzero coefficient is then used as if no other orders were present.

For example, suppose that the given list contains six glue nodes with the respective stretchabilities 3pt, 8fill, 5fil, 6pt, −3fil, −8fill. Then the total is essentially 2fil; and if a total additional space of 6pt is to be achieved by stretching, the actual amounts of stretch will be 0pt, 0pt, 15pt, 0pt, −9pt, and 0pt, since only 'fil' glue will be considered. (The 'fill' glue is therefore not really stretching infinitely with respect to 'fil'; nobody would actually want that to happen.)

The arrays *total_stretch* and *total_shrink* are used to determine how much glue of each kind is present.

⟨ Global variables 13 ⟩ +≡
total_stretch, *total_shrink*: **array** [*glue_ord*] **of** *scaled*;   { glue found by *hpack* or *vpack* }

647.   If the global variable *adjust_tail* is non-null, the *hpack* routine also removes all occurrences of *ins_node*, *mark_node*, and *adjust_node* items and appends the resulting material onto the list that ends at location *adjust_tail*.

⟨ Global variables 13 ⟩ +≡
adjust_tail: *pointer*;   { tail of adjustment list }

648.   ⟨ Set initial values of key variables 21 ⟩ +≡
    adjust_tail ← *null*;

649. Here now is *hpack*, which contains few if any surprises.

function *hpack*(*p* : *pointer*; *w* : *scaled*; *m* : *small_number*): *pointer*;
  label *reswitch*, *common_ending*, *exit*;
  var *r*: *pointer*; { the box node that will be returned }
    q: *pointer*; { trails behind *p* }
    h, d, x: *scaled*; { height, depth, and natural width }
    s: *scaled*; { shift amount }
    g: *pointer*; { points to a glue specification }
    o: *glue_ord*; { order of infinity }
    f: *internal_font_number*; { the font in a *char_node* }
    i: *four_quarters*; { font information about a *char_node* }
    hd: *eight_bits*; { height and depth indices for a character }
    b: *integer*; { badness of the new box }
  begin *r* ← *get_node*(*box_node_size*); *type*(*r*) ← *hlist_node*; *subtype*(*r*) ← *min_quarterword*;
  shift_amount(*r*) ← 0; *q* ← *r* + *list_offset*; *link*(*q*) ← *p*;
  h ← 0; ⟨ Clear dimensions to zero 650 ⟩;
  while *p* ≠ *null* **do** ⟨ Examine node *p* in the hlist, taking account of its effect on the dimensions of the
      new box, or moving it to the adjustment list; then advance *p* to the next node 651 ⟩;
  if *adjust_tail* ≠ *null* **then** *link*(*adjust_tail*) ← *null*;
  height(*r*) ← *h*; *depth*(*r*) ← *d*;
  ⟨ Determine the value of *width*(*r*) and the appropriate glue setting; then **return** or **goto**
    common_ending 657 ⟩;
common_ending: ⟨ Finish issuing a diagnostic message for an overfull or underfull hbox 663 ⟩;
exit: *hpack* ← *r*;
  end;

650. ⟨ Clear dimensions to zero 650 ⟩ ≡
  d ← 0; *x* ← 0; *total_stretch*[*normal*] ← 0; *total_shrink*[*normal*] ← 0; *total_stretch*[*fil*] ← 0;
  total_shrink[*fil*] ← 0; *total_stretch*[*fill*] ← 0; *total_shrink*[*fill*] ← 0; *total_stretch*[*filll*] ← 0;
  total_shrink[*filll*] ← 0

This code is used in sections 649 and 668.

651. ⟨ Examine node *p* in the hlist, taking account of its effect on the dimensions of the new box, or
    moving it to the adjustment list; then advance *p* to the next node 651 ⟩ ≡
  begin *reswitch*: **while** *is_char_node*(*p*) **do** ⟨ Incorporate character dimensions into the dimensions of
    the hbox that will contain it, then move to the next node 654 ⟩;
  if *p* ≠ *null* **then**
    begin case *type*(*p*) **of**
    hlist_node, *vlist_node*, *rule_node*, *unset_node*: ⟨ Incorporate box dimensions into the dimensions of
        the hbox that will contain it 653 ⟩;
    ins_node, *mark_node*, *adjust_node*: **if** *adjust_tail* ≠ *null* **then**
      ⟨ Transfer node *p* to the adjustment list 655 ⟩;
    whatsit_node: ⟨ Incorporate a whatsit node into an hbox 1360 ⟩;
    glue_node: ⟨ Incorporate glue into the horizontal totals 656 ⟩;
    kern_node, *math_node*: *x* ← *x* + *width*(*p*);
    ligature_node: ⟨ Make node *p* look like a *char_node* and **goto** *reswitch* 652 ⟩;
    othercases *do_nothing*
    endcases;

$p \leftarrow link(p);$
        end;
    end

This code is used in section 649.

652. $\langle$ Make node p look like a *char_node* and **goto** *reswitch* 652 $\rangle \equiv$
    begin $mem[lig\_trick] \leftarrow mem[lig\_char(p)];$ $link(lig\_trick) \leftarrow link(p);$ $p \leftarrow lig\_trick;$ **goto** *reswitch*;
    end

This code is used in sections 622, 651, and 1147.

653. The code here implicitly uses the fact that running dimensions are indicated by *null_flag*, which will be ignored in the calculations becase it is a highly negative number.

$\langle$ Incorporate box dimensions into the dimensions of the hbox that will contain it 653 $\rangle \equiv$
    begin $x \leftarrow x + width(p);$
    if $type(p) \geq rule\_node$ **then** $s \leftarrow 0$ **else** $s \leftarrow shift\_amount(p);$
    if $height(p) - s > h$ **then** $h \leftarrow height(p) - s;$
    if $depth(p) + s > d$ **then** $d \leftarrow depth(p) + s;$
    end

This code is used in section 651.

654. The following code is part of TEX's inner loop; i.e., adding another character of text to the user's input will cause each of these instructions to be exercised one more time.

$\langle$ Incorporate character dimensions into the dimensions of the hbox that will contain it, then move to
        the next node 654 $\rangle \equiv$
    begin $f \leftarrow font(p);$ $i \leftarrow char\_info(f)(character(p));$ $hd \leftarrow height\_depth(i);$
    $x \leftarrow x + char\_width(f)(i);$
    $s \leftarrow char\_height(f)(hd);$ **if** $s > h$ **then** $h \leftarrow s;$
    $s \leftarrow char\_depth(f)(hd);$ **if** $s > d$ **then** $d \leftarrow s;$
    $p \leftarrow link(p);$
    end

This code is used in section 651.

---

adjust_node = 5, §142.
adjust_tail: *pointer*, §647.
box_node_size = 7, §135.
char_depth = macro, §554.
char_height = macro, §554.
char_info = macro, §554.
char_node, §134.
char_width = macro, §554.
character = macro, §134.
common_ending = 50, §15.
depth = macro, §135.
do_nothing = macro, §16.
eight_bits = 0 .. 255, §25.
exit = 10, §15.
fil = 1, §150.
fill = 2, §150.
filll = 3, §150.
font = macro, §134.
four_quarters = **packed record**,

§113.
get_node: **function**, §125.
glue_node = 10, §149.
glue_ord = 0 .. 3, §150.
height = macro, §135.
height_depth = macro, §554.
hlist_node = 0, §135.
ins_node = 3, §140.
internal_font_number = 0 .. *font_max*,
    §548.
is_char_node = macro, §134.
kern_node = 11, §155.
lig_char = macro, §143.
lig_trick = macro, §162.
ligature_node = 6, §143.
link = macro, §118.
list_offset = 5, §135.
mark_node = 4, §141.
math_node = 9, §147.

mem: **array**, §116.
min_quarterword = 0, §110.
normal = 0, §135.
null = macro, §115.
null_flag = macro, §138.
pointer = macro, §115.
reswitch = 21, §15.
rule_node = 2, §138.
scaled = *integer*, §101.
shift_amount = macro, §135.
small_number = 0 .. 63, §101.
subtype = macro, §133.
total_shrink: **array**, §646.
total_stretch: **array**, §646.
type = macro, §133.
unset_node = 13, §159.
vlist_node = 1, §137.
whatsit_node = 8, §146.
width = macro, §135.

655.   Although node q is not necessarily the immediate predecessor of node p, it always points to some node in the list preceding p. Thus, we can delete nodes by moving q when necessary. The algorithm takes linear time, and the extra computation does not intrude on the inner loop unless it is necessary to make a deletion.

⟨ Transfer node p to the adjustment list 655 ⟩ ≡
    begin while $link(q) \neq p$ **do** $q \leftarrow link(q)$;
    if $type(p) = adjust\_node$ **then**
        begin $link(adjust\_tail) \leftarrow adjust\_ptr(p)$;
        while $link(adjust\_tail) \neq null$ **do** $adjust\_tail \leftarrow link(adjust\_tail)$;
        $p \leftarrow link(p)$; $free\_node(link(q), small\_node\_size)$;
        end
    else begin $link(adjust\_tail) \leftarrow p$; $adjust\_tail \leftarrow p$; $p \leftarrow link(p)$;
        end;
    $link(q) \leftarrow p$; $p \leftarrow q$;
    end

This code is used in section 651.

656.   ⟨ Incorporate glue into the horizontal totals 656 ⟩ ≡
    begin $g \leftarrow glue\_ptr(p)$; $x \leftarrow x + width(g)$;
    $o \leftarrow stretch\_order(g)$; $total\_stretch[o] \leftarrow total\_stretch[o] + stretch(g)$; $o \leftarrow shrink\_order(g)$;
    $total\_shrink[o] \leftarrow total\_shrink[o] + shrink(g)$;
    if $subtype(p) \geq a\_leaders$ **then**
        begin $g \leftarrow leader\_ptr(p)$;
        if $height(g) > h$ **then** $h \leftarrow height(g)$;
        if $depth(g) > d$ **then** $d \leftarrow depth(g)$;
        end;
    end

This code is used in section 651.

657.   When we get to the present part of the program, x is the natural width of the box being packaged.

⟨ Determine the value of $width(r)$ and the appropriate glue setting; then **return** or **goto**
        $common\_ending$ 657 ⟩ ≡
    if $m = additional$ **then** $w \leftarrow x + w$;
    $width(r) \leftarrow w$; $x \leftarrow w - x$;   { now x is the excess to be made up }
    if $x = 0$ **then**
        begin $glue\_sign(r) \leftarrow normal$; $glue\_order(r) \leftarrow normal$; $set\_glue\_ratio\_zero(glue\_set(r))$; **return**;
        end
    else if $x > 0$ **then**
        ⟨ Determine horizontal glue stretch setting, then **return** or **goto** $common\_ending$ 658 ⟩
        else ⟨ Determine horizontal glue shrink setting, then **return** or **goto** $common\_ending$ 664 ⟩

This code is used in section 649.

658.   ⟨ Determine horizontal glue stretch setting, then **return** or **goto** $common\_ending$ 658 ⟩ ≡
    begin ⟨ Determine the stretch order 659 ⟩;
    $glue\_order(r) \leftarrow o$; $glue\_sign(r) \leftarrow stretching$;
    if $total\_stretch[o] \neq 0$ **then** $glue\_set(r) \leftarrow unfloat(x/total\_stretch[o])$
    else begin $glue\_sign(r) \leftarrow normal$; $set\_glue\_ratio\_zero(glue\_set(r))$;   { there's nothing to stretch }

end;
if $(hbadness < inf\_bad) \wedge (o = normal) \wedge (list\_ptr(r) \neq null)$ **then**
⟨ Report an underfull hbox and **goto** $common\_ending$, if this box is sufficiently bad 660 ⟩;
return;
end

This code is used in section 657.

659. ⟨ Determine the stretch order 659 ⟩ ≡
if $total\_stretch[filll] \neq 0$ **then** $o \leftarrow filll$
else if $total\_stretch[fill] \neq 0$ **then** $o \leftarrow fill$
  else if $total\_stretch[fil] \neq 0$ **then** $o \leftarrow fil$
    else $o \leftarrow normal$

This code is used in sections 658, 673, and 796.

660. ⟨ Report an underfull hbox and **goto** $common\_ending$, if this box is sufficiently bad 660 ⟩ ≡
begin $b \leftarrow badness(x, total\_stretch[normal])$;
if $b > hbadness$ **then**
  begin $print\_ln$;
  if $b > 100$ **then** $print\_nl(\texttt{"Underfull"})$ **else** $print\_nl(\texttt{"Loose"})$;
  $print(\texttt{"\_\textbackslash hbox\_(badness\_"})$; $print\_int(b)$; **goto** $common\_ending$;
  end;
end

This code is used in section 658.

661. In order to provide a decent indication of where an overfull or underfull box originated, we use a global variable $pack\_begin\_line$ that is set nonzero only when $hpack$ is being called by the paragraph builder or the alignment finishing routine.

⟨ Global variables 13 ⟩ +≡
$pack\_begin\_line$: $integer$;   { source file line where the current paragraph or alignment began; a negative
    value denotes alignment }

662. ⟨ Set initial values of key variables 21 ⟩ +≡
$pack\_begin\_line \leftarrow 0$;

$a\_leaders = 100$, §149.
$additional = 1$, §644.
$adjust\_node = 5$, §142.
$adjust\_ptr$ = macro, §142.
$adjust\_tail$: $pointer$, §647.
b: $integer$, §649.
$badness$: **function**, §108.
$common\_ending = 50$, §15.
d: $scaled$, §649.
$depth$ = macro, §135.
$fil = 1$, §150.
$fill = 2$, §150.
$filll = 3$, §150.
$free\_node$: **procedure**, §130.
g: $pointer$, §649.
$glue\_order$ = macro, §135.
$glue\_ptr$ = macro, §149.
$glue\_set$ = macro, §135.

$glue\_sign$ = macro, §135.
h: $scaled$, §649.
$hbadness$ = macro, §236.
$height$ = macro, §135.
$hpack$: **function**, §649.
$inf\_bad = 10000$, §108.
$leader\_ptr$ = macro, §149.
$link$ = macro, §118.
$list\_ptr$ = macro, §135.
m: $small\_number$, §649.
$normal = 0$, §135.
$null$ = macro, §115.
o: $glue\_ord$, §649.
p: $pointer$, §649.
$print$: **procedure**, §59.
$print\_int$: **procedure**, §65.
$print\_ln$: **procedure**, §57.
$print\_nl$: **procedure**, §62.

q: $pointer$, §649.
r: $pointer$, §649.
$set\_glue\_ratio\_zero$ = macro, §109.
$shrink$ = macro, §150.
$shrink\_order$ = macro, §150.
$small\_node\_size = 2$, §141.
$stretch$ = macro, §150.
$stretch\_order$ = macro, §150.
$stretching = 1$, §135.
$subtype$ = macro, §133.
$total\_shrink$: **array**, §646.
$total\_stretch$: **array**, §646.
$type$ = macro, §133.
$unfloat$ = macro, §109.
w: $scaled$, §649.
$width$ = macro, §135.
x: $scaled$, §649.

663. ⟨Finish issuing a diagnostic message for an overfull or underfull hbox 663⟩ ≡
  if *output_active* **then** *print*(")␣has␣occurred␣while␣\output␣is␣active")
  else begin if *pack_begin_line* ≠ 0 **then**
      begin if *pack_begin_line* > 0 **then** *print*(")␣in␣paragraph␣at␣lines␣")
      else *print*(")␣in␣alignment␣at␣lines␣");
      print_int(*abs*(*pack_begin_line*)); *print*("--");
      end
    else *print*(")␣detected␣at␣line␣");
    print_int(*line*);
    end;
  print_ln;
  font_in_short_display ← *null_font*; *short_display*(*list_ptr*(*r*)); *print_ln*;
  begin_diagnostic; *show_box*(*r*); *end_diagnostic*(*true*)

This code is used in section 649.

664. ⟨Determine horizontal glue shrink setting, then **return** or **goto** *common_ending* 664⟩ ≡
  begin ⟨Determine the shrink order 665⟩;
  glue_order(*r*) ← *o*; *glue_sign*(*r*) ← *shrinking*;
  if *total_shrink*[*o*] ≠ 0 **then** *glue_set*(*r*) ← *unfloat*((−*x*)/*total_shrink*[*o*])
  else begin *glue_sign*(*r*) ← *normal*; *set_glue_ratio_zero*(*glue_set*(*r*)); { there's nothing to shrink }
    end;
  if (*total_shrink*[*o*] < −*x*) ∧ (*o* = *normal*) ∧ (*list_ptr*(*r*) ≠ *null*) **then**
    begin *set_glue_ratio_one*(*glue_set*(*r*)); { this is the maximum shrinkage }
    ⟨Report an overfull hbox and **goto** *common_ending*, if this box is sufficiently bad 666⟩;
    end
  else if (*hbadness* < 100) ∧ (*o* = *normal*) ∧ (*list_ptr*(*r*) ≠ *null*) **then**
      ⟨Report a tight hbox and **goto** *common_ending*, if this box is sufficiently bad 667⟩;
  return;
  end

This code is used in section 657.

665. ⟨Determine the shrink order 665⟩ ≡
  if *total_shrink*[*filll*] ≠ 0 **then** *o* ← *filll*
  else if *total_shrink*[*fill*] ≠ 0 **then** *o* ← *fill*
    else if *total_shrink*[*fil*] ≠ 0 **then** *o* ← *fil*
      else *o* ← *normal*

This code is used in sections 664, 676, and 796.

666. ⟨Report an overfull hbox and **goto** *common_ending*, if this box is sufficiently bad 666⟩ ≡
  if (−*x* − *total_shrink*[*normal*] > *hfuzz*) ∨ (*hbadness* < 100) **then**
    begin if (*overfull_rule* > 0) ∧ (−*x* − *total_shrink*[*normal*] > *hfuzz*) **then**
      begin while *link*(*q*) ≠ *null* **do** *q* ← *link*(*q*);
      link(*q*) ← *new_rule*; *width*(*link*(*q*)) ← *overfull_rule*;
      end;
    print_ln; *print_nl*("Overfull␣\hbox␣("); *print_scaled*(−*x* − *total_shrink*[*normal*]);
    print("pt␣too␣wide"); **goto** *common_ending*;
    end

This code is used in section 664.

667. ⟨ Report a tight hbox and **goto** *common_ending*, if this box is sufficiently bad 667 ⟩ ≡
    begin $b \leftarrow badness(-x, total\_shrink[normal])$;
  if $b > hbadness$ **then**
    begin *print_ln*; *print_nl*("Tight␣\hbox␣(badness␣"); *print_int*(b); **goto** *common_ending*;
    end;
  end

This code is used in section 664.

668. The *vpack* subroutine is actually a special case of a slightly more general routine called *vpackage*, which has four parameters. The fourth parameter, which is *max_dimen* in the case of *vpack*, specifies the maximum depth of the page box that is constructed. The depth is first computed by the normal rules; if it exceeds this limit, the reference point is simply moved down until the limiting depth is attained.

define $vpack(\#) \equiv vpackage(\#, max\_dimen)$ { special case of unconstrained depth }

function $vpackage(p : pointer; h : scaled; m : small\_number; l : scaled): pointer;$
  label $common\_ending, exit;$
  var $r: pointer;$ { the box node that will be returned }
    $w, d, x: scaled;$ { width, depth, and natural height }
    $s: scaled;$ { shift amount }
    $g: pointer;$ { points to a glue specification }
    $o: glue\_ord;$ { order of infinity }
    $b: integer;$ { badness of the new box }
  begin $r \leftarrow get\_node(box\_node\_size);$ $type(r) \leftarrow vlist\_node;$ $subtype(r) \leftarrow min\_quarterword;$
  $shift\_amount(r) \leftarrow 0;$ $list\_ptr(r) \leftarrow p;$
  $w \leftarrow 0;$ ⟨ Clear dimensions to zero 650 ⟩;
  while $p \neq null$ **do** ⟨ Examine node p in the vlist, taking account of its effect on the dimensions of the
       new box; then advance p to the next node 669 ⟩;
  $width(r) \leftarrow w;$
  if $d > l$ **then**
    begin $x \leftarrow x + d - l;$ $depth(r) \leftarrow l;$
    end
  else $depth(r) \leftarrow d;$
  ⟨ Determine the value of $height(r)$ and the appropriate glue setting; then **return** or **goto**
    $common\_ending$ 672 ⟩;
$common\_ending:$ ⟨ Finish issuing a diagnostic message for an overfull or underfull vbox 675 ⟩;
$exit:$ $vpackage \leftarrow r;$
  end;

669. ⟨ Examine node p in the vlist, taking account of its effect on the dimensions of the new box;
    then advance p to the next node 669 ⟩ ≡
  begin if $is\_char\_node(p)$ **then** $confusion("vpack")$
  else case $type(p)$ **of**
    $hlist\_node, vlist\_node, rule\_node, unset\_node:$ ⟨ Incorporate box dimensions into the dimensions of
       the vbox that will contain it 670 ⟩;
    $whatsit\_node:$ ⟨ Incorporate a whatsit node into a vbox 1359 ⟩;
    $glue\_node:$ ⟨ Incorporate glue into the vertical totals 671 ⟩;
    $kern\_node:$ **begin** $x \leftarrow x + d + width(p);$ $d \leftarrow 0;$
      end;
    othercases $do\_nothing$
    endcases;
  $p \leftarrow link(p);$
  end

This code is used in section 668.

670. ⟨ Incorporate box dimensions into the dimensions of the vbox that will contain it 670 ⟩ ≡
  begin $x \leftarrow x + d + height(p);$ $d \leftarrow depth(p);$

if $type(p) \geq rule\_node$ **then** $s \leftarrow 0$ **else** $s \leftarrow shift\_amount(p)$;
if $width(p) + s > w$ **then** $w \leftarrow width(p) + s$;
end

This code is used in section 669.

671. ⟨ Incorporate glue into the vertical totals 671 ⟩ ≡
  begin $x \leftarrow x + d$; $d \leftarrow 0$;
  $g \leftarrow glue\_ptr(p)$; $x \leftarrow x + width(g)$;
  $o \leftarrow stretch\_order(g)$; $total\_stretch[o] \leftarrow total\_stretch[o] + stretch(g)$; $o \leftarrow shrink\_order(g)$;
  $total\_shrink[o] \leftarrow total\_shrink[o] + shrink(g)$;
  if $subtype(p) \geq a\_leaders$ **then**
    begin $g \leftarrow leader\_ptr(p)$;
    if $width(g) > w$ **then** $w \leftarrow width(g)$;
    end;
  end

This code is used in section 669.

672. When we get to the present part of the program, x is the natural height of the box being packaged.

⟨ Determine the value of $height(r)$ and the appropriate glue setting; then **return** or **goto**
    common_ending 672 ⟩ ≡
  if $m = additional$ **then** $h \leftarrow x + h$;
  $height(r) \leftarrow h$; $x \leftarrow h - x$; { now x is the excess to be made up }
  if $x = 0$ **then**
    begin $glue\_sign(r) \leftarrow normal$; $glue\_order(r) \leftarrow normal$; $set\_glue\_ratio\_zero(glue\_set(r))$; **return**;
    end
  else if $x > 0$ **then**
      ⟨ Determine vertical glue stretch setting, then **return** or **goto** *common_ending* 673 ⟩
      else ⟨ Determine vertical glue shrink setting, then **return** or **goto** *common_ending* 676 ⟩

This code is used in section 668.

---

673. ⟨Determine vertical glue stretch setting, then **return** or **goto** $common\_ending$ 673⟩ ≡
  begin ⟨Determine the stretch order 659⟩;
  $glue\_order(r) \leftarrow o$; $glue\_sign(r) \leftarrow stretching$;
  if $total\_stretch[o] \neq 0$ **then** $glue\_set(r) \leftarrow unfloat(x/total\_stretch[o])$
  else begin $glue\_sign(r) \leftarrow normal$; $set\_glue\_ratio\_zero(glue\_set(r))$;   { there's nothing to stretch }
    end;
  if $(vbadness < inf\_bad) \wedge (o = normal) \wedge (list\_ptr(r) \neq null)$ **then**
    ⟨Report an underfull vbox and **goto** $common\_ending$, if this box is sufficiently bad 674⟩;
  return;
  end

This code is used in section 672.

674. ⟨Report an underfull vbox and **goto** $common\_ending$, if this box is sufficiently bad 674⟩ ≡
  begin $b \leftarrow badness(x, total\_stretch[normal])$;
  if $b > vbadness$ **then**
    begin $print\_ln$;
    if $b > 100$ **then** $print\_nl(\texttt{"Underfull"})$ **else** $print\_nl(\texttt{"Loose"})$;
    $print(\texttt{"␣\textbackslash vbox␣(badness␣"})$; $print\_int(b)$; **goto** $common\_ending$;
    end;
  end

This code is used in section 673.

675. ⟨Finish issuing a diagnostic message for an overfull or underfull vbox 675⟩ ≡
  if $output\_active$ **then** $print(\texttt{")␣has␣occurred␣while␣\textbackslash output␣is␣active"})$
  else begin if $pack\_begin\_line \neq 0$ **then**   { it's actually negative }
    begin $print(\texttt{")␣in␣alignment␣at␣lines␣"})$; $print\_int(abs(pack\_begin\_line))$; $print(\texttt{"--"})$;
    end
    else $print(\texttt{")␣detected␣at␣line␣"})$;
    $print\_int(line)$; $print\_ln$;
    end;
  $begin\_diagnostic$; $show\_box(r)$; $end\_diagnostic(true)$

This code is used in section 668.

676. ⟨Determine vertical glue shrink setting, then **return** or **goto** $common\_ending$ 676⟩ ≡
  begin ⟨Determine the shrink order 665⟩;
  $glue\_order(r) \leftarrow o$; $glue\_sign(r) \leftarrow shrinking$;
  if $total\_shrink[o] \neq 0$ **then** $glue\_set(r) \leftarrow unfloat((-x)/total\_shrink[o])$
  else begin $glue\_sign(r) \leftarrow normal$; $set\_glue\_ratio\_zero(glue\_set(r))$;   { there's nothing to shrink }
    end;
  if $(total\_shrink[o] < -x) \wedge (o = normal) \wedge (list\_ptr(r) \neq null)$ **then**
    begin $set\_glue\_ratio\_one(glue\_set(r))$;   { this is the maximum shrinkage }
    ⟨Report an overfull vbox and **goto** $common\_ending$, if this box is sufficiently bad 677⟩;
    end
  else if $(vbadness < 100) \wedge (o = normal) \wedge (list\_ptr(r) \neq null)$ **then**
    ⟨Report a tight vbox and **goto** $common\_ending$, if this box is sufficiently bad 678⟩;
  return;
  end

This code is used in section 672.

677. ⟨ Report an overfull vbox and **goto** *common_ending*, if this box is sufficiently bad 677 ⟩ ≡
  if $(-x - total\_shrink\,[normal] > vfuzz\,) \vee (vbadness < 100)$ **then**
    begin *print_ln*; *print_nl*("Overfull␣\vbox␣("); *print_scaled*$(-x - total\_shrink\,[normal])$;
    print("pt␣too␣high"); **goto** *common_ending*;
    end

This code is used in section 676.

678. ⟨ Report a tight vbox and **goto** *common_ending*, if this box is sufficiently bad 678 ⟩ ≡
  begin $b \leftarrow badness\,(-x, total\_shrink\,[normal])$;
  if $b > vbadness$ **then**
    begin *print_ln*; *print_nl*("Tight␣\vbox␣(badness␣"); *print_int*(b); **goto** *common_ending*;
    end;
  end

This code is used in section 676.

679.   When a box is being appended to the current vertical list, the baselineskip calculation is
handled by the *append_to_vlist* routine.

procedure *append_to_vlist*$(b : pointer\,)$;
  var *d*: *scaled*;   { deficiency of space between baselines }
    p: *pointer*;   { a new glue specification }
  begin if $prev\_depth > ignore\_depth$ **then**
    begin $d \leftarrow width\,(baseline\_skip\,) - prev\_depth - height\,(b)$;
    if $d < line\_skip\_limit$ **then** $p \leftarrow new\_param\_glue\,(line\_skip\_code\,)$
    else begin $p \leftarrow new\_skip\_param\,(baseline\_skip\_code\,)$; $width\,(temp\_ptr\,) \leftarrow d$;
        { $temp\_ptr = glue\_ptr\,(p)$ }
      end;
    $link\,(tail\,) \leftarrow p$; $tail \leftarrow p$;
    end;
  $link\,(tail\,) \leftarrow b$; $tail \leftarrow b$; $prev\_depth \leftarrow depth\,(b)$;
  end;

---

b: *integer*, §668.
badness: **function**, §108.
baseline_skip = macro, §224.
baseline_skip_code = 1, §224.
begin_diagnostic: **procedure**, §245.
common_ending = 50, §15.
depth = macro, §135.
end_diagnostic: **procedure**, §245.
glue_order = macro, §135.
glue_ptr = macro, §149.
glue_set = macro, §135.
glue_sign = macro, §135.
height = macro, §135.
ignore_depth = macro, §212.
inf_bad = 10000, §108.
line: *integer*, §304.
line_skip_code = 0, §224.

line_skip_limit = macro, §247.
link = macro, §118.
list_ptr = macro, §135.
new_param_glue: **function**, §152.
new_skip_param: **function**, §154.
normal = 0, §135.
null = macro, §115.
o: *glue_ord*, §668.
output_active: *boolean*, §989.
pack_begin_line: *integer*, §661.
pointer = macro, §115.
prev_depth = macro, §213.
print: **procedure**, §59.
print_int: **procedure**, §65.
print_ln: **procedure**, §57.
print_nl: **procedure**, §62.
print_scaled: **procedure**, §103.

r: *pointer*, §668.
scaled = *integer*, §101.
set_glue_ratio_one = macro, §109.
set_glue_ratio_zero = macro, §109.
show_box: **procedure**, §198.
shrinking = 2, §135.
stretching = 1, §135.
tail = macro, §213.
temp_ptr: *pointer*, §115.
total_shrink: **array**, §646.
total_stretch: **array**, §646.
unfloat = macro, §109.
vbadness = macro, §236.
vfuzz = macro, §247.
width = macro, §135.
x: *scaled*, §668.

680. Data structures for math mode. When TeX reads a formula that is enclosed between $'s, it constructs an *mlist*, which is essentially a tree structure representing that formula. An mlist is a linear sequence of items, but we can regard it as a tree structure because mlists can appear within mlists. For example, many of the entries can be subscripted or superscripted, and such "scripts" are mlists in their own right.

An entire formula is parsed into such a tree before any of the actual typesetting is done, because the current style of type is usually not known until the formula has been fully scanned. For example, when the formula '$a+b \over c+d$' is being read, there is no way to tell that 'a+b' will be in script size until '\over' has appeared.

During the scanning process, each element of the mlist being built is classified as a relation, a binary operator, an open parenthesis, etc., or as a construct like '\sqrt' that must be built up. This classification appears in the mlist data structure.

After a formula has been fully scanned, the mlist is converted to an hlist so that it can be incorporated into the surrounding text. This conversion is controlled by a recursive procedure that decides all of the appropriate styles by a "top-down" process starting at the outermost level and working in towards the subformulas. The formula is ultimately pasted together using combinations of horizontal and vertical boxes, with glue and penalty nodes inserted as necessary.

An mlist is represented internally as a linked list consisting chiefly of "noads" (pronounced "no-adds"), to distinguish them from the somewhat similar "nodes" in hlists and vlists. Certain kinds of ordinary nodes are allowed to appear in mlists together with the noads; TeX tells the difference by means of the *type* field, since a noad's *type* is always greater than that of a node. An mlist does not contain character nodes, hlist nodes, vlist nodes, math nodes, ligature nodes, mark nodes, insert nodes, adjust nodes, or unset nodes; in particular, each mlist item appears in the variable-size part of *mem*, so the *type* field is always present.

681. Each noad is four or more words long. The first word contains the *type* and *subtype* and *link* fields that are already so familiar to us; the second, third, and fourth words are called the noad's *nucleus*, *subscr*, and *supscr* fields.

Consider, for example, the simple formula 'x^2', which would be parsed into an mlist containing a single element called an *ord_noad*. The *nucleus* of this noad is a representation of 'x', the *subscr* is empty, and the *supscr* is a representation of '2'.

The *nucleus*, *subscr*, and *supscr* fields are further broken into subfields. If p points to a noad, and if q is one of its principal fields (e.g., $q = subscr(p)$), there are several possibilities for the subfields, depending on the *math_type* of q.

$math\_type(q) = math\_char$ means that $fam(q)$ refers to one of the sixteen font families, and $character(q)$ is the number of a character within a font of that family, as in a character node.

$math\_type(q) = math\_text\_char$ is similar, but the character is unsubscripted and unsuperscripted and it is followed immediately by another character from the same font. (This *math_type* setting appears only briefly during the processing; it is used to suppress unwanted italic corrections.)

$math\_type(q) = empty$ indicates a field with no value (the corresponding attribute of noad p is not present).

$math\_type(q) = sub\_box$ means that $info(q)$ points to a box node (either an *hlist_node* or a *vlist_node*) that should be used as the value of the field. The *shift_amount* in the subsidiary box node is the amount by which that box will be shifted downward.

$math\_type(q) = sub\_mlist$ means that $info(q)$ points to an mlist; the mlist must be converted to an hlist in order to obtain the value of this field.

In the latter case, we might have $info(q) = null$. This is not the same as $math\_type(q) = empty$; for example, '$P_{}$' and 'P' produce different results (the former will not have the "italic correction" added to the width of P, but the "script skip" will be added).

The definitions of subfields given here are evidently wasteful of space, since a halfword is being used for the *math_type* although only three bits would be needed. However, there are hardly ever many noads present at once, since they are soon converted to nodes that take up even more space, so we can afford to represent them in whatever way simplifies the programming.

define $noad\_size = 4$ { number of words in a normal noad }
define $nucleus(\#) \equiv \# + 1$ { the *nucleus* field of a noad }
define $supscr(\#) \equiv \# + 2$ { the *supscr* field of a noad }
define $subscr(\#) \equiv \# + 3$ { the *subscr* field of a noad }
define $math\_type \equiv link$ { a *halfword* in *mem* }
define $fam \equiv font$ { a *quarterword* in *mem* }
define $math\_char = 1$ { *math_type* when the attribute is simple }
define $sub\_box = 2$ { *math_type* when the attribute is a box }
define $sub\_mlist = 3$ { *math_type* when the attribute is a formula }
define $math\_text\_char = 4$ { *math_type* when italic correction is dubious }

$character$ = macro, §134.
$empty = 0$, §16.
$font$ = macro, §134.
$halfword = min\_halfword\ ..$
    $max\_halfword$, §113.
$hlist\_node = 0$, §135.

$info$ = macro, §118.
$link$ = macro, §118.
mem: **array**, §116.
$null$ = macro, §115.
$ord\_noad = 16$, §682.

$quarterword = 0\ ..\ 255$, §113.
$shift\_amount$ = macro, §135.
$subtype$ = macro, §133.
$type$ = macro, §133.
$vlist\_node = 1$, §137.

682. Each portion of a formula is classified as Ord, Op, Bin, Rel, Ope, Clo, Pun, or Inn, for purposes of spacing and line breaking. An *ord_noad*, *op_noad*, *bin_noad*, *rel_noad*, *open_noad*, *close_noad*, *punct_noad*, or *inner_noad* is used to represent portions of the various types. For example, an '=' sign in a formula leads to the creation of a *rel_noad* whose *nucleus* field is a representation of an equals sign (usually *fam* = 0, *character* = '75). A formula preceded by \mathrel also results in a *rel_noad*. When a *rel_noad* is followed by an *op_noad*, say, and possibly separated by one or more ordinary nodes (not noads), TEX will insert a penalty node (with the current *rel_penalty*) just after the formula that corresponds to the *rel_noad*, unless there already was a penalty immediately following; and a "thick space" will be inserted just before the formula that corresponds to the *op_noad*.

A noad of type *ord_noad*, *op_noad*, ..., *inner_noad* usually has a *subtype* = *normal*. The only exception is that an *op_noad* might have *subtype* = *limits* or *no_limits*, if the normal positioning of limits has been overridden for this operator.

> **define** *ord_noad* = *unset_node* + 3   { *type* of a noad classified Ord }
> **define** *op_noad* = *ord_noad* + 1   { *type* of a noad classified Op }
> **define** *bin_noad* = *ord_noad* + 2   { *type* of a noad classified Bin }
> **define** *rel_noad* = *ord_noad* + 3   { *type* of a noad classified Rel }
> **define** *open_noad* = *ord_noad* + 4   { *type* of a noad classified Ope }
> **define** *close_noad* = *ord_noad* + 5   { *type* of a noad classified Clo }
> **define** *punct_noad* = *ord_noad* + 6   { *type* of a noad classified Pun }
> **define** *inner_noad* = *ord_noad* + 7   { *type* of a noad classified Inn }
> **define** *limits* = 1   { *subtype* of *op_noad* whose scripts are to be above, below }
> **define** *no_limits* = 2   { *subtype* of *op_noad* whose scripts are to be normal }

683. A *radical_noad* is five words long; the fifth word is the *left_delimiter* field, which usually represents a square root sign.

A *fraction_noad* is six words long; it has a *right_delimiter* field as well as a *left_delimiter*.

Delimiter fields are of type *four_quarters*, and they have four subfields called *small_fam*, *small_char*, *large_fam*, *large_char*. These subfields represent variable-size delimiters by giving the "small" and "large" starting characters, as explained in Chapter 17 of *The TEXbook*.

A *fraction_noad* is actually quite different from all other noads. Not only does it have six words, it has *thickness*, *denominator*, and *numerator* fields instead of *nucleus*, *subscr*, and *supscr*. The *thickness* is a scaled value that tells how thick to make a fraction rule; however, the special value *default_code* is used to stand for the *default_rule_thickness* of the current size. The *numerator* and *denominator* point to mlists that define a fraction; we always have

$$math\_type(numerator) = math\_type(denominator) = sub\_mlist.$$

The *left_delimiter* and *right_delimiter* fields specify delimiters that will be placed at the left and right of the fraction. In this way, a *fraction_noad* is able to represent all of TEX's operators \over, \atop, \above, \overwithdelims, \atopwithdelims, and \abovewithdelims.

> **define** *left_delimiter*(#) ≡ # + 4   { first delimiter field of a noad }
> **define** *right_delimiter*(#) ≡ # + 5   { second delimiter field of a fraction noad }
> **define** *radical_noad* = *inner_noad* + 1   { *type* of a noad for square roots }
> **define** *radical_noad_size* = 5   { number of *mem* words in a radical noad }
> **define** *fraction_noad* = *radical_noad* + 1   { *type* of a noad for generalized fractions }

define *fraction_noad_size* = 6   { number of *mem* words in a fraction noad }
define *small_fam*(#) ≡ *mem*[#].*qqqq*.*b0*   { *fam* for "small" delimiter }
define *small_char*(#) ≡ *mem*[#].*qqqq*.*b1*   { *character* for "small" delimiter }
define *large_fam*(#) ≡ *mem*[#].*qqqq*.*b2*   { *fam* for "large" delimiter }
define *large_char*(#) ≡ *mem*[#].*qqqq*.*b3*   { *character* for "large" delimiter }
define *thickness* ≡ *width*   { *thickness* field in a fraction noad }
define *default_code* ≡ ´10000000000   { denotes *default_rule_thickness* }
define *numerator* ≡ *supscr*   { *numerator* field in a fraction noad }
define *denominator* ≡ *subscr*   { *denominator* field in a fraction noad }

684.   The global variable *empty_field* is set up for initialization of empty fields in new noads. Similarly, *null_delimiter* is for the initialization of delimiter fields.

⟨ Global variables 13 ⟩ +≡
empty_field: *two_halves*;
null_delimiter: *four_quarters*;

685.   ⟨ Set initial values of key variables 21 ⟩ +≡
empty_field.*rh* ← *empty*; *empty_field*.*lh* ← *null*;
null_delimiter.*b0* ← 0; *null_delimiter*.*b1* ← *min_quarterword*;
null_delimiter.*b2* ← 0; *null_delimiter*.*b3* ← *min_quarterword*;

686.   The *new_noad* function creates an *ord_noad* that is completely null.

function *new_noad*: *pointer*;
   var *p*: *pointer*;
   begin *p* ← *get_node*(*noad_size*); *type*(*p*) ← *ord_noad*; *subtype*(*p*) ← *normal*;
   mem[*nucleus*(*p*)].*hh* ← *empty_field*; *mem*[*subscr*(*p*)].*hh* ← *empty_field*;
   mem[*supscr*(*p*)].*hh* ← *empty_field*; *new_noad* ← *p*;
   end;

---

b0: *quarterword*, §113.
b1: *quarterword*, §113.
b2: *quarterword*, §113.
b3: *quarterword*, §113.
character = macro, §134.
default_rule_thickness = macro, §701.
empty = 0, §16.
fam = macro, §681.
four_quarters = **packed record**, §113.

get_node: **function**, §125.
hh: *two_halves*, §113.
lh: *halfword*, §560.
math_type = macro, §681.
mem: **array**, §116.
min_quarterword = 0, §110.
noad_size = 4, §681.
normal = 0, §135.
nucleus = macro, §681.
null = macro, §115.
pointer = macro, §115.

qqqq: *four_quarters*, §113.
rel_penalty = macro, §236.
rh: *halfword*, §113.
sub_mlist = 3, §681.
subscr = macro, §681.
subtype = macro, §133.
supscr = macro, §681.
two_halves = **packed record**, §113.
type = macro, §133.
unset_node = 13, §159.
width = macro, §135.

687. A few more kinds of noads will complete the set: An *under_noad* has its nucleus underlined; an *over_noad* has it overlined. An *accent_noad* places an accent over its nucleus; the accent character appears as $fam(accent\_chr(p))$ and $character(accent\_chr(p))$. A *vcenter_noad* centers its nucleus vertically with respect to the axis of the formula; in such noads we always have $math\_type(nucleus(p)) = sub\_box$.

And finally, we have *left_noad* and *right_noad* types, to implement TeX's \left and \right. The *nucleus* of such noads is replaced by a *delimiter* field; thus, for example, '\left(' produces a *left_noad* such that $delimiter(p)$ holds the family and character codes for all left parentheses. A *left_noad* never appears in an mlist except as the first element, and a *right_noad* never appears in an mlist except as the last element; furthermore, we either have both a *left_noad* and a *right_noad*, or neither one is present. The *subscr* and *supscr* fields are always *empty* in a *left_noad* and a *right_noad*.

define $under\_noad = fraction\_noad + 1$ { *type* of a noad for underlining }
define $over\_noad = under\_noad + 1$ { *type* of a noad for overlining }
define $accent\_noad = over\_noad + 1$ { *type* of a noad for accented subformulas }
define $accent\_noad\_size = 5$ { number of *mem* words in an accent noad }
define $accent\_chr(\#) \equiv \# + 4$ { the *accent_chr* field of an accent noad }
define $vcenter\_noad = accent\_noad + 1$ { *type* of a noad for \vcenter }
define $left\_noad = vcenter\_noad + 1$ { *type* of a noad for \left }
define $right\_noad = left\_noad + 1$ { *type* of a noad for \right }
define $delimiter \equiv nucleus$ { *delimiter* field in left and right noads }
define $scripts\_allowed(\#) \equiv (type(\#) \geq ord\_noad) \wedge (type(\#) < left\_noad)$

688. Math formulas can also contain instructions like \textstyle that override TeX's normal style rules. A *style_node* is inserted into the data structure to record such instructions; it is three words long, so it is considered a node instead of a noad. The *subtype* is either *display_style* or *text_style* or *script_style* or *script_script_style*. The second and third words of a *style_node* are not used, but they are present because a *choice_node* is converted to a *style_node*.

TeX uses even numbers 0, 2, 4, 6 to encode the basic styles *display_style*, ..., *script_script_style*, and adds 1 to get the "cramped" versions of these styles. This gives a numerical order that is backwards from the convention of Appendix G in *The TeXbook*; i.e., a smaller style has a larger numerical value.

define $style\_node = unset\_node + 1$ { *type* of a style node }
define $style\_node\_size = 3$ { number of words in a style node }
define $display\_style = 0$ { *subtype* for \displaystyle }
define $text\_style = 2$ { *subtype* for \textstyle }
define $script\_style = 4$ { *subtype* for \scriptstyle }
define $script\_script\_style = 6$ { *subtype* for \scriptscriptstyle }
define $cramped = 1$ { add this to an uncramped style if you want to cramp it }

function $new\_style(s : small\_number)$: *pointer*; { create a style node }
  var p: *pointer*; { the new node }
  begin $p \leftarrow get\_node(style\_node\_size)$; $type(p) \leftarrow style\_node$; $subtype(p) \leftarrow s$; $width(p) \leftarrow 0$;
  $depth(p) \leftarrow 0$; { the *width* and *depth* are not used }
  $new\_style \leftarrow p$;
  end;

689. Finally, the `\mathchoice` primitive creates a *choice_node*, which has special subfields *display_mlist*, *text_mlist*, *script_mlist*, and *script_script_mlist* pointing to the mlists for each style.

define *choice_node* = *unset_node* + 2   { *type* of a choice node }
define *display_mlist*(**#**) ≡ *info*(**#** + 1)   { mlist to be used in display style }
define *text_mlist*(**#**) ≡ *link*(**#** + 1)   { mlist to be used in text style }
define *script_mlist*(**#**) ≡ *info*(**#** + 2)   { mlist to be used in script style }
define *script_script_mlist*(**#**) ≡ *link*(**#** + 2)   { mlist to be used in scriptscript style }

function *new_choice*: *pointer*;   { create a choice node }
 var p: *pointer*;   { the new node }
 begin $p \leftarrow get\_node(style\_node\_size)$; $type(p) \leftarrow choice\_node$; $subtype(p) \leftarrow 0$;
   { the *subtype* is not used }
 $display\_mlist(p) \leftarrow null$; $text\_mlist(p) \leftarrow null$; $script\_mlist(p) \leftarrow null$; $script\_script\_mlist(p) \leftarrow null$;
 $new\_choice \leftarrow p$;
 end;

690. Let's consider now the previously unwritten part of *show_node_list* that displays the things that can only be present in mlists; this program illustrates how to access the data structures just defined.

In the context of the following program, p points to a node or noad that should be displayed, and the current string contains the "recursion history" that leads to this point. The recursion history consists of a dot for each outer level in which p is subsidiary to some node, or in which p is subsidiary to the *nucleus* field of some noad; the dot is replaced by '[' or '(' or '/' or '\' if p is descended from the *subscr* or *supscr* or *denominator* or *numerator* fields of noads. For example, the current string would be '. (. [/' if p points to the *ord_noad* for x in the (ridiculous) formula '`$\sqrt{a^{{b_{c\over x+y} }}}$`'.

⟨ Cases of *show_node_list* that arise in mlists only 690 ⟩ ≡
style_node: *print_style*(*subtype*(p));
choice_node: ⟨ Display choice node p 695 ⟩;
ord_noad, *op_noad*, *bin_noad*, *rel_noad*, *open_noad*, *close_noad*, *punct_noad*, *inner_noad*,
   radical_noad, *over_noad*, *under_noad*, *vcenter_noad*, *accent_noad*, *left_noad*, *right_noad*: ⟨ Display
   normal noad p 696 ⟩;
fraction_noad: ⟨ Display fraction noad p 697 ⟩;

This code is used in section 183.

---

bin_noad = 18, §682.
character = macro, §134.
close_noad = 21, §682.
denominator = macro, §683.
depth = macro, §135.
empty = 0, §16.
fam = macro, §681.
fraction_noad = 25, §683.
get_node: **function**, §125.
info = macro, §118.
inner_noad = 23, §682.
link = macro, §118.

math_type = macro, §681.
mem: **array**, §116.
nucleus = macro, §681.
null = macro, §115.
numerator = macro, §683.
op_noad = 17, §682.
open_noad = 20, §682.
ord_noad = 16, §682.
p: *pointer*, §182.
pointer = macro, §115.
print_style: **procedure**, §694.
punct_noad = 22, §682.

radical_noad = 24, §683.
rel_noad = 19, §682.
show_node_list: **procedure**, §182.
small_number = 0 .. 63, §101.
sub_box = 2, §681.
subscr = macro, §681.
subtype = macro, §133.
supscr = macro, §681.
type = macro, §133.
unset_node = 13, §159.
width = macro, §135.

691. Here are some simple routines used in the display of noads.

⟨ Declare procedures needed for displaying the elements of mlists 691 ⟩ ≡
procedure *print_fam_and_char*(*p* : *pointer*); { prints family and character }
  begin *print_esc*("fam"); *print_int*(*fam*(*p*)); *print_char*("␣"); *print_ASCII*(*qo*(*character*(*p*)));
  end;

procedure *print_delimiter*(*p* : *pointer*); { prints a delimiter as 24-bit hex value }
  var *a*: *integer*; { accumulator }
  begin *a* ← *small_fam*(*p*) * 256 + *qo*(*small_char*(*p*));
  a ← *a* * "1000 + *large_fam*(*p*) * 256 + *qo*(*large_char*(*p*));
  if *a* < 0 **then** *print_int*(*a*) { this should never happen }
  else *print_hex*(*a*);
  end;

See also sections 692 and 694.

This code is used in section 179.

692. The next subroutine will descend to another level of recursion when a subsidiary mlist needs to be displayed. The parameter *c* indicates what character is to become part of the recursion history. An empty mlist is distinguished from a field with *math_type*(*p*) = *empty*, because these are not equivalent (as explained above).

⟨ Declare procedures needed for displaying the elements of mlists 691 ⟩ +≡
procedure *show_info*; *forward*; { *show_node_list*(*info*(*temp_ptr*)) }
procedure *print_subsidiary_data*(*p* : *pointer*; *c* : *ASCII_code*); { display a noad field }
  begin if *cur_length* ≥ *depth_threshold* **then**
    begin if *math_type*(*p*) ≠ *empty* **then** *print*("␣[]");
    end
  else begin *append_char*(*c*); { include *c* in the recursion history }
    temp_ptr ← *p*; { prepare for *show_info* if recursion is needed }
    case *math_type*(*p*) **of**
    math_char: **begin** *print_ln*; *print_current_string*; *print_fam_and_char*(*p*);
      end;
    sub_box: *show_info*; { recursive call }
    sub_mlist: **if** *info*(*p*) = *null* **then**
        begin *print_ln*; *print_current_string*; *print*("{}");
        end
      else *show_info*; { recursive call }
    othercases *do_nothing* { empty }
    endcases;
    flush_char; { remove *c* from the recursion history }
    end;
  end;

693. The inelegant introduction of *show_info* in the code above seems better than the alternative of using Pascal's strange *forward* declaration for a procedure with parameters. The Pascal convention about dropping parameters from a post-*forward* procedure is, frankly, so intolerable to the author of TEX that he would rather stoop to communication via a global temporary variable. (A similar stoopidity occurred with respect to *hlist_out* and *vlist_out* above, and it will occur with respect to *mlist_to_hlist* below.)

procedure *show_info*;   { the reader will kindly forgive this }
  begin *show_node_list*(*info*(*temp_ptr*));
  end;

694. ⟨ Declare procedures needed for displaying the elements of mlists 691 ⟩ +≡
procedure *print_style*(*c* : *integer*);
  begin case *c* **div** 2 **of**
  0: *print_esc*("displaystyle");   { *display_style* = 0 }
  1: *print_esc*("textstyle");   { *text_style* = 2 }
  2: *print_esc*("scriptstyle");   { *script_style* = 4 }
  3: *print_esc*("scriptscriptstyle");   { *script_script_style* = 6 }
  othercases *print*("Unknown␣style!")
  endcases;
  end;

695. ⟨ Display choice node *p* 695 ⟩ ≡
  begin *print_esc*("mathchoice"); *append_char*("D"); *show_node_list*(*display_mlist*(*p*)); *flush_char*;
  append_char("T"); *show_node_list*(*text_mlist*(*p*)); *flush_char*; *append_char*("S");
  show_node_list(*script_mlist*(*p*)); *flush_char*; *append_char*("s");
  show_node_list(*script_script_mlist*(*p*)); *flush_char*;
  end

This code is used in section 690.

696. ⟨Display normal noad p 696⟩ ≡
　begin case $type(p)$ **of**
　ord_noad: $print\_esc($"mathord"$)$;
　op_noad: $print\_esc($"mathop"$)$;
　bin_noad: $print\_esc($"mathbin"$)$;
　rel_noad: $print\_esc($"mathrel"$)$;
　$open\_noad$: $print\_esc($"mathopen"$)$;
　$close\_noad$: $print\_esc($"mathclose"$)$;
　$punct\_noad$: $print\_esc($"mathpunct"$)$;
　$inner\_noad$: $print\_esc($"mathinner"$)$;
　$over\_noad$: $print\_esc($"overline"$)$;
　$under\_noad$: $print\_esc($"underline"$)$;
　$vcenter\_noad$: $print\_esc($"vcenter"$)$;
　$radical\_noad$: **begin** $print\_esc($"radical"$)$; $print\_delimiter(left\_delimiter(p))$;
　　end;
　$accent\_noad$: **begin** $print\_esc($"accent"$)$; $print\_fam\_and\_char(accent\_chr(p))$;
　　end;
　$left\_noad$: **begin** $print\_esc($"left"$)$; $print\_delimiter(nucleus(p))$;
　　end;
　$right\_noad$: **begin** $print\_esc($"right"$)$; $print\_delimiter(nucleus(p))$;
　　end;
　end;
　if $subtype(p) \neq normal$ **then**
　　if $subtype(p) = limits$ **then** $print\_esc($"limits"$)$
　　else $print\_esc($"nolimits"$)$;
　if $type(p) < left\_noad$ **then** $print\_subsidiary\_data(nucleus(p),$"."$)$;
　$print\_subsidiary\_data(supscr(p),$"^"$)$; $print\_subsidiary\_data(subscr(p),$"_"$)$;
　end
This code is used in section 690.

697. ⟨Display fraction noad p 697⟩ ≡
　begin $print\_esc($"fraction,␣thickness␣"$)$;
　if $thickness(p) = default\_code$ **then** $print($"=␣default"$)$
　else $print\_scaled(thickness(p))$;
　if $(small\_fam(left\_delimiter(p)) \neq 0) \vee (small\_char(left\_delimiter(p)) \neq min\_quarterword) \vee$
　　　$(large\_fam(left\_delimiter(p)) \neq 0) \vee (large\_char(left\_delimiter(p)) \neq min\_quarterword)$ **then**
　begin $print($",␣left-delimiter␣"$)$; $print\_delimiter(left\_delimiter(p))$;
　end;
　if $(small\_fam(right\_delimiter(p)) \neq 0) \vee (small\_char(right\_delimiter(p)) \neq min\_quarterword) \vee$
　　　$(large\_fam(right\_delimiter(p)) \neq 0) \vee (large\_char(right\_delimiter(p)) \neq min\_quarterword)$ **then**
　　begin $print($",␣right-delimiter␣"$)$; $print\_delimiter(right\_delimiter(p))$;
　　end;
　$print\_subsidiary\_data(numerator(p),$"\"$)$; $print\_subsidiary\_data(denominator(p),$"/"$)$;
　end
This code is used in section 690.

698. That which can be displayed can also be destroyed.

⟨ Cases of *flush_node_list* that arise in mlists only 698 ⟩ ≡

style_node: **begin** *free_node*(*p*, *style_node_size*); **goto** *done*;
   end;

choice_node: **begin** *flush_node_list*(*display_mlist*(*p*)); *flush_node_list*(*text_mlist*(*p*));
   flush_node_list(*script_mlist*(*p*)); *flush_node_list*(*script_script_mlist*(*p*)); *free_node*(*p*, *style_node_size*);
   goto *done*;
   end;

ord_noad, *op_noad*, *bin_noad*, *rel_noad*, *open_noad*, *close_noad*, *punct_noad*, *inner_noad*, *radical_noad*,
      over_noad, *under_noad*, *vcenter_noad*, *accent_noad*:
   begin if *math_type*(*nucleus*(*p*)) ≥ *sub_box* **then** *flush_node_list*(*info*(*nucleus*(*p*)));
   if *math_type*(*supscr*(*p*)) ≥ *sub_box* **then** *flush_node_list*(*info*(*supscr*(*p*)));
   if *math_type*(*subscr*(*p*)) ≥ *sub_box* **then** *flush_node_list*(*info*(*subscr*(*p*)));
   if *type*(*p*) = *radical_noad* **then** *free_node*(*p*, *radical_noad_size*)
   else if *type*(*p*) = *accent_noad* **then** *free_node*(*p*, *accent_noad_size*)
     else *free_node*(*p*, *noad_size*);
   goto *done*;
   end;

left_noad, *right_noad*: **begin** *free_node*(*p*, *noad_size*); **goto** *done*;
   end;

fraction_noad: **begin** *flush_node_list*(*info*(*numerator*(*p*))); *flush_node_list*(*info*(*denominator*(*p*)));
   free_node(*p*, *fraction_noad_size*); **goto** *done*;
   end;

This code is used in section 202.

---

accent_chr = macro, §687.
accent_noad = 28, §687.
accent_noad_size = 5, §687.
bin_noad = 18, §682.
close_noad = 21, §682.
default_code = macro, §683.
denominator = macro, §683.
display_mlist = macro, §689.
done = 30, §15.
flush_node_list: **procedure**, §202.
fraction_noad = 25, §683.
fraction_noad_size = 6, §683.
free_node: **procedure**, §130.
info = macro, §118.
inner_noad = 23, §682.
large_char = macro, §683.
large_fam = macro, §683.
left_delimiter = macro, §683.
left_noad = 30, §687.
limits = 1, §682.
math_type = macro, §681.

min_quarterword = 0, §110.
noad_size = 4, §681.
normal = 0, §135.
nucleus = macro, §681.
numerator = macro, §683.
op_noad = 17, §682.
open_noad = 20, §682.
ord_noad = 16, §682.
over_noad = 27, §687.
p: *pointer*, §182.
p: *pointer*, §202.
print: **procedure**, §59.
print_delimiter: **procedure**, §691.
print_esc: **procedure**, §63.
print_fam_and_char: **procedure**,
  §691.
print_scaled: **procedure**, §103.
print_subsidiary_data: **procedure**,
  §692.
punct_noad = 22, §682.

radical_noad = 24, §683.
radical_noad_size = 5, §683.
rel_noad = 19, §682.
right_delimiter = macro, §683.
right_noad = 31, §687.
script_mlist = macro, §689.
script_script_mlist = macro, §689.
small_char = macro, §683.
small_fam = macro, §683.
style_node = 14, §688.
style_node_size = 3, §688.
sub_box = 2, §681.
subscr = macro, §681.
subtype = macro, §133.
supscr = macro, §681.
text_mlist = macro, §689.
thickness = macro, §683.
type = macro, §133.
under_noad = 26, §687.
vcenter_noad = 29, §687.

699.   Subroutines for math mode.   In order to convert mlists to hlists, i.e., noads to nodes, we need several subroutines that are conveniently dealt with now.

Let us first introduce the macros that make it easy to get at the parameters and other font information. A size code, which is a multiple of 16, is added to a family number to get an index into the table of internal font numbers for each combination of family and size. (Be alert: Size codes get larger as the type gets smaller.)

> **define** $text\_size = 0$ { size code for the largest size in a family }
> **define** $script\_size = 16$ { size code for the medium size in a family }
> **define** $script\_script\_size = 32$ { size code for the smallest size in a family }

⟨ Basic printing procedures 57 ⟩ +≡
procedure $print\_size(s : integer)$;
> **begin if** $s = 0$ **then** $print\_esc(\texttt{"textfont"})$
> **else if** $s = script\_size$ **then** $print\_esc(\texttt{"scriptfont"})$
>> **else** $print\_esc(\texttt{"scriptscriptfont"})$;
> **end**;

700.   Before an mlist is converted to an hlist, TeX makes sure that the fonts in family 2 have enough parameters to be math-symbol fonts, and that the fonts in family 3 have enough parameters to be math-extension fonts. The math-symbol parameters are referred to by using the following macros, which take a size code as their parameter; for example, $num1(cur\_size)$ gives the value of the $num1$ parameter for the current size.

> **define** $mathsy\_end(\texttt{\#}) \equiv fam\_fnt(2 + \texttt{\#})\ ]\ ]\ .sc$
> **define** $mathsy(\texttt{\#}) \equiv font\_info\ [\ \texttt{\#} + param\_base\ [\ mathsy\_end$
> **define** $math\_x\_height \equiv mathsy(5)$ { height of 'x' }
> **define** $math\_quad \equiv mathsy(6)$ { 18mu }
> **define** $num1 \equiv mathsy(8)$ { numerator shift-up in display styles }
> **define** $num2 \equiv mathsy(9)$ { numerator shift-up in non-display, non-\atop }
> **define** $num3 \equiv mathsy(10)$ { numerator shift-up in non-display \atop }
> **define** $denom1 \equiv mathsy(11)$ { denominator shift-down in display styles }
> **define** $denom2 \equiv mathsy(12)$ { denominator shift-down in non-display styles }
> **define** $sup1 \equiv mathsy(13)$ { superscript shift-up in uncramped display style }
> **define** $sup2 \equiv mathsy(14)$ { superscript shift-up in uncramped non-display }
> **define** $sup3 \equiv mathsy(15)$ { superscript shift-up in cramped styles }
> **define** $sub1 \equiv mathsy(16)$ { subscript shift-down if superscript is absent }
> **define** $sub2 \equiv mathsy(17)$ { subscript shift-down if superscript is present }
> **define** $sup\_drop \equiv mathsy(18)$ { superscript baseline below top of large box }
> **define** $sub\_drop \equiv mathsy(19)$ { subscript baseline below bottom of large box }
> **define** $delim1 \equiv mathsy(20)$ { size of \atopwithdelims delimiters in display styles }
> **define** $delim2 \equiv mathsy(21)$ { size of \atopwithdelims delimiters in non-displays }
> **define** $axis\_height \equiv mathsy(22)$ { height of fraction lines above the baseline }
> **define** $total\_mathsy\_params = 22$

701.   The math-extension parameters have similar macros, but the size code is omitted (since it is always cur_size when we refer to such parameters).

> **define** $mathex(\texttt{\#}) \equiv font\_info\,[\texttt{\#} + param\_base\,[fam\_fnt(3 + cur\_size)]].sc$
> **define** $default\_rule\_thickness \equiv mathex(8)$ { thickness of \over bars }
> **define** $big\_op\_spacing1 \equiv mathex(9)$ { minimum clearance above a displayed op }

define $big\_op\_spacing2 \equiv mathex(10)$ { minimum clearance below a displayed op }
define $big\_op\_spacing3 \equiv mathex(11)$ { minimum baselineskip above displayed op }
define $big\_op\_spacing4 \equiv mathex(12)$ { minimum baselineskip below displayed op }
define $big\_op\_spacing5 \equiv mathex(13)$ { padding above and below displayed limits }
define $total\_mathex\_params = 13$

702.   We also need to compute the change in style between mlists and their subsidiaries. The following macros define the subsidiary style for an overlined nucleus (*cramped_style*), for a subscript or a superscript (*sub_style* or *sup_style*), or for a numerator or denominator (*num_style* or *denom_style*).

define $cramped\_style(\texttt{\#}) \equiv 2 * (\texttt{\#}\ \textbf{div}\ 2) + cramped$ { cramp the style }
define $sub\_style(\texttt{\#}) \equiv 2 * (\texttt{\#}\ \textbf{div}\ 4) + script\_style + cramped$ { smaller and cramped }
define $sup\_style(\texttt{\#}) \equiv 2 * (\texttt{\#}\ \textbf{div}\ 4) + script\_style + (\texttt{\#}\ \textbf{mod}\ 2)$ { smaller }
define $num\_style(\texttt{\#}) \equiv \texttt{\#} + 2 - 2 * (\texttt{\#}\ \textbf{div}\ 6)$ { smaller unless already script-script }
define $denom\_style(\texttt{\#}) \equiv 2 * (\texttt{\#}\ \textbf{div}\ 2) + cramped + 2 - 2 * (\texttt{\#}\ \textbf{div}\ 6)$ { smaller, cramped }

703.   When the style changes, the following piece of program computes associated information:

$\langle$ Set up the values of *cur_size* and *cur_mu*, based on *cur_style* 703 $\rangle \equiv$
  begin if $cur\_style < script\_style$ **then** $cur\_size \leftarrow text\_size$
  else $cur\_size \leftarrow 16 * ((cur\_style - text\_style)\ \textbf{div}\ 2)$;
  $cur\_mu \leftarrow x\_over\_n(math\_quad(cur\_size), 18)$;
  end

This code is used in sections 720, 726, 730, 754, 760, and 763.

704.   Here is a function that returns a pointer to a rule node having a given thickness t. The rule will extend horizontally to the boundary of the vlist that eventually contains it.

function $fraction\_rule(t : scaled)$: *pointer*;   { construct the bar for a fraction }
  var p: *pointer*;   { the new node }
  begin $p \leftarrow new\_rule$; $height(p) \leftarrow t$; $depth(p) \leftarrow 0$; $fraction\_rule \leftarrow p$;
  end;

705.   The *overbar* function returns a pointer to a vlist box that consists of a given box b, above which has been placed a kern of height k under a fraction rule of thickness t under additional space of height t.

function $overbar(b : pointer; k, t : scaled)$: *pointer*;
  var p, q: *pointer*;   { nodes being constructed }
  begin $p \leftarrow new\_kern(k)$; $link(p) \leftarrow b$; $q \leftarrow fraction\_rule(t)$; $link(q) \leftarrow p$; $p \leftarrow new\_kern(t)$;
  $link(p) \leftarrow q$; $overbar \leftarrow vpack(p, natural)$;
  end;

$cramped = 1$, §688.
cur_mu: *scaled*, §719.
cur_size: *small_number*, §719.
cur_style: *small_number*, §719.
$depth$ = macro, §135.
fam_fnt = macro, §230.
$font\_info$: **array**, §549.

$height$ = macro, §135.
$link$ = macro, §118.
$natural$ = macro, §644.
new_kern: **function**, §156.
new_rule: **function**, §139.
$param\_base$: **array**, §550.
$pointer$ = macro, §115.

$print\_esc$: **procedure**, §63.
sc = macro, §113.
$scaled = integer$, §101.
$script\_style = 4$, §688.
$text\_style = 2$, §688.
$vpack$ = macro, §668.
x_over_n: **function**, §106.

706. The *var_delimiter* function, which finds or constructs a sufficiently large delimiter, is the most interesting of the auxiliary functions that currently concern us. Given a pointer d to a delimiter field in some noad, together with a size code s and a vertical distance v, this function returns a pointer to a box that contains the smallest variant of d whose height plus depth is v or more. (And if no variant is large enough, it returns the largest available variant.) In particular, this routine will construct arbitrarily large delimiters from extensible components, if d leads to such characters.

The value returned is a box whose *shift_amount* has been set so that the box is vertically centered with respect to the axis in the given size. If a built-up symbol is returned, the height of the box before shifting will be the height of its topmost component.

$\langle$ Declare subprocedures for *var_delimiter* 709 $\rangle$
function *var_delimiter*(d : *pointer*; s : *small_number*; v : *scaled*): *pointer*;
  label *found*, *continue*;
  var b: *pointer*; { the box that will be constructed }
    f, g: *internal_font_number*; { best-so-far and tentative font codes }
    c, x, y: *quarterword*; { best-so-far and tentative character codes }
    m, n: *integer*; { the number of extensible pieces }
    u: *scaled*; { height-plus-depth of a tentative character }
    w: *scaled*; { largest height-plus-depth so far }
    q: *four_quarters*; { character info }
    hd: *eight_bits*; { height-depth byte }
    r: *four_quarters*; { extensible pieces }
    z: *small_number*; { runs through font family members }
    large_attempt: *boolean*; { are we trying the "large" variant? }
  begin $f \leftarrow null\_font$; $w \leftarrow 0$; *large_attempt* $\leftarrow false$; $z \leftarrow small\_fam(d)$; $x \leftarrow small\_char(d)$;
  loop begin $\langle$ Look at the variants of (z, x); set f and c whenever a better character is found; **goto**
      found as soon as a large enough variant is encountered 707 $\rangle$;
    if *large_attempt* **then goto** *found*; { there were none large enough }
    large_attempt $\leftarrow true$; $z \leftarrow large\_fam(d)$; $x \leftarrow large\_char(d)$;
    end;
found: **if** $f \neq null\_font$ **then** $\langle$ Make variable b point to a box for (f, c) 710 $\rangle$
  else begin $b \leftarrow new\_null\_box$; $width(b) \leftarrow null\_delimiter\_space$;
    { use this width if no delimiter was found }
    end;
  $shift\_amount(b) \leftarrow half(height(b) - depth(b)) - axis\_height(s)$; *var_delimiter* $\leftarrow b$;
  end;

707. The search process is complicated slightly by the facts that some of the characters might not be present in some of the fonts, and they might not be probed in increasing order of height.

$\langle$ Look at the variants of (z, x); set f and c whenever a better character is found; **goto** *found* as soon as
    a large enough variant is encountered 707 $\rangle$ $\equiv$
  if $(z \neq 0) \vee (x \neq min\_quarterword)$ **then**
    begin $z \leftarrow z + s + 16$;
    repeat $z \leftarrow z - 16$; $g \leftarrow fam\_fnt(z)$;
      if $g \neq null\_font$ **then** $\langle$ Look at the list of characters starting with x in font g; set f and c
        whenever a better character is found; **goto** *found* as soon as a large enough variant is
        encountered 708 $\rangle$;

until $z < 16$;
end

This code is used in section 706.

708. ⟨ Look at the list of characters starting with x in font g; set f and c whenever a better character
    is found; **goto** *found* as soon as a large enough variant is encountered 708 ⟩ ≡
  begin $y \leftarrow x$;
continue: **if** $(qo(y) \geq font\_bc[g]) \wedge (qo(y) \leq font\_ec[g])$ **then**
    begin $q \leftarrow char\_info(g)(y)$;
    if $char\_exists(q)$ **then**
      begin if $char\_tag(q) = ext\_tag$ **then**
        begin $f \leftarrow g$; $c \leftarrow y$; **goto** *found*;
        end;
      $hd \leftarrow height\_depth(q)$; $u \leftarrow char\_height(g)(hd) + char\_depth(g)(hd)$;
      if $u > w$ **then**
        begin $f \leftarrow g$; $c \leftarrow y$; $w \leftarrow u$;
        if $u \geq v$ **then goto** *found*;
        end;
      if $char\_tag(q) = list\_tag$ **then**
        begin $y \leftarrow rem\_byte(q)$; **goto** *continue*;
        end;
      end;
    end;
  end

This code is used in section 707.

$axis\_height$ = macro, §700.
$char\_depth$ = macro, §554.
$char\_exists$ = macro, §554.
$char\_height$ = macro, §554.
$char\_info$ = macro, §554.
$char\_tag$ = macro, §554.
$continue$ = 22, §15.
$depth$ = macro, §135.
$eight\_bits$ = 0 .. 255, §25.
ext_tag = 3, §544.
fam_fnt = macro, §230.
$font\_bc$: **array**, §549.
$font\_ec$: **array**, §549.

$found$ = 40, §15.
$four\_quarters$ = **packed record**,
  §113.
$half$: **function**, §100.
$height$ = macro, §135.
$height\_depth$ = macro, §554.
$internal\_font\_number$ = 0 .. $font\_max$,
  §548.
$large\_char$ = macro, §683.
$large\_fam$ = macro, §683.
$list\_tag$ = 2, §544.
$min\_quarterword$ = 0, §110.
new_null_box: **function**, §136.

$null\_delimiter\_space$ = macro, §247.
$null\_font$ = macro, §232.
$pointer$ = macro, §115.
qo = macro, §112.
$quarterword$ = 0 .. 255, §113.
rem_byte = macro, §545.
$scaled$ = $integer$, §101.
$shift\_amount$ = macro, §135.
$small\_char$ = macro, §683.
$small\_fam$ = macro, §683.
$small\_number$ = 0 .. 63, §101.
$width$ = macro, §135.

709. Here is a subroutine that creates a new box, whose list contains a single character, and whose width includes the italic correction for that character. The height or depth of the box will be negative, if the height or depth of the character is negative; thus, this routine may deliver a slightly different result than *hpack* would produce.

⟨ Declare subprocedures for *var_delimiter* 709 ⟩ ≡
function *char_box*(f : *internal_font_number*; c : *quarterword*): *pointer*;
　　var q: *four_quarters*; *hd*: *eight_bits*;　{ *height_depth* byte }
　　　b, p: *pointer*;　　{ the new box and its character node }
　　begin $q \leftarrow char\_info(f)(c)$; *hd* $\leftarrow height\_depth(q)$; $b \leftarrow new\_null\_box$;
　　width(b) $\leftarrow char\_width(f)(q) + char\_italic(f)(q)$; *height*($b$) $\leftarrow char\_height(f)(hd)$;
　　depth(b) $\leftarrow char\_depth(f)(hd)$; $p \leftarrow get\_avail$; *character*(p) $\leftarrow c$; *font*(p) $\leftarrow f$; *list_ptr*(b) $\leftarrow p$;
　　char_box $\leftarrow b$;
　　end;

See also sections 711 and 712.

This code is used in section 706.

710. When the following code is executed, *char_tag*(q) will be equal to *ext_tag* if and only if a built-up symbol is supposed to be returned.

⟨ Make variable b point to a box for (f, c) 710 ⟩ ≡
　if *char_tag*(q) = *ext_tag* **then**
　　⟨ Construct an extensible character in a new box b, using recipe *rem_byte*(q) and font f 713 ⟩
　else $b \leftarrow char\_box(f, c)$

This code is used in section 706.

711. When we build an extensible character, it's handy to have the following subroutine, which puts a given character on top of the characters already in box b:

⟨ Declare subprocedures for *var_delimiter* 709 ⟩ +≡
procedure *stack_into_box*(b : *pointer*; f : *internal_font_number*; c : *quarterword*);
　　var p: *pointer*;　　{ new node placed into b }
　　begin $p \leftarrow char\_box(f, c)$; *link*($p$) $\leftarrow list\_ptr(b)$; *list_ptr*(b) $\leftarrow p$; *height*(b) $\leftarrow height(p)$;
　　end;

712. Another handy subroutine computes the height plus depth of a given character:

⟨ Declare subprocedures for *var_delimiter* 709 ⟩ +≡
function *height_plus_depth*(f : *internal_font_number*; c : *quarterword*): *scaled*;
　　var q: *four_quarters*; *hd*: *eight_bits*;　{ *height_depth* byte }
　　begin $q \leftarrow char\_info(f)(c)$; *hd* $\leftarrow height\_depth(q)$;
　　height_plus_depth $\leftarrow char\_height(f)(hd) + char\_depth(f)(hd)$;
　　end;

713. ⟨ Construct an extensible character in a new box b, using recipe *rem_byte*(q) and font f 713 ⟩ ≡
　begin $b \leftarrow new\_null\_box$; *type*($b$) $\leftarrow vlist\_node$; $r \leftarrow font\_info[exten\_base[f] + rem\_byte(q)].qqqq$;
　⟨ Compute the minimum suitable height, w, and the corresponding number of extension steps, n; also
　　set *width*(b) 714 ⟩;
　$c \leftarrow ext\_bot(r)$;
　if $c \neq min\_quarterword$ **then** *stack_into_box*(b, f, c);
　$c \leftarrow ext\_rep(r)$;
　for $m \leftarrow 1$ **to** n **do** *stack_into_box*(b, f, c);

$c \leftarrow \mathit{ext\_mid}(r)$;
if $c \neq \mathit{min\_quarterword}$ **then**
    begin $\mathit{stack\_into\_box}(b, f, c)$; $c \leftarrow \mathit{ext\_rep}(r)$;
    for $m \leftarrow 1$ **to** n **do** $\mathit{stack\_into\_box}(b, f, c)$;
    end;
$c \leftarrow \mathit{ext\_top}(r)$;
if $c \neq \mathit{min\_quarterword}$ **then** $\mathit{stack\_into\_box}(b, f, c)$;
$\mathit{depth}(b) \leftarrow w - \mathit{height}(b)$;
end

This code is used in section 710.

714. The width of an extensible character is the width of the repeatable module. If this module does not have positive height plus depth, we don't use any copies of it, otherwise we use as few as possible (in groups of two if there is a middle part).

⟨ Compute the minimum suitable height, w, and the corresponding number of extension steps, n; also set $\mathit{width}(b)$ 714 ⟩ ≡
$c \leftarrow \mathit{ext\_rep}(r)$; $u \leftarrow \mathit{height\_plus\_depth}(f, c)$; $w \leftarrow 0$; $q \leftarrow \mathit{char\_info}(f)(c)$;
$\mathit{width}(b) \leftarrow \mathit{char\_width}(f)(q) + \mathit{char\_italic}(f)(q)$;
$c \leftarrow \mathit{ext\_bot}(r)$; **if** $c \neq \mathit{min\_quarterword}$ **then** $w \leftarrow w + \mathit{height\_plus\_depth}(f, c)$;
$c \leftarrow \mathit{ext\_mid}(r)$; **if** $c \neq \mathit{min\_quarterword}$ **then** $w \leftarrow w + \mathit{height\_plus\_depth}(f, c)$;
$c \leftarrow \mathit{ext\_top}(r)$; **if** $c \neq \mathit{min\_quarterword}$ **then** $w \leftarrow w + \mathit{height\_plus\_depth}(f, c)$;
$n \leftarrow 0$;
if $u > 0$ **then**
    while $w < v$ **do**
        begin $w \leftarrow w + u$; $\mathit{incr}(n)$;
        if $\mathit{ext\_mid}(r) \neq \mathit{min\_quarterword}$ **then** $w \leftarrow w + u$;
        end

This code is used in section 713.

---

b: *pointer*, §706.
c: *quarterword*, §706.
char_depth = macro, §554.
char_height = macro, §554.
char_info = macro, §554.
char_italic = macro, §554.
char_tag = macro, §554.
char_width = macro, §554.
character = macro, §134.
depth = macro, §135.
eight_bits = 0 .. 255, §25.
ext_bot = macro, §546.
ext_mid = macro, §546.
ext_rep = macro, §546.
ext_tag = 3, §544.
ext_top = macro, §546.
exten_base: **array**, §550.

f: *internal_font_number*, §706.
font = macro, §134.
font_info: **array**, §549.
four_quarters = **packed record**, §113.
get_avail: **function**, §120.
height = macro, §135.
height_depth = macro, §554.
hpack: **function**, §649.
incr = macro, §16.
internal_font_number = 0 .. *font_max*, §548.
link = macro, §118.
list_ptr = macro, §135.
m: *integer*, §706.
min_quarterword = 0, §110.

n: *integer*, §706.
new_null_box: **function**, §136.
pointer = macro, §115.
q: *four_quarters*, §706.
qqqq: *four_quarters*, §113.
quarterword = 0 .. 255, §113.
r: *four_quarters*, §706.
rem_byte = macro, §545.
scaled = *integer*, §101.
type = macro, §133.
u: *scaled*, §706.
v: *scaled*, §706.
var_delimiter: **function**, §706.
vlist_node = 1, §137.
w: *scaled*, §706.
width = macro, §135.

715. The next subroutine is much simpler; it is used for numerators and denominators of fractions as well as for displayed operators and their limits above and below. It takes a given hlist box b and changes it so that the new box is centered in a box of width w. The centering is done by putting \hss glue at the left and right of the list inside b, then packaging the new box; thus, the actual box might not really be centered, if it already contains infinite glue.

The given box might contain a single character whose italic correction has been added to the width of the box; in this case a compensating kern is inserted.

function $rebox(b : pointer; w : scaled)$: $pointer$;
  var p: $pointer$; { temporary register for list manipulation }
    f: $internal\_font\_number$; { font in a one-character box }
    v: $scaled$; { width of a character without italic correction }
  begin if $(width(b) \neq w) \wedge (list\_ptr(b) \neq null)$ **then**
    begin if $type(b) = vlist\_node$ **then** $b \leftarrow hpack(b, natural)$;
    $p \leftarrow list\_ptr(b)$;
    if $(is\_char\_node(p)) \wedge (link(p) = null)$ **then**
      begin $f \leftarrow font(p)$; $v \leftarrow char\_width(f)(char\_info(f)(character(p)))$;
      if $v \neq width(b)$ **then** $link(p) \leftarrow new\_kern(width(b) - v)$;
      end;
    $free\_node(b, box\_node\_size)$; $b \leftarrow new\_glue(ss\_glue)$; $link(b) \leftarrow p$;
    while $link(p) \neq null$ **do** $p \leftarrow link(p)$;
    $link(p) \leftarrow new\_glue(ss\_glue)$; $rebox \leftarrow hpack(b, w, exactly)$;
    end
  else begin $width(b) \leftarrow w$; $rebox \leftarrow b$;
    end;
  end;

716. Here is a subroutine that creates a new glue specification from another one that is expressed in 'mu', given the value of the math unit.

  define $mu\_mult(\#) \equiv nx\_plus\_y(n, \#, xn\_over\_d(\#, f, '200000))$

function $math\_glue(g : pointer; m : scaled)$: $pointer$;
  var p: $pointer$; { the new glue specification }
    n: $integer$; { integer part of m }
    f: $scaled$; { fraction part of m }
  begin $n \leftarrow x\_over\_n(m, '200000)$; $f \leftarrow remainder$;
  $p \leftarrow get\_node(glue\_spec\_size)$; $width(p) \leftarrow mu\_mult(width(g))$; { convert mu to pt }
  $stretch\_order(p) \leftarrow stretch\_order(g)$;
  if $stretch\_order(p) = normal$ **then** $stretch(p) \leftarrow mu\_mult(stretch(g))$
  else $stretch(p) \leftarrow stretch(g)$;
  $shrink\_order(p) \leftarrow shrink\_order(g)$;
  if $shrink\_order(p) = normal$ **then** $shrink(p) \leftarrow mu\_mult(shrink(g))$
  else $shrink(p) \leftarrow shrink(g)$;
  $math\_glue \leftarrow p$;
  end;

717. The $math\_kern$ subroutine removes mu_glue from a kern node, given the value of the math unit.

procedure $math\_kern(p : pointer; m : scaled)$;

var n: $integer$; { integer part of m }
   f: $scaled$; { fraction part of m }
begin if $subtype(p) = mu\_glue$ **then**
   begin $n \leftarrow x\_over\_n(m, \ '200000)$; $f \leftarrow remainder$;
   $width(p) \leftarrow mu\_mult(width(p))$; $subtype(p) \leftarrow normal$;
   end;
  end;

718. Sometimes it is necessary to destroy an mlist. The following subroutine empties the current list, assuming that $abs(mode) = mmode$.

procedure $flush\_math$;
  begin $flush\_node\_list(link(head))$; $flush\_node\_list(incompleat\_noad)$; $link(head) \leftarrow null$;
  $tail \leftarrow head$; $incompleat\_noad \leftarrow null$;
  end;

719.   Typesetting math formulas.   TeX's most important routine for dealing with formulas is called *mlist_to_hlist*. After a formula has been scanned and represented as an mlist, this routine converts it to an hlist that can be placed into a box or incorporated into the text of a paragraph. There are three implicit parameters, passed in global variables: *cur_mlist* points to the first node or noad in the given mlist (and it might be *null*); *cur_style* is a style code; and *mlist_penalties* is *true* if penalty nodes for potential line breaks are to be inserted into the resulting hlist. After *mlist_to_hlist* has acted, *link*(*temp_head*) points to the translated hlist.

Since mlists can be inside mlists, the procedure is recursive. And since this is not part of TeX's inner loop, the program has been written in a manner that stresses compactness over efficiency.

⟨ Global variables 13 ⟩ +≡
cur_mlist: *pointer*;   { beginning of mlist to be translated }
cur_style: *small_number*;   { style code at current place in the list }
cur_size: *small_number*;   { size code corresponding to *cur_style* }
cur_mu: *scaled*;   { the math unit width corresponding to *cur_size* }
mlist_penalties: *boolean*;   { should *mlist_to_hlist* insert penalties? }

720.   The recursion in *mlist_to_hlist* is due primarily to a subroutine called *clean_box* that puts a given noad field into a box using a given math style; *mlist_to_hlist* can call *clean_box*, which can call *mlist_to_hlist*.

The box returned by *clean_box* is "clean" in the sense that its *shift_amount* is zero.

procedure *mlist_to_hlist*; *forward*;
function *clean_box*(*p* : *pointer*; *s* : *small_number*): *pointer*;
  label *found*;
  var *q*: *pointer*;   { beginning of a list to be boxed }
    save_style: *small_number*;   { *cur_style* to be restored }
    x: *pointer*;   { box to be returned }
    r: *pointer*;   { temporary pointer }
  begin case *math_type*(*p*) **of**
  math_char: **begin** *cur_mlist* ← *new_noad*; *mem*[*nucleus*(*cur_mlist*)] ← *mem*[*p*];
    end;
  sub_box: **begin** *q* ← *info*(*p*); **goto** *found*;
    end;
  sub_mlist: *cur_mlist* ← *info*(*p*);
  othercases begin *q* ← *new_null_box*; **goto** *found*;
    end
  endcases;
  save_style ← *cur_style*; *cur_style* ← *s*; *mlist_penalties* ← *false*;
  mlist_to_hlist; *q* ← *link*(*temp_head*);   { recursive call }
  cur_style ← *save_style*;   { restore the style }
  ⟨ Set up the values of *cur_size* and *cur_mu*, based on *cur_style* 703 ⟩;
found: **if** *is_char_node*(*q*) ∨ (*q* = *null*) **then** *x* ← *hpack*(*q*, *natural*)
  else if (*link*(*q*) = *null*) ∧ (*type*(*q*) ≤ *vlist_node*) ∧ (*shift_amount*(*q*) = 0) **then** *x* ← *q*
        { it's already clean }
    else *x* ← *hpack*(*q*, *natural*);
  ⟨ Simplify a trivial box 721 ⟩;
  clean_box ← *x*;
  end;

721.   Here we save memory space in a common case.

⟨ Simplify a trivial box 721 ⟩ ≡
  $q \leftarrow list\_ptr(x)$;
  if $is\_char\_node(q)$ **then**
    begin $r \leftarrow link(q)$;
    if $r \neq null$ **then**
      if $link(r) = null$ **then**
        if $\neg is\_char\_node(r)$ **then**
          if $type(r) = kern\_node$ **then**
            begin $free\_node(r, small\_node\_size)$; $link(q) \leftarrow null$;
            end;
  end

This code is used in section 720.

722.   It is convenient to have a procedure that converts a *math_char* field to an "unpacked" form. The *fetch* routine sets *cur_f*, *cur_c*, and *cur_i* to the font code, character code, and character information bytes of a given noad field. It also takes care of issuing error messages for nonexistent characters; in such cases, $char\_exists(cur\_i)$ will be *false* after *fetch* has acted, and the field will also have been reset to *empty*.

procedure $fetch(a : pointer)$;   { unpack the *math_char* field a }
  begin $cur\_c \leftarrow character(a)$; $cur\_f \leftarrow fam\_fnt(fam(a) + cur\_size)$;
  if $cur\_f = null\_font$ **then** ⟨ Complain about an undefined family and set *cur_i* null 723 ⟩
  else begin if $(qo(cur\_c) \geq font\_bc[cur\_f]) \wedge (qo(cur\_c) \leq font\_ec[cur\_f])$ **then**
      $cur\_i \leftarrow char\_info(cur\_f)(cur\_c)$
    else $cur\_i \leftarrow null\_character$;
    if $\neg(char\_exists(cur\_i))$ **then**
      begin $char\_warning(cur\_f, qo(cur\_c))$; $math\_type(a) \leftarrow empty$;
      end;
    end;
  end;

---

char_exists = macro, §554.
char_info = macro, §554.
char_warning: **procedure**, §581.
character = macro, §134.
cur_c: *quarterword*, §724.
cur_f: *internal_font_number*, §724.
cur_i: *four_quarters*, §724.
empty = 0, §16.
fam = macro, §681.
fam_fnt = macro, §230.
font_bc: **array**, §549.
font_ec: **array**, §549.
found = 40, §15.
free_node: **procedure**, §130.

hpack: **function**, §649.
info = macro, §118.
is_char_node = macro, §134.
kern_node = 11, §155.
link = macro, §118.
list_ptr = macro, §135.
math_char = 1, §681.
math_type = macro, §681.
mem: **array**, §116.
mlist_to_hlist: **procedure**, §726.
natural = macro, §644.
new_noad: **function**, §686.
new_null_box: **function**, §136.
nucleus = macro, §681.

null = macro, §115.
null_character: *four_quarters*, §555.
null_font = macro, §232.
pointer = macro, §115.
qo = macro, §112.
scaled = *integer*, §101.
shift_amount = macro, §135.
small_node_size = 2, §141.
small_number = 0 .. 63, §101.
sub_box = 2, §681.
sub_mlist = 3, §681.
temp_head = macro, §162.
type = macro, §133.
vlist_node = 1, §137.

723. ⟨ Complain about an undefined family and set cur_i null 723 ⟩ ≡
   begin $print\_err$(""); $print\_size$(cur_size); $print\_char$("␣"); $print\_int$($fam(a)$);
   $print$("␣is␣undefined␣(character␣"); $print\_ASCII$($qo(cur\_c)$); $print\_char$(")");
   $help4$("Somewhere␣in␣the␣math␣formula␣just␣ended,␣you␣used␣the")
   ("stated␣character␣from␣an␣undefined␣font␣family.␣For␣example,")
   ("plain␣TeX␣doesn´t␣allow␣\it␣or␣\sl␣in␣subscripts.␣Proceed,")
   ("and␣I´ll␣try␣to␣forget␣that␣I␣needed␣that␣character."); $error$; $cur\_i \leftarrow null\_character$;
   $math\_type(a) \leftarrow empty$;
   end

This code is used in section 722.

724. The outputs of *fetch* are placed in global variables.

⟨ Global variables 13 ⟩ +≡
cur_f: $internal\_font\_number$;   { the *font* field of a $math\_char$ }
cur_c: $quarterword$;   { the *character* field of a $math\_char$ }
cur_i: $four\_quarters$;   { the *char_info* of a $math\_char$, or a lig/kern instruction }

725. We need to do a lot of different things, so $mlist\_to\_hlist$ makes two passes over the given mlist.

The first pass does most of the processing: It removes "mu" spacing from glue, it recursively evaluates all subsidiary mlists so that only the top-level mlist remains to be handled, it puts fractions and square roots and such things into boxes, it attaches subscripts and superscripts, and it computes the overall height and depth of the top-level mlist so that the size of delimiters for a *left_noad* and a *right_noad* will be known. The hlist resulting from each noad is recorded in that noad's *new_hlist* field, an integer field that replaces the *nucleus* or *thickness*.

The second pass eliminates all noads and inserts the correct glue and penalties between nodes.

   define $new\_hlist(\#) \equiv mem[nucleus(\#)].int$ { the translation of an mlist }

726. Here is the overall plan of $mlist\_to\_hlist$, and the list of its local variables.

   define $done\_with\_noad = 80$ { go here when a noad has been fully translated }
   define $done\_with\_node = 81$ { go here when a node has been fully converted }
   define $check\_dimensions = 82$ { go here to update max_h and max_d }
   define $delete\_q = 83$ { go here to delete q and move to the next node }
⟨ Declare math construction procedures 734 ⟩
procedure $mlist\_to\_hlist$;
   label $reswitch$, $check\_dimensions$, $done\_with\_noad$, $done\_with\_node$, $delete\_q$, $done$;
   var $mlist$: $pointer$;   { beginning of the given list }
      $penalties$: $boolean$;   { should penalty nodes be inserted? }
      $style$: $small\_number$;   { the given style }
      $save\_style$: $small\_number$;   { holds cur_style during recursion }
      q: $pointer$;   { runs through the mlist }
      r: $pointer$;   { the most recent noad preceding q }
      r_type: $small\_number$;   { the *type* of noad r, or op_noad if $r = null$ }
      t: $small\_number$;   { the effective *type* of noad q during the second pass }
      p, x, y, z: $pointer$;   { temporary registers for list construction }
      pen: $integer$;   { a penalty to be inserted }
      s: $small\_number$;   { the size of a noad to be deleted }

max_h, max_d: *scaled*;   { maximum height and depth of the list translated so far }

$delta$: *scaled*;   { offset between subscript and superscript }

begin $mlist \leftarrow cur\_mlist$; $penalties \leftarrow mlist\_penalties$; $style \leftarrow cur\_style$;

{ tuck global parameters away as local variables }

$q \leftarrow mlist$; $r \leftarrow null$; $r\_type \leftarrow op\_noad$; $max\_h \leftarrow 0$; $max\_d \leftarrow 0$;

⟨ Set up the values of *cur_size* and *cur_mu*, based on *cur_style* 703 ⟩;

while $q \neq null$ **do** ⟨ Process node-or-noad q as much as possible in preparation for the second pass of
 mlist_to_hlist, then move to the next item in the mlist 727 ⟩;

⟨ Convert a final *bin_noad* to an *ord_noad* 729 ⟩;

⟨ Make a second pass over the mlist, removing all noads and inserting the proper spacing and
 penalties 760 ⟩;

end;

727.   We use the fact that no character nodes appear in an mlist, hence the field $type(q)$ is always present.

⟨ Process node-or-noad q as much as possible in preparation for the second pass of *mlist_to_hlist*, then
 move to the next item in the mlist 727 ⟩ ≡

begin ⟨ Do first-pass processing based on $type(q)$; **goto** *done_with_noad* if a noad has been
 fully processed, **goto** *check_dimensions* if it has been translated into $new\_hlist(q)$, or **goto**
 done_with_node if a node has been fully processed 728 ⟩;

check_dimensions: $z \leftarrow hpack(new\_hlist(q), natural)$;

if $height(z) > max\_h$ **then** $max\_h \leftarrow height(z)$;

if $depth(z) > max\_d$ **then** $max\_d \leftarrow depth(z)$;

$free\_node(z, box\_node\_size)$;

done_with_noad: $r \leftarrow q$; $r\_type \leftarrow type(r)$;

done_with_node: $q \leftarrow link(q)$;

end

This code is used in section 726.

---

a: *pointer*, §722.
bin_noad = 18, §682.
box_node_size = 7, §135.
char_info = macro, §554.
character = macro, §134.
cur_mlist: *pointer*, §719.
cur_mu: *scaled*, §719.
cur_size: *small_number*, §719.
cur_style: *small_number*, §719.
depth = macro, §135.
done = 30, §15.
empty = 0, §16.
error: **procedure**, §82.
fam = macro, §681.
fetch: **procedure**, §722.
font = macro, §134.
four_quarters = **packed record**, §113.

free_node: **procedure**, §130.
height = macro, §135.
help4 = macro, §79.
hpack: **function**, §649.
int: *integer*, §113.
internal_font_number = 0 .. *font_max*, §548.
left_noad = 30, §687.
link = macro, §118.
math_char = 1, §681.
math_type = macro, §681.
mem: **array**, §116.
mlist_penalties: *boolean*, §719.
natural = macro, §644.
nucleus = macro, §681.
null = macro, §115.
null_character: *four_quarters*, §555.

op_noad = 17, §682.
ord_noad = 16, §682.
pointer = macro, §115.
print: **procedure**, §59.
print_ASCII: **procedure**, §68.
print_char: **procedure**, §58.
print_err = macro, §73.
print_int: **procedure**, §65.
print_size: **procedure**, §699.
qo = macro, §112.
quarterword = 0 .. 255, §113.
reswitch = 21, §15.
right_noad = 31, §687.
scaled = *integer*, §101.
small_number = 0 .. 63, §101.
thickness = macro, §683.
type = macro, §133.

728. One of the things we must do on the first pass is change a *bin_noad* to an *ord_noad* if the *bin_noad* is not in the context of a binary operator. The values of r and *r_type* make this fairly easy.

⟨ Do first-pass processing based on *type*(*q*); **goto** *done_with_noad* if a noad has been fully processed, **goto** *check_dimensions* if it has been translated into *new_hlist*(*q*), or **goto** *done_with_node* if a node has been fully processed 728 ⟩ ≡
reswitch: *delta* ← 0;
  case *type*(*q*) **of**
  bin_noad: **case** *r_type* **of**
    bin_noad, *op_noad*, *rel_noad*, *open_noad*, *punct_noad*, *left_noad*: **begin** *type*(*q*) ← *ord_noad*;
    goto *reswitch*;
    end;
    othercases *do_nothing*
    endcases;
  rel_noad, *close_noad*, *punct_noad*, *right_noad*:
    begin ⟨ Convert a final *bin_noad* to an *ord_noad* 729 ⟩;
    if *type*(*q*) = *right_noad* **then goto** *done_with_noad*;
    end;
  ⟨ Cases for noads that can follow a *bin_noad* 733 ⟩
  ⟨ Cases for nodes that can appear in an mlist, after which we **goto** *done_with_node* 730 ⟩
  othercases *confusion*("mlist1")
  endcases;
⟨ Convert *nucleus*(*q*) to an hlist and attach the sub/superscripts 754 ⟩

This code is used in section 727.

729. ⟨ Convert a final *bin_noad* to an *ord_noad* 729 ⟩ ≡
  if *r_type* = *bin_noad* **then** *type*(*r*) ← *ord_noad*

This code is used in sections 726 and 728.

730. ⟨ Cases for nodes that can appear in an mlist, after which we **goto** *done_with_node* 730 ⟩ ≡
style_node: **begin** *cur_style* ← *subtype*(*q*);
  ⟨ Set up the values of *cur_size* and *cur_mu*, based on *cur_style* 703 ⟩;
  goto *done_with_node*;
  end;
choice_node: ⟨ Change this node to a style node followed by the correct choice, then **goto** *done_with_node* 731 ⟩;
ins_node, *mark_node*, *adjust_node*, *whatsit_node*, *penalty_node*, *disc_node*: **goto** *done_with_node*;
rule_node: **begin if** *height*(*q*) > *max_h* **then** *max_h* ← *height*(*q*);
  if *depth*(*q*) > *max_d* **then** *max_d* ← *depth*(*q*);
  goto *done_with_node*;
  end;
glue_node: **begin** ⟨ Convert math glue to ordinary glue 732 ⟩;
  goto *done_with_node*;
  end;
kern_node: **begin** *math_kern*(*q*, *cur_mu*); **goto** *done_with_node*;
  end;

This code is used in section 728.

731.   define *choose_mlist*(**#**) ≡
           begin $p \leftarrow$ **#**(q); **#**$(q) \leftarrow null$; **end**
⟨ Change this node to a style node followed by the correct choice, then **goto** *done_with_node* 731 ⟩ ≡
  begin case *cur_style* **div** 2 **of**
  0: *choose_mlist*(*display_mlist*);   { *display_style* = 0 }
  1: *choose_mlist*(*text_mlist*);   { *text_style* = 2 }
  2: *choose_mlist*(*script_mlist*);   { *script_style* = 4 }
  3: *choose_mlist*(*script_script_mlist*);   { *script_script_style* = 6 }
  end;   { there are no other cases }
  flush_node_list(*display_mlist*(q)); *flush_node_list*(*text_mlist*(q)); *flush_node_list*(*script_mlist*(q));
  flush_node_list(*script_script_mlist*(q));
  type(q) ← *style_node*; *subtype*(q) ← *cur_style*; *width*(q) ← 0; *depth*(q) ← 0;
  if $p \neq null$ **then**
      begin $z \leftarrow link(q)$; $link(q) \leftarrow p$;
      while $link(p) \neq null$ **do** $p \leftarrow link(p)$;
      $link(p) \leftarrow z$;
      end;
  goto *done_with_node*;
  end
This code is used in section 730.

732. Conditional math glue ('\nonscript') results in a *glue_node* pointing to *zero_glue*, with $subtype(q) = cond\_math\_glue$; in such a case the node following will be eliminated if it is a glue or kern node and if the current size is different from *text_size*. Unconditional math glue ('\muskip') is converted to normal glue by multiplying the dimensions by *cur_mu*.

⟨ Convert math glue to ordinary glue 732 ⟩ ≡
  if $subtype(q) = mu\_glue$ **then**
    begin $x \leftarrow glue\_ptr(q);\ y \leftarrow math\_glue(x, cur\_mu);\ delete\_glue\_ref(x);\ glue\_ptr(q) \leftarrow y;$
    $subtype(q) \leftarrow normal;$
    end
  else if $(cur\_size \neq text\_size) \wedge (subtype(q) = cond\_math\_glue)$ **then**
      begin $p \leftarrow link(q);$
      if $p \neq null$ **then**
        if $(type(p) = glue\_node) \vee (type(p) = kern\_node)$ **then**
          begin $link(q) \leftarrow link(p);\ link(p) \leftarrow null;\ flush\_node\_list(p);$
          end;
      end

This code is used in section 730.

733. ⟨ Cases for noads that can follow a *bin_noad* 733 ⟩ ≡
left_noad: **goto** *done_with_noad*;
fraction_noad: **begin** $make\_fraction(q);$ **goto** *check_dimensions*;
  end;
op_noad: **begin** $delta \leftarrow make\_op(q);$
  if $subtype(q) = limits$ **then goto** *check_dimensions*;
  end;
ord_noad: $make\_ord(q);$
open_noad, *inner_noad*: *do_nothing*;
radical_noad: $make\_radical(q);$
over_noad: $make\_over(q);$
under_noad: $make\_under(q);$
accent_noad: $make\_math\_accent(q);$
vcenter_noad: $make\_vcenter(q);$

This code is used in section 728.

734. Most of the actual construction work of *mlist_to_hlist* is done by procedures with names like *make_fraction*, *make_radical*, etc. To illustrate the general setup of such procedures, let's begin with a couple of simple ones.

⟨ Declare math construction procedures 734 ⟩ ≡
procedure $make\_over(q : pointer);$
  begin $info(nucleus(q)) \leftarrow overbar(clean\_box(nucleus(q), cramped\_style(cur\_style)),$
    $3 * default\_rule\_thickness, default\_rule\_thickness);\ math\_type(nucleus(q)) \leftarrow sub\_box;$
  end;

See also sections 735, 736, 737, 738, 743, 749, 752, 756, and 762.

This code is used in section 726.

735. ⟨Declare math construction procedures 734⟩ +≡
procedure $make\_under(q : pointer)$;
 var p, x, y: $pointer$; { temporary registers for box construction }
  $delta$: $scaled$; { overall height plus depth }
 begin $x \leftarrow clean\_box(nucleus(q), cur\_style)$; $p \leftarrow new\_kern(3 * default\_rule\_thickness)$; $link(x) \leftarrow p$;
 $link(p) \leftarrow fraction\_rule(default\_rule\_thickness)$; $y \leftarrow vpack(x, natural)$;
 $delta \leftarrow height(y) + depth(y) + default\_rule\_thickness$; $height(y) \leftarrow height(x)$;
 $depth(y) \leftarrow delta - height(y)$; $info(nucleus(q)) \leftarrow y$; $math\_type(nucleus(q)) \leftarrow sub\_box$;
 end;

736. ⟨Declare math construction procedures 734⟩ +≡
procedure $make\_vcenter(q : pointer)$;
 var v: $pointer$; { the box that should be centered vertically }
  $delta$: $scaled$; { its height plus depth }
 begin $v \leftarrow info(nucleus(q))$;
 if $type(v) \neq vlist\_node$ **then** $confusion(\texttt{"vcenter"})$;
 $delta \leftarrow height(v) + depth(v)$; $height(v) \leftarrow axis\_height(cur\_size) + half(delta)$;
 $depth(v) \leftarrow delta - height(v)$;
 end;

$accent\_noad = 28$, §687.
$axis\_height =$ macro, §700.
$bin\_noad = 18$, §682.
$check\_dimensions = 82$, §726.
$clean\_box$: **function**, §720.
$cond\_math\_glue = 98$, §149.
$confusion$: **procedure**, §95.
$cramped\_style =$ macro, §702.
cur_mu: $scaled$, §719.
cur_size: $small\_number$, §719.
cur_style: $small\_number$, §719.
$default\_rule\_thickness =$ macro, §701.
$delete\_glue\_ref$: **procedure**, §201.
$delta$: $scaled$, §726.
$depth =$ macro, §135.
$do\_nothing =$ macro, §16.
$done\_with\_noad = 80$, §726.
$flush\_node\_list$: **procedure**, §202.
$fraction\_noad = 25$, §683.
$fraction\_rule$: **function**, §704.
$glue\_node = 10$, §149.

$glue\_ptr =$ macro, §149.
$half$: **function**, §100.
$height =$ macro, §135.
$info =$ macro, §118.
$inner\_noad = 23$, §682.
$kern\_node = 11$, §155.
$left\_noad = 30$, §687.
$limits = 1$, §682.
$link =$ macro, §118.
$make\_fraction$: **procedure**, §743.
$make\_math\_accent$: **procedure**, §738.
$make\_op$: **function**, §749.
$make\_ord$: **procedure**, §752.
$make\_radical$: **procedure**, §737.
$math\_glue$: **function**, §716.
$math\_type =$ macro, §681.
$mu\_glue = 99$, §149.
$natural =$ macro, §644.
new_kern: **function**, §156.
$normal = 0$, §135.
$nucleus =$ macro, §681.

$null =$ macro, §115.
$op\_noad = 17$, §682.
$open\_noad = 20$, §682.
$ord\_noad = 16$, §682.
$over\_noad = 27$, §687.
$overbar$: **function**, §705.
p: $pointer$, §726.
$pointer =$ macro, §115.
q: $pointer$, §726.
$radical\_noad = 24$, §683.
$scaled = integer$, §101.
$sub\_box = 2$, §681.
$subtype =$ macro, §133.
$text\_size = 0$, §699.
$type =$ macro, §133.
$under\_noad = 26$, §687.
$vcenter\_noad = 29$, §687.
$vlist\_node = 1$, §137.
$vpack =$ macro, §668.
x: $pointer$, §726.
y: $pointer$, §726.
$zero\_glue =$ macro, §162.

737. According to the rules in the DVI file specifications, we ensure alignment between a square root sign and the rule above its nucleus by assuming that the baseline of the square-root symbol is the same as the bottom of the rule. The height of the square-root symbol will be the thickness of the rule, and the depth of the square-root symbol should exceed or equal the height-plus-depth of the nucleus plus a certain minimum clearance clr. The symbol will be placed so that the actual clearance is clr plus half the excess.

⟨ Declare math construction procedures 734 ⟩ +≡

procedure $make\_radical(q : pointer)$;
   var x, y: $pointer$; { temporary registers for box construction }
     $delta, clr$: $scaled$; { dimensions involved in the calculation }
   begin $x \leftarrow clean\_box(nucleus(q), cramped\_style(cur\_style))$;
   if $cur\_style < text\_style$ **then** { display style }
     $clr \leftarrow default\_rule\_thickness + (abs(math\_x\_height(cur\_size))$ **div** $4)$
   else begin $clr \leftarrow default\_rule\_thickness$; $clr \leftarrow clr + (abs(clr)$ **div** $4)$;
     end;
   $y \leftarrow var\_delimiter(left\_delimiter(q), cur\_size, height(x) + depth(x) + clr + default\_rule\_thickness)$;
   $delta \leftarrow depth(y) - (height(x) + depth(x) + clr)$;
   if $delta > 0$ **then** $clr \leftarrow clr + half(delta)$; { increase the actual clearance }
   $shift\_amount(y) \leftarrow -(height(x) + clr)$; $link(y) \leftarrow overbar(x, clr, height(y))$;
   $info(nucleus(q)) \leftarrow hpack(y, natural)$; $math\_type(nucleus(q)) \leftarrow sub\_box$;
   end;

738. Slants are not considered when placing accents in math mode. The accenter is centered over the accentee, and the accent width is treated as zero with respect to the size of the final box.

⟨ Declare math construction procedures 734 ⟩ +≡

procedure $make\_math\_accent(q : pointer)$;
   label $done, done1$;
   var p, x, y: $pointer$; { temporary registers for box construction }
     a: $integer$; { address of lig/kern instruction }
     c: $quarterword$; { accent character }
     f: $internal\_font\_number$; { its font }
     i: $four\_quarters$; { its $char\_info$ }
     s: $scaled$; { amount to skew the accent to the right }
     h: $scaled$; { height of character being accented }
     $delta$: $scaled$; { space to remove between accent and accentee }
     w: $scaled$; { width of the accentee, not including sub/superscripts }
   begin $fetch(accent\_chr(q))$;
   if $char\_exists(cur\_i)$ **then**
     begin $i \leftarrow cur\_i$; $c \leftarrow cur\_c$; $f \leftarrow cur\_f$;
     ⟨ Compute the amount of skew 741 ⟩;
     $x \leftarrow clean\_box(nucleus(q), cramped\_style(cur\_style))$; $w \leftarrow width(x)$; $h \leftarrow height(x)$;
     ⟨ Switch to a larger accent if available and appropriate 740 ⟩;
     if $h < x\_height(f)$ **then** $delta \leftarrow h$ **else** $delta \leftarrow x\_height(f)$;
     if $(math\_type(supscr(q)) \neq empty) \vee (math\_type(subscr(q)) \neq empty)$ **then**
       if $math\_type(nucleus(q)) = math\_char$ **then**
         ⟨ Swap the subscript and superscript into box x 742 ⟩;

$y \leftarrow char\_box(f,c)$; $shift\_amount(y) \leftarrow s + half(w - width(y))$; $width(y) \leftarrow 0$;
$p \leftarrow new\_kern(-delta)$; $link(p) \leftarrow x$; $link(y) \leftarrow p$; $y \leftarrow vpack(y, natural)$; $width(y) \leftarrow width(x)$;
if $height(y) < h$ **then** ⟨ Make the height of box y equal to h 739 ⟩;
$info(nucleus(q)) \leftarrow y$; $math\_type(nucleus(q)) \leftarrow sub\_box$;
    end;
  end;

739. ⟨ Make the height of box y equal to h 739 ⟩ ≡
  begin $p \leftarrow new\_kern(h - height(y))$; $link(p) \leftarrow list\_ptr(y)$; $list\_ptr(y) \leftarrow p$; $height(y) \leftarrow h$;
  end

This code is used in section 738.

740. ⟨ Switch to a larger accent if available and appropriate 740 ⟩ ≡
  loop begin if $char\_tag(i) \neq list\_tag$ **then goto** *done*;
    $y \leftarrow rem\_byte(i)$; $i \leftarrow char\_info(f)(y)$;
    if $char\_width(f)(i) > w$ **then goto** *done*;
    $c \leftarrow y$;
    end;
done:

This code is used in section 738.

---

accent_chr = macro, §687.
char_box: **function**, §709.
char_exists = macro, §554.
char_info = macro, §554.
char_tag = macro, §554.
char_width = macro, §554.
clean_box: **function**, §720.
cramped_style = macro, §702.
cur_f: *internal_font_number*, §724.
cur_size: *small_number*, §719.
cur_style: *small_number*, §719.
default_rule_thickness = macro, §701.
depth = macro, §135.
done = 30, §15.
done1 = 31, §15.
empty = 0, §16.

fetch: **procedure**, §722.
four_quarters = **packed record**, §113.
half: **function**, §100.
height = macro, §135.
hpack: **function**, §649.
info = macro, §118.
internal_font_number = 0 .. *font_max*, §548.
left_delimiter = macro, §683.
link = macro, §118.
list_ptr = macro, §135.
list_tag = 2, §544.
math_char = 1, §681.
math_type = macro, §681.
math_x_height = macro, §700.
natural = macro, §644.

new_kern: **function**, §156.
nucleus = macro, §681.
overbar: **function**, §705.
pointer = macro, §115.
quarterword = 0 .. 255, §113.
rem_byte = macro, §545.
scaled = *integer*, §101.
shift_amount = macro, §135.
sub_box = 2, §681.
subscr = macro, §681.
supscr = macro, §681.
text_style = 2, §688.
var_delimiter: **function**, §706.
vpack = macro, §668.
width = macro, §135.
x_height = macro, §558.

741. ⟨Compute the amount of skew 741⟩ ≡
$s \leftarrow 0;$
if $math\_type(nucleus(q)) = math\_char$ **then**
  begin $fetch(nucleus(q));$
  if $char\_tag(cur\_i) = lig\_tag$ **then**
    begin $a \leftarrow lig\_kern\_start(cur\_f)(cur\_i);$
    repeat $cur\_i \leftarrow font\_info[a].qqqq;$
      if $qo(next\_char(cur\_i)) = skew\_char[cur\_f]$ **then**
        begin if $op\_bit(cur\_i) \geq kern\_flag$ **then** $s \leftarrow char\_kern(cur\_f)(cur\_i);$
        goto $done1;$
        end;
      $incr(a);$
    until $stop\_bit(cur\_i) \geq stop\_flag;$
    end;
  end;
$done1:$

This code is used in section 738.

742. ⟨Swap the subscript and superscript into box x 742⟩ ≡
begin $flush\_node\_list(x);$ $x \leftarrow new\_noad;$ $mem[nucleus(x)] \leftarrow mem[nucleus(q)];$
$mem[supscr(x)] \leftarrow mem[supscr(q)];$ $mem[subscr(x)] \leftarrow mem[subscr(q)];$
$mem[supscr(q)].hh \leftarrow empty\_field;$ $mem[subscr(q)].hh \leftarrow empty\_field;$
$math\_type(nucleus(q)) \leftarrow sub\_mlist;$ $info(nucleus(q)) \leftarrow x;$ $x \leftarrow clean\_box(nucleus(q), cur\_style);$
$delta \leftarrow delta + height(x) - h;$ $h \leftarrow height(x);$
end

This code is used in section 738.

743. The $make\_fraction$ procedure is a bit different because it sets $new\_hlist(q)$ directly rather than making a sub-box.
⟨Declare math construction procedures 734⟩ +≡
procedure $make\_fraction(q : pointer);$
  var $p, v, x, y, z:$ $pointer;$ { temporary registers for box construction }
    $delta, delta1, delta2, shift\_up, shift\_down, clr:$ $scaled;$ { dimensions for box calculations }
  begin if $thickness(q) = default\_code$ **then** $thickness(q) \leftarrow default\_rule\_thickness;$
  ⟨Create equal-width boxes x and z for the numerator and denominator, and compute the default
    amounts $shift\_up$ and $shift\_down$ by which they are displaced from the baseline 744⟩;
  if $thickness(q) = 0$ **then** ⟨Adjust $shift\_up$ and $shift\_down$ for the case of no fraction line 745⟩
  else ⟨Adjust $shift\_up$ and $shift\_down$ for the case of a fraction line 746⟩;
  ⟨Construct a vlist box for the fraction, according to $shift\_up$ and $shift\_down$ 747⟩;
  ⟨Put the fraction into a box with its delimiters, and make $new\_hlist(q)$ point to it 748⟩;
  end;

744. ⟨Create equal-width boxes x and z for the numerator and denominator, and compute the
  default amounts $shift\_up$ and $shift\_down$ by which they are displaced from the baseline 744⟩ ≡
$x \leftarrow clean\_box(numerator(q), num\_style(cur\_style));$
$z \leftarrow clean\_box(denominator(q), denom\_style(cur\_style));$
if $width(x) < width(z)$ **then** $x \leftarrow rebox(x, width(z))$
else $z \leftarrow rebox(z, width(x));$
if $cur\_style < text\_style$ **then** { text style }

begin $shift\_up \leftarrow num1\,(cur\_size)$; $shift\_down \leftarrow denom1\,(cur\_size)$;
end
else begin $shift\_down \leftarrow denom2\,(cur\_size)$;
  if $thickness(q) \neq 0$ **then** $shift\_up \leftarrow num2\,(cur\_size)$
  else $shift\_up \leftarrow num3\,(cur\_size)$;
end

This code is used in section 743.

745. The numerator and denominator must be separated by a certain minimum clearance, called *clr* in the following program. The difference between *clr* and the actual clearance is $2delta$.

$\langle$ Adjust *shift_up* and *shift_down* for the case of no fraction line 745 $\rangle \equiv$
  begin if $cur\_style < text\_style$ **then** $clr \leftarrow 7 * default\_rule\_thickness$
  else $clr \leftarrow 3 * default\_rule\_thickness$;
  $delta \leftarrow half\,(clr - ((shift\_up - depth(x)) - (height(z) - shift\_down)))$;
  if $delta > 0$ **then**
    begin $shift\_up \leftarrow shift\_up + delta$; $shift\_down \leftarrow shift\_down + delta$;
    end;
  end

This code is used in section 743.

746. In the case of a fraction line, the minimum clearance depends on the actual thickness of the line.

⟨ Adjust *shift_up* and *shift_down* for the case of a fraction line 746 ⟩ ≡
    begin if *cur_style* < *text_style* **then** *clr* ← 3 * *thickness*(*q*)
    else *clr* ← *thickness*(*q*);
    delta ← *half*(*thickness*(*q*)); *delta1* ← *clr* − ((*shift_up* − *depth*(*x*)) − (*axis_height*(*cur_size*) + *delta*));
    delta2 ← *clr* − ((*axis_height*(*cur_size*) − *delta*) − (*height*(*z*) − *shift_down*));
    if *delta1* > 0 **then** *shift_up* ← *shift_up* + *delta1*;
    if *delta2* > 0 **then** *shift_down* ← *shift_down* + *delta2*;
    end

This code is used in section 743.

747. ⟨ Construct a vlist box for the fraction, according to *shift_up* and *shift_down* 747 ⟩ ≡
    v ← *new_null_box*; *type*(*v*) ← *vlist_node*; *height*(*v*) ← *shift_up* + *height*(*x*);
    depth(*v*) ← *depth*(*z*) + *shift_down*; *width*(*v*) ← *width*(*x*); { this also equals *width*(*z*) }
    if *thickness*(*q*) = 0 **then**
        begin *p* ← *new_kern*((*shift_up* − *depth*(*x*)) − (*height*(*z*) − *shift_down*)); *link*(*p*) ← *z*;
        end
    else begin *y* ← *fraction_rule*(*thickness*(*q*));
        p ← *new_kern*((*axis_height*(*cur_size*) − *delta*) − (*height*(*z*) − *shift_down*));
        link(*y*) ← *p*; *link*(*p*) ← *z*;
        p ← *new_kern*((*shift_up* − *depth*(*x*)) − (*axis_height*(*cur_size*) + *delta*)); *link*(*p*) ← *y*;
        end;
    link(*x*) ← *p*; *list_ptr*(*v*) ← *x*

This code is used in section 743.

748. ⟨ Put the fraction into a box with its delimiters, and make *new_hlist*(*q*) point to it 748 ⟩ ≡
    if *cur_style* < *text_style* **then** *delta* ← *delim1*(*cur_size*)
    else *delta* ← *delim2*(*cur_size*);
    x ← *var_delimiter*(*left_delimiter*(*q*), *cur_size*, *delta*); *link*(*x*) ← *v*;
    z ← *var_delimiter*(*right_delimiter*(*q*), *cur_size*, *delta*); *link*(*v*) ← *z*;
    new_hlist(*q*) ← *hpack*(*x*, *natural*)

This code is used in section 743.

749. If the nucleus of an *op_noad* is a single character, it is to be centered vertically with respect to the axis, after first being enlarged (via a character list in the font) if we are in display style. The normal convention for placing displayed limits is to put them above and below the operator in display style.

The italic correction is removed from the character if there is a subscript and the limits are not being displayed. The *make_op* routine returns the value that should be used as an offset between subscript and superscript.

After *make_op* has acted, *subtype*(*q*) will be *limits* if and only if the limits have been set above and below the operator. In that case, *new_hlist*(*q*) will already contain the desired final box.

⟨ Declare math construction procedures 734 ⟩ +≡

function $make\_op(q : pointer)$: $scaled$;

   var $delta$: $scaled$;   { offset between subscript and superscript }

     p, v, x, y, z: $pointer$;   { temporary registers for box construction }

     $shift\_up, shift\_down$: $scaled$;   { dimensions for box calculation }

   begin if $(subtype(q) = normal) \wedge (cur\_style < text\_style)$ **then** $subtype(q) \leftarrow limits$;

   if $math\_type(nucleus(q)) = math\_char$ **then**

     begin $fetch(nucleus(q))$;

     if $(cur\_style < text\_style) \wedge (char\_tag(cur\_i) = list\_tag)$ **then**   { make it larger }

       begin $cur\_c \leftarrow rem\_byte(cur\_i)$; $character(nucleus(q)) \leftarrow cur\_c$;

       $cur\_i \leftarrow char\_info(cur\_f)(cur\_c)$;

       end;

     $delta \leftarrow char\_italic(cur\_f)(cur\_i)$; $x \leftarrow clean\_box(nucleus(q), cur\_style)$;

     if $(math\_type(subscr(q)) \neq empty) \wedge (subtype(q) \neq limits)$ **then** $width(x) \leftarrow width(x) - delta$;

       { remove italic correction }

     $shift\_amount(x) \leftarrow half(height(x) - depth(x)) - axis\_height(cur\_size)$;   { center vertically }

     $math\_type(nucleus(q)) \leftarrow sub\_box$; $info(nucleus(q)) \leftarrow x$;

     end

   else $delta \leftarrow 0$;

   if $subtype(q) = limits$ **then** ⟨ Construct a box with limits above and below it, skewed by $delta$ 750 ⟩;

   $make\_op \leftarrow delta$;

   end;

$axis\_height$ = macro, §700.
$char\_info$ = macro, §554.
$char\_italic$ = macro, §554.
$char\_tag$ = macro, §554.
$character$ = macro, §134.
$clean\_box$: **function**, §720.
clr: $scaled$, §743.
cur_f: $internal\_font\_number$, §724.
cur_size: $small\_number$, §719.
cur_style: $small\_number$, §719.
$delim1$ = macro, §700.
$delim2$ = macro, §700.
$delta$: $scaled$, §743.
$delta1$: $scaled$, §743.
$delta2$: $scaled$, §743.
$depth$ = macro, §135.
$empty$ = 0, §16.
$fetch$: **procedure**, §722.
$fraction\_rule$: **function**, §704.
$half$: **function**, §100.

$height$ = macro, §135.
$hpack$: **function**, §649.
$info$ = macro, §118.
$left\_delimiter$ = macro, §683.
$limits$ = 1, §682.
$link$ = macro, §118.
$list\_ptr$ = macro, §135.
$list\_tag$ = 2, §544.
$math\_char$ = 1, §681.
$math\_type$ = macro, §681.
$natural$ = macro, §644.
new_hlist = macro, §725.
new_kern: **function**, §156.
new_null_box: **function**, §136.
$normal$ = 0, §135.
$nucleus$ = macro, §681.
op_noad = 17, §682.
p: $pointer$, §743.
$pointer$ = macro, §115.
q: $pointer$, §743.

rem_byte = macro, §545.
$right\_delimiter$ = macro, §683.
$scaled$ = $integer$, §101.
$shift\_amount$ = macro, §135.
$shift\_down$: $scaled$, §743.
$shift\_up$: $scaled$, §743.
sub_box = 2, §681.
$subscr$ = macro, §681.
$subtype$ = macro, §133.
$text\_style$ = 2, §688.
$thickness$ = macro, §683.
$type$ = macro, §133.
v: $pointer$, §743.
$var\_delimiter$: **function**, §706.
$vlist\_node$ = 1, §137.
$width$ = macro, §135.
x: $pointer$, §743.
y: $pointer$, §743.
z: $pointer$, §743.

750. The following program builds a vlist box v for displayed limits. The width of the box is not affected by the fact that the limits may be skewed.

⟨ Construct a box with limits above and below it, skewed by $delta$ 750 ⟩ ≡

> **begin** $x \leftarrow clean\_box(supscr(q), sup\_style(cur\_style))$; $y \leftarrow clean\_box(nucleus(q), cur\_style)$;
> $z \leftarrow clean\_box(subscr(q), sub\_style(cur\_style))$; $v \leftarrow new\_null\_box$; $type(v) \leftarrow vlist\_node$;
> $width(v) \leftarrow width(y)$;
> **if** $width(x) > width(v)$ **then** $width(v) \leftarrow width(x)$;
> **if** $width(z) > width(v)$ **then** $width(v) \leftarrow width(z)$;
> $x \leftarrow rebox(x, width(v))$; $y \leftarrow rebox(y, width(v))$; $z \leftarrow rebox(z, width(v))$;
> $shift\_amount(x) \leftarrow half(delta)$; $shift\_amount(z) \leftarrow -shift\_amount(x)$; $height(v) \leftarrow height(y)$;
> $depth(v) \leftarrow depth(y)$;
> ⟨ Attach the limits to y and adjust $height(v)$, $depth(v)$ to account for their presence 751 ⟩;
> $new\_hlist(q) \leftarrow v$;
> **end**

This code is used in section 749.

751. We use $shift\_up$ and $shift\_down$ in the following program for the amount of glue between the displayed operator y and its limits x and z. The vlist inside box v will consist of x followed by y followed by z, with kern nodes for the spaces between and around them.

⟨ Attach the limits to y and adjust $height(v)$, $depth(v)$ to account for their presence 751 ⟩ ≡

> **if** $math\_type(supscr(q)) = empty$ **then**
> > **begin** $free\_node(x, box\_node\_size)$; $list\_ptr(v) \leftarrow y$;
> > **end**
> **else begin** $shift\_up \leftarrow big\_op\_spacing3 - depth(x)$;
> > **if** $shift\_up < big\_op\_spacing1$ **then** $shift\_up \leftarrow big\_op\_spacing1$;
> > $p \leftarrow new\_kern(shift\_up)$; $link(p) \leftarrow y$; $link(x) \leftarrow p$;
> > $p \leftarrow new\_kern(big\_op\_spacing5)$; $link(p) \leftarrow x$; $list\_ptr(v) \leftarrow p$;
> > $height(v) \leftarrow height(v) + big\_op\_spacing5 + height(x) + depth(x) + shift\_up$;
> > **end**;
> **if** $math\_type(subscr(q)) = empty$ **then** $free\_node(z, box\_node\_size)$
> **else begin** $shift\_down \leftarrow big\_op\_spacing4 - height(z)$;
> > **if** $shift\_down < big\_op\_spacing2$ **then** $shift\_down \leftarrow big\_op\_spacing2$;
> > $p \leftarrow new\_kern(shift\_down)$; $link(y) \leftarrow p$; $link(p) \leftarrow z$;
> > $p \leftarrow new\_kern(big\_op\_spacing5)$; $link(z) \leftarrow p$;
> > $depth(v) \leftarrow depth(v) + big\_op\_spacing5 + height(z) + depth(z) + shift\_down$;
> > **end**

This code is used in section 750.

752. A ligature found in a math formula does not create a *ligature_node*, because there is no question of hyphenation afterwards; the ligature will simply be stored in an ordinary *char_node*, after residing in an *ord_noad*.

The *math_type* is converted to *math_text_char* here if we would not want to apply an italic correction to the current character unless it belongs to a math font (i.e., a font with $space = 0$).

⟨ Declare math construction procedures 734 ⟩ +≡
procedure *make_ord* (*q* : *pointer*);
   label *restart*, *exit*;
   var *a*: *integer*;   { address of lig/kern instruction }
     p: *pointer*;   { temporary register for list manipulation }
   begin *restart*:
   if (*math_type*(*subscr*(*q*)) = *empty*) ∧ (*math_type*(*supscr*(*q*)) = *empty*) ∧
       (*math_type*(*nucleus*(*q*)) = *math_char*) **then**
     begin *p* ← *link*(*q*);
     if *p* ≠ *null* **then**
       if (*type*(*p*) ≥ *ord_noad*) ∧ (*type*(*p*) ≤ *punct_noad*) **then**
         if *math_type*(*nucleus*(*p*)) = *math_char* **then**
           if *fam*(*nucleus*(*p*)) = *fam*(*nucleus*(*q*)) **then**
             begin *math_type*(*nucleus*(*q*)) ← *math_text_char*; *fetch*(*nucleus*(*q*));
             if *char_tag*(*cur_i*) = *lig_tag* **then**
               begin *a* ← *lig_kern_start*(*cur_f*)(*cur_i*); *cur_c* ← *character*(*nucleus*(*p*));
               repeat *cur_i* ← *font_info*[*a*].*qqqq*;
                 ⟨ If instruction *cur_i* is a kern with *cur_c*, attach the kern after *q* and **return**; or if
                    it is a ligature with *cur_c*, combine noads *q* and *p* and **goto** *restart* 753 ⟩;
                 incr(*a*);
               until *stop_bit*(*cur_i*) ≥ *stop_flag*;
               end;
             end;
     end;
exit: **end**;

---

big_op_spacing1 = macro, §701.
big_op_spacing2 = macro, §701.
big_op_spacing3 = macro, §701.
big_op_spacing4 = macro, §701.
big_op_spacing5 = macro, §701.
box_node_size = 7, §135.
char_node, §134.
char_tag = macro, §554.
character = macro, §134.
clean_box: **function**, §720.
cur_f: *internal_font_number*, §724.
cur_style: *small_number*, §719.
delta: *scaled*, §749.
depth = macro, §135.
empty = 0, §16.
exit = 10, §15.
fam = macro, §681.
fetch: **procedure**, §722.
font_info: **array**, §549.
free_node: **procedure**, §130.
half: **function**, §100.

height = macro, §135.
incr = macro, §16.
lig_kern_start = macro, §557.
lig_tag = 1, §544.
ligature_node = 6, §143.
link = macro, §118.
list_ptr = macro, §135.
math_char = 1, §681.
math_text_char = 4, §681.
math_type = macro, §681.
new_hlist = macro, §725.
new_kern: **function**, §156.
new_null_box: **function**, §136.
nucleus = macro, §681.
null = macro, §115.
ord_noad = 16, §682.
p: *pointer*, §749.
pointer = macro, §115.
punct_noad = 22, §682.
q: *pointer*, §749.

qqqq: *four_quarters*, §113.
rebox: **function**, §715.
restart = 20, §15.
shift_amount = macro, §135.
shift_down: *scaled*, §749.
shift_up: *scaled*, §749.
space = macro, §558.
stop_bit = macro, §545.
stop_flag = 128, §545.
sub_style = macro, §702.
subscr = macro, §681.
sup_style = macro, §702.
supscr = macro, §681.
type = macro, §133.
v: *pointer*, §749.
vlist_node = 1, §137.
width = macro, §135.
x: *pointer*, §749.
y: *pointer*, §749.
z: *pointer*, §749.

753. Note that a ligature between an *ord_noad* and another kind of noad is replaced by an *ord_noad*. Presumably a font designer will define such ligatures only when this convention makes sense.

⟨ If instruction *cur_i* is a kern with *cur_c*, attach the kern after q and **return**; or if it is a ligature with *cur_c*, combine noads q and p and **goto** *restart* 753 ⟩ ≡
  if *next_char*(*cur_i*) = *cur_c* **then**
    if *op_bit*(*cur_i*) ≥ *kern_flag* **then**
      begin $p \leftarrow$ *new_kern*(*char_kern*(*cur_f*)(*cur_i*)); *link*(p) ← *link*(q); *link*(q) ← p; **return**;
      end
    else begin *link*(q) ← *link*(p); *math_type*(*nucleus*(q)) ← *math_char*;
      character(*nucleus*(q)) ← *rem_byte*(*cur_i*);
      mem[*subscr*(q)] ← *mem*[*subscr*(p)]; *mem*[*supscr*(q)] ← *mem*[*supscr*(p)];
      free_node(p, *noad_size*); **goto** *restart*;
      end

This code is used in section 752.

754. When we get to the following part of the program, we have "fallen through" from cases that did not lead to *check_dimensions* or *done_with_noad* or *done_with_node*. Thus, q points to a noad whose nucleus may need to be converted to an hlist, and whose subscripts and superscripts need to be appended if they are present.

If *nucleus*(q) is not a *math_char*, the variable *delta* is the amount by which a superscript should be moved right with respect to a subscript when both are present.

⟨ Convert *nucleus*(q) to an hlist and attach the sub/superscripts 754 ⟩ ≡
  case *math_type*(*nucleus*(q)) **of**
  math_char, *math_text_char*: ⟨ Create a character node p for *nucleus*(q), possibly followed by a kern node for the italic correction, and set *delta* to the italic correction if a subscript is present 755 ⟩;
  empty: $p \leftarrow$ *null*;
  sub_box: $p \leftarrow$ *info*(*nucleus*(q));
  sub_mlist: **begin** *cur_mlist* ← *info*(*nucleus*(q)); *save_style* ← *cur_style*; *mlist_penalties* ← *false*;
    mlist_to_hlist; { recursive call }
    cur_style ← *save_style*; ⟨ Set up the values of *cur_size* and *cur_mu*, based on *cur_style* 703 ⟩;
    $p \leftarrow$ *hpack*(*link*(*temp_head*), *natural*);
    end;
  othercases *confusion*("mlist2")
  endcases;
  new_hlist(q) ← p;
  if (*math_type*(*subscr*(q)) = *empty*) ∧ (*math_type*(*supscr*(q)) = *empty*) **then goto** *check_dimensions*;
  make_scripts(q, *delta*)

This code is used in section 728.

755. ⟨ Create a character node p for *nucleus*(q), possibly followed by a kern node for the italic correction, and set *delta* to the italic correction if a subscript is present 755 ⟩ ≡
  begin *fetch*(*nucleus*(q));
  if *char_exists*(*cur_i*) **then**
    begin *delta* ← *char_italic*(*cur_f*)(*cur_i*); $p \leftarrow$ *new_character*(*cur_f*, *qo*(*cur_c*));
    if (*math_type*(*nucleus*(q)) = *math_text_char*) ∧ (*space*(*cur_f*) ≠ 0) **then** *delta* ← 0;
      { no italic correction in mid-word of text font }

> **if** $(math\_type(subscr(q)) = empty) \wedge (delta \neq 0)$ **then**
> $\quad$ **begin** $link(p) \leftarrow new\_kern(delta);\ \ delta \leftarrow 0;$
> $\quad$ **end**;
> **end**
> **else** $p \leftarrow null;$
> **end**

This code is used in section 754.

756. The purpose of $make\_scripts(q, delta)$ is to attach the subscript and/or superscript of noad q to the list that starts at $new\_hlist(q)$, given that subscript and superscript aren't both empty. The superscript will appear to the right of the subscript by a given distance $delta$.

We set $shift\_down$ and $shift\_up$ to the minimum amounts to shift the baseline of subscripts and superscripts based on the given nucleus.

⟨ Declare math construction procedures 734 ⟩ +≡
procedure $make\_scripts(q : pointer;\ delta : scaled)$;
    var p, x, y, z: *pointer*;   { temporary registers for box construction }
      $shift\_up, shift\_down, clr$: *scaled*;   { dimensions in the calculation }
      t: *small_number*;   { subsidiary size code }
    begin $p \leftarrow new\_hlist(q)$;
    if $is\_char\_node(p)$ **then**
      begin $shift\_up \leftarrow 0$; $shift\_down \leftarrow 0$;
      end
    else begin $z \leftarrow hpack(p, natural)$;
      if $cur\_style < script\_style$ **then** $t \leftarrow script\_size$ **else** $t \leftarrow script\_script\_size$;
      $shift\_up \leftarrow height(z) - sup\_drop(t)$; $shift\_down \leftarrow depth(z) + sub\_drop(t)$;
      $free\_node(z, box\_node\_size)$;
      end;
    if $math\_type(supscr(q)) = empty$ **then**
      ⟨ Construct a subscript box x when there is no superscript 757 ⟩
    else begin ⟨ Construct a superscript box x 758 ⟩;
      if $math\_type(subscr(q)) = empty$ **then** $shift\_amount(x) \leftarrow -shift\_up$
      else ⟨ Construct a sub/superscript combination box x, with the superscript offset by $delta$ 759 ⟩;
      end;
    if $new\_hlist(q) = null$ **then** $new\_hlist(q) \leftarrow x$
    else begin $p \leftarrow new\_hlist(q)$;
      while $link(p) \neq null$ **do** $p \leftarrow link(p)$;
      $link(p) \leftarrow x$;
      end;
    end;

757. When there is a subscript without a superscript, the top of the subscript should not exceed the baseline plus four-fifths of the x-height.

⟨ Construct a subscript box x when there is no superscript 757 ⟩ ≡
    begin $x \leftarrow clean\_box(subscr(q), sub\_style(cur\_style))$; $width(x) \leftarrow width(x) + script\_space$;
    if $shift\_down < sub1(cur\_size)$ **then** $shift\_down \leftarrow sub1(cur\_size)$;
    $clr \leftarrow height(x) - (abs(math\_x\_height(cur\_size) * 4)\ \textbf{div}\ 5)$;
    if $shift\_down < clr$ **then** $shift\_down \leftarrow clr$;
    $shift\_amount(x) \leftarrow shift\_down$;
    end

This code is used in section 756.

758. The bottom of a superscript should never descend below the baseline plus one-fourth of the x-height.

⟨ Construct a superscript box x 758 ⟩ ≡
   begin $x \leftarrow clean\_box(supscr(q), sup\_style(cur\_style))$; $width(x) \leftarrow width(x) + script\_space$;
   if $odd(cur\_style)$ **then** $clr \leftarrow sup3(cur\_size)$
   else if $cur\_style < text\_style$ **then** $clr \leftarrow sup1(cur\_size)$
      else $clr \leftarrow sup2(cur\_size)$;
   if $shift\_up < clr$ **then** $shift\_up \leftarrow clr$;
   $clr \leftarrow depth(x) + (abs(math\_x\_height(cur\_size))$ **div** $4)$;
   if $shift\_up < clr$ **then** $shift\_up \leftarrow clr$;
   end

This code is used in section 756.

759. When both subscript and superscript are present, the subscript must be separated from the superscript by at least four times $default\_rule\_thickness$. If this condition would be violated, the subscript moves down, after which both subscript and superscript move up so that the bottom of the superscript is at least as high as the baseline plus four-fifths of the x-height.

⟨ Construct a sub/superscript combination box x, with the superscript offset by $delta$ 759 ⟩ ≡
   begin $y \leftarrow clean\_box(subscr(q), sub\_style(cur\_style))$; $width(y) \leftarrow width(y) + script\_space$;
   if $shift\_down < sub2(cur\_size)$ **then** $shift\_down \leftarrow sub2(cur\_size)$;
   $clr \leftarrow 4 * default\_rule\_thickness - ((shift\_up - depth(x)) - (height(y) - shift\_down))$;
   if $clr > 0$ **then**
     begin $shift\_down \leftarrow shift\_down + clr$;
     $clr \leftarrow (abs(math\_x\_height(cur\_size) * 4)$ **div** $5) - (shift\_up - depth(x))$;
     if $clr > 0$ **then**
       begin $shift\_up \leftarrow shift\_up + clr$; $shift\_down \leftarrow shift\_down - clr$;
       end;
     end;
   $shift\_amount(x) \leftarrow delta$; { superscript is $delta$ to the right of the subscript }
   $p \leftarrow new\_kern((shift\_up - depth(x)) - (height(y) - shift\_down))$; $link(x) \leftarrow p$; $link(p) \leftarrow y$;
   $x \leftarrow vpack(x, natural)$; $shift\_amount(x) \leftarrow shift\_down$;
   end

This code is used in section 756.

$box\_node\_size = 7$, §135.
$clean\_box$: **function**, §720.
cur_size: $small\_number$, §719.
cur_style: $small\_number$, §719.
$default\_rule\_thickness$ = macro, §701.
$depth$ = macro, §135.
$empty = 0$, §16.
$free\_node$: **procedure**, §130.
$height$ = macro, §135.
$hpack$: **function**, §649.
is_char_node = macro, §134.
$link$ = macro, §118.
$math\_type$ = macro, §681.

$math\_x\_height$ = macro, §700.
$natural$ = macro, §644.
new_hlist = macro, §725.
new_kern: **function**, §156.
$null$ = macro, §115.
$pointer$ = macro, §115.
$scaled = integer$, §101.
$script\_script\_size = 32$, §699.
$script\_size = 16$, §699.
$script\_space$ = macro, §247.
$script\_style = 4$, §688.
$shift\_amount$ = macro, §135.
$small\_number = 0 .. 63$, §101.
sub_drop = macro, §700.

sub_style = macro, §702.
$sub1$ = macro, §700.
$sub2$ = macro, §700.
$subscr$ = macro, §681.
sup_drop = macro, §700.
sup_style = macro, §702.
$sup1$ = macro, §700.
$sup2$ = macro, §700.
$sup3$ = macro, §700.
$supscr$ = macro, §681.
$text\_style = 2$, §688.
$vpack$ = macro, §668.
$width$ = macro, §135.

760. We have now tied up all the loose ends of the first pass of *mlist_to_hlist*. The second pass simply goes through and hooks everything together with the proper glue and penalties. It also handles the *left_noad* and *right_noad* that might be present, since *max_h* and *max_d* are now known. Variable *p* points to a node at the current end of the final hlist.

⟨ Make a second pass over the mlist, removing all noads and inserting the proper spacing and penalties 760 ⟩ ≡
  $p \leftarrow temp\_head$; $link(p) \leftarrow null$; $q \leftarrow mlist$; $r\_type \leftarrow 0$; $cur\_style \leftarrow style$;
  ⟨ Set up the values of *cur_size* and *cur_mu*, based on *cur_style* 703 ⟩;
  while $q \neq null$ **do**
    begin ⟨ If node *q* is a style node, change the style and **goto** *delete_q*; otherwise if it is not a noad,
        put it into the hlist, advance *q*, and **goto** *done*; otherwise set *s* to the size of noad *q*, set *t* to
        the associated type (*ord_noad .. inner_noad*), and set *pen* to the associated penalty 761 ⟩;
    ⟨ Append inter-element spacing based on *r_type* and *t* 766 ⟩;
    ⟨ Append any *new_hlist* entries for *q*, and any appropriate penalties 767 ⟩;
    $r\_type \leftarrow t$;
  delete_q: $r \leftarrow q$; $q \leftarrow link(q)$; $free\_node(r, s)$;
  done: **end**

This code is used in section 726.

761. Just before doing the big **case** switch in the second pass, the program sets up default values so that most of the branches are short.

⟨ If node *q* is a style node, change the style and **goto** *delete_q*; otherwise if it is not a noad, put it into
    the hlist, advance *q*, and **goto** *done*; otherwise set *s* to the size of noad *q*, set *t* to the associated
    type (*ord_noad .. inner_noad*), and set *pen* to the associated penalty 761 ⟩ ≡
  $t \leftarrow ord\_noad$; $s \leftarrow noad\_size$; $pen \leftarrow inf\_penalty$;
  case $type(q)$ **of**
  op_noad, *open_noad*, *close_noad*, *punct_noad*, *inner_noad*: $t \leftarrow type(q)$;
  bin_noad: **begin** $t \leftarrow bin\_noad$; $pen \leftarrow bin\_op\_penalty$;
    end;
  rel_noad: **begin** $t \leftarrow rel\_noad$; $pen \leftarrow rel\_penalty$;
    end;
  ord_noad, *vcenter_noad*, *over_noad*, *under_noad*: *do_nothing*;
  radical_noad: $s \leftarrow radical\_noad\_size$;
  accent_noad: $s \leftarrow accent\_noad\_size$;
  fraction_noad: **begin** $t \leftarrow inner\_noad$; $s \leftarrow fraction\_noad\_size$;
    end;
  left_noad, *right_noad*: $t \leftarrow make\_left\_right(q, style, max\_d, max\_h)$;
  style_node: ⟨ Change the current style and **goto** *delete_q* 763 ⟩;
  whatsit_node, *penalty_node*, *rule_node*, *disc_node*, *adjust_node*, *ins_node*, *mark_node*,
    glue_node, *kern_node*:
    begin $link(p) \leftarrow q$; $p \leftarrow q$; $q \leftarrow link(q)$; $link(p) \leftarrow null$; **goto** *done*;
    end;
  othercases $confusion(\texttt{"mlist3"})$
  endcases

This code is used in section 760.

762.   The *make_left_right* function constructs a left or right delimiter of the required size and returns the value *open_noad* or *close_noad*. The *right_noad* and *left_noad* will both be based on the original *style*, so they will have consistent sizes.

We use the fact that *right_noad* − *left_noad* = *close_noad* − *open_noad*.

⟨ Declare math construction procedures 734 ⟩ +≡
function *make_left_right*(*q* : *pointer*; *style* : *small_number*; *max_d*, *max_h* : *scaled*): *small_number*;
    var *delta*, *delta1*, *delta2*: *scaled*;   { dimensions used in the calculation }
    begin if *style* < *script_style* **then**   *cur_size* ← *text_size*
    else *cur_size* ← 16 ∗ ((*style* − *text_style*) **div** 2);
    delta2 ← *max_d* + *axis_height*(*cur_size*);   *delta1* ← *max_h* + *max_d* − *delta2*;
    if *delta2* > *delta1* **then** *delta1* ← *delta2*;   { *delta1* is max distance from axis }
    delta ← (*delta1* **div** 500) ∗ *delimiter_factor*;   *delta2* ← *delta1* + *delta1* − *delimiter_shortfall*;
    if *delta* < *delta2* **then** *delta* ← *delta2*;
    new_hlist(*q*) ← *var_delimiter*(*delimiter*(*q*), *cur_size*, *delta*);
    make_left_right ← *type*(*q*) − (*left_noad* − *open_noad*);   { *open_noad* or *close_noad* }
    end;

763.   ⟨ Change the current style and **goto** *delete_q* 763 ⟩ ≡
    begin *cur_style* ← *subtype*(*q*);   *s* ← *style_node_size*;
    ⟨ Set up the values of *cur_size* and *cur_mu*, based on *cur_style* 703 ⟩;
    goto *delete_q*;
    end

This code is used in section 761.

764. The inter-element spacing in math formulas depends on a 8×8 table that TEX preloads as a 64-digit string. The elements of this string have the following significance:

>   0 means no space;
>   1 means a conditional thin space (\nonscript\mskip\thinmuskip);
>   2 means a thin space (\mskip\thinmuskip);
>   3 means a conditional medium space (\nonscript\mskip\medmuskip);
>   4 means a conditional thick space (\nonscript\mskip\thickmuskip);
>   * means an impossible case.

This is all pretty cryptic, but *The TEXbook* explains what is supposed to happen, and the string makes it happen.

A global variable *magic_offset* is computed so that if a and b are in the range *ord_noad .. inner_noad*, then *str_pool*$[a * 8 + b + magic\_offset]$ is the digit for spacing between noad types a and b.

If Pascal had provided a good way to preload constant arrays, this part of the program would not have been so strange.

define *math_spacing* =
"0234000122*4000133**3**344*0400400*000000234000111*1111112341011"

⟨ Global variables 13 ⟩ +≡
magic_offset: *integer*; { used to find inter-element spacing }

765. ⟨ Compute the magic offset 765 ⟩ ≡
magic_offset ← *str_start*[*math_spacing*] − 9 ∗ *ord_noad*
This code is used in section 1337.

766. ⟨ Append inter-element spacing based on *r_type* and *t* 766 ⟩ ≡
  if *r_type* > 0 **then**   { not the first noad }
    begin case *str_pool*[*r_type* ∗ 8 + *t* + *magic_offset*] **of**
    "0": $x \leftarrow 0$;
    "1": **if** *cur_style* < *script_style* **then** $x \leftarrow$ *thin_mu_skip_code* **else** $x \leftarrow 0$;
    "2": $x \leftarrow$ *thin_mu_skip_code*;
    "3": **if** *cur_style* < *script_style* **then** $x \leftarrow$ *med_mu_skip_code* **else** $x \leftarrow 0$;
    "4": **if** *cur_style* < *script_style* **then** $x \leftarrow$ *thick_mu_skip_code* **else** $x \leftarrow 0$;
    othercases *confusion*("mlist4")
    endcases;
    if $x \neq 0$ **then**
      begin $y \leftarrow$ *math_glue*(*glue_par*(x), *cur_mu*); $z \leftarrow$ *new_glue*(y); *glue_ref_count*(y) ← *null*;
      link(p) ← z; $p \leftarrow z$;
      subtype(z) ← $x + 1$;   { store a symbolic subtype }
      end;
    end
This code is used in section 760.

767.   We insert a penalty node after the hlist entries of noad q if *pen* is not an "infinite" penalty, and if the node immediately following q is not a penalty node or a *rel_noad* or absent entirely.

⟨ Append any *new_hlist* entries for q, and any appropriate penalties 767 ⟩ ≡

 if $new\_hlist(q) \neq null$ **then**
  begin $link(p) \leftarrow new\_hlist(q)$;
  repeat $p \leftarrow link(p)$;
  until $link(p) = null$;
  end;
 if *penalties* **then**
  if $link(q) \neq null$ **then**
   if $pen < inf\_penalty$ **then**
    begin $r\_type \leftarrow type(link(q))$;
    if $r\_type \neq penalty\_node$ **then**
     if $r\_type \neq rel\_noad$ **then**
      begin $z \leftarrow new\_penalty(pen)$; $link(p) \leftarrow z$; $p \leftarrow z$;
      end;
    end

This code is used in section 760.

768. Alignment. It's sort of a miracle whenever \halign and \valign work, because they cut across so many of the control structures of TEX.

Therefore the present page is probably not the best place for a beginner to start reading this program; it is better to master everything else first.

Let us focus our thoughts on an example of what the input might be, in order to get some idea about how the alignment miracle happens. The example doesn't do anything useful, but it is sufficiently general to indicate all of the special cases that must be dealt with; please do not be disturbed by its apparent complexity and meaninglessness.

```
\tabskip 2pt plus 3pt
\halign to 300pt{u1#v1&
        \tabskip 1pt plus 1fil u2#v2&
        u3#v3\cr
    a1&\omit a2&\vrule\cr
    \noalign{\vskip 3pt}
    b1\span b2\cr
    \omit&c2\span\omit\cr}
```

Here's what happens:

(0) When '\halign to 300pt{' is scanned, the *scan_spec* routine places the 300pt dimension onto the *save_stack*, and an *align_group* code is placed above it. This will make it possible to complete the alignment when the matching '}' is found.

(1) The preamble is scanned next. Macros in the preamble are not expanded, except as part of a tabskip specification. For example, if u2 had been a macro in the preamble above, it would have been expanded, since TEX must look for 'minus...' as part of the tabskip glue. A "preamble list" is constructed based on the user's preamble; in our case it contains the following seven items:

\glue 2pt plus 3pt	(the tabskip preceding column 1)
\alignrecord, width $-\infty$	(preamble info for column 1)
\glue 2pt plus 3pt	(the tabskip between columns 1 and 2)
\alignrecord, width $-\infty$	(preamble info for column 2)
\glue 1pt plus 1fil	(the tabskip between columns 2 and 3)
\alignrecord, width $-\infty$	(preamble info for column 3)
\glue 1pt plus 1fil	(the tabskip following column 3)

These "alignrecord" entries have the same size as an *unset_node*, since they will later be converted into such nodes. However, at the moment they have no *type* or *subtype* fields; they have *info* fields instead, and these *info* fields are initially set to the value *end_span*, for reasons explained below. Furthermore, the alignrecord nodes have no *height* or *depth* fields; these are renamed *u_part* and *v_part*, and they point to token lists for the templates of the alignment. For example, the *u_part* field in the first alignrecord points to the token list 'u1', i.e., the template preceding the '#' for column 1.

(2) TEX now looks at what follows the \cr that ended the preamble. It is not '\noalign' or '\omit', so this input is put back to be read again, and the template 'u1' is fed to the scanner.

Just before reading 'u1', TeX goes into restricted horizontal mode. Just after reading 'u1', TeX will see 'a1', and then (when the & is sensed) TeX will see 'v1'. Then TeX scans an *endv* token, indicating the end of a column. At this point an *unset_node* is created, containing the contents of the current hlist (i.e., 'u1a1v1'). The natural width of this unset node replaces the *width* field of the alignrecord for column 1; in general, the alignrecords will record the maximum natural width that has occurred so far in a given column.

(3) Since '\omit' follows the '&', the templates for column 2 are now bypassed. Again TeX goes into restricted horizontal mode and makes an *unset_node* from the resulting hlist; but this time the hlist contains simply 'a2'. The natural width of the new unset box is remembered in the *width* field of the alignrecord for column 2.

(4) A third *unset_node* is created for column 3, using essentially the mechanism that worked for column 1; this unset box contains 'u3\vrule v3'. The vertical rule in this case has running dimensions that will later extend to the height and depth of the whole first row, since each *unset_node* in a row will eventually inherit the height and depth of its enclosing box.

(5) The first row has now ended; it is made into a single unset box comprising the following seven items:

```
\glue 2pt plus 3pt
\unsetbox for 1 column:   u1a1v1
\glue 2pt plus 3pt
\unsetbox for 1 column:   a2
\glue 1pt plus 1fil
\unsetbox for 1 column:   u3|v3
\glue 1pt plus 1fil
```

The width of this unset row is unimportant, but it has the correct height and depth, so the correct baselineskip glue will be computed as the row is inserted into a vertical list.

(6) Since '\noalign' follows the current \cr, TeX appends additional material (in this case \vskip 3pt) to the vertical list. While processing this material, TeX will be in internal vertical mode, and *no_align_group* will be on *save_stack*.

align_group = 6, §269.	*info* = macro, §118.	*type* = macro, §133.
depth = macro, §135.	*no_align_group* = 7, §269.	*u_part* = macro, §769.
end_span = macro, §162.	*save_stack*: **array**, §271.	*unset_node* = 13, §159.
endv = 9, §207.	*scan_spec*: **procedure**, §645.	*v_part* = macro, §769.
height = macro, §135.	*subtype* = macro, §133.	*width* = macro, §135.

768. (continued)

(7) The next row produces an unset box that looks like this:

```
\glue 2pt plus 3pt
\unsetbox for 2 columns:   u1b1v1u2b2v2
\glue 1pt plus 1fil
\unsetbox for 1 column:    (empty)
\glue 1pt plus 1fil
```

The natural width of the unset box that spans columns 1 and 2 is stored in a "span node," which we will explain later; the *info* field of the alignrecord for column 1 now points to the new span node, and the *info* of the span node points to *end_span*.

(8) The final row produces the unset box

```
\glue 2pt plus 3pt
\unsetbox for 1 column:    (empty)
\glue 2pt plus 3pt
\unsetbox for 2 columns:   u2c2v2
\glue 1pt plus 1fil
```

A new span node is attached to the alignrecord for column 2.

(9) The last step is to compute the true column widths and to change all the unset boxes to hboxes, appending the whole works to the vertical list that encloses the \halign. The rules for deciding on the final widths of each unset column box will be explained below.

Note that as \halign is being processed, we fearlessly give up control to the rest of TeX. At critical junctures, an alignment routine is called upon to step in and do some little action, but most of the time these routines just lurk in the background. It's something like post-hypnotic suggestion.

769. We have mentioned that alignrecords contain no *height* or *depth* fields. Their *glue_sign* and *glue_order* are pre-empted as well, since it is necessary to store information about what to do when a template ends. This information is called the *extra_info* field.

define $u\_part(\#) \equiv mem[\# + height\_offset].int$ { pointer to $\langle u_j \rangle$ token list }
define $v\_part(\#) \equiv mem[\# + depth\_offset].int$ { pointer to $\langle v_j \rangle$ token list }
define $extra\_info(\#) \equiv info(\# + list\_offset)$ { info to remember during template }

770. Alignments can occur within alignments, so a small stack is used to access the alignrecord information. At each level we have a *preamble* pointer, indicating the beginning of the preamble list; a *cur_align* pointer, indicating the current position in the preamble list; a *cur_span* pointer, indicating the value of *cur_align* at the beginning of a sequence of spanned columns; a *cur_loop* pointer, indicating the tabskip glue before an alignrecord that should be copied next if the current list is extended; and the *align_state* variable, which indicates the nesting of braces so that \cr and \span and tab marks are properly intercepted. There also are pointers *cur_head* and *cur_tail* to the head and tail of a list of adjustments being moved out from horizontal mode to vertical mode.

The current values of these seven quantities appear in global variables; when they have to be pushed down, they are stored in 5-word nodes, and *align_ptr* points to the topmost such node.

> **define** *preamble* $\equiv$ *link*(*align_head*) { the current preamble list }
> **define** *align_stack_node_size* = 5 { number of *mem* words to save alignment states }

⟨ Global variables 13 ⟩ +≡
cur_align: *pointer*; { current position in preamble list }
cur_span: *pointer*; { start of currently spanned columns in preamble list }
cur_loop: *pointer*; { place to copy when extending a periodic preamble }
align_ptr: *pointer*; { most recently pushed-down alignment stack node }
cur_head, *cur_tail*: *pointer*; { adjustment list pointers }

771. The *align_state* and *preamble* variables are initialized elsewhere.

⟨ Set initial values of key variables 21 ⟩ +≡
  align_ptr ← *null*; *cur_align* ← *null*; *cur_span* ← *null*; *cur_loop* ← *null*; *cur_head* ← *null*;
  cur_tail ← *null*;

772. Alignment stack maintenance is handled by a pair of trivial routines called *push_alignment* and *pop_alignment*.

> **procedure** *push_alignment*;
>   **var** *p*: *pointer*; { the new alignment stack node }
>   **begin** *p* ← *get_node*(*align_stack_node_size*); *link*(*p*) ← *align_ptr*; *info*(*p*) ← *cur_align*;
>   *llink*(*p*) ← *preamble*; *rlink*(*p*) ← *cur_span*; *mem*[*p*+2].*int* ← *cur_loop*; *mem*[*p*+3].*int* ← *align_state*;
>   *info*(*p* + 4) ← *cur_head*; *link*(*p* + 4) ← *cur_tail*; *align_ptr* ← *p*; *cur_head* ← *get_avail*;
>   **end**;

> **procedure** *pop_alignment*;
>   **var** *p*: *pointer*; { the top alignment stack node }
>   **begin** *free_avail*(*cur_head*); *p* ← *align_ptr*; *cur_tail* ← *link*(*p* + 4); *cur_head* ← *info*(*p* + 4);
>   *align_state* ← *mem*[*p* + 3].*int*; *cur_loop* ← *mem*[*p* + 2].*int*; *cur_span* ← *rlink*(*p*);
>   *preamble* ← *llink*(*p*); *cur_align* ← *info*(*p*); *align_ptr* ← *link*(*p*); *free_node*(*p*, *align_stack_node_size*);
>   **end**;

773. TeX has eight procedures that govern alignments: *init_align* and *fin_align* are used at the very beginning and the very end; *init_row* and *fin_row* are used at the beginning and end of individual rows; *init_span* is used at the beginning of a sequence of spanned columns (possibly involving only one column); *init_col* and *fin_col* are used at the beginning and end of individual columns; and *align_peek* is used after \cr to see whether the next item is \noalign.

We shall consider these routines in the order they are first used during the course of a complete \halign, namely *init_align*, *align_peek*, *init_row*, *init_span*, *init_col*, *fin_col*, *fin_row*, *fin_align*.

---

align_head = macro, §162.
align_peek: **procedure**, §785.
align_state: *integer*, §309.
depth = macro, §135.
depth_offset = 2, §135.
end_span = macro, §162.
fin_align: **procedure**, §800.
fin_col: **function**, §791.
fin_row: **procedure**, §799.
free_avail = macro, §121.

free_node: **procedure**, §130.
get_avail: **function**, §120.
get_node: **function**, §125.
glue_order = macro, §135.
glue_sign = macro, §135.
height = macro, §135.
height_offset = 3, §135.
info = macro, §118.
init_align: **procedure**, §774.
init_col: **procedure**, §788.

init_row: **procedure**, §786.
init_span: **procedure**, §787.
int: *integer*, §113.
link = macro, §118.
list_offset = 5, §135.
llink = macro, §124.
mem: **array**, §116.
null = macro, §115.
pointer = macro, §115.
rlink = macro, §124.

774. When \halign or \valign has been scanned in an appropriate mode, TₑX calls *init_align*, whose task is to get everything off to a good start. This mostly involves scanning the preamble and putting its information into the preamble list.

⟨ Declare the procedure called *get_preamble_token* 782 ⟩
procedure *align_peek*; *forward*;
procedure *normal_paragraph*; *forward*;
procedure *init_align*;
  label *done*, *done1*, *done2*, *continue*;
  var *save_cs_ptr*: *pointer*; { *warning_index* value for error messages }
    p: *pointer*; { for short-term temporary use }
  begin *save_cs_ptr* ← *cur_cs*; { \halign or \valign, usually }
  push_alignment; *align_state* ← −1000000; { enter a new alignment level }
  ⟨ Check for improper alignment in displayed math 776 ⟩;
  push_nest; { enter a new semantic level }
  ⟨ Change current mode to −*vmode* for \halign, −*hmode* for \valign 775 ⟩;
  scan_spec; *new_save_level*(*align_group*);
  ⟨ Scan the preamble and record it in the *preamble* list 777 ⟩;
  new_save_level(*align_group*);
  if *every_cr* ≠ *null* **then** *begin_token_list*(*every_cr*, *every_cr_text*);
  align_peek; { look for \noalign or \omit }
  end;

775. In vertical modes, *prev_depth* already has the correct value. But if we are in *mmode* (displayed formula mode), we reach out to the enclosing vertical mode for the *prev_depth* value that produces the correct baseline calculations.

⟨ Change current mode to −*vmode* for \halign, −*hmode* for \valign 775 ⟩ ≡
  if *mode* = *mmode* **then**
    begin *mode* ← −*vmode*; *prev_depth* ← *nest*[*nest_ptr* − 2].*aux_field*;
    end
  else if *mode* > 0 **then** *negate*(*mode*)
This code is used in section 774.

776. When \halign is used as a displayed formula, there should be no other pieces of mlists present.

⟨ Check for improper alignment in displayed math 776 ⟩ ≡
  if (*mode* = *mmode*) ∧ ((*tail* ≠ *head*) ∨ (*incompleat_noad* ≠ *null*)) **then**
    begin *print_err*("Improper␣"); *print_esc*("halign"); *print*("␣inside␣$$´s");
    help3("Displays␣can␣use␣special␣alignments␣(like␣\eqalignno)")
    ("only␣if␣nothing␣but␣the␣alignment␣itself␣is␣between␣$$´s.")
    ("So␣I´ve␣deleted␣the␣formulas␣that␣preceded␣this␣alignment."); *error*; *flush_math*;
    end
This code is used in section 774.

777. ⟨ Scan the preamble and record it in the *preamble* list 777 ⟩ ≡
  preamble ← *null*; *cur_align* ← *align_head*; *cur_loop* ← *null*; *scanner_status* ← *aligning*;
  warning_index ← *save_cs_ptr*; *align_state* ← −1000000; { at this point, *cur_cmd* = *left_brace* }
  loop begin ⟨ Append the current tabskip glue to the preamble list 778 ⟩;
    if *cur_cmd* = *car_ret* **then goto** *done*; { \cr ends the preamble }

⟨ Scan preamble text until *cur_cmd* is *tab_mark* or *car_ret*, looking for changes in the tabskip glue;
      append an alignrecord to the preamble list 779 ⟩;
   end;
done: *scanner_status* ← *normal*

This code is used in section 774.

778.   ⟨ Append the current tabskip glue to the preamble list 778 ⟩ ≡
   link(*cur_align*) ← *new_param_glue*(*tab_skip_code*);   *cur_align* ← *link*(*cur_align*)

This code is used in section 777.

779.   ⟨ Scan preamble text until *cur_cmd* is *tab_mark* or *car_ret*, looking for changes in the tabskip
      glue; append an alignrecord to the preamble list 779 ⟩ ≡
   ⟨ Scan the template ⟨u_j⟩, putting the resulting token list in *hold_head* 783 ⟩;
   link(*cur_align*) ← *new_null_box*;   *cur_align* ← *link*(*cur_align*);   { a new alignrecord }
   info(*cur_align*) ← *end_span*;   *width*(*cur_align*) ← *null_flag*;   *u_part*(*cur_align*) ← *link*(*hold_head*);
   ⟨ Scan the template ⟨v_j⟩, putting the resulting token list in *hold_head* 784 ⟩;
   v_part(*cur_align*) ← *link*(*hold_head*)

This code is used in section 777.

---

align_group = 6, §269.
align_head = macro, §162.
align_peek: **procedure**, §785.
align_state: *integer*, §309.
aligning = 4, §305.
aux_field: *integer*, §212.
begin_token_list: **procedure**, §323.
car_ret = 5, §207.
continue = 22, §15.
cur_align: *pointer*, §770.
cur_cmd: *eight_bits*, §297.
cur_cs: *pointer*, §297.
cur_loop: *pointer*, §770.
done = 30, §15.
done1 = 31, §15.
done2 = 32, §15.
end_span = macro, §162.
error: **procedure**, §82.
every_cr = macro, §230.
every_cr_text = 13, §307.
flush_math: **procedure**, §718.

get_preamble_token: **procedure**,
   §782.
head = macro, §213.
help3 = macro, §79.
hmode = 101, §211.
hold_head = macro, §162.
incompleat_noad = macro, §213.
info = macro, §118.
left_brace = 1, §207.
link = macro, §118.
mmode = 201, §211.
mode = macro, §213.
negate = macro, §16.
nest: **array**, §213.
nest_ptr: 0 . . *nest_size*, §213.
new_null_box: **function**, §136.
new_param_glue: **function**, §152.
new_save_level: **procedure**, §274.
normal = 0, §135.
normal_paragraph: **procedure**,
   §1070.

null = macro, §115.
null_flag = macro, §138.
pointer = macro, §115.
preamble = macro, §770.
prev_depth = macro, §213.
print: **procedure**, §59.
print_err = macro, §73.
print_esc: **procedure**, §63.
push_alignment: **procedure**, §772.
push_nest: **procedure**, §216.
scan_spec: **procedure**, §645.
scanner_status: 0 . . 5, §305.
tab_mark = 4, §207.
tab_skip_code = 11, §224.
tail = macro, §213.
u_part = macro, §769.
v_part = macro, §769.
vmode = 1, §211.
warning_index: *pointer*, §305.
width = macro, §135.

780. We enter '\span' into *eqtb* with *tab_mark* as its command code, and with *span_code* as the command modifier. This makes TEX interpret it essentially the same as an alignment delimiter like '&', yet it is recognizably different when we need to distinguish it from a normal delimiter. It also turns out to be useful to give a special *cr_code* to '\cr', and an even larger *cr_cr_code* to '\crcr'.

The end of a template is represented by two "frozen" control sequences called \endtemplate. The first has the command code *end_template*, which is > *outer_call*, so it will not easily disappear in the presence of errors. The *get_x_token* routine converts the first into the second, which has *endv* as its command code.

> **define** *span_code* = 128   { distinct from any character }
> **define** *cr_code* = 129   { distinct from *span_code* and from any character }
> **define** *cr_cr_code* = *cr_code* + 1   { this distinguishes \crcr from \cr }
> **define** *end_template_token* ≡ *cs_token_flag* + *frozen_end_template*

⟨ Put each of TEX's primitives into the hash table 226 ⟩ +≡
> *primitive*("span", *tab_mark*, *span_code*);
> *primitive*("cr", *car_ret*, *cr_code*); *text*(*frozen_cr*) ← "cr"; *eqtb*[*frozen_cr*] ← *eqtb*[*cur_val*];
> *primitive*("crcr", *car_ret*, *cr_cr_code*); *text*(*frozen_end_template*) ← "endtemplate";
> *text*(*frozen_endv*) ← "endtemplate"; *eq_type*(*frozen_endv*) ← *endv*; *equiv*(*frozen_endv*) ← *null_list*;
> *eq_level*(*frozen_endv*) ← *level_one*;
> *eqtb*[*frozen_end_template*] ← *eqtb*[*frozen_endv*]; *eq_type*(*frozen_end_template*) ← *end_template*;

781. ⟨ Cases of *print_cmd_chr* for symbolic printing of primitives 227 ⟩ +≡
tab_mark: **if** *chr_code* = *span_code* **then** *print_esc*("span")
> **else** *chr_cmd*("alignment⎵tab⎵character⎵");

car_ret: **if** *chr_code* = *cr_code* **then** *print_esc*("cr")
> **else** *print_esc*("crcr");

782. The preamble is copied directly, except that \tabskip causes a change to the tabskip glue, thereby possibly expanding macros that immediately follow it. An appearance of \span also causes such an expansion.

Note that if the preamble contains '\global\tabskip', the '\global' token survives in the preamble and the '\tabskip' defines new tabskip glue (locally).

⟨ Declare the procedure called *get_preamble_token* 782 ⟩ ≡
procedure *get_preamble_token*;
> **label** *restart*;
> **begin** *restart*: *get_token*;
> **while** (*cur_chr* = *span_code*) ∧ (*cur_cmd* = *tab_mark*) **do**
>   **begin** *get_token*;   { this token will be expanded once }
>   **if** *cur_cmd* > *max_command* **then**
>   **begin** *expand*; *get_token*;
>   **end**;
>   **end**;

if $(cur\_cmd = assign\_glue) \wedge (cur\_chr = glue\_base + tab\_skip\_code)$ **then**
 begin $scan\_optional\_equals$; $scan\_glue(glue\_val)$;
 if $global\_defs > 0$ **then** $geq\_define(glue\_base + tab\_skip\_code, glue\_ref, cur\_val)$
 else $eq\_define(glue\_base + tab\_skip\_code, glue\_ref, cur\_val)$;
 goto $restart$;
 end;
end;

This code is used in section 774.

783. Spaces are eliminated from the beginning of a template.

⟨ Scan the template ⟨u_j⟩, putting the resulting token list in $hold\_head$ 783 ⟩ ≡
 $p \leftarrow hold\_head$; $link(p) \leftarrow null$;
 loop begin $get\_preamble\_token$;
  if $cur\_cmd = mac\_param$ **then goto** $done1$;
  if $(cur\_cmd \leq car\_ret) \wedge (cur\_cmd \geq tab\_mark) \wedge (align\_state = -1000000)$ **then**
   if $(p = hold\_head) \wedge (cur\_loop = null) \wedge (cur\_cmd = tab\_mark)$ **then** $cur\_loop \leftarrow cur\_align$
   else begin $print\_err($"Missing␣#␣inserted␣in␣alignment␣preamble"$)$;
    $help3($"There␣should␣be␣exactly␣one␣#␣between␣&´s,␣when␣an"$)$
    $($"\halign␣or␣\valign␣is␣being␣set␣up.␣In␣this␣case␣you␣had"$)$
    $($"none,␣so␣I´ve␣put␣one␣in;␣maybe␣that␣will␣work."$)$; $back\_error$; **goto** $done1$;
   end
  else if $(cur\_cmd \neq spacer) \vee (p \neq hold\_head)$ **then**
   begin $link(p) \leftarrow get\_avail$; $p \leftarrow link(p)$; $info(p) \leftarrow cur\_tok$;
   end;
  end;
$done1$:

This code is used in section 779.

$align\_state$: $integer$, §309.
$assign\_glue = 74$, §209.
$back\_error$: **procedure**, §327.
$car\_ret = 5$, §207.
chr_cmd = macro, §298.
chr_code: $halfword$, §298.
cs_token_flag = macro, §289.
cur_align: $pointer$, §770.
cur_chr: $halfword$, §297.
cur_cmd: $eight\_bits$, §297.
cur_loop: $pointer$, §770.
cur_tok: $halfword$, §297.
cur_val: $integer$, §410.
$done1 = 31$, §15.
$end\_template = 114$, §210.
$endv = 9$, §207.
eq_define: **procedure**, §277.
eq_level = macro, §221.
eq_type = macro, §221.

$eqtb$: **array**, §253.
$equiv$ = macro, §221.
$expand$: **procedure**, §366.
$frozen\_cr = 2359$, §222.
$frozen\_end\_template = 2363$, §222.
$frozen\_endv = 2364$, §222.
geq_define: **procedure**, §279.
get_avail: **function**, §120.
get_token: **procedure**, §365.
get_x_token: **procedure**, §380.
$global\_defs$ = macro, §236.
$glue\_base = 2626$, §222.
$glue\_ref = 116$, §210.
$glue\_val = 2$, §410.
$help3$ = macro, §79.
$hold\_head$ = macro, §162.
$info$ = macro, §118.
$level\_one = 1$, §221.
$link$ = macro, §118.

$mac\_param = 6$, §207.
$max\_command = 99$, §209.
$null$ = macro, §115.
$null\_list$ = macro, §162.
$outer\_call = 112$, §210.
p: $pointer$, §774.
$primitive$: **procedure**, §264.
$print\_cmd\_chr$: **procedure**, §298.
$print\_err$ = macro, §73.
$print\_esc$: **procedure**, §63.
$restart = 20$, §15.
$scan\_glue$: **procedure**, §461.
$scan\_optional\_equals$: **procedure**,
 §405.
$spacer = 10$, §207.
$tab\_mark = 4$, §207.
$tab\_skip\_code = 11$, §224.
$text$ = macro, §256.

784. ⟨ Scan the template ⟨v_j⟩, putting the resulting token list in *hold_head* 784 ⟩ ≡
   $p \leftarrow hold\_head$; $link(p) \leftarrow null$;
   loop begin *continue*: *get_preamble_token*;
      if $(cur\_cmd \leq car\_ret) \wedge (cur\_cmd \geq tab\_mark) \wedge (align\_state = -1000000)$ **then goto** *done2*;
      if $cur\_cmd = mac\_param$ **then**
         begin *print_err*("Only␣one␣#␣is␣allowed␣per␣tab");
         help3("There␣should␣be␣exactly␣one␣#␣between␣&´s,␣when␣an")
         ("\halign␣or␣\valign␣is␣being␣set␣up.␣In␣this␣case␣you␣had")
         ("more␣than␣one,␣so␣I´m␣ignoring␣all␣but␣the␣first."); *error*; **goto** *continue*;
         end;
      $link(p) \leftarrow get\_avail$; $p \leftarrow link(p)$; $info(p) \leftarrow cur\_tok$;
      end;
   done2: $link(p) \leftarrow get\_avail$; $p \leftarrow link(p)$; $info(p) \leftarrow end\_template\_token$
         { put \endtemplate at the end }
This code is used in section 779.

785. The tricky part about alignments is getting the templates into the scanner at the right time, and recovering control when a row or column is finished.

We usually begin a row after each \cr has been sensed, unless that \cr is followed by \noalign or by the right brace that terminates the alignment. The *align_peek* routine is used to look ahead and do the right thing; it either gets a new row started, or gets a \noalign started, or finishes off the alignment.

⟨ Declare the procedure called *align_peek* 785 ⟩ ≡
procedure *align_peek*;
   label *restart*;
   begin *restart*: $align\_state \leftarrow 1000000$; ⟨ Get the next non-blank non-call token 406 ⟩;
   if $cur\_cmd = no\_align$ **then**
      begin *scan_left_brace*; *new_save_level*(*no_align_group*);
      if $mode = -vmode$ **then** *normal_paragraph*;
      end
   else if $cur\_cmd = right\_brace$ **then** *fin_align*
      else if $(cur\_cmd = car\_ret) \wedge (cur\_chr = cr\_cr\_code)$ **then goto** *restart*   { ignore \crcr }
         else begin *init_row*;   { start a new row }
            init_col;   { start a new column and replace what we peeked at }
            end;
   end;
This code is used in section 800.

786. To start a row (i.e., a 'row' that rhymes with 'dough' but not with 'bough'), we enter a new semantic level, copy the first tabskip glue, and change from internal vertical mode to restricted horizontal mode or vice versa. The *space_factor* and *prev_depth* are not used on this semantic level, but we clear *aux* to zero just to be tidy.

⟨ Declare the procedure called *init_span* 787 ⟩
procedure *init_row*;
   begin *push_nest*; $mode \leftarrow (-hmode - vmode) - mode$; $aux \leftarrow 0$;
   tail_append(*new_glue*(*glue_ptr*(*preamble*))); $subtype(tail) \leftarrow tab\_skip\_code + 1$;
   $cur\_align \leftarrow link(preamble)$; $cur\_tail \leftarrow cur\_head$; *init_span*(*cur_align*);
   end;

787. The parameter to *init_span* is a pointer to the alignrecord where the next column or group of columns will begin. A new semantic level is entered, so that the columns will generate a list for subsequent packaging.

⟨ Declare the procedure called *init_span* 787 ⟩ ≡
procedure *init_span*(*p* : *pointer*);
  begin *push_nest*;
  if *mode* = −*hmode* **then** *space_factor* ← 1000
  else begin *prev_depth* ← *ignore_depth*; *normal_paragraph*;
    end;
  cur_span ← *p*;
  end;

This code is used in section 786.

788. When a column begins, we assume that *cur_cmd* is either *omit* or else the current token should be put back into the input until the ⟨*u_j*⟩ template has been scanned. (Note that *cur_cmd* might be *tab_mark* or *car_ret*.) We also assume that *align_state* is approximately 1000000 at this time. We remain in the same mode, and start the template if it is called for.

procedure *init_col*;
  begin *extra_info*(*cur_align*) ← *cur_cmd*;
  if *cur_cmd* = *omit* **then** *align_state* ← 0
  else begin *back_input*; *begin_token_list*(*u_part*(*cur_align*), *u_template*);
    end; { now *align_state* = 1000000 }
  end;

---

align_state: *integer*, §309.
aux = macro, §213.
back_input: **procedure**, §325.
begin_token_list: **procedure**, §323.
car_ret = 5, §207.
continue = 22, §15.
cr_cr_code = 130, §780.
cur_align: *pointer*, §770.
cur_chr: *halfword*, §297.
cur_cmd: *eight_bits*, §297.
cur_head: *pointer*, §770.
cur_span: *pointer*, §770.
cur_tail: *pointer*, §770.
cur_tok: *halfword*, §297.
done2 = 32, §15.
end_template_token = macro, §780.
error: **procedure**, §82.
extra_info = macro, §769.
fin_align: **procedure**, §800.

get_avail: **function**, §120.
get_preamble_token: **procedure**, §782.
glue_ptr = macro, §149.
help3 = macro, §79.
hmode = 101, §211.
hold_head = macro, §162.
ignore_depth = macro, §212.
info = macro, §118.
link = macro, §118.
mac_param = 6, §207.
mode = macro, §213.
new_glue: **function**, §153.
new_save_level: **procedure**, §274.
no_align = 34, §208.
no_align_group = 7, §269.
normal_paragraph: **procedure**, §1070.
null = macro, §115.

omit = 63, §208.
p: *pointer*, §774.
pointer = macro, §115.
preamble = macro, §770.
prev_depth = macro, §213.
print_err = macro, §73.
push_nest: **procedure**, §216.
restart = 20, §15.
right_brace = 2, §207.
scan_left_brace: **procedure**, §403.
space_factor = macro, §213.
subtype = macro, §133.
tab_mark = 4, §207.
tab_skip_code = 11, §224.
tail = macro, §213.
tail_append = macro, §214.
u_part = macro, §769.
u_template = 1, §307.
vmode = 1, §211.

789. The scanner sets *align_state* to zero when the $\langle u_j \rangle$ template ends. When a subsequent \cr or \span or tab mark occurs with *align_state* = 0, the scanner activates the following code, which fires up the $\langle v_j \rangle$ template. We need to remember the *cur_chr*, which is either *cr_cr_code*, *cr_code*, *span_code*, or a character code, depending on how the column text has ended.

This part of the program had better not be activated when the preamble to another alignment is being scanned.

⟨ Insert the $\langle v_j \rangle$ template and **goto** *restart* 789 ⟩ ≡
  begin if *scanner_status* = *aligning* **then**
    fatal_error("(interwoven␣alignment␣preambles␣are␣not␣allowed)");
  cur_cmd ← *extra_info*(*cur_align*); *extra_info*(*cur_align*) ← *cur_chr*;
  if *cur_cmd* = *omit* **then** *begin_token_list*(*omit_template*, *v_template*)
  else *begin_token_list*(*v_part*(*cur_align*), *v_template*);
  align_state ← 1000000; **goto** *restart*;
  end

This code is used in section 342.

790. The token list *omit_template* just referred to is a constant token list that contains the special control sequence \endtemplate only.

⟨ Initialize the special list heads and constant nodes 790 ⟩ ≡
  info(*omit_template*) ← *end_template_token*;   { *link*(*omit_template*) = *null* }

See also sections 797, 820, 981, and 988.

This code is used in section 164.

791. When the *endv* command at the end of a $\langle v_j \rangle$ template comes through the scanner, things really start to happen; and it is the *fin_col* routine that makes them happen. This routine returns *true* if a row as well as a column has been finished.

function *fin_col*: *boolean*;
  label *exit*;
  var *p*: *pointer*;   { the alignrecord after the current one }
    q, *r*: *pointer*;   { temporary pointers for list manipulation }
    s: *pointer*;   { a new span node }
    u: *pointer*;   { a new unset box }
    w: *scaled*;   { natural width }
    o: *glue_ord*;   { order of infinity }
    n: *halfword*;   { span counter }
  begin *q* ← *link*(*cur_align*);
  if (*cur_align* = *null*) ∨ (*q* = *null*) **then** *confusion*("endv");
  p ← *link*(*q*); ⟨ If the preamble list has been traversed, check that the row has ended 792 ⟩;
  if *extra_info*(*cur_align*) ≠ *span_code* **then**
    begin *unsave*; *new_save_level*(*align_group*);
    ⟨ Package an unset box for the current column and record its width 796 ⟩;
    ⟨ Copy the tabskip glue between columns 795 ⟩;
    if *extra_info*(*cur_align*) ≥ *cr_code* **then**
      begin *fin_col* ← *true*; **return**;
      end;
    init_span(*p*);
    end;

$align\_state \leftarrow 1000000$; ⟨Get the next non-blank non-call token 406⟩;
$cur\_align \leftarrow p$; $init\_col$; $fin\_col \leftarrow false$;
exit: **end**;

792. ⟨If the preamble list has been traversed, check that the row has ended 792⟩ ≡
 if $(p = null) \wedge (extra\_info(cur\_align) < cr\_code)$ **then**
  if $cur\_loop \neq null$ **then** ⟨Lengthen the preamble periodically 793⟩
  else begin $print\_err($"Extra␣alignment␣tab␣has␣been␣changed␣to␣"$)$; $print\_esc($"cr"$)$;
   $help3($"You␣have␣given␣more␣\span␣or␣&␣marks␣than␣there␣were"$)$
   $($"in␣the␣preamble␣to␣the␣\halign␣or␣\valign␣now␣in␣progress."$)$
   $($"So␣I´ll␣assume␣that␣you␣meant␣to␣type␣\cr␣instead."$)$; $extra\_info(cur\_align) \leftarrow cr\_code$;
   error;
   end

This code is used in section 791.

793. ⟨Lengthen the preamble periodically 793⟩ ≡
 begin $link(q) \leftarrow new\_null\_box$; $p \leftarrow link(q)$; { a new alignrecord }
 $info(p) \leftarrow end\_span$; $width(p) \leftarrow null\_flag$; $cur\_loop \leftarrow link(cur\_loop)$;
 ⟨Copy the templates from node cur_loop into node p 794⟩;
 $cur\_loop \leftarrow link(cur\_loop)$; $link(p) \leftarrow new\_glue(glue\_ptr(cur\_loop))$;
 end

This code is used in section 792.

794. ⟨Copy the templates from node cur_loop into node p 794⟩ ≡
 $q \leftarrow hold\_head$; $r \leftarrow u\_part(cur\_loop)$;
 while $r \neq null$ **do**
  begin $link(q) \leftarrow get\_avail$; $q \leftarrow link(q)$; $info(q) \leftarrow info(r)$; $r \leftarrow link(r)$;
  end;
 $link(q) \leftarrow null$; $u\_part(p) \leftarrow link(hold\_head)$; $q \leftarrow hold\_head$; $r \leftarrow v\_part(cur\_loop)$;
 while $r \neq null$ **do**
  begin $link(q) \leftarrow get\_avail$; $q \leftarrow link(q)$; $info(q) \leftarrow info(r)$; $r \leftarrow link(r)$;
  end;
 $link(q) \leftarrow null$; $v\_part(p) \leftarrow link(hold\_head)$

This code is used in section 793.

---

align_group = 6, §269.
align_state: **integer**, §309.
aligning = 4, §305.
begin_token_list: **procedure**, §323.
confusion: **procedure**, §95.
cr_code = 129, §780.
cr_cr_code = 130, §780.
cur_align: **pointer**, §770.
cur_chr: **halfword**, §297.
cur_cmd: **eight_bits**, §297.
cur_loop: **pointer**, §770.
end_span = **macro**, §162.
end_template_token = **macro**, §780.
endv = 9, §207.
error: **procedure**, §82.
exit = 10, §15.

extra_info = **macro**, §769.
fatal_error: **procedure**, §93.
get_avail: **function**, §120.
glue_ord = 0 .. 3, §150.
glue_ptr = **macro**, §149.
halfword = *min_halfword* ..
 max_halfword, §113.
help3 = **macro**, §79.
hold_head = **macro**, §162.
info = **macro**, §118.
link = **macro**, §118.
new_glue: **function**, §153.
new_null_box: **function**, §136.
new_save_level: **procedure**, §274.
null = **macro**, §115.

null_flag = **macro**, §138.
omit = 63, §208.
omit_template = **macro**, §162.
pointer = **macro**, §115.
print_err = **macro**, §73.
print_esc: **procedure**, §63.
restart = 20, §15.
scaled = **integer**, §101.
scanner_status: 0 .. 5, §305.
span_code = 128, §780.
u_part = **macro**, §769.
unsave: **procedure**, §281.
v_part = **macro**, §769.
v_template = 2, §307.
width = **macro**, §135.

795. ⟨ Copy the tabskip glue between columns 795 ⟩ ≡
  $tail\_append(new\_glue(glue\_ptr(link(cur\_align))))$; $subtype(tail) \leftarrow tab\_skip\_code + 1$

This code is used in section 791.

796. ⟨ Package an unset box for the current column and record its width 796 ⟩ ≡
  begin if $mode = -hmode$ **then**
    begin $adjust\_tail \leftarrow cur\_tail$; $u \leftarrow hpack(link(head), natural)$; $w \leftarrow width(u)$;
    $cur\_tail \leftarrow adjust\_tail$; $adjust\_tail \leftarrow null$;
    end
  else begin $u \leftarrow vpackage(link(head), natural, 0)$; $w \leftarrow height(u)$;
    end;
  $n \leftarrow min\_quarterword$; { this represents a span count of 1 }
  if $cur\_span \neq cur\_align$ **then** ⟨ Update width entry for spanned columns 798 ⟩
  else if $w > width(cur\_align)$ **then** $width(cur\_align) \leftarrow w$;
  $type(u) \leftarrow unset\_node$; $span\_count(u) \leftarrow n$;
  ⟨ Determine the stretch order 659 ⟩;
  $glue\_order(u) \leftarrow o$; $glue\_stretch(u) \leftarrow total\_stretch[o]$;
  ⟨ Determine the shrink order 665 ⟩;
  $glue\_sign(u) \leftarrow o$; $glue\_shrink(u) \leftarrow total\_shrink[o]$;
  pop_nest; $link(tail) \leftarrow u$; $tail \leftarrow u$;
  end

This code is used in section 791.

797. A span node is a 2-word record containing *width*, *info*, and *link* fields. The *link* field is not really a link, it indicates the number of spanned columns; the *info* field points to a span node for the same starting column, having a greater extent of spanning, or to *end_span*, which has the largest possible *link* field; the *width* field holds the largest natural width corresponding to a particular set of spanned columns.

A list of the maximum widths so far, for spanned columns starting at a given column, begins with the *info* field of the alignrecord for that column.

  define $span\_node\_size = 2$ { number of *mem* words for a span node }

⟨ Initialize the special list heads and constant nodes 790 ⟩ +≡
  $link(end\_span) \leftarrow max\_quarterword + 1$; $info(end\_span) \leftarrow null$;

798. ⟨ Update width entry for spanned columns 798 ⟩ ≡
  begin $q \leftarrow cur\_span$;
  repeat $incr(n)$; $q \leftarrow link(link(q))$;
  until $q = cur\_align$;
  if $n > max\_quarterword$ **then** $confusion("256_{\sqcup}spans")$;   { this can happen, but won't }
  $q \leftarrow cur\_span$;
  while $link(info(q)) < n$ **do** $q \leftarrow info(q)$;
  if $link(info(q)) > n$ **then**
    begin $s \leftarrow get\_node(span\_node\_size)$; $info(s) \leftarrow info(q)$; $link(s) \leftarrow n$; $info(q) \leftarrow s$; $width(s) \leftarrow w$;
    end
  else if $width(info(q)) < w$ **then** $width(info(q)) \leftarrow w$;
  end

This code is used in section 796.

799. At the end of a row, we append an unset box to the current vlist (for \halign) or the current hlist (for \valign). This unset box contains the unset boxes for the columns, separated by the tabskip glue. Everything will be set later.

procedure *fin_row*;
  var *p*: *pointer*; { the new unset box }
  begin if *mode* = −*hmode* **then**
    begin *p* ← *hpack*(*link*(*head*), *natural*); *pop_nest*; *append_to_vlist*(*p*);
    if *cur_head* ≠ *cur_tail* **then**
      begin *link*(*tail*) ← *link*(*cur_head*); *tail* ← *cur_tail*;
      end;
    end
  else begin *p* ← *vpack*(*link*(*head*), *natural*); *pop_nest*; *link*(*tail*) ← *p*; *tail* ← *p*; *space_factor* ← 1000;
    end;
  type(*p*) ← *unset_node*; *glue_stretch*(*p*) ← 0;
  if *every_cr* ≠ *null* **then** *begin_token_list*(*every_cr*, *every_cr_text*);
  align_peek;
  end; { note that *glue_shrink*(*p*) = 0 since *glue_shrink* ≡ *shift_amount* }

800. Finally, we will reach the end of the alignment, and we can breathe a sigh of relief that memory hasn't overflowed. All the unset boxes will now be set so that the columns line up, taking due account of spanned columns.

procedure *do_assignments*; *forward*;
procedure *resume_after_display*; *forward*;
procedure *build_page*; *forward*;
procedure *fin_align*;
  var p, q, r, s, u, v: *pointer*; { registers for the list operations }
    t, w: *scaled*; { width of column }
    o: *scaled*; { shift offset for unset boxes }
    n: *halfword*; { matching span amount }
    rule_save: *scaled*; { temporary storage for *overfull_rule* }
  begin if *cur_group* $\neq$ *align_group* **then** *confusion*("align1");
  unsave; { that *align_group* was for individual entries }
  if *cur_group* $\neq$ *align_group* **then** *confusion*("align0");
  unsave; { that *align_group* was for the whole alignment }
  if *nest*[*nest_ptr* $-$ 1].*mode_field* $=$ *mmode* **then** $o \leftarrow$ *display_indent*
  else $o \leftarrow 0$;
  ⟨ Go through the preamble list, determining the column widths and changing the alignrecords to
      dummy unset boxes 801 ⟩;
  ⟨ Package the preamble list, to determine the actual tabskip glue amounts, and let p point to this
      prototype box 804 ⟩;
  ⟨ Set the glue in all the unset boxes of the current list 805 ⟩;
  flush_node_list(p); *pop_alignment*; ⟨ Insert the current list into its environment 812 ⟩;
  end;
⟨ Declare the procedure called *align_peek* 785 ⟩

801. It's time now to dismantle the preamble list and to compute the column widths. Let w_{ij} be the maximum of the natural widths of all entries that span columns i through j, inclusive. The alignrecord for column i contains w_{ii} in its *width* field, and there is also a linked list of the nonzero w_{ij} for increasing j, accessible via the *info* field; these span nodes contain the value $j - i - 1 + min\_quarterword$ in their *link* fields. The values of w_{ii} were initialized to *null_flag*, which we regard as $-\infty$.

The final column widths are defined by the formula

$$w_j = \max_{1 \leq i \leq j} \left(w_{ij} - \sum_{i \leq k < j} (t_k + w_k) \right),$$

where t_k is the natural width of the tabskip glue between columns k and $k + 1$. However, if $w_{ij} = -\infty$ for all i in the range $1 \leq i \leq j$ (i.e., if every entry that involved column j also involved column $j + 1$), we let $w_j = 0$, and we zero out the tabskip glue after column j.

TeX computes these values by using the following scheme: First $w_1 = w_{11}$. Then replace w_{2j} by $\max(w_{2j}, w_{1j} - t_1 - w_1)$, for all $j > 1$. Then $w_2 = w_{22}$. Then replace w_{3j} by $\max(w_{3j}, w_{2j} - t_2 - w_2)$ for all $j > 2$; and so on. If any w_j turns out to be $-\infty$, its value is changed to zero and so is the next tabskip.

⟨ Go through the preamble list, determining the column widths and changing the alignrecords to dummy
      unset boxes 801 ⟩ ≡
  $q \leftarrow link(preamble)$;
  repeat $flush\_list(u\_part(q))$; $flush\_list(v\_part(q))$; $p \leftarrow link(link(q))$;
      if $width(q) = null\_flag$ **then** ⟨ Nullify $width(q)$ and the tabskip glue following this column 802 ⟩;
      if $info(q) \neq end\_span$ **then**
          ⟨ Merge the widths in the span nodes of q with those of p, destroying the span nodes of q 803 ⟩;
      $type(q) \leftarrow unset\_node$; $span\_count(q) \leftarrow min\_quarterword$; $height(q) \leftarrow 0$; $depth(q) \leftarrow 0$;
      $glue\_order(q) \leftarrow normal$; $glue\_sign(q) \leftarrow normal$; $glue\_stretch(q) \leftarrow 0$; $glue\_shrink(q) \leftarrow 0$; $q \leftarrow p$;
  until $q = null$

This code is used in section 800.

802. ⟨ Nullify $width(q)$ and the tabskip glue following this column 802 ⟩ ≡
  begin $width(q) \leftarrow 0$; $r \leftarrow link(q)$; $s \leftarrow glue\_ptr(r)$;
  if $s \neq zero\_glue$ **then**
      begin $add\_glue\_ref(zero\_glue)$; $delete\_glue\_ref(s)$; $glue\_ptr(r) \leftarrow zero\_glue$;
      end;
  end

This code is used in section 801.

---

add_glue_ref = macro, §203.
$align\_group$ = 6, §269.
$align\_peek$: **procedure**, §785.
$build\_page$: **procedure**, §994.
$confusion$: **procedure**, §95.
cur_group: $group\_code$, §271.
$delete\_glue\_ref$: **procedure**, §201.
$depth$ = macro, §135.
$display\_indent$ = macro, §247.
$do\_assignments$: **procedure**, §1270.
end_span = macro, §162.
$flush\_list$: **procedure**, §123.
$flush\_node\_list$: **procedure**, §202.
$glue\_order$ = macro, §135.
$glue\_ptr$ = macro, §149.
$glue\_shrink$ = macro, §159.

$glue\_sign$ = macro, §135.
$glue\_stretch$ = macro, §159.
$halfword$ = $min\_halfword$ ..
    $max\_halfword$, §113.
$height$ = macro, §135.
$info$ = macro, §118.
$link$ = macro, §118.
$min\_quarterword$ = 0, §110.
$mmode$ = 201, §211.
$mode\_field$: −201 .. 201, §212.
$nest$: **array**, §213.
$nest\_ptr$: 0 .. $nest\_size$, §213.
$normal$ = 0, §135.
$null$ = macro, §115.
$null\_flag$ = macro, §138.

$overfull\_rule$ = macro, §247.
$pointer$ = macro, §115.
$pop\_alignment$: **procedure**, §772.
$preamble$ = macro, §770.
$resume\_after\_display$: **procedure**,
    §1200.
$scaled$ = $integer$, §101.
$span\_count$ = macro, §159.
$type$ = macro, §133.
u_part = macro, §769.
$unsave$: **procedure**, §281.
$unset\_node$ = 13, §159.
v_part = macro, §769.
$width$ = macro, §135.
$zero\_glue$ = macro, §162.

803. Merging of two span-node lists is a typical exercise in the manipulation of linearly linked data structures. The essential invariant in the following **repeat** loop is that we want to dispense with node r, in q's list, and u is its successor; all nodes of p's list up to and including s have been processed, and the successor of s matches r or precedes r or follows r, according as $link(r) = n$ or $link(r) > n$ or $link(r) < n$.

⟨ Merge the widths in the span nodes of q with those of p, destroying the span nodes of q 803 ⟩ ≡
> **begin** $t \leftarrow width(q) + width(glue\_ptr(link(q)))$; $r \leftarrow info(q)$; $s \leftarrow end\_span$; $info(s) \leftarrow p$;
> $n \leftarrow min\_quarterword + 1$;
> **repeat** $width(r) \leftarrow width(r) - t$; $u \leftarrow info(r)$;
> > **while** $link(r) > n$ **do**
> > > **begin** $s \leftarrow info(s)$; $n \leftarrow link(info(s)) + 1$;
> > > **end**;
> > **if** $link(r) < n$ **then**
> > > **begin** $info(r) \leftarrow info(s)$; $info(s) \leftarrow r$; $decr(link(r))$; $s \leftarrow r$;
> > > **end**
> > **else begin if** $width(r) > width(info(s))$ **then** $width(info(s)) \leftarrow width(r)$;
> > > $free\_node(r, span\_node\_size)$;
> > > **end**;
> > $r \leftarrow u$;
> **until** $r = end\_span$;
> **end**

This code is used in section 801.

804. Now the preamble list has been converted to a list of alternating unset boxes and tabskip glue, where the box widths are equal to the final column sizes. In case of \valign, we change the widths to heights, so that a correct error message will be produced if the alignment is overfull or underfull.

⟨ Package the preamble list, to determine the actual tabskip glue amounts, and let p point to this
        prototype box 804 ⟩ ≡
> $save\_ptr \leftarrow save\_ptr - 2$; $pack\_begin\_line \leftarrow -mode\_line$;
> **if** $mode = -vmode$ **then**
> > **begin** $rule\_save \leftarrow overfull\_rule$; $overfull\_rule \leftarrow 0$;   { prevent rule from being packaged }
> > $p \leftarrow hpack(preamble, saved(1), saved(0))$; $overfull\_rule \leftarrow rule\_save$;
> > **end**
> **else begin** $q \leftarrow link(preamble)$;
> > **repeat** $height(q) \leftarrow width(q)$; $width(q) \leftarrow 0$; $q \leftarrow link(link(q))$;
> > **until** $q = null$;
> > $p \leftarrow vpack(preamble, saved(1), saved(0))$; $q \leftarrow link(preamble)$;
> > **repeat** $width(q) \leftarrow height(q)$; $height(q) \leftarrow 0$; $q \leftarrow link(link(q))$;
> > **until** $q = null$;
> > **end**;
> $pack\_begin\_line \leftarrow 0$

This code is used in section 800.

805. ⟨ Set the glue in all the unset boxes of the current list 805 ⟩ ≡
> $q \leftarrow link(head)$;
> **while** $q \neq null$ **do**

begin if $type(q) = unset\_node$ **then** ⟨ Set the unset box q and the unset boxes in it 807 ⟩
    else if $type(q) = rule\_node$ **then**
        ⟨ Make the running dimensions in rule q extend to the boundaries of the alignment 806 ⟩;
    $q \leftarrow link(q)$;
    end

This code is used in section 800.

806.   ⟨ Make the running dimensions in rule q extend to the boundaries of the alignment 806 ⟩ ≡
    begin if $is\_running(width(q))$ **then** $width(q) \leftarrow width(p)$;
    if $is\_running(height(q))$ **then** $height(q) \leftarrow height(p)$;
    if $is\_running(depth(q))$ **then** $depth(q) \leftarrow depth(p)$;
    end

This code is used in section 805.

807.   The unset box q represents a row that contains one or more unset boxes, depending on how soon \cr occurred in that row.

⟨ Set the unset box q and the unset boxes in it 807 ⟩ ≡
    begin if $mode = -vmode$ **then**
        begin $type(q) \leftarrow hlist\_node$; $width(q) \leftarrow width(p)$;
        end
    else begin $type(q) \leftarrow vlist\_node$; $height(q) \leftarrow height(p)$;
        end;
    $glue\_order(q) \leftarrow glue\_order(p)$; $glue\_sign(q) \leftarrow glue\_sign(p)$; $glue\_set(q) \leftarrow glue\_set(p)$;
    $shift\_amount(q) \leftarrow o$; $r \leftarrow link(list\_ptr(q))$; $s \leftarrow link(list\_ptr(p))$;
    repeat ⟨ Set the glue in node r and change it from an unset node 808 ⟩;
        $r \leftarrow link(link(r))$; $s \leftarrow link(link(s))$;
    until $r = null$;
    end

This code is used in section 805.

808. A box made from spanned columns will be followed by tabskip glue nodes and by empty boxes as if there were no spanning. This permits perfect alignment of subsequent entries, and it prevents values that depend on floating point arithmetic from entering into the dimensions of any boxes.

⟨ Set the glue in node r and change it from an unset node 808 ⟩ ≡
   $n \leftarrow span\_count(r)$; $t \leftarrow width(s)$; $w \leftarrow t$; $u \leftarrow hold\_head$;
   while $n > min\_quarterword$ **do**
      begin $decr(n)$; ⟨ Append tabskip glue and an empty box to list u, and update s and t as the
         prototype nodes are passed 809 ⟩;
      end;
   if $mode = -vmode$ **then**
      ⟨ Make the unset node r into an *hlist_node* of width w, setting the glue as if the width were t 810 ⟩
   else ⟨ Make the unset node r into a *vlist_node* of height w, setting the glue as if the height were t 811 ⟩;
   $shift\_amount(r) \leftarrow 0$;
   if $u \neq hold\_head$ **then**   { append blank boxes to account for spanned nodes }
      begin $link(u) \leftarrow link(r)$; $link(r) \leftarrow link(hold\_head)$; $r \leftarrow u$;
      end

This code is used in section 807.

809. ⟨ Append tabskip glue and an empty box to list u, and update s and t as the prototype nodes are passed 809 ⟩ ≡
   $s \leftarrow link(s)$; $v \leftarrow glue\_ptr(s)$; $link(u) \leftarrow new\_glue(v)$; $u \leftarrow link(u)$; $subtype(u) \leftarrow tab\_skip\_code + 1$;
   $t \leftarrow t + width(v)$;
   if $glue\_sign(p) = stretching$ **then**
      begin if $stretch\_order(v) = glue\_order(p)$ **then** $t \leftarrow t + round(float(glue\_set(p)) * stretch(v))$;
      end
   else if $glue\_sign(p) = shrinking$ **then**
      begin if $shrink\_order(v) = glue\_order(p)$ **then** $t \leftarrow t - round(float(glue\_set(p)) * shrink(v))$;
      end;
   $s \leftarrow link(s)$; $link(u) \leftarrow new\_null\_box$; $u \leftarrow link(u)$; $t \leftarrow t + width(s)$;
   if $mode = -vmode$ **then** $width(u) \leftarrow width(s)$ **else begin** $type(u) \leftarrow vlist\_node$;
      $height(u) \leftarrow width(s)$;
      end

This code is used in section 808.

810. ⟨ Make the unset node r into an *hlist_node* of width w, setting the glue as if the width were t 810 ⟩ ≡
begin $height(r) \leftarrow height(q)$; $depth(r) \leftarrow depth(q)$;
if $t = width(r)$ **then**
   begin $glue\_sign(r) \leftarrow normal$; $glue\_order(r) \leftarrow normal$; $set\_glue\_ratio\_zero(glue\_set(r))$;
   end
else if $t > width(r)$ **then**
      begin $glue\_sign(r) \leftarrow stretching$;
      if $glue\_stretch(r) = 0$ **then** $set\_glue\_ratio\_zero(glue\_set(r))$
      else $glue\_set(r) \leftarrow unfloat((t - width(r))/glue\_stretch(r))$;
      end
   else begin $glue\_order(r) \leftarrow glue\_sign(r)$; $glue\_sign(r) \leftarrow shrinking$;
      if $glue\_shrink(r) = 0$ **then** $set\_glue\_ratio\_zero(glue\_set(r))$

      else if $(glue\_order(r) = normal) \wedge (width(r) - t > glue\_shrink(r))$ **then**
         $set\_glue\_ratio\_one(glue\_set(r))$
        else $glue\_set(r) \leftarrow unfloat((width(r) - t)/glue\_shrink(r))$;
     end;
  $width(r) \leftarrow w$; $type(r) \leftarrow hlist\_node$;
  end

This code is used in section 808.

811. ⟨ Make the unset node r into a *vlist_node* of height w, setting the glue as if the height were
     t 811 ⟩ ≡
begin $width(r) \leftarrow width(q)$;
if $t = height(r)$ **then**
  begin $glue\_sign(r) \leftarrow normal$; $glue\_order(r) \leftarrow normal$; $set\_glue\_ratio\_zero(glue\_set(r))$;
  end
else if $t > height(r)$ **then**
    begin $glue\_sign(r) \leftarrow stretching$;
    if $glue\_stretch(r) = 0$ **then** $set\_glue\_ratio\_zero(glue\_set(r))$
    else $glue\_set(r) \leftarrow unfloat((t - height(r))/glue\_stretch(r))$;
    end
  else begin $glue\_order(r) \leftarrow glue\_sign(r)$; $glue\_sign(r) \leftarrow shrinking$;
    if $glue\_shrink(r) = 0$ **then** $set\_glue\_ratio\_zero(glue\_set(r))$
    else if $(glue\_order(r) = normal) \wedge (height(r) - t > glue\_shrink(r))$ **then**
       $set\_glue\_ratio\_one(glue\_set(r))$
      else $glue\_set(r) \leftarrow unfloat((height(r) - t)/glue\_shrink(r))$;
    end;
  $height(r) \leftarrow w$; $type(r) \leftarrow vlist\_node$;
  end

This code is used in section 808.

$decr$ = macro, §16.
$depth$ = macro, §135.
$float$ = macro, §109.
$glue\_order$ = macro, §135.
$glue\_ptr$ = macro, §149.
$glue\_set$ = macro, §135.
$glue\_shrink$ = macro, §159.
$glue\_sign$ = macro, §135.
$glue\_stretch$ = macro, §159.
$height$ = macro, §135.
$hlist\_node = 0$, §135.
$hold\_head$ = macro, §162.
$link$ = macro, §118.
$min\_quarterword = 0$, §110.
$mode$ = macro, §213.

n: *halfword*, §800.
new_glue: **function**, §153.
new_null_box: **function**, §136.
$normal = 0$, §135.
p: *pointer*, §800.
q: *pointer*, §800.
r: *pointer*, §800.
s: *pointer*, §800.
$set\_glue\_ratio\_one$ = macro, §109.
$set\_glue\_ratio\_zero$ = macro, §109.
$shift\_amount$ = macro, §135.
$shrink$ = macro, §150.
$shrink\_order$ = macro, §150.
$shrinking = 2$, §135.
$span\_count$ = macro, §159.

$stretch$ = macro, §150.
$stretch\_order$ = macro, §150.
$stretching = 1$, §135.
$subtype$ = macro, §133.
t: *scaled*, §800.
$tab\_skip\_code = 11$, §224.
$type$ = macro, §133.
u: *pointer*, §800.
$unfloat$ = macro, §109.
v: *pointer*, §800.
$vlist\_node = 1$, §137.
$vmode = 1$, §211.
w: *scaled*, §800.
$width$ = macro, §135.

812. We now have a completed alignment, in the list that starts at *head* and ends at *tail*. This list will be merged with the one that encloses it. (In case the enclosing mode is *mmode*, for displayed formulas, we will need to insert glue before and after the display: that part of the program will be deferred until we're more familiar with such operations.)

⟨ Insert the current list into its environment 812 ⟩ ≡
> $t \leftarrow aux$; $p \leftarrow link(head)$; $q \leftarrow tail$; *pop_nest*;
> **if** $mode = mmode$ **then** ⟨ Finish an alignment in a display 1206 ⟩
> **else begin** $aux \leftarrow t$; $link(tail) \leftarrow p$;
> > **if** $p \neq null$ **then** $tail \leftarrow q$;
> > **if** $mode = vmode$ **then** *build_page*;
> **end**

This code is used in section 800.

813.   Breaking paragraphs into lines.   We come now to what is probably the most interesting algorithm of TeX: the mechanism for choosing the "best possible" breakpoints that yield the individual lines of a paragraph. TeX's line-breaking algorithm takes a given horizontal list and converts it to a sequence of boxes that are appended to the current vertical list. In the course of doing this, it creates a special data structure containing three kinds of records that are not used elsewhere in TeX. Such nodes are created while a paragraph is being processed, and they are destroyed afterwards; thus, the other parts of TeX do not need to know anything about how line-breaking is done.

The method used here is based on an approach devised by Michael F. Plass and the author in 1977, subsequently generalized and improved by the same two people in 1980. A detailed discussion appears in *SOFTWARE—Practice & Experience* **11** (1981), 1119–1184, where it is shown that the line-breaking problem can be regarded as a special case of the problem of computing the shortest path in an acyclic network. The cited paper includes numerous examples and describes the history of line breaking as it has been practiced by printers through the ages. The present implementation adds two new ideas to the algorithm of 1980: memory space requirements are considerably reduced by using smaller records for inactive nodes than for active ones, and arithmetic overflow is avoided by using "delta distances" instead of keeping track of the total distance from the beginning of the paragraph to the current point.

814.   The *line_break* procedure should be invoked only in horizontal mode; it leaves that mode and places its output into the current vlist of the enclosing vertical mode (or internal vertical mode). There is one explicit parameter: *final_widow_penalty* is the amount of additional penalty to be inserted before the final line of the paragraph.

There are also a number of implicit parameters: The hlist to be broken starts at *link*(*head*), and it is nonempty. The value of *prev_graf* in the enclosing semantic level tells where the paragraph should begin in the sequence of line numbers, in case hanging indentation or \parshape are in use; *prev_graf* is zero unless this paragraph is being continued after a displayed formula. Other implicit parameters, such as the *par_shape_ptr* and various penalties to use for hyphenation, etc., appear in *eqtb*.

After *line_break* has acted, it will have updated the current vlist and the value of *prev_graf*. Furthermore, the global variable *just_box* will point to the final box created by *line_break*, so that the width of this line can be ascertained when it is necessary to decide whether to use *above_display_skip* or *above_display_short_skip* before a displayed formula.

⟨ Global variables 13 ⟩ +≡
just_box: *pointer*;   { the *hlist_node* for the last line of the new paragraph }

---

above_display_short_skip = macro, §224.
above_display_skip = macro, §224.
aux = macro, §213.
build_page: **procedure**, §994.
eqtb: **array**, §253.
final_widow_penalty: *integer*, §815.
head = macro, §213.

hlist_node = 0, §135.
line_break: **procedure**, §815.
link = macro, §118.
mmode = 201, §211.
mode = macro, §213.
null = macro, §115.
p: *pointer*, §800.
par_shape_ptr = macro, §230.

pointer = macro, §115.
pop_nest: **procedure**, §217.
prev_graf = macro, §213.
q: *pointer*, §800.
t: *scaled*, §800.
tail = macro, §213.
vmode = 1, §211.

815. Since *line_break* is a rather lengthy procedure—sort of a small world unto itself—we must build it up little by little, somewhat more cautiously than we have done with the simpler procedures of TEX. Here is the general outline.

⟨ Declare subprocedures for *line_break* 826 ⟩
procedure *line_break*(*final_widow_penalty* : *integer*);
  label *done*, *done1*, *done2*, *done3*, *done4*;
  var ⟨ Local variables for line breaking 862 ⟩
  begin *pack_begin_line* ← *mode_line*; { this is for over/underfull box messages }
  ⟨ Get ready to start line breaking 816 ⟩;
  ⟨ Find optimal breakpoints 863 ⟩;
  ⟨ Break the paragraph at the chosen breakpoints, justify the resulting lines to the correct widths, and
      append them to the current vertical list 876 ⟩;
  ⟨ Clean up the memory by removing the break nodes 865 ⟩;
  pack_begin_line ← 0;
  end;

816. The first task is to move the list from *head* to *temp_head* and go into the enclosing semantic level. We also append the \parfillskip glue to the end of the paragraph, removing a space (or other glue node) if it was there, since spaces usually precede blank lines and instances of '$$'. The *par_fill_skip* is preceded by an infinite penalty, so it will never be considered as a potential breakpoint.

This code assumes that a *glue_node* and a *penalty_node* occupy the same number of words in *mem*.

⟨ Get ready to start line breaking 816 ⟩ ≡
  link(*temp_head*) ← *link*(*head*);
  if *is_char_node*(*tail*) **then** *tail_append*(*new_penalty*(*inf_penalty*))
  else if *type*(*tail*) ≠ *glue_node* **then** *tail_append*(*new_penalty*(*inf_penalty*))
    else begin *type*(*tail*) ← *penalty_node*; *delete_glue_ref*(*glue_ptr*(*tail*));
      flush_node_list(*leader_ptr*(*tail*)); *penalty*(*tail*) ← *inf_penalty*;
    end;
  link(*tail*) ← *new_param_glue*(*par_fill_skip_code*); *pop_nest*;
See also sections 827, 834, and 848.
This code is used in section 815.

817. When looking for optimal line breaks, TEX creates a "break node" for each break that is *feasible*, in the sense that there is a way to end a line at the given place without requiring any line to stretch more than a given tolerance. A break node is characterized by three things: the position of the break (which is a pointer to a *glue_node*, *math_node*, *penalty_node*, or *disc_node*); the ordinal number of the line that will follow this breakpoint; and the fitness classification of the line that has just ended, i.e., *tight_fit*, *decent_fit*, *loose_fit*, or *very_loose_fit*.

  define *tight_fit* = 3 { fitness classification for lines shrinking 0.5 to 1.0 of their shrinkability }
  define *loose_fit* = 1 { fitness classification for lines stretching 0.5 to 1.0 of their stretchability }
  define *very_loose_fit* = 0 { fitness classification for lines stretching more than their stretchability }
  define *decent_fit* = 2 { fitness classification for all other lines }

818. The algorithm essentially determines the best possible way to achieve each feasible combination of position, line, and fitness. Thus, it answers questions like, "What is the best way to break the opening part of the paragraph so that the fourth line is a tight line ending at such-and-such a place?" However, the fact that all lines are to be the same length after a certain point makes it possible to regard all sufficiently large line numbers as equivalent, when the looseness parameter is zero, and this makes it possible for the algorithm to save space and time.

An "active node" and a "passive node" are created in *mem* for each feasible breakpoint that needs to be considered. Active nodes are three words long and passive nodes are two words long. We need active nodes only for breakpoints near the place in the paragraph that is currently being examined, so they are recycled within a comparatively short time after they are created.

819. An active node for a given breakpoint contains six fields:

link points to the next node in the list of active nodes; the last active node has *link* = *last_active*.

break_node points to the passive node associated with this breakpoint.

line_number is the number of the line that follows this breakpoint.

fitness is the fitness classification of the line ending at this breakpoint.

type is either *hyphenated* or *unhyphenated*, depending on whether this breakpoint is a *disc_node*.

total_demerits is the minimum possible sum of demerits over all lines leading from the beginning of the paragraph to this breakpoint.

The value of *link*(*active*) points to the first active node on a linked list of all currently active nodes. This list is in order by *line_number*, except that nodes with *line_number* > *easy_line* may be in any order relative to each other.

> **define** *active_node_size* = 3 { number of words in active nodes }
> **define** *fitness* ≡ *subtype* { *very_loose_fit* .. *tight_fit* on final line for this break }
> **define** *break_node* ≡ *rlink* { pointer to the corresponding passive node }
> **define** *line_number* ≡ *llink* { line that begins at this breakpoint }
> **define** *total_demerits*(#) ≡ *mem*[# + 2].*int* { the quantity that TeX minimizes }
> **define** *unhyphenated* = 0 { the *type* of a normal active break node }
> **define** *hyphenated* = 1 { the *type* of an active node that breaks at a *disc_node* }
> **define** *last_active* ≡ *active* { the active list ends where it begins }

820. ⟨ Initialize the special list heads and constant nodes 790 ⟩ +≡
> *type*(*last_active*) ← *hyphenated*; *line_number*(*last_active*) ← *max_halfword*; *subtype*(*last_active*) ← 0;
> { the *subtype* is never examined by the algorithm }

---

active = macro, §162.
delete_glue_ref: **procedure**, §201.
disc_node = 7, §145.
done = 30, §15.
done1 = 31, §15.
done2 = 32, §15.
done3 = 33, §15.
done4 = 34, §15.
easy_line: *halfword*, §847.
flush_node_list: **procedure**, §202.
glue_node = 10, §149.
glue_ptr = macro, §149.
head = macro, §213.

inf_penalty = 10000, §157.
int: *integer*, §113.
is_char_node = macro, §134.
leader_ptr = macro, §149.
link = macro, §118.
llink = macro, §124.
math_node = 9, §147.
max_halfword = macro, §110.
mem: **array**, §116.
mode_line = macro, §213.
new_param_glue: **function**, §152.
new_penalty: **function**, §158.

pack_begin_line: *integer*, §661.
par_fill_skip = macro, §224.
par_fill_skip_code = 14, §224.
penalty = macro, §157.
penalty_node = 12, §157.
pop_nest: **procedure**, §217.
rlink = macro, §124.
subtype = macro, §133.
tail = macro, §213.
tail_append = macro, §214.
temp_head = macro, §162.
type = macro, §133.

821. The passive node for a given breakpoint contains only four fields:

link points to the passive node created just before this one, if any, otherwise it is *null*.

cur_break points to the position of this breakpoint in the horizontal list for the paragraph being broken.

prev_break points to the passive node that should precede this one in an optimal path to this breakpoint.

serial is equal to n if this passive node is the nth one created during the current pass. (This field is used only when printing out detailed statistics about the line-breaking calculations.)

There is a global variable called *passive* that points to the most recently created passive node. Another global variable, *printed_node*, is used to help print out the paragraph when detailed information about the line-breaking computation is being displayed.

> **define** *passive_node_size* = 2 { number of words in passive nodes }
> **define** *cur_break* ≡ *rlink*   { in passive node, points to position of this breakpoint }
> **define** *prev_break* ≡ *llink*   { points to passive node that should precede this one }
> **define** *serial* ≡ *info*   { serial number for symbolic identification }

⟨ Global variables 13 ⟩ +≡
passive: *pointer*;   { most recent node on passive list }
printed_node: *pointer*;   { most recent node that has been printed }
pass_number: *pointer*;   { the number of passive nodes allocated on this pass }

822. The active list also contains "delta" nodes that help the algorithm compute the badness of individual lines. Such nodes appear only between two active nodes, and they have *type* = *delta_node*. If p and r are active nodes and if q is a delta node between them, so that $link(p) = q$ and $link(q) = r$, then q tells the space difference between lines in the horizontal list that start after breakpoint p and lines that start after breakpoint r. In other words, if we know the length of the line that starts after p and ends at our current position, then the corresponding length of the line that starts after r is obtained by adding the amounts in node q. A delta node contains six scaled numbers, since it must record the net change in glue stretchability with respect to all orders of infinity. The natural width difference appears in $mem[q+1].sc$; the stretch differences in units of pt, fil, fill, and filll appear in $mem[q+2 .. q+5].sc$; and the shrink difference appears in $mem[q+6].sc$. The *subtype* field of a delta node is not used.

> **define** *delta_node_size* = 7   { number of words in a delta node }
> **define** *delta_node* = 2   { *type* field in a delta node }

823. As the algorithm runs, it maintains a set of six delta-like registers for the length of the line following the first active breakpoint to the current position in the given hlist. When it makes a pass through the active list, it also maintains a similar set of six registers for the length following the active breakpoint of current interest. A third set holds the length of an empty line (namely, the sum of \leftskip and \rightskip); and a fourth set is used to create new delta nodes.

When we pass a delta node we want to do operations like

$$\textbf{for } k \leftarrow 1 \textbf{ to } 6 \textbf{ do } cur\_active\_width[k] \leftarrow cur\_active\_width[k] + mem[q+k].sc;$$

and we want to do this without the overhead of **for** loops. The *do_all_six* macro makes such six-tuples convenient.

define $do\_all\_six(\#) \equiv \#(1); \; \#(2); \; \#(3); \; \#(4); \; \#(5); \; \#(6)$

⟨ Global variables 13 ⟩ +≡
$active\_width$: **array** $[1 .. 6]$ **of** $scaled$; { distance from first active node to cur_p }
cur_active_width: **array** $[1 .. 6]$ **of** $scaled$; { distance from current active node }
$background$: **array** $[1 .. 6]$ **of** $scaled$; { length of an "empty" line }
$break\_width$: **array** $[1 .. 6]$ **of** $scaled$; { length being computed after current break }

824. Let's state the principles of the delta nodes more precisely and concisely, so that the following programs will be less obscure. For each legal breakpoint p in the paragraph, we define two quantities $\alpha(p)$ and $\beta(p)$ such that the length of material in a line from breakpoint p to breakpoint q is $\gamma + \beta(q) - \alpha(p)$, for some fixed γ. Intuitively, $\alpha(p)$ and $\beta(q)$ are the total length of material from the beginning of the paragraph to a point "after" a break at p and to a point "before" a break at q; and γ is the width of an empty line, namely the length contributed by \leftskip and \rightskip.

Suppose, for example, that the paragraph consists entirely of alternating boxes and glue skips; let the boxes have widths $x_1 \ldots x_n$ and let the skips have widths $y_1 \ldots y_n$, so that the paragraph can be represented by $x_1 y_1 \ldots x_n y_n$. Let p_i be the legal breakpoint at y_i; then $\alpha(p_i) = x_1 + y_1 + \cdots + x_i + y_i$, and $\beta(p_i) = x_1 + y_1 + \cdots + x_i$. To check this, note that the length of material from p_2 to p_5, say, is $\gamma + x_3 + y_3 + x_4 + y_4 + x_5 = \gamma + \beta(p_5) - \alpha(p_2)$.

The quantities α, β, γ involve glue stretchability and shrinkability as well as a natural width. If we were to compute $\alpha(p)$ and $\beta(p)$ for each p, we would need multiple precision arithmetic, and the multiprecise numbers would have to be kept in the active nodes. TeX avoids this problem by working entirely with relative differences or "deltas." Suppose, for example, that the active list contains $a_1 \, \delta_1 \, a_2 \, \delta_2 \, a_3$, where the a's are active breakpoints and the δ's are delta nodes. Then $\delta_1 = \alpha(a_1) - \alpha(a_2)$ and $\delta_2 = \alpha(a_2) - \alpha(a_3)$. If the line breaking algorithm is currently positioned at some other breakpoint p, the $active\_width$ array contains the value $\gamma + \beta(p) - \alpha(a_1)$. If we are scanning through the list of active nodes and considering a tentative line that runs from a_2 to p, say, the cur_active_width array will contain the value $\gamma + \beta(p) - \alpha(a_2)$. Thus, when we move from a_2 to a_3, we want to add $\alpha(a_2) - \alpha(a_3)$ to cur_active_width; and this is just δ_2, which appears in the active list between a_2 and a_3. The $background$ array contains γ. The $break\_width$ array will be used to calculate values of new delta nodes when the active list is being updated.

cur_p: $pointer$, §828.
$info$ = macro, §118.
$link$ = macro, §118.
$llink$ = macro, §124.

mem: **array**, §116.
$null$ = macro, §115.
$pointer$ = macro, §115.
$rlink$ = macro, §124.

sc = macro, §113.
$scaled$ = $integer$, §101.
$subtype$ = macro, §133.
$type$ = macro, §133.

825. Glue nodes in a horizontal list that is being paragraphed are not supposed to include "infinite" shrinkability; that is why the algorithm maintains four registers for stretching but only one for shrinking. If the user tries to introduce infinite shrinkability, the shrinkability will be reset to finite and an error message will be issued. A boolean variable *no_shrink_error_yet* prevents this error message from appearing more than once per paragraph.

define *check_shrinkage*(**#**) ≡
        if (*shrink_order*(**#**) ≠ *normal*) ∧ (*shrink*(**#**) ≠ 0) **then**
           begin # ← *finite_shrink*(**#**);
           end

⟨ Global variables 13 ⟩ +≡
no_shrink_error_yet: *boolean*;   { have we complained about infinite shrinkage? }

826. ⟨ Declare subprocedures for *line_break* 826 ⟩ ≡
function *finite_shrink*(*p* : *pointer*): *pointer*;   { recovers from infinite shrinkage }
  var *q*: *pointer*;   { new glue specification }
  begin if *no_shrink_error_yet* **then**
    begin *no_shrink_error_yet* ← *false*;
    print_err("Infinite␣glue␣shrinkage␣found␣in␣a␣paragraph");
    help5("The␣paragraph␣just␣ended␣includes␣some␣glue␣that␣has")
        ("infinite␣shrinkability,␣e.g.,␣`\hskip␣0pt␣minus␣1fil´.")
        ("Such␣glue␣doesn´t␣belong␣there---it␣allows␣a␣paragraph")
        ("of␣any␣length␣to␣fit␣on␣one␣line.␣But␣it´s␣safe␣to␣proceed,")
        ("since␣the␣offensive␣shrinkability␣has␣been␣made␣finite."); *error*;
    end;
  q ← *new_spec*(*p*); *shrink_order*(*q*) ← *normal*; *delete_glue_ref*(*p*); *finite_shrink* ← *q*;
  end;
See also sections 829, 877, and 895.
This code is used in section 815.

827. ⟨ Get ready to start line breaking 816 ⟩ +≡
  no_shrink_error_yet ← *true*;
  check_shrinkage(*left_skip*); *check_shrinkage*(*right_skip*);
  q ← *left_skip*; *r* ← *right_skip*; *background*[1] ← *width*(*q*) + *width*(*r*);
  background[2] ← 0; *background*[3] ← 0; *background*[4] ← 0; *background*[5] ← 0;
  background[2 + *stretch_order*(*q*)] ← *stretch*(*q*);
  background[2 + *stretch_order*(*r*)] ← *background*[2 + *stretch_order*(*r*)] + *stretch*(*r*);
  background[6] ← *shrink*(*q*) + *shrink*(*r*);

828. A pointer variable *cur_p* runs through the given horizontal list as we look for breakpoints. This variable is global, since it is used both by *line_break* and by its subprocedure *try_break*.

Another global variable called *threshold* is used to determine the feasibility of individual lines: breakpoints are feasible if there is a way to reach them without creating lines whose badness exceeds *threshold*. (The badness is compared to *threshold* before penalties are added, so that penalty values do not affect the feasibility of breakpoints, except that no break is allowed when the penalty is 10000 or more.) If *threshold* is 10000 or more, all legal breaks are considered feasible, since the *badness* function specified above never returns a value greater than 10000.

Two passes might be made through the paragraph in an attempt to find at least one set of feasible breakpoints. On the first pass, we have *threshold* = *pretolerance* and *second_pass* = *false*.

If this pass fails to find a feasible solution, *threshold* is set to *tolerance*, *second_pass* is set *true*, and an attempt is made to hyphenate as many words as possible.

⟨ Global variables 13 ⟩ +≡

cur_p: *pointer*;   { the current breakpoint under consideration }

second_pass: *boolean*;   { is this our second attempt to break this paragraph? }

threshold: *integer*;   { maximum badness on feasible lines }

829. The heart of the line-breaking procedure is '*try_break*', a subroutine that tests if the current breakpoint *cur_p* is feasible, by running through the active list to see what lines of text can be made from active nodes to *cur_p*. If feasible breaks are possible, new break nodes are created. If *cur_p* is too far from an active node, that node is deactivated.

The parameter *pi* to *try_break* is the penalty associated with a break at *cur_p*; we have *pi* = *eject_penalty* if the break is forced, and *pi* = *inf_penalty* if the break is illegal.

The other parameter, *break_type*, is set to *hyphenated* or *unhyphenated*, depending on whether or not the current break is at a *disc_node*. The end of a paragraph is also regarded as '*hyphenated*'; this case is distinguishable by the condition *cur_p* = *null*.

> **define** *copy_to_cur_active*(#) ≡ *cur_active_width*[#] ← *active_width*[#]
> **define** *deactivate* = 60   { go here when node *r* should be deactivated }

⟨ Declare subprocedures for *line_break* 826 ⟩ +≡
procedure *try_break*(*pi* : *integer*; *break_type* : *small_number*);
  label *exit*, *done*, *done1*, *continue*, *deactivate*;
  var *r*: *pointer*;   { runs through the active list }
    prev_r: *pointer*;   { stays a step behind *r* }
    old_l: *halfword*;   { maximum line number in current equivalence class of lines }
    no_break_yet: *boolean*;   { have we found a feasible break at *cur_p*? }
    ⟨ Other local variables for *try_break* 830 ⟩
  begin ⟨ Make sure that *pi* is in the proper range 831 ⟩;
  no_break_yet ← *true*; *prev_r* ← *active*; *old_l* ← 0; *do_all_six*(*copy_to_cur_active*);
  loop begin *continue*: *r* ← *link*(*prev_r*); ⟨ If node *r* is of type *delta_node*, update *cur_active_width*,
        set *prev_r* and *prev_prev_r*, then **goto** *continue* 832 ⟩;
    ⟨ If a line number class has ended, create new active nodes for the best feasible breaks in that class;
        then **return** if *r* = *last_active*, otherwise compute the new *line_width* 835 ⟩;
    ⟨ Consider the demerits for a line from *r* to *cur_p*; deactivate node *r* if it should no longer be active;
        then **goto** *continue* if a line from *r* to *cur_p* is infeasible, otherwise record a new feasible
        break 851 ⟩;
  end;
exit: **stat** ⟨ Update the value of *printed_node* for symbolic displays 858 ⟩ **tats**
  end;

830. ⟨ Other local variables for *try_break* 830 ⟩ ≡
prev_prev_r: *pointer*;   { a step behind *prev_r*, if *type*(*prev_r*) = *delta_node* }
s: *pointer*;   { runs through nodes ahead of *cur_p* }
q: *pointer*;   { points to a new node being created }
v: *pointer*;   { points to a glue specification }
t: *quarterword*;   { replacement count, if *cur_p* is a discretionary node }
f: *internal_font_number*;   { used in character width calculation }
l: *halfword*;   { line number of current active node }
node_r_stays_active: *boolean*;   { should node *r* remain in the active list? }
line_width: *scaled*;   { the current line will be justified to this width }
fit_class: *very_loose_fit* .. *tight_fit*;   { possible fitness class of test line }
b: *halfword*;   { badness of test line }
d: *integer*;   { demerits of test line }
artificial_badness: *boolean*;   { has *b* been forced to zero? }
save_link: *pointer*;   { temporarily holds value of *link*(*cur_p*) }

shortfall: *scaled*;   { used in badness calculations }

This code is used in section 829.

831. ⟨ Make sure that *pi* is in the proper range 831 ⟩ ≡
  if *abs*(*pi*) ≥ *inf_penalty* **then**
    if *pi* > 0 **then return**   { this breakpoint is inhibited by infinite penalty }
    else *pi* ← *eject_penalty*   { this breakpoint will be forced }

This code is used in section 829.

832.   The following code uses the fact that *type*(*last_active*) ≠ *delta_node*.
  define *update_width*(**#**) ≡ *cur_active_width*[**#**] ← *cur_active_width*[**#**] + *mem*[*r* + **#**].*sc*
⟨ If node *r* is of type *delta_node*, update *cur_active_width*, set *prev_r* and *prev_prev_r*, then **goto**
    continue 832 ⟩ ≡
  if *type*(*r*) = *delta_node* **then**
    begin *do_all_six*(*update_width*); *prev_prev_r* ← *prev_r*; *prev_r* ← *r*; **goto** *continue*;
    end

This code is used in section 829.

833.   As we consider various ways to end a line at *cur_p*, in a given line number class, we
keep track of the best total demerits known, in an array with one entry for each of the fitness
classifications. For example, *minimal_demerits*[*tight_fit*] contains the fewest total demerits of
feasible line breaks ending at *cur_p* with a *tight_fit* line; *best_place*[*tight_fit*] points to the passive
node for the break before *cur_p* that achieves such an optimum; and *best_pl_line*[*tight_fit*] is the
line_number field in the active node corresponding to *best_place*[*tight_fit*]. When no feasible break
sequence is known, the *minimal_demerits* entries will be equal to *awful_bad*, which is $2^{30} - 1$.
Another variable, *minimum_demerits*, keeps track of the smallest value in the *minimal_demerits*
array.

  define *awful_bad* ≡ ´7777777777´   { more than a billion demerits }
⟨ Global variables 13 ⟩ +≡
minimal_demerits: **array** [*very_loose_fit* .. *tight_fit*] **of** *scaled*;
        { best total demerits known for current line class and position, given the fitness }
minimum_demerits: *scaled*;   { best total demerits known for current line class and position }
best_place: **array** [*very_loose_fit* .. *tight_fit*] **of** *pointer*;   { how to achieve *minimal_demerits* }
best_pl_line: **array** [*very_loose_fit* .. *tight_fit*] **of** *halfword*;   { corresponding line number }

---

active = macro, §162.
active_width: **array**, §823.
continue = 22, §15.
cur_active_width: **array**, §823.
cur_p: *pointer*, §828.
delta_node = 2, §822.
disc_node = 7, §145.
do_all_six = macro, §823.
done = 30, §15.
done1 = 31, §15.
eject_penalty = −10000, §157.
exit = 10, §15.
halfword = *min_halfword* ..
  max_halfword, §113.
hyphenated = 1, §819.
inf_penalty = 10000, §157.
internal_font_number = 0 .. *font_max*,
  §548.
last_active = macro, §819.
line_break: **procedure**, §815.
line_number = macro, §819.
link = macro, §118.
mem: **array**, §116.
null = macro, §115.
pointer = macro, §115.
printed_node: *pointer*, §821.
quarterword = 0 .. 255, §113.
sc = macro, §113.
scaled = *integer*, §101.
small_number = 0 .. 63, §101.
tight_fit = 3, §817.
type = macro, §133.
unhyphenated = 0, §819.
very_loose_fit = 0, §817.

834. ⟨Get ready to start line breaking 816⟩ +≡
  $minimum\_demerits \leftarrow awful\_bad$; $minimal\_demerits[tight\_fit] \leftarrow awful\_bad$;
  $minimal\_demerits[decent\_fit] \leftarrow awful\_bad$; $minimal\_demerits[loose\_fit] \leftarrow awful\_bad$;
  $minimal\_demerits[very\_loose\_fit] \leftarrow awful\_bad$;

835. The first part of the following code is part of TeX's inner loop, so we don't want to waste any time. The current active node, namely node r, contains the line number that will be considered next. At the end of the list we have arranged the data structure so that $r = last\_active$ and $line\_number(last\_active) > old\_l$.

⟨If a line number class has ended, create new active nodes for the best feasible breaks in that class;
      then **return** if $r = last\_active$, otherwise compute the new $line\_width$ 835⟩ ≡
  begin $l \leftarrow line\_number(r)$;
  if $l > old\_l$ **then**
    begin   { now we are no longer in the inner loop }
    if $(minimum\_demerits < awful\_bad) \wedge ((old\_l \neq easy\_line) \vee (r = last\_active))$ **then**
      ⟨Create new active nodes for the best feasible breaks just found 836⟩;
    if $r = last\_active$ **then return**;
    ⟨Compute the new line width 850⟩;
    end;
  end

This code is used in section 829.

836. It is not necessary to create new active nodes having $minimal\_demerits$ greater than $minimum\_demerits + abs(adj\_demerits)$, since such active nodes will never be chosen in the final paragraph breaks. This observation allows us to omit a substantial number of feasible breakpoints from further consideration.

⟨Create new active nodes for the best feasible breaks just found 836⟩ ≡
  begin if no_break_yet **then** ⟨Compute the values of $break\_width$ 837⟩;
  ⟨Insert a delta node to prepare for breaks at cur_p 843⟩;
  $minimum\_demerits \leftarrow minimum\_demerits + abs(adj\_demerits)$;
  for $fit\_class \leftarrow very\_loose\_fit$ **to** $tight\_fit$ **do**
    begin if $minimal\_demerits[fit\_class] \leq minimum\_demerits$ **then**
      ⟨Insert a new active node from $best\_place[fit\_class]$ to cur_p 845⟩;
    $minimal\_demerits[fit\_class] \leftarrow awful\_bad$;
    end;
  $minimum\_demerits \leftarrow awful\_bad$; ⟨Insert a delta node to prepare for the next active node 844⟩;
  end

This code is used in section 835.

837. When we insert a new active node for a break at cur_p, suppose this new node is to be placed just before active node a; then we essentially want to insert '$\delta\ cur\_p\ \delta'$' before a, where $\delta = \alpha(a) - \alpha(cur\_p)$ and $\delta' = \alpha(cur\_p) - \alpha(a)$ in the notation explained above. The cur_active_width array now holds $\gamma + \beta(cur\_p) - \alpha(a)$; so δ can be obtained by subtracting cur_active_width from the quantity $\gamma + \beta(cur\_p) - \alpha(cur\_p)$. The latter quantity can be regarded as the length of a line "from cur_p to cur_p"; we call it the $break\_width$ at cur_p.

The $break\_width$ is usually negative, since it consists of the background (which is normally zero) minus the width of nodes following cur_p that are eliminated after a break. If, for example, node *cur_p* is a glue node, the width of this glue is subtracted from the background; and we also look ahead to eliminate all subsequent glue and penalty and kern and math nodes, subtracting their widths as well.

Kern nodes for accents are treated specially: They do not disappear at a line break.

define *set_break_width_to_background*(**#**) ≡ *break_width*[**#**] ← *background*[**#**]

⟨ Compute the values of *break_width* 837 ⟩ ≡
 begin *no_break_yet* ← *false*; *do_all_six*(*set_break_width_to_background*);
 if (*break_type* = *unhyphenated*) ∨ (*cur_p* = *null*) **then**
  begin *s* ← *cur_p*;
  while *s* ≠ *null* **do**
   begin if *is_char_node*(*s*) **then goto** *done*;
   case *type*(*s*) **of**
   glue_node: ⟨ Subtract glue from *break_width* 838 ⟩;
   penalty_node: *do_nothing*;
   math_node, *kern_node*: **if** *subtype*(*s*) = *acc_kern* **then goto** *done*
    else *break_width*[1] ← *break_width*[1] − *width*(*s*);
   othercases goto *done*
   endcases;
   s ← *link*(*s*);
   end;
  end
 else ⟨ Compute the discretionary *break_width* values 840 ⟩;
done: **end**

This code is used in section 836.

838. ⟨ Subtract glue from *break_width* 838 ⟩ ≡
 begin *v* ← *glue_ptr*(*s*); *break_width*[1] ← *break_width*[1] − *width*(*v*);
 break_width[2 + *stretch_order*(*v*)] ← *break_width*[2 + *stretch_order*(*v*)] − *stretch*(*v*);
 break_width[6] ← *break_width*[6] − *shrink*(*v*);
 end

This code is used in section 837.

839. When *cur_p* is a discretionary break, the length of a line "from *cur_p* to *cur_p*" has to be defined properly so that the other calculations work out. Suppose that the pre-break text at *cur_p* has length l_0, the post-break text has length l_1, and the replacement text has length l. Suppose also that q is the node following the replacement text. Then length of a line from *cur_p* to q will be computed as $\gamma + \beta(q) - \alpha(cur\_p)$, where $\beta(q) = \beta(cur\_p) - l_0 + l$. The actual length will be the background plus l_1, so the length from *cur_p* to *cur_p* should be $\gamma + l_0 + l_1 - l$.

The value of l_0 need not be computed, since *line_break* will put it into the global variable *disc_width* before calling *try_break*.

⟨ Global variables 13 ⟩ +≡
disc_width: *scaled*;   { the length of discretionary material preceding a break }

840.   ⟨ Compute the discretionary *break_width* values 840 ⟩ ≡
  begin $t \leftarrow replace\_count(cur\_p)$; $s \leftarrow cur\_p$;
  while $t > 0$ **do**
    begin $decr(t)$; $s \leftarrow link(s)$; ⟨ Subtract the width of node s from *break_width* 841 ⟩;
    end;
  $s \leftarrow post\_break(cur\_p)$;
  while $s \neq null$ **do**
    begin ⟨ Add the width of node s to *break_width* 842 ⟩;
    $s \leftarrow link(s)$;
    end;
  $break\_width[1] \leftarrow break\_width[1] + disc\_width$;
  end

This code is used in section 837.

841.   Replacement texts and discretionary texts are supposed to contain only character nodes, kern nodes, ligature nodes, and box or rule nodes.

⟨ Subtract the width of node s from *break_width* 841 ⟩ ≡
  if *is_char_node*(s) **then**
    begin $f \leftarrow font(s)$; $break\_width[1] \leftarrow break\_width[1] - char\_width(f)(char\_info(f)(character(s)))$;
    end
  else case *type*(s) **of**
    ligature_node: **begin** $f \leftarrow font(lig\_char(s))$;
      $break\_width[1] \leftarrow break\_width[1] - char\_width(f)(char\_info(f)(character(lig\_char(s))))$;
      end;
    hlist_node, *vlist_node*, *rule_node*, *kern_node*: $break\_width[1] \leftarrow break\_width[1] - width(s)$;
    othercases *confusion*("disc1")
    endcases

This code is used in section 840.

842.   ⟨ Add the width of node s to *break_width* 842 ⟩ ≡
  if *is_char_node*(s) **then**
    begin $f \leftarrow font(s)$; $break\_width[1] \leftarrow break\_width[1] + char\_width(f)(char\_info(f)(character(s)))$;
    end
  else case *type*(s) **of**
    ligature_node: **begin** $f \leftarrow font(lig\_char(s))$;
      $break\_width[1] \leftarrow break\_width[1] + char\_width(f)(char\_info(f)(character(lig\_char(s))))$;
      end;

hlist_node, *vlist_node*, *rule_node*, *kern_node*: $break\_width[1] \leftarrow break\_width[1] + width(s)$;
othercases *confusion*("disc2")
endcases

This code is used in section 840.

843. We use the fact that $type(active) \neq delta\_node$.

define *convert_to_break_width*(**#**) $\equiv mem[prev\_r + \#].sc \leftarrow$
$\qquad\qquad mem[prev\_r + \#].sc - cur\_active\_width[\#] + break\_width[\#]$
define *store_break_width*(**#**) $\equiv active\_width[\#] \leftarrow break\_width[\#]$
define *new_delta_to_break_width*(**#**) $\equiv mem[q + \#].sc \leftarrow break\_width[\#] - cur\_active\_width[\#]$

⟨ Insert a delta node to prepare for breaks at *cur_p* 843 ⟩ ≡
  if $type(prev\_r) = delta\_node$ **then**   { modify an existing delta node }
    begin $do\_all\_six(convert\_to\_break\_width)$;
    end
  else if $prev\_r = active$ **then**   { no delta node needed at the beginning }
      begin $do\_all\_six(store\_break\_width)$;
      end
    else begin $q \leftarrow get\_node(delta\_node\_size)$; $link(q) \leftarrow r$; $type(q) \leftarrow delta\_node$; $subtype(q) \leftarrow 0$;
        { the *subtype* is not used }
      $do\_all\_six(new\_delta\_to\_break\_width)$; $link(prev\_r) \leftarrow q$; $prev\_prev\_r \leftarrow prev\_r$; $prev\_r \leftarrow q$;
    end

This code is used in section 836.

844. When the following code is performed, we will have just inserted at least one active node before *r*, so $type(prev\_r) \neq delta\_node$.

define *new_delta_from_break_width*(**#**) $\equiv mem[q + \#].sc \leftarrow cur\_active\_width[\#] - break\_width[\#]$

⟨ Insert a delta node to prepare for the next active node 844 ⟩ ≡
  if $r \neq last\_active$ **then**
    begin $q \leftarrow get\_node(delta\_node\_size)$; $link(q) \leftarrow r$; $type(q) \leftarrow delta\_node$; $subtype(q) \leftarrow 0$;
        { the *subtype* is not used }
    $do\_all\_six(new\_delta\_from\_break\_width)$; $link(prev\_r) \leftarrow q$; $prev\_prev\_r \leftarrow prev\_r$; $prev\_r \leftarrow q$;
    end

This code is used in section 836.

---

active = macro, §162.
active_width: **array**, §823.
break_width: **array**, §823.
char_info = macro, §554.
char_width = macro, §554.
character = macro, §134.
confusion: **procedure**, §95.
cur_active_width: **array**, §823.
cur_p: *pointer*, §828.
decr = macro, §16.
delta_node = 2, §822.
delta_node_size = 7, §822.
do_all_six = macro, §823.
f: *internal_font_number*, §830.

font = macro, §134.
get_node: **function**, §125.
hlist_node = 0, §135.
is_char_node = macro, §134.
kern_node = 11, §155.
last_active = macro, §819.
lig_char = macro, §143.
ligature_node = 6, §143.
line_break: **procedure**, §815.
link = macro, §118.
mem: **array**, §116.
null = macro, §115.
post_break = macro, §145.
prev_r: *pointer*, §829.

q: *pointer*, §830.
r: *pointer*, §829.
replace_count = macro, §145.
rule_node = 2, §138.
s: *pointer*, §830.
sc = macro, §113.
scaled = *integer*, §101.
subtype = macro, §133.
t: *quarterword*, §830.
try_break: **procedure**, §829.
type = macro, §133.
vlist_node = 1, §137.
width = macro, §135.

845. When we create an active node, we also create the corresponding passive node.

⟨ Insert a new active node from $best\_place[fit\_class]$ to cur_p 845 ⟩ ≡
> **begin** $q \leftarrow get\_node(passive\_node\_size)$; $link(q) \leftarrow passive$; $passive \leftarrow q$; $cur\_break(q) \leftarrow cur\_p$;
> **stat** $incr(pass\_number)$; $serial(q) \leftarrow pass\_number$; **tats**
> $prev\_break(q) \leftarrow best\_place[fit\_class]$;
> $q \leftarrow get\_node(active\_node\_size)$; $break\_node(q) \leftarrow passive$;
> $line\_number(q) \leftarrow best\_pl\_line[fit\_class] + 1$; $fitness(q) \leftarrow fit\_class$; $type(q) \leftarrow break\_type$;
> $total\_demerits(q) \leftarrow minimal\_demerits[fit\_class]$; $link(q) \leftarrow r$; $link(prev\_r) \leftarrow q$; $prev\_r \leftarrow q$;
> **stat if** $tracing\_paragraphs > 0$ **then** ⟨ Print a symbolic description of the new break node 846 ⟩;
> **tats**
> **end**

This code is used in section 836.

846. ⟨ Print a symbolic description of the new break node 846 ⟩ ≡
> **begin** $print\_nl("@@")$; $print\_int(serial(passive))$; $print(":_line_")$; $print\_int(line\_number(q) - 1)$;
> $print\_char(".")$; $print\_int(fit\_class)$;
> **if** $break\_type = hyphenated$ **then** $print\_char("-")$;
> $print("_t=")$; $print\_int(total\_demerits(q))$; $print("_->_@@")$;
> **if** $prev\_break(passive) = null$ **then** $print\_char("0")$
> **else** $print\_int(serial(prev\_break(passive)))$;
> **end**

This code is used in section 845.

847. The length of lines depends on whether the user has specified \parshape or \hangindent. If par_shape_ptr is not null, it points to a $(2n+1)$-word record in mem, where the $info$ in the first word contains the value of n, and the other $2n$ words contain the left margins and line lengths for the first n lines of the paragraph; the specifications for line n apply to all subsequent lines. If $par\_shape\_ptr = null$, the shape of the paragraph depends on the value of $n = hang\_after$; if $n \geq 0$, hanging indentation takes place on lines $n+1$, $n+2$, ..., otherwise it takes place on lines 1, ..., $|n|$. When hanging indentation is active, the left margin is $hang\_indent$, if $hang\_indent \geq 0$, else it is 0; the line length is $hsize - |hang\_indent|$. The normal setting is $par\_shape\_ptr = null$, $hang\_after = 0$, and $hang\_indent = 1$. Note that if $hang\_indent = 0$, the value of $hang\_after$ is irrelevant.

⟨ Global variables 13 ⟩ +≡
$easy\_line$: $halfword$;   { line numbers > $easy\_line$ are equivalent in break nodes }
$last\_special\_line$: $halfword$;   { line numbers > $last\_special\_line$ all have the same width }
$first\_width$: $scaled$;   { the width of all lines ≤ $last\_special\_line$, if no \parshape has been specified }
$second\_width$: $scaled$;   { the width of all lines > $last\_special\_line$ }
$first\_indent$: $scaled$;   { left margin to go with $first\_width$ }
$second\_indent$: $scaled$;   { left margin to go with $second\_width$ }

848.   We compute the values of *easy_line* and the other local variables relating to line length when the *line_break* procedure is initializing itself.

⟨ Get ready to start line breaking 816 ⟩ +≡
  if *par_shape_ptr* = *null* **then**
    if *hang_indent* = 0 **then**
      begin *last_special_line* ← 0; *second_width* ← *hsize*; *second_indent* ← 0;
      end
    else ⟨ Set line length parameters in preparation for hanging indentation 849 ⟩
  else begin *last_special_line* ← *info*(*par_shape_ptr*) − 1;
    second_width ← *mem*[*par_shape_ptr* + 2 * (*last_special_line* + 1)].*sc*;
    second_indent ← *mem*[*par_shape_ptr* + 2 * *last_special_line* + 1].*sc*;
    end;
  if *looseness* = 0 **then** *easy_line* ← *last_special_line*
  else *easy_line* ← *max_halfword*

849.   ⟨ Set line length parameters in preparation for hanging indentation 849 ⟩ ≡
  begin *last_special_line* ← *abs*(*hang_after*);
  if *hang_after* < 0 **then**
    begin *first_width* ← *hsize* − *abs*(*hang_indent*);
    if *hang_indent* ≥ 0 **then** *first_indent* ← *hang_indent*
    else *first_indent* ← 0;
    second_width ← *hsize*; *second_indent* ← 0;
    end
  else begin *first_width* ← *hsize*; *first_indent* ← 0; *second_width* ← *hsize* − *abs*(*hang_indent*);
    if *hang_indent* ≥ 0 **then** *second_indent* ← *hang_indent*
    else *second_indent* ← 0;
    end;
  end

This code is used in section 848.

---

active_node_size = 3, §819.
best_pl_line: **array**, §833.
best_place: **array**, §833.
break_node = macro, §819.
break_type: *small_number*, §829.
cur_break = macro, §821.
cur_p: *pointer*, §828.
fit_class: 0 .. 3, §830.
fitness = macro, §819.
get_node: **function**, §125.
halfword = *min_halfword* ..
  max_halfword, §113.
hang_after = macro, §236.
hang_indent = macro, §247.
hsize = macro, §247.

hyphenated = 1, §819.
incr = macro, §16.
info = macro, §118.
line_break: **procedure**, §815.
line_number = macro, §819.
link = macro, §118.
looseness = macro, §236.
max_halfword = macro, §110.
mem: **array**, §116.
minimal_demerits: **array**, §833.
null = macro, §115.
par_shape_ptr = macro, §230.
pass_number: *pointer*, §821.
passive: *pointer*, §821.
passive_node_size = 2, §821.

prev_break = macro, §821.
prev_r: *pointer*, §829.
print: **procedure**, §59.
print_char: **procedure**, §58.
print_int: **procedure**, §65.
print_nl: **procedure**, §62.
q: *pointer*, §830.
r: *pointer*, §829.
sc = macro, §113.
scaled = *integer*, §101.
serial = macro, §821.
total_demerits = macro, §819.
tracing_paragraphs = macro, §236.
type = macro, §133.

850. When we come to the following code, we have just encountered the first active node r whose *line_number* field contains l. Thus we want to compute the length of the lth line of the current paragraph. Furthermore, we want to set *old_l* to the last number in the class of line numbers equivalent to l.

⟨ Compute the new line width 850 ⟩ ≡
  if $l > easy\_line$ **then**
    begin *line_width* ← *second_width*; *old_l* ← *max_halfword* − 1;
    end
  else begin *old_l* ← l;
    if $l > last\_special\_line$ **then** *line_width* ← *second_width*
    else if *par_shape_ptr* = *null* **then** *line_width* ← *first_width*
      else *line_width* ← *mem*[*par_shape_ptr* + 2 ∗ l].*sc*;
    end

This code is used in section 835.

851. The remaining part of *try_break* deals with the calculation of demerits for a break from r to *cur_p*.

The first thing to do is calculate the badness, b. This value will always be between zero and *inf_bad* + 1; the latter value occurs only in the case of lines from r to *cur_p* that cannot shrink enough to fit the necessary width. In such cases, node r will be deactivated. We also deactivate node r when a break at *cur_p* is forced, since future breaks must go through a forced break.

⟨ Consider the demerits for a line from r to *cur_p*; deactivate node r if it should no longer be active; then
    goto *continue* if a line from r to *cur_p* is infeasible, otherwise record a new feasible break 851 ⟩ ≡
  begin stat *artificial_badness* ← *false*; **tats**
  shortfall ← *line_width* − *cur_active_width*[1];   { we're this much too short }
  if *shortfall* > 0 **then** ⟨ Set the value of b to the badness for stretching the line, and compute the
        corresponding *fit_class* 852 ⟩
  else ⟨ Set the value of b to the badness for shrinking the line, and compute the corresponding
        fit_class 853 ⟩;
  if $(b > inf\_bad) \lor (pi = eject\_penalty)$ **then** ⟨ Prepare to deactivate node r, and **goto** *deactivate*
        unless there is a reason to consider lines of text from r to *cur_p* 854 ⟩
  else begin *prev_r* ← r;
    if $b > threshold$ **then goto** *continue*;
    node_r_stays_active ← *true*;
    end;
  ⟨ Record a new feasible break 855 ⟩;
  if *node_r_stays_active* **then goto** *continue*;   { *prev_r* has been set to r }
deactivate: ⟨ Deactivate node r 860 ⟩;
  end

This code is used in section 829.

852. When a line must stretch, the available stretchability can be found in the subarray *cur_active_width*[2 .. 5], in units of points, fil, fill, and filll.

The present section is part of TeX's inner loop, and it is most often performed when the badness is infinite; therefore it is worth while to make a quick test for large width excess and small stretchability, before calling the *badness* subroutine.

⟨ Set the value of b to the badness for stretching the line, and compute the corresponding *fit_class* 852 ⟩ ≡
   if (*cur_active_width*[3] ≠ 0) ∨ (*cur_active_width*[4] ≠ 0) ∨ (*cur_active_width*[5] ≠ 0) **then**
      begin $b \leftarrow 0$; *fit_class* ← *decent_fit*; { infinite stretch }
      end
   else begin if *shortfall* > 7230584 **then**
        if *cur_active_width*[2] < 1663497 **then**
          begin $b \leftarrow$ *inf_bad*; *fit_class* ← *very_loose_fit*; **goto** *done1*;
          end;
     $b \leftarrow$ *badness*(*shortfall*, *cur_active_width*[2]);
     if $b > 12$ **then**
        if $b > 99$ **then** *fit_class* ← *very_loose_fit*
        else *fit_class* ← *loose_fit*
     else *fit_class* ← *decent_fit*;
   done1: **end**

This code is used in section 851.

853. Shrinkability is never infinite in a paragraph; we can shrink the line from r to *cur_p* by at most *cur_active_width*[6].

⟨ Set the value of b to the badness for shrinking the line, and compute the corresponding *fit_class* 853 ⟩ ≡
   begin if −*shortfall* > *cur_active_width*[6] **then** $b \leftarrow$ *inf_bad* + 1
   else $b \leftarrow$ *badness*(−*shortfall*, *cur_active_width*[6]);
   if $b > 12$ **then** *fit_class* ← *tight_fit* **else** *fit_class* ← *decent_fit*;
   end

This code is used in section 851.

---

artificial_badness: **boolean**, §830.
b: *halfword*, §830.
badness: **function**, §108.
continue = 22, §15.
cur_active_width: **array**, §823.
cur_p: *pointer*, §828.
deactivate = 60, §829.
decent_fit = 2, §817.
done1 = 31, §15.
easy_line: *halfword*, §847.
eject_penalty = −10000, §157.
first_width: *scaled*, §847.

fit_class: 0 .. 3, §830.
inf_bad = 10000, §108.
l: *halfword*, §830.
last_special_line: *halfword*, §847.
line_number = macro, §819.
loose_fit = 1, §817.
max_halfword = macro, §110.
mem: **array**, §116.
node_r_stays_active: *boolean*, §830.
null = macro, §115.
old_l: *halfword*, §829.

par_shape_ptr = macro, §230.
pi: *integer*, §829.
prev_r: *pointer*, §829.
r: *pointer*, §829.
sc = macro, §113.
second_width: *scaled*, §847.
shortfall: *scaled*, §830.
threshold: *integer*, §828.
tight_fit = 3, §817.
try_break: **procedure**, §829.
very_loose_fit = 0, §817.

854. During the second pass, we dare not lose all active nodes, lest we lose touch with the line breaks already found. The code shown here makes sure that such a catastrophe does not happen, by permitting overfull boxes as a last resort. This particular part of TeX was a source of several subtle bugs before the correct program logic was finally discovered; readers who seek to "improve" TeX should therefore think thrice before daring to make any changes here.

⟨ Prepare to deactivate node r, and **goto** *deactivate* unless there is a reason to consider lines of text from r to *cur_p* 854 ⟩ ≡
  begin if *second_pass* $\wedge$ (*minimum_demerits* $=$ *awful_bad*) $\wedge$ (*link*(*r*) $=$ *last_active*) $\wedge$ (*prev_r* $=$ *active*)
      then
    begin $b \leftarrow 0$;   { set badness zero, this break is forced }
    stat *artificial_badness* $\leftarrow$ *true*; **tats**
    end
  else if $b >$ *threshold* **then goto** *deactivate*;
  node_r_stays_active $\leftarrow$ *false*;
  end

This code is used in section 851.

855. When we get to this part of the code, the line from r to *cur_p* is feasible, its badness is b, and its fitness classification is *fit_class*. We don't want to make an active node for this break yet, but we will compute the total demerits and record them in the *minimal_demerits* array, if such a break is the current champion among all ways to get to *cur_p* in a given line-number class and fitness class.

⟨ Record a new feasible break 855 ⟩ ≡
  ⟨ Compute the demerits, d, from r to *cur_p* 859 ⟩;
  stat if *tracing_paragraphs* > 0 **then** ⟨ Print a symbolic description of this feasible break 856 ⟩;
  tats
  $d \leftarrow d + total\_demerits(r)$;   { this is the minimum total demerits from the beginning to *cur_p* via r }
  if $d \leq minimal\_demerits[fit\_class]$ **then**
    begin *minimal_demerits*[*fit_class*] $\leftarrow d$; *best_place*[*fit_class*] $\leftarrow$ *break_node*(*r*);
    best_pl_line[*fit_class*] $\leftarrow l$;
    if $d < minimum\_demerits$ **then** *minimum_demerits* $\leftarrow d$;
    end

This code is used in section 851.

856. ⟨ Print a symbolic description of this feasible break 856 ⟩ ≡
  begin if *printed_node* $\neq$ *cur_p* **then**
    ⟨ Print the list between *printed_node* and *cur_p*, then set *printed_node* $\leftarrow$ *cur_p* 857 ⟩;
  print_nl("@");
  if *cur_p* $=$ *null* **then** *print_esc*("par")
  else if *type*(*cur_p*) $\neq$ *glue_node* **then**
      begin if *type*(*cur_p*) $=$ *penalty_node* **then** *print_esc*("penalty")
      else if *type*(*cur_p*) $=$ *disc_node* **then** *print_esc*("discretionary")
        else if *type*(*cur_p*) $=$ *kern_node* **then** *print_esc*("kern")
          else *print_esc*("math");
      end;
  print("␣via␣@@");
  if *break_node*(*r*) $=$ *null* **then** *print_char*("0")

```
else print_int(serial(break_node(r)));
print("␣b=");
if artificial_badness then print_char("*") else print_int(b);
print("␣p="); print_int(pi); print("␣d="); print_int(d);
end
```

This code is used in section 855.

857. ⟨ Print the list between *printed_node* and *cur_p*, then set *printed_node* ← *cur_p* 857 ⟩ ≡
```
begin print_nl("");
if cur_p = null then short_display(link(printed_node))
else begin save_link ← link(cur_p); link(cur_p) ← null; print_nl("");
  short_display(link(printed_node)); link(cur_p) ← save_link;
  end;
printed_node ← cur_p;
end
```

This code is used in section 856.

858.   When the data for a discretionary break is being displayed, we will have printed the *pre_break* and *post_break* lists; we want to skip over the third list, so that the discretionary data will not appear twice. The following code is performed at the very end of *try_break*.

⟨ Update the value of *printed_node* for symbolic displays 858 ⟩ ≡
```
if cur_p = printed_node then
  if cur_p ≠ null then
    if type(cur_p) = disc_node then
      begin t ← replace_count(cur_p);
      while t > 0 do
        begin decr(t); printed_node ← link(printed_node);
        end;
      end
```

This code is used in section 829.

---

active = macro, §162.
artificial_badness: boolean, §830.
awful_bad = macro, §833.
b: halfword, §830.
best_pl_line: **array**, §833.
best_place: **array**, §833.
break_node = macro, §819.
cur_p: pointer, §828.
d: integer, §830.
deactivate = 60, §829.
decr = macro, §16.
disc_node = 7, §145.
fit_class: 0 . . 3, §830.
glue_node = 10, §149.
kern_node = 11, §155.

l: halfword, §830.
last_active = macro, §819.
link = macro, §118.
minimal_demerits: **array**, §833.
minimum_demerits: scaled, §833.
node_r_stays_active: boolean, §830.
null = macro, §115.
penalty_node = 12, §157.
pi: integer, §829.
post_break = macro, §145.
pre_break = macro, §145.
prev_r: pointer, §829.
print: **procedure**, §59.
print_char: **procedure**, §58.
print_esc: **procedure**, §63.

print_int: **procedure**, §65.
print_nl: **procedure**, §62.
printed_node: pointer, §821.
r: pointer, §829.
replace_count = macro, §145.
save_link: pointer, §830.
second_pass: boolean, §828.
serial = macro, §821.
short_display: **procedure**, §174.
t: quarterword, §830.
threshold: integer, §828.
total_demerits = macro, §819.
tracing_paragraphs = macro, §236.
try_break: **procedure**, §829.
type = macro, §133.

859. ⟨ Compute the demerits, d, from r to cur_p 859 ⟩ ≡
  $d \leftarrow line\_penalty + b$; $d \leftarrow d * d$;
  if $pi \neq 0$ **then**
    if $pi > 0$ **then** $d \leftarrow d + pi * pi$
    else if $pi > eject\_penalty$ **then** $d \leftarrow d - pi * pi$;
  if $(break\_type = hyphenated) \wedge (type(r) = hyphenated)$ **then**
    if $cur\_p \neq null$ **then** $d \leftarrow d + double\_hyphen\_demerits$
    else $d \leftarrow d + final\_hyphen\_demerits$;
  if $abs(fit\_class - fitness(r)) > 1$ **then** $d \leftarrow d + adj\_demerits$
This code is used in section 855.

860. When an active node disappears, we must delete an adjacent delta node if the active node was at the beginning or the end of the active list, or if it was surrounded by delta nodes. We also must preserve the property that cur_active_width represents the length of material from $link(prev\_r)$ to cur_p.

  define $combine\_two\_deltas(\#) \equiv mem[prev\_r + \#].sc \leftarrow mem[prev\_r + \#].sc + mem[r + \#].sc$
  define $downdate\_width(\#) \equiv cur\_active\_width[\#] \leftarrow cur\_active\_width[\#] - mem[prev\_r + \#].sc$

⟨ Deactivate node r 860 ⟩ ≡
  $link(prev\_r) \leftarrow link(r)$; $free\_node(r, active\_node\_size)$;
  if $prev\_r = active$ **then** ⟨ Update the active widths, since the first active node has been deleted 861 ⟩
  else if $type(prev\_r) = delta\_node$ **then**
    begin $r \leftarrow link(prev\_r)$;
    if $r = last\_active$ **then**
      begin $do\_all\_six(downdate\_width)$; $link(prev\_prev\_r) \leftarrow last\_active$;
      $free\_node(prev\_r, delta\_node\_size)$; $prev\_r \leftarrow prev\_prev\_r$;
      end
    else if $type(r) = delta\_node$ **then**
      begin $do\_all\_six(update\_width)$; $do\_all\_six(combine\_two\_deltas)$; $link(prev\_r) \leftarrow link(r)$;
      $free\_node(r, delta\_node\_size)$;
      end;
    end
This code is used in section 851.

861. The following code uses the fact that $type(last\_active) \neq delta\_node$. If the active list has just become empty, we do not need to update the $active\_width$ array, since it will be initialized when an active node is next inserted.

  define $update\_active(\#) \equiv active\_width[\#] \leftarrow active\_width[\#] + mem[r + \#].sc$

⟨ Update the active widths, since the first active node has been deleted 861 ⟩ ≡
  begin $r \leftarrow link(active)$;
  if $type(r) = delta\_node$ **then**
    begin $do\_all\_six(update\_active)$; $do\_all\_six(copy\_to\_cur\_active)$; $link(active) \leftarrow link(r)$;
    $free\_node(r, delta\_node\_size)$;
    end;
  end
This code is used in section 860.

active = macro, §162.
active_node_size = 3, §819.
active_width: **array**, §823.
adj_demerits = macro, §236.
b: *halfword*, §830.
break_type: *small_number*, §829.
copy_to_cur_active = macro, §829.
cur_active_width: **array**, §823.
cur_p: *pointer*, §828.
d: *integer*, §830.
delta_node = 2, §822.

delta_node_size = 7, §822.
do_all_six = macro, §823.
double_hyphen_demerits = macro,
    §236.
eject_penalty = −10000, §157.
final_hyphen_demerits = macro,
    §236.
fit_class: 0 .. 3, §830.
fitness = macro, §819.
free_node: **procedure**, §130.
hyphenated = 1, §819.

last_active = macro, §819.
line_penalty = macro, §236.
link = macro, §118.
mem: **array**, §116.
null = macro, §115.
pi: *integer*, §829.
prev_r: *pointer*, §829.
r: *pointer*, §829.
sc = macro, §113.
type = macro, §133.
update_width = macro, §832.

862. Breaking paragraphs into lines, continued. So far we have gotten a little way into the *line_break* routine, having covered its important *try_break* subroutine. Now let's consider the rest of the process.

The main loop of *line_break* traverses the given hlist, starting at *link*(*temp_head*), and calls *try_break* at each legal breakpoint. A variable called *auto_breaking* is set to true except within math formulas, since glue nodes are not legal breakpoints when they appear in formulas.

The current node of interest in the hlist is pointed to by *cur_p*. Another variable, *prev_p*, is usually one step behind *cur_p*, but the real meaning of *prev_p* is this: If *type*(*cur_p*) = *glue_node* then *cur_p* is a legal breakpoint if and only if *auto_breaking* is true and *prev_p* does not point to a glue node, penalty node, kern node, or math node.

The following declarations provide for a few other local variables that are used in special calculations.

⟨ Local variables for line breaking 862 ⟩ ≡
auto_breaking: *boolean*; { is node *cur_p* outside a formula? }
prev_p: *pointer*; { helps to determine when glue nodes are breakpoints }
q, r, s: *pointer*; { miscellaneous nodes of temporary interest }
f: *internal_font_number*; { used when calculating character widths }
See also section 893.

This code is used in section 815.

863. The 'loop' in the following code is performed at most twice per call of *line_break*, since it is actually a pass over the entire paragraph.

⟨ Find optimal breakpoints 863 ⟩ ≡
  threshold ← *pretolerance*;
  if *threshold* ≥ 0 **then**
    begin stat if *tracing_paragraphs* > 0 **then**
      begin *begin_diagnostic*; *print_nl*("@firstpass"); **end**; **tats**
    second_pass ← *false*;
    end
  else begin *threshold* ← *tolerance*; *second_pass* ← *true*;
    stat if *tracing_paragraphs* > 0 **then** *begin_diagnostic*; **tats**
    end;
  loop begin ⟨ Create an active breakpoint representing the beginning of the paragraph 864 ⟩;
    cur_p ← *link*(*temp_head*); *auto_breaking* ← *true*;
    prev_p ← *cur_p*; { glue at beginning is not a legal breakpoint }
    while (*cur_p* ≠ *null*) ∧ (*link*(*active*) ≠ *last_active*) **do**
      ⟨ Call *try_break* if *cur_p* is a legal breakpoint; on the second pass, also try to hyphenate the next
        word, if *cur_p* is a glue node; then advance *cur_p* to the next node of the paragraph that
        could possibly be a legal breakpoint 866 ⟩;
    if *cur_p* = *null* **then** ⟨ Try the final line break at the end of the paragraph, and **goto** *done* if the
        desired breakpoints have been found 873 ⟩;
    ⟨ Clean up the memory by removing the break nodes 865 ⟩;
    stat if *tracing_paragraphs* > 0 **then** *print_nl*("@secondpass"); **tats**
    threshold ← *tolerance*; *second_pass* ← *true*; { if at first you don't succeed, ... }
    end;
done: **stat if** *tracing_paragraphs* > 0 **then** *end_diagnostic*(*true*); **tats**

This code is used in section 815.

864.   The active node that represents the starting point does not need a corresponding passive node.

$\quad$ **define** $\mathit{store\_background}\,(\texttt{\#}) \equiv \mathit{active\_width}\,[\texttt{\#}] \leftarrow \mathit{background}\,[\texttt{\#}]$

⟨ Create an active breakpoint representing the beginning of the paragraph 864 ⟩ ≡
$\quad q \leftarrow \mathit{get\_node}(\mathit{active\_node\_size});\ \mathit{type}(q) \leftarrow \mathit{unhyphenated};\ \mathit{fitness}(q) \leftarrow \mathit{decent\_fit};$
$\quad \mathit{link}(q) \leftarrow \mathit{last\_active};\ \mathit{break\_node}(q) \leftarrow \mathit{null};\ \mathit{line\_number}(q) \leftarrow \mathit{prev\_graf} + 1;\ \mathit{total\_demerits}(q) \leftarrow 0;$
$\quad \mathit{link}(\mathit{active}) \leftarrow q;\ \mathit{do\_all\_six}(\mathit{store\_background});$
$\quad \mathit{passive} \leftarrow \mathit{null};\ \mathit{printed\_node} \leftarrow \mathit{temp\_head};\ \mathit{pass\_number} \leftarrow 0;\ \mathit{font\_in\_short\_display} \leftarrow \mathit{null\_font}$

This code is used in section 863.

865.   ⟨ Clean up the memory by removing the break nodes 865 ⟩ ≡
$\quad q \leftarrow \mathit{link}(\mathit{active});$
$\quad$ **while** $q \neq \mathit{last\_active}$ **do**
$\quad\quad$ **begin** $\mathit{cur\_p} \leftarrow \mathit{link}(q);$
$\quad\quad$ **if** $\mathit{type}(q) = \mathit{delta\_node}$ **then** $\mathit{free\_node}(q, \mathit{delta\_node\_size})$
$\quad\quad$ **else** $\mathit{free\_node}(q, \mathit{active\_node\_size});$
$\quad\quad q \leftarrow \mathit{cur\_p};$
$\quad\quad$ **end**;
$\quad q \leftarrow \mathit{passive};$
$\quad$ **while** $q \neq \mathit{null}$ **do**
$\quad\quad$ **begin** $\mathit{cur\_p} \leftarrow \mathit{link}(q);\ \mathit{free\_node}(q, \mathit{passive\_node\_size});\ q \leftarrow \mathit{cur\_p};$
$\quad\quad$ **end**

This code is used in sections 815 and 863.

---

active = macro, §162.
active_node_size = 3, §819.
active_width: **array**, §823.
background: **array**, §823.
begin_diagnostic: **procedure**, §245.
break_node = macro, §819.
cur_p: *pointer*, §828.
decent_fit = 2, §817.
delta_node = 2, §822.
delta_node_size = 7, §822.
do_all_six = macro, §823.
done = 30, §15.
end_diagnostic: **procedure**, §245.
fitness = macro, §819.
font_in_short_display: *integer*, §173.

free_node: **procedure**, §130.
get_node: **function**, §125.
glue_node = 10, §149.
internal_font_number = 0 .. *font_max*,
$\quad$§548.
last_active = macro, §819.
line_break: **procedure**, §815.
line_number = macro, §819.
link = macro, §118.
null = macro, §115.
null_font = macro, §232.
pass_number: *pointer*, §821.
passive: *pointer*, §821.
passive_node_size = 2, §821.

pointer = macro, §115.
pretolerance = macro, §236.
prev_graf = macro, §213.
print_nl: **procedure**, §62.
printed_node: *pointer*, §821.
second_pass: *boolean*, §828.
temp_head = macro, §162.
threshold: *integer*, §828.
tolerance = macro, §236.
total_demerits = macro, §819.
tracing_paragraphs = macro, §236.
try_break: **procedure**, §829.
type = macro, §133.
unhyphenated = 0, §819.

866. Here is the main switch in the *line_break* routine, where legal breaks are determined. As we move through the hlist, we need to keep the *active_width* array up to date, so that the badness of individual lines is readily calculated by *try_break*. It is convenient to use the short name *act_width* for the component of active width that represents real width as opposed to glue.

> **define** *act_width* ≡ *active_width*[1]   { length from first active node to current node }
> **define** *kern_break* ≡
>   **begin**
>   **if** ¬*is_char_node*(*link*(*cur_p*)) ∧ *auto_breaking* **then**
>   **if** *type*(*link*(*cur_p*)) = *glue_node* **then** *try_break*(0, *unhyphenated*);
>   *act_width* ← *act_width* + *width*(*cur_p*);
>   **end**

⟨ Call *try_break* if *cur_p* is a legal breakpoint; on the second pass, also try to hyphenate the next word, if
      cur_p is a glue node; then advance *cur_p* to the next node of the paragraph that could possibly
      be a legal breakpoint 866 ⟩ ≡
  begin if *is_char_node*(*cur_p*) **then**
    ⟨ Advance *cur_p* to the node following the present string of characters 867 ⟩;
  case *type*(*cur_p*) **of**
  hlist_node, *vlist_node*, *rule_node*: *act_width* ← *act_width* + *width*(*cur_p*);
  whatsit_node: ⟨ Advance past a whatsit node in the *line_break* loop 1362 ⟩;
  glue_node: **begin** ⟨ If node *cur_p* is a legal breakpoint, call *try_break* 868 ⟩;
        ⟨ Update the active widths by including the glue in *glue_ptr*(*cur_p*) 869 ⟩;
        if *second_pass* ∧ *auto_breaking* **then** ⟨ Try to hyphenate the following word 894 ⟩;
        end;
  kern_node: *kern_break*;
  ligature_node: **begin** *f* ← *font*(*lig_char*(*cur_p*));
        act_width ← *act_width* + *char_width*(*f*)(*char_info*(*f*)(*character*(*lig_char*(*cur_p*)))));
        end;
  disc_node: ⟨ Try to break after a discretionary fragment 870 ⟩;
  math_node: **begin** *auto_breaking* ← (*subtype*(*cur_p*) = *after*); *kern_break*;
        end;
  penalty_node: *try_break*(*penalty*(*cur_p*), *unhyphenated*);
  mark_node, *ins_node*, *adjust_node*: *do_nothing*;
  othercases *confusion*("paragraph")
  endcases;
  prev_p ← *cur_p*; *cur_p* ← *link*(*cur_p*);
  end

This code is used in section 863.

867. The code that passes over the characters of words in a paragraph is part of TeX's inner loop, so it has been streamlined for speed. We use the fact that '\parfillskip' glue appears at the end of each paragraph; it is therefore unnecessary to check if *link*(*cur_p*) = *null* when *cur_p* is a character node.

⟨ Advance *cur_p* to the node following the present string of characters 867 ⟩ ≡
  begin *prev_p* ← *cur_p*;
  repeat *f* ← *font*(*cur_p*); *act_width* ← *act_width* + *char_width*(*f*)(*char_info*(*f*)(*character*(*cur_p*)));
    cur_p ← *link*(*cur_p*);
  until ¬*is_char_node*(*cur_p*);

end

This code is used in section 866.

868.   When node *cur_p* is a glue node, we look at *prev_p* to see whether or not a breakpoint is legal at *cur_p*, as explained above.

⟨ If node *cur_p* is a legal breakpoint, call *try_break* 868 ⟩ ≡
    if *auto_breaking* **then**
        begin if *is_char_node*(*prev_p*) **then** *try_break*(0, *unhyphenated*)
        else if *precedes_break*(*prev_p*) **then** *try_break*(0, *unhyphenated*);
        end

This code is used in section 866.

869.   ⟨ Update the active widths by including the glue in *glue_ptr*(*cur_p*) 869 ⟩ ≡
    begin *check_shrinkage*(*glue_ptr*(*cur_p*)); *q* ← *glue_ptr*(*cur_p*); *act_width* ← *act_width* + *width*(*q*);
    active_width[2 + *stretch_order*(*q*)] ← *active_width*[2 + *stretch_order*(*q*)] + *stretch*(*q*);
    active_width[6] ← *active_width*[6] + *shrink*(*q*);
    end

This code is used in section 866.

870.   The following code knows that discretionary texts contain only character nodes, kern nodes, box nodes, rule nodes, and ligature nodes.

⟨ Try to break after a discretionary fragment 870 ⟩ ≡
    begin *s* ← *pre_break*(*cur_p*); *disc_width* ← 0;
    if *s* = *null* **then** *try_break*(*ex_hyphen_penalty*, *hyphenated*)
    else begin repeat ⟨ Add the width of node *s* to *disc_width* 871 ⟩;
        s ← *link*(*s*);
    until *s* = *null*;
    act_width ← *act_width* + *disc_width*; *try_break*(*hyphen_penalty*, *hyphenated*);
    act_width ← *act_width* − *disc_width*;
    end;
    end

This code is used in section 866.

---

active_width: **array**, §823.
adjust_node = 5, §142.
after = 1, §147.
auto_breaking: *boolean*, §862.
char_info = macro, §554.
char_width = macro, §554.
character = macro, §134.
check_shrinkage = macro, §825.
confusion: **procedure**, §95.
cur_p: *pointer*, §828.
disc_node = 7, §145.
disc_width: *scaled*, §839.
do_nothing = macro, §16.
ex_hyphen_penalty = macro, §236.
f: *internal_font_number*, §862.
font = macro, §134.
glue_node = 10, §149.

glue_ptr = macro, §149.
hlist_node = 0, §135.
hyphen_penalty = macro, §236.
hyphenated = 1, §819.
ins_node = 3, §140.
is_char_node = macro, §134.
kern_node = 11, §155.
lig_char = macro, §143.
ligature_node = 6, §143.
line_break: **procedure**, §815.
link = macro, §118.
mark_node = 4, §141.
math_node = 9, §147.
null = macro, §115.
penalty = macro, §157.
penalty_node = 12, §157.
pre_break = macro, §145.

precedes_break = macro, §148.
prev_p: *pointer*, §862.
q: *pointer*, §862.
rule_node = 2, §138.
s: *pointer*, §862.
second_pass: *boolean*, §828.
shrink = macro, §150.
stretch = macro, §150.
stretch_order = macro, §150.
subtype = macro, §133.
try_break: **procedure**, §829.
type = macro, §133.
unhyphenated = 0, §819.
vlist_node = 1, §137.
whatsit_node = 8, §146.
width = macro, §135.

871. ⟨ Add the width of node s to $disc\_width$ 871 ⟩ ≡

  if $is\_char\_node(s)$ **then**
    begin $f \leftarrow font(s)$; $disc\_width \leftarrow disc\_width + char\_width(f)(char\_info(f)(character(s)))$;
    end
  else case $type(s)$ **of**
    $ligature\_node$: **begin** $f \leftarrow font(lig\_char(s))$;
      $disc\_width \leftarrow disc\_width + char\_width(f)(char\_info(f)(character(lig\_char(s))))$;
      end;
    $hlist\_node, vlist\_node, rule\_node, kern\_node$: $disc\_width \leftarrow disc\_width + width(s)$;
    othercases $confusion(\texttt{"disc3"})$
    endcases

This code is used in section 870.

872. The forced line break at the paragraph's end will reduce the list of breakpoints so that all active nodes represent breaks at $cur\_p = null$. On the first pass, we insist on finding an active node that has the correct "looseness." On the second pass, there will be at least one active node, and we will match the desired looseness as well as we can.

The global variable $best\_bet$ will be set to the active node for the best way to break the paragraph, and a few other variables are used to help determine what is best.

⟨ Global variables 13 ⟩ +≡

$best\_bet$: $pointer$; { use this passive node and its predecessors }
$fewest\_demerits$: $integer$; { the demerits associated with $best\_bet$ }
$best\_line$: $halfword$; { line number following the last line of the new paragraph }
$actual\_looseness$: $integer$; { the difference between $line\_number(best\_bet)$ and the optimum $best\_line$ }
$line\_diff$: $integer$; { the difference between the current line number and the optimum $best\_line$ }

873. ⟨ Try the final line break at the end of the paragraph, and **goto** *done* if the desired breakpoints have been found 873 ⟩ ≡

  begin $try\_break(eject\_penalty, hyphenated)$;
  if $link(active) \neq last\_active$ **then**
    begin ⟨ Find an active node with fewest demerits 874 ⟩;
    if $looseness = 0$ **then** **goto** *done*;
    ⟨ Find the best active node for the desired looseness 875 ⟩;
    if $(actual\_looseness = looseness) \vee second\_pass$ **then** **goto** *done*;
    end;
  end

This code is used in section 863.

874. ⟨ Find an active node with fewest demerits 874 ⟩ ≡

  $r \leftarrow link(active)$; $fewest\_demerits \leftarrow awful\_bad$;
  repeat if $type(r) \neq delta\_node$ **then**
    if $total\_demerits(r) < fewest\_demerits$ **then**
      begin $fewest\_demerits \leftarrow total\_demerits(r)$; $best\_bet \leftarrow r$;
      end;
    $r \leftarrow link(r)$;
  until $r = last\_active$;
  $best\_line \leftarrow line\_number(best\_bet)$

This code is used in section 873.

875. The adjustment for a desired looseness is a slightly more complicated version of the loop just considered. Note that if a paragraph is broken into segments by displayed equations, each segment will be subject to the looseness calculation, independently of the other segments.

⟨ Find the best active node for the desired looseness 875 ⟩ ≡
    begin $r \leftarrow link(active);\ actual\_looseness \leftarrow 0;$
    repeat if $type(r) \neq delta\_node$ **then**
        begin $line\_diff \leftarrow line\_number(r) - best\_line;$
        if $((line\_diff < actual\_looseness) \wedge (looseness \leq line\_diff)) \vee$
                $((line\_diff > actual\_looseness) \wedge (looseness \geq line\_diff))$ **then**
            begin $best\_bet \leftarrow r;\ actual\_looseness \leftarrow line\_diff;\ fewest\_demerits \leftarrow total\_demerits(r);$
        end
        else if $(line\_diff = actual\_looseness) \wedge (total\_demerits(r) < fewest\_demerits)$ **then**
            begin $best\_bet \leftarrow r;\ fewest\_demerits \leftarrow total\_demerits(r);$
            end;
        end;
      $r \leftarrow link(r);$
    until $r = last\_active;$
    $best\_line \leftarrow line\_number(best\_bet);$
    end

This code is used in section 873.

876. Once the best sequence of breakpoints has been found (hurray), we call on the procedure *post_line_break* to finish the remainder of the work. (By introducing this subprocedure, we are able to keep *line_break* from getting extremely long.)

⟨ Break the paragraph at the chosen breakpoints, justify the resulting lines to the correct widths, and
    append them to the current vertical list 876 ⟩ ≡
    $post\_line\_break(final\_widow\_penalty)$

This code is used in section 815.

---

active = macro, §162.	*font* = macro, §134.	*looseness* = macro, §236.
awful_bad = macro, §833.	*halfword* = *min_halfword* . .	*null* = macro, §115.
char_info = macro, §554.	*max_halfword*, §113.	*pointer* = macro, §115.
char_width = macro, §554.	*hlist_node* = 0, §135.	*post_line_break*: **procedure**, §877.
character = macro, §134.	*hyphenated* = 1, §819.	*r*: *pointer*, §862.
confusion: **procedure**, §95.	*is_char_node* = macro, §134.	*rule_node* = 2, §138.
cur_p: *pointer*, §828.	*kern_node* = 11, §155.	*s*: *pointer*, §862.
delta_node = 2, §822.	*last_active* = macro, §819.	*second_pass*: *boolean*, §828.
disc_width: *scaled*, §839.	*lig_char* = macro, §143.	*total_demerits* = macro, §819.
done = 30, §15.	*ligature_node* = 6, §143.	*try_break*: **procedure**, §829.
eject_penalty = −10000, §157.	*line_break*: **procedure**, §815.	*type* = macro, §133.
f: *internal_font_number*, §862.	*line_number* = macro, §819.	*vlist_node* = 1, §137.
final_widow_penalty: *integer*, §815.	*link* = macro, §118.	*width* = macro, §135.

877. The total number of lines that will be set by *post_line_break* is *best_line* − *prev_graf* − 1. The last breakpoint is specified by *break_node*(*best_bet*), and this passive node points to the other breakpoints via the *prev_break* links. The finishing-up phase starts by linking the relevant passive nodes in forward order, changing *prev_break* to *next_break*. (The *next_break* fields actually reside in the same memory space as the *prev_break* fields did, but we give them a new name because of their new significance.) Then the lines are justified, one by one.

define *next_break* ≡ *prev_break*   { new name for *prev_break* after links are reversed }

⟨ Declare subprocedures for *line_break* 826 ⟩ +≡
procedure *post_line_break*(*final_widow_penalty* : *integer*);
  label *done*, *done1*;
  var *q*, *r*, *s*: *pointer*;   { temporary registers for list manipulation }
    disc_break: *boolean*;   { was the current break at a discretionary node? }
    cur_width: *scaled*;   { width of line number *cur_line* }
    cur_indent: *scaled*;   { left margin of line number *cur_line* }
    t: *quarterword*;   { used for replacement counts in discretionary nodes }
    pen: *integer*;   { use when calculating penalties between lines }
    cur_line: *halfword*;   { the current line number being justified }
  begin ⟨ Reverse the links of the relevant passive nodes, setting *cur_p* to the first breakpoint 878 ⟩;
  cur_line ← *prev_graf* + 1;
  repeat ⟨ Justify the line ending at breakpoint *cur_p*, and append it to the current vertical list,
       together with associated penalties and other insertions 880 ⟩;
    incr(*cur_line*);   *cur_p* ← *next_break*(*cur_p*);
    if *cur_p* ≠ *null* **then** ⟨ Prune unwanted nodes at the beginning of the next line 879 ⟩;
  until *cur_p* = *null*;
  if (*cur_line* ≠ *best_line*) ∨ (*link*(*temp_head*) ≠ *null*) **then** *confusion*("line␣breaking");
  prev_graf ← *best_line* − 1;
  end;

878. The job of reversing links in a list is conveniently regarded as the job of taking items off one stack and putting them on another. In this case we take them off a stack pointed to by *q* and having *prev_break* fields; we put them on a stack pointed to by *cur_p* and having *next_break* fields. Node *r* is the passive node being moved from stack to stack.

⟨ Reverse the links of the relevant passive nodes, setting *cur_p* to the first breakpoint 878 ⟩ ≡
  q ← *break_node*(*best_bet*);   *cur_p* ← *null*;
  repeat *r* ← *q*;   *q* ← *prev_break*(*q*);   *next_break*(*r*) ← *cur_p*;   *cur_p* ← *r*;
  until *q* = *null*
This code is used in section 877.

879. Glue and penalty and kern and math nodes are deleted at the beginning of a line, except in the unusual case that the node to be deleted is actually one of the chosen breakpoints. The pruning done here is designed to match the lookahead computation in *try_break*, where the *break_width* values are computed for non-discretionary breakpoints.

⟨ Prune unwanted nodes at the beginning of the next line 879 ⟩ ≡
  begin *r* ← *temp_head*;
  loop begin *q* ← *link*(*r*);
    if *q* = *cur_break*(*cur_p*) **then goto** *done1*;   { *cur_break*(*cur_p*) is the next breakpoint }
      { now *q* cannot be *null* }

> **if** *is_char_node*(*q*) **then goto** *done1*;
> **if** *non_discardable*(*q*) **then goto** *done1*;
> **if** *subtype*(*q*) = *acc_kern* **then**
>   **if** *type*(*q*) = *kern_node* **then goto** *done1*;
> *r* ← *q*;   { now *type*(*q*) = *glue_node*, *kern_node*, *math_node* or *penalty_node* }
> **end**;
> *done1*: **if** *r* ≠ *temp_head* **then**
>   **begin** *link*(*r*) ← *null*; *flush_node_list*(*link*(*temp_head*)); *link*(*temp_head*) ← *q*;
>   **end**;
> **end**

This code is used in section 877.

880.   The current line to be justified appears in a horizontal list starting at *link*(*temp_head*) and ending at *cur_break*(*cur_p*). If *cur_break*(*cur_p*) is a glue node, we reset the glue to equal the *right_skip* glue; otherwise we append the *right_skip* glue at the right. If *cur_break*(*cur_p*) is a discretionary node, we modify the list so that the discretionary break is compulsory, and we set *disc_break* to *true*. We also append the *left_skip* glue at the left of the line, unless it is zero.

⟨ Justify the line ending at breakpoint *cur_p*, and append it to the current vertical list, together with associated penalties and other insertions 880 ⟩ ≡
  ⟨ Modify the end of the line to reflect the nature of the break and to include \rightskip; also set the proper value of *disc_break* 881 ⟩;
  ⟨ Put the \leftskip glue at the left and detach this line 887 ⟩;
  ⟨ Call the packaging subroutine, setting *just_box* to the justified box 889 ⟩;
  ⟨ Append the new box to the current vertical list, followed by the list of special nodes taken out of the box by the packager 888 ⟩;
  ⟨ Append a penalty node, if a nonzero penalty is appropriate 890 ⟩

This code is used in section 877.

881. At the end of the following code, q will point to the final node on the list about to be justified.

⟨ Modify the end of the line to reflect the nature of the break and to include \rightskip; also set the proper value of *disc_break* 881 ⟩ ≡
  $q \leftarrow cur\_break(cur\_p)$; *disc_break* $\leftarrow false$;
  if $q \neq null$ **then**   { q cannot be a *char_node* }
    if $type(q) = glue\_node$ **then**
      begin $delete\_glue\_ref(glue\_ptr(q))$; $glue\_ptr(q) \leftarrow right\_skip$; $subtype(q) \leftarrow right\_skip\_code + 1$;
      $add\_glue\_ref(right\_skip)$; **goto** *done*;
      end
    else begin if $type(q) = disc\_node$ **then**
        ⟨ Change discretionary to compulsory and set *disc_break* $\leftarrow true$ 882 ⟩;
      if $\neg is\_char\_node(q)$ **then**
        if $(type(q) = math\_node) \vee (type(q) = kern\_node)$ **then** $width(q) \leftarrow 0$;
      end
    else begin $q \leftarrow temp\_head$;
      while $link(q) \neq null$ **do** $q \leftarrow link(q)$;
      end;
  ⟨ Put the \rightskip glue after node q 886 ⟩;
done:

This code is used in section 880.

882. ⟨ Change discretionary to compulsory and set *disc_break* $\leftarrow true$ 882 ⟩ ≡
  begin $t \leftarrow replace\_count(q)$; ⟨ Destroy the t nodes following q, but save the last one if it is a necessary
    kern; make r point to the following node 883 ⟩;
  if $post\_break(q) \neq null$ **then** ⟨ Transplant the post-break list 884 ⟩;
  if $pre\_break(q) \neq null$ **then** ⟨ Transplant the pre-break list 885 ⟩;
  $link(q) \leftarrow r$; *disc_break* $\leftarrow true$;
  end

This code is used in section 881.

883. A subtle bug that would perhaps never have been detected is avoided here by preserving a kern node that just might equal $cur\_break(next\_break(cur\_p))$.

⟨ Destroy the t nodes following q, but save the last one if it is a necessary kern; make r point to the following node 883 ⟩ ≡
  if $t = 0$ **then** $r \leftarrow link(q)$
  else begin $r \leftarrow q$;
    while $t > 1$ **do**
      begin $r \leftarrow link(r)$; $decr(t)$;
      end;
    $s \leftarrow link(r)$;
    if $\neg is\_char\_node(s)$ **then**
      if $next\_break(cur\_p) \neq null$ **then**
        if $cur\_break(next\_break(cur\_p)) = s$ **then** $s \leftarrow r$;
    $r \leftarrow link(s)$; $link(s) \leftarrow null$; $flush\_node\_list(link(q))$; $replace\_count(q) \leftarrow 0$;
    end

This code is used in section 882.

884.   We move the post-break list from inside node q to the main list by reattaching it just before the present node r, then resetting r.

⟨ Transplant the post-break list 884 ⟩ ≡
   begin $s \leftarrow post\_break(q)$;
   while $link(s) \neq null$ **do** $s \leftarrow link(s)$;
   $link(s) \leftarrow r$; $r \leftarrow post\_break(q)$; $post\_break(q) \leftarrow null$;
   end

This code is used in section 882.

885.   We move the pre-break list from inside node q to the main list by reattaching it just after the present node q, then resetting q.

⟨ Transplant the pre-break list 885 ⟩ ≡
   begin $s \leftarrow pre\_break(q)$; $link(q) \leftarrow s$;
   while $link(s) \neq null$ **do** $s \leftarrow link(s)$;
   $pre\_break(q) \leftarrow null$; $q \leftarrow s$;
   end

This code is used in section 882.

886.   ⟨ Put the \rightskip glue after node q 886 ⟩ ≡
   $r \leftarrow new\_param\_glue(right\_skip\_code)$; $link(r) \leftarrow link(q)$; $link(q) \leftarrow r$; $q \leftarrow r$
This code is used in section 881.

887.   The following code begins with q at the end of the list to be justified. It ends with q at the beginning of that list, and with $link(temp\_head)$ pointing to the remainder of the paragraph, if any.

⟨ Put the \leftskip glue at the left and detach this line 887 ⟩ ≡
   $r \leftarrow link(q)$; $link(q) \leftarrow null$; $q \leftarrow link(temp\_head)$; $link(temp\_head) \leftarrow r$;
   if $left\_skip \neq zero\_glue$ **then**
      begin $r \leftarrow new\_param\_glue(left\_skip\_code)$; $link(r) \leftarrow q$; $q \leftarrow r$;
      end

This code is used in section 880.

---

add_glue_ref = macro, §203.
$char\_node$, §134.
cur_break = macro, §821.
cur_p: $pointer$, §828.
$decr$ = macro, §16.
$delete\_glue\_ref$: **procedure**, §201.
$disc\_break$: $boolean$, §877.
$disc\_node$ = 7, §145.
$done$ = 30, §15.
$flush\_node\_list$: **procedure**, §202.
$glue\_node$ = 10, §149.
$glue\_ptr$ = macro, §149.

is_char_node = macro, §134.
$kern\_node$ = 11, §155.
$left\_skip$ = macro, §224.
$left\_skip\_code$ = 7, §224.
$link$ = macro, §118.
$math\_node$ = 9, §147.
new_param_glue: **function**, §152.
$next\_break$ = macro, §877.
$null$ = macro, §115.
$post\_break$ = macro, §145.
pre_break = macro, §145.
q: $pointer$, §877.

r: $pointer$, §877.
$replace\_count$ = macro, §145.
$right\_skip$ = macro, §224.
$right\_skip\_code$ = 8, §224.
s: $pointer$, §877.
$subtype$ = macro, §133.
t: $quarterword$, §877.
$temp\_head$ = macro, §162.
$type$ = macro, §133.
$width$ = macro, §135.
$zero\_glue$ = macro, §162.

888. ⟨ Append the new box to the current vertical list, followed by the list of special nodes taken out of the box by the packager 888 ⟩ ≡

  append_to_vlist(*just_box*);
  if *adjust_head* ≠ *adjust_tail* **then**
    begin *link*(*tail*) ← *link*(*adjust_head*); *tail* ← *adjust_tail*;
    end;
  adjust_tail ← *null*

This code is used in section 880.

889. Now *q* points to the hlist that represents the current line of the paragraph. We need to compute the appropriate line width, pack the line into a box of this size, and shift the box by the appropriate amount of indentation.

⟨ Call the packaging subroutine, setting *just_box* to the justified box 889 ⟩ ≡

  if *cur_line* > *last_special_line* **then**
    begin *cur_width* ← *second_width*; *cur_indent* ← *second_indent*;
    end
  else if *par_shape_ptr* = *null* **then**
      begin *cur_width* ← *first_width*; *cur_indent* ← *first_indent*;
      end
    else begin *cur_width* ← *mem*[*par_shape_ptr* + 2 ∗ *cur_line*].*sc*;
      cur_indent ← *mem*[*par_shape_ptr* + 2 ∗ *cur_line* − 1].*sc*;
      end;
  adjust_tail ← *adjust_head*; *just_box* ← *hpack*(*q*, *cur_width*, *exactly*);
  shift_amount(*just_box*) ← *cur_indent*

This code is used in section 880.

890. Penalties between the lines of a paragraph come from club and widow lines, from the *inter_line_penalty* parameter, and from lines that end at discretionary breaks. Breaking between lines of a two-line paragraph gets both club-line and widow-line penalties. The local variable *pen* will be set to the sum of all relevant penalties for the current line, except that the final line is never penalized.

⟨ Append a penalty node, if a nonzero penalty is appropriate 890 ⟩ ≡

  if *cur_line* + 1 ≠ *best_line* **then**
    begin *pen* ← *inter_line_penalty*;
    if *cur_line* = *prev_graf* + 1 **then** *pen* ← *pen* + *club_penalty*;
    if *cur_line* + 2 = *best_line* **then** *pen* ← *pen* + *final_widow_penalty*;
    if *disc_break* **then** *pen* ← *pen* + *broken_penalty*;
    if *pen* ≠ 0 **then**
      begin *r* ← *new_penalty*(*pen*); *link*(*tail*) ← *r*; *tail* ← *r*;
      end;
    end

This code is used in section 880.

891. Pre-hyphenation.   When the line-breaking routine is unable to find a feasible sequence of breakpoints, it makes a second pass over the paragraph, attempting to hyphenate the hyphenatable words. The goal of hyphenation is to insert discretionary material into the paragraph so that there are more potential places to break.

The general rules for hyphenation are somewhat complex and technical, because we want to be able to hyphenate words that are preceded or followed by punctuation marks, and because we want the rules to work for languages other than English. We also must contend with the fact that hyphens might radically alter the ligature and kerning structure of a word.

A sequence of characters will be considered for hyphenation only if it belongs to a "potentially hyphenatable part" of the current paragraph. This is a sequence of nodes $p_0 p_1 \ldots p_m$ where p_0 is a glue node, $p_1 \ldots p_{m-1}$ are either character or ligature or whatsit or implicit kern nodes, and p_m is a glue or penalty or insertion or adjust or mark or whatsit or explicit kern node. (Therefore hyphenation is disabled by boxes, math formulas, and discretionary nodes already inserted by the user.) The ligature nodes among $p_1 \ldots p_{m-1}$ are effectively expanded into the original non-ligature characters; the kern nodes and whatsits are ignored. Each character c is now classified as either a nonletter (if $c \geq 128$ or $lc\_code(c) = 0$), a lowercase letter (if $lc\_code(c) = c$), or an uppercase letter (otherwise); an uppercase letter is treated as if it were $lc\_code(c)$ for purposes of hyphenation. The characters generated by $p_1 \ldots p_{m-1}$ may begin with nonletters; let c_1 be the first letter that is not in the middle of a ligature. Whatsit nodes preceding c_1 are ignored; a whatsit found after c_1 will be the terminating node p_m. All characters that do not have the same font as c_1 will be treated as nonletters. The *hyphen_char* for that font must be between 0 and 255, otherwise hyphenation will not be attempted. TeX looks ahead for as many consecutive letters $c_1 \ldots c_n$ as possible; however, n must be less than 64, so a character that would otherwise be c_{64} is effectively not a letter. Furthermore c_n must not be in the middle of a ligature. In this way we obtain a string of letters $c_1 \ldots c_n$ that are generated by nodes $p_a \ldots p_b$, where $1 \leq a \leq b+1 \leq m$. If $n \geq 5$, this string qualifies for hyphenation; however, *uc_hyph* must be positive, if c_1 is uppercase.

The hyphenation process takes place in three stages. First, the candidate sequence $c_1 \ldots c_n$ is found; then potential positions for hyphens are determined by referring to hyphenation tables; and finally, the nodes $p_a \ldots p_b$ are replaced by a new sequence of nodes that includes the discretionary breaks found.

Fortunately, we do not have to do all this calculation very often, because of the way it has been taken out of TeX's inner loop. For example, when the second edition of the author's 700-page book *Seminumerical Algorithms* was typeset by TeX, only about 1.2 hyphenations needed to be tried per paragraph, since the line breaking algorithm needed to use two passes on only about 5 per cent of the paragraphs.

892. The letters $c_1 \ldots c_n$ that are candidates for hyphenation are placed into an array called hc; the number n is placed into hn; pointers to nodes p_a and p_b in the description above are placed into variables ha and hb; and the font number is placed into hf.

⟨ Global variables 13 ⟩ +≡
hc: **array** [0 .. 65] **of** *halfword*;   { word to be hyphenated }
hn: *small_number*;   { the number of positions occupied in hc }
ha, hb: *pointer*;   { nodes ha .. hb should be replaced by the hyphenated result }
hf: *internal_font_number*;   { font number of the letters in hc }
hu: **array** [1 .. 63] **of** *ASCII_code*;   { like hc, before conversion to lowercase }
hyf_char: *integer*;   { hyphen character of the relevant font }

893. Hyphenation routines need a few more local variables.

⟨ Local variables for line breaking 862 ⟩ +≡
j: *small_number*;   { an index into hc or hu }
c: 0 .. 255;   { character being considered for hyphenation }

894. When the following code is activated, the *line_break* procedure is in its second pass, and *cur_p* points to a glue node.

⟨ Try to hyphenate the following word 894 ⟩ ≡
  begin $s \leftarrow link(cur\_p)$;
  if $s \neq null$ **then**
    begin ⟨ Skip to node ha, or **goto** *done1* if no hyphenation should be attempted 896 ⟩;
    ⟨ Skip to node hb, putting letters into hu and hc 897 ⟩;
    ⟨ Check that the nodes following hb permit hyphenation and that at least five letters have been
        found, otherwise **goto** *done1* 899 ⟩;
    hyphenate;
    end;
done1: **end**

This code is used in section 866.

895. ⟨ Declare subprocedures for *line_break* 826 ⟩ +≡
⟨ Declare the function called *reconstitute* 906 ⟩
procedure *hyphenate*;
  label *done*, *found*, *not_found*, *found1*, *exit*;
  var ⟨ Local variables for hyphenation 901 ⟩
  begin ⟨ Find hyphen locations for the word in hc 923 ⟩;
  ⟨ If no hyphens were found, **return** 902 ⟩;
  ⟨ Replace nodes ha .. hb by a sequence of nodes that includes the discretionary hyphens 903 ⟩;
exit: **end**;

ASCII_code = 0 .. 127, §18.
cur_p: *pointer*, §828.
done = 30, §15.
done1 = 31, §15.
exit = 10, §15.
found = 40, §15.
found1 = 41, §15.
halfword = *min_halfword* ..

max_halfword, §113.
hyphen_char: **array**, §549.
internal_font_number = 0 .. *font_max*,
    §548.
lc_code = macro, §230.
line_break: **procedure**, §815.
link = macro, §118.

not_found = 45, §15.
null = macro, §115.
pointer = macro, §115.
reconstitute: **function**, §906.
s: *pointer*, §862.
small_number = 0 .. 63, §101.
uc_hyph = macro, §236.

896. The first thing we need to do is find the node ha that contains the first letter.

⟨Skip to node ha, or **goto** $done1$ if no hyphenation should be attempted 896⟩ ≡
  loop begin if $is\_char\_node(s)$ **then**
      begin $c \leftarrow qo(character(s))$; $hf \leftarrow font(s)$;
      end
    else if $type(s) = ligature\_node$ **then**
        begin $q \leftarrow lig\_ptr(s)$; $c \leftarrow qo(character(q))$; $hf \leftarrow font(q)$;
        end
      else if $(type(s) = kern\_node) \wedge (subtype(s) = normal)$ **then** $c \leftarrow 128$
        else if $type(s) = whatsit\_node$ **then** $c \leftarrow 128$
          else goto $done1$;
    if $c < 128$ **then**
      if $lc\_code(c) \neq 0$ **then**
        if $(lc\_code(c) = c) \vee (uc\_hyph > 0)$ **then goto** $done2$
        else goto $done1$;
    $s \leftarrow link(s)$;
    end;
$done2$: $hyf\_char \leftarrow hyphen\_char[hf]$;
  if $hyf\_char < 0$ **then goto** $done1$;
  if $hyf\_char > 255$ **then goto** $done1$;
  $ha \leftarrow s$

This code is used in section 894.

897. The word to be hyphenated is now moved to the hu and hc arrays.

⟨Skip to node hb, putting letters into hu and hc 897⟩ ≡
  $hn \leftarrow 0$;
  loop begin if $is\_char\_node(s)$ **then**
      begin if $font(s) \neq hf$ **then goto** $done3$;
      $c \leftarrow qo(character(s))$;
      if $c \geq 128$ **then goto** $done3$;
      if $(lc\_code(c) = 0) \vee (hn = 63)$ **then goto** $done3$;
      $hb \leftarrow s$; $incr(hn)$; $hu[hn] \leftarrow c$; $hc[hn] \leftarrow lc\_code(c) - 1$;
      end
    else if $type(s) = ligature\_node$ **then** ⟨Move the characters of a ligature node to hu and hc; but
        goto $done3$ if they are not all letters 898⟩
      else if $(type(s) \neq kern\_node) \vee (subtype(s) \neq normal)$ **then goto** $done3$;
    $s \leftarrow link(s)$;
    end;
$done3$:

This code is used in section 894.

898. We let j be the index of the character being stored when a ligature node is being expanded, since we do not want to advance hn until we are sure that the entire ligature consists of letters. Note that it is possible to get to *done3* with $hn = 0$ and hb not set to any value.

⟨ Move the characters of a ligature node to hu and hc; but **goto** *done3* if they are not all letters 898 ⟩ ≡
> **begin** $j \leftarrow hn$; $q \leftarrow lig\_ptr(s)$;
> **if** $font(q) \neq hf$ **then goto** *done3*;
> **repeat** $c \leftarrow qo(character(q))$;
> > **if** $c \geq 128$ **then goto** *done3*;
> > **if** $(lc\_code(c) = 0) \vee (j = 63)$ **then goto** *done3*;
> > $incr(j)$; $hu[j] \leftarrow c$; $hc[j] \leftarrow lc\_code(c) - 1$;
> > $q \leftarrow link(q)$;
> **until** $q = null$;
> $hb \leftarrow s$; $hn \leftarrow j$;
> **end**

This code is used in section 897.

899. ⟨ Check that the nodes following hb permit hyphenation and that at least five letters have been found, otherwise **goto** *done1* 899 ⟩ ≡
> **if** $hn < 5$ **then goto** *done1*;
> **loop begin if** $\neg(is\_char\_node(s))$ **then**
> > **case** $type(s)$ **of**
> > *ligature_node*: *do_nothing*;
> > *kern_node*: **if** $subtype(s) \neq normal$ **then goto** *done4*;
> > *whatsit_node*, *glue_node*, *penalty_node*, *ins_node*, *adjust_node*, *mark_node*: **goto** *done4*;
> > **othercases goto** *done1*
> > **endcases**;
> > $s \leftarrow link(s)$;
> **end**;
> *done4*:

This code is used in section 894.

$adjust\_node = 5$, §142.
c: $0 \mathinner{\ldotp\ldotp} 255$, §893.
$character$ = macro, §134.
$do\_nothing$ = macro, §16.
$done1 = 31$, §15.
$done2 = 32$, §15.
$done3 = 33$, §15.
$done4 = 34$, §15.
$font$ = macro, §134.
$glue\_node = 10$, §149.
ha: *pointer*, §892.
hb: *pointer*, §892.
hc: **array**, §892.

hf: *internal_font_number*, §892.
hn: *small_number*, §892.
hu: **array**, §892.
hyf_char: *integer*, §892.
$hyphen\_char$: **array**, §549.
$incr$ = macro, §16.
$ins\_node = 3$, §140.
is_char_node = macro, §134.
j: *small_number*, §893.
$kern\_node = 11$, §155.
lc_code = macro, §230.
lig_ptr = macro, §143.
$ligature\_node = 6$, §143.

$link$ = macro, §118.
$mark\_node = 4$, §141.
$normal = 0$, §135.
$null$ = macro, §115.
$penalty\_node = 12$, §157.
q: *pointer*, §862.
qo = macro, §112.
s: *pointer*, §862.
$subtype$ = macro, §133.
$type$ = macro, §133.
uc_hyph = macro, §236.
$whatsit\_node = 8$, §146.

900.   Post-hyphenation.   If a hyphen may be inserted between $hc[j]$ and $hc[j + 1]$, the hyphenation procedure will set $hyf[j]$ to some small odd number. But before we look at TeX's hyphenation procedure, which is independent of the rest of the line-breaking algorithm, let us consider what we will do with the hyphens it finds, since it is better to work on this part of the program before forgetting what ha and hb, etc., are all about.

⟨ Global variables 13 ⟩ +≡
hyf: **array** [0 .. 64] **of** 0 .. 9;   { odd values indicate discretionary hyphens }

901.   ⟨ Local variables for hyphenation 901 ⟩ ≡
i, j, l: 0 .. 65;   { indices into hc or hu }
q, r, s: *pointer*;   { temporary registers for list manipulation }
See also sections 912, 922, and 929.
This code is used in section 895.

902.   TeX will never insert a hyphen that has fewer than two letters before it or fewer than three after it; hence, a five-letter word has comparatively little chance of being hyphenated. If no hyphens have been found, we can save time by not having to make any changes to the paragraph.

⟨ If no hyphens were found, **return** 902 ⟩ ≡
   for $j \leftarrow 2$ **to** $hn - 3$ **do**
     if $odd(hyf[j])$ **then goto** *found1*;
   return;
found1:
This code is used in section 895.

903.   If hyphens are in fact going to be inserted, TeX first deletes the subsequence of nodes $ha .. hb$. The variable s will point to the node preceding ha, and q will point to the node following hb, so that things can be hooked up after we reconstitute the hyphenated word.

⟨ Replace nodes $ha .. hb$ by a sequence of nodes that includes the discretionary hyphens 903 ⟩ ≡
   $q \leftarrow link(hb)$; $link(hb) \leftarrow null$; $s \leftarrow cur\_p$;
   while $link(s) \neq ha$ **do** $s \leftarrow link(s)$;
   $link(s) \leftarrow null$; $flush\_node\_list(ha)$;
   ⟨ Reconstitute nodes for the hyphenated word, inserting discretionary hyphens 913 ⟩
This code is used in section 895.

904.   We must now face the fact that the battle is not over, even though the hyphens have been found: The process of reconstituting a word can be nontrivial because ligatures might change when a hyphen is present. *The TeXbook* discusses the difficulties of the word "difficult", but since fonts can include highly general ligatures, the discretionary material surrounding a hyphen can be even more complex than that. For example, suppose that abcdef is a word in a font for which the only ligatures are bc, cd, de, and ef. If this word is to permit hyphenation between b and c, the two patterns with and without hyphenation are a bc de f and a b - cd ef. Thus the insertion of a hyphen might cause effects to ripple arbitrarily far into the rest of the word. A further complication arises if additional hyphens appear together with such rippling, e.g., if the word in the example just given could also be hyphenated between c and d; TeX avoids this by simply ignoring the additional hyphens in such weird cases.

905.   The processing is facilitated by a subroutine called *reconstitute*. Given an index j, this function creates a node for the next character or ligature found in the *hu* array starting at $hu[j]$, using font *hf*. For example, if $hu[j .. j + 2]$ contains the three letters 'f', 'i', and 'x', and if font *hf* contains an 'fi' ligature but no 'fix' ligature, then *reconstitute* will create a ligature node for 'fi'. The index of the last character consumed, in this case $j + 1$, will be returned. Furthermore, a kern node is created and appended, if kerning is called for between the consumed character or ligature and the next (unconsumed) character.

A second parameter, n, gives the limit beyond which this procedure does not advance. In other words, $hu[n]$ might be consumed, but $hu[n + 1]$ is never accessed.

The global variable *hyphen_passed* is set to k if this procedure consumes two characters $hu[k]$ and $hu[k + 1]$ such that $hyf[k]$ is odd, i.e., if the ligature might have to be broken by a hyphen, or if a kern is inserted between $hu[k]$ and $hu[k + 1]$. If this condition holds for more than one value of k, the smallest value is used; and if the condition holds for no values of k, *hyphen_passed* is set to zero.

After *reconstitute* has acted, *link*(*hold_head*) points to the character or ligature node that was created, and *link*(*link*(*hold_head*)) will either be *null* or a pointer to the kern node that was appended.

⟨ Global variables 13 ⟩ +≡
hyphen_passed: *small_number*;   { first hyphen in a ligature, if any }

906.   ⟨ Declare the function called *reconstitute* 906 ⟩ ≡
function *reconstitute*(j, n : *small_number*): *small_number*;
   label *continue*, *done*;
   var *p*: *pointer*;   { a node being created }
     s: *pointer*;   { a node being appended to }
     q: *four_quarters*;   { character information or a lig/kern instruction }
     c: *quarterword*;   { current character }
     d: *quarterword*;   { current character or ligature }
     w: *scaled*;   { amount of kerning }
     r: 0 .. *font_mem_size*;   { position of current lig/kern instruction }
   begin ⟨ Build a list of characters in a maximal ligature, and set w to the amount of kerning that
      should follow 907 ⟩;
   ⟨ If the list has more than one element, create a ligature node 910 ⟩;
   ⟨ Attach kerning, if $w \neq 0$ 911 ⟩;
   reconstitute ← *j*;
   end;
This code is used in section 895.

---

continue = 22, §15.
cur_p: *pointer*, §828.
done = 30, §15.
flush_node_list: **procedure**, §202.
font_mem_size = **const**, §11.
found1 = 41, §15.
four_quarters = **packed record**,

§113.
ha: *pointer*, §892.
hb: *pointer*, §892.
hc: **array**, §892.
hf: *internal_font_number*, §892.
hn: *small_number*, §892.
hold_head = macro, §162.

hu: **array**, §892.
link = macro, §118.
null = macro, §115.
pointer = macro, §115.
quarterword = 0 .. 255, §113.
scaled = *integer*, §101.
small_number = 0 .. 63, §101.

907. ⟨ Build a list of characters in a maximal ligature, and set w to the amount of kerning that should follow 907 ⟩ ≡

  $hyphen\_passed \leftarrow 0$; $s \leftarrow hold\_head$; $w \leftarrow 0$; $d \leftarrow qi(hu[j])$; $c \leftarrow d$;

  loop begin $continue$: $p \leftarrow get\_avail$; $font(p) \leftarrow hf$; $character(p) \leftarrow c$; $link(s) \leftarrow p$;

    ⟨ Look for a ligature or kern between d and the following character; update the data structure and
      goto $continue$ if a ligature is found, otherwise update w and **goto** $done$ 908 ⟩;

    end;

$done$:

This code is used in section 906.

908. ⟨ Look for a ligature or kern between d and the following character; update the data structure
    and **goto** $continue$ if a ligature is found, otherwise update w and **goto** $done$ 908 ⟩ ≡

  if $j = n$ **then goto** $done$;

  $q \leftarrow char\_info(hf)(d)$;

  if $char\_tag(q) \neq lig\_tag$ **then goto** $done$;

  $r \leftarrow lig\_kern\_start(hf)(q)$; $c \leftarrow qi(hu[j+1])$;

  loop begin $q \leftarrow font\_info[r].qqqq$;

    if $next\_char(q) = c$ **then**

      begin if $odd(hyf[j]) \wedge (hyphen\_passed = 0)$ **then** $hyphen\_passed \leftarrow j$;

      if $op\_bit(q) < kern\_flag$ **then** ⟨ Append to the ligature and **goto** $continue$ 909 ⟩

      else begin $w \leftarrow char\_kern(hf)(q)$; **goto** $done$;

        end;

      end

    else if $stop\_bit(q) < stop\_flag$ **then** $incr(r)$

      else goto $done$;

    end

This code is used in section 907.

909. ⟨ Append to the ligature and **goto** $continue$ 909 ⟩ ≡

  begin $d \leftarrow rem\_byte(q)$; $incr(j)$; $s \leftarrow p$; **goto** $continue$;

  end

This code is used in section 908.

910. After the list has been built, $link(s)$ points to the final list element.

⟨ If the list has more than one element, create a ligature node 910 ⟩ ≡

  if $s \neq hold\_head$ **then**

    begin $p \leftarrow new\_ligature(hf, d, link(hold\_head))$; $link(hold\_head) \leftarrow p$;

    end

This code is used in section 906.

911. ⟨ Attach kerning, if $w \neq 0$ 911 ⟩ ≡

  if $w \neq 0$ **then** $link(link(hold\_head)) \leftarrow new\_kern(w)$

This code is used in section 906.

912. Okay, we're ready to insert the potential hyphenations that were found. When the following program is executed, we want to append the word $hu[1 .. hn]$ after node s, and node q should be appended to the result. During this process, the variable i will be a temporary counter or an index into hu; the variable j will be an index to our current position in hu; the variable

l will be the counterpart of j, in a discretionary branch; the variable r will point to new nodes being created; and we need a few new local variables:

⟨ Local variables for hyphenation 901 ⟩ +≡
major_tail, *minor_tail*: *pointer*;
          { the end of lists in the main and discretionary branches being reconstructed }
c: *ASCII_code*; { character temporarily replaced by a hyphen }
hyf_node: *pointer*; { the hyphen, if it exists }

913.   When the following code is performed, $hyf[j]$ will be zero for $j = 1$ and for $j \geq hn - 2$.

⟨ Reconstitute nodes for the hyphenated word, inserting discretionary hyphens 913 ⟩ ≡
    $j \leftarrow 0$;
    repeat $l \leftarrow j$; $j \leftarrow reconstitute(j + 1, hn)$;
        if *hyphen_passed* $\neq 0$ **then** ⟨ Create and append a discretionary node as an alternative to the
                ligature, and continue to develop both branches until they become equivalent 914 ⟩
        else begin $link(s) \leftarrow link(hold\_head)$; $s \leftarrow link(s)$;
            if $link(s) \neq null$ **then** $s \leftarrow link(s)$;
            end;
        if $odd(hyf[j])$ **then** ⟨ Insert a discretionary hyphen after s 918 ⟩;
    until $j = hn$;
    $link(s) \leftarrow q$

This code is used in section 903.

ASCII_code = 0 .. 127, §18.
c: *quarterword*, §906.
char_info = macro, §554.
char_kern = macro, §557.
char_tag = macro, §554.
character = macro, §134.
continue = 22, §15.
d: *quarterword*, §906.
done = 30, §15.
font = macro, §134.
font_info: **array**, §549.
get_avail: **function**, §120.
hf: *internal_font_number*, §892.
hn: *small_number*, §892.
hold_head = macro, §162.
hu: **array**, §892.

hyf: **array**, §900.
hyphen_passed: *small_number*, §905.
i: 0 .. 65, §901.
incr = macro, §16.
j: 0 .. 65, §901.
j: *small_number*, §906.
kern_flag = 128, §545.
l: 0 .. 65, §901.
lig_kern_start = macro, §557.
lig_tag = 1, §544.
link = macro, §118.
n: *small_number*, §906.
new_kern: **function**, §156.
new_ligature: **function**, §144.
next_char = macro, §545.
null = macro, §115.

op_bit = macro, §545.
p: *pointer*, §906.
pointer = macro, §115.
q: *pointer*, §901.
q: *four_quarters*, §906.
qi = macro, §112.
qqqq: *four_quarters*, §113.
r: *pointer*, §901.
r: 0 .. *font_mem_size*, §906.
rem_byte = macro, §545.
s: *pointer*, §901.
s: *pointer*, §906.
stop_bit = macro, §545.
stop_flag = 128, §545.
w: *scaled*, §906.

914. ⟨Create and append a discretionary node as an alternative to the ligature, and continue to develop both branches until they become equivalent 914⟩ ≡

begin $r \leftarrow get\_node(small\_node\_size)$; $link(s) \leftarrow r$; $link(r) \leftarrow link(hold\_head)$; $type(r) \leftarrow disc\_node$; $major\_tail \leftarrow link(hold\_head)$;

if $link(major\_tail) \neq null$ **then** $major\_tail \leftarrow link(major\_tail)$;

$i \leftarrow hyphen\_passed$; ⟨Put the characters $hu[l+1 .. i]$ and a hyphen into $pre\_break(r)$ 915⟩;

⟨Put the characters $hu[i+1 ..]$ into $post\_break(r)$, appending to this list and to $major\_tail$ until synchronization has been achieved 916⟩;

⟨Move pointer s to the end of the current list, and set $replace\_count(r)$ appropriately 917⟩;

end

This code is used in section 913.

915. The new hyphen might combine with the previous character via ligature or kern. At this point we have $l < i \leq j$ and $i \leq hn - 3$.

⟨Put the characters $hu[l+1 .. i]$ and a hyphen into $pre\_break(r)$ 915⟩ ≡

$minor\_tail \leftarrow null$; $hyf\_node \leftarrow new\_character(hf, hyf\_char)$;

if $hyf\_node \neq null$ **then**

  begin $incr(i)$; $c \leftarrow hu[i]$; $hu[i] \leftarrow hyf\_char$;

  end;

repeat $l \leftarrow reconstitute(l+1, i)$;

  if $minor\_tail = null$ **then** $pre\_break(r) \leftarrow link(hold\_head)$

  else $link(minor\_tail) \leftarrow link(hold\_head)$;

  $minor\_tail \leftarrow link(hold\_head)$;

  if $link(minor\_tail) \neq null$ **then** $minor\_tail \leftarrow link(minor\_tail)$;

until $l = i$;

if $hyf\_node \neq null$ **then**

  begin $hu[i] \leftarrow c$; { restore the character in the hyphen position }

  $free\_avail(hyf\_node)$; $decr(i)$; $l \leftarrow i$;

  end;

$hyf[i] \leftarrow 0$

This code is used in section 914.

916. The synchronization algorithm begins with $l = i \leq j$.

⟨Put the characters $hu[i+1 ..]$ into $post\_break(r)$, appending to this list and to $major\_tail$ until synchronization has been achieved 916⟩ ≡

$minor\_tail \leftarrow null$; $post\_break(r) \leftarrow null$;

while $l < j$ **do**

  begin repeat $l \leftarrow reconstitute(l+1, hn)$;

    if $minor\_tail = null$ **then** $post\_break(r) \leftarrow link(hold\_head)$

    else $link(minor\_tail) \leftarrow link(hold\_head)$;

    $minor\_tail \leftarrow link(hold\_head)$;

    if $link(minor\_tail) \neq null$ **then**

      begin $hyf[l] \leftarrow 0$; $minor\_tail \leftarrow link(minor\_tail)$; { kern present }

      end;

  until $l \geq j$;

  while $l > j$ **do**

    begin $j \leftarrow reconstitute(j+1, hn)$; $link(major\_tail) \leftarrow link(hold\_head)$;

    $major\_tail \leftarrow link(hold\_head)$;

> if $link(major\_tail) \neq null$ then
>> begin $hyf[j] \leftarrow 0$; $major\_tail \leftarrow link(major\_tail)$; { kern present }
>> end;
> end;
end

This code is used in section 914.

917. ⟨ Move pointer s to the end of the current list, and set $replace\_count(r)$ appropriately 917 ⟩ ≡
> $i \leftarrow 0$; $s \leftarrow r$;
> while $link(s) \neq null$ do
>> begin $incr(i)$; $s \leftarrow link(s)$;
>> end;
> $replace\_count(r) \leftarrow i$

This code is used in section 914.

918. At this point $link(s)$ is $null$.

⟨ Insert a discretionary hyphen after s 918 ⟩ ≡
> begin $r \leftarrow new\_disc$; $pre\_break(r) \leftarrow new\_character(hf, hyf\_char)$; $link(s) \leftarrow r$; $s \leftarrow r$;
> end

This code is used in section 913.

---

c: $ASCII\_code$, §912.
$decr$ = macro, §16.
$disc\_node = 7$, §145.
$free\_avail$ = macro, §121.
get_node: **function**, §125.
hf: $internal\_font\_number$, §892.
hn: $small\_number$, §892.
$hold\_head$ = macro, §162.
hu: **array**, §892.
hyf: **array**, §900.

hyf_char: $integer$, §892.
hyf_node: $pointer$, §912.
$hyphen\_passed$: $small\_number$, §905.
i: $0 .. 65$, §901.
$incr$ = macro, §16.
j: $0 .. 65$, §901.
l: $0 .. 65$, §901.
$link$ = macro, §118.
$major\_tail$: $pointer$, §912.
$minor\_tail$: $pointer$, §912.

$new\_character$: **function**, §582.
new_disc: **function**, §145.
$null$ = macro, §115.
$post\_break$ = macro, §145.
pre_break = macro, §145.
r: $pointer$, §901.
$replace\_count$ = macro, §145.
s: $pointer$, §901.
$small\_node\_size = 2$, §141.
$type$ = macro, §133.

919.   Hyphenation. When a word $hc[1 .. hn]$ has been set up to contain a candidate for hyphenation, TeX first looks to see if it is in the user's exception dictionary. If not, hyphens are inserted based on patterns that appear within the given word, using an algorithm due to Frank M. Liang.

Let's consider Liang's method first, since it is much more interesting than the exception-lookup routine. The algorithm begins by setting $hyf[j]$ to zero for all j, and invalid characters are inserted into $hc[0]$ and $hc[hn+1]$ to serve as delimiters. Then a reasonably fast method is used to see which of a given set of patterns occurs in the word $hc[0 .. (hn+1)]$. Each pattern $p_1 \ldots p_k$ of length k has an associated sequence of $k+1$ numbers $n_0 \ldots n_k$; and if the pattern occurs in $hc[(j+1) .. (j+k)]$, TeX will set $hyf[j+i] \leftarrow \max(hyf[j+i], n_i)$ for $0 \le i \le k$. After this has been done for each pattern that occurs, a discretionary hyphen will be inserted between $hc[j]$ and $hc[j+1]$ when $hyf[j]$ is odd, as we have already seen.

The set of patterns $p_1 \ldots p_k$ and associated numbers $n_0 \ldots n_k$ depends, of course, on the language whose words are being hyphenated, and on the degree of hyphenation that is desired. A method for finding appropriate p's and n's, from a given dictionary of words and acceptable hyphenations, is discussed in Liang's Ph.D. thesis (Stanford University, 1983); TeX simply starts with the patterns and works from there.

920.   The patterns are stored in a compact table that is also efficient for retrieval, using a variant of "trie memory" [cf. *The Art of Computer Programming* **3** (1973), 481–505]. We can find each pattern $p_1 \ldots p_k$ by setting $z_1 \leftarrow p_1$ and then, for $1 < i \le k$, setting $z_i \leftarrow trie\_link(z_{i-1}) + p_i$; the pattern will be identified by the number z_k. Since all the pattern information is packed together into a single $trie\_link$ array, it is necessary to prevent confusion between the data from inequivalent patterns, so another table is provided such that $trie\_char(z_i) = p_i$ for all i. There is also a table $trie\_op(z_k)$ to identify the numbers $n_0 \ldots n_k$ associated with $p_1 \ldots p_k$.

Comparatively few different number sequences $n_0 \ldots n_k$ actually occur, since most of the n's are generally zero. Therefore the number sequences are encoded in such a way that $trie\_op(z_k)$ is only one byte long. If $trie\_op(z_k) \ne min\_quarterword$, when $p_1 \ldots p_k$ has matched the letters in $hc[(l-k+1) .. l]$, we perform all of the required operations for this pattern by carrying out the following little program: Set $v \leftarrow trie\_op(z_k)$. Then set $hyf[l - hyf\_distance[v]] \leftarrow \max(hyf[l - hyf\_distance[v]], hyf\_num[v])$, and $v \leftarrow hyf\_next[v]$; repeat, if necessary, until $v = min\_quarterword$.

⟨ Types in the outer block 18 ⟩ +≡
  $trie\_pointer = 0 .. trie\_size$;   { an index into *trie* }

921.   **define** $trie\_link(\#) \equiv trie[\#].rh$ { "downward" link in a trie }
  define $trie\_char(\#) \equiv trie[\#].b1$ { character matched at this trie location }
  define $trie\_op(\#) \equiv trie[\#].b0$ { program for hyphenation at this trie location }
⟨ Global variables 13 ⟩ +≡
trie: **array** [*trie_pointer*] **of** *two_halves*;   { *trie_link*, *trie_char*, *trie_op* }
hyf_distance: **array** [*quarterword*] **of** *small_number*;   { position $k-j$ of n_j }
hyf_num: **array** [*quarterword*] **of** *small_number*;   { value of n_j }
hyf_next: **array** [*quarterword*] **of** *quarterword*;   { continuation of this *trie_op* }

922.   ⟨ Local variables for hyphenation 901 ⟩ +≡
z: *trie_pointer*;   { an index into *trie* }
v: *quarterword*;   { an index into *hyf_distance*, etc. }

923.   Assuming that these auxiliary tables have been set up properly, the hyphenation algorithm is quite short. In the following code we set $hc[hn + 2]$ to the impossible value 256, in order to guarantee that $hc[hn + 3]$ will never be fetched.

⟨ Find hyphen locations for the word in hc 923 ⟩ ≡
  for $j \leftarrow 0$ **to** hn **do** $hyf[j] \leftarrow 0$;
  ⟨ Look for the word $hc[1 .. hn]$ in the exception table, and **goto** *found* (with hyf containing the
      hyphens) if an entry is found 930 ⟩;
  $hc[0] \leftarrow 127$; $hc[hn + 1] \leftarrow 127$; $hc[hn + 2] \leftarrow 256$;   { insert delimiters }
  for $j \leftarrow 0$ **to** $hn - 2$ **do**
    begin $z \leftarrow hc[j]$; $l \leftarrow j$;
    while $hc[l] = trie\_char(z)$ **do**
      begin if $trie\_op(z) \neq min\_quarterword$ **then** ⟨ Store maximum values in the hyf table 924 ⟩;
      $incr(l)$; $z \leftarrow trie\_link(z) + hc[l]$;
      end;
    end;
found: $hyf[1] \leftarrow 0$; $hyf[hn - 2] \leftarrow 0$; $hyf[hn - 1] \leftarrow 0$; $hyf[hn] \leftarrow 0$

This code is used in section 895.

924.   ⟨ Store maximum values in the hyf table 924 ⟩ ≡
  begin $v \leftarrow trie\_op(z)$;
  repeat $i \leftarrow l - hyf\_distance[v]$;
    if $hyf\_num[v] > hyf[i]$ **then** $hyf[i] \leftarrow hyf\_num[v]$;
    $v \leftarrow hyf\_next[v]$;
  until $v = min\_quarterword$;
  end

This code is used in section 923.

$b0$: *quarterword*, §113.
$b1$: *quarterword*, §113.
found = 40, §15.
hc: **array**, §892.
hn: *small_number*, §892.
hyf: **array**, §900.

i: 0 .. 65, §901.
incr = macro, §16.
j: 0 .. 65, §901.
l: 0 .. 65, §901.
min_quarterword = 0, §110.

quarterword = 0 .. 255, §113.
rh: *halfword*, §113.
small_number = 0 .. 63, §101.
trie_size = **const**, §11.
two_halves = **packed record**, §113.

925. The exception table that is built by TeX's \hyphenation primitive is organized as an ordered hash table [cf. Amble and Knuth, *The Computer Journal* **17** (1974), 135–142] using linear probing. If α and β are words, we will say that $\alpha < \beta$ if $|\alpha| < |\beta|$ or if $|\alpha| = |\beta|$ and α is lexicographically smaller than β. (The notation $|\alpha|$ stands for the length of α.) The idea of ordered hashing is to arrange the table so that a given word α can be sought by computing a hash address $h = h(\alpha)$ and then looking in table positions $h, h - 1, \ldots$, until encountering the first word $\leq \alpha$. If this word is different from α, we can conclude that α is not in the table.

The words in the table point to lists in *mem* that specify hyphen positions in their *info* fields. The list for $c_1 \ldots c_n$ contains the number k if the word $c_1 \ldots c_n$ has a discretionary hyphen between c_k and c_{k+1}.

⟨ Types in the outer block 18 ⟩ +≡
    hyph_pointer $= 0 \mathrel{..} hyph\_size$;   { an index into the ordered hash table }

926. ⟨ Global variables 13 ⟩ +≡
hyph_word: **array** [*hyph_pointer*] **of** *str_number*;   { exception words }
hyph_list: **array** [*hyph_pointer*] **of** *pointer*;   { list of hyphen positions }
hyph_count: *hyph_pointer*;   { the number of words in the exception dictionary }

927. ⟨ Local variables for initialization 19 ⟩ +≡
z: *hyph_pointer*;   { runs through the exception dictionary }

928. ⟨ Set initial values of key variables 21 ⟩ +≡
    for $z \leftarrow 0$ **to** *hyph_size* **do**
       begin *hyph_word*[*z*] $\leftarrow 0$; *hyph_list*[*z*] $\leftarrow$ *null*;
       end;
    hyph_count $\leftarrow 0$;

929. The algorithm for exception lookup is quite simple, as soon as we have a few more local variables to work with.

⟨ Local variables for hyphenation 901 ⟩ +≡
h: *hyph_pointer*;   { an index into *hyph_word* and *hyph_list* }
k: *str_number*;   { an index into *str_start* }
u: *pool_pointer*;   { an index into *str_pool* }

930. First we compute the hash code h, then we search until we either find the word or we don't.

⟨ Look for the word *hc*[1 .. *hn*] in the exception table, and **goto** *found* (with *hyf* containing the hyphens) if an entry is found 930 ⟩ ≡
    $h \leftarrow hc[1]$;
    for $j \leftarrow 2$ **to** *hn* **do** $h \leftarrow (h + h + hc[j])$ **mod** *hyph_size*;
    loop begin ⟨ If the string *hyph_word*[*h*] is less than *hc*[1 .. *hn*], **goto** *not_found*; but if the two strings
       are equal, set *hyf* to the hyphen positions and **goto** *found* 931 ⟩;
       if $h > 0$ **then** *decr*(*h*) **else** $h \leftarrow$ *hyph_size*;
       end;
not_found:

This code is used in section 923.

931. ⟨ If the string *hyph_word*[*h*] is less than *hc*[1 .. *hn*], **goto** *not_found*; but if the two strings are equal, set *hyf* to the hyphen positions and **goto** *found* 931 ⟩ ≡

k ← *hyph_word*[*h*];
if *k* = 0 **then goto** *not_found*;
if *length*(*k*) < *hn* **then goto** *not_found*;
if *length*(*k*) = *hn* **then**
    begin *j* ← 1; *u* ← *str_start*[*k*];
    repeat if *str_pool*[*u*] < *hc*[*j*] **then goto** *not_found*;
      if *str_pool*[*u*] > *hc*[*j*] **then goto** *done*;
      incr(*j*); *incr*(*u*);
    until *j* > *hn*;
    ⟨ Insert hyphens as specified in *hyph_list*[*h*] 932 ⟩;
    goto *found*;
    end;
done:

This code is used in section 930.

932. ⟨ Insert hyphens as specified in *hyph_list*[*h*] 932 ⟩ ≡

s ← *hyph_list*[*h*];
while *s* ≠ *null* **do**
    begin *hyf*[*info*(*s*)] ← 1; *s* ← *link*(*s*);
    end

This code is used in section 931.

933. ⟨ Search *hyph_list* for pointers to *p* 933 ⟩ ≡

for *q* ← 0 **to** *hyph_size* **do**
    begin if *hyph_list*[*q*] = *p* **then**
      begin *print_nl*("HYPH("); *print_int*(*q*); *print_char*(")");
      end;
    end

This code is used in section 172.

---

decr = macro, §16.
done = 30, §15.
found = 40, §15.
hc: **array**, §892.
hn: *small_number*, §892.
hyf: **array**, §900.
hyph_size = 307, §12.
incr = macro, §16.
info = macro, §118.

j: 0 .. 65, §901.
length = macro, §40.
link = macro, §118.
mem: **array**, §116.
not_found = 45, §15.
null = macro, §115.
p: *pointer*, §906.
pointer = macro, §115.
pool_pointer = 0 .. *pool_size*, §38.

print_char: **procedure**, §58.
print_int: **procedure**, §65.
print_nl: **procedure**, §62.
q: *four_quarters*, §906.
s: *pointer*, §901.
str_number = 0 .. *max_strings*, §38.
str_pool: **packed array**, §39.
str_start: **array**, §39.

934. We have now completed the hyphenation routine, so the *line_break* procedure is finished at last. Since the hyphenation exception table is fresh in our minds, it's a good time to deal with the routine that adds new entries to it.

When TEX has scanned '\hyphenation', it calls on a procedure named *new_hyph_exceptions* to do the right thing.

procedure *new_hyph_exceptions*;   { enters new exceptions }
  label *reswitch, exit, found, not_found, done*;
  var *n: small_number*;   { length of current word }
    j: small_number;   { an index into *hc* }
    h: hyph_pointer;   { an index into *hyph_word* and *hyph_list* }
    k: str_number;   { an index into *str_start* }
    p: pointer;   { head of a list of hyphen positions }
    q: pointer;   { used when creating a new node for list *p* }
    s, t: str_number;   { strings being compared or stored }
    u, v: pool_pointer;   { indices into *str_pool* }
  begin *scan_left_brace*;   { a left brace must follow \hyphenation }
  ⟨ Enter as many hyphenation exceptions as are listed, until coming to a right brace; then skip an
      optional space and **return** 935 ⟩;
exit: **end**;

935. ⟨ Enter as many hyphenation exceptions as are listed, until coming to a right brace; then skip
    an optional space and **return** 935 ⟩ ≡
n ← 0; *p* ← *null*;
loop begin *get_x_token*;
reswitch: **case** *cur_cmd* **of**
    letter, other_char, char_given: ⟨ Append a new letter or hyphen 937 ⟩;
    char_num: **begin** *scan_char_num*; *cur_chr* ← *cur_val*; *cur_cmd* ← *char_given*; **goto** *reswitch*;
      end;
    spacer, right_brace: **begin if** *n* > 4 **then** ⟨ Enter a hyphenation exception 939 ⟩;
      if *cur_cmd* = *right_brace* **then return**;
      n ← 0; *p* ← *null*;
      end;
    othercases ⟨ Give improper \hyphenation error 936 ⟩
    endcases;
    end
This code is used in section 934.

936. ⟨ Give improper \hyphenation error 936 ⟩ ≡
  begin *print_err*("Improper␣"); *print_esc*("hyphenation"); *print*("␣will␣be␣flushed");
  help2("Hyphenation␣exceptions␣must␣contain␣only␣letters")
  ("and␣hyphens.␣But␣continue;␣I´ll␣forgive␣and␣forget."); *error*;
  end
This code is used in section 935.

937. ⟨ Append a new letter or hyphen 937 ⟩ ≡
  if *cur_chr* = "-" **then** ⟨ Append the value *n* to list *p* 938 ⟩
  else begin if (*cur_chr* > 127) ∨ (*lc_code*(*cur_chr*) = 0) **then**
      begin *print_err*("Not␣a␣letter");
      help2("Letters␣in␣\hyphenation␣words␣must␣have␣\lccode>0.")

("Proceed;␣I´ll␣ignore␣the␣character␣I␣just␣read."); *error*;
  end
else if $n < 63$ **then**
    begin $incr(n)$; $hc[n] \leftarrow lc\_code(cur\_chr) - 1$;
    end;
  end

This code is used in section 935.

938. $\langle$ Append the value n to list p 938 $\rangle \equiv$
  begin if $n > 1$ **then**
    begin $q \leftarrow get\_avail$; $link(q) \leftarrow p$; $info(q) \leftarrow n$; $p \leftarrow q$;
    end;
  end

This code is used in section 937.

939. $\langle$ Enter a hyphenation exception 939 $\rangle \equiv$
  begin $str\_room(n)$; $h \leftarrow 0$;
  for $j \leftarrow 1$ **to** n **do**
    begin $h \leftarrow (h + h + hc[j])$ **mod** $hyph\_size$; $append\_char(hc[j])$;
    end;
  $s \leftarrow make\_string$;
  loop begin if $p = null$ **then goto** *done*;
    if $info(p) < n - 2$ **then goto** *done*;
    $q \leftarrow link(p)$; $free\_avail(p)$; $p \leftarrow q$;   { eliminate hyphens that TEX doesn't like }
    end;
done: $\langle$ Insert the pair (s, p) into the exception table 940 $\rangle$;
  end

This code is used in section 935.

·

append_char = macro, §42.
char_given = 67, §208.
char_num = 16, §208.
cur_chr: *halfword*, §297.
cur_cmd: *eight_bits*, §297.
cur_val: *integer*, §410.
done = 30, §15.
error: **procedure**, §82.
exit = 10, §15.
found = 40, §15.
free_avail = macro, §121.
get_avail: **function**, §120.
get_x_token: **procedure**, §380.
hc: **array**, §892.
help2 = macro, §79.

hyph_list: **array**, §926.
hyph_pointer = 0 .. 307, §925.
hyph_size = 307, §12.
hyph_word: **array**, §926.
incr = macro, §16.
info = macro, §118.
lc_code = macro, §230.
letter = 11, §207.
line_break: **procedure**, §815.
link = macro, §118.
make_string: **function**, §43.
not_found = 45, §15.
null = macro, §115.
other_char = 12, §207.
pointer = macro, §115.

pool_pointer = 0 .. *pool_size*, §38.
print: **procedure**, §59.
print_err = macro, §73.
print_esc: **procedure**, §63.
reswitch = 21, §15.
right_brace = 2, §207.
scan_char_num: **procedure**, §435.
scan_left_brace: **procedure**, §403.
small_number = 0 .. 63, §101.
spacer = 10, §207.
str_number = 0 .. *max_strings*, §38.
str_pool: **packed array**, §39.
str_room = macro, §42.
str_start: **array**, §39.

940. ⟨Insert the pair (s, p) into the exception table 940⟩ ≡
    if $hyph\_count = hyph\_size$ **then** $overflow(\texttt{"exception\_dictionary"}, hyph\_size)$;
    $incr(hyph\_count)$;
    while $hyph\_word[h] \neq 0$ **do**
        begin ⟨If the string $hyph\_word[h]$ is less than or equal to s, interchange $(hyph\_word[h], hyph\_list[h])$
            with (s, p) 941⟩;
        if $h > 0$ **then** $decr(h)$ **else** $h \leftarrow hyph\_size$;
        end;
    $hyph\_word[h] \leftarrow s$; $hyph\_list[h] \leftarrow p$

This code is used in section 939.

941. ⟨If the string $hyph\_word[h]$ is less than or equal to s, interchange $(hyph\_word[h], hyph\_list[h])$
    with (s, p) 941⟩ ≡
  $k \leftarrow hyph\_word[h]$;
  if $length(k) < length(s)$ **then goto** *found*;
  if $length(k) > length(s)$ **then goto** *not_found*;
  $u \leftarrow str\_start[k]$; $v \leftarrow str\_start[s]$;
  repeat if $str\_pool[u] < str\_pool[v]$ **then goto** *found*;
    if $str\_pool[u] > str\_pool[v]$ **then goto** *not_found*;
    $incr(u)$; $incr(v)$;
  until $u = str\_start[k + 1]$;
found: $q \leftarrow hyph\_list[h]$; $hyph\_list[h] \leftarrow p$; $p \leftarrow q$;
  $t \leftarrow hyph\_word[h]$; $hyph\_word[h] \leftarrow s$; $s \leftarrow t$;
not_found:

This code is used in section 940.

942. Initializing the hyphenation tables.   The trie for TEX's hyphenation algorithm is built from a sequence of patterns following a \patterns specification. Such a specification is allowed only in INITEX, since the extra memory for auxiliary tables and for the initialization program itself would only clutter up the production version of TEX with a lot of deadwood.

The initialization first builds a trie that is linked instead of packed into sequential storage, so that insertions are readily made. Then it compresses the linked trie by identifying common subtries, and finally the trie is packed into the efficient sequential form that the hyphenation algorithm actually uses.

    init ⟨ Declare procedures for preprocessing hyphenation patterns 944 ⟩
    tini

943.   Before we discuss trie building in detail, let's consider the simpler problem of creating the *hyf_distance*, *hyf_num*, and *hyf_next* arrays.

Suppose, for example, that TEX reads the pattern 'ab2cde1'. This is a pattern of length 5, with $n_0 \ldots n_5 = 0\,0\,2\,0\,0\,1$ in the notation above. We want the corresponding *trie_op* code v to have $hyf\_distance[v] = 3$, $hyf\_num[v] = 2$, and $hyf\_next[v] = v'$, where the auxiliary *trie_op* code v' has $hyf\_distance[v'] = 0$, $hyf\_num[v'] = 1$, and $hyf\_next[v'] = min\_quarterword$.

TEX computes an appropriate value v with the *new_trie_op* subroutine below, by setting

$$v' \leftarrow new\_trie\_op(0, 1, min\_quarterword), \qquad v \leftarrow new\_trie\_op(3, 2, v').$$

This subroutine looks up its three parameters in a special hash table, assigning a new value only if these three have not appeared before.

The hash table is called *trie_op_hash*, and the number of entries it contains is *trie_op_ptr*. If the table overflows, the excess ops are ignored.

    define *quarterword_diff* = *max_quarterword* − *min_quarterword*
    define *trie_op_hash_size* = *quarterword_diff* + *quarterword_diff*   { double }
⟨ Global variables 13 ⟩ +≡
    init *trie_op_hash*: **array** [0 .. *trie_op_hash_size*] **of** *quarterword*;   { trie op codes for triples }
    tini
    trie_op_ptr: *quarterword*;   { highest *trie_op* assigned }

---

decr = macro, §16.
found = 40, §15.
h: *hyph_pointer*, §934.
hyph_count: *hyph_pointer*, §926.
hyph_list: **array**, §926.
hyph_size = 307, §12.
hyph_word: **array**, §926.
incr = macro, §16.

k: *str_number*, §934.
length = macro, §40.
max_quarterword = 255, §110.
min_quarterword = 0, §110.
new_trie_op: **function**, §944.
not_found = 45, §15.
overflow: **procedure**, §94.
p: *pointer*, §934.

q: *pointer*, §934.
quarterword = 0 .. 255, §113.
s: *str_number*, §934.
str_pool: **packed array**, §39.
str_start: **array**, §39.
t: *str_number*, §934.
u: *pool_pointer*, §934.
v: *pool_pointer*, §934.

944. The hash function used by *new_trie_op* is based on the observation that $313/510$ is an approximation to the golden ratio [cf. *The Art of Computer Programming* **3** (1973), 510–512]; *trie_op_hash_size* is usually a multiple of 510. But the choice is comparatively unimportant in this particular application.

⟨ Declare procedures for preprocessing hyphenation patterns 944 ⟩ ≡
function *new_trie_op*(*d*, *n* : *small_number*; *v* : *quarterword*): *quarterword*;
  label *exit*;
  var *h*: 0 .. *trie_op_hash_size*; { trial hash location }
    u: *quarterword*; { trial op code }
  begin $h \leftarrow abs(n + 313 * d + 361 * v) \bmod \mathit{trie\_op\_hash\_size}$;
  loop begin $u \leftarrow \mathit{trie\_op\_hash}[h]$;
    if $u = \mathit{min\_quarterword}$ **then** { empty position found }
      begin if $\mathit{trie\_op\_ptr} = \mathit{max\_quarterword}$ **then** { overflow }
        begin $\mathit{new\_trie\_op} \leftarrow \mathit{min\_quarterword}$; **return**;
        end;
      $incr(\mathit{trie\_op\_ptr})$; $\mathit{hyf\_distance}[\mathit{trie\_op\_ptr}] \leftarrow d$; $\mathit{hyf\_num}[\mathit{trie\_op\_ptr}] \leftarrow n$;
      $\mathit{hyf\_next}[\mathit{trie\_op\_ptr}] \leftarrow v$; $\mathit{trie\_op\_hash}[h] \leftarrow \mathit{trie\_op\_ptr}$; $\mathit{new\_trie\_op} \leftarrow \mathit{trie\_op\_ptr}$; **return**;
      end;
    if $(\mathit{hyf\_distance}[u] = d) \wedge (\mathit{hyf\_num}[u] = n) \wedge (\mathit{hyf\_next}[u] = v)$ **then**
      begin $\mathit{new\_trie\_op} \leftarrow u$; **return**;
      end;
    if $h > 0$ **then** $decr(h)$ **else** $h \leftarrow \mathit{trie\_op\_hash\_size}$;
    end;
exit: **end**;

See also sections 947, 948, 949, 951, 953, 957, 959, and 960.

This code is used in section 942.

945. The linked trie that is used to preprocess hyphenation patterns appears in several global arrays. Each node represents an instruction of the form "if you see character *c*, then perform operation *o*, move to the next character, and go to node *l*; otherwise go to node *r*." The four quantities *c*, *o*, *l*, and *r* are stored in four arrays *trie_c*, *trie_o*, *trie_l*, and *trie_r*. The root of the trie is *trie_l*[0], and the number of nodes is *trie_ptr*. Null trie pointers are represented by zero. To initialize the trie, we simply set *trie_l*[0] and *trie_ptr* to zero. We also set *trie_c*[0] to some arbitrary value, since the algorithm may access it.

    The algorithms maintain the condition

$$\mathit{trie\_c}[\mathit{trie\_r}[z]] > \mathit{trie\_c}[z] \qquad \text{whenever } z \neq 0 \text{ and } \mathit{trie\_r}[z] \neq 0;$$

in other words, sibling nodes are ordered by their *c* fields.

    define *trie_root* ≡ *trie_l*[0] { root of the linked trie }
⟨ Global variables 13 ⟩ +≡
  init *trie_c*: **packed array** [*trie_pointer*] **of** *ASCII_code*; { characters to match }
  trie_o: **packed array** [*trie_pointer*] **of** *quarterword*; { operations to perform }
  trie_l: **packed array** [*trie_pointer*] **of** *trie_pointer*; { left subtrie links }
  trie_r: **packed array** [*trie_pointer*] **of** *trie_pointer*; { right subtrie links }
  trie_ptr: *trie_pointer*; { the number of nodes in the trie }
  tini

946. Let us suppose that a linked trie has already been constructed. Experience shows that we can often reduce its size by recognizing common subtries; therefore another hash table is introduced for this purpose, somewhat similar to *trie_op_hash*. The new hash table will be initialized to zero.

⟨ Global variables 13 ⟩ +≡
    init *trie_hash*: **packed array** [*trie_pointer*] **of** *trie_pointer*;
    tini { to identify equivalent subtries }

947. The function *trie_node*(p) returns *p* if *p* is distinct from other nodes that it has seen, otherwise it returns the number of the first equivalent node that it has seen.

⟨ Declare procedures for preprocessing hyphenation patterns 944 ⟩ +≡
function *trie_node*(p : *trie_pointer*): *trie_pointer*; { converts to a canonical form }
  label *exit*;
  var *h*: *trie_pointer*; { trial hash location }
    q: *trie_pointer*; { trial trie node }
  begin $h \leftarrow abs(trie\_c[p] + 1009 * trie\_o[p] + 2718 * trie\_l[p] + 3142 * trie\_r[p])$ **mod** *trie_size*;
  loop begin $q \leftarrow trie\_hash[h]$;
    if $q = 0$ **then**
      begin $trie\_hash[h] \leftarrow p$; $trie\_node \leftarrow p$; **return**;
      end;
    if $(trie\_c[q] = trie\_c[p]) \wedge (trie\_o[q] = trie\_o[p]) \wedge (trie\_l[q] = trie\_l[p]) \wedge (trie\_r[q] = trie\_r[p])$ **then**
      begin $trie\_node \leftarrow q$; **return**;
      end;
    if $h > 0$ **then** *decr*(h) **else** $h \leftarrow trie\_size$;
    end;
exit: **end**;

948. A neat recursive procedure is now able to compress a trie by traversing it and applying *trie_node* to its nodes in "bottom up" fashion. We will compress the entire trie by clearing *trie_hash* to zero and then saying '*trie_root* ← *compress_trie*(*trie_root*)'.

⟨ Declare procedures for preprocessing hyphenation patterns 944 ⟩ +≡
function *compress_trie*(p : *trie_pointer*): *trie_pointer*;
  begin if $p = 0$ **then** *compress_trie* ← 0
  else begin $trie\_l[p] \leftarrow compress\_trie(trie\_l[p])$; $trie\_r[p] \leftarrow compress\_trie(trie\_r[p])$;
    $compress\_trie \leftarrow trie\_node(p)$;
    end;
  end;

ASCII_code = 0 .. 127, §18.
decr = macro, §16.
exit = 10, §15.
incr = macro, §16.
max_quarterword = 255, §110.

min_quarterword = 0, §110.
quarterword = 0 .. 255, §113.
small_number = 0 .. 63, §101.
trie_op_hash: **array**, §943.

trie_op_hash_size = 510, §943.
trie_op_ptr: *quarterword*, §943.
trie_pointer = 0 .. *trie_size*, §920.
trie_size = **const**, §11.

949.   Before we forget how to initialize the data structures that have been mentioned so far, let's write a procedure that does the initialization.

⟨ Declare procedures for preprocessing hyphenation patterns 944 ⟩ +≡
procedure *init_pattern_memory*;   { gets ready to build a linked trie }
   var *h*: 0 .. *trie_op_hash_size*;   { an index into *trie_op_hash* }
     p: *trie_pointer*;   { an index into *trie_hash* }
   begin for *h* ← 0 **to** *trie_op_hash_size* **do** *trie_op_hash*[*h*] ← *min_quarterword*;
   trie_op_ptr ← *min_quarterword*; *trie_root* ← 0; *trie_c*[0] ← 0; *trie_ptr* ← 0;
   for *p* ← 0 **to** *trie_size* **do** *trie_hash*[*p*] ← 0;
   end;

950.   The compressed trie will be packed into the *trie* array using a "top-down first-fit" procedure. This is a little tricky, so the reader should pay close attention: The *trie_hash* array is cleared to zero again and renamed *trie_ref* for this phase of the operation; later on, *trie_ref*[*p*] will be nonzero if the linked trie node *p* is the oldest sibling in a family and if the characters *c* of that family have been allocated to locations *trie_ref*[*p*] + *c* in the *trie* array. Locations of *trie* that are in use will have *trie_link* = 0, while the unused holes in *trie* will be doubly linked with *trie_link* pointing to the next larger vacant location and *trie_back* pointing to the next smaller one. This double linking will have been carried out only as far as *trie_max*, where *trie_max* is the largest index of *trie* that will be needed. Another array *trie_taken* tells whether or not a given location is equal to *trie_ref*[*p*] for some *p*; this array is used to ensure that distinct nodes in the compressed trie will have distinct *trie_ref* entries.

   define *trie_ref* ≡ *trie_hash*   { where linked trie families go into *trie* }
   define *trie_back*(#) ≡ *trie*[#].*lh*   { backward links in *trie* holes }

⟨ Global variables 13 ⟩ +≡
   init *trie_taken*: **packed array** [*trie_pointer*] **of** *boolean*;   { does a family start here? }
   trie_min: *trie_pointer*;   { all locations ≤ *trie_min* are vacant in *trie* }
   tini
   trie_max: *trie_pointer*;   { largest location used in *trie* }

951.   Here is how these data structures are initialized.

⟨ Declare procedures for preprocessing hyphenation patterns 944 ⟩ +≡
procedure *init_trie_memory*;   { gets ready to pack into *trie* }
   var *p*: *trie_pointer*;   { index into *trie_ref*, *trie*, *trie_taken* }
   begin for *p* ← 0 **to** *trie_ptr* **do** *trie_ref*[*p*] ← 0;
   trie_max ← 128; *trie_min* ← 128; *trie_link*(0) ← 1; *trie_taken*[0] ← *false*;
   for *p* ← 1 **to** 128 **do**
     begin *trie_back*(*p*) ← *p* − 1; *trie_link*(*p*) ← *p* + 1; *trie_taken*[*p*] ← *false*;
     end;
   end;

952.   Each time \patterns appears, it overrides any patterns that were entered earlier, so the arrays are not initialized until TeX sees \patterns. However, some of the global variables must be initialized when INITEX is loaded, in case the user never mentions any \patterns.

⟨ Initialize table entries (done by INITEX only) 164 ⟩ +≡
   trie_op_ptr ← *min_quarterword*;
   trie_link(0) ← 0; *trie_char*(0) ← 0; *trie_op*(0) ← 0;

for $k \leftarrow 1$ **to** 127 **do** $trie[k] \leftarrow trie[0]$;
$trie\_max \leftarrow 127$;

953. The *first_fit* procedure finds the smallest hole z in *trie* such that a trie family starting at a given node p will fit into vacant positions starting at z. If $c = trie\_c[p]$, this means that location $z - c$ must not already be taken by some other family, and that $z - c + c'$ must be vacant for all characters c' in the family. The procedure sets $trie\_ref[p]$ to $z - c$ when the first fit has been found.

$\langle$ Declare procedures for preprocessing hyphenation patterns 944 $\rangle$ $+\equiv$
procedure *first_fit*($p : trie\_pointer$);   { packs a family into *trie* }
  label *not_found*, *found*;
  var h: *trie_pointer*;   { candidate for $trie\_ref[p]$ }
    z: *trie_pointer*;   { runs through holes }
    q: *trie_pointer*;   { runs through the family starting at p }
    c: *ASCII_code*;   { smallest character in the family }
  begin $c \leftarrow trie\_c[p]$;   { we have $c > 0$ }
  if $c < trie\_min$ **then** $trie\_min \leftarrow c$;
  $z \leftarrow trie\_link(trie\_min - 1)$;   { get the first conceivably good hole }
  loop begin if $z < c$ **then goto** *not_found*;
    $h \leftarrow z - c$;
    $\langle$ Ensure that $trie\_max \geq h + 128$ 954 $\rangle$;
    if $trie\_taken[h]$ **then goto** *not_found*;
    $\langle$ If all characters of the family fit relative to h, then **goto** *found*, otherwise **goto** *not_found* 955 $\rangle$;
  not_found: $z \leftarrow trie\_link(z)$;   { move to the next hole }
    end;
found: $\langle$ Pack the family into *trie* relative to h 956 $\rangle$;
  end;

954. By making sure that $trie\_max$ is at least $h + 128$, we can be sure that $trie\_max > z$, since $h = z + c$. It follows that location $trie\_max$ will never be occupied in *trie*, and we will have $trie\_max \geq trie\_link(z)$.

$\langle$ Ensure that $trie\_max \geq h + 128$ 954 $\rangle$ $\equiv$
  if $trie\_max < h + 128$ **then**
    begin if $trie\_size \leq h + 128$ **then** *overflow*("pattern␣memory", $trie\_size$);
    repeat *incr*($trie\_max$); $trie\_taken[trie\_max] \leftarrow false$; $trie\_link(trie\_max) \leftarrow trie\_max + 1$;
      $trie\_back(trie\_max) \leftarrow trie\_max - 1$;
    until $trie\_max = h + 128$;
    end
This code is used in section 953.

$ASCII\_code = 0 .. 127$, §18.
found $= 40$, §15.
incr $=$ **macro**, §16.
k: *integer*, §163.
lh: *halfword*, §560.
min_quarterword $= 0$, §110.

not_found $= 45$, §15.
overflow: **procedure**, §94.
trie_c: **packed array**, §945.
trie_hash: **packed array**, §946.
trie_op_hash: **array**, §943.
trie_op_hash_size $= 510$, §943.

trie_op_ptr: *quarterword*, §943.
trie_pointer $= 0 .. trie\_size$, §920.
trie_ptr: *trie_pointer*, §945.
trie_root $=$ **macro**, §945.
trie_size $=$ **const**, §11.

955. ⟨If all characters of the family fit relative to h, then **goto** *found*, otherwise **goto** *not_found* 955⟩ ≡
$q \leftarrow trie\_r[p]$;
while $q > 0$ **do**
  begin if $trie\_link(h + trie\_c[q]) = 0$ **then goto** *not_found*;
  $q \leftarrow trie\_r[q]$;
  end;
goto *found*

This code is used in section 953.

956. ⟨Pack the family into *trie* relative to h 956⟩ ≡
  $trie\_taken[h] \leftarrow true$; $trie\_ref[p] \leftarrow h$; $q \leftarrow p$;
  repeat $z \leftarrow h + trie\_c[q]$; $trie\_back(trie\_link(z)) \leftarrow trie\_back(z)$;
    $trie\_link(trie\_back(z)) \leftarrow trie\_link(z)$; $trie\_link(z) \leftarrow 0$; $q \leftarrow trie\_r[q]$;
  until $q = 0$

This code is used in section 953.

957. To pack the entire linked trie, we use the following recursive procedure.

⟨Declare procedures for preprocessing hyphenation patterns 944⟩ +≡
procedure $trie\_pack(p : trie\_pointer)$; { pack subtries of a family }
  var q: $trie\_pointer$; { a local variable that need not be saved on recursive calls }
  begin repeat $q \leftarrow trie\_l[p]$;
    if $(q > 0) \wedge (trie\_ref[q] = 0)$ **then**
      begin $first\_fit(q)$; $trie\_pack(q)$;
      end;
    $p \leftarrow trie\_r[p]$;
  until $p = 0$;
  end;

958. When the whole trie has been allocated into the sequential table, we must go through it once again so that *trie* contains the correct information. Null pointers in the linked trie will be replaced by the first untaken position r in *trie*, since this properly implements an "empty" family. The value of r is stored in $trie\_ref[0]$ just before the fixup process starts. Note that $trie\_max$ will always be at least as large as $r + 127$, since it is always at least 128 more than each location that is taken.

⟨Move the data into *trie* 958⟩ ≡
  $r \leftarrow 0$;
  while $trie\_taken[r]$ **do** $incr(r)$;
  $trie\_ref[0] \leftarrow r$; { r will be used for null pointers }
  $trie\_fix(trie\_root)$ { this fixes the non-holes in *trie* }

This code is used in section 966.

959. The fixing-up procedure is, of course, recursive. Since the linked trie usually has overlapping subtries, the same data may be moved several times; but that causes no harm, and at most as much work is done as it took to build the uncompressed trie.

⟨Declare procedures for preprocessing hyphenation patterns 944⟩ +≡
procedure $trie\_fix(p : trie\_pointer)$; { moves p and its siblings into *trie* }
  var q: $trie\_pointer$; { a local variable that need not be saved on recursive calls }

c: $ASCII\_code$;   { another one that need not be saved }
z: $trie\_pointer$;   { $trie$ reference; this local variable must be saved }
begin $z \leftarrow trie\_ref[p]$;
while $p \neq 0$ **do**
   begin $q \leftarrow trie\_l[p]$; $c \leftarrow trie\_c[p]$; $trie\_link(z+c) \leftarrow trie\_ref[q]$; $trie\_char(z+c) \leftarrow c$;
   $trie\_op(z+c) \leftarrow trie\_o[p]$;
   if $q > 0$ **then** $trie\_fix(q)$;
   $p \leftarrow trie\_r[p]$;
   end;
end;

960.   Now let's put all these routines together. When INITEX has scanned the '\patterns'
control sequence, it calls on *new_patterns* to do the right thing. After *new_patterns* has acted,
the compacted pattern data will appear in the array $trie[1 .. trie\_max]$, and the associated
numeric hyphenation data will appear in locations $[(min\_quarterword + 1) .. trie\_op\_ptr]$ of the
arrays *hyf_distance*, *hyf_num*, *hyf_next*.

⟨ Declare procedures for preprocessing hyphenation patterns 944 ⟩ +≡
procedure *new_patterns*;   { initializes the hyphenation pattern data }
   label *done*, *done1*;
   var k, l: *small_number*;   { indices into *hc* and *hyf* }
      digit_sensed: *boolean*;   { should the next digit be treated as a letter? }
      v: *quarterword*;   { trie op code }
      p, q: *trie_pointer*;   { nodes of trie traversed during insertion }
      first_child: *boolean*;   { is $p = trie\_l[q]$? }
      c: *ASCII_code*;   { character being inserted }
      r, s: *trie_pointer*;   { used to clean up the packed *trie* }
      h: *two_halves*;   { template used to zero out *trie*'s holes }
   begin *scan_left_brace*;   { a left brace must follow \patterns }
   init_pattern_memory;
   ⟨ Enter all of the patterns into a linked trie, until coming to a right brace; then skip an optional
      space 961 ⟩;
   $trie\_root \leftarrow compress\_trie(trie\_root)$;   { compress the trie }
   ⟨ Pack the trie 966 ⟩;
   end;

$ASCII\_code = 0 .. 127$, §18.
compress_trie: **function**, §948.
$done = 30$, §15.
$done1 = 31$, §15.
first_fit: **procedure**, §953.
$found = 40$, §15.
h: *trie_pointer*, §953.
hc: **array**, §892.
hyf: **array**, §900.
$incr$ = macro, §16.
init_pattern_memory: **procedure**,

§949.
$min\_quarterword = 0$, §110.
$not\_found = 45$, §15.
p: *trie_pointer*, §953.
q: *trie_pointer*, §953.
$quarterword = 0 .. 255$, §113.
scan_left_brace: **procedure**, §403.
$small\_number = 0 .. 63$, §101.
trie_back = macro, §950.
trie_c: **packed array**, §945.
trie_l: **packed array**, §945.

trie_max: *trie_pointer*, §950.
trie_o: **packed array**, §945.
trie_op_ptr: *quarterword*, §943.
trie_pointer = $0 .. trie\_size$, §920.
trie_r: **packed array**, §945.
trie_ref = macro, §950.
trie_root = macro, §945.
trie_taken: **packed array**, §950.
two_halves = **packed record**, §113.
z: *trie_pointer*, §953.

961. Novices are not supposed to be using \patterns, so the error messages are terse. (Note that all error messages appear in TEX's string pool, even if they are used only by INITEX.)

⟨Enter all of the patterns into a linked trie, until coming to a right brace; then skip an optional
        space 961⟩ ≡
  $k \leftarrow 0$; $hyf[0] \leftarrow 0$; $digit\_sensed \leftarrow false$;
  loop begin get_x_token;
    case cur_cmd **of**
    $letter, other\_char$: ⟨Append a new letter or a hyphen level 962⟩;
    $spacer, right\_brace$: **begin if** $k > 0$ **then** ⟨Insert a new pattern into the linked trie 963⟩;
      if $cur\_cmd = right\_brace$ **then goto** $done$;
      $k \leftarrow 0$; $hyf[0] \leftarrow 0$; $digit\_sensed \leftarrow false$;
      end;
    othercases begin $print\_err("Bad_\sqcup")$; $print\_esc("patterns")$; $help1("(See_\sqcup Appendix_\sqcup H.)")$;
      $error$;
      end
    endcases;
    end;
$done$:
This code is used in section 960.

962. ⟨Append a new letter or a hyphen level 962⟩ ≡
  if $digit\_sensed \lor (cur\_chr < "0") \lor (cur\_chr > "9")$ **then**
    begin if $cur\_chr = "."$ **then** $cur\_chr \leftarrow 128$ {edge-of-word delimiter}
    else begin $cur\_chr \leftarrow lc\_code(cur\_chr)$;
      if $cur\_chr = 0$ **then**
        begin $print\_err("Nonletter")$; $help1("(See_\sqcup Appendix_\sqcup H.)")$; $error$; $cur\_chr \leftarrow 128$;
        end;
      end;
    if $k < 63$ **then**
      begin $incr(k)$; $hc[k] \leftarrow cur\_chr - 1$; $hyf[k] \leftarrow 0$; $digit\_sensed \leftarrow false$;
      end;
    end
  else begin $hyf[k] \leftarrow cur\_chr - "0"$;
    if $k < 63$ **then** $digit\_sensed \leftarrow true$;
    end
This code is used in section 961.

963. When the following code comes into play, the pattern $p_1 \ldots p_k$ appears in $hc[1 .. k]$, and the corresponding sequence of numbers $n_0 \ldots n_k$ appears in $hyf[0 .. k]$.

⟨Insert a new pattern into the linked trie 963⟩ ≡
  begin ⟨Compute the trie op code, v, and set $l \leftarrow 0$ 965⟩;
  $q \leftarrow 0$;
  while $l < k$ **do**
    begin $incr(l)$; $c \leftarrow hc[l]$; $p \leftarrow trie\_l[q]$; $first\_child \leftarrow true$;
    while $(p > 0) \land (c > trie\_c[p])$ **do**
      begin $q \leftarrow p$; $p \leftarrow trie\_r[q]$; $first\_child \leftarrow false$;
      end;

> **if** $(p = 0) \vee (c < trie\_c[p])$ **then**
>   ⟨Insert a new trie node between q and p, and make p point to it 964⟩;
> $q \leftarrow p$; { now node q represents $p_1 \dots p_l$ }
> **end**;
> **if** $trie\_o[q] \neq min\_quarterword$ **then**
>   **begin** $print\_err($"Duplicate␣pattern"$)$; $help1($"(See␣Appendix␣H.)"$)$; $error$;
>   **end**;
> $trie\_o[q] \leftarrow v$;
> **end**

This code is used in section 961.

964. ⟨Insert a new trie node between q and p, and make p point to it 964⟩ ≡
  begin if $trie\_ptr = trie\_size$ **then** $overflow($"pattern␣memory"$, trie\_size)$;
  $incr(trie\_ptr)$; $trie\_r[trie\_ptr] \leftarrow p$; $p \leftarrow trie\_ptr$; $trie\_l[p] \leftarrow 0$;
  if $first\_child$ **then** $trie\_l[q] \leftarrow p$ **else** $trie\_r[q] \leftarrow p$;
  $trie\_c[p] \leftarrow c$; $trie\_o[p] \leftarrow min\_quarterword$;
  end

This code is used in section 963.

965. ⟨Compute the trie op code, v, and set $l \leftarrow 0$ 965⟩ ≡
  if $hc[1] = 127$ **then** $hyf[0] \leftarrow 0$;
  if $hc[k] = 127$ **then** $hyf[k] \leftarrow 0$;
  $l \leftarrow k$; $v \leftarrow min\_quarterword$;
  loop begin if $hyf[l] \neq 0$ **then** $v \leftarrow new\_trie\_op(k - l, hyf[l], v)$;
    if $l > 0$ **then** $decr(l)$ **else goto** $done1$;
    end;
$done1$:

This code is used in section 963.

---

c: $ASCII\_code$, §960.
cur_chr: $halfword$, §297.
cur_cmd: $eight\_bits$, §297.
$decr$ = macro, §16.
$digit\_sensed$: $boolean$, §960.
$done = 30$, §15.
$done1 = 31$, §15.
$error$: **procedure**, §82.
$first\_child$: $boolean$, §960.
get_x_token: **procedure**, §380.
hc: **array**, §892.
$help1$ = macro, §79.

hyf: **array**, §900.
$incr$ = macro, §16.
k: $small\_number$, §960.
l: $small\_number$, §960.
lc_code = macro, §230.
$letter = 11$, §207.
$min\_quarterword = 0$, §110.
new_trie_op: **function**, §944.
$other\_char = 12$, §207.
$overflow$: **procedure**, §94.
p: $trie\_pointer$, §960.
$print\_err$ = macro, §73.

$print\_esc$: **procedure**, §63.
q: $trie\_pointer$, §960.
$right\_brace = 2$, §207.
$spacer = 10$, §207.
$trie\_c$: **packed array**, §945.
$trie\_l$: **packed array**, §945.
$trie\_o$: **packed array**, §945.
$trie\_ptr$: $trie\_pointer$, §945.
$trie\_r$: **packed array**, §945.
$trie\_size$ = **const**, §11.
v: $quarterword$, §960.

966. The following packing routine is rigged so that the root of the linked tree gets mapped into location 0 of *trie*, as required by the hyphenation algorithm. This happens because the first call of *first_fit* will "take" location 0.

⟨ Pack the trie 966 ⟩ ≡
  init_trie_memory;
  if *trie_root* ≠ 0 **then**
    begin *first_fit*(*trie_root*); *trie_pack*(*trie_root*);
    end;
  ⟨ Move the data into *trie* 958 ⟩;
  r ← 0;   { finally, we will zero out the holes }
  h.rh ← 0; *h.b0* ← *min_quarterword*; *h.b1* ← 0;
      { *trie_link* ← 0, *trie_op* ← *min_quarterword*, *trie_char* ← 0 }
  repeat *s* ← *trie_link*(*r*); *trie*[*r*] ← *h*; *r* ← *s*;
  until *r* > *trie_max*

This code is used in section 960.

967. Breaking vertical lists into pages. The *vsplit* procedure, which implements TℇX's \vsplit operation, is considerably simpler than *line_break* because it doesn't have to worry about hyphenation, and because its mission is to discover a single break instead of an optimum sequence of breakpoints. But before we get into the details of *vsplit*, we need to consider a few more basic things.

968. A subroutine called *prune_page_top* takes a pointer to a vlist and returns a pointer to a modified vlist in which all glue, kern, and penalty nodes have been deleted before the first box or rule node. However, the first box or rule is actually preceded by a newly created glue node designed so that the topmost baseline will be at distance *split_top_skip* from the top, whenever this is possible without backspacing.

In this routine and those that follow, we make use of the fact that a vertical list contains no character nodes, hence the *type* field exists for each node in the list.

function *prune_page_top*(*p* : *pointer*): *pointer*;   { adjust top after page break }
   var *prev_p*: *pointer*;   { lags one step behind *p* }
     q: *pointer*;   { temporary variable for list manipulation }
   begin *prev_p* ← *temp_head*; *link*(*temp_head*) ← *p*;
  while *p* ≠ *null* **do**
    case *type*(*p*) **of**
    hlist_node, *vlist_node*, *rule_node*: ⟨ Insert glue for *split_top_skip* and set *p* ← *null* 969 ⟩;
    whatsit_node, *mark_node*, *ins_node*: **begin** *prev_p* ← *p*; *p* ← *link*(*prev_p*);
      end;
    glue_node, *kern_node*, *penalty_node*: **begin** *q* ← *p*; *p* ← *link*(*q*); *link*(*q*) ← *null*; *link*(*prev_p*) ← *p*;
      flush_node_list(*q*);
      end;
    othercases *confusion*("pruning")
    endcases;
   prune_page_top ← *link*(*temp_head*);
   end;

969. ⟨Insert glue for *split_top_skip* and set $p \leftarrow null$ 969⟩ ≡
> **begin** $q \leftarrow new\_skip\_param(split\_top\_skip\_code)$; $link(prev\_p) \leftarrow q$; $link(q) \leftarrow p$;
> > { now $temp\_ptr = glue\_ptr(q)$ }
> **if** $width(temp\_ptr) > height(p)$ **then** $width(temp\_ptr) \leftarrow width(temp\_ptr) - height(p)$
> **else** $width(temp\_ptr) \leftarrow 0$;
> $p \leftarrow null$;
> **end**

This code is used in section 968.

970. The next subroutine finds the best place to break a given vertical list so as to obtain a box of height h, with maximum depth d. A pointer to the beginning of the vertical list is given, and a pointer to the optimum breakpoint is returned. The list is effectively followed by a forced break, i.e., a penalty node with the *eject_penalty*; if the best break occurs at this artificial node, the value *null* is returned.

An array of six *scaled* distances is used to keep track of the height from the beginning of the list to the current place, just as in *line_break*. In fact, we use one of the same arrays, only changing its name to reflect its new significance.

> **define** $active\_height \equiv active\_width$ { new name for the six distance variables }
> **define** $cur\_height \equiv active\_height[1]$ { the natural height }
> **define** $set\_height\_zero(\#) \equiv active\_height[\#] \leftarrow 0$ { initialize the height to zero }
> **define** $update\_heights = 90$ { go here to record glue in the *active_height* table }

function $vert\_break(p : pointer; h, d : scaled): pointer$; { finds optimum page break }
> **label** $done, not\_found, update\_heights$;
> **var** $prev\_p$: *pointer*; { if p is a glue node, $type(prev\_p)$ determines whether p is a legal breakpoint }
> > q, r: *pointer*; { glue specifications }
> > pi: *integer*; { penalty value }
> > b: *integer*; { badness at a trial breakpoint }
> > $least\_cost$: *integer*; { the smallest badness plus penalties found so far }
> > $best\_place$: *pointer*; { the most recent break that leads to *least_cost* }
> > $prev\_dp$: *scaled*; { depth of previous box in the list }
> > t: *small_number*; { *type* of the node following a kern }
> **begin** $prev\_p \leftarrow p$; { an initial glue node is not a legal breakpoint }
> $least\_cost \leftarrow awful\_bad$; $do\_all\_six(set\_height\_zero)$; $prev\_dp \leftarrow 0$;
> **loop begin** ⟨If node p is a legal breakpoint, check if this break is the best known, and **goto** *done* if
> > p is null or if the page-so-far is already too full to accept more stuff 972⟩;
> > $prev\_p \leftarrow p$; $p \leftarrow link(prev\_p)$;
> > **end**;
> $done$: $vert\_break \leftarrow best\_place$;
> **end**;

971. A global variable *best_height_plus_depth* will be set to the natural size of the box that corresponds to the optimum breakpoint found by *vert_break*. (This value is used by the insertion-splitting algorithm of the page builder.)

⟨Global variables 13⟩ +≡
$best\_height\_plus\_depth$: *scaled*; { height of the best box, without stretching or shrinking }

972. A subtle point to be noted here is that the maximum depth d might be negative, so *cur_height* and *prev_dp* might need to be corrected even after a glue or kern node.

⟨If node p is a legal breakpoint, check if this break is the best known, and **goto** *done* if p is null or if
        the page-so-far is already too full to accept more stuff 972⟩ ≡
    if $p = null$ **then** $pi \leftarrow eject\_penalty$
    else ⟨Use node p to update the current height and depth measurements; if this node is not a legal
            breakpoint, **goto** *not_found* or *update_heights*, otherwise set pi to the associated penalty at
            the break 973⟩;
    ⟨Check if node p is a new champion breakpoint; then **goto** *done* if p is a forced break or if the
            page-so-far is already too full 974⟩;
    if $(type(p) < glue\_node) \vee (type(p) > kern\_node)$ **then goto** *not_found*;
update_heights: ⟨Update the current height and depth measurements with respect to a glue or kern
        node p 976⟩;
not_found: **if** $prev\_dp > d$ **then**
        begin $cur\_height \leftarrow cur\_height + prev\_dp - d$; $prev\_dp \leftarrow d$;
        end;
This code is used in section 970.

973.   ⟨Use node p to update the current height and depth measurements; if this node is not a legal
        breakpoint, **goto** *not_found* or *update_heights*, otherwise set pi to the associated penalty at the
        break 973⟩ ≡
    case $type(p)$ **of**
    $hlist\_node$, $vlist\_node$, $rule\_node$: **begin**
        $cur\_height \leftarrow cur\_height + prev\_dp + height(p)$; $prev\_dp \leftarrow depth(p)$; **goto** *not_found*;
        end;
    $whatsit\_node$: ⟨Process whatsit p in $vert\_break$ loop, **goto** *not_found* 1364⟩;
    $glue\_node$: **if** $precedes\_break(prev\_p)$ **then** $pi \leftarrow 0$
        else goto *update_heights*;
    $kern\_node$: **begin if** $link(p) = null$ **then** $t \leftarrow penalty\_node$
        else $t \leftarrow type(link(p))$;
        if $t = glue\_node$ **then** $pi \leftarrow 0$ **else goto** *update_heights*;
        end;
    $penalty\_node$: $pi \leftarrow penalty(p)$;
    $mark\_node$, ins_node: **goto** *not_found*;
    othercases $confusion($"vertbreak"$)$
    endcases
This code is used in section 972.

974. **define** *deplorable* ≡ 100000   { more than *inf_bad*, but less than *awful_bad* }

⟨ Check if node p is a new champion breakpoint; then **goto** *done* if p is a forced break or if the page-so-far is already too full 974 ⟩ ≡

  if $pi < inf\_penalty$ **then**
    begin ⟨ Compute the badness, b, using *awful_bad* if the box is too full 975 ⟩;
    if $b < awful\_bad$ **then**
      if $pi \leq eject\_penalty$ **then** $b \leftarrow pi$
      else if $b < inf\_bad$ **then** $b \leftarrow b + pi$
        else $b \leftarrow deplorable$;
    if $b \leq least\_cost$ **then**
      begin $best\_place \leftarrow p$; $least\_cost \leftarrow b$; $best\_height\_plus\_depth \leftarrow cur\_height + prev\_dp$;
      end;
    if $(b = awful\_bad) \vee (pi \leq eject\_penalty)$ **then goto** *done*;
    end

This code is used in section 972.

975. ⟨ Compute the badness, b, using *awful_bad* if the box is too full 975 ⟩ ≡
  if $cur\_height < h$ **then**
    if $(active\_height[3] \neq 0) \vee (active\_height[4] \neq 0) \vee (active\_height[5] \neq 0)$ **then** $b \leftarrow 0$
    else $b \leftarrow badness(h - cur\_height, active\_height[2])$
  else if $cur\_height - h > active\_height[6]$ **then** $b \leftarrow awful\_bad$
    else $b \leftarrow badness(cur\_height - h, active\_height[6])$

This code is used in section 974.

976. Vertical lists that are subject to the *vert_break* procedure should not contain infinite shrinkability, since that would permit any amount of information to "fit" on one page.

⟨ Update the current height and depth measurements with respect to a glue or kern node p 976 ⟩ ≡
  if $type(p) = kern\_node$ **then** $q \leftarrow p$
  else begin $q \leftarrow glue\_ptr(p)$;
    $active\_height[2 + stretch\_order(q)] \leftarrow active\_height[2 + stretch\_order(q)] + stretch(q)$;
    $active\_height[6] \leftarrow active\_height[6] + shrink(q)$;
    if $(shrink\_order(q) \neq normal) \wedge (shrink(q) \neq 0)$ **then**
      begin
      $print\_err($"Infinite␣glue␣shrinkage␣found␣in␣box␣being␣split"$)$;
      $help4($"The␣box␣you␣are␣\vsplitting␣contains␣some␣infinitely"$)$
      ($"shrinkable␣glue,␣e.g.,␣`\vss´␣or␣`\vskip␣0pt␣minus␣1fil´."$)
      ($"Such␣glue␣doesn´t␣belong␣there;␣but␣you␣can␣safely␣proceed,"$)
      ($"since␣the␣offensive␣shrinkability␣has␣been␣made␣finite."$); *error*; $r \leftarrow new\_spec(q)$;
      $shrink\_order(r) \leftarrow normal$; $delete\_glue\_ref(q)$; $glue\_ptr(p) \leftarrow r$;
      end;
    end;
  $cur\_height \leftarrow cur\_height + prev\_dp + width(q)$; $prev\_dp \leftarrow 0$

This code is used in section 972.

977. Now we are ready to consider *vsplit* itself. Most of its work is accomplished by the two subroutines that we have just considered.

Given the number of a vlist box n, and given a desired page height h, the *vsplit* function finds the best initial segment of the vlist and returns a box for a page of height h. The remainder of

the vlist, if any, replaces the original box, after removing glue and penalties and adjusting for
split_top_skip. Mark nodes in the split-off box are used to set the values of *split_first_mark* and
split_bot_mark; we use the fact that *split_first_mark* = *null* if and only if *split_bot_mark* = *null*.

The original box becomes "void" if and only if it has been entirely extracted. The extracted
box is "void" if and only if the original box was void (or if it was, erroneously, an hlist box).

function *vsplit*(*n* : *eight_bits*; *h* : *scaled*): *pointer*;   { extracts a page of height *h* from box *n* }
  label *exit*, *done*;
  var *v*: *pointer*;   { the box to be split }
    p: *pointer*;   { runs through the vlist }
    q: *pointer*;   { points to where the break occurs }
  begin *v* ← *box*(*n*);
  if *split_first_mark* ≠ *null* **then**
    begin *delete_token_ref*(*split_first_mark*); *split_first_mark* ← *null*; *delete_token_ref*(*split_bot_mark*);
    split_bot_mark ← *null*;
    end;
  ⟨ Dispense with trivial cases of void or bad boxes 978 ⟩;
  q ← *vert_break*(*list_ptr*(*v*), *h*, *split_max_depth*);
  ⟨ Look at all the marks in nodes before the break, and set the final link to *null* at the break 979 ⟩;
  q ← *prune_page_top*(*q*); *p* ← *list_ptr*(*v*); *free_node*(*v*, *box_node_size*);
  if *q* = *null* **then** *box*(*n*) ← *null*   { the *eq_level* of the box stays the same }
  else *box*(*n*) ← *vpack*(*q*, *natural*);
  vsplit ← *vpackage*(*p*, *h*, *exactly*, *split_max_depth*);
exit: **end**;

---

active_height = macro, §970.
awful_bad = macro, §833.
b: *integer*, §970.
badness: **function**, §108.
best_height_plus_depth: *scaled*, §971.
best_place: *pointer*, §970.
box = macro, §230.
box_node_size = 7, §135.
cur_height = macro, §970.
delete_glue_ref: **procedure**, §201.
delete_token_ref: **procedure**, §200.
done = 30, §15.
eight_bits = 0 .. 255, §25.
eject_penalty = −10000, §157.
eq_level = macro, §221.
error: **procedure**, §82.
exactly = 0, §644.
exit = 10, §15.

free_node: **procedure**, §130.
glue_ptr = macro, §149.
h: *scaled*, §970.
help4 = macro, §79.
inf_bad = 10000, §108.
inf_penalty = 10000, §157.
kern_node = 11, §155.
least_cost: *integer*, §970.
list_ptr = macro, §135.
natural = macro, §644.
new_spec: **function**, §151.
normal = 0, §135.
null = macro, §115.
p: *pointer*, §970.
pi: *integer*, §970.
pointer = macro, §115.
prev_dp: *scaled*, §970.
print_err = macro, §73.

prune_page_top: **function**, §968.
q: *pointer*, §970.
r: *pointer*, §970.
scaled = *integer*, §101.
shrink = macro, §150.
shrink_order = macro, §150.
split_bot_mark = macro, §382.
split_first_mark = macro, §382.
split_max_depth = macro, §247.
split_top_skip = macro, §224.
stretch = macro, §150.
stretch_order = macro, §150.
type = macro, §133.
vert_break: **function**, §970.
vpack = macro, §668.
vpackage: **function**, §668.
width = macro, §135.

978. ⟨Dispense with trivial cases of void or bad boxes 978⟩ ≡

  if $v = null$ **then**
    begin $vsplit \leftarrow null$; **return**;
    end;
  if $type(v) \neq vlist\_node$ **then**
    begin $print\_err("")$; $print\_esc("vsplit")$; $print("\_needs\_a\_")$; $print\_esc("vbox")$;
    $help2("The\_box\_you\_are\_trying\_to\_split\_is\_an\_\backslash hbox.")$
    $("I\_can\'t\_split\_such\_a\_box,\_so\_I\'ll\_leave\_it\_alone.")$; $error$; $vsplit \leftarrow null$; **return**;
    end

This code is used in section 977.

979. It's possible that the box begins with a penalty node that is the "best" break, so we must be careful to handle this special case correctly.

⟨Look at all the marks in nodes before the break, and set the final link to *null* at the break 979⟩ ≡

  $p \leftarrow list\_ptr(v)$;
  if $p = q$ **then** $list\_ptr(v) \leftarrow null$
  else loop begin if $type(p) = mark\_node$ **then**
      if $split\_first\_mark = null$ **then**
        begin $split\_first\_mark \leftarrow mark\_ptr(p)$; $split\_bot\_mark \leftarrow split\_first\_mark$;
        $token\_ref\_count(split\_first\_mark) \leftarrow token\_ref\_count(split\_first\_mark) + 2$;
        end
      else begin $delete\_token\_ref(split\_bot\_mark)$; $split\_bot\_mark \leftarrow mark\_ptr(p)$;
        $add\_token\_ref(split\_bot\_mark)$;
        end;
    if $link(p) = q$ **then**
      begin $link(p) \leftarrow null$; **goto** *done*;
      end;
    $p \leftarrow link(p)$;
    end;
done:

This code is used in section 977.

980.   The page builder.   When TEX appends new material to its main vlist in vertical mode, it uses a method something like *vsplit* to decide where a page ends, except that the calculations are done "on line" as new items are placed on the list. The main complication in this process is that insertions have to be put into their boxes and removed from the vlist, in a more-or-less optimum manner.

We shall use the term "current page" for that part of the main vlist that is being considered as a candidate for being broken off and sent to the user's output routine. The current page starts at *link*(*page_head*), and it ends at *page_tail*. We have *page_head* = *page_tail* if this list is empty.

Utter chaos would reign if the user kept changing page specifications while a page is being constructed, so the page builder keeps the pertinent specifications frozen as soon as the page receives its first box or insertion. The global variable *page_contents* is *empty* when the current page contains only mark nodes and content-less whatsit nodes; it is *inserts_only* if the page contains only insertion nodes in addition to marks and whatsits. Glue nodes, kern nodes, and penalty nodes are discarded until a box or rule node appears, at which time *page_contents* changes to *box_there*. As soon as *page_contents* becomes non-*empty*, the current *vsize* and *max_depth* are squirreled away into *page_goal* and *page_max_depth*; the latter values will be used until the page has been forwarded to the user's output routine. The \topskip adjustment is made when *page_contents* changes to *box_there*.

Although *page_goal* starts out equal to *vsize*, it is decreased by the scaled natural height-plus-depth of the insertions considered so far, and by the \skip corrections for those insertions. Therefore it represents the size into which the non-inserted material should fit, assuming that all insertions in the current page have been made.

The global variables *best_page_break* and *least_page_cost* correspond respectively to the local variables *best_place* and *least_cost* in the *vert_break* routine that we have already studied; i.e., they record the location and value of the best place currently known for breaking the current page. The value of *page_goal* at the time of the best break is stored in *best_size*.

define *inserts_only* = 1   { *page_contents* when an insert node has been contributed, but no boxes }
define *box_there* = 2   {*page_contents* when a box or rule has been contributed }
⟨ Global variables 13 ⟩ +≡
page_tail: *pointer*;   { the final node on the current page }
page_contents: *empty* .. *box_there*;   { what is on the current page so far? }
page_max_depth: *scaled*;   { maximum box depth on page being built }
best_page_break: *pointer*;   { break here to get the best page known so far }
least_page_cost: *integer*;   { the score for this currently best page }
best_size: *scaled*;   { its *page_goal* }

---

add_token_ref = macro, §203.
best_place: *pointer*, §970.
delete_token_ref: **procedure**, §200.
done = 30, §15.
empty = 0, §16.
error: **procedure**, §82.
help2 = macro, §79.
least_cost: *integer*, §970.
link = macro, §118.
list_ptr = macro, §135.
mark_node = 4, §141.

mark_ptr = macro, §141.
max_depth = macro, §247.
null = macro, §115.
p: *pointer*, §970.
page_goal = macro, §982.
page_head = macro, §162.
pointer = macro, §115.
print: **procedure**, §59.
print_err = macro, §73.
print_esc: **procedure**, §63.
q: *pointer*, §970.

scaled = *integer*, §101.
split_bot_mark = macro, §382.
split_first_mark = macro, §382.
token_ref_count = macro, §200.
type = macro, §133.
v: *pointer*, §977.
vert_break: **function**, §970.
vlist_node = 1, §137.
vsize = macro, §247.
vsplit: **function**, §977.

981.   The page builder has another data structure to keep track of insertions. This is a list of four-word nodes, starting and ending at *page_ins_head*. That is, the first element of the list is node $r_1 = link(page\_ins\_head)$; node r_j is followed by $r_{j+1} = link(r_j)$; and if there are n items we have $r_{n+1} = page\_ins\_head$. The *subtype* field of each node in this list refers to an insertion number; for example, '\insert 250' would correspond to a node whose *subtype* is $qi(250)$ (the same as the *subtype* field of the relevant *ins_node*). These *subtype* fields are in increasing order, and $subtype(page\_ins\_head) = qi(255)$, so *page_ins_head* serves as a convenient sentinel at the end of the list. A record is present for each insertion number that appears in the current page.

The *type* field in these nodes distinguishes two possibilities that might occur as we look ahead before deciding on the optimum page break. If $type(r) = inserting$, then $height(r)$ contains the total of the height-plus-depth dimensions of the box and all its inserts seen so far. If $type(r) = split\_up$, then no more insertions will be made into this box, because at least one previous insertion was too big to fit on the current page; $broken\_ptr(r)$ points to the node where that insertion will be split, if TeX decides to split it, $broken\_ins(r)$ points to the insertion node that was tentatively split, and $height(r)$ includes also the natural height plus depth of the part that would be split off.

In both cases, $last\_ins\_ptr(r)$ points to the last *ins_node* encountered for box $qo(subtype(r))$ that would be at least partially inserted on the next page; and $best\_ins\_ptr(r)$ points to the last such *ins_node* that should actually be inserted, to get the page with minimum badness among all page breaks considered so far. We have $best\_ins\_ptr(r) = null$ if and only if no insertion for this box should be made to produce this optimum page.

The data structure definitions here use the fact that the *height* field appears in the fourth word of a box node.

> **define** *page_ins_node_size* = 4   { number of words for a page insertion node }
> **define** *inserting* = 0   { an insertion class that has not yet overflowed }
> **define** *split_up* = 1   { an overflowed insertion class }
> **define** *broken_ptr*(#) ≡ *link*(# + 1)   { an insertion for this class will break here if anywhere }
> **define** *broken_ins*(#) ≡ *info*(# + 1)   { this insertion might break at *broken_ptr* }
> **define** *last_ins_ptr*(#) ≡ *link*(# + 2)   { the most recent insertion for this *subtype* }
> **define** *best_ins_ptr*(#) ≡ *info*(# + 2)   { the optimum most recent insertion }

⟨ Initialize the special list heads and constant nodes 790 ⟩ +≡
  $subtype(page\_ins\_head) \leftarrow qi(255)$; $type(page\_ins\_head) \leftarrow split\_up$;
  $link(page\_ins\_head) \leftarrow page\_ins\_head$;

982.   An array *page_so_far* records the heights and depths of everything on the current page. This array contains six *scaled* numbers, like the similar arrays already considered in *line_break* and *vert_break*; and it also contains *page_goal* and *page_depth*, since these values are all accessible to the user via *set_page_dimen* commands. The value of *page_so_far*[1] is also called *page_total*. The stretch and shrink components of the \skip corrections for each insertion are included in *page_so_far*, but the natural space components of these corrections are not, since they have been subtracted from *page_goal*.

The variable *page_depth* records the depth of the current page; it has been adjusted so that it is at most *page_max_depth*. The variable *last_glue* points to the glue specification of the most recent node contributed from the contribution list, if this was a glue node; otherwise $last\_glue = max\_halfword$. (If the contribution list is nonempty, however, the value of *last_glue* is not necessarily accurate.) The variables *last_penalty* and *last_kern* are similar. And finally, *insert_penalties* holds the sum of the penalties associated with all split and floating insertions.

> **define** *page_goal* ≡ *page_so_far*[0]   { desired height of information on page being built }
> **define** *page_total* ≡ *page_so_far*[1]   { height of the current page }
> **define** *page_shrink* ≡ *page_so_far*[6]   { shrinkability of the current page }
> **define** *page_depth* ≡ *page_so_far*[7]   { depth of the current page }

⟨ Global variables 13 ⟩ +≡
page_so_far: **array** [0 .. 7] **of** *scaled*;   { height and glue of the current page }
last_glue: *pointer*;   { used to implement \lastskip }
last_penalty: *integer*;   { used to implement \lastpenalty }
last_kern: *scaled*;   { used to implement \lastkern }
insert_penalties: *integer*;   { sum of the penalties for held-over insertions }

983. ⟨ Put each of TEX's primitives into the hash table 226 ⟩ +≡
> *primitive*("pagegoal", *set_page_dimen*, 0); *primitive*("pagetotal", *set_page_dimen*, 1);
> *primitive*("pagestretch", *set_page_dimen*, 2); *primitive*("pagefilstretch", *set_page_dimen*, 3);
> *primitive*("pagefillstretch", *set_page_dimen*, 4); *primitive*("pagefilllstretch", *set_page_dimen*, 5);
> *primitive*("pageshrink", *set_page_dimen*, 6); *primitive*("pagedepth", *set_page_dimen*, 7);

984. ⟨ Cases of *print_cmd_chr* for symbolic printing of primitives 227 ⟩ +≡
set_page_dimen: **case** *chr_code* **of**
> 0: *print_esc*("pagegoal");
> 1: *print_esc*("pagetotal");
> 2: *print_esc*("pagestretch");
> 3: *print_esc*("pagefilstretch");
> 4: *print_esc*("pagefillstretch");
> 5: *print_esc*("pagefilllstretch");
> 6: *print_esc*("pageshrink");
> **othercases** *print_esc*("pagedepth")
> **endcases**;

---

chr_code: *halfword*, §298.
info = macro, §118.
ins_node = 3, §140.
line_break: **procedure**, §815.
link = macro, §118.
max_halfword = macro, §110.
null = macro, §115.

page_ins_head = macro, §162.
page_max_depth: *scaled*, §980.
pointer = macro, §115.
primitive: **procedure**, §264.
print_cmd_chr: **procedure**, §298.
print_esc: **procedure**, §63.
qi = macro, §112.

qo = macro, §112.
scaled = *integer*, §101.
set_page_dimen = 80, §209.
subtype = macro, §133.
type = macro, §133.
vert_break: **function**, §970.

985. **define** *print_plus_end*(#) ≡ *print*(#); **end**
  define *print_plus*(#) ≡
       if *page_so_far*[#] ≠ 0 **then**
          begin *print*("␣plus␣"); *print_scaled*(*page_so_far*[#]); *print_plus_end*

procedure *print_totals*;
  begin *print_scaled*(*page_total*); *print_plus*(2)(""); *print_plus*(3)("fil"); *print_plus*(4)("fill");
  print_plus(5)("filll");
  if *page_shrink* ≠ 0 **then**
    begin *print*("␣minus␣"); *print_scaled*(*page_shrink*);
    end;
  end;

986. ⟨ Show the status of the current page 986 ⟩ ≡
  if *page_head* ≠ *page_tail* **then**
    begin *print_nl*("###␣current␣page:");
    if *output_active* **then** *print*("␣(held␣over␣for␣next␣output)");
    show_box(*link*(*page_head*));
    if *page_contents* > *empty* **then**
      begin *print_nl*("total␣height␣"); *print_totals*; *print_nl*("␣goal␣height␣");
      print_scaled(*page_goal*); *r* ← *link*(*page_ins_head*);
      while *r* ≠ *page_ins_head* **do**
        begin *print_ln*; *print_esc*("insert"); *t* ← *qo*(*subtype*(*r*)); *print_int*(*t*); *print*("␣adds␣");
        t ← *x_over_n*(*height*(*r*), 1000) * *count*(*t*); *print_scaled*(*t*);
        if *type*(*r*) = *split_up* **then**
          begin *q* ← *page_head*; *t* ← 0;
          repeat *q* ← *link*(*q*);
            if (*type*(*q*) = *ins_node*) ∧ (*subtype*(*q*) = *subtype*(*r*)) **then** *incr*(*t*);
          until *q* = *broken_ins*(*r*);
          print(",␣#"); *print_int*(*t*); *print*("␣might␣split");
          end;
        r ← *link*(*r*);
        end;
      end;
    end

This code is used in section 218.

987. Here is a procedure that is called when the *page_contents* is changing from *empty* to *inserts_only* or *box_there*.

  define *set_page_so_far_zero*(#) ≡ *page_so_far*[#] ← 0

procedure *freeze_page_specs*(*s* : *small_number*);
  begin *page_contents* ← *s*; *page_goal* ← *vsize*; *page_max_depth* ← *max_depth*; *page_depth* ← 0;
  do_all_six(*set_page_so_far_zero*); *least_page_cost* ← *awful_bad*;
  stat if *tracing_pages* > 0 **then**
    begin *begin_diagnostic*; *print_nl*("%%␣goal␣height="); *print_scaled*(*page_goal*);
    print(",␣max␣depth="); *print_scaled*(*page_max_depth*); *end_diagnostic*(*false*);
    end; **tats**
  end;

988.   Pages are built by appending nodes to the current list in TₑX's vertical mode, which is at the outermost level of the semantic nest. This vlist is split into two parts; the "current page" that we have been talking so much about already, and the "contribution list" that receives new nodes as they are created. The current page contains everything that the page builder has accounted for in its data structures, as described above, while the contribution list contains other things that have been generated by other parts of TₑX but have not yet been seen by the page builder. The contribution list starts at $link(contrib\_head)$, and it ends at the current node in TₑX's vertical mode.

When TₑX has appended new material in vertical mode, it calls the procedure $build\_page$, which tries to catch up by moving nodes from the contribution list to the current page. This procedure will succeed in its goal of emptying the contribution list, unless a page break is discovered, i.e., unless the current page has grown to the point where the optimum next page break has been determined. In the latter case, the nodes after the optimum break will go back onto the contribution list, and control will effectively pass to the user's output routine.

We make $type(page\_head) = glue\_node$, so that an initial glue node on the current page will not be considered a valid breakpoint.

⟨ Initialize the special list heads and constant nodes 790 ⟩ +≡
    $type(page\_head) \leftarrow glue\_node;\ subtype(page\_head) \leftarrow normal;$

989.   The global variable $output\_active$ is true during the time the user's output routine is driving TₑX.

⟨ Global variables 13 ⟩ +≡
$output\_active: boolean;$ { are we in the midst of an output routine? }

990.   ⟨ Set initial values of key variables 21 ⟩ +≡
    $output\_active \leftarrow false;\ insert\_penalties \leftarrow 0;$

---

991.   The page builder is ready to start a fresh page if we initialize the following state variables. (However, the page insertion list is initialized elsewhere.)

⟨ Start a new current page 991 ⟩ ≡
    $page\_contents \leftarrow empty$; $page\_tail \leftarrow page\_head$; $link(page\_head) \leftarrow null$;
    $last\_glue \leftarrow max\_halfword$; $last\_penalty \leftarrow 0$; $last\_kern \leftarrow 0$; $page\_depth \leftarrow 0$; $page\_max\_depth \leftarrow 0$
This code is used in sections 215 and 1017.

992.   At certain times box 255 is supposed to be void (i.e., *null*), or an insertion box is supposed to be ready to accept a vertical list. If not, an error message is printed, and the following subroutine flushes the unwanted contents, reporting them to the user.

procedure *box_error*(n : *eight_bits*);
    begin *error*; *begin_diagnostic*; *print_nl*("The␣following␣box␣has␣been␣deleted:");
    show_box(*box*(n)); *end_diagnostic*(*true*); *flush_node_list*(*box*(n)); *box*(n) ← *null*;
    end;

993.   The following procedure guarantees that a given box register does not contain an \hbox.

procedure *ensure_vbox*(n : *eight_bits*);
    var p: *pointer*;   { the box register contents }
    begin $p \leftarrow box(n)$;
    if $p \neq null$ **then**
        if $type(p) = hlist\_node$ **then**
            begin *print_err*("Insertions␣can␣only␣be␣added␣to␣a␣vbox");
            help3("Tut␣tut:␣You´re␣trying␣to␣\insert␣into␣a")
            ("\box␣register␣that␣now␣contains␣an␣\hbox.")
            ("Proceed,␣and␣I´ll␣discard␣its␣present␣contents."); *box_error*(n);
            end;
    end;

994.   TₑX is not always in vertical mode at the time *build_page* is called; the current mode reflects what TₑX should return to, after the contribution list has been emptied. A call on *build_page* should be immediately followed by '**goto** *big_switch*', which is TₑX's central control point.

    define *contribute* = 80   { go here to link a node into the current page }

⟨ Declare the procedure called *fire_up* 1012 ⟩
procedure *build_page*;   { append contributions to the current page }
    label *exit*, *done*, *done1*, *continue*, *contribute*, *update_heights*;
    var p: *pointer*;   { the node being appended }
        q, r: *pointer*;   { nodes being examined }
        b, c: *integer*;   { badness and cost of current page }
        pi: *integer*;   { penalty to be added to the badness }
        n: *min_quarterword* .. 255;   { insertion box number }
        delta, h, w: *scaled*;   { sizes used for insertion calculations }
    begin if ($link(contrib\_head) = null$) ∨ *output_active* **then return**;
    repeat *continue*: $p \leftarrow link(contrib\_head)$;
        ⟨ Update the values of *last_glue*, *last_penalty*, and *last_kern* 996 ⟩;
        ⟨ Move node p to the current page; if it is time for a page break, put the nodes following the break
            back onto the contribution list, and **return** to the user's output routine if there is one 997 ⟩;

until $link(contrib\_head) = null$;
⟨ Make the contribution list empty by setting its tail to $contrib\_head$ 995 ⟩;
$exit$: **end**;

995.   define $contrib\_tail \equiv nest[0].tail\_field$ { tail of the contribution list }
⟨ Make the contribution list empty by setting its tail to $contrib\_head$ 995 ⟩ ≡
    if $nest\_ptr = 0$ **then** $tail \leftarrow contrib\_head$ { vertical mode }
    else $contrib\_tail \leftarrow contrib\_head$ { other modes }

This code is used in section 994.

**996.   ** ⟨ Update the values of $last\_glue$, $last\_penalty$, and $last\_kern$ 996 ⟩ ≡
    if $last\_glue \neq max\_halfword$ **then** $delete\_glue\_ref(last\_glue)$;
    $last\_penalty \leftarrow 0$; $last\_kern \leftarrow 0$;
    if $type(p) = glue\_node$ **then**
        begin $last\_glue \leftarrow glue\_ptr(p)$; $add\_glue\_ref(last\_glue)$;
        end
    else begin $last\_glue \leftarrow max\_halfword$;
        if $type(p) = penalty\_node$ **then** $last\_penalty \leftarrow penalty(p)$
        else if $type(p) = kern\_node$ **then** $last\_kern \leftarrow width(p)$;
        end

This code is used in section 994.

997.   The code here is an example of a many-way switch into routines that merge together in different places. Some people call this unstructured programming, but the author doesn't see much wrong with it, as long as the various labels have a well-understood meaning.

⟨ Move node p to the current page; if it is time for a page break, put the nodes following the break back onto the contribution list, and **return** to the user's output routine if there is one 997 ⟩ ≡

  ⟨ If the current page is empty and node p is to be deleted, **goto** *done1*; otherwise use node p to update the state of the current page; if this node is an insertion, **goto** *contribute*; otherwise if this node is not a legal breakpoint, **goto** *contribute* or *update_heights*; otherwise set pi to the penalty associated with this breakpoint 1000 ⟩;

  ⟨ Check if node p is a new champion breakpoint; then if it is time for a page break, prepare for output, and either fire up the user's output routine and **return** or ship out the page and **goto** *done* 1005 ⟩;

  if $(type(p) < glue\_node) \vee (type(p) > kern\_node)$ **then goto** *contribute*;

update_heights: ⟨ Update the current page measurements with respect to the glue or kern specified by node p 1004 ⟩;

contribute: ⟨ Make sure that *page_max_depth* is not exceeded 1003 ⟩;

  ⟨ Link node p into the current page and **goto** *done* 998 ⟩;

done1: ⟨ Recycle node p 999 ⟩;

done:

This code is used in section 994.

998.   ⟨ Link node p into the current page and **goto** *done* 998 ⟩ ≡

  $link(page\_tail) \leftarrow p$; $page\_tail \leftarrow p$; $link(contrib\_head) \leftarrow link(p)$; $link(p) \leftarrow null$; **goto** *done*

This code is used in section 997.

999.   ⟨ Recycle node p 999 ⟩ ≡

  $link(contrib\_head) \leftarrow link(p)$; $link(p) \leftarrow null$; $flush\_node\_list(p)$

This code is used in section 997.

1000.   The title of this section is already so long, it seems best to avoid making it more accurate but still longer, by mentioning the fact that a kern node at the end of the contribution list will not be contributed until we know its successor.

⟨ If the current page is empty and node p is to be deleted, **goto** *done1*; otherwise use node p to update the state of the current page; if this node is an insertion, **goto** *contribute*; otherwise if this node is not a legal breakpoint, **goto** *contribute* or *update_heights*; otherwise set pi to the penalty associated with this breakpoint 1000 ⟩ ≡

  case $type(p)$ **of**

  hlist_node, *vlist_node*, *rule_node*: **if** $page\_contents < box\_there$ **then**

      ⟨ Initialize the current page, insert the \topskip glue ahead of p, and **goto** *continue* 1001 ⟩

    else ⟨ Prepare to move a box or rule node to the current page, then **goto** *contribute* 1002 ⟩;

  whatsit_node: ⟨ Prepare to move whatsit p to the current page, then **goto** *contribute* 1363 ⟩;

  glue_node: **if** $page\_contents < box\_there$ **then goto** *done1*

    else if $precedes\_break(page\_tail)$ **then** $pi \leftarrow 0$

      else goto *update_heights*;

  kern_node: **if** $page\_contents < box\_there$ **then goto** *done1*

    else if $link(p) = null$ **then return**

      else if $type(link(p)) = glue\_node$ **then** $pi \leftarrow 0$

        else goto *update_heights*;

penalty_node: **if** *page_contents* < *box_there* **then goto** *done1* **else** *pi* ← *penalty*(*p*);
mark_node: **goto** *contribute*;
ins_node: ⟨Append an insertion to the current page and **goto** *contribute* 1008⟩;
othercases *confusion*("page")
endcases

This code is used in section 997.

1001. ⟨Initialize the current page, insert the \topskip glue ahead of *p*, and **goto** *continue* 1001⟩ ≡
   begin if *page_contents* = *empty* **then** *freeze_page_specs*(*box_there*)
   else *page_contents* ← *box_there*;
   q ← *new_skip_param*(*top_skip_code*); *link*(*q*) ← *p*;   { now *temp_ptr* = *glue_ptr*(*q*) }
   if *width*(*temp_ptr*) > *height*(*p*) **then** *width*(*temp_ptr*) ← *width*(*temp_ptr*) − *height*(*p*)
   else *width*(*temp_ptr*) ← 0;
   link(*q*) ← *p*; *link*(*contrib_head*) ← *q*; **goto** *continue*;
   end

This code is used in section 1000.

1002. ⟨Prepare to move a box or rule node to the current page, then **goto** *contribute* 1002⟩ ≡
   begin *page_total* ← *page_total* + *page_depth* + *height*(*p*); *page_depth* ← *depth*(*p*); **goto** *contribute*;
   end

This code is used in section 1000.

1003. ⟨Make sure that *page_max_depth* is not exceeded 1003⟩ ≡
   if *page_depth* > *page_max_depth* **then**
      begin *page_total* ← *page_total* + *page_depth* − *page_max_depth*;
      page_depth ← *page_max_depth*;
      end;

This code is used in section 997.

---

box_there = 2, §980.
confusion: **procedure**, §95.
continue = 22, §15.
contrib_head = macro, §162.
contribute = 80, §994.
depth = macro, §135.
done = 30, §15.
done1 = 31, §15.
empty = 0, §16.
flush_node_list: **procedure**, §202.
freeze_page_specs: **procedure**, §987.
glue_node = 10, §149.
glue_ptr = macro, §149.
height, §981.

hlist_node = 0, §135.
ins_node = 3, §140.
kern_node = 11, §155.
link = macro, §118.
mark_node = 4, §141.
new_skip_param: **function**, §154.
null = macro, §115.
p: *pointer*, §994.
page_contents: 0 .. 2, §980.
page_depth = macro, §982.
page_max_depth: *scaled*, §980.
page_tail: *pointer*, §980.
page_total = macro, §982.

penalty = macro, §157.
penalty_node = 12, §157.
pi: *integer*, §994.
precedes_break = macro, §148.
q: *pointer*, §994.
rule_node = 2, §138.
temp_ptr: *pointer*, §115.
top_skip_code = 9, §224.
type = macro, §133.
update_heights = 90, §970.
vlist_node = 1, §137.
whatsit_node = 8, §146.
width = macro, §135.

1004. ⟨ Update the current page measurements with respect to the glue or kern specified by node p 1004 ⟩ ≡

if $type(p) = kern\_node$ **then** $q \leftarrow p$
else begin $q \leftarrow glue\_ptr(p)$;
$\quad page\_so\_far[2 + stretch\_order(q)] \leftarrow page\_so\_far[2 + stretch\_order(q)] + stretch(q)$;
$\quad page\_shrink \leftarrow page\_shrink + shrink(q)$;
$\quad$ **if** $(shrink\_order(q) \neq normal) \wedge (shrink(q) \neq 0)$ **then**
$\qquad$ **begin**
$\qquad print\_err($"Infinite␣glue␣shrinkage␣found␣on␣current␣page"$)$;
$\qquad help4 ($"The␣page␣about␣to␣be␣output␣contains␣some␣infinitely"$)$
$\qquad ($"shrinkable␣glue,␣e.g.,␣`\vss´␣or␣`\vskip␣0pt␣minus␣1fil´."$)$
$\qquad ($"Such␣glue␣doesn´t␣belong␣there;␣but␣you␣can␣safely␣proceed,"$)$
$\qquad ($"since␣the␣offensive␣shrinkability␣has␣been␣made␣finite."$)$; $error$; $r \leftarrow new\_spec(q)$;
$\qquad shrink\_order(r) \leftarrow normal$; $delete\_glue\_ref(q)$; $glue\_ptr(p) \leftarrow r$;
$\qquad$ **end**;
$\quad$ **end**;
$page\_total \leftarrow page\_total + page\_depth + width(q)$; $page\_depth \leftarrow 0$

This code is used in section 997.

1005. ⟨ Check if node p is a new champion breakpoint; then if it is time for a page break, prepare for output, and either fire up the user's output routine and **return** or ship out the page and **goto** *done* 1005 ⟩ ≡

if $pi < inf\_penalty$ **then**
$\quad$ **begin** ⟨ Compute the badness, b, of the current page, using $awful\_bad$ if the box is too full 1007 ⟩;
$\quad$ **if** $b < awful\_bad$ **then**
$\qquad$ **if** $pi \leq eject\_penalty$ **then** $c \leftarrow pi$
$\qquad$ **else if** $b < inf\_bad$ **then** $c \leftarrow b + pi + insert\_penalties$
$\qquad\quad$ **else** $c \leftarrow deplorable$
$\quad$ **else** $c \leftarrow b$;
$\quad$ **if** $insert\_penalties \geq 10000$ **then** $c \leftarrow awful\_bad$;
$\quad$ **stat if** $tracing\_pages > 0$ **then** ⟨ Display page break cost 1006 ⟩;
$\quad$ **tats**
$\quad$ **if** $c \leq least\_page\_cost$ **then**
$\qquad$ **begin** $best\_page\_break \leftarrow p$; $best\_size \leftarrow page\_goal$; $least\_page\_cost \leftarrow c$;
$\qquad r \leftarrow link(page\_ins\_head)$;
$\qquad$ **while** $r \neq page\_ins\_head$ **do**
$\qquad\quad$ **begin** $best\_ins\_ptr(r) \leftarrow last\_ins\_ptr(r)$; $r \leftarrow link(r)$;
$\qquad\quad$ **end**;
$\qquad$ **end**;
$\quad$ **if** $(c = awful\_bad) \vee (pi \leq eject\_penalty)$ **then**
$\qquad$ **begin** $fire\_up(p)$; { output the current page at the best place }
$\qquad$ **if** $output\_active$ **then return**; { user's output routine will act }
$\qquad$ **goto** *done*; { the page has been shipped out by default output routine }
$\qquad$ **end**;
$\quad$ **end**

This code is used in section 997.

1006. ⟨ Display page break cost 1006 ⟩ ≡
    begin *begin_diagnostic*; *print_nl*("%"); *print*("␣t="); *print_totals*;
    print("␣g="); *print_scaled*(*page_goal*);
    print("␣b=");
    if *b* = *awful_bad* **then** *print_char*("*") **else** *print_int*(*b*);
    print("␣p="); *print_int*(*pi*); *print*("␣c=");
    if *c* = *awful_bad* **then** *print_char*("*") **else** *print_int*(*c*);
    if *c* ≤ *least_page_cost* **then** *print_char*("#");
    end_diagnostic(*false*);
    end

This code is used in section 1005.

1007. ⟨ Compute the badness, *b*, of the current page, using *awful_bad* if the box is too full 1007 ⟩ ≡
    if *page_total* < *page_goal* **then**
        if (*page_so_far*[3] ≠ 0) ∨ (*page_so_far*[4] ≠ 0) ∨ (*page_so_far*[5] ≠ 0) **then** *b* ← 0
        else *b* ← *badness*(*page_goal* − *page_total*, *page_so_far*[2])
    else if *page_total* − *page_goal* > *page_shrink* **then** *b* ← *awful_bad*
        else *b* ← *badness*(*page_total* − *page_goal*, *page_shrink*)

This code is used in section 1005.

---

awful_bad = macro, §833.
b: *integer*, §994.
badness: **function**, §108.
begin_diagnostic: **procedure**, §245.
best_ins_ptr = macro, §981.
best_page_break: *pointer*, §980.
best_size: *scaled*, §980.
c: *ASCII_code*, §960.
delete_glue_ref: **procedure**, §201.
deplorable = macro, §974.
done = 30, §15.
eject_penalty = −10000, §157.
end_diagnostic: **procedure**, §245.
error: **procedure**, §82.
fire_up: **procedure**, §1012.
glue_ptr = macro, §149.
help4 = macro, §79.

inf_bad = 10000, §108.
inf_penalty = 10000, §157.
insert_penalties: *integer*, §982.
kern_node = 11, §155.
last_ins_ptr = macro, §981.
least_page_cost: *integer*, §980.
link = macro, §118.
new_spec: **function**, §151.
normal = 0, §135.
p: *pointer*, §994.
page_depth = macro, §982.
page_goal = macro, §982.
page_ins_head = macro, §162.
page_shrink = macro, §982.
page_so_far: **array**, §982.
page_total = macro, §982.
pi: *integer*, §994.

print: **procedure**, §59.
print_char: **procedure**, §58.
print_err = macro, §73.
print_int: **procedure**, §65.
print_nl: **procedure**, §62.
print_scaled: **procedure**, §103.
print_totals: **procedure**, §985.
q: *pointer*, §994.
r: *pointer*, §994.
shrink = macro, §150.
shrink_order = macro, §150.
stretch = macro, §150.
stretch_order = macro, §150.
tracing_pages = macro, §236.
type = macro, §133.
width = macro, §135.

1008. ⟨Append an insertion to the current page and **goto** *contribute* 1008⟩ ≡
  begin if *page_contents* = *empty* **then** *freeze_page_specs*(*inserts_only*);
  $n \leftarrow subtype(p)$; $r \leftarrow page\_ins\_head$;
  while $n \geq subtype(link(r))$ **do** $r \leftarrow link(r)$;
  $n \leftarrow qo(n)$;
  if $subtype(r) \neq qi(n)$ **then** ⟨Create a page insertion node with $subtype(r) = qi(n)$, and include the
      glue correction for box n in the current page state 1009⟩;
  if $type(r) = split\_up$ **then** $insert\_penalties \leftarrow insert\_penalties + float\_cost(p)$
  else begin $last\_ins\_ptr(r) \leftarrow p$; $delta \leftarrow page\_goal - page\_total - page\_depth + page\_shrink$;
      { this much room is left if we shrink the maximum }
    if $count(n) = 1000$ **then** $h \leftarrow height(p)$
    else $h \leftarrow x\_over\_n(height(p), 1000) * count(n)$;   { this much room is needed }
    if $((h \leq 0) \vee (h \leq delta)) \wedge (height(p) + height(r) \leq dimen(n))$ **then**
      begin $page\_goal \leftarrow page\_goal - h$; $height(r) \leftarrow height(r) + height(p)$;
      end
    else ⟨Find the best way to split the insertion, and change $type(r)$ to $split\_up$ 1010⟩;
    end;
  goto *contribute*;
  end

This code is used in section 1000.

1009. We take note of the value of \skip n and the height plus depth of \box n only when the first \insert n node is encountered for a new page. A user who changes the contents of \box n after that first \insert n had better be either extremely careful or extremely lucky, or both.

⟨Create a page insertion node with $subtype(r) = qi(n)$, and include the glue correction for box n in the
      current page state 1009⟩ ≡
  begin $q \leftarrow get\_node(page\_ins\_node\_size)$; $link(q) \leftarrow link(r)$; $link(r) \leftarrow q$; $r \leftarrow q$;
  $subtype(r) \leftarrow qi(n)$; $type(r) \leftarrow inserting$; $ensure\_vbox(n)$;
  if $box(n) = null$ **then** $height(r) \leftarrow 0$
  else $height(r) \leftarrow height(box(n)) + depth(box(n))$;
  $best\_ins\_ptr(r) \leftarrow null$;
  $q \leftarrow skip(n)$;
  if $count(n) = 1000$ **then** $h \leftarrow height(r)$
  else $h \leftarrow x\_over\_n(height(r), 1000) * count(n)$;
  $page\_goal \leftarrow page\_goal - h - width(q)$;
  $page\_so\_far[2 + stretch\_order(q)] \leftarrow page\_so\_far[2 + stretch\_order(q)] + stretch(q)$;
  $page\_shrink \leftarrow page\_shrink + shrink(q)$;
  if $(shrink\_order(q) \neq normal) \wedge (shrink(q) \neq 0)$ **then**
    begin $print\_err($"Infinite␣glue␣shrinkage␣inserted␣from␣"$)$; $print\_esc($"skip"$)$; $print\_int(n)$;
    $help3($"The␣correction␣glue␣for␣page␣breaking␣with␣insertions"$)$
    $($"must␣have␣finite␣shrinkability.␣But␣you␣may␣proceed,"$)$
    $($"since␣the␣offensive␣shrinkability␣has␣been␣made␣finite."$)$; *error*;
    end;
  end

This code is used in section 1008.

1010. Here is the code that will split a long footnote between pages, in an emergency. The current situation deserves to be recapitulated: Node p is an insertion into box n; the insertion will not fit, in its entirety, either because it would make the total contents of box n greater than \dimen n, or because it would make the incremental amount of growth h greater than the available space *delta*, or both. (This amount h has been weighted by the insertion scaling factor, i.e., by \count n over 1000.) Now we will choose the best way to break the vlist of the insertion, using the same criteria as in the \vsplit operation.

⟨ Find the best way to split the insertion, and change $type(r)$ to $split\_up$ 1010 ⟩ ≡
  begin if $count(n) \leq 0$ **then** $w \leftarrow max\_dimen$
  else begin $w \leftarrow page\_goal - page\_total - page\_depth$;
    if $count(n) \neq 1000$ **then** $w \leftarrow x\_over\_n(w, count(n)) * 1000$;
    end;
  if $w > dimen(n) - height(r)$ **then** $w \leftarrow dimen(n) - height(r)$;
  $q \leftarrow vert\_break(ins\_ptr(p), w, depth(p))$; $height(r) \leftarrow height(r) + best\_height\_plus\_depth$;
  stat if $tracing\_pages > 0$ **then** ⟨ Display insertion split cost 1011 ⟩;
  tats
  if $count(n) \neq 1000$ **then** $best\_height\_plus\_depth \leftarrow x\_over\_n(best\_height\_plus\_depth, 1000) * count(n)$;
  $page\_goal \leftarrow page\_goal - best\_height\_plus\_depth$; $type(r) \leftarrow split\_up$; $broken\_ptr(r) \leftarrow q$;
  $broken\_ins(r) \leftarrow p$;
  if $q = null$ **then** $insert\_penalties \leftarrow insert\_penalties + eject\_penalty$
  else if $type(q) = penalty\_node$ **then** $insert\_penalties \leftarrow insert\_penalties + penalty(q)$;
  end

This code is used in section 1008.

1011. ⟨Display insertion split cost 1011⟩ ≡
  begin *begin_diagnostic*; *print_nl*("%␣split"); *print_int*(n); *print*("␣to␣"); *print_scaled*(w);
  print_char(","); *print_scaled*(best_height_plus_depth); *print*("␣p=");
  if q = null **then** *print_int*(eject_penalty)
  else if *type*(q) = penalty_node **then** *print_int*(penalty(q))
    else *print_char*("0");
  end_diagnostic(false);
  end

This code is used in section 1010.

1012. When the page builder has looked at as much material as could appear before the next page break, it makes its decision. The break that gave minimum badness will be used to put a completed "page" into box 255, with insertions appended to their other boxes.

We also set the values of *top_mark*, *first_mark*, and *bot_mark*. The program uses the fact that *bot_mark* ≠ *null* implies *first_mark* ≠ *null*; it also knows that *bot_mark* = *null* implies *top_mark* = *first_mark* = *null*.

The *fire_up* subroutine prepares to output the current page at the best place; then it fires up the user's output routine, if there is one, or it simply ships out the page. There is one parameter, c, which represents the node that was being contributed to the page when the decision to force an output was made.

⟨Declare the procedure called *fire_up* 1012⟩ ≡
procedure *fire_up*(c : pointer);
  label *exit*;
  var p, q, r, s: pointer;   { nodes being examined and/or changed }
    prev_p: pointer;   { precedessor of p }
    n: min_quarterword .. 255;   { insertion box number }
    wait: boolean;   { should the present insertion be held over? }
    save_vbadness: integer;   { saved value of vbadness }
    save_vfuzz: scaled;   { saved value of vfuzz }
    save_split_top_skip: pointer;   { saved value of split_top_skip }
  begin ⟨Set the value of *output_penalty* 1013⟩;
  if bot_mark ≠ null **then**
    begin if top_mark ≠ null **then** *delete_token_ref*(top_mark);
    top_mark ← bot_mark; *add_token_ref*(top_mark); *delete_token_ref*(first_mark); first_mark ← null;
    end;
  ⟨Put the optimal current page into box 255, update *first_mark* and *bot_mark*, append insertions to
    their boxes, and put the remaining nodes back on the contribution list 1014⟩;
  if (top_mark ≠ null) ∧ (first_mark = null) **then**
    begin first_mark ← top_mark; *add_token_ref*(top_mark);
    end;
  if output_routine ≠ null **then**
    if dead_cycles ≥ max_dead_cycles **then**
      ⟨Explain that too many dead cycles have occurred in a row 1024⟩
    else ⟨Fire up the user's output routine and **return** 1025⟩;
  ⟨Perform the default output routine 1023⟩;
exit: **end**;

This code is used in section 994.

1013. ⟨Set the value of *output_penalty* 1013⟩ ≡
  if *type*(*best_page_break*) = *penalty_node* **then**
    begin *geq_word_define*(*int_base* + *output_penalty_code*, *penalty*(*best_page_break*));
    penalty(*best_page_break*) ← *inf_penalty*;
    end
  else *geq_word_define*(*int_base* + *output_penalty_code*, *inf_penalty*)
This code is used in section 1012.

1014. As the page is finally being prepared for output, pointer *p* runs through the vlist, with *prev_p* trailing behind; pointer *q* is the tail of a list of insertions that are being held over for a subsequent page.

⟨Put the optimal current page into box 255, update *first_mark* and *bot_mark*, append insertions to their
      boxes, and put the remaining nodes back on the contribution list 1014⟩ ≡
  if *c* = *best_page_break* **then** *best_page_break* ← *null*;   { *c* not yet linked in }
  ⟨Ensure that box 255 is empty before output 1015⟩;
  insert_penalties ← 0;   { this will count the number of insertions held over }
  save_split_top_skip ← *split_top_skip*;
  ⟨Prepare all the boxes involved in insertions to act as queues 1018⟩;
  q ← *hold_head*; *link*(*q*) ← *null*; *prev_p* ← *page_head*; *p* ← *link*(*prev_p*);
  while *p* ≠ *best_page_break* **do**
    begin if *type*(*p*) = *ins_node* **then** ⟨Either insert the material specified by node *p* into the
          appropriate box, or hold it for the next page; also delete node *p* from the current page 1020⟩
    else if *type*(*p*) = *mark_node* **then** ⟨Update the values of *first_mark* and *bot_mark* 1016⟩;
    prev_p ← *p*; *p* ← *link*(*prev_p*);
    end;
  split_top_skip ← *save_split_top_skip*; ⟨Break the current page at node *p*, put it in box 255, and put
      the remaining nodes on the contribution list 1017⟩;
  ⟨Delete the page-insertion nodes 1019⟩
This code is used in section 1012.

1015. ⟨ Ensure that box 255 is empty before output 1015 ⟩ ≡
   if $box(255) \neq null$ **then**
      begin $print\_err("")$; $print\_esc("box")$; $print("255_{\sqcup}is_{\sqcup}not_{\sqcup}void")$;
      $help2("You_{\sqcup}shouldn't_{\sqcup}use_{\sqcup}\backslash box255_{\sqcup}except_{\sqcup}in_{\sqcup}\backslash output_{\sqcup}routines.")$
      $("Proceed,_{\sqcup}and_{\sqcup}I'll_{\sqcup}discard_{\sqcup}its_{\sqcup}present_{\sqcup}contents.")$; $box\_error(255)$;
      end

This code is used in section 1014.

1016. ⟨ Update the values of *first_mark* and *bot_mark* 1016 ⟩ ≡
   begin if $first\_mark = null$ **then**
      begin $first\_mark \leftarrow mark\_ptr(p)$; $add\_token\_ref(first\_mark)$;
      end;
   if $bot\_mark \neq null$ **then** $delete\_token\_ref(bot\_mark)$;
   $bot\_mark \leftarrow mark\_ptr(p)$; $add\_token\_ref(bot\_mark)$;
   end

This code is used in section 1014.

1017. When the following code is executed, the current page runs from node $link(page\_head)$ to node *prev_p*, and the nodes from p to *page_tail* are to be placed back at the front of the contribution list. Furthermore the heldover insertions appear in a list from $link(hold\_head)$ to q; we will put them into the current page list for safekeeping while the user's output routine is active. We might have $q = hold\_head$; and $p = null$ if and only if $prev\_p = page\_tail$. Error messages are suppressed within *vpackage*, since the box might appear to be overfull or underfull simply because the stretch and shrink from the \skip registers for inserts are not actually present in the box.

⟨ Break the current page at node p, put it in box 255, and put the remaining nodes on the contribution
      list 1017 ⟩ ≡
   if $p \neq null$ **then**
      begin if $link(contrib\_head) = null$ **then**
         if $nest\_ptr = 0$ **then** $tail \leftarrow page\_tail$
         else $contrib\_tail \leftarrow page\_tail$;
      $link(page\_tail) \leftarrow link(contrib\_head)$; $link(contrib\_head) \leftarrow p$; $link(prev\_p) \leftarrow null$;
      end;
   $save\_vbadness \leftarrow vbadness$; $vbadness \leftarrow inf\_bad$; $save\_vfuzz \leftarrow vfuzz$; $vfuzz \leftarrow max\_dimen$;
      { inhibit error messages }
   $box(255) \leftarrow vpackage(link(page\_head), best\_size, exactly, page\_max\_depth)$; $vbadness \leftarrow save\_vbadness$;
   $vfuzz \leftarrow save\_vfuzz$;
   if $last\_glue \neq max\_halfword$ **then** $delete\_glue\_ref(last\_glue)$;
   ⟨ Start a new current page 991 ⟩;   { this sets $last\_glue \leftarrow max\_halfword$ }
   if $q \neq hold\_head$ **then**
      begin $link(page\_head) \leftarrow link(hold\_head)$; $page\_tail \leftarrow q$;
      end

This code is used in section 1014.

1018. If many insertions are supposed to go into the same box, we want to know the position of the last node in that box, so that we don't need to waste time when linking further information into it. The *last_ins_ptr* fields of the page insertion nodes are therefore used for this purpose during the packaging phase.

⟨ Prepare all the boxes involved in insertions to act as queues 1018 ⟩ ≡
  r ← *link*(*page_ins_head*);
  while *r* ≠ *page_ins_head* **do**
    begin if *best_ins_ptr*(*r*) ≠ *null* **then**
      begin *n* ← *qo*(*subtype*(*r*)); *ensure_vbox*(*n*);
      if *box*(*n*) = *null* **then** *box*(*n*) ← *new_null_box*;
      p ← *box*(*n*) + *list_offset*;
      while *link*(*p*) ≠ *null* **do** *p* ← *link*(*p*);
      last_ins_ptr(*r*) ← *p*;
      end;
    r ← *link*(*r*);
    end

This code is used in section 1014.

1019. ⟨ Delete the page-insertion nodes 1019 ⟩ ≡
  r ←- *link*(*page_ins_head*);
  while *r* ≠ *page_ins_head* **do**
    begin *q* ← *link*(*r*); *free_node*(*r*, *page_ins_node_size*); *r* ← *q*;
    end;
  link(*page_ins_head*) ← *page_ins_head*

This code is used in section 1014.

---

add_token_ref = macro, §203.
best_ins_ptr = macro, §981.
best_size: *scaled*, §980.
bot_mark = macro, §382.
box = macro, §230.
box_error: **procedure**, §992.
contrib_head = macro, §162.
contrib_tail = macro, §995.
delete_glue_ref: **procedure**, §201.
delete_token_ref: **procedure**, §200.
ensure_vbox: **procedure**, §993.
exactly = 0, §644.
first_mark = macro, §382.
free_node: **procedure**, §130.
help2 = macro, §79.
hold_head = macro, §162.

inf_bad = 10000, §108.
last_glue: *pointer*, §982.
last_ins_ptr = macro, §981.
link = macro, §118.
list_offset = 5, §135.
mark_ptr = macro, §141.
max_dimen = macro, §421.
max_halfword = macro, §110.
n: 0 .. 255, §1012.
nest_ptr: 0 .. *nest_size*, §213.
new_null_box: **function**, §136.
null = macro, §115.
p: *pointer*, §1012.
page_head = macro, §162.
page_ins_head = macro, §162.
page_ins_node_size = 4, §981.

page_max_depth: *scaled*, §980.
page_tail: *pointer*, §980.
prev_p: *pointer*, §1012.
print: **procedure**, §59.
print_err = macro, §73.
print_esc: **procedure**, §63.
q: *pointer*, §1012.
qo = macro, §112.
r: *pointer*, §1012.
save_vbadness: *integer*, §1012.
save_vfuzz: *scaled*, §1012.
subtype = macro, §133.
tail = macro, §213.
vbadness = macro, §236.
vfuzz = macro, §247.
vpackage: **function**, §668.

1020. We will set $best\_ins\_ptr \leftarrow null$ and package the box corresponding to insertion node r, just after making the final insertion into that box. If this final insertion is '$split\_up$', the remainder after splitting and pruning (if any) will be carried over to the next page.

$\langle$ Either insert the material specified by node p into the appropriate box, or hold it for the next page; also delete node p from the current page $1020 \rangle \equiv$

> **begin** $r \leftarrow link(page\_ins\_head)$;
> **while** $subtype(r) \neq subtype(p)$ **do** $r \leftarrow link(r)$;
> **if** $best\_ins\_ptr(r) = null$ **then** $wait \leftarrow true$
> **else begin** $wait \leftarrow false$; $s \leftarrow ins\_ptr(p)$; $link(last\_ins\_ptr(r)) \leftarrow s$; $s \leftarrow last\_ins\_ptr(r)$;
> > **if** $best\_ins\_ptr(r) = p$ **then** $\langle$ Wrap up the box specified by node r, splitting node p if called for; set $wait \leftarrow true$ if node p holds a remainder after splitting $1021 \rangle$
> > **else begin while** $link(s) \neq null$ **do** $s \leftarrow link(s)$;
> > > $last\_ins\_ptr(r) \leftarrow s$;
> > > **end**;
> > **end**;
> $\langle$ Either append the insertion node p after node q, and remove it from the current page, or delete $node(p)$ $1022 \rangle$;
> **end**

This code is used in section 1014.

1021. $\langle$ Wrap up the box specified by node r, splitting node p if called for; set $wait \leftarrow true$ if node p holds a remainder after splitting $1021 \rangle \equiv$

> **begin if** $type(r) = split\_up$ **then**
> > **if** $(broken\_ins(r) = p) \wedge (broken\_ptr(r) \neq null)$ **then**
> > > **begin while** $link(s) \neq broken\_ptr(r)$ **do** $s \leftarrow link(s)$;
> > > $split\_top\_skip \leftarrow split\_top\_ptr(p)$; $ins\_ptr(p) \leftarrow prune\_page\_top(broken\_ptr(r))$;
> > > **if** $ins\_ptr(p) \neq null$ **then**
> > > > **begin** $temp\_ptr \leftarrow vpack(ins\_ptr(p), natural)$;
> > > > $height(p) \leftarrow height(temp\_ptr) + depth(temp\_ptr)$; $free\_node(temp\_ptr, box\_node\_size)$;
> > > > $wait \leftarrow true$;
> > > > **end**;
> > > $link(s) \leftarrow null$;
> > > **end**;
> $best\_ins\_ptr(r) \leftarrow null$; $n \leftarrow qo(subtype(r))$; $temp\_ptr \leftarrow list\_ptr(box(n))$;
> $free\_node(box(n), box\_node\_size)$; $box(n) \leftarrow vpack(temp\_ptr, natural)$;
> **end**

This code is used in section 1020.

1022. $\langle$ Either append the insertion node p after node q, and remove it from the current page, or delete $node(p)$ $1022 \rangle \equiv$

> $link(prev\_p) \leftarrow link(p)$; $link(p) \leftarrow null$;
> **if** $wait$ **then**
> > **begin** $link(q) \leftarrow p$; $q \leftarrow p$; $incr(insert\_penalties)$;
> > **end**
> **else begin** $delete\_glue\_ref(split\_top\_ptr(p))$; $free\_node(p, ins\_node\_size)$;
> > **end**;
> $p \leftarrow prev\_p$

This code is used in section 1020.

1023.　The list of heldover insertions, running from $link(page\_head)$ to $page\_tail$, must be moved to the contribution list when the user has specified no output routine.

⟨ Perform the default output routine 1023 ⟩ ≡
　　begin if $link(page\_head) \neq null$ **then**
　　　begin if $link(contrib\_head) = null$ **then**
　　　　if $nest\_ptr = 0$ **then**　$tail \leftarrow page\_tail$ **else** $contrib\_tail \leftarrow page\_tail$
　　　else $link(page\_tail) \leftarrow link(contrib\_head)$;
　　　$link(contrib\_head) \leftarrow link(page\_head)$; $link(page\_head) \leftarrow null$; $page\_tail \leftarrow page\_head$;
　　　end;
　　$ship\_out(box(255))$; $box(255) \leftarrow null$;
　　end

This code is used in section 1012.

1024.　⟨ Explain that too many dead cycles have occurred in a row 1024 ⟩ ≡
　　begin $print\_err($"Output␣loop---"$)$; $print\_int(dead\_cycles)$; $print($"␣consecutive␣dead␣cycles"$)$;
　　$help3($"I´ve␣concluded␣that␣your␣\output␣is␣awry;␣it␣never␣does␣a"$)$
　　$($"\shipout,␣so␣I´m␣shipping␣\box255␣out␣myself.␣Next␣time"$)$
　　$($"increase␣\maxdeadcycles␣if␣you␣want␣me␣to␣be␣more␣patient!"$)$; $error$;
　　end

This code is used in section 1012.

1025.　⟨ Fire up the user's output routine and **return** 1025 ⟩ ≡
　　begin $output\_active \leftarrow true$; $incr(dead\_cycles)$; $push\_nest$; $mode \leftarrow -vmode$;
　　$prev\_depth \leftarrow ignore\_depth$; $mode\_line \leftarrow -line$; $begin\_token\_list(output\_routine, output\_text)$;
　　$new\_save\_level(output\_group)$; $normal\_paragraph$; $scan\_left\_brace$; **return**;
　　end

This code is used in section 1012.

$begin\_token\_list$: **procedure**, §323.
$best\_ins\_ptr$ = macro, §981.
box = macro, §230.
box_node_size = 7, §135.
$broken\_ins$ = macro, §981.
$broken\_ptr$ = macro, §981.
$contrib\_head$ = macro, §162.
$contrib\_tail$ = macro, §995.
$dead\_cycles$: *integer*, §592.
$delete\_glue\_ref$: **procedure**, §201.
$depth$ = macro, §135.
$error$: **procedure**, §82.
$free\_node$: **procedure**, §130.
$height$, §981.
$help3$ = macro, §79.
$ignore\_depth$ = macro, §212.
$incr$ = macro, §16.
ins_node_size = 5, §140.
ins_ptr = macro, §140.
$insert\_penalties$: *integer*, §982.
$last\_ins\_ptr$ = macro, §981.

$line$: *integer*, §304.
$link$ = macro, §118.
$list\_ptr$ = macro, §135.
$mode$ = macro, §213.
$mode\_line$ = macro, §213.
n: 0 .. 255, §1012.
$natural$ = macro, §644.
$nest\_ptr$: 0 .. $nest\_size$, §213.
new_save_level: **procedure**, §274.
$normal\_paragraph$: **procedure**, §1070.
$null$ = macro, §115.
$output\_group$ = 8, §269.
$output\_routine$ = macro, §230.
$output\_text$ = 6, §307.
p: *pointer*, §1012.
$page\_head$ = macro, §162.
$page\_ins\_head$ = macro, §162.
$page\_tail$: *pointer*, §980.
$prev\_depth$ = macro, §213.
$prev\_p$: *pointer*, §1012.

$print$: **procedure**, §59.
$print\_err$ = macro, §73.
$print\_int$: **procedure**, §65.
$prune\_page\_top$: **function**, §968.
$push\_nest$: **procedure**, §216.
q: *pointer*, §1012.
qo = macro, §112.
r: *pointer*, §1012.
s: *pointer*, §1012.
$scan\_left\_brace$: **procedure**, §403.
$ship\_out$: **procedure**, §638.
$split\_top\_ptr$ = macro, §140.
$split\_top\_skip$ = macro, §224.
$split\_up$ = 1, §981.
$subtype$ = macro, §133.
$tail$ = macro, §213.
$temp\_ptr$: *pointer*, §115.
$type$ = macro, §133.
$vmode$ = 1, §211.
$vpack$ = macro, §668.
$wait$: *boolean*, §1012.

1026. When the user's output routine finishes, it has constructed a vlist in internal vertical mode, and TeX will do the following:

⟨ Resume the page builder after an output routine has come to an end 1026 ⟩ ≡
> **begin if** *loc* ≠ *null* **then** ⟨ Recover from an unbalanced output routine 1027 ⟩;
> *end_token_list*;   { conserve stack space in case more outputs are triggered }
> *end_graf*; *unsave*; *output_active* ← *false*; *insert_penalties* ← 0;
> ⟨ Ensure that box 255 is empty after output 1028 ⟩;
> **if** *tail* ≠ *head* **then**   { current list goes after heldover insertions }
> > **begin** *link*(*page_tail*) ← *link*(*head*); *page_tail* ← *tail*;
> > **end**;
> **if** *link*(*page_head*) ≠ *null* **then**   { and both go before heldover contributions }
> > **begin if** *link*(*contrib_head*) = *null* **then** *contrib_tail* ← *page_tail*;
> > *link*(*page_tail*) ← *link*(*contrib_head*); *link*(*contrib_head*) ← *link*(*page_head*);
> > *link*(*page_head*) ← *null*; *page_tail* ← *page_head*;
> > **end**;
> *pop_nest*; *build_page*;
> **end**

This code is used in section 1100.

1027.   ⟨ Recover from an unbalanced output routine 1027 ⟩ ≡
> **begin** *print_err*("Unbalanced␣output␣routine");
> *help2*("Your␣sneaky␣output␣routine␣has␣fewer␣real␣{´s␣than␣}´s.")
> ("I␣can´t␣handle␣that␣very␣well;␣good␣luck."); *error*;
> **repeat** *get_token*;
> **until** *loc* = *null*;
> **end**

This code is used in section 1026.

1028.   ⟨ Ensure that box 255 is empty after output 1028 ⟩ ≡
> **if** *box*(255) ≠ *null* **then**
> > **begin** *print_err*("Output␣routine␣didn´t␣use␣all␣of␣"); *print_esc*("box"); *print_int*(255);
> > *help3*("Your␣\output␣commands␣should␣empty␣\box255,")
> > ("e.g.,␣by␣saying␣`\shipout\box255´.")
> > ("Proceed;␣I´ll␣discard␣its␣present␣contents."); *box_error*(255);
> > **end**

This code is used in section 1026.

box = macro, §230.
box_error: **procedure**, §992.
$build\_page$: **procedure**, §994.
$contrib\_head$ = macro, §162.
$contrib\_tail$ = macro, §995.
end_graf: **procedure**, §1096.
end_token_list: **procedure**, §324.
$error$: **procedure**, §82.

get_token: **procedure**, §365.
$head$ = macro, §213.
$help2$ = macro, §79.
$help3$ = macro, §79.
$insert\_penalties$: $integer$, §982.
$link$ = macro, §118.
loc = macro, §36.
$null$ = macro, §115.

$page\_head$ = macro, §162.
$page\_tail$: $pointer$, §980.
pop_nest: **procedure**, §217.
$print\_err$ = macro, §73.
$print\_esc$: **procedure**, §63.
$print\_int$: **procedure**, §65.
$tail$ = macro, §213.
$unsave$: **procedure**, §281.

1029.   The chief executive.   We come now to the *main_control* routine, which contains the master switch that causes all the various pieces of TeX to do their things, in the right order.

In a sense, this is the grand climax of the program: It applies all the tools that we have worked so hard to construct. In another sense, this is the messiest part of the program: It necessarily refers to other pieces of code all over the place, so that a person can't fully understand what is going on without paging back and forth to be reminded of conventions that are defined elsewhere. We are now at the hub of the web, the central nervous system that touches most of the other parts and ties them together.

The structure of *main_control* itself is quite simple. There's a label called *big_switch*, at which point the next token of input is fetched using *get_x_token*. Then the program branches at high speed into one of about 100 possible directions, based on the value of the current mode and the newly fetched command code; the sum $abs(mode) + cur\_cmd$ indicates what to do next. For example, the case '*vmode + letter*' arises when a letter occurs in vertical mode (or internal vertical mode); this case leads to instructions that initialize a new paragraph and enter horizontal mode.

The big **case** statement that contains this multiway switch has been labeled *reswitch*, so that the program can **goto** *reswitch* when the next token has already been fetched. Most of the cases are quite short; they call an "action procedure" that does the work for that case, and then they either **goto** *reswitch* or they "fall through" to the end of the **case** statement, which returns control back to *big_switch*. Thus, *main_control* is not an extremely large procedure, in spite of the multiplicity of things it must do; it is small enough to be handled by Pascal compilers that put severe restrictions on procedure size.

One case is singled out for special treatment, because it accounts for most of TeX's activities in typical applications. The process of reading simple text and converting it into *char_node* records, while looking for ligatures and kerns, is part of TeX's "inner loop"; the whole program runs efficiently when its inner loop is fast, so this part has been written with particular care.

1030.   We shall concentrate first on the inner loop of *main_control*, deferring consideration of the other cases until later.

    define *big_switch* = 60   { go here to branch on the next token of input }
    define *main_loop* = 70   { go here to typeset *cur_chr* in the current font }
    define *main_loop_1* = 71   { like *main_loop*, but (f, c) = current font and char }
    define *main_loop_2* = 72   { like *main_loop_1*, but *c* is known to be in range }
    define *main_loop_3* = 73   { like *main_loop_2*, but several variables are set up }
    define *append_normal_space* = 74   { go here to append a normal space between words }
⟨ Declare action procedures for use by *main_control* 1043 ⟩
⟨ Declare the procedure called *handle_right_brace* 1068 ⟩
procedure *main_control*;   { governs TeX's activities }
    label *big_switch*, *reswitch*, *main_loop*, *main_loop_1*, *main_loop_2*, *main_loop_3*, *append_normal_space*,
        exit;
    var *t*: *integer*;   { general-purpose temporary variable }
    ⟨ Local variables for the inner loop of *main_control* 1032 ⟩
    begin if *every_job* ≠ *null* **then** *begin_token_list*(*every_job*, *every_job_text*);
big_switch: *get_x_token*;
reswitch: ⟨ Give diagnostic information, if requested 1031 ⟩;
    case $abs(mode) + cur\_cmd$ **of**
    hmode + letter, *hmode + other_char*, *hmode + char_given*: **goto** *main_loop*;

hmode + *char_num*: **begin** *scan_char_num*; *cur_chr* ← *cur_val*; **goto** *main_loop*;
  end;
hmode + *spacer*: **if** *space_factor* = 1000 **then goto** *append_normal_space*
  else *app_space*;
hmode + *ex_space*, *mmode* + *ex_space*: **goto** *append_normal_space*;
⟨ Cases of *main_control* that are not part of the inner loop 1045 ⟩
end;   { of the big **case** statement }
goto *big_switch*;
main_loop: ⟨ Append character *cur_chr* and the following characters (if any) to the current hlist in the
    current font; **goto** *reswitch* when a non-character has been fetched 1033 ⟩;
append_normal_space: ⟨ Append a normal inter-word space to the current list, then **goto** *big_switch* 1041 ⟩;
exit: **end**;

1031.   When a new token has just been fetched at *big_switch*, we have an ideal place to monitor
TeX's activity.

⟨ Give diagnostic information, if requested 1031 ⟩ ≡
  if *interrupt* ≠ 0 **then**
    if *OK_to_interrupt* **then**
      begin *back_input*; *check_interrupt*; **goto** *big_switch*;
      end;
  debug if *panicking* **then** *check_mem*(*false*); **gubed**
  if *tracing_commands* > 0 **then** *show_cur_cmd_chr*

This code is used in section 1030.

1032. In the following program, l is the current character or ligature; it might grow into a longer ligature. One or more characters has been used to define l, and the last of these was c. The chief use of c will be to modify *space_factor* and to insert discretionary nodes after explicit hyphens in the text.

⟨ Local variables for the inner loop of *main_control* 1032 ⟩ ≡
l: *quarterword*; { the current character or ligature }
c: *eight_bits*; { the most recent character }
f: *internal_font_number*; { the current font }
r: *halfword*; { the next character for ligature/kern matching }
p: *pointer*; { the current *char_node* }
k: $0 .. font\_mem\_size$; { index into *font_info* }
q: *pointer*; { where a ligature should be detached }
i: *four_quarters*; { character information bytes for l }
j: *four_quarters*; { ligature/kern command }
s: *integer*; { space factor code }
ligature_present: *boolean*; { should a ligature node be made? }

This code is used in section 1030.

1033. ⟨ Append character *cur_chr* and the following characters (if any) to the current hlist in the current font; **goto** *reswitch* when a non-character has been fetched 1033 ⟩ ≡
  $f \leftarrow cur\_font$; $c \leftarrow cur\_chr$;
main_loop_1: **if** $(c < font\_bc[f]) \lor (c > font\_ec[f])$ **then**
    begin *char_warning*(f, c); **goto** *big_switch*;
    end;
main_loop_2: $q \leftarrow tail$; *ligature_present* $\leftarrow$ *false*; $l \leftarrow qi(c)$;
main_loop_3: ⟨ Adjust the space factor, based on its current value and c 1034 ⟩;
  ⟨ Append character l and the following characters (if any) to the current hlist, in font f; if
    ligature_present, detach a ligature node starting at *link*(q); if c is a hyphen, append a null
    disc_node; finally **goto** *reswitch* 1035 ⟩

This code is used in section 1030.

1034. We leave *space_factor* unchanged if *sf_code*$(c) = 0$; otherwise we set it to *sf_code*(c), except that the space factor never changes from a value less than 1000 to a value exceeding 1000. If $c \geq 128$, its *sf_code* is implicitly 1000. The most common case is *sf_code*$(c) = 1000$, so we want that case to be fast.

⟨ Adjust the space factor, based on its current value and c 1034 ⟩ ≡
  if $c < 128$ **then**
    begin $s \leftarrow sf\_code(c)$;
    if $s = 1000$ **then** *space_factor* $\leftarrow 1000$
    else if $s < 1000$ **then**
        begin if $s > 0$ **then** *space_factor* $\leftarrow s$;
        end
      else if *space_factor* < 1000 **then** *space_factor* $\leftarrow 1000$
        else *space_factor* $\leftarrow s$;
    end
  else *space_factor* $\leftarrow 1000$

This code is used in section 1033.

1035. Now we come to the inner loop, in which the characters of a word are gathered at (hopefully) high speed.

⟨ Append character l and the following characters (if any) to the current hlist, in font f; if
       ligature_present, detach a ligature node starting at *link*(*q*); if *c* is a hyphen, append a null
       disc_node; finally **goto** *reswitch* 1035 ⟩ ≡
  $i \leftarrow char\_info(f)(l)$;
  if *char_exists*(*i*) **then**
    begin *fast_get_avail*(*p*); *font*(*p*) ← *f*; *character*(*p*) ← *qi*(*c*); *link*(*tail*) ← *p*; *tail* ← *p*;
    end
  else *char_warning*(*f*, *qo*(*l*));
⟨ Look ahead for ligature or kerning, either continuing the main loop or going to *reswitch* 1036 ⟩
This code is used in section 1033.

1036. The result of \char can participate in a ligature or kern, so we must look ahead for it.

⟨ Look ahead for ligature or kerning, either continuing the main loop or going to *reswitch* 1036 ⟩ ≡
  get_next;   { set only *cur_cmd* and *cur_chr* }
  if *cur_cmd* = *letter* **then** $r \leftarrow qi(cur\_chr)$
  else if *cur_cmd* = *other_char* **then** $r \leftarrow qi(cur\_chr)$
    else if *cur_cmd* = *char_given* **then** $r \leftarrow qi(cur\_chr)$
      else begin *x_token*;   { set *cur_cmd*, *cur_chr*, *cur_tok* }
        if (*cur_cmd* = *letter*) ∨ (*cur_cmd* = *other_char*) ∨ (*cur_cmd* = *char_given*) **then**
          $r \leftarrow qi(cur\_chr)$
        else if *cur_cmd* = *char_num* **then**
          begin *scan_char_num*; $r \leftarrow qi(cur\_val)$;
          end
        else $r \leftarrow qi(256)$;   { this flag means that no character follows }
      end;
  if *char_tag*(*i*) = *lig_tag* **then**
    if $r \neq qi(256)$ **then** ⟨ Follow the lig/kern program; **goto** *main_loop_3* if scoring a hit 1037 ⟩;
  ⟨ Make a ligature node, if *ligature_present*; insert a discretionary node for an explicit hyphen, if *c* is
     the current *hyphen_char* 1039 ⟩;
  if $r = qi(256)$ **then goto** *reswitch*;   { *cur_cmd*, *cur_chr*, *cur_tok* are untouched }
  $c \leftarrow qo(r)$; **goto** *main_loop_1*   { *f* is still valid }
This code is used in section 1035.

---

char_exists = macro, §554.	*font* = macro, §134.	*link* = macro, §118.
char_given = 67, §208.	*font_bc*: **array**, §549.	*main_loop_1* = 71, §1030.
char_info = macro, §554.	*font_ec*: **array**, §549.	*main_loop_2* = 72, §1030.
char_node, §134.	*font_info*: **array**, §549.	*main_loop_3* = 73, §1030.
char_num = 16, §208.	*font_mem_size* = **const**, §11.	*other_char* = 12, §207.
char_tag = macro, §554.	*four_quarters* = **packed record**,	*pointer* = macro, §115.
char_warning: **procedure**, §581.	§113.	*qi* = macro, §112.
character = macro, §134.	*get_next*: **procedure**, §341.	*qo* = macro, §112.
cur_chr: *halfword*, §297.	*halfword* = *min_halfword* ..	*quarterword* = 0 .. 255, §113.
cur_cmd: *eight_bits*, §297.	*max_halfword*, §113.	*reswitch* = 21, §15.
cur_font = macro, §230.	*hyphen_char*: **array**, §549.	*scan_char_num*: **procedure**, §435.
cur_tok: *halfword*, §297.	*internal_font_number* = 0 .. *font_max*,	*sf_code* = macro, §230.
cur_val: *integer*, §410.	§548.	*space_factor* = macro, §213.
disc_node = 7, §145.	*letter* = 11, §207.	*tail* = macro, §213.
eight_bits = 0 .. 255, §25.	*lig_tag* = 1, §544.	*x_token*: **procedure**, §381.
fast_get_avail = macro, §122.		

1037. Even though comparatively few characters have a lig/kern program, the **repeat** construction here counts as part of TEX's inner loop, since it involves a potentially long sequential search. For example, tests with one commonly used font showed that about 40 per cent of all characters had a lig/kern program, and the **repeat** loop was performed about four times for every such character.

⟨ Follow the lig/kern program; **goto** $main\_loop\_3$ if scoring a hit 1037 ⟩ ≡
  begin $k \leftarrow lig\_kern\_start(f)(i)$;
  repeat $j \leftarrow font\_info[k].qqqq$;   { fetch a lig/kern command }
    if $next\_char(j) = r$ **then**
      if $op\_bit(j) < kern\_flag$ **then** ⟨ Extend a ligature, **goto** $main\_loop\_3$ 1040 ⟩
      else ⟨ Append a kern, **goto** $main\_loop\_2$ 1038 ⟩;
    $incr(k)$;
  until $stop\_bit(j) \geq stop\_flag$;
  end

This code is used in section 1036.

1038. ⟨ Append a kern, **goto** $main\_loop\_2$ 1038 ⟩ ≡
  begin ⟨ Make a ligature node, if $ligature\_present$; insert a discretionary node for an explicit hyphen,
    if c is the current $hyphen\_char$ 1039 ⟩;
  $tail\_append(new\_kern(char\_kern(f)(j)))$; $c \leftarrow qo(r)$; **goto** $main\_loop\_2$;
  end

This code is used in section 1037.

1039. A discretionary break is not inserted for an explicit hyphen when we are in restricted horizontal mode. In particular, this avoids putting discretionary nodes inside of other discretionaries.

⟨ Make a ligature node, if $ligature\_present$; insert a discretionary node for an explicit hyphen, if c is the
    current $hyphen\_char$ 1039 ⟩ ≡
  if $ligature\_present$ **then**
    begin $p \leftarrow new\_ligature(f, l, link(q))$; $link(q) \leftarrow p$; $tail \leftarrow p$;
    end;
  if $c = hyphen\_char[f]$ **then**
    if $mode = hmode$ **then** $tail\_append(new\_disc)$

This code is used in sections 1036 and 1038.

1040. ⟨ Extend a ligature, **goto** $main\_loop\_3$ 1040 ⟩ ≡
  begin $ligature\_present \leftarrow true$; $l \leftarrow rem\_byte(j)$; $c \leftarrow qo(r)$; **goto** $main\_loop\_3$;
  end

This code is used in section 1037.

1041. The occurrence of blank spaces is almost part of TEX's inner loop, since we usually encounter about one space for every five non-blank characters. Therefore $main\_control$ gives second-highest priority to ordinary spaces.

When a glue parameter like \spaceskip is set to '0pt', we will see to it later that the corresponding glue specification is precisely $zero\_glue$, not merely a pointer to some other specification that happens to be full of zeroes. Therefore it is simple to test whether a glue parameter is zero or not.

⟨ Append a normal inter-word space to the current list, then **goto** *big_switch* 1041 ⟩ ≡
 if *space_skip* = *zero_glue* **then**
  begin ⟨ Find the glue specification, *p*, for text spaces in the current font 1042 ⟩;
  q ← *new_glue*(*p*);
  end
 else *q* ← *new_param_glue*(*space_skip_code*);
 link(*tail*) ← *q*; *tail* ← *q*; **goto** *big_switch*
This code is used in section 1030.

1042. Having *font_glue* allocated for each text font saves both time and memory. If any of the three spacing parameters are subsequently changed by the use of \fontdimen, the *find_font_dimen* procedure deallocates the *font_glue* specification allocated here.

⟨ Find the glue specification, *p*, for text spaces in the current font 1042 ⟩ ≡
 begin *p* ← *font_glue*[*cur_font*];
 if *p* = *null* **then**
  begin *f* ← *cur_font*; *p* ← *new_spec*(*zero_glue*); *k* ← *param_base*[*f*] + *space_code*;
  width(*p*) ← *font_info*[*k*].*sc*; *stretch*(*p*) ← *font_info*[*k* + 1].*sc*; *shrink*(*p*) ← *font_info*[*k* + 2].*sc*;
  font_glue[*f*] ← *p*;
  end;
 end
This code is used in sections 1041 and 1043.

---

c: *eight_bits*, §1032.
char_kern = macro, §557.
cur_font = macro, §230.
f: *internal_font_number*, §1032.
find_font_dimen: **procedure**, §578.
font_glue: **array**, §549.
font_info: **array**, §549.
hmode = 101, §211.
hyphen_char: **array**, §549.
i: *four_quarters*, §1032.
incr = macro, §16.
j: *four_quarters*, §1032.
k: 0 .. *font_mem_size*, §1032.
kern_flag = 128, §545.
l: *quarterword*, §1032.
lig_kern_start = macro, §557.
ligature_present: *boolean*, §1032.

link = macro, §118.
main_loop_2 = 72, §1030.
main_loop_3 = 73, §1030.
mode = macro, §213.
new_disc: **function**, §145.
new_glue: **function**, §153.
new_kern: **function**, §156.
new_ligature: **function**, §144.
new_param_glue: **function**, §152.
new_spec: **function**, §151.
next_char = macro, §545.
null = macro, §115.
op_bit = macro, §545.
p: *pointer*, §1032.
param_base: **array**, §550.
q: *pointer*, §1032.

qo = macro, §112.
qqqq: *four_quarters*, §113.
r: *halfword*, §1032.
rem_byte = macro, §545.
sc = macro, §113.
shrink = macro, §150.
space_code = 2, §547.
space_skip = macro, §224.
space_skip_code = 12, §224.
stop_bit = macro, §545.
stop_flag = 128, §545.
stretch = macro, §150.
tail = macro, §213.
tail_append = macro, §214.
width = macro, §135.
zero_glue = macro, §162.

1043. ⟨ Declare action procedures for use by *main_control* 1043 ⟩ ≡
procedure *app_space*;   { handle spaces when *space_factor* ≠ 1000 }
   var *p*: *pointer*;   { glue specification }
      q: *pointer*;   { glue node }
      f: *internal_font_number*;   { the current font }
      k: 0 .. *font_mem_size*;   { index into *font_info* }
   begin if (*space_factor* ≥ 2000) ∧ (*xspace_skip* ≠ *zero_glue*) **then**
      q ← *new_param_glue*(*xspace_skip_code*)
   else begin if *space_skip* ≠ *zero_glue* **then** *p* ← *space_skip*
      else ⟨ Find the glue specification, *p*, for text spaces in the current font 1042 ⟩;
      p ← *new_spec*(*p*); ⟨ Modify the glue specification in *p* according to the space factor 1044 ⟩;
      q ← *new_glue*(*p*); *glue_ref_count*(*p*) ← *null*;
      end;
   link(*tail*) ← *q*; *tail* ← *q*;
   end;

See also sections 1047, 1049, 1050, 1051, 1054, 1060, 1061, 1064, 1069, 1070, 1075, 1079, 1084, 1086, 1091, 1093, 1095, 1096, 1099, 1101, 1103, 1105, 1110, 1113, 1117, 1119, 1123, 1127, 1129, 1131, 1135, 1136, 1138, 1142, 1151, 1155, 1159, 1160, 1163, 1165, 1172, 1174, 1176, 1181, 1191, 1194, 1200, 1211, 1270, 1275, 1279, 1288, 1293, 1302, and 1348.

This code is used in section 1030.

1044. ⟨ Modify the glue specification in *p* according to the space factor 1044 ⟩ ≡
   if *space_factor* ≥ 2000 **then** *width*(*p*) ← *width*(*p*) + *extra_space*(*cur_font*);
   stretch(*p*) ← *xn_over_d*(*stretch*(*p*), *space_factor*, 1000);
   shrink(*p*) ← *xn_over_d*(*shrink*(*p*), 1000, *space_factor*)

This code is used in section 1043.

1045.   Whew—that covers the main loop. We can now proceed at a leisurely pace through the other combinations of possibilities.

   define *any_mode*(**#**) ≡ *vmode* + **#**, *hmode* + **#**, *mmode* + **#**   { for mode-independent commands }

⟨ Cases of *main_control* that are not part of the inner loop 1045 ⟩ ≡
any_mode(*relax*), *vmode* + *spacer*, *mmode* + *spacer*: *do_nothing*;
any_mode(*ignore_spaces*): **begin** ⟨ Get the next non-blank non-call token 406 ⟩;
   goto *reswitch*;
   end;
vmode + *stop*: **if** *its_all_over* **then return**;   { this is the only way out }
⟨ Forbidden cases detected in *main_control* 1048 ⟩ *any_mode*(*mac_param*): *report_illegal_case*;
⟨ Math-only cases in non-math modes, or vice versa 1046 ⟩: *insert_dollar_sign*;
⟨ Cases of *main_control* that build boxes and lists 1056 ⟩
⟨ Cases of *main_control* that don't depend on *mode* 1210 ⟩
⟨ Cases of *main_control* that are for extensions to TeX 1347 ⟩

This code is used in section 1030.

1046.   Here is a list of cases where the user has probably gotten into or out of math mode by mistake. TeX will insert a dollar sign and rescan the current token.

   define *non_math*(**#**) ≡ *vmode* + **#**, *hmode* + **#**

⟨ Math-only cases in non-math modes, or vice versa 1046 ⟩ ≡
  non_math(*sup_mark*), *non_math*(*sub_mark*), *non_math*(*math_char_num*), *non_math*(*math_given*),
      non_math(*math_comp*), *non_math*(*delim_num*), *non_math*(*left_right*), *non_math*(*above*),
      non_math(*radical*), *non_math*(*math_style*), *non_math*(*math_choice*), *non_math*(*vcenter*),
      non_math(*non_script*), *non_math*(*mkern*), *non_math*(*limit_switch*), *non_math*(*mskip*),
      non_math(*math_accent*), *mmode* + *endv*, *mmode* + *par_end*, *mmode* + *stop*, *mmode* + *vskip*,
      mmode + *un_vbox*, *mmode* + *valign*, *mmode* + *hrule*
This code is used in section 1045.

1047.   ⟨ Declare action procedures for use by *main_control* 1043 ⟩ +≡
procedure *insert_dollar_sign*;
    begin *back_input*; *cur_tok* ← *math_shift_token* + "$"; *print_err*("Missing␣$␣inserted");
    help2("I´ve␣inserted␣a␣begin-math/end-math␣symbol␣since␣I␣think")
    ("you␣left␣one␣out.␣Proceed,␣with␣fingers␣crossed."); *ins_error*;
    end;

1048.   When erroneous situations arise, TEX usually issues an error message specific to the
particular error. For example, '\noalign' should not appear in any mode, since it is recognized
by the *align_peek* routine in all of its legitimate appearances; a special error message is given when
'\noalign' occurs elsewhere. But sometimes the most appropriate error message is simply that
the user is not allowed to do what he or she has attempted. For example, '\moveleft' is allowed
only in vertical mode, and '\lower' only in non-vertical modes. Such cases are enumerated here
and in the other sections referred to under 'See also . . . .'

⟨ Forbidden cases detected in *main_control* 1048 ⟩ ≡
  vmode + *vmove*, *hmode* + *hmove*, *mmode* + *hmove*, *any_mode*(*last_item*),
See also sections 1098, 1111, and 1144.

This code is used in section 1045.

---

above = 52, §208.
align_peek: **procedure**, §785.
back_input: **procedure**, §325.
cur_font = macro, §230.
cur_tok: **halfword**, §297.
delim_num = 15, §207.
do_nothing = macro, §16.
endv = 9, §207.
extra_space = macro, §558.
font_info: **array**, §549.
font_mem_size = **const**, §11.
glue_ref_count = macro, §150.
help2 = macro, §79.
hmode = 101, §211.
hmove = 21, §208.
hrule = 36, §208.
ignore_spaces = 39, §208.
ins_error: **procedure**, §327.
internal_font_number = 0 .. *font_max*,
    §548.
its_all_over: **function**, §1054.
last_item = 69, §208.
left_right = 49, §208.
limit_switch = 51, §208.

link = macro, §118.
mac_param = 6, §207.
math_accent = 46, §208.
math_char_num = 17, §208.
math_choice = 54, §208.
math_comp = 50, §208.
math_given = 68, §208.
math_shift_token = 768, §289.
math_style = 53, §208.
mkern = 30, §208.
mmode = 201, §211.
mode = macro, §213.
mskip = 28, §208.
new_glue: **function**, §153.
new_param_glue: **function**, §152.
new_spec: **function**, §151.
non_script = 55, §208.
null = macro, §115.
par_end = 13, §207.
pointer = macro, §115.
print_err = macro, §73.
radical = 65, §208.
relax = 0, §207.

report_illegal_case: **procedure**,
    §1050.
reswitch = 21, §15.
shrink = macro, §150.
space_factor = macro, §213.
space_skip = macro, §224.
spacer = 10, §207.
stop = 14, §207.
stretch = macro, §150.
sub_mark = 8, §207.
sup_mark = 7, §207.
tail = macro, §213.
un_vbox = 24, §208.
valign = 33, §208.
vcenter = 56, §208.
vmode = 1, §211.
vmove = 22, §208.
vskip = 27, §208.
width = macro, §135.
xn_over_d: **function**, §107.
xspace_skip = macro, §224.
xspace_skip_code = 13, §224.
zero_glue = macro, §162.

1049. The '*you_cant*' procedure prints a line saying that the current command is illegal in the current mode; it identifies these things symbolically.

⟨ Declare action procedures for use by *main_control* 1043 ⟩ +≡
procedure *you_cant*;
  begin *print_err*("You␣can´t␣use␣`"); *print_cmd_chr*(*cur_cmd*, *cur_chr*); *print*("´␣in␣");
  print_mode(*mode*);
  end;

1050. ⟨ Declare action procedures for use by *main_control* 1043 ⟩ +≡
procedure *report_illegal_case*;
  begin *you_cant*; *help4*("Sorry,␣but␣I´m␣not␣programmed␣to␣handle␣this␣case;")
  ("I´ll␣just␣pretend␣that␣you␣didn´t␣ask␣for␣it.")
  ("If␣you´re␣in␣the␣wrong␣mode,␣you␣might␣be␣able␣to")
  ("return␣to␣the␣right␣one␣by␣typing␣`I}´␣or␣`I\$´␣or␣`I\par´.");
  error;
  end;

1051. Some operations are allowed only in privileged modes, i.e., in cases that $mode > 0$. The *privileged* function is used to detect violations of this rule; it issues an error message and returns *false* if the current *mode* is negative.

⟨ Declare action procedures for use by *main_control* 1043 ⟩ +≡
function *privileged*: *boolean*;
  begin if $mode > 0$ **then** *privileged* ← *true*
  else begin *report_illegal_case*; *privileged* ← *false*;
    end;
  end;

1052. Either \dump or \end will cause *main_control* to enter the endgame, since both of them have '*stop*' as their command code.

⟨ Put each of TEX's primitives into the hash table 226 ⟩ +≡
  primitive("end", *stop*, 0);
  primitive("dump", *stop*, 1);

1053. ⟨ Cases of *print_cmd_chr* for symbolic printing of primitives 227 ⟩ +≡
stop: **if** *chr_code* = 1 **then** *print_esc*("dump") **else** *print_esc*("end");

1054. We don't want to leave *main_control* immediately when a *stop* command is sensed, because it may be necessary to invoke an \output routine several times before things really grind to a halt. (The output routine might even say '\gdef\end{...}', to prolong the life of the job.) Therefore *its_all_over* is *true* only when the current page and contribution list are empty, and when the last output was not a "dead cycle."

⟨ Declare action procedures for use by *main_control* 1043 ⟩ +≡
function *its_all_over*: *boolean*;   { do this when \end or \dump occurs }
  label *exit*;
  begin if *privileged* **then**
    begin if (*page_head* = *page_tail*) ∧ (*head* = *tail*) ∧ (*dead_cycles* = 0) **then**
      begin *its_all_over* ← *true*; **return**;
      end;

$back\_input$;   { we will try to end again after ejecting residual material }
$tail\_append(new\_null\_box)$; $width(tail) \leftarrow hsize$; $tail\_append(new\_glue(fill\_glue))$;
$tail\_append(new\_penalty(-\,{}'10000000000))$;
$build\_page$;   { append \hbox to \hsize{}\vss\penalty-'10000000000 }
end;
$its\_all\_over \leftarrow false$;
$exit$: **end**;

1055.   Building boxes and lists.   The most important parts of *main_control* are concerned with TEX's chief mission of box-making. We need to control the activities that put entries on vlists and hlists, as well as the activities that convert those lists into boxes. All of the necessary machinery has already been developed; it remains for us to "push the buttons" at the right times.

1056.   As an introduction to these routines, let's consider one of the simplest cases: What happens when '\hrule' occurs in vertical mode, or '\vrule' in horizontal mode or math mode? The code in *main_control* is short, since the *scan_rule_spec* routine already does most of what is required; thus, there is no need for a special action procedure.

Note that baselineskip calculations are disabled after a rule in vertical mode, by setting $prev\_depth \leftarrow ignore\_depth$.

⟨ Cases of *main_control* that build boxes and lists 1056 ⟩ ≡

$vmode + hrule, hmode + vrule, mmode + vrule$: **begin** *tail_append*(*scan_rule_spec*);

　　if $abs(mode) = vmode$ **then** $prev\_depth \leftarrow ignore\_depth$

　　else if $abs(mode) = hmode$ **then** $space\_factor \leftarrow 1000$;

　　end;

See also sections 1057, 1063, 1067, 1073, 1090, 1092, 1094, 1097, 1102, 1104, 1109, 1112, 1116, 1122, 1126, 1130, 1134, 1137, 1140, 1150, 1154, 1158, 1162, 1164, 1167, 1171, 1175, 1180, 1190, and 1193.

This code is used in section 1045.

1057.   The processing of things like \hskip and \vskip is slightly more complicated. But the code in *main_control* is very short, since it simply calls on the action routine *append_glue*. Similarly, \kern activates *append_kern*.

⟨ Cases of *main_control* that build boxes and lists 1056 ⟩ +≡

$vmode + vskip, hmode + hskip, mmode + hskip, mmode + mskip$: *append_glue*;

$any\_mode(kern), mmode + mkern$: *append_kern*;

1058.   The *hskip* and *vskip* command codes are used for control sequences like \hss and \vfil as well as for \hskip and \vskip. The difference is in the value of *cur_chr*.

　　define $fil\_code = 0$　{ identifies \hfil and \vfil }

　　define $fill\_code = 1$　{ identifies \hfill and \vfill }

　　define $ss\_code = 2$　{ identifies \hss and \vss }

　　define $fil\_neg\_code = 3$　{ identifies \hfilneg and \vfilneg }

　　define $skip\_code = 4$　{ identifies \hskip and \vskip }

　　define $mskip\_code = 5$　{ identifies \mskip }

⟨ Put each of TEX's primitives into the hash table 226 ⟩ +≡

　　primitive("hskip", *hskip*, *skip_code*);

　　primitive("hfil", *hskip*, *fil_code*);　*primitive*("hfill", *hskip*, *fill_code*);

　　primitive("hss", *hskip*, *ss_code*);　*primitive*("hfilneg", *hskip*, *fil_neg_code*);

　　primitive("vskip", *vskip*, *skip_code*);

　　primitive("vfil", *vskip*, *fil_code*);　*primitive*("vfill", *vskip*, *fill_code*);

　　primitive("vss", *vskip*, *ss_code*);　*primitive*("vfilneg", *vskip*, *fil_neg_code*);

　　primitive("mskip", *mskip*, *mskip_code*);

　　primitive("kern", *kern*, *explicit*);　*primitive*("mkern", *mkern*, *mu_glue*);

1059.   ⟨ Cases of *print_cmd_chr* for symbolic printing of primitives 227 ⟩ +≡
hskip: **case** *chr_code* **of**
   skip_code: *print_esc*("hskip");
   fil_code: *print_esc*("hfil");
   fill_code: *print_esc*("hfill");
   ss_code: *print_esc*("hss");
   othercases *print_esc*("hfilneg")
   endcases;
vskip: **case** *chr_code* **of**
   skip_code: *print_esc*("vskip");
   fil_code: *print_esc*("vfil");
   fill_code: *print_esc*("vfill");
   ss_code: *print_esc*("vss");
   othercases *print_esc*("vfilneg")
   endcases;
mskip: *print_esc*("mskip");
kern: *print_esc*("kern");
mkern: *print_esc*("mkern");

---

any_mode = macro, §1045.
append_glue: **procedure**, §1060.
append_kern: **procedure**, §1061.
chr_code: *halfword*, §298.
cur_chr: *halfword*, §297.
explicit = 1, §155.
hmode = 101, §211.
hrule = 36, §208.
hskip = 26, §208.

ignore_depth = macro, §212.
kern, §545.
mkern = 30, §208.
mmode = 201, §211.
mode = macro, §213.
mskip = 28, §208.
mu_glue = 99, §149.
prev_depth = macro, §213.
primitive: **procedure**, §264.

print_cmd_chr: **procedure**, §298.
print_esc: **procedure**, §63.
scan_rule_spec: **function**, §463.
space_factor = macro, §213.
tail_append = macro, §214.
vmode = 1, §211.
vrule = 35, §208.
vskip = 27, §208.

1060. All the work relating to glue creation has been relegated to the following subroutine. It does not call *build_page*, because it is used in at least one place where that would be a mistake.

⟨Declare action procedures for use by *main_control* 1043⟩ +≡

procedure *append_glue*;

  var *s*: *small_number*;   { modifier of skip command }

  begin *s* ← *cur_chr*;

  case *s* **of**

  fil_code: *cur_val* ← *fil_glue*;

  fill_code: *cur_val* ← *fill_glue*;

  ss_code: *cur_val* ← *ss_glue*;

  fil_neg_code: *cur_val* ← *fil_neg_glue*;

  skip_code: *scan_glue*(*glue_val*);

  mskip_code: *scan_glue*(*mu_val*);

  end;   { now *cur_val* points to the glue specification }

  tail_append(*new_glue*(*cur_val*));

  if *s* ≥ *skip_code* **then**

    begin *decr*(*glue_ref_count*(*cur_val*));

    if *s* > *skip_code* **then** *subtype*(*tail*) ← *mu_glue*;

    end;

  end;

1061. ⟨Declare action procedures for use by *main_control* 1043⟩ +≡

procedure *append_kern*;

  var *s*: *quarterword*;   { *subtype* of the kern node }

  begin *s* ← *cur_chr*; *scan_dimen*(*s* = *mu_glue*, *false*, *false*); *tail_append*(*new_kern*(*cur_val*));

  subtype(*tail*) ← *s*;

  end;

1062. Many of the actions related to box-making are triggered by the appearance of braces in the input. For example, when the user says '\hbox to 100pt{⟨hlist⟩}' in vertical mode, the information about the box size (100pt, *exactly*) is put onto *save_stack* with a level boundary word just above it, and *cur_group* ← *adjusted_hbox_group*; TeX enters restricted horizontal mode to process the hlist. The right brace eventually causes *save_stack* to be restored to its former state, at which time the information about the box size (100pt, *exactly*) is available once again; a box is packaged and we leave restricted horizontal mode, appending the new box to the current list of the enclosing mode (in this case to the current list of vertical mode), followed by any vertical adjustments that were removed from the box by *hpack*.

The next few sections of the program are therefore concerned with the treatment of left and right curly braces.

1063. If a left brace occurs in the middle of a page or paragraph, it simply introduces a new level of grouping, and the matching right brace will not have such a drastic effect. Such grouping affects neither the mode nor the current list.

⟨Cases of *main_control* that build boxes and lists 1056⟩ +≡

non_math(*left_brace*): *new_save_level*(*simple_group*);

any_mode(*begin_group*): *new_save_level*(*semi_simple_group*);

any_mode(*end_group*): **if** *cur_group* = *semi_simple_group* **then** *unsave*

  else *off_save*;

1064. We have to deal with errors in which braces and such things are not properly nested. Sometimes the user makes an error of commission by inserting an extra symbol, but sometimes the user makes an error of omission. TEX can't always tell one from the other, so it makes a guess and tries to avoid getting into a loop.

The *off_save* routine is called when the current group code is wrong. It tries to insert something into the user's input that will help clean off the top level.

⟨ Declare action procedures for use by *main_control* 1043 ⟩ +≡
procedure *off_save*;
    var *p*: *pointer*; { inserted token }
    begin if *cur_group* = *bottom_level* **then**
        ⟨ Drop current token and complain that it was unmatched 1066 ⟩
    else begin *back_input*; *p* ← *get_avail*; *link*(*temp_head*) ← *p*; *print_err*("Missing␣");
        ⟨ Prepare to insert a token that matches *cur_group*, and print what it is 1065 ⟩;
        print("␣inserted"); *ins_list*(*link*(*temp_head*));
        help5("I´ve␣inserted␣something␣that␣you␣may␣have␣forgotten.")
        ("(See␣the␣<inserted␣text>␣above.)")
        ("With␣luck,␣this␣will␣get␣me␣unwedged.␣␣But␣if␣you")
        ("really␣didn´t␣forget␣anything,␣try␣typing␣`2´␣now;␣then")
        ("my␣insertion␣and␣my␣current␣dilemma␣will␣both␣disappear."); *error*;
        end;
    end;

---

adjusted_hbox_group = 3, §269.
any_mode = macro, §1045.
back_input: **procedure**, §325.
begin_group = 61, §208.
bottom_level = 0, §269.
build_page: **procedure**, §994.
cur_chr: *halfword*, §297.
cur_group: *group_code*, §271.
cur_val: *integer*, §410.
decr = macro, §16.
end_group = 62, §208.
error: **procedure**, §82.
exactly = 0, §644.
fil_code = 0, §1058.
fil_glue = macro, §162.
fil_neg_code = 3, §1058.
fil_neg_glue = macro, §162.
fill_code = 1, §1058.

fill_glue: macro, §162.
get_avail: **function**, §120.
glue_ref_count = macro, §150.
glue_val = 2, §410.
help5 = macro, §79.
hpack: **function**, §649.
ins_list = macro, §323.
left_brace = 1, §207.
link = macro, §118.
mskip_code = 5, §1058.
mu_glue = 99, §149.
mu_val = 3, §410.
new_glue: **function**, §153.
new_kern: **function**, §156.
new_save_level: **procedure**, §274.
non_math = macro, §1046.
pointer = macro, §115.

print: **procedure**, §59.
print_err = macro, §73.
quarterword = 0 . . 255, §113.
save_stack: **array**, §271.
scan_dimen: **procedure**, §448.
scan_glue: **procedure**, §461.
semi_simple_group = 14, §269.
simple_group = 1, §269.
skip_code = 4, §1058.
small_number = 0 . . 63, §101.
ss_code = 2, §1058.
ss_glue = macro, §162.
subtype = macro, §133.
tail = macro, §213.
tail_append = macro, §214.
temp_head = macro, §162.
unsave: **procedure**, §281.

1065. At this point, $link(temp\_head) = p$, a pointer to an empty one-word node.

⟨ Prepare to insert a token that matches cur_group, and print what it is 1065 ⟩ ≡
  case cur_group **of**
  $semi\_simple\_group$: **begin** $info(p) \leftarrow cs\_token\_flag + frozen\_end\_group$; $print\_esc("endgroup")$;
    end;
  $math\_shift\_group$: **begin** $info(p) \leftarrow math\_shift\_token + "\$"$; $print\_char("\$")$;
    end;
  $math\_left\_group$: **begin** $info(p) \leftarrow cs\_token\_flag + frozen\_right$; $link(p) \leftarrow get\_avail$; $p \leftarrow link(p)$;
    $info(p) \leftarrow other\_token + "."$; $print\_esc("right.")$;
    end;
  othercases begin $info(p) \leftarrow right\_brace\_token + "}"$; $print\_char("}")$;
    end
  endcases

This code is used in section 1064.

1066. It's very hard to get this error message; indeed, the case didn't arise until more than two years after it had been programmed.

⟨ Drop current token and complain that it was unmatched 1066 ⟩ ≡
  begin $print\_err("Extra_\sqcup")$; $print\_cmd\_chr(cur\_cmd, cur\_chr)$;
  $help1("Things_\sqcup are_\sqcup pretty_\sqcup mixed_\sqcup up,_\sqcup but_\sqcup I_\sqcup think_\sqcup the_\sqcup worst_\sqcup is_\sqcup over.")$;
  $error$;
  end

This code is used in section 1064.

1067. The routine for a $right\_brace$ character branches into many subcases, since a variety of things may happen, depending on cur_group. Some types of groups are not supposed to be ended by a right brace; error messages are given in hopes of pinpointing the problem. Most branches of this routine will be filled in later, when we are ready to understand them; meanwhile, we must prepare ourselves to deal with such errors.

⟨ Cases of $main\_control$ that build boxes and lists 1056 ⟩ +≡
$any\_mode(right\_brace)$: $handle\_right\_brace$;

1068. ⟨ Declare the procedure called $handle\_right\_brace$ 1068 ⟩ ≡
procedure $handle\_right\_brace$;
  var p, q: $pointer$; { for short-term use }
    d: $scaled$; { holds $split\_max\_depth$ in $insert\_group$ }
    f: $integer$; { holds $floating\_penalty$ in $insert\_group$ }
  begin case cur_group **of**
  $simple\_group$: $unsave$;
  $bottom\_level$: **begin** $print\_err("Too_\sqcup many_\sqcup}`s")$;
    $help2("You've_\sqcup closed_\sqcup more_\sqcup groups_\sqcup than_\sqcup you_\sqcup opened.")$
    $("Such_\sqcup booboos_\sqcup are_\sqcup generally_\sqcup harmless,_\sqcup so_\sqcup keep_\sqcup going.")$; $error$;
    end;
  $semi\_simple\_group, math\_shift\_group, math\_left\_group$: $extra\_right\_brace$;
  ⟨ Cases of $handle\_right\_brace$ where a $right\_brace$ triggers a delayed action 1085 ⟩
  othercases $confusion("rightbrace")$
  endcases;

end;

This code is used in section 1030.

1069. ⟨ Declare action procedures for use by *main_control* 1043 ⟩ +≡
procedure *extra_right_brace*;
  begin *print_err*("Extra␣},␣or␣forgotten␣");
  case *cur_group* **of**
  semi_simple_group: *print_esc*("endgroup");
  math_shift_group: *print_char*("$");
  math_left_group: *print_esc*("right");
  end;
  help5("I´ve␣deleted␣a␣group-closing␣symbol␣because␣it␣seems␣to␣be")
  ("spurious,␣as␣in␣`$x}$´.␣But␣perhaps␣the␣}␣is␣legitimate␣and")
  ("you␣forgot␣something␣else,␣as␣in␣`\hbox{$x}´.␣In␣such␣cases")
  ("the␣way␣to␣recover␣is␣to␣insert␣both␣the␣forgotten␣and␣the")
  ("deleted␣material,␣e.g.,␣by␣typing␣`I$}´."); *error*; *incr*(*align_state*);
  end;

1070. Here is where we clear the parameters that are supposed to revert to their default values after every paragraph and when internal vertical mode is entered.

⟨ Declare action procedures for use by *main_control* 1043 ⟩ +≡
procedure *normal_paragraph*;
  begin if *looseness* ≠ 0 **then** *eq_word_define*(*int_base* + *looseness_code*, 0);
  if *hang_indent* ≠ 0 **then** *eq_word_define*(*dimen_base* + *hang_indent_code*, 0);
  if *hang_after* ≠ 1 **then** *eq_word_define*(*int_base* + *hang_after_code*, 1);
  if *par_shape_ptr* ≠ *null* **then** *eq_define*(*par_shape_loc*, *shape_ref*, *null*);
  end;

---

align_state: *integer*, §309.
any_mode = macro, §1045.
bottom_level = 0, §269.
confusion: **procedure**, §95.
cs_token_flag = macro, §289.
cur_chr: *halfword*, §297.
cur_cmd: *eight_bits*, §297.
cur_group: *group_code*, §271.
dimen_base = 4801, §236.
eq_define: **procedure**, §277.
eq_word_define: **procedure**, §278.
error: **procedure**, §82.
floating_penalty = macro, §236.
frozen_end_group = 2360, §222.
frozen_right = 2361, §222.
get_avail: **function**, §120.
hang_after = macro, §236.
hang_after_code = 41, §236.

hang_indent = macro, §247.
hang_indent_code = 17, §247.
help1 = macro, §79.
help2 = macro, §79.
help5 = macro, §79.
incr = macro, §16.
info = macro, §118.
insert_group = 11, §269.
int_base = 4367, §230.
link = macro, §118.
looseness = macro, §236.
looseness_code = 19, §236.
math_left_group = 16, §269.
math_shift_group = 15, §269.
math_shift_token = 768, §289.
null = macro, §115.
other_token = 3072, §289.

p: *pointer*, §1064.
par_shape_loc = 3156, §230.
par_shape_ptr = macro, §230.
pointer = macro, §115.
print_char: **procedure**, §58.
print_cmd_chr: **procedure**, §298.
print_err = macro, §73.
print_esc: **procedure**, §63.
right_brace = 2, §207.
right_brace_token = 512, §289.
scaled = *integer*, §101.
semi_simple_group = 14, §269.
shape_ref = 117, §210.
simple_group = 1, §269.
split_max_depth = macro, §247.
temp_head = macro, §162.
unsave: **procedure**, §281.

1071.   Now let's turn to the question of how \hbox is treated. We actually need to consider also a slightly larger context, since constructions like '\setbox3=\hbox...' and '\leaders\hbox...' and '\lower3.8pt\hbox...' are supposed to invoke quite different actions after the box has been packaged. Conversely, constructions like '\setbox3=' can be followed by a variety of different kinds of boxes, and we would like to encode such things in an efficient way.

In other words, there are two problems: To represent the context of a box, and to represent its type.

The first problem is solved by putting a "context code" on the *save_stack*, just below the two entries that give the dimensions produced by *scan_spec*. The context code is either a (signed) shift amount, or it is a large integer $\geq$ *box_flag*, where *box_flag* = 2^{30}. Codes *box_flag* through *box_flag* + 255 represent '\setbox0' through '\setbox255'; codes *box_flag* + 256 through *box_flag* + 511 represent '\global\setbox0' through '\global\setbox255'; code *box_flag* + 512 represents '\shipout'; and codes *box_flag* + 513 through *box_flag* + 515 represent '\leaders', '\cleaders', and '\xleaders'.

The second problem is solved by giving the command code *make_box* to all control sequences that produce a box, and by using the following *chr_code* values to distinguish between them: *box_code*, *copy_code*, *last_box_code*, *vsplit_code*, *vtop_code*, *vtop_code* + *vmode*, and *vtop_code* + *hmode*, where the latter two are used denote \vbox and \hbox, respectively.

> **define** *box_flag* ≡ ´10000000000   { context code for '\setbox0' }
> **define** *ship_out_flag* ≡ *box_flag* + 512   { context code for '\shipout' }
> **define** *leader_flag* ≡ *box_flag* + 513   { context code for '\leaders' }
> **define** *box_code* = 0   { *chr_code* for '\box' }
> **define** *copy_code* = 1   { *chr_code* for '\copy' }
> **define** *last_box_code* = 2   { *chr_code* for '\lastbox' }
> **define** *vsplit_code* = 3   { *chr_code* for '\vsplit' }
> **define** *vtop_code* = 4   { *chr_code* for '\vtop' }

⟨ Put each of TEX's primitives into the hash table 226 ⟩ +≡
> *primitive*("moveleft", *hmove*, 1); *primitive*("moveright", *hmove*, 0);
> *primitive*("raise", *vmove*, 1); *primitive*("lower", *vmove*, 0);
>
> *primitive*("box", *make_box*, *box_code*); *primitive*("copy", *make_box*, *copy_code*);
> *primitive*("lastbox", *make_box*, *last_box_code*); *primitive*("vsplit", *make_box*, *vsplit_code*);
> *primitive*("vtop", *make_box*, *vtop_code*);
> *primitive*("vbox", *make_box*, *vtop_code* + *vmode*); *primitive*("hbox", *make_box*, *vtop_code* + *hmode*);
> *primitive*("shipout", *leader_ship*, *a_leaders* − 1);   { *ship_out_flag* = *leader_flag* − 1 }
> *primitive*("leaders", *leader_ship*, *a_leaders*); *primitive*("cleaders", *leader_ship*, *c_leaders*);
> *primitive*("xleaders", *leader_ship*, *x_leaders*);

1072.   ⟨ Cases of *print_cmd_chr* for symbolic printing of primitives 227 ⟩ +≡
hmove: **if** *chr_code* = 1 **then** *print_esc*("moveleft") **else** *print_esc*("moveright");
vmove: **if** *chr_code* = 1 **then** *print_esc*("raise") **else** *print_esc*("lower");
make_box: **case** *chr_code* **of**
>   *box_code*: *print_esc*("box");
>   *copy_code*: *print_esc*("copy");
>   *last_box_code*: *print_esc*("lastbox");
>   *vsplit_code*: *print_esc*("vsplit");
>   *vtop_code*: *print_esc*("vtop");

$vtop\_code + vmode$: $print\_esc(\texttt{"vbox"})$;
  othercases $print\_esc(\texttt{"hbox"})$
  endcases;
$leader\_ship$: **if** $chr\_code = a\_leaders$ **then** $print\_esc(\texttt{"leaders"})$
  else if $chr\_code = c\_leaders$ **then** $print\_esc(\texttt{"cleaders"})$
    else if $chr\_code = x\_leaders$ **then** $print\_esc(\texttt{"xleaders"})$
      else $print\_esc(\texttt{"shipout"})$;

1073. Constructions that require a box are started by placing a context code on *save_stack* and calling *scan_box*. The *scan_box* routine verifies that a *make_box* command comes next and then it calls *begin_box*.

⟨ Cases of *main_control* that build boxes and lists 1056 ⟩ +≡
$vmode + hmove, hmode + vmove, mmode + vmove$: **begin** $t \leftarrow cur\_chr$; $scan\_normal\_dimen$;
  if $t = 0$ **then** $saved(0) \leftarrow cur\_val$ **else** $saved(0) \leftarrow -cur\_val$;
  $scan\_box$;
  end;
$any\_mode(leader\_ship)$: **begin** $saved(0) \leftarrow leader\_flag - a\_leaders + cur\_chr$; $scan\_box$;
  end;
$any\_mode(make\_box)$: **begin** $saved(0) \leftarrow 0$; $begin\_box$;
  end;

1074. The global variable *cur_box* will point to a newly-made box. If the box is void, we will have *cur_box* = *null*. Otherwise we will have *type(cur_box)* = *hlist_node* or *vlist_node* or *rule_node*; the *rule_node* case can occur only with leaders.

⟨ Global variables 13 ⟩ +≡
cur_box: *pointer*;   { box to be placed into its context }

1075. The *box_end* procedure does the right thing with *cur_box*, if *saved*(0) represents the context as explained above.

⟨ Declare action procedures for use by *main_control* 1043 ⟩ +≡

procedure *box_end*;
   var *p*: *pointer*; { *ord_noad* for new box in math mode }
   begin if *saved*(0) < *box_flag* **then**
     ⟨ Append box *cur_box* to the current list, shifted by *saved*(0) 1076 ⟩
   else if *saved*(0) < *ship_out_flag* **then** ⟨ Store *cur_box* in a box register 1077 ⟩
     else if *cur_box* ≠ *null* **then**
       if *saved*(0) > *ship_out_flag* **then** ⟨ Append a new leader node that uses *cur_box* 1078 ⟩
       else *ship_out*(*cur_box*);
   end;

1076. The global variable *adjust_tail* will be non-null if and only if the current box might include adjustments that should be appended to the current vertical list.

⟨ Append box *cur_box* to the current list, shifted by *saved*(0) 1076 ⟩ ≡

   begin if *cur_box* ≠ *null* **then**
     begin *shift_amount*(*cur_box*) ← *saved*(0);
     if *abs*(*mode*) = *vmode* **then**
       begin *append_to_vlist*(*cur_box*);
       if *adjust_tail* ≠ *null* **then**
         begin if *adjust_head* ≠ *adjust_tail* **then**
           begin *link*(*tail*) ← *link*(*adjust_head*); *tail* ← *adjust_tail*;
           end;
         adjust_tail ← *null*;
         end;
       if *mode* > 0 **then** *build_page*;
       end
     else begin if *abs*(*mode*) = *hmode* **then** *space_factor* ← 1000
       else begin *p* ← *new_noad*; *math_type*(*nucleus*(*p*)) ← *sub_box*; *info*(*nucleus*(*p*)) ← *cur_box*;
        cur_box ← *p*;
       end;
       link(*tail*) ← *cur_box*; *tail* ← *cur_box*;
      end;
     end;
   end

This code is used in section 1075.

1077. ⟨ Store *cur_box* in a box register 1077 ⟩ ≡
   if *saved*(0) < *box_flag* + 256 **then** *eq_define*(*box_base* − *box_flag* + *saved*(0), *box_ref*, *cur_box*)
   else *geq_define*(*box_base* − *box_flag* − 256 + *saved*(0), *box_ref*, *cur_box*)

This code is used in section 1075.

1078. ⟨Append a new leader node that uses *cur_box* 1078⟩ ≡

    begin ⟨Get the next non-blank non-relax non-call token 404⟩;

    if ((*cur_cmd* = *hskip*) ∧ (*abs*(*mode*) ≠ *vmode*)) ∨ ((*cur_cmd* = *vskip*) ∧ (*abs*(*mode*) = *vmode*)) ∨

        ((*cur_cmd* = *mskip*) ∧ (*abs*(*mode*) = *mmode*)) **then**

        begin *append_glue*; *subtype*(*tail*) ← *saved*(0) − (*leader_flag* − *a_leaders*);

        leader_ptr(*tail*) ← *cur_box*;

        end

    else begin *print_err*("Leaders␣not␣followed␣by␣proper␣glue");

        help3("You␣should␣say␣`\leaders␣<box␣or␣rule><hskip␣or␣vskip>´.")

        ("I␣found␣the␣<box␣or␣rule>,␣but␣there´s␣no␣suitable")

        ("<hskip␣or␣vskip>,␣so␣I´m␣ignoring␣these␣leaders."); *back_error*; *flush_node_list*(*cur_box*);

        end;

    end

This code is used in section 1075.

---

a_leaders = 100, §149.
adjust_head = macro, §162.
adjust_tail: *pointer*, §647.
append_glue: **procedure**, §1060.
append_to_vlist: **procedure**, §679.
back_error: **procedure**, §327.
box_base = 3422, §230.
box_flag = macro, §1071.
box_ref = 118, §210.
build_page: **procedure**, §994.
cur_box: *pointer*, §1074.
cur_cmd: *eight_bits*, §297.
eq_define: **procedure**, §277.
flush_node_list: **procedure**, §202.

geq_define: **procedure**, §279.
help3 = macro, §79.
hmode = 101, §211.
hskip = 26, §208.
info = macro, §118.
leader_flag = macro, §1071.
leader_ptr = macro, §149.
link = macro, §118.
math_type = macro, §681.
mmode = 201, §211.
mode = macro, §213.
mskip = 28, §208.
new_noad: **function**, §686.
nucleus = macro, §681.

null = macro, §115.
ord_noad = 16, §682.
pointer = macro, §115.
print_err = macro, §73.
saved = macro, §274.
shift_amount = macro, §135.
ship_out: **procedure**, §638.
ship_out_flag = macro, §1071.
space_factor = macro, §213.
sub_box = 2, §681.
subtype = macro, §133.
tail = macro, §213.
vmode = 1, §211.
vskip = 27, §208.

1079. Now that we can see what eventually happens to boxes, we can consider the first steps in their creation. The *begin_box* routine is called when *saved*(0) is a context specification, *cur_chr* specifies the type of box desired, and *cur_cmd* = *make_box*.

⟨ Declare action procedures for use by *main_control* 1043 ⟩ +≡
procedure *begin_box*;
 label *exit*, *done*;
 var *p*, *q*: *pointer*; { run through the current list }
  m: *quarterword*; { the length of a replacement list }
  k: *halfword*; { 0 or *vmode* or *hmode* }
  n: *eight_bits*; { a box number }
 begin case *cur_chr* **of**
 box_code: **begin** *scan_eight_bit_int*; *cur_box* ← *box*(*cur_val*); *box*(*cur_val*) ← *null*;
   { the box becomes void, at the same level }
  end;
 copy_code: **begin** *scan_eight_bit_int*; *cur_box* ← *copy_node_list*(*box*(*cur_val*));
  end;
 last_box_code: ⟨ If the current list ends with a box node, delete it from the list and make *cur_box*
   point to it; otherwise set *cur_box* ← *null* 1080 ⟩;
 vsplit_code: ⟨ Split off part of a vertical box, make *cur_box* point to it 1082 ⟩;
 othercases ⟨ Initiate the construction of an hbox or vbox, then **return** 1083 ⟩
 endcases;
 box_end; { in simple cases, we use the box immediately }
exit: **end**;

1080. Note that the condition ¬*is_char_node*(*tail*) implies that *head* ≠ *tail*, since *head* is a one-word node.

⟨ If the current list ends with a box node, delete it from the list and make *cur_box* point to it; otherwise set *cur_box* ← *null* 1080 ⟩ ≡
 begin *cur_box* ← *null*;
 if *abs*(*mode*) = *mmode* **then**
  begin *you_cant*; *help1*("Sorry;␣this␣\lastbox␣will␣be␣void."); *error*;
  end
 else if (*mode* = *vmode*) ∧ (*head* = *tail*) **then**
  begin *you_cant*; *help2*("Sorry...I␣usually␣can´t␣take␣things␣from␣the␣current␣page.")
  ("This␣\lastbox␣will␣therefore␣be␣void."); *error*;
  end
  else begin if ¬*is_char_node*(*tail*) **then**
   if (*type*(*tail*) = *hlist_node*) ∨ (*type*(*tail*) = *vlist_node*) **then**
    ⟨ Remove the last box, unless it's part of a discretionary 1081 ⟩;
  end;
 end

This code is used in section 1079.

1081.   ⟨Remove the last box, unless it's part of a discretionary 1081⟩ ≡
  begin $q \leftarrow head$;
  repeat $p \leftarrow q$;
    if $\neg is\_char\_node(q)$ **then**
      if $type(q) = disc\_node$ **then**
        begin for $m \leftarrow 1$ **to** $replace\_count(q)$ **do** $p \leftarrow link(p)$;
        if $p = tail$ **then goto** $done$;
        end;
    $q \leftarrow link(p)$;
  until $q = tail$;
  $cur\_box \leftarrow tail$; $shift\_amount(cur\_box) \leftarrow 0$; $tail \leftarrow p$; $link(p) \leftarrow null$;
$done$: **end**

This code is used in section 1080.

1082.   Here we deal with things like '\vsplit 13 to 100pt'.

⟨Split off part of a vertical box, make cur_box point to it 1082⟩ ≡
  begin $scan\_eight\_bit\_int$; $n \leftarrow cur\_val$;
  if $\neg scan\_keyword("to")$ **then**
    begin $print\_err("Missing␣`to´␣inserted")$;
    $help2("I´m␣working␣on␣`\vsplit<box␣number>␣to␣<dimen>´;")$
    $("will␣look␣for␣the␣<dimen>␣next.")$; $error$;
    end;
  $scan\_normal\_dimen$; $cur\_box \leftarrow vsplit(n, cur\_val)$;
  end

This code is used in section 1079.

---

box = macro, §230.
box_code = 0, §1071.
box_end: **procedure**, §1075.
$copy\_code$ = 1, §1071.
$copy\_node\_list$: **function**, §204.
cur_box: $pointer$, §1074.
cur_chr: $halfword$, §297.
cur_cmd: $eight\_bits$, §297.
cur_val: $integer$, §410.
$disc\_node$ = 7, §145.
$done$ = 30, §15.
$eight\_bits$ = 0 .. 255, §25.
$error$: **procedure**, §82.
$exit$ = 10, §15.
$halfword = min\_halfword$ ..

$max\_halfword$, §113.
$head$ = macro, §213.
$help1$ = macro, §79.
$help2$ = macro, §79.
$hlist\_node$ = 0, §135.
$hmode$ = 101, §211.
is_char_node = macro, §134.
$last\_box\_code$ = 2, §1071.
$link$ = macro, §118.
$make\_box$ = 20, §208.
$mmode$ = 201, §211.
$mode$ = macro, §213.
$null$ = macro, §115.
$pointer$ = macro, §115.
$print\_err$ = macro, §73.

$quarterword$ = 0 .. 255, §113.
$replace\_count$ = macro, §145.
$saved$ = macro, §274.
$scan\_eight\_bit\_int$: **procedure**,
  §433.
$scan\_keyword$: **function**, §407.
$scan\_normal\_dimen$ = macro, §448.
$shift\_amount$ = macro, §135.
$tail$ = macro, §213.
$type$ = macro, §133.
$vlist\_node$ = 1, §137.
$vmode$ = 1, §211.
$vsplit$: **function**, §977.
$vsplit\_code$ = 3, §1071.
you_cant: **procedure**, §1049.

1083. Here is where we enter restricted horizontal mode or internal vertical mode, in order to make a box.

⟨ Initiate the construction of an hbox or vbox, then **return** 1083 ⟩ ≡
  begin $k \leftarrow cur\_chr - vtop\_code$; $incr(save\_ptr)$; $scan\_spec$;
  if $k = hmode$ **then**
    if $(saved(-3) < box\_flag) \wedge (abs(mode) = vmode)$ **then** $new\_save\_level(adjusted\_hbox\_group)$
    else $new\_save\_level(hbox\_group)$
  else begin if $k = vmode$ **then** $new\_save\_level(vbox\_group)$
    else begin $new\_save\_level(vtop\_group)$; $k \leftarrow vmode$;
      end;
    $normal\_paragraph$;
    end;
  $push\_nest$; $mode \leftarrow -k$;
  if $k = vmode$ **then**
    begin $prev\_depth \leftarrow ignore\_depth$;
    if $every\_vbox \neq null$ **then** $begin\_token\_list(every\_vbox, every\_vbox\_text)$;
    end
  else begin $space\_factor \leftarrow 1000$;
    if $every\_hbox \neq null$ **then** $begin\_token\_list(every\_hbox, every\_hbox\_text)$;
    end;
  return;
  end

This code is used in section 1079.

1084. ⟨ Declare action procedures for use by $main\_control$ 1043 ⟩ +≡
procedure $scan\_box$;   { the next input should specify a box or perhaps a rule }
  begin ⟨ Get the next non-blank non-relax non-call token 404 ⟩;
  if $cur\_cmd = make\_box$ **then** $begin\_box$
  else if $(saved(0) \geq leader\_flag) \wedge ((cur\_cmd = hrule) \vee (cur\_cmd = vrule))$ **then**
    begin $cur\_box \leftarrow scan\_rule\_spec$; box_end;
    end
  else begin
    $print\_err("A_\sqcup<box>_\sqcup was_\sqcup supposed_\sqcup to_\sqcup be_\sqcup here")$;
    $help3("I_\sqcup was_\sqcup expecting_\sqcup to_\sqcup see_\sqcup \backslash hbox_\sqcup or_\sqcup \backslash vbox_\sqcup or_\sqcup \backslash copy_\sqcup or_\sqcup \backslash box_\sqcup or")$
    $("something_\sqcup like_\sqcup that._\sqcup So_\sqcup you_\sqcup might_\sqcup find_\sqcup something_\sqcup missing_\sqcup in")$
    $("your_\sqcup output._\sqcup But_\sqcup keep_\sqcup trying;_\sqcup you_\sqcup can_\sqcup fix_\sqcup this_\sqcup later.")$; $back\_error$;
    end;
  end;

1085. When the right brace occurs at the end of an \hbox or \vbox or \vtop construction, the *package* routine comes into action. We might also have to finish a paragraph that hasn't ended.

⟨ Cases of $handle\_right\_brace$ where a $right\_brace$ triggers a delayed action 1085 ⟩ ≡
$hbox\_group$: $package(0)$;
$adjusted\_hbox\_group$: **begin** $adjust\_tail \leftarrow adjust\_head$; $package(0)$;
  end;
$vbox\_group$: **begin** end_graf; $package(0)$;
  end;
$vtop\_group$: **begin** end_graf; $package(vtop\_code)$;

end;

See also sections 1100, 1118, 1132, 1133, 1168, 1173, and 1186.

This code is used in section 1068.

1086. ⟨ Declare action procedures for use by *main_control* 1043 ⟩ +≡
procedure *package*(*c* : *small_number*);
  var *h*: *scaled*; { height of box }
    p: *pointer*; { first node in a box }
    d: *scaled*; { max depth }
  begin *d* ← *box_max_depth*; *unsave*; *save_ptr* ← *save_ptr* − 3;
  if *mode* = −*hmode* **then** *cur_box* ← *hpack*(*link*(*head*), *saved*(2), *saved*(1))
  else begin *cur_box* ← *vpackage*(*link*(*head*), *saved*(2), *saved*(1), *d*);
    if *c* = *vtop_code* **then** ⟨ Readjust the height and depth of *cur_box*, for \vtop 1087 ⟩;
    end;
  pop_nest; *box_end*;
  end;

1087. The height of a '\vtop' box is inherited from the first item on its list, if that item is an *hlist_node*, *vlist_node*, or *rule_node*; otherwise the \vtop height is zero.

⟨ Readjust the height and depth of *cur_box*, for \vtop 1087 ⟩ ≡
  begin *h* ← 0; *p* ← *list_ptr*(*cur_box*);
  if *p* ≠ *null* **then**
    if *type*(*p*) ≤ *rule_node* **then** *h* ← *height*(*p*);
  depth(*cur_box*) ← *depth*(*cur_box*) − *h* + *height*(*cur_box*); *height*(*cur_box*) ← *h*;
  end

This code is used in section 1086.

1088. A paragraph begins when horizontal-mode material occurs in vertical mode, or when the paragraph is explicitly started by '\indent' or '\noindent'.

⟨ Put each of TEX's primitives into the hash table 226 ⟩ +≡
  primitive("indent", *start_par*, 1); *primitive*("noindent", *start_par*, 0);

1089. ⟨ Cases of *print_cmd_chr* for symbolic printing of primitives 227 ⟩ +≡
start_par: **if** *chr_code* = 0 **then** *print_esc*("noindent") **else** *print_esc*("indent");

1090. ⟨ Cases of *main_control* that build boxes and lists 1056 ⟩ +≡
vmode + *start_par*: *new_graf*(*cur_chr* > 0);
vmode + *letter*, *vmode* + *other_char*, *vmode* + *char_num*, *vmode* + *char_given*, *vmode* + *math_shift*,
    vmode + *un_hbox*, *vmode* + *vrule*, *vmode* + *accent*, *vmode* + *discretionary*, *vmode* + *hskip*,
    vmode + *valign*, *vmode* + *ex_space*:
  begin *back_input*; *new_graf*(*true*);
  end;

1091. ⟨ Declare action procedures for use by *main_control* 1043 ⟩ +≡
procedure *new_graf*(*indented* : *boolean*);
  begin *prev_graf* ← 0;
  if (*mode* = *vmode*) ∨ (*head* ≠ *tail*) **then** *tail_append*(*new_param_glue*(*par_skip_code*));
  push_nest; *mode* ← *hmode*; *space_factor* ← 1000;
  if *indented* **then**
    begin *tail* ← *new_null_box*; *link*(*head*) ← *tail*; *width*(*tail*) ← *par_indent*;
    end;
  if *every_par* ≠ *null* **then** *begin_token_list*(*every_par*, *every_par_text*);
  if *nest_ptr* = 1 **then** *build_page*; { put *par_skip* glue on current page }
  end;

1092. ⟨ Cases of *main_control* that build boxes and lists 1056 ⟩ +≡
hmode + *start_par*, *mmode* + *start_par*: *indent_in_hmode*;

1093. ⟨ Declare action procedures for use by *main_control* 1043 ⟩ +≡
procedure *indent_in_hmode*;
  var *p*, *q*: *pointer*;
  begin if *cur_chr* > 0 **then** { \indent }
    begin *p* ← *new_null_box*; *width*(*p*) ← *par_indent*;
    if *abs*(*mode*) = *hmode* **then** *space_factor* ← 1000
    else begin *q* ← *new_noad*; *math_type*(*nucleus*(*q*)) ← *sub_box*; *info*(*nucleus*(*q*)) ← *p*; *p* ← *q*;
      end;
    tail_append(*p*);
    end;
  end;

1094. A paragraph ends when a *par_end* command is sensed, or when we are in horizontal mode when reaching the right brace of vertical-mode routines like \vbox, \insert, or \output.

⟨ Cases of *main_control* that build boxes and lists 1056 ⟩ +≡
vmode + *par_end*: **begin** *normal_paragraph*;
  if *mode* > 0 **then** *build_page*;
  end;

$hmode + par\_end$: **begin if** $align\_state < 0$ **then** off_save;
        { this tries to recover from an alignment that didn't end properly }
    end_graf;   { this takes us to the enclosing mode, if $mode > 0$ }
    if $mode = vmode$ **then** $build\_page$;
    end;
$hmode + stop, hmode + vskip, hmode + hrule, hmode + un\_vbox, hmode + halign$: $head\_for\_vmode$;

1095.   ⟨ Declare action procedures for use by $main\_control$ 1043 ⟩ $+\equiv$
procedure $head\_for\_vmode$;
  begin if $mode < 0$ **then**
    if $cur\_cmd \neq hrule$ **then** off_save
    else begin $print\_err($"You␣can´t␣use␣`"$)$; $print\_esc($"hrule"$)$;
      $print($"´␣here␣except␣with␣leaders"$)$;
      $help2($"To␣put␣a␣horizontal␣rule␣in␣an␣hbox␣or␣an␣alignment,"$)$
      ($"you␣should␣use␣\leaders␣or␣\hrulefill␣(see␣The␣TeXbook)."$)$; $error$;
      end
  else begin $back\_input$; $cur\_tok \leftarrow par\_token$; $back\_input$; $token\_type \leftarrow inserted$;
    end;
  end;

1096.   ⟨ Declare action procedures for use by $main\_control$ 1043 ⟩ $+\equiv$
procedure end_graf;
  begin if $mode = hmode$ **then**
    begin if $head = tail$ **then** pop_nest { null paragraphs are ignored }
    else $line\_break(widow\_penalty)$;
    $normal\_paragraph$; $error\_count \leftarrow 0$;
    end;
  end;

1097. Insertion and adjustment and mark nodes are constructed by the following pieces of the program.

⟨ Cases of *main_control* that build boxes and lists 1056 ⟩ +≡
any_mode(*insert*), *hmode* + *vadjust*, *mmode* + *vadjust*: *begin_insert_or_adjust*;
any_mode(*mark*): *make_mark*;

1098. ⟨ Forbidden cases detected in *main_control* 1048 ⟩ +≡
  vmode + *vadjust*,

1099. ⟨ Declare action procedures for use by *main_control* 1043 ⟩ +≡
procedure *begin_insert_or_adjust*;
  begin if *cur_cmd* = *vadjust* **then** *cur_val* ← 255
  else begin *scan_eight_bit_int*;
    if *cur_val* = 255 **then**
      begin *print_err*("You␣can´t␣"); *print_esc*("insert"); *print_int*(255);
      help1("I´m␣changing␣to␣\insert0;␣box␣255␣is␣special."); *error*; *cur_val* ← 0;
      end;
    end;
  saved(0) ← *cur_val*; *incr*(*save_ptr*); *new_save_level*(*insert_group*); *scan_left_brace*;
  normal_paragraph; *push_nest*; *mode* ← −*vmode*; *prev_depth* ← *ignore_depth*;
  end;

1100. ⟨ Cases of *handle_right_brace* where a *right_brace* triggers a delayed action 1085 ⟩ +≡
insert_group: **begin** *end_graf*; *q* ← *split_top_skip*; *add_glue_ref*(*q*); *d* ← *split_max_depth*;
  f ← *floating_penalty*; *unsave*; *decr*(*save_ptr*);
        { now *saved*(0) is the insertion number, or 255 for *vadjust* }
  p ← *vpack*(*link*(*head*), *natural*); *pop_nest*;
  if *saved*(0) < 255 **then**
    begin *tail_append*(*get_node*(*ins_node_size*)); *type*(*tail*) ← *ins_node*; *subtype*(*tail*) ← *qi*(*saved*(0));
    height(*tail*) ← *height*(*p*) + *depth*(*p*); *ins_ptr*(*tail*) ← *list_ptr*(*p*); *split_top_ptr*(*tail*) ← *q*;
    depth(*tail*) ← *d*; *float_cost*(*tail*) ← *f*;
    end
  else begin *tail_append*(*get_node*(*small_node_size*)); *type*(*tail*) ← *adjust_node*;
    subtype(*tail*) ← 0;   { the *subtype* is not used }
    adjust_ptr(*tail*) ← *list_ptr*(*p*); *delete_glue_ref*(*q*);
    end;
  free_node(*p*, *box_node_size*);
  if *nest_ptr* = 0 **then** *build_page*;
  end;
output_group: ⟨ Resume the page builder after an output routine has come to an end 1026 ⟩;

1101. ⟨ Declare action procedures for use by *main_control* 1043 ⟩ +≡
procedure *make_mark*;
  var *p*: *pointer*;   { new node }
  begin *p* ← *scan_toks*(*false*, *true*); *p* ← *get_node*(*small_node_size*); *type*(*p*) ← *mark_node*;
  subtype(*p*) ← 0;   { the *subtype* is not used }
  mark_ptr(*p*) ← *def_ref*; *link*(*tail*) ← *p*; *tail* ← *p*;
  end;

1102.   Penalty nodes get into a list via the *break_penalty* command.

⟨ Cases of *main_control* that build boxes and lists 1056 ⟩ +≡
any_mode(*break_penalty*): *append_penalty*;

1103.   ⟨ Declare action procedures for use by *main_control* 1043 ⟩ +≡
procedure *append_penalty*;
　　begin *scan_int*; *tail_append*(*new_penalty*(*cur_val*));
　　if *mode* = *vmode* **then** *build_page*;
　　end;

1104.   The *remove_item* command removes a penalty, kern, or glue node if it appears at the tail
of the current list, using a brute-force linear scan. Like \lastbox, this command is not allowed
in vertical mode (except internal vertical mode), since the current list in vertical mode is sent to
the page builder. But if we happen to be able to implement it in vertical mode, we do.

⟨ Cases of *main_control* that build boxes and lists 1056 ⟩ +≡
any_mode(*remove_item*): *delete_last*;

1105. When *delete_last* is called, *cur_chr* is the *type* of node that will be deleted, if present.

⟨ Declare action procedures for use by *main_control* 1043 ⟩ +≡
procedure *delete_last*;
  label *exit*;
  var *p, q*: *pointer*;   { run through the current list }
    m: *quarterword*;   { the length of a replacement list }
  begin if (*mode* = *vmode*) ∧ (*tail* = *head*) **then**
    ⟨ Apologize for inability to do the operation now, unless \unskip follows non-glue 1106 ⟩
  else begin if ¬*is_char_node*(*tail*) **then**
      if *type*(*tail*) = *cur_chr* **then**
        begin *q* ← *head*;
        repeat *p* ← *q*;
          if ¬*is_char_node*(*q*) **then**
            if *type*(*q*) = *disc_node* **then**
              begin for *m* ← 1 **to** *replace_count*(*q*) **do** *p* ← *link*(*p*);
              if *p* = *tail* **then return**;
              end;
            q ← *link*(*p*);
          until *q* = *tail*;
          link(*p*) ← *null*; *flush_node_list*(*tail*); *tail* ← *p*;
        end;
    end;
exit: **end**;

1106. ⟨ Apologize for inability to do the operation now, unless \unskip follows non-glue 1106 ⟩ ≡
  begin if (*cur_chr* ≠ *glue_node*) ∨ (*last_glue* ≠ *max_halfword*) **then**
    begin *you_cant*; *help2*("Sorry...I␣usually␣can´t␣take␣things␣from␣the␣current␣page.")
    ("Try␣`I\vskip-\lastskip´␣instead.");
    if *cur_chr* = *kern_node* **then** *help_line*[0] ← ("Try␣`I\kern-\lastkern´␣instead.")
    else if *cur_chr* ≠ *glue_node* **then**
        help_line[0] ← ("Perhaps␣you␣can␣make␣the␣output␣routine␣do␣it.");
    error;
    end;
  end
This code is used in section 1105.

1107. ⟨ Put each of TeX's primitives into the hash table 226 ⟩ +≡
  primitive("unpenalty", *remove_item*, *penalty_node*);
  primitive("unkern", *remove_item*, *kern_node*);
  primitive("unskip", *remove_item*, *glue_node*);
  primitive("unhbox", *un_hbox*, *box_code*);
  primitive("unhcopy", *un_hbox*, *copy_code*);
  primitive("unvbox", *un_vbox*, *box_code*);
  primitive("unvcopy", *un_vbox*, *copy_code*);

1108. ⟨ Cases of *print_cmd_chr* for symbolic printing of primitives 227 ⟩ +≡
remove_item: **if** *chr_code* = *glue_node* **then** *print_esc*("unskip")
  else if *chr_code* = *kern_node* **then** *print_esc*("unkern")
    else *print_esc*("unpenalty");

un_hbox: **if** *chr_code* = *copy_code* **then** *print_esc*("unhcopy")
   else *print_esc*("unhbox");
un_vbox: **if** *chr_code* = *copy_code* **then** *print_esc*("unvcopy")
   else *print_esc*("unvbox");

1109.   The *un_hbox* and *un_vbox* commands unwrap one of the 256 current boxes.

⟨ Cases of *main_control* that build boxes and lists 1056 ⟩ +≡
vmode + *un_vbox*, *hmode* + *un_hbox*, *mmode* + *un_hbox*: *unpackage*;

1110.   ⟨ Declare action procedures for use by *main_control* 1043 ⟩ +≡
procedure *unpackage*;
  label *exit*;
  var *p*: *pointer*; { the box }
    c: *box_code* .. *copy_code*; { should we copy? }
  begin *c* ← *cur_chr*; *scan_eight_bit_int*; *p* ← *box*(*cur_val*);
  if *p* = *null* **then return**;
  if (*abs*(*mode*) = *mmode*) ∨ ((*abs*(*mode*) = *vmode*) ∧ (*type*(*p*) ≠ *vlist_node*)) ∨
      ((*abs*(*mode*) = *hmode*) ∧ (*type*(*p*) ≠ *hlist_node*)) **then**
    begin *print_err*("Incompatible␣list␣can´t␣be␣unboxed");
    help3("Sorry,␣Pandora.␣(You␣sneaky␣devil.)")
    ("I␣refuse␣to␣unbox␣an␣\hbox␣in␣vertical␣mode␣or␣vice␣versa.")
    ("And␣I␣can´t␣open␣any␣boxes␣in␣math␣mode.");
    error; **return**;
    end;
  if *c* = *copy_code* **then** *link*(*tail*) ← *copy_node_list*(*list_ptr*(*p*))
  else begin *link*(*tail*) ← *list_ptr*(*p*); *box*(*cur_val*) ← *null*; *free_node*(*p*, *box_node_size*);
    end;
  while *link*(*tail*) ≠ *null* **do** *tail* ← *link*(*tail*);
exit: **end**;

1111.   ⟨ Forbidden cases detected in *main_control* 1048 ⟩ +≡
  vmode + *ital_corr*,

---

box = macro, §230.
box_code = 0, §1071.
box_node_size = 7, §135.
chr_code: *halfword*, §298.
copy_code = 1, §1071.
copy_node_list: **function**, §204.
cur_chr: *halfword*, §297.
cur_val: *integer*, §410.
disc_node = 7, §145.
error: **procedure**, §82.
exit = 10, §15.
flush_node_list: **procedure**, §202.
free_node: **procedure**, §130.
glue_node = 10, §149.
head = macro, §213.
help_line: **array**, §79.

help2 = macro, §79.
help3 = macro, §79.
hlist_node = 0, §135.
hmode = 101, §211.
is_char_node = macro, §134.
ital_corr = 44, §208.
kern_node = 11, §155.
last_glue: *pointer*, §982.
link = macro, §118.
list_ptr = macro, §135.
max_halfword = macro, §110.
mmode = 201, §211.
mode = macro, §213.
null = macro, §115.
penalty_node = 12, §157.
pointer = macro, §115.

primitive: **procedure**, §264.
print_cmd_chr: **procedure**, §298.
print_err = macro, §73.
print_esc: **procedure**, §63.
quarterword = 0 .. 255, §113.
remove_item = 25, §208.
replace_count = macro, §145.
scan_eight_bit_int: **procedure**,
  §433.
tail = macro, §213.
type = macro, §133.
un_hbox = 23, §208.
un_vbox = 24, §208.
vlist_node = 1, §137.
vmode = 1, §211.
you_cant: **procedure**, §1049.

1112. Italic corrections are converted to kern nodes when the *ital_corr* command follows a character. In math mode the same effect is achieved by appending a kern of zero here, since italic corrections are supplied later.

⟨ Cases of *main_control* that build boxes and lists 1056 ⟩ +≡
hmode + *ital_corr*: *append_italic_correction*;
mmode + *ital_corr*: *tail_append*(*new_kern*(0));

1113. ⟨ Declare action procedures for use by *main_control* 1043 ⟩ +≡
procedure *append_italic_correction*;
  label *exit*;
  var *p*: *pointer*;   { *char_node* at the tail of the current list }
    f: *internal_font_number*;   { the font in the *char_node* }
  begin if *tail* ≠ *head* **then**
    begin if *is_char_node*(*tail*) **then** *p* ← *tail*
    else if *type*(*tail*) = *ligature_node* **then** *p* ← *lig_char*(*tail*)
      else return;
    f ← *font*(*p*); *tail_append*(*new_kern*(*char_italic*(*f*)(*char_info*(*f*)(*character*(*p*)))));
    subtype(*tail*) ← *explicit*;
    end;
exit: **end**;

1114. Discretionary nodes are easy in the common case '\-', but in the general case we must process three braces full of items.

⟨ Put each of TeX's primitives into the hash table 226 ⟩ +≡
  primitive("-", *discretionary*, 1); *primitive*("discretionary", *discretionary*, 0);

1115. ⟨ Cases of *print_cmd_chr* for symbolic printing of primitives 227 ⟩ +≡
discretionary: **if** *chr_code* = 1 **then** *print_esc*("-") **else** *print_esc*("discretionary");

1116. ⟨ Cases of *main_control* that build boxes and lists 1056 ⟩ +≡
hmode + *discretionary*, *mmode* + *discretionary*: *append_discretionary*;

1117. The space factor does not change when we append a discretionary node, but it starts out as 1000 in the subsidiary lists.

⟨ Declare action procedures for use by *main_control* 1043 ⟩ +≡
procedure *append_discretionary*;
  var *c*: *integer*;   { hyphen character }
  begin *tail_append*(*new_disc*);
  if *cur_chr* = 1 **then**
    begin *c* ← *hyphen_char*[*cur_font*];
    if *c* ≥ 0 **then**
      if *c* < 256 **then** *pre_break*(*tail*) ← *new_character*(*cur_font*, *c*);
    end
  else begin *incr*(*save_ptr*); *saved*(−1) ← 0; *scan_left_brace*; *new_save_level*(*disc_group*); *push_nest*;
    mode ← −*hmode*; *space_factor* ← 1000;
    end;
  end;

1118.   The three discretionary lists are constructed somewhat as if they were hboxes. A subroutine called *build_discretionary* handles the transitions. (This is sort of fun.)

⟨ Cases of *handle_right_brace* where a *right_brace* triggers a delayed action 1085 ⟩ +≡
disc_group: *build_discretionary*;

1119.   ⟨ Declare action procedures for use by *main_control* 1043 ⟩ +≡
procedure *build_discretionary*;
  label *done*, *exit*;
  var *p*, *q*: *pointer*;   { for link manipulation }
    n: *integer*;   { length of discretionary list }
  begin *unsave*; ⟨ Prune the current list, if necessary, until it contains only *char_node*, *kern_node*,
      hlist_node, *vlist_node*, *rule_node*, and *ligature_node* items; set *n* to the length of the list, and set
      q to the list's tail 1121 ⟩;
  p ← *link*(*head*); *pop_nest*;
  case *saved*(−1) **of**
  0: *pre_break*(*tail*) ← *p*;
  1: *post_break*(*tail*) ← *p*;
  2: ⟨ Attach list *p* to the current list, and record its length; then finish up and **return** 1120 ⟩;
  end;   { there are no other cases }
  incr(*saved*(−1)); *scan_left_brace*; *new_save_level*(*disc_group*); *push_nest*; *mode* ← −*hmode*;
  space_factor ← 1000;
exit: **end**;

---

char_info = macro, §554.
char_italic = macro, §554.
char_node, §134.
character = macro, §134.
chr_code: *halfword*, §298.
cur_chr: *halfword*, §297.
cur_font = macro, §230.
disc_group = 10, §269.
discretionary = 47, §208.
done = 30, §15.
exit = 10, §15.
explicit = 1, §155.
font = macro, §134.
head = macro, §213.
hlist_node = 0, §135.
hmode = 101, §211.
hyphen_char: **array**, §549.
incr = macro, §16.

internal_font_number = 0 .. *font_max*,
  §548.
is_char_node = macro, §134.
ital_corr = 44, §208.
kern_node = 11, §155.
lig_char = macro, §143.
ligature_node = 6, §143.
link = macro, §118.
mmode = 201, §211.
mode = macro, §213.
new_character: **function**, §582.
new_disc: **function**, §145.
new_kern: **function**, §156.
new_save_level: **procedure**, §274.
pointer = macro, §115.
pop_nest: **procedure**, §217.
post_break = macro, §145.

pre_break = macro, §145.
primitive: **procedure**, §264.
print_cmd_chr: **procedure**, §298.
print_esc: **procedure**, §63.
push_nest: **procedure**, §216.
right_brace = 2, §207.
rule_node = 2, §138.
save_ptr: 0 .. *save_size*, §271.
saved = macro, §274.
scan_left_brace: **procedure**, §403.
space_factor = macro, §213.
subtype = macro, §133.
tail = macro, §213.
tail_append = macro, §214.
type = macro, §133.
unsave: **procedure**, §281.
vlist_node = 1, §137.

1120. ⟨Attach list p to the current list, and record its length; then finish up and **return** 1120⟩ ≡
  begin if $(n > 0) \wedge (abs(mode) = mmode)$ **then**
    begin $print\_err($"Illegal␣math␣"$);$ $print\_esc($"discretionary"$);$
    $help2($"Sorry:␣The␣third␣part␣of␣a␣discretionary␣break␣must␣be"$)$
    ("empty,␣in␣math␣formulas.␣I␣had␣to␣delete␣your␣third␣part."$);$ $flush\_node\_list(p);$ $n \leftarrow 0;$
    $error;$
    end
  else $link(tail) \leftarrow p;$
  if $n \le max\_quarterword$ **then** $replace\_count(tail) \leftarrow n$
  else begin $print\_err($"Discretionary␣list␣is␣too␣long"$);$
    $help2($"Wow---I␣never␣thought␣anybody␣would␣tweak␣me␣here."$)$
    ("You␣can´t␣seriously␣need␣such␣a␣huge␣discretionary␣list?"$);$ $error;$
    end;
  if $n > 0$ **then** $tail \leftarrow q;$
  $decr(save\_ptr);$ **return**;
  end

This code is used in section 1119.

1121. During this loop, $p = link(q)$ and there are n items preceding p.

⟨Prune the current list, if necessary, until it contains only *char_node*, *kern_node*, *hlist_node*, *vlist_node*,
    rule_node, and *ligature_node* items; set n to the length of the list, and set q to the list's
    tail 1121⟩ ≡
  $q \leftarrow head;$ $p \leftarrow link(q);$ $n \leftarrow 0;$
  while $p \ne null$ **do**
    begin if $\neg is\_char\_node(p)$ **then**
      if $type(p) > rule\_node$ **then**
        if $type(p) \ne kern\_node$ **then**
          if $type(p) \ne ligature\_node$ **then**
            begin $print\_err($"Improper␣discretionary␣list"$);$
            $help1($"Discretionary␣lists␣must␣contain␣only␣boxes␣and␣kerns."$);$
            $error;$ $begin\_diagnostic;$
            $print\_nl($"The␣following␣discretionary␣sublist␣has␣been␣deleted:"$);$ $show\_box(p);$
            $end\_diagnostic(true);$ $flush\_node\_list(p);$ $link(q) \leftarrow null;$ **goto** $done;$
            end;
    $q \leftarrow p;$ $p \leftarrow link(q);$ $incr(n);$
    end;
$done$:

This code is used in section 1119.

1122. We need only one more thing to complete the horizontal mode routines, namely the
\accent primitive.

⟨Cases of *main_control* that build boxes and lists 1056⟩ +≡
$hmode + accent$: $make\_accent;$

1123. The positioning of accents is straightforward but tedious. Given an accent of width
a, designed for characters of height x and slant s; and given a character of width w, height
h, and slant t: We will shift the accent down by $x - h$, and we will insert kern nodes that
have the effect of centering the accent over the character and shifting the accent to the right by

$\delta = \frac{1}{2}(w - a) + h \cdot t - x \cdot s$. If either character is absent from the font, we will simply use the other, without shifting.

⟨ Declare action procedures for use by *main_control* 1043 ⟩ +≡
procedure *make_accent*;
  var *s, t*: *real*; { amount of slant }
    p, q, r: *pointer*; { character, box, and kern nodes }
    f: *internal_font_number*; { relevant font }
    a, h, x, w, delta: *scaled*; { heights and widths, as explained above }
    i: *four_quarters*; { character information }
  begin *scan_char_num*; *f* ← *cur_font*; *p* ← *new_character*(*f, cur_val*);
  if *p* ≠ *null* **then**
    begin *x* ← *x_height*(*f*); *s* ← *slant*(*f*)/*float_constant*(65536);
    a ← *char_width*(*f*)(*char_info*(*f*)(*character*(*p*)));
    do_assignments;
    ⟨ Create a character node *q* for the next character, but set *q* ← *null* if problems arise 1124 ⟩;
    if *q* ≠ *null* **then** ⟨ Append the accent with appropriate kerns, then set *p* ← *q* 1125 ⟩;
    link(*tail*) ← *p*; *tail* ← *p*; *space_factor* ← 1000;
    end;
  end;

1124. ⟨ Create a character node *q* for the next character, but set *q* ← *null* if problems arise 1124 ⟩ ≡
  q ← *null*; *f* ← *cur_font*;
  if (*cur_cmd* = *letter*) ∨ (*cur_cmd* = *other_char*) ∨ (*cur_cmd* = *char_given*) **then**
    q ← *new_character*(*f, cur_chr*)
  else if *cur_cmd* = *char_num* **then**
      begin *scan_char_num*; *q* ← *new_character*(*f, cur_val*);
      end
    else *back_input*

This code is used in section 1123.

---

accent = 45, §208.
back_input: **procedure**, §325.
begin_diagnostic: **procedure**, §245.
char_given = 67, §208.
char_info = macro, §554.
char_node, §134.
char_num = 16, §208.
char_width = macro, §554.
character = macro, §134.
cur_chr: *halfword*, §297.
cur_cmd: *eight_bits*, §297.
cur_font = macro, §230.
cur_val: *integer*, §410.
decr = macro, §16.
do_assignments: **procedure**, §1270.
done = 30, §15.
end_diagnostic: **procedure**, §245.
error: **procedure**, §82.
float_constant = macro, §109.
flush_node_list: **procedure**, §202.

four_quarters = **packed record**, §113.
head = macro, §213.
help1 = macro, §79.
help2 = macro, §79.
hlist_node = 0, §135.
hmode = 101, §211.
incr = macro, §16.
internal_font_number = 0 . . *font_max*, §548.
is_char_node = macro, §134.
kern_node = 11, §155.
letter = 11, §207.
ligature_node = 6, §143.
link = macro, §118.
max_quarterword = 255, §110.
mmode = 201, §211.
mode = macro, §213.
n: *integer*, §1119.
new_character: **function**, §582.

null = macro, §115.
other_char = 12, §207.
p: *pointer*, §1119.
pointer = macro, §115.
print_err = macro, §73.
print_esc: **procedure**, §63.
print_nl: **procedure**, §62.
q: *pointer*, §1119.
replace_count = macro, §145.
rule_node = 2, §138.
save_ptr: 0 . . *save_size*, §271.
scaled = *integer*, §101.
scan_char_num: **procedure**, §435.
show_box: **procedure**, §198.
slant = macro, §558.
space_factor = macro, §213.
tail = macro, §213.
type = macro, §133.
vlist_node = 1, §137.
x_height = macro, §558.

1125. The kern nodes appended here must be distinguished from other kerns, lest they be wiped away by the hyphenation algorithm or by a previous line break.

The two kerns are computed with (machine-dependent) *real* arithmetic, but their sum is machine-independent; the net effect is machine-independent, because the user cannot remove these nodes nor access them via \lastkern.

⟨ Append the accent with appropriate kerns, then set $p \leftarrow q$ 1125 ⟩ ≡
begin $t \leftarrow slant(f)/float\_constant(65536)$; $i \leftarrow char\_info(f)(character(q))$; $w \leftarrow char\_width(f)(i)$;
$h \leftarrow char\_height(f)(height\_depth(i))$;
if $h \neq x$ **then** { the accent must be shifted up or down }
  begin $p \leftarrow hpack(p, natural)$; $shift\_amount(p) \leftarrow x - h$;
  end;
$delta \leftarrow round((w - a)/float\_constant(2) + h * t - x * s)$; $r \leftarrow new\_kern(delta)$;
$subtype(r) \leftarrow acc\_kern$; $link(tail) \leftarrow r$; $link(r) \leftarrow p$; $tail \leftarrow new\_kern(-a - delta)$;
$subtype(tail) \leftarrow acc\_kern$; $link(p) \leftarrow tail$; $p \leftarrow q$;
end

This code is used in section 1123.

1126. When '\cr' or '\span' or a tab mark comes through the scanner into *main_control*, it might be that the user has foolishly inserted one of them into something that has nothing to do with alignment. But it is far more likely that a left brace or right brace has been omitted, since *get_next* takes actions appropriate to alignment only when '\cr' or '\span' or tab marks occur with *align_state* = 0. The following program attempts to make an appropriate recovery.

⟨ Cases of *main_control* that build boxes and lists 1056 ⟩ +≡
$any\_mode(car\_ret)$, $any\_mode(tab\_mark)$: $align\_error$;
$any\_mode(no\_align)$: no_align_error;
$any\_mode(omit)$: $omit\_error$;

1127. ⟨ Declare action procedures for use by *main_control* 1043 ⟩ +≡
procedure *align_error*;
  begin if $abs(align\_state) > 2$ **then**
    ⟨ Express consternation over the fact that no alignment is in progress 1128 ⟩
  else begin *back_input*;
    if $align\_state < 0$ **then**
      begin $print\_err($"Missing␣{␣inserted"$)$; $incr(align\_state)$; $cur\_tok \leftarrow left\_brace\_token +$ "{";
      end
    else begin $print\_err($"Missing␣}␣inserted"$)$; $decr(align\_state)$;
      $cur\_tok \leftarrow right\_brace\_token +$ "}";
      end;
    $help3($"I´ve␣put␣in␣what␣seems␣to␣be␣necessary␣to␣fix"$)$
    ($"the␣current␣column␣of␣the␣current␣alignment."$)
    ($"Try␣to␣go␣on,␣since␣this␣might␣almost␣work."$)$; ins_error;
    end;
  end;

1128. ⟨ Express consternation over the fact that no alignment is in progress 1128 ⟩ ≡
  begin $print\_err($"Misplaced␣"$)$; $print\_cmd\_chr(cur\_cmd, cur\_chr)$;
  if $cur\_tok = tab\_token +$ "&" **then**
    begin $help6($"I␣can´t␣figure␣out␣why␣you␣would␣want␣to␣use␣a␣tab␣mark"$)$

```
    ("here.␣If␣you␣just␣want␣an␣ampersand,␣the␣remedy␣is")
    ("simple:␣Just␣type␣`I\&´␣now.␣But␣if␣some␣right␣brace")
    ("up␣above␣has␣ended␣a␣previous␣alignment␣prematurely,")
    ("you´re␣probably␣due␣for␣more␣error␣messages,␣and␣you")
    ("might␣try␣typing␣`S´␣now␣just␣to␣see␣what␣is␣salvageable.");
  end
else begin help5("I␣can´t␣figure␣out␣why␣you␣would␣want␣to␣use␣a␣tab␣mark")
    ("or␣\cr␣or␣\span␣just␣now.␣If␣something␣like␣a␣right␣brace")
    ("up␣above␣has␣ended␣a␣previous␣alignment␣prematurely,")
    ("you´re␣probably␣due␣for␣more␣error␣messages,␣and␣you")
    ("might␣try␣typing␣`S´␣now␣just␣to␣see␣what␣is␣salvageable.");
  end;
error;
end
```

This code is used in section 1127.

1129. The help messages here contain a little white lie, since \noalign and \omit are allowed also after '\noalign{...}'.

⟨ Declare action procedures for use by *main_control* 1043 ⟩ +≡
procedure *no_align_error*;
  begin *print_err*("Misplaced␣"); *print_esc*("noalign");
  help2("I␣expect␣to␣see␣\noalign␣only␣after␣the␣\cr␣of")
  ("an␣alignment.␣Proceed,␣and␣I´ll␣ignore␣this␣case."); *error*;
  end;
procedure *omit_error*;
  begin *print_err*("Misplaced␣"); *print_esc*("omit");
  help2("I␣expect␣to␣see␣\omit␣only␣after␣tab␣marks␣or␣the␣\cr␣of")
  ("an␣alignment.␣Proceed,␣and␣I´ll␣ignore␣this␣case."); *error*;
  end;

---

a: *scaled*, §1123.
acc_kern = 2, §155.
align_state: *integer*, §309.
any_mode = macro, §1045.
back_input: **procedure**, §325.
car_ret = 5, §207.
char_height = macro, §554.
char_info = macro, §554.
char_width = macro, §554.
character = macro, §134.
cur_chr: *halfword*, §297.
cur_cmd: *eight_bits*, §297.
cur_tok: *halfword*, §297.
decr = macro, §16.
delta: *scaled*, §1123.
error: **procedure**, §82.
f: *internal_font_number*, §1123.
float_constant = macro, §109.

get_next: **procedure**, §341.
h: *scaled*, §1123.
height_depth = macro, §554.
help2 = macro, §79.
help3 = macro, §79.
help5 = macro, §79.
help6 = macro, §79.
hpack: **function**, §649.
i: *four_quarters*, §1123.
incr = macro, §16.
ins_error: **procedure**, §327.
left_brace_token = 256, §289.
link = macro, §118.
natural = macro, §644.
new_kern: **function**, §156.
no_align = 34, §208.
omit = 63, §208.

p: *pointer*, §1123.
print_cmd_chr: **procedure**, §298.
print_err = macro, §73.
print_esc: **procedure**, §63.
q: *pointer*, §1123.
r: *pointer*, §1123.
right_brace_token = 512, §289.
s: *real*, §1123.
shift_amount = macro, §135.
slant = macro, §558.
subtype = macro, §133.
t: *real*, §1123.
tab_mark = 4, §207.
tab_token = 1024, §289.
tail = macro, §213.
w: *scaled*, §1123.
x: *scaled*, §1123.

1130. We've now covered most of the abuses of \halign and \valign. Let's take a look at what happens when they are used correctly.

⟨ Cases of *main_control* that build boxes and lists 1056 ⟩ +≡
vmode + *halign*, *hmode* + *valign*: *init_align*;
mmode + *halign*: **if** *privileged* **then** *init_align*;
vmode + *endv*, *hmode* + *endv*: *do_endv*;

1131. An *align_group* code is supposed to remain on the *save_stack* during an entire alignment, until *fin_align* removes it.

⟨ Declare action procedures for use by *main_control* 1043 ⟩ +≡
procedure *do_endv*;
  begin if *cur_group* = *align_group* **then**
    begin *end_graf*;
    if *fin_col* **then** *fin_row*;
    end
  else *off_save*;
  end;

1132. ⟨ Cases of *handle_right_brace* where a *right_brace* triggers a delayed action 1085 ⟩ +≡
align_group: **begin** *back_input*; *cur_tok* ← *cs_token_flag* + *frozen_cr*; *print_err*("Missing␣");
  print_esc("cr"); *print*("␣inserted");
  help1("I´m␣guessing␣that␣you␣meant␣to␣end␣an␣alignment␣here."); *ins_error*;
  end;

1133. ⟨ Cases of *handle_right_brace* where a *right_brace* triggers a delayed action 1085 ⟩ +≡
no_align_group: **begin** *end_graf*; *unsave*; *align_peek*;
  end;

1134. Finally, \endcsname is not supposed to get through to *main_control*.

⟨ Cases of *main_control* that build boxes and lists 1056 ⟩ +≡
any_mode(*end_cs_name*): *cs_error*;

1135. ⟨ Declare action procedures for use by *main_control* 1043 ⟩ +≡
procedure *cs_error*;
  begin *print_err*("Extra␣"); *print_esc*("endcsname");
  help1("I´m␣ignoring␣this,␣since␣I␣wasn´t␣doing␣a␣\csname."); *error*;
  end;

1136.   Building math lists.   The routines that TeX uses to create mlists are similar to those we have just seen for the generation of hlists and vlists. But it is necessary to make "noads" as well as nodes, so the reader should review the discussion of math mode data structures before trying to make sense out of the following program.

Here is a little routine that needs to be done whenever a subformula is about to be processed. The parameter is a code like *math_group*.

⟨ Declare action procedures for use by *main_control* 1043 ⟩ +≡
procedure *push_math*(*c* : *group_code*);
    begin *push_nest*; *mode* ← −*mmode*; *incompleat_noad* ← *null*; *new_save_level*(*c*);
    end;

1137.   We get into math mode from horizontal mode when a '**\$**' (i.e., a *math_shift* character) is scanned. We must check to see whether this '**\$**' is immediately followed by another, in case display math mode is called for.

⟨ Cases of *main_control* that build boxes and lists 1056 ⟩ +≡
hmode + *math_shift*: *init_math*;

1138. ⟨Declare action procedures for use by *main_control* 1043⟩ +≡
procedure *init_math*;
  label *reswitch*, *found*, *not_found*, *done*;
  var *w*: *scaled*;   { new or partial *pre_display_size* }
    l: *scaled*;   { new *display_width* }
    s: *scaled*;   { new *display_indent* }
    p: *pointer*;   { current node when calculating *pre_display_size* }
    q: *pointer*;   { glue specification when calculating *pre_display_size* }
    f: *internal_font_number*;   { font in current *char_node* }
    n: *integer*;   { scope of paragraph shape specification }
    v: *scaled*;   { *w* plus possible glue amount }
    d: *scaled*;   { increment to *v* }
  begin *get_token*;   { *get_x_token* would fail on \ifmmode! }
  if ($cur\_cmd = math\_shift$) ∧ ($mode > 0$) **then** ⟨Go into display math mode 1145⟩
  else begin *back_input*; ⟨Go into ordinary math mode 1139⟩;
    end;
  end;

1139. ⟨Go into ordinary math mode 1139⟩ ≡
  begin *push_math*(*math_shift_group*); *eq_word_define*($int\_base + cur\_fam\_code, -1$);
  if $every\_math \neq null$ **then** *begin_token_list*(*every_math*, *every_math_text*);
  end
This code is used in sections 1138 and 1142.

1140. We get into ordinary math mode from display math mode when '\eqno' or '\leqno' appears. In such cases *cur_chr* will be 0 or 1, respectively; the value of *cur_chr* is placed onto *save_stack* for safe keeping.

⟨Cases of *main_control* that build boxes and lists 1056⟩ +≡
$mmode + eq\_no$: **if** *privileged* **then** *start_eq_no*;

1141. ⟨Put each of TEX's primitives into the hash table 226⟩ +≡
  primitive("eqno", *eq_no*, 0); *primitive*("leqno", *eq_no*, 1);

1142. When TEX is in display math mode, $cur\_group = math\_shift\_group$, so it is not necessary for the *start_eq_no* procedure to test for this condition.

⟨Declare action procedures for use by *main_control* 1043⟩ +≡
procedure *start_eq_no*;
  begin $saved(0) \leftarrow cur\_chr$; *incr*(*save_ptr*); ⟨Go into ordinary math mode 1139⟩;
  end;

1143. ⟨Cases of *print_cmd_chr* for symbolic printing of primitives 227⟩ +≡
eq_no: **if** $chr\_code = 1$ **then** *print_esc*("leqno") **else** *print_esc*("eqno");

1144. ⟨Forbidden cases detected in *main_control* 1048⟩ +≡
  non_math(*eq_no*),

1145. When we enter display math mode, we need to call *line_break* to process the partial paragraph that has just been interrupted by the display. Then we can set the proper values of *display_width* and *display_indent* and *pre_display_size*.

⟨ Go into display math mode 1145 ⟩ ≡
  begin if *head* = *tail* **then**   { '\noindent$$' or '$$ $$' }
    begin *pop_nest*; *w* ← −*max_dimen*;
    end
  else begin *line_break*(*display_widow_penalty*);
    ⟨ Calculate the natural width, *w*, by which the characters of the final line extend to the right of the
        reference point, plus two ems; or set *w* ← *max_dimen* if the non-blank information on that
        line is affected by stretching or shrinking 1146 ⟩;
    end;   { Now we are in vertical mode, working on the list that will contain the display }
  ⟨ Calculate the length, *l*, and the shift amount, *s*, of the display lines 1149 ⟩;
  push_math(*math_shift_group*); *mode* ← *mmode*; *eq_word_define*(*int_base* + *cur_fam_code*, −1);
  eq_word_define(*dimen_base* + *pre_display_size_code*, *w*);
  eq_word_define(*dimen_base* + *display_width_code*, *l*);
  eq_word_define(*dimen_base* + *display_indent_code*, *s*);
  if *every_display* ≠ *null* **then** *begin_token_list*(*every_display*, *every_display_text*);
  if *nest_ptr* = 1 **then** *build_page*;
  end

This code is used in section 1138.

---

back_input: **procedure**, §325.
begin_token_list: **procedure**, §323.
build_page: **procedure**, §994.
char_node, §134.
chr_code: *halfword*, §298.
cur_chr: *halfword*, §297.
cur_cmd: *eight_bits*, §297.
cur_fam_code = 44, §236.
cur_group: *group_code*, §271.
dimen_base = 4801, §236.
display_indent = macro, §247.
display_indent_code = 15, §247.
display_widow_penalty = macro, §236.
display_width = macro, §247.
display_width_code = 14, §247.
done = 30, §15.
eq_no = 48, §208.
eq_word_define: **procedure**, §278.

every_display = macro, §230.
every_display_text = 9, §307.
every_math = macro, §230.
every_math_text = 8, §307.
found = 40, §15.
get_token: **procedure**, §365.
get_x_token: **procedure**, §380.
head = macro, §213.
incr = macro, §16.
int_base = 4367, §230.
internal_font_number = 0 .. *font_max*, §548.
line_break: **procedure**, §815.
math_shift = 3, §207.
math_shift_group = 15, §269.
max_dimen = macro, §421.
mmode = 201, §211.
mode = macro, §213.
nest_ptr: 0 .. *nest_size*, §213.

non_math = macro, §1046.
not_found = 45, §15.
null = macro, §115.
pointer = macro, §115.
pop_nest: **procedure**, §217.
pre_display_size = macro, §247.
pre_display_size_code = 13, §247.
primitive: **procedure**, §264.
print_cmd_chr: **procedure**, §298.
print_esc: **procedure**, §63.
privileged: **function**, §1051.
push_math: **procedure**, §1136.
reswitch = 21, §15.
save_ptr: 0 .. *save_size*, §271.
save_stack: **array**, §271.
saved = macro, §274.
scaled = *integer*, §101.
tail = macro, §213.

1146. ⟨ Calculate the natural width, w, by which the characters of the final line extend to the right of the reference point, plus two ems; or set $w \leftarrow max\_dimen$ if the non-blank information on that line is affected by stretching or shrinking 1146 ⟩ ≡

$v \leftarrow shift\_amount(just\_box) + 2 * quad(cur\_font)$; $w \leftarrow -max\_dimen$; $p \leftarrow list\_ptr(just\_box)$;

while $p \neq null$ **do**

    begin ⟨ Let d be the natural width of node p; if the node is "visible," **goto** *found*; if the node is glue that stretches or shrinks, set $v \leftarrow max\_dimen$ 1147 ⟩;

    if $v < max\_dimen$ **then** $v \leftarrow v + d$;

    goto *not_found*;

found: **if** $v < max\_dimen$ **then**

      begin $v \leftarrow v + d$; $w \leftarrow v$;

      end

    else begin $w \leftarrow max\_dimen$; **goto** *done*;

      end;

not_found: $p \leftarrow link(p)$;

    end;

done:

This code is used in section 1145.

1147. ⟨ Let d be the natural width of node p; if the node is "visible," **goto** *found*; if the node is glue that stretches or shrinks, set $v \leftarrow max\_dimen$ 1147 ⟩ ≡

reswitch: **if** $is\_char\_node(p)$ **then**

    begin $f \leftarrow font(p)$; $d \leftarrow char\_width(f)(char\_info(f)(character(p)))$; **goto** *found*;

    end;

case $type(p)$ **of**

hlist_node, vlist_node, rule_node: **begin** $d \leftarrow width(p)$; **goto** *found*;

    end;

ligature_node: ⟨ Make node p look like a *char_node* and **goto** *reswitch* 652 ⟩;

kern_node, math_node: $d \leftarrow width(p)$;

glue_node: ⟨ Let d be the natural width of this glue; if stretching or shrinking, set $v \leftarrow max\_dimen$;

    goto *found* in the case of leaders 1148 ⟩;

whatsit_node: ⟨ Let d be the width of the whatsit p 1361 ⟩;

othercases $d \leftarrow 0$

endcases

This code is used in section 1146.

1148. We need to be careful that w, v, and d do not depend on any *glue_set* values, since such values are subject to system-dependent rounding. System-dependent numbers are not allowed to infiltrate parameters like *pre_display_size*, since TEX82 is supposed to make the same decisions on all machines.

⟨ Let d be the natural width of this glue; if stretching or shrinking, set $v \leftarrow max\_dimen$; **goto** *found* in the case of leaders 1148 ⟩ ≡

    begin $q \leftarrow glue\_ptr(p)$; $d \leftarrow width(q)$;

    if $glue\_sign(just\_box) = stretching$ **then**

      begin if $(glue\_order(just\_box) = stretch\_order(q)) \wedge (stretch(q) \neq 0)$ **then** $v \leftarrow max\_dimen$;

      end

    else if $glue\_sign(just\_box) = shrinking$ **then**

      begin if $(glue\_order(just\_box) = shrink\_order(q)) \wedge (shrink(q) \neq 0)$ **then** $v \leftarrow max\_dimen$;

```
      end;
  if subtype(p) ≥ a_leaders then goto found;
  end
```

This code is used in section 1147.

1149.   A displayed equation is considered to be three lines long, so we calculate the length and offset of line number $prev\_graf + 2$.

⟨ Calculate the length, l, and the shift amount, s, of the display lines 1149 ⟩ ≡
```
  if par_shape_ptr = null then
      if (hang_indent ≠ 0) ∧ (((hang_after ≥ 0) ∧ (prev_graf + 2 > hang_after)) ∨
            (prev_graf + 1 < −hang_after)) then
          begin l ← hsize − abs(hang_indent);
          if hang_indent > 0 then  s ← hang_indent else s ← 0;
          end
      else begin l ← hsize;  s ← 0;
          end
  else begin n ← info(par_shape_ptr);
      if prev_graf + 2 ≥ n then  p ← par_shape_ptr + 2 ∗ n
      else p ← par_shape_ptr + 2 ∗ (prev_graf + 2);
      s ← mem[p − 1].sc;  l ← mem[p].sc;
      end
```

This code is used in section 1145.

$a\_leaders = 100$, §149.
$char\_info$ = macro, §554.
$char\_node$, §134.
$char\_width$ = macro, §554.
$character$ = macro, §134.
cur_font = macro, §230.
d: $scaled$, §1138.
$done = 30$, §15.
f: $internal\_font\_number$, §1138.
$font$ = macro, §134.
$found = 40$, §15.
$glue\_node = 10$, §149.
$glue\_order$ = macro, §135.
$glue\_ptr$ = macro, §149.
$glue\_set$ = macro, §135.
$glue\_sign$ = macro, §135.
$hang\_after$ = macro, §236.
$hang\_indent$ = macro, §247.
$hlist\_node = 0$, §135.
$hsize$ = macro, §247.

$info$ = macro, §118.
is_char_node = macro, §134.
$just\_box$: $pointer$, §814.
$kern\_node = 11$, §155.
l: $scaled$, §1138.
$ligature\_node = 6$, §143.
$link$ = macro, §118.
$list\_ptr$ = macro, §135.
$math\_node = 9$, §147.
max_dimen = macro, §421.
mem: **array**, §116.
n: $integer$, §1138.
$not\_found = 45$, §15.
$null$ = macro, §115.
p: $pointer$, §1138.
par_shape_ptr = macro, §230.
$pre\_display\_size$ = macro, §247.
$prev\_graf$ = macro, §213.
q: $pointer$, §1138.

$quad$ = macro, §558.
$reswitch = 21$, §15.
$rule\_node = 2$, §138.
s: $scaled$, §1138.
sc = macro, §113.
$shift\_amount$ = macro, §135.
$shrink$ = macro, §150.
$shrink\_order$ = macro, §150.
$shrinking = 2$, §135.
$stretch$ = macro, §150.
$stretch\_order$ = macro, §150.
$stretching = 1$, §135.
$subtype$ = macro, §133.
$type$ = macro, §133.
v: $scaled$, §1138.
$vlist\_node = 1$, §137.
w: $scaled$, §1138.
$whatsit\_node = 8$, §146.
$width$ = macro, §135.

1150. Subformulas of math formulas cause a new level of math mode to be entered, on the semantic nest as well as the save stack. These subformulas arise in several ways: (1) A left brace by itself indicates the beginning of a subformula that will be put into a box, thereby freezing its glue and preventing line breaks. (2) A subscript or superscript is treated as a subformula if it is not a single character; the same applies to the nucleus of things like \underline. (3) The \left primitive initiates a subformula that will be terminated by a matching \right. The group codes placed on *save_stack* in these three cases are *math_group*, *math_group*, and *math_left_group*, respectively.

Here is the code that handles case (1); the other cases are not quite as trivial, so we shall consider them later.

⟨ Cases of *main_control* that build boxes and lists 1056 ⟩ +≡
mmode + *left_brace*: **begin** *tail_append*(*new_noad*); *back_input*; *scan_math*(*nucleus*(*tail*));
   end;

1151. Recall that the *nucleus*, *subscr*, and *supscr* fields in a noad are broken down into subfields called *math_type* and either *info* or (*fam*, *character*). The job of *scan_math* is to figure out what to place in one of these principal fields; it looks at the subformula that comes next in the input, and places an encoding of that subformula into a given word of *mem*.

   define *fam_in_range* ≡ ((*cur_fam* ≥ 0) ∧ (*cur_fam* < 16))

⟨ Declare action procedures for use by *main_control* 1043 ⟩ +≡
procedure *scan_math*(*p* : *pointer*);
  label *restart*, *reswitch*, *exit*;
  var *c*: *integer*; { math character code }
  begin *restart*: ⟨ Get the next non-blank non-relax non-call token 404 ⟩;
reswitch: **case** *cur_cmd* **of**
  letter, *other_char*, *char_given*: **if** *cur_chr* ≥ 128 **then** *c* ← *cur_chr*
    else begin *c* ← *ho*(*math_code*(*cur_chr*));
      if *c* = ′100000 **then**
        begin ⟨ Treat *cur_chr* as an active character 1152 ⟩;
        goto *restart*;
        end;
      end;
  char_num: **begin** *scan_char_num*; *cur_chr* ← *cur_val*; *cur_cmd* ← *char_given*; **goto** *reswitch*;
    end;
  math_char_num: **begin** *scan_fifteen_bit_int*; *c* ← *cur_val*;
    end;
  math_given: *c* ← *cur_chr*;
  delim_num: **begin** *scan_twenty_seven_bit_int*; *c* ← *cur_val* **div** ′10000;
    end;
  othercases ⟨ Scan a subformula enclosed in braces and **return** 1153 ⟩
  endcases;
  math_type(*p*) ← *math_char*; *character*(*p*) ← *qi*(*c* **mod** 256);
  if (*c* ≥ *var_code*) ∧ *fam_in_range* **then** *fam*(*p*) ← *cur_fam*
  else *fam*(*p*) ← (*c* **div** 256) **mod** 16;
exit: **end**;

1152. An active character that is an *outer_call* is allowed here.

⟨ Treat *cur_chr* as an active character 1152 ⟩ ≡
   begin *cur_cs* ← *cur_chr* + *active_base*; *cur_cmd* ← *eq_type*(*cur_cs*); *cur_chr* ← *equiv*(*cur_cs*);
   x_token; *back_input*;
   end

This code is used in sections 1151 and 1155.

1153. The pointer *p* is placed on *save_stack* while a complex subformula is being scanned.

⟨ Scan a subformula enclosed in braces and **return** 1153 ⟩ ≡
   begin *back_input*; *scan_left_brace*;
   saved(0) ← *p*; *incr*(*save_ptr*); *push_math*(*math_group*); **return**;
   end

This code is used in section 1151.

1154. The simplest math formula is, of course, '\$ \$', when no noads are generated. The next simplest cases involve a single character, e.g., '\$x\$'. Even though such cases may not seem to be very interesting, the reader can perhaps understand how happy the author was when '\$x\$' was first properly typeset by TₑX. The code in this section was used.

⟨ Cases of *main_control* that build boxes and lists 1056 ⟩ +≡
mmode + *letter*, *mmode* + *other_char*, *mmode* + *char_given*: **if** *cur_chr* < 128 **then**
    set_math_char(*ho*(*math_code*(*cur_chr*)))
  else *set_math_char*(*cur_chr*);
mmode + *char_num*: **begin** *scan_char_num*; *cur_chr* ← *cur_val*;
  if *cur_chr* < 128 **then** *set_math_char*(*ho*(*math_code*(*cur_chr*)))
  else *set_math_char*(*cur_chr*);
  end;
mmode + *math_char_num*: **begin** *scan_fifteen_bit_int*; *set_math_char*(*cur_val*);
  end;
mmode + *math_given*: *set_math_char*(*cur_chr*);
mmode + *delim_num*: **begin** *scan_twenty_seven_bit_int*; *set_math_char*(*cur_val* **div** ´10000);
  end;

---

active_base = 1, §222.
back_input: **procedure**, §325.
char_given = 67, §208.
char_num = 16, §208.
character = macro, §134.
cur_chr: *halfword*, §297.
cur_cmd: *eight_bits*, §297.
cur_cs: *pointer*, §297.
cur_fam = macro, §236.
cur_val: *integer*, §410.
delim_num = 15, §207.
eq_type = macro, §221.
equiv = macro, §221.
exit = 10, §15.
fam = macro, §681.
ho = macro, §112.
incr = macro, §16.
info = macro, §118.

left_brace = 1, §207.
letter = 11, §207.
math_char = 1, §681.
math_char_num = 17, §208.
math_code = macro, §230.
math_given = 68, §208.
math_group = 9, §269.
math_left_group = 16, §269.
math_type = macro, §681.
mem: **array**, §116.
mmode = 201, §211.
new_noad: **function**, §686.
nucleus = macro, §681.
other_char = 12, §207.
outer_call = 112, §210.
pointer = macro, §115.
push_math: **procedure**, §1136.
qi = macro, §112.

restart = 20, §15.
reswitch = 21, §15.
save_ptr: 0 .. *save_size*, §271.
save_stack: **array**, §271.
saved = macro, §274.
scan_char_num: **procedure**, §435.
scan_fifteen_bit_int: **procedure**,
  §436.
scan_left_brace: **procedure**, §403.
scan_twenty_seven_bit_int:
  procedure, §437.
set_math_char: **procedure**, §1155.
subscr = macro, §681.
supscr = macro, §681.
tail = macro, §213.
tail_append = macro, §214.
var_code = macro, §232.
x_token: **procedure**, §381.

1155. The *set_math_char* procedure creates a new noad appropriate to a given math code, and appends it to the current mlist. However, if the math code is sufficiently large, the *cur_chr* is treated as an active character and nothing is appended.

⟨Declare action procedures for use by *main_control* 1043⟩ +≡

procedure *set_math_char*(*c* : *integer*);
  var *p*: *pointer*; { the new noad }
  begin if $c \geq$ ´100000 **then** ⟨Treat *cur_chr* as an active character 1152⟩
  else begin $p \leftarrow new\_noad$; $math\_type(nucleus(p)) \leftarrow math\_char$;
    $character(nucleus(p)) \leftarrow qi(c \bmod 256)$; $fam(nucleus(p)) \leftarrow (c \operatorname{div} 256) \bmod 16$;
    if $c \geq var\_code$ **then**
      begin if *fam_in_range* **then** $fam(nucleus(p)) \leftarrow cur\_fam$;
      $type(p) \leftarrow ord\_noad$;
      end
    else $type(p) \leftarrow ord\_noad + (c \operatorname{div}$ ´10000);
    $link(tail) \leftarrow p$; $tail \leftarrow p$;
    end;
  end;

1156. Primitive math operators like \mathop and \underline are given the command code *math_comp*, supplemented by the noad type that they generate.

⟨Put each of TEX's primitives into the hash table 226⟩ +≡
  primitive("mathord", *math_comp*, *ord_noad*); *primitive*("mathop", *math_comp*, *op_noad*);
  primitive("mathbin", *math_comp*, *bin_noad*); *primitive*("mathrel", *math_comp*, *rel_noad*);
  primitive("mathopen", *math_comp*, *open_noad*); *primitive*("mathclose", *math_comp*, *close_noad*);
  primitive("mathpunct", *math_comp*, *punct_noad*); *primitive*("mathinner", *math_comp*, *inner_noad*);
  primitive("underline", *math_comp*, *under_noad*); *primitive*("overline", *math_comp*, *over_noad*);
  primitive("displaylimits", *limit_switch*, *normal*); *primitive*("limits", *limit_switch*, *limits*);
  primitive("nolimits", *limit_switch*, *no_limits*);

1157. ⟨Cases of *print_cmd_chr* for symbolic printing of primitives 227⟩ +≡
math_comp: **case** *chr_code* **of**
  ord_noad: *print_esc*("mathord");
  op_noad: *print_esc*("mathop");
  bin_noad: *print_esc*("mathbin");
  rel_noad: *print_esc*("mathrel");
  open_noad: *print_esc*("mathopen");
  close_noad: *print_esc*("mathclose");
  punct_noad: *print_esc*("mathpunct");
  inner_noad: *print_esc*("mathinner");
  under_noad: *print_esc*("underline");
  othercases *print_esc*("overline")
  endcases;
limit_switch: **if** $chr\_code = limits$ **then** *print_esc*("limits")
  else if $chr\_code = no\_limits$ **then** *print_esc*("nolimits")
    else *print_esc*("displaylimits");

1158. ⟨Cases of *main_control* that build boxes and lists 1056⟩ +≡
mmode + *math_comp*: **begin** *tail_append*(*new_noad*); $type(tail) \leftarrow cur\_chr$; *scan_math*(*nucleus*(*tail*));

end;
$mmode + limit\_switch$: $math\_limit\_switch$;

1159. ⟨ Declare action procedures for use by $main\_control$ 1043 ⟩ +≡
procedure $math\_limit\_switch$;
    label $exit$;
    begin if $head \neq tail$ **then**
       if $type(tail) = op\_noad$ **then**
         begin $subtype(tail) \leftarrow cur\_chr$; **return**;
         end;
    $print\_err($"Limit␣controls␣must␣follow␣a␣math␣operator"$)$;
    $help1($"I´m␣ignoring␣this␣misplaced␣\limits␣or␣\nolimits␣command."$)$; $error$;
$exit$: **end**;

1160. Delimiter fields of noads are filled in by the $scan\_delimiter$ routine. The first parameter of this procedure is the mem address where the delimiter is to be placed; the second tells if this delimiter follows \radical or not.

⟨ Declare action procedures for use by $main\_control$ 1043 ⟩ +≡
procedure $scan\_delimiter(p : pointer; r : boolean)$;
    begin if r **then** $scan\_twenty\_seven\_bit\_int$
    else begin ⟨ Get the next non-blank non-relax non-call token 404 ⟩;
       case cur_cmd **of**
       $letter, other\_char$: $cur\_val \leftarrow del\_code(cur\_chr)$;
       $delim\_num$: $scan\_twenty\_seven\_bit\_int$;
       othercases $cur\_val \leftarrow -1$
       endcases;
       end;
    if $cur\_val < 0$ **then**
       ⟨ Report that an invalid delimiter code is being changed to null; set $cur\_val \leftarrow 0$ 1161 ⟩;
    $small\_fam(p) \leftarrow (cur\_val$ **div** $'4000000)$ **mod** 16; $small\_char(p) \leftarrow qi((cur\_val$ **div** $'10000)$ **mod** $256)$;
    $large\_fam(p) \leftarrow (cur\_val$ **div** $256)$ **mod** 16; $large\_char(p) \leftarrow qi(cur\_val$ **mod** $256)$;
    end;

$bin\_noad = 18$, §682.
$character =$ **macro**, §134.
chr_code: $halfword$, §298.
$close\_noad = 21$, §682.
cur_chr: $halfword$, §297.
cur_cmd: $eight\_bits$, §297.
$cur\_fam =$ **macro**, §236.
cur_val: $integer$, §410.
$del\_code =$ **macro**, §236.
$delim\_num = 15$, §207.
$error$: **procedure**, §82.
$exit = 10$, §15.
$fam =$ **macro**, §681.
$fam\_in\_range =$ **macro**, §1151.
$head =$ **macro**, §213.
$help1 =$ **macro**, §79.
$inner\_noad = 23$, §682.
$large\_char =$ **macro**, §683.
$large\_fam =$ **macro**, §683.

$letter = 11$, §207.
$limit\_switch = 51$, §208.
$limits = 1$, §682.
$link =$ **macro**, §118.
$math\_char = 1$, §681.
$math\_comp = 50$, §208.
$math\_type =$ **macro**, §681.
mem: **array**, §116.
$mmode = 201$, §211.
new_noad: **function**, §686.
$no\_limits = 2$, §682.
$normal = 0$, §135.
$nucleus =$ **macro**, §681.
$op\_noad = 17$, §682.
$open\_noad = 20$, §682.
$ord\_noad = 16$, §682.
$other\_char = 12$, §207.
$over\_noad = 27$, §687.

$pointer =$ **macro**, §115.
$primitive$: **procedure**, §264.
$print\_cmd\_chr$: **procedure**, §298.
$print\_err =$ **macro**, §73.
$print\_esc$: **procedure**, §63.
$punct\_noad = 22$, §682.
$qi =$ **macro**, §112.
$rel\_noad = 19$, §682.
$scan\_twenty\_seven\_bit\_int$:
    procedure, §437.
$small\_char =$ **macro**, §683.
$small\_fam =$ **macro**, §683.
$subtype =$ **macro**, §133.
$tail =$ **macro**, §213.
$tail\_append =$ **macro**, §214.
$type =$ **macro**, §133.
$under\_noad = 26$, §687.
$var\_code =$ **macro**, §232.

1161. ⟨Report that an invalid delimiter code is being changed to null; set $cur\_val \leftarrow 0$ 1161⟩ ≡
  begin $print\_err$("Missing␣delimiter␣(.␣inserted)");
  $help6$("I␣was␣expecting␣to␣see␣something␣like␣`(␣or␣\{␣or")
  ("`\}´␣here.␣If␣you␣typed,␣e.g.,␣`{␣instead␣of␣\{´,␣you")
  ("should␣probably␣delete␣the␣`{´␣by␣typing␣`1´␣now,␣so␣that")
  ("braces␣don´t␣get␣unbalanced.␣Otherwise␣just␣proceed.")
  ("Acceptable␣delimiters␣are␣characters␣whose␣\delcode␣is")
  ("nonnegative,␣or␣you␣can␣use␣`\delimiter␣<delimiter␣code>´."); $back\_error$; $cur\_val \leftarrow 0$;
  end

This code is used in section 1160.

1162. ⟨Cases of $main\_control$ that build boxes and lists 1056⟩ +≡
$mmode + radical$: $math\_radical$;

1163. ⟨Declare action procedures for use by $main\_control$ 1043⟩ +≡
procedure $math\_radical$;
  begin $tail\_append(get\_node(radical\_noad\_size))$; $type(tail) \leftarrow radical\_noad$; $subtype(tail) \leftarrow normal$;
  $mem[nucleus(tail)].hh \leftarrow empty\_field$; $mem[subscr(tail)].hh \leftarrow empty\_field$;
  $mem[supscr(tail)].hh \leftarrow empty\_field$; $scan\_delimiter(left\_delimiter(tail), true)$;
  $scan\_math(nucleus(tail))$;
  end;

1164. ⟨Cases of $main\_control$ that build boxes and lists 1056⟩ +≡
$mmode + accent$, $mmode + math\_accent$: $math\_ac$;

1165. ⟨Declare action procedures for use by $main\_control$ 1043⟩ +≡
procedure $math\_ac$;
  begin if $cur\_cmd = accent$ **then** ⟨Complain that the user should have said \mathaccent 1166⟩;
  $tail\_append(get\_node(accent\_noad\_size))$; $type(tail) \leftarrow accent\_noad$; $subtype(tail) \leftarrow normal$;
  $mem[nucleus(tail)].hh \leftarrow empty\_field$; $mem[subscr(tail)].hh \leftarrow empty\_field$;
  $mem[supscr(tail)].hh \leftarrow empty\_field$; $math\_type(accent\_chr(tail)) \leftarrow math\_char$; $scan\_fifteen\_bit\_int$;
  $character(accent\_chr(tail)) \leftarrow qi(cur\_val \bmod 256)$;
  if $(cur\_val \geq var\_code) \wedge fam\_in\_range$ **then** $fam(accent\_chr(tail)) \leftarrow cur\_fam$
  else $fam(accent\_chr(tail)) \leftarrow (cur\_val \bmod 256) \bmod 16$;
  $scan\_math(nucleus(tail))$;
  end;

1166. ⟨Complain that the user should have said \mathaccent 1166⟩ ≡
  begin $print\_err$("Please␣use␣"); $print\_esc$("mathaccent"); $print$("␣for␣accents␣in␣math␣mode");
  $help2$("I´m␣changing␣\accent␣to␣\mathaccent␣here;␣wish␣me␣luck.")
  ("(Accents␣are␣not␣the␣same␣in␣formulas␣as␣they␣are␣in␣text.)"); $error$;
  end

This code is used in section 1165.

1167. ⟨Cases of $main\_control$ that build boxes and lists 1056⟩ +≡
$mmode + vcenter$: **begin** $scan\_spec$; $new\_save\_level(vcenter\_group)$; $normal\_paragraph$; $push\_nest$;
  $mode \leftarrow -vmode$; $prev\_depth \leftarrow ignore\_depth$;
  if $every\_vbox \neq null$ **then** $begin\_token\_list(every\_vbox, every\_vbox\_text)$;
  end;

1168. ⟨Cases of *handle_right_brace* where a *right_brace* triggers a delayed action 1085⟩ +≡
vcenter_group: **begin** *end_graf*; *unsave*; *save_ptr* ← *save_ptr* − 2;
  p ← *vpack*(*link*(*head*), *saved*(1), *saved*(0)); *pop_nest*; *tail_append*(*new_noad*);
  type(*tail*) ← *vcenter_noad*; *math_type*(*nucleus*(*tail*)) ← *sub_box*; *info*(*nucleus*(*tail*)) ← *p*;
  end;

1169. The routine that inserts a *style_node* holds no surprises.
⟨Put each of TEX's primitives into the hash table 226⟩ +≡
  primitive("displaystyle", *math_style*, *display_style*); *primitive*("textstyle", *math_style*, *text_style*);
  primitive("scriptstyle", *math_style*, *script_style*);
  primitive("scriptscriptstyle", *math_style*, *script_script_style*);

1170. ⟨Cases of *print_cmd_chr* for symbolic printing of primitives 227⟩ +≡
math_style: *print_style*(*chr_code*);

1171. ⟨Cases of *main_control* that build boxes and lists 1056⟩ +≡
mmode + *math_style*: *tail_append*(*new_style*(*cur_chr*));
mmode + *non_script*: **begin** *tail_append*(*new_glue*(*zero_glue*)); *subtype*(*tail*) ← *cond_math_glue*;
  end;
mmode + *math_choice*: *append_choices*;

---

accent = 45, §208.
accent_chr = macro, §687.
accent_noad = 28, §687.
accent_noad_size = 5, §687.
append_choices: **procedure**, §1172.
back_error: **procedure**, §327.
begin_token_list: **procedure**, §323.
character = macro, §134.
chr_code: *halfword*, §298.
cond_math_glue = 98, §149.
cur_chr: *halfword*, §297.
cur_cmd: *eight_bits*, §297.
cur_fam = macro, §236.
cur_val: *integer*, §410.
display_style = 0, §688.
empty_field: *two_halves*, §684.
error: **procedure**, §82.
every_vbox = macro, §230.
every_vbox_text = 11, §307.
fam = macro, §681.
fam_in_range = macro, §1151.
get_node: **function**, §125.
head = macro, §213.
help2 = macro, §79.
help6 = macro, §79.
hh: *two_halves*, §113.
ignore_depth = macro, §212.
info = macro, §118.
left_delimiter = macro, §683.
link = macro, §118.

math_accent = 46, §208.
math_char = 1, §681.
math_choice = 54, §208.
math_style = 53, §208.
math_type = macro, §681.
mem: *array*, §116.
mmode = 201, §211.
mode = macro, §213.
new_glue: **function**, §153.
new_noad: **function**, §686.
new_save_level: **procedure**, §274.
new_style: **function**, §688.
non_script = 55, §208.
normal = 0, §135.
normal_paragraph: **procedure**,
  §1070.
nucleus = macro, §681.
null = macro, §115.
p: *pointer*, §1068.
pop_nest: **procedure**, §217.
prev_depth = macro, §213.
primitive: **procedure**, §264.
print: **procedure**, §59.
print_cmd_chr: **procedure**, §298.
print_err = macro, §73.
print_esc: **procedure**, §63.
print_style: **procedure**, §694.
push_nest: **procedure**, §216.
qi = macro, §112.

radical = 65, §208.
radical_noad = 24, §683.
radical_noad_size = 5, §683.
right_brace = 2, §207.
save_ptr: 0 .. *save_size*, §271.
saved = macro, §274.
scan_delimiter: **procedure**, §1160.
scan_fifteen_bit_int: **procedure**,
  §436.
scan_spec: **procedure**, §645.
script_script_style = 6, §688.
script_style = 4, §688.
style_node = 14, §688.
sub_box = 2, §681.
subscr = macro, §681.
subtype = macro, §133.
supscr = macro, §681.
tail = macro, §213.
tail_append = macro, §214.
text_style = 2, §688.
type = macro, §133.
unsave: **procedure**, §281.
var_code = macro, §232.
vcenter = 56, §208.
vcenter_group = 12, §269.
vcenter_noad = 29, §687.
vmode = 1, §211.
vpack = macro, §668.
zero_glue = macro, §162.

1172.   The routine that scans the four mlists of a \mathchoice is very much like the routine that builds discretionary nodes.

⟨ Declare action procedures for use by *main_control* 1043 ⟩ +≡
procedure *append_choices*;
  begin *tail_append*(*new_choice*); *incr*(*save_ptr*); *saved*(−1) ← 0; *scan_left_brace*;
  push_math(*math_choice_group*);
  end;

1173.   ⟨ Cases of *handle_right_brace* where a *right_brace* triggers a delayed action 1085 ⟩ +≡
math_choice_group: *build_choices*;

1174.   ⟨ Declare action procedures for use by *main_control* 1043 ⟩ +≡
⟨ Declare the function called *fin_mlist* 1184 ⟩
procedure *build_choices*;
  label *exit*;
  var *p*: *pointer*;   { the current mlist }
  begin *unsave*; *p* ← *fin_mlist*(*null*);
  case *saved*(−1) **of**
  0: *display_mlist*(*tail*) ← *p*;
  1: *text_mlist*(*tail*) ← *p*;
  2: *script_mlist*(*tail*) ← *p*;
  3: **begin** *script_script_mlist*(*tail*) ← *p*; *decr*(*save_ptr*); **return**;
    end;
  end;   { there are no other cases }
  incr(*saved*(−1)); *scan_left_brace*; *push_math*(*math_choice_group*);
exit: **end**;

1175.   Subscripts and superscripts are attached to the previous nucleus by the action procedure called *sub_sup*. We use the facts that $sub\_mark = sup\_mark + 1$ and $subscr(p) = supscr(p) + 1$.

⟨ Cases of *main_control* that build boxes and lists 1056 ⟩ +≡
$mmode + sub\_mark$, $mmode + sup\_mark$: *sub_sup*;

1176.   ⟨ Declare action procedures for use by *main_control* 1043 ⟩ +≡
procedure *sub_sup*;
  var *t*: *small_number*;   { type of previous sub/superscript }
    p: *pointer*;   { field to be filled by *scan_math* }
  begin *t* ← *empty*; *p* ← *null*;
  if *tail* ≠ *head* **then**
    if *scripts_allowed*(*tail*) **then**
      begin *p* ← *supscr*(*tail*) + *cur_cmd* − *sup_mark*;   { *supscr* or *subscr* }
      t ← *math_type*(*p*);
      end;
  if (*p* = *null*) ∨ (*t* ≠ *empty*) **then** ⟨ Insert a dummy noad to be sub/superscripted 1177 ⟩;
  scan_math(*p*);
  end;

1177. ⟨Insert a dummy noad to be sub/superscripted 1177⟩ ≡
    begin *tail_append*(*new_noad*); $p \leftarrow supscr(tail) + cur\_cmd - sup\_mark$;   { *supscr* or *subscr* }
    if $t \neq empty$ **then**
        begin if *cur_cmd* = *sup_mark* **then**
            begin *print_err*("Double␣superscript");
            help1("I␣treat␣`x^1^2´␣essentially␣like␣`x^1{}^2´.");
            end
        else begin *print_err*("Double␣subscript");
            help1("I␣treat␣`x_1_2´␣essentially␣like␣`x_1{}_2´.");
            end;
        error;
        end;
    end

This code is used in section 1176.

1178. An operation like '\over' causes the current mlist to go into a state of suspended animation: *incompleat_noad* points to a *fraction_noad* that contains the mlist-so-far as its numerator, while the denominator is yet to come. Finally when the mlist is finished, the denominator will go into the incompleat fraction noad, and that noad will become the whole formula, unless it is surrounded by '\left' and '\right' delimiters.

    define *above_code* = 0   { '\above' }
    define *over_code* = 1   { '\over' }
    define *atop_code* = 2   { '\atop' }
    define *delimited_code* = 3   { '\abovewithdelims', etc. }
⟨Put each of TeX's primitives into the hash table 226⟩ +≡
    primitive("above", *above*, *above_code*);
    primitive("over", *above*, *over_code*);
    primitive("atop", *above*, *atop_code*);
    primitive("abovewithdelims", *above*, *delimited_code* + *above_code*);
    primitive("overwithdelims", *above*, *delimited_code* + *over_code*);
    primitive("atopwithdelims", *above*, *delimited_code* + *atop_code*);

---

above = 52, §208.
cur_cmd: *eight_bits*, §297.
decr = macro, §16.
display_mlist = macro, §689.
empty = 0, §16.
error: **procedure**, §82.
exit = 10, §15.
fin_mlist: **function**, §1184.
fraction_noad = 25, §683.
head = macro, §213.
help1 = macro, §79.
incompleat_noad = macro, §213.
incr = macro, §16.

math_choice_group = 13, §269.
math_type = macro, §681.
mmode = 201, §211.
new_choice: **function**, §689.
new_noad: **function**, §686.
null = macro, §115.
pointer = macro, §115.
primitive: **procedure**, §264.
print_err = macro, §73.
push_math: **procedure**, §1136.
right_brace = 2, §207.
save_ptr: 0 .. *save_size*, §271.
saved = macro, §274.

scan_left_brace: **procedure**, §403.
script_mlist = macro, §689.
script_script_mlist = macro, §689.
scripts_allowed = macro, §687.
small_number = 0 .. 63, §101.
sub_mark = 8, §207.
subscr = macro, §681.
sup_mark = 7, §207.
supscr = macro, §681.
tail = macro, §213.
tail_append = macro, §214.
text_mlist = macro, §689.
unsave: **procedure**, §281.

1179. ⟨ Cases of *print_cmd_chr* for symbolic printing of primitives 227 ⟩ +≡
above: **case** *chr_code* **of**
  over_code: *print_esc*("over");
  atop_code: *print_esc*("atop");
  delimited_code + *above_code*: *print_esc*("abovewithdelims");
  delimited_code + *over_code*: *print_esc*("overwithdelims");
  delimited_code + *atop_code*: *print_esc*("atopwithdelims");
  othercases *print_esc*("above")
  endcases;

1180. ⟨ Cases of *main_control* that build boxes and lists 1056 ⟩ +≡
mmode + *above*: *math_fraction*;

1181. ⟨ Declare action procedures for use by *main_control* 1043 ⟩ +≡
procedure *math_fraction*;
  var *c*: *small_number*; { the type of generalized fraction we are scanning }
  begin *c* ← *cur_chr*;
  if *incompleat_noad* ≠ *null* **then**
    ⟨ Ignore the fraction operation and complain about this ambiguous case 1183 ⟩
  else begin *incompleat_noad* ← *get_node*(*fraction_noad_size*); *type*(*incompleat_noad*) ← *fraction_noad*;
    subtype(*incompleat_noad*) ← *normal*; *math_type*(*numerator*(*incompleat_noad*)) ← *sub_mlist*;
    info(*numerator*(*incompleat_noad*)) ← *link*(*head*);
    mem[*denominator*(*incompleat_noad*)].*hh* ← *empty_field*;
    mem[*left_delimiter*(*incompleat_noad*)].*qqqq* ← *null_delimiter*;
    mem[*right_delimiter*(*incompleat_noad*)].*qqqq* ← *null_delimiter*;
    link(*head*) ← *null*; *tail* ← *head*; ⟨ Use code *c* to distinguish between generalized fractions 1182 ⟩;
    end;
  end;

1182. ⟨ Use code *c* to distinguish between generalized fractions 1182 ⟩ ≡
  if *c* ≥ *delimited_code* **then**
    begin *scan_delimiter*(*left_delimiter*(*incompleat_noad*), *false*);
    scan_delimiter(*right_delimiter*(*incompleat_noad*), *false*);
    end;
  case *c* **mod** *delimited_code* **of**
  above_code: **begin** *scan_normal_dimen*; *thickness*(*incompleat_noad*) ← *cur_val*;
    end;
  over_code: *thickness*(*incompleat_noad*) ← *default_code*;
  atop_code: *thickness*(*incompleat_noad*) ← 0;
  end { there are no other cases }
This code is used in section 1181.

1183. ⟨ Ignore the fraction operation and complain about this ambiguous case 1183 ⟩ ≡
  begin if *c* ≥ *delimited_code* **then**
    begin *scan_delimiter*(*garbage*, *false*); *scan_delimiter*(*garbage*, *false*);
    end;
  if *c* **mod** *delimited_code* = *above_code* **then** *scan_normal_dimen*;
  print_err("Ambiguous;␣you␣need␣another␣{␣and␣}");
  help3("I´m␣ignoring␣this␣fraction␣specification,␣since␣I␣don´t")

```
("know␣whether␣a␣construction␣like␣`x␣\over␣y␣\over␣z´")
("means␣`{x␣\over␣y}␣\over␣z´␣or␣`x␣\over␣{y␣\over␣z}´.");  error;
end
```
This code is used in section 1181.

1184.   At the end of a math formula or subformula, the *fin_mlist* routine is called upon to return a pointer to the newly completed mlist, and to pop the nest back to the enclosing semantic level. The parameter to *fin_mlist*, if not null, points to a *right_noad* that ends the current mlist; this *right_noad* has not yet been appended.

⟨ Declare the function called *fin_mlist* 1184 ⟩ ≡
function *fin_mlist*(*p* : *pointer*): *pointer*;
   var *q*: *pointer*;   { the mlist to return }
   begin if *incompleat_noad* ≠ *null* **then** ⟨ Compleat the incompleat noad 1185 ⟩
   else begin *link*(*tail*) ← *p*; *q* ← *link*(*head*);
      end;
   pop_nest; *fin_mlist* ← *q*;
   end;

This code is used in section 1174.

1185.   ⟨ Compleat the incompleat noad 1185 ⟩ ≡
   begin *math_type*(*denominator*(*incompleat_noad*)) ← *sub_mlist*;
   info(*denominator*(*incompleat_noad*)) ← *link*(*head*);
   if *p* = *null* **then** *q* ← *incompleat_noad*
   else begin *q* ← *info*(*numerator*(*incompleat_noad*));
      if *type*(*q*) ≠ *left_noad* **then** *confusion*("right");
      info(*numerator*(*incompleat_noad*)) ← *link*(*q*); *link*(*q*) ← *incompleat_noad*;
      link(*incompleat_noad*) ← *p*;
      end;
   end

This code is used in section 1184.

---

above = 52, §208.
above_code = 0, §1178.
atop_code = 2, §1178.
chr_code: *halfword*, §298.
confusion: **procedure**, §95.
cur_chr: *halfword*, §297.
cur_val: *integer*, §410.
default_code = macro, §683.
delimited_code = 3, §1178.
denominator = macro, §683.
empty_field: *two_halves*, §684.
error: **procedure**, §82.
fraction_noad = 25, §683.
fraction_noad_size = 6, §683.
garbage = macro, §162.
get_node: **function**, §125.

head = macro, §213.
help3 = macro, §79.
hh: *two_halves*, §113.
incompleat_noad = macro, §213.
info = macro, §118.
left_delimiter = macro, §683.
left_noad = 30, §687.
link = macro, §118.
math_type = macro, §681.
mem: **array**, §116.
mmode = 201, §211.
normal = 0, §135.
null = macro, §115.
null_delimiter: *four_quarters*, §684.
numerator = macro, §683.
over_code = 1, §1178.

pointer = macro, §115.
pop_nest: **procedure**, §217.
print_cmd_chr: **procedure**, §298.
print_err = macro, §73.
print_esc: **procedure**, §63.
qqqq: *four_quarters*, §113.
right_delimiter = macro, §683.
right_noad = 31, §687.
scan_delimiter: **procedure**, §1160.
scan_normal_dimen = macro, §448.
small_number = 0 .. 63, §101.
sub_mlist = 3, §681.
subtype = macro, §133.
tail = macro, §213.
thickness = macro, §683.
type = macro, §133.

1186. Now at last we're ready to see what happens when a right brace occurs in a math formula. Two special cases are simplified here: Braces are effectively removed when they surround a single Ord character or, when they surround an accent that is the nucleus of an Ord atom.

⟨ Cases of *handle_right_brace* where a *right_brace* triggers a delayed action 1085 ⟩ +≡
math_group: **begin** *unsave*; *decr*(*save_ptr*);
  math_type(*saved*(0)) ← *sub_mlist*; *p* ← *fin_mlist*(*null*); *info*(*saved*(0)) ← *p*;
  if *p* ≠ *null* **then**
    if *link*(*p*) = *null* **then**
      if *type*(*p*) = *ord_noad* **then**
        begin if *math_type*(*subscr*(*p*)) = *empty* **then**
          if *math_type*(*supscr*(*p*)) = *empty* **then**
            begin *mem*[*saved*(0)].*hh* ← *mem*[*nucleus*(*p*)].*hh*; *free_node*(*p*, *noad_size*);
            end;
        end
      else if *type*(*p*) = *accent_noad* **then**
        if *saved*(0) = *nucleus*(*tail*) **then**
          if *type*(*tail*) = *ord_noad* **then** ⟨ Replace the tail of the list by *p* 1187 ⟩;
  end;

1187. ⟨ Replace the tail of the list by *p* 1187 ⟩ ≡
  begin *q* ← *head*;
  while *link*(*q*) ≠ *tail* **do** *q* ← *link*(*q*);
  link(*q*) ← *p*; *free_node*(*tail*, *noad_size*); *tail* ← *p*;
  end
This code is used in section 1186.

1188. We have dealt with all constructions of math mode except '\left' and '\right', so the picture is completed by the following sections of the program.

⟨ Put each of TeX's primitives into the hash table 226 ⟩ +≡
  primitive("left", *left_right*, *left_noad*); *primitive*("right", *left_right*, *right_noad*);
  text(*frozen_right*) ← "right"; *eqtb*[*frozen_right*] ← *eqtb*[*cur_val*];

1189. ⟨ Cases of *print_cmd_chr* for symbolic printing of primitives 227 ⟩ +≡
left_right: **if** *chr_code* = *left_noad* **then** *print_esc*("left")
  else *print_esc*("right");

1190. ⟨ Cases of *main_control* that build boxes and lists 1056 ⟩ +≡
mmode + *left_right*: *math_left_right*;

1191. ⟨Declare action procedures for use by *main_control* 1043⟩ +≡
procedure *math_left_right*;
  var *t*: *small_number*; {*left_noad* or *right_noad*}
    p: *pointer*; {new noad}
  begin *t* ← *cur_chr*;
  if (*t* = *right_noad*) ∧ (*cur_group* ≠ *math_left_group*) **then**
    ⟨Try to recover from mismatched \right 1192⟩
  else begin *p* ← *new_noad*; *type*(*p*) ← *t*; *scan_delimiter*(*delimiter*(*p*), *false*);
    if *t* = *left_noad* **then**
      begin *push_math*(*math_left_group*); *link*(*head*) ← *p*; *tail* ← *p*;
      end
    else begin *p* ← *fin_mlist*(*p*); *unsave*; {end of *math_left_group*}
      tail_append(*new_noad*); *type*(*tail*) ← *inner_noad*; *math_type*(*nucleus*(*tail*)) ← *sub_mlist*;
      info(*nucleus*(*tail*)) ← *p*;
      end;
    end;
  end;

1192. ⟨Try to recover from mismatched \right 1192⟩ ≡
begin if *cur_group* = *math_shift_group* **then**
  begin *scan_delimiter*(*garbage*, *false*); *print_err*("Extra␣"); *print_esc*("right");
  help1("I´m␣ignoring␣a␣\right␣that␣had␣no␣matching␣\left."); *error*;
  end
else *off_save*;
end
This code is used in section 1191.

1193. Here is the only way out of math mode.

⟨Cases of *main_control* that build boxes and lists 1056⟩ +≡
mmode + *math_shift*: **if** *cur_group* = *math_shift_group* **then** *after_math*
  else *off_save*;

1194. ⟨Declare action procedures for use by *main_control* 1043⟩ +≡
procedure *after_math*;
  var *l*: *boolean*;   { '\leqno' instead of '\eqno' }
    danger: *boolean*;   { not enough symbol fonts are present }
    m: *integer*;   { *mmode* or −*mmode* }
    p: *pointer*;   { the formula }
    a: *pointer*;   { box containing equation number }
    ⟨Local variables for finishing a displayed formula 1198⟩
  begin *danger* ← *false*; ⟨Check that the necessary fonts for math symbols are present; if not, flush
      the current math lists and set *danger* ← *true* 1195⟩;
  m ← *mode*; *l* ← *false*; *p* ← *fin_mlist*(*null*);   { this pops the nest }
  if *mode* = −*m* **then**   { end of equation number }
    begin *cur_mlist* ← *p*; *cur_style* ← *text_style*; *mlist_penalties* ← *false*; *mlist_to_hlist*;
    a ← *hpack*(*link*(*temp_head*), *natural*); *unsave*; *decr*(*save_ptr*);
      { now *cur_group* = *math_shift_group* }
    if *saved*(0) = 1 **then** *l* ← *true*;
    if *danger* **then** *flush_math*;
    m ← *mode*; *p* ← *fin_mlist*(*null*);
    end
  else *a* ← *null*;
  if *m* < 0 **then** ⟨Finish math in text 1196⟩
  else begin ⟨Check that another **$** follows 1197⟩;
    ⟨Finish displayed math 1199⟩;
    end;
  end;

1195. ⟨Check that the necessary fonts for math symbols are present; if not, flush the current math
    lists and set *danger* ← *true* 1195⟩ ≡
if (*font_params*[*fam_fnt*(2 + *text_size*)] < *total_mathsy_params*) ∨
    (*font_params*[*fam_fnt*(2 + *script_size*)] < *total_mathsy_params*) ∨
    (*font_params*[*fam_fnt*(2 + *script_script_size*)] < *total_mathsy_params*) **then**
  begin *print_err*("Math␣formula␣deleted:␣Insufficient␣symbol␣fonts");
  help3("Sorry,␣but␣I␣can´t␣typeset␣math␣unless␣\textfont␣2")
  ("and␣\scriptfont␣2␣and␣\scriptscriptfont␣2␣have␣all")
  ("the␣\fontdimen␣values␣needed␣in␣math␣symbol␣fonts."); *error*; *flush_math*; *danger* ← *true*;
  end
  else if (*font_params*[*fam_fnt*(3 + *text_size*)] < *total_mathex_params*) ∨
      (*font_params*[*fam_fnt*(3 + *script_size*)] < *total_mathex_params*) ∨
      (*font_params*[*fam_fnt*(3 + *script_script_size*)] < *total_mathex_params*) **then**
    begin *print_err*("Math␣formula␣deleted:␣Insufficient␣extension␣fonts");
    help3("Sorry,␣but␣I␣can´t␣typeset␣math␣unless␣\textfont␣3")
    ("and␣\scriptfont␣3␣and␣\scriptscriptfont␣3␣have␣all")
    ("the␣\fontdimen␣values␣needed␣in␣math␣extension␣fonts."); *error*; *flush_math*;
    danger ← *true*;
    end
This code is used in section 1194.

1196. The *unsave* is done after everything else here; hence an appearance of '\mathsurround'
inside of '**$**...**$**' affects the spacing at these particular **$**'s. This is consistent with the conventions

of '`$$...$$`', since '`\abovedisplayskip`' inside a display affects the space above that display.

⟨ Finish math in text 1196 ⟩ ≡
    begin *tail_append*(*new_math*(*math_surround*, *before*)); *cur_mlist* ← *p*; *cur_style* ← *text_style*;
    mlist_penalties ← (*mode* > 0); *mlist_to_hlist*; *link*(*tail*) ← *link*(*temp_head*);
    while *link*(*tail*) ≠ *null* **do** *tail* ← *link*(*tail*);
    tail_append(*new_math*(*math_surround*, *after*)); *space_factor* ← 1000; *unsave*;
    end

This code is used in section 1194.

1197. TₑX gets to the following part of the program when the first '`$`' ending a display has been scanned.

⟨ Check that another `$` follows 1197 ⟩ ≡
    begin *get_x_token*;
    if *cur_cmd* ≠ *math_shift* **then**
        begin *print_err*("Display␣math␣should␣end␣with␣$$");
        help2("The␣`$´␣that␣I␣just␣saw␣supposedly␣matches␣a␣previous␣`$$´.")
        ("So␣I␣shall␣assume␣that␣you␣typed␣`$$´␣both␣times."); *back_error*;
        end;
    end

This code is used in sections 1194 and 1206.

---

after = 1, §147.
back_error: **procedure**, §327.
before = 0, §147.
cur_cmd: *eight_bits*, §297.
cur_group: *group_code*, §271.
cur_mlist: *pointer*, §719.
cur_style: *small_number*, §719.
decr = macro, §16.
error: **procedure**, §82.
fam_fnt = macro, §230.
fin_mlist: **function**, §1184.
flush_math: **procedure**, §718.
font_params: **array**, §549.
get_x_token: **procedure**, §380.
help2 = macro, §79.

help3 = macro, §79.
hpack: **function**, §649.
link = macro, §118.
math_shift = 3, §207.
math_shift_group = 15, §269.
math_surround = macro, §247.
mlist_penalties: *boolean*, §719.
mlist_to_hlist: **procedure**, §726.
mmode = 201, §211.
mode = macro, §213.
natural = macro, §644.
new_math: **function**, §147.
null = macro, §115.
pointer = macro, §115.

print_err = macro, §73.
save_ptr: 0 .. *save_size*, §271.
saved = macro, §274.
script_script_size = 32, §699.
script_size = 16, §699.
space_factor = macro, §213.
tail = macro, §213.
tail_append = macro, §214.
temp_head = macro, §162.
text_size = 0, §699.
text_style = 2, §688.
total_mathex_params = 13, §701.
total_mathsy_params = 22, §700. ·
unsave: **procedure**, §281.

1198. We have saved the worst for last: The fussiest part of math mode processing occurs when a displayed formula is being centered and placed with an optional equation number.

⟨ Local variables for finishing a displayed formula 1198 ⟩ ≡
b: *pointer*; { box containing the equation }
w: *scaled*; { width of the equation }
z: *scaled*; { width of the line }
e: *scaled*; { width of equation number }
q: *scaled*; { width of equation number plus space to separate from equation }
d: *scaled*; { displacement of equation in the line }
s: *scaled*; { move the line right this much }
g1, *g2*: *small_number*; { glue parameter codes for before and after }
r: *pointer*; { kern node used to position the display }
t: *pointer*; { tail of adjustment list }
This code is used in section 1194.

1199. At this time p points to the mlist for the formula; a is either *null* or it points to a box containing the equation number; and we are in vertical mode (or internal vertical mode).

⟨ Finish displayed math 1199 ⟩ ≡
  cur_mlist ← *p*; *cur_style* ← *display_style*; *mlist_penalties* ← *false*; *mlist_to_hlist*;
  p ← *link*(*temp_head*);
  adjust_tail ← *adjust_head*; *b* ← *hpack*(*p, natural*); *t* ← *adjust_tail*; *adjust_tail* ← *null*;
  w ← *width*(*b*); *z* ← *display_width*; *s* ← *display_indent*;
  if (*a* = *null*) ∨ *danger* **then**
    begin *e* ← 0; *q* ← 0;
    end
  else begin *e* ← *width*(*a*); *q* ← *e* + *math_quad*(*text_size*);
    end;
  if *w* + *q* > *z* **then** ⟨ Squeeze the equation as much as possible; if there is an equation number that
      should go on a separate line by itself, set *e* ← 0 1201 ⟩;
  ⟨ Determine the displacement, *d*, of the left edge of the equation, with respect to the line size *z*,
      assuming that *l* = *false* 1202 ⟩;
  ⟨ Append the glue or equation number preceding the display 1203 ⟩;
  ⟨ Append the display and perhaps also the equation number 1204 ⟩;
  ⟨ Append the glue or equation number following the display 1205 ⟩;
  resume_after_display
This code is used in section 1194.

1200. ⟨ Declare action procedures for use by *main_control* 1043 ⟩ +≡
procedure *resume_after_display*;
  begin if *cur_group* ≠ *math_shift_group* **then** *confusion*("display");
  unsave; *prev_graf* ← *prev_graf* + 3; *push_nest*; *mode* ← *hmode*; *space_factor* ← 1000;
  ⟨ Scan an optional space 443 ⟩;
  if *nest_ptr* = 1 **then** *build_page*;
  end;

1201. The user can force the equation number to go on a separate line by making its width zero.

⟨ Squeeze the equation as much as possible; if there is an equation number that should go on a separate
      line by itself, set *e* ← 0 1201 ⟩ ≡

begin if $(e \neq 0) \wedge ((w - total\_shrink[normal] + q \leq z) \vee$
$\quad (total\_shrink[fil] \neq 0) \vee (total\_shrink[fill] \neq 0) \vee (total\_shrink[filll] \neq 0))$ **then**
$\quad$ **begin** $free\_node(b, box\_node\_size)$; $b \leftarrow hpack(p, z - q, exactly)$;
$\quad$ **end**
else begin $e \leftarrow 0$;
$\quad$ **if** $w > z$ **then**
$\quad\quad$ **begin** $free\_node(b, box\_node\_size)$; $b \leftarrow hpack(p, z, exactly)$;
$\quad\quad$ **end**;
$\quad$ **end**;
$w \leftarrow width(b)$;
end

This code is used in section 1199.

1202. We try first to center the display without regard to the existence of the equation number. If that would make it too close (where "too close" means that the space between display and equation number is less than the width of the equation number), we either center it in the remaining space or move it as far from the equation number as possible. The latter alternative is taken only if the display begins with glue, since we assume that the user put glue there to control the spacing precisely.

$\langle$ Determine the displacement, d, of the left edge of the equation, with respect to the line size z, assuming
$\quad$ that $l = false$ 1202 $\rangle \equiv$
$d \leftarrow half(z - w)$;
if $(e > 0) \wedge (d < 2 * e)$ **then** $\quad$ { too close }
$\quad$ **begin** $d \leftarrow half(z - w - e)$;
$\quad$ **if** $p \neq null$ **then**
$\quad\quad$ **if** $type(p) = glue\_node$ **then** $d \leftarrow 0$;
$\quad$ **end**

This code is used in section 1199.

---

a: *pointer*, §1194.
adjust_head = macro, §162.
adjust_tail: *pointer*, §647.
box_node_size = 7, §135.
build_page: **procedure**, §994.
confusion: **procedure**, §95.
cur_group: *group_code*, §271.
cur_mlist: *pointer*, §719.
cur_style: *small_number*, §719.
danger: *boolean*, §1194.
display_indent = macro, §247.
display_style = 0, §688.
display_width = macro, §247.
exactly = 0, §644.
fil = 1, §150.
fill = 2, §150.

filll = 3, §150.
free_node: **procedure**, §130.
glue_node = 10, §149.
half: **function**, §100.
hmode = 101, §211.
hpack: **function**, §649.
l: *boolean*, §1194.
link = macro, §118.
math_quad = macro, §700.
math_shift_group = 15, §269.
mlist_penalties: *boolean*, §719.
mlist_to_hlist: **procedure**, §726.
mode = macro, §213.
natural = macro, §644.
nest_ptr: 0 .. *nest_size*, §213.

normal = 0, §135.
null = macro, §115.
p: *pointer*, §1194.
pointer = macro, §115.
prev_graf = macro, §213.
push_nest: **procedure**, §216.
scaled = *integer*, §101.
small_number = 0 .. 63, §101.
space_factor = macro, §213.
temp_head = macro, §162.
text_size = 0, §699.
total_shrink: **array**, §646.
type = macro, §133.
unsave: **procedure**, §281.
width = macro, §135.

1203. If the equation number is set on a line by itself, either before or after the formula, we append an infinite penalty so that no page break will separate the display from its number; and we use the same size and displacement for all three potential lines of the display, even though '\parshape' may specify them differently.

⟨ Append the glue or equation number preceding the display 1203 ⟩ ≡
   $tail\_append(new\_penalty(pre\_display\_penalty))$;
   if $(d + s \leq pre\_display\_size) \vee l$ **then**   { not enough clearance }
     begin $g1 \leftarrow above\_display\_skip\_code$; $g2 \leftarrow below\_display\_skip\_code$;
     end
   else begin $g1 \leftarrow above\_display\_short\_skip\_code$; $g2 \leftarrow below\_display\_short\_skip\_code$;
     end;
   if $l \wedge (e = 0)$ **then**   { it follows that $type(a) = hlist\_node$ }
     begin $shift\_amount(a) \leftarrow s$; $append\_to\_vlist(a)$; $tail\_append(new\_penalty(inf\_penalty))$;
     end
   else $tail\_append(new\_param\_glue(g1))$

This code is used in section 1199.

1204. ⟨ Append the display and perhaps also the equation number 1204 ⟩ ≡
   if $e \neq 0$ **then**
     begin $r \leftarrow new\_kern(z - w - e - d)$;
     if l **then**
       begin $link(a) \leftarrow r$; $link(r) \leftarrow b$; $b \leftarrow a$; $d \leftarrow 0$;
       end
     else begin $link(b) \leftarrow r$; $link(r) \leftarrow a$;
       end;
     $b \leftarrow hpack(b, natural)$;
     end;
   $shift\_amount(b) \leftarrow s + d$; $append\_to\_vlist(b)$;
   if $t \neq adjust\_head$ **then**
     begin $link(tail) \leftarrow link(adjust\_head)$; $tail \leftarrow t$;
     end

This code is used in section 1199.

1205. ⟨ Append the glue or equation number following the display 1205 ⟩ ≡
   if $(a \neq null) \wedge (e = 0) \wedge \neg l$ **then**
     begin $tail\_append(new\_penalty(inf\_penalty))$; $shift\_amount(a) \leftarrow s + z - width(a)$;
     $append\_to\_vlist(a)$; $tail\_append(new\_penalty(post\_display\_penalty))$;
     end
   else begin $tail\_append(new\_penalty(post\_display\_penalty))$; $tail\_append(new\_param\_glue(g2))$;
     end

This code is used in section 1199.

1206. When \halign appears in a display, the alignment routines operate essentially as they do in vertical mode. Then the following program is activated, with p and q pointing to the beginning and end of the resulting list, and with t the $prev\_depth$ value.

⟨ Finish an alignment in a display 1206 ⟩ ≡
   begin $do\_assignments$;
   if $cur\_cmd \neq math\_shift$ **then** ⟨ Pontificate about improper alignment in display 1207 ⟩

else ⟨ Check that another **\$** follows 1197 ⟩;
pop_nest; *tail_append*(*new_penalty*(*pre_display_penalty*));
tail_append(*new_param_glue*(*above_display_skip_code*)); *link*(*tail*) ← *p*;
if *p* ≠ *null* **then** *tail* ← *q*;
tail_append(*new_penalty*(*post_display_penalty*));
tail_append(*new_param_glue*(*below_display_skip_code*)); *prev_depth* ← *t*; *resume_after_display*;
end

This code is used in section 812.

1207.   ⟨ Pontificate about improper alignment in display 1207 ⟩ ≡
begin *print_err*("Missing␣\$\$␣inserted");
help2("Displays␣can␣use␣special␣alignments␣(like␣\eqalignno)")
("only␣if␣nothing␣but␣the␣alignment␣itself␣is␣between␣\$\$´s."); *back_error*;
end

This code is used in section 1206.

---

a: *pointer*, §1194.
above_display_short_skip_code = 5, §224.
above_display_skip_code = 3, §224.
adjust_head = macro, §162.
append_to_vlist: **procedure**, §679.
b: *pointer*, §1198.
back_error: **procedure**, §327.
below_display_short_skip_code = 6, §224.
below_display_skip_code = 4, §224.
cur_cmd: *eight_bits*, §297.
d: *scaled*, §1198.
do_assignments: **procedure**, §1270.
e: *scaled*, §1198.
g1: *small_number*, §1198.

g2: *small_number*, §1198.
help2 = macro, §79.
hlist_node = 0, §135.
hpack: **function**, §649.
inf_penalty = 10000, §157.
l: *boolean*, §1194.
link = macro, §118.
math_shift = 3, §207.
natural = macro, §644.
new_kern: **function**, §156.
new_param_glue: **function**, §152.
new_penalty: **function**, §158.
null = macro, §115.
p: *pointer*, §800.
pop_nest: **procedure**, §217.
post_display_penalty = macro, §236.

pre_display_penalty = macro, §236.
pre_display_size = macro, §247.
prev_depth = macro, §213.
print_err = macro, §73.
q: *pointer*, §800.
r: *pointer*, §1198.
s: *scaled*, §1198.
shift_amount = macro, §135.
t: *scaled*, §800.
t: *pointer*, §1198.
tail = macro, §213.
tail_append = macro, §214.
type = macro, §133.
w: *scaled*, §1198.
width = macro, §135.
z: *scaled*, §1198.

1208. Mode-independent processing. The long *main_control* procedure has now been fully specified, except for certain activities that are independent of the current mode. These activities do not change the current vlist or hlist or mlist; if they change anything, it is the value of a parameter or the meaning of a control sequence.

Assignments to values in *eqtb* can be global or local. Furthermore, a control sequence can be defined to be '\long' or '\outer', and it might or might not be expanded. The prefixes '\global', '\long', and '\outer' can occur in any order. Therefore we assign binary numeric codes, making it possible to accumulate the union of all specified prefixes by adding the corresponding codes. (Pascal's **set** operations could also have been used.)

⟨ Put each of TeX's primitives into the hash table 226 ⟩ +≡
  primitive("long", *prefix*, 1); *primitive*("outer", *prefix*, 2); *primitive*("global", *prefix*, 4);
  primitive("def", *def*, 0); *primitive*("gdef", *def*, 1); *primitive*("edef", *def*, 2);
  primitive("xdef", *def*, 3);

1209. ⟨ Cases of *print_cmd_chr* for symbolic printing of primitives 227 ⟩ +≡
prefix: **if** *chr_code* = 1 **then** *print_esc*("long")
  else if *chr_code* = 2 **then** *print_esc*("outer")
    else *print_esc*("global");
def: **if** *chr_code* = 0 **then** *print_esc*("def")
  else if *chr_code* = 1 **then** *print_esc*("gdef")
    else if *chr_code* = 2 **then** *print_esc*("edef")
      else *print_esc*("xdef");

1210. Every prefix, and every command code that might or might not be prefixed, calls the action procedure *prefixed_command*. This routine accumulates a sequence of prefixes until coming to a non-prefix, then it carries out the command.

⟨ Cases of *main_control* that don't depend on *mode* 1210 ⟩ ≡
any_mode(*toks_register*), *any_mode*(*assign_toks*), *any_mode*(*assign_int*), *any_mode*(*assign_dimen*),
    any_mode(*assign_glue*), *any_mode*(*assign_mu_glue*), *any_mode*(*assign_font_dimen*),
    any_mode(*assign_font_int*), *any_mode*(*set_aux*), *any_mode*(*set_prev_graf*),
    any_mode(*set_page_dimen*), *any_mode*(*set_page_int*), *any_mode*(*set_box_dimen*),
    any_mode(*set_shape*), *any_mode*(*def_code*), *any_mode*(*def_family*), *any_mode*(*set_font*),
    any_mode(*def_font*), *any_mode*(*register*), *any_mode*(*advance*), *any_mode*(*multiply*),
    any_mode(*divide*), *any_mode*(*prefix*), *any_mode*(*let*), *any_mode*(*shorthand_def*),
    any_mode(*read_to_cs*), *any_mode*(*def*), *any_mode*(*set_box*), *any_mode*(*hyph_data*),
    any_mode(*set_interaction*): *prefixed_command*;
See also sections 1268, 1271, 1274, 1276, 1285, and 1290.
This code is used in section 1045.

1211. If the user says, e.g., '\global\global', the redundancy is silently accepted.
⟨ Declare action procedures for use by *main_control* 1043 ⟩ +≡
⟨ Declare subprocedures for *prefixed_command* 1215 ⟩
procedure *prefixed_command*;
  label *done*, *exit*;
  var *a*: *small_number*; { accumulated prefix codes so far }
    f: *internal_font_number*; { identifies a font }
    j: *halfword*; { index into a \parshape specification }

k: $0 .. font\_mem\_size$; { index into *font_info* }
p, q: *pointer*; { for temporary short-term use }
n: *integer*; { ditto }
e: *boolean*; { should a definition be expanded? or was \let not done? }
begin $a \leftarrow 0$;
while $cur\_cmd = prefix$ **do**
  begin if $\neg odd(a \mathbf{\ div\ } cur\_chr)$ **then** $a \leftarrow a + cur\_chr$;
  ⟨ Get the next non-blank non-relax non-call token 404 ⟩;
  if $cur\_cmd \leq max\_non\_prefixed\_command$ **then** ⟨ Discard erroneous prefixes and **return** 1212 ⟩;
  end;
⟨ Discard the prefixes \long and \outer if they are irrelevant 1213 ⟩;
⟨ Adjust for the setting of \globaldefs 1214 ⟩;
case cur_cmd **of**
⟨ Assignments 1217 ⟩
othercases $confusion("prefix")$
endcases;
done: ⟨ Insert a token saved by \afterassignment, if any 1269 ⟩;
exit: **end**;

1212.   ⟨ Discard erroneous prefixes and **return** 1212 ⟩ ≡
begin $print\_err("You␣can´t␣use␣a␣prefix␣with␣`")$; $print\_cmd\_chr(cur\_cmd, cur\_chr)$;
$print\_char("´")$; $help1("I´ll␣pretend␣you␣didn´t␣say␣\long␣or␣\outer␣or␣\global.")$;
$back\_error$; **return**;
end

This code is used in section 1211.

$advance = 89$, §209.
$any\_mode =$ macro, §1045.
$assign\_dimen = 73$, §209.
$assign\_font\_dimen = 76$, §209.
$assign\_font\_int = 77$, §209.
$assign\_glue = 74$, §209.
$assign\_int = 72$, §209.
$assign\_mu\_glue = 75$, §209.
$assign\_toks = 71$, §209.
$back\_error$: **procedure**, §327.
chr_code: *halfword*, §298.
$confusion$: **procedure**, §95.
cur_chr: *halfword*, §297.
cur_cmd: *eight_bits*, §297.
$def = 96$, §209.
$def\_code = 84$, §209.
$def\_family = 85$, §209.
$def\_font = 87$, §209.
$divide = 91$, §209.

$done = 30$, §15.
$eqtb$: **array**, §253.
$exit = 10$, §15.
$font\_info$: **array**, §549.
$font\_mem\_size =$ **const**, §11.
$halfword = min\_halfword ..$
  $max\_halfword$, §113.
$help1 =$ macro, §79.
$hyph\_data = 98$, §209.
$internal\_font\_number = 0 .. font\_max$,
  §548.
$let = 93$, §209.
$main\_control$: **procedure**, §1030.
$max\_non\_prefixed\_command = 69$,
  §208.
$mode =$ macro, §213.
$multiply = 90$, §209.
$pointer =$ macro, §115.
$prefix = 92$, §209.

$primitive$: **procedure**, §264.
$print\_char$: **procedure**, §58.
$print\_cmd\_chr$: **procedure**, §298.
$print\_err =$ macro, §73.
$print\_esc$: **procedure**, §63.
$read\_to\_cs = 95$, §209.
$register = 88$, §209.
$set\_aux = 78$, §209.
$set\_box = 97$, §209.
$set\_box\_dimen = 82$, §209.
$set\_font = 86$, §209.
$set\_interaction = 99$, §209.
$set\_page\_dimen = 80$, §209.
$set\_page\_int = 81$, §209.
$set\_prev\_graf = 79$, §209.
$set\_shape = 83$, §209.
$shorthand\_def = 94$, §209.
$small\_number = 0 .. 63$, §101.
$toks\_register = 70$, §209.

1213. ⟨ Discard the prefixes \long and \outer if they are irrelevant 1213 ⟩ ≡
  if (*cur_cmd* ≠ *def*) ∧ (*a* **mod** 4 ≠ 0) **then**
     begin *print_err*("You␣can´t␣use␣`"); *print_esc*("long"); *print*("´␣or␣`"); *print_esc*("outer");
     print("´␣with␣`"); *print_cmd_chr*(*cur_cmd*, *cur_chr*); *print_char*("´");
     help1("I´ll␣pretend␣you␣didn´t␣say␣\long␣or␣\outer␣here."); *error*;
     end

This code is used in section 1211.

1214. The previous routine does not have to adjust *a* so that *a* **mod** 4 = 0, since the following routines test for the \global prefix as follows.

  define *global* ≡ (*a* ≥ 4)
  define *define*(#) ≡
          if *global* **then** *geq_define*(#) **else** *eq_define*(#)
  define *word_define*(#) ≡
          if *global* **then** *geq_word_define*(#) **else** *eq_word_define*(#)

⟨ Adjust for the setting of \globaldefs 1214 ⟩ ≡
  if *global_defs* ≠ 0 **then**
     if *global_defs* < 0 **then**
        begin if *global* **then** *a* ← *a* − 4;
        end
     else begin if ¬*global* **then** *a* ← *a* + 4;
        end

This code is used in section 1211.

1215. When a control sequence is to be defined, by \def or \let or something similar, the *get_r_token* routine will substitute a special control sequence for a token that is not redefinable.

⟨ Declare subprocedures for *prefixed_command* 1215 ⟩ ≡
procedure *get_r_token*;
  label *restart*;
  begin *restart*: **repeat** *get_token*;
  until *cur_tok* ≠ *space_token*;
  if (*cur_cs* = 0) ∨ (*cur_cs* > *frozen_control_sequence*) **then**
     begin *print_err*("Missing␣control␣sequence␣inserted");
     help5("Please␣don´t␣say␣`\def␣cs{...}´,␣say␣`\def\cs{...}´.")
     ("I´ve␣inserted␣an␣inaccessible␣control␣sequence␣so␣that␣your")
     ("definition␣will␣be␣completed␣without␣mixing␣me␣up␣too␣badly.")
     ("You␣can␣recover␣graciously␣from␣this␣error,␣if␣you´re")
     ("careful;␣see␣exercise␣27.2␣in␣The␣TeXbook.");
     if *cur_cs* = 0 **then** *back_input*;
     cur_tok ← *cs_token_flag* + *frozen_protection*; *ins_error*; **goto** *restart*;
     end;
  end;

See also sections 1229, 1236, 1243, 1244, 1245, 1246, 1247, 1257, and 1265.

This code is used in section 1211.

1216. ⟨ Initialize table entries (done by INITEX only) 164 ⟩ +≡
  text(*frozen_protection*) ← "inaccessible";

1217. Here's an example of the way many of the following routines operate. (Unfortunately, they aren't all as simple as this.)

⟨ Assignments 1217 ⟩ ≡

set_font: *define*(*cur_font_loc*, *data*, *cur_chr*);

See also sections 1218, 1221, 1224, 1225, 1226, 1228, 1232, 1234, 1235, 1241, 1242, 1248, 1252, 1253, 1256, and 1264.

This code is used in section 1211.

1218. When a *def* command has been scanned, *cur_chr* is odd if the definition is supposed to be global, and *cur_chr* ≥ 2 if the definition is supposed to be expanded.

⟨ Assignments 1217 ⟩ +≡

def: **begin if** *odd*(*cur_chr*) ∧ ¬*global* ∧ (*global_defs* ≥ 0) **then** $a \leftarrow a + 4$;
  $e \leftarrow (cur\_chr \geq 2)$; *get_r_token*; $p \leftarrow cur\_cs$; $q \leftarrow scan\_toks(true, e)$;
  define(*p*, *call* + (*a* **mod** 4), *def_ref*);
  end;

1219. Both \let and \futurelet share the command code *let*.

⟨ Put each of TeX's primitives into the hash table 226 ⟩ +≡

  primitive("let", *let*, *normal*);
  primitive("futurelet", *let*, *normal* + 1);

1220. ⟨ Cases of *print_cmd_chr* for symbolic printing of primitives 227 ⟩ +≡

let: **if** *chr_code* ≠ *normal* **then** *print_esc*("futurelet") **else** *print_esc*("let");

---

a: *small_number*, §1211.
back_input: **procedure**, §325.
call = 110, §210.
chr_code: *halfword*, §298.
cs_token_flag = macro, §289.
cur_chr: *halfword*, §297.
cur_cmd: *eight_bits*, §297.
cur_cs: *pointer*, §297.
cur_font_loc = 3678, §230.
cur_tok: *halfword*, §297.
data = 119, §210.
def = 96, §209.
def_ref: *pointer*, §305.
e: *boolean*, §1211.

eq_define: **procedure**, §277.
eq_word_define: **procedure**, §278.
error: **procedure**, §82.
frozen_control_sequence = 2358, §222.
frozen_protection = 2358, §222.
geq_define: **procedure**, §279.
geq_word_define: **procedure**, §279.
get_token: **procedure**, §365.
global_defs = macro, §236.
help1 = macro, §79.
help5 = macro, §79.
ins_error: **procedure**, §327.
let = 93, §209.

normal = 0, §135.
p: *pointer*, §1211.
primitive: **procedure**, §264.
print: **procedure**, §59.
print_char: **procedure**, §58.
print_cmd_chr: **procedure**, §298.
print_err = macro, §73.
print_esc: **procedure**, §63.
q: *pointer*, §1211.
restart = 20, §15.
scan_toks: **function**, §473.
set_font = 86, §209.
space_token = 2592, §289.
text = macro, §256.

1221. ⟨ Assignments 1217 ⟩ +≡

let: **begin** $n \leftarrow cur\_chr$; get_r_token; $p \leftarrow cur\_cs$;
  if $n = normal$ **then**
    begin repeat get_token;
    until $cur\_cmd \neq spacer$;
    if $cur\_tok = other\_token +$ "=" **then**
      begin get_token;
      if $cur\_cmd = spacer$ **then** get_token;
      end;
    end
  else begin get_token; $q \leftarrow cur\_tok$; get_token; $back\_input$; $cur\_tok \leftarrow q$; $back\_input$;
      { look ahead, then back up }
    end;   { note that $back\_input$ doesn't affect cur_cmd, cur_chr }
  if $cur\_cmd \geq call$ **then** $add\_token\_ref(cur\_chr)$;
  $define(p, cur\_cmd, cur\_chr)$;
  end;

1222. A \chardef creates a control sequence whose cmd is $char\_given$; a \mathchardef creates a control sequence whose cmd is $math\_given$; and the corresponding chr is the character code or math code. A \countdef or \dimendef or \skipdef or \muskipdef creates a control sequence whose cmd is $assign\_int$ or ... or $assign\_mu\_glue$, and the corresponding chr is the $eqtb$ location of the internal register in question.

define $char\_def\_code = 0$ { $shorthand\_def$ for \chardef }
define $math\_char\_def\_code = 1$ { $shorthand\_def$ for \mathchardef }
define $count\_def\_code = 2$ { $shorthand\_def$ for \countdef }
define $dimen\_def\_code = 3$ { $shorthand\_def$ for \dimendef }
define $skip\_def\_code = 4$ { $shorthand\_def$ for \skipdef }
define $mu\_skip\_def\_code = 5$ { $shorthand\_def$ for \muskipdef }
define $toks\_def\_code = 6$ { $shorthand\_def$ for \toksdef }

⟨ Put each of TeX's primitives into the hash table 226 ⟩ +≡
  $primitive($"chardef"$, shorthand\_def, char\_def\_code)$;
  $primitive($"mathchardef"$, shorthand\_def, math\_char\_def\_code)$;
  $primitive($"countdef"$, shorthand\_def, count\_def\_code)$;
  $primitive($"dimendef"$, shorthand\_def, dimen\_def\_code)$;
  $primitive($"skipdef"$, shorthand\_def, skip\_def\_code)$;
  $primitive($"muskipdef"$, shorthand\_def, mu\_skip\_def\_code)$;
  $primitive($"toksdef"$, shorthand\_def, toks\_def\_code)$;

1223. ⟨ Cases of $print\_cmd\_chr$ for symbolic printing of primitives 227 ⟩ +≡

$shorthand\_def$: **case** chr_code **of**
  $char\_def\_code$: $print\_esc($"chardef"$)$;
  $math\_char\_def\_code$: $print\_esc($"mathchardef"$)$;
  $count\_def\_code$: $print\_esc($"countdef"$)$;
  $dimen\_def\_code$: $print\_esc($"dimendef"$)$;
  $skip\_def\_code$: $print\_esc($"skipdef"$)$;
  $mu\_skip\_def\_code$: $print\_esc($"muskipdef"$)$;
  othercases $print\_esc($"toksdef"$)$
  endcases;

char_given: **begin** *print_esc*("char"); *print_hex*(*chr_code*);
  end;
math_given: **begin** *print_esc*("mathchar"); *print_hex*(*chr_code*);
  end;

1224. We temporarily define *p* to be *relax*, so that an occurrence of *p* while scanning the definition will simply stop the scanning instead of producing an "undefined control sequence" error or expanding the previous meaning. This allows, for instance, '\chardef\foo=123\foo'.

⟨ Assignments 1217 ⟩ +≡
shorthand_def: **begin** $n \leftarrow cur\_chr$; *get_r_token*; $p \leftarrow cur\_cs$; *define*(*p*, *relax*, 256);
  scan_optional_equals;
  case *n* **of**
  char_def_code: **begin** *scan_char_num*; *define*(*p*, *char_given*, *cur_val*);
    end;
  math_char_def_code: **begin** *scan_fifteen_bit_int*; *define*(*p*, *math_given*, *cur_val*);
    end;
  othercases begin *scan_eight_bit_int*;
    case *n* **of**
    char_def_code: *define*(*p*, *char_given*, *cur_val*);
    math_char_def_code: *define*(*p*, *math_given*, *cur_val*);
    count_def_code: *define*(*p*, *assign_int*, *count_base* + *cur_val*);
    dimen_def_code: *define*(*p*, *assign_dimen*, *scaled_base* + *cur_val*);
    skip_def_code: *define*(*p*, *assign_glue*, *skip_base* + *cur_val*);
    mu_skip_def_code: *define*(*p*, *assign_mu_glue*, *mu_skip_base* + *cur_val*);
    toks_def_code: *define*(*p*, *assign_toks*, *toks_base* + *cur_val*);
    end;   { there are no other cases }
    end
  endcases;
  end;

---

add_token_ref = macro, §203.
assign_dimen = 73, §209.
assign_glue = 74, §209.
assign_int = 72, §209.
assign_mu_glue = 75, §209.
assign_toks = 71, §209.
back_input: **procedure**, §325.
call = 110, §210.
char_given = 67, §208.
chr_code: **halfword**, §298.
cmd: *quarterword*, §298.
count_base = 4417, §236.
cur_chr: *halfword*, §297.
cur_cmd: *eight_bits*, §297.
cur_cs: *pointer*, §297.
cur_tok: *halfword*, §297.

cur_val: *integer*, §410.
define = macro, §1214.
eqtb: **array**, §253.
get_r_token: **procedure**, §1215.
get_token: **procedure**, §365.
let = 93, §209.
math_given = 68, §208.
mu_skip_base = 2900, §224.
n: *integer*, §1211.
normal = 0, §135.
other_token = 3072, §289.
p: *pointer*, §1211.
primitive: **procedure**, §264.
print_cmd_chr: **procedure**, §298.
print_esc: **procedure**, §63.

print_hex: **procedure**, §67.
q: *pointer*, §1211.
relax = 0, §207.
scaled_base = 4821, §247.
scan_char_num: **procedure**, §435.
scan_eight_bit_int: **procedure**, §433.
scan_fifteen_bit_int: **procedure**, §436.
scan_optional_equals: **procedure**, §405.
shorthand_def = 94, §209.
skip_base = 2644, §224.
spacer = 10, §207.
toks_base = 3166, §230.

1225. ⟨Assignments 1217⟩ +≡

read_to_cs: **begin** *scan_int*; *n* ← *cur_val*;
  if ¬*scan_keyword*("to") **then**
    begin *print_err*("Missing␣`to´␣inserted");
    help2("You␣should␣have␣said␣`\read<number>␣to␣\cs´.")
    ("I´m␣going␣to␣look␣for␣the␣\cs␣now."); *error*;
    end;
  get_r_token; *p* ← *cur_cs*; *read_toks*(*n*, *p*); *define*(*p*, *call*, *cur_val*);
  end;

1226. The token-list parameters, \output and \everypar, etc., receive their values in the following way. (For safety's sake, we place an enclosing pair of braces around an \output list.)

⟨Assignments 1217⟩ +≡

toks_register, *assign_toks*: **begin** *q* ← *cur_cs*;
  if *cur_cmd* = *toks_register* **then**
    begin *scan_eight_bit_int*; *p* ← *toks_base* + *cur_val*;
    end
  else *p* ← *cur_chr*; { *p* = *every_par_loc* or *output_routine_loc* or … }
  scan_optional_equals; ⟨Get the next non-blank non-relax non-call token 404⟩;
  if *cur_cmd* ≠ *left_brace* **then** ⟨If the right-hand side is a token parameter or token register, finish the assignment and **goto** *done* 1227⟩;
  back_input; *cur_cs* ← *q*; *q* ← *scan_toks*(*false*, *false*);
  if *link*(*def_ref*) = *null* **then** { empty list: revert to the default }
    begin *define*(*p*, *undefined_cs*, *null*); *free_avail*(*def_ref*);
    end
  else begin if *p* = *output_routine_loc* **then** { enclose in curlies }
      begin *link*(*q*) ← *get_avail*; *q* ← *link*(*q*); *info*(*q*) ← *right_brace_token* + "}"; *q* ← *get_avail*;
      info(*q*) ← *left_brace_token* + "{"; *link*(*q*) ← *link*(*def_ref*); *link*(*def_ref*) ← *q*;
      end;
    define(*p*, *call*, *def_ref*);
    end;
  end;

1227. ⟨If the right-hand side is a token parameter or token register, finish the assignment and **goto** *done* 1227⟩ ≡

  begin if *cur_cmd* = *toks_register* **then**
    begin *scan_eight_bit_int*; *cur_cmd* ← *assign_toks*; *cur_chr* ← *toks_base* + *cur_val*;
    end;
  if *cur_cmd* = *assign_toks* **then**
    begin *q* ← *equiv*(*cur_chr*);
    if *q* = *null* **then** *define*(*p*, *undefined_cs*, *null*)
    else begin *add_token_ref*(*q*); *define*(*p*, *call*, *q*);
      end;
    goto *done*;
    end;
  end

This code is used in section 1226.

1228.   Similar routines are used to assign values to the numeric parameters.

⟨ Assignments 1217 ⟩ +≡

assign_int: **begin** $p \leftarrow cur\_chr$; *scan_optional_equals*; *scan_int*; *word_define*(p, cur_val);
    end;

assign_dimen: **begin** $p \leftarrow cur\_chr$; *scan_optional_equals*; *scan_normal_dimen*; *word_define*(p, cur_val);
    end;

assign_glue, *assign_mu_glue*: **begin** $p \leftarrow cur\_chr$; $n \leftarrow cur\_cmd$; *scan_optional_equals*;
    if $n = assign\_mu\_glue$ **then** *scan_glue*(mu_val) **else** *scan_glue*$(glue\_val)$;
    trap_zero_glue; *define*$(p, glue\_ref, cur\_val)$;
    end;

1229.   When a glue register or parameter becomes zero, it will always point to *zero_glue* because of the following procedure.

⟨ Declare subprocedures for *prefixed_command* 1215 ⟩ +≡

procedure *trap_zero_glue*;
    begin if $(width(cur\_val) = 0) \wedge (stretch(cur\_val) = 0) \wedge (shrink(cur\_val) = 0)$ **then**
       begin *add_glue_ref*$(zero\_glue)$; *delete_glue_ref*(cur_val); $cur\_val \leftarrow zero\_glue$;
       end;
    end;

---

add_glue_ref = macro, §203.
add_token_ref = macro, §203.
assign_dimen = 73, §209.
assign_glue = 74, §209.
assign_int = 72, §209.
assign_mu_glue = 75, §209.
assign_toks = 71, §209.
back_input: **procedure**, §325.
call = 110, §210.
cur_chr: *halfword*, §297.
cur_cmd: *eight_bits*, §297.
cur_cs: *pointer*, §297.
cur_val: *integer*, §410.
def_ref: *pointer*, §305.
define = macro, §1214.
delete_glue_ref: **procedure**, §201.
done = 30, §15.
equiv = macro, §221.
error: **procedure**, §82.

every_par_loc = 3158, §230.
free_avail = macro, §121.
get_avail: **function**, §120.
get_r_token: **procedure**, §1215.
glue_ref = 116, §210.
glue_val = 2, §410.
help2 = macro, §79.
info = macro, §118.
left_brace = 1, §207.
left_brace_token = 256, §289.
link = macro, §118.
mu_val = 3, §410.
n: *integer*, §1211.
null = macro, §115.
output_routine_loc = 3157, §230.
p: *pointer*, §1211.
print_err = macro, §73.
q: *pointer*, §1211.
read_to_cs = 95, §209.

read_toks: **procedure**, §482.
right_brace_token = 512, §289.
scan_eight_bit_int: **procedure**, §433.
scan_glue: **procedure**, §461.
scan_int: **procedure**, §440.
scan_keyword: **function**, §407.
scan_normal_dimen = macro, §448.
scan_optional_equals: **procedure**, §405.
scan_toks: **function**, §473.
shrink = macro, §150.
stretch = macro, §150.
toks_base = 3166, §230.
toks_register = 70, §209.
undefined_cs = 100, §210.
width = macro, §135.
word_define = macro, §1214.
zero_glue = macro, §162.

1230. The various character code tables are changed by the *def_code* commands, and the font families are declared by *def_family*.

⟨ Put each of TEX's primitives into the hash table 226 ⟩ +≡
  primitive("catcode", *def_code*, *cat_code_base*); *primitive*("mathcode", *def_code*, *math_code_base*);
  primitive("lccode", *def_code*, *lc_code_base*); *primitive*("uccode", *def_code*, *uc_code_base*);
  primitive("sfcode", *def_code*, *sf_code_base*); *primitive*("delcode", *def_code*, *del_code_base*);
  primitive("textfont", *def_family*, *math_font_base*);
  primitive("scriptfont", *def_family*, *math_font_base* + *script_size*);
  primitive("scriptscriptfont", *def_family*, *math_font_base* + *script_script_size*);

1231. ⟨ Cases of *print_cmd_chr* for symbolic printing of primitives 227 ⟩ +≡
def_code: **if** *chr_code* = *cat_code_base* **then** *print_esc*("catcode")
  else if *chr_code* = *math_code_base* **then** *print_esc*("mathcode")
    else if *chr_code* = *lc_code_base* **then** *print_esc*("lccode")
      else if *chr_code* = *uc_code_base* **then** *print_esc*("uccode")
        else if *chr_code* = *sf_code_base* **then** *print_esc*("sfcode")
          else *print_esc*("delcode");
def_family: *print_size*(*chr_code* − *math_font_base*);

1232. The different types of code values have different legal ranges; the following program is careful to check each case properly.

⟨ Assignments 1217 ⟩ +≡
def_code: **begin** ⟨ Let *n* be the largest legal code value, based on *cur_chr* 1233 ⟩;
  p ← *cur_chr*; *scan_seven_bit_int*; *p* ← *p* + *cur_val*; *scan_optional_equals*; *scan_int*;
  if ((*cur_val* < 0) ∧ (*p* < *del_code_base*)) ∨ (*cur_val* > *n*) **then**
    begin *print_err*("Invalid␣code␣("); *print_int*(*cur_val*);
    if *p* < *del_code_base* **then** *print*("),␣should␣be␣in␣the␣range␣0..")
    else *print*("),␣should␣be␣at␣most␣");
    print_int(*n*); *help1*("I´m␣going␣to␣use␣0␣instead␣of␣that␣illegal␣code␣value.");
    error; *cur_val* ← 0;
    end;
  if *p* < *math_code_base* **then** *define*(*p*, *data*, *cur_val*)
  else if *p* < *del_code_base* **then** *define*(*p*, *data*, *hi*(*cur_val*))
    else *word_define*(*p*, *cur_val*);
  end;

1233. ⟨ Let *n* be the largest legal code value, based on *cur_chr* 1233 ⟩ ≡
  if *cur_chr* = *cat_code_base* **then** *n* ← *max_char_code*
  else if *cur_chr* = *math_code_base* **then** *n* ← ´100000
    else if *cur_chr* = *sf_code_base* **then** *n* ← ´77777
      else if *cur_chr* = *del_code_base* **then** *n* ← ´77777777
        else *n* ← 127

This code is used in section 1232.

1234. ⟨ Assignments 1217 ⟩ +≡
def_family: **begin** *p* ← *cur_chr*; *scan_four_bit_int*; *p* ← *p* + *cur_val*; *scan_optional_equals*;
  scan_font_ident; *define*(*p*, *data*, *cur_val*);
  end;

1235.   Next we consider changes to TeX's numeric registers.

⟨ Assignments 1217 ⟩ +≡

register, advance, multiply, divide: *do_register_command*(*a*);

1236.   We use the fact that *register* < *advance* < *multiply* < *divide*.

⟨ Declare subprocedures for *prefixed_command* 1215 ⟩ +≡
procedure *do_register_command*(*a* : *small_number*);
 label *found, exit*;
 var *l, q, r, s*: *pointer*;   { for list manipulation }
  p: *int_val* .. *mu_val*;   { type of register involved }
 begin *q* ← *cur_cmd*; ⟨ Compute the register location *l* and its type *p*; but **return** if invalid 1237 ⟩;
 if *q* = *register* **then** *scan_optional_equals*
 else if *scan_keyword*("by") **then** *do_nothing*;   { optional 'by' }
 arith_error ← *false*;
 if *q* < *multiply* **then** ⟨ Compute result of *register* or *advance*, put it in *cur_val* 1238 ⟩
 else ⟨ Compute result of *multiply* or *divide*, put it in *cur_val* 1240 ⟩;
 if *arith_error* **then**
  begin *print_err*("Arithmetic⎵overflow");
  help2("I⎵can´t⎵carry⎵out⎵that⎵multiplication⎵or⎵division,")
  ("since⎵the⎵result⎵is⎵out⎵of⎵range."); *error*; **return**;
  end;
 if *p* < *glue_val* **then** *word_define*(*l, cur_val*)
 else begin *trap_zero_glue*; *define*(*l, glue_ref, cur_val*);
  end;
exit: **end**;

---

a: *small_number*, §1211.
advance = 89, §209.
arith_error: *boolean*, §104.
cat_code_base = 3727, §230.
chr_code: *halfword*, §298.
cur_chr: *halfword*, §297.
cur_cmd: *eight_bits*, §297.
cur_val: *integer*, §410.
data = 119, §210.
def_code = 84, §209.
def_family = 85, §209.
define = macro, §1214.
del_code_base = 4673, §236.
divide = 91, §209.
do_nothing = macro, §16.
error: **procedure**, §82.
exit = 10, §15.
found = 40, §15.
glue_ref = 116, §210.

glue_val = 2, §410.
help1 = macro, §79.
help2 = macro, §79.
hi = macro, §112.
int_val = 0, §410.
lc_code_base = 3855, §230.
math_code_base = 4239, §230.
math_font_base = 3679, §230.
max_char_code = 15, §207.
mu_val = 3, §410.
multiply = 90, §209.
n: *integer*, §1211.
p: *pointer*, §1211.
pointer = macro, §115.
primitive: **procedure**, §264.
print: **procedure**, §59.
print_cmd_chr: **procedure**, §298.
print_err = macro, §73.

print_esc: **procedure**, §63.
print_int: **procedure**, §65.
print_size: **procedure**, §699.
register = 88, §209.
scan_font_ident: **procedure**, §577.
scan_four_bit_int: **procedure**, §434.
scan_int: **procedure**, §440.
scan_keyword: **function**, §407.
scan_optional_equals: **procedure**, §405.
scan_seven_bit_int: **procedure**, §432.
script_script_size = 32, §699.
script_size = 16, §699.
sf_code_base = 4111, §230.
small_number = 0 .. 63, §101.
uc_code_base = 3983, §230.
word_define = macro, §1214.

1237. Here we use the fact that the consecutive codes int_val .. .mu_val and $assign\_int$ .. $assign\_mu\_glue$ correspond to each other nicely.

⟨ Compute the register location l and its type p; but **return** if invalid 1237 ⟩ ≡

  begin if $q \neq register$ **then**

    begin get_x_token;

    if $(cur\_cmd \geq assign\_int) \wedge (cur\_cmd \leq assign\_mu\_glue)$ **then**

      begin $l \leftarrow cur\_chr$; $p \leftarrow cur\_cmd - assign\_int$; **goto** $found$;

      end;

    if $cur\_cmd \neq register$ **then**

      begin $print\_err($"You␣can´t␣use␣`"$)$; $print\_cmd\_chr(cur\_cmd, cur\_chr)$; $print($"´␣after␣"$)$;

      $print\_cmd\_chr(q, 0)$; $help1($"I´m␣forgetting␣what␣you␣said␣and␣not␣changing␣anything."$)$;

      $error$; **return**;

      end;

    end;

  $p \leftarrow cur\_chr$; $scan\_eight\_bit\_int$;

  case p **of**

  int_val: $l \leftarrow cur\_val + count\_base$;

  $dimen\_val$: $l \leftarrow cur\_val + scaled\_base$;

  $glue\_val$: $l \leftarrow cur\_val + skip\_base$;

  mu_val: $l \leftarrow cur\_val + mu\_skip\_base$;

  end; { there are no other cases }

  end;

$found$:

This code is used in section 1236.

1238. ⟨ Compute result of $register$ or $advance$, put it in cur_val 1238 ⟩ ≡

  if $p < glue\_val$ **then**

    begin if $p = int\_val$ **then** $scan\_int$ **else** $scan\_normal\_dimen$;

    if $q = advance$ **then** $cur\_val \leftarrow cur\_val + eqtb[l].int$;

    end

  else begin $scan\_glue(p)$;

    if $q = advance$ **then** ⟨ Compute the sum of two glue specs 1239 ⟩;

    end

This code is used in section 1236.

1239. ⟨ Compute the sum of two glue specs 1239 ⟩ ≡

  begin $q \leftarrow new\_spec(cur\_val)$; $r \leftarrow equiv(l)$; $delete\_glue\_ref(cur\_val)$;

  $width(q) \leftarrow width(q) + width(r)$;

  if $stretch(q) = 0$ **then** $stretch\_order(q) \leftarrow normal$;

  if $stretch\_order(q) = stretch\_order(r)$ **then** $stretch(q) \leftarrow stretch(q) + stretch(r)$

  else if $(stretch\_order(q) < stretch\_order(r)) \wedge (stretch(r) \neq 0)$ **then**

    begin $stretch(q) \leftarrow stretch(r)$; $stretch\_order(q) \leftarrow stretch\_order(r)$;

    end;

  if $shrink(q) = 0$ **then** $shrink\_order(q) \leftarrow normal$;

  if $shrink\_order(q) = shrink\_order(r)$ **then** $shrink(q) \leftarrow shrink(q) + shrink(r)$

  else if $(shrink\_order(q) < shrink\_order(r)) \wedge (shrink(r) \neq 0)$ **then**

    begin $shrink(q) \leftarrow shrink(r)$; $shrink\_order(q) \leftarrow shrink\_order(r)$;

    end;

$cur\_val \leftarrow q;$
end

This code is used in section 1238.

1240. ⟨ Compute result of *multiply* or *divide*, put it in *cur_val* 1240 ⟩ ≡
 begin *scan_int*;
 if $p < glue\_val$ **then**
  if $q = multiply$ **then** $cur\_val \leftarrow nx\_plus\_y(eqtb[l].int, cur\_val, 0)$
  else $cur\_val \leftarrow x\_over\_n(eqtb[l].int, cur\_val)$
 else begin $s \leftarrow equiv(l);\ r \leftarrow new\_spec(s);$
  if $q = multiply$ **then**
   begin $width(r) \leftarrow nx\_plus\_y(width(s), cur\_val, 0);\ stretch(r) \leftarrow nx\_plus\_y(stretch(s), cur\_val, 0);$
   $shrink(r) \leftarrow nx\_plus\_y(shrink(s), cur\_val, 0);$
   end
  else begin $width(r) \leftarrow x\_over\_n(width(s), cur\_val);\ stretch(r) \leftarrow x\_over\_n(stretch(s), cur\_val);$
   $shrink(r) \leftarrow x\_over\_n(shrink(s), cur\_val);$
   end;
  $cur\_val \leftarrow r;$
  end;
 end

This code is used in section 1236.

1241. The processing of boxes is somewhat different, because it may be necessary to scan and create an entire box before we actually change the value of the old one.

⟨ Assignments 1217 ⟩ +≡
set_box: **begin** $scan\_eight\_bit\_int$;
 if $global$ **then** $saved(0) \leftarrow box\_flag + 256 + cur\_val$
 else $saved(0) \leftarrow box\_flag + cur\_val;$
 $scan\_optional\_equals;\ scan\_box;$
 end;

---

advance = 89, §209.
assign_int = 72, §209.
assign_mu_glue = 75, §209.
box_flag = macro, §1071.
count_base = 4417, §236.
cur_chr: *halfword*, §297.
cur_cmd: *eight_bits*, §297.
cur_val: *integer*, §410.
delete_glue_ref: **procedure**, §201.
dimen_val = 1, §410.
divide = 91, §209.
eqtb: **array**, §253.
equiv = macro, §221.
error: **procedure**, §82.
found = 40, §15.
get_x_token: **procedure**, §380.
global = macro, §1214.
glue_val = 2, §410.

help1 = macro, §79.
int: *integer*, §113.
int_val = 0, §410.
l: *pointer*, §1236.
mu_skip_base = 2900, §224.
mu_val = 3, §410.
multiply = 90, §209.
new_spec: **function**, §151.
normal = 0, §135.
nx_plus_y: **function**, §105.
p: 0 .. 3, §1236.
print: **procedure**, §59.
print_cmd_chr: **procedure**, §298.
print_err = macro, §73.
q: *pointer*, §1236.
r: *pointer*, §1236.
register = 88, §209.
s: *pointer*, §1236.

saved = macro, §274.
scaled_base = 4821, §247.
scan_box: **procedure**, §1084.
scan_eight_bit_int: **procedure**,
 §433.
scan_glue: **procedure**, §461.
scan_int: **procedure**, §440.
scan_normal_dimen = macro, §448.
scan_optional_equals: **procedure**,
 §405.
set_box = 97, §209.
shrink = macro, §150.
shrink_order = macro, §150.
skip_base = 2644, §224.
stretch = macro, §150.
stretch_order = macro, §150.
width = macro, §135.
x_over_n: **function**, §106.

1242. The *space_factor* or *prev_depth* settings are changed when a *set_aux* command is sensed. Similarly, *prev_graf* is changed in the presence of *set_prev_graf*, and *dead_cycles* or *insert_penalties* in the presence of *set_page_int*. These definitions are always global.

When some dimension of a box register is changed, the change isn't exactly global; but TeX does not look at the \global switch.

⟨ Assignments 1217 ⟩ +≡
set_aux: *alter_aux*;
set_prev_graf: *alter_prev_graf*;
set_page_dimen: *alter_page_so_far*;
set_page_int: *alter_integer*;
set_box_dimen: *alter_box_dimen*;

1243. ⟨ Declare subprocedures for *prefixed_command* 1215 ⟩ +≡
procedure *alter_aux*;
  var *c*: *halfword*; { *hmode* or *vmode* }
  begin if *cur_chr* ≠ *abs*(*mode*) **then** *report_illegal_case*
  else begin *c* ← *cur_chr*; *scan_optional_equals*;
    if *c* = *vmode* **then**
      begin *scan_normal_dimen*; *prev_depth* ← *cur_val*;
      end
    else begin *scan_int*;
      if (*cur_val* ≤ 0) ∨ (*cur_val* > 32767) **then**
        begin *print_err*("Bad␣space␣factor");
        help1("I␣allow␣only␣values␣in␣the␣range␣1..32767␣here."); *int_error*(*cur_val*);
        end
      else *space_factor* ← *cur_val*;
      end;
    end;
  end;

1244. ⟨ Declare subprocedures for *prefixed_command* 1215 ⟩ +≡
procedure *alter_prev_graf*;
  var *p*: 0 .. *nest_size*; { index into *nest* }
  begin *nest*[*nest_ptr*] ← *cur_list*; *p* ← *nest_ptr*;
  while *abs*(*nest*[*p*].*mode_field*) ≠ *vmode* **do** *decr*(*p*);
  scan_optional_equals; *scan_int*;
  if *cur_val* < 0 **then**
    begin *print_err*("Bad␣"); *print_esc*("prevgraf");
    help1("I␣allow␣only␣nonnegative␣values␣here."); *int_error*(*cur_val*);
    end
  else begin *nest*[*p*].*pg_field* ← *cur_val*; *cur_list* ← *nest*[*nest_ptr*];
    end;
  end;

1245. ⟨ Declare subprocedures for *prefixed_command* 1215 ⟩ +≡
procedure *alter_page_so_far*;
  var *c*: 0 .. 7; { index into *page_so_far* }
  begin *c* ← *cur_chr*; *scan_optional_equals*; *scan_normal_dimen*; *page_so_far*[*c*] ← *cur_val*;
  end;

1246. ⟨Declare subprocedures for *prefixed_command* 1215⟩ +≡
procedure *alter_integer*;
   var *c*: 0 .. 1; { 0 for \deadcycles, 1 for \insertpenalties }
   begin *c* ← *cur_chr*; *scan_optional_equals*; *scan_int*;
   if *c* = 0 **then** *dead_cycles* ← *cur_val*
   else *insert_penalties* ← *cur_val*;
   end;

1247. ⟨Declare subprocedures for *prefixed_command* 1215⟩ +≡
procedure *alter_box_dimen*;
   var *c*: *small_number*; { *width_offset* or *height_offset* or *depth_offset* }
     b: *eight_bits*; { box number }
   begin *c* ← *cur_chr*; *scan_eight_bit_int*; *b* ← *cur_val*; *scan_optional_equals*; *scan_normal_dimen*;
   if *box*(*b*) ≠ *null* **then** *mem*[*box*(*b*) + *c*].*sc* ← *cur_val*;
   end;

1248. Paragraph shapes are set up in the obvious way.
⟨Assignments 1217⟩ +≡
set_shape: **begin** *scan_optional_equals*; *scan_int*; *n* ← *cur_val*;
   if *n* ≤ 0 **then** *p* ← *null*
   else begin *p* ← *get_node*(2 ∗ *n* + 1); *info*(*p*) ← *n*;
     for *j* ← 1 **to** *n* **do**
       begin *scan_normal_dimen*; *mem*[*p* + 2 ∗ *j* − 1].*sc* ← *cur_val*; { indentation }
       scan_normal_dimen; *mem*[*p* + 2 ∗ *j*].*sc* ← *cur_val*; { width }
       end;
     end;
  define(*par_shape_loc*, *shape_ref*, *p*);
  end;

---

box = macro, §230.
cur_chr: *halfword*, §297.
cur_list: *list_state_record*, §213.
cur_val: *integer*, §410.
dead_cycles: *integer*, §592.
decr = macro, §16.
define = macro, §1214.
depth_offset = 2, §135.
eight_bits = 0 .. 255, §25.
get_node: **function**, §125.
halfword = *min_halfword* ..
  max_halfword, §113.
height_offset = 3, §135.
help1 = macro, §79.
hmode = 101, §211.
info = macro, §118.
insert_penalties: *integer*, §982.
int_error: **procedure**, §91.
j: *halfword*, §1211.

mem: **array**, §116.
mode = macro, §213.
mode_field: −201 .. 201, §212.
n: *integer*, §1211.
nest: **array**, §213.
nest_ptr: 0 .. *nest_size*, §213.
nest_size = **const**, §11.
null = macro, §115.
p: *pointer*, §1211.
page_so_far: **array**, §982.
par_shape_loc = 3156, §230.
pg_field: *integer*, §212.
prev_depth = macro, §213.
prev_graf = macro, §213.
print_err = macro, §73.
print_esc: **procedure**, §63.
report_illegal_case: **procedure**,
  §1050.

sc = macro, §113.
scan_eight_bit_int: **procedure**,
  §433.
scan_int: **procedure**, §440.
scan_normal_dimen = macro, §448.
scan_optional_equals: **procedure**,
  §405.
set_aux = 78, §209.
set_box_dimen = 82, §209.
set_page_dimen = 80, §209.
set_page_int = 81, §209.
set_prev_graf = 79, §209.
set_shape = 83, §209.
shape_ref = 117, §210.
small_number = 0 .. 63, §101.
space_factor = macro, §213.
vmode = 1, §211.
width_offset = 1, §135.

1249. Here's something that isn't quite so obvious. It guarantees that $info(par\_shape\_ptr)$ can hold any positive n such $get\_node(2*n+1)$ doesn't overflow the memory capacity.

⟨ Check the "constant" values for consistency 14 ⟩ +≡
  if $2*max\_halfword < mem\_top - mem\_min$ **then** $bad \leftarrow 41$;

1250. New hyphenation data is loaded by the $hyph\_data$ command.

⟨ Put each of TEX's primitives into the hash table 226 ⟩ +≡
  $primitive(\texttt{"hyphenation"}, hyph\_data, 0)$; $primitive(\texttt{"patterns"}, hyph\_data, 1)$;

1251. ⟨ Cases of $print\_cmd\_chr$ for symbolic printing of primitives 227 ⟩ +≡
$hyph\_data$: **if** $chr\_code = 1$ **then** $print\_esc(\texttt{"patterns"})$
  else $print\_esc(\texttt{"hyphenation"})$;

1252. ⟨ Assignments 1217 ⟩ +≡
$hyph\_data$: **if** $cur\_chr = 1$ **then**
    begin init $new\_patterns$; **goto** $done$; **tini**
    $print\_err(\texttt{"Patterns␣can␣be␣loaded␣only␣by␣INITEX"})$; $help0$; $error$;
    repeat get_token;
    until $cur\_cmd = right\_brace$; { flush the patterns }
    return;
    end
  else begin $new\_hyph\_exceptions$; **goto** $done$;
    end;

1253. All of TEX's parameters are kept in $eqtb$ except the font information, the interaction mode, and the hyphenation tables; these are strictly global.

⟨ Assignments 1217 ⟩ +≡
$assign\_font\_dimen$: **begin** $find\_font\_dimen(true)$; $k \leftarrow cur\_val$; $scan\_optional\_equals$;
  $scan\_normal\_dimen$; $font\_info[k].sc \leftarrow cur\_val$;
  end;
$assign\_font\_int$: **begin** $n \leftarrow cur\_chr$; $scan\_font\_ident$; $f \leftarrow cur\_val$; $scan\_optional\_equals$; $scan\_int$;
  if $n = 0$ **then** $hyphen\_char[f] \leftarrow cur\_val$ **else** $skew\_char[f] \leftarrow cur\_val$;
  end;

1254. ⟨ Put each of TEX's primitives into the hash table 226 ⟩ +≡
  $primitive(\texttt{"hyphenchar"}, assign\_font\_int, 0)$; $primitive(\texttt{"skewchar"}, assign\_font\_int, 1)$;

1255. ⟨ Cases of $print\_cmd\_chr$ for symbolic printing of primitives 227 ⟩ +≡
$assign\_font\_int$: **if** $chr\_code = 0$ **then** $print\_esc(\texttt{"hyphenchar"})$
  else $print\_esc(\texttt{"skewchar"})$;

1256. Here is where the information for a new font gets loaded.

⟨ Assignments 1217 ⟩ +≡
def_font: $new\_font(a)$;

1257. ⟨ Declare subprocedures for $prefixed\_command$ 1215 ⟩ +≡
procedure $new\_font(a : small\_number)$;
  label $common\_ending$;
  var u: $pointer$; { user's font identifier }
    s: $scaled$; { stated "at" size, or negative of scaled magnification }

f: *internal_font_number*;   { runs through existing fonts }
t: *str_number*;   { name for the frozen font identifier }
old_setting: $0 .. max\_selector$;   { holds *selector* setting }
begin if *job_name* $= 0$ **then** *open_log_file*;   { avoid confusing texput with the font name }
get_r_token; $u \leftarrow cur\_cs$;
if $u \geq hash\_base$ **then** $t \leftarrow text(u)$
else if $u \geq single\_base$ **then**
      if $u = null\_cs$ **then** $t \leftarrow$ "FONT" **else** $t \leftarrow u - single\_base$
    else begin *old_setting* $\leftarrow$ *selector*; *selector* $\leftarrow$ *new_string*; *print*("FONT"); *print*($u - active\_base$);
        selector $\leftarrow$ *old_setting*; *str_room*(1); $t \leftarrow$ *make_string*;
    end;
define($u, set\_font, null\_font$); *scan_optional_equals*; *scan_file_name*;
⟨ Scan the font size specification 1258 ⟩;
⟨ If this font has already been loaded, set f to the internal font number and **goto** *common_ending* 1260 ⟩;
$f \leftarrow$ *read_font_info*(u, cur_name, cur_area, s);
common_ending: *equiv*(u) $\leftarrow f$; *eqtb*[*font_id_base* $+ f$] $\leftarrow$ *eqtb*[u]; *font_id_text*(f) $\leftarrow t$;
  end;

---

a: *small_number*, §1211.
active_base $= 1$, §222.
assign_font_dimen $= 76$, §209.
assign_font_int $= 77$, §209.
bad: *integer*, §13.
chr_code: *halfword*, §298.
common_ending $= 50$, §15.
cur_area: *str_number*, §512.
cur_chr: *halfword*, §297.
cur_cmd: *eight_bits*, §297.
cur_cs: *pointer*, §297.
cur_name: *str_number*, §512.
cur_val: *integer*, §410.
def_font $= 87$, §209.
define = macro, §1214.
done $= 30$, §15.
eqtb: **array**, §253.
equiv = macro, §221.
error: **procedure**, §82.
f: *internal_font_number*, §1211.
find_font_dimen: **procedure**, §578.
font_id_base $= 2368$, §222.
font_id_text = macro, §256.
font_info: **array**, §549.
get_node: **function**, §125.

get_r_token: **procedure**, §1215.
get_token: **procedure**, §365.
hash_base $= 258$, §222.
help0 = macro, §79.
hyph_data $= 98$, §209.
hyphen_char: **array**, §549.
info = macro, §118.
internal_font_number $= 0 .. font\_max$,
  §548.
job_name: *str_number*, §527.
k: $0 .. font\_mem\_size$, §1211.
make_string: **function**, §43.
max_halfword = macro, §110.
max_selector $= 21$, §54.
mem_min = **const**, §11.
mem_top = macro, §12.
n: *integer*, §1211.
new_hyph_exceptions: **procedure**,
  §934.
new_patterns: **procedure**, §960.
new_string $= 21$, §54.
null_cs $= 257$, §222.
null_font = macro, §232.
open_log_file: **procedure**, §534.
par_shape_ptr = macro, §230.

pointer = macro, §115.
primitive: **procedure**, §264.
print: **procedure**, §59.
print_cmd_chr: **procedure**, §298.
print_err = macro, §73.
print_esc: **procedure**, §63.
read_font_info: **function**, §560.
right_brace $= 2$, §207.
sc = macro, §113.
scaled = *integer*, §101.
scan_file_name: **procedure**, §526.
scan_font_ident: **procedure**, §577.
scan_int: **procedure**, §440.
scan_normal_dimen = macro, §448.
scan_optional_equals: **procedure**,
  §405.
selector: $0 .. 21$, §54.
set_font $= 86$, §209.
single_base $= 129$, §222.
skew_char: **array**, §549.
small_number $= 0 .. 63$, §101.
str_number $= 0 .. max\_strings$, §38.
str_room = macro, §42.
text = macro, §256.

1258. ⟨ Scan the font size specification 1258 ⟩ ≡
  name_in_progress ← *true*;   { this keeps *cur_name* from being changed }
  if *scan_keyword*("at") **then** ⟨ Put the (positive) 'at' size into *s* 1259 ⟩
  else if *scan_keyword*("scaled") **then**
      begin *scan_int*; *s* ← −*cur_val*;
      if (*cur_val* ≤ 0) ∨ (*cur_val* > 32768) **then**
        begin *print_err*("Illegal␣magnification␣has␣been␣changed␣to␣1000");
        help1("The␣magnification␣ratio␣must␣be␣between␣1␣and␣32768."); *int_error*(*cur_val*);
        s ← −1000;
        end;
      end
    else *s* ← −1000;
  name_in_progress ← *false*

This code is used in section 1257.

1259. ⟨ Put the (positive) 'at' size into *s* 1259 ⟩ ≡
  begin *scan_normal_dimen*; *s* ← *cur_val*;
  if ($s \le 0$) ∨ ($s \ge$ ′1000000000) **then**
    begin *print_err*("Improper␣`at`␣size␣("); *print_scaled*(*s*); *print*("pt"),␣replaced␣by␣10pt");
    help2("I␣can␣only␣handle␣fonts␣at␣positive␣sizes␣that␣are")
    ("less␣than␣2048pt,␣so␣I´ve␣changed␣what␣you␣said␣to␣10pt."); *error*; *s* ← 10 ∗ *unity*;
    end;
  end

This code is used in section 1258.

1260. When the user gives a new identifier to a font that was previously loaded, the new name becomes the font identifier of record. Font names 'xyz' and 'XYZ' are considered to be different.
⟨ If this font has already been loaded, set *f* to the internal font number and **goto** *common_ending* 1260 ⟩ ≡
  for *f* ← *font_base* + 1 **to** *font_ptr* **do**
    if *str_eq_str*(*font_name*[*f*], *cur_name*) ∧ *str_eq_str*(*font_area*[*f*], *cur_area*) **then**
      begin if *s* > 0 **then**
        begin if *s* = *font_size*[*f*] **then goto** *common_ending*;
        end
      else if *font_size*[*f*] = *xn_over_d*(*font_dsize*[*f*], −*s*, 1000) **then goto** *common_ending*;
      end

This code is used in section 1257.

1261. ⟨ Cases of *print_cmd_chr* for symbolic printing of primitives 227 ⟩ +≡
  set_font: **begin** *print*("select␣font␣"); *print*(*font_name*[*chr_code*]);
    if *font_size*[*chr_code*] ≠ *font_dsize*[*chr_code*] **then**
      begin *print*("␣at␣"); *print_scaled*(*font_size*[*chr_code*]); *print*("pt");
      end;
    end;

1262. ⟨ Put each of TeX's primitives into the hash table 226 ⟩ +≡
  primitive("batchmode", *set_interaction*, *batch_mode*);
  primitive("nonstopmode", *set_interaction*, *nonstop_mode*);
  primitive("scrollmode", *set_interaction*, *scroll_mode*);
  primitive("errorstopmode", *set_interaction*, *error_stop_mode*);

1263. ⟨ Cases of *print_cmd_chr* for symbolic printing of primitives 227 ⟩ +≡
set_interaction: **case** *chr_code* **of**
  batch_mode: *print_esc*("batchmode");
  nonstop_mode: *print_esc*("nonstopmode");
  scroll_mode: *print_esc*("scrollmode");
  othercases *print_esc*("errorstopmode")
  endcases;

1264. ⟨ Assignments 1217 ⟩ +≡
set_interaction: *new_interaction*;

1265. ⟨ Declare subprocedures for *prefixed_command* 1215 ⟩ +≡
procedure *new_interaction*;
  begin *print_ln*; *interaction* ← *cur_chr*; ⟨ Initialize the print *selector* based on *interaction* 75 ⟩;
  if *job_name* ≠ 0 **then** *selector* ← *selector* + 2;
  end;

1266. The \afterassignment command puts a token into the global variable *after_token*. This global variable is examined just after every assignment has been performed.

⟨ Global variables 13 ⟩ +≡
after_token: *halfword*;   { zero, or a saved token }

1267. ⟨ Set initial values of key variables 21 ⟩ +≡
  after_token ← 0;

1268. ⟨ Cases of *main_control* that don't depend on *mode* 1210 ⟩ +≡
any_mode(*after_assignment*): **begin** *get_token*; *after_token* ← *cur_tok*;
  end;

1269. ⟨ Insert a token saved by \afterassignment, if any 1269 ⟩ ≡
  if *after_token* ≠ 0 **then**
    begin *cur_tok* ← *after_token*; *back_input*; *after_token* ← 0;
    end
This code is used in section 1211.

---

after_assignment = 40, §208.
any_mode = macro, §1045.
back_input: **procedure**, §325.
batch_mode = 0, §73.
chr_code: *halfword*, §298.
common_ending = 50, §15.
cur_area: *str_number*, §512.
cur_chr: *halfword*, §297.
cur_name: *str_number*, §512.
cur_tok: *halfword*, §297.
cur_val: *integer*, §410.
error: **procedure**, §82.
error_stop_mode = 3, §73.
f: *internal_font_number*, §1257.
font_area: **array**, §549.
font_base = 0, §12.
font_dsize: **array**, §549.

font_name: **array**, §549.
font_ptr: *internal_font_number*, §549.
font_size: **array**, §549.
get_token: **procedure**, §365.
halfword = *min_halfword* .. *max_halfword*, §113.
help1 = macro, §79.
help2 = macro, §79.
int_error: **procedure**, §91.
interaction: 0 .. 3, §73.
job_name: *str_number*, §527.
main_control: **procedure**, §1030.
mode = macro, §213.
name_in_progress: *boolean*, §527.
nonstop_mode = 1, §73.
primitive: **procedure**, §264.

print: **procedure**, §59.
print_cmd_chr: **procedure**, §298.
print_err = macro, §73.
print_esc: **procedure**, §63.
print_ln: **procedure**, §57.
print_scaled: **procedure**, §103.
s: *scaled*, §1257.
scan_int: **procedure**, §440.
scan_keyword: **function**, §407.
scan_normal_dimen = macro, §448.
scroll_mode = 2, §73.
selector: 0 .. 21, §54.
set_font = 86, §209.
set_interaction = 99, §209.
str_eq_str: **function**, §46.
unity = macro, §101.
xn_over_d: **function**, §107.

1270.   Here is a procedure that might be called 'Get the next non-blank non-relax non-call non-assignment token'.

⟨ Declare action procedures for use by *main_control* 1043 ⟩ +≡
procedure *do_assignments*;
  label *exit*;
  begin loop
    begin ⟨ Get the next non-blank non-relax non-call token 404 ⟩;
    if *cur_cmd* ≤ *max_non_prefixed_command* **then return**;
    prefixed_command;
    end;
exit: **end**;

1271.   ⟨ Cases of *main_control* that don't depend on *mode* 1210 ⟩ +≡
any_mode(*after_group*): **begin** *get_token*; *save_for_after*(*cur_tok*);
  end;

1272.   Files for \read are opened and closed by the *in_stream* command.

⟨ Put each of TEX's primitives into the hash table 226 ⟩ +≡
  primitive("openin", *in_stream*, 1); *primitive*("closein", *in_stream*, 0);

1273.   ⟨ Cases of *print_cmd_chr* for symbolic printing of primitives 227 ⟩ +≡
in_stream: **if** *chr_code* = 0 **then** *print_esc*("closein")
  else *print_esc*("openin");

1274.   ⟨ Cases of *main_control* that don't depend on *mode* 1210 ⟩ +≡
any_mode(*in_stream*): *open_or_close_in*;

1275.   ⟨ Declare action procedures for use by *main_control* 1043 ⟩ +≡
procedure *open_or_close_in*;
  var *c*: 0 .. 1;   { 1 for \openin, 0 for \closein }
    n: 0 .. 15;   { stream number }
  begin *c* ← *cur_chr*; *scan_four_bit_int*; *n* ← *cur_val*;
  if *read_open*[*n*] ≠ *closed* **then**
    begin *a_close*(*read_file*[*n*]); *read_open*[*n*] ← *closed*;
    end;
  if *c* ≠ 0 **then**
    begin *scan_optional_equals*; *scan_file_name*;
    if *cur_ext* = "" **then** *cur_ext* ← ".tex";
    pack_cur_name;
    if *a_open_in*(*read_file*[*n*]) **then** *read_open*[*n*] ← *just_open*;
    end;
  end;

1276.   The user can issue messages to the terminal, regardless of the current mode.

⟨ Cases of *main_control* that don't depend on *mode* 1210 ⟩ +≡
any_mode(*message*): *issue_message*;

1277.   ⟨ Put each of TEX's primitives into the hash table 226 ⟩ +≡
  primitive("message", *message*, 0); *primitive*("errmessage", *message*, 1);

1278. ⟨ Cases of *print_cmd_chr* for symbolic printing of primitives 227 ⟩ +≡
message: **if** *chr_code* = 0 **then** *print_esc*("message")
    else *print_esc*("errmessage");

1279. ⟨ Declare action procedures for use by *main_control* 1043 ⟩ +≡
procedure *issue_message*;
    var *old_setting*: 0 .. *max_selector*;   { holds *selector* setting }
        c: 0 .. 1;   { identifies \message and \errmessage }
        s: *str_number*;   { the message }
    begin *c* ← *cur_chr*; *link*(*garbage*) ← *scan_toks*(*false*, *true*); *old_setting* ← *selector*;
    selector ← *new_string*; *token_show*(*def_ref*); *selector* ← *old_setting*; *flush_list*(*def_ref*); *str_room*(1);
    s ← *make_string*;
    if *c* = 0 **then** ⟨ Print string *s* on the terminal 1280 ⟩
    else ⟨ Print string *s* as an error message 1283 ⟩;
    flush_string;
    end;

1280. ⟨ Print string *s* on the terminal 1280 ⟩ ≡
    begin if *term_offset* + *length*(*s*) > *max_print_line* − 2 **then** *print_ln*
    else if (*term_offset* > 0) ∨ (*file_offset* > 0) **then** *print_char*("␣");
    print(*s*); *update_terminal*;
    end
This code is used in section 1279.

1281. If \errmessage occurs often in *scroll_mode*, without user-defined \errhelp, we don't want to give a long help message each time. So we give a verbose explanation only once.
⟨ Global variables 13 ⟩ +≡
long_help_seen: *boolean*;   { has the long \errmessage help been used? }

1282. ⟨ Set initial values of key variables 21 ⟩ +≡
    long_help_seen ← *false*;

---

a_close: **procedure**, §28.
a_open_in: **function**, §27.
after_group = 41, §208.
any_mode = macro, §1045.
chr_code: *halfword*, §298.
closed = 2, §480.
cur_chr: *halfword*, §297.
cur_cmd: *eight_bits*, §297.
cur_ext: *str_number*, §512.
cur_tok: *halfword*, §297.
cur_val: *integer*, §410.
def_ref: *pointer*, §305.
exit = 10, §15.
file_offset: 0 .. *max_print_line*, §54.
flush_list: **procedure**, §123.
flush_string = macro, §44.
garbage = macro, §162.
get_token: **procedure**, §365.

in_stream = 60, §208.
just_open = 1, §480.
length = macro, §40.
link = macro, §118.
main_control: **procedure**, §1030.
make_string: **function**, §43.
max_non_prefixed_command = 69, §208.
max_print_line = **const**, §11.
max_selector = 21, §54.
message = 58, §208.
mode = macro, §213.
new_string = 21, §54.
pack_cur_name = macro, §529.
primitive: **procedure**, §264.
print: **procedure**, §59.
print_char: **procedure**, §58.
print_cmd_chr: **procedure**, §298.

print_esc: **procedure**, §63.
print_ln: **procedure**, §57.
read_file: **array**, §480.
read_open: **array**, §480.
save_for_after: **procedure**, §280.
scan_file_name: **procedure**, §526.
scan_four_bit_int: **procedure**, §434.
scan_optional_equals: **procedure**, §405.
scan_toks: **function**, §473.
scroll_mode = 2, §73.
selector: 0 .. 21, §54.
str_number = 0 .. *max_strings*, §38.
str_room = macro, §42.
term_offset: 0 .. *max_print_line*, §54.
token_show: **procedure**, §295.
update_terminal = macro, §34.

1283. ⟨ Print string s as an error message 1283 ⟩ ≡
  begin *print_err*(*s*);
  if *err_help* ≠ *null* **then** *use_err_help* ← *true*
  else if *long_help_seen* **then** *help1*("(That␣was␣another␣\errmessage.)")
    else begin if *interaction* < *error_stop_mode* **then** *long_help_seen* ← *true*;
      help4("This␣error␣message␣was␣generated␣by␣an␣\errmessage")
      ("command,␣so␣I␣can´t␣give␣any␣explicit␣help.")
      ("Pretend␣that␣you´re␣Hercule␣Poirot,␣examine␣all␣clues,")
      ("and␣deduce␣the␣truth␣by␣order␣and␣method.");
      end;
  error; *use_err_help* ← *false*;
  end
This code is used in section 1279.

1284. The *error* routine calls on *give_err_help* if help is requested from the *err_help* parameter.
procedure *give_err_help*;
  begin *token_show*(*err_help*);
  end;

1285. The \uppercase and \lowercase commands are implemented by building a token list and then changing the cases of the letters in it.
⟨ Cases of *main_control* that don't depend on *mode* 1210 ⟩ +≡
any_mode(*case_shift*): *shift_case*;

1286. ⟨ Put each of TEX's primitives into the hash table 226 ⟩ +≡
  primitive("lowercase", *case_shift*, *lc_code_base*); *primitive*("uppercase", *case_shift*, *uc_code_base*);

1287. ⟨ Cases of *print_cmd_chr* for symbolic printing of primitives 227 ⟩ +≡
case_shift: **if** *chr_code* = *lc_code_base* **then** *print_esc*("lowercase")
  else *print_esc*("uppercase");

1288. ⟨ Declare action procedures for use by *main_control* 1043 ⟩ +≡
procedure *shift_case*;
  var *b*: *pointer*; { *lc_code_base* or *uc_code_base* }
    p: *pointer*; { runs through the token list }
    t: *halfword*; { token }
    c: *eight_bits*; { character code }
  begin *b* ← *cur_chr*; *p* ← *scan_toks*(*false*, *false*); *p* ← *link*(*def_ref*);
  while *p* ≠ *null* **do**
    begin ⟨ Change the case of the token in *p*, if a change is appropriate 1289 ⟩;
    p ← *link*(*p*);
    end;
  back_list(*link*(*def_ref*)); *free_avail*(*def_ref*); { omit reference count }
  end;

1289.   When the case of a *chr_code* changes, we don't change the *cmd*. We also change active characters, using the fact that *cs_token_flag* is a multiple of 256.

⟨ Change the case of the token in *p*, if a change is appropriate 1289 ⟩ ≡
> $t \leftarrow info(p)$;
> **if** $t < cs\_token\_flag + single\_base$ **then**
> > **begin if** $t \geq cs\_token\_flag$ **then** $t \leftarrow t - active\_base$;
> > $c \leftarrow t \bmod 256$;
> > **if** $c < 128$ **then**
> > > **if** $equiv(b + c) \neq 0$ **then** $t \leftarrow 256 * (t \text{ div } 256) + equiv(b + c)$;
> > **if** $t \geq cs\_token\_flag$ **then** $info(p) \leftarrow t + active\_base$
> > **else** $info(p) \leftarrow t$;
> > **end**

This code is used in section 1288.

1290.   We come finally to the last pieces missing from *main_control*, namely the '\show' commands that are useful when debugging.

⟨ Cases of *main_control* that don't depend on *mode* 1210 ⟩ +≡
any_mode(*xray*): *show_whatever*;

1291.   **define** *show_code* = 0   { \show }
> **define** *show_box_code* = 1   { \showbox }
> **define** *show_the_code* = 2   { \showthe }
> **define** *show_lists* = 3   { \showlists }

⟨ Put each of TeX's primitives into the hash table 226 ⟩ +≡
> *primitive*("show", *xray*, *show_code*); *primitive*("showbox", *xray*, *show_box_code*);
> *primitive*("showthe", *xray*, *show_the_code*); *primitive*("showlists", *xray*, *show_lists*);

1292.   ⟨ Cases of *print_cmd_chr* for symbolic printing of primitives 227 ⟩ +≡
xray: **case** *chr_code* **of**
> *show_box_code*: *print_esc*("showbox");
> *show_the_code*: *print_esc*("showthe");
> *show_lists*: *print_esc*("showlists");
> **othercases** *print_esc*("show")
> **endcases**;

---

active_base = 1, §222.
any_mode = macro, §1045.
back_list = macro, §323.
case_shift = 57, §208.
chr_code: *halfword*, §298.
cmd: *quarterword*, §298.
cs_token_flag = macro, §289.
cur_chr: *halfword*, §297.
def_ref: *pointer*, §305.
eight_bits = 0 . . 255, §25.
equiv = macro, §221.
err_help = macro, §230.
error: **procedure**, §82.
error_stop_mode = 3, §73.

free_avail = macro, §121.
halfword = *min_halfword* . .
   max_halfword, §113.
help1 = macro, §79.
help4 = macro, §79.
info = macro, §118.
interaction: 0 . . 3, §73.
lc_code_base = 3855, §230.
link = macro, §118.
long_help_seen: *boolean*, §1281.
main_control: **procedure**, §1030.
mode = macro, §213.
null = macro, §115.

pointer = macro, §115.
primitive: **procedure**, §264.
print_cmd_chr: **procedure**, §298.
print_err = macro, §73.
print_esc: **procedure**, §63.
s: *str_number*, §1279.
scan_toks: **function**, §473.
show_whatever: **procedure**, §1293.
single_base = 129, §222.
token_show: **procedure**, §295.
uc_code_base = 3983, §230.
use_err_help: *boolean*, §79.
xray = 19, §208.

1293. ⟨ Declare action procedures for use by *main_control* 1043 ⟩ +≡
procedure *show_whatever*;
  label *common_ending*;
  var *p*: *pointer*;   { tail of a token list to show }
  begin case *cur_chr* **of**
  show_lists: **begin** *begin_diagnostic*; *show_activities*;
    end;
  show_box_code: ⟨ Show the current contents of a box 1296 ⟩;
  show_code: ⟨ Show the current meaning of a token, then **goto** *common_ending* 1294 ⟩;
  othercases ⟨ Show the current value of some parameter or register, then **goto** *common_ending* 1297 ⟩
  endcases;
  ⟨ Complete a potentially long \show command 1298 ⟩;
common_ending: **if** *interaction* < *error_stop_mode* **then**
    begin *help0*; *decr*(*error_count*);
    end
  else if *tracing_online* > 0 **then**
    begin
    help3("This␣isn´t␣an␣error␣message;␣I´m␣just␣\showing␣something.")
    ("Type␣`I\show...´␣to␣show␣more␣(e.g.,␣\show\cs,")
    ("\showthe\count10,␣\showbox255,␣\showlists).");
    end
  else begin
    help5("This␣isn´t␣an␣error␣message;␣I´m␣just␣\showing␣something.")
    ("Type␣`I\show...´␣to␣show␣more␣(e.g.,␣\show\cs,")
    ("\showthe\count10,␣\showbox255,␣\showlists).")
    ("And␣type␣`I\tracingonline=1\show...´␣to␣show␣boxes␣and")
    ("lists␣on␣your␣terminal␣as␣well␣as␣in␣the␣transcript␣file.");
    end;
  error;
  end;

1294. ⟨ Show the current meaning of a token, then **goto** *common_ending* 1294 ⟩ ≡
  begin *get_token*;
  if *interaction* = *error_stop_mode* **then** *wake_up_terminal*;
  print_nl(">␣");
  if *cur_cs* ≠ 0 **then**
    begin *sprint_cs*(*cur_cs*); *print_char*("=");
    end;
  print_meaning; **goto** *common_ending*;
  end
This code is used in section 1293.

1295. ⟨Cases of *print_cmd_chr* for symbolic printing of primitives 227⟩ +≡
undefined_cs: *print*("undefined");
call: *print*("macro");
long_call: *print_esc*("long␣macro");
outer_call: *print_esc*("outer␣macro");
long_outer_call: **begin** *print_esc*("long"); *print_esc*("outer␣macro");
  end;
end_template: *print_esc*("outer␣endtemplate");

1296. ⟨Show the current contents of a box 1296⟩ ≡
  begin *scan_eight_bit_int*; *begin_diagnostic*; *print_nl*(">␣\box"); *print_int*(*cur_val*); *print_char*("=");
  if *box*(*cur_val*) = *null* **then** *print*("void")
  else *show_box*(*box*(*cur_val*));
  end

This code is used in section 1293.

1297. ⟨Show the current value of some parameter or register, then **goto** *common_ending* 1297⟩ ≡
  begin *p* ← *the_toks*;
  if *interaction* = *error_stop_mode* **then** *wake_up_terminal*;
  print_nl(">␣"); *token_show*(*temp_head*); *flush_list*(*link*(*temp_head*)); **goto** *common_ending*;
  end

This code is used in section 1293.

1298. ⟨Complete a potentially long \show command 1298⟩ ≡
  end_diagnostic(*true*); *print_err*("OK");
  if *selector* = *term_and_log* **then**
    if *tracing_online* ≤ 0 **then**
      begin *selector* ← *term_only*; *print*("␣(see␣the␣transcript␣file)"); *selector* ← *term_and_log*;
      end

This code is used in section 1293.

1299.   Dumping and undumping the tables.   After INITEX has seen a collection of fonts and macros, it can write all the necessary information on an auxiliary file so that production versions of TeX are able to initialize their memory at high speed. The present section of the program takes care of such output and input. We shall consider simultaneously the processes of storing and restoring, so that the inverse relation between them is clear.

The global variable *format_ident* is a string that is printed right after the *banner* line when TeX is ready to start. For INITEX this string says simply '(INITEX)'; for other versions of TeX it says, for example, '(preloaded format=plain 82.11.19)', showing the year, month, and day that the format file was created. We have *format_ident* = 0 before TeX's tables are loaded.

⟨ Global variables 13 ⟩ +≡
format_ident: *str_number*;

1300.   ⟨ Set initial values of key variables 21 ⟩ +≡
format_ident ← 0;

1301.   ⟨ Initialize table entries (done by INITEX only) 164 ⟩ +≡
format_ident ← "␣(INITEX)";

1302.   ⟨ Declare action procedures for use by *main_control* 1043 ⟩ +≡
init procedure *store_fmt_file*;
label *found1*, *found2*, *done1*, *done2*;
var *j*, *k*, *l*: *integer*;   { all-purpose indices }
   p, *q*: *pointer*;   { all-purpose pointers }
   x: *integer*;   { something to dump }
   w: *four_quarters*;   { four ASCII codes }
begin ⟨ If dumping is not allowed, abort 1304 ⟩;
⟨ Create the *format_ident*, open the format file, and inform the user that dumping has begun 1328 ⟩;
⟨ Dump constants for consistency check 1307 ⟩;
⟨ Dump the string pool 1309 ⟩;
⟨ Dump the dynamic memory 1311 ⟩;
⟨ Dump the table of equivalents 1313 ⟩;
⟨ Dump the font information 1320 ⟩;
⟨ Dump the hyphenation tables 1324 ⟩;
⟨ Dump a couple more things and the closing check word 1326 ⟩;
⟨ Close the format file 1329 ⟩;
end;
tini

1303.   Corresponding to the procedure that dumps a format file, we have a function that reads one in. The function returns *false* if the dumped format is incompatible with the present TeX table sizes, etc.

define *bad_fmt* = 6666   { go here if the format file is unacceptable }
define *too_small*(#) ≡
         begin *wake_up_terminal*; *wterm_ln*(´---!␣Must␣increase␣the␣´, #); **goto** *bad_fmt*;
         end
⟨ Declare the function called *open_fmt_file* 524 ⟩
function *load_fmt_file*: *boolean*;
   label *bad_fmt*, *exit*;

> **var** j, k: *integer*;   { all-purpose indices }
> p, q: *pointer*;   { all-purpose pointers }
> x: *integer*;   { something undumped }
> w: *four_quarters*;   { four ASCII codes }
> **begin** ⟨ Undump constants for consistency check 1308 ⟩;
> ⟨ Undump the string pool 1310 ⟩;
> ⟨ Undump the dynamic memory 1312 ⟩;
> ⟨ Undump the table of equivalents 1314 ⟩;
> ⟨ Undump the font information 1321 ⟩;
> ⟨ Undump the hyphenation tables 1325 ⟩;
> ⟨ Undump a couple more things and the closing check word 1327 ⟩;
> $load\_fmt\_file \leftarrow true$; **return**;   { it worked! }
> *bad_fmt*: *wake_up_terminal*; *wterm_ln*(´(Fatal␣format␣file␣error;␣I´´m␣stymied)´);
> $load\_fmt\_file \leftarrow false$;
> *exit*: **end**;

1304. The user is not allowed to dump a format file unless $save\_ptr = 0$. This condition implies that $cur\_level = level\_one$, hence the xeq_level array is constant and it need not be dumped.

⟨ If dumping is not allowed, abort 1304 ⟩ ≡
> **if** $save\_ptr \neq 0$ **then**
>   **begin** *print_err*("You␣can´t␣dump␣inside␣a␣group"); *help1*("`{...\dump}´␣is␣a␣no-no.");
>   *succumb*;
>   **end**

This code is used in section 1302.

1305. Format files consist of *memory_word* items, and we use the following macros to dump words of different types:

> **define** $dump\_wd$(#) ≡
>   **begin** $fmt\_file\uparrow \leftarrow$ **#**; put(*fmt_file*); **end**
> **define** $dump\_int$(#) ≡
>   **begin** $fmt\_file\uparrow.int \leftarrow$ **#**; put(*fmt_file*); **end**
> **define** $dump\_hh$(#) ≡
>   **begin** $fmt\_file\uparrow.hh \leftarrow$ **#**; put(*fmt_file*); **end**
> **define** $dump\_qqqq$(#) ≡
>   **begin** $fmt\_file\uparrow.qqqq \leftarrow$ **#**; put(*fmt_file*); **end**

⟨ Global variables 13 ⟩ +≡
fmt_file: *word_file*;   { for input or output of format information }

---

banner = macro, §2.
cur_level: *quarterword*, §271.
done1 = 31, §15.
done2 = 32, §15.
exit = 10, §15.
found1 = 41, §15.
found2 = 42, §15.
four_quarters = **packed record**, §113.

help1 = macro, §79.
hh: *two_halves*, §113.
int: *integer*, §113.
level_one = 1, §221.
main_control: **procedure**, §1030.
memory_word = **record**, §113.
open_fmt_file: **function**, §524.
pointer = macro, §115.
print_err = macro, §73.

qqqq: *four_quarters*, §113.
save_ptr: 0 .. *save_size*, §271.
str_number = 0 .. *max_strings*, §38.
succumb = macro, §93.
wake_up_terminal = macro, §34.
word_file = **file**, §113.
wterm_ln = macro, §56.
xeq_level: **array**, §253.

1306. The inverse macros are slightly more complicated, since we need to check the range of the values we are reading in. We say '*undump*(a)(b)(x)' to read an integer value x that is supposed to be in the range $a \le x \le b$.

> **define** *undump_wd*(#) ≡
>   **begin** *get*(*fmt_file*); # ← *fmt_file*↑; **end**
> **define** *undump_int*(#) ≡
>   **begin** *get*(*fmt_file*); # ← *fmt_file*↑.*int*; **end**
> **define** *undump_hh*(#) ≡
>   **begin** *get*(*fmt_file*); # ← *fmt_file*↑.*hh*; **end**
> **define** *undump_qqqq*(#) ≡
>   **begin** *get*(*fmt_file*); # ← *fmt_file*↑.*qqqq*; **end**
> **define** *undump_end_end*(#) ≡ # ← *x*; **end**
> **define** *undump_end*(#) ≡ (*x* > #) **then goto** *bad_fmt* **else** *undump_end_end*
> **define** *undump*(#) ≡
>   **begin** *undump_int*(*x*);
>   **if** (*x* < #) ∨ *undump_end*
> **define** *undump_size_end_end*(#) ≡ *too_small*(#) **else** *undump_end_end*
> **define** *undump_size_end*(#) ≡
>   **if** *x* > # **then** *undump_size_end_end*
> **define** *undump_size*(#) ≡
>   **begin** *undump_int*(*x*);
>   **if** *x* < # **then goto** *bad_fmt*;
>   *undump_size_end*

1307. The next few sections of the program should make it clear how we use the dump/undump macros.

⟨ Dump constants for consistency check 1307 ⟩ ≡
  dump_int(@$);
  dump_int(*mem_bot*);
  dump_int(*mem_top*);
  dump_int(*eqtb_size*);
  dump_int(*hash_prime*);
  dump_int(*hyph_size*)

This code is used in section 1302.

1308. Sections of a WEB program that are "commented out" still contribute strings to the string pool; therefore INITEX and TEX will have the same strings. (And it is, of course, a good thing that they do.)

⟨ Undump constants for consistency check 1308 ⟩ ≡
  x ← *fmt_file*↑.*int*;
  if *x* ≠ @$ **then goto** *bad_fmt*;   { check that strings are the same }
  undump_int(*x*);
  if *x* ≠ *mem_bot* **then goto** *bad_fmt*;
  undump_int(*x*);
  if *x* ≠ *mem_top* **then goto** *bad_fmt*;
  undump_int(*x*);
  if *x* ≠ *eqtb_size* **then goto** *bad_fmt*;

$undump\_int(x)$;

if $x \neq hash\_prime$ **then goto** *bad_fmt*;

$undump\_int(x)$;

if $x \neq hyph\_size$ **then goto** *bad_fmt*

This code is used in section 1303.

1309.   **define** $dump\_four\_ASCII \equiv w.b0 \leftarrow str\_pool[k]$; $w.b1 \leftarrow str\_pool[k+1]$;
$\quad\quad\quad w.b2 \leftarrow str\_pool[k+2]$; $w.b3 \leftarrow str\_pool[k+3]$; $dump\_qqqq(w)$

$\langle$ Dump the string pool 1309 $\rangle \equiv$

$\quad dump\_int(pool\_ptr)$; $dump\_int(str\_ptr)$;

$\quad$ **for** $k \leftarrow 0$ **to** str_ptr **do** $dump\_int(str\_start[k])$;

$\quad k \leftarrow 0$;

$\quad$ **while** $k + 4 < pool\_ptr$ **do**

$\quad\quad$ **begin** $dump\_four\_ASCII$; $k \leftarrow k + 4$;

$\quad\quad$ **end**;

$\quad k \leftarrow pool\_ptr - 4$; $dump\_four\_ASCII$; $print\_ln$; $print\_int(str\_ptr)$;

$\quad print(\texttt{"\_strings\_of\_total\_length\_"})$; $print\_int(pool\_ptr)$

This code is used in section 1302.

1310.   **define** $undump\_four\_ASCII \equiv undump\_qqqq(w)$; $str\_pool[k] \leftarrow w.b0$; $str\_pool[k+1] \leftarrow w.b1$;
$\quad\quad\quad str\_pool[k+2] \leftarrow w.b2$; $str\_pool[k+3] \leftarrow w.b3$

$\langle$ Undump the string pool 1310 $\rangle \equiv$

$\quad undump\_size(0)(pool\_size)(\texttt{\`{}string\_pool\_size\'{}})(pool\_ptr)$;

$\quad undump\_size(0)(max\_strings)(\texttt{\`{}max\_strings\'{}})(str\_ptr)$;

$\quad$ **for** $k \leftarrow 0$ **to** str_ptr **do** $undump(0)(pool\_ptr)(str\_start[k])$;

$\quad k \leftarrow 0$;

$\quad$ **while** $k + 4 < pool\_ptr$ **do**

$\quad\quad$ **begin** $undump\_four\_ASCII$; $k \leftarrow k + 4$;

$\quad\quad$ **end**;

$\quad k \leftarrow pool\_ptr - 4$; $undump\_four\_ASCII$

This code is used in section 1303.

$b0$: *quarterword*, §113.
$b1$: *quarterword*, §113.
$b2$: *quarterword*, §113.
$b3$: *quarterword*, §113.
bad_fmt = 6666, §1303.
$dump\_int$ = macro, §1305.
$dump\_qqqq$ = macro, §1305.
$eqtb\_size$ = 5076, §247.
fmt_file: *word_file*, §1305.
hash_prime = 1777, §12.
hh: *two_halves*, §113.

hyph_size = 307, §12.
int: *integer*, §113.
k: *integer*, §1302.
k: *integer*, §1303.
max_strings = **const**, §11.
mem_bot = 0, §12.
mem_top = macro, §12.
pool_ptr: *pool_pointer*, §39.
pool_size = **const**, §11.
print: **procedure**, §59.

print_int: **procedure**, §65.
print_ln: **procedure**, §57.
qqqq: *four_quarters*, §113.
str_pool: **packed array**, §39.
str_ptr: *str_number*, §39.
str_start: **array**, §39.
too_small = macro, §1303.
w: *four_quarters*, §1302.
w: *four_quarters*, §1303.
x: *integer*, §1303.

1311.   By sorting the list of available spaces in the variable-size portion of mem, we are usually able to get by without having to dump very much of the dynamic memory.

We recompute var_used and dyn_used, so that INITEX dumps valid information even when it has not been gathering statistics.

$\langle$ Dump the dynamic memory $1311 \rangle \equiv$
   $sort\_avail$; $var\_used \leftarrow 0$; $dump\_int(lo\_mem\_max)$; $dump\_int(rover)$; $p \leftarrow mem\_bot$; $q \leftarrow rover$;
   $x \leftarrow 0$;
   repeat for $k \leftarrow p$ **to** $q + 1$ **do** $dump\_wd(mem[k])$;
     $x \leftarrow x + q + 2 - p$; $var\_used \leftarrow var\_used + q - p$; $p \leftarrow q + node\_size(q)$; $q \leftarrow rlink(q)$;
   until $q = rover$;
   $var\_used \leftarrow var\_used + lo\_mem\_max - p$; $dyn\_used \leftarrow mem\_end + 1 - hi\_mem\_min$;
   for $k \leftarrow p$ **to** lo_mem_max **do** $dump\_wd(mem[k])$;
   $x \leftarrow x + lo\_mem\_max + 1 - p$; $dump\_int(hi\_mem\_min)$; $dump\_int(avail)$;
   for $k \leftarrow hi\_mem\_min$ **to** mem_end **do** $dump\_wd(mem[k])$;
   $x \leftarrow x + mem\_end + 1 - hi\_mem\_min$; $p \leftarrow avail$;
   while $p \neq null$ **do**
     begin $decr(dyn\_used)$; $p \leftarrow link(p)$;
     end;
   $dump\_int(var\_used)$; $dump\_int(dyn\_used)$; $print\_ln$; $print\_int(x)$;
   $print("\textvisiblespace memory\textvisiblespace locations\textvisiblespace dumped;\textvisiblespace current\textvisiblespace usage\textvisiblespace is\textvisiblespace ")$; $print\_int(var\_used)$; $print\_char("\&")$;
   $print\_int(dyn\_used)$

This code is used in section 1302.

1312. $\langle$ Undump the dynamic memory $1312 \rangle \equiv$
  $undump(lo\_mem\_stat\_max + 1000)(hi\_mem\_stat\_min - 1)(lo\_mem\_max)$;
  $undump(lo\_mem\_stat\_max + 1)(lo\_mem\_max)(rover)$; $p \leftarrow mem\_bot$; $q \leftarrow rover$; $x \leftarrow 0$;
  repeat for $k \leftarrow p$ **to** $q + 1$ **do** $undump\_wd(mem[k])$;
    $p \leftarrow q + node\_size(q)$;
    if $(p > lo\_mem\_max) \lor ((q \geq rlink(q)) \land (rlink(q) \neq rover))$ **then goto** bad_fmt;
    $q \leftarrow rlink(q)$;
  until $q = rover$;
  for $k \leftarrow p$ **to** lo_mem_max **do** $undump\_wd(mem[k])$;
  if $mem\_min < mem\_bot - 2$ **then**   {make more low memory available}
    begin $p \leftarrow llink(rover)$; $q \leftarrow mem\_min + 1$; $link(mem\_min) \leftarrow null$; $info(mem\_min) \leftarrow null$;
       {we don't use the bottom word}
    $rlink(p) \leftarrow q$; $llink(rover) \leftarrow q$;
    $rlink(q) \leftarrow rover$; $llink(q) \leftarrow p$; $link(q) \leftarrow empty\_flag$; $node\_size(q) \leftarrow mem\_bot - q$;
    end;
  $undump(lo\_mem\_max + 1)(hi\_mem\_stat\_min)(hi\_mem\_min)$; $undump(null)(mem\_top)(avail)$;
  $mem\_end \leftarrow mem\_top$;
  for $k \leftarrow hi\_mem\_min$ **to** mem_end **do** $undump\_wd(mem[k])$;
  $undump\_int(var\_used)$; $undump\_int(dyn\_used)$

This code is used in section 1303.

1313.   ⟨ Dump the table of equivalents 1313 ⟩ ≡
    ⟨ Dump regions 1 to 4 of *eqtb* 1315 ⟩;
    ⟨ Dump regions 5 and 6 of *eqtb* 1316 ⟩;
    dump_int(*par_loc*); *dump_int*(*write_loc*);
    ⟨ Dump the hash table 1318 ⟩
This code is used in section 1302.

1314.   ⟨ Undump the table of equivalents 1314 ⟩ ≡
    ⟨ Undump regions 1 to 6 of *eqtb* 1317 ⟩;
    undump(*hash_base*)(*frozen_control_sequence*)(*par_loc*); *par_token* ← *cs_token_flag* + *par_loc*;
    undump(*hash_base*)(*frozen_control_sequence*)(*write_loc*);
    ⟨ Undump the hash table 1319 ⟩
This code is used in section 1303.

---

avail: *pointer*, §118.
bad_fmt = 6666, §1303.
cs_token_flag = macro, §289.
decr = macro, §16.
dump_int = macro, §1305.
dump_wd = macro, §1305.
dyn_used: *integer*, §117.
empty_flag = macro, §124.
eqtb: **array**, §253.
frozen_control_sequence = 2358, §222.
hash_base = 258, §222.
hi_mem_min: *pointer*, §116.
hi_mem_stat_min = macro, §162.
info = macro, §118.
k: *integer*, §1302.

k: *integer*, §1303.
link = macro, §118.
llink = macro, §124.
lo_mem_max: *pointer*, §116.
lo_mem_stat_max = macro, §162.
mem: **array**, §116.
mem_bot = 0, §12.
mem_end: *pointer*, §118.
mem_min = **const**, §11.
mem_top = macro, §12.
node_size = macro, §124.
null = macro, §115.
p: *pointer*, §1302.
p: *pointer*, §1303.
par_loc: *pointer*, §333.
par_token: *halfword*, §333.

print: **procedure**, §59.
print_char: **procedure**, §58.
print_int: **procedure**, §65.
print_ln: **procedure**, §57.
q: *pointer*, §1302.
q: *pointer*, §1303.
rlink = macro, §124.
rover: *pointer*, §124.
sort_avail: **procedure**, §131.
undump = macro, §1306.
undump_int = macro, §1306.
undump_wd = macro, §1306.
var_used: *integer*, §117.
write_loc: *pointer*, §1345.
x: *integer*, §1302.
x: *integer*, §1303.

1315. The table of equivalents usually contains repeated information, so we dump it in compressed form: The sequence of $n+2$ values $(n, x_1, \ldots, x_n, m)$ in the format file represents $n+m$ consecutive entries of $eqtb$, with m extra copies of x_n, namely $(x_1, \ldots, x_n, x_n, \ldots, x_n)$.

$\langle$ Dump regions 1 to 4 of $eqtb$ 1315 $\rangle \equiv$

  $k \leftarrow active\_base$;

  repeat $j \leftarrow k$;

    while $j < int\_base - 1$ **do**

      begin if $(equiv(j) = equiv(j+1)) \wedge (eq\_type(j) = eq\_type(j+1)) \wedge (eq\_level(j) = eq\_level(j+1))$

          then goto $found1$;

      $incr(j)$;

      end;

    $l \leftarrow int\_base$; **goto** $done1$; $\{ j = int\_base - 1 \}$

  $found1$: $incr(j)$; $l \leftarrow j$;

    while $j < int\_base - 1$ **do**

      begin if $(equiv(j) \neq equiv(j+1)) \vee (eq\_type(j) \neq eq\_type(j+1)) \vee (eq\_level(j) \neq eq\_level(j+1))$

          then goto $done1$;

      $incr(j)$;

      end;

  $done1$: $dump\_int(l - k)$;

    while $k < l$ **do**

      begin $dump\_wd(eqtb[k])$; $incr(k)$;

      end;

    $k \leftarrow j + 1$; $dump\_int(k - l)$;

  until $k = int\_base$

This code is used in section 1313.

1316. $\langle$ Dump regions 5 and 6 of $eqtb$ 1316 $\rangle \equiv$

  repeat $j \leftarrow k$;

    while $j < eqtb\_size$ **do**

      begin if $eqtb[j].int = eqtb[j+1].int$ **then goto** $found2$;

      $incr(j)$;

      end;

    $l \leftarrow eqtb\_size + 1$; **goto** $done2$; $\{ j = eqtb\_size \}$

  $found2$: $incr(j)$; $l \leftarrow j$;

    while $j < eqtb\_size$ **do**

      begin if $eqtb[j].int \neq eqtb[j+1].int$ **then goto** $done2$;

      $incr(j)$;

      end;

  $done2$: $dump\_int(l - k)$;

    while $k < l$ **do**

      begin $dump\_wd(eqtb[k])$; $incr(k)$;

      end;

    $k \leftarrow j + 1$; $dump\_int(k - l)$;

  until $k > eqtb\_size$

This code is used in section 1313.

1317. ⟨ Undump regions 1 to 6 of *eqtb* 1317 ⟩ ≡

  $k \leftarrow active\_base$;

  repeat *undump_int*(*x*);

    if $(x < 1) \lor (k + x > eqtb\_size + 1)$ **then goto** *bad_fmt*;

    for $j \leftarrow k$ **to** $k + x - 1$ **do** *undump_wd*(*eqtb*[*j*]);

    $k \leftarrow k + x$; *undump_int*(*x*);

    if $(x < 0) \lor (k + x > eqtb\_size + 1)$ **then goto** *bad_fmt*;

    for $j \leftarrow k$ **to** $k + x - 1$ **do** *eqtb*[*j*] $\leftarrow$ *eqtb*[*k* − 1];

    $k \leftarrow k + x$;

  until $k > eqtb\_size$

This code is used in section 1314.

1318. A different scheme is used to compress the hash table, since its lower region is usually sparse. When $text(p) \neq 0$ for $p \leq hash\_used$, we output two words, p and $hash[p]$. The hash table is, of course, densely packed for $p \geq hash\_used$, so the remaining entries are output in a block.

⟨ Dump the hash table 1318 ⟩ ≡

  dump_int(*hash_used*); $cs\_count \leftarrow frozen\_control\_sequence - 1 - hash\_used$;

  for $p \leftarrow hash\_base$ **to** *hash_used* **do**

    if $text(p) \neq 0$ **then**

      begin *dump_int*(*p*); *dump_hh*(*hash*[*p*]); *incr*(*cs_count*);

      end;

  for $p \leftarrow hash\_used + 1$ **to** $undefined\_control\_sequence - 1$ **do** *dump_hh*(*hash*[*p*]);

  dump_int(*cs_count*);

  print_ln; *print_int*(*cs_count*); *print*("␣multiletter␣control␣sequences")

This code is used in section 1313.

1319. ⟨ Undump the hash table 1319 ⟩ ≡

  undump(*hash_base*)(*frozen_control_sequence*)(*hash_used*); $p \leftarrow hash\_base - 1$;

  repeat *undump*(*p* + 1)(*hash_used*)(*p*); *undump_hh*(*hash*[*p*]);

  until $p = hash\_used$;

  for $p \leftarrow hash\_used + 1$ **to** $undefined\_control\_sequence - 1$ **do** *undump_hh*(*hash*[*p*]);

  undump_int(*cs_count*)

This code is used in section 1314.

---

active_base = 1, §222.

bad_fmt = 6666, §1303.

cs_count: *integer*, §256.

done1 = 31, §15.

done2 = 32, §15.

dump_hh = macro, §1305.

dump_int = macro, §1305.

dump_wd = macro, §1305.

eq_level = macro, §221.

eq_type = macro, §221.

eqtb: **array**, §253.

eqtb_size = 5076, §247.

equiv = macro, §221.

found1 = 41, §15.

found2 = 42, §15.

frozen_control_sequence = 2358, §222.

hash: **array**, §256.

hash_base = 258, §222.

hash_used: *pointer*, §256.

incr = macro, §16.

int: *integer*, §113.

int_base = 4367, §230.

j: *integer*, §1302.

j: *integer*, §1303.

k: *integer*, §1302.

k: *integer*, §1303.

l: *integer*, §1302.

p: *pointer*, §1302.

p: *pointer*, §1303.

print: **procedure**, §59.

print_int: **procedure**, §65.

print_ln: **procedure**, §57.

text = macro, §256.

undefined_control_sequence = 2625, §222.

undump = macro, §1306.

undump_hh = macro, §1306.

undump_int = macro, §1306.

undump_wd = macro, §1306.

x: *integer*, §1303.

1320. ⟨ Dump the font information 1320 ⟩ ≡
$dump\_int(fmem\_ptr)$;
for $k \leftarrow 0$ **to** $fmem\_ptr - 1$ **do** $dump\_wd(font\_info[k])$;
$dump\_int(font\_ptr)$;
for $k \leftarrow null\_font$ **to** $font\_ptr$ **do** ⟨ Dump the array info for internal font number k 1322 ⟩;
$print\_ln$; $print\_int(fmem\_ptr - 7)$; $print("\_words\_of\_font\_info\_for\_")$;
$print\_int(font\_ptr - font\_base)$; $print("\_preloaded\_font")$;
if $font\_ptr \neq font\_base + 1$ **then** $print\_char("s")$

This code is used in section 1: · 2.

1321. ⟨ Undump the font information 1321 ⟩ ≡
$undump\_size(7)(font\_mem\_size)(\´font\_mem\_size\´)(fmem\_ptr)$;
for $k \leftarrow 0$ **to** $fmem\_ptr - 1$ **do** $undump\_wd(font\_info[k])$;
$undump\_size(font\_base)(font\_max)(\´font\_max\´)(font\_ptr)$;
for $k \leftarrow null\_font$ **to** $font\_ptr$ **do** ⟨ Undump the array info for internal font number k 1323 ⟩

This code is used in section 1303.

1322. ⟨ Dump the array info for internal font number k 1322 ⟩ ≡
begin $dump\_qqqq(font\_check[k])$; $dump\_int(font\_size[k])$; $dump\_int(font\_dsize[k])$;
$dump\_int(font\_params[k])$;
$dump\_int(hyphen\_char[k])$; $dump\_int(skew\_char[k])$;
$dump\_int(font\_name[k])$; $dump\_int(font\_area[k])$;
$dump\_int(font\_bc[k])$; $dump\_int(font\_ec[k])$;
$dump\_int(char\_base[k])$; $dump\_int(width\_base[k])$; $dump\_int(height\_base[k])$;
$dump\_int(depth\_base[k])$; $dump\_int(italic\_base[k])$; $dump\_int(lig\_kern\_base[k])$;
$dump\_int(kern\_base[k])$; $dump\_int(exten\_base[k])$; $dump\_int(param\_base[k])$;
$dump\_int(font\_glue[k])$;
$print\_nl("\font")$; $print\_esc(font\_id\_text(k))$; $print\_char("=")$;
$print\_file\_name(font\_name[k], font\_area[k], "")$;
if $font\_size[k] \neq font\_dsize[k]$ **then**
    begin $print("\_at\_")$; $print\_scaled(font\_size[k])$; $print("pt")$;
    end;
end

This code is used in section 1320.

1323. ⟨ Undump the array info for internal font number k 1323 ⟩ ≡
begin $undump\_qqqq(font\_check[k])$;
$undump\_int(font\_size[k])$; $undump\_int(font\_dsize[k])$;
$undump(min\_halfword)(max\_halfword)(font\_params[k])$;
$undump\_int(hyphen\_char[k])$; $undump\_int(skew\_char[k])$;
$undump(0)(str\_ptr)(font\_name[k])$; $undump(0)(str\_ptr)(font\_area[k])$;
$undump(0)(255)(font\_bc[k])$; $undump(0)(255)(font\_ec[k])$;
$undump\_int(char\_base[k])$; $undump\_int(width\_base[k])$; $undump\_int(height\_base[k])$;
$undump\_int(depth\_base[k])$; $undump\_int(italic\_base[k])$; $undump\_int(lig\_kern\_base[k])$;
$undump\_int(kern\_base[k])$; $undump\_int(exten\_base[k])$; $undump\_int(param\_base[k])$;
$undump(min\_halfword)(lo\_mem\_max)(font\_glue[k])$;
end

This code is used in section 1321.

1324. ⟨ Dump the hyphenation tables 1324 ⟩ ≡

$dump\_int(hyph\_count)$;

for $k \leftarrow 0$ **to** $hyph\_size$ **do**

  if $hyph\_word[k] \neq 0$ **then**

    begin $dump\_int(k)$; $dump\_int(hyph\_word[k])$; $dump\_int(hyph\_list[k])$;

    end;

$dump\_int(trie\_max)$;

for $k \leftarrow 0$ **to** $trie\_max$ **do** $dump\_hh(trie[k])$;

$dump\_int(trie\_op\_ptr)$;

for $k \leftarrow min\_quarterword + 1$ **to** $trie\_op\_ptr$ **do**

  begin $dump\_int(hyf\_distance[k])$; $dump\_int(hyf\_num[k])$; $dump\_int(hyf\_next[k])$;

  end;

$print\_ln$; $print\_int(hyph\_count)$; $print("\textvisiblespace hyphenation\textvisiblespace exception")$;

if $hyph\_count \neq 1$ **then** $print\_char("s")$;

$print\_nl("Hyphenation\textvisiblespace trie\textvisiblespace of\textvisiblespace length\textvisiblespace ")$; $print\_int(trie\_max)$; $print("\textvisiblespace has\textvisiblespace ")$;

$print\_int(qo(trie\_op\_ptr))$; $print("\textvisiblespace op")$;

if $trie\_op\_ptr \neq min\_quarterword + 1$ **then** $print\_char("s")$

This code is used in section 1302.

$char\_base$: **array**, §550.
$depth\_base$: **array**, §550.
$dump\_hh$ = macro, §1305.
$dump\_int$ = macro, §1305.
$dump\_qqqq$ = macro, §1305.
$dump\_wd$ = macro, §1305.
$exten\_base$: **array**, §550.
$fmem\_ptr$: $0 .. font\_mem\_size$, §549.
$font\_area$: **array**, §549.
$font\_base = 0$, §12.
$font\_bc$: **array**, §549.
$font\_check$: **array**, §549.
$font\_dsize$: **array**, §549.
$font\_ec$: **array**, §549.
$font\_glue$: **array**, §549.
$font\_id\_text$ = macro, §256.
$font\_info$: **array**, §549.
$font\_max$ = **const**, §11.
$font\_mem\_size$ = **const**, §11.
$font\_name$: **array**, §549.
$font\_params$: **array**, §549.
$font\_ptr$: $internal\_font\_number$,

§549.
$font\_size$: **array**, §549.
$height\_base$: **array**, §550.
$hyf\_distance$: **array**, §921.
hyf_next: **array**, §921.
hyf_num: **array**, §921.
$hyph\_count$: $hyph\_pointer$, §926.
$hyph\_list$: **array**, §926.
$hyph\_size = 307$, §12.
$hyph\_word$: **array**, §926.
$hyphen\_char$: **array**, §549.
$italic\_base$: **array**, §550.
k: $integer$, §1302.
k: $integer$, §1303.
$kern\_base$: **array**, §550.
lig_kern_base: **array**, §550.
lo_mem_max: $pointer$, §116.
$max\_halfword$ = macro, §110.
$min\_halfword$ = macro, §110.
$min\_quarterword = 0$, §110.
$null\_font$ = macro, §232.

$param\_base$: **array**, §550.
$print$: **procedure**, §59.
$print\_char$: **procedure**, §58.
$print\_esc$: **procedure**, §63.
$print\_file\_name$: **procedure**, §518.
$print\_int$: **procedure**, §65.
$print\_ln$: **procedure**, §57.
$print\_nl$: **procedure**, §62.
$print\_scaled$: **procedure**, §103.
qo = macro, §112.
$skew\_char$: **array**, §549.
str_ptr: str_number, §39.
$trie$: **array**, §921.
$trie\_max$: $trie\_pointer$, §950.
$trie\_op\_ptr$: $quarterword$, §943.
$undump$ = macro, §1306.
$undump\_int$ = macro, §1306.
$undump\_qqqq$ = macro, §1306.
$undump\_size$ = macro, §1306.
$undump\_wd$ = macro, §1306.
$width\_base$: **array**, §550.

1325. ⟨Undump the hyphenation tables 1325⟩ ≡

$undump(0)(hyph\_size)(hyph\_count)$;

for $k \leftarrow 1$ **to** $hyph\_count$ **do**

    begin $undump(0)(hyph\_size)(j)$; $undump(0)(str\_ptr)(hyph\_word[j])$;

    $undump(min\_halfword)(max\_halfword)(hyph\_list[j])$;

    end;

$undump\_size(0)(trie\_size)(\text{`trie}_\sqcup\text{size'})(trie\_max)$;

for $k \leftarrow 0$ **to** $trie\_max$ **do** $undump\_hh(trie[k])$;

$undump(min\_quarterword)(max\_quarterword)(trie\_op\_ptr)$;

for $k \leftarrow min\_quarterword + 1$ **to** $trie\_op\_ptr$ **do**

    begin $undump(0)(63)(hyf\_distance[k])$; { a $small\_number$ }

    $undump(0)(63)(hyf\_num[k])$; $undump(min\_quarterword)(max\_quarterword)(hyf\_next[k])$;

    end

This code is used in section 1303.

1326. We have already printed a lot of statistics, so we set $tracing\_stats \leftarrow 0$ to prevent them appearing again.

⟨Dump a couple more things and the closing check word 1326⟩ ≡

  $dump\_int(interaction)$; $dump\_int(format\_ident)$; $dump\_int(69069)$; $tracing\_stats \leftarrow 0$

This code is used in section 1302.

1327. ⟨Undump a couple more things and the closing check word 1327⟩ ≡

  $undump(batch\_mode)(error\_stop\_mode)(interaction)$; $undump(0)(str\_ptr)(format\_ident)$;

  $undump\_int(x)$;

  if $(x \neq 69069) \vee eof(fmt\_file)$ **then goto** bad_fmt

This code is used in section 1303.

1328. ⟨Create the $format\_ident$, open the format file, and inform the user that dumping has begun 1328⟩ ≡

$selector \leftarrow new\_string$; $print("_\sqcup(\textbf{preloaded}_\sqcup\textbf{format}=")$; $print(job\_name)$; $print\_char("_\sqcup")$;

$print\_int(year \textbf{ mod } 100)$; $print\_char(".")$; $print\_int(month)$; $print\_char(".")$; $print\_int(day)$;

$print\_char(")")$;

if $interaction = batch\_mode$ **then** $selector \leftarrow log\_only$

else $selector \leftarrow term\_and\_log$;

$str\_room(1)$; $format\_ident \leftarrow make\_string$; $pack\_job\_name(".fmt")$;

while $\neg w\_open\_out(fmt\_file)$ **do** $prompt\_file\_name("format_\sqcup file_\sqcup name", ".fmt")$;

$print\_nl("Beginning_\sqcup to_\sqcup dump_\sqcup on_\sqcup file_\sqcup")$; $print(w\_make\_name\_string(fmt\_file))$; $flush\_string$;

$print\_nl(format\_ident)$

This code is used in section 1302.

1329. ⟨Close the format file 1329⟩ ≡

  $w\_close(fmt\_file)$

This code is used in section 1302.

1330.   The main program.   This is it: the part of TeX that executes all those procedures
we have written.

Well—almost. Let's leave space for a few more routines that we may have forgotten.

⟨ Last-minute procedures 1333 ⟩

1331. We have noted that there are two versions of TₑX82. One, called INITEX, has to be run first; it initializes everything from scratch, without reading a format file, and it has the capability of dumping a format file. The other one is called 'VIRTEX'; it is a "virgin" program that needs to input a format file in order to get started. VIRTEX typically has more memory capacity than INITEX, because it does not need the space consumed by the auxiliary hyphenation tables and the numerous calls on *primitive*, etc.

The VIRTEX program cannot read a format file instantaneously, of course; the best implementations therefore allow for production versions of TₑX that not only avoid the loading routine for Pascal object code, they also have a format file pre-loaded. This is impossible to do if we stick to standard Pascal; but there is a simple way to fool many systems into avoiding the initialization, as follows: (1) We declare a global integer variable called *ready_already*. The probability is negligible that this variable holds any particular value like 314159 when VIRTEX is first loaded. (2) After we have read in a format file and initialized everything, we set *ready_already* ← 314159. (3) Soon VIRTEX will print '*', waiting for more input; and at this point we interrupt the program and save its core image in some form that the operating system can reload speedily. (4) When that core image is activated, the program starts again at the beginning; but now *ready_already* = 314159 and all the other global variables have their initial values too. The former chastity has vanished!

In other words, if we allow ourselves to test the condition *ready_already* = 314159, before *ready_already* has been assigned a value, we can avoid the lengthy initialization. Dirty tricks rarely pay off so handsomely.

On systems that allow such preloading, the standard program called TeX should be the one that has **plain** format preloaded, since that agrees with *The TₑXbook*. Other versions, e.g., AmSTeX, should also be provided for commonly used formats.

⟨ Global variables 13 ⟩ +≡
ready_already: *integer*;   { a sacrifice of purity for economy }

1332. Now this is really it: TₑX starts and ends here.

The initial test involving *ready_already* should be deleted if the Pascal runtime system is smart enough to detect such a "mistake."

begin   { *start_here* }
history ← *fatal_error_stop*;   { in case we quit during initialization }
t_open_out;   { open the terminal for output }
if *ready_already* = 314159 **then goto** *start_of_TₑX*;
⟨ Check the "constant" values for consistency 14 ⟩
if *bad* > 0 **then**
    begin *wterm_ln*(´Ouch---my␣internal␣constants␣have␣been␣clobbered!´, ´---case␣´, *bad* : 1);
    goto *final_end*;
    end;
initialize;   { set global variables to their starting values }
init if ¬*get_strings_started* **then goto** *final_end*;
init_prim;   { call *primitive* for each primitive }
tini
ready_already ← 314159;
start_of_TₑX: ⟨ Initialize the output routines 55 ⟩;
⟨ Get the first line of input and prepare to start 1337 ⟩;
init_str_ptr ← *str_ptr*; *init_pool_ptr* ← *pool_ptr*;

$history \leftarrow spotless;$ { ready to go! }
$main\_control;$ { come to life }
$final\_cleanup;$ { prepare for death }
$end\_of\_T_{\!E}\!X:$ $close\_files\_and\_terminate;$
$final\_end:$ $ready\_already \leftarrow 0;$
end.

1333. Here we do whatever is needed to complete T$_{\!E}$X's job gracefully on the local operating system. The code here might come into play after a fatal error; it must therefore consist entirely of "safe" operations that cannot produce error messages. For example, it would be a mistake to call *str_room* or *make_string* at this time, because a call on *overflow* might lead to an infinite loop.

Actually there's one way to get error messages, via *prepare_mag*; but that can't cause infinite recursion.

⟨ Last-minute procedures 1333 ⟩ ≡
procedure *close_files_and_terminate*;
   var k: *integer*; { all-purpose index }
   begin ⟨ Finish the extensions 1367 ⟩;
   stat if *tracing_stats* > 0 **then** ⟨ Output statistics about this job 1334 ⟩; **tats**
   wake_up_terminal; ⟨ Finish the DVI file 642 ⟩;
   if *job_name* > 0 **then**
      begin *wlog_cr*; *a_close*(*log_file*); *selector* $\leftarrow$ *selector* $- 2$;
      if *selector* $=$ *term_only* **then**
         begin *print_nl*("Transcript␣written␣on␣"); *print*(*log_name*); *print_char*(".");
         end;
      end;
   end;

See also sections 1335, 1336, and 1338.

This code is used in section 1330.

---

a_close: **procedure**, §28.
bad: *integer*, §13.
end_of_T$_{\!E}$X $= 9998$, §6.
fatal_error_stop $= 3$, §76.
final_cleanup: **procedure**, §1335.
final_end $= 9999$, §6.
get_strings_started: **function**, §47.
history: $0 .. 3$, §76.
init_pool_ptr: *pool_pointer*, §39.
init_prim: **procedure**, §1336.
init_str_ptr: *str_number*, §39.
initialize: **procedure**, §4.

job_name: *str_number*, §527.
log_file: *alpha_file*, §54.
log_name: *str_number*, §532.
main_control: **procedure**, §1030.
make_string: **function**, §43.
overflow: **procedure**, §94.
pool_ptr: *pool_pointer*, §39.
prepare_mag: **procedure**, §288.
primitive: **procedure**, §264.
print: **procedure**, §59.
print_char: **procedure**, §58.
print_nl: **procedure**, §62.

selector: $0 .. 21$, §54.
spotless $= 0$, §76.
start_of_T$_{\!E}$X $= 1$, §6.
str_ptr: *str_number*, §39.
str_room $=$ macro, §42.
t_open_out $=$ macro, §33.
term_only $= 17$, §54.
tracing_stats $=$ macro, §236.
wake_up_terminal $=$ macro, §34.
wlog_cr $=$ macro, §56.
wterm_ln $=$ macro, §56.

1334. The present section goes directly to the log file instead of using *print* commands, because there's no need for these strings to take up *str_pool* memory when a non-**stat** version of TₑX is being used.

⟨ Output statistics about this job 1334 ⟩ ≡

  if *job_name* > 0 **then** { the log file is open }

    begin *wlog_ln*(´␣´); *wlog_ln*(´Here␣is␣how␣much␣of␣TeX´´s␣memory´, ´␣you␣used:´);

    wlog(´␣´, *str_ptr* − *init_str_ptr* : 1, ´␣string´);

    if *str_ptr* ≠ *init_str_ptr* + 1 **then** *wlog*(´s´);

    wlog_ln(´␣out␣of␣´, *max_strings* − *init_str_ptr* : 1);

    wlog_ln(´␣´, *pool_ptr* − *init_pool_ptr* : 1, ´␣string␣characters␣out␣of␣´, *pool_size* − *init_pool_ptr* : 1);

    wlog_ln(´␣´, *lo_mem_max* − *mem_min* + *mem_end* − *hi_mem_min* + 2 : 1,

        ´␣words␣of␣memory␣out␣of␣´, *mem_end* + 1 − *mem_min* : 1);

    wlog_ln(´␣´, *cs_count* : 1, ´␣multiletter␣control␣sequences␣out␣of␣´, *hash_size* : 1);

    wlog(´␣´, *fmem_ptr* : 1, ´␣words␣of␣font␣info␣for␣´, *font_ptr* − *font_base* : 1, ´␣font´);

    if *font_ptr* ≠ *font_base* + 1 **then** *wlog*(´s´);

    wlog_ln(´,␣out␣of␣´, *font_mem_size* : 1, ´␣for␣´, *font_max* − *font_base* : 1);

    wlog(´␣´, *hyph_count* : 1, ´␣hyphenation␣exception´);

    if *hyph_count* ≠ 1 **then** *wlog*(´s´);

    wlog_ln(´␣out␣of␣´, *hyph_size* : 1);

    wlog_ln(´␣´, *max_in_stack* : 1, ´i,´, *max_nest_stack* : 1, ´n,´, *max_param_stack* : 1, ´p,´,

        max_buf_stack + 1 : 1, ´b,´, *max_save_stack* + 6 : 1, ´s␣stack␣positions␣out␣of␣´,

        stack_size : 1, ´i,´, *nest_size* : 1, ´n,´, *param_size* : 1, ´p,´, *buf_size* : 1, ´b,´, *save_size* : 1, ´s´);

  end

This code is used in section 1333.

1335. We get to the *final_cleanup* routine when \end or \dump has been scanned and *its_all_over*.

⟨ Last-minute procedures 1333 ⟩ +≡

procedure *final_cleanup*;

  label *exit*;

  var *c*: *small_number*; { 0 for \end, 1 for \dump }

  begin *c* ← *cur_chr*;

  if *job_name* = 0 **then** *open_log_file*;

  if *cur_level* > *level_one* **then**

    begin *print_nl*("("); *print_esc*("end␣occurred␣"); *print*("inside␣a␣group␣at␣level␣");

    print_int(*cur_level* − *level_one*); *print_char*(")");

    end;

  while *cond_ptr* ≠ *null* **do**

    begin *print_nl*("("); *print_esc*("end␣occurred␣"); *print*("when␣"); *print_cmd_chr*(*if_test*, *cur_if*);

    if *if_line* ≠ 0 **then**

      begin *print*("␣on␣line␣"); *print_int*(*if_line*);

      end;

    print("␣was␣incomplete)"); *if_line* ← *if_line_field*(*cond_ptr*); *cur_if* ← *subtype*(*cond_ptr*);

    cond_ptr ← *link*(*cond_ptr*);

    end;

if *history* ≠ *spotless* **then**
　　if ((*history* = *warning_issued*) ∨ (*interaction* < *error_stop_mode*)) **then**
　　　if *selector* = *term_and_log* **then**
　　　　begin *selector* ← *term_only*;
　　　　print_nl("(see␣the␣transcript␣file␣for␣additional␣information)");
　　　　selector ← *term_and_log*;
　　　　end;
　　if *c* = 1 **then**
　　　begin init *store_fmt_file*; **return**; **tini**
　　　print_nl("(\dump␣is␣performed␣only␣by␣INITEX)"); **return**;
　　　end;
exit: **end**;

1336. ⟨Last-minute procedures 1333⟩ +≡
　init procedure *init_prim*;　{ initialize all the primitives }
　begin *no_new_control_sequence* ← *false*; ⟨Put each of TEX's primitives into the hash table 226⟩;
　no_new_control_sequence ← *true*;
　end;
　tini

---

buf_size = **const**, §11.
cond_ptr: *pointer*, §489.
cs_count: *integer*, §256.
cur_chr: *halfword*, §297.
cur_if: *small_number*, §489.
cur_level: *quarterword*, §271.
error_stop_mode = 3, §73.
exit = 10, §15.
fmem_ptr: 0 .. *font_mem_size*, §549.
font_base = 0, §12.
font_max = **const**, §11.
font_mem_size = **const**, §11.
font_ptr: *internal_font_number*,
　§549.
hash_size = 2100, §12.
hi_mem_min: *pointer*, §116.
history: 0 .. 3, §76.
hyph_count: *hyph_pointer*, §926.
hyph_size = 307, §12.
if_line: *integer*, §489.
if_line_field = macro, §489.
if_test = 104, §210.
init_pool_ptr: *pool_pointer*, §39.

init_str_ptr: *str_number*, §39.
interaction: 0 .. 3, §73.
its_all_over: **function**, §1054.
job_name: *str_number*, §527.
level_one = 1, §221.
link = macro, §118.
lo_mem_max: *pointer*, §116.
max_buf_stack: 0 .. *buf_size*, §30.
max_in_stack: 0 .. *stack_size*, §301.
max_nest_stack: 0 .. *nest_size*, §213.
max_param_stack: *integer*, §308.
max_save_stack: 0 .. *save_size*,
　§271.
max_strings = **const**, §11.
mem_end: *pointer*, §118.
mem_min = **const**, §11.
nest_size = **const**, §11.
no_new_control_sequence: *boolean*,
　§256.
null = macro, §115.
open_log_file: **procedure**, §534.
param_size = **const**, §11.

pool_ptr: *pool_pointer*, §39.
pool_size = **const**, §11.
print: **procedure**, §59.
print_char: **procedure**, §58.
print_cmd_chr: **procedure**, §298.
print_esc: **procedure**, §63.
print_int: **procedure**, §65.
print_nl: **procedure**, §62.
save_size = **const**, §11.
selector: 0 .. 21, §54.
small_number = 0 .. 63, §101.
spotless = 0, §76.
stack_size = **const**, §11.
store_fmt_file: **procedure**, §1302.
str_pool: **packed array**, §39.
str_ptr: *str_number*, §39.
subtype = macro, §133.
term_and_log = 19, §54.
term_only = 17, §54.
warning_issued = 1, §76.
wlog = macro, §56.
wlog_ln = macro, §56.

1337. When we begin the following code, TeX's tables may still contain garbage; the strings might not even be present. Thus we must proceed cautiously to get bootstrapped in.

But when we finish this part of the program, TeX is ready to call on the *main_control* routine to do its work.

⟨ Get the first line of input and prepare to start 1337 ⟩ ≡
 begin ⟨ Initialize the input routines 331 ⟩;
 if (*format_ident* = 0) ∨ (*buffer*[*loc*] = "&") **then**
  begin if *format_ident* ≠ 0 **then** *initialize*; { erase preloaded format }
  if ¬*open_fmt_file* **then goto** *final_end*;
  if ¬*load_fmt_file* **then**
   begin *w_close*(*fmt_file*); **goto** *final_end*;
   end;
  w_close(*fmt_file*);
  while (*loc* < *limit*) ∧ (*buffer*[*loc*] = "␣") **do** *incr*(*loc*);
  end;
 if (*end_line_char* < 0) ∨ (*end_line_char* > 127) **then** *decr*(*limit*)
 else *buffer*[*limit*] ← *end_line_char*;
 fix_date_and_time;
 ⟨ Compute the magic offset 765 ⟩;
 ⟨ Initialize the print *selector* based on *interaction* 75 ⟩;
 if (*loc* < *limit*) ∧ (*cat_code*(*buffer*[*loc*]) ≠ *escape*) **then** *start_input*; { \input assumed }
 end

This code is used in section 1332.

1338. Debugging. Once TeX is working, it should be possible to diagnose most errors with the `\show` commands and other diagnostic features. But for the initial stages of debugging, and for the revelation of really deep mysteries, you can compile TeX with a few more aids, including the Pascal runtime checks and its debugger. An additional routine called *debug_help* will also come into play when you type 'D' after an error message; *debug_help* also occurs just before a fatal error causes TeX to succumb.

The interface to *debug_help* is primitive, but it is good enough when used with a Pascal debugger that allows you to set breakpoints and to read variables and change their values. After getting the prompt 'debug #', you type either a negative number (this exits *debug_help*), or zero (this goes to a location where you can set a breakpoint, thereby entering into dialog with the Pascal debugger), or a positive number m followed by an argument n. The meaning of m and n will be clear from the program below. (If $m = 13$, there is an additional argument, l.)

define *breakpoint* = 888   { place where a breakpoint is desirable }

⟨ Last-minute procedures 1333 ⟩ +≡
    debug procedure *debug_help*;   { routine to display various things }
    label *breakpoint, exit*;
    var k, l, m, n: *integer*;
    begin loop
        begin *wake_up_terminal*; *print_nl*("debug␣#␣(-1␣to␣exit):"); *update_terminal*;
        read(*term_in, m*);
        if $m < 0$ **then return**
        else if $m = 0$ **then**
                begin goto *breakpoint*; @\   { go to every label at least once }
            breakpoint: $m \leftarrow 0$; @{´BREAKPOINT´@}@\
                end
            else begin *read*(*term_in, n*);
                case m **of**
                ⟨ Numbered cases for *debug_help* 1339 ⟩
                othercases *print*("?")
                endcases;
                end;
        end;
    exit: **end**;
    gubed

1339. ⟨ Numbered cases for *debug_help* 1339 ⟩ ≡

1: *print_word* (*mem*[*n*]);   { display *mem*[*n*] in all forms }

2: *print_int* (*info* (*n*));

3: *print_int* (*link* (*n*));

4: *print_word* (*eqtb*[*n*]);

5: *print_word* (*font_info*[*n*]);

6: *print_word* (*save_stack*[*n*]);

7: *show_box* (*n*);   { show a box, abbreviated by *show_box_depth* and *show_box_breadth* }

8: **begin** *breadth_max* ← 10000; *depth_threshold* ← *pool_size* − *pool_ptr* − 10; *show_node_list* (*n*);

      { show a box in its entirety }

  end;

9: *show_token_list* (*n*, *null*, 1000);

10: *print* (*n*);

11: *check_mem* (*n* > 0);   { check wellformedness; print new busy locations if *n* > 0 }

12: *search_mem* (*n*);   { look for pointers to *n* }

13: **begin** *read* (*term_in*, *l*); *print_cmd_chr* (*n*, *l*);

  end;

14: **for** *k* ← 0 **to** *n* **do**   *print* (*buffer* [*k*]);

15: **begin** *font_in_short_display* ← *null_font*; *short_display* (*n*);

  end;

16: *panicking* ← ¬*panicking*;

This code is used in section 1338.

---

breadth_max: *integer*, §181.
buffer: **array**, §30.
check_mem: **procedure**, §167.
depth_threshold: *integer*, §181.
eqtb: **array**, §253.
exit = 10, §15.
font_in_short_display: *integer*, §173.
font_info: **array**, §549.
info = macro, §118.
link = macro, §118.
mem: **array**, §116.

null = macro, §115.
null_font = macro, §232.
panicking: *boolean*, §165.
pool_ptr: *pool_pointer*, §39.
pool_size = **const**, §11.
print: **procedure**, §59.
print_cmd_chr: **procedure**, §298.
print_int: **procedure**, §65.
print_nl: **procedure**, §62.
print_word: **procedure**, §114.
save_stack: **array**, §271.

search_mem: **procedure**, §172.
short_display: **procedure**, §174.
show_box: **procedure**, §198.
show_box_breadth = macro, §236.
show_box_depth = macro, §236.
show_node_list: **procedure**, §182.
show_token_list: **procedure**, §292.
term_in: *alpha_file*, §32.
update_terminal = macro, §34.
wake_up_terminal = macro, §34.

1340.   Extensions.   The program above includes a bunch of "hooks" that allow further capabilities to be added without upsetting TeX's basic structure. Most of these hooks are concerned with "whatsit" nodes, which are intended to be used for special purposes; whenever a new extension to TeX involves a new kind of whatsit node, a corresponding change needs to be made to the routines below that deal with such nodes, but it will usually be unnecessary to make many changes to the other parts of this program.

In order to demonstrate how extensions can be made, we shall treat '`\write`', '`\openout`', '`\closeout`', '`\immediate`', and '`\special`' as if they were extensions. These commands are actually primitives of TeX82, and they should appear in all implementations of the system; but let's try to imagine that they aren't. Then the program below illustrates how a person could add them.

Sometimes, of course, an extension will require changes to TeX itself; no system of hooks could be complete enough for all conceivable extensions. The features associated with '`\write`' are almost all confined to the following paragraphs, but there are small parts of the *print_ln* and *print_char* procedures that were introduced specifically to \write characters. Furthermore one of the token lists recognized by the scanner is a *write_text*; and there are a few other miscellaneous places where we have already provided for some aspect of \write. The goal of a TeX extender should be to minimize alterations to the standard parts of the program, and to avoid them completely if possible. He or she should also be quite sure that there's no easy way to accomplish the desired goals with the standard features that TeX already has. "Think thrice before extending," because that may save a lot of work, and it will also keep incompatible extensions of TeX from proliferating.

1341.   First let's consider the format of whatsit nodes that are used to represent the data associated with \write and its relatives. Recall that a whatsit has $type = whatsit\_node$, and the *subtype* is supposed to distinguish different kinds of whatsits. Each node occupies two or more words; the exact number is immaterial, as long as it is readily determined from the *subtype* or other data.

We shall introduce four *subtype* values here, corresponding to the control sequences \openout, \write, \closeout, and \special. The second word of such whatsits has a *write_stream* field that identifies the write-stream number (0 to 15, or 16 for out-of-range and positive, or 17 for out-of-range and negative). In the case of \write and \special, there is also a field that points to the reference count of a token list that should be sent. In the case of \openout, we need three words and three auxiliary subfields to hold the string numbers for name, area, and extension.

define $write\_node\_size = 2$ { number of words in a write/whatsit node }
define $open\_node\_size = 3$ { number of words in an open/whatsit node }
define $open\_node = 0$ { *subtype* in whatsits that represent files to \openout }
define $write\_node = 1$ { *subtype* in whatsits that represent things to \write }
define $close\_node = 2$ { *subtype* in whatsits that represent streams to \closeout }
define $special\_node = 3$ { *subtype* in whatsits that represent \special things }
define $write\_tokens(\#) \equiv link(\# + 1)$ { reference count of token list to write }
define $write\_stream(\#) \equiv info(\# + 1)$ { stream number (0 to 16) }
define $open\_name(\#) \equiv link(\# + 1)$ { string number of file name to open }
define $open\_area(\#) \equiv info(\# + 2)$ { string number of file area for *open_name* }
define $open\_ext(\#) \equiv link(\# + 2)$ { string number of file extension for *open_name* }

1342. The sixteen possible \write streams are represented by the *write_file* array. The *j*th file is open if and only if *write_open*[*j*] = *true*. The last two streams are special; *write_open*[16] represents a stream number greater than 15, while *write_open*[17] represents a negative stream number, and both of these variables are always *false*.

⟨ Global variables 13 ⟩ +≡
write_file: **array** [0 .. 15] **of** *alpha_file*;
write_open: **array** [0 .. 17] **of** *boolean*;

1343. ⟨ Set initial values of key variables 21 ⟩ +≡
    for *k* ← 0 **to** 17 **do** *write_open*[*k*] ← *false*;

1344. Extensions might introduce new command codes; but it's best to use *extension* with a modifier, whenever possible, so that *main_control* stays the same.

    define *immediate_code* = 4   { command modifier for \immediate }

⟨ Put each of TEX's primitives into the hash table 226 ⟩ +≡
    primitive("openout", *extension*, *open_node*);
    primitive("write", *extension*, *write_node*); *write_loc* ← *cur_val*;
    primitive("closeout", *extension*, *close_node*);
    primitive("special", *extension*, *special_node*);
    primitive("immediate", *extension*, *immediate_code*);

1345. The variable *write_loc* just introduced is used to provide an appropriate error message in case of "runaway" write texts.

⟨ Global variables 13 ⟩ +≡
write_loc: *pointer*; { *eqtb* address of \write }

1346. ⟨ Cases of *print_cmd_chr* for symbolic printing of primitives 227 ⟩ +≡
extension: **case** *chr_code* **of**
    open_node: *print_esc*("openout");
    write_node: *print_esc*("write");
    close_node: *print_esc*("closeout");
    special_node: *print_esc*("special");
    immediate_code: *print_esc*("immediate");
    othercases *print*("[unknown␣extension!]")
    endcases;

---

alpha_file = **packed file**, §25.
chr_code: *halfword*, §298.
cur_val: *integer*, §410.
eqtb: **array**, §253.
extension = 59, §208.
info = macro, §118.
k: *integer*, §163.

link = macro, §118.
main_control: **procedure**, §1030.
pointer = macro, §115.
primitive: **procedure**, §264.
print: **procedure**, §59.
print_char: **procedure**, §58.
print_cmd_chr: **procedure**, §298.

print_esc: **procedure**, §63.
print_ln: **procedure**, §57.
subtype = macro, §133.
type = macro, §133.
whatsit_node = 8, §146.
write_text = 15, §307.

1347. When an *extension* command occurs in *main_control*, in any mode, the *do_extension* routine is called.

⟨ Cases of *main_control* that are for extensions to TEX 1347 ⟩ ≡
any_mode(*extension*): *do_extension*;

This code is used in section 1045.

1348. ⟨ Declare action procedures for use by *main_control* 1043 ⟩ +≡
⟨ Declare procedures needed in *do_extension* 1349 ⟩
procedure *do_extension*;
   var *i, j, k*: *integer*; { all-purpose integers }
     p, q, r: *pointer*; { all-purpose pointers }
   begin case *cur_chr* **of**
   open_node: ⟨ Implement \openout 1351 ⟩;
   write_node: ⟨ Implement \write 1352 ⟩;
   close_node: ⟨ Implement \closeout 1353 ⟩;
   special_node: ⟨ Implement \special 1354 ⟩;
   immediate_code: ⟨ Implement \immediate 1375 ⟩;
   othercases *confusion*("ext1")
   endcases;
   end;

1349. Here is a subroutine that creates a whatsit node having a given *subtype* and a given number of words. It initializes only the first word of the whatsit, and appends it to the current list.

⟨ Declare procedures needed in *do_extension* 1349 ⟩ ≡
procedure *new_whatsit*(*s* : *small_number*; *w* : *small_number*);
   var *p*: *pointer*; { the new node }
   begin *p* ← *get_node*(*w*); *type*(*p*) ← *whatsit_node*; *subtype*(*p*) ← *s*; *link*(*tail*) ← *p*; *tail* ← *p*;
   end;

See also section 1350.

This code is used in section 1348.

1350. The next subroutine uses *cur_chr* to decide what sort of whatsit is involved, and also inserts a *write_stream* number.

⟨ Declare procedures needed in *do_extension* 1349 ⟩ +≡
procedure *new_write_whatsit*(*w* : *small_number*);
   begin *new_whatsit*(*cur_chr*, *w*);
   if *w* ≠ *write_node_size* **then** *scan_four_bit_int*
   else begin *scan_int*;
     if *cur_val* < 0 **then** *cur_val* ← 17
     else if *cur_val* > 15 **then** *cur_val* ← 16;
     end;
   write_stream(*tail*) ← *cur_val*;
   end;

1351. ⟨ Implement \openout 1351 ⟩ ≡
   begin *new_write_whatsit*(*open_node_size*); *scan_optional_equals*; *scan_file_name*;
   open_name(*tail*) ← *cur_name*; *open_area*(*tail*) ← *cur_area*; *open_ext*(*tail*) ← *cur_ext*;

end

This code is used in section 1348.

1352. When '`\write 12{...}`' appears, we scan the token list '`{...}`' without expanding its macros; the macros will be expanded later when this token list is rescanned.

⟨ Implement `\write` 1352 ⟩ ≡
 begin $k \leftarrow \mathit{cur\_cs}$; $\mathit{new\_write\_whatsit}(\mathit{write\_node\_size})$;
 $\mathit{cur\_cs} \leftarrow k$; $p \leftarrow \mathit{scan\_toks}(\mathit{false}, \mathit{false})$; $\mathit{write\_tokens}(\mathit{tail}) \leftarrow \mathit{def\_ref}$;
 end

This code is used in section 1348.

1353. ⟨ Implement `\closeout` 1353 ⟩ ≡
 begin $\mathit{new\_write\_whatsit}(\mathit{write\_node\_size})$; $\mathit{write\_tokens}(\mathit{tail}) \leftarrow \mathit{null}$;
 end

This code is used in section 1348.

1354. When '`\special{...}`' appears, we expand the macros in the token list as in `\xdef` and `\mark`.

⟨ Implement `\special` 1354 ⟩ ≡
 begin $\mathit{new\_whatsit}(\mathit{special\_node}, \mathit{write\_node\_size})$; $\mathit{write\_stream}(\mathit{tail}) \leftarrow \mathit{null}$;
 $p \leftarrow \mathit{scan\_toks}(\mathit{false}, \mathit{true})$; $\mathit{write\_tokens}(\mathit{tail}) \leftarrow \mathit{def\_ref}$;
 end

This code is used in section 1348.

1355. Each new type of node that appears in our data structure must be capable of being displayed, copied, destroyed, and so on. The routines that we need for write-oriented whatsits are somewhat like those for mark nodes; other extensions might, of course, involve more subtlety here.

⟨ Basic printing procedures 57 ⟩ +≡
procedure $\mathit{print\_write\_whatsit}(s : \mathit{str\_number}; p : \mathit{pointer})$;
 begin $\mathit{print\_esc}(s)$;
 if $\mathit{write\_stream}(p) < 16$ **then** $\mathit{print\_int}(\mathit{write\_stream}(p))$
 else if $\mathit{write\_stream}(p) = 16$ **then** $\mathit{print\_char}(\texttt{"*"})$
  else $\mathit{print\_char}(\texttt{"-"})$;
 end;

---

any_mode = macro, §1045.
close_node = 2, §1341.
confusion: **procedure**, §95.
cur_area: *str_number*, §512.
cur_chr: *halfword*, §297.
cur_cs: *pointer*, §297.
cur_ext: *str_number*, §512.
cur_name: *str_number*, §512.
cur_val: *integer*, §410.
def_ref: *pointer*, §305.
extension = 59, §208.
get_node: **function**, §125.
immediate_code = 4, §1344.
link = macro, §118.

main_control: **procedure**, §1030.
null = macro, §115.
open_area = macro, §1341.
open_ext = macro, §1341.
open_name = macro, §1341.
open_node = 0, §1341.
open_node_size = 3, §1341.
pointer = macro, §115.
print_char: **procedure**, §58.
print_esc: **procedure**, §63.
print_int: **procedure**, §65.
scan_file_name: **procedure**, §526.
scan_four_bit_int: **procedure**, §434.
scan_int: **procedure**, §440.

scan_optional_equals: **procedure**, §405.
scan_toks: **function**, §473.
small_number = 0 .. 63, §101.
special_node = 3, §1341.
str_number = 0 .. *max_strings*, §38.
subtype = macro, §133.
tail = macro, §213.
type = macro, §133.
whatsit_node = 8, §146.
write_node = 1, §1341.
write_node_size = 2, §1341.
write_stream = macro, §1341.
write_tokens = macro, §1341.

1356.   ⟨ Display the whatsit node p 1356 ⟩ ≡
  case $subtype(p)$ **of**
  $open\_node$: **begin** $print\_write\_whatsit($"openout"$, p)$; $print\_char($"="$)$;
    $print\_file\_name(open\_name(p), open\_area(p), open\_ext(p))$;
    end;
  $write\_node$: **begin** $print\_write\_whatsit($"write"$, p)$; $print\_mark(write\_tokens(p))$;
    end;
  $close\_node$: $print\_write\_whatsit($"closeout"$, p)$;
  $special\_node$: **begin** $print\_esc($"special"$)$; $print\_mark(write\_tokens(p))$;
    end;
  othercases $print($"whatsit?"$)$
  endcases

This code is used in section 183.

1357.   ⟨ Make a partial copy of the whatsit node p and make r point to it; set $words$ to the number of
      initial words not yet copied 1357 ⟩ ≡
  case $subtype(p)$ **of**
  $open\_node$: **begin** $r \leftarrow get\_node(open\_node\_size)$; $words \leftarrow open\_node\_size$;
    end;
  $write\_node, special\_node$: **begin** $r \leftarrow get\_node(write\_node\_size)$; $add\_token\_ref(write\_tokens(p))$;
    $words \leftarrow write\_node\_size$;
    end;
  $close\_node$: **begin** $r \leftarrow get\_node(small\_node\_size)$; $words \leftarrow small\_node\_size$;
    end;
  othercases $confusion($"ext2"$)$
  endcases

This code is used in section 206.

1358.   ⟨ Wipe out the whatsit node p and **goto** $done$ 1358 ⟩ ≡
  begin case $subtype(p)$ **of**
  $open\_node$: $free\_node(p, open\_node\_size)$;
  $write\_node, special\_node$: **begin** $delete\_token\_ref(write\_tokens(p))$; $free\_node(p, write\_node\_size)$;
    goto $done$;
    end;
  $close\_node$: $free\_node(p, small\_node\_size)$;
  othercases $confusion($"ext3"$)$
  endcases;
  goto $done$;
  end

This code is used in section 202.

1359.   ⟨ Incorporate a whatsit node into a vbox 1359 ⟩ ≡
  $do\_nothing$

This code is used in section 669.

1360.   ⟨ Incorporate a whatsit node into an hbox 1360 ⟩ ≡
  $do\_nothing$

This code is used in section 651.

1361. ⟨ Let d be the width of the whatsit p 1361 ⟩ ≡
   $d \leftarrow 0$
This code is used in section 1147.

1362. ⟨ Advance past a whatsit node in the *line_break* loop 1362 ⟩ ≡
   do_nothing
This code is used in section 866.

1363. ⟨ Prepare to move whatsit p to the current page, then **goto** *contribute* 1363 ⟩ ≡
   goto *contribute*
This code is used in section 1000.

1364. ⟨ Process whatsit p in *vert_break* loop, **goto** *not_found* 1364 ⟩ ≡
   goto *not_found*
This code is used in section 973.

1365. ⟨ Output the whatsit node p in a vlist 1365 ⟩ ≡
   out_what(p)
This code is used in section 631.

1366. ⟨ Output the whatsit node p in an hlist 1366 ⟩ ≡
   out_what(p)
This code is used in section 622.

1367. ⟨ Finish the extensions 1367 ⟩ ≡
   for $k \leftarrow 0$ **to** 15 **do**
     if *write_open*[k] **then** *a_close*(*write_file*[k])
This code is used in section 1333.

---

a_close: **procedure**, §28.
add_token_ref = macro, §203.
close_node = 2, §1341.
confusion: **procedure**, §95.
contribute = 80, §994.
d: *scaled*, §1138.
delete_token_ref: **procedure**, §200.
do_nothing = macro, §16.
done = 30, §15.
free_node: **procedure**, §130.
get_node: **function**, §125.
k: *integer*, §1333.
line_break: **procedure**, §815.
not_found = 45, §15.
open_area = macro, §1341.
open_ext = macro, §1341.

open_name = macro, §1341.
open_node = 0, §1341.
open_node_size = 3, §1341.
out_what: **procedure**, §1373.
p: *pointer*, §182.
p: *pointer*, §202.
p: *pointer*, §204.
p: *pointer*, §619.
p: *pointer*, §629.
p: *pointer*, §970.
p: *pointer*, §994.
p: *pointer*, §1138.
print: **procedure**, §59.
print_char: **procedure**, §58.
print_esc: **procedure**, §63.

print_file_name: **procedure**, §518.
print_mark: **procedure**, §176.
print_write_whatsit: **procedure**,
  §1355.
r: *pointer*, §204.
small_node_size = 2, §141.
special_node = 3, §1341.
subtype = macro, §133.
vert_break: **function**, §970.
words: 0 .. 5, §204.
write_file: **array**, §1342.
write_node = 1, §1341.
write_node_size = 2, §1341.
write_open: **array**, §1342.
write_tokens = macro, §1341.

1368. After all this preliminary shuffling, we come finally to the routines that actually send out the requested data. Let's do \special first (it's easier).

⟨ Declare procedures needed in *hlist_out*, *vlist_out* 1368 ⟩ ≡
procedure *special_out*(*p* : *pointer*);
  var *old_setting*: 0 .. *max_selector*; { holds print *selector* }
    k: *pool_pointer*; { index into *str_pool* }
  begin *synch_h*; *synch_v*;
  old_setting ← *selector*; *selector* ← *new_string*;
  show_token_list(*link*(*write_tokens*(*p*)), *null*, *pool_size* − *pool_ptr*); *selector* ← *old_setting*; *str_room*(1);
  if *cur_length* < 256 **then**
    begin *dvi_out*(*xxx1*); *dvi_out*(*cur_length*);
    end
  else begin *dvi_out*(*xxx4*); *dvi_four*(*cur_length*);
    end;
  for *k* ← *str_start*[*str_ptr*] **to** *pool_ptr* − 1 **do** *dvi_out*(*str_pool*[*k*]);
  pool_ptr ← *str_start*[*str_ptr*]; { erase the string }
  end;

See also sections 1370 and 1373.

This code is used in section 619.

1369. To write a token list, we must run it through TeX's scanner, expanding macros and \the and \number, etc. This might cause runaways, if a delimited macro parameter isn't matched, and runaways would be extremely confusing since we are calling on TeX's scanner in the middle of a \shipout command. Therefore we will put a dummy control sequence as a "stopper," right after the token list. This control sequence is artificially defined to be \outer.

⟨ Initialize table entries (done by **INITEX** only) 164 ⟩ +≡
  text(*end_write*) ← "endwrite"; *eq_level*(*end_write*) ← *level_one*; *eq_type*(*end_write*) ← *outer_call*;
  equiv(*end_write*) ← *null*;

1370. ⟨ Declare procedures needed in *hlist_out*, *vlist_out* 1368 ⟩ +≡
procedure *write_out*(*p* : *pointer*);
  var *old_setting*: 0 .. *max_selector*; { holds print *selector* }
    old_mode: *integer*; { saved *mode* }
    j: *small_number*; { write stream number }
    q, *r*: *pointer*; { temporary variables for list manipulation }
  begin ⟨ Expand macros in the token list and make *link*(*def_ref*) point to the result 1371 ⟩;
  old_setting ← *selector*; *j* ← *write_stream*(*p*);
  if *write_open*[*j*] **then** *selector* ← *j*
  else begin { write to the terminal if file isn't open }
    if (*j* = 17) ∧ (*selector* = *term_and_log*) **then** *selector* ← *log_only*;
    print_nl("");
    end;
  show_token_list(*link*(*def_ref*), *null*, 10000000); *print_ln*; *flush_list*(*def_ref*); *selector* ← *old_setting*;
  end;

1371. The final line of this routine is slightly subtle; at least, the author didn't think about it until getting burnt! There is a used-up token list on the stack, namely the one that contained *end_write_token*. (We insert this artificial '\endwrite' to prevent runaways, as explained above.)

If it were not removed, and if there were numerous writes on a single page, the stack would overflow.

define $end\_write\_token \equiv cs\_token\_flag + end\_write$

$\langle$ Expand macros in the token list and make $link(def\_ref)$ point to the result 1371 $\rangle \equiv$
$\quad q \leftarrow get\_avail;\ info(q) \leftarrow right\_brace\_token + "\}";$
$\quad r \leftarrow get\_avail;\ link(q) \leftarrow r;\ info(r) \leftarrow end\_write\_token;\ ins\_list(q);$
$\quad begin\_token\_list(write\_tokens(p), write\_text);$
$\quad q \leftarrow get\_avail;\ info(q) \leftarrow left\_brace\_token + "\{";\ ins\_list(q);$
$\quad\quad \{$ now we're ready to scan '$\{\langle$ token list $\rangle\}$ \endwrite' $\}$
$\quad old\_mode \leftarrow mode;\ mode \leftarrow 0;\ \{$ disable \prevdepth, \spacefactor, \lastskip $\}$
$\quad cur\_cs \leftarrow write\_loc;\ q \leftarrow scan\_toks(false, true);\ \{$ expand macros, etc. $\}$
$\quad get\_token;$ **if** $cur\_tok \neq end\_write\_token$ **then** $\langle$ Recover from an unbalanced write command 1372 $\rangle;$
$\quad mode \leftarrow old\_mode;\ end\_token\_list\quad \{$ conserve stack space $\}$

This code is used in section 1370.

1372. $\langle$ Recover from an unbalanced write command 1372 $\rangle \equiv$
$\quad$ **begin** $print\_err("Unbalanced_{\sqcup}write_{\sqcup}command");$
$\quad help2("On_{\sqcup}this_{\sqcup}page_{\sqcup}there's_{\sqcup}a_{\sqcup}\backslash write_{\sqcup}with_{\sqcup}fewer_{\sqcup}real_{\sqcup}\{'s_{\sqcup}than_{\sqcup}}'s.")$
$\quad ("I_{\sqcup}can't_{\sqcup}handle_{\sqcup}that_{\sqcup}very_{\sqcup}well;_{\sqcup}good_{\sqcup}luck.");\ error;$
$\quad$ **repeat** $get\_token;$
$\quad$ **until** $cur\_tok = end\_write\_token;$
$\quad$ **end**

This code is used in section 1371.

1373.   The *out_what* procedure takes care of outputting whatsit nodes for *vlist_out* and *hlist_out*.

⟨ Declare procedures needed in *hlist_out*, *vlist_out* 1368 ⟩ +≡

procedure *out_what*(*p* : *pointer*);
  var *j*: *small_number*;   { write stream number }
  begin case *subtype*(*p*) **of**
  open_node, *write_node*, *close_node*: ⟨ Do some work that has been queued up for \write 1374 ⟩;
  special_node: *special_out*(*p*);
  othercases *confusion*("ext4")
  endcases;
  end;

1374.   We don't implement \write inside of leaders. (The reason is that the number of times a leader box appears might be different in different implementations, due to machine-dependent rounding in the glue calculations.)

⟨ Do some work that has been queued up for \write 1374 ⟩ ≡
  if ¬*doing_leaders* **then**
    begin *j* ← *write_stream*(*p*);
    if *subtype*(*p*) = *write_node* **then** *write_out*(*p*)
    else begin if *write_open*[*j*] **then** *a_close*(*write_file*[*j*]);
      if *subtype*(*p*) = *close_node* **then** *write_open*[*j*] ← *false*
      else if *j* < 16 **then**
        begin *cur_name* ← *open_name*(*p*); *cur_area* ← *open_area*(*p*); *cur_ext* ← *open_ext*(*p*);
        if *cur_ext* = "" **then** *cur_ext* ← ".tex";
        pack_cur_name;
        while ¬*a_open_out*(*write_file*[*j*]) **do** *prompt_file_name*("output␣file␣name", ".tex");
        write_open[*j*] ← *true*;
        end;
      end;
    end

This code is used in section 1373.

1375.   The presence of '\immediate' causes the *do_extension* procedure to descend to one level of recursion. Nothing happens unless \immediate is followed by '\openout', '\write', or '\closeout'.

⟨ Implement \immediate 1375 ⟩ ≡
  begin *get_x_token*;
  if (*cur_cmd* = *extension*) ∧ (*cur_chr* ≤ *close_node*) **then**
    begin *p* ← *tail*; *do_extension*;   { append a whatsit node }
    out_what(*tail*);   { do the action immediately }
    flush_node_list(*tail*); *tail* ← *p*; *link*(*p*) ← *null*;
    end
  else *back_input*;
  end

This code is used in section 1348.

1376. System-dependent changes. This section should be replaced, if necessary, by any special alterations to the program that are necessary to make TeX work at a particular installation. It is usually best to design your change file so that all changes to previous sections preserve the section numbering; then everybody's version will be consistent with the published program. More extensive changes, which introduce new sections, can be inserted here; then only the index itself will get a new section number.

a_close: **procedure**, §28.
a_open_out: **function**, §27.
back_input: **procedure**, §325.
close_node = 2, §1341.
confusion: **procedure**, §95.
cur_area: *str_number*, §512.
cur_chr: *halfword*, §297.
cur_cmd: *eight_bits*, §297.
cur_ext: *str_number*, §512.
cur_name: *str_number*, §512.
doing_leaders: *boolean*, §592.
extension = 59, §208.
flush_node_list: **procedure**, §202.

get_x_token: **procedure**, §380.
hlist_out: **procedure**, §619.
link = macro, §118.
null = macro, §115.
open_area = macro, §1341.
open_ext = macro, §1341.
open_name = macro, §1341.
open_node = 0, §1341.
p: *pointer*, §1348.
pack_cur_name = macro, §529.
pointer = macro, §115.
prompt_file_name: **procedure**,

§530.
small_number = 0 .. 63, §101.
special_node = 3, §1341.
special_out: **procedure**, §1368.
subtype = macro, §133.
tail = macro, §213.
vlist_out: **procedure**, §629.
write_file: **array**, §1342.
write_node = 1, §1341.
write_open: **array**, §1342.
write_out: **procedure**, §1370.
write_stream = macro, §1341.

1377.   Index.   Here is where you can find all uses of each identifier in the program, with underlined entries pointing to where the identifier was defined. If the identifier is only one letter long, however, you get to see only the underlined entries. *All references are to section numbers instead of page numbers.*

This index also lists error messages and other aspects of the program that you might want to look up some day. For example, the entry for "system dependencies" lists all sections that should receive special attention from people who are installing TeX in a new operating environment. A list of various things that can't happen appears under "this can't happen". Approximately 40 sections are listed under "inner loop"; these account for about 60% of TeX's running time, exclusive of input and output.

`#`: 1006.
`*`: 174, 176, 178, 313, 360, 856, 1006, 1355.
`**`: 37, 534.
`->`: 294.
`=>`: 363.
`?`: 83.
`???`: 59–60.
`@`: 856.
`@@`: 846.
a: 47, 102, 218, 518, 519, 523, 560, 597, 691, 722, 738, 752, 1123, 1194, 1211, 1236, 1257.
`A <box> was supposed to...`: 1084.
a_close: 28, 51, 329, 485–486, 1275, 1333, 1367, 1374.
a_leaders: 149, 189, 625, 627, 634, 636, 656, 671, 1071–1073, 1078, 1148.
a_make_name_string: 525, 534, 537.
a_open_in: 27, 51, 537, 1275.
a_open_out: 27, 534, 1374.
A_token: 445.
abort: 560, 563–565, 568–571, 573, 575.
above: 208, 1046, 1178–1180.
`\above` primitive: 1178.
above_code: 1178, 1179, 1182–1183.
above_display_short_skip: 224, 814.
`\abovedisplayshortskip` primitive: 226.
above_display_short_skip_code: 224, 225–226, 1203.
above_display_skip: 224, 814.
`\abovedisplayskip` primitive: 226.
above_display_skip_code: 224, 225–226, 1203, 1206.
`\abovewithdelims` primitive: 1178.
abs: 66, 186, 211, 218–219, 418, 422, 448, 501, 610, 663, 675, 718, 737, 757–759, 831, 836, 849, 859, 944, 947, 1029–1030, 1056, 1076, 1078, 1080, 1083, 1093, 1110, 1120, 1127, 1149, 1243–1244.
absorbing: 305, 306, 339, 473.
acc_kern: 155, 191, 837, 879, 1125.
accent: 208, 265–266, 1090, 1122, 1164–1165.
`\accent` primitive: 265.
accent_chr: 687, 696, 738, 1165.
accent_noad: 687, 690, 696, 698, 733, 761, 1165, 1186.
accent_noad_size: 687, 698, 761, 1165.
act_width: 866, 867, 869–870.
action procedure: 1029.

active: 162, 819, 829, 843, 854, 860–861, 863–865, 873–875.
active_base: 220, 222, 252–253, 255, 262–263, 353, 442, 506, 1152, 1257, 1289, 1315, 1317.
active_char: 207, 344, 506.
active_height: 970, 975–976.
active_node_size: 819, 845, 860, 864–865.
active_width: 823, 824, 829, 843, 861, 864, 866, 869, 970.
actual_looseness: 872, 873, 875.
add_delims_to: 347.
add_glue_ref: 203, 206, 430, 802, 881, 996, 1100, 1229.
add_token_ref: 203, 206, 323, 979, 1012, 1016, 1221, 1227, 1357.
additional: 644, 645, 657, 672.
adj_demerits: 236, 836, 859.
`\adjdemerits` primitive: 238.
adj_demerits_code: 236, 237–238.
adjust: 576.
adjust_head: 162, 888–889, 1076, 1085, 1199, 1204.
adjust_node: 142, 148, 175, 183, 202, 206, 647, 651, 655, 730, 761, 866, 899, 1100.
adjust_ptr: 142, 197, 202, 206, 655, 1100.
adjust_tail: 647, 648–649, 651, 655, 796, 888–889, 1076, 1085, 1199.
adjusted_hbox_group: 269, 1062, 1083, 1085.
advance: 209, 265–266, 1210, 1235–1236, 1238.
`\advance` primitive: 265.
after: 147, 866, 1196.
after_assignment: 208, 265–266, 1268.
`\afterassignment` primitive: 265.
after_group: 208, 265–266, 1271.
`\aftergroup` primitive: 265.
after_math: 1193, 1194.
after_token: 1266, 1267–1269.
aire: 560, 561, 563, 576.
align_error: 1126, 1127.
align_group: 269, 768, 774, 791, 800, 1131–1132.
align_head: 162, 770, 777.
align_peek: 773–774, 785, 799, 1048, 1133.
align_ptr: 770, 771–772.
align_stack_node_size: 770, 772.

⟨ Accumulate the constant until *cur_tok* is not a suitable digit 445 ⟩   Used in section 444.

⟨ Add the width of node *s* to *break_width* 842 ⟩   Used in section 840.

⟨ Add the width of node *s* to *disc_width* 871 ⟩   Used in section 870.

⟨ Adjust for the magnification ratio 457 ⟩   Used in section 453.

⟨ Adjust for the setting of \globaldefs 1214 ⟩   Used in section 1211.

⟨ Adjust *shift_up* and *shift_down* for the case of a fraction line 746 ⟩   Used in section 743.

⟨ Adjust *shift_up* and *shift_down* for the case of no fraction line 745 ⟩   Used in section 743.

⟨ Adjust the space factor, based on its current value and *c* 1034 ⟩   Used in section 1033.

⟨ Advance *cur_p* to the node following the present string of characters 867 ⟩   Used in section 866.

⟨ Advance past a whatsit node in the *line_break* loop 1362 ⟩   Used in section 866.

⟨ Advance *r*; **goto** *found* if the parameter delimiter has been fully matched, otherwise **goto** *continue* 394 ⟩   Used in section 392.

⟨ Allocate entire node *p* and **goto** *found* 129 ⟩   Used in section 127.

⟨ Allocate from the top of node *p* and **goto** *found* 128 ⟩   Used in section 127.

⟨ Apologize for inability to do the operation now, unless \unskip follows non-glue 1106 ⟩   Used in section 1105.

⟨ Apologize for not loading the font, **goto** *done* 567 ⟩   Used in section 566.

⟨ Append a kern, **goto** *main_loop_2* 1038 ⟩   Used in section 1037.

⟨ Append a new leader node that uses *cur_box* 1078 ⟩   Used in section 1075.

⟨ Append a new letter or a hyphen level 962 ⟩   Used in section 961.

⟨ Append a new letter or hyphen 937 ⟩   Used in section 935.

⟨ Append a normal inter-word space to the current list, then **goto** *big_switch* 1041 ⟩   Used in section 1030.

⟨ Append a penalty node, if a nonzero penalty is appropriate 890 ⟩   Used in section 880.

⟨ Append an insertion to the current page and **goto** *contribute* 1008 ⟩   Used in section 1000.

⟨ Append any *new_hlist* entries for *q*, and any appropriate penalties 767 ⟩   Used in section 760.

⟨ Append box *cur_box* to the current list, shifted by *saved*(0) 1076 ⟩   Used in section 1075.

⟨ Append character *cur_chr* and the following characters (if any) to the current hlist in the current font; **goto** *reswitch* when a non-character has been fetched 1033 ⟩   Used in section 1030.

⟨ Append character *l* and the following characters (if any) to the current hlist, in font *f*; if *ligature_present*, detach a ligature node starting at *link*(*q*); if *c* is a hyphen, append a null *disc_node*; finally **goto** *reswitch* 1035 ⟩   Used in section 1033.

⟨ Append inter-element spacing based on *r_type* and *t* 766 ⟩   Used in section 760.

⟨ Append tabskip glue and an empty box to list *u*, and update *s* and *t* as the prototype nodes are passed 809 ⟩   Used in section 808.

⟨ Append the accent with appropriate kerns, then set *p* ← *q* 1125 ⟩   Used in section 1123.

⟨ Append the current tabskip glue to the preamble list 778 ⟩   Used in section 777.

⟨ Append the display and perhaps also the equation number 1204 ⟩   Used in section 1199.

⟨ Append the glue or equation number following the display 1205 ⟩   Used in section 1199.

⟨ Append the glue or equation number preceding the display 1203 ⟩   Used in section 1199.

⟨ Append the new box to the current vertical list, followed by the list of special nodes taken out of the box by the packager 888 ⟩   Used in section 880.

⟨ Append the value *n* to list *p* 938 ⟩   Used in section 937.

⟨ Append to the ligature and **goto** *continue* 909 ⟩   Used in section 908.

⟨ Assign the values *depth_threshold* ← *show_box_depth* and *breadth_max* ← *show_box_breadth* 236 ⟩   Used in section 198.

⟨ Assignments 1217, 1218, 1221, 1224, 1225, 1226, 1228, 1232, 1234, 1235, 1241, 1242, 1248, 1252, 1253, 1256, 1264 ⟩   Used in section 1211.

⟨ Attach kerning, if *w* ≠ 0 911 ⟩   Used in section 906.

⟨ Attach list p to the current list, and record its length; then finish up and **return** 1120 ⟩
    Used in section 1119.

⟨ Attach the limits to y and adjust $height(v)$, $depth(v)$ to account for their presence 751 ⟩
    Used in section 750.

⟨ Back up an outer control sequence so that it can be reread 337 ⟩   Used in section 336.

⟨ Basic printing procedures 57, 58, 59, 60, 62, 63, 64, 65, 262, 263, 518, 699, 1355 ⟩   Used in section 4.

⟨ Break the current page at node p, put it in box 255, and put the remaining nodes on the contribution list 1017 ⟩   Used in section 1014.

⟨ Break the paragraph at the chosen breakpoints, justify the resulting lines to the correct widths, and append them to the current vertical list 876 ⟩   Used in section 815.

⟨ Build a list of characters in a maximal ligature, and set w to the amount of kerning that should follow 907 ⟩   Used in section 906.

⟨ Calculate the length, l, and the shift amount, s, of the display lines 1149 ⟩   Used in section 1145.

⟨ Calculate the natural width, w, by which the characters of the final line extend to the right of the reference point, plus two ems; or set $w \leftarrow max\_dimen$ if the non-blank information on that line is affected by stretching or shrinking 1146 ⟩   Used in section 1145.

⟨ Call the packaging subroutine, setting $just\_box$ to the justified box 889 ⟩   Used in section 880.

⟨ Call try_break if cur_p is a legal breakpoint; on the second pass, also try to hyphenate the next word, if cur_p is a glue node; then advance cur_p to the next node of the paragraph that could possibly be a legal breakpoint 866 ⟩   Used in section 863.

⟨ Case statement to copy different types and set $words$ to the number of initial words not yet copied 206 ⟩
    Used in section 205.

⟨ Cases for noads that can follow a bin_noad 733 ⟩   Used in section 728.

⟨ Cases for nodes that can appear in an mlist, after which we **goto** $done\_with\_node$ 730 ⟩
    Used in section 728.

⟨ Cases of $flush\_node\_list$ that arise in mlists only 698 ⟩   Used in section 202.

⟨ Cases of $handle\_right\_brace$ where a $right\_brace$ triggers a delayed action 1085, 1100, 1118, 1132, 1133, 1168, 1173, 1186 ⟩   Used in section 1068.

⟨ Cases of $main\_control$ that are for extensions to TeX 1347 ⟩   Used in section 1045.

⟨ Cases of $main\_control$ that are not part of the inner loop 1045 ⟩   Used in section 1030.

⟨ Cases of $main\_control$ that build boxes and lists 1056, 1057, 1063, 1067, 1073, 1090, 1092, 1094, 1097, 1102, 1104, 1109, 1112, 1116, 1122, 1126, 1130, 1134, 1137, 1140, 1150, 1154, 1158, 1162, 1164, 1167, 1171, 1175, 1180, 1190, 1193 ⟩   Used in section 1045.

⟨ Cases of $main\_control$ that don't depend on $mode$ 1210, 1268, 1271, 1274, 1276, 1285, 1290 ⟩
    Used in section 1045.

⟨ Cases of $print\_cmd\_chr$ for symbolic printing of primitives 227, 231, 239, 249, 266, 335, 377, 385, 412, 417, 469, 488, 492, 781, 984, 1053, 1059, 1072, 1089, 1108, 1115, 1143, 1157, 1170, 1179, 1189, 1209, 1220, 1223, 1231, 1251, 1255, 1261, 1263, 1273, 1278, 1287, 1292, 1295, 1346 ⟩   Used in section 298.

⟨ Cases of $show\_node\_list$ that arise in mlists only 690 ⟩   Used in section 183.

⟨ Cases where character is ignored 345 ⟩   Used in section 344.

⟨ Change buffered instruction to y or w and **goto** $found$ 613 ⟩   Used in section 612.

⟨ Change buffered instruction to z or x and **goto** $found$ 614 ⟩   Used in section 612.

⟨ Change current mode to $-vmode$ for \halign, $-hmode$ for \valign 775 ⟩   Used in section 774.

⟨ Change discretionary to compulsory and set $disc\_break \leftarrow true$ 882 ⟩   Used in section 881.

⟨ Change font dvi_f to f 621 ⟩   Used in section 620.

⟨ Change state if necessary, and **goto** $switch$ if the current character should be ignored, or **goto** $reswitch$ if the current character changes to another 344 ⟩   Used in section 343.

⟨ Change the case of the token in p, if a change is appropriate 1289 ⟩   Used in section 1288.

⟨ Change the current style and **goto** *delete_q* 763 ⟩   Used in section 761.

⟨ Change the interaction level and **return** 86 ⟩   Used in section 84.

⟨ Change this node to a style node followed by the correct choice, then **goto** *done_with_node* 731 ⟩
  Used in section 730.

⟨ Character *k* cannot be printed 49 ⟩   Used in section 48.

⟨ Character *s* is the current new-line character 244 ⟩   Used in sections 58, 59, and 60.

⟨ Check flags of unavailable nodes 170 ⟩   Used in section 167.

⟨ Check for charlist cycle 570 ⟩   Used in section 569.

⟨ Check for improper alignment in displayed math 776 ⟩   Used in section 774.

⟨ Check if node *p* is a new champion breakpoint; then **goto** *done* if *p* is a forced break or if the page-so-far
  is already too full 974 ⟩   Used in section 972.

⟨ Check if node *p* is a new champion breakpoint; then if it is time for a page break, prepare for output,
  and either fire up the user's output routine and **return** or ship out the page and **goto** *done* 1005 ⟩
  Used in section 997.

⟨ Check single-word *avail* list 168 ⟩   Used in section 167.

⟨ Check that another $ follows 1197 ⟩   Used in sections 1194 and 1206.

⟨ Check that the necessary fonts for math symbols are present; if not, flush the current math lists and
  set *danger* ← *true* 1195 ⟩   Used in section 1194.

⟨ Check that the nodes following *hb* permit hyphenation and that at least five letters have been found,
  otherwise **goto** *done1* 899 ⟩   Used in section 894.

⟨ Check the "constant" values for consistency 14, 111, 290, 522, 1249 ⟩   Used in section 1332.

⟨ Check the pool check sum 53 ⟩   Used in section 52.

⟨ Check variable-size *avail* list 169 ⟩   Used in section 167.

⟨ Clean up the memory by removing the break nodes 865 ⟩   Used in sections 815 and 863.

⟨ Clear dimensions to zero 650 ⟩   Used in sections 649 and 668.

⟨ Clear off top level from *save_stack* 282 ⟩   Used in section 281.

⟨ Close the format file 1329 ⟩   Used in section 1302.

⟨ Coerce glue to a dimension 451 ⟩   Used in sections 449 and 455.

⟨ Compiler directives 9 ⟩   Used in section 4.

⟨ Complain about an undefined family and set *cur_i* null 723 ⟩   Used in section 722.

⟨ Complain about an undefined macro 370 ⟩   Used in section 367.

⟨ Complain about missing **\endcsname** 373 ⟩   Used in section 372.

⟨ Complain about unknown unit and **goto** *done2* 459 ⟩   Used in section 458.

⟨ Complain that **\the** can't do this; give zero result 428 ⟩   Used in section 413.

⟨ Complain that the user should have said **\mathaccent** 1166 ⟩   Used in section 1165.

⟨ Compleat the incompleat noad 1185 ⟩   Used in section 1184.

⟨ Complete a potentially long **\show** command 1298 ⟩   Used in section 1293.

⟨ Compute result of *multiply* or *divide*, put it in *cur_val* 1240 ⟩   Used in section 1236.

⟨ Compute result of *register* or *advance*, put it in *cur_val* 1238 ⟩   Used in section 1236.

⟨ Compute the amount of skew 741 ⟩   Used in section 738.

⟨ Compute the badness, *b*, of the current page, using *awful_bad* if the box is too full 1007 ⟩
  Used in section 1005.

⟨ Compute the badness, *b*, using *awful_bad* if the box is too full 975 ⟩   Used in section 974.

⟨ Compute the demerits, *d*, from *r* to *cur_p* 859 ⟩   Used in section 855.

⟨ Compute the discretionary *break_width* values 840 ⟩   Used in section 837.

⟨ Compute the hash code *h* 261 ⟩   Used in section 259.

⟨ Compute the magic offset 765 ⟩   Used in section 1337.

⟨ Compute the minimum suitable height, w, and the corresponding number of extension steps, n; also set $width(b)$ 714 ⟩   Used in section 713.

⟨ Compute the new line width 850 ⟩   Used in section 835.

⟨ Compute the register location l and its type p; but **return** if invalid 1237 ⟩   Used in section 1236.

⟨ Compute the sum of two glue specs 1239 ⟩   Used in section 1238.

⟨ Compute the trie op code, v, and set $l \leftarrow 0$ 965 ⟩   Used in section 963.

⟨ Compute the values of $break\_width$ 837 ⟩   Used in section 836.

⟨ Consider a node with matching width; **goto** *found* if it's a hit 612 ⟩   Used in section 611.

⟨ Consider the demerits for a line from r to cur_p; deactivate node r if it should no longer be active; then **goto** *continue* if a line from r to cur_p is infeasible, otherwise record a new feasible break 851 ⟩   Used in section 829.

⟨ Constants in the outer block 11 ⟩   Used in section 4.

⟨ Construct a box with limits above and below it, skewed by $delta$ 750 ⟩   Used in section 749.

⟨ Construct a sub/superscript combination box x, with the superscript offset by $delta$ 759 ⟩   Used in section 756.

⟨ Construct a subscript box x when there is no superscript 757 ⟩   Used in section 756.

⟨ Construct a superscript box x 758 ⟩   Used in section 756.

⟨ Construct a vlist box for the fraction, according to $shift\_up$ and $shift\_down$ 747 ⟩   Used in section 743.

⟨ Construct an extensible character in a new box b, using recipe $rem\_byte(q)$ and font f 713 ⟩   Used in section 710.

⟨ Contribute an entire group to the current parameter 399 ⟩   Used in section 392.

⟨ Contribute the recently matched tokens to the current parameter, and **goto** *continue* if a partial match is still in effect; but abort if $s = null$ 397 ⟩   Used in section 392.

⟨ Convert a final bin_noad to an ord_noad 729 ⟩   Used in sections 726 and 728.

⟨ Convert cur_val to a lower level 429 ⟩   Used in section 413.

⟨ Convert math glue to ordinary glue 732 ⟩   Used in section 730.

⟨ Convert $nucleus(q)$ to an hlist and attach the sub/superscripts 754 ⟩   Used in section 728.

⟨ Copy the tabskip glue between columns 795 ⟩   Used in section 791.

⟨ Copy the templates from node cur_loop into node p 794 ⟩   Used in section 793.

⟨ Copy the token list 466 ⟩   Used in section 465.

⟨ Create a character node p for $nucleus(q)$, possibly followed by a kern node for the italic correction, and set $delta$ to the italic correction if a subscript is present 755 ⟩   Used in section 754.

⟨ Create a character node q for the next character, but set $q \leftarrow null$ if problems arise 1124 ⟩   Used in section 1123.

⟨ Create a new glue specification whose width is cur_val; scan for its stretch and shrink components 462 ⟩   Used in section 461.

⟨ Create a page insertion node with $subtype(r) = qi(n)$, and include the glue correction for box n in the current page state 1009 ⟩   Used in section 1008.

⟨ Create an active breakpoint representing the beginning of the paragraph 864 ⟩   Used in section 863.

⟨ Create and append a discretionary node as an alternative to the ligature, and continue to develop both branches until they become equivalent 914 ⟩   Used in section 913.

⟨ Create equal-width boxes x and z for the numerator and denominator, and compute the default amounts $shift\_up$ and $shift\_down$ by which they are displaced from the baseline 744 ⟩   Used in section 743.

⟨ Create new active nodes for the best feasible breaks just found 836 ⟩   Used in section 835.

⟨ Create the $format\_ident$, open the format file, and inform the user that dumping has begun 1328 ⟩   Used in section 1302.

⟨ Current mem equivalent of glue parameter number n 224 ⟩   Used in sections 152 and 154.

⟨ Deactivate node r 860 ⟩   Used in section 851.

⟨ Declare action procedures for use by *main_control* 1043, 1047, 1049, 1050, 1051, 1054, 1060, 1061, 1064, 1069, 1070, 1075, 1079, 1084, 1086, 1091, 1093, 1095, 1096, 1099, 1101, 1103, 1105, 1110, 1113, 1117, 1119, 1123, 1127, 1129, 1131, 1135, 1136, 1138, 1142, 1151, 1155, 1159, 1160, 1163, 1165, 1172, 1174, 1176, 1181, 1191, 1194, 1200, 1211, 1270, 1275, 1279, 1288, 1293, 1302, 1348 ⟩   Used in section 1030.

⟨ Declare math construction procedures 734, 735, 736, 737, 738, 743, 749, 752, 756, 762 ⟩   Used in section 726.

⟨ Declare procedures for preprocessing hyphenation patterns 944, 947, 948, 949, 951, 953, 957, 959, 960 ⟩   Used in section 942.

⟨ Declare procedures needed for displaying the elements of mlists 691, 692, 694 ⟩   Used in section 179.

⟨ Declare procedures needed in *do_extension* 1349, 1350 ⟩   Used in section 1348.

⟨ Declare procedures needed in *hlist_out*, *vlist_out* 1368, 1370, 1373 ⟩   Used in section 619.

⟨ Declare procedures that scan font-related stuff 577, 578 ⟩   Used in section 409.

⟨ Declare procedures that scan restricted classes of integers 432, 433, 434, 435, 436, 437 ⟩   Used in section 409.

⟨ Declare subprocedures for *line_break* 826, 829, 877, 895 ⟩   Used in section 815.

⟨ Declare subprocedures for *prefixed_command* 1215, 1229, 1236, 1243, 1244, 1245, 1246, 1247, 1257, 1265 ⟩   Used in section 1211.

⟨ Declare subprocedures for *var_delimiter* 709, 711, 712 ⟩   Used in section 706.

⟨ Declare the function called *fin_mlist* 1184 ⟩   Used in section 1174.

⟨ Declare the function called *open_fmt_file* 524 ⟩   Used in section 1303.

⟨ Declare the function called *reconstitute* 906 ⟩   Used in section 895.

⟨ Declare the procedure called *align_peek* 785 ⟩   Used in section 800.

⟨ Declare the procedure called *fire_up* 1012 ⟩   Used in section 994.

⟨ Declare the procedure called *get_preamble_token* 782 ⟩   Used in section 774.

⟨ Declare the procedure called *handle_right_brace* 1068 ⟩   Used in section 1030.

⟨ Declare the procedure called *init_span* 787 ⟩   Used in section 786.

⟨ Declare the procedure called *insert_relax* 379 ⟩   Used in section 366.

⟨ Declare the procedure called *macro_call* 389 ⟩   Used in section 366.

⟨ Declare the procedure called *print_cmd_chr* 298 ⟩   Used in section 252.

⟨ Declare the procedure called *print_skip_param* 225 ⟩   Used in section 179.

⟨ Declare the procedure called *restore_trace* 284 ⟩   Used in section 281.

⟨ Declare the procedure called *runaway* 306 ⟩   Used in section 119.

⟨ Declare the procedure called *show_token_list* 292 ⟩   Used in section 119.

⟨ Decry the invalid character and **goto** *restart* 346 ⟩   Used in section 344.

⟨ Delete the page-insertion nodes 1019 ⟩   Used in section 1014.

⟨ Delete $c -$ "0" tokens and **goto** *continue* 88 ⟩   Used in section 84.

⟨ Destroy the t nodes following q, but save the last one if it is a necessary kern; make r point to the following node 883 ⟩   Used in section 882.

⟨ Determine horizontal glue shrink setting, then **return** or **goto** *common_ending* 664 ⟩   Used in section 657.

⟨ Determine horizontal glue stretch setting, then **return** or **goto** *common_ending* 658 ⟩   Used in section 657.

⟨ Determine the displacement, d, of the left edge of the equation, with respect to the line size z, assuming that $l = false$ 1202 ⟩   Used in section 1199.

⟨ Determine the shrink order 665 ⟩   Used in sections 664, 676, and 796.

⟨ Determine the stretch order 659 ⟩   Used in sections 658, 673, and 796.

⟨ Determine the value of *height*(r) and the appropriate glue setting; then **return** or **goto** *common_ending* 672 ⟩   Used in section 668.

⟨Determine the value of *width*(*r*) and the appropriate glue setting; then **return** or **goto** *common_ending* 657⟩   Used in section 649.

⟨Determine vertical glue shrink setting, then **return** or **goto** *common_ending* 676⟩   Used in section 672.

⟨Determine vertical glue stretch setting, then **return** or **goto** *common_ending* 673⟩   Used in section 672.

⟨Discard erroneous prefixes and **return** 1212⟩   Used in section 1211.

⟨Discard the prefixes \long and \outer if they are irrelevant 1213⟩   Used in section 1211.

⟨Dispense with trivial cases of void or bad boxes 978⟩   Used in section 977.

⟨Display adjustment *p* 197⟩   Used in section 183.

⟨Display box *p* 184⟩   Used in section 183.

⟨Display choice node *p* 695⟩   Used in section 690.

⟨Display discretionary *p* 195⟩   Used in section 183.

⟨Display fraction noad *p* 697⟩   Used in section 690.

⟨Display glue *p* 189⟩   Used in section 183.

⟨Display insertion *p* 188⟩   Used in section 183.

⟨Display insertion split cost 1011⟩   Used in section 1010.

⟨Display kern *p* 191⟩   Used in section 183.

⟨Display leaders *p* 190⟩   Used in section 189.

⟨Display ligature *p* 193⟩   Used in section 183.

⟨Display mark *p* 196⟩   Used in section 183.

⟨Display math node *p* 192⟩   Used in section 183.

⟨Display node *p* 183⟩   Used in section 182.

⟨Display normal noad *p* 696⟩   Used in section 690.

⟨Display page break cost 1006⟩   Used in section 1005.

⟨Display penalty *p* 194⟩   Used in section 183.

⟨Display rule *p* 187⟩   Used in section 183.

⟨Display special fields of the unset node *p* 185⟩   Used in section 184.

⟨Display the current context 312⟩   Used in section 311.

⟨Display the token (*m*, *c*) 294⟩   Used in section 293.

⟨Display the value of *b* 502⟩   Used in section 498.

⟨Display the value of *glue_set*(*p*) 186⟩   Used in section 184.

⟨Display the whatsit node *p* 1356⟩   Used in section 183.

⟨Display token *p*, and **return** if there are problems 293⟩   Used in section 292.

⟨Do first-pass processing based on *type*(*q*); **goto** *done_with_noad* if a noad has been fully processed, **goto** *check_dimensions* if it has been translated into *new_hlist*(*q*), or **goto** *done_with_node* if a node has been fully processed 728⟩   Used in section 727.

⟨Do magic computation 320⟩   Used in section 292.

⟨Do some work that has been queued up for \write 1374⟩   Used in section 1373.

⟨Drop current token and complain that it was unmatched 1066⟩   Used in section 1064.

⟨Dump a couple more things and the closing check word 1326⟩   Used in section 1302.

⟨Dump constants for consistency check 1307⟩   Used in section 1302.

⟨Dump regions 1 to 4 of *eqtb* 1315⟩   Used in section 1313.

⟨Dump regions 5 and 6 of *eqtb* 1316⟩   Used in section 1313.

⟨Dump the array info for internal font number *k* 1322⟩   Used in section 1320.

⟨Dump the dynamic memory 1311⟩   Used in section 1302.

⟨Dump the font information 1320⟩   Used in section 1302.

⟨Dump the hash table 1318⟩   Used in section 1313.

⟨Dump the hyphenation tables 1324⟩   Used in section 1302.

⟨ Dump the string pool 1309 ⟩   Used in section 1302.

⟨ Dump the table of equivalents 1313 ⟩   Used in section 1302.

⟨ Either append the insertion node p after node q, and remove it from the current page, or delete *node*(p) 1022 ⟩   Used in section 1020.

⟨ Either insert the material specified by node p into the appropriate box, or hold it for the next page; also delete node p from the current page 1020 ⟩   Used in section 1014.

⟨ Either process \ifcase or set b to the value of a boolean condition 501 ⟩   Used in section 498.

⟨ Empty the last bytes out of *dvi_buf* 599 ⟩   Used in section 642.

⟨ Ensure that box 255 is empty after output 1028 ⟩   Used in section 1026.

⟨ Ensure that box 255 is empty before output 1015 ⟩   Used in section 1014.

⟨ Ensure that $trie\_max \geq h + 128$ 954 ⟩   Used in section 953.

⟨ Enter a hyphenation exception 939 ⟩   Used in section 935.

⟨ Enter all of the patterns into a linked trie, until coming to a right brace; then skip an optional space 961 ⟩   Used in section 960.

⟨ Enter as many hyphenation exceptions as are listed, until coming to a right brace; then skip an optional space and **return** 935 ⟩   Used in section 934.

⟨ Enter *skip_blanks* state, emit a space 349 ⟩   Used in section 347.

⟨ Error handling procedures 78, 81, 82, 93, 94, 95 ⟩   Used in section 4.

⟨ Examine node p in the hlist, taking account of its effect on the dimensions of the new box, or moving it to the adjustment list; then advance p to the next node 651 ⟩   Used in section 649.

⟨ Examine node p in the vlist, taking account of its effect on the dimensions of the new box; then advance p to the next node 669 ⟩   Used in section 668.

⟨ Expand a nonmacro 367 ⟩   Used in section 366.

⟨ Expand macros in the token list and make *link*(*def_ref*) point to the result 1371 ⟩   Used in section 1370.

⟨ Expand the next part of the input 478 ⟩   Used in section 477.

⟨ Expand the token after the next token 368 ⟩   Used in section 367.

⟨ Explain that too many dead cycles have occurred in a row 1024 ⟩   Used in section 1012.

⟨ Express astonishment that no number was here 446 ⟩   Used in section 444.

⟨ Express consternation over the fact that no alignment is in progress 1128 ⟩   Used in section 1127.

⟨ Express shock at the missing left brace; **goto** *found* 475 ⟩   Used in section 474.

⟨ Extend a ligature, **goto** *main_loop_3* 1040 ⟩   Used in section 1037.

⟨ Feed the macro body and its parameters to the scanner 390 ⟩   Used in section 389.

⟨ Fetch a box dimension 420 ⟩   Used in section 413.

⟨ Fetch a character code from some table 414 ⟩   Used in section 413.

⟨ Fetch a font dimension 425 ⟩   Used in section 413.

⟨ Fetch a font integer 426 ⟩   Used in section 413.

⟨ Fetch a register 427 ⟩   Used in section 413.

⟨ Fetch a token list or font identifier, provided that $level = tok\_val$ 415 ⟩   Used in section 413.

⟨ Fetch an internal dimension and **goto** *attach_sign*, or fetch an internal integer 449 ⟩   Used in section 448.

⟨ Fetch an item in the current node, if appropriate 424 ⟩   Used in section 413.

⟨ Fetch something on the *page_so_far* 421 ⟩   Used in section 413.

⟨ Fetch the *dead_cycles* or the *insert_penalties* 419 ⟩   Used in section 413.

⟨ Fetch the *par_shape* size 423 ⟩   Used in section 413.

⟨ Fetch the *prev_graf* 422 ⟩   Used in section 413.

⟨ Fetch the *space_factor* or the *prev_depth* 418 ⟩   Used in section 413.

⟨ Find an active node with fewest demerits 874 ⟩   Used in section 873.

⟨ Find hyphen locations for the word in *hc* 923 ⟩   Used in section 895.

⟨ Find optimal breakpoints 863 ⟩   Used in section 815.
⟨ Find the best active node for the desired looseness 875 ⟩   Used in section 873.
⟨ Find the best way to split the insertion, and change $type(r)$ to $split\_up$ 1010 ⟩   Used in section 1008.
⟨ Find the glue specification, p, for text spaces in the current font 1042 ⟩   Used in sections 1041 and 1043.
⟨ Finish an alignment in a display 1206 ⟩   Used in section 812.
⟨ Finish displayed math 1199 ⟩   Used in section 1194.
⟨ Finish issuing a diagnostic message for an overfull or underfull hbox 663 ⟩   Used in section 649.
⟨ Finish issuing a diagnostic message for an overfull or underfull vbox 675 ⟩   Used in section 668.
⟨ Finish line, emit a \par 351 ⟩   Used in section 347.
⟨ Finish line, emit a space 348 ⟩   Used in section 347.
⟨ Finish line, **goto** *switch* 350 ⟩   Used in section 347.
⟨ Finish math in text 1196 ⟩   Used in section 1194.
⟨ Finish the DVI file 642 ⟩   Used in section 1333.
⟨ Finish the extensions 1367 ⟩   Used in section 1333.
⟨ Fire up the user's output routine and **return** 1025 ⟩   Used in section 1012.
⟨ Fix the reference count, if any, and negate cur_val if *negative* 430 ⟩   Used in section 413.
⟨ Flush the box from memory, showing statistics if requested 639 ⟩   Used in section 638.
⟨ Follow the lig/kern program; **goto** $main\_loop\_3$ if scoring a hit 1037 ⟩   Used in section 1036.
⟨ Forbidden cases detected in $main\_control$ 1048, 1098, 1111, 1144 ⟩   Used in section 1045.
⟨ Generate a *down* or *right* command for w and **return** 610 ⟩   Used in section 607.
⟨ Generate a $y0$ or $z0$ command in order to reuse a previous appearance of w 609 ⟩   Used in section 607.
⟨ Get ready to start line breaking 816, 827, 834, 848 ⟩   Used in section 815.
⟨ Get the first line of input and prepare to start 1337 ⟩   Used in section 1332.
⟨ Get the next non-blank non-call token 406 ⟩
    Used in sections 405, 441, 455, 503, 526, 577, 785, 791, and 1045.
⟨ Get the next non-blank non-relax non-call token 404 ⟩
    Used in sections 403, 1078, 1084, 1151, 1160, 1211, 1226, and 1270.
⟨ Get the next non-blank non-sign token; set *negative* appropriately 441 ⟩
    Used in sections 440, 448, and 461.
⟨ Get the next token, suppressing expansion 358 ⟩   Used in section 357.
⟨ Get user's advice and **return** 83 ⟩   Used in section 82.
⟨ Give diagnostic information, if requested 1031 ⟩   Used in section 1030.
⟨ Give improper \hyphenation error 936 ⟩   Used in section 935.
⟨ Global variables 13, 20, 26, 30, 32, 39, 50, 54, 73, 76, 79, 96, 104, 115, 116, 117, 118, 124, 165, 173, 181, 213, 246,
    253, 256, 271, 286, 297, 301, 304, 305, 308, 309, 310, 333, 361, 382, 387, 388, 410, 438, 447, 480, 489, 493, 512, 513,
    520, 527, 532, 539, 549, 550, 555, 592, 595, 605, 616, 646, 647, 661, 684, 719, 724, 764, 770, 814, 821, 823, 825, 828,
    833, 839, 847, 872, 892, 900, 905, 921, 926, 943, 945, 946, 950, 971, 980, 982, 989, 1074, 1266, 1281, 1299, 1305,
    1331, 1342, 1345 ⟩   Used in section 4.
⟨ Go into display math mode 1145 ⟩   Used in section 1138.
⟨ Go into ordinary math mode 1139 ⟩   Used in sections 1138 and 1142.
⟨ Go through the preamble list, determining the column widths and changing the alignrecords to dummy
    unset boxes 801 ⟩   Used in section 800.
⟨ Grow more variable-size memory and **goto** *restart* 126 ⟩   Used in section 125.
⟨ Handle situations involving spaces, braces, changes of state 347 ⟩   Used in section 344.
⟨ If a line number class has ended, create new active nodes for the best feasible breaks in that class; then
    return if $r = last\_active$, otherwise compute the new $line\_width$ 835 ⟩   Used in section 829.
⟨ If all characters of the family fit relative to h, then **goto** *found*, otherwise **goto** *not_found* 955 ⟩
    Used in section 953.

⟨ If an alignment entry has just ended, take appropriate action 342 ⟩   Used in section 341.

⟨ If an expanded control code is present, reduce it and **goto** *start_cs* 355 ⟩   Used in sections 354 and 356.

⟨ If dumping is not allowed, abort 1304 ⟩   Used in section 1302.

⟨ If instruction *cur_i* is a kern with *cur_c*, attach the kern after *q* and **return**; or if it is a ligature with *cur_c*, combine noads *q* and *p* and **goto** *restart* 753 ⟩   Used in section 752.

⟨ If no hyphens were found, **return** 902 ⟩   Used in section 895.

⟨ If node *cur_p* is a legal breakpoint, call *try_break* 868 ⟩   Used in section 866.

⟨ If node *p* is a legal breakpoint, check if this break is the best known, and **goto** *done* if *p* is null or if the page-so-far is already too full to accept more stuff 972 ⟩   Used in section 970.

⟨ If node *q* is a style node, change the style and **goto** *delete_q*; otherwise if it is not a noad, put it into the hlist, advance *q*, and **goto** *done*; otherwise set *s* to the size of noad *q*, set *t* to the associated type (*ord_noad* .. *inner_noad*), and set *pen* to the associated penalty 761 ⟩   Used in section 760.

⟨ If node *r* is of type *delta_node*, update *cur_active_width*, set *prev_r* and *prev_prev_r*, then **goto** *continue* 832 ⟩   Used in section 829.

⟨ If the current list ends with a box node, delete it from the list and make *cur_box* point to it; otherwise set *cur_box* ← *null* 1080 ⟩   Used in section 1079.

⟨ If the current page is empty and node *p* is to be deleted, **goto** *done1*; otherwise use node *p* to update the state of the current page; if this node is an insertion, **goto** *contribute*; otherwise if this node is not a legal breakpoint, **goto** *contribute* or *update_heights*; otherwise set *pi* to the penalty associated with this breakpoint 1000 ⟩   Used in section 997.

⟨ If the list has more than one element, create a ligature node 910 ⟩   Used in section 906.

⟨ If the next character is a parameter number, make *cur_tok* a *match* token; but if it is a left brace, store '*left_brace*, *end_match*', set *hash_brace*, and **goto** *done* 476 ⟩   Used in section 474.

⟨ If the preamble list has been traversed, check that the row has ended 792 ⟩   Used in section 791.

⟨ If the right-hand side is a token parameter or token register, finish the assignment and **goto** *done* 1227 ⟩   Used in section 1226.

⟨ If the string *hyph_word*[*h*] is less than *hc*[1 .. *hn*], **goto** *not_found*; but if the two strings are equal, set *hyf* to the hyphen positions and **goto** *found* 931 ⟩   Used in section 930.

⟨ If the string *hyph_word*[*h*] is less than or equal to *s*, interchange (*hyph_word*[*h*], *hyph_list*[*h*]) with (*s*, *p*) 941 ⟩   Used in section 940.

⟨ If this font has already been loaded, set *f* to the internal font number and **goto** *common_ending* 1260 ⟩   Used in section 1257.

⟨ If this *sup_mark* starts a control character like ^^A, then **goto** *reswitch*, otherwise set *state* ← *mid_line* 352 ⟩   Used in section 344.

⟨ Ignore the fraction operation and complain about this ambiguous case 1183 ⟩   Used in section 1181.

⟨ Implement \closeout 1353 ⟩   Used in section 1348.

⟨ Implement \immediate 1375 ⟩   Used in section 1348.

⟨ Implement \openout 1351 ⟩   Used in section 1348.

⟨ Implement \special 1354 ⟩   Used in section 1348.

⟨ Implement \write 1352 ⟩   Used in section 1348.

⟨ Incorporate a whatsit node into a vbox 1359 ⟩   Used in section 669.

⟨ Incorporate a whatsit node into an hbox 1360 ⟩   Used in section 651.

⟨ Incorporate box dimensions into the dimensions of the hbox that will contain it 653 ⟩   Used in section 651.

⟨ Incorporate box dimensions into the dimensions of the vbox that will contain it 670 ⟩   Used in section 669.

⟨ Incorporate character dimensions into the dimensions of the hbox that will contain it, then move to the next node 654 ⟩   Used in section 651.

⟨ Incorporate glue into the horizontal totals 656 ⟩   Used in section 651.

⟨ Incorporate glue into the vertical totals 671 ⟩   Used in section 669.

⟨ Increase the number of parameters in the last font 580 ⟩   Used in section 578.

⟨ Initialize table entries (done by INITEX only) 164, 222, 228, 232, 240, 250, 258, 552, 952, 1216, 1301, 1369 ⟩   Used in section 8.

⟨ Initialize the current page, insert the \topskip glue ahead of p, and **goto** *continue* 1001 ⟩   Used in section 1000.

⟨ Initialize the input routines 331 ⟩   Used in section 1337.

⟨ Initialize the output routines 55, 61, 528, 533 ⟩   Used in section 1332.

⟨ Initialize the print *selector* based on *interaction* 75 ⟩   Used in sections 1265 and 1337.

⟨ Initialize the special list heads and constant nodes 790, 797, 820, 981, 988 ⟩   Used in section 164.

⟨ Initialize variables as *ship_out* begins 617 ⟩   Used in section 640.

⟨ Initialize whatever TeX might access 8 ⟩   Used in section 4.

⟨ Initiate or terminate input from a file 378 ⟩   Used in section 367.

⟨ Initiate the construction of an hbox or vbox, then **return** 1083 ⟩   Used in section 1079.

⟨ Input and store tokens from the next line of the file 483 ⟩   Used in section 482.

⟨ Input for \read from the terminal 484 ⟩   Used in section 483.

⟨ Input from external file, **goto** *restart* if no input found 343 ⟩   Used in section 341.

⟨ Input from token list, **goto** *restart* if end of list or if a parameter needs to be expanded 357 ⟩   Used in section 341.

⟨ Input the first line of *read_file* [m] 485 ⟩   Used in section 483.

⟨ Input the next line of *read_file* [m] 486 ⟩   Used in section 483.

⟨ Insert a delta node to prepare for breaks at *cur_p* 843 ⟩   Used in section 836.

⟨ Insert a delta node to prepare for the next active node ε44 ⟩   Used in section 836.

⟨ Insert a discretionary hyphen after s 918 ⟩   Used in section 913.

⟨ Insert a dummy noad to be sub/superscripted 1177 ⟩   Used in section 1176.

⟨ Insert a *frozen_endv* token 375 ⟩   Used in section 366.

⟨ Insert a new active node from *best_place* [*fit_class*] to *cur_p* 845 ⟩   Used in section 836.

⟨ Insert a new control sequence after p, then make p point to it 260 ⟩   Used in section 259.

⟨ Insert a new pattern into the linked trie 963 ⟩   Used in section 961.

⟨ Insert a new trie node between q and p, and make p point to it 964 ⟩   Used in section 963.

⟨ Insert a token saved by \afterassignment, if any 1269 ⟩   Used in section 1211.

⟨ Insert glue for *split_top_skip* and set $p \leftarrow null$ 969 ⟩   Used in section 968.

⟨ Insert hyphens as specified in *hyph_list* [h] 932 ⟩   Used in section 931.

⟨ Insert macro parameter and **goto** *restart* 359 ⟩   Used in section 357.

⟨ Insert the appropriate mark text into the scanner 386 ⟩   Used in section 367.

⟨ Insert the current list into its environment 812 ⟩   Used in section 800.

⟨ Insert the pair (s, p) into the exception table 940 ⟩   Used in section 939.

⟨ Insert the ⟨v_j⟩ template and **goto** *restart* 789 ⟩   Used in section 342.

⟨ Insert token p into TeX's input 326 ⟩   Used in section 282.

⟨ Interpret code c and **return** if done 84 ⟩   Used in section 83.

⟨ Introduce new material from the terminal and **return** 87 ⟩   Used in section 84.

⟨ Issue an error message if *cur_val* = *fmem_ptr* 579 ⟩   Used in section 578.

⟨ Justify the line ending at breakpoint *cur_p*, and append it to the current vertical list, together with associated penalties and other insertions 880 ⟩   Used in section 877.

⟨ Labels in the outer block 6 ⟩   Used in section 4.

⟨ Last-minute procedures 1333, 1335, 1336, 1338 ⟩   Used in section 1330.

⟨ Lengthen the preamble periodically 793 ⟩   Used in section 792.

⟨ Let cur_h be the position of the first box, and set $leader\_wd + lx$ to the spacing between corresponding parts of boxes 627 ⟩   Used in section 626.

⟨ Let cur_v be the position of the first box, and set $leader\_ht + lx$ to the spacing between corresponding parts of boxes 636 ⟩   Used in section 635.

⟨ Let d be the natural width of node p; if the node is "visible," **goto** *found*; if the node is glue that stretches or shrinks, set $v \leftarrow max\_dimen$ 1147 ⟩   Used in section 1146.

⟨ Let d be the natural width of this glue; if stretching or shrinking, set $v \leftarrow max\_dimen$; **goto** *found* in the case of leaders 1148 ⟩   Used in section 1147.

⟨ Let d be the width of the whatsit p 1361 ⟩   Used in section 1147.

⟨ Let n be the largest legal code value, based on cur_chr 1233 ⟩   Used in section 1232.

⟨ Link node p into the current page and **goto** *done* 998 ⟩   Used in section 997.

⟨ Local variables for dimension calculations 450 ⟩   Used in section 448.

⟨ Local variables for finishing a displayed formula 1198 ⟩   Used in section 1194.

⟨ Local variables for formatting calculations 315 ⟩   Used in section 311.

⟨ Local variables for hyphenation 901, 912, 922, 929 ⟩   Used in section 895.

⟨ Local variables for initialization 19, 163, 927 ⟩   Used in section 4.

⟨ Local variables for line breaking 862, 893 ⟩   Used in section 815.

⟨ Local variables for the inner loop of $main\_control$ 1032 ⟩   Used in section 1030.

⟨ Look ahead for ligature or kerning, either continuing the main loop or going to *reswitch* 1036 ⟩ Used in section 1035.

⟨ Look at all the marks in nodes before the break, and set the final link to *null* at the break 979 ⟩ Used in section 977.

⟨ Look at the list of characters starting with x in font g; set f and c whenever a better character is found; **goto** *found* as soon as a large enough variant is encountered 708 ⟩   Used in section 707.

⟨ Look at the other stack entries until deciding what sort of DVI command to generate; **goto** *found* if node p is a "hit" 611 ⟩   Used in section 607.

⟨ Look at the variants of (z, x); set f and c whenever a better character is found; **goto** *found* as soon as a large enough variant is encountered 707 ⟩   Used in section 706.

⟨ Look for a ligature or kern between d and the following character; update the data structure and **goto** *continue* if a ligature is found, otherwise update w and **goto** *done* 908 ⟩   Used in section 907.

⟨ Look for parameter number or ## 479 ⟩   Used in section 477.

⟨ Look for the word $hc[1 .. hn]$ in the exception table, and **goto** *found* (with *hyf* containing the hyphens) if an entry is found 930 ⟩   Used in section 923.

⟨ Look up the characters of list r in the hash table, and set cur_cs 374 ⟩   Used in section 372.

⟨ Make a copy of node p in node r 205 ⟩   Used in section 204.

⟨ Make a ligature node, if $ligature\_present$; insert a discretionary node for an explicit hyphen, if c is the current $hyphen\_char$ 1039 ⟩   Used in sections 1036 and 1038.

⟨ Make a partial copy of the whatsit node p and make r point to it; set *words* to the number of initial words not yet copied 1357 ⟩   Used in section 206.

⟨ Make a second pass over the mlist, removing all noads and inserting the proper spacing and penalties 760 ⟩   Used in section 726.

⟨ Make final adjustments and **goto** *done* 576 ⟩   Used in section 562.

⟨ Make node p look like a $char\_node$ and **goto** *reswitch* 652 ⟩   Used in sections 622, 651, and 1147.

⟨ Make sure that $page\_max\_depth$ is not exceeded 1003 ⟩   Used in section 997.

⟨ Make sure that pi is in the proper range 831 ⟩   Used in section 829.

⟨ Make the contribution list empty by setting its tail to $contrib\_head$ 995 ⟩   Used in section 994.

⟨ Make the first 128 strings 48 ⟩   Used in section 47.

⟨ Make the height of box y equal to h 739 ⟩   Used in section 738.

⟨ Output the whatsit node p in a vlist 1365 ⟩   Used in section 631.

⟨ Output the whatsit node p in an hlist 1366 ⟩   Used in section 622.

⟨ Pack the family into *trie* relative to h 956 ⟩   Used in section 953.

⟨ Pack the trie 966 ⟩   Used in section 960.

⟨ Package an unset box for the current column and record its width 796 ⟩   Used in section 791.

⟨ Package the preamble list, to determine the actual tabskip glue amounts, and let p point to this prototype box 804 ⟩   Used in section 800.

⟨ Perform the default output routine 1023 ⟩   Used in section 1012.

⟨ Pontificate about improper alignment in display 1207 ⟩   Used in section 1206.

⟨ Pop the condition stack 496 ⟩   Used in sections 498, 500, 509, and 510.

⟨ Prepare all the boxes involved in insertions to act as queues 1018 ⟩   Used in section 1014.

⟨ Prepare to deactivate node r, and **goto** *deactivate* unless there is a reason to consider lines of text from r to *cur_p* 854 ⟩   Used in section 851.

⟨ Prepare to insert a token that matches *cur_group*, and print what it is 1065 ⟩   Used in section 1064.

⟨ Prepare to move a box or rule node to the current page, then **goto** *contribute* 1002 ⟩   Used in section 1000.

⟨ Prepare to move whatsit p to the current page, then **goto** *contribute* 1363 ⟩   Used in section 1000.

⟨ Print a short indication of the contents of node p 175 ⟩   Used in section 174.

⟨ Print a symbolic description of the new break node 846 ⟩   Used in section 845.

⟨ Print a symbolic description of this feasible break 856 ⟩   Used in section 855.

⟨ Print either 'definition' or 'use' or 'preamble' or 'text', and insert tokens that should lead to recovery 339 ⟩   Used in section 338.

⟨ Print location of current line 313 ⟩   Used in section 312.

⟨ Print newly busy locations 171 ⟩   Used in section 167.

⟨ Print string s as an error message 1283 ⟩   Used in section 1279.

⟨ Print string s on the terminal 1280 ⟩   Used in section 1279.

⟨ Print the banner line, including the date and time 536 ⟩   Used in section 534.

⟨ Print the font identifier for $font(p)$ 267 ⟩   Used in sections 174 and 176.

⟨ Print the help information and **goto** *continue* 89 ⟩   Used in section 84.

⟨ Print the list between *printed_node* and *cur_p*, then set *printed_node* ← *cur_p* 857 ⟩   Used in section 856.

⟨ Print the menu of available options 85 ⟩   Used in section 84.

⟨ Print the result of command c 472 ⟩   Used in section 470.

⟨ Print two lines using the tricky pseudoprinted information 317 ⟩   Used in section 312.

⟨ Print type of token list 314 ⟩   Used in section 312.

⟨ Process an active-character control sequence and set *state* ← *mid_line* 353 ⟩   Used in section 344.

⟨ Process node-or-noad q as much as possible in preparation for the second pass of *mlist_to_hlist*, then move to the next item in the mlist 727 ⟩   Used in section 726.

⟨ Process whatsit p in *vert_break* loop, **goto** *not_found* 1364 ⟩   Used in section 973.

⟨ Prune the current list, if necessary, until it contains only *char_node*, *kern_node*, *hlist_node*, *vlist_node*, *rule_node*, and *ligature_node* items; set n to the length of the list, and set q to the list's tail 1121 ⟩   Used in section 1119.

⟨ Prune unwanted nodes at the beginning of the next line 879 ⟩   Used in section 877.

⟨ Pseudoprint the line 318 ⟩   Used in section 312.

⟨ Pseudoprint the token list 319 ⟩   Used in section 312.

⟨ Push the condition stack 495 ⟩   Used in section 498.

⟨ Put each of TeX's primitives into the hash table 226, 230, 238, 248, 265, 334, 376, 384, 411, 416, 468, 487, 491, 553, 780, 983, 1052, 1058, 1071, 1088, 1107, 1114, 1141, 1156, 1169, 1178, 1188, 1208, 1219, 1222, 1230, 1250, 1254,

1262, 1272, 1277, 1286, 1291, 1344⟩   Used in section 1336.

⟨ Put help message on the transcript file 90 ⟩   Used in section 82.

⟨ Put the (positive) 'at' size into s 1259 ⟩   Used in section 1258.

⟨ Put the characters $hu[i + 1 \; ..]$ into $post\_break(r)$, appending to this list and to $major\_tail$ until synchronization has been achieved 916 ⟩   Used in section 914.

⟨ Put the characters $hu[l + 1 \; .. \; i]$ and a hyphen into $pre\_break(r)$ 915 ⟩   Used in section 914.

⟨ Put the fraction into a box with its delimiters, and make $new\_hlist(q)$ point to it 748 ⟩
   Used in section 743.

⟨ Put the \leftskip glue at the left and detach this line 887 ⟩   Used in section 880.

⟨ Put the optimal current page into box 255, update $first\_mark$ and bot_mark, append insertions to their boxes, and put the remaining nodes back on the contribution list 1014 ⟩   Used in section 1012.

⟨ Put the \rightskip glue after node q 886 ⟩   Used in section 881.

⟨ Read and check the font data; *abort* if the TFM file is malformed; if there's no room for this font, say so and **goto** *done*; otherwise $incr(font\_ptr)$ and **goto** *done* 562 ⟩   Used in section 560.

⟨ Read box dimensions 571 ⟩   Used in section 562.

⟨ Read character data 569 ⟩   Used in section 562.

⟨ Read extensible character recipes 574 ⟩   Used in section 562.

⟨ Read font parameters 575 ⟩   Used in section 562.

⟨ Read ligature/kern program 573 ⟩   Used in section 562.

⟨ Read next line of file into *buffer*, or **goto** *restart* if the file has ended 362 ⟩   Used in section 360.

⟨ Read one string, but return *false* if the string memory space is getting too tight for comfort 52 ⟩
   Used in section 51.

⟨ Read the first line of the new file 538 ⟩   Used in section 537.

⟨ Read the other strings from the TEX.POOL file and return *true*, or give an error message and return *false* 51 ⟩   Used in section 47.

⟨ Read the TFM header 568 ⟩   Used in section 562.

⟨ Read the TFM size fields 565 ⟩   Used in section 562.

⟨ Readjust the height and depth of cur_box, for \vtop 1087 ⟩   Used in section 1086.

⟨ Reconstitute nodes for the hyphenated word, inserting discretionary hyphens 913 ⟩   Used in section 903.

⟨ Record a new feasible break 855 ⟩   Used in section 851.

⟨ Recover from an unbalanced output routine 1027 ⟩   Used in section 1026.

⟨ Recover from an unbalanced write command 1372 ⟩   Used in section 1371.

⟨ Recycle node p 999 ⟩   Used in section 997.

⟨ Remove the last box, unless it's part of a discretionary 1081 ⟩   Used in section 1080.

⟨ Replace nodes $ha \; .. \; hb$ by a sequence of nodes that includes the discretionary hyphens 903 ⟩
   Used in section 895.

⟨ Replace the tail of the list by p 1187 ⟩   Used in section 1186.

⟨ Replace z by z' and compute α, β 572 ⟩   Used in section 571.

⟨ Report a runaway argument and abort 396 ⟩   Used in sections 392 and 399.

⟨ Report a tight hbox and **goto** *common_ending*, if this box is sufficiently bad 667 ⟩   Used in section 664.

⟨ Report a tight vbox and **goto** *common_ending*, if this box is sufficiently bad 678 ⟩   Used in section 676.

⟨ Report an extra right brace and **goto** *continue* 395 ⟩   Used in section 392.

⟨ Report an improper use of the macro and abort 398 ⟩   Used in section 397.

⟨ Report an overfull hbox and **goto** *common_ending*, if this box is sufficiently bad 666 ⟩
   Used in section 664.

⟨ Report an overfull vbox and **goto** *common_ending*, if this box is sufficiently bad 677 ⟩
   Used in section 676.

⟨Report an underfull hbox and **goto** *common_ending*, if this box is sufficiently bad 660⟩
    Used in section 658.
⟨Report an underfull vbox and **goto** *common_ending*, if this box is sufficiently bad 674⟩
    Used in section 673.
⟨Report that an invalid delimiter code is being changed to null; set *cur_val* ← 0 1161⟩
    Used in section 1160.
⟨Report that the font won't be loaded 561⟩   Used in section 560.
⟨Report that this dimension is out of range 460⟩   Used in section 448.
⟨Resume the page builder after an output routine has come to an end 1026⟩   Used in section 1100.
⟨Reverse the links of the relevant passive nodes, setting *cur_p* to the first breakpoint 878⟩
    Used in section 877.
⟨Scan a control sequence and set *state* ← *skip_blanks* or *mid_line* 354⟩   Used in section 344.
⟨Scan a numeric constant 444⟩   Used in section 440.
⟨Scan a parameter until its delimiter string has been found; or, if *s* = *null*, simply scan the delimiter
    string 392⟩   Used in section 391.
⟨Scan a subformula enclosed in braces and **return** 1153⟩   Used in section 1151.
⟨Scan ahead in the buffer until finding a nonletter; if an expanded control code is encountered, reduce it
    and **goto** *start_cs*; otherwise if a multiletter control sequence is found, adjust *cur_cs* and *loc*, and
    goto *found* 356⟩   Used in section 354.
⟨Scan an alphabetic character code into *cur_val* 442⟩   Used in section 440.
⟨Scan an optional space 443⟩   Used in sections 442, 448, 455, and 1200.
⟨Scan and build the body of the token list; **goto** *found* when finished 477⟩   Used in section 473.
⟨Scan and build the parameter part of the macro definition 474⟩   Used in section 473.
⟨Scan decimal fraction 452⟩   Used in section 448.
⟨Scan file name in the buffer 531⟩   Used in section 530.
⟨Scan for all other units and adjust *cur_val* and *f* accordingly; **goto** *done* in the case of scaled
    points 458⟩   Used in section 453.
⟨Scan for `fil` units; **goto** *attach_fraction* if found 454⟩   Used in section 453.
⟨Scan for `mu` units and **goto** *attach_fraction* 456⟩   Used in section 453.
⟨Scan for units that are internal dimensions; **goto** *attach_sign* with *cur_val* set if found 455⟩
    Used in section 453.
⟨Scan preamble text until *cur_cmd* is *tab_mark* or *car_ret*, looking for changes in the tabskip glue;
    append an alignrecord to the preamble list 779⟩   Used in section 777.
⟨Scan the argument for command *c* 471⟩   Used in section 470.
⟨Scan the font size specification 1258⟩   Used in section 1257.
⟨Scan the parameters and make *link*(*r*) point to the macro body; but **return** if an illegal \par is
    detected 391⟩   Used in section 389.
⟨Scan the preamble and record it in the *preamble* list 777⟩   Used in section 774.
⟨Scan the template ⟨*u_j*⟩, putting the resulting token list in *hold_head* 783⟩   Used in section 779.
⟨Scan the template ⟨*v_j*⟩, putting the resulting token list in *hold_head* 784⟩   Used in section 779.
⟨Scan units and set *cur_val* to $x \cdot (cur\_val + f/2^{16})$, where there are *x* units per sp; **goto** *attach_sign* if
    the units are internal 453⟩   Used in section 448.
⟨Search *eqtb* for equivalents equal to *p* 255⟩   Used in section 172.
⟨Search *hyph_list* for pointers to *p* 933⟩   Used in section 172.
⟨Search *save_stack* for equivalents that point to *p* 285⟩   Used in section 172.
⟨Select the appropriate case and **return** or **goto** *common_ending* 509⟩   Used in section 501.
⟨Set initial values of key variables 21, 23, 24, 74, 77, 80, 97, 166, 215, 254, 257, 272, 287, 383, 439, 481, 490, 521,
    551, 556, 593, 596, 606, 648, 662, 685, 771, 928, 990, 1267, 1282, 1300, 1343⟩   Used in section 8.

⟨ Set line length parameters in preparation for hanging indentation 849 ⟩   Used in section 848.

⟨ Set the glue in all the unset boxes of the current list 805 ⟩   Used in section 800.

⟨ Set the glue in node r and change it from an unset node 808 ⟩   Used in section 807.

⟨ Set the unset box q and the unset boxes in it 807 ⟩   Used in section 805.

⟨ Set the value of b to the badness for shrinking the line, and compute the corresponding fit_class 853 ⟩   Used in section 851.

⟨ Set the value of b to the badness for stretching the line, and compute the corresponding fit_class 852 ⟩   Used in section 851.

⟨ Set the value of $output\_penalty$ 1013 ⟩   Used in section 1012.

⟨ Set up the values of cur_size and cur_mu, based on cur_style 703 ⟩   Used in sections 720, 726, 730, 754, 760, and 763.

⟨ Set variable c to the current escape character 243 ⟩   Used in section 63.

⟨ Ship box p out 640 ⟩   Used in section 638.

⟨ Show equivalent n, in region 1 or 2 223 ⟩   Used in section 252.

⟨ Show equivalent n, in region 3 229 ⟩   Used in section 252.

⟨ Show equivalent n, in region 4 233 ⟩   Used in section 252.

⟨ Show equivalent n, in region 5 242 ⟩   Used in section 252.

⟨ Show equivalent n, in region 6 251 ⟩   Used in section 252.

⟨ Show the auxiliary field, a 219 ⟩   Used in section 218.

⟨ Show the current contents of a box 1296 ⟩   Used in section 1293.

⟨ Show the current meaning of a token, then **goto** $common\_ending$ 1294 ⟩   Used in section 1293.

⟨ Show the current value of some parameter or register, then **goto** $common\_ending$ 1297 ⟩   Used in section 1293.

⟨ Show the font identifier in $eqtb[n]$ 234 ⟩   Used in section 233.

⟨ Show the halfword code in $eqtb[n]$ 235 ⟩   Used in section 233.

⟨ Show the status of the current page 986 ⟩   Used in section 218.

⟨ Show the text of the macro being expanded 401 ⟩   Used in section 389.

⟨ Simplify a trivial box 721 ⟩   Used in section 720.

⟨ Skip to \else or \fi, then **goto** $common\_ending$ 500 ⟩   Used in section 498.

⟨ Skip to node ha, or **goto** $done1$ if no hyphenation should be attempted 896 ⟩   Used in section 894.

⟨ Skip to node hb, putting letters into hu and hc 897 ⟩   Used in section 894.

⟨ Sort p into the list starting at $rover$ and advance p to $rlink(p)$ 132 ⟩   Used in section 131.

⟨ Split off part of a vertical box, make cur_box point to it 1082 ⟩   Used in section 1079.

⟨ Squeeze the equation as much as possible; if there is an equation number that should go on a separate line by itself, set $e \leftarrow 0$ 1201 ⟩   Used in section 1199.

⟨ Start a new current page 991 ⟩   Used in sections 215 and 1017.

⟨ Store cur_box in a box register 1077 ⟩   Used in section 1075.

⟨ Store maximum values in the hyf table 924 ⟩   Used in section 923.

⟨ Store $save\_stack[save\_ptr]$ in $eqtb[p]$, unless $eqtb[p]$ holds a global value 283 ⟩   Used in section 282.

⟨ Store the current token, but **goto** $continue$ if it is a blank space that would become an undelimited parameter 393 ⟩   Used in section 392.

⟨ Subtract glue from $break\_width$ 838 ⟩   Used in section 837.

⟨ Subtract the width of node s from $break\_width$ 841 ⟩   Used in section 840.

⟨ Suppress expansion of the next token 369 ⟩   Used in section 367.

⟨ Swap the subscript and superscript into box x 742 ⟩   Used in section 738.

⟨ Switch to a larger accent if available and appropriate 740 ⟩   Used in section 738.

⟨ Tell the user what has run away and try to recover 338 ⟩   Used in section 336.

⟨ Terminate the current conditional and skip to \fi 510 ⟩   Used in section 367.

⟨ Test box register status 505 ⟩   Used in section 501.

⟨ Test if an integer is odd 504 ⟩   Used in section 501.

⟨ Test if two characters match 506 ⟩   Used in section 501.

⟨ Test if two macro texts match 508 ⟩   Used in section 507.

⟨ Test if two tokens match 507 ⟩   Used in section 501.

⟨ Test relation between integers or dimensions 503 ⟩   Used in section 501.

⟨ The em width for *cur_font* 558 ⟩   Used in section 455.

⟨ The x-height for *cur_font* 559 ⟩   Used in section 455.

⟨ Tidy up the parameter just scanned, and tuck it away 400 ⟩   Used in section 392.

⟨ Transfer node p to the adjustment list 655 ⟩   Used in section 651.

⟨ Transplant the post-break list 884 ⟩   Used in section 882.

⟨ Transplant the pre-break list 885 ⟩   Used in section 882.

⟨ Treat *cur_chr* as an active character 1152 ⟩   Used in sections 1151 and 1155.

⟨ Try the final line break at the end of the paragraph, and **goto** *done* if the desired breakpoints have been found 873 ⟩   Used in section 863.

⟨ Try to allocate within node p and its physical successors, and **goto** *found* if allocation was possible 127 ⟩   Used in section 125.

⟨ Try to break after a discretionary fragment 870 ⟩   Used in section 866.

⟨ Try to get a different log file name 535 ⟩   Used in section 534.

⟨ Try to hyphenate the following word 894 ⟩   Used in section 866.

⟨ Try to recover from mismatched \right 1192 ⟩   Used in section 1191.

⟨ Types in the outer block 18, 25, 38, 101, 109, 113, 150, 212, 269, 300, 548, 594, 920, 925 ⟩   Used in section 4.

⟨ Undump a couple more things and the closing check word 1327 ⟩   Used in section 1303.

⟨ Undump constants for consistency check 1308 ⟩   Used in section 1303.

⟨ Undump regions 1 to 6 of *eqtb* 1317 ⟩   Used in section 1314.

⟨ Undump the array info for internal font number k 1323 ⟩   Used in section 1321.

⟨ Undump the dynamic memory 1312 ⟩   Used in section 1303.

⟨ Undump the font information 1321 ⟩   Used in section 1303.

⟨ Undump the hash table 1319 ⟩   Used in section 1314.

⟨ Undump the hyphenation tables 1325 ⟩   Used in section 1303.

⟨ Undump the string pool 1310 ⟩   Used in section 1303.

⟨ Undump the table of equivalents 1314 ⟩   Used in section 1303.

⟨ Update the active widths by including the glue in *glue_ptr*(*cur_p*) 869 ⟩   Used in section 866.

⟨ Update the active widths, since the first active node has been deleted 861 ⟩   Used in section 860.

⟨ Update the current height and depth measurements with respect to a glue or kern node p 976 ⟩   Used in section 972.

⟨ Update the current page measurements with respect to the glue or kern specified by node p 1004 ⟩   Used in section 997.

⟨ Update the value of *printed_node* for symbolic displays 858 ⟩   Used in section 829.

⟨ Update the values of *first_mark* and *bot_mark* 1016 ⟩   Used in section 1014.

⟨ Update the values of *last_glue*, *last_penalty*, and *last_kern* 996 ⟩   Used in section 994.

⟨ Update the values of *max_h* and *max_v*; but if the page is too large, **goto** *done* 641 ⟩   Used in section 640.

⟨ Update width entry for spanned columns 798 ⟩   Used in section 796.

⟨ Use code c to distinguish between generalized fractions 1182 ⟩   Used in section 1181.

⟨ Use node p to update the current height and depth measurements; if this node is not a legal breakpoint, **goto** *not_found* or *update_heights*, otherwise set *pi* to the associated penalty at the break 973 ⟩   Used in section 972.

⟨ Use size fields to allocate font information 566 ⟩   Used in section 562.

⟨ Wipe out the whatsit node p and **goto** *done* 1358 ⟩   Used in section 202.

⟨ Wrap up the box specified by node r, splitting node p if called for; set *wait* ← *true* if node p holds a
   remainder after splitting 1021 ⟩   Used in section 1020.

CHART   594

Here is a diagram that shows the major components of TeX as rectangles. Components that interact strongly have been placed next to each other.

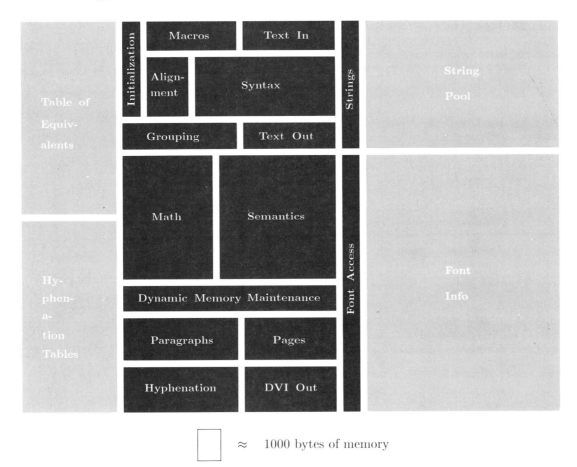

$\approx$ 1000 bytes of memory

In addition to the components shown, a large rectangle labeled 'Dynamic Memory' should be imagined underneath all the darker areas in the center of the chart; this is *mem*, which is used extensively by almost all components of the program.

The rectangles have been drawn to scale according to the approximate amount of memory space they occupy in a typical production system. In this way the chart indicates a total of about $12 \times 22 = 264K$ bytes of memory, plus $12 \times 10 = 120K$ for the dynamic memory region not shown explicitly. The dynamic memory is often considerably larger in practice, because it is desirable to accommodate large macro packages and large pages; hence we can estimate TeX's total memory requirements to be about 500K bytes.

To "Sis & P.J.
for a Christmas chuckle
(1963), — and, perhaps, an
occasional one thereafter!
Frank

Bennett Cerf's Houseful of Laughter

Bennett Cerf's
Houseful

Random House **New York**

of **Laughter**

Illustrated by Arnold Roth , Walt Kelly, and Roger Price

The editor thanks the following for permission to reprint copyrighted material: McGraw-Hill Book Co., Inc., for an excerpt from *It All Started With Columbus*, revised edition, by Richard Armour, copyright, 1953 © 1961, by Richard Armour; Heywood Hale Broun and Constance Broun for "The Fifty-First Dragon," copyright, 1921, 1941, by Heywood Hale Broun; Simon and Schuster, Inc., for "The Story of Chicken Little," copyright, 1953, by Walt Kelly; Helen Thurber for "The Little Girl and the Wolf" by James Thurber, copyright, 1939, by The New Yorker Magazine, Inc.; Doubleday & Company, Inc., for "The Ransom of Red Chief" from *Whirligigs* by O. Henry, copyright, 1907, by Doubleday & Company, Inc.; Random House, Inc., for "How Beautiful With Mud" from *We Shook the Family Tree* by Hildegarde Dolson, copyright, 1941, 1942, 1946, by Hildegarde Dolson; McIntosh and Otis, Inc., for "The Affair at 7, Rue de M—," copyright © 1955, by John Steinbeck; Alfred A. Knopf, Inc., for "Father Opens My Mail" from *Life With Father*, copyright, 1934, by Clarence Day; Dodd, Mead & Company for "How We Kept Mother's Day" from *Laugh With Leacock* by Stephen Leacock, copyright, 1930, by Dodd, Mead & Company; Harper & Row, Publishers, Incorporated, for "Your Boy and His Dog" from *Chips Off the Old Benchley* by Robert Benchley, copyright, 1932, by The Hearst Corporation, New York Mirror Division; Simon and Schuster, Inc., for droodles from *The Rich Sardine*, copyright, 1954, by Roger Price; World Publishing Company for "Pay the Two Francs," copyright ©1960, by Art Buchwald, from *Don't Forget to Write*; Billy Rose for "Learning to Drive" from *Wine, Women, and Words*, copyright, 1946, 1947, 1948, by Glenmore Productions, Inc.; Hughes Mearns for "The Little Man Who Wasn't There"; John Schaffner Literary Agent for "Miniature" from *For Partly Proud Parents* (Harper & Brothers), copyright, 1950, by Richard Armour; Simon and Schuster, Inc., for "Infant Prodigy" from *Look Who's a Mother*, copyright, 1945, by Margaret Fishback; E. P. Dutton & Co., Inc., for "Habits of the Hippopotamus" from *Gaily the Troubadour* by Arthur Guiterman, copyright, 1936, by E. P. Dutton & Co., Inc.; Little, Brown and Co. for "Eletelephony" from *Tirra Lirra* by Laura E. Richards; Liveright, Publishers, New York, for three poems from *Poems in Praise of Practically Nothing* by Samuel Hoffenstein, copyright ©R-1956, by David Hoffenstein; The Dial Press, Inc., for "Song of the Pop-Bottlers" from *A Bowl of Bishop* by Morris Bishop, copyright, 1954, by Morris Bishop; Little, Brown and Co. for "The Lama," copyright, 1931, by Ogden Nash (originally published in *The New Yorker*), "Song of the Open Road," copyright, 1932, by Ogden Nash (originally published in *The New Yorker*), "Reflections on Babies," copyright, 1940, by Ogden Nash, and "The Termite," "The Fly," and "The Eel," copyright, 1942, by Ogden Nash; Harper & Row, Publishers, Incorporated, for limericks from *Out on a Limerick*, copyright © 1960, by Bennett Cerf; Epstein and Carroll, Associates, for "The Word Market" from *The Phantom Tollbooth* by Norton Juster, copyright © 1961, by Norton Juster; Helen Thurber for "The Night the Bed Fell" by James Thurber, copyright, 1933, © 1961, by The New Yorker Magazine, Inc.; Doubleday & Company, Inc., for "The Face Is Familiar But—" copyright, 1945, by Max Shulman, from *The Many Loves of Dobie Gillis* by Max Shulman; Random House, Inc., for "Practice Mission" from *No Time for Sergeants* by Mac Hyman, copyright, 1954, by Mac Hyman.

The riddles in "Riddle-de-Dee" are reprinted from *Riddle-de-Dee* by Bennett Cerf (Random House), copyright © 1962, by Bennett Cerf.

Contents

Foreword

HOUSEFUL OF LAUGHTER is one anthology that changed stories in midstream—and is, I promise you, very much the better for it. Originally, it consisted of material *I* believed would tickle the fancies of boys and girls in their early teens. Several mothers and fathers approved my selections. "Off to the printers with the script!" I cried happily.

Then, at the last moment, I had a revolutionary idea. Why not, I suggested at an editorial meeting, astonishing associates with my ingenuity, test our material on the boys and girls *themselves*—to find out if they still respond to stories that once convulsed their tottering old parents?

Testers proved easy to come by. Anthologists and critics evidently mature early in life—with opinions that are frighteningly definite. Nary a 12-to-15-year-old did we encounter who didn't know *exactly* what should be included in HOUSEFUL OF LAUGHTER—and, equally important, what should be left out. Kitty Hart's lovely daughter, Cathy, and precocious and persuasive Tommy and Peter Bernstein were particularly helpful. My own two boys remembered stories they had loved when they were younger. Everybody got into the act. *And did we listen?*

As the book changed form, I grew so enthusiastic about the help of my young collaborators that my wife predicted I'd wind up in schoolyards hissing at teenagers, "Psst! Want to help edit an anthology of humor?"

The fact is that everybody *wants* to laugh more in this world today—and everybody *needs* to if he is to preserve his sanity. HOUSEFUL OF LAUGHTER in its final form, will, I hope, at least point some thousands of young readers in the right direction.

BENNETT CERF

Bennett Cerf's Houseful of Laughter

It All Started With Columbus

by Richard Armour

The Discovery of America

America was founded by Columbus in 1492. This is an easy date to remember because it rhymes with "ocean blue," which was the color of the Atlantic in those days. If he had sailed a year later the date would still be easy to remember because it would rhyme with "boundless sea."

Columbus fled to this country because of persecution by Ferdinand and Isabella, who refused to believe the world was round, even when Columbus showed them an egg. Ferdinand later became famous because he objected to bullfights and said he preferred to smell flowers if he had to smell anything. He was stung in the end by a bee.

Before Columbus reached America, which he named after a man called American Vesuvius, he cried "Ceylon! Ceylon!" because he wanted to see India, which was engraved on his heart, before he died. When he arrived, he cried again. This time he cried "Excelsior!" meaning "I have founded it." Excelsior has been widely used ever since by persons returning with chinaware from China, with indiaware from India, and with underware from Down Under.

Columbus was mistaken in thinking he had reached India when actually he had not got even as far as Indiana. There is still a great

From the book *It All Started With Columbus*.

deal of confusion about the East and the West. As Columbus discovered, if you go west long enough you find yourself in the east, and vice versa. The East and the West are kept apart by the Date Line, just as the North and South are kept apart by the Masons' Dixon Line. In the New World most of the eastern half of the country is called the Middle West, although it is known as the East by those who live in the Far West.

Columbus, who was as confused as anybody who has been at sea for a long time, called the first people he saw "Indians." It is not known what they called Columbus. His unfortunate error has been perpetuated through the centuries. The original Americans are still known as "Indians," while all manner of immigrants from England, Ireland, Angora, and Lichtenstein are referred to as "Americans."[1]

Accompanied by his devoted followers, the Knights of Columbus, Columbus made several other voyages in search of India. Try as he might, however, he kept discovering America, and finally returned to Spain to die. He lived for a time in Madrid, but spent his last days in Disgrace.

---

[1] Or, by their mathematically inclined friends, "100 percent Americans."

A MINORITY OPINION

Some say it was not Columbus who discovered America but a man named Leaf Ericson. Leaf came from one of the Scandinavian countries with a shipload of people, all of whom were called Yon Yonson or Ole Olson or Big Swede, and went straight to Wisconsin, where he unloaded his passengers and went back for more.

On his next trip he went to Minnesota.

We know all this from some undecipherable remarks he made on a piece of stone. This stone has since become an utter rune.

FURTHER EXPLORATIONS

After Columbus proved the world was round, a great many people went around it. Marco Polo, who was one of the earlier explorers, had the misfortune to live several centuries before Columbus. Therefore, although he got around a good deal, he did not get completely around. He went far to the north, however, and is remembered for his discovery of the Polo regions.

The chief rivals in exploration were England and Spain. England had men like Cabot, who spoke only to a man named Lowell, and Sir Francis Drake, who had a singed beard and a ship called the *Golden Behind.*

Nor should we forget Sir Martin Fourflusher.[1]

The struggle between England and Spain came to a climax in an epic sea battle off the Azores known as the Last Fight of the Revenge. In this decisive conflict, Sir Richard Grenville and Alfred Lord Tennyson proved conclusively that the lighter English warships could get more miles to the galleon.

England has ruled the waves ever since and has kept the sun from

---

[1] A direct descendant of the early Saxons, who knew all the Angles.

setting anywhere on her empire, thus providing a longer working day than in other countries.

Other explorers included Bilbo, Cabbage de Vaca, Cortez (known as The Stout, who traveled much in realms looking for gold), and Pantsy de Lion, a thirsty old man who was looking for a drinking fountain.[1] He never found it, but he founded Florida, to which a great many thirsty old men have gone ever since.

The Virginia Colony

All this time there was not much happening in the New World, except that it was steadily growing older.

This period, known as the Doldrums, came to an end in fifteen-something-or-other when Sir Walter Raleigh, a man with a pointed beard and a pointless way of muddying his cloak, established a colony in America in the hope of pleasing the Queen, whose favor he had been in but was temporarily out of.

Although he claimed the new land in the name of Elizabeth, he called it Virginia, which aroused suspicions in Elizabeth's mind and caused her to confine Sir Walter in a tower. While imprisoned, Sir Walter made good use of his time by writing a history of the world on such scraps of paper as he could find, and filling other scraps of paper with a weed brought back from Virginia.

He had barely completed his history when he lost his head. Had he been permitted to keep it a few years longer he might have become the first man to roll a cigarette with one hand.

The Virginia Colony was lost for a time, and its name was

---

[1] Some historians say that in his wanderings through the South he invented the Dixie cup, just in case.

changed to The Lost Colony, but it was subsequently found at about the place where it was last seen. Its original name of Virginia was restored because Elizabeth no longer cared, being dead.[1]

THE INDIANS

The people who were already in the New World when the white men arrived were the first Americans, or America Firsters. They were also referred to as the First Families of Virginia.

The early colonists found the Indians living in toupees, or wigwams, and sending up smoke signals, or wigwags, with piece pipes. Apparently because of a shortage of pipes, they sat in a circle and passed one pipe around, each biting off a piece as it passed. The chief Indian was named Hiawatha, and his squaw, whose name was Evangeline, did all the work. This was later to become an Old American Custom.

The Chiefs, it must be said in all fairness, were too busy to work. They were engaged in making wampum, or whoopee, when they were not mixing war paint or scattering arrowheads about, to be found centuries later.

In order to have their hands free to work, the squaws carried their babies, or cabooses, on their back, very much as kangaroos carry their babies on their front, only different.

The Indians were stern, silent people who never showed their feelings, even while being scalped. They crept up on their enemies without breaking a twig and were familiar with all the warpaths. Despite their savage ways, they sincerely loved peace, and were called Nobel Savages.

Their favorite word was "How," which the colonists soon learned was not a question.

The whites feared the redskins and considered them the forest's

---

[1] The end of Elizabeth is known as the Elizabethan Period.

prime evil. Some went so far as to say that "The only good Indian is a wooden Indian." The redskins resented the whiteskins because they thought they had come to take their lands away from them, and their fears were well grounded.

Captain John Smith was the first of a long line of Smiths who came to this country to keep up with the Joneses.

He was captured by the great Indian Chief, Powhatan, and was about to be killed when Popocatepetl, the fiery young daughter of the Chief, stepped in. We are not told what she stepped in, but she saved Captain John Smith's life, for which he thanked her. Later she married an Englishman, which improved relations.

The Pilgrims

The Pilgrims were a branch of the Puritans, and were proud of their family tree. They wore tall hats, which they had to take off when they went inside because they attended a low church. This displeased King James, who raised the roof. He demanded that they attend the same church as he did. At least this is his side of the story, which became known as the King James Version.

Although the King insisted, the Puritans, who were very stiff-necked from years of wearing truffles on their collars, stubbornly declined. They would probably still be declining if they had not left England and gone to Leyden, a city in Holland noted for the discovery of electricity in a jar. (Electricity was subsequently lost for a while, but was rediscovered, by accident, when Benjamin Franklin was told to go fly a kite, and did.)

While in Holland, the Pilgrims suffered from pangs of sin, and sent their children to Dutch Reform Schools when they misbehaved. These children, naturally enough, became Protestants, but their protests were ignored.

THE PLYMOUTH COLONY

After several years in Holland, the Pilgrims decided to set out for the New World. This decision to move is known as Pilgrims' Progress.

The ship on which they sailed was the *Mayflower*. In stormy weather the women and children descended below the heaving decks, thus becoming the *Mayflower* descendants. There they huddled with the Colonial Dames and other early settlers and passed the weary hours comparing genealogies.

It was a long and perilous voyage across the Atlantic. Several times they were blown off their course. But finally, in 1620, which was a doubly Memorable Year because it was also the year in which they set sail, they sighted the rocky coast. The rock on which they landed they called Plymouth Rock because it reminded them of another rock of the same name in England. They built a small picket fence around it and made it a national shrine.

The first four men ashore became our fourfathers.

THE FIRST WINTER

After a short stay on Plymouth Rock, which was windy and damp, the Pilgrims sought a more sheltered place to build a town. One party went in one direction and one went in another. This was the beginning of the two-party system. When the two parties met, they held the first town meeting.

The first winter was cold, which was a distinct surprise to the Pilgrims. Indeed, they might not have survived but for the corn that was given them by friendly Indians. By a curious quirk of history, it has since become illegal for white men to give Indians either corn or rye.

The next spring the crops were good, and in the fall the Pilgrims celebrated their first Thanksgiving, which fell, that fall, on a Thursday. The friendly Indians were invited, and the unfriendly Indians stayed in the background, muttering.

One of the leaders of the little band[1] at Plymouth was Captain Miles Standish. He was known throughout the township for his courtship.

He was an exceptional man. Except for him, almost all the Pilgrims were named William or John. One of the latter was Miles Standish's friend, quiet John Alden, a man who did not speak for himself until spoken to. He was spoken to, and sharply, by the fair Priscilla, whom he married, much to the annoyance of Miles Standish, who thought he was stood up by his stand-in.

The Colonies Grow

Let us leave the Pilgrims in Plymouth and see what was happening elsewhere in New England.

Education took a forward step with the founding of Harvard in a yard near the Charles River. Among the early benefactors of Harvard was a plantation owner from the South known as "Cotton" Mather. The first library was only a five-foot shelf, given to the college by T. S. Eliot, a graduate who no longer had need of it. The books on this shelf are known as the Great Books and have grown to one hundred.

With the founding of two other old colleges, Old Eli and Old

---

[1] A precursor of such bandleaders as Paul Whiteman and Benny Goodman.

Nassau, the educational system was complete. Because of the ivory towers which were a distinctive feature of many of the early buildings, the three colleges became known as the Ivory League.

To provide recreational facilities for students at Harvard, the city of Boston was established. Boston became famous for its two famous hills, Beacon and Bunker, its two famous churches, North and South, and its two famous bays, Back and Front.

The people of Boston became wealthy by exporting baked beans and codfish, which they were smart enough not to eat themselves. Many, who were pillars of the churches and pillars of society, came to be known as Propper Bostonians.

WILLIAMS AND PENN

One who was unhappy with life in Plymouth was Roger Williams, who thought the Pilgrims were intolerable. The Pilgrims, in turn, thought Williams was impossible. He proposed that they pay the Indians for their land instead of simply taking it from them. This utopian suggestion was dismissed by the Pilgrims as economically unsound.

Because of his unorthodox views, the Pilgrims branded him. They branded him a heretic, and drove him from town to town, although he preferred to walk. This was why Roger Williams reluctantly left Plymouth and founded Rhode Island, which is really not an island and is so small that it is usually indicated on maps by the letters "R.I." out in the Atlantic Ocean. It was once densely wooded. It is now densely populated.

William Penn, on the other hand, came to America to collect some land the King owed his father. He belonged to a frightened religious sect known as the Quakers. So that he would not be forgotten, he gave his name to the Pennsylvania Railroad, the Pennsylvania Station, and the state prison, which is known as the Penn.

MASSACHUSETTS BAY

The English had always been a seafaring race, ever since they were Danes. Therefore one of their first acts in the New World was to make Massachusetts Bay a colony. From Massachusetts Bay and the nearby bayous they went out in their high-masted vessels looking for whale oil, which they found mostly in whales. The men who went away on voyages to capture whales were called whalers. So, by coincidence, were their sturdy ships. This is more confusing to us now than it was then.

The most famous whale, in those days, was an ill-tempered, unpredictable old whale called Moody Dick. Everyone was on the lookout for him, especially whalers whose legs he had bitten off in one of his nastier moods. The one-legged whaler who was most resentful was Captain A. Hab, who persisted until he finally managed to harpoon Moody Dick where it hurt the most. The whale had the last word, however, for he overturned Captain A. Hab's ship, the *Peapod*, which went down with all hands, including both of Captain A. Hab's.

CONNECTICUT

Fortunately for those who liked to visit New York but preferred not to live there, Connecticut was founded within commuting distance.

It was founded by Thomas Hooker, a clergyman who, in a dim church, interpreted the Gospel according to his own lights. He would also accept no money for his preaching, which set a low wage standard for others; he was therefore scorned as a free thinker. So he left under a cloud. Many of his parishioners believed his stern words about hell and followed him to Hartford, where he guaranteed them protection in the hereafter and sold them the first fire-insurance policies.

Connecticut is usually spelled Conn, which is easier.

Life in Old New England

Most of the Puritans were ministers. Each week they could hardly wait until Sunday, when they preached for several hours on such subjects as "Hellfire" and "Damnation." In those days, church attendance was as good every Sunday as it is today on Easter.

The homes of the Puritans were simple and austere, but their furniture was antique and therefore frightfully expensive. The chairs were as straight and stiff as the Puritans themselves, and had hard bottoms. They became known as period pieces because they went to pieces after a short period of sitting on them.

Stores were known as Shoppes, or Ye Olde Shoppes. Prices were somewhat higher at the latter.

The Puritans believed in justice. A woman who was a witch, or a man who was a son of a witch, was punished by being stuck in the stocks. These were wooden devices that had holes to put the arms and legs through, and were considered disgraceful. They were also considered uncomfortable.

Every day the men went out into the fields in their blunderbusses and sowed corn. The women, meanwhile, were busy at home embroidering the alphabet and the date on a piece of cloth.

Other amusements were pillories, whipping posts, and Indian massacres.

THE LAND

The land was stony and hilly, except in places where it was hilly and stony. The stones were useful for making millstones and milestones. The Indians sharpened them and used them for scalping and other social purposes.

The hills were useful to watch for Indians from, unless the Indians were already on them. They were hard to plow up, but they were relatively easy to plow down.

THE CLIMATE

The winters in New England were long. Largely for this reason, the summers were short. In keeping with the seasons, long underwear was worn in the winter and short underwear in the summer.

The Dutch and the French Come to America

Many believed there was a shorter way to get to Asia than around America. Not yet having discovered the Panama Canal, they were looking for the next best thing, which was the Northwest Passage. Since it did not exist, it was, of course, hard to find. Nevertheless many Intrepid Explorers made their reputation hunting for it.

One of those who sought the Northwest Passage was Henry Hudson. In a ship of which he was part owner, called the *Half Mine*, he led a crew of Dutchmen to the mouth of the Hudson River, which he was pleased to find named after himself.

Stopping only to make friends with the Indians and to buy the island of Manhattan from an Indian named Minnehaha (or "Laughing Minnie") for a handful of beads,[1] he pushed on up the river. When he stopped pushing he was in Albany, and he was disappointed. The water was getting shallower and shallower and it was clear. It was clear that this was not the Northwest Passage, and that instead of founding an important route to the Orient, he was about to founder at the state capital. The choice was also clear. He must remain in Albany or make the hard and perilous voyage back across the Atlantic. Without hesitation he chose the latter.

On a second trip to the New World in search of the elusive Passage, Henry Hudson sailed into Hudson Bay. This, again, was not the Northwest Passage, but its name had a familiar ring.

It is not known what became of this Able Navigator who had not been able to find what he was looking for. One theory is that Hudson met Cadillac and De Soto, and that together they discovered Detroit.

NEW AMSTERDAM

Because of Henry Hudson's explorations, the Dutch laid claim to the mouth of the Hudson River, which in their systematic way they divided into the North River and the East River. A stubborn race, they named Manhattan New Amsterdam, although it was obviously New York.

New Amsterdam was soon swarming with wealthy Dutch traitors known as poltroons. These were bluff, hearty men who smoked long pipes and loved to eat burghers. They frequently had their pictures painted, and one of the most picturesque was their Governor, Rip Van Winkle, a one-legged gentleman who fell into a deep sleep while watching a bowling game.

The English also claimed Manhattan, in view of the fact the beads with which it was purchased were plainly stamped "Made in

---

[1] Beads were then selling at $24 a handful.

England." The Dutch could not see the merits of their claim, but they could see that the English had more guns on their warships, so they left.

This was a turning point.

The clever English changed the name Amsterdam to York, but they retained the New.[1]

LA SALLE

The French, although exhausted by the Hundred Years' War, were not too tired to try to establish themselves in the New World. There were still mountains which had not been planted with flags, and there were still rivers that had not been sailed up. So they sailed up them. Many of these still rivers ran deep and led into fastnesses where no white man had ever trod and very few had walked.

At last the only river remaining to be sailed up was the Mississippi. In this instance the French explorer La Salle defied convention. A headstrong young man, he began at the headwaters of the mighty river and sailed down it. He thus not only opened up a vast new territory but discovered an easier means of navigating the rivers of America. La Salle's interesting account of his trip down the river, called *Life on the Mississippi,* is available in an English translation by Mark Twain.

Thanks to La Salle, the Mississippi basin remained in French hands until they grew tired of holding it and sold it for $15,000,000, which many thought was a high price for a second-hand basin.

It is to the French also that we owe the establishment of the beautiful city of Quebec, which was named, according to custom, after the King of France, whose name, according to custom, was Louis (pronounced kwĕ-bĕk'). The English later seized Quebec and

---

[1] The city was later called New York, New York, for the sake of those who did not catch it the first time.

its outskirts, called Canada, from the French, but not without a struggle.

Henceforth the French were dominated by the English, who became our Good Neighbors to the north. We have had amicable relations ever since by agreeing that there are two sides to everything, for example Niagara Falls, which has an American side and a Canadian side.

Test

1. Why do you think Columbus was so interested in traveling to distant places? What else do you know about his home life?

2. Are you really convinced that the world is round? Do you worry much about it?

3. To what extent would the course of American history have been altered if America had never been discovered?

4. What would you say about the Puritans? Would you say the same if they were listening?

5. Can the passengers on the *Mayflower* be considered immigrants? With their strong sense of duty, do you suppose they tried to conceal anything from the customs officials?

6. Have you ever thought how much of a Pilgrim was wasted when an Indian kept only his scalp?

7. Trace on a map the voyages of Henry Hudson. Use a solid line to show where he went and a dotted line to show where he thought he was going. Sign on the dotted line.

8. What would you have done if you had been in La Salle's shoes? How do you know he wore any?

The Fifty-First Dragon

by Heywood Broun

Of all the pupils at the knight school Gawaine Le Coeur-Hardy was among the least promising. He was tall and sturdy, but his instructors soon discovered that he lacked spirit. He would hide in the woods when the jousting class was called, although his companions and members of the faculty sought to appeal to his better nature by shouting to him to come out and break his neck like a man. Even when they told him that the lances were padded, the horses no more than ponies and the field unusually soft for late autumn, Gawaine refused to grow enthusiastic. The Headmaster and the Assistant Professor of Pleasaunce were discussing the case one spring afternoon and the Assistant Professor could see no remedy but expulsion.

"No," said the Headmaster, as he looked out at the purple hills which ringed the school, "I think I'll train him to slay dragons."

"He might be killed," objected the Assistant Professor.

"So he might," replied the Headmaster brightly. But he added, more soberly, "We must consider the greater good. We are responsible for the formation of this lad's character."

"Are the dragons particularly bad this year?" interrupted the Assistant Professor. This was characteristic. He always seemed restive when the head of the school began to talk ethics and the ideals of the institution.

"I've never known them worse," replied the headmaster. "Up in the hills to the south last week they killed a number of peasants, two cows and a prize pig. And if this dry spell holds there's no telling

---

From *Seeing Things at Night*.

when they may start a forest fire simply by breathing around indiscriminately."

"Would any refund on the tuition fee be necessary in case of an accident to young Coeur-Hardy?"

"No," the principal answered, judicially, "that's all covered in the contract. But as a matter of fact he wouldn't be killed. Before I send him up in the hills I'm going to give him a magic word."

"That's a good idea," said the Professor. "Sometimes they work wonders."

From that day on Gawaine specialized in dragons. His course included both theory and practice. In the morning there were long lectures on the history, anatomy, manners and customs of dragons. Gawaine did not distinguish himself in these studies. He had a marvelously versatile gift for forgetting things. In the afternoon he showed to better advantage, for then he would go down to the South Meadow and practice with a battle-ax. In this exercise he was truly impressive, for he had enormous strength as well as speed and grace. He even developed a deceptive display of ferocity. Old alumni say that it was a thrilling sight to see Gawaine charging across the field toward the dummy paper dragon which had been set up for his practice. As he ran he would brandish his ax and shout "A murrain on thee!" or some other vivid bit of campus slang. It never took him more than one stroke to behead the dummy dragon.

Gradually his task was made more difficult. Paper gave way to papier-mâché and finally to wood, but even the toughest of these dummy dragons had no terrors for Gawaine. One sweep of the ax always did the business. There were those who said that when the practice was protracted until dusk and the dragons threw long, fantastic shadows across the meadow Gawaine did not charge so impetuously nor shout so loudly. It is possible there was malice in this charge. At any rate, the Headmaster decided by the end of June that it was time for the test. Only the night before a dragon had come close to the school grounds and had eaten some of the lettuce from the garden. The faculty decided that Gawaine was ready. They gave him a diploma and a new battle-ax and the Head-master summoned him to a private conference.

"Sit down," said the Headmaster. "Have a cigarette."

Gawaine hesitated.

"Oh, I know it's against the rules," said the Headmaster. "But after all, you have received your preliminary degree. You are no longer a boy. You are a man. Tomorrow you will go out into the world, the great world of achievement."

Gawaine took a cigarette. The Headmaster offered him a match but he produced one of his own and began to puff away with a dexterity which quite amazed the principal.

"Here you have learned the theories of life," continued the Headmaster, resuming the thread of his discourse, "but after all, life is not a matter of theories. Life is a matter of facts. It calls on the young and the old alike to face these facts, even though they are hard and sometimes unpleasant. Your problem, for example, is to slay dragons."

"They say that those dragons down in the south wood are five hundred feet long," ventured Gawaine, timorously.

"Stuff and nonsense!" said the Headmaster. "The curate saw one last week from the top of Arthur's Hill. The dragon was sunning himself down in the valley. The curate didn't have an opportunity to look at him very long because he felt it was his duty to hurry back to make a report to me. He said the monster—or shall I say, the big lizard?—wasn't an inch over two hundred feet. But the size has nothing at all to do with it. You'll find the big ones even easier than the little ones. They're far slower on their feet and less aggressive, I'm told. Besides, before you go I'm going to equip you in such fashion that you need have no fear of all the dragons in the world."

"I'd like an enchanted cap," said Gawaine.

"What's that?" answered the Headmaster, testily.

"A cap to make me disappear," explained Gawaine.

The Headmaster laughed indulgently. "You mustn't believe all those old wives' stories," he said. "There isn't any such thing. A cap to make you disappear, indeed! What would you do with it? You haven't even appeared yet. Why, my boy, you could walk from here to London, and nobody would so much as look at you. You're nobody. You couldn't be more invisible than that."

Gawaine seemed dangerously close to a relapse into his old habit of whimpering. The Headmaster reassured him: "Don't worry; I'll give you something much better than an enchanted cap. I'm going to give you a magic word. All you have to do is to repeat the magic charm once and no dragon can possibly harm a hair of your head. You can cut off his head at your leisure."

He took a heavy book from the shelf behind his desk and began to run through it. "Sometimes," he said, "the charm is a whole phrase or even a sentence. I might, for instance, give you 'To make the'—no, that might not do. I think a single word would be best for dragons."

"A short word," suggested Gawaine.

"It can't be too short or it wouldn't be potent. There isn't so much hurry as all that. Here's a splendid magic word: 'Rumplesnitz.' Do you think you can learn that?"

Gawaine tried and in an hour or so he seemed to have the word well in hand. Again and again he interrupted the lesson to inquire, "And if I say 'Rumplesnitz,' the dragon can't possibly hurt me?" And always the Headmaster replied, "If you only say 'Rumplesnitz,' you are perfectly safe."

Toward morning Gawaine seemed resigned to his career. At daybreak the Headmaster saw him to the edge of the forest and pointed him to the direction on which he should proceed. About a mile away to the southwest a cloud of steam hovered over an open meadow in the woods and the Headmaster assured Gawaine that under the steam he would find whether it would be best to approach the dragon on the run as he did in his practice in the South Meadow or to walk slowly toward him, shouting "Rumplesnitz" all the way.

The problem was decided for him. No sooner had he come to the fringe of the meadow than the dragon spied him and began to charge. It was a large dragon and yet it seemed decidedly aggressive in spite of the Headmaster's statement to the contrary. As the dragon charged it released huge clouds of hissing steam through its nostrils. It was almost as if a gigantic teapot had gone mad. The

dragon came forward so fast and Gawaine was so frightened that he had time to say "Rumplesnitz" only once. As he said it, he swung his battle-ax and off popped the head of the dragon. Gawaine had to admit that it was even easier to kill a real dragon than a wooden one if only you said "Rumplesnitz."

Gawaine brought the ears home and a small section of the tail. His school mates and the faculty made much of him, but the Headmaster wisely kept him from being spoiled by insisting that he go on with his work. Every clear day Gawaine rose at dawn and went out to kill dragons. The Headmaster kept him at home when it rained, because he said the woods were damp and unhealthy at such times and that he didn't want the boy to run needless risks. Few good days passed in which Gawaine failed to get a dragon. On one particularly fortunate day he killed three, a husband and wife and a visiting relative. Gradually he developed a technique. Pupils who sometimes watched him from the hilltops a long way off said that he often allowed the dragon to come within a few feet before he said "Rumplesnitz." He came to say it with a mocking sneer. Occasionally he did stunts. Once when an excursion party from London was watching him he went into action with his right hand tied behind his neck. The dragon's head came off just as easily.

As Gawaine's record of killings mounted higher the Headmaster found it impossible to keep him completely in hand. He fell into the habit of stealing out at night and engaging in long drinking bouts at the village tavern. It was after such a debauch that he rose a little before dawn one fine August morning and started out after his fiftieth dragon. His head was heavy and his mind sluggish. He was heavy in other respects as well, for he had adopted the somewhat vulgar practice of wearing his medals, ribbons and all, when he went out dragon hunting. The decorations began on his chest and ran all the way down to his abdomen. They must have weighed at least eight pounds.

Gawaine found a dragon in the same meadow where he had killed the first one. It was a fair-sized dragon, but evidently an old one. Its face was wrinkled and Gawaine thought he had never seen so hideous a countenance. Much to the lad's disgust, the monster refused to charge and Gawaine was obliged to walk toward him. He whistled as he went. The dragon regarded him hopelessly, but craftily. Of course it had heard of Gawaine. Even when the lad raised his battle-ax the dragon made no move. It knew that there was no salvation in the quickest thrust of the head, for it had been informed that this hunter was protected by an enchantment. It merely waited, hoping something would turn up. Gawaine raised the battle-ax and suddenly lowered it again. He had grown very pale and he trembled violently. The dragon suspected a trick. "What's the matter?" it asked, with false solicitude.

"I've forgotten the magic word," stammered Gawaine.

"What a pity," said the dragon. "So that was the secret. It doesn't seem quite sporting to me, all this magic stuff, you know. Not cricket, as we used to say when I was a little dragon; but after all, that's a matter of opinion."

Gawaine was so helpless with terror that the dragon's confidence rose immeasurably and it could not resist the temptation to show off a bit.

"Could I possibly be of any assistance?" it asked. "What's the first letter of the magic word?"

"It begins with an 'r,'" said Gawaine weakly.

"Let's see," mused the dragon, "that doesn't tell us much, does it? What sort of a word is this? Is it an epithet, do you think?"

Gawaine could do no more than nod.

"Why, of course," exclaimed the dragon, "reactionary Republican."

Gawaine shook his head.

"Well, then," said the dragon, "we'd better get down to business. Will you surrender?"

With the suggestion of a compromise Gawaine mustered up enough courage to speak.

"What will you do if I surrender?" he asked.

"Why, I'll eat you," said the dragon.

"And if I don't surrender?"

"I'll eat you just the same."

"Then it doesn't make any difference, does it?" moaned Gawaine.

"It does to me," said the dragon with a smile. "I'd rather you didn't surrender. You'd taste much better if you didn't."

The dragon waited for a long time for Gawaine to ask "Why?" but the boy was too frightened to speak. At last the dragon had to give the explanation without his cue line. "You see," he said, "if you don't surrender you'll taste better because you'll die game."

This was an old and ancient trick of the dragon's. By means of some such quip he was accustomed to paralyze his victims with laughter and then to destroy them. Gawaine was sufficiently paralyzed as it was, but laughter had no part in his helplessness. With the last word of the joke the dragon drew back his head and struck. In that second there flashed into the mind of Gawaine the magic word "Rumplesnitz," but there was no time to say it. There was time only to strike and, without a word, Gawaine met the onrush of the dragon with a full swing. He put all his back and shoulders into it. The impact was terrific and the head of the dragon flew away almost a hundred yards and landed in a thicket.

Gawaine did not remain frightened very long after the death of the dragon. His mood was one of wonder. He was enormously puzzled. He cut off the ears of the monster almost in a trance. Again and again he thought to himself, "I didn't say 'Rumplesnitz'!" He was sure of that and yet there was no question that he had killed the dragon. In fact, he had never killed one so utterly. Never before had he driven a head for anything like the same distance. Twenty-five yards was perhaps his best previous record. All the way back to the knight school he kept rumbling about in his mind seeking an explanation for what had occurred. He went to the Headmaster immediately and after closing the door told him what had happened. "I didn't say 'Rumplesnitz,'" he explained with great earnestness.

The Headmaster laughed. "I'm glad you've found out," he said. "It makes you ever so much more of a hero. Don't you see that? Now you know that it was you who killed all these dragons and not that foolish little word 'Rumplesnitz.'"

Gawaine frowned. "Then it wasn't a magic word after all?" he asked.

"Of course not," said the Headmaster. "You ought to be too old for such foolishness. There isn't any such thing as a magic word."

"But you told me it was magic," protested Gawaine. "You said it was magic and now you say it isn't."

"It wasn't magic in a literal sense," answered the Headmaster, "but it was much more wonderful than that. The word gave you confidence. It took away fears. If I hadn't told you that you might have been killed the very first time. It was your battle-ax did the trick."

Gawaine surprised the Headmaster by his attitude. He was obviously distressed by the explanation. He interrupted a long philosophic and ethical discourse by the Headmaster with, "If I hadn't of hit 'em all mighty hard and fast any one of 'em might have crushed me like a, like a—" He fumbled for a word.

"Egg shell," suggested the Headmaster.

"Like a egg shell," assented Gawaine, and he said it many times. All through the evening meal people who sat near him heard him muttering. "Like a egg shell, like a egg shell."

The next day was clear, but Gawaine did not get up at dawn. Indeed, it was almost noon when the Headmaster found him cowering in bed, with the clothes pulled over his head. The principal called the Assistant Professor of Pleasaunce, and together they dragged the boy toward the forest.

"He'll be all right as soon as he gets a couple more dragons under his belt," explained the Headmaster.

The Assistant Professor of Pleasaunce agreed. "It would be a shame to stop such a fine run," he said. "Why, counting that one yesterday, he's killed fifty dragons."

They pushed the boy into a thicket above which hung a meager cloud of steam. It was obviously quite a small dragon. But Gawaine did not come back that night or the next. In fact, he never came back. Some weeks afterward brave spirits from the school explored the thicket, but they could find nothing to remind them of Gawaine except the metal parts of his medals. Even the ribbons had been devoured.

The Headmaster and the Assistant Professor of Pleasaunce agreed that it would be just as well not to tell the school how Gawaine had achieved his record and still less how he came to die. They held that it might have a bad effect on school spirit. Accordingly, Gawaine has lived in the memory of the school as its greatest hero. No visitor succeeds in leaving the building today without seeing a great shield which hangs on the wall of the dining hall. Fifty pairs of dragons' ears are mounted upon the shield and underneath in gilt letters is "Gawaine Le Coeur-Hardy," followed by the simple inscription, "He killed fifty dragons." The record has never been equaled.

The STORY of CHICKEN Little

by Walt Kelly

One day Chicken Little was standing by his own self out in the woods and a-mindin' of his own business.

What you doin' out here, son?

Like it say in the story, I is mindin' my own business.

Smart li'l sprat!

Plunk!

Ooh!

From *Uncle Pogo So-So Stories*.

The Little Girl and the Wolf

by James Thurber

James Thurber grew up to be one of America's greatest and most popular humorists. (His superb story, "The Night the Bed Fell," is reprinted in this volume.) But when he was a little boy there was one nursery tale that invariably scared the daylights out of him. That was the account of Little Red Riding Hood's trouble with the Big, Bad Wolf. So just as soon as Mr. Thurber grew up he wrote his own version of the affair—and here it is.—B.C.

One afternoon a big wolf waited in a dark forest for a little girl to come along carrying a basket of food for her grandmother. Finally a little girl did come along and she was carrying a basket of food.

From *The New Yorker*.

"Are you carrying that basket to your grandmother?" asked the wolf. The little girl said, yes, she was. So the wolf asked her where her grandmother lived and the little girl told him and he disappeared into the woods.

When the little girl opened the door of her grandmother's house she saw that there was somebody in bed with a nightcap and nightgown on. She had approached no nearer than twenty-five feet from the bed when she saw that it was not her grandmother but the wolf, for even in a nightcap a wolf does not look any more like your grandmother than the Metro-Goldwyn-Mayer lion looks like Calvin Coolidge. So the little girl took an automatic out of her basket and shot the wolf dead.

MORAL: IT IS NOT SO EASY TO FOOL LITTLE GIRLS NOWADAYS AS IT USED TO BE.

The Ransom of Red Chief

by O. Henry

It looked like a good thing: but wait till I tell you. We were down South, in Alabama—Bill Driscoll and myself—when this kidnapping idea struck us. It was, as Bill afterward expressed it, "during a moment of temporary mental apparition"; but we didn't find that out till later.

There was a town down there, as flat as a flannel-cake, and called Summit, of course. It contained inhabitants of as undeleterious and self-satisfied a class of peasantry as ever clustered around a Maypole.

Bill and me had a joint capital of about six hundred dollars, and we needed just two thousand dollars more to pull off a fraudulent town-lot scheme in Western Illinois with. We talked it over on the front steps of the Hotel. Philoprogenitiveness, says we, is strong in semi-rural communities; therefore, and for other reasons, a kidnapping project ought to do better there than in the radius of newspapers that send reporters out in plain clothes to stir up talk about such things. We knew that Summit couldn't get after us with anything stronger than constables and, maybe, some lackadaisical bloodhounds and a diatribe or two in the *Weekly Farmers' Budget.* So, it looked good.

We selected for our victim the only child of a prominent citizen named Ebenezer Dorset. The father was respectable and tight, a mortgage fancier and a stern, upright collection-plate passer and forecloser. The kid was a boy of ten, with bas-relief freckles, and hair the color of the cover of the magazine you buy at the news-

---

From *Whirligigs.*

stand when you want to catch a train. Bill and me figured that Ebenezer would melt down for a ransom of two thousand dollars to a cent. But wait till I tell you.

About two miles from Summit was a little mountain, covered with a dense cedar brake. On the rear elevation of this mountain was a cave. There we stored provisions.

One evening after sundown, we drove in a buggy past old Dorset's house. The kid was in the street, throwing rocks at a kitten on the opposite fence.

"Hey, little boy!" says Bill, "would you like to have a bag of candy and a nice ride?"

The boy catches Bill neatly in the eye with a piece of brick.

"That will cost the old man an extra five hundred dollars," says Bill, climbing over the wheel.

That boy put up a fight like a welter-weight cinnamon bear; but, at last, we got him down in the bottom of the buggy and drove away. We took him up to the cave, and I hitched the horse in the cedar brake. After dark I drove the buggy to the little village, three miles away, where we had hired it, and walked back to the mountain.

Bill was pasting court-plaster over the scratches and bruises on his features. There was a fire burning behind the big rock at the entrance of the cave, and the boy was watching a pot of boiling coffee, with two buzzard tail-feathers stuck in his red hair. He points a stick at me when I come up, and says:

"Ha! cursed paleface, do you dare to enter the camp of Red Chief, the terror of the plains?"

"He's all right now," says Bill, rolling up his trousers and examining some bruises on his shins. "We're playing Indian. We're making Buffalo Bill's show look like magic-lantern views of Palestine in the town hall. I'm Old Hank, the Trapper, Red Chief's captive, and I'm to be scalped at daybreak. By Geronimo! that kid can kick hard."

Yes, sir, that boy seemed to be having the time of his life. The fun of camping out in a cave had made him forget that he was a captive himself. He immediately christened me Snake-eye, the Spy, and announced that, when his braves returned from the warpath, I was to be broiled at the stake at the rising of the sun.

Then we had supper; and he filled his mouth full of bacon and bread and gravy, and began to talk. He made a during-dinner speech something like this:

"I like this fine. I never camped out before; but I had a pet 'possum once, and I was nine last birthday. I hate to go to school. Rats ate up sixteen of Jimmy Talbot's aunt's speckled hen's eggs. Are there any real Indians in these woods? I want some more gravy. Does the trees moving make the wind blow? We had five puppies. What makes your nose so red, Hank? My father has lots of money. Are the stars hot? I whipped Ed Walker twice, Saturday. I don't like girls. You dassent catch toads unless with a string. Do oxen make any noise? Why are oranges round? Have you got beds to sleep on in this cave? Amos Murray has got six toes. A parrot can talk, but a monkey or a fish can't. How many does it take to make twelve?"

Every few minutes he would remember that he was a pesky redskin, and pick up his stick rifle and tiptoe to the mouth of the cave to rubber for the scouts of the hated paleface. Now and then he would let out a war-whoop that made Old Hank the Trapper shiver. That boy had Bill terrorized from the start.

"Red Chief," says I to the kid, "would you like to go home?"

"Aw, what for?" says he. "I don't have any fun at home. I hate to go to school. I like to camp out. You won't take me back home again, Snake-eye, will you?"

"Not right away," says I. "We'll stay here in the cave awhile."

"All right!" says he. "That'll be fine. I never had such fun in all my life."

We went to bed about eleven o'clock. We spread down some wide blankets and quilts and put Red Chief between us. We weren't afraid he'd run away. He kept us awake for three hours, jumping up and reaching for his rifle and screeching: "Hist! pard," in mine and Bill's ears, as the fancied crackle of a twig or the rustle of a leaf revealed to his young imagination the stealthy approach of the outlaw band. At last, I fell into a troubled sleep, and dreamed that I had been kidnapped and chained to a tree by a ferocious pirate with red hair.

Just at daybreak, I was awakened by a series of awful screams from Bill. They weren't yells, or howls, or shouts, or whoops, or yawps, such as you'd expect from a manly set of vocal organs— they were simply indecent, terrifying, humiliating screams, such as women emit when they see ghosts or caterpillars. It's an awful thing to hear a strong, desperate, fat man scream incontinently in a cave at daybreak.

I jumped up to see what the matter was. Red Chief was sitting on Bill's chest, with one hand twined in Bill's hair. In the other he had the sharp case-knife we used for slicing bacon; and he was industriously and realistically trying to take Bill's scalp, according to the sentence that had been pronounced upon him the evening before.

I got the knife away from the kid and made him lie down again. But, from that moment, Bill's spirit was broken. He laid down on his side of the bed, but he never closed an eye again in sleep as long as that boy was with us. I dozed off for a while, but along toward sun-up I remembered that Red Chief had said I was to be burned at the stake at the rising of the sun. I wasn't nervous or afraid; but I sat up and lit my pipe and leaned against a rock.

"What you getting up so soon for, Sam?" asked Bill.

"Me?" says I. "Oh, I got a kind of pain in my shoulder. I thought sitting up would rest it."

"You're a liar!" says Bill. "You're afraid. You was to be burned at sunrise, and you was afraid he'd do it. And he would, too, if he could find a match. Ain't it awful, Sam? Do you think anybody will pay out money to get a little imp like that back home?"

"Sure," said I. "A rowdy kid like that is just the kind that parents dote on. Now, you and the Chief get up and cook breakfast, while I go up on the top of this mountain and reconnoitre."

I went up on the peak of the little mountain and ran my eye over the contiguous vicinity. Over towards Summit I expected to see the sturdy yeomanry of the village armed with scythes and pitchforks beating the countryside for the dastardly kidnappers. But what I saw was a peaceful landscape dotted with one man ploughing with a dun mule. Nobody was dragging the creek; no couriers dashed hither and yon, bringing tidings of no news to the distracted parents. There was a sylvan attitude of somnolent sleepiness pervading that section of the external outward surface of Alabama that lay exposed to my view. "Perhaps," says I to myself, "it has not yet been discovered that the wolves have borne away the tender lambkin from the fold. Heaven help the wolves!" says I, and I went down the mountain to breakfast.

When I got to the cave I found Bill backed up against the side of it, breathing hard, and the boy threatening to smash him with a rock half as big as a cocoanut.

"He put a red-hot boiled potato down my back," explained Bill, "and then mashed it with his foot; and I boxed his ears. Have you got a gun about you, Sam?"

I took the rock away from the boy and kind of patched up the argument. "I'll fix you," says the kid to Bill. "No man ever yet struck the Red Chief but he got paid for it. You better beware!"

After breakfast the kid takes a piece of leather with strings wrapped around it out of his pocket and goes outside the cave unwinding it.

"What's he up to now?" says Bill, anxiously. "You don't think he'll run away, do you, Sam?"

"No fear of it," says I. "He don't seem to be much of a home body. But we've got to fix up some plan about the ransom. There don't seem to be much excitement around Summit on account of his disappearance; but maybe they haven't realized yet that he's gone. His folks may think he's spending the night with Aunt Jane or one of the neighbors. Anyhow, he'll be missed today. Tonight we must get a message to his father demanding the two thousand dollars for his return."

Just then we heard a kind of war-whoop, such as David might have emitted when he knocked out the champion Goliath. It was a sling that Red Chief had pulled out of his pocket, and he was whirling it around his head.

I dodged, and heard a heavy thud and a kind of a sigh from Bill, like a horse gives out when you take his saddle off. A rock the size of an egg had caught Bill just behind his left ear. He loosened himself all over and fell in the fire across the frying pan of hot water for washing the dishes. I dragged him out and poured cold water on his head for half an hour.

By and by, Bill sits up and feels behind his ear and says: "Sam, do you know who my favorite Biblical character is?"

"Take it easy," says I. "You'll come to your senses presently."

"King Herod," says he. "You won't go away and leave me here alone, will you, Sam?"

I went out and caught that boy and shook him until his freckles rattled.

"If you don't behave," says I, "I'll take you straight home. Now, are you going to be good, or not?"

"I was only funning," says he, sullenly, "I didn't mean to hurt Old Hank. But what did he hit me for? I'll behave, Snake-eye, if you won't send me home, and if you'll let me play the Black Scout today."

"I don't know the game," says I. "That's for you and Mr. Bill to decide. He's your playmate for the day. I'm going away for a while, on business. Now, you come in and make friends with him and say you are sorry for hurting him, or home you go, at once."

I made him and Bill shake hands, and then I took Bill aside and told him I was going to Poplar Grove, a little village three miles from the cave, and find out what I could about how the kidnapping had been regarded in Summit. Also, I thought it best to send a peremptory letter to old man Dorset that day, demanding the ransom and dictating how it should be paid.

"You know, Sam," says Bill, "I've stood by you without batting an eye in earthquakes, fire and flood—in poker games, dynamite outrages, police raids, train robberies, and cyclones. I never lost my nerve yet till we kidnapped that two-legged skyrocket of a kid. He's got me going. You won't leave me long with him, will you, Sam?"

"I'll be back some time this afternoon," says I. "You must keep the boy amused and quiet till I return. And now we'll write the letter to old Dorset."

Bill and I got paper and pencil and worked on the letter while Red Chief, with a blanket wrapped around him, strutted up and down, guarding the mouth of the cave. Bill begged me tearfully to make the ransom fifteen hundred dollars instead of two thousand. "I ain't attempting," says he, "to decry the celebrated moral aspect of parental affection, but we're dealing with humans, and it ain't human for anybody to give up two thousand dollars for that forty-pound chunk of freckled wildcat. I'm willing to take a chance at fifteen hundred dollars. You can charge the difference up to me."

So, to relieve Bill, I acceded, and we collaborated a letter that ran this way:

Ebenezer Dorset, Esq.:

We have your boy concealed in a place far from Summit. It is useless for you or the most skillful detectives to attempt to find him. Absolutely, the only terms on which you can have him restored to you are these: We demand fifteen hundred dollars in large bills for his return; the money to be left at midnight tonight at the same spot and in the same box as your reply—as hereinafter described. If you agree to these terms, send your answer in writing by a solitary messenger tonight at half-past eight o'clock. After crossing Owl Creek on the road to Poplar Grove, there are three large trees about a hundred yards apart, close to the fence of the wheat field on the right-hand side. At the bottom of the fence-post, opposite the third tree, will be found a small pasteboard box.

The messenger will place the answer in this box and return immediately to Summit.

If you attempt any treachery or fail to comply with our demand as stated, you will never see your boy again.

If you pay the money as demanded, he will be returned to you safe and well within three hours. These terms are final, and if you do not accede to them no further communication will be attempted.

TWO DESPERATE MEN

I addressed this letter to Dorset, and put it in my pocket. As I was about to start, the kid comes up to me and says:

"Aw, Snake-eye, you said I could play the Black Scout while you was gone."

"Play it, of course," says I. "Mr. Bill will play with you. What kind of a game is it?"

"I'm the Black Scout," says Red Chief, "and I have to ride to the stockade to warn the settlers that the Indians are coming. I'm tired of playing Indian myself. I want to be the Black Scout."

"All right," says I. "It sounds harmless to me. I guess Mr. Bill will help you foil the pesky savages."

"What am I to do?" asks Bill, looking at the kid suspiciously.

"You are the hoss," says Black Scout. "Get down on your hands and knees. How can I ride to the stockade without a hoss?"

"You'd better keep him interested," said I, "till we get the scheme going. Loosen up."

Bill gets down on his all fours, and a look comes in his eye like a rabbit's when you catch it in a trap.

"How far is it to the stockade, kid?" he asks, in a husky manner of voice.

"Ninety miles," says the Black Scout. "And you have to hump yourself to get there on time. Whoa, now!"

The Black Scout jumps on Bill's back and digs his heels in his side.

"For Heaven's sake," says Bill, "hurry back, Sam, as soon as you can. I wish we hadn't made the ransom more than a thousand. Say, you quit kicking me or I'll get up and warm you good."

I walked over to Poplar Grove and sat around the post office and store, talking with the chaw-bacons that came in to trade. One whiskerando says that he hears Summit is all upset on account of Elder Ebenezer Dorset's boy having been lost or stolen. That was all I wanted to know. I bought some smoking tobacco, referred casually to the price of black-eyed peas, posted my letter surreptitiously, and came away. The postmaster said the mail-carrier would come by in an hour to take the mail to Summit.

When I got back to the cave Bill and the boy were not to be found. I explored the vicinity of the cave, and risked a yodel or two, but there was no response.

So I lighted my pipe and sat down on a mossy bank to await developments.

In about half an hour I heard the bushes rustle, and Bill wabbled out into the little glade in front of the cave. Behind him was the kid, stepping softly like a scout, with a broad grin on his face. Bill stopped, took off his hat, and wiped his face with a red handkerchief. The kid stopped about eight feet behind him.

"Sam," says Bill, "I suppose you'll think I'm a renegade, but I couldn't help it. I'm a grown person with masculine proclivities and habits of self-defense, but there is a time when all systems of egotism and predominance fail. The boy is gone. I sent him home.

All is off. There was martyrs in old times," goes on Bill, "that suffered death rather than give up the particular graft they enjoyed. None of 'em ever was subjugated to such supernatural tortures as I have been. I tried to be faithful to our articles of depredation; but there came a limit."

"What's the trouble, Bill?" I asks him.

"I was rode," says Bill, "the ninety miles to the stockade, not barring an inch. Then, when the settlers was rescued, I was given oats. Sand ain't a palatable substitute. And then, for an hour I had to try to explain to him why there was nothin' in holes, how a road can run both ways, and what makes the grass green. I tell you, Sam, a human can only stand so much. I takes him by the neck of his clothes and drags him down the mountain. On the way he kicks my legs black and blue from the knees down; and I've got to have two or three bites on my thumb and hand cauterized.

"But he's gone"—continues Bill—"gone home. I showed him the road to Summit and kicked him about eight feet nearer there at one kick. I'm sorry we lose the ransom; but it was either that or Bill Driscoll to the madhouse."

Bill is puffing and blowing, but there is a look of ineffable peace and growing content on his rose-pink features.

"Bill," says I, "there isn't any heart disease in your family, is there?"

"No," says Bill, "nothing chronic except malaria and accidents. Why?"

"Then you might turn around," says I, "and have a look behind you."

Bill turns and sees the boy, and loses his complexion and sits down plump on the ground and begins to pluck aimlessly at grass and little sticks. For an hour I was afraid of his mind. And then I told him that my scheme was to put the whole job through immediately and that we would get the ransom and be off with it by midnight if old Dorset fell in with our proposition. So Bill braced up enough to give the kid a weak sort of a smile and a promise to play the Russian in a Japanese war with him as soon as he felt a little better.

I had a scheme for collecting that ransom without danger of being caught by counterplots that ought to commend itself to professional kidnappers. The tree under which the answer was to be left—and the money later on—was close to the road fence with

big, bare fields on all sides. If a gang of constables should be watching for anyone to come for the note, they could see him a long way off crossing the fields or in the road. But no, sirree! At half-past eight I was up in that tree as well hidden as a tree toad, waiting for the messenger to arrive.

Exactly on time, a half-grown boy rides up the road on a bicycle, locates the pasteboard box at the foot of the fencepost, slips a folded piece of paper into it, and pedals away again back toward Summit.

I waited an hour and then concluded the thing was square. I

THE RANSOM OF RED CHIEF

slid down the tree, got the note, slipped along the fence till I struck the woods, and was back at the cave in another half an hour. I opened the note, got near the lantern, and read it to Bill. It was written with a pen in a crabbed hand, and the sum and substance of it was this:

> Two Desperate Men.
>
> *Gentlemen:* I received your letter today by post, in regard to the ransom you ask for the return of my son. I think you are a little high in your demands, and I hereby make you a counterproposition, which I am inclined to believe you will accept. You bring Johnny home and pay me two hundred and fifty dollars in cash, and I agree to take him off your hands. You had better come at night, for the neighbors believe he is lost, and I couldn't be responsible for what they would do to anybody they saw bringing him back. Very respectfully,
>
> EBENEZER DORSET

"Great Pirates of Penzance," says I; "of all the impudent—"

But I glanced at Bill, and hesitated. He had the most appealing look in his eyes I ever saw on the face of a dumb or a talking brute.

"Sam," says he, "what's two hundred and fifty dollars, after all? We've got the money. One more night of this kid will send me to a bed in Bedlam. Besides being a thorough gentleman, I think Mr. Dorset is a spendthrift for making us such a liberal offer. You ain't going to let the chance go, are you?"

"Tell you the truth, Bill," says I, "this little he ewe lamb has somewhat got on my nerves too. We'll take him home, pay the ransom, and make our getaway."

We took him home that night. We got him to go by telling him that his father had bought a silver-mounted rifle and a pair of moccasins for him, and we were to hunt bears the next day.

It was just twelve o'clock when we knocked at Ebenezer's front door. Just at the moment when I should have been abstracting the fifteen hundred dollars from the box under the tree, according to the original proposition, Bill was counting out two hundred and fifty dollars into Dorset's hand.

When the kid found out we were going to leave him at home he started up a howl like a calliope and fastened himself as tight as a leech to Bill's leg. His father peeled him away gradually, like a porous plaster.

"How long can you hold him?" asks Bill.

"I'm not as strong as I used to be," says old Dorset. "But I think I can promise you ten minutes."

"Enough," says Bill. "In ten minutes I shall cross the Central, Southern, and Middle Western States, and be legging it trippingly for the Canadian border."

And, as dark as it was, and as fat as Bill was, and as good a runner as I am, he was a good mile and a half out of Summit before I could catch up with him.

Riddle-de-Dee

Collected by Bennett Cerf

Q. What did the duck say when it laid a square egg?
A. "Ouch!"

Q. Why is a pig's tail like getting up at 4:40 A.M.?
A. It's twirly.

Q. What's black and white and red all over?
A. A blushing zebra.

Q. When do giraffes have eight legs?
A. When there are two of them.

Q. A man fell out of a tenth-story window but was barely scratched. Why?
A. He was wearing a light fall suit.

Q. Four men fell into the water, but only three of them got their hair wet. Why?
A. One of them was bald.

Q. What are the three most common causes of forest fires?
A. Men, women, and children.

Q. How can you divide sixteen apples among seventeen hungry people?
A. Make applesauce.

Q. What time is it when the clock strikes thirteen?
A. Time to get the clock fixed.

From the book *Riddle-de-Dee.*

Q. How can you tell a male hippopotamus from a female hippo-
    potamus?
A. Ask it a question. If *he* answers, it's a male; if *she* answers,
    it's a female.

Q. Why do they have mirrors on chewing-gum machines?
A. So you can see how you look when the gum doesn't come out.

Q. Which is bigger: Mr. Bigger or Mr. Bigger's baby?
A. The baby is a little Bigger.

Q. How can you stop a small child from spilling food at the table?
A. Feed him on the floor.

Q. When should a boy kick about something he gets for his
    birthday?
A. When he gets a football.

Q. Why did a mother knit her G.I. son three socks?
A. Because he wrote that he had grown another foot.

Q. Who has the most friends for lunch?
A. A cannibal.

Q. What's worse than finding a worm in an apple?
A. Finding half a worm.

Q. When should a baker quit making doughnuts?
A. When he gets sick of the hole business.

Q. What's the best way to keep milk from turning sour?
A. Keep it inside the cow.

Q. Name a product raised in countries where there's lots of rain.
A. Umbrellas.

Q. What has four legs and one foot?
A. A bed.

Q. What was the largest island in the world before Australia was discovered?
A. Australia.

Q. Is it harmful to write on an empty stomach?
A. No, but paper is better.

Q. How can you live to be one hundred years old?
A. Drink a glass of milk every morning for twelve hundred months.

Q. Why is a traffic cop the strongest man in the world?
A. Because he can hold up a ten-ton truck with one hand.

Q. What has eighteen legs and catches flies?
A. A baseball team.

Q. What contains more feet in winter than in summer?
A. A skating rink.

Q. Why did Robin Hood rob only the rich?
A. Because the poor had no money.

Q. Why is it useless to send a letter to Washington?
A. Because he died in 1799.

Q. Where was the Declaration of Independence signed?
A. At the bottom.

Q. What did the big toe say to the little toe?
A. "Don't look now, but there's a heel following us."

Q. Which is faster: heat or cold?
A. Heat. You can catch cold.

Q. What animal drops from the clouds?
A. The rain, dear.

Q. What question can *never* be answered "Yes"?
A. "Are you asleep?"

Q. What question must *always* be answered "Yes"?
A. "What does Y-E-S spell?"

Q. What word is always pronounced wrong?
A. Wrong.

Q. What did the rake say to the hoe?
A. Hi, hoe!

Q. How can you find a rabbit that is lost in the woods?
A. Make a noise like a carrot.

Q. Why do humming birds hum?
A. Because they don't know the words.

How Beautiful with Mud

by Hildegarde Dolson

Perhaps the surest way to tell when a female goes over the boundary from childhood into meaningful adolescence is to watch how long it takes her to get to bed at night. My own cross-over, which could be summed up in our family as "What on earth is Hildegarde *doing* in the bathroom?" must have occurred when I was a freshman in high school. Until then, I fell into bed dog-tired each night, after the briefest possible bout with toothbrush and washcloth. But once I'd become aware of the Body Beautiful, as portrayed in advertisements in women's magazines, my absorption was complete and my attitude highly optimistic. I too would be beautiful. I would also be Flower-Fresh, Fastidious and Dainty—a triple-threat virtue obviously prized above pearls by the entire male sex, as depicted in the *Ladies' Home Journal*.

Somehow, out of my dollar-a-week allowance, I managed to buy Mum, Odorono, Listerine and something called Nipso, the latter guaranteed to remove excess hair from arms and legs, and make a man think, "Oooo, what a flawless surface." It's true that I had no men, nor was I a particularly hairy child, having only a light yellow down on my angular appendages. Nevertheless, I applied the Nipso painstakingly in the bathroom one night with Sally as my interested audience. I had noticed the stuff had a rather overpowering, sickish sweet scent, but this was a very minor drawback, considering the goal I had in mind. After Sally had been watching me for a few minutes, she began holding her nose. Finally she asked me to unlock the door and let her out. "Don't you want to see me wash it

---

From *We Shook the Family Tree.*

off?" I asked, rather hurt.

"No," Sally said. "It smells funny."

In the next hour, as my father, mother and brothers followed their noses to the upstairs hall, there were far more detailed descriptions of just how Nipso affected the olfactory senses. Jimmy, being a simple child, merely said "Pugh" and went away. My father thought it was most like the odor of rotten eggs, but Bobby said No, it was more like a mouse that's been dead quite a while. Mother was more tactful, only remarking that Nipso obviously wasn't meant to be applied in a house people lived in. Since it certainly wasn't meant to be applied in a wooded dell, either, I was prevailed upon to throw the rest of the tube away.

I didn't mind too much, because I already had my eye on something that sounded far more fascinating than Nipso. This was a miraculous substance called Beauty Clay, and every time I read about it in a magazine advertisement, the words enveloped me in rapture. Even the story of its discovery was a masterpiece in lyrical prose. Seems this girl was traveling in an obscure European country (name on request) and ran out of those things ladies always run out of at the wrong time, such as powder and make-up lotion. The worse part was that the girl really *needed* such artifices to cover up bumps. Through some intuitive process which escapes me at the moment, she had the presence of mind to go to a near-by hamlet, pick up a handful of mud, and plaster it on her face. Then she lay dozing in the sun, by a brook. When she came to, washed the claylike mud off her face, and looked at her reflection in the brook, she knew she had hit the jackpot. Boy, she was beautiful. Looking at the Before-and-After pictures, I could see that *this* beauty was more than skin-deep, having benefited even her nose, eyes and hair.

After pondering all this, I could well understand why a jar of the imported Beauty Clay cost $4.98. In fact, it was dirt cheap at the price, and my only problem was how to lay my hands on $4.98. Certainly I had no intention of enlisting financial support from my parents. For one thing, it was too much money, and for another thing, parents ask too many questions. Far better, I thought, to let the transformation of their oldest daughter come as a dazzling surprise.

Due to the fact that I had such important things as Beauty Clay on my mind, it was understandable that my monthly marks in algebra should cause even more distress than usual in the bosom of my family. Each month, the high-school honor roll, consisting of the names of the ten highest students in each class, was published in the *Franklin News-Herald.* And each month, my own name was prominently absent. Appeals to my better nature, my pride, and the honor of the Dolsons did no good. I honestly meant well, and I even went so far as to carry books home from school and carry them back again the next morning. But freshman algebra, implying as it did that X equals Y, was simply beyond me. Finally my father said that if I got on the Honor Roll he'd give me five dollars. Wobbly as I was in mathematics, it took me only a flash to realize this sum was approximately equal to $4.98, or the piddling price of the Beauty Clay. From there on in, I was straining every muscle. When I say that I got 89 in algebra and climbed to the bottom rung of the Honor Roll, I am stating a miracle simply. What is more important, I got the five bucks.

My father said that if I liked, he'd put most of it in my savings account. Bobby said, with even more enthusiasm, that he knew where I could get a bargain in a second-hand pistol. I declined both offers, marveling at the things men could think of to do with money, and made my way, on foot, to Riesenman's drugstore. When Mr. Riesenman said he had no Beauty Clay, I was grieved. When he said he'd never even heard of the stuff, I was appalled. It took three trips to convince him that he must order it immediately, money on the line.

Then I went home and waited. With admirable restraint, I waited five days. After that, I made daily inquiries on my way home from school. If I was with friends, I'd say I had to do an errand for Mother and would catch up to them later. They must often have wondered, in the next thirty days, at the number of unobtainable items my mother demanded of a drugstore. Finally came the wonderful afternoon when Mr. Riesenman said, "Here you are, Hildegarde." His jovial air may have been due to the fact that he was rid of me at last. My own joy was primitive and unconfined. At last I'd got hold of a rainbow.

It took a week more before I could achieve the needed privacy for my quick-change act. Mother was taking Jimmy and Sally downtown to get new shoes, Bobby was going skiing, and my father, as usual, would be at the office. I got home to the empty house at twenty minutes of four, and made a beeline for the Beauty Clay. According to the directions, I then washed off all make-up, which in my own case was a faint dash of powder on my nose, and wrapped myself in a sheet "To protect that pretty frock," or, more accurately, my blue-serge middy blouse. Then I took a small wooden spatula the manufacturer had thoughtfully provided, and dug into the jar.

The Beauty Clay was a rather peculiar shade of grayish-green, and I spread this all over my face and neck—"even to the hairline where tell-tale wrinkles hide." The directions also urged me not to talk or smile during the twenty minutes it would take the clay to dry. The last thing in the world I wanted to do was talk or smile. That could come later. For now, a reverent silence would suffice. In fact, as the thick green clay dried firmly in place, it had to suffice. Even though my face and neck felt as if they'd been cast in cement, the very sensation reassured me. Obviously, something was happening. I sat bolt upright in a chair and let it happen.

After fifteen minutes of this, the doorbell rang. I decided to ignore it. The doorbell rang again and again, jangling at my conscience. Nobody at our house ever ignored doorbells, and I was relieved when it stopped. In my eagerness to see who had been calling on us, I ran to my window, opened it, and leaned out. The departing guest was only the man who brought us country butter each week, I was glad to note. Hearing the sound of the window opening above him, he looked up. When he saw me leaning out, his mouth dropped open and he let out a hoarse, awful sound. Then he turned and ran down the steep hill at incredible speed. I couldn't imagine what had struck him, to act so foolish.

It wasn't until I'd remembered the clay and went to look in a mirror that I understood. Swathed in a sheet, and with every visible millimeter of skin a sickly gray-green, I scared even myself.

According to the clock, the Beauty Clay had been on the required twenty minutes, and was now ready to be washed off. It occurred to me that if twenty minutes was enough to make me beautiful, thirty minutes or even forty minutes would make me twice as beautiful. Besides, it would give me more lovely moments of anticipation, and Mother wouldn't be home until after five.

By the time my face was so rigid that even my eyeballs felt yanked from their sockets, I knew I must be done, on both sides. As I started back to the bathroom, I heard Bobby's voice downstairs yelling "Mom!" With the haste born of horror I ran back and just managed to bolt myself inside the bathroom as Bobby leaped up the stairs and came down the hall toward his room. Then I turned on the faucet and set to work. The directions had particularly warned "Use only gentle splashes to remove the mask—No rubbing or washcloth." It took several minutes of gentle splashing to make me realize this was getting me nowhere fast. Indeed, it was like splashing playfully at the Rock of Gibraltar. I decided that maybe it wouldn't hurt if I rubbed the beauty mask just a little, with a nailbrush. This hurt only the nailbrush. I myself remained embedded in Beauty Clay.

By this time, I was getting worried. Mother would be home very soon and I needed a face—even any old face. Suddenly it occurred to me that a silver knife would be a big help, although I wasn't sure just how. When I heard Bobby moving around in his room, I yelled at him to bring me a knife from the dining-room sideboard. Rather, that's what I intended to yell, but my facial muscles were still cast in stone, and the most I could do was grunt. In desperation, I ran down to the sideboard, tripping over my sheet as I went, and got the knife. Unfortunately, just as I was coming back through the dusky upstairs hall, Bobby walked out of his room and met me, face to face. The mental impact, on Bobby, was terrific. To do him justice, he realized almost instantly that this was his own sister, and not, as he at first imagined, a sea monster. But even this realization was not too reassuring.

I had often imagined how my family would look at me after the Beauty Clay had taken effect. Now it had taken effect—or even permanent possession of me—and Bobby was certainly reacting, but not quite as I'd pictured it.

"Wh—what?" he finally managed to croak, pointing at my face.

His concern was so obvious and even comforting that I tried to explain what had happened. The sounds that came out alarmed him even more.

Not having the time or the necessary freedom of speech to explain any further, I dashed into the bathroom and began hitting the handle of the knife against my rocky visage. To my heavenly relief, it began to crack. After repeated blows, which made me a little groggy, the stuff had broken up enough to allow me to wriggle my jaw. Meanwhile, Bobby stood at the door watching, completely bemused.

Taking advantage of the cracks in my surface, I dug the blade of the knife in, and by scraping, gouging, digging and prying, I got part of my face clear. As soon as I could talk, I turned on Bobby. "If you tell anybody about this, I'll kill you," I said fiercely.

Whether it was the intensity of my threat or a latent chivalry aroused by seeing a lady tortured before his very eyes, I still don't know, but Bobby said, "Cross my heart and hope to die."

He then pointed out that spots of the gray-green stuff were still very much with me. As I grabbed up the nailbrush again, to tackle these remnants, he asked in a hushed voice, "But what *is* it?"

"Beauty Clay," I said. "I sent away for it."

Bobby looked as though he couldn't understand why anyone would deliberately send away for such punishment, when there was already enough trouble in the world. However, for the first time in a long, hideous half-hour, I remembered why I'd gone through this ordeal, and now I looked into the mirror expecting to see results that would wipe out all memory of suffering. The reflection that met my eye was certainly changed all right, varying as it did between an angry scarlet where the skin had been rubbed off, to the greenish splotches still clinging.

Maybe if I got it all off, I thought. When it was all off, except those portions wedded to my hair, I gazed at myself wearily, all hope abandoned. My face was my own—but raw. Instead of the Body Beautiful I looked like the Body Boiled. Even worse, my illusions had been cracked wide open, and not by a silver knife.

"You look awfully red," Bobby said. I did indeed. To add to my troubles, we could now hear the family assembling downstairs, and Mother's voice came up, "Hildegarde, will you come set the table right away, dear?"

I moved numbly.

"You'd better take off the sheet," Bobby said.

I took off the sheet.

Just as I reached the stairs, he whispered, "Why don't you say you were frostbitten and rubbed yourself with snow?"

I looked at him with limp gratitude.

When Mother saw my scarlet, splotched face, she exclaimed in concern. "Why, Hildegarde, are you feverish?" She made a move as if to feel my forehead, but I backed away. I was burning up, but not with fever.

"I'm all right," I said, applying myself to setting the table. With my face half in the china cupboard, I mumbled that I'd been frostbitten and had rubbed myself with snow.

"Oh, Cliff," Mother called. "Little Hildegarde was frostbitten."

My father immediately came out to the kitchen. "How could she be frostbitten?" he asked reasonably. "It's thirty-four above zero."

"But her ears still look white," Mother said.

They probably did, too, compared to the rest of my face. By some oversight, I had neglected to put Beauty Clay on my ears. "I'm all right," I insisted again. "I rubbed hard to get the circulation going."

This at least was true. Anyone could tell at a glance that my circulation was going full blast, from the neck up.

Bobby had followed me out to the kitchen to see how the frostbite story went over. As mother kept exclaiming over my condition he now said staunchly, "Sure she's all right. Let her alone."

My father and mother both stared at him, in this new role of Big Brother Galahad. In fact, my father reacted rather cynically. "Bobby, did you and your friends knock Hildegarde down and rub her face with snow?" he asked.

"Me?" Bobby squeaked. He gave me a dirty look, as if to say, "You'd better talk fast."

I denied hotly that Bobby had done any such thing. In fact, I proceeded to build him up as my sole rescuer, a great big St. Bernard of a brother who had come bounding through the snowdrifts to bring me life and hope.

Bobby looked so gratified at what he'd been through in my story that I knew my secret was safe.

Sally, always an affectionate child, began to sob. "She might have died. Bobby saved her from freezing."

My father and mother remained dry-eyed. Against this new set-up of Brother Loves Sister they were suspicious, but inclined to do nothing.

And in a way I *had* been frostbitten, to the quick. Lying in bed that night, still smarting, I tried to think up ways to get even. It wasn't clear to me exactly whom or what I had to get even with. All I knew was that I was sore and unbeautiful, and mulcted of five dollars. With the hot and cold fury of a woman stung, I suddenly conceived my plan for revenge. It was so simple and logical and yet brilliant that my mind relaxed at last. Someday I, too, would write advertisements.

The Affair at 7, Rue de M——

by John Steinbeck

I had hoped to withhold from public scrutiny those rather curious events which have given me some concern for the past month. I knew of course that there was talk in the neighborhood. I have even heard some of the distortions current in my district, stories, I hasten to add, in which there is no particle of truth. However, my desire for privacy was shattered yesterday by a visit of two members of the fourth estate who assured me that the story, or rather a story, had escaped the boundaries of my *arrondisement.*

In the light of impending publicity I think it only fair to issue the true details of those happenings which have come to be known as The Affair at 7, rue de M——, in order that nonsense may not be added to a set of circumstances which are not without their *bizarrerie.* I shall set down the events as they happened without comment, thereby allowing the public to judge of the situation.

At the beginning of the summer I carried my family to Paris and took up residence in a pretty little house at 7, rue de M——, a building which in another period had been the mews of the great house beside it. The whole property is now owned and part of it inhabited by a noble French family of such age and purity that its members still consider the Bourbons unacceptable as claimants to the throne of France.

From *Harper's Bazaar.*

To this pretty little converted stable with three floors of rooms above a well-paved courtyard, I brought my immediate family, consisting of my wife, my three children, two small boys and a grown daughter, and of course myself. Our domestic arrangement, in addition to the concierge who, as you might say, came with the house, consists of a French cook of great ability, a Spanish maid and my own secretary, a girl of Swiss nationality whose high attainments and ambitions are only equaled by her moral altitude. This then was our little family group when the events I am about to chronicle were ushered in.

If one must have an agency in this matter, I can find no alternative to placing not the blame but rather the authorship, albeit innocent, on my younger son John, a lively child of singular beauty and buck teeth.

This young man has, during the last several years in America, become not so much an addict as an aficionado of that curious American practice, the chewing of bubble gum, and one of the pleasanter aspects of the early summer in Paris lay in the fact that the Cadet John had neglected to bring any of the atrocious substance with him from America. The child's speech became clear and unobstructed and the hypnotized look went out of his eyes. Alas, this delightful situation was not long to continue. An old family friend traveling in Europe brought as a present to the children a more than adequate supply of this beastly gum, thinking to do them a kindness. Thereupon the old familiar situation reasserted itself. Speech fought its damp way past a huge wad of the gum and emerged with the sound of a faulty water trap. The jaws were in constant motion, giving the face at best a look of agony while the eyes took on a glaze like those of a pig with a recently severed jugular. Since I do not believe in inhibiting my children I resigned myself to a summer not quite so pleasant as I had at first hoped.

On occasion I do not follow my ordinary practice of laissez-faire.

When I am composing the material for a book or play or essay, in a word, when the utmost of concentration is required, I am prone to establish tyrannical· rules for my own comfort and effectiveness. One of these rules is that there shall be neither chewing nor bubbling while I am trying to concentrate. This rule is so thoroughly understood by the Cadet John that he accepts it as one of the laws of nature and does not either complain or attempt to evade the ruling. It is his pleasure and my solace for my son to come sometimes into my workroom, there to sit quietly beside me for a time. He knows he must be silent and when he has remained so for as long a time as his character permits, he goes out quietly, leaving us both enriched by the wordless association.

Two weeks ago in the late afternoon, I sat at my desk composing a short essay for *Figaro Littéraire,* an essay which later aroused some controversy when it was printed under the title "Sartre Resartus." I had come to that passage concerning the proper clothing for the soul when to my astonishment and chagrin I heard the unmistakable soft plopping sound of a bursting balloon of bubble gum. I looked sternly at my offspring and saw him chewing away. His cheeks were colored with embarrassment and the muscles of his jaw stood rigidly out.

"You know the rule," I said coldly.

To my amazement tears came into his eyes and while his jaws continued to masticate hugely, his blubbery voice forced its way past the huge lump of bubble gum in his mouth.

"I didn't do it," he cried.

"What do you mean, you didn't do it?" I demanded in a rage. "I distinctly heard and now I distinctly see."

"Oh, sir!" he moaned. "I really didn't. I'm not chewing it, sir. It's chewing me."

For a moment I inspected him closely. He is an honest child, only under the greatest pressure of gain permitting himself an untruth. I had the horrible thought that the bubble gum had finally had its way and that my son's reason was tottering. If this were so, it were better to tread softly. Quietly I put out my hand. "Lay it here," I said kindly.

My child tried manfully to disengage the gum from his jaws. "It won't let me go," he sputtered.

"Open up," I said and then inserting my fingers in his mouth I seized hold of the large lump of gum and after a struggle in which my fingers slipped again and again, managed to drag it forth and to deposit the ugly blob on my desk on top of a pile of white manuscript paper.

For a moment it seemed to shudder there on the paper and then with an easy slowness it began to undulate, to swell and recede with the exact motion of being chewed while my son and I regarded it with popping eyes.

For a long time we watched it while I drove through my mind for some kind of explanation. Either I was dreaming or some principle as yet unknown had taken its seat in the pulsing bubble gum on the desk. I am not unintelligent. While I considered the indecent thing, a hundred little thoughts and glimmerings of understanding raced through my brain. At last I asked, "How long has it been chewing you?"

"Since last night," he replied.

"And when did you first notice, this, this propensity on its part?"

He spoke with perfect candor. "I will ask you to believe me, sir," he said. "Last night before I went to sleep I put it under my pillow as is my invariable custom. In the night I was awakened to find that it was in my mouth. I again placed it under my pillow and this morning it was again in my mouth, lying very quietly. When, however, I became thoroughly awakened, I was conscious of a slight motion and shortly afterward the situation dawned on me that I was no longer master of the gum. It had taken its head. I tried to remove it, sir, and could not. You yourself with all of your strength have seen how difficult it was to extract. I came to your workroom to await your first disengagement, wishing to acquaint you with my difficulty. Oh, Daddy, what do you think has happened?"

The cancerous thing held my complete attention.

"I must think," I said. "This is something a little out of the ordinary, and I do not believe it should be passed over without some investigation."

As I spoke a change came over the gum. It ceased to chew itself and seemed to rest for a while, and then with a flowing movement like those monocellular animals of the order *Paramecium,* the gum slid across the desk straight in the direction of my son. For a moment I was stricken with astonishment and for an even longer time I failed to discern its intent. It dropped to his knee, climbed horribly up his shirt front. Only then did I understand. It was trying to get back into his mouth. He looked down on it paralyzed with fright.

"Stop," I cried, for I realized that my third-born was in danger and at such times I am capable of a violence which verges on the murderous. I seized the monster from his chin and striding from my workroom, entered the salon, opened the window, and hurled the thing into the busy traffic on the rue de M———.

I believe it is the duty of a parent to ward off those shocks which may cause dreams or trauma whenever possible. I went back to my study to find young John sitting where I had left him. He was staring into space. There was a troubled line between his brows.

"Son," I said, "you and I have seen something which, while we know it to have happened, we might find difficult to describe with any degree of success to others. I ask you to imagine the scene if we should tell this story to the other members of the family. I greatly fear we should be laughed out of the house."

"Yes, sir," he said passively.

"Therefore I am going to propose to you, my son, that we lock the episode deep in our memories and never mention it to a soul

as long as we live." I waited for his assent and when it did not
come, glanced up at his face to see it a ravaged field of terror. His
eyes were starting out of his head. I turned in the direction of his
gaze. Under the door there crept a paper-thin sheet which, once it
had entered the room, grew to a gray blob and rested on the rug,
pulsing and chewing. After a moment it moved again by pseudo-
podian progression toward my son.

I fought down panic as I rushed at it. I grabbed it up and flung it
on my desk, then seizing an African war club from among the
trophies on the wall, a dreadful instrument studded with brass, I
beat the gum until I was breathless and it a torn piece of plastic
fabric. The moment I rested, it drew itself together and for a few
moments chewed very rapidly as though it chuckled at my impo-
tence, and then inexorably it moved toward my son, who by this
time was crouched in a corner moaning with terror.

Now a coldness came over me. I picked up the filthy thing and
wrapped it in my handkerchief, strode out of the house, walked
three blocks to the Seine and flung the handkerchief into the slowly
moving current.

I spent a good part of the afternoon soothing my son and trying
to reassure him that his fears were over. But such was his nervous-
ness that I had to give him half a barbiturate tablet to get him to
sleep that night, while my wife insisted that I call a doctor. I did not
at that time dare to tell her why I could not obey her wish.

I was awakened, indeed the whole house was awakened, in the
night by a terrified muffled scream from the children's room. I took
the stairs two at a time and burst in the room, flicking the light
switch as I went. John sat up in bed squalling, while with his fingers
he dug at his half-opened mouth, a mouth which horrifyingly went
right on chewing. As I looked a bubble emerged between his fingers
and burst with a wet plopping sound.

What chance of keeping our secret now! All had to be explained, but with the plopping gum pinned to a breadboard with an ice pick the explanation was easier than it might have been. And I am proud of the help and comfort given me. There is no strength like that of the family. Our French cook solved the problem by refusing to believe it even when she saw it. It was not reasonable, she explained, and she was a reasonable member of a reasonable people. The Spanish maid ordered and paid for an exorcism by the parish priest who, poor man, after two hours of strenuous effort went away muttering that this was more a matter of the stomach than the soul.

For two weeks we were besieged by the monster. We burned it in the fireplace, causing it to splutter in blue flames and melt in a nasty mess among the ashes. Before morning it had crawled through the keyhole of the children's room, leaving a trail of wood ash on the door, and again we were awakened by screams from the Cadet.

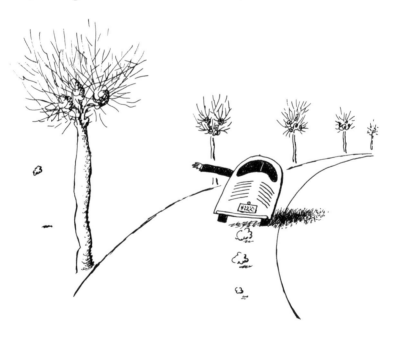

In despair I drove far into the country and threw it from my automobile. It was back before morning. Apparently it had crept to the highway and placed itself in the Paris traffic until picked up by a truck tire. When we tore it from John's mouth it had still the nonskid marks of Michelin imprinted in its side.

Fatigue and frustration will take their toll. In exhaustion, with my will to fight back sapped, and after we had tried every possible method to lose or destroy the bubble gum, I placed it at last under a bell jar which I ordinarily use to cover my microscope. I collapsed in a chair to gaze at it with weary defeated eyes. John slept in his little bed under the influence of sedatives backed by my assurance that I would not let the Thing out of my sight.

I lighted a pipe and settled back to watch it. Inside the bell jar the gray tumorous lump moved restlessly about searching for some means of exit from its prison. Now and then it paused as though in thought and emitted a bubble in my direction. I could feel the hatred it had for me. In my weariness I found my mind slipping into an analysis which had so far escaped me.

The background I had been over hurriedly. It must be that from constant association with the lambent life which is my son, the magic of life had been created in the bubble gum. And with life had come intelligence, not the manly open intelligence of the boy, but an evil calculating wiliness.

How could it be otherwise? Intelligence without the soul to balance it must of necessity be evil. The gum had not absorbed any part of John's soul.

Very well, said my mind, now we have a hypothesis of its origin, let us consider its nature. What does it think? What does it want? What does it need? My mind leaped like a terrier. It needs and wants to get back to its host, my son. It wants to be chewed. It must be chewed to survive.

Inside the bell jar the gum inserted a thin wedge of itself under the heavy glass foot and constricted so that the whole jar lifted a fraction of an inch. I laughed as I drove it back. I laughed with almost insane triumph. I had the answer.

In the dining room I procured a clear plastic plate, one of a dozen my wife had bought for picnics in the country. Then turning the bell jar over and securing the monster in its bottom, I smeared the mouth of it with a heavy plastic cement guaranteed to be water-, alcohol-, and acid-proof. I forced the plate over the opening and pressed it down until the glue took hold and bound the plate to the glass, making an airtight container. And last I turned the jar upright again and adjusted the reading light so that I could observe every movement of my prisoner.

Again it searched the circle for escape. Then it faced me and emitted a great number of bubbles very rapidly. I could hear the little bursting plops through the glass.

"I have you, my beauty," I cried. "I have you at last."

That was a week ago. I have not left the side of the bell jar since, and have only turned my head to accept a cup of coffee. When I go to the bathroom, my wife takes my place. I can now report the following hopeful news.

During the first day and night, the bubble gum tried every means to escape. Then for a day and a night it seemed to be agitated and nervous as though it had for the first time realized its predicament. The third day it went to work with its chewing motion, only the action was speeded up greatly, like the chewing of a baseball fan. On the fourth day it began to weaken and I observed with joy a kind of dryness on its once slick and shiny exterior.

I am now in the seventh day and I believe it is almost over. The gum is lying in the center of the plate. At intervals it heaves and subsides. Its color has turned to a nasty yellow. Once today when my son entered the room, it leaped up excitedly, then seemed to realize its hopelessness and collapsed on the plate. It will die tonight I think and only then will I dig a deep hole in the garden, and I will deposit the sealed bell jar and cover it up and plant geraniums over it.

It is my hope that this account will set straight some of the silly tales that are being hawked in the neighborhood.

Father Opens My Mail

by Clarence Day

There was a time in my boyhood when I felt that Father had handicapped me severely in life by naming me after him, "Clarence." All literature, so far as I could see, was thronged with objectionable persons named Clarence. Percy was bad enough, but there had been some good fighters named Percy. The only Clarence in history was a duke who did something dirty at Tewkesbury, and who died a ridiculous death afterwards in a barrel of malmsey.

As for the Clarences in the fiction I read, they were horrible. In one story, for instance, there were two brothers, Clarence and Frank. Clarence was a "vain, disagreeable little fellow," who was proud of his curly hair and fine clothes, while Frank was a "rollicking boy who was ready to play games with anybody." Clarence didn't like to play games, of course. He just minced around looking on.

One day when the mother of these boys had gone out, this story went on, Clarence "tempted" Frank to disobey her and fly their kite on the roof. Frank didn't want to, but Clarence kept taunting him and daring him until Frank was stung into doing it. After the two boys went up to the roof, Frank got good and dirty, running up and down and stumbling over scuttles, while Clarence sat there, giving him orders, and kept his natty clothes tidy. To my horror, he even spread out his handkerchief on the trapdoor to sit on. And to crown all, this sneak told on Frank as soon as their mother came in.

This wasn't an exceptionally mean Clarence, either. He was just run-of-the-mill. Some were worse.

From *Life With Father*.

So far as I could ever learn, however, Father had never heard of these stories, and had never dreamed of there being anything objectionable in his name. Quite the contrary. And yet as a boy he had lived a good rough-and-tumble boy's life. He had played and fought on the city streets, and kept a dog in Grandpa's stable, and stolen rides to Greenpoint Ferry on the high, lurching bus. In the summer he had gone to West Springfield and had run down Shad Lane through the trees to the house where Grandpa was born, and had gone barefoot and driven the cows home just as though he had been named Tom or Bill.

He had the same character as a boy, I suppose, that he had as a man, and he was too independent to care if people thought his name fancy. He paid no attention to the prejudices of others, except to disapprove of them. He had plenty of prejudices himself, of course, but they were his own. He was humorous and confident and level-headed, and I imagine that if any boy had tried to make fun of him for being named Clarence, Father would simply have laughed and told him he didn't know what he was talking about.

I asked Mother how this name had ever happened to spring up in our family. She explained that my great-great-grandfather was Benjamin Day, and my great-grandfather was Henry, and consequently my grandfather had been named Benjamin Henry. He in turn had named his eldest son Henry and his second son Benjamin. The result was that when Father was born there was no family name left. The privilege of choosing a name for Father had thereupon been given to Grandma, and unluckily for the Day family she had been reading a novel, the hero of which was named Clarence.

I knew that Grandma, though very like Grandpa in some respects, had a dreamy side which he hadn't, a side that she usually kept to herself, in her serene, quiet way. Her romantic choice of this name probably made Grandpa smile, but he was a detached sort of man who didn't take small matters seriously, and who drew a good deal of private amusement from the happenings of everyday life. Besides, he was partly to blame in this case, because that novel was one he had published himself in his magazine.

I asked Mother, when she had finished, why I had been named Clarence too.

It hadn't been her choice, Mother said. She had suggested all sorts of names to Father, but there seemed to be something wrong with each one. When she had at last spoken of naming me after him, he had said at once that that was the best suggestion yet—he said it sounded just right.

Father and I would have had plenty of friction in any case. This identity of names made things worse. Every time that I had been more of a fool than he liked, Father would try to impress on me my responsibilities as his eldest son, and above all as the son to whom he had given his name, as he put it. A great deal was expected, it seemed to me, of a boy who was named after his father. I used to envy my brothers, who didn't have anything expected of them on this score at all.

I envied them still more after I was old enough to begin getting letters. I then discovered that when Father "gave" me his name, he had also, not unnaturally, I had to admit, retained it himself, and when anything came for Clarence S. Day he opened it, though it was sometimes for me.

He also opened everything that came addressed to Clarence S. Day, Jr. He didn't do this intentionally, but unless the "Jr." was clearly written, it looked like "Esq.," and anyhow Father was too accustomed to open all Clarence Day letters to remember about looking carefully every time for a "Jr." So far as mail and express went, I had no name at all of my own.

For the most part nobody wrote to me when I was a small boy except firms whose advertisements I had read in the *Youth's Companion* and to whom I had written requesting them to send me their circulars. These circulars described remarkable bargains in magicians' card outfits, stamps and coins, pocket knives, trick spiders, and imitation fried eggs, and they seemed interesting and valuable to me when I got them. The trouble was that Father usually got them and at once tore them up. I then had to write for such circulars again, and if Father got the second one too, he would sometimes explode with annoyance. He became particularly indignant one year, I remember, when he was repeatedly urged to take advantage of a special bargain sale of false whiskers. He said he couldn't understand why these offerings kept pouring in. I knew why, in this case, but at other times I was often surprised myself at the number he got, not realizing that as a result of my postcard request my or our name had been automatically put on several large general mailing lists.

During this period I got more of my mail out of Father's wastebasket than I did from the postman.

At the age of twelve or thirteen, I stopped writing for these childish things and turned to a new field. Father and I, whichever of us got at the mail first, then began to receive not merely circulars but personal letters beginning:

Dear Friend Day:

In reply to your valued request for one of our Mammoth Agents' Outfits, kindly forward postoffice order for $1.49 to cover cost of postage and packing, and we will put you in a position to earn a large income in your spare time with absolutely no labor on your part, by taking subscriptions for *The Secret Handbook of Mesmerism,* and our *Tales of Blood* series.

And one spring, I remember, as the result of what I had intended to be a secret application on my part, Father was assigned "the exclusive rights for Staten Island and Hoboken of selling the Gem Home Popper for Pop Corn. Housewives buy it at sight."

After Father had stormily endured these afflictions for a while, he and I began to get letters from girls. Fortunately for our feelings, these were rare, but they were ordeals for both of us. Father had forgotten, if he ever knew, how silly young girls can sound, and I got my first lesson in how unsystematic they were. No matter how private and playful they meant their letters to be, they forgot to put "Jr." on the envelope every once in so often. When Father opened these letters, he read them all the way through, sometimes twice, muttering to himself over and over: "This is very peculiar. I don't understand this at all. Here's a letter to me from some person I never heard of. I can't see what it's about." By the time it had occurred to him that possibly the letter might be for me, I was red and embarrassed and even angrier at the girl than at Father. And on days when he had read some of the phrases aloud to the family, it nearly killed me to claim it.

Lots of fellows whom I knew had been named after their fathers without having such troubles. But although Father couldn't have been kinder-hearted or had any better intentions, when he saw his name on a package or envelope it never dawned on him that it might not be for him. He was too active in his habits to wait until I had a chance to get at it. And as he was also single-minded and prompt to attend to unfinished business, he opened everything automatically and then did his best to dispose of it.

This went on even after I grew up, until I had a home of my own. Father was always perfectly decent about it, but he never changed. When he saw I felt sulky, he was genuinely sorry and said so, but he couldn't see why all this should annoy me, and he was surprised and amused that it did. I used to get angry once in a while when something came for me which I particularly hadn't wished him to see and which I would find lying, opened, on the hall table marked

"For Jr.?" when I came in; but nobody could stay angry with Father—he was too utterly guiltless of having meant to offend.

He often got angry himself, but it was mostly at things, not at persons, and he didn't mind a bit (as a rule) when persons got angry at him. He even declared, when I got back from college, feeling dignified, and told him that I wished he'd be more careful, that he suffered from these mistakes more than I did. It wasn't *his* fault, he pointed out, if my stupid correspondents couldn't remember my name, and it wasn't any pleasure to him to be upset at his breakfast by finding that a damned lunatic company in Battle Creek had sent him a box of dry bread crumbs, with a letter asserting that this rubbish would be good for his stomach. "I admit I threw it into the fireplace, Clarence, but what else could I do? If you valued this preposterous concoction, my dear boy, I'm sorry. I'll buy another box for you today, if you'll tell me where I can get it. Don't feel badly. I'll buy you a barrel. Only I hope you won't eat it."

In the days when Mrs. Pankhurst and her friends were chaining themselves to lamp-posts in London, in their campaign for the vote, a letter came from Frances Hand trustfully asking "Dear Clarence" to do something to help Woman Suffrage—speak at a meeting, I think. Father got red in the face. "Speak at one of their meetings!" he roared at Mother. "I'd like nothing better! You can tell Mrs. Hand that it would give me great pleasure to inform all those crackpots in petticoats exactly what I think of their antics."

"Now, Clare," Mother said, "you mustn't talk that way. I like that nice Mrs. Hand, and anyhow this letter must be for Clarence."

One time I asked Father for his opinion of a low-priced stock I'd been watching. His opinion was that it was not worth a damn. I thought this over, but I still wished to buy it, so I placed a scale order with another firm instead of with Father's office, and said nothing about it. At the end of the month this other firm sent me a statement, setting forth each of my little transactions in full, and of course they forgot to put the "Jr." at the end of my name. When Father opened the envelope, he thought at first in his excitement that this firm had actually opened an account for him without being asked. I found him telling Mother that he'd like to wring their damned necks.

"That must be for me, Father," I said, when I took in what had happened.

We looked at each other.

"You bought this stuff?" he said incredulously. "After all I said about it?"

"Yes, Father."

He handed over the statement and walked out of the room.

Both he and I felt offended and angry. We stayed so for several days, too, but we then made it up.

Once in a while when I got a letter that I had no time to answer I used to address an envelope to the sender and then put anything in it that happened to be lying around on my desk—a circular about books, a piece of newspaper, an old laundry bill—anything at all, just to be amiable, and yet at the same time to save myself the trouble of writing. I happened to tell several people about this private habit of mine at a dinner one night—a dinner at which Alice Duer Miller and one or two other writers were present. A little later she wrote me a criticism of Henry James and ended by saying that I needn't send her any of my old laundry bills because she wouldn't stand it. And she forgot to put on the "Jr."

"In the name of God," Father said bleakly, "this is the worst yet. Here's a woman who says I'd better not read *The Golden Bowl*, which I have no intention whatever of doing, and she also warns me for some unknown reason not to send her my laundry bills."

The good part of all these experiences, as I realize now, was that in the end they drew Father and me closer together. My brothers had only chance battles with him. I had a war. Neither he nor I relished its clashes, but they made us surprisingly intimate.

Child's Play

A Selection of Anecdotes as Told by Bennett Cerf

A young mother in Milwaukee, exhausted from her daily chores, lay down on her couch to steal forty winks. Half asleep, she felt one of her youngsters patting her face and was drowsily pleased by this unexpected display of affection.

Then the doorbell rang. She jumped up with a start to admit a delivery man from her husband's favorite tobacco shop. He looked at her so queerly that when he had gone, she rushed over to a mirror to inspect herself.

Her face was completely plastered with green trading stamps!

There's a lady in the suburbs who is determined that, when her twelve-year-old son Herbert grows up, he will be not only a superb dancer, but a brilliant conversationalist as well. With that end in view, she marches him to dancing school every Wednesday afternoon, and furthermore sits grimly at the ringside to see that he not only pushes little girls around the room, more or less in tune with the music, but talks to them brightly at the same time. Herbert takes an exceedingly dim view of the entire procedure.

Last Wednesday, Herbert was executing what he fondly believed to be a foxtrot with a brand-new dancing partner when he caught his mother's signal: "Engage her in conversation!" He took a deep breath, and gallantly informed his lady fair, "Say, you sweat less than any fat girl I've ever danced with!"

A fond mother was pleased with her son. "You see, Jerry," she

---

From *Try and Stop Me* and other books by Bennett Cerf.

beamed, "I told you that was a nice little boy next door. I was glad to see from the window just now that you had made friends with him and were helping him pick up his marbles."

"Marbles!" scoffed Jerry. "I socked him in the jaw. Those weren't marbles; those were teeth."

A girl in the booth at a big movie theatre hesitated when a youngster sought to buy a ticket for the early afternoon show. "Why aren't you in school?" she asked sharply. "It's okay, lady," he assured her. "I've got the measles."

CHILDREN OF DISTINCTION

BOYS

1. Peter, who, like all six-year-olds, abhorred washing, came to the dinner table one evening with elbows black as pitch. Sent back to the bathroom for repairs, he dawdled there so long that his mother called, "How are you coming, Pete? Elbows clean yet?" "Not clean," he called back triumphantly, "but I've got them to match."

2. The 150-pound ten-year-old who won the part of Cleopatra in a school play. "But why," asked his mother, "did they give such a part to the huskiest lad in the class?" "They had to," explained the boy cheerfully. "It was my snake!"

3. The boy scout who admitted to his father that his daily good deed was not quite good enough this once. "I helped an old lady across the street like you suggested," he said, "but she got hit by a taxi."

4. The nine-year-old who, asked by his teacher to name the four seasons of the year, came up with "Football, Basketball, Baseball, and Vacation."

5. The kid from Texas who got all the way to the finals of a national spelling bee but then lost out because he couldn't spell "small."

GIRLS

1. Lucinda, who, at the age of ten was given a check for twenty dollars by her parents and told to open an account at the savings bank. Officials there gave her an application blank that included the question, "Have you had an account previously elsewhere, and if so, will you please print here the name of the bank?"

Lucinda gave the problem due thought, then laboriously spelled out, "Yes. Piggy."

2. The little girl at camp who asked her tentmate, "Do you ever get homesick?" "Yes, I do," admitted the tentmate, "but only when I'm home."

3. The honest seven-year-old who admitted calmly to her parents that Billy Brown had kissed her after class. "How did that happen?" gasped her mother. "It wasn't easy," admitted the young lady, "but three girls helped me catch him."

4. The little girl who assured her teacher, "Of *course* I know how to spell banana. I just never know when to stop."

5. Judy, who was leading her young friends in the kitchen in a symphony banged out on pots and pans. "I wish Mom would hurry

and make us stop," she grumbled. "This noise is killing me."

AND THEIR PARENTS

1. The mother who demanded of her son, just turned seven, "What are you reading?" "A story about a cow jumping over the moon," was the answer. "Throw that book away at once," commanded the mother. "How often have I told you you're too young to read science fiction?"

2. The proud mother who bragged, "My son Arthur is smarter than Abraham Lincoln. Arthur could recite the Gettysburg Address when he was ten years old. Lincoln didn't say it till he was fifty."

3. The dapper New Yorker—one of the ten best-dressed men in America—who came to collect his six-year-old daughter at a birthday party. Taking hold of her hand to guide her across the street, he observed, "Goodness, Vicki, your hands seem mighty sticky today." "Yours would be, too," she informed him, "if you had a piece of lemon pie and a chocolate eclair in your pocket."

4. Will Rogers' ma. When he was ten, she had trouble persuading him to tuck in his shirttails in school or when company came to dinner. Then she sewed lace around the bottom of every shirt he owned. It worked wonders.

5. The mother of little John Charles, who found his first report card distinctly encouraging. "John Charles is a bright, alert lad," was the teacher's comment, "but I believe he spends too much time playing with the girls. However, I am working on a plan which I believe will break him of the habit."

John Charles' mother acknowledged receipt of the report and added this note of her own: "Let me know if your plan works, and I'll try it on his father."

Five-year-old Christopher went to a party in a brand-new suit. When he came home, ragged holes had been cut into it with a pair of scissors. His shocked mother exclaimed, "What did you do to your expensive new suit?"

"We decided to play grocery store," explained Christopher. "I was a piece of Swiss cheese."

A famous film producer's son came home from his freshman year at college with a set of grades so dazzling that the whole family glowed with pride. His brother Jonathan, aged five, finally felt it was time for him to get into the act, however, and declared loudly, "I got an 'A' in arithmetic today."

His father indulgently replied, "I didn't know they taught arithmetic in kindergarten. What's one and one?" Jonathan pondered a moment, then reported, "We haven't gotten that far yet."

A young blueblood from Boston was showing her family album to some friends from the Midwest. "Isn't this one a scream?" she asked. "It's my Aunt Dorothy. She's the fattest lady who ever lived on Pinckney Street." One of the visitors, duly impressed, said, "And who is that standing behind her?" The little girl said, "Don't be silly. That's still Aunt Dorothy."

A little boy had been pawing over a stationer's stock of greeting cards for some time when a clerk asked, "Just what is it you're looking for, Sonny? Birthday greeting? Message to a sick friend? Anniversary congratulations to your ma and dad?"

The boy shook his head "No" and answered wistfully, "Got anything in the line of blank report cards?"

A bank robber was reported driving like mad somewhere in Virginia, and every sheriff in the state was alerted to watch for him. Taking no chances, one conscientious sheriff decided to stop every car on the road and cross-examine its occupants. The dowager in a sleek limousine took this amiss. "By what authority do you presume to stop this car?" she demanded angrily.

The sheriff took his badge out of his pocket to show the lady—and blushed violently. The badge was a tin affair marked "Space

Ship Patrol." His nine-year-old son had switched badges.

Kids dearly love receiving presents—but hate even more having to write thank-you letters therefor. My own Jonny got around to thanking his Uncle Herbert for a Christmas gift along about March 25. What he wrote was, "I'm sorry I didn't thank you for my present, and it would serve me right if you forgot about my birthday next Thursday. . . ."

Here are a couple of noteworthy letters received by fond parents from their children in summer camp:

1. "Dear Mom: Please bring some food when you come to visit me. All we get here is breakfast, lunch, and supper."

2. "Dear Dad: Please write often even if it is only a couple of dollars."

It was Mrs. Abernathy's eleven-year-old daughter, Nell, incidentally, who came home from camp with a gold medal for packing her trunk more neatly than any other girl. "How did you do it?" marveled Mrs. Abernathy, "when at home we can never get you to clean up the mess you leave behind."

"It was cinchy," explained Nell. "I just never unpacked all summer."

A San Francisco six-year-old, obviously impeccably reared, came home from a party in fine spirits, to be asked by his mother, "Were you the youngest one there?"

"Not at all," he answered loftily. "There was another gentleman present who was wheeled in in a baby carriage."

Eight-year-old Claudia was packed off to Charlevoix for a visit with her old-maid aunt. Her last-minute instructions were, "Remember, Aunt Hester is a bit on the prissy side. If you have to go to the bathroom, be sure to say, 'I'd like to powder my nose.'"

Claudia made such a hit with Aunt Hester that when the time came for her to leave she was told, "I certainly loved having you here, my dear. On your next visit you must bring your little sister Sue with you." "I better not," said Claudia hastily. "Sue still powders her nose in bed."

Boys and girls have adopted enthusiastically a game introduced by Steve Allen. Steve provides you with the answer; you must figure out the question.
Examples:
1. *Answer:* Mount Whitney, Mount Olympus, and Mount Sinai.
   Question: Name two mountains and a hospital.
2. *Answer:* Cleopatra, Pocahontas, and Florence Nightingale.
   Question: Name three dead women.
3. *Answer:* Washington Irving.
   Question: Who was the first President, Sam?

Television has changed schoolboys and girls a lot—but they've never come up with a substitute for that good old kissing game of post office. A group of enthusiastic kids were playing it recently at a party, when a boy and girl shut themselves in a closet and didn't come out. "Come out of there," ordered the host's mother finally. "We can't," the boy called back. "We have our braces hooked!"

Nine-year-old Marian, taken by her parents for her first transcontinental rail journey, was thrilled when the train plunged into a long tunnel in the Rockies. When it finally emerged at the other end, she peered out of the vista-dome window, and exclaimed, "Look, Mom! It's tomorrow!"

Herman Hickman, late football coach and commentator, had a sentimental streak almost as wide as he was. Here's his favorite poem, authorship unknown, which he was ready to recite at the drop of a referee's whistle:

A LITTLE BOY PRAYS FOR HIS DOG

Dear God,

> They say my dog is dead;
> He had the softest little head;
> He was so good, he'd always do
> Most anything I told him to.

Kind God,

> Sometimes he'd chase a cat,
> (He wasn't often bad like that),
> And if I called him back, he came
> The minute that I said his name.

Please God,

> If he feels scared up there,
> Won't You please let him sleep somewhere
> Near You? Oh, please take care of him,
> I love him so! His name is Tim.

An amiable gentleman paused to watch some kids in a sandlot baseball game. "What's the score, son?" he asked one of the players. "28 to 0 against us right now," said the kid. "My!" said the gentleman, "Aren't you a bit discouraged?" "Discouraged nothing," enthused the kid. "We haven't been to bat yet."

Never in real life was there a baseball star to compare with one invented by Ed Gardner. His name was Gruskin and he was called Two-Top for the very good reason that he had two heads. This not only enabled him to watch first base and third base at the same time, but made him a great man to pitch double-headers.

When Two-Top Gruskin first reported to the Dodgers he was wearing a white sweater. "What are you fellows staring at?" he asked his new teammates angrily. "Haven't any of you seen a white sweater before?" "Two-Top," interrupted the manager, "I'm a man of few words. There's a uniform and two caps waiting for you. Waiter, bring my new pitcher two glasses of milk."

Two-Top had pitched six hitless innings in his first game when the umpire suddenly threw off his mask and yelled to the manager, "Hey, do you realize this pitcher of yours has two heads?" "Yeah," chimed in the catcher, Gorilla Hogan, "and I'm sick and tired of him already. When I signal for a high fast one, he nods 'yes' with one head, but shakes the other 'no.' Either he goes or I go, Mr. Manager—and don't forget who owns the ball."

That marked the end of Two-Top Gruskin's big-league career, but that very night he won first prize at a masquerade party by disguising himself as a pair of bookends. Then he enlisted in the army. The doctor took his chart to the colonel. "Let's see," said the colonel. "Eyes—brown and blue. Hair—blonde and brunette. Mustache—yes and no. This fellow sounds as if he's got two heads." "He has," said the doctor. "Oh," said the colonel.

Two-Top was a big success in the army as soon as he made up his mind which head to salute.

How We Kept Mother's Day

by Stephen Leacock

Of all the different ideas that have been started lately, I think that the very best is the notion of celebrating once a year "Mother's Day." I don't wonder that this is becoming such a popular day all over America and I am sure the idea will spread to England too.

It is especially in a big family like ours that such an idea takes hold. So we decided to have a special celebration of Mother's Day. We thought it a fine idea. It made us all realize how much Mother had done for us for years, and all the efforts and sacrifice that she had made for our sake.

So we decided that we'd make it a great day, a holiday for all the family, and do everything we could to make Mother happy. Father decided to take a holiday from his office so as to help in celebrating the day, and my sister Anne and I stayed home from college classes, and Mary and my brother Will stayed home from High School.

It was our plan to make it a day just like Xmas or any big holiday, and so we decided to decorate the house with flowers and with mottoes over the mantelpieces, and all that kind of thing. We got Mother to make mottoes and arrange the decorations, because she always does it at Xmas.

The two girls thought it would be a nice thing to dress in our very best for such a big occasion, and so they both got new hats. Mother trimmed both the hats, and they looked fine, and Father

---

From *Laugh With Leacock*.

had bought four-in-hand silk ties for himself and us boys as a souvenir of the day to remember Mother by. We were going to get Mother a new hat too, but it turned out that she seemed to really like her old grey bonnet better than a new one, and both the girls said that it was awfully becoming to her.

Well, after breakfast we had it arranged as a surprise for Mother that we would hire a motor car and take her for a beautiful drive away into the country. Mother is hardly ever able to have a treat like that, because we can only afford to keep one maid, and so Mother is busy in the house nearly all the time. And of course the country is so lovely now that it would be just grand for her to have a lovely morning, driving for miles and miles.

But on the very morning of the day we changed the plan a little bit, because it occurred to Father that a thing it would be better to do even than to take Mother for a motor drive would be to take her fishing. Father said that as the car was hired and paid for, we might just as well use it for a drive up into hills where the streams are. As Father said, if you just go out driving without any object, you have a sense of aimlessness, but if you are going to fish, there is a definite purpose in front of you to heighten the enjoyment.

So we all felt that it would be nicer for Mother to have a definite purpose; and anyway, it turned out that Father had just got a new rod the day before, which made the idea of fishing all the more appropriate, and he said that Mother could use it if she wanted to; in fact, he said it was practically for her, only Mother said she would much rather watch him fish and not try to fish herself.

So we got everything arranged for the trip, and we got Mother to cut up some sandwiches and make up a sort of lunch in case we got hungry, though of course we were to come back home to a big dinner in the middle of the day, just like Xmas or New Year's Day. Mother packed it all up in a basket for us ready to go in the motor.

Well, when the car came to the door, it turned out that there hardly seemed as much room in it as we had supposed, because we hadn't reckoned on Father's fishing basket and the rods and the lunch, and it was plain enough that we couldn't all get in.

Father said not to mind him, he said that he could just as well stay home, and that he was sure that he could put in the time working in the garden; he said that there was a lot of rough dirty work that he could do, like digging a trench for the garbage, that would save hiring a man, and so he said that he'd stay home; he said that we were not to let the fact of his not having had a real holiday for three years stand in our way; he wanted us to go right ahead and be happy and have a big day, and not to mind him. He said that he could plug away all day, and in fact he said he'd been a fool to think there'd be any holiday for him.

But of course we all felt that it would never do to let Father stay home, especially as we knew he would make trouble if he did. The two girls, Anne and Mary, would gladly have stayed and helped the maid get dinner, only it seemed such a pity to, on a lovely day like this, having their new hats. But they both said that Mother had only to say the word, and they'd gladly stay home and work. Will and I would have dropped out, but unfortunately we wouldn't have been any use in getting the dinner.

So in the end it was decided that Mother would stay home and just have a lovely restful day round the house, and get the dinner. It turned out anyway that Mother doesn't care for fishing, and also it was just a little bit cold and fresh out of doors, though it was lovely and sunny, and Father was rather afraid that Mother might take cold if she came.

He said he would never forgive himself if he dragged Mother round the country and let her take a severe cold at a time when she might be having a beautiful rest. He said it was our duty to try and let Mother get all the rest and quiet that she could, after all that she had done for all of us, and he said that that was principally why he had fallen in with this idea of a fishing trip, so as to give Mother a little quiet. He said that young people seldom realize how much quiet means to people who are getting old. As to himself, he could still stand the racket, but he was glad to shelter Mother from it.

So we all drove away with three cheers for Mother, and Mother stood and watched us from the verandah for as long as she could see us, and Father waved his hand back to her every few minutes till he hit his hand on the back edge of the car, and then said that he didn't think that Mother could see us any longer.

Well, we had the loveliest day up among the hills that you could possibly imagine, and Father caught such big specimens that he felt sure that Mother couldn't have landed them anyway, if she had been fishing for them, and Will and I fished too, though we didn't get so many as Father, and the two girls met quite a lot of people that they knew as we drove along, and there were some young men friends of theirs that they met along the stream and talked to, and so we all had a splendid time.

It was quite late when we got back, nearly seven o'clock in the evening, but Mother had guessed that we would be late, so she had kept back the dinner so as to have it just nicely ready and hot for us. Only first she had to get towels and soap for Father and clean things for him to put on, because he always gets so messed up with fishing, and that kept Mother busy for a little while, that and helping the girls get ready.

But at last everything was ready, and we sat down to the grandest kind of dinner—roast turkey and all sorts of things like on Xmas Day. Mother had to get up and down a good bit during the meal fetching things back and forward, but at the end Father noticed it and said she simply mustn't do it, that he wanted her to spare herself, and he got up and fetched the walnuts over from the sideboard himself.

The dinner lasted a long while, and was great fun, and when it was over all of us wanted to help clear the things up and wash the dishes, only Mother said that she would really much rather do it, and so we let her, because we wanted just for once to humor her.

It was quite late when it was all over, and when we all kissed Mother before going to bed, she said it had been the most wonderful day in her life, and I think there were tears in her eyes. So we all felt awfully repaid for all that we had done.

Your Boy and His Dog

by Robert Benchley

People are constantly writing in to this department and asking: "What kind of dog shall I give my boy?" or sometimes: "What kind of boy shall I give my dog?" And although we are always somewhat surprised to get a query like this, ours really being the Jam and Fern Question Box, we usually give the same answer to both forms of inquiry: "Are you quite sure that you want to do either?" This confuses them, and we are able to snatch a few more minutes for our regular work.

But the question of Boy and Dog is one which will not be downed. There is no doubt that every healthy, normal boy (if there is such a thing in these days of Child Study) should own a dog at some time in his life, preferably between the ages of forty-five and fifty. Give a dog to a boy who is much younger and his parents will find themselves obliged to pack up and go to the Sailors' Snug Harbor to live until the dog runs away—which he will do as soon as the first pretty face comes along.

But a dog teaches a boy fidelity, perseverance, and to turn around three times before lying down—very important traits in times like these. In fact, just as soon as a dog comes along who, in addition to these qualities, also knows when to buy and sell stocks, he can be moved right up to the boy's bedroom and the boy can sleep in the doghouse.

In buying a dog for a very small child, attention must be paid to one or two essential points. In the first place, the dog must be one which will come apart easily or of such a breed that the sizing will

---

From *Chips Off the Old Benchley*.

get pasty and all gummed up when wet. Dachshunds are ideal dogs for small children, as they are already stretched and pulled to such a length that the child cannot do much harm one way or the other. The dachshund being so long also makes it difficult for a very small child to go through with the favorite juvenile maneuver of lifting the dog's hind legs up in the air and wheeling it along like a barrow, cooing, "Diddy-app!" Any small child trying to lift a dachshund's hind legs up very high is going to find itself flat on its back.

For the very small child who likes to pick animals up around the middle and carry them over to the fireplace, mastiffs, St. Bernards, or Russian wolfhounds are not indicated—that is, not if the child is of any value at all. It is not that the larger dogs resent being carried around the middle and dropped in the fireplace (in fact, the smaller the dog, the more touchy it is in matters of dignity, as is so often the case with people and nations); but, even though a mastiff does everything that it can to help the child in carrying it by the diaphragm, there are matters of gravity to be reckoned with which make it impossible to carry the thing through without something being broken. If a dog could be trained to wrestle and throw the child immediately, a great deal of time could be saved.

But, as we have suggested, the ideal age for a boy to own a dog is between forty-five and fifty. By this time the boy ought to have attained his full growth and, provided he is ever going to, ought to know more or less what he wants to make of himself in life. At this age the dog will be more of a companion than a chattel, and, if necessary, can be counted upon to carry the boy by the middle and drop him into bed in case sleep overcomes him at a dinner or camp meeting or anything. It can also be counted upon to tell him he has made a fool of himself and embarrassed all his friends. A wife could do no more.

The training of the dog is something which should be left to the boy, as this teaches him responsibility and accustoms him to the use of authority, probably the only time he will ever have a chance to use it. If, for example, the dog insists on following the boy when he is leaving the house, even after repeated commands to "Go on back home!" the boy must decide on one of two courses. He must either take the dog back to the house and lock it in the cellar, or, as an alternate course, he can give up the idea of going out himself and stay with the dog. The latter is the better way, especially if the dog is in good voice and given to screaming the house down.

There has always been considerable difference of opinion as to whether or not a dog really thinks. I, personally, have no doubt that distinct mental processes do go on inside the dog's brain, although many times these processes are hardly worthy of the name. I have known dogs, especially puppies, who were almost as stupid as humans in their mental reactions.

The only reason that puppies do not get into more trouble than they do (if there *is* any more trouble than that which puppies get into) is that they are so small. A child, for instance, should not expect to be able to fall as heavily, eat as heartily of shoe leather, or throw up as casually as a puppy does, for there is more bulk to a child and the results of these practices will be more serious in exact proportion to the size and capacity. Whereas, for example, a puppy might be able to eat only the toe of a slipper, a child might well succeed in eating the whole shoe—which, considering the nails and everything, would not be wise.

One of the reasons why dogs are given credit for serious thinking is the formation of their eyebrows. A dog lying in front of a fire and looking up at his master may appear pathetic, disapproving, sage, or amused, according to the angle at which its eyebrows are set by nature.

It is quite possible, and even probable, that nothing at all is going on behind the eyebrows. In fact, one dog who had a great reputation for sagacity once told me in confidence that most of the time when he was supposed to be regarding a human with an age-old philosophical rumination he was really asleep behind his shaggy overhanging brows. "You could have knocked me over with a feather," he said, "when I found out that people were talking about my wisdom and suggesting running me for President."

This, of course, offers a possibility for the future of the child itself. As soon as the boy makes up his mind just what type of man he wants to be, he could buy some crêpe hair and a bottle of spirit gum and make himself a pair of eyebrows to suit the role: converging toward the nose if he wants to be a judge or savant; pointing upward from the edge of the eyes if he wants to be a worried-looking man, like a broker; elevated to his forehead if he plans on simulating surprise as a personal characteristic; and in red patches if he intends being a stage Irishman.

In this way he may be able to get away with a great deal, as his pal the dog does.

At any rate, the important thing is to get a dog for the boy and see what each can teach the other. The way things are going now with our Younger Generation, the chances are that before long the dog will be smoking, drinking gin, and wearing a soft hat pulled over one eye.

The Rich Sardine

Seven Droodles by Roger Price

Droodles, explains Roger Price, are "little drawings that make a complete picture using the fewest possible lines. They are contrived doodles that you don't understand until you ask, and then it's too late to wish you hadn't."

For example, here is an example:

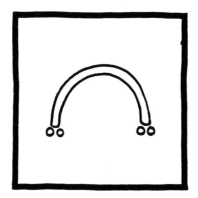

Puzzled? You shouldn't be. Obviously, this is

A WORM ROLLERSKATING

Here is example number 2:

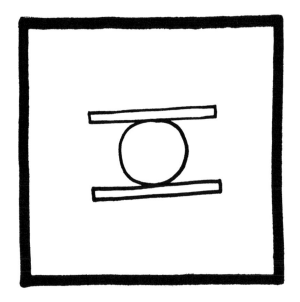

Examined closely, this can be nothing but

TOMATO SANDWICH MADE BY AN

AMATEUR TOMATO SANDWICH MAKER

Example 3:

This really could be nothing else than

DETERMINED WORM

CRAWLING OVER A RAZOR BLADE

Example 4:

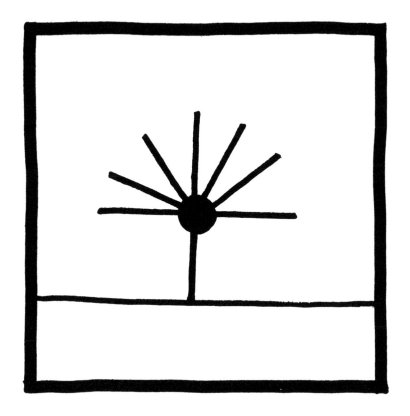

The correct title of this great work of art is

TOTAL ECLIPSE OF THE SUN ON A STICK

although two stubborn dissenters hold out, respectively, for FAMILY
OF WORMS STUCK IN A CANDIED APPLE and A FRIGHTENED MOP.

Example 5:

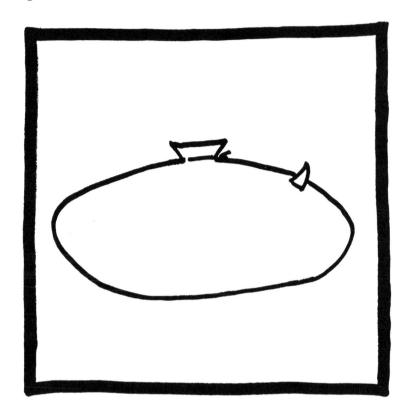

This, of course, is

A RHINOCEROS IN A PAPER BAG

although Mr. Price is apprehensive lest the suggestion of putting rhinoceroses in paper bags start a fad.

Example 6:

The title of this masterpiece is

OCTOPUS SIGNALING FOR A LEFT TURN

Finally, here is Example 7, which gave Roger Price the title for the book from which these droodles have been copied (with the kind permission of the maestro):

Yes, it's

THE RICH SARDINE

Tom's Whitewash

by Mark Twain

Saturday morning was come, and all the summer world was bright and fresh, and brimming with life. There was a song in every heart; and if the heart was young the music issued at the lips. There was cheer in every face and a spring in every step. The locust trees were in bloom and the fragrance of the blossoms filled the air. Cardiff Hill, beyond the village and above it, was green with vegetation; and it lay just far enough away to seem a Delectable Land, dreamy, reposeful, and inviting.

Tom appeared on the sidewalk with a bucket of whitewash and a long-handled brush. He surveyed the fence, and all gladness left him and a deep melancholy settled down upon his spirit. Thirty yards of board fence nine feet high. Life to him seemed hollow, and existence but a burden. Sighing he dipped his brush and passed it along the topmost plank; repeated the operation; did it again; compared the insignificant whitewashed streak with the far-reaching continent of unwhitewashed fence, and sat down on a tree-box discouraged. Jim came skipping out at the gate with a tin pail, and singing "Buffalo Gals." Bringing water from the town pump had always been hateful work in Tom's eyes before, but now it did not strike him so. He remembered that there was company at the pump. White, mulatto, and Negro boys and girls were always there waiting their turns, resting, trading playthings, quarreling, fighting, skylarking. And he remembered that, although the pump was only a hundred and fifty yards off, Jim never got back with a bucket of water under an hour—and even then somebody generally

---

From *The Adventures of Tom Sawyer.*

had to go after him. Tom said:

"Say, Jim, I'll fetch the water if you'll whitewash some."

Jim shook his head and said:

"Can't, Marse Tom. Ole missis, she tole me I got to go an' git dis water an' not stop foolin' roun' wid anybody. She say she spec' Marse Tom gwine to ax me to whitewash, an' so she tole me go 'long an' 'tend to my own business—she 'lowed *she'd* 'tend to de whitewashin'."

"Oh, never mind what she said, Jim. That's the way she always talks. Gimme the bucket—I won't be gone only a minute. *She* won't ever know."

"Oh, I dasn't, Marse Tom. Ole missis she'd take an' tar de head off'n me. 'Deed she would."

"*She!* She never licks anybody—whacks 'em over the head with her thimble—and who cares for that, I'd like to know. She talks awful, but talk don't hurt—anyways it don't if she don't cry. Jim, I'll give you a marvel. I'll give you a white alley!"

Jim began to waver.

"White alley, Jim! And its a bully taw."

"My! Dat's a mighty gay marvel, I tell you! But Marse Tom, I's powerful 'fraid ole missis—"

"And besides, if you will I'll show you my sore toe."

Jim was only human—this attraction was too much for him. He put down his pail, took the white alley, and bent over the toe with absorbing interest while the bandage was being unwound. In another moment he was flying down the street with his pail and a tingling rear, Tom was whitewashing with vigor, and Aunt Polly was retiring from the field with a slipper in her hand and triumph in her eye.

But Tom's energy did not last. He began to think of the fun he had planned for this day, and his sorrows multiplied. Soon the free boys would come tripping along on all sorts of delicious expeditions, and they would make a world of fun of him for having to work—the very thought of it burnt him like fire. He got out his worldly wealth and examined it—bits of toys, marbles, and trash; enough to buy an exchange of *work*, maybe, but not half enough to buy so much as half an hour of pure freedom. So he returned his straitened means to his pocket and gave up the idea of trying to buy the boys. At this dark and hopeless moment an inspiration burst upon him! Nothing less than a great, magnificent inspiration.

He took up his brush and went tranquilly to work. Ben Rogers hove in sight presently—the very boy, of all boys, whose ridicule he had been dreading. Ben's gait was the hop-skip-and-jump—proof enough that his heart was light and his anticipations high. He was eating an apple, and giving a long, melodious whoop, at intervals, followed by a deep-toned ding-dong-dong, ding-dong-dong, for he was personating a steamboat. As he drew near, he slackened speed, took the middle of the street, leaned far over to starboard and rounded to ponderously and with laborious pomp and circumstance —for he was personating the *Big Missouri*, and considered himself to be drawing nine feet of water. He was boat and captain and engine bells combined, so he had to imagine himself standing on his own hurricane deck giving the orders and executing them:

"Stop her, sir! Ting-a-ling-ling!" The headway ran almost out and he drew up slowly toward the sidewalk.

"Ship up to back! Ting-a-ling-ling!" His arms straightened and stiffened down his sides.

"Set her back on the stabboard! Ting-a-ling-ling! Chow! Ch-chow-wow! Chow!" His right hand, meantime, describing stately circles—for it was representing a forty-foot wheel.

"Let her go back on the labboard! Ting-a-ling-ling! Chow-ch-chow-chow!" The left hand began to describe circles.

"Stop the stabboard! Ting-a-ling-ling! Stop the labboard! Come ahead on the stabboard! Stop her! Let your outside turn over slow! Ting-a-ling-ling! Chow-ow-ow! Get out that head line! *Lively* now! Come—out with your spring line—what're you about there! Take a turn round that stump with the bight of it! Stand by that stage, now —let her go! Done with the engines, sir! Ting-a-ling-ling! *Sh't! sh't!*

sh't!" (trying the gauge cocks).

Tom went on whitewashing—paid no attention to the steamboat. Ben stared a moment and then said:

"Hi-*yi! You're* up a stump, ain't you!"

No answer. Tom surveyed his last touch with the eye of an artist, then he gave his brush another gentle sweep and surveyed the result, as before. Ben ranged up alongside of him. Tom's mouth watered for the apple, but he stuck to his work. Ben said:

"Hello, old chap, you got to work, hey?"

Tom wheeled suddenly and said:

"Why, it's you, Ben! I warn't noticing."

"*Say*—I'm going in a-swimming, I am. Don't you wish you could? But of course you'd druther *work*—wouldn't you? Course you would!"

Tom contemplated the boy a bit, and said:

"What do you call work?"

"Why, ain't *that* work?"

Tom resumed his whitewashing, and answered carelessly:

"Well, maybe it is, and maybe it ain't. All I know is, it suits Tom Sawyer."

"Oh come, now, you don't mean to let on that you *like* it?"

The brush continued to move.

"Like it? Well, I don't see why I oughtn't to like it. Does a boy get a chance to whitewash a fence every day?"

That put the thing in a new light. Ben stopped nibbling his apple. Tom swept his brush daintily back and forth—stepped back to note the effect—added a touch here and there—criticized the effect again—Ben watching every move and getting more and more interested, more and more absorbed. Presently he said:

"Say, Tom let *me* whitewash a little."

Tom considered, was about to consent; but he altered his mind:

"No—no—I reckon it wouldn't hardly do, Ben. You see, Aunt Polly's awful particular about this fence—right here on the street, you know—but if it was the back fence I wouldn't mind and *she* wouldn't. Yes, she's awful particular about this fence; it's got to be done very careful; I reckon there ain't one boy in a thousand, maybe two thousand that can do it the way it's got to be done."

"No—is that so? Oh come, now—lemme just try. Only just a little—I'd let *you*, if you was me, Tom."

"Ben, I'd like to, honest Injun; but Aunt Polly—well, Jim wanted to do it, but she wouldn't let him; Sid wanted to do it, and she wouldn't let Sid. Now don't you see how I'm fixed? If you was to tackle this fence and anything was to happen to it—"

"Oh, shucks, I'll be just as careful. Now lemme try. Say—I'll give you the core of my apple."

"Well, here— No, Ben, now don't. I'm afeared—"

"I'll give you *all* of it!"

Tom gave up the brush with reluctance in his face, but alacrity in his heart. And while the late steamer *Big Missouri* worked and sweated in the sun, the retired artist sat on a barrel in the shade close by, dangled his legs, munched his apple, and planned the slaughter of more innocents. There was no lack of material; boys happened along every little while; they came to jeer, but remained to whitewash. By the time Ben was fagged out, Tom had traded the next chance to Billy Fisher for a kite, in good repair; and when *he* played out, Johnny Miller bought in for a dead rat and a string to swing it with—and so on, and so on, hour after hour. And when the middle of the afternoon came, from being a poor poverty-stricken boy in the morning, Tom was literally rolling in wealth. He had besides the things before mentioned, twelve marbles, part of a jew's-harp, a piece of blue bottle glass to look through, a spool cannon, a key that wouldn't unlock anything, a fragment of chalk, a glass stopper of a decanter, a tin soldier, a couple of tadpoles, six firecrackers, a kitten with only one eye, a brass doorknob, a dog collar—but no dog—the handle of a knife, four pieces of orange peel, and a dilapidated old window sash.

He had had a nice, good, idle time all the while—plenty of company—and the fence had three coats of whitewash on it! If he hadn't run out of whitewash, he would have bankrupted every boy in the village.

Tom said to himself that it was not such a hollow world, after all. He had discovered a great law of human action, without knowing it —namely, that in order to make a man or a boy covet a thing, it is only necessary to make the thing difficult to attain. If he had been a great and wise philosopher, like the writer of this book, he would now have comprehended that Work consists of whatever a body is *obliged* to do and that Play consists of whatever a body is not obliged to do. And this would help him to understand why constructing artificial flowers or performing on a treadmill is work, while rolling tenpins or climbing Mont Blanc is only amusement. There are wealthy gentlemen in England who drive four-horse passenger coaches twenty or thirty miles on a daily line, in the summer, because the privilege costs them considerable money; but if they were offered wages for the service, that would turn it into work and then they would resign.

The boy mused awhile over the substantial change which had taken place in his worldly circumstances, and then wended toward headquarters to report.

Pay the Two Francs

by Art Buchwald

Like I said, we had this party with chopped chicken liver, turkey, ham, and various salads. But since we were giving the party with another couple, the Bernheims, we had to share with them the left-over food and also return a large, silver tray which we borrowed for the party.

So we called a taxi and carried all the food downstairs to go to the Bernheims. Every once in a while you get a taxi driver in Paris who talks to other chauffeurs. In his opinion, every driver on the road is an idiot, and also yellow. To prove it, our driver challenged every car on the Champs Elysées. All of them did prove yellow except one, another taxi driver. They both put on their brakes at the same time, avoiding a smashup, but the tray with the chopped chicken liver, ham, turkey, and salad went flying on to the floor of the taxi.

This was too much for my nerves, and I told the driver to stop the cab and let us off at the Hotel California, on the Rue de Berri. Insulted because we didn't trust his driving, he blamed us for not holding on to the tray when he had to stop to avoid an accident. He said we didn't know how to ride in a taxi. I said he didn't know how to drive one.

At the California I told my wife to get out of the cab. Then I bent down in the cab to pick up the food and the tray.

The driver said, "Pay me now."

I replied, "After I take the food out of the taxi."

He said, "I want my money right now."

From *Don't Forget to Write.*

I said, "You'll get it after I take the food out of the cab."

"Then we're going to the police," he said. And with the door open he put the cab into gear, and away we went, leaving my wife standing on the sidewalk.

"Nobody refuses to pay me," he said, as he drove madly in search of a police station. Unfortunately he didn't know where one was, and we kept driving around in circles. Finally he arrived not at a police station, but a police barracks where they round up Algerian terrorists.

Four policemen with submachine guns greeted us at the entrance.

It didn't seem like the place for two people who were having an argument about a taxi to get it settled, and it turned out I was right. A police captain came charging out of the barracks, furious that he was bothered. He started bawling out the taxi driver for coming there.

I was enjoying the show when he turned on me and bawled me

out for not paying the taxi driver. He demanded my identification papers and told one of the policemen to take me and the driver to a commissariat—a regular police station.

The nearest one was located in the basement of the Grand Palais, where the Paris Automobile Show is held. When we arrived the police lieutenant demanded to know what was wrong.

"Well, we had this chopped chicken liver," I said.

"You had what?" he asked in amazement.

"Chopped chicken liver in the taxi."

Everyone in the station looked up from their work.

"And we had turkey and ham and salad, and he's a lousy driver," I said.

"He won't pay me," the taxi driver said. "He had all the food on the seat, and he didn't hold on to it. Is this my fault?"

The lieutenant scratched his head. "Ça, c'est extraordinaire."

"I wanted to pay him, but I wanted to get the chicken liver out of the taxi first," I said.

"It is not true," the taxi driver said. "His wife knows it's not true."

"Where is his wife?"

"He left her standing in front of the Hotel California," I screamed.

"Calm down," the lieutenant said. "Nothing can happen to her in front of the Hotel California. Where is the chicken liver now?"

"In the bottom of the taxicab where he put it," I said accusingly.

"No," the taxi driver said, "where he let it fall."

Everyone in the police station was breaking up with laughter, and I could see I was losing the battle.

"Do you want to pay him, or not?" the lieutenant asked.

"I'll pay him after I take the food out of the taxi."

"All right," the lieutenant said. "Take the food out of the taxi and pay him."

I went back outside, and while a dozen gendarmes looked on with interest, I put the food back on the silver tray. I heard one say to another, "C'est extraordinaire. Foie de volaille haché. C'est plutôt cannibale." ("Chopped chicken liver. It's extraordinary— almost cannibal.")

I paid the taxi driver, refusing to give him a tip, and he drove off, screaming.

I didn't have the nerve to ask the lieutenant to call me another taxi, so I picked up the silver tray and, with the laughter of the police still in my ears, I walked up the Champs Elysées for five blocks.

It will be the last time we give a party with somebody else.

Learning to Drive

by Billy Rose

On the way back from Mt. Kisco, my wife said, "I wish you'd learn how to drive. Every time you want something, somebody's got to stop what he's doing and chauffeur you into the village."

"Okay," I said, "if you'll play teacher."

Next morning I crawled into the car beside my wife. "Just turn this jigger over," she began, "push in this dingus, pull out this doohickey, step on this wingdoodle, press down on this thingama-bob, and you're all set to go."

"What's this gizmo?" I asked.

"The hand brake," she said. "You throw it on quickly in case of emergency."

"What happens if the brakes don't work?"

"Hit something cheap," advised my spouse.

A moment later the car went hiccuping down the road. Then for a mile it went smooth as you please. A feeling of confidence came over me, the same feeling all new drivers get just before the lights go out. I pressed down on the gas.

"The pistons seem to be knocking," I said professionally.

"Pistons nothing," said my mate. "Those are my knees."

Everything went fine until we got to the traffic light in the village. I forgot to press the hickey-madoodle on the gilhooley, and the car stalled. The lights changed from green to red, and from red back to green. A cop came over.

"What's the matter?" he asked. "Haven't we got any colors you like?"

From *Wine, Women, and Song.*

After switching the radio on and off, I suddenly pressed the right thing. In the order of the way it happened, I grazed the cop, skidded through the safety zone, clipped the fender on a bus, and came to rest with my bumper against a fire plug. The cop stalked over. He took a handkerchief out of his pocket and dropped it in front of the car.

"Lookit, Gene Autry," he said. "I wanna see you do that all over again, and this time pick up the handkerchief with your teeth."

My wife gave him the big smile. "He's learning to drive," she said.

"No kidding!" said the cop. "How long is this class going to last? Some other drivers would like to use this road when Sonny Boy gets through with it."

"What did I do wrong?" I asked the officer.

"Didn't you hear my whistle? Didn't you see my signal?" he demanded.

I shook my head.

The cop sighed. "I'd better go home. I don't seem to be doing much good around here."

I threw the car into reverse and backed away from the fire plug.

"If you're going to drive much," yelled the cop, "I'd have the car painted red on one side and blue on the other, so the witnesses will contradict one another."

"What kind of cops do they have in Mt. Kisco?" I asked my wife as we headed for home.

"I wouldn't know," she deadpanned. "Maybe he's Milton Berle's brother."

There are two stone posts flanking the drive which leads up to my house. I got past them without a scratch—also without the rear bumper. That did it.

Since then, I've never been behind a wheel. When we go driving, I sit in the back seat and read the Burma Shave signs. The only concession I've made to the Automotive Age is to learn how to fold a road map.

A Turn for the Verse

MISCELLANEOUS POEMS

The Purple Cow
by Gelett Burgess

I never saw a Purple Cow,
I never hope to see one,
But I can tell you, anyhow,
I'd rather see than be one!

O I C
Anonymous

I'm in a 10der mood today
& feel poetic, 2;
4 fun I'll just — off a line
& send it off 2 U.

I'm sorry you've been 6 o long;
Don't B disconsol8;
But bear your ills with 42de,
& they won't seem so gr8.

The Little Man Who Wasn't There

by Hughes Mearns

As I was going up the stair
I met a man who wasn't there!
He wasn't there again today!
I wish, I *wish* he'd stay away!

Miniature

by Richard Armour

My day-old son is plenty scrawny,
His mouth is wide with screams, or yawny.
His ears seem larger than he's needing,
His nose is flat, his chin's receding.
His skin is very, very red
He has no hair upon his head.
And yet I'm proud as proud can be
To hear you say he looks like me.

"Miniature" from *For Partly Proud Parents.*

Infant Prodigy

by Margaret Fishback

At six weeks Baby grinned a grin
That spread from mouth to eyes to chin.
And Doc, the smartie, had the brass
To tell me it was only gas!

Note to a Persistent Pest

from Groucho Marx

Although I never yet have forgotten a face,
I'm willing to make an exception in your case.

"Infant Prodigy" from *Look Who's a Mother*.

Habits of the Hippopotamus

by Arthur Guiterman

The hippopotamus is strong
   And huge of head and broad of bustle;
The limbs on which he rolls along
   Are big with hippopotomuscle.

He does not greatly care for sweets
   Like ice cream, apple pie, or custard,
But takes to flavor what he eats
   A little hippopotomustard.

The hippopotamus is true
   To all his principles, and just;
He always tries his best to do
   The things one hippopotomust.

He never rides in trucks or trams,
   In taxicabs or omnibuses,
And so keeps out of traffic jams
   And other hippopotomusses.

From *Gaily the Troubadour.*

How to Tell the Wild Animals

by Carolyn Wells

If ever you should go by chance
   To jungles in the East;
And if there should to you advance
   A large and tawny beast,
If he roars at you as you're dyin'
You'll know it is the Asian Lion.

Or if some time when roaming round,
   A noble wild beast greets you,
With black stripes on a yellow ground,
   Just notice if he eats you.
This simple rule may help you learn
The Bengal Tiger to discern.

If strolling forth, a beast you view,
   Whose hide with spots is peppered,
As soon as he has lept on you,
   You'll know it is the Leopard.
'Twill do no good to roar with pain,
He'll only lep and lep again.

If when you're walking round your yard,
  You meet a creature there,
Who hugs you very, very hard,
  Be sure it is the Bear.
If you have any doubt, I guess,
He'll give you just one more caress.

Though to distinguish beasts of prey
  A novice might nonplus,
The Crocodiles you always may
  Tell from Hyenas thus:
Hyenas come with merry smiles;
But if they weep, they're Crocodiles.

The true Chameleon is small,
  A lizard sort of thing;
He hasn't any ears at all,
  And not a single wing.
If there is nothing in the tree,
'Tis the Chameleon you see.

Eletelephony

by Laura E. Richards

Once there was an elephant,
Who tried to use the telephant—
No! no! I mean an elephone
Who tried to use the telephone—
(Dear me! I am not certain quite
That even now I've got it right.)

Howe'er it was, he got his trunk
Entangled in the telephunk;
The more he tried to get it free,
The louder buzzed the telephee—
(I fear I'd better drop the song
Of elephop and telephong!)

From *Tirra Lirra.*

Poems in Praise of Practically Nothing

by Samuel Hoffenstein

You buy some flowers for your table;
You tend them tenderly as you're able.
You fetch them water from hither and thither—
What thanks do you get for it all? They wither.

You buy yourself a new suit of clothes;
The care you give it, God only knows.
The material, of course, is the very best yet;
You get it pressed and pressed and pressed yet.
You keep it free from specks so tiny—
What thanks do you get? The pants get shiny.

You leap out of bed; you start to get ready;
You dress and you dress till you feel unsteady.
Hours go by, and you're still busy
Putting on clothes, till your brain is dizzy.
Do you flinch, do you quit, do you go out naked?
The least little button, you don't forsake it.
What thanks do you get? Well, for all this mess, yet
When night comes around you've got to undress yet.

From the book *Poems in Praise of Practically Nothing.*

Father William

by Lewis Carroll

"You are old, Father William," the young man said,
  "And your hair has become very white;
And yet you incessantly stand on your head—
  Do you think, at your age, it is right?"

"In my youth," Father William replied to his son,
  "I feared it might injure the brain;
But now that I'm perfectly sure I have none,
  Why, I do it again and again."

"You are old," said the youth, "as I mentioned before,
  And have grown most uncommonly fat;
Yet you turned a back-somersault in at the door—
  Pray, what is the reason for that?"

"In my youth," said the sage, as he shook his gray locks,
  "I kept all my limbs very supple
By the use of this ointment—one shilling the box—
  Allow me to sell you a couple?"

"You are old," said the youth, "and your jaws are too weak
  For anything tougher than suet;
Yet you finished the goose, with the bones and the beak—
  Pray, how did you manage to do it?"

"In my youth," said his father, "I took to the law,
  And argued each case with my wife;
And the muscular strength which it gave to my jaw
  Has lasted the rest of my life."

"You are old," said the youth; "one would hardly suppose
    That your eye was as steady as ever;
Yet you balanced an eel on the end of your nose—
    What made you so awfully clever?"

"I have answered three questions, and that is enough,"
    Said his father, "don't give yourself airs!
Do you think I can listen all day to such stuff?
    Be off, or I'll kick you downstairs!"

Song of the Pop-Bottlers

by Morris Bishop

Pop bottles pop-bottles
    In pop shops;
The pop-bottles Pop bottles
    Poor Pop drops.

When Pop drops pop-bottles,
    Pop-bottles plop!
Pop-bottle-tops topple!
    Pop mops slop!

Stop! Pop'll drop bottle!
    Stop, Pop, stop!
When Pop bottles pop-bottles,
    Pop-bottles pop!

From *A Bowl of Bishop*.

SIX POEMS BY OGDEN NASH

REFLECTIONS ON BABIES
A bit of talcum
Is always walcum.

SONG OF THE OPEN ROAD
I think that I shall never see
A billboard lovely as a tree.
Indeed, unless the billboards fall,
I'll never see a tree at all.

THE EEL
I don't mind eels
Except at meals—
And the way they feels.

THE LAMA
The one-L lama,
He's a priest.
The two-L llama,
He's a beast.
And I will bet
A silk pajama
There isn't any
Three-L lllama.

From *Verses From 1929 On.*

THE FLY
The Lord in His wisdom made the fly
And then forgot to tell us why.

THE TERMITE
Some primal termite knocked on wood
And tasted it, and found it good,
And that is why your cousin May
Fell through the parlor floor today.

LITTLE WILLIE POEMS

The monstrous—and celebrated—"Little Willie" probably owed his original fame to Charles H. Clark, who wrote, way back in the 1870's:

> Little Willie had a purple monkey climbing up
>   a stick
> And when he licked the paint all off, it made
>   him very sick.
> And in his latest hours he clasped the monkey in
>   his hand,
> And said goodbye to earth and went to a better land.
> Oh, no more he'll shoot his sister with his little
>   wooden gun,
> And no more he'll twist the pussy's tail and
>   make her yowl for fun.
> The pussy's tail now stands up straight; the
>   gun is laid aside;
> The monkey doesn't jump around since Little
>   Willie died.

Here are a few of the other countless outrageous activities engaged in by Little Willie since that time:

> In the family drinking well
> Willie pushed his sister Nell.
> Said his mother, drawing water,
> "It's mighty tough to raise a daughter."

> Little Willie with a curse,
> Threw a coffeepot at nurse.
> When it struck her on the nose,
> Father cheered, "How straight he throws!"

Little Willie on a farm
Fell off a horse and broke his arm
All the neighbors cried, "What fun!
Bad luck that it was only one!"

Little Willie, on one of his dashes,
Fell in the fire and was burned to ashes.
Soon the room got very chilly
But nobody liked to poke up Willie.

Willie, with a thirst for gore,
Nailed his sister to a door.
Mother said, with humor quaint,
"Willie dear! Don't scratch the paint!"

Little Willie, feeling bright,
Bought a stick of dynamite.
Curiosity seldom pays:
It rained Willie for seven days.

TWO-LINERS

The shortest poem in the English language probably is Strickland
Gillian's "Lines on the Antiquity of Fleas":

Adam
Had 'em.

Equally terse is William Benet's "Maid's Day Out."

Thurs.
Hers.

Humorist George Ade once mourned:

Last night at twelve I felt immense,
But now I feel like thirty cents.

Richard Armour made this discovery:
>Shake and shake the catsup bottle:
>None will come, and then a lot'll.

A man who didn't like guests posted this notice at the entrance
of his driveway:
>The road isn't passable;
>Not even jackassable.

Begged an irritable lady at a tea party:
>Please diet
>In quiet.

A Seattle driver hung this sign on the back of his pick-up truck:
>Spring has sprung and grass has rizz
>Where last year's reckless driver is.

And a henpecked husband observed:
>Women do not talk all day:
>It only seems to sound that way.

OUT ON A LIMERICK

>There was a young lady named Bright,
>Whose speed was much faster than light.
>>She went out one day
>>In a relative way
>And returned on the previous night.

>There was a young lady of Niger
>Who smiled as she rode on a tiger.
>>They returned from the ride
>>With the lady inside
>And the smile on the face of the tiger.

From the book *Out on a Limerick* by Bennett Cerf.

I wish that my room had a floor;
I don't so much care for a door,
    But this walking around
    Without touching the ground
Is getting to be quite a bore!
              —GELETT BURGESS

The bottle of perfume that Willie sent
Was highly displeasing to Millicent.
    Her thanks were so cold
    That they quarreled, I'm told,
Through that silly scent Willie sent Millicent.

There was an old man in a boat,
Who said, "I'm afloat! I'm afloat!"
    When they said, "No, you ain't,"
    He was ready to faint,
That unhappy old man in a boat.
              —EDWARD LEAR

As a beauty I am not a star.
There are others more handsome, by far.
    But my face, I don't mind it
    For I am behind it.
It's the people in front get the jar!
              —WOODROW WILSON

There was a young lady of Crete
Who was so exceedingly neat,
    When she got out of bed
    She stood on her head
To make sure of not soiling her feet.

A cat in despondency sighed
And resolved to commit suicide.
   She passed under the wheels
   Of eight automobiles
And under the ninth one she died.

There once was a lady named Harris
That nothing seemed apt to embarrass
   Till the bathsalts she shook
   In a tub that she took
Turned out to be plaster-of-Paris.

Said an envious, erudite ermine,
"There's one thing I cannot determine:
   When a dame wears my coat
   She's a person of note;
When I wear it, I'm called only vermin."

There was a sightseer named Sue
Who saw a strange beast at the zoo.
   When she asked, "Is it old?"
   She was smilingly told,
"It's not an old beast, but a gnu."

The fabulous wizard of Oz
Retired from business becoz
   What with up-to-date science,
   To most of his clients
He wasn't the wiz that he woz.

There was an old man on the Rhine
Who was asked at what hour he'd dine.
   He replied, "At eleven,
   Four, six, three, and seven.
Not to mention a quarter to nine."

There was a young man so benighted
He didn't know when he was slighted.
   He went to a party
   And ate just as hearty
As if he'd been really invited.

The fact is that Rome needed money
And, further, the Gauls got too funny.
   So they sent out some legions
   To clean up them regions.
J. Caesar? Yep, he was there, sonny.

A fellow named Crosby (not Bing)
Was asked by a hostess to sing.
   He replied, "Though it's odd,
   I can never tell 'God
Save the Weasel' from 'Pop Goes the King.'"

There was an old man of Tarentum
Who gnashed his false teeth till he bent 'em.
　　When they asked him the cost
　　Of what he had lost,
He replied, "I can't say, 'cause I rent 'em."

There was a young fellow of Perth
Who was born on the day of his birth.
　　He was married, they say,
　　On his wife's wedding day,
And he died when he quitted the earth.

A newspaper writer named Fling
Could make copy from most anything.
　　But the copy he wrote
　　Of a ten-dollar note
Was so good he is now in Sing Sing.

I'd rather have fingers than toes;
I'd rather have ears than a nose;
　　And as for my hair,
　　I'm glad it's all there.
I'll be awfully sad when it goes.

　　　　　　　　　　—GELETT BURGESS

When twins came, their father, Dan Dunn,
Gave "Edward" as name to each son.
　　When folks said, "Absurd!"
　　He replied, "Ain't you heard
That two Eds are better than one?"

　　　　　　　　　　—BERTON BRALEY

Said a foolish young lady in Wales,
"A smell of escaped gas prevails."
   Then she searched with a light
   And later that night
Was collected—in seventeen pails.

A barber who lived in Moravia
Was renowned for his fearless behavia.
   An enormous baboon
   Broke into his saloon,
But he murmured, "I'm darned if I'll shavia."

A tutor who tooted a flute
Tried to teach two young tooters to toot.
   Said the two to the tutor,
   "Is it harder to toot, or
To tutor two tooters to toot?"

                    —CAROLYN WELLS

A certain young chap named Bill Beebee
Was in love with a lady named Phoebe.
   "But," he said, "I must see
   What the clerical fee
Be before Phoebe be Phoebe Beebee."

In Iceland, a supple young miss
Enthused, "I think skating is bliss."
   This no more will she state
   For a slip of her skate
Left her ending up something like this.

The Word Market

by Norton Juster

In The Phantom Tollbooth, *a boy named Milo finds his way to a strange and fascinating land. His traveling companion is Tock—a watchdog who (naturally) ticks. "The Word Market" describes one of their most entertaining adventures.—*B.C.

As they approached the market, Milo could see crowds of people pushing and shouting their way among the stalls, buying and selling, trading and bargaining. Huge wood-wheeled carts streamed into the market square from the orchards, and long caravans bound for the four corners of the kingdom made ready to leave. Sacks and boxes were piled high waiting to be delivered to the ships that sailed the Sea of Knowledge, and off to one side a group of minstrels sang songs to the delight of those either too young or too old to engage in trade. But above all the noise and tumult of the crowd could be heard the merchants' voices loudly advertising their products.

"Get your fresh-picked ifs, ands, and buts."

"Hey-yaa, hey-yaa, hey-yaa, nice ripe wheres and whens."

"Juicy, tempting words for sale."

So many words and so many people! They were from every place imaginable and some places even beyond that, and they were all busy sorting, choosing, and stuffing things into cases. As soon as one was filled, another was begun. There seemed to be no end to the bustle and activity.

Milo and Tock wandered up and down the aisles looking at the wonderful assortment of words for sale. There were short ones and easy ones for everyday use, and long and very important ones for special occasions, and even some marvelously fancy ones packed in individual gift boxes for use in royal decrees and pronouncements.

"Step right up, step right up—fancy, best-quality words right here," announced one man in a booming voice. "Step right up—ah, what can I do for you, little boy? How about a nice bagful of pronouns—or maybe you'd like our special assortment of names?"

Milo had never thought much about words before, but these looked so good that he longed to have some.

"Look, Tock," he cried, "aren't they wonderful?"

"They're fine, if you have something to say," replied Tock in a tired voice, for he was much more interested in finding a bone than in shopping for new words.

"Maybe if I buy some I can learn how to use them," said Milo eagerly as he began to pick through the words in the stall. Finally he chose three which looked particularly good to him—"quagmire," "flabbergast," and "upholstery." He had no idea what they meant, but they looked very grand and elegant.

"How much are these?" he inquired, and when the man whispered the answer he quickly put them back on the shelf and started to walk on.

"Why not take a few pounds of 'happys'?" advised the salesman. "They're much more practical—and very useful for Happy Birthday, Happy New Year, happy days, and happy-go-lucky."

"I'd like to very much," began Milo, "but—"

"Or perhaps you'd be interested in a package of 'goods'—always handy for good morning, good afternoon, good evening, and good-by," he suggested.

Milo did want to buy something, but the only money he had was the coin he needed to get back through the tollbooth, and Tock, of course, had nothing but the time.

"No, thank you," replied Milo. "We're just looking." And they continued on through the market.

As they turned down the last aisle of stalls, Milo noticed a wagon that seemed different from the rest. On its side was a small neatly lettered sign that said "DO IT YOURSELF," and inside were twenty-six bins filled with all the letters of the alphabet from A to Z.

"These are for people who like to make their own words," the man in charge informed him. "You can pick any assortment you like or buy a special box complete with all letters, punctuation marks, and a book of instructions. Here, taste an A; they're very good."

Milo nibbled carefully at the letter and discovered that it was quite sweet and delicious—just the way you'd expect an A to taste.

"I knew you'd like it," laughed the letter man, popping two G's and an R into his mouth and letting the juice drip down his chin. "A's are one of our most popular letters. All of them aren't that good," he confided in a low voice. "Take the Z, for instance—very dry and sawdusty. And the X? Why, it tastes like a trunkful of stale air. That's why people hardly ever use them. But most of the others are quite tasty. Try some more."

He gave Milo an I, which was icy and refreshing, and Tock a crisp, crunchy C.

"Most people are just too lazy to make their own words," he continued, "but it's much more fun."

"Is it difficult? I'm not much good at making words," admitted Milo, spitting the pits from a P.

"Perhaps I can be of some assistance—a-s-s-i-s-t-a-n-c-e," buzzed an unfamiliar voice, and when Milo looked up he saw an enormous bee, at least twice his size, sitting on top of the wagon.

"I am the Spelling Bee," announced the Spelling Bee. "Don't be alarmed—a-l-a-r-m-e-d."

Tock ducked under the wagon, and Milo, who was not overly fond of normal-sized bees, began to back away slowly.

"I can spell anything—a-n-y-t-h-i-n-g," he boasted, testing his wings. "Try me, try me!"

"Can you spell good-by?" suggested Milo as he continued to back away.

The bee gently lifted himself into the air and circled lazily over Milo's head.

"Perhaps—p-e-r-h-a-p-s—you are under the misapprehension—m-i-s-a-p-p-r-e-h-e-n-s-i-o-n—that I am dangerous," he said, turning a smart loop to the left. "Let me assure—a-s-s-u-r-e—you that my intentions are peaceful—p-e-a-c-e-f-u-l." And with that he settled back on top of the wagon and fanned himself with one wing. "Now," he panted, "think of the most difficult word you can and I'll spell it. Hurry up, hurry up!" And he jumped up and down impatiently.

"He looks friendly enough," thought Milo, not sure just how friendly a friendly bumblebee should be, and tried to think of a very difficult word. "Spell 'vegetable'," he suggested, for it was one that always troubled him at school.

"That is a difficult one," said the bee, winking at the letter man. "Let me see now . . . hmmmmmmm . . ." He frowned and wiped his brow and paced slowly back and forth on top of the wagon. "How much time do I have?"

"Just ten seconds," cried Milo excitedly. "Count them off, Tock."

"Oh dear, oh dear, oh dear, oh dear," the bee repeated, continuing to pace nervously. Then, just as the time ran out, he spelled as fast as he could—"v-e-g-e-t-a-b-l-e."

"Correct," shouted the letter man, and everyone cheered.

"Can you spell everything?" asked Milo admiringly.

"Just about," replied the bee with a hint of pride in his voice. "You see, years ago I was just an ordinary bee minding my own business, smelling flowers all day, and occasionally picking up part-time work in people's bonnets. Then one day I realized that I'd never amount to anything without an education and, being naturally adept at spelling, I decided that—"

"BALDERDASH!" shouted a booming voice. And from around the wagon stepped a large beetlelike insect dressed in a lavish coat, striped pants, checked vest, spats, and a high silk hat. "Let me repeat—BALDERDASH!" he shouted again, swinging his cane and clicking his heels in mid-air. "Come now, don't be ill-mannered. Isn't someone going to introduce me to the little boy?"

"This," said the bee with complete disdain, "is the Humbug. A very dislikable fellow."

"NONSENSE! Everyone loves a Humbug," shouted the Humbug. "As I was saying to the king just the other day—"

"You've never met the king," accused the bee angrily. Then, turning to Milo, he said, "Don't believe a thing this old fraud says."

"BOSH!" replied the Humbug. "We're an old and noble family, honorable to the core—Insecticus Humbugium, if I may use the

Latin. Why, we fought in the crusades with Richard the Lion Heart, crossed the Atlantic with Columbus, blazed trails with the pioneers, and today many members of the family hold prominent government positions throughout the world. History is full of Humbugs."

"A very pretty speech—s-p-e-e-c-h," sneered the bee. "Now why don't you go away? I was just advising the lad of the importance of proper spelling."

"BAH!" said the bug, putting an arm around Milo. "As soon as you learn to spell one word, they ask you to spell another. You can never catch up—so why bother? Take my advice, my boy, and forget about it. As my great-great-great-grandfather George Washington Humbug used to say—"

"You, sir," shouted the bee very excitedly, "are an impostor—i-m-p-o-s-t-o-r—who can't even spell his own name."

"A slavish concern for the composition of words is the sign of a bankrupt intellect," roared the Humbug, waving his cane furiously.

Milo didn't have any idea what this meant, but it seemed to infuriate the Spelling Bee, who flew down and knocked off the Humbug's hat with his wing.

"Be careful," shouted Milo as the bug swung his cane again, catching the bee on the foot and knocking over the box of W's.

"My foot!" shouted the bee.

"My hat!" shouted the bug—and the fight was on.

The Spelling Bee buzzed dangerously in and out of range of the Humbug's wildly swinging cane as they menaced and threatened each other, and the crowd stepped back out of danger.

"There must be some other way to—" began Milo. And then he yelled, "WATCH OUT," but it was too late.

There was a tremendous crash as the Humbug in his great fury tripped into one of the stalls, knocking it into another, then another, then another, then another, until every stall in the market place had been upset and the words lay scrambled in great confusion all over the square.

The bee, who had tangled himself in some bunting, toppled to the ground, knocking Milo over on top of him, and lay there shouting, "Help! Help! There's a little boy on me." The bug sprawled untidily on a mound of squashed letters and Tock, his alarm ringing persistently, was buried under a pile of words.

"Done what you've looked," angrily shouted one of the salesmen. He meant to say "Look what you've done," but the words had gotten so hopelessly mixed up that no one could make any sense at all.

"Do going to we what are!" complained another, as everyone set about straightening things up as well as they could.

For several minutes no one spoke an understandable sentence, which added greatly to the confusion. As soon as possible, however, the stalls were righted and the words swept into one large pile for sorting.

The Spelling Bee, who was quite upset by the whole affair, had flown off in a huff, and just as Milo got to his feet the entire police force of Dictionopolis appeared—loudly blowing his whistle.

"Now we'll get to the bottom of this," he heard someone say. "Here comes Officer Shrift."

Striding across the square was the shortest policeman Milo had ever seen. He was scarcely two feet tall and almost twice as wide, and he wore a blue uniform with white belt and gloves, a peaked cap, and a very fierce expression. He continued blowing the whistle until his face was beet red, stopping only long enough to shout, "You're guilty, you're guilty," at everyone he passed. "I've never seen anyone so guilty," he said as he reached Milo. Then, turning towards Tock, who was still ringing loudly, he said, "Turn off that dog; it's disrespectful to sound your alarm in the presence of a policeman."

He made a careful note of that in his black book and strode up and down, his hands clasped behind his back, surveying the wreckage in the market place.

"Very pretty, very pretty." He scowled. "Who's responsible for all this? Speak up or I'll arrest the lot of you."

There was a long silence. Since hardly anybody had actually seen what had happened, no one spoke.

"You," said the policeman, pointing an accusing finger at the Humbug, who was brushing himself off and straightening his hat, "you look suspicious to me."

The startled Humbug dropped his cane and nervously replied, "Let me assure you, sir, on my honor as a gentleman, that I was merely an innocent bystander, minding my own business, enjoying the stimulating sights and sounds of the world of commerce, when this young lad—"

"AHA!" interrupted Officer Shrift, making another note in his little book. "Just as I thought: boys are the cause of everything."

"Pardon me," insisted the Humbug, "but I in no way meant to imply that—"

"SILENCE!" thundered the policeman, pulling himself up to full height and glaring menacingly at the terrified bug. "And now," he continued, speaking to Milo, "where were you on the night of July 27?"

"What does that have to do with it?" asked Milo.

"It's my birthday, that's what," said the policeman as he entered "Forgot my birthday" in his little book. "Boys always forget other people's birthdays.

"You have committed the following crimes," he continued: "having a dog with an unauthorized alarm, sowing confusion, upsetting the applecart, wreaking havoc, and mincing words."

"Now see here," growled Tock angrily.

"And illegal barking," he added, frowning at the watchdog. "It's against the law to bark without using the barking meter. Are you ready to be sentenced?"

"Only a judge can sentence you," said Milo, who remembered reading that in one of his schoolbooks.

"Good point," replied the policeman, taking off his cap and putting on a long black robe. "I am also the judge. Now would you like a long or a short sentence?"

"A short one, if you please," said Milo.

"Good," said the judge, rapping his gavel three times. "I always have trouble remembering the long ones. How about 'I am'? That's the shortest sentence I know."

Everyone agreed that it was a very fair sentence, and the judge continued: "There will also be a small additional penalty of six million years in prison. Case closed," he pronounced, rapping his gavel again. "Come with me. I'll take you to the dungeon."

"Only a jailer can put you in prison," offered Milo, quoting the same book.

"Good point," said the judge, removing his robe and taking out a large bunch of keys. "I am also the jailer." And with that he led them away.

"Keep your chin up," shouted the Humbug. "Maybe they'll take a million years off for good behavior."

The heavy prison door swung back slowly and Milo and Tock followed Officer Shrift down a long dark corridor lit by only an occasional flickering candle.

"Watch the steps," advised the policeman as they started down a steep circular staircase.

The air was dank and musty—like the smell of wet blankets— and the massive stone walls were slimy to the touch. Down and down they went until they arrived at another door even heavier and stronger-looking than the first. A cobweb brushed across Milo's face and he shuddered.

"You'll find it quite pleasant here," chuckled the policeman as he slid the bolt back and pushed the door open with a screech and a squeak. "Not much company, but you can always chat with the witch."

"The witch?" trembled Milo.

"Yes, she's been here for a long time," he said, starting along another corridor.

In a few more minutes they had gone through three other doors, across a narrow footbridge, down two more corridors and another stairway, and stood finally in front of a small cell door.

"This is it," said the policeman, "All the comforts of home."

The door opened and then shut and Milo and Tock found themselves in a high vaulted cell with two tiny windows halfway up on the wall.

"See you in six million years," said Officer Shrift, and the sound of his footsteps grew fainter and fainter until it wasn't heard at all.

"It looks serious, doesn't it, Tock?" said Milo very sadly.

"It certainly does," the dog replied, sniffing around to see what their new quarters were like.

"I don't know what we're going to do for all that time; we don't even have a checker set or a box of crayons."

"Don't worry," growled Tock, raising one paw assuringly, "something will turn up. Here, wind me, will you please? I'm beginning to run down."

"You know something, Tock?" he said as he wound up the dog. "You can get in a lot of trouble mixing up words or just not knowing how to spell them. If we ever get out of here, I'm going to make sure to learn all about them."

"A very commendable ambition, young man," said a small voice from across the cell.

Milo looked up, very surprised, and noticed for the first time, in the half-light of the room, a pleasant-looking old lady quietly knitting and rocking.

"Hello," he said.

"How do you do?" she replied.

"You'd better be very careful," Milo advised. "I understand there's a witch somewhere in here."

"I am she," the old lady answered casually, and pulled her shawl a little closer around her shoulders.

Milo jumped back in fright and quickly grabbed Tock to make sure that his alarm didn't go off—for he knew how much witches hate loud noises.

"Don't be frightened," she laughed. "I'm not a witch—I'm a Which."

"Oh," said Milo, because he couldn't think of anything else to say.

"I'm Faintly Macabre, the not-so-wicked Which," she continued, "and I'm certainly not going to harm you."

"What's a Which?" asked Milo, releasing Tock and stepping a little closer.

"Well," said the old lady, just as a rat scurried across her foot, "I am the king's great aunt. For years and years I was in charge of choosing which words were to be used for all occasions, which ones to say and which ones not to say, which ones to write and which ones not to write. As you can well imagine, with all the thousands to choose from, it was a most important and responsible job. I was given the title of 'Official Which,' which made me very proud and happy.

"At first I did my best to make sure that only the most proper and fitting words were used. Everything was said clearly and simply and no words were wasted. I had signs posted all over the palace and market place which said: BREVITY IS THE SOUL OF WIT.

"But power corrupts, and soon I grew miserly and chose fewer and fewer words, trying to keep as many as possible for myself. I had new signs posted which said: AN ILL-CHOSEN WORD IS THE FOOL'S MESSENGER.

"Soon sales began to fall off in the market. The people were afraid to buy as many words as before, and hard times came to the kingdom. But still I grew more and more miserly. Soon there were so few words chosen that hardly anything could be said, and even casual conversation became difficult. Again I had new signs posted, which said: SPEAK FITLY OR BE SILENT WISELY.

"And finally I had even these replaced by ones which read simply: SILENCE IS GOLDEN.

"All talk stopped. No words were sold, the market place closed down, and the people grew poor and disconsolate. When the king saw what had happened, he became furious and had me cast into this dungeon where you see me now, an older and wiser woman.

"That was all many years ago," she continued, "but they never appointed a new Which, and that explains why today people use as many words as they can and think themselves very wise for doing so. For always remember that while it is wrong to use too few, it is often far worse to use too many."

When she had finished, she sighed deeply, patted Milo gently on the shoulder, and began knitting once again.

"And have you been down here ever since then?" asked Milo sympathetically.

"Yes," she said sadly. "Most people have forgotten me entirely, or remember me wrongly as a witch not a Which. But it matters not, it matters not," she went on unhappily, "for they are equally frightened of both."

"I don't think you're frightening," said Milo, and Tock wagged his tail in agreement.

"I thank you very much," said Faintly Macabre. "You may call me Aunt Faintly. Here, have a punctuation mark." And she held out a box of sugar-coated question marks, periods, commas, and exclamation points. "That's all I get to eat now."

"Well, when I get out of here, I'm going to help you," Milo declared forcefully.

"I'm afraid there's not much a little boy and a dog can do," she said, "but never you mind; it's not so bad. I've grown quite used to it here. But you must be going or else you'll waste the whole day."

"Oh, we're here for six million years," sighed Milo, "and I don't see any way to escape."

"Nonsense," scolded the Which, "you mustn't take Officer Shrift so seriously. He loves to put people in prison, but he doesn't care about keeping them there. Now just press the button in the wall and be on your way."

Milo pressed the button and a door swung open, letting in a shaft of brilliant sunshine.

"Good-by; come again," shouted the Which as they stepped outside and the door slammed shut.

The Night the Bed Fell

by James Thurber

I suppose that the high-water mark of my youth in Columbus, Ohio, was the night the bed fell on my father. It makes a better recitation (unless, as some friends of mine have said, one has heard it five or six times) than it does a piece of writing, for it is almost necessary to throw furniture around, shake doors, and bark like a dog, to lend the proper atmosphere and verisimilitude to what is admittedly a somewhat incredible tale. Still, it did take place.

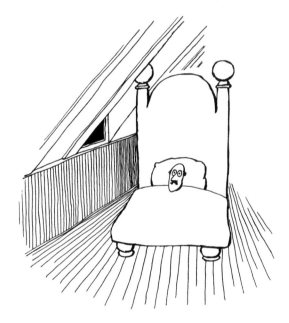

It happened, then, that my father had decided to sleep in the attic one night, to be away where he could think. My mother opposed the notion strongly because, she said, the old wooden bed

From *The New Yorker*.

up there was unsafe: it was wobbly and the heavy headboard would crash down on father's head in case the bed fell, and kill him. There was no dissuading him, however, and at a quarter past ten he closed the attic door behind him and went up the narrow twisting stairs. We later heard ominous creakings as he crawled into bed. Grandfather, who usually slept in the attic bed when he was with us, had disappeared some days before. (On these occasions he was usually gone six or eight days and returned growling and out of temper, with the news that the federal Union was run by a passel of blockheads and that the Army of the Potomac didn't have any more chance than a fiddler's bitch.)

We had visiting us at this time a nervous first cousin of mine named Briggs Beall, who believed that he was likely to cease breathing when he was asleep. It was his feeling that if he were not awakened every hour during the night, he might die of suffocation. He had been accustomed to setting an alarm clock to ring at intervals until morning, but I persuaded him to abandon this. He slept in my room and I told him that I was such a light sleeper that if anybody quit breathing in the same room with me, I would wake instantly. He tested me the first night—which I had suspected he would—by holding his breath after my regular breathing had convinced him I was asleep. I was not asleep, however, and called to him. This seemed to allay his fears a little, but he took the precaution of putting a glass of spirits of camphor on a little table at the head of his bed. In case I didn't arouse him until he was almost gone, he said, he would sniff the camphor, a powerful reviver.

Briggs was not the only member of his family who had his crotchets. Old Aunt Melissa Beall (who could whistle like a man, with two fingers in her mouth) suffered under the premonition that she was destined to die on South High Street, because she had been born on South High Street and married on South High Street.

Then there was Aunt Sarah Shoaf, who never went to bed at night without the fear that a burglar was going to get in and blow chloroform under her door through a tube. To avert this calamity—

for she was in greater dread of anesthetics than of losing her household goods—she always piled her money, silverware, and other valuables in a neat stack just outside her bedroom with a note reading: "This is all I have. Please take it and do not use your chloroform, as this is all I have."

Aunt Gracie Shoaf also had a burglar phobia, but she met it with more fortitude. She was confident that burglars had been getting into her house every night for forty years. The fact that she never missed anything was to her no proof to the contrary. She always claimed that she scared them off before they could take anything, by throwing shoes down the hallway. When she went to bed she piled, where she could get at them handily, all the shoes there were about her house. Five minutes after she had turned off the light, she would sit up in bed and say "Hark!" Her husband, who had learned to ignore the whole situation as long ago as 1903, would either be sound asleep or pretend to be sound asleep. In either case he would not respond to her tugging and pulling, so that presently she would arise, tiptoe to the door, open it slightly and heave a shoe down the hall in one direction and its mate down the hall in the other direction. Some nights she threw them all, some nights only a couple of pair.

But I am straying from the remarkable incidents that took place during the night that the bed fell on father. By midnight we were all in bed. The layout of the rooms and the disposition of their occupants is important to an understanding of what later occurred. In the front room upstairs (just under father's attic bedroom) were my mother and my brother, Herman, who sometimes sang in his sleep, usually "Marching Through Georgia" or "Onward, Christian Soldiers." Briggs Beall and myself were in a room adjoining this one. My brother Roy was in a room across the hall from ours. Our bull terrier, Rex, slept in the hall.

My bed was an army cot, one of those affairs which are made wide enough to sleep on comfortably only by putting up, flat with the middle section, the two sides which ordinarily hang down like the sideboards of a drop-leaf table. When these sides are up, it is perilous to roll too far toward the edge, for then the cot is likely to tip completely over, bringing the whole bed down on top of one with a tremendous banging crash. This, in fact, is precisely what happened, about two o'clock in the morning. (It was my mother who, in recalling the scene later, first referred to it as "the night the bed fell on your father.")

Always a deep sleeper, slow to arouse (I had lied to Briggs), I was at first unconscious of what had happened when the iron cot rolled me onto the floor and toppled over on me. It left me still warmly bundled up and unhurt, for the bed rested above me like a canopy. Hence I did not wake up, only reached the edge of consciousness and went back. The racket, however, instantly awakened my mother, in the next room, who came to the immediate conclusion that her worst dread was realized: the big wooden bed upstairs had fallen on father. She therefore screamed, "Let's go to your poor father!" It was this shout, rather than the noise of my cot falling, that awakened my brother Herman, in the same room with her. He thought that mother had become, for no apparent reason, hysterical. "You're all right, mamma!" he shouted, trying to calm her. They exchanged shout for shout for perhaps ten seconds: "Let's go to your poor father!" and "You're all right!" That woke up Briggs. By this time I was conscious of what was going on, in a vague way, but did not yet realize that I was under my bed instead of on it. Briggs, awakening in the midst of loud shouts of fear and apprehension, came to the quick conclusion that he was suffocating and that we were all trying to "bring him out." With a low moan, he grasped the glass of camphor at the head of his bed and instead of sniffing it poured it over himself. The room reeked of camphor. "Ugf, ahfg!" choked Briggs, like a drowning man, for he had almost succeeded in stopping his breath under the deluge of pungent spirits. He leaped out of bed and groped toward the open window, but he came up against one that was closed. With his hand, he beat out the glass, and I could hear it crash and tinkle in the alleyway below. It was at this juncture that I, in trying to get up, had the uncanny sensation of feeling my bed above me! Foggy with sleep, I now suspected, in my turn, that the whole uproar was being made in a frantic endeavor to extricate me from what must be an unheard-of and perilous situation. "Get me out of this!" I bawled. "Get me out!" I think I had the nightmarish belief that I was entombed in a mine. "Gugh!" gasped Briggs, floundering in his camphor.

By this time my mother, still shouting, pursued by Herman, still shouting, was trying to open the door to the attic, in order to go up and get my father's body out of the wreckage. The door was stuck, however, and wouldn't yield. Her frantic pulls on it only added to the general banging and confusion. Roy and the dog were now up, the one shouting questions, the other barking.

Father, farthest away and soundest sleeper of all, had by this time been awakened by the battering on the attic door. He decided that the house was on fire. "I'm coming, I'm coming!" he wailed in a slow, sleepy voice—it took him many minutes to regain full consciousness. My mother, still believing he was caught under the bed, detected in his "I'm coming!" the mournful, resigned note of one who is preparing to meet his Maker. "He's dying!" she shouted.

"I'm all right!" Briggs yelled, to reassure her. "I'm all right!" He still believed that it was his own closeness to death that was worrying mother. I found at last the light switch in my room, unlocked the door, and Briggs and I joined the others at the attic door. The dog, who never did like Briggs, jumped for him—assuming that he was the culprit in whatever was going on—and Roy had to throw Rex and hold him. We could hear father crawling out of bed upstairs. Roy pulled the attic door open, with a mighty jerk, and father came down the stairs, sleepy and irritable but safe and sound. My mother began to weep when she saw him. Rex began to howl. "What in the name of God is going on here?" asked father.

The situation was finally put together like a gigantic jigsaw puzzle. Father caught a cold from prowling around in his bare feet but there were no other bad results. "I'm glad," said mother, who always looked on the bright side of things, "that your grandfather wasn't here."

The Face Is Familiar But——

by Max Shulman

You can never tell. Citizens, you can never tell. Take the week end of May 18. From all indications it was going to be a dreamboat. Saturday night was the fraternity formal, and Sunday night Petey Burch was taking me to the Dr. Askit quiz broadcast. Every prospect pleased.

At 7:30 Saturday night I got into my rented tux and picked up my rented car. At 8:30 I called for my date and was told that she had come down with the measles at 7:30. So I shugged my rented shoulders, got into my rented car, and went to the dance alone.

I had taken my place in the stag line when Petey Burch rushed up to me, his face flushed with excitement. He waved a letter at me. "I've got it!" he cried. "Here's a letter from my parents saying I can join the Navy." Petey, like me, was seventeen years old and needed permission from home to enlist.

"That's swell, Petey," I said. "I've got some news too. My date has the measles."

"Tough," he said sympathetically. Then he suddenly got more excited than ever and hollered: "No! No, that's perfect. Listen, Dobie, the recruiting station is still open. I can go right down and enlist now."

"But what about the dance? What about your date?"

"The Navy," said Petey, snapping to attention, "needs men now. Every minute counts. How can I think of staying at a dance when there's a war to be won? I've got to get out of here, Dobie. I owe it to the boys Over There."

From *The Many Loves of Dobie Gillis.*

"What are you going to tell your date?"

"That's where you come in, Dobie. You take my girl; I go catch a bus. I won't tell her anything. I'll just disappear and you explain it to her later."

"Won't she mind?"

"I suppose she will, but it doesn't really matter. This is the first date I've ever had with her and I'll probably never see her again." He set his jaw. "God knows when I'll be coming back from Over There."

"I understand," I said simply.

"Thanks, old man," he said simply.

We shook hands.

"By the way," I said, "what about those two tickets you've got for the Dr. Askit broadcast tomorrow night?"

"They're yours," he said, handing them to me.

"Thanks, old man," I said simply.

"Here comes my date now," Petey said, pointing at the powder-room door. I took one look at her and knew what a patriot he must be to run out on a smooth operator like that. She was strictly on the side of angels.

"Where'd you find her?" I drooled.

"Just met her the other night. She's new around here. Now. I'll introduce you and you dance with her while I make my get-away."

"Solid," I agreed.

She walked over to us, making pink-taffeta noises. The timing was perfect. The orchestra was tuning up for the first number just as she reached us.

"Hi," said Petey. "I want you to meet a friend of mine. Dobie Gillis, this is——"

At that instant the orchestra started to play and I didn't catch her name. And no wonder. The orchestra was led by a trumpeter who had a delusion that good trumpeting and loud trumpeting are the same thing. Between him and Harry James, he figured, were only a few hundred decibels of volume. Every time he played he narrowed the gap.

"Excuse me," shouted Petey, and left.

"Dance?" I yelled.

"What?" she screamed.

I made dancing motions and she nodded. We moved out on the floor. I tried to tell her while we were dancing that I hadn't caught her name, but it was impossible. The trumpeter, feeling himself gaining on Harry James, was pursuing his advantage hard. At last there came a short trumpet break, and I made a determined stab at it.

"I don't like to seem dull," I said to the girl, "but when Petey

introduced us, I didn't catch your——"

But the trumpeter was back on the job, stronger than ever after his little rest. The rest of the song made the "Anvil Chorus" sound like a lullaby. I gave up then, and we just danced.

Came the intermission and I tried again. "I know this is going to sound silly, but when we were intro——"

"I wonder where Petey is," she interrupted. "He's been gone an awfully long time."

"Oh, not so long really. Well, as I was saying, it makes me feel foolish to ask, but I didn't——"

"It has, too, been a long time. I think that's an awfully funny way

for a boy to act when he takes a girl out for the first time. Where do
you suppose he is?"

"Oh, I don't know. Probably just—oh well, I suppose I might as
well tell you now." So I told her.

She bit her lip. "Dobie," she quavered, "will you please take me
home?"

"Home? It's so early."

"Please, Dobie."

Seventeen years of experience had taught me not to argue with a
woman whose eyes are full of tears. I went and got my Driv-Ur-Self
limousine, packed her into it, and started off.

"I—live—at—2123—Fremont—Avenue," she wailed.

"There, there," I cooed. "Try to look at it this way. The Navy
needs men now. The longer he stayed around the dance tonight, the
longer the war would last. Believe me, if my parents would sign a
letter for me, I'd be Over There plenty quick, believe me."

"You mean," she wept, "that you would run off and stand up a
girl at a formal affair?"

"Well," I said, "maybe not that. I mean I would hardly run out
on a girl like you." I took her hand. "A girl so beautiful and lovely
and pretty."

She smiled through tears. "You're sweet, Dobie."

"Oh, pshaw," I pshawed. "Say, I've got a couple of tickets to the
Dr. Askit quiz broadcast tomorrow night. How about it?"

"Oh, Dobie, I'd love to. Only I don't know if Daddy will let me.
He wants me to stay in and study tomorrow night. But I'll see what
I can do. You call me."

"All right," I said, "but first there's something you have to tell
me." I turned to her. "Now, please don't think that I'm a jerk, but
it wasn't my fault. When Petey introduced us, I didn't——"

At this point I ran into the rear end of a bus. There followed a
period of unpleasantness with the bus driver, during which I got a
pithy lecture on traffic regulations. I don't know what he had to be
sore about. His bus wasn't even nicked. The radiator grill of my car,

on the other hand, was a total loss.

And when I got back in the car, there was more grief. The sudden stop had thrown the girl against the windshield head first, and her hat, a little straw number with birds, bees, flowers, and a patch of real grass, was now a heap of rubble. She howled all the way home.

"I'm afraid this evening hasn't been much fun," I said truly as I walked her to her door.

"I'm sorry, Dobie," she sniffled. "I'm sorry all this had to happen to you. You've been so nice to me."

"Oh, it's nothing any young American wouldn't have done," I said.

"You've been very sweet," she repeated. "I hope we'll get to be very good friends."

"Oh, we will. We certainly will."

She was putting her key in the lock.

"Just one more thing," I said. "Before you go in, there's something I have to know———"

"Of course," she said. "I asked you to call and didn't give you my number. It's Kenwood 6817."

"No," I said, "it's not that. I mean yes, I wanted that too. But there's another thing."

"Certainly, Dobie," she whispered and kissed me quickly. Then the door was closed behind her.

"Nuts," I mumbled, got into the car, returned it to the Driv-Ur-Self service, where I left a month's allowance to pay for the broken grille, and went back to the fraternity house.

A few of the guys were sitting in the living room. "Hi, Dobie," called one. "How'd you come out with that smooth operator? Petey sure picked the right night to run off and join the Navy, eh?"

"Oh, she was fine," I answered. "Say, do any of you fellows know her name?"

"No, you lucky dog. She's all yours. Petey just met her this week and you're the only one he introduced her to. No competition. You lucky dog."

"Yeah, sure," I said. "Lucky dog." And I went upstairs to bed.

It was a troubled night, but I had a headful of plans when I got up in the morning. After all, the problem wasn't so difficult. Finding out a girl's name should be no task for a college freshman, a crossword-puzzle expert, and the senior-class poet of the Salmon P. Chase High School, Blue Earth, Minnesota.

First I picked up the phone and dialed the operator. "Hello," I said, "I'd like to find out the name of the people who live at 2123 Fremont Avenue. The number is Kenwood 6817."

"I'm sorry. We're not allowed to give out that information."

I hung up. Then I tried plan No. 2. I dialed Kenwood 6817. A gruff male voice answered, "Hello."

"Hello," I said, "Who is this?"

"Who is *this?*" he said.

"This is Dobie Gillis. Who is this?"

"Who did you wish to speak to?"

Clearly, I was getting nowhere. I hung up.

Then I went and knocked on the door of Ed Beasley's room. Ed was a new pledge of the fraternity, and he was part of my third plan. He opened the door. "Enter, master," he said in the manner required of new pledges.

"Varlet," I said, "I have a task for you. Take yon telephone book and look through it until you find the name of the people who have telephone number Kenwood 6817."

"But, master——" protested Ed.

"I have spoken," I said sharply and walked off briskly, rubbing my palms.

In ten minutes Ed was in my room with Roger Goodhue, the president of the fraternity. "Dobie," said Roger, "you are acquainted with the university policy regarding the hazing of pledges."

"Hazing?"

"You know very well that hazing was outlawed this year by the Dean of Student Affairs. And yet you go right ahead and haze poor

Ed. Do you think more of your own amusement than the good of
the fraternity? Do you know that if Ed had gone to the dean instead
of me we would have had our charter taken away? I am going to
insist on an apology right here and now."

Ed got his apology and walked off briskly, rubbing his palms.

"We'll have no more of that," said Roger, and he left too.

I took the phone book myself and spent four blinding hours
looking for Kenwood 6817. Then I remembered that Petey had
said the girl was new around here. The phone book was six months
old; obviously her number would not be listed until a new edition
was out.

The only course left to me was to try calling the number again in
the hope that she would answer the phone herself. This time I was
lucky. It was her voice.

"Hello," I cried, "who is this?"

"Why, it's Dobie Gillis," she said. "Daddy said you called before.
Why didn't you ask to talk to me?"

"We were cut off," I said.

"About tonight: I can go to the broadcast with you. I told Daddy
we were going to the library to study. So be sure you tell the same
story when you get here. I better hang up now. I hear Daddy
coming downstairs. See you at eight. 'Bye."

"Goodbye," I said.

And goodbye to some lovely ideas. But I was far from licked.
When I drove up to her house at eight in a car I had borrowed from
a fraternity brother (I wisely decided not to try the Driv-Ur-Self
people again), I still had a few aces up my sleeve. It was now a
matter of pride with me. I thought of the day I had recited the
senior-class poem at Salmon P. Chase High School and I said to
myself, "By George, a man who could do that can find a simple
girl's name, by George." And I wasn't going to be stupid about it
either. I wasn't going to just ask her. After all this trouble, I was
going to be sly about it. Sly, see?

I walked up to the porch, looking carefully for some marker with the family name on it. There was nothing. Even on the mailbox there was no name.

But in the mailbox was a letter! Quickly I scooped it out of the box, just in time to be confronted by a large, hostile man framed in a suddenly open doorway.

"And what, pray, are you doing in our mailbox?" he asked with dangerous calmness.

"I'm Dobie Gillis," I squeaked. "I'm here to call on your daughter. I just saw the mail in the box and thought I'd bring it in to you." I gave him a greenish smile.

"So you're the one who hung up on me this afternoon." He placed a very firm hand on my shoulder. "Come inside, please, young man," he said.

The girl was sitting in the living room. "Do you know this fellow?" asked her father.

"Of course, Daddy. That's Dobie Gillis, the boy who is going to take me over to the library to study tonight. Dobie, this my father."

"How do you do, Mr. Zzzzzm," I mumbled.

"What?" he said.

"Well, we better run along," I said, taking the girl's hand.

"Just a moment, young man. I'd like to ask you a few things," said her father.

"Can't wait," I chirped. "Every minute counts. Stitch in time saves nine. Starve a cold and stuff a fever. Spare the rod and spoil the child." Meanwhile I was pulling the girl closer and closer to the door. "A penny saved is a penny earned," I said and got her out on the porch.

"It's such a nice night," I cried. "Let's run to the car." I had her in the car and the car in low and picking up speed fast before she could say a word.

"Dobie, you've been acting awfully strange tonight," she said with perfect justification. "I think I want to go home."

"Oh no, no, no. Not that. I'm just excited about our first real date, that's all."

"Sometimes you're so strange, and then sometimes you're so sweet. I can't figure you out."

"I'm a complex type," I admitted. And then I went to work. "How do you spell your name?" I asked.

"Just the way it sounds. What did you think?"

"Oh, I thought so. I just was wondering." I rang up a "No Sale" and started again. "Names are my hobby," I confessed. "Just before I came to get you tonight I was looking through a dictionary of names. Do you know, for instance, that Dorothy means 'gift of God'?"

"No. Really?"

"Yes. And Beatrice means 'making happy,' and Gertrude means 'spear maiden.'"

"Wonderful. Do you know any more?"

"Thousands," I said. "Abigail means 'my father's joy,' Margaret means 'a pearl,' Phyllis means 'a green bough,' and Beulah means 'she who is to be married.'" My eyes narrowed craftily; I was about to spring the trap. "Do you know what your name means?"

"Sure," she said. "It doesn't mean anything. I looked it up once, and it just said that it was from the Hebrew and didn't mean anything."

We were in front of the broadcasting studio. "Curses," I cursed and parked the car.

We went inside and were given tickets to hold. In a moment Dr. Askit took the stage and the broadcast began. "Everyone who came in here tonight was given a ticket," said Dr. Askit. "Each ticket has a number. I will now draw numbers out of this fishbowl here and call them off. If your number is called, please come up on the stage and be a contestant." He reached into the fishbowl. "The first number is 174. Will the person holding 174 please come up here?"

"That's you," said the girl excitedly.

I thought fast. If I went upon the stage, I had a chance to win $64. Not a very good chance, because I'm not very bright about these things. But if I gave the girl my ticket and had her go up, Dr.

Askit would make her give him her name and I would know what it
was and all this nonsense would be over. It was the answer to my
problem. "You go," I told her. "Take my ticket and go."

"But, Dobie——"

"Go ahead." I pushed her out in the aisle.

"And here comes a charming young lady," said Dr. Askit. He
helped her to the microphone. "A very lucky young lady, I might
add. Miss, do you know what you are?"

"What?"

"You are the ten thousandth contestant that has appeared on the
Dr. Askit quiz program. And do you know what I am going to do in
honor of this occasion?"

"What?"

"I am going to pay you ten times as much as I ordinarily pay
contestants. Instead of a $64 maximum, you have a chance to win
$640!"

"I may have to pay $640 to learn this girl's name," I thought, and
waves of blackness passed before my eyes.

"Now," said Dr. Askit, "what would you like to talk about? Here
is a list of subjects."

Without hesitation she said, "Number Six. The meaning of names
of girls."

I tore two handfuls of upholstery from my seat.

"The first one is Dorothy," said Dr. Askit.

"Gift of God," replied the girl.

"Right! You now have $10. Would you like to try for $20? All
right? The next one is Beatrice."

Two real tears ran down my cheeks. The woman sitting next to
me moved over one seat.

"Making happy," said the girl.

"Absolutely correct!" crowed Dr. Askit. "Now would you care to
try for $40?"

"You'll be sorry!" sang someone.

"Like hell she will!" I hollered.

"I'll try," she said.

"Gertrude," said Dr. Askit.

"Forty dollars," I mourned silently. A sports coat. A good rod and reel. A new radiator grille for a Driv-Ur-Self car.

"Spear maiden," said the girl.

"Wonderful! There's no stopping this young lady tonight. How about the $80 question? Yes? All right. Abigail. Think now. This is a toughie."

"Oh, that's easy. My father's joy."

"Easy, she said. Easy. Go ahead," I wept, as I pommeled the arm of my seat, "rub it in. Easy!"

"You certainly know your names," said Dr. Askit admiringly. "What do you say to the $160 question? All right? Margaret."

"A pearl."

The usher came over to my seat and asked if anything was wrong. I shook my head mutely. "Are you sure?" he said. I nodded. He left, but kept looking at me.

"In all my years in radio," said Dr. Askit, "I have never known such a contestant. The next question, my dear, is for $320. Will you try?"

"Shoot," she said gaily.

"Phyllis."

"A green bough."

"Right! Correct! Absolutely correct!"

Two ushers were beside me now. "I see them epileptics before," one whispered to the other. "We better get him out of here."

"Go away," I croaked, flecking everyone near me with light foam.

"Now," said Dr. Askit, "will you take the big chance? The $640 question?"

She gulped and nodded.

"For $640—Beulah."

"She who is to be married," she said.

The ushers were tugging at my sleeves.

"And the lady wins $640! Congratulations! And now, may I ask you your name?"

"Come quietly, bud," said the ushers to me. "Please don't make us use no force."

"Great balls of fire, don't make me go now!" I cried. "Not now! I paid $640 to hear this."

"My name," she said, "is Mary Brown."

"You were sweet," she said to me as we drove home, "to let me go up there tonight instead of you."

"Think nothing of it, Mary Brown," I said bitterly.

She threw back her head and laughed. "You're so funny, Dobie. I think I like you more than any boy I've ever met."

"Well, that's something to be thankful for, Mary Brown," I replied.

She laughed some more. Then she leaned over and kissed my cheek. "Oh, Dobie, you're marvelous."

So Mary Brown kissed me and thought I was marvelous. Well, that was just dandy.

"Marvelous," she repeated and kissed me again.

"Thank you, Mary Brown," I said.

No use being bitter about it. After all, $640 wasn't all the money in the world. Not quite, anyhow. I had Mary Brown, now. Maybe I could learn to love her after a while. She looked easy enough to love. Maybe someday we would get married. Maybe there would even be a dowry. A large dowry. About $640.

I felt a little better. But just a little.

I parked in front of her house. "I'll never forget this evening as long as I live," she said as we walked to the porch.

"Nor I, Mary Brown," I said truthfully.

She giggled. She put her key in the front door. "Would you like to come in, Dobie—dear?"

"No thanks, Mary Brown. I have a feeling your father doesn't care for me." Then it dawned on me. "Look!" I cried. "Your father.

You told him you were at the library tonight. What if he was listening to the radio tonight and heard you on the Dr. Askit program?"

"Oh, don't worry. People's voices sound different over the radio."

"But the name! You gave your name!"

She looked at me curiously. "Are you kiddin'? You know very well I didn't give my right name. . . . DOBIE! WHY ARE YOU BEATING YOUR HEAD AGAINST THE WALL?"

Practice Mission

by Mac Hyman

Ever since No Time for Sergeants *was published in 1954, readers old and young have been laughing over the misadventures of Mac Hyman's blundering, well-meaning hillbilly, Will Stockdale—first in book form, then on Broadway, in television, and on the screen. There follows one of the hilarious highlights of Stockdale's wild and woolly military career.—*B.C.

After we got assigned to gunnery, me and Ben both got to be airmans-third-class which means you wear a stripe on your arm, only we didnt get to wear it long because of this Captain that was in charge of our crew in transition. He was the pilot of the plane and was always real particular, wanting you to wear neckties and such most of the time, which I didnt care nothing about. Anyhow, he stopped me and Ben up town one day and I didnt have my tie on, and we had a few words about that when I tried to explain to him how it was, which I found out later I warnt supposed to do—Ben said all I was supposed to do was stand there and say "No excuse, sir," which sounded like a kind of foolish way to talk to a man—so one thing led to another and we was recruits again; and besides that he changed us off his crew and put us in another crew. And Ben didnt like that too much because he said we was now on the *sorriest* crew on the base. He said everybody knowed it was the worst crew there, but I didnt think so myself because I got along with them pretty good. They was real easygoing compared to the other one; it didnt make much difference with them whether you showed up for a mission or not. Lieutenant Bridges was the pilot and he was a Reserve and was the only one of the officers I knowed much at first because the planes was so monstrously big and because we flew in the back and they flew in the front so that we didnt see much of the others, and didnt know them usually when we did. But Lieutenant Bridges was a mighty easygoing fellow and didnt care much what you done; he went around most of the time with his eyes about half-opened and half-closed, just kind of dragging himself around like he was walking in his sleep, only he just seemed that way, I think; he warnt really asleep but probably only half drunk, even though it was kind of hard to tell the difference most of the time. And as far as I was concerned, I had ruther been on his crew than the first one because he was so easy to work for. If you took it in your head you didnt want to go on a mission, he never would notice you warnt there nohow. I mean like this one fellow we had; he didnt fly hardly any and one day when he come out to the plane, Lieutenant Bridges didnt remember him and wouldnt let him fly with us until he went back to Operations and got a card showing he was supposed to be on our crew.

Anyhow, Sergeant King got back to being a sergeant again by that time and had got himself a job in the Orderly Room, and me and Ben hung around a good bit, not doing much but going on practice missions, and Ben finally quit worrying about losing his stripe, and we had a right nice time. Ben still didn't like the crew much—he was mighty disappointed in them most of the time and said it was a good thing most of the officers warnt like them and all that, but he liked flying a lot, so we went on most of the missions, not skipping them the way about half the crew did. And I didn't mind it much myself—it warnt much trouble because there warnt nothing to do in the back of the plane but sleep or play cards or set there and watch the country go under you. Finally I got a checkerboard and took that along, and me and Ben and this other fellow took turns playing each other, only the other fellow didn't play much because he was working on a model airplane that he took along with him. We never did get to know him too good, though, because he finally just quit coming altogether, and I guess he must have dropped off the crew because we didn't see him around nowhere for a long time.

Anyhow, there warnt much to it; when we was scheduled for a mission, me and Ben went and crawled in the back of the plane, and when it landed, we crawled back out, and never had anything to say to anybody except sometimes when Lieutenant Bridges would call back to see if anybody else was around, and I was kind of enjoying it. And then one day I happened to meet the co-pilot up in Operations, which was a right peculiar thing because we was just standing there talking together and his voice sounded familiar and he said mine did too, and finally we found out we was on the same crew together. His name was Lieutenant Gardella and he seemed like a real nice fellow, and when I asked him what they done up in the front of the plane, he said, "Nothing much. What do yall do in the back?"

So I told him about the checkers and the cards that we played sometimes and he said that sounded mighty good to him and that he would come back and play with us sometimes, and I told him I would like to have him and that I wanted him to meet Ben besides. I asked him what his job was and he said, "Oh, I do different things. Mainly, I just let the wheels up and down and I stick to that pretty much as I dont care to take on anything more right now."

"How long you been letting them up and down?"

"A pretty good while," he said. "About six weeks now, ever since I got out of cadets. Next time we fly I'm going to let the flaps up and down too. Say, why dont you come up front and fly with us next time? Why dont you ask Bridges about it?"

"Well, that's mighty nice of you. I'd sho like to see you let them wheels up and down."

"Sure," he said. "I'll show you all about it."

He was a real obliging kind of fellow that way and you wouldnt think he was an officer at all just to look at him—he looked like he was only about thirteen years old and you would probably think he was a Boy Scout instead of an officer if you seen him, only he always had this big cigar in his mouth and usually didnt seem real sober neither, which of course aint like most Boy Scouts as they usually seem right sober most of the time.

So I went out and finally found Lieutenant Bridges in the BOQ and he was lying down on his bunk and I had to stand around a while before I could tell whether he was asleep or awake with his eyes half open the way they always was, but finally he set up and looked at me, and I told him what I wanted. And he said, "Look here, you cant just go around flying here and there. Why dont you ask your own pilot?"

And I told him *he* was my pilot, and so he looked at me for a while and finally said, "Oh, yeah, I thought I had seen you around somewhere before. What did you say your name was now?"

So we talked for a while and he said I could ride up front with them on the next trip, and then I asked about Ben, and he said, "Ben who?" and I explained to him that Ben was another one of his gunners, and he said it was all right by him, that it didnt make no difference to him one way or the other.

But when I went back and told Ben about it, Ben said, "No, I'll stay in the back where I'm supposed to stay. I never seen officers care as little about things as this bunch does. I wish we had never got off the other crew myself."

So I told him I would ride in the back too, but he said, "No, there aint any use in that. After all, the pilot is in charge of the plane and what he says goes, I guess, even if he dont seem to know what he is talking about half the time."

But they warnt all that bad, I didnt think, and I really enjoyed watching them work when I flew up front. We took off that day about dark and Lieutenant Bridges got the plane off the ground real good and Lieutenant Gardella let the wheels up and done a right good job of it too, right smack up in the sides like he had been borned doing it; we went skimming out over the end of the runway and then Lieutenant Gardella got out a cigar and stuck it in his mouth and rared back and begun reading a magazine, while Lieutenant Bridges flew back over the field and then set it on the automatic, and then propped his feet up and leaned his seat back to go to sleep. I watched it all and it seemed like they done right good, and then I went·back to talk with Lieutenant Kendall, the engineer, only he said he was sleepy and was getting his parachute under his head and sticking his feet out in the aisle trying to get comfortable. So I finally went back and set in the radio operators seat, because he hadnt showed up, and watched Lieutenant Cover while he navigated; and he was the one I wished Ben could have seen because he was probably the hardest-working man I ever seen in my life. He was bounding all over the back of the plane navigating even before it was over the end of the runway, peeping down tubes and looking out the window and writing things down on maps that he had scattered all over the desk, then grabbing up one of them three watches that he had scattered around and checking the time, and writing that down, and then taking this camera-looking thing he

had, and running back to the dome and pointing it out at the stars that was just coming out, and then running back to write that down too. He wrote so fast and so hard that twice the lead flew off the pencil and flipped across the plane and nearly hit me in the eye; and another time he snatched up a map that had this weight on it that sailed across the desk and caught me right beside the head; so I got up and moved down a ways after that as it did seem right dangerous being close to him working that hard but I still watched him a good while and got a kick out of it.

Anyhow, I wished Ben could have seen it the way he went at things; he was so busy most of the time he wouldn't even talk to me. Most people that work hard usually like to talk about it a good bit, but when I asked him where he was navigating to, he snapped real quick, "Biloxi, Mississippi. Dont bother me, I'm busy," and wouldnt even look at me. After a little bit, we was well on the way and it was dark and the plane was quiet the way it gets at night, with only the sounds of the engines and no lights to speak of except little blue dials and the lamp that come down over Lieutenant Cover's head; but watching him work was enough to wear you out, so I got a little bit sleepy, and must have dozed off for a good while because when I woke up there was a big disturbance going on with people walking around and talking, and I didnt know what was going on.

Anyhow, I woke up and felt the plane going in these big circles, and then I looked over to the desk and there was Lieutenant Bridges standing holding one of the maps in his hand and looking at it, and Lieutenant Cover arguing with him, rattling papers around and trying to show him how he had figured this and that. Lieutenant Kendall was setting over there watching them with his chin propped up on his hands, and Lieutenant Gardella was up front flying the plane in these big circles, looking around every once in a while to see what was going on with the big cigar stuck out of his mouth; they was talking loud and everybody seemed real interested in it, and it seemed like Lieutenant Bridges knowed a lot about navigation himself even though he was the pilot. He was waving the map around saying, "I dont care what your figures show. I guess I can look out the window and *see,* can't I?"

"Well, you just check the figures for yourself," Lieutenant Cover said. "I got a fix about thirty minutes ago and that showed us right here, and thirty minutes later, we're supposed to be right *here.* You can check every figure down there. I figured that position by Dead

Reckoning and I figured it thirty minutes from that fix, and I know it's right!"

But Lieutenant Bridges kept on shaking his head and saying, "Well, by God, I can *see*, cant I? I can look right out the window and *see*, cant I?"

So they talked a good bit about navigation that way and both took a lot of interest in it, it seemed like. Lieutenant Kendall was setting back there listening to the whole thing and he was right interested too, even though he was the engineer, and so I stepped back there and asked him what the discussion was all about. And he said, "What do you think it's about? They're lost again naturally. I been in this plane seven times and five of them we been lost. All I know is how much gas we got and if they want to know that, I'll be glad to tell them, but I aint going to worry about it anymore. They can ditch the plane or jump out for all I care; the only thing I know is about how much gas we got."

Then Lieutenant Gardella called back and asked how much gas *did* we have, and Lieutenant Kendall said, "Tell him we can fly another forty minutes. I dont want to talk with him because every time we do, we get in an argument over where we are, and I'm tired of talking about it."

"I know what you mean," I said. "I dont like to argue about things neither, but it is good to see everybody taking such an interest in things; old Ben would be surprised to see it."

"Who is Ben?"

"He's one of the gunners," I said. "He rides in the back of the plane."

"Well," Lieutenant Kendall said. "I hope he knows how to use a parachute."

"Sho," I said. "I bet Ben knows about as much about parachutes as anybody you ever seen."

Anyhow we chatted a while and then I went back and listened to Lieutenant Bridges and Lieutenant Cover some more. Lieutenant Cover was still talking about his DR position where he said we ought to be; he turned to Lieutenant Bridges and said, "Well, who's been navigating, you or me? I got a fix no moren thirty minutes ago and that means our DR position is right here, about a hundred miles out over the Gulf of Mexico . . ."

And then Lieutenant Bridges came in with *his* side of the argument, saying, "Well, I might not have been navigating but I got eyes in my head, and I guess I can look out the window right now and see we're circling over a town half the size of New York; and according to this map or none I ever saw in my life, there aint a town at *all* in the middle of the Gulf of Mexico, much less one half the size of New York and . . ."

"Well, just look then," Lieutenant Cover said. "Dont argue with me, just look. You can check every figure I got here. My DR position puts . . ."

"Well, I dont care anything about that," Lieutenant Bridges said. "All I want to know is what town we're circling over, and if you can tell me that, we can land this thing because we cant fly here all night long while you try to tell me there is a town of that size in the middle of the Gulf of Mexico!"

So they took on that way for a while, and then Lieutenant Gardella and Lieutenant Kendall had a pretty good argument about one of the engines going out; so they discussed that a good while too until Lieutenant Kendall said, "Well, there's not any sense in arguing about it; I'm going to feather the thing." And after a little bit, they changed positions, and Lieutenant Bridges come up front and looked out and seen that one of the engines warnt working, and went back to see Lieutenant Kendall and they had a long talk over the engine being feathered too. Lieutenant Bridges said, "You are not supposed to go around feathering engines like that. I'm the one that's supposed to feather the engine. I'm the pilot, aint I?"

"Yeah, but you was too busy trying to navigate the plane when you're supposed to be up there flying it and . . ."

"All right," Lieutenant Bridges said, "But at least you could have *told* me we had lost an engine. I am the *pilot*, aint I?"

So they talked about that a good while too, and I set back and watched and listened, only I must have dozed off again because when I woke up, we was coming in for a landing. We hit and bounced once pretty hard so that I got throwed halfway across the plane, and then bounced again so that it throwed me back where I started from, but then I grabbed on and didnt get throwed no more on the rest of the bounces. We taxied up the runway with the wheels squeaking and finally stopped and started getting out, but nobody was talking much by then except Lieutenant Gardella—he kept telling Lieutenant Bridges that he thought the *third* bounce was the smoothest of all, but Lieutenant Bridges didnt seem to care about talking about it none, and I noticed in a minute that none of the others did either.

Anyhow, we got out and they had this truck waiting for us and we got on that, and nobody was discussing nothing by this time, and I was right sorry for that because I wanted Ben to hear them because they was right interesting to listen to. But everybody just set there and then Lieutenant Cover come out with all his maps and everything folded up, and he got in and didnt say a word to nobody either. The truck finally started up and we headed across the ramp with everybody real quiet until finally Lieutenant Bridges leaned over and tapped Lieutenant Cover on the shoulder and said, "Look, Cover, I dont mean to run this thing into the ground, but I would appreciate it if you would try to find out where this place is. I mean if it is in the middle of the Gulf of Mexico, we've damn well dis*cov*ered something."

And then Lieutenant Cover said, "Well, the way you fly, it's a wonder we didnt end up there anyhow."

So we drove up and got off and everybody stood around for a while hemming and hawing, and Lieutenant Bridges went over and asked Lieutenant Cover again if he had figured out where we was, and Lieutenant Cover said, "I thought you was the one who knew so much about it. If you want to find out, why dont you ask the driver?"

But then Lieutenant Bridges said, "Ask the driver? You expect me to land a plane and then go over and ask a truck driver where I landed it?" and got right stubborn about it. But then he turned to me and said, "Hey, what was your name now?"

"Stockdale," I said.

"Look, Stockdale," he said. "How about scouting around here somewhere and see if you cant find out what place this is, will you? Be kind of casual about it, you know."

So I went down the way and asked a fellow and he told me Houston, Texas, and I come back and told Lieutenant Bridges and he seemed to feel much better about things then. "Well, Houston aint such a bad town after all," he said. "By gosh, Cover, you're getting better every day. You didn't miss the field but about four hundred and fifty miles this time."

Then Lieutenant Cover said, "Well, what I figured was that you would bounce the rest of the way—it looked like it from the way we landed . . ."

And then Lieutenant Bridges had something to say to that, and after a while they begun squabbling a little bit, which I didnt like to hear. Me and Ben stood around waiting while they went at it and Ben said to me, "I never heered a bunch of officers argue so much in my life!"

"Yeah, Ben, they do now, but you ought to have been in the front of that plane and seen the way they worked. That was something else. If you could have seen that, you would have thought a lot more of them. Why, I'll bet they are about as good a crew as you can find, when they're sober like that."

"Which aint often," Ben said.

Anyhow, I hated for Ben to hear the squabbling and kept on talking to him until they had finished up with it because he got so disgusted about things like that. But they was finally finished; all of them heading across the ramp except Lieutenant Cover who had lost the argument because they had all jumped on him together before it was over—he was getting all his charts and stuff up and mumbling to himself. And I felt right sorry for him the way he had lost out on the argument and everything; I went over to him and said, "Well, I wouldn't worry about it none. I dont see how it amounts to too much. I had just as soon land at this field as any other one, and we aint going to be here but one day nohow. . . ."

But he was right down on things and turned around and looked at me like he was almost mad with me, and said, "Look, do you want to check my figures? Do you want to check them and see for yourself? I got them all right here!"

"Well, I dont know nothing about it," I said. "If you say they're right, I guess they is."

"I can show you my DR position," he said. "It shows us right out in the Gulf."

"Well, I wouldnt know about that," I said. "If you say your DR position is out in the Gulf, I reckon that's where it is all right. How long do you expect it to be out there?"

But he was pretty much down on things; he turned away and stomped off without even answering me—nothing you could say would make him feel any better.